ORACLE®

Oracle Press™

Oracle Database 12c
The Complete Reference

About the Authors

Bob Bryla is an Oracle 9*i*, 10*g*, and 11*g* Certified Professional with more than 20 years of experience in database design, database application development, training, and Oracle database administration. He is the primary Oracle DBA and database systems engineer at Epic in Verona, Wisconsin.

He is a technical editor for a number of Oracle Press books, including several certification study guides for Oracle Database 10*g*, 11*g*, and 12*c*. He has also been known to watch science fiction movies and tinker with Android devices in his spare time.

Kevin Loney is an internationally recognized expert in the design, development, administration, and tuning of Oracle databases. A technology and project group leader in the financial industry, he was named Consultant of the Year by *Oracle Magazine* in 2002. His best-selling books include *Oracle Database 11g DBA Handbook*, *Oracle Advanced Tuning and Administration*, and *Oracle SQL & PL/SQL Annotated Archives*. He is the author of numerous technical articles in industry magazines and presents at Oracle user conferences in North America and Europe, where he is regularly among the highest-rated presenters.

About the Contributor and Technical Editor

Scott Gossett (contributing author, technical editor) is a technical director in the Oracle Advanced Technologies Solutions organization with more than 20 years' experience specializing in RAC, performance tuning, and high-availability databases. Prior to becoming a technical director, Scott was a senior principal instructor for Oracle Education for over 12 years, primarily teaching Oracle internals, performance tuning, RAC, and database administration. In addition, Scott is one of the architects and primary authors of the Oracle Certified Master exam. Scott has been a technical editor for nine Oracle Press books.

ORACLE®

Oracle Press™

Oracle Database 12c
The Complete Reference

Bob Bryla
Kevin Loney

New York   Chicago   San Francisco
Lisbon   London   Madrid   Mexico City
Milan   New Delhi   San Juan
Seoul   Singapore   Sydney   Toronto

Cataloging-in-Publication Data is on file with the Library of Congress

McGraw-Hill Education books are available at special quantity discounts to use as premiums and sales promotions, or for use in corporate training programs. To contact a representative, please visit the Contact Us pages at www.mhprofessional.com.

Oracle Database 12c: The Complete Reference

1234567890 DOC DOC 109876543

ISBN: Book p/n 978-0-07-180172-0 and CD p/n 978-0-07-180173-7
of set 978-0-07-180175-1

MHID: Book p/n 0-07-180172-3 and CD p/n 0-07-180173-1
of set 0-07-180175-8

Sponsoring Editor Paul Carlstroem	**Copy Editor** LeeAnn Pickrell	**Illustration** Apollo Publishing Services and Howie Severson, Fortuitous Publishing Services
Editorial Supervisor Jody McKenzie	**Proofreader** Susie Elkind	
Project Editor LeeAnn Pickrell	**Indexer** Rebecca Plunkett	**Art Director, Cover** Jeff Weeks
Acquisitions Coordinator Amanda Russell	**Production Supervisor** George Anderson	
Technical Editor Scott Gossett	**Composition** Apollo Publishing Services	

To the gang at home: I couldn't have done it without you!
And the pizzas. And the rock 'n' roll.

—Bob Bryla

Contents at a Glance

PART VI
Java in Oracle

PART VII
Hitchhiker's Guides

PART VIII

Contents

PART I
Critical Database Concepts

PART II
SQL and SQL*Plus

PART III
Beyond the Basics

PART IV
PL/SQL

PART V
Object-Relational Databases

PART VI
Java in Oracle

PART VII
Hitchhiker's Guides

Acknowledgments

M any technical books need the expertise of more than one person, and this one is no exception. Thanks to Kevin for his expertise on the previous editions of this book, making it a success.

Thanks also go out to all of the people at McGraw-Hill Education who kept this book on a reasonable schedule and learned to be even more patient with me than ever before, including Paul Carlstroem, Amanda Russell, and Jody McKenzie. Thanks also to Scott Gossett who gave me good advice when the theoretical met the practical. I would also be remiss if I didn't thank LeeAnn Pickrell who inspired flashbacks to my college writing courses.

Many of my professional colleagues at Epic were a source of both inspiration and guidance: Chris Tyne, Scott Hinman, and Lonny Niederstadt. In this case, the whole is truly greater than the sum of its parts.

If you have any questions or comments about any part of this book, please do not hesitate to contact me at rjbdba@gmail.com.

—Bob Bryla

PART

I

Critical Database
Concepts

CHAPTER
1

Oracle Database 12c
Architecture Options

Oracle Database 12*c* is a significant upgrade from prior releases of Oracle, even from the groundbreaking and somewhat revolutionary 11*g*. New features give developers, database administrators, and end users greater control over the storage, processing, and retrieval of their data. In this chapter, you will see highlights of the Oracle Database 12*c* architecture. You will read detailed discussions of enhanced 11*g* features, such as SQL replay, change management, partition management, and result caching, in later chapters, in addition to discussions of several major features new to 12*c*, such as pluggable databases and the consolidation features 12*c* brings to the table. The goal of this chapter is to present a high-level overview of the capabilities you can feature in your Oracle applications and provide an introduction to the chapters that describe them.

This book is divided into eight major sections.

In Part I, "Critical Database Concepts," you will see an overview of Oracle Database 12*c*'s options, learn how to install the Oracle software and how to create or upgrade a database, and get advice on planning your application implementation. These chapters establish the common vocabulary that both end users and developers can use to coherently and intelligently share concepts and ensure the success of any development effort. This introductory chapter and Chapter 4 are intended for both developers and end users of Oracle; Chapters 2 and 3 are intended for database administrators.

Part II, "SQL and SQL*Plus," teaches the theory and techniques of relational database systems and applications, including SQL (Structured Query Language) and SQL*Plus. The section begins with relatively few assumptions about data-processing knowledge on the part of the reader and then advances, step by step, through some very deep issues and complex techniques. The method very consciously uses clear, conversational English, with unique and interesting examples, and strictly avoids the use of undefined terms or jargon. This section is aimed primarily at developers and end users who are new to Oracle or need a quick review of certain Oracle features. It moves step by step through the basic capabilities of SQL and Oracle's interactive query facility, SQL*Plus, which is still vital to an organization's toolset even with the proliferation of GUI-based tools such as SQL Developer. When you've completed this section, you should have a thorough understanding of all SQL keywords, functions, and operators. Within an Oracle database, you should be able to produce complex queries, create tables, and insert, update, and delete data.

Part III, "Beyond the Basics," covers advanced options, including virtual private databases, Data Pump, replication (including tools like GoldenGate), text indexing, external tables, change replay, pluggable databases, and the use of the flashback options for developers and database administrators. Most of the features described in this section will not be directly used by end users, but the applications they use can be based on these features.

Part IV, "PL/SQL," provides coverage of PL/SQL. The topics include a review of PL/SQL structures, plus triggers, stored procedures, and packages. Both standard and native dynamic PL/SQL are covered.

Part V, "Object-Relational Databases," provides extensive coverage of object-oriented features such as abstract datatypes, methods, object views, object tables, nested tables, varying arrays, and large objects.

Part VI, "Java in Oracle," provides coverage of the Java features in the Oracle database. This section includes an overview of Java syntax as well as chapters on JDBC and Java stored procedures.

Part VII, "Hitchhiker's Guides," provides an overview of the Real Application Cluster and grid architecture available in Oracle Database 12*c* as well as case studies in using Oracle's tuning tools, features such as the client-side cache, an overview of database administration, and a high-level description of the use of XML in Oracle.

Part VIII, Alphabetical Reference, is a reference for the Oracle server—a book unto itself. Reading the introductory pages to this reference will make its use much more effective and understandable. These pages explain in greater detail what is and is not included and how to read the entries. This section contains references for most major Oracle commands, keywords, products, features, and functions, with extensive cross-referencing of topics. The reference is intended for use by both Oracle developers and users but assumes some familiarity with the products. On the Downloads page at www.oraclepressbooks.com, you will find the table-creation statements and row insertions for all the tables used in this book. For anyone learning Oracle, having these tables available on your own Oracle ID, or on a practice ID, will make trying or expanding on the examples very easy.

Databases and Instances

An Oracle database is a collection of data in one or more files. The database contains physical and logical structures. In the course of developing an application, you create structures such as tables and indexes to store rows and speed their retrieval. You can create synonyms for the object names, view objects in different databases (across database links), and restrict access to the objects. You can even use *external tables* to access files outside the database as if the rows in the files were rows in tables. In this book, you will see how to create these objects and develop applications based on them.

An Oracle *instance* comprises a memory area called the *System Global Area (SGA)* and the background processes that interact between the SGA and the database files on disk. In an Oracle Real Application Cluster (RAC), more than one instance will use the same database (see Chapter 50). The instances generally are on separate servers connected by a high-speed interconnect.

Inside the Database

Within the Oracle database, the basic structure is a table. Oracle Database 12*c* supports many types of tables, including the following:

- **Relational tables**   Using the Oracle-supplied datatypes (see "Datatypes" in the Alphabetical Reference), you can create tables to store the rows inserted and manipulated by your applications. Tables have column definitions, and you can add or drop columns as the application requirements change. Tables are created via the CREATE TABLE command.

- **Object-relational tables**   To take advantage of features such as type inheritance, you can use Oracle's object-relational capabilities. You can define your own datatypes and then use them as the basis for column definitions, object tables, nested tables, varying arrays, and more. See Part V of this book.

- **Index-organized tables**   You can create a table that stores its data within an index structure, allowing the data to be sorted within the table while dramatically reducing storage requirements and I/O usage. See Chapter 17.

- **External tables**   Data stored in flat files may be treated as a table that users can query directly and join to other tables in queries. You can use external tables to access large volumes of data without ever loading them into your database. See Chapter 28. Note that Oracle also supports *BFILE datatypes,* a pointer to an external binary file. Before creating a BFILE or an external table, you must create a directory alias within Oracle (via the CREATE DIRECTORY command) pointing to the physical location of the file. See Chapter 40 for details on BFILEs and other large object datatypes.

■ **Partitioned tables** You can divide a table into multiple partitions, which allows you to separately manage each part of the table. You can add new partitions to a table, split existing partitions, and administer a partition apart from the other partitions of the table. Partitioning may simplify or improve the performance of maintenance activities and user queries. You can partition tables on ranges of values, on lists of values, on hashes of column values, or on combinations of those options. The significant expansion of partition types in Oracle Database 11*g* continues with more flexible online maintenance of individual table partitions in Oracle Database 12*c*. See Chapter 18.

■ **Materialized views** A materialized view is a replica of data retrieved by a query. User queries may be redirected to the materialized views to avoid large tables during execution—the optimizer will rewrite the queries automatically. You can establish and manage refresh schedules to keep the data in the materialized views fresh enough for business needs. See Chapter 26.

■ **Temporary tables** You can use the CREATE GLOBAL TEMPORARY TABLE command to create a table in which multiple users can insert rows. Each user sees only his or her rows in the table. See Chapter 14.

■ **Clustered tables** If two tables are commonly queried together, you can physically store them together via a structure called a *cluster*. See Chapter 17.

■ **Dropped tables** You can quickly recover dropped tables via the FLASHBACK TABLE TO BEFORE DROP command. You can flash back multiple tables at once or flash back the entire database to a prior point in time. Oracle supports *flashback queries,* which return earlier versions of rows from an existing table.

To support access to tables, you can use views that perform joins and aggregations, limit the rows returned, or alter the columns displayed. Views may be read-only or updatable, and they can reference local or remote tables. Remote tables can be accessed via database links. You can use synonyms to mask the physical location of the tables. See Chapter 17 for details on views and Chapter 25 for details on database links.

To tune the accesses to these tables, Oracle supports many types of indexes, including the following:

■ **B*-tree indexes** A B*-tree index is the standard type of index available in Oracle, and it's very useful for selecting rows that meet an equivalence criteria or a range criteria. Indexes are created via the CREATE INDEX command.

■ **Bitmap indexes** For columns that have few unique values, a bitmap index may be able to improve query performance. Bitmap indexes should only be used when the data is batch loaded (as in many data warehousing or reporting applications) and is rarely updated or deleted.

■ **Reverse key indexes** If there are I/O contention issues during the inserts of sequential values, Oracle can dynamically reverse the indexed values prior to storing them.

■ **Function-based indexes** Instead of indexing a column, such as NAME, you can index a function-based column, such as UPPER(NAME). The function-based index gives the Oracle optimizer additional options when selecting an execution path.

■ **Partitioned indexes** You can partition indexes to support partitioned tables or to simplify index management. Index partitions can be local to table partitions or may globally apply to all rows in the table.

■ **Text indexes** You can index text values to support enhanced searching capabilities, such as expanding word stems or searching for phrases. Text indexes are sets of tables and indexes maintained by Oracle to support complex text-searching requirements. Oracle Database 12c offers enhancements to text indexes that simplify their administration and maintenance.

See Chapters 17 and 46 for further details on the index types listed here (excluding text indexes). For text indexes, see Chapter 27.

Storing the Data

All of these logical structures in the database must be stored somewhere in the database. Oracle maintains a data dictionary (see Chapter 45) that records *metadata* about each object—the object owner, a definition, related privileges, and so on. For objects that require physical storage space of their own, Oracle will allocate space within a *tablespace*.

Tablespaces

A tablespace consists of one or more *datafiles*; a datafile can be a part of one and only one tablespace. Oracle Database 12c creates at least two tablespaces for each database—SYSTEM and SYSAUX—to support its internal management needs. You can use Oracle managed files (OMF) to simplify the creation and maintenance of datafiles in conjunction with Automatic Storage Management (ASM).

You can create a special kind of tablespace, called a *bigfile* tablespace, that can be many thousands of terabytes in size. Along with OMF, the management of bigfiles makes tablespace management completely transparent to the DBA; the DBA can manage the tablespace as a unit without worrying about the size and structure of the underlying datafiles.

If a tablespace is designated as a *temporary* tablespace, the tablespace itself is permanent; only the segments saved in the tablespace are temporary. Oracle uses temporary tablespaces to support sorting operations such as index creations and join processing. Temporary segments should not be stored in the same tablespaces as permanent objects.

Tablespaces can be either *dictionary managed* or *locally managed*. In a dictionary-managed tablespace, space management is recorded in the data dictionary. In a locally managed tablespace (the default since Oracle Database 10g), Oracle maintains a bitmap in each datafile of the tablespace to track space availability. Only quotas are managed in the data dictionary, dramatically reducing the contention for data dictionary tables.

Automatic Storage Management

Automatic Storage Management (ASM) automates the layout of datafiles and other operating system–level files used by the database by distributing them across all available disks. When new disks are added to the ASM instance, the database files are automatically redistributed across all disks in the defined disk group for optimal performance. The multiplexing features of an ASM instance minimize the possibility of data loss and are generally more effective than a manual scheme that places critical files and backups on different physical drives. Oracle Database 12c makes ASM even more robust by proactively validating mirrored data in disk groups for logical consistency before the corruption is detected in the application. See Chapter 51.

Automatic Undo Management

To support your transactions, Oracle can dynamically create and manage *undo segments,* which help maintain prior images of the changed blocks and rows. Users who have previously queried the rows you are changing will still see the rows as they existed when their queries began.

Automatic Undo Management (AUM) allows Oracle to manage the undo segments directly with no database administrator intervention required. The use of AUM also simplifies the use of flashback queries. You can execute *flashback version queries* to see the different versions of a row as it changed during a specified time interval. See Chapters 29 and 30 for further details on the use of undo segments, flashback queries, and flashback version queries.

Dropped Data

The *recycle bin* concept introduced with Oracle Database 10*g* impacts the space requirements for your tablespaces and datafiles. The default behavior for the drop of a table is for the table to retain its space allocation; you can see its space usage via the RECYCLEBIN data dictionary view. If you create and drop a table twice, you will have two copies of the table in the recycle bin. Although this architecture greatly simplifies recoveries of accidentally dropped tables, it may considerably increase the space used in your database. Use the PURGE command to remove old entries from your recycle bin. See the Alphabetical Reference for the PURGE command's syntax.

Guarding the Data

You can fully control the access to your data. You can grant other users privileges to perform specific functions (such as SELECT, INSERT, and so on) on your objects. You can pass along the right to execute further grants. You can grant privileges to roles, which are then granted to users, grouping privileges into manageable sets.

Oracle supports a very detailed level of privileges; you can control which rows are accessible and, during auditing, which rows trigger audit events to be recorded. When you use the Virtual Private Database (VPD) option, users' queries of tables are always limited regardless of the method by which they access the tables.

You can enable column masking for sensitive data, and you can encrypt the data as it is stored on disk. See Chapter 20 for details on the implementation of VPD.

In addition to securing access to the data, you can audit activities in the database. Auditable events include privileged actions (such as creating users), changes to data structures, and access of specific rows and tables.

Programmatic Structures

Oracle supports a wide array of programmatic access methods. The SQL language, described in detail throughout this book, is key to any application development effort. Other access methods include the following:

- **PL/SQL** As described in Part IV of this book, PL/SQL is a critical component of most application implementations. You can use PL/SQL to create stored procedures and functions, and you can call your functions within queries. Procedures and functions can be collected into packages. You can also create triggers, telling the database what steps to take when different events occur within the database. Triggers may occur during database events (such as database startup), changes to structures (such as attempts to drop tables), or changes to rows. In each case, you will use PL/SQL to control the behavior of the database or application when the triggering event occurs.

- **Dynamic SQL** You can generate SQL at run time and pass it to procedures that execute it via dynamic SQL. See Chapter 36.

- **SQL*Plus**   As shown throughout this book, SQL*Plus provides a simple interface to the Oracle database. SQL*Plus can support rudimentary reporting requirements, but it is better known for its support of scripting. It provides a consistent interface for retrieving data from the data dictionary and creating database objects.

- **Java and JDBC**   As shown in Part VI of this book, Oracle's support for Java and JDBC allows you to use Java in place of PL/SQL for many operations. You can even write Java-based stored procedures. Oracle's Java offerings have been expanded and enhanced with each new release.

- **XML**   As described in Chapter 52, you can use Oracle's XML interfaces and XML types to support inserting and retrieving data via XML.

- **Object-oriented SQL and PL/SQL**   You can use Oracle to create and access object-oriented structures, including user-defined datatypes, methods, large objects (LOBs), object tables, and nested tables. See Part V.

- **Data Pump**   Data Pump Import and Data Pump Export, both introduced in Oracle Database 10*g*, greatly enhance the manageability and performance of the earlier Import and Export utilities. You can use Data Pump to extract data quickly and move it to different databases while altering the schema and changing the rows. Enhancements since Oracle Database 10*g* make it even easier to transport schemas, tablespaces, and even entire databases from one database to another, even if the destination database is on a different operating system and hardware platform. See Chapter 24 for details on the use of Data Pump.

- **SQL*Loader**   You can use SQL*Loader to quickly load flat files into Oracle tables. A single flat file can be loaded into multiple tables during the same load, and loads can be parallelized. See Chapter 23.

- **External programs and procedures**   You can embed SQL within external programs, or you can create procedural libraries that are later linked to Oracle. See Chapter 35.

- **UTL_MAIL**   A package introduced in Oracle Database 10*g*, UTL_MAIL allows a PL/SQL application developer to send e-mails without having to know how to use the underlying SMTP protocol stack.

Choosing Architectures and Options

Oracle provides a full array of tools for developing applications based on Oracle Database 12*c*. Many of the features introduced with Oracle Database 12*c* will be available to you regardless of the application architecture you select.

If you have previously implemented applications in earlier versions of Oracle, you should review your database to identify areas where new features will benefit your application. For example, if you have previously implemented materialized views, you may be able to take advantage of new features that expand the possibilities for incremental ("fast") refreshes of the materialized views. Oracle provides a set of procedures that help you manage your materialized view refresh schedule. For example, you can execute a procedure that will generate a description of your refresh possibilities and the configuration issues (if any) that prevent you from using the fastest options possible. You can use another Oracle-provided procedure to generate recommendations for tuning materialized view structures based on a provided set of sample queries.

Some of the new features may contain small changes that can have a dramatic impact on your application or your coding approach. For example, you can use the change replay features to capture commands executed on one database and replay them on another. Some of the significant new and enhanced features of Oracle Database 12c include "invisible" indexes, multiple index types on the same set of table columns, simplified table maintenance, enhanced native support for left outer joins, and editioned objects. You should evaluate your previous architecture decisions in light of the new features available.

In the next several chapters, you will learn how to install Oracle Database 12c and how to upgrade to Oracle Database 12c from prior releases. Following those chapters, you will see an overview of application planning, followed by many chapters on the use of SQL, PL/SQL, Java, object-oriented features, and XML to help you get the most out of your Oracle database. Your application architecture may change over time as the business process changes. During those changes, you should be sure to review the latest features to determine how your application can best exploit them for functionality and performance.

CHAPTER
2

Installing Oracle Database 12c and Creating a Database

A s Oracle's installation software becomes easier to use with each release, it is very tempting to unzip the six or seven downloaded zip files and start the installation right away. Although this is fine if you're going to experiment with some new database features, much more planning is required to perform a successful installation without having to rework or even reinstall Oracle a month from now. Although the complete details of an Oracle Database 12*c* installation are beyond the scope of this book, you will see the basics of an Oracle install using the Oracle Database Installer or the Grid Infrastructure Installer, both initiated by the **runInstaller** command in the database or grid installation directories, respectively. Grid Infrastructure installation is required if you want to use Automatic Storage Management (ASM) or if you are installing a Real Application Cluster (RAC) database. In any case, a thorough review of the installation guide for your specific platform is key to a successful Oracle database deployment.

NOTE
Although this chapter is intended for beginning database administrators, the planning process should include end users, application developers, and system administrators, so the workload and space requirements will be as accurate as possible.

The following issues should be addressed or resolved before you start the installation:

■ Decide on the local database name and which domain will contain this database.

■ For the first project to use the database, estimate the number of tables and indexes as well as their size to plan for disk space estimates beyond what is required for the Oracle SYSTEM tablespace and the associated Oracle software and tools.

■ Plan the locations of the physical datafiles on the server's disk to maximize performance and recoverability. In general, the more physical disks, the better. If a RAID or a shared storage area will be used for the datafiles, consider Oracle Managed Files (OMF) to manage the placement of the datafiles. You can use Automatic Storage Management (ASM) to simplify your storage management. See Chapter 51 for details on ASM.

■ Review and understand the basic initialization parameters. These parameters are identified by a value of TRUE in the ISBASIC column of the dynamic performance view V$PARAMETER.

■ Select the database character set, along with an alternate character set. Although it's easy to let the character sets default on install, you may need to consider where the database users are located and their language requirements. Character sets can be changed after installation only if the new character set is a superset of the existing character set.

■ Decide on the best default database block size. The default block size defined by DB_BLOCK_SIZE cannot be changed later without reinstalling the database. Note that Oracle can support multiple block sizes within a single database, but the SYSTEM tablespace will always have the default block size unless you reinstall. An online transaction processing (OLTP) database might rarely have a 4K or even a 2K block size, but usually 8K aligns with Oracle best practices. A decision support system (DSS) or data warehouse database will have a block size of at least 8K and as large as 32K if the circumstances warrant it.

■ Ensure that you're storing non-SYSTEM user objects in non-SYSTEM tablespaces. Make sure that all nonadministrative users are assigned a non-SYSTEM tablespace as their default tablespace. This setting should be the default in Oracle Database 11*g* and 12*c*.

- Use Automatic Undo Management (AUM) to ease administration of transaction undo information. This setting defaults to AUTO in Oracle Database 11*g* and 12*c*.

- Plan a backup and recovery strategy. Decide how the database needs to be backed up and how often. Plan to use more than one method to back up the database.

Familiarity with a couple of key websites is a must. Oracle Technology Network (OTN), at www.oracle.com/technetwork, has a wealth of information, including white papers, free tools, sample code, and the online version of *Oracle Magazine*. There is no charge for using OTN, other than registering on the site. You can download the latest version of the Oracle software from the OTN site.

Purchasing a license for Oracle database software is a good start, but an Oracle support contract may be the key to a successful installation and deployment. Using Oracle's support site (https://support.oracle.com) means you might never have to leave the friendly confines of your web browser to keep your database up and running. Through Oracle Support, you can submit a support request, search through other support requests, download patches, download white papers, and search the bug database.

Overview of Licensing and Installation Options

A successful initial software installation is the first step. Regardless of the software and hardware platform on which you're installing Oracle, the types of installations you can perform are the same. Although these may change with product releases, they generally include the following:

- **Enterprise Edition**   This edition is the most feature rich and extensible version of the Oracle database. It includes features such as Flashback Database and allows you to add additional pieces of licensed functionality, such as Oracle Spatial, Partitioning, Advanced Compression, Oracle OLAP, Oracle Label Security, and Oracle Data Mining.

- **Standard Edition**   This edition provides a good subset of the features of the Enterprise Edition, generally including the features that a small business will need, in addition to clustering services such as RAC.

- **Standard Edition One**   This edition provides the same features as Standard Edition without the Enterprise features such as RAC. All applications developed on this edition are fully compatible with Enterprise Edition.

- **Personal Edition**   This edition allows for development of applications that will run on either the Standard Edition, Standard Edition One, or Enterprise Edition. This edition cannot be used in a production environment.

- **Express Edition**   This edition is free and includes a preconfigured Application Express GUI. Some limitations on RAM, CPU, and disk space are imposed, but any applications developed on this edition can be deployed on any other edition with no changes.

Licensing for the Oracle database is only by named user or CPU, and there is no longer a concurrent user licensing option. Therefore, the DBA should use the initialization parameter LICENSE_MAX_USERS to specify the maximum number of users that can be created in the database. In addition, the Oracle Management Server (the backend for an Oracle Enterprise Manager, or OEM, client) can be installed during a server- or client-side installation.

Installing the Oracle Software

The process of installing Oracle on a Windows or Linux server is similar, other than the executable you use to launch the installer. In either case, you want to install Grid Infrastructure first so you can support RAC and ASM for an enterprise environment.

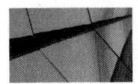

NOTE
*For Unix environments, you will need to set a proper value for the DISPLAY environment variable and run **xhost +** in your terminal session prior to starting the installation via the **runInstaller** script.*

Installing the Grid Infrastructure

The Grid Infrastructure installation begins with an option to connect to Oracle Support to get any software updates not included with the installation files. Figure 2-1 shows the option to register this installation with Oracle and download any available updates.

![Oracle Grid Infrastructure Setup screen - Step 1 of 10, Download Software Updates]

FIGURE 2-1. *Grid Infrastructure initial screen*

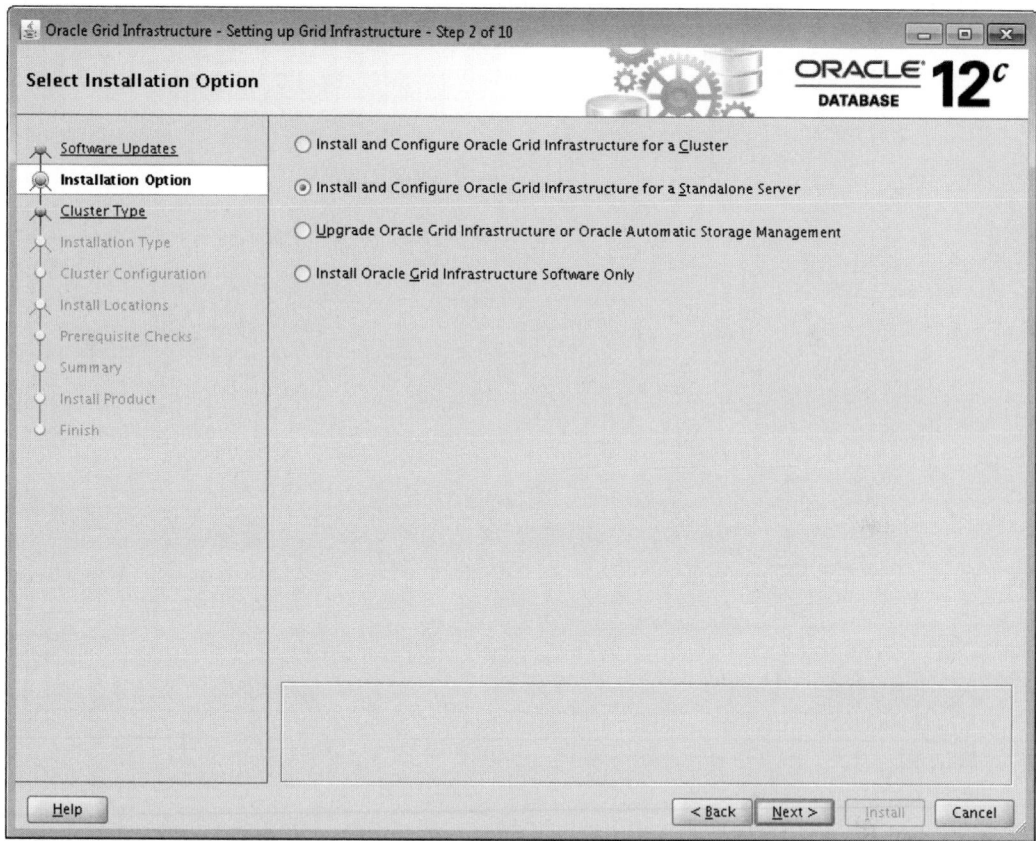

FIGURE 2-2.   *Grid Infrastructure installation options*

The next page gives you the option to configure a standalone server or to just install the software. In Figure 2-2, the installation will include ASM storage but will not share the storage in a clustered environment.

The next page gives you the language options. Then comes the storage option page: in Figure 2-3, you create an ASM disk group (see Chapter 51) to store the datafiles, control files, and undo tablespace and redo log files.

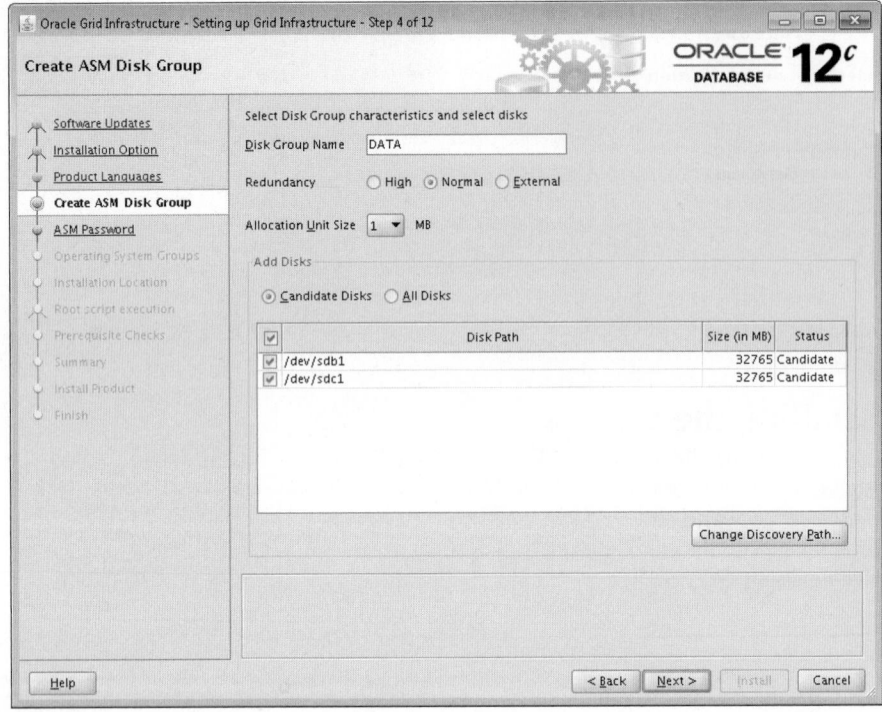

FIGURE 2-3. *Grid Infrastructure storage options*

After all of the configuration options have been selected, Grid Infrastructure is installed. At completion, the background services required to support Grid-enabled databases are started:

```
. . .
Now product-specific root actions will be performed.

Using configuration parameter file:
/u01/app/oracle/product/12.1.0/grid/crs/install/crsconfig_params

LOCAL ADD MODE

Creating OCR keys for user 'oracle', privgrp 'oinstall'..

Operation successful.

LOCAL ONLY MODE

Successfully accumulated necessary OCR keys.

Creating OCR keys for user 'root', privgrp 'root'..

Operation successful.
```

```
CRS-4664: Node oel58 successfully pinned.

2012/05/06 14:48:07 CLSRSC-330: Adding Clusterware
   entries to file '/etc/inittab'

oel58      2012/05/06 14:48:36
  /u01/app/oracle/product/12.1.0/grid/cdata/oel58/backup_20120506_144836.olr
2012/05/06 14:48:36 CLSRSC-327: Successfully configured

   Oracle Grid Infrastructure for a Standalone Server

[root@oel58 dev]#
```

Grid Infrastructure is now running, making storage available to any database installed on that server.

Installing the Database

The Database installation process starts much the same as the Grid Infrastructure process. The initial installation pages prompt you for your Oracle Support account (which is highly recommended) to provide security and other updates via Oracle Support. For a production database, you'll specify a Server Class installation, as you can see in Figure 2-4. This installation option provides you with more flexibility in configuring a database that will run in an enterprise environment.

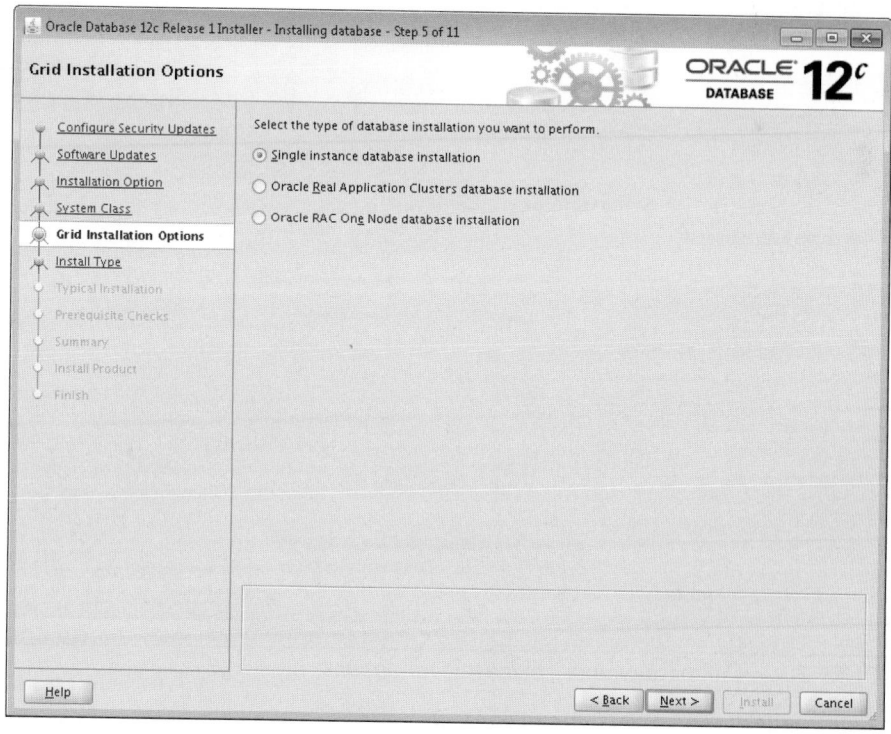

FIGURE 2-4.   *Database Server Class option*

On a subsequent page, you'll specify what version you're installing that coincides with the license you purchased: Enterprise Edition, Standard Edition, Standard Edition One, or other options. Subsequent pages prompt you for the destination of the executable files, the type of database, and the name of the database. You configure the amount of memory and the memory management scheme for the database in Figure 2-5.

It is strongly recommended that you create the sample schemas in Figure 2-5. Creating the starter database is a good way to make sure the server environment is set up correctly, as well as to review any new features of Oracle Database 12c. The starter database may also be a good candidate as a repository for Recovery Manager (RMAN).

In Figure 2-6, you specify the location of database storage, which in this case is the ASM disk group you created in the Grid Infrastructure Installation process. You may use multiple disk groups within a single database instance to ease management, improve manageability, or segregate database backups for recovery purposes.

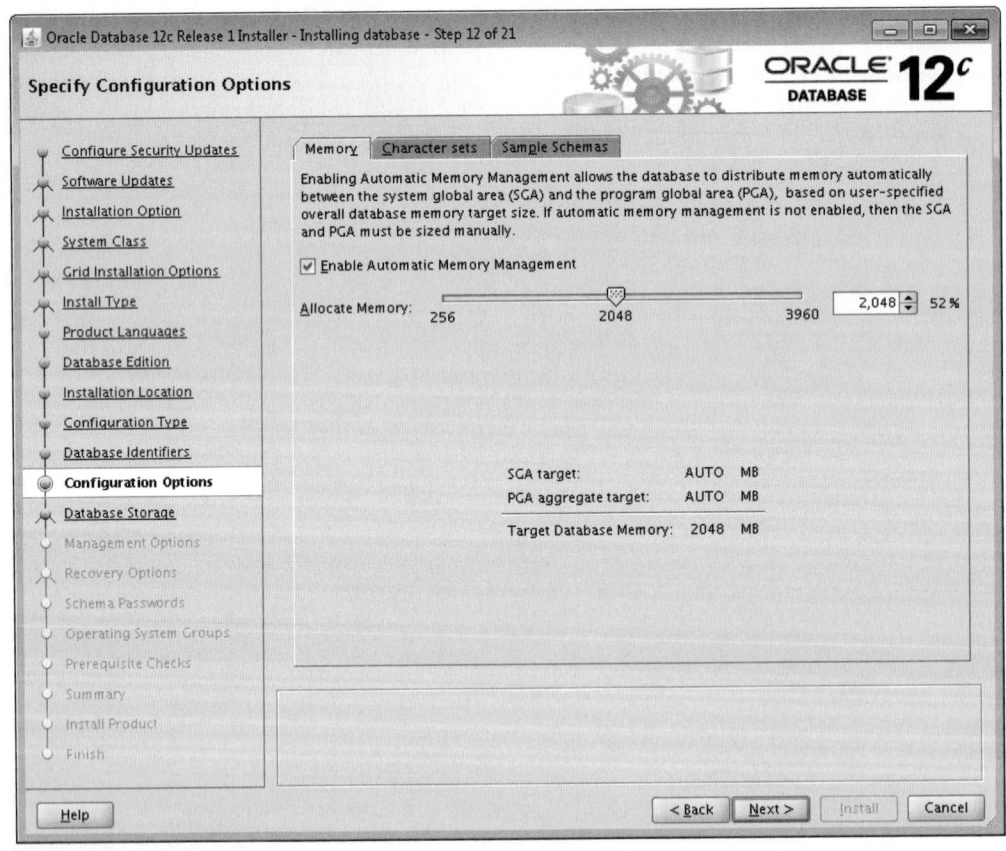

FIGURE 2-5.   *Database memory management options*

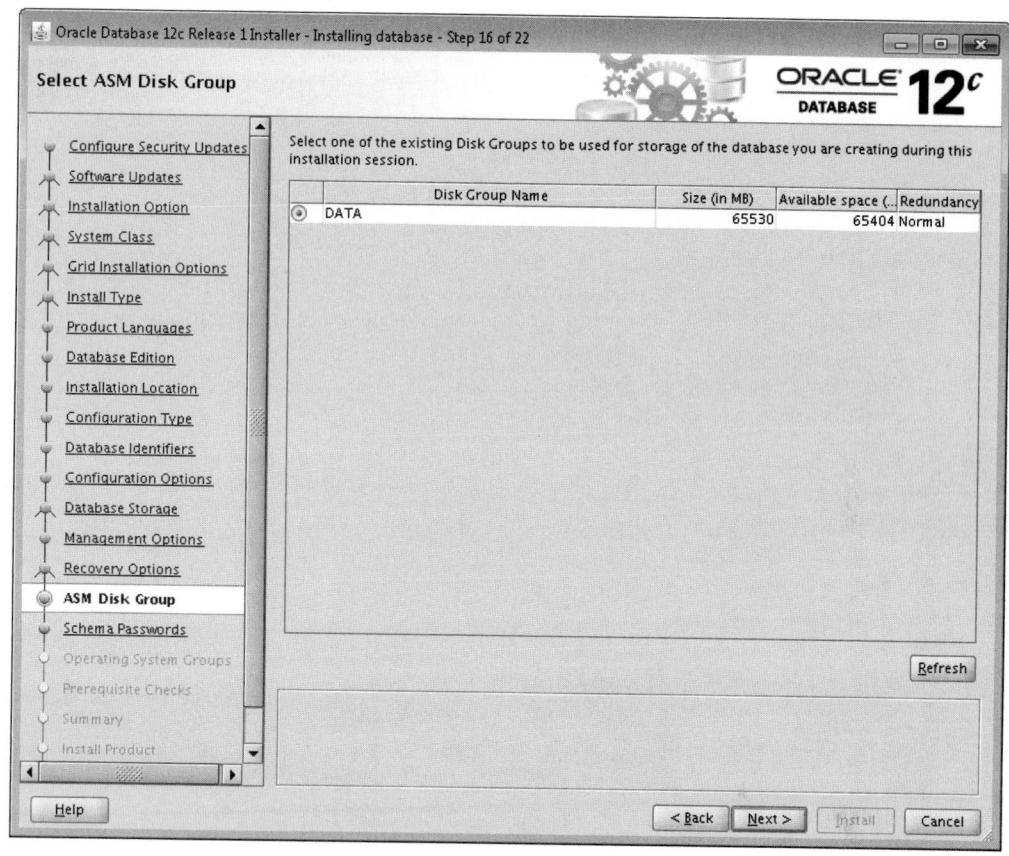

FIGURE 2-6.   *Database storage options*

After specifying additional security and management options, the database installation proceeds as shown in Figure 2-7 and is then available for use.

If you need to relaunch the database installation process (for example, to create another database on the same server), you can use the Database Configuration Assistant (**dbca**) at the Unix prompt or from the Configuration and Migration tools menu in Windows. Optionally, you can execute the CREATE DATABASE command to create a new database. The syntax for the CREATE DATABASE command is provided in the Alphabetical Reference section of this book.

FIGURE 2-7. *Database installation progress*

CHAPTER
3

Upgrading to Oracle Database 12c

I f you have previously installed an earlier version of the Oracle database server, you can upgrade your database to Oracle Database 12c. Multiple upgrade paths are supported; the right choice for you will depend on factors such as your current Oracle software version and your database size. In this chapter, you will see descriptions of these methods along with guidelines for their use.

If you have not used a version of Oracle prior to Oracle Database 12c, you can skip this chapter for now. However, you will likely need to refer to it when you upgrade from Oracle Database 12c to a later version or when you migrate data from a different database into your database.

Prior to beginning the upgrade, you should read the Oracle Database 12c Installation Guide for your operating system. A successful installation is dependent on a properly configured environment—including operating system patch levels and system parameter settings. Plan to get the installation and upgrade right the first time, rather than attempting to restart a partially successful installation. Even though the Oracle Universal Installer (OUI) checks for minimum values of system parameter settings, you should adjust those parameters upward to match your expected database load and growth.

This chapter assumes that your installation of the Oracle Database 12c software (see Chapter 2) completed successfully and that you have an Oracle database that uses an earlier version of the Oracle software. To upgrade that database, you have four options:

- *Use the Database Upgrade Assistant to guide and perform the upgrade in place.* The old database will become an Oracle 12c database during this process.

- *Perform a manual upgrade of the database.* The old database will become an Oracle 12c database during this process.

- *Use the Data Pump Export and Data Pump Import utilities to move data from an earlier version of Oracle to the Oracle 12c database.* Two separate databases will be used—the old database as the source for the export and the new database as the target for the import.

- *Copy data from an earlier version of Oracle to an Oracle 12c database.* Two separate databases will be used—the old database as the source for the copy and the new database as the target for the copy.

Upgrading a database in place—via either the Database Upgrade Assistant or the manual upgrade path—is called a *direct upgrade*. In the examples in this chapter, both the Oracle Grid Infrastructure and Database installation will be upgraded in place.

NOTE
Direct upgrade of the database to version 12c is only supported if your present database is release 10.2.0.5, 11.1.0.7, or release 11.2.0.2 or later. If you are using any other release, you will have to first upgrade the database to one of those releases, or you will need to use a different upgrade option.

Because a direct upgrade does not involve creating a second database for the one being upgraded, it may complete faster and require less disk space than an indirect upgrade.

NOTE
Plan your upgrades carefully; you may need to allow time for multiple incremental upgrades (such as from 9.2.0.3 to 10.2.0.5) prior to upgrading to Oracle Database 12c.

Choosing an Upgrade Method

As described in the previous section, two direct upgrade paths and two indirect upgrade paths are available. This section contains a more detailed description of the options, followed by usage descriptions.

In general, the direct upgrade paths perform the upgrade the fastest because they upgrade the database in place. The other methods involve copying data, either to a Data Pump Export dump file on the file system or across a database link. For very large databases, the time required to re-create the database completely via the indirect methods may exclude them as viable options.

The first direct method relies on the *Database Upgrade Assistant (DBUA)*. DBUA is an interactive tool that guides you through the upgrade process. DBUA evaluates your present database configuration and recommends modifications that can be implemented during the upgrade process. These recommendations may include the sizing of files and the specifications for the new SYSAUX tablespace (if upgrading from a pre-Oracle 10g database). After you accept the recommendations, DBUA performs the upgrade in the background while displaying a progress panel. DBUA is similar in approach to the Database Configuration Assistant (DBCA). As discussed in Chapter 2, DBCA is a graphical interface to the steps and parameters required to make the upgrade a success.

The second direct method is called a *manual upgrade*. Whereas DBUA runs scripts in the background, the manual upgrade path involves database administrators running the scripts themselves. The manual upgrade approach gives you a great deal of control, but it also adds to the level of risk in the upgrade because you must perform the steps in the proper order.

You can use Data Pump Export and Data Pump Import as an indirect method for upgrading a database. In this method, you export the data from the old version of the database and then import it into a database that uses the new version of the Oracle software. This process may require disk space for multiple copies of the data—in the source database, in the dump file, and in the target database. In exchange for these costs, this method gives you great flexibility in choosing which data to migrate. You can select specific tablespaces, schemas, tables, and rows to be exported.

In the Data Pump Export/Import method, the original database is not upgraded; its data is extracted and moved, and the database can then either be deleted or be run in parallel with the new database until testing of the new database has been completed. In the process of performing the export/import, you are selecting and reinserting each row of the database. If the database is very large, the import process may take a long time, impacting your ability to provide the upgraded database to your users in a timely fashion. See Chapters 24 and 51 for details on the Data Pump Export and Import utilities.

In the data-copying method, you issue a series of CREATE TABLE AS SELECT or INSERT AS SELECT commands that cross database links (see Chapter 25) to retrieve the source data. The tables are created in the Oracle 12c database based on queries of data from a separate source database. This method allows you to bring over data incrementally and to limit the rows and columns migrated. However, you need to be careful that the copied data maintains all the necessary relationships among tables. As with the Data Pump Export/Import method, this method may require a significant amount of time for large databases.

Selecting the proper upgrade method requires you to evaluate the technical expertise of your team, the data that is to be migrated, and the allowable downtime for the database during the migration. In general, DBUA is the method preferred for very large databases, whereas smaller databases may use an indirect method.

Before Upgrading

Prior to beginning the migration, you should back up the existing database and database software. If the migration fails for some reason and you are unable to revert the database or software to its earlier version, you will be able to restore your backup and re-create your database.

You should develop and test scripts that will allow you to evaluate the performance and functionality of the database following the upgrade. This evaluation may include the performance of specific database operations or the overall performance of the database under a significant user load.

Prior to executing the upgrade process on a production database, you should attempt the upgrade on a test database so that any missing components (such as operating system patches) can be identified and the time required for the upgrade can be measured.

Prior to performing a direct upgrade, you should analyze the data dictionary tables. During the upgrade process to Oracle Database 12c, the data dictionary will be analyzed if it has not been analyzed already, so performing this step in advance will aid the performance of the upgrade.

Upgrading the Grid Infrastructure and Database

With each successive release of Oracle Grid Infrastructure and Database software, the installation and upgrade steps become easier and easier. You can have both Oracle Grid Infrastructure and Oracle Database up and running when you start the upgrade process. You can even continue to use a previous version of the database with the 12c version of the Grid Infrastructure if you cannot perform both parts of the upgrade in the same time period.

The following two sections describe in-place upgrades of both Grid Infrastructure and Database using the Oracle Universal Installer (OUI) in the installation media for each product. You launch the Installer from the command line as follows after setting up your DISPLAY environment variable if required (see Chapter 2):

```
[oracle@lap01 grid]$ ./runInstaller &
[1] 13489
Starting Oracle Universal Installer...
Checking Temp space: must be greater than 120 MB.   Actual 3689 MB    Passed
Checking swap space: must be greater than 150 MB.   Actual 3688 MB    Passed
Checking monitor: must be configured to display at least 256 colors.
      Actual 16777216     Passed
Preparing to launch Oracle Universal Installer from
   /tmp/OraInstall2012-12-06_08-30-12PM. Please wait ...
```

Grid Infrastructure Upgrade

After starting the Grid Infrastructure Installer with the **runInstaller** command, you are presented with the Installer options shown in Figure 3-1. In this chapter, we're performing an in-place upgrade.

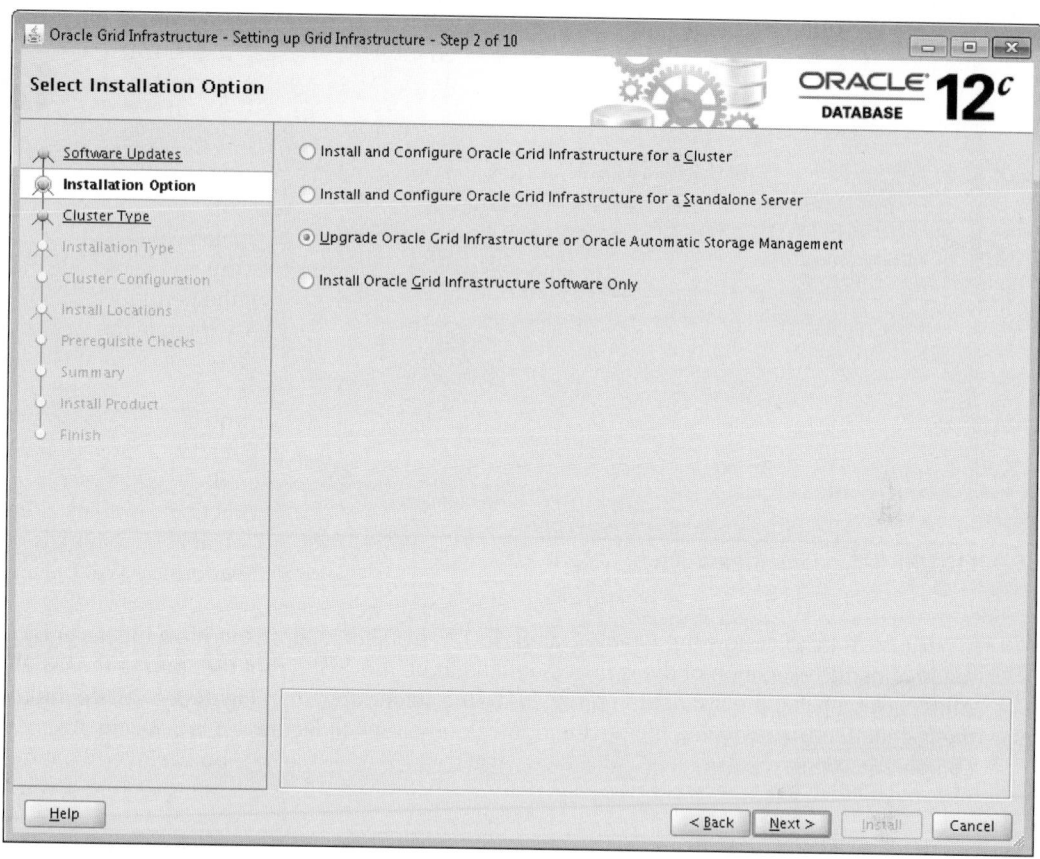

FIGURE 3-1.   *Grid Infrastructure setup screen—upgrade*

In Figure 3-2, you specify the Linux OS groups whose users will have privileges to manage the disk storage and disk groups for the Grid Infrastructure instance. Since Oracle Database 11*g*, privileges are more finely grained to permit separation of duties for different job roles in an Oracle environment. For example, the SYSASM privilege was added in Oracle Database 11*g* to give specific privileges for a DBA to manage only the ASM instance. Future versions of Grid Infrastructure will not permit SYSDBA privileges for an ASM instance.

Even though this installation is "in place," that does not necessarily mean the software must be placed in the same directory. In fact, leaving the previous version of the software in its original location is probably a good idea in case you have to downgrade. Oracle recommends that the installation files reside under the existing ORACLE_BASE, but it is not required. In Figure 3-3, the new Grid Infrastructure files will reside in **/u02** instead of **/u01**.

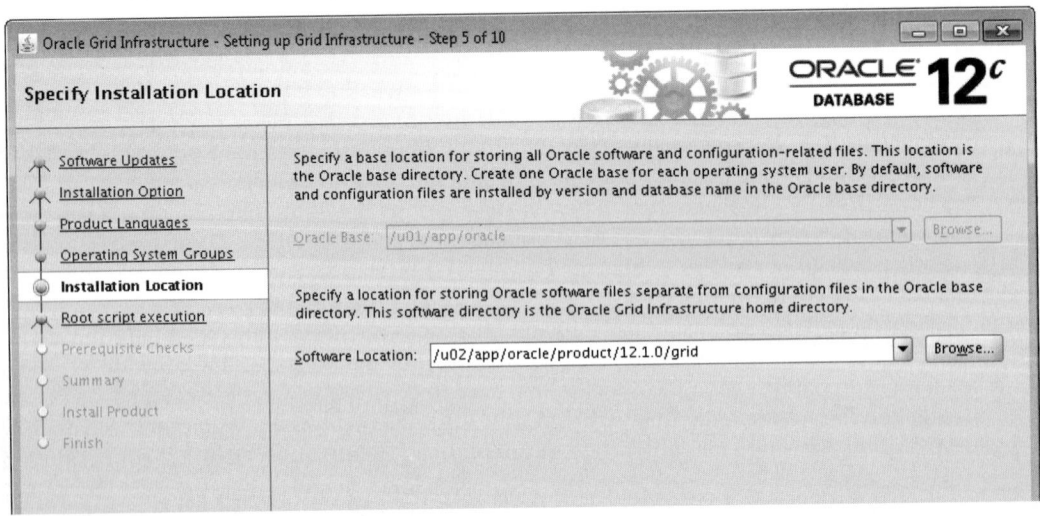

FIGURE 3-2. *Grid Infrastructure OS groups*

Figure 3-4 shows how the Oracle Database 12c Installer makes your life a bit easier by automating the execution of the scripts that need to be run as the root user during the installation. After clicking Next, the installation proceeds to the screen shown in Figure 3-5. Since the rest of the installation is automated, the next window you will see in Figure 3-6 is a successful completion status.

FIGURE 3-3 *Destination for installation files*

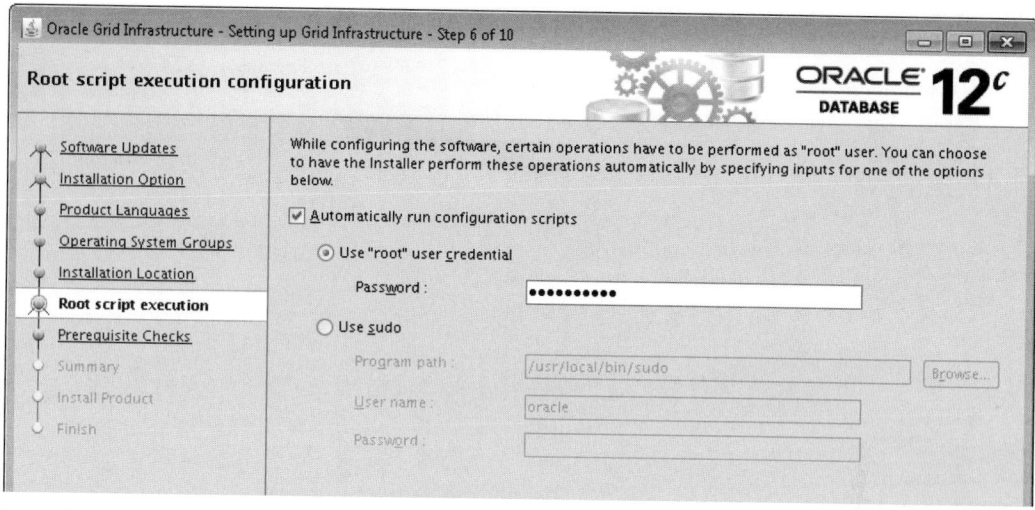

FIGURE 3-4.   *Credentials for root user*

FIGURE 3-5.   *Grid Infrastructure installation progress*

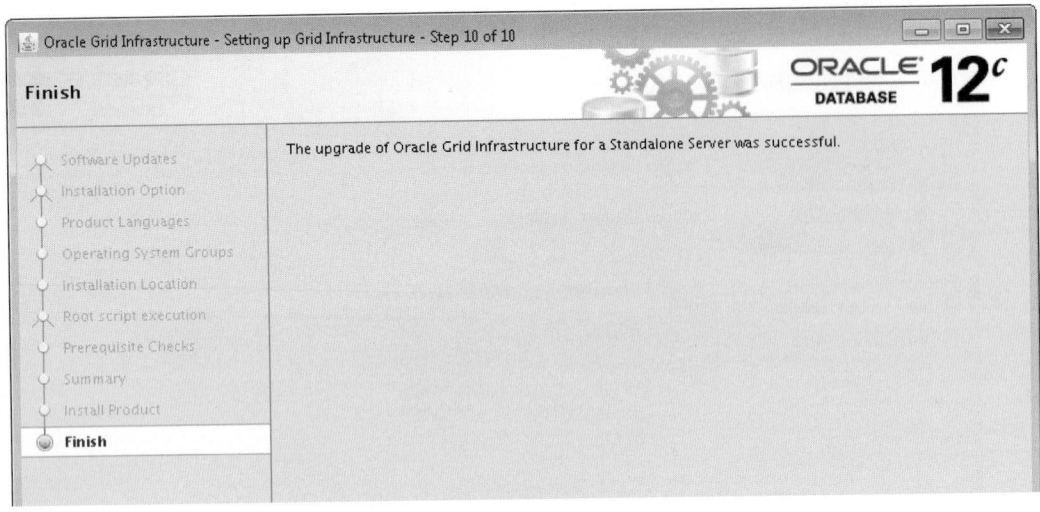

FIGURE 3-6.   *Grid Infrastructure installation complete*

The ASM instance is restarted and is running Oracle Database 12c. All databases using this instance are still on their previous version, and can be used as-is until they are upgraded as well. The database upgrade is in the next section.

Database Upgrade

You should use the Pre-Upgrade Information Tool to analyze the database prior to upgrading. This tool is provided in a SQL script that is installed with the Oracle Database 12c software; you need to run it against the database to be upgraded. The file, named **utlu121i.sql**, is located in the **/rdbms/admin** subdirectory under the Oracle Database 12c software home directory. You should run that file in the database to be upgraded as a SYSDBA-privileged user, spooling the results to a log file. The results will show you any potential problems that should be addressed prior to the upgrade.

If there are no issues to resolve prior to the upgrade, shut down the database and perform an offline backup before continuing with the upgrade process.

The database upgrade itself takes a bit more work, but is still extremely automated. Most of your time will be spent waiting for the Installer to upgrade the database in place. Figure 3-7 is where you select the Upgrade option.

Depending on what features your Oracle software is licensed for, you'll choose the database edition you want to install in Figure 3-8.

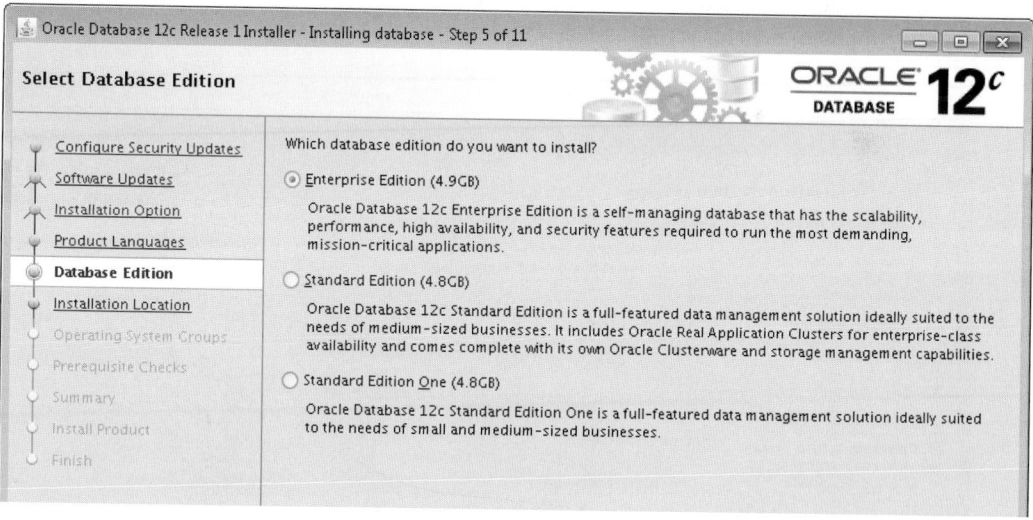

FIGURE 3-7. *Selecting the database Upgrade option*

FIGURE 3-8. *Selecting the database edition to install*

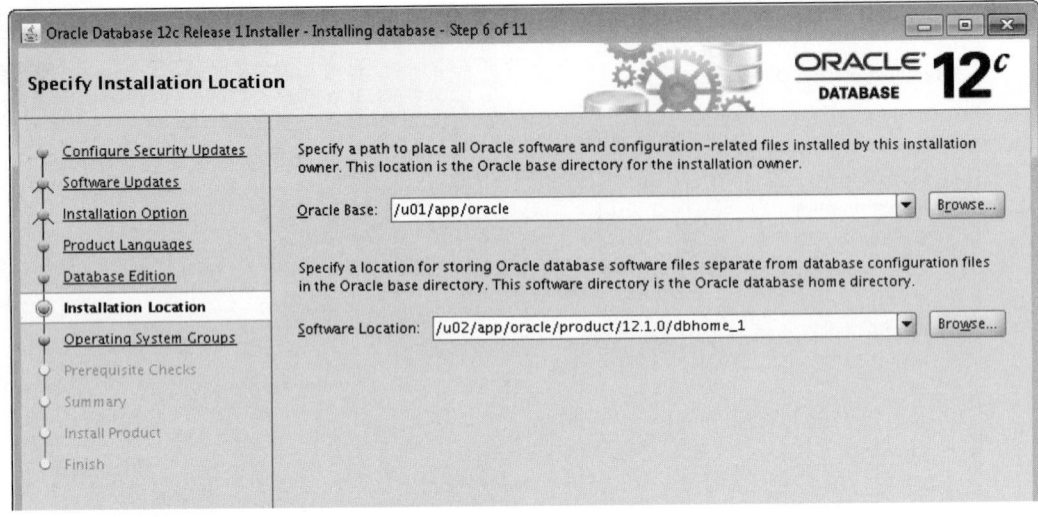

FIGURE 3-9. *Software installation directory location*

In Figure 3-9, you specify the directory for the new database software much as you did previously when you updated the Grid Infrastructure software.

The options for separation of duties in an Oracle shop are evident in Figure 3-10. For a smaller shop, you may have your Oracle DBAs in the same OS group.

FIGURE 3-10. *Linux groups for DBA roles and privileges*

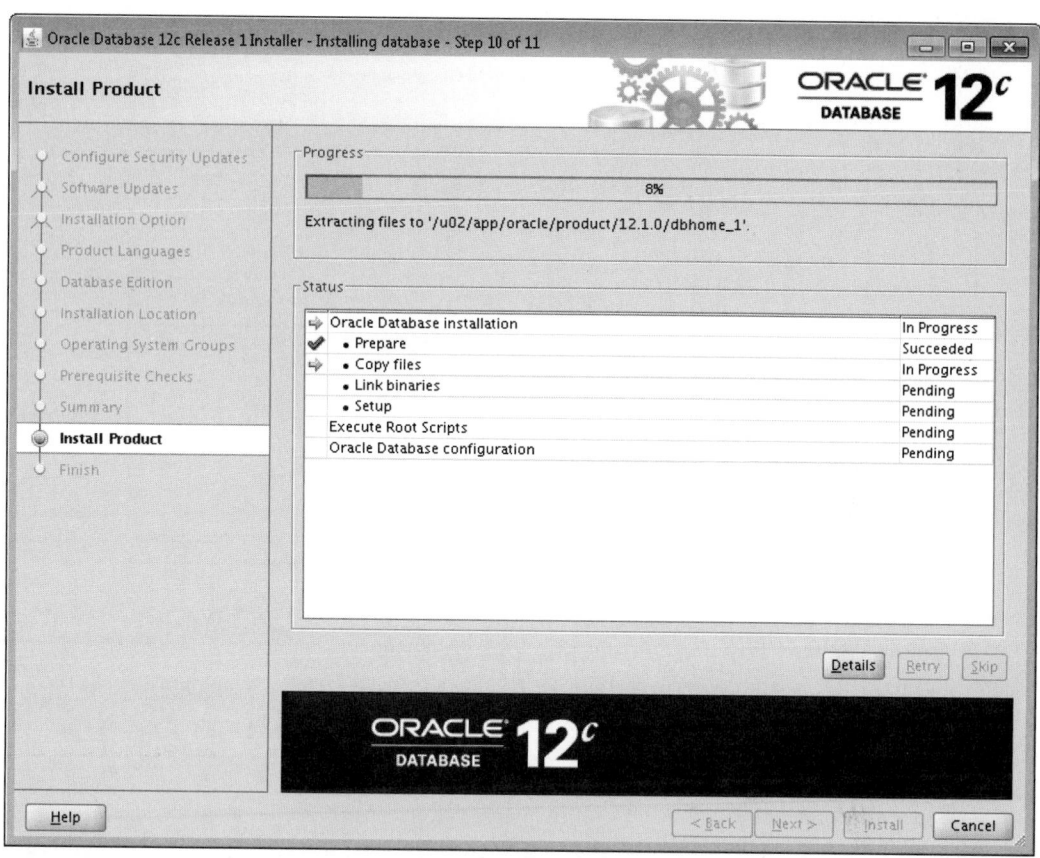

FIGURE 3-11.   *Database software installation progress*

The installation of the new database software proceeds in Figure 3-11. Figure 3-12 is a pop-up window that specifies any additional scripts that must be run as the root user since the installation itself was likely initiated by the **oracle** user.

After the script(s) in Figure 3-12 have completed successfully, Figure 3-13 shows the remaining database software installation tasks.

FIGURE 3-12. *Scripts to run as root user*

FIGURE 3-13. *Finishing the database software installation*

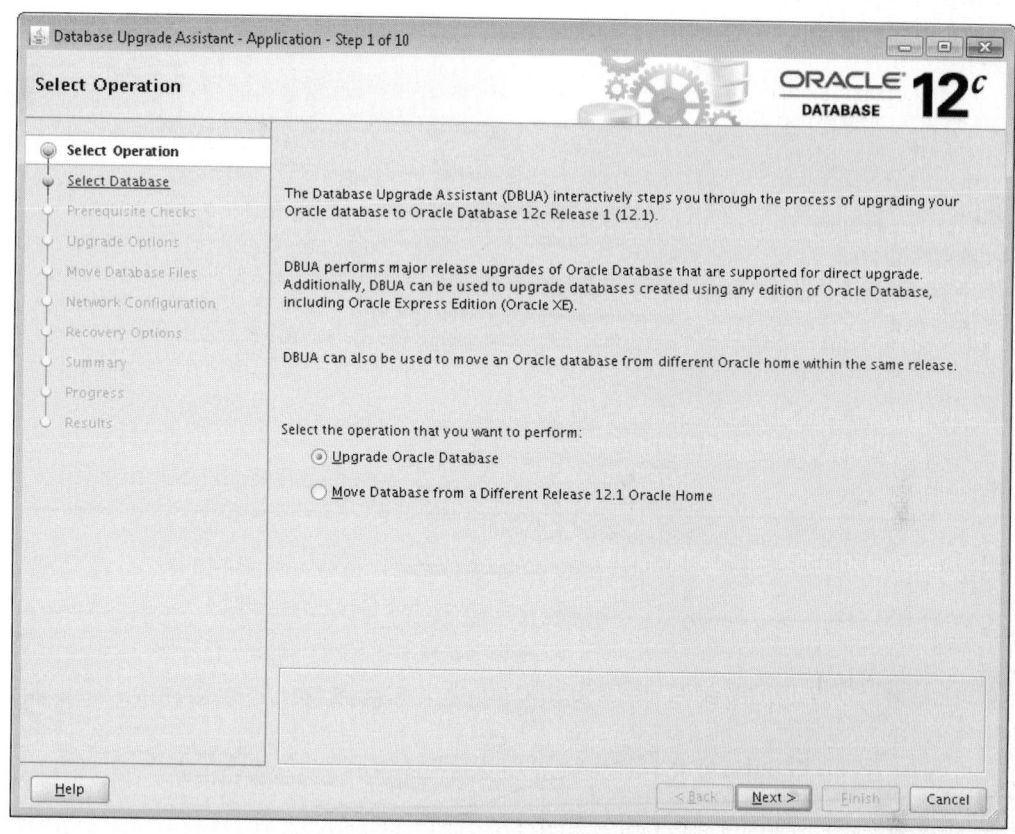

FIGURE 3-14.   *Database Upgrade Assistant (DBUA)*

Now that the upgraded database software is in place, the database itself must be upgraded, so the Database Upgrade Assistant (DBUA) is automatically launched next. The first DBUA window is shown in Figure 3-14.

For one reason or another, you may not want to upgrade all databases on a server at once. Therefore, the DBUA window in Figure 3-15 lets you choose which database to upgrade next.

In Figure 3-16, you see the results of the Pre-Upgrade Utility Checks. Most, if not all of these warnings, should be addressed before proceeding with the upgrade.

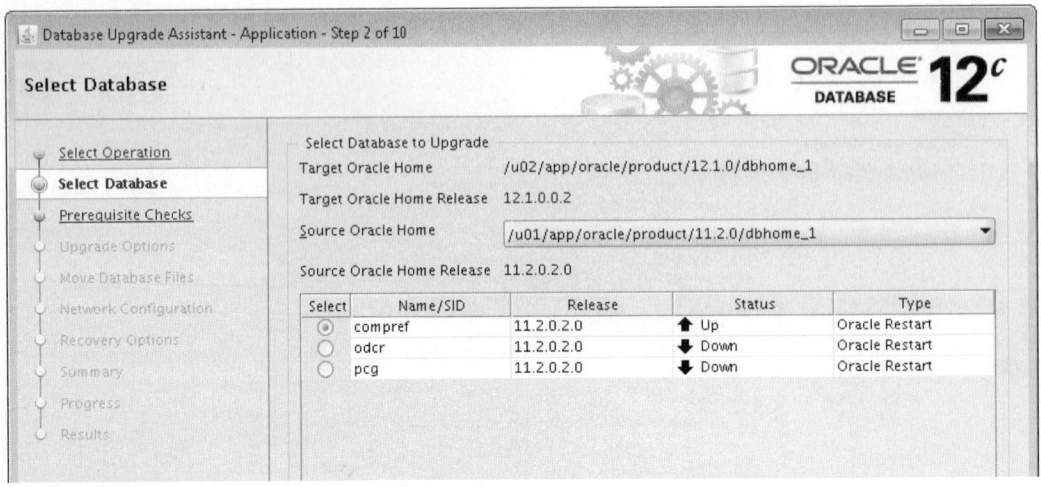

FIGURE 3-15. *Choosing a database to upgrade*

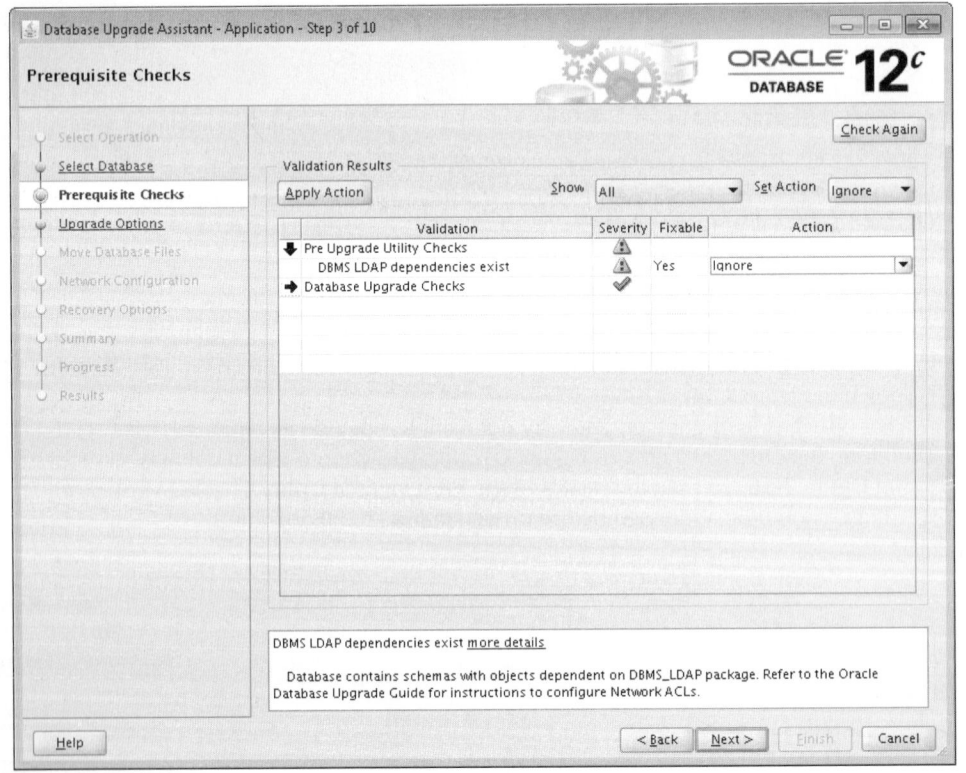

FIGURE 3-16. *Database upgrade checks*

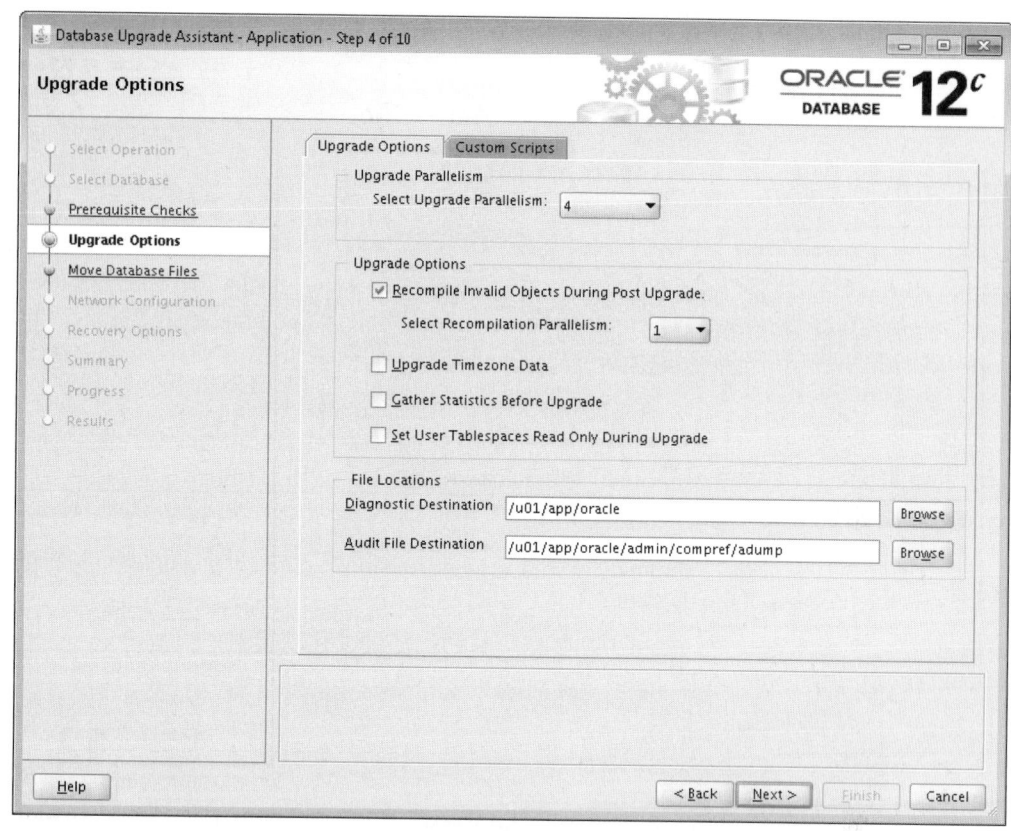

FIGURE 3-17.   *Upgrade options*

Figure 3-17 shows various tasks that you may or may not want to automate or include as part of the upgrade process. If your server has multiple CPUs and I/O channels, you can leverage them during the upgrade to reduce the time needed to complete the upgrade dramatically. If you are not doing an in-place upgrade, Figure 3-18 gives you the opportunity to specify a new destination.

FIGURE 3-18.   *File migration options*

Figure 3-19 provides a summary of what is going to happen during the upgrade, and Figure 3-20 shows the progress of the upgrade.

FIGURE 3-19.   *Upgrade options summary*

FIGURE 3-20.   *Upgrade progress*

If the upgrade is successful, you'll see the window in Figure 3-21. When you click the Close button, DBUA is complete and you'll return to the Installer where, as shown in Figure 3-22, you are notified that the entire database upgrade process is complete.

Once both the Grid Infrastructure and Oracle Database software have been upgraded, your **/etc/oratab** file will reflect the new home directories for the upgraded Grid and Database software:

```
+ASM:/u02/app/oracle/product/12.1.0/grid:N:        # line added by Agent
odcr:/u01/app/oracle/product/11.2.0/dbhome_1:N:    # line added by Agent
pcg:/u01/app/oracle/product/11.2.0/dbhome_1:N:     # line added by Agent
compref:/u02/app/oracle/product/12.1.0/dbhome_1:N: # line added by Agent
```

After Upgrading

Following the upgrade, you should double-check the configuration and parameter files related to the database, particularly if the instance name changed in the migration process. These files include

- The **tnsnames.ora** file
- The **listener.ora** file
- Programs that may have hard-coded instance names in them

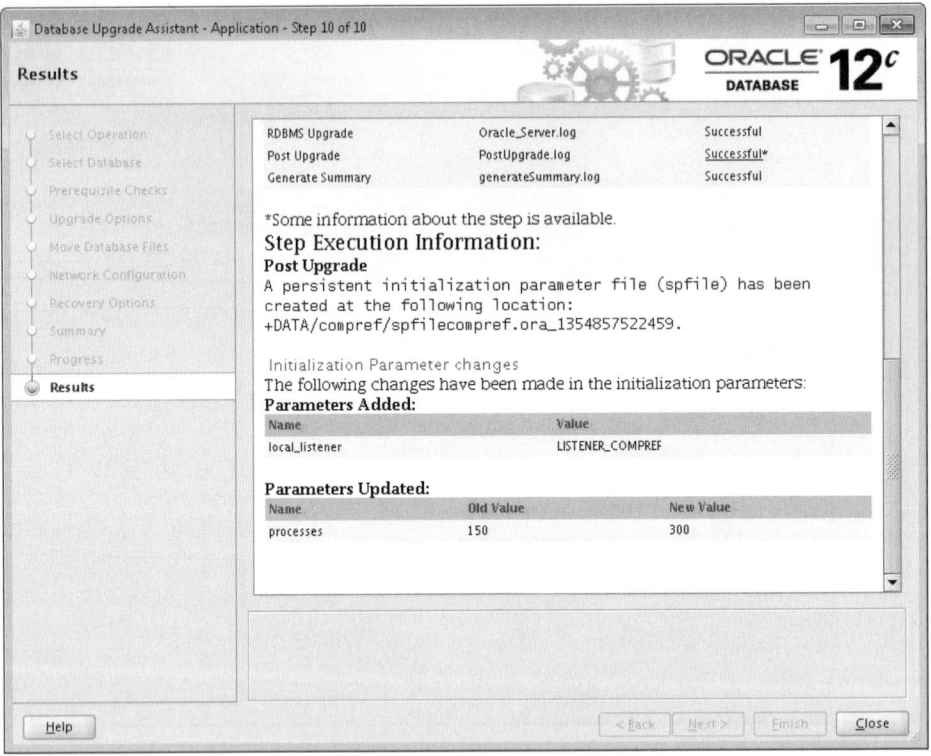

FIGURE 3-21. *DBUA summary*

FIGURE 3-22. *Installer summary*

NOTE
*You will need to manually reload the modified **listener.ora** file if you are not using DBUA to perform the upgrade.*

Additional post-upgrade steps should include verifying the values for all environment variables (such as **ORACLE_HOME** and **PATH**) and upgrading the Recovery Manager (RMAN) recovery catalog.

You should review your database initialization parameters to make sure deprecated and obsolete parameters have been removed; these should have been identified during the migration process. Be sure to recompile any programs you have written that rely on the database software libraries.

Once the upgrade has completed, perform the functional and performance tests identified before the upgrade began. If there are issues with the database functionality, attempt to identify any parameter settings or missing objects that may be impacting the test results. You may want to leave the COMPATIBLE initialization parameter at the previous release until you've confirmed that the upgrade was successful. In addition, you may want to leave the OPTIMIZER_FEATURES_ ENABLE parameter at the previous release number until you can ensure that execution plans are stable and have not regressed. As an added measure of caution, and if you have an extra server or enough disk space and CPU resources on the current server, you can also clone the existing database and upgrade the clone to the current release. In this way, you can more thoroughly test the new optimizer and other features before committing to the new release.

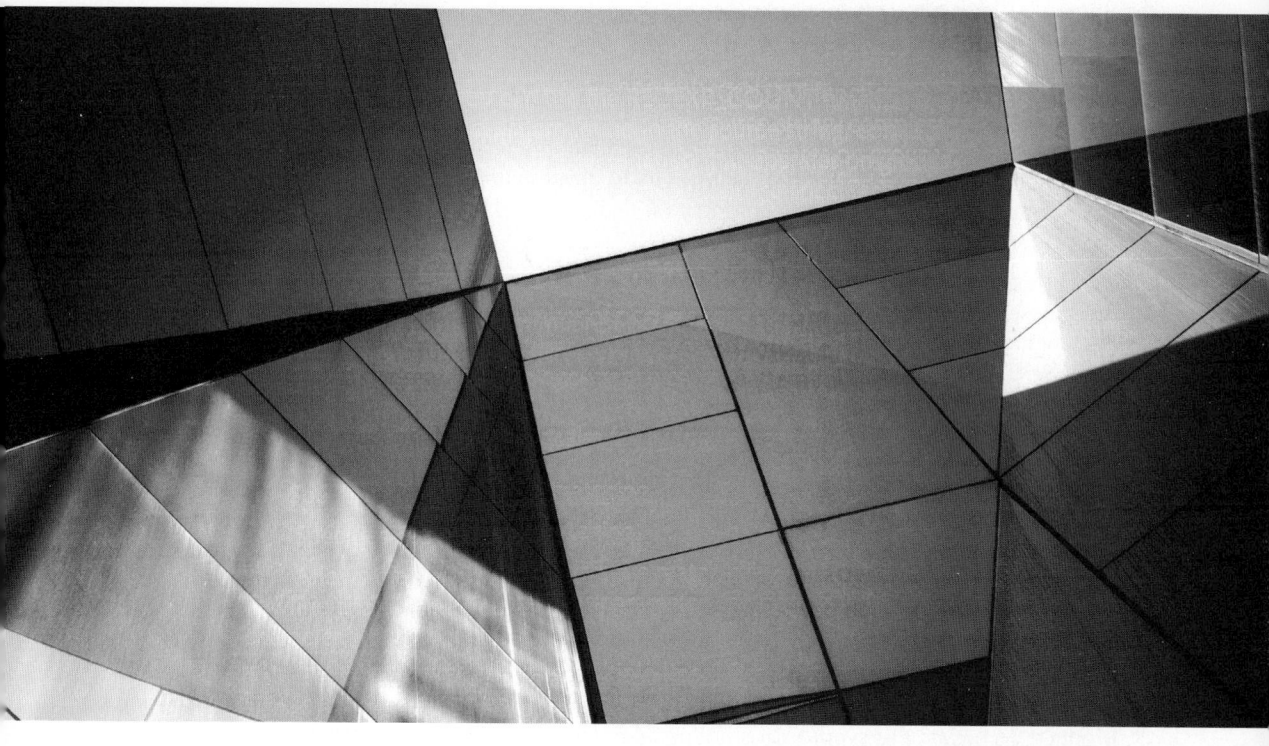

CHAPTER
4

Planning Oracle
Applications—Approaches,
Risks, and Standards

F or an Oracle application to be built and used rapidly and effectively, users and developers must share a common language and a deep and common understanding of both the business application and the Oracle tools. In the preceding chapters, you have seen the overall Oracle product descriptions and the installation/upgrade steps involved. Now that the software is installed, you have the opportunity to develop applications that build on the shared business and data understanding among your technical and business area staff members.

Historically, the systems analyst studied the business requirements and built an application to meet those needs. The user was involved only in describing the business and, perhaps, in reviewing the functionality of the application after it was completed.

With the new tools and approaches available, and especially with Oracle, applications can be built that more closely match the needs and work habits of the business—but only if a common understanding and language exists. This book is aimed specifically at fostering this understanding and providing the means for both user and developer to exploit Oracle Database 12*c*'s full potential. The end user knows details about the business that the developer does not comprehend. The developer understands internal functions and features of Oracle and about the computer environment that are too technically complex for the end user. But these areas of exclusive expertise are minor compared with what both end users and developers can share in using Oracle. There is a remarkable opportunity here.

It is no secret that "business" people and "systems" or "technical" people have been in conflict for decades. Reasons for this include differences in knowledge, culture, professional interests, and goals, and the alienation that simple physical separation between groups can often produce. To be fair, this syndrome is not peculiar to data processing. The same thing occurs among people in accounting, personnel, or senior management, as members of each group gather apart from other groups on a separate floor or in a separate building or city. Relations between the individuals from one group and another become formalized, strained, and abnormal. Artificial barriers and procedures that stem from this isolationism become established, and these also contribute to the syndrome.

This is all very well, you say, and may be interesting to sociologists, but what does it have to do with Oracle?

Because Oracle isn't cloaked in arcane language that only systems professionals can comprehend, it fundamentally changes the nature of the relationship between business and systems people. Anybody can understand it. Anybody can use it. Information that previously was trapped in computer systems until someone in systems created a new report and released it now is accessible, instantly, to a business person, simply by typing an English-like query. This changes the rules of the game.

Where Oracle is used, it has radically improved the understanding between the two camps, has increased their knowledge of one another, and has even begun to normalize relations between them. This has also produced superior applications and end results.

Since its first release, Oracle has been based on the easily understood relational model (explained shortly), so non-programmers can readily understand what Oracle does and how it does it. This makes it approachable and unimposing.

Some individuals neither accept nor understand this yet, nor do they realize just how vital it is that the dated and artificial barriers between "users" and "systems" continue to fall. But the advent of cooperative development will profoundly affect applications and their usefulness.

However, many application developers have fallen into an easy trap with Oracle: carrying forward unhelpful methods from previous-generation system designs. There is a lot to unlearn. Many of the techniques (and limitations) that were indispensable to a previous generation of systems are not only unnecessary in designing applications with Oracle, but also positively counterproductive. In the process of explaining Oracle, the burden of these old habits and approaches must be lifted. Refreshing new possibilities are available.

Throughout this book, the intent will be to explain Oracle in a way that is clear and simple, in terms that both users and developers can understand and share. Outdated or inappropriate design and management techniques will be exposed and replaced.

The Cooperative Approach

The Oracle database is an *object-relational database management system*. A relational database is an extremely simple way of thinking about and managing the data used in a business. It is nothing more than a collection of tables of data. We all encounter tables every day—weather reports, stock charts, sports scores, and so on. These are all tables, with column headings and rows of information simply presented. Even so, the relational approach can be sophisticated and powerful enough for even the most complex of businesses. An object-relational database supports all the features of a relational database while also supporting object-oriented concepts and features. You can use Oracle as a relational database management system (RDBMS) or take advantage of its object-oriented features—or a mixture of both where appropriate.

Unfortunately, the very people who can benefit most from a relational database—the business users—generally understand it the least. Application developers, who must build systems that these users need to do their jobs, often find relational concepts difficult to explain in simple terms. A common language is needed to make this cooperative approach work.

The first two parts of this book explain, in readily understandable terms, just what a relational database is and how to use it effectively in business. It may seem that this discussion is for the benefit of "users" only. An experienced relational application designer may be inclined to skip these early chapters and simply use the book as a primary source Oracle reference. Although much of this material may seem like elementary review, it is an opportunity for an application designer to acquire a clear, consistent, and workable terminology with which to talk to users about their needs and how these needs might be quickly met. If you are an application designer, this discussion may also help you unlearn some unnecessary and probably unconscious design habits. Many of these habits will be uncovered in the course of introducing the relational approach. It is important to realize that even Oracle's power can be diminished considerably by design methods appropriate only to nonrelational development.

If you are an end user, understanding the basic ideas behind object-relational databases will help you express your needs cogently to application developers and comprehend how those needs can be met. An average person working in a business role can go from beginner to expert in short order. With Oracle, you have the power to get and use information; you have hands-on control over reports and data; and you possess a clear-eyed understanding of what the application does and how it does it. Oracle gives you, the user, the ability to control an application or query facility expertly and *know* whether you are getting all the available flexibility and power.

You also will be able to unburden programmers of their least favorite task: writing new reports. In large organizations, as much as 95 percent of all programming backlog is composed of new report requests. Because you can write your own reports, in minutes instead of months, you will be delighted to have the responsibility.

Everyone Has "Data"

A library keeps lists of members, books, and fines. The owner of a baseball-card collection keeps track of players' names, dates, averages, and card values. In any business, certain pieces of information about customers, products, prices, financial status, and so on, must be saved. These pieces of information are called *data.*

Information philosophers like to say that data is just data until it is organized in a meaningful way, at which point it becomes "information." If this is true, then Oracle is also a means of easily turning data into information. Oracle will sort through and manipulate data to reveal pieces of knowledge—such as totals, buying trends, or other relationships—that are as yet undiscovered. You will learn how to make these discoveries. The main point here is that you have data, and you do three basic things with it: acquire it, store it, and retrieve it.

Once you've achieved the basics, you can make computations with data, move it from one place to another, or modify it. This is called *processing,* and, fundamentally, it involves the same three steps that affect how information is organized.

You could do all this with a cigar box, pencil, and paper, but as the volume of data increases, your tools tend to change. You may use a file cabinet, calculators, pencils, and paper. Although at some point, making the leap to computers makes sense, your tasks remain the same.

A *relational database management system (RDBMS)* such as Oracle gives you a way of doing these tasks in an understandable and reasonably uncomplicated way. Oracle basically does three things, as shown in Figure 4-1.

- Lets you put data into it
- Keeps the data
- Lets you get the data out and work with it

Oracle supports this in/keep/out approach and provides clever tools that allow you considerable sophistication in how the data is captured, edited, modified, and put in; how you keep it secure; and how you get it out to manipulate and report on it.

FIGURE 4-1. *Shows how simple the process is*

The Familiar Language of Oracle

The information stored in Oracle is kept in tables—much like the weather table from a daily newspaper, shown in Figure 4-2.

This table has four columns: CITY, TEMPERATURE, HUMIDITY, and CONDITION. It also has a row for each city from Athens to Sydney. Lastly, it has a table name: WEATHER.

These are the three major characteristics of most tables you see in print: *columns, rows,* and a *name*. The same is true in a relational database. Anyone can understand the words and the ideas they represent because the words used to describe the parts of a table in an Oracle database are the same words used in everyday conversation. The words have no special, unusual, or esoteric meanings. What you see is what you get.

Tables of Information

Oracle stores information in tables, an example of which is shown in Figure 4-3. Each of these tables has one or more columns. The column headings—such as CITY, TEMPERATURE, HUMIDITY, and CONDITION in Figure 4-3—describe the kind of information kept in the column. The information is stored row after row (city after city). Each unique set of data, such as the temperature, humidity, and condition for the city of Manchester, gets its own row.

Oracle avoids specialized, academic terminology in order to make the product more approachable. In research papers on relational theory, a column may be called an "attribute," a row may be called a "tuple" (rhymes with "couple"), and a table may be called an "entity." For an end user, however, these terms are confusing. More than anything, they are an unnecessary renaming of things for which there are already commonly understood names in our shared everyday language. Oracle takes advantage of this shared language, and developers can too. It is imperative to recognize the wall of mistrust and misunderstanding that the use of unnecessary technical jargon produces. Like Oracle, this book will stick with "tables," "columns," and "rows."

	WEATHER		
CITY	**TEMPERATURE**	**HUMIDITY**	**CONDITION**
Athens.......	97	89	Sunny
Chicago......	66	88	Rain
Lima.........	45	79	Rain
Manchester...	66	98	Fog
Paris........	81	62	Cloudy
Sparta.......	74	63	Cloudy
Sydney.......	69	99	Sunny

FIGURE 4-2. *A weather table from a newspaper*

Table name

A column ↓ **WEATHER**

CITY	TEMPERATURE	HUMIDITY	CONDITION	
Athens	97	89	Sunny	← A row
Chicago	66	88	Rain	
Lima	45	79	Rain	
Manchester	66	98	Fog	
Paris	81	62	Cloudy	
Sparta	74	63	Cloudy	
Sydney	69	99	Sunny	

FIGURE 4-3. *A WEATHER table from Oracle*

Structured Query Language

Oracle was the first company to release a product that used the English-based *Structured Query Language,* or *SQL*. This language allows end users to extract information themselves, without using a systems group for every little report.

Oracle's query language has structure, just as English or any other language has structure. It has rules of grammar and syntax, but they are basically the normal rules of careful English speech and can be readily understood.

SQL, pronounced either "sequel" or "S-Q-L," is an astonishingly capable tool, as you will see. Using it does not require any programming experience.

Here's an example of how you might use SQL. If someone asked you to select from the preceding WEATHER table the city where the humidity is 89, you would quickly respond "Athens." If you were asked to select cities where the temperature is 66, you would respond "Chicago and Manchester."

Oracle is able to answer these same questions nearly as easily as you are and in response to simple queries very much like the ones you were just asked. The keywords used in a query to Oracle are SELECT, FROM, WHERE, and ORDER BY. They are clues to Oracle to help it understand your request and respond with the correct answer.

A Simple Oracle Query

If Oracle had the example WEATHER table in its database, your first query (with a semicolon to tell Oracle to execute the command) would be simply this:

```
select city from weather where humidity = 89 ;
```

Oracle would respond as follows:

```
CITY
----------
Athens
```

Your second query would be this:

```
select city from weather where temperature = 66 ;
```

For this query, Oracle would respond with the following:

```
CITY
-----------
Manchester
Chicago
```

As you can see, each of these queries uses the keywords SELECT, FROM, and WHERE. What about ORDER BY? Suppose you wanted to see all the cities listed in order by temperature. You'd simply type this:

```
select city, temperature
from weather
order by temperature;
```

and Oracle would instantly respond with this:

```
CITY          TEMPERATURE
-----------   -----------
Lima                   45
Manchester             66
Chicago                66
Sydney                 69
Sparta                 74
Paris                  81
Athens                 97
```

Oracle has quickly reordered your table by temperature. (This table lists lowest temperatures first; in the next chapter, you'll learn how to specify whether you want low numbers or high numbers first.)

You can ask many other questions using Oracle's query facility, but these examples show how easy it is to obtain the information you need from an Oracle database in the form that is most useful to you. You can build complicated requests from simple pieces of information, but the method used to do this will always be understandable. For instance, you can combine the WHERE and ORDER BY keywords, both simple by themselves, to tell Oracle to select those cities where the temperature is greater than 80 and to show them in order by increasing temperature. You would type this:

```
select city, temperature from weather
where temperature > 80
order by temperature;
```

and Oracle would instantly respond with this:

```
CITY          TEMPERATURE
-----------   -----------
Paris                  81
Athens                 97
```

Or, to be even more specific, you could request cities where the temperature is greater than 80 and the humidity is less than 70:

```
select city, temperature, humidity from weather
where temperature > 80
   and humidity < 70
order by temperature ;
```

and Oracle would respond with this:

```
CITY          TEMPERATURE HUMIDITY
-----------   ----------- --------
Paris                  81       62
```

Why It Is Called "Relational"

Notice that the WEATHER table lists cities from several countries, and some countries have more than one city listed. Suppose you need to know in which country a particular city is located. You could create a separate LOCATION table of cities and their countries, as shown in Figure 4-4.

For any city in the WEATHER table, you can simply look at the LOCATION table, find the name in the CITY column, look over to the COUNTRY column in the same row, and see the country's name. (For simplicity's sake, we'll ignore the fact that there are also cities named Moscow and Paris in the United States.)

These are two completely separate and independent tables. Each contains its own information in columns and rows. The tables have one significant thing in common: the CITY column. For each city name in the WEATHER table, there is an identical city name in the LOCATION table.

For instance, what are the current temperature, humidity, and condition in an Australian city? Look at the two tables, figure it out, and then resume reading this.

How did you solve it? You found just one AUSTRALIA entry, under the COUNTRY column, in the LOCATION table. Next to it, in the CITY column of the same row, was the name of the city, SYDNEY. You took this name, SYDNEY, and then looked for it in the CITY column of the WEATHER table. When you found it, you moved across the row and found the TEMPERATURE, HUMIDITY, and CONDITION: 69, 99, and SUNNY.

LOCATION	
CITY	**COUNTRY**
----------	--------
Athens	Greece
Chicago	United States
Conakry	Guinea
Lima	Peru
Madras	India
Madrid	Spain
Manchester	England
Moscow	Russia
Paris	France
Rome	Italy
Shenyang	China
Sparta	Greece
Sydney	Australia
Tokyo	Japan

WEATHER			
CITY	**TEMPERATURE**	**HUMIDITY**	**CONDITION**
----------	-----------	--------	---------
Athens	97	89	Sunny
Chicago	66	88	Rain
Lima	45	79	Rain
Manchester	66	98	Fog
Paris	81	62	Cloudy
Sparta	74	63	Cloudy
Sydney	69	99	Sunny

FIGURE 4-4. *WEATHER and LOCATION tables*

Even though the tables are independent, you can easily see that they are related. The city name in one table is *related* to the city name in the other (see Figure 4-5). This relationship is the basis for the name *relational* database.

This is the basic idea of a relational database (sometimes called a *relational model*). Data is stored in tables. Tables have columns, rows, and names. Tables can be related to each other if each has a column with a common type of information.

That's it. It's as simple as it seems.

LOCATION

CITY	COUNTRY
Athens	Greece
Chicago	United States
Conakry	Guinea
Lima	Peru
Madras	India
Madrid	Spain
Manchester	England
Moscow	Russia
Paris	France
Rome	Italy
Shenyang	China
Sparta	Greece
Sydney	Australia
Tokyo	Japan

WEATHER

CITY	TEMPERATURE	HUMIDITY	CONDITION
Athens	97	89	Sunny
Chicago	66	88	Rain
Lima	45	79	Rain
Manchester	66	98	Fog
Paris	81	62	Cloudy
Sparta	74	63	Cloudy
Sydney	69	99	Sunny

———— Relationship ————

FIGURE 4-5. *The relationship between the WEATHER and LOCATION tables*

Some Common, Everyday Examples

Once you understand the basic idea of relational databases, you'll begin to see tables, rows, and columns everywhere. Not that you didn't see them before, but you probably didn't think about them in quite the same way. Many of the tables you are accustomed to seeing could be stored in Oracle. They could be used to answer questions quickly that would take you quite some time to answer using nearly any other method.

A typical stock market report in the paper might look like the one in Figure 4-6. This is a small portion of a dense, alphabetical listing that fills several narrow columns on several pages in a newspaper. Which stock traded the most shares? Which had the biggest percentage change in its price, either positively or negatively? The answers to these questions can be obtained through simple English queries in Oracle, which can find the answers much faster than you could by searching the columns on the newspaper page.

Figure 4-7 is an index to a newspaper. What's in section F? If you read the paper from front to back, in what order would you read the articles? The answers to these questions are obtainable via simple English queries in Oracle. You will learn how to do all these queries, and even build the tables to store the information, in the course of using this reference.

Throughout this book, the examples use data and objects encountered frequently in business and everyday life. Similar data to use for your exercises should be as easy to find as your nearest bookshelf. You will learn how to enter and retrieve data in the pages ahead, using examples based on these everyday data sources.

Company	Close Yesterday	Close Today	Shares Traded
Ad Specialty	31.75	31.75	18,333,876
Apple Cannery	33.75	36.50	25,787,229
AT Space	46.75	48.00	11,398,323
August Enterprises	15.00	15.00	12,221,711
Brandon Ellipsis	32.75	33.50	25,789,769
General Entropy	64.25	66.00	7,598,562
Geneva Rocketry	22.75	27.25	22,533,944
Hayward Antiseptic	104.25	106.00	3,358,561
IDK	95.00	95.25	9,443,523
India Cosmetics	30.75	30.75	8,134,878
Isaiah James Storage	13.25	13.75	22,112,171
KDK Airlines	80.00	85.25	7,481,566
Kentgen Biophysics	18.25	19.50	6,636,863
LaVay Cosmetics	21.50	22.00	3,341,542
Local Development	26.75	27.25	2,596,934
Maxtide	8.25	8.00	2,836,893
MBK Communications	43.25	41.00	10,022,980
Memory Graphics	15.50	14.25	4,557,992
Micro Token	77.00	76.50	25,205,667
Nancy Lee Features	13.50	14.25	14,222,692
Northern Boreal	26.75	28.00	1,348,323
Ockham Systems	21.50	22.00	7,052,990
Oscar Coal Drayage	87.00	88.50	25,798,992
Robert James Apparel	23.25	24.00	19,032,481
Soup Sensations	16.25	16.75	22,574,879
Wonder Labs	5.00	5.00	2,553,712

FIGURE 4-6.   *A stock market table*

As with any new technology or new venture, thinking through not only the benefits and opportunities that are presented, but also the costs and risks, is sensible. Combine a relational database with a series of powerful and easy-to-use tools, as Oracle does, and the possibility of being seduced into disaster by its simplicity becomes real. Add in object-oriented and web capabilities, and the dangers increase. The following sections discuss some of the dangers that both developers and users need to consider.

Feature	Section	Page
Births	F	7
Bridge	B	2
Business	E	1
Classified	F	8
Comics	C	4
Doctor's In	F	6
Editorials	A	12
Modern Life	B	1
Movies	B	4
National News	A	1
Obituaries	F	6
Sports	D	1
Television	B	7
Weather	C	2

FIGURE 4-7. *A table based on sections of a newspaper*

What Are the Risks?

The primary risk in developing relational database applications is that it *is* as easy as they say. Understanding tables, columns, and rows isn't difficult. The relationship between two tables is conceptually simple. Even *normalization,* the process of analyzing the inherent or "normal" relationships among the various elements of a company's data, is fairly easy to learn.

Unfortunately, this simplicity often produces instant "experts," full of confidence but with little experience in building real, production-quality applications. For a tiny marketing database or a home inventory application, this doesn't matter very much. The mistakes made will reveal themselves in time, the lessons will be learned, and the errors will be avoided the next time around. In an important application, however, this overconfidence is a sure formula for disaster. This lack of experience is usually behind the press's stories of major project failures.

Fourth- and fifth-generation tools seduce developers into rushing into production. Changes can be made and implemented so quickly that testing is given short shrift. The elimination of virtually all desk-checking compounds the problem. When the negative incentive (the long cycle) that encouraged desk-checking disappeared, desk-checking went with it. The attitude of many seems to be, "If the application isn't quite right, we can fix it quickly. If the data gets corrupted, we can patch it with a quick update. If it's not fast enough, we can tune it on the fly. Let's get it in ahead of schedule and show the stuff we're made of."

The testing cycle in an important Oracle project should be longer and more thorough than in a traditional project. This is true even if proper project controls are in place, and even if seasoned project managers are guiding the project, because there will be less desk-checking and an inherent overconfidence. This testing must check the correctness of data-entry screens and reports, of data loads and updates, of data integrity and concurrence, and particularly of transaction and storage volumes during peak loads.

Because it really is as easy as Oracle says, application development with Oracle's tools can be breathtakingly rapid. Web-based application development environments such as Oracle's Application Express can get you from spreadsheet to database to end user in a matter of minutes. But this automatically reduces the amount of testing done as a normal part of development, and the planned testing and quality assurance must be consciously lengthened to compensate. This need is not usually foreseen by those new to either Oracle or fourth- and fifth-generation tools, but you must budget for it in your project plan.

The Importance of the New Vision

Many of us look forward to the day when we can simply type a "natural" language query in English, and have the answer back, on our screen, in seconds.

We are closer to this goal than most of us realize. The limiting factor is no longer technology, but rather the rigor of thought in our application designs. Oracle can straightforwardly build English-based systems that are easily understood and exploited by unsophisticated users. The potential is there, already available in Oracle's database and tools, but only a few have understood and used it.

Clarity and understandability should be the hallmarks of any Oracle application. Applications can operate in English, be understood readily by end users who have no programming background, and provide information based on a simple English query.

How? First of all, a major goal of the design effort must be to make the application easy to understand and simple to use. If you err, it must always be in this direction, even if it means consuming more CPU or disk space. The limitation of this approach is that you could make an application exceptionally easy to use by creating overly complex programs that are nearly impossible to maintain or enhance. This is an equally bad mistake. All things being equal, however, an end-user orientation should never be sacrificed for clever coding.

Changing Environments

Consider that the cost to run a computer, expressed as the cost per million instructions per second (MIPS), has historically declined at the rate of 20 percent per year. Labor costs, on the other hand, have risen steadily. This means that any work that can be shifted from human laborers to machines may represent a cost savings.

Have we factored this incredible shift into our application designs? The answer is "somewhat" but terribly unevenly. The real progress has been in *environments,* such as the visionary work first done at Xerox Palo Alto Research Center (PARC), and then on the Macintosh, and now in web-based browsers and other graphical icon-based systems. These environments are much easier to learn and understand than the older, character-based environments, and people who use them can produce in minutes what previously took days. The improvement in some cases has been so huge that we've entirely lost sight of how hard some tasks used to be.

Unfortunately, this concept of an accommodating and friendly environment hasn't been grasped by many application developers. Even when they work in these environments, they continue old habits that are just no longer appropriate.

Codes, Abbreviations, and Naming Standards

The problem of old programming habits is most pronounced in codes, abbreviations, and naming standards, which are almost completely ignored when the needs of end users are considered. When these three issues are thought about at all, usually only the needs and conventions of the systems groups are considered. This may seem like a dry and uninteresting problem to be forced to think through, but it can make the difference between great success and grudging acceptance, between an order-of-magnitude leap in productivity and a marginal gain, between interested, effective users and bored, harried users who make continual demands on the developers.

Here's what happened. Business records used to be kept in ledgers and journals. Each event or transaction was written down, line by line, in English. As we developed applications, codes were added to replace data values (such as "01" for "Accounts Receivable," "02" for "Accounts Payable," and so on). Key-entry clerks would actually have to know or look up most of these codes and type them in at the appropriately labeled fields on their screens. This is an extreme example, but literally thousands of applications take exactly this approach and are every bit as difficult to learn or understand.

This problem has been most pronounced in large, conventional mainframe systems development. As relational databases are introduced into these groups, they are used simply as replacements for older input/output methods such as Virtual Storage Access Method (VSAM) and Information Management System (IMS). The power and features of the relational database are virtually wasted when used in such a fashion.

Why Are Codes Used Instead of English?

Why use codes at all? Two primary justifications are usually offered:

- A category has so many items in it that all of them can't reasonably be represented or remembered in English.
- To save space in the computer.

The second point is an anachronism. Memory and permanent storage were once so expensive and CPUs so slow (with less power than a modern hand-held calculator) that programmers had to cram every piece of information into the smallest possible space. Numbers, character for character, take half of the computer storage space of letters, and codes reduce the demands on the machine even more.

Because machines were expensive, developers had to use codes for *everything* to make *anything* work at all. It was a technical solution to an economic problem. For users, who had to learn all sorts of meaningless codes, the demands were terrible. Machines were too slow and too expensive to accommodate the humans, so the humans were trained to accommodate the machines. It was a necessary evil.

This economic justification for codes vanished years ago. Computers are now fast enough and cheap enough to accommodate the way people work and to use words that people understand. It's high time they did so. Yet, without really thinking through the justifications, developers and designers continue to use codes.

The first point—that of too many items per category—is more substantive, but much less so than it first appears. One idea is that it takes less effort (and is, therefore, less expensive) for someone to key in the numeric codes than actual text string values such as book titles. This justification is untrue in Oracle. Not only is it more costly to train people to know the correct customer, product, transaction, and other codes, and more expensive because of the cost of mistakes (which are high with code-based systems), but also using codes means not using Oracle fully; Oracle is able to take the first few characters of a title and fill in the rest of the name itself. It can do the same thing with product names, transactions (a "b" automatically fills in with "buy," an "s" with "sell"), and so on, throughout an application. It does this with very robust pattern-matching capabilities.

Internally, of course, your tables will likely use codes to enforce referential integrity and to join tables, both of which are discussed in this and subsequent chapters. The codes satisfy normalization rules and do save quite a bit of space; the codes are decoded by another table. On web forms or in applications, the end user may never see the actual codes.

The Benefit of User Feedback

There is an immediate additional benefit to using words: Key-entry errors drop almost to zero because the users get immediate feedback, in English, of the business information they're entering. Digits don't get transposed; codes don't get remembered incorrectly; and, in financial applications, money rarely is lost in accounts due to entry errors, with significant savings.

Applications also become much more comprehensible. Screens and reports are transformed from arcane arrays of numbers and codes into a readable and understandable format. The change of application design from code-oriented to English-oriented has a profound and invigorating effect on a company and its employees. For users who have been burdened by code manuals, an English-based application produces a tremendous psychological release.

How to Reduce the Confusion

Another version of the "too many items per category" justification is that the number of products, customers, or transaction types is just too great to differentiate each by name, or there are too many identical or very similar items in a category (customers named "John Smith," for instance). A category can contain too many entries to make the options easy to remember or differentiate, but more often this is evidence of an incomplete job of categorizing information: Too many dissimilar things are crammed into too broad a category. Developing an application with a strong English-based (or French, German, Spanish, and so on) orientation, as opposed to code-based, requires time spent with users and developers—taking apart the information about the business, understanding its natural relationships and categories, and then carefully constructing a database and naming scheme that simply and accurately reflect these discoveries.

There are three basic steps to doing this:

1. Normalize the data.
2. Choose English names for the tables and columns.
3. Choose English words for the data.

Each of these steps will be explained in order. The goal is to design an application in which the data is sensibly organized, is stored in tables and columns whose names are familiar to the user, and is described in familiar terms, not codes.

Normalization

Relations between countries, or between departments in a company, or between users and developers, are usually the product of particular historical circumstances, which may define current relations even though the circumstances have long since passed. The result of this can be abnormal relations, or, in current parlance, *dysfunctional* relations. History and circumstance often have the same effect on data—on how it is collected, organized, and reported. And data, too, can become abnormal and dysfunctional.

Normalization is the process of putting things right, making them normal. The origin of the term is *norma,* the Latin word for a carpenter's square that's used for ensuring a right angle. In geometry, when a line is at a right angle to another line, it is said to be "normal" to it. In a relational database, the term also has a specific mathematical meaning having to do with separating elements of data (such as names, addresses, or skills) into *affinity groups* and defining the normal, or "right," relationships between them.

The basic concepts of normalization are being introduced here so users can contribute to the design of an application they will be using or better understand one that has already been built. It would be a mistake, however, to think that this process is really only applicable to designing a database or a computer application. Normalization results in deep insights into the information used in a business and how the various elements of that information are related to each other. This will prove to be educational in areas apart from databases and computers.

The Logical Model

An early step in the analysis process is the building of a *logical model,* which is simply a normalized diagram of the data used by the business. Knowing why and how the data gets broken apart and segregated is essential to understanding the model, and the model is essential to building an application that will support the business for a long time, without requiring extraordinary support.

Normalization is usually discussed in terms of *form:* First, Second, and Third Normal Form are the most common terms, with Third representing the most highly normalized state. There are Fourth and Fifth normalization levels defined as well, but they are beyond the scope of this discussion.

Consider a bookshelf: For each book, you can store information about it—the title, publisher, authors, and multiple categories or descriptive terms for the book. Assume that this book-level data becomes the table design in Oracle. The table might be called BOOKSHELF, and the columns might be TITLE, PUBLISHER, AUTHOR1, AUTHOR2, AUTHOR3, and CATEGORY1, CATEGORY2, CATEGORY3. The users of this table already have a problem: In the BOOKSHELF table, users are limited to listing just three authors or categories for a single book.

What happens when the list of acceptable categories changes? Someone has to go through every row in the BOOKSHELF table and correct all the old values. And what if one of the authors changes his or her name? Again, all the related records must be changed. What will you do when a fourth author contributes to a book?

These are not really computer or technical issues, even though they became apparent because you were designing a database. These are much more basic issues about how to sensibly and logically organize the information of a business. These are the issues that normalization addresses. Normalization is done with a step-by-step reorganization of the elements of the data into affinity groups, by eliminating dysfunctional relationships and by ensuring normal relationships.

Normalizing the Data

Step one of the reorganization is to put the data into First Normal Form. You do this by moving data into separate tables, where the data in each table is of a similar type, and giving each table a *primary key*—a unique label or identifier. This eliminates repeating groups of data, such as the authors on the bookshelf.

Instead of having only three authors allowed per book, each author's data is placed in a separate table, with a row per name and description. Doing this eliminates the need for a variable number of authors in the BOOKSHELF table and is a better design than limiting the BOOKSHELF table to just three authors.

Next, you define the primary key to each table: What will uniquely identify and allow you to extract one row of information? For simplicity's sake, assume the titles and authors' names are unique, so AUTHOR_NAME is the primary key to the AUTHOR table.

You now have split BOOKSHELF into two tables: AUTHOR, with columns AUTHOR_NAME (the primary key) and COMMENTS, and BOOKSHELF, with a primary key of TITLE, and with columns PUBLISHER, CATEGORY1, CATEGORY2, CATEGORY3, RATING, and RATING_ DESCRIPTION. A third table, BOOKSHELF_AUTHOR, provides the associations: Multiple authors can be listed for a single book and an author can write multiple books—known as a *many-to-many* relationship. Figure 4-8 shows these relationships and primary keys.

The next step in the normalization process, Second Normal Form, entails taking out data that's only dependent on a part of the key. If there are attributes that do not depend on the entire key, those attributes should be moved to a new table. In this case, RATING_DESCRIPTION is not really dependent on TITLE—it's based on the RATING column value, so it should be moved to a separate table.

The final step, Third Normal Form, means getting rid of anything in the tables that doesn't depend solely on the primary key. In this example, the categories are interrelated; you would not list a title as both Fiction and Nonfiction, and you would have different subcategories under the Adult category than you would have under the Children category. Category information is, therefore, moved to a separate table. Figure 4-9 shows the tables in Third Normal Form.

Anytime the data is in Third Normal Form, it is already automatically in Second and First Normal Form. The whole process can, therefore, actually be accomplished less tediously than by going from form to form. Simply arrange the data so the columns in each table, other than the primary key, are dependent only on the *whole primary key*. Third Normal Form is sometimes described as "the key, the whole key, and nothing but the key."

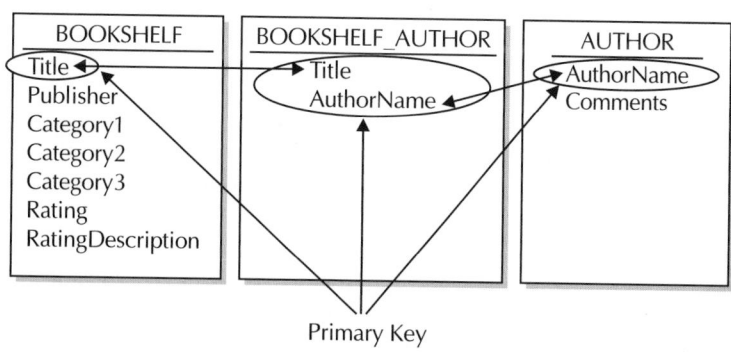

FIGURE 4-8.   *The BOOKSHELF, AUTHOR, and BOOKSHELF_AUTHOR tables*

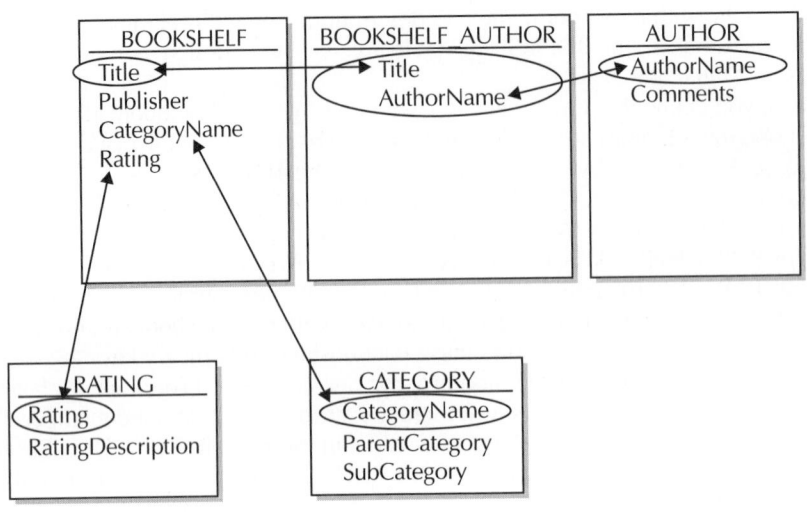

FIGURE 4-9. *BOOKSHELF and related tables*

Navigating Through the Data

The BOOKSHELF database is now in Third Normal Form. Figure 4-10 shows a sample of what these tables might contain. It's easy to see how these tables are related. You navigate from one to the other to pull out information on a particular author, based on the keys to each table. The primary key in each table is able to uniquely identify a single row. Choose Stephen Jay Gould, for instance, and you can readily discover his record in the AUTHOR table, because AUTHOR_NAME is the primary key.

Look up Harper Lee in the AUTHOR_NAME column of the BOOKSHELF_AUTHOR table and you'll see that she has published one novel, whose title is *To Kill a Mockingbird*. You can then check the PUBLISHER, CATEGORY, and RATING for that book in the BOOKSHELF table. You can check the RATING table for a description of the rating.

When you looked up *To Kill a Mockingbird* in the BOOKSHELF table, you were searching by the primary key for the table. To find the author of that book, you could reverse your earlier search path, looking through BOOKSHELF_AUTHOR for the records that have that value in the TITLE column—the column TITLE is a foreign key in the BOOKSHELF_AUTHOR table. When the primary key for BOOKSHELF appears in another table, as it does in the BOOKSHELF_AUTHOR table, it is called a *foreign key* to that table.

These tables also show real-world characteristics: There are ratings and categories that are not yet used by books on the bookshelf. Because the data is organized logically, you can keep a record of potential categories, ratings, and authors even if none of the current books use those values.

This is a sensible and logical way to organize information, even if the "tables" are written in a ledger book or on scraps of paper kept in cigar boxes. Of course, there is still some work to do to · turn this into a real database. For instance, AUTHOR_NAME probably ought to be broken into FIRST_NAME and LAST_NAME, and you might want to find a way to show which author is the primary author, or if one is an editor rather than an author.

```
AUTHOR
AUTHOR_NAME                   COMMENTS
--------------------          -------------------------------------------
Dietrich Bonhoeffer          German theologian, killed in a war camp
Robert Bretall               Kierkegaard anthologist
Alexandra Day                Author of picture books for children
Stephen Jay Gould            Science columnist, Harvard professor
Soren Kierkegaard            Danish philosopher and theologian
Harper Lee                   American novelist, published only one novel
Lucy Maud Montgomery         Canadian novelist
John Allen Paulos            Mathematics professor
J. Rodale                    Organic gardening expert
```

```
RATING
RATING        RATING_DESCRIPTION
----------    -----------------
1             Entertainment
2             Background information
3             Recommended
4             Strongly recommended
5             Required reading
```

```
CATEGORY
CATEGORY_NAME                 PARENT_CATEGORY      SUBCATEGORY
--------------                ---------------      -----------
ADULTREF                      ADULT                REFERENCE
ADULTFIC                      ADULT                FICTION
ADULTNF                       ADULT                NONFICTION
CHILDRENPIC                   CHILDREN             PICTURE BOOK
CHILDRENFIC                   CHILDREN             FICTION
CHILDRENNF                    CHILDREN             NONFICTION
```

FIGURE 4-10. *Sample data from the BOOKSHELF tables*

BOOKSHELF_AUTHOR TITLE	AUTHOR_NAME
To Kill a Mockingbird	Harper Lee
Wonderful Life	Stephen Jay Gould
Innumeracy	John Allen Paulos
Kierkegaard Anthology	Robert Bretall
Kierkegaard Anthology	Soren Kierkegaard
Anne of Green Gables	Lucy Maud Montgomery
Good Dog, Carl	Alexandra Day
Letters and Papers From Prison	Dietrich Bonhoeffer

BOOKSHELF TITLE	PUBLISHER	CATEGORY_NAME	RATING
To Kill a Mockingbird	Harpercollins	ADULTFIC	5
Wonderful Life	W.W. Norton & Co.	ADULTNF	5
Innumeracy	Vintage Books	ADULTNF	4
Kierkegaard Anthology	Princeton Univ Pr	ADULTREF	3
Anne of Green Gables	Grammercy	CHILDRENFIC	3
Good Dog, Carl	Little Simon	CHILDRENPIC	1
Letters and Papers From Prison	Scribner	ADULTNF	4

FIGURE 4-10. *Sample data from the BOOKSHELF tables* (continued)

This whole process is called *normalization*. It really isn't any trickier than this. Although some other issues are involved in a good design, the basics of analyzing the "normal" relationships among the various elements of data are just as simple and straightforward as I've explained. It makes sense regardless of whether a relational database or a computer is involved at all.

One caution needs to be raised, however. Normalization is a part of the process of analysis. It is not design. Design of a database application includes many other considerations, and it is a fundamental mistake to believe that the normalized tables of the logical model are the "design" for the actual database. This fundamental confusion of analysis and design contributes to the stories in the press about the failure of major relational applications. These issues are addressed for developers more fully later in this chapter.

English Names for Tables and Columns

Once the relationships between the various elements of the data in an application are understood and the data elements are segregated appropriately, considerable thought must be devoted to choosing names for the tables and columns into which the data will be placed. This is an area given too little attention, even by those who should know better. Table and column names are often developed without consulting end users and without rigorous review. Both of these failings have serious consequences when it comes to actually using an application.

For example, consider the tables shown in Figure 4-10. The table and column names are virtually all self-explanatory. An end user, even one new to relational ideas and SQL, would have little difficulty understanding or even replicating a query such as this:

```
select title, publisher
from bookshelf
order by publisher;
```

Users understand this because the words are all familiar. There are no obscure or ill-defined terms. When tables with many more columns in them must be defined, naming the columns can be more difficult, but a few consistently enforced rules will help immensely. Consider some of the difficulties commonly caused by a lack of naming conventions. What if you had chosen these names instead?

```
BOOKSHELF        B_A         AUTHS           CATEGORIES
-------------    --------    ------------    ---------------
title            title       anam            cat
pub              anam        comms           p_cat
cat                                          s_cat
rat
```

The naming techniques in this table, as bizarre as they look, are unfortunately very common. They represent tables and columns named by following the conventions (and lack of conventions) used by several well-known vendors and developers.

Here are a few of the more obvious difficulties in the list of names:

- *Abbreviations are used without good reason.* This makes remembering the "spelling" of a table or column name virtually impossible. The names may as well be codes because the users will have to look them up.

- *Abbreviations are inconsistent.*

- *The purpose or meaning of a column or table is not apparent from the name.* In addition to abbreviations making the spelling of names difficult to remember, they obscure the nature of the data that the column or table contains. What is P_CAT? COMMS?

- *Underscores are used inconsistently.* Sometimes they are used to separate words in a name, but other times they are not. How will anyone remember which name does or doesn't have an underscore?

- *Use of plurals is inconsistent.* Is it CATEGORY or CATEGORIES? COMM or COMMS? Standard design practice dictates that table and column names should be singular.

- *Rules apparently used have immediate limitations.* If the first letter of the table name is to be used for a name column, as in ANAM for a table whose table name starts with *A*, what happens when a second table beginning with the letter *A* becomes necessary? Does the name column in that table also get called ANAM? If so, why isn't the column in both simply called NAME?

These are only a few of the most obvious difficulties. Users subjected to poor naming of tables and columns will not be able to simply type English queries. The queries won't have the intuitive and familiar "feel" that the BOOKSHELF table query has, and this affects the acceptance and usefulness of the application significantly.

Programmers used to be required to create names that were a maximum of six to eight characters in length. As a result, names unavoidably were confused mixes of letters, numbers, and cryptic abbreviations. Like so many other restrictions forced on users by older technology, this restriction is just no longer applicable. Oracle allows table and column names up to 30 characters long, giving designers plenty of room to create full, unambiguous, and descriptive names.

The difficulties outlined here imply solutions, such as avoiding abbreviations and plurals, and either eliminating underscores or using them consistently. These quick rules of thumb will go a long way toward solving the naming confusion so prevalent today. At the same time, naming conventions need to be simple, easily understood, and easily remembered. In a sense, what is called for is a normalization of names. In much the same way that data is analyzed logically, segregated by purpose, and thereby normalized, the same sort of logical attention needs to be given to naming standards. The job of building an application is improperly done without it.

English Words for the Data

Having raised the important issue of naming conventions for tables and columns, the next step is to look at the data itself. After all, when the data from the tables is printed on a report, how self-evident the data is determines how understandable the report is. In the BOOKSHELF example, RATING is a code value, and CATEGORY is a concatenation of multiple values. Is this an improvement? If you asked another person about a book, would you want to hear that it was rated a 4 in AdultNF? Why should a machine be permitted to be less clear?

Additionally, keeping the information in English makes writing and understanding queries much simpler. The query should be as English-like as possible:

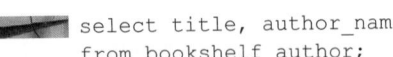

```
select title, author_name
from bookshelf_author;
```

Capitalization in Names and Data

Oracle makes it slightly easier to remember table and column names by ignoring whether you type in capital letters, small letters, or a mixture of the two. It stores table and column names in its internal data dictionary in uppercase. When you type a query, it instantly converts the table and column names to uppercase, and then checks for them in the dictionary. Some other relational systems are case sensitive. If users type a column name as **Ability**, but the database thinks it is "ability" or "ABILITY" (depending on what it was told when the table was created), it will not understand the query.

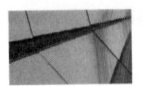

NOTE
You can force Oracle to create tables and columns with mixed-case names, but doing so will make querying and working with the data difficult. Use the default uppercase behavior.

The ability to create case-sensitive table names is promoted as a benefit because it allows programmers to create many tables with, for instance, similar names. They can make a worker table, a Worker table, a wORker table, and so on. These will all be separate tables. How is anyone, including the programmer, supposed to remember the differences? This is a drawback, not a benefit, and Oracle was wise not to fall into this trap.

Looking back over this chapter, you'll see that this practice was not followed. Rather, it was delayed until the subject could be introduced and put in its proper context. From here on, with the exception of one or two tables and a few isolated instances, data in the database will be in mixed case as you'd expect and all uppercase when consistency is important or it's a code set.

Normalizing Names

Several query tools have come on the market whose purpose is to let you make queries using common English words instead of odd conglomerations. These products work by building a logical map between the common English words and the hard-to-remember, non-English column names, table names, and codes. The mapping takes careful thought, but once completed, it makes the user's interaction with the application easy. But why not put the care in at the beginning? Why create a need for yet another layer, another product, and more work, when much of the confusion can be avoided simply by naming things better the first time around?

For performance reasons, it may be that some of an application's data must still be stored in a coded fashion within the computer's database. These codes should not be exposed to users, during either data entry or retrieval, and Oracle allows them to be easily hidden.

The instant that data entry requires codes, key-entry errors increase. When reports contain codes instead of English, errors of interpretation begin. And when users need to create new or ad hoc reports, their ability to do so quickly and accurately is severely impaired both by codes and by not being able to remember strange column and table names.

Oracle gives users the power to see and work with English throughout the entire application. It is a waste of Oracle's power to ignore this opportunity, and it will without question produce a less understandable and less productive application. Developers should seize the opportunity. Users should demand it. Both will benefit immeasurably.

Good Design Has a Human Touch

At this point, if you are new to Oracle you may want to go right into working with Oracle and the SQL language. That is covered in the next chapter; the remainder of this chapter focuses on performance, naming, and design considerations. You can refer back to this section later when you are ready to design and implement an application.

This section looks at a method of approaching a development project that takes into account the real business tasks your end users have to accomplish. This focus distinguishes this method from the more common data orientation of many developers and development methodologies. Data normalization and Computer Aided Software Engineering (CASE) technologies have become so much the center of attention with relational application development that a focus on the data and the issues of referential integrity, keys, normalization, and table diagrams has become almost an obsession. These issues are so often confused with design—and even believed to *be* design—that the reminder that they are analysis is often met with surprise.

Normalization is analysis, not design. And it is only a part of the analysis necessary to understand a business and build a useful application. The goal of application development, after all, is to help the business run more successfully by improving the speed and efficiency with which business tasks are done and by making the environment in which people work as meaningful and supportive as possible. Give people control over their information, and intuitive, straightforward access to it, and they will respond gratefully and productively. Assign the control to a remote group, cloud the information in codes and user-hostile interfaces, and they will be unhappy and unproductive.

The methods outlined in this section are not intended to be a rigorous elucidation of the process, and the tools you use and are familiar with for data structures or flows are probably sufficient for the task. The purpose here is to disclose an approach that is effective in creating responsive, appropriate, and accommodating applications.

Understanding the Application Tasks

One of the often-neglected steps in building software is understanding the end user's job—the tasks that computer automation is intended to support. Occasionally, this is because the application itself is quite specialized; more often, it is because the approach to design tends to be data oriented. Frequently, these are the major questions asked in the analysis:

- What data should be captured?
- How should the data be processed?
- How should the data be reported?

These questions expand into a series of subquestions, and they include issues such as input forms, codes, screen layouts, computations, postings, corrections, audit trails, retention, storage volumes, processing cycles, report formatting, distribution, and maintenance. These are all vitally important areas. One difficulty, however, is that they all focus solely on data.

People *use* data, but they *do* tasks. One might argue that although this may be true of professional workers, key-entry clerks really only transfer data from an input form to a keyboard; their tasks are very data oriented. This is a fair portrayal of these jobs today. But is this a consequence of the real job that needs to get done, or is it a symptom of the design of the computer application? Using humans as input devices, particularly for data that is voluminous, consistent in format (as on forms), and in a limited range of variability, is an expensive and antiquated, not to mention dehumanizing, method of capturing data. Like the use of codes to accommodate machine limitations, it's an idea whose time has passed.

This may sound like so much philosophy, but it has practical import in the way application design is done. People use data, but they do tasks. And they don't do tasks through to completion one at a time. They do several tasks that are subsets of or in intersection with each other, and they do them all at once, in parallel.

When designers allow this idea to direct the analysis and creation of an application, rather than focusing on the data orientation that has been historically dominant, the very nature of the effort changes significantly. Why have windowing and web environments been so successful? Because they allow a user to jump quickly among small tasks, keeping them all active without having to shut down and exit one in order to begin another. The windowing environment comes closer to mapping the way people really think and work than the old "one thing at a time" approach ever did. This lesson should not be lost. It should be built upon.

Understanding the application tasks means going far beyond identifying the data elements, normalizing them, and creating screens, processing programs, and reports. It means really understanding what the users do and what their tasks are, and designing the application to be responsive to those tasks, not just to capture the data associated with them. In fact, when the orientation is toward the data, the resulting design will inevitably *distort* the users' tasks rather than support them.

How do you design an application that is responsive to tasks rather than data? The biggest hurdle is simply understanding that focusing on tasks is necessary. This allows you to approach the analysis of the business from a fresh perspective.

The first step in the analysis process is to understand the tasks. For which tasks do the members of this group really need to use computers? What is the real service or product produced? This seems like a fundamental and even simplistic first question, but you'll find that a surprising number of business people are quite unclear about the answer. An amazing number of businesses, from healthcare to banking, from shipping to manufacturing, used to think they were in the data processing business. After all, they input data, processed it, and reported it, didn't they? This delusion is yet another symptom of the data orientation our systems designs have had that has led dozens of companies to attempt to market their imagined "real" product, data processing, with disastrous consequences for most of them.

Hence the importance of learning about a business application: You have to keep an open mind, and may often have to challenge pet notions about what the business is in order to learn what it really is. This is a healthy, if sometimes difficult, process.

And, just as it is essential that business people become literate users of SQL and understand the basics of the relational model, so it is important that application designers really understand the service or product being delivered, and the tasks *necessary* to make that happen. A project team that includes end users who have been introduced to the essentials of SQL and the relational approach, such as by reading this book, and designers who are sensitive to end users' needs and understand the value of a task-oriented, readable application environment, will turn out extraordinarily good systems. The members of such a project team check, support, and enhance each other's efforts.

One approach to this process is to develop two converging documents: a task document and a data document. It is in the process of preparing the task document that the deep understanding of the application comes about. The data document will help implement the vision and ensure that the details and rules are all accounted for, but the task document defines the vision of what the business is.

Outline of Tasks

The task document is a joint effort of the business users and the application designers. It lists the tasks associated with the business from the top down. It begins with a basic description of the business. This should be a simple declarative sentence of three to ten words, in the active voice, without commas, and with a minimum of adjectives:

We sell insurance.

It should not be:

Amalgamated Diversified is a leading international supplier of financial resources, training, information processing, transaction capture and distribution, communications, customer support, and industry direction in the field of shared risk funding for health care maintenance, property preservation, and automobile liability.

There is a tremendous temptation to cram every little detail about a business and its dreams about itself into this first sentence. Don't do it. The effort of trimming the descriptive excesses down to a simple sentence focuses the mind wonderfully. If you can't get the business down to ten words, you haven't understood it yet.

But, as an application designer, creating this sentence isn't your task alone; it is a joint effort with the business user, and it initiates the task documentation process. It provides you with the opportunity to begin serious questioning about what the business does and how it does it. This is a valuable process for the business itself, quite independent of the fact that an application is being built. You will encounter numerous tasks and subtasks, procedures, and rules that will prove to be meaningless or of marginal use. Typically, these are artifacts of either a previous problem, long since solved, or of information or reporting requests from managers long since departed.

Some wags have suggested that the way to deal with too many reports being created, whether manually or by computer, is simply to stop producing them and see if anyone notices. This is a humorous notion, but the seed of truth it contains needs to be a part of the task documentation process. In fact, it proved quite useful in Y2K remediation efforts—many programs and reports didn't have to be fixed, simply because they were no longer used!

Your approach to the joint effort of documenting tasks allows you to ask skeptical questions and look at (and reevaluate the usefulness of) what may be mere artifacts. Be aware, however, that you need to proceed with the frank acknowledgment that you, as a designer, cannot understand the business as thoroughly as the user does. There is an important line between seizing the opportunity of an application development project to rationalize what tasks are done and why, and possibly offending the users by presuming to understand the "real" business better than they do.

Ask the user to describe a task in detail and explain to you the reason for each step. If the reason is a weak one, such as "We've always done it this way," or "I think they use this upstairs for something," red flags should go up. Say that you don't understand, and ask again for an explanation. If the response is still unsatisfactory, put the task and your question on a separate list for resolution. Some of these questions will be answered simply by someone who knows the subject better; others will require talking to senior management; and many tasks will end up eliminated because they are no longer needed. One of the evidences of a good analysis process is the improvement of existing procedures, independent of, and generally long before, the implementation of a new computer application.

General Format of the Task Document

This is the general format for the task document:

- Summary sentence describing the business (three to ten words)
- Summary sentences describing and numbering the major tasks of the business (short sentences, short words)
- Additional levels of task detail, as needed, within each of the major tasks

By all means, follow the summary sentence for every level with a short, descriptive paragraph, if you want, but don't use this as an excuse to avoid the effort of making the summary sentence clear and crisp. Major tasks are typically numbered 1.0, 2.0, 3.0, and so on, and are sometimes referred to as *zero-level tasks*. The levels below each of these are numbered using additional dots, as in 3.1 and 3.1.14. Each major task is taken down to the level where it is a collection of *atomic tasks*—tasks for which no subtask is meaningful in itself and that, once started, is either taken to completion or dropped entirely. Atomic tasks are never left half-finished.

Writing a check is an atomic task; filling in the dollar amount is not. Answering the telephone as a customer service representative is not an atomic task; answering the phone and fulfilling the customer's request is atomic. Atomic tasks must be meaningful and must complete an action.

The level at which a task is atomic will vary by task. The task represented by 3.1.14 may be atomic yet still have several additional sublevels. The task 3.2 may be atomic, or 3.1.16.4 may be. What is important is not the numbering scheme (which is nothing more than a method for outlining a hierarchy of tasks) but the decomposition to the atomic level. The atomic tasks are the fundamental building blocks of the business. Two tasks can still be atomic if one occasionally depends on the other, but only if each can and does get completed independently. If two tasks always depend on each other, they are not atomic. The real atomic task includes them both.

In most businesses, you will quickly discover that many tasks do not fit neatly into just one of the major (zero-level) tasks, but seem to span two or more, and work in a network or "dotted-line" fashion. This is nearly always evidence of improper definition of the major tasks or incomplete atomization of the lower tasks. The goal is to turn each task into a conceptual "object," with a well-defined idea of what it does (its goal in life) and what resources (data, computation, thinking, paper, pencil, and so on) it uses to accomplish its goal.

Insights Resulting from the Task Document

Several insights come out of the task document. First, because the task document is task oriented rather than data oriented, it is likely to substantially change the way user screens are designed. It will affect what data is captured, how it is presented, how help is implemented, and how users switch from one task to another. The task orientation will help ensure that the most common kinds of jumping between tasks will not require inordinate effort from the user.

Second, the categorization of major tasks will change as conflicts are discovered; this will affect how both the designers and the business users understand the business.

Third, even the summary sentence itself will probably change. Rationalizing a business into atomic task "objects" forces a clearing out of artifacts, misconceptions, and unneeded dependencies that have long weighed down the business unnecessarily.

This is not a painless process, but the benefits in terms of the business's self-understanding, the cleanup of procedures, and the automation of the tasks will usually far exceed the emotional costs and time spent. It helps immensely if there is general understanding going into the project that uncomfortable questions will be asked, incorrect assumptions will be corrected, and step-by-step adjustments will be made to the task document until it is completed.

Understanding the Data

In conjunction with the decomposition and description of the tasks, the resources required at each step are described in the task document, especially in terms of the data required. This is done on a task-by-task basis, and the data requirements are then included in the data document. This is a conceptually different approach from the classical view of the data. You will not simply take the forms and screens currently used by each task and record the elements they contain. The flaw in this "piece of paper in a cigar box" approach lies in our tendency (even though we don't like to admit it) to accept anything printed on paper as necessary or true.

In looking at each task, you should determine what data is necessary to do the task, rather than what data elements are on the form you use to do the task. By requiring that the definition of the data needed come from the task rather than from any existing forms or screens, you force an examination of the true purpose of the task and the real data requirements. If the person doing the task doesn't know how the data is used, the element goes on the list for resolution. An amazing amount of garbage is eliminated by this process.

Once the current data elements have been identified, they must be carefully scrutinized. Numeric and letter codes are always suspect. They disguise real information behind counterintuitive, meaningless symbols. There are times and tasks for which codes are handy, easily remembered, or made necessary by sheer volume. But, in your final design, these cases should be rare and obvious. If they are not, you've lost your way.

In the scrutiny of existing data elements, codes should be set aside for special attention. In each case, ask yourself whether the element should be a code. Its continued use as a code should be viewed suspiciously. There must be good arguments and compelling reasons for perpetuating the disguise. The process for converting codes back into English is fairly simple, but it's a joint effort. The codes are first listed by data element, along with their meanings. These are then examined by users and designers, and short English versions of the meanings are proposed, discussed, and tentatively approved. Keep the code value itself for internal database use, such as joining tables, though.

In this same discussion, designers and end users should decide on names for the data elements. These will become column names in the database and will be regularly used in English queries, so the names should be descriptive (avoiding abbreviations, other than those common to the business) and singular. Because of the intimate relationship between the column name and the data it contains, the two should be specified simultaneously. A thoughtful choice of a column name will vastly simplify determining its new English contents.

Data elements that are not codes also must be rigorously examined. By this point, you have good reason to believe that all the data elements you've identified are necessary to the business tasks, but they are not necessarily well organized. What appears to be one data element in the existing task may, in fact, be several elements mixed together that require separation. Names, addresses, and phone numbers are very common examples of this, but every application has a wealth of others.

First and last names were mixed together, for example, in the AUTHOR table. The AUTHOR_NAME column held both first and last names, even though the tables were in Third Normal Form. This would be an extremely burdensome way actually to implement an application, in spite of the fact that the normalization rules were technically met. To make the application practical and prepare it for English queries, the AUTHOR_NAME column needs to be decomposed into at least two new columns, LAST_NAME and FIRST_NAME. This same categorization process is regularly needed in rationalizing other data elements, and it's often quite independent of normalization.

The degree of decomposition depends on how the particular data elements are likely to be used. It is possible to go too far and decompose categories that, although made up of separable pieces, provide no additional value in their new state. Decomposition is application dependent on an element-by-element basis. Once decomposition has been done, these new elements, which will become columns, need to be thoughtfully named, and the data they will contain needs to be scrutinized. Text data that will fall into a definable number of values should be reviewed for naming. These column names and values, like those of the codes, are tentative.

The Atomic Data Models

Now the process of normalization begins, and with it the drawing of the atomic data models. There are many good texts on the subject and a wide variety of analysis and design tools that can speed the process, so this book doesn't suggest any particular method, because recommending one method may hinder rather than help.

Each atomic transaction should be modeled, and it should be labeled with the task number to which it applies. Included in the model are table names, primary and foreign keys, and major columns. Each normalized relationship should have a descriptive name, and estimated row counts and transaction rates should appear with each table. Accompanying each model is an additional sheet with all the columns and datatypes, their ranges of value, and the tentative names for the tables, columns, and named values in the columns.

The Atomic Business Model

This data document is now combined with the task document. The combined document is a business model. It's reviewed jointly by the application designers and end users for accuracy and completeness.

The Business Model

At this point, both the application designers and the end users should possess a clear vision of the business, its tasks, and its data. Once the business model is corrected and approved, the process of synthesizing the tasks and data models into an overall business model begins. This part of the process sorts common data elements between tasks, completes final, large-scale normalization, and resolves consistent, definitive names for all the parts.

This can be quite a large drawing for major applications, with supporting documentation that includes the tasks, the data models (with corrected element names, based on the full model), and a list of all the full-scale tables and their column names, datatypes, and contents. A final check is made by tracing the data access paths of each transaction in the full business model to determine that all the data the transaction requires is available for selection or insertion, and that no tasks insert data with elements missing that are essential to the model's referential integrity.

With the exception of the effort spent to name the various tables, columns, and common values properly, virtually everything to this point has been analysis, *not* design. The aim has been to promote understanding of the business and its components.

Data Entry

Screen design does not proceed from the business model. It is not focused on tables, but rather on tasks, so screens or web pages are created that support the task orientation and the need to jump between subtasks when necessary. In practical terms, this will often map readily to a primary table used by the task and to other tables that can be queried for values or updated as the primary table is accessed.

But there will also be occasions when there simply is no main table, but instead a variety of related tables, all of which will supply or receive data to support the task. These screens will look and act quite differently from the typical table-oriented screens developed in many applications, but they will significantly amplify the effectiveness of their users and their contribution to the business. And that's the whole purpose of this approach.

The interaction between the user and the machine is critical; the input and query screens should consistently be task oriented and descriptive in English. The use of icons and graphical interfaces plays an important role as well. Screens must reflect the way work is actually done and be built to respond in the language in which business is conducted.

Query and Reporting

If anything sets the relational approach, and SQL, apart from more traditional application environments, it is the ability for end users to learn and execute ad hoc queries easily. These are those reports and one-time queries that are outside of the basic set usually developed and delivered along with the application code.

With Oracle's SQL*Plus or SQL Developer utilities, end users are given unprecedented control over their own data. Both the users and developers benefit from this ability: the users because they can build reports, analyze information, modify their queries, and reexecute them, all in a matter of minutes, and the developers because they are relieved of the undesirable requirement of creating new reports.

Users are granted the power to look into their data, analyze it, and respond with a speed and thoroughness unimaginable just a few years ago. This leap in productivity is greatly extended if the tables, columns, and data values are carefully crafted in English; it is greatly foreshortened if bad naming conventions and meaningless codes and abbreviations are permitted to infect the design. The time spent in the design process to name the objects consistently and descriptively will pay off quickly for the users and, therefore, for the business.

Some people, typically those who have not built major relational applications, fear that turning query facilities over to end users will cripple the machine on which the facilities are used. The fear is that users will write inefficient queries that will consume overwhelming numbers of CPU cycles, slowing the machine and every other user. Experience shows that this generally is not true. Users quickly learn which kinds of queries run fast and which do not. Further, most business intelligence and reporting tools available today can estimate the amount of time a query will take and restrict access—by user, time of day, or both—to queries that would consume a disproportionate amount of resources. In practice, the demands users make on a machine only occasionally get out of hand, but the benefits they derive far exceed the cost of the processing. Virtually any time you can move effort from a person to a machine, you save money.

The real goal of design is to clarify and satisfy the needs of the business and business users. If there is a bias, it must always be toward making the application easier to understand and use, particularly at the expense of CPU or disk, but less so if the cost is an internal complexity so great that maintenance and change become difficult and slow.

Toward Object Name Normalization

The basic approach to naming is to choose meaningful, memorable, and descriptive readable names, avoiding abbreviations and codes, and using underscores either consistently or not at all. In a large application, table, column, and data names will often be multiword, as in the case of REVERSED_EXPENSE_ACCOUNT or LAST_GL_CLOSE_DATE. The goal of thoughtful naming methods is ease of use: The names must be easy to remember and must follow rules that are easily explained and applied. In the pages ahead, a somewhat more rigorous approach to naming is presented, with the ultimate goal of developing a formal process of object name normalization.

Level-Name Integrity

In a relational database system, the hierarchy of objects ranges from the database, to the table owners, to the tables, to the columns, to the data values. In very large systems, there may even be multiple databases, and these may be distributed within locations. For the sake of brevity, the higher levels will be ignored for now, but what is said will apply to them as well.

Each level in this hierarchy is defined within the level above it, and each level should be given names appropriate to its own level and should not incorporate names from outside its own level. For example, a table cannot have two columns called NAME, and the account named George cannot own two tables named AUTHOR.

There is no requirement that each of George's tables have a name that is unique throughout the entire database. Other owners may have AUTHOR tables as well. Even if George is granted access to those tables, there is no confusion because he can identify each table uniquely by prefixing its owner's name to the table name, as in DIETRICH.AUTHOR. It would not be logically consistent to incorporate George's owner name into the name of each of his tables, as in

GEOAUTHOR, GEOBOOKSHELF, and so on. This confuses and complicates the table name by placing part of its parent's name in its own, in effect a violation of *level-name integrity*.

Brevity should never be favored over clarity. Including pieces of table names in column names is a bad technique, because it violates the logical idea of levels and the level-name integrity that this requires. It is also confusing, requiring users to look up column names virtually every time they want to write a query. Object names must be unique within their parent, but no incorporation of names from outside an object's own level should be permitted.

The support for abstract datatypes in Oracle strengthens your ability to create consistent names for attributes. If you create a datatype called ADDRESS_TY, it will have the same attributes each time it is used. Each of the attributes will have a consistent name, datatype, and length, making their implementation more consistent across the enterprise. However, using abstract datatypes in this manner requires that you do both of the following:

- Properly define the datatypes at the start so you can avoid having to modify the datatype later.

- Support the syntax requirements of abstract datatypes.

Foreign Keys

The one area of difficulty with using brief column names is the occasional appearance of a foreign key in a table in which another column has the same name that the foreign key column has in its home table. One possible long-term solution is to allow the use of the full foreign key name, including the table name of its home table, as a column name in the local table (such as BOOKSHELF.TITLE as a column name).

The practical need to solve the same-name column problem requires one of the following actions:

- Invent a name that incorporates the source table of the foreign key in its name without using the dot (using an underscore, for instance).

- Invent a name that incorporates an abbreviation of the source table of the foreign key in its name.

- Invent a name different from its name in its source table.

- Change the name of the conflicting column.

None of these is particularly attractive, but if you come across the same-name dilemma, you'll need to take one of these actions.

Singular Names

One area of great inconsistency and confusion is the question of whether objects should have singular or plural names. Should it be the AUTHOR table or the AUTHORS table? Should it be the NAME column or the NAMES column?

There are two helpful ways to think about this issue. First, consider some columns common to nearly every database: NAME, ADDRESS, CITY, STATE, and ZIP. Other than the first column, does it ever occur to anyone to make these names plural? It is nearly self-evident when considering these names that they each describe the contents of a single row—a record. Even though relational databases are "set oriented," clearly the fundamental unit of a set is a row, and it is the content of that row that is well-described by singular column names. When designing a data-entry screen to capture a person's name and address, should it look like this?

```
Names:     _____

Addresses: _____

Cities: _____  States ___  Zips _____-_____
```

Or will you make these column names singular on the screen because you're capturing *one* name and address at a time, but tell the users that when they write queries they must all be converted to plural? It is simply more intuitive and straightforward to restrict column names to singular.

If all objects are named consistently, neither you nor a user has to try to remember the rules for what is plural and what isn't. The benefit of this should be obvious. Suppose we decide that all objects will henceforth be plural. We now have "s" or "es" on the end of virtually every object, perhaps even on the end of each word in a long multiword object name. Of what possible benefit is it to key all these extra letters all the time? Is it easier to use? Is it easier to understand? Is it easier to remember? Obviously, it is none of these.

Therefore, the best solution is this: All object names are always singular. The sole exception to this rule is any widely accepted term already commonly used in the business, such as "sales."

Brevity

As mentioned earlier, clarity should never be sacrificed for brevity, but given two equally meaningful, memorable, and descriptive names, always choose the shorter. During application development, propose alternative column and table names such as these to a group of users and developers and get their input on choosing the clearest name. How do you build lists of alternatives? Use a thesaurus and a dictionary. On a project team dedicated to developing superior, productive applications, every team member should be given a thesaurus and a dictionary as basic equipment and then should be reminded over and over again of the importance of careful object naming.

Object Name Thesaurus

Ultimately, relational databases should include an object name thesaurus, just as they include a data dictionary. This thesaurus should enforce the company's naming standards and ensure consistency of name choice and abbreviation (where used).

Such standards may require the use of underscores in object naming to make the parsing of the name into component parts a straightforward task. This also helps enforce the consistent use of underscores, rather than the scattered, inconsistent usage within an application that underscores frequently receive now.

If you work directly with a government agency or large firm, that organization may already have object-naming standards. The object-naming standards of large organizations have over the years radiated into the rest of the commercial marketplace, and they may form the basis for the naming standards used at your company. For example, those standards may provide the direction to choose between "Corporation" and "Firm." If they do not, you should develop your naming standards to be consistent, both with those base standards and with the guidelines put forth in this chapter.

Intelligent Keys and Column Values

Intelligent keys are so named because they contain nontrivial combinations of information. The term is misleading in the extreme because it implies something positive or worthwhile. A more meaningful term might be *overloaded* keys. General ledger and product codes often fall into this category and contain all the difficulties associated with other codes, and more. Further, the difficulties found in overloaded keys also apply to non-key columns that are packed with more than one piece of meaningful data.

Typical of an overloaded key or column value is this description: "The first character is the region code. The next four characters are the catalog number. The final digit is the cost center code, unless this is an imported part, in which case an *I* is tagged onto the end of the number, or unless it is a high-volume item, such as screws, in which case only three digits are used for catalog number, and the region code is HD."

Eliminating overloaded key and column values is essential in good relational design. The dependencies built on pieces of these keys (usually foreign keys into other tables) are all at risk if the structure is maintained. Unfortunately, many application areas have overloaded keys that have been used for years and are deeply embedded in the company's tasks. Some of them were created during earlier efforts at automation, using databases that could not support multiple key columns for composite keys. Others came about through historical accretion, by forcing a short code, usually numeric, to mean more and to cover more cases than it was ever intended to at the beginning. Eliminating the existing overloaded keys may have practical ramifications that make it impossible to do immediately. This makes building a new relational application more difficult.

The solution to this problem is to create a new set of keys, both primary and foreign, that properly normalizes the data; then, make sure people can access tables only through these new keys. The overloaded key is then kept as an additional, and unique, table column. Access to it is still possible using historical methods (matching the overloaded key in a query, for instance), but the newly structured keys are promoted as the preferred access method. Over time, with proper training, users will gravitate to the new keys. Eventually, the overloaded keys (and other overloaded column values) can simply be NULLed out or dropped from the table.

Failing to eliminate overloaded keys and values makes extracting information from the database, validating the values, ensuring data integrity, and modifying the structure all extremely difficult and costly.

The Commandments

All the major issues in designing for productivity have now been discussed. It probably is worthwhile to sum these up in a single place—thus "The Commandments" (or perhaps "The Suggestions"). Their presentation does not assume that you need to be told what to do, but rather that you are capable of making rational judgments and can benefit from the experience of others facing the same challenges. The purpose here is not to describe the development cycle, which you probably understand better than you want to, but rather to bias that development with an orientation that will radically change how the application will look, feel, and be used. Careful attention to these ideas can dramatically improve the productivity and happiness of an application's users.

The ten commandments of humane database application design:

1. Include users. Put them on the project team and teach them the relational model and SQL.

2. Name tables, columns, keys, and data jointly with the users. Develop an application thesaurus to ensure name consistency.

3. Use English words that are meaningful, memorable, descriptive, short, and singular. Use underscores consistently or not at all.

4. Don't mix levels in naming.

5. Avoid codes and abbreviations.

6. Use meaningful keys where possible.

7. Decompose overloaded keys.

8. Analyze and design from the tasks, not just the data. Remember that normalization is not design.

9. Move tasks from users to the machine. It is profitable to spend cycles and storage to gain ease of use.

10. Don't be seduced by development speed. Take time and care in analyses, design, testing, and tuning.

There's a reason why this chapter precedes the ones on the commands and functions—if you have a poor design, your application will suffer no matter what commands you use. Plan for functionality, plan for performance, plan for recoverability, plan for security, and plan for availability. Plan for success.

PART
II

SQL and SQL*Plus

CHAPTER
5

The Basic Parts of
Speech in SQL

W ith the Structured Query Language (SQL), you tell Oracle which information you want it to SELECT, INSERT, UPDATE, or DELETE. In fact, these four verbs are the primary words you will use to give Oracle instructions. You can use an additional command, MERGE, to perform INSERT, UPDATE, and even DELETE operations with a single command. As described in later chapters, these basic commands support flashback version queries and other advanced features.

In Part I, you saw what is meant by "relational," how tables are organized into columns and rows, and how to instruct Oracle to select certain columns from a table and show you the information in them, row by row. In this and the following chapters, you will learn how to do this more completely for the different datatypes supported by Oracle. In this part, you will learn how to interact with SQL*Plus, a powerful Oracle command-line tool that can take your instructions for Oracle, check them for correctness, submit them to Oracle, and then modify or reformat the response Oracle gives, based on orders or directions you've set in place. Even with the recent proliferation of GUI tools such as SQL Developer from Oracle, the SQL*Plus tool lives on, not only in batch jobs but also as a text-based tool that is often faster and more succinct than using one of the GUI tools.

It may be a little confusing at first to understand the difference between what SQL*Plus is doing and what Oracle is doing, especially because the error messages that Oracle produces are simply passed on to you by SQL*Plus, but you will see as you work through this book where the differences lie. As you get started, just think of SQL*Plus as a coworker—an assistant who follows your instructions and helps you do your work more quickly. You interact with this coworker by typing on your keyboard.

You may follow the examples in this and subsequent chapters by typing the commands shown. Your Oracle and SQL*Plus programs should respond just as they do in these examples. However, you do need to make certain that the tables used in this book have been loaded into your copy of Oracle.

You can understand what is described in this book without actually typing it in yourself; for example, you can use the commands shown with your own tables. It will probably be clearer and easier, though, if you have the same tables loaded into Oracle as the ones used here and practice using the same queries. Visit www.OraclePressBooks.com for downloadable files. Assuming that you have loaded the demo tables into an Oracle database, you can connect to SQL*Plus and begin working by typing this at the operating system prompt (Windows or Unix):

```
[oracle@srvr1 ~]$ sqlplus
```

(If you want to run SQL*Plus from your desktop client machine, select the SQL Plus program option from the Application Development menu option under the Oracle software menu option under Windows; otherwise, type **sqlplus** as the Windows or Unix command line.) This starts SQL*Plus. (Note that you don't type the * that is in the middle of the official product name, and the asterisk doesn't appear in the program name, either.) Because Oracle is careful to guard who can access the data it stores, it requires that you enter an ID and password to connect to it. Oracle will display a copyright message and then ask for your username and password. Log into your database using the account and password you created to hold the sample tables (such as **practice/practice**). If you provide a valid username and password, SQL*Plus will announce that you're connected to Oracle and then will display this prompt:

```
SQL>
```

You are now in SQL*Plus, and it awaits your instructions.

NOTE
*Many application development environments provide direct SQL access to Oracle databases. The SQL commands shown in this chapter will work from within those tools, but some commands specific to SQL*Plus (such as DESCRIBE) might not.*

If the command fails, there are several potential reasons: Oracle is not in your path; you are not authorized to use SQL*Plus; or Oracle hasn't been installed properly on your computer. If you get the message

```
ERROR: ORA-1017: invalid username/password; logon denied
```

either you've entered the username or password incorrectly or your username has not yet been set up properly on your copy of Oracle. After three unsuccessful attempts to enter a username and password that Oracle recognizes, SQL*Plus terminates the attempt to log on, showing this message:

```
unable to CONNECT to ORACLE after 3 attempts, exiting SQL*Plus
```

If you get this message, contact your company's database administrator. Assuming everything is in order, and the SQL> prompt has appeared, you may now begin working with SQL*Plus.
When you want to quit working and leave SQL*Plus, type this:

```
quit
```

or

```
exit
```

Style

First, some comments on style. SQL*Plus doesn't care whether the SQL commands you type are in uppercase or lowercase. For example, the command

```
SeLeCt feaTURE, section, PAGE FROM newsPaPeR;
```

will produce exactly the same result as this one:

```
select Feature, Section, Page from NEWSPAPER;
```

Case matters only when SQL*Plus or Oracle is checking an alphanumeric value for equality. If you tell Oracle to find a row where SECTION = 'f', and SECTION is really equal to 'F', Oracle won't find it (because *f* and *F* are not identical). Aside from this usage, case is completely irrelevant. (Incidentally, 'F', as used here, is called a *literal,* meaning that you want SECTION to be tested literally against the letter *F,* not a column *named* F. The single quote marks enclosing the letter tell Oracle that this is a literal and not a column name.)

NOTE
Oracle can create identifiers for tables and columns that are case sensitive if you enclose them in double quotes. This usage is rare and can cause confusion among database administrators and database users alike. Its use is strongly discouraged without good justification.

As a matter of style, this book follows certain conventions about case to make the text easier to read and to distinguish between the SQL commands and the rest of the text:

- SQL keywords and clauses such as SELECT, FROM, WHERE, ORDER BY, HAVING, and GROUP BY, along with SQL operators such as IN, BETWEEN, and UPPER will always be uppercase in the body of the text.

- SQL*Plus commands also will be uppercase (for example, COLUMN, SET, SAVE, TTITLE, and so on) in the body of the text.

- SQL and SQL*Plus code listings will generally be in lowercase, as you might type them in a command.

You may want to follow similar conventions in creating your own queries, or your company already may have standards it would like you to use. You may even choose to invent your own. Regardless, the goal of any such standards should always be to make your work simple to read and understand.

Creating the NEWSPAPER Table

The examples in this book are based on the tables created by the scripts located on the CD or from the sample code on the Oracle Press website. Each table is created via the CREATE TABLE command, which specifies the names of the columns in the table, as well as the characteristics of those columns. Here is the CREATE TABLE command for the NEWSPAPER table, which is used in many of the examples in this chapter:

```
create table newspaper (
feature        varchar2(15) not null,
section        char(1),
page           number
);
```

In later chapters in this book, you'll see how to interpret all the clauses of this command. For now, you can read it as, "Create a table called NEWSPAPER. It will have three columns, named FEATURE (a variable-length character column), SECTION (a fixed-length character column), and PAGE (a numeric column). The values in the FEATURE column can be up to 15 characters long, and every row must have a value for FEATURE. SECTION values will all be 1 character long."

In later chapters, you'll see how to extend this simple command to add constraints, indexes, and storage clauses. For now, the NEWSPAPER table will be kept simple so the examples can focus on SQL.

Using SQL to Select Data from Tables

Figure 5-1 shows a table of features from a local newspaper. If this were an Oracle table, rather than just paper and ink on the front of the local paper, SQL*Plus would display it for you if you typed this:

```
select feature, section, page from newspaper;
```

```
FEATURE            S       PAGE
---------------    -    ----------
National News      A         1
Sports             D         1
Editorials         A        12
Business           E         1
Weather            C         2
Television         B         7
Births             F         7
Classified         F         8
Modern Life        B         1
Comics             C         4
Movies             B         4
Bridge             B         2
Obituaries         F         6
Doctor Is In       F         6

14 rows selected.
```

NOTE

Depending on your configuration, the listing may have a page break in it. If that happens, use the SET PAGESIZE command to increase the size of each displayed page of results. See the Alphabetical Reference for details on this command.

What's the difference between the table you created and the one shown in the output in Figure 5-1? Both tables have the same information, but the format differs and the order of rows may be different. For example, the column headings differ slightly. In fact, they even differ slightly from the columns you just asked for in the SELECT statement.

Notice that the column named SECTION shows up in SQL*Plus as just the letter *S*. Also, although you used all lowercase letters to type the column headings in the command

```
select feature, section, page from newspaper;
```

the column headings came back with all the letters in uppercase.

These changes are the result of the assumptions SQL*Plus makes about how information should be presented. You can change these assumptions, and you probably will, but until you give SQL*Plus different orders, this is how it changes what you input:

- It changes all the column headings to uppercase.
- It allows columns to be only as wide as a column is defined to be in Oracle.
- It squeezes out any spaces if the column heading is a function. (This will be demonstrated in Chapter 7.)

FEATURE	SECTION	PAGE
Births	F	7
Bridge	B	2
Business	E	1
Classified	F	8
Comic	C	4
Doctor Is In	F	6
Editorials	A	12
Modern Life	B	1
Movies	B	4
National News	A	1
Obituaries	F	6
Sports	D	1
Television	B	7
Weather	C	2

FIGURE 5-1. *A NEWSPAPER table*

The first point is obvious. The column names you used were shifted to uppercase. The second point is not obvious. How *are* the columns defined? To find out, ask Oracle. Simply tell SQL*Plus to DESCRIBE the table, as shown here:

```
describe newspaper
```

```
Name                               Null?     Type
---------------------------------  --------  ------------
FEATURE                            NOT NULL  VARCHAR2(15)
SECTION                                      CHAR(1)
PAGE                                         NUMBER
```

This display is a descriptive table that lists the columns and their definitions for the NEWSPAPER table; the DESCRIBE command works for any table. Note that the details in this description match the CREATE TABLE command given earlier in this chapter.

The first column tells the names of the columns in the table being described.

The second column (Null?) is really a rule about the column named to its left. When the NEWSPAPER table was created, the NOT NULL rule instructed Oracle not to allow any user to add a new row to the table if he or she left the FEATURE column empty (NULL means empty). Of course, in a table such as NEWSPAPER, it probably would have been worthwhile to use the same rule for all three columns. What good is it to know the title of a feature without also knowing what section it's in and what page it's on? But, for the sake of this example, only FEATURE was created with the rule that it could not be NULL.

Because SECTION and PAGE have nothing in the Null? column, they are allowed to be empty in any row of the NEWSPAPER table.

The third column (TYPE) tells the basic nature of the individual columns. Feature is a VARCHAR2 (variable-length character) column that can be up to 15 characters (letters, numbers, symbols, or spaces) long.

SECTION is a character column as well, but it is only one character long. The creator of the table knew that newspaper sections in the local paper are only a single letter, so the column was defined to be only as wide as it needed to be. It was defined using the CHAR datatype, which is used for fixed-length character strings. When SQL*Plus went to display the results of your query

```
select feature, section, page from newspaper;
```

it knew from Oracle that SECTION was a maximum of only one character. It assumed that you did not want to use up more space than this, so it displayed a column just one character wide and used as much of the column name as it could—in this case, just the letter *S*.

The third column in the NEWSPAPER table is PAGE, which is simply a number. Notice that the PAGE column shows up as ten spaces wide, even though no pages use more than two digits—numbers usually are not defined as having a maximum width, so SQL*Plus assumes a maximum just to get started.

You also may have noticed that the heading for the only column composed solely of numbers, PAGE, was *right-justified*—that is, it sits over on the right side of the column, whereas the headings for columns that contain characters sit over on the left. This is standard alignment for column headings in SQL*Plus. As with other column features, you'll see in Chapter 6 how to change alignment as needed.

Finally, SQL*Plus tells you how many rows it found in Oracle's NEWSPAPER table. (Notice the "14 rows selected" notation at the bottom of the display.) This is called *feedback*. You can make SQL*Plus stop giving feedback by setting the FEEDBACK option, as shown here:

```
set feedback off
```

Alternatively, you can set a minimum number of rows for FEEDBACK to work:

```
set feedback 25
```

This last example tells Oracle that you don't want to know how many rows have been displayed until at least 25 have been displayed. Unless you tell SQL*Plus differently, FEEDBACK is set to 6.

The SET command is a SQL*Plus command, which means that it is an instruction telling SQL*Plus how to act. There are many SQL*Plus options, such as FEEDBACK, that you can set. Several of these will be shown and used in this chapter and in the chapters to follow. For a complete list, look up SET in the Alphabetical Reference section of this book.

The SET command has a counterpart named SHOW that allows you to see what instructions you've given to SQL*Plus. For instance, you can check the setting of FEEDBACK by typing

```
show feedback
```

SQL*Plus will respond with the following:

```
FEEDBACK ON for 25 or more rows
```

The width used to display numbers also is changed by the SET command. You check it by typing

```
show numwidth
```

SQL*Plus will reply as shown here:

```
numwidth 10
```

Because 10 is a wide width for displaying page numbers that never contain more than two digits, shrink the display by typing

```
set numwidth 5
```

However, this means that all number columns will be five digits wide. If you anticipate having numbers with more than five digits, you must use a number greater than 5. Individual columns in the display also can be set independently. This will be covered in Chapter 6.

If NUMWIDTH is at least 7, Oracle displays the number in exponential format:

```
set numwidth 6

select 123456789123456789 num from DUAL;

   NUM
------
######

set numwidth 7

/

    NUM
-------
1.2E+17
```

SELECT, FROM, WHERE, and ORDER BY

You will use four primary keywords in SQL when selecting information from an Oracle table: SELECT, FROM, WHERE, and ORDER BY. You will use SELECT and FROM in every Oracle query you write.

The SELECT keyword tells Oracle which columns you want, and FROM tells Oracle the name(s) of the table(s) those columns are in. The NEWSPAPER table example showed how these keywords are used. In the first line that you entered, a comma follows each column name except the last. You'll notice that a correctly typed SQL query reads pretty much like an English sentence. A query in SQL*Plus usually ends with a semicolon (sometimes called the *SQL terminator*). The

WHERE keyword tells Oracle what qualifiers you'd like to put on the information it is selecting. For example, if you input

```
select feature, section, page from newspaper
where section = 'F';
```

```
FEATURE          S  PAGE
---------------  -  -----
Births           F     7
Classified       F     8
Obituaries       F     6
Doctor Is In     F     6
```

Oracle checks each row in the NEWSPAPER table before sending the row back to you. It skips over those without the single letter *F* in their SECTION column. It returns those where the SECTION entry is 'F', and SQL*Plus displays them for you.

To tell Oracle that you want the information it returns sorted in the order you specify, use ORDER BY. You can be as elaborate as you like about the order you request. Consider these examples:

```
select feature, section, page from newspaper
where section = 'F'
order by feature;
```

```
FEATURE          S  PAGE
---------------  -  -----
Births           F     7
Classified       F     8
Doctor Is In     F     6
Obituaries       F     6
```

They are nearly reversed when ordered by page, as shown here:

```
select feature, section, page from newspaper
where section = 'F'
order by page;
```

```
FEATURE          S  PAGE
---------------  -  -----
Obituaries       F     6
Doctor Is In     F     6
Births           F     7
Classified       F     8
```

In the next example, Oracle first puts the features in order by page (see the previous listing to observe the order they are in when they are ordered only by page). It then puts them in further order by feature, listing "Doctor Is In" ahead of "Obituaries".

```
select feature, section, page from newspaper
where section = 'F'
order by page, feature;
```

```
FEATURE           S   PAGE
---------------   -   -----
Doctor Is In      F     6
Obituaries        F     6
Births            F     7
Classified        F     8
```

Using ORDER BY also can reverse the normal order like this:

```
select feature, section, page from newspaper
where section = 'F'
order by page desc, feature;
```

```
FEATURE           S   PAGE
---------------   -   -----
Classified        F     8
Births            F     7
Doctor Is In      F     6
Obituaries        F     6
```

The DESC keyword stands for *descending.* Because it followed the word PAGE in the ORDER BY line, it put the page numbers in descending order. It would have the same effect on the FEATURE column if it followed the word FEATURE in the ORDER BY line.

Notice that each of these keywords—SELECT, FROM, WHERE, and ORDER BY—has its own way of structuring the words that follow it. The groups of words including these keywords are often called *clauses,* as shown in Figure 5-2.

Logic and Value

Just as the ORDER BY clause can have several parts, so can the WHERE clause, but with a significantly greater degree of sophistication. You control the extent to which you use WHERE through the careful use of logical instructions to Oracle on what you expect it to return to you. These instructions are expressed using mathematical symbols called *logical operators.* These are explained shortly, and they also are listed in the Alphabetical Reference section of this book.

`select feature, section, page`	←SELECT clause
`from newspaper`	←FROM clause
`where section = 'F'`	←WHERE clause

FIGURE 5-2. *Clauses*

The following is a simple example in which the values in the PAGE column are tested to see if any equals 6. Every row where this is true is returned to you. Any row in which PAGE is not equal to 6 is skipped (in other words, those rows for which PAGE = 6 is false).

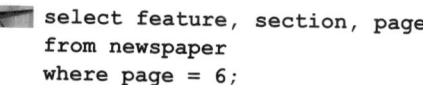

```
select feature, section, page
from newspaper
where page = 6;
```

```
FEATURE           S   PAGE
---------------   -   -----
Obituaries        F      6
Doctor Is In      F      6
```

The equal sign is called a *logical operator* because it operates by making a logical test that compares the values on either side of it—in this case, the value of PAGE and the value 6—to see if they are equal.

In this example, no quotes are placed around the value being checked because the column the value is compared to (the PAGE column) is defined as a NUMBER datatype. Numeric values do not require quotes around them during comparisons.

Single-Value Tests

You can use one of several logical operators to test against a single value, as shown in the next section, "Logical Tests Against a Single Value." Take a few examples from any of the expressions listed in this section. They all work similarly and can be combined at will, although they must follow certain rules about how they'll act together.

Logical Tests Against a Single Value

All these operators work with letters, numbers, or date values, and with columns or literals.

Equal, Greater Than, Less Than, Not Equal

page = 6	PAGE is equal to 6.
page > 6	PAGE is greater than 6.
page >= 6	PAGE is greater than or equal to 6.
page < 6	PAGE is less than 6.
page <= 6	PAGE is less than or equal to 6.
page != 6	PAGE is not equal to 6.
page ^= 6	PAGE is not equal to 6.
page <> 6	PAGE is not equal to 6.

Because some keyboards lack an exclamation mark (!) or a caret (^), Oracle gives you three ways to type the not-equal operator. The final alternative, <>, qualifies as a not-equal operator because it permits only numbers less than 6 (in this example) or greater than 6, but not 6 itself.

LIKE

`feature like 'Mo%'`	FEATURE begins with the letters "Mo".
`feature like '_ _ I%'`	FEATURE has an "I" in the third position.
`feature like '%o%o%'`	FEATURE has two "o"s in it.

LIKE performs pattern matching. An underline character (_) represents exactly one character. A percent sign (%) represents any number of characters, including zero characters.

IS NULL, IS NOT NULL

`precipitation is null`	PRECIPITATION is unknown.
`precipitation is not null`	PRECIPITATION is known.

NULL tests to see if data exists in a column for a row. If the column is completely empty and does not have any value at all, it is said to be "null." The word IS must be used with NULL and NOT NULL; equal, greater-than, and less-than signs do not work with NULL and NOT NULL.

Equal, Greater Than, Less Than, Not Equal

Logical tests can compare values both for equality and for relative value. Here, a simple test is made for all sections equal to "B":

```
select feature, section, page
from newspaper
where section = 'B';
```

```
FEATURE          S  PAGE
---------------  -  -----
Television       B    7
Modern Life      B    1
Movies           B    4
Bridge           B    2
```

The following is the test for all pages greater than 4:

```
select feature, section, page
from newspaper
where page > 4;
```

```
FEATURE          S  PAGE
---------------  -  -----
Editorials       A   12
Television       B    7
Births           F    7
Classified       F    8
Obituaries       F    6
Doctor Is In     F    6
```

The following is the test for sections greater than "B" (this means later in the alphabet than the letter "B"):

```
select feature, section, page
from newspaper
where section > 'B';
```

```
FEATURE           S  PAGE
---------------   - -----
Sports            D    1
Business          E    1
Weather           C    2
Births            F    7
Classified        F    8
Comics            C    4
Obituaries        F    6
Doctor Is In      F    6
```

Just as a test can be made for greater than, so can a test be made for less than, as shown here (all page numbers less than 8):

```
select feature, section, page
from newspaper
where page < 8;
```

```
FEATURE           S      PAGE
---------------   - ----------
National News     A         1
Sports            D         1
Business          E         1
Weather           C         2
Television        B         7
Births            F         7
Modern Life       B         1
Comics            C         4
Movies            B         4
Bridge            B         2
Obituaries        F         6
Doctor Is In      F         6
```

The opposite of the test for equality is the not-equal test, as given here:

```
select feature, section, page
from newspaper
where page <> 1;
```

```
FEATURE           S      PAGE
---------------   - ----------
Editorials        A        12
Weather           C         2
Television        B         7
Births            F         7
Classified        F         8
Comics            C         4
```

```
Movies         B      4
Bridge         B      2
Obituaries     F      6
Doctor Is In   F      6
```

NOTE
Be careful when using the greater-than and less-than operators against numbers that are stored in character datatype columns. All values in VARCHAR2 and CHAR columns are treated as character strings during comparisons. Therefore, numbers that are stored in those types of columns will be compared as if they were character strings, not numbers. If the column's datatype is NUMBER, then 12 is greater than 9. If it is a character column, then 9 is greater than 12, because the character '9' is greater than the character '1' in every character set's collating sequence.

LIKE

One of the commonly used features of SQL is a pattern-matching operator called LIKE, which is able to search through the rows of a database column for values that look like a pattern you describe. It uses two special characters to denote which kind of matching to do: a percent sign, called a *wildcard,* and an underline, called a *position marker.* To look for all the features that begin with the letters *Mo,* use the following:

```
select feature, section, page from newspaper
where feature like 'Mo%';
```

```
FEATURE         S     PAGE
--------------- - ----------
Modern Life     B        1
Movies          B        4
```

The percent sign (%) means anything is acceptable here: one character, a hundred characters, or no characters. If the first letters are "Mo", LIKE will find the feature. If the query had used 'MO%' as its search condition instead, then no rows would have been returned, owing to Oracle's case-sensitivity in data values.

If you want to find those features that have the letter "" in the third position of their titles, and you don't care which two characters precede the "i" or what set of characters follows, using two underscores (__) specifies that any character in those two positions is acceptable. Position three must have a lowercase "i", and the percent sign after that says anything is okay.

```
select feature, section, page from newspaper
where feature like '__i%';
```

```
FEATURE         S     PAGE
--------------- - ----------
Editorials      A       12
Bridge          B        2
Obituaries      F        6
```

Multiple percent signs also can be used. To find those words with two lowercase "o"s anywhere in the FEATURE title, three percent signs are used, as shown here:

```
select feature, section, page from newspaper
where feature like '%o%o%';
```

```
FEATURE          S    PAGE
--------------   -   ----------
Doctor Is In     F         6
```

For the sake of comparison, the following is the same query, but it is looking for two "i"s:

```
select feature, section, page from newspaper
where feature like '%i%i%';
```

```
FEATURE          S    PAGE
--------------   -   ----------
Editorials       A        12
Television       B         7
Classified       F         8
Obituaries       F         6
```

This pattern-matching feature can play an important role in making an application friendlier by simplifying searches for names, products, addresses, and other partially remembered items. In Chapter 8, you will see how to use advanced Unix-style regular expression searches.

NULL and NOT NULL

The NEWSPAPER table has no columns in it that are NULL, even though the DESCRIBE you performed on it showed that they are allowed. The following query on the COMFORT table contains, among other data, the precipitation for San Francisco, California, and Keene, New Hampshire, for four sample dates during 2011:

```
select city, sample_date, precipitation
from comfort;
```

```
CITY            SAMPLE_DA  PRECIPITATION
-------------   ---------  -------------
San Francisco   21-MAR-11           .5
San Francisco   22-JUN-11           .1
San Francisco   23-SEP-11           .1
San Francisco   22-DEC-11          2.3
Keene           21-MAR-11          4.4
Keene           22-JUN-11          1.3
Keene           23-SEP-11
Keene           22-DEC-11          3.9
```

You can find out the city and dates on which precipitation was not measured with this query:

```
select city, sample_date, precipitation
from comfort
where precipitation is null;
```

```
CITY            SAMPLE_DA  PRECIPITATION
-------------   ---------  -------------
Keene           23-SEP-11
```

IS NULL essentially instructs Oracle to identify rows whose columns are missing data. You don't know for that day whether the value should be 0, 1, or 5 inches. Because it is unknown, the value in the column is not set to 0; it stays empty. By using NOT with this query, you also can find those cities and dates for which data exists:

```
select city, sample_date, precipitation
from comfort
where precipitation is not null;


CITY          SAMPLE_DA PRECIPITATION
------------- --------- -------------
San Francisco 21-MAR-11           .5
San Francisco 22-JUN-11           .1
San Francisco 23-SEP-11           .1
San Francisco 22-DEC-11          2.3
Keene         21-MAR-11          4.4
Keene         22-JUN-11          1.3
Keene         22-DEC-11          3.9
```

Oracle lets you use the relational operators (=, !=, and so on) with NULL, but this kind of comparison will not return the expected results. Use IS or IS NOT for comparing values to NULL.

Simple Tests Against a List of Values

There are logical operators that test against a single value, and there others that test against many values, such as a list. The following tables show just such a group of operators.

Logical tests with numbers

page in (1,2,3)	PAGE is in the list (1,2,3).
page not in (1,2,3)	PAGE is not in the list (1,2,3).
page between 6 and 10	PAGE is equal to 6, 10, or anything in between.
page not between 6 and 10	PAGE is less than 6 or greater than 10.

With letters (or characters)

section in ('A','C','F')	SECTION is in the list ('A','C','F').
section not in ('A','C','F'))	SECTION is not in the list ('A','C','F').
section between 'B' and 'D'	SECTION is equal to 'B', 'D', or anything in between (alphabetically).
section not between 'B' AND 'D'	SECTION is below 'B' or above 'D' (alphabetically).

Here are a few examples of how these logical operators are used:

```
select feature, section, page
from newspaper
where section in ('A','B','F');
```

```
FEATURE           S      PAGE
--------------- - ----------
National News     A         1
Editorials        A        12
Television        B         7
Births            F         7
Classified        F         8
Modern Life       B         1
Movies            B         4
Bridge            B         2
Obituaries        F         6
Doctor Is In      F         6
```

```
select feature, section, page
from newspaper
where section not in ('A','B','F');
```

```
FEATURE           S      PAGE
--------------- - ----------
Sports            D         1
Business          E         1
Weather           C         2
Comics            C         4
```

```
select feature, section, page
from newspaper
where page between 7 and 10;
```

```
FEATURE           S      PAGE
--------------- - ----------
Television        B         7
Births            F         7
Classified        F         8
```

These logical tests also can be combined, as in this case:

```
select feature, section, page
from newspaper
where section = 'F'
  and page > 7;
```

```
FEATURE           S      PAGE
--------------- - ----------
Classified        F         8
```

The AND operator can be used to combine two logical expressions and requires any row Oracle examines to pass *both* tests; both SECTION = 'F' and PAGE > 7 must be true for a row to be returned from the query. Alternatively, OR can be used, which will return rows to you if *either* logical expression turns out to be true:

```
select feature, section, page
from newspaper
where section = 'F'
   or page > 7;
```

```
FEATURE          S  PAGE
---------------  -  -----
Editorials       A   12
Births           F    7
Classified       F    8
Obituaries       F    6
Doctor Is In     F    6
```

There are some SECTIONs (table rows) here that qualify even though they are not equal to "F" because their PAGE is greater than 7, and there are others whose PAGE is less than or equal to 7 but whose SECTION is equal to "F".

Finally, choose those features in Section F between pages 7 and 10 with this query:

```
select feature, section, page
from newspaper
where section = 'F'
  and  page between 7 and 10;
```

```
FEATURE          S  PAGE
---------------  -  -----
Births           F    7
Classified       F    8
```

There are a few additional *many-value operators* whose use is more complex; they will be covered in Chapter 9. They also can be found, along with those just discussed, in the Alphabetical Reference section of this book.

Combining Logic

Both AND and OR follow the common sense meanings of the words. They can be combined in a virtually unlimited number of ways, but you must use care, because ANDs and ORs get convoluted very easily.

Suppose you want to find the features in the paper that the editors tend to bury, those that are placed somewhere past page 2 of Section A or B. You might try this:

```
select feature, section, page
from newspaper
where section = 'A'
   or section = 'B'
  and  page > 2;
```

```
FEATURE          S  PAGE
---------------  -  -----
National News    A    1
Editorials       A   12
Television       B    7
Movies           B    4
```

Note that the result you got back from Oracle is not what you wanted. Somehow, page 1 of section A was included. Why is this happening? Is there a way to get Oracle to answer the question correctly? Although both AND and OR are logical connectors, AND is stronger. It binds the logical expressions on either side of it more strongly than OR does (technically, AND is said to have higher *precedence* or priority), which means the WHERE clause

```
where section = 'A'
   or section = 'B'
  and page > 2;
```

is interpreted to read, "where section is A, or where section is B *and* page is greater than 2." If you look at the failed example just given, you'll see how this interpretation affected the result. The AND is always evaluated first.

You can break this default precedence order by using parentheses that enclose those expressions you want to be interpreted together. Parentheses override the normal precedence:

```
select feature, section, page
from newspaper
where page > 2
  and ( section = 'A' or section = 'B' );
```

```
FEATURE            S PAGE
------------------ - ----
Editorials         A   12
Television         B    7
Movies             B    4
```

The result is exactly what you wanted in the first place. Note that although you can type this with the sections listed first, the result is identical because the parentheses tell Oracle what to interpret together. Compare this to the different results caused by changing the order in the first example, where parentheses were not used.

Another Use for WHERE: Subqueries

What if the logical operators in the earlier sections, "Logical Tests Against a Single Value" and "Logical Tests Against a List of Values," could be used not just with a single literal value (such as 'F') or a typed list of values (such as 4,2,7 or 'A','C','F'), but with values brought back by an Oracle query? In fact, this is a powerful SQL feature: using queries within other queries.

Imagine that you are the author of the "Doctor Is In" feature, and each newspaper that publishes your column sends along a copy of the table of contents that includes your piece. Of course, each editor rates your importance a little differently and places you in a section he or she deems suited to your feature. Without knowing ahead of time where your feature is, or with what other features you are placed, how could you write a query to find out where a particular local paper places your feature? You might do this:

```
select section from newspaper
where feature = 'Doctor Is In';
```

```
S
-
F
```

The result is "F". Knowing this, you could do this query:

```
select feature from newspaper
where section = 'F';
```

```
FEATURE
---------------
Births
Classified
Obituaries
Doctor Is In
```

You're in there with births, deaths, and classified ads. Could the two separate queries have been combined into one? Yes, as shown here:

```
select feature from newspaper
where section = (select section from newspaper
                where feature = 'Doctor Is In');
```

```
FEATURE
---------------
Births
Classified
Obituaries
Doctor Is In
```

Single Values from a Subquery

In effect, the SELECT statement in parentheses (called a *subquery*) brought back a single value, "F". The main query then treated this value as if it were a literal "F", as was used in the previous query. Remember that the equal sign is a single-value test. It can't work with lists, so if your subquery returned more than one row, you'd get an error message like this:

```
select * from newspaper
where section = (select section from newspaper
                where page = 1);
where section = (select section from newspaper
                 *
ERROR at line 2:
ORA-01427:  single-row subquery returns more than one row
```

All the logical operators that test single values can work with subqueries as long as the subquery returns a single row. For instance, you can ask for all the features in the paper where the section is *less than* (that is, earlier in the alphabet) the section that carries your column. The asterisk in this SELECT statement shows a shorthand way to request all the columns in a table without listing them individually. They will be displayed in the order in which they were created in the table.

```
select * from newspaper
where section < (select section from newspaper
                where Feature = 'Doctor Is In');
```

```
FEATURE         S  PAGE
--------------- -  -----
National News   A     1
Sports          D     1
Editorials      A    12
Business        E     1
Weather         C     2
Television      B     7
Modern Life     B     1
Comics          C     4
Movies          B     4
Bridge          B     2

10 rows selected.
```

Ten other features rank ahead of your medical advice in this local paper.

Lists of Values from a Subquery

Just as the single-value logical operators can be used on a subquery, so can the many-value operators. If a subquery returns one or more rows, the value in the column for each row will be stacked up in a list. For example, suppose you want to know the cities and countries where it is cloudy. You could have a table of complete weather information for all cities and a LOCATION table for all cities and their countries, as shown here:

```
select city, country from location;
```

```
CITY                          COUNTRY
----------------------------  ----------------------------
Athens                        Greece
Chicago                       United States
Conakry                       Guinea
Lima                          Peru
Madras                        India
Manchester                    England
Moscow                        Russia
Paris                         France
Shenyang                      China
Rome                          Italy
Tokyo                         Japan
Sydney                        Australia
Sparta                        Greece
Madrid                        Spain
```

```
select city, condition from weather;
```

```
CITY        CONDITION
----------- -----------
Lima        Rain
Paris       Cloudy
Manchester  Fog
Athens      Sunny
```

```
Chicago      Rain
Sydney       Sunny
Sparta       Cloudy
```

First, you'd discover which cities were cloudy:

```
select city from weather
where condition = 'Cloudy';

CITY
-----------
Paris
Sparta
```

Then, you would build a list including those cities and use it to query the LOCATION table:

```
select city, country from location
where city in ('Paris', 'Sparta');

CITY                           COUNTRY
------------------------       --------------------------
Paris                          France
Sparta                         Greece
```

The same task can be accomplished by a subquery, where the SELECT in parentheses builds a list of cities that are tested by the IN operator, as shown here:

```
select city, country from location
where city in (select city from weather
               where condition = 'Cloudy');

CITY                           COUNTRY
------------------------       --------------------------
Paris                          France
Sparta                         Greece
```

The other many-value operators work similarly. The fundamental task is to build a subquery that produces a list that can be logically tested. The following are some relevant points:

- The subquery must either have only one column or compare its selected columns to the same number of columns in parentheses in the main query (covered in Chapter 13).
- The subquery must be enclosed in parentheses.
- Subqueries that produce only one row can be used with *either* single- or many-value operators.
- Subqueries that produce more than one row can be used *only* with many-value operators.

Combining Tables

If you've normalized your data, you'll probably need to combine two or more tables to get all the information you want.

Suppose you are the oracle at Delphi. The Athenians come to ask about the forces of nature that might affect the expected attack by the Spartans, as well as the direction from which they are likely to appear:

```
select city, condition, temperature from weather;
```

```
CITY         CONDITION    TEMPERATURE
-----------  -----------  -----------
Lima         Rain                  45
Paris        Cloudy                81
Manchester   Fog                   66
Athens       Sunny                 97
Chicago      Rain                  66
Sydney       Sunny                 69
Sparta       Cloudy                74
```

You realize your geography is rusty, so you query the LOCATION table:

```
select city, longitude, eastwest, latitude, northsouth
from location;
```

```
CITY                     LONGITUDE E LATITUDE N
-----------------------  --------- - -------- -
Athens                       23.43 E    37.58 N
Chicago                      87.38 W    41.53 N
Conakry                      13.43 W     9.31 N
Lima                         77.11 W    12.11 S
Madras                       80.17 E    13.05 N
Manchester                    2.15 W    53.3  N
Moscow                       37.35 E    55.45 N
Paris                         2.2  E    48.52 N
Shenyang                    123.27 E    41.48 N
Rome                         12.29 E    41.54 N
Tokyo                       139.46 E    35.42 N
Sydney                      151.13 E    33.52 S
Sparta                       22.27 E    37.05 N
Madrid                        3.41 W    40.24 N
```

This is much more than you need, and it doesn't have any weather information. Yet these two tables, WEATHER and LOCATION, have a column in common: CITY. You can, therefore, put the information from the two tables together by joining them. You merely use the WHERE clause to tell Oracle what the two tables have in common:

```
select weather.city, condition, temperature, latitude,
       northsouth, longitude, eastwest
from weather, location
where weather.city = location.city;
```

```
CITY         CONDITION    TEMPERATURE LATITUDE N LONGITUDE E
-----------  -----------  ----------- -------- - --------- -
Athens       Sunny                 97    37.58 N    23.43 E
```

Chicago	Rain	66	41.53 N	87.38 W
Lima	Rain	45	12.11 S	77.11 W
Manchester	Fog	66	53.3 N	2.15 W
Paris	Cloudy	81	48.52 N	2.2 E
Sydney	Sunny	69	33.52 S	151.13 E
Sparta	Cloudy	74	37.05 N	22.27 E

Notice that the only rows in this combined table are those where the same city is in *both* tables. The WHERE clause is still executing your logic, as it did earlier in the case of the NEWSPAPER table. The logic you gave described the relationship between the two tables. It says, "Select those rows in the WEATHER table and the LOCATION table where the cities are equal." If a city is only in one table, it would have nothing to be equal to in the other table. The notation used in the SELECT statement is TABLE.COLUMN_NAME—in this case, WEATHER.CITY.

The SELECT clause has chosen those columns from the two tables that you'd like to see displayed; any columns in either table that you did not ask for are simply ignored. If the first line had simply said

```
select city, condition, temperature, latitude
```

then Oracle would not have known to which city you were referring. Oracle would tell you that the column name CITY was ambiguous. The correct wording in the SELECT clause is WEATHER.CITY or LOCATION.CITY. In this example, it won't make a bit of difference which of these alternatives is used, but you will encounter cases where the choice of identically named columns from two or more tables will contain very different data. In addition, if you're testing for an equality condition, you can specify the join column between two tables such that you won't have to qualify the column name in the SELECT clause; we'll cover this method in Chapter 13.

The WHERE clause also requires the names of the tables to accompany the identical column name by which the tables are combined: "where weather dot city equals location dot city" (that is, where the CITY column in the WEATHER table equals the CITY column in the LOCATION table).

Consider that the combination of the two tables looks like a single table with seven columns and seven rows. Everything that you excluded is gone. There is no HUMIDITY column here, even though it is a part of the WEATHER table. There is no COUNTRY column here, even though it is a part of the LOCATION table. And of the 14 cities in the LOCATION table, only those that are in the WEATHER table are included in this table. Your WHERE clause didn't allow the other columns to be selected.

A table that is built from columns in one or more tables is sometimes called a *projection table,* or a *result table.*

Creating a View

There is even more here than meets the eye. Not only does this look like a new table, but you can give it a name and treat it like one. This is called "creating a view." A *view* provides a way of hiding the logic that created the joined table just displayed. It works this way:

```
create view invasion as
select weather.city, condition, temperature, latitude,
    northsouth, longitude, eastwest
from weather, location
where weather.city = location.city;

View created.
```

Now you can act as if INVASION were a real table with its own rows and columns. You can even ask Oracle to describe it to you:

`describe invasion`

```
Name                               Null?     Type
-------------------------------    -------   -----------
CITY                                         VARCHAR2(11)
CONDITION                                    VARCHAR2(9)
TEMPERATURE                                  NUMBER
LATITUDE                                     NUMBER
NORTHSOUTH                                   CHAR(1)
LONGITUDE                                    NUMBER
EASTWEST                                     CHAR(1)
```

You can query it, too (note that you will not have to specify which table the CITY columns were from because that logic is hidden inside the view):

```
select city, condition, temperature, latitude, northsouth,
    longitude, eastwest
from invasion;
```

```
CITY          CONDITION    TEMPERATURE LATITUDE N LONGITUDE E
-----------   -----------  ----------- -------- - --------- -
Athens        Sunny                 97    37.58 N     23.43 E
Chicago       Rain                  66    41.53 N     87.38 W
Lima          Rain                  45    12.11 S     77.11 W
Manchester    Fog                   66     53.3 N      2.15 W
Paris         Cloudy                81    48.52 N      2.2 E
Sydney        Sunny                 69    33.52 S    151.13 E
Sparta        Cloudy                74    37.05 N     22.27 E
```

There will be some Oracle functions you won't be able to use on a view that you can use on a plain table, but they are few and mostly involve modifying rows and indexing tables, which will be discussed in later chapters. For the most part, a view behaves and can be manipulated just like any other table.

NOTE
Views do not contain any data. Tables contain data. Although you can create "materialized views" that contain data, they are truly tables, not views.

Suppose now you realize that you don't really need information about Chicago or other cities outside of Greece, so you change the query. Will the following work?

```
select city, condition, temperature, latitude, northsouth,
    longitude, eastwest
from invasion
where country = 'Greece';
```

SQL*Plus passes back this message from Oracle:

```
where country = 'Greece'
          *
ERROR at line 4:
ORA-00904: "COUNTRY": invalid identifier
```

Why? Because even though COUNTRY is a real column in one of the tables behind the view called INVASION, it was not included in the SELECT clause when the view was created. It is as if it does not exist. So, you must go back to the CREATE VIEW statement and include only the country of Greece there or add the COUNTRY column:

```
create or replace view invasion as
select weather.city, condition, temperature, latitude,
    northsouth, longitude, eastwest
from weather, location
where weather.city = location.city
  and country = 'Greece';
```

```
View created.
```

Using the CREATE OR REPLACE VIEW command allows you to create a new version of a view without first dropping the old one. This command makes it easier to administer users' privileges to access the view, as will be described in Chapter 19.

The logic of the WHERE clause has now been expanded to include both joining two tables and a single-value test on a column in one of those tables. Now, query Oracle. You'll get this response:

```
select city, condition, temperature, latitude, northsouth,
    longitude, eastwest
from invasion;
```

```
CITY        CONDITION   TEMPERATURE LATITUDE N LONGITUDE E
----------- ----------- ----------- -------- - --------- -
Athens      Sunny                97    37.58 N    23.43 E
Sparta      Cloudy               74    37.05 N    22.27 E
```

These results allow you to warn the Athenians that the Spartans are likely to appear from the southwest but will be overheated and tired from their march. With a little trigonometry, you could even make Oracle calculate how far they will have marched.

Expanding the View

The power of views to hide or even modify data can be used for a variety of useful purposes. Very complex reports can be built up by the creation of a series of simple views, and specific individuals or groups can be restricted to seeing only certain pieces of the whole table.

In fact, any qualifications you can put into a query can become part of a view. You could, for instance, let supervisors looking at a payroll table see only their own salaries and those of the people working for them, or you could restrict operating divisions in a company to seeing only their own financial results, even though the table actually contains results for all divisions. Most importantly, views are *not* snapshots of the data at a certain point in the past. They are dynamic and always reflect the data in the underlying tables. The instant data in a table is changed, any views created with that table change as well.

For example, you may create a view that restricts values based on column values. As shown here, a query that restricts the LOCATION table on the COUNTRY column could be used to limit the rows that are visible via the view:

```
create or replace view peru_locations as
select * from location
where country = 'Peru';
```

A user querying PERU_LOCATIONS would not be able to see any rows from any country other than Peru.

The queries used to define views may also reference *pseudo-columns*. A pseudo-column is a "column" that returns a value when it is selected, but is not an actual column in a table. The USER pseudo-column, when selected, will always return the Oracle username that executed the query. So, if a column in the table contains usernames, those values can be compared against the USER pseudo-column to restrict its rows, as shown in the following listing. In this example, the NAME table is queried. If the value of its NAME column is the same as the name of the user entering the query, then rows will be returned.

```
create or replace view restricted_names as
select * from name
where name = user;
```

This type of view is very useful when users require access to selected rows in a table. It prevents them from seeing any rows that do not match their Oracle username.

Views are powerful tools. There will be more to come on the subject of views in Chapter 17.

In summary, the WHERE clause can be used to join two tables based on a common column or columns. The resulting set of data can be turned into a view (with its own name), which can be treated as if it were a regular table itself. The power of a view is in its ability to limit or change the way data is seen by a user, even though the underlying tables themselves are not affected.

CHAPTER

6

Basic SQL*Plus Reports and Commands

S QL*Plus is usually thought of as a tool to manipulate data and perform ad hoc queries against the database; it can also function as an interactive report writer when a GUI tool might be overkill or not even available. It uses SQL commands to get information from the Oracle database, and it lets you create reports by giving you easy control over titles, column headings, subtotals and totals, reformatting of numbers and text, and much more. It also can be used to change the database through the INSERT, UPDATE, MERGE, and DELETE commands in SQL. SQL*Plus can even be used as a code generator, where a series of commands in SQL*Plus can dynamically build a program and then execute it.

In most production applications, more advanced report writers are used—such as Web-based parameter-driven reports using tools such as Oracle Application Express (APEX). SQL*Plus is most commonly used for simple queries and printed reports. Getting SQL*Plus to format information in reports according to your tastes and needs requires only a handful of *commands*—keywords that instruct SQL*Plus how to behave. These are listed in Table 6-1. Detailed explanations, examples, and additional features of each of these commands are given in the Alphabetical Reference section of this book.

In this chapter, you will see a basic report that was written using SQL*Plus, along with an explanation of the features used to create it. If building a report seems a bit daunting at first, don't worry. Once you try the steps, you'll find them simple to understand, and they will soon become familiar.

You can write SQL*Plus reports while working interactively with SQL*Plus—that is, you can type commands about page headings, column titles, formatting, breaks, totals, and so on, and then execute a SQL query, and SQL*Plus will immediately produce the report formatted to your specifications. For quick answers to simple questions that aren't likely to recur, this is a fine approach. More common, however, are complex reports that need to be produced periodically and that you'll want to print or save to a file rather than just view on the screen. Unfortunately, when you quit SQL*Plus, it promptly forgets every instruction you've given it. If you were restricted to using SQL*Plus only in this interactive way, then running the same report at a later time would require typing everything all over again.

The alternative is very straightforward. You simply type the commands, line by line, into a file. SQL*Plus can then read this file as if it were a script, and execute your commands just as if you were typing them. In effect, you create a report program, but you do it without a programmer or a compiler. You create this file using any of the popular editor programs available, or even (given certain restrictions) a word processor.

The editor is not a part of Oracle. Editors come in hundreds of varieties, and every company or person seems to have a favorite. Most editors are native to a particular operating system as well, whereas SQL*Plus is the same regardless of the OS. Oracle realized this and decided to let you choose which editor program to use, rather than packaging a program with Oracle and forcing you to use it. When you're ready to use your editor program, you suspend SQL*Plus, jump over to the editor program, create or change your SQL*Plus report program or script (also called a *start file*), and then jump back to SQL*Plus, right at the spot you left, and run the report (see Figure 6-1).

Command	Definition
REMARK	Tells SQL*Plus that the words to follow are to be treated as comments, not instructions.
SET HEADSEP	Acts as a heading separator; identifies the single character that tells SQL*Plus to split a title into two or more lines.
TTITLE	Sets the top title for each page of a report.
BTITLE	Sets the bottom title for each page of a report.
COLUMN	Gives SQL*Plus a variety of instructions on the heading, format, and treatment of a column.
BREAK ON	Tells SQL*Plus where to put spaces between sections of a report, or where to break for subtotals and totals.
COMPUTE SUM	Makes SQL*Plus calculate subtotals.
SET LINESIZE	Sets the maximum number of characters allowed on any line of the report.
SET PAGESIZE	Sets the maximum number of lines per page.
SET NEWPAGE	Sets the number of blank lines between pages.
SPOOL	Moves a report you would normally see displayed on the screen into a file, so you can print it.
/* */	Marks the beginning and ending of a comment within a SQL entry. Similar to remark.
--	Marks the beginning of an inline comment within a SQL entry. Treats everything from the mark to the end of the line as a comment. Similar to remark.
SET PAUSE	Makes the screen display stop between pages of output.
SAVE	Saves the SQL query you're creating into the file of your choice.
HOST	Sends any command to the host operating system.
START OR @	Tells SQL*Plus to follow (execute) the instructions you've saved in a text file.
EDIT	Pops you out of SQL*Plus and into the editor of your choice.
DEFINE _EDITOR	Tells SQL*Plus the name of the editor of your choice.
EXIT OR QUIT	Terminates SQL*Plus.

TABLE 6-1.   *Basic SQL*Plus Commands*

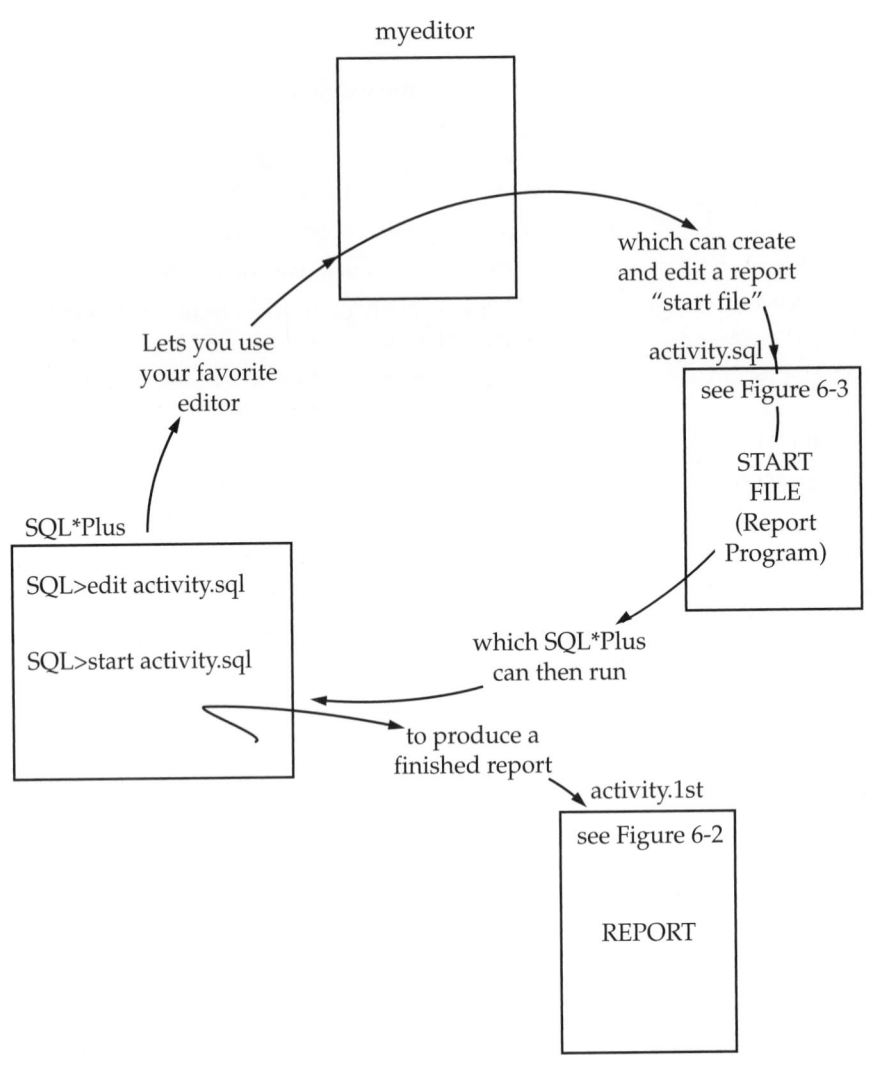

FIGURE 6-1. *Report-creation process*

SQL*Plus also has a built-in editor of its own, sometimes called the *command line editor,* that allows you to quickly modify a SQL query without leaving SQL*Plus. Using this editor will be covered later in this chapter.

Building a Simple Report
Figure 6-2 provides a quick-and-easy report showing the dates books were checked out and returned during a three-month time period.

```
Thu Apr 04                                                      page 1

              Checkout Log for 1/1/12-3/31/12


                                                              Days
     NAME                   TITLE            CHECKOUTD RETURNEDD  Out
     -------------------- -------------------- --------- --------- -------
     Dorah Talbot           Either/Or          02-Jan-12 10-Jan-12   8.00
                            Polar Express      01-Feb-12 15-Feb-12  14.00
                            Good Dog, Carl     01-Feb-12 15-Feb-12  14.00
                            My Ledger          15-Feb-12 03-Mar-12  16.00
     ********************                                        -------
     Avg                                                          13.00


     Angie Talbot           Anne Of Green Gables 02-Jan-12 20-Jan-12  18.00
                            Midnight Magic     20-Jan-12 03-Feb-12  14.00
                            Harry Potter And The 03-Feb-12 14-Feb-12  11.00
                            Prisoner Of Azkaban
     ********************                                        -------
     Avg                                                          14.33


     Fred Fuller            John Adams         01-Feb-12 01-Mar-12  28.00
                            Truman             01-Mar-12 20-Mar-12  19.00
     ********************                                        -------
     Avg                                                          23.50


     Gerhardt Kentgen       Wonderful Life     02-Jan-12 02-Feb-12  31.00
                            Midnight Magic     05-Feb-12 10-Feb-12   5.00
                            The Mismeasure Of  13-Feb-12 05-Mar-12  20.00
                            Man
     ********************                                        -------
     Avg                                                          18.67


     Jed Hopkins            Innumeracy         01-Jan-12 22-Jan-12  21.00
                            To Kill A          15-Feb-12 01-Mar-12  14.00
                            Mockingbird
     ********************                                        -------
     Avg                                                          17.50


     Pat Lavay              The Shipping News  02-Jan-12 12-Jan-12  10.00
                            The Mismeasure Of  12-Jan-12 12-Feb-12  31.00
                            Man
     ********************                                        -------
     Avg                                                          20.50


     Roland Brandt          The Shipping News  12-Jan-12 12-Mar-12  59.00
                            The Discoverers    12-Jan-12 01-Mar-12  48.00
                            West With The Night 12-Jan-12 01-Mar-12  48.00
     ********************                                        -------
     Avg                                                          51.67


                                                              -------
     Avg                                                          22.58

                         From The Bookshelf
```

FIGURE 6-2.   *Bookshelf checkout report output*

① **REMARK**

The first line of Figure 6-3, at Circle 1, is documentation about the start file itself. Documentation lines begin with

REM

which stands for REMARK. SQL*Plus ignores anything on a line that begins with REM, thus allowing you to add comments, documentation, and explanations to any start file you create. It is always a good idea to place remarks at the top of a start file, giving the filename, its creator and date of creation, the name of anyone who has modified it, the date of modification, what was modified, and an explanation of the purpose of the file. This information will prove invaluable later on, as you develop more complex reports or when dozens of reports begin to accumulate.

FIGURE 6-3. *The activity .sql file*

SQL*Plus and SQL

The SELECT statement toward the bottom of Figure 6-3, beginning with the word SELECT and ending with the semicolon (;), is *Structured Query Language*—the language you use to talk to the Oracle database. Every other command on the page is a SQL*Plus command, used to format the results of a SQL query into a report.

The SQL*Plus START command causes SQL*Plus to read the file **activity.sql** and execute the instructions you've placed in it. Reviewing this start file will show you the basic SQL*Plus instructions you can use to produce reports or change the way SQL*Plus interacts with you. Depending on your experience, this may seem formidable or elementary. It is made up of a series of simple instructions to SQL*Plus.

Figure 6-3 shows the SQL*Plus start file that produced this report (in this case, named **activity.sql**). To run this report program in SQL*Plus, type the following:

```
start activity.sql
```

② SET HEADSEP

The punctuation that follows SET HEADSEP (for HEADing SEParator) at Circle 2 in Figure 6-3 tells SQL*Plus how you will indicate where you want to break a page title or a column heading that runs longer than one line. When you first activate SQL*Plus, the default HEADSEP character is the vertical bar (|), but if you want to use vertical bars in your titles, you may find it simpler to use a different HEADSEP character. The heading separator command only works for the COLUMN command, not as part of a SELECT statement.

```
set headsep !
```

CAUTION
Choosing a character that may otherwise appear in a title or column heading will cause unexpected line splitting.

③ TTITLE and BTITLE

The line

```
ttitle 'Checkout Log for 1/1/12-3/31/12'
```

at Circle 3 in Figure 6-3 instructs SQL*Plus to put this "TOP TITLE" at the top of each page of the report. The title you choose must be enclosed in single quotation marks. The line

```
btitle 'From The Bookshelf'
```

works similarly to TTITLE, except that it goes at the bottom of each page (as the *B* indicates), and it also must be in single quotation marks. Because single quotes are used to enclose the entire title, an apostrophe (the same character on your keyboard) would trick SQL*Plus into believing the title had ended.

NOTE
Put two single quotation marks right next to each other when you want to print an apostrophe or a single quotation mark. Because both SQL and SQL*Plus rely on single quotation marks to enclose strings of characters, this technique is used throughout SQL and SQL*Plus whenever an apostrophe needs to be printed or displayed.

When using TTITLE this way, SQL*Plus will always center the title you choose based on the LINESIZE you set (LINESIZE will be discussed later in the chapter), and it will always place the weekday, month, and the day of the month on which the report was run in the upper-left corner and the page number in the upper-right corner.

You can use the REPHEADER and REPFOOTER commands to create headers and footers for reports. See the Alphabetical Reference section of this book for descriptions of REPHEADER and REPFOOTER.

COLUMN

COLUMN allows you to change the heading and format of any column in a SELECT statement. Look at the report shown earlier in Figure 6-2. The fifth column, Days Out, is not a column in the database, and it's called DAYSOUT in the query shown in Figure 6-3. The line

```
column DaysOut heading 'Days!Out'
```

relabels the column and gives it a new heading. This heading breaks into two lines because it has the HEADSEP character (!) embedded in it. The line

```
column Name format a20
```

 at Circle 4 sets the width for the NAME column's display at 20. The *a* tells SQL*Plus that this is an alphabetic column, as opposed to a numeric column. The width can be set to virtually any value, irrespective of how the column is defined in the database.

 The NAME column is defined as 25 characters wide, so it's possible that some names will have more than 20 characters. If you did nothing else in defining this column on the report, any name more than 20 characters long would wrap onto the next line. Looking at Figure 6-2 again, you can see that four of the titles have wrapped; the TITLE column is defined as VARCHAR2(100) but is formatted as a20 (see Circle 5).

Instead of using theWORD_WRAPPED format, you could choose TRUNCATED, eliminating the display of any characters that exceed the specified format length for the column.

 Circle 6 in Figure 6-3 shows an example of formatting a number:

```
column DaysOut format 999.99
```

This defines a column with room for five digits and a decimal point. If you count the spaces in the report for the DAYSOUT column, you'll see seven spaces. Just looking at the COLUMN command might lead you to believe the column would be six spaces wide, but this would leave no room for a minus sign if the number were negative, so an extra space on the left is always provided for numbers.

 Circle 7 in Figure 6-3 refers to a column that didn't appear in the table when we had SQL*Plus describe it:

```
column DaysOut heading 'Days!Out'
```

What is DAYSOUT? Look at the SELECT statement at the bottom of Figure 6-3. DAYSOUT appears in the following line:

```
returned_date-checkout_date as daysout /*count days*/
```

This tells SQL to perform date arithmetic—count the number of days between two dates—and give the computation a simpler column name. As a consequence, SQL*Plus sees a column named DAYSOUT, and all its formatting and other commands will act as if it were a real column in the table. The COLUMN command for DAYSOUT is an example. "DAYSOUT" is referred to as a *column alias*—another name to use when referring to a column.

⑧ BREAK ON

Look at Circle 8 in Figure 6-3. Note on the report in Figure 6-2 how the checkout records for each name are grouped together. This effect was produced by the line

```
break on Name skip 1 on report
```

as well as by the line

```
order by name, checkout_date;
```

in the SELECT statement near the end of the start file.

SQL*Plus looks at each row as it is brought back from Oracle and keeps track of the value in NAME. For the first four rows, this value is Dorah Talbot, so SQL*Plus displays the rows it has retrieved so far. On the fifth row, NAME changes to Emily Talbot. SQL*Plus remembers your break instructions, which tell it that when NAME changes, it should break away from the normal display of row after row and skip one line. You'll notice one line between the NAME sections on the report. Unless the names were collected together because of the ORDER by clause, it wouldn't make sense for BREAK on to skip one line every time NAME changed. This is why the BREAK on command and the ORDER BY clause must be coordinated.

You also may notice that the name Dorah Talbot is only printed on the first line of its section, as are the rest of the names. This eliminates the duplicate printing of each of these names for every row in each section, which is visually unattractive. If you want, you can force SQL*Plus to duplicate the name on each row of its section by altering the BREAK on command to read

```
break on name duplicate skip 1
```

The report output in Figure 6-2 shows an average for DAYSOUT for the entire report. To be able to get a grand total for a report, add an additional break using the BREAK ON report command. Be careful when adding breaks because they all need to be created by a single command; entering two consecutive BREAK ON commands will cause the first command's instructions to be replaced by the second command. See Circle 8 for the BREAK ON command used for the report:

```
break on name skip 1 on report
```

⑨ COMPUTE AVG

The averages calculated for each section on the report were produced by the COMPUTE AVG command at Circle 9. This command always works in conjunction with the BREAK ON command, and the totals computed are always for the section specified by BREAK ON. It is probably wise to consider these two related commands as a single unit:

```
break on Name skip 1 on report
compute avg of DaysOut on Name
compute avg of DaysOut on report
```

In other words, this tells SQL*Plus to compute the average of the DAYSOUT for each NAME. SQL*Plus does this first for Dorah Talbot and then for each successive name. Every time SQL*Plus sees a new name, it calculates and prints an average for the previous DAYSOUT values. COMPUTE avg also puts a row of asterisks below the column that BREAK ON is using, and it prints "Avg" underneath. For reports with many columns that need to be added, a separate COMPUTE avg (or COMPUTE sum if you're calculating sums) statement is used for each calculation. It also is possible to have several different kinds of breaks on a large report (for NAME, TITLE, and dates, for example), along with coordinated COMPUTE avg commands.

You can use a BREAK ON command without a COMPUTE sum command, such as for organizing your report into sections where no totals are needed (addresses with a BREAK ON CITY would be an example), but the reverse is not true.

NOTE
Every COMPUTE AVG command must have a BREAK ON command to guide it, and the ON portion of both commands must match (such as ON NAME in the preceding example: BREAK ON NAME SKIP 1 ON REPORT AND COMPUTE AVG OF DAYSOUT ON NAME).

The following are the basic rules:

- Every BREAK ON must have a related ORDER BY.
- Every COMPUTE AVG must have a related BREAK ON.

This makes sense, of course, but it's easy to forget one of the pieces. In addition to COMPUTE AVG, you can also use COMPUTE SUM, COMPUTE COUNT, COMPUTE MAX, or any other of Oracle's grouping functions on the set of records.

⑩ SET LINESIZE

The four commands at Circle 10 in Figure 6-3 control the gross dimensions of your report. The command SET LINESIZE governs the maximum number of characters that will appear on a single line. For letter-size paper or smaller terminal windows, this number is usually around 75 or 80, unless your printer uses a very compressed (narrow) character font.

If you put more columns of information in your SQL query than will fit into the LINESIZE you've allotted, SQL*Plus will wrap the additional columns down onto the next line and stack columns under each other. You actually can use this to very good effect when a lot of data needs to be presented.

SQL*Plus also uses LINESIZE to determine where to center the TTITLE, and where to place the date and page number. Both the date and page number appear on the top line, and the distance between the first letter of the date and the last digit of the page number will always equal the LINESIZE you set.

SET PAGESIZE

The SET PAGESIZE command sets the total number of lines SQL*Plus will place on each page, including the TTITLE, BTITLE, COLUMN HEADINGS, and any blank lines it prints. The value for PAGESIZE can be from 0 (do not show headings) to 50000, depending on what device or window you'll use to view the report. SET PAGESIZE is coordinated with SET NEWPAGE. The default PAGESIZE is 14.

NOTE
SET PAGESIZE does not set the size of the body of the report (the number of printed lines from the date down to the BTITLE); instead, it sets the total length of the page, measured in lines.

SET NEWPAGE

A better name for SET NEWPAGE might have been "set blank lines" because what it really does is print blank lines before the top line (date, page number) of each page in your report. This command is useful both for adjusting the position of reports coming out on single pages on a laser printer and for skipping over the perforations between the pages of continuous-form computer paper (that is, if you still print reports!).

Therefore, if you type

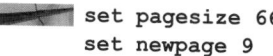
```
set pagesize 66
set newpage 9
```

SQL*Plus produces a report starting with nine blank lines, followed by 57 lines of information (counting from the date down to the BTITLE). If you increase the size of NEWPAGE, SQL*Plus puts fewer rows of information on each page, but produces more pages altogether.

That's understandable, you say, but what has been done at Circle 10 on Figure 6-3?

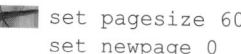
```
set pagesize 60
set newpage 0
```

This is a strange size for a report page. Is SQL*Plus to put zero blank lines between pages? No. Instead, the 0 after NEWPAGE switches on a special property: SET NEWPAGE 0 produces a *top-of-form* character (usually a hex 13) just before the date on each page. Most modern printers respond to this by moving immediately to the top of the next page, where the printing of the report will begin. The combination of SET PAGESIZE 60 and SET NEWPAGE 0 produces a report whose body of information is exactly 60 lines long and which has a top-of-form character at the beginning of each page. This is a cleaner and simpler way to control page printing than jockeying around with blank lines and lines per page. You can also use the SET NEWPAGE none command, which results in no blank lines and no form feeds between report pages.

NOTE
*Directives such as PAGESIZE and NEWPAGE become obsolete if you use XML as your output format. Using SQL*Plus with XML formatting is covered in subsequent chapters.*

(11) SPOOL

In the early days of computers, most file storage was done on spools of either magnetic wire or tape (yes, that would be in the mid- to late-20th century). Writing information into a file and spooling a file were virtually synonymous. The term has survived, and *spooling* now generally refers to any process of moving information from one place to another. In SQL*Plus,

```
spool activity.lst
```

tells SQL to take all the output from SQL*Plus and write it to the file named activity.lst. Once you've told SQL*Plus to spool, it continues to do so until you tell it to stop, which you do by exiting or by inputting the following:

```
spool off
```

This means, for instance, that you could type

```
spool work.fil
```

and then type a SQL query, such as

```
select feature, section, page from newspaper
where section = 'F';
```

```
FEATURE          S   PAGE
---------------  -   ----
Births           F      7
Classified       F      8
Obituaries       F      6
Doctor Is In     F      6
```

or a series of SQL*Plus commands, such as

```
set pagesize 60
column section heading 'My Favorites'
```

or anything else. Whatever prompts SQL*Plus produces, whatever error messages you get, whatever appears on the computer screen while spooling—it all ends up in the file work.fil. Spooling doesn't discriminate. It records everything that happens from the instant you use the SPOOL command until you use SPOOL OFF, which brings us back to the report at Circle 11 of Figure 6-3:

```
spool activity.lst
```

This phrase is carefully placed as the command just before the SELECT statement, and SPOOL off immediately follows. Had SPOOL activity.lst appeared any earlier, the SQL*Plus commands you were issuing would have ended up on the first page of your report file. Instead, they go into the file **activity.lst**, which is what you see in Figure 6-2: the results of the SQL query, formatted according to your instructions, and nothing more. You are now free to print the file, confident that a clean report will show up on your printer or in a PDF document.

This set of commands prints the SQL query on the first page of the output, followed by the data starting on the second page. To not show the SQL query with the output, you can also change the order of commands: Type in the SQL query but without the concluding semicolon. Press ENTER twice, and the command is still in SQL*Plus's buffer, unexecuted. You can then start spooling and execute the command:

```
(SQL command typed here)

spool activity.lst
/
spool off
```

You can append data to existing spool files. The default is (as in prior versions) to create a new output file. You can now use the APPEND or REPLACE option of the SPOOL command to either append data to an existing file that matches the name you give, or replace that existing file with your new output, respectively.

(12) */* */*

Circle 12 of Figure 6-3 shows how a comment can be embedded in a SQL statement. This is different in method and use from the REMARK statement discussed earlier. REMARK (or REM) must appear at the beginning of a line, and it works only for the single line on which it appears. Furthermore, a multiple-line SQL statement is not permitted to have a REMARK within it. For example, the following is wrong:

```
select feature, section, page
rem this is just a comment
from newspaper
where section = 'F';
```

This will not work, and you'll get an error message. However, you can embed remarks in SQL following the method shown at Circle 12, or like this:

```
select feature, section, page
 /* this is just a comment */
from newspaper
where section = 'F';
```

The secret lies in knowing that /* tells SQL*Plus a comment has begun. Everything it sees from that point forward, even if it continues for many words and lines, is regarded as a comment, until SQL*Plus sees */, which tells it that the comment has ended. You can also use the characters – – to begin a comment. The end of the line ends the comment. This kind of comment works just like a single-line version of /* */, except that you use –– (two dashes) instead.

Some Clarification on Column Headings

It's possible that the difference between the renaming that occurs in

```
returned_date-checkout_date as daysout
```

and the new heading given the column heading specified in

```
column DaysOut heading 'Days!Out'
```

is not quite clear, particularly if you look at this command:

```
compute avg of daysout on name
```

SQL*Plus commands are aware only of columns that actually appear in the SELECT statement. Every COLUMN command refers to a column in the SELECT statement. Both BREAK ON and COMPUTE refer only to columns in the SELECT statement. The only reason a COLUMN command or a COMPUTE command is aware of the column DAYSOUT is that it got its name in the SELECT statement itself. The renaming of "RETURNED_DATE-CHECKOUT_DATE" to "DAYSOUT" is something done by SQL, *not* by SQL*Plus.

Other Features

It's not terribly difficult to look at a start file and the report it produces and see how all the formatting and computation was accomplished. It's possible to begin by creating the start file, typing into it each of the commands you expect you'll need and then running it in SQL*Plus to see if it is correct. But when you're creating reports for the first time, it is often much simpler to experiment interactively with SQL*Plus, adjusting column formats, the SQL query, the titles, and the totals, until what you really want begins to take shape.

Command Line Editor

When you type a SQL statement, SQL*Plus remembers each line as you enter it, storing it in what is called the *SQL buffer* (a fancy name for a computer scratchpad where your SQL statements are kept). Suppose you've entered this query:

```
select featuer, section, page
from newspaper
where section = 'F';
```

SQL*Plus responds with the following:

```
select featuer, section, page
       *
ERROR at line 1:
ORA-00904: "FEATUER": invalid identifier
```

You now realize you've misspelled "Feature." You do not have to retype the entire query. The command line editor is already present and waiting for instructions. First, ask it to list your query:

```
list
```

SQL*Plus immediately responds with this:

```
1    select featuer, section, page
2    from newspaper
3*   where section = 'F'
```

Notice that SQL*Plus shows all three lines and numbers them. It also places an asterisk next to line 3, which means it is the line your editing commands are able to affect. But you want to change line 1, so you type and SQL*Plus lists the following:

list 1

```
     1* select featuer, section, page
```

Line 1 is displayed and is now the current line. You can change it by typing this:

change /featuer/feature

```
  1* select feature, section, page
```

You can use C in place of CHANGE.
You can check the whole query again with either LIST or just the letter L:

list

```
  1  select feature, section, page
  2  from newspaper
  3* where section = 'F'
```

If you believe this is correct, enter a single slash after the prompt. This slash has nothing to do with the CHANGE command or the editor. Instead, it tells SQL*Plus to execute the SQL statement in the buffer again:

/

```
FEATURE          S   PAGE
---------------  -   ----
Births           F     7
Classified       F     8
Obituaries       F     6
Doctor Is In     F     6
```

The CHANGE command requires that you mark the start and end of the text to be changed with a slash (/) or some other character. The line

c $featuer$feature

would have worked just as well. SQL*Plus looks at the first character after the word CHANGE (which can be abbreviated to C as in this example) and assumes that is the character you've chosen to use to mark the start and end of the incorrect text (these markers are usually called *delimiters*). You can also delete the current line, as shown here:

list

```
  1  select feature, section, page
  2  from newspaper
  3* where section = 'F'
```

del

list

```
  1  select feature, section, page
  2  from newspaper
```

DEL will delete just what is on the current line. You can pass the DEL command a range of line numbers, to delete multiple lines at once, by specifying the first and last line numbers for the range of lines to delete. To delete lines 3 through 7, use DEL 3 7. Note you include a space before the number of the first line to delete (3) and another space before the number of the last line to delete (7). If you leave out the space between the 3 and the 7, SQL*Plus will try to delete line 37. To delete from line 2 to the end of the buffer, use DEL 2 LAST. You can use the same kind of syntax with the LIST command; for example, LIST 3 7 will list the lines 3 through 7. See the entries for the DEL and LIST commands in the Alphabetical Reference for the full syntax options.

The command DELETE (spelled out) will erase all the lines and put the word DELETE as line 1. This will only cause problems, so avoid typing the whole word DELETE and just type DEL. If your goal is to clear out the SELECT statement completely, type this:

```
clear buffer
```

If you'd like to append something to the current line, you can use the APPEND command (or just the letter A):

```
list 1
```

```
1* select feature, section, page
```

```
a  "whereitis"
```

```
1* select feature, section, page "whereitis"
```

APPEND places its text right up against the end of the current line, with no spaces in between. To put a space in, as was done here, type *two* spaces between the word APPEND and the text.

You may also INPUT a whole new line after the current line, as shown here:

```
list
```

```
1  select feature, section, page "whereitis"
2* from newspaper
```

```
input where section = 'A'
```

```
list
```

```
1  select feature, section, page "whereitis"
2  from newspaper
3* where section = 'A'
```

Then you can set the column heading for the WHEREITIS column:

```
column whereitis heading "Where It Is"
```

And then you can run the query:

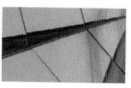 /

```
FEATURE          S Where It Is
--------------   - -----------
National News    A           1
Editorials       A          12
```

To review, the command line editor can LIST the SQL statement you've typed, CHANGE or DELETE the current line (marked by the asterisk), APPEND something onto the end of the current line, or INPUT an entire line after the current line. Once your corrections are made, the SQL statement will execute if you type a slash at the SQL> prompt.

CAUTION
Each of these commands can be abbreviated to its own first letter, except DEL, which must be exactly the three letters: DEL.

The command line editor can edit only your SQL statement. It cannot edit SQL*Plus commands. If you've typed COLUMN Name format a18, for instance, and want to change it to COLUMN Name format a20, you must retype the whole thing (this is in the SQL*Plus interactive mode—if you've got the commands in a file, you obviously can change them with your own editor). Also note that in interactive mode, once you've started to type a SQL statement, you must complete it before you can enter any additional SQL*Plus commands, such as COLUMN formats or TTITLE. As soon as SQL*Plus sees the word SELECT, it assumes everything to follow is part of the SELECT statement until it sees *either* a semicolon (;) at the end of the last SQL statement line *or* a slash (/) at the beginning of the line after the last SQL statement line.
Either of these is correct:

```
select * from ledger;

select * from ledger
/
```

This, however, is not:

```
select * from ledger/
```

SET PAUSE
During the development of a new report or when using SQL*Plus for quick queries of the database, it's usually helpful to set the LINESIZE at 79 or 80, the PAGESIZE at 24 (the default is 14), and NEWPAGE at 1. You accompany this with two related commands, as shown here:

```
set pause 'More. . .'
set pause on
```

From Legacy to Leading Edge

Although SQL*Plus has been and always will be adept at formatting output to fit monospaced on an 8.5" by 11" piece of paper, it will always keep up with the needs of the latest version of the database it connects to. Thousands of Oracle shops with thousands of SQL*Plus scripts that work just fine every day will likely still be using hundreds of them several Oracle versions from now.

For example, SQL*Plus for Oracle Database 12*c* has a new SET command, SET COLINVISIBLE, to allow invisible column metadata to be displayed in a DESCRIBE command. Invisible columns were introduced in Oracle Database 11*g*.

The SQL*Plus STARTUP command supports Oracle 12*c* pluggable databases along with new SHOW commands to display information about pluggable databases and their containers.

This combination produces exactly one full screen of information for each page of the report that is produced and pauses at each page for viewing ("More. . ." will appear in the lower-left corner) until you press ENTER. After the various column headings and titles are worked out, the PAGESIZE can be readjusted for a page of paper and the pause eliminated with this:

```
set pause off
```

SAVE

If the changes you want to make to your SQL statement are extensive, or if you simply want to work in your own editor, save the SQL you've created so far, in interactive mode, by writing the SQL to a file, like this:

```
save fred.sql
```

SQL*Plus responds with

```
Created file fred.sql
```

Your SQL (but not any COLUMN, TTITLE, or other SQL*Plus commands) is now in a file named **fred.sql** (or a name of your choice), which you can edit using your own editor.

If the file already exists, you must use the REPLACE option (abbreviated REP) of the SAVE command to save the new query in a file with that name. For this example, the syntax would be

```
save fred.sql rep
```

Alternatively, you could append to the **fred.sql** file with the command **save fred.sql app**.

Store

You can use the STORE command to save your current SQL*Plus environment settings to a file. The following creates a file called **my_settings.sql** and stores the settings in that file:

```
store set my_settings.sql create
```

If the **my_settings.sql** file already exists, you can use the REPLACE option instead of CREATE, replacing the old file with the new settings. You could also use the APPEND option to append the new settings to an existing file.

Editing

Everyone has a favorite editor. Word processing programs can be used with SQL*Plus, but only if you save the files created in them in ASCII format (see your word processor manual for details on how to do this). Editors are just programs themselves. They are normally invoked simply by typing their name at the operating system prompt. On Linux or Unix, it usually looks something like this:

```
$ vi fred.sql
```

In this example, vi is your editor's name, and fred.sql represents the file you want to edit (the start file described previously was used here only as an example—you would enter the real name of whatever file you want to edit). Other kinds of computers won't necessarily have the $ prompt, but they will have something equivalent. If you can invoke an editor this way on your computer, it is nearly certain you can do the same from within SQL*Plus, *except* that you don't type the name of your editor, but rather the word EDIT:

```
SQL> edit fred.sql
```

You should first tell SQL*Plus your editor's name. You do this while in SQL*Plus by *defining* the editor, like this:

```
define _editor = "vi"
```

(That's an underscore before the e in editor.) SQL*Plus will then remember the name of your editor (until you QUIT SQL*Plus) and allow you to use it anytime you want. See the sidebar "Using **login.sql** to Define the Editor" for directions on making this happen automatically.

HOST

In the unlikely event that none of the editing commands described in the preceding section work, but you do have an editor you'd like to use, you can invoke it by typing this:

```
host vi fred.sql
```

HOST tells SQL*Plus that this is a command to simply hand back to the operating system for execution. It's the equivalent of typing **vi fred.sql** at the operating system prompt. Incidentally, this same HOST command can be used to execute almost any operating system command from within SQL*Plus, including **dir, copy, move, erase, cls**, and others.

Using login.sql to Define the Editor

If you'd like SQL*Plus to define your editor automatically, put the DEFINE _EDITOR command in a file named **login.sql**. This is a special filename that SQL*Plus always looks for whenever it starts up. If it finds **login.sql** in the directory from which you started SQL*Plus, it executes any commands in the file as if you had entered them by hand.

You can put virtually any command in **login.sql** that you can use in SQL*Plus, including both SQL*Plus commands and SQL statements; all of them will be executed before SQL*Plus gives you the SQL prompt. This can be a convenient way to set up your own individual SQL*Plus environment, with all the basic layouts the way you prefer them. Here's an example of a typical **login.sql** file:

```
prompt login.sql loaded.
set feedback off
set sqlprompt 'What now, boss? '
set sqlnumber off
set numwidth 5
set pagesize 24
set linesize 79
define _editor="vi"
```

Since Oracle Database 10g, Oracle provides three new predefined environment variables: _DATE, _PRIVILEGE ('AS SYSDBA', 'AS SYSOPER', or blank), and _USER (same value as show user returns).

Another file, named **glogin.sql**, is used to establish default SQL*Plus settings for all database users. This file, usually stored in the administrative directory for SQL*Plus, is useful in enforcing column and environment settings for multiple users. As of Oracle 11g, SQL*Plus settings previously stored in **glogin.sql** are now embedded in the executable.

The meaning of each of these commands can be found in the Alphabetical Reference section of this book.

Adding SQL*Plus Commands

Once you've saved a SQL statement into a file, such as **fred.sql**, you can add to the file any SQL*Plus commands you want. Essentially, you can build this file in a similar fashion to **activity .sql** in Figure 6-3. When you've finished working on it, you can exit your editor and be returned to SQL*Plus.

START

Once you are back in SQL*Plus, test your editing work by executing the file you've just edited:

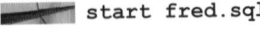

```
start fred.sql
```

All the SQL*Plus and SQL commands in that file will execute, line by line, just as if you'd entered each one of them by hand. If you've included a SPOOL and a SPOOL OFF command in

the file, you can use your editor to view the results of your work. This is just what was shown in Figure 6-2—the product of starting **activity.sql** and spooling its results into **activity.lst**.
To develop a report, use steps like these, in cycles:

1. Use SQL*Plus to build a SQL query interactively. When it appears close to being satisfactory, save it under a name such as **test.sql**. (The extension **.sql** is usually reserved for start files, scripts that execute to produce a report.)

2. Edit the file **test.sql** using a favorite editor. Add COLUMN, BREAK, COMPUTE, SET, and SPOOL commands to the file. You usually spool to a file with the extension **.lst**, such as **test.lst**. Exit the editor.

3. Back in SQL*Plus, the file **test.sql** is STARTED. Its results fly past on the screen, but also go into the file **test.lst**. The editor examines this file.

4. Incorporate any necessary changes into **test.sql** and run it again.

5. Continue this process until the report is correct and polished.

Checking the SQL*Plus Environment

You saw earlier that the command line editor can't change SQL*Plus commands because it can affect only SQL statements—those lines stored in the SQL buffer. You also saw that you can SAVE SQL statements and STORE environment settings in files, where they can be modified using your own editor.

If you'd like to check how a particular column is defined, type

```
column daysout
```

without anything following the column name. SQL*Plus will then list all the instructions you've given about that column, as shown here:

```
COLUMN   DaysOut ON
HEADING  'Days!Out' headsep '!'
FORMAT   999.99
```

If you type just the word **COLUMN**, without any column name following it, then *all* the columns will be listed. You will see all the columns Oracle sets up by default, plus the ones that you've defined:

```
COLUMN   Title ON
FORMAT   a20
word_wrap

COLUMN   DaysOut ON
HEADING  'Days!Out' headsep '!'
FORMAT   999.99

COLUMN   Name ON
FORMAT   a20
```

TTITLE, BTITLE, BREAK, and COMPUTE are displayed simply by typing their names, with nothing following. SQL*Plus answers back immediately with the current definitions. The first line in each of the next examples is what you type; the following lines show SQL*Plus's replies:

```
ttitle
ttitle ON and is the following 31 characters:
Checkout Log for 1/1/12-3/31/12
```

```
btitle
btitle ON and is the following 18 characters:
From the Bookshelf
```

```
break
break on report nodup
        on name skip 1 nodup
```

```
compute
compute avg label 'avg' of daysout on name
compute avg label 'avg' of daysout on report
```

Looking at those settings (also called *parameters*) that follow the SET command requires the use of the SHOW command:

```
show headsep
headsep "!" (hex 21)
```

```
show linesize
linesize 80
```

```
show pagesize
pagesize 60
```

```
show newpage
newpage 0
```

See the Alphabetical Reference section of this book under SET and SHOW for a complete list of parameters.

The TTITLE and BTITLE settings can be disabled by using the BTITLE OFF and TTITLE OFF commands. The following listing shows these commands (note that SQL*Plus does not reply to the commands):

```
ttitle off
```

```
btitle off
```

The settings for columns, breaks, and computes can be disabled via the CLEAR COLUMNS, CLEAR BREAKS, and CLEAR COMPUTES commands. The first line in each example in the following listing is what you type; the lines that follow show how SQL*Plus replies:

```
clear columns
columns cleared

clear breaks
breaks cleared

clear computes
computes cleared
```

Building Blocks

This has been a fairly dense chapter, particularly if SQL*Plus is new to you; yet on reflection, you'll probably agree that what was introduced here is not really difficult. If Figure 6-3 looked daunting when you began the chapter, look at it again now. Is there any line that you don't understand, or don't have a sense for what is being done and why? You could, if you wanted, simply copy this file (**activity.sql**) into another file with a different name and then begin to modify it to suit your own tastes and to query against your own tables. The structure of any reports you produce will, after all, be very similar.

There is a lot going on in **activity.sql**, but it is made up of simple building blocks. This will be the approach used throughout the book. Oracle provides building blocks, and lots of them, but each separate block is understandable and useful.

In the previous chapters, you learned how to select data out of the database, choosing certain columns and ignoring others, choosing certain rows based on logical restrictions you set up, and combining two tables to give you information not available from either one on its own.

In this chapter, you learned how to give orders that SQL*Plus can follow in formatting and producing the pages and headings of polished reports.

In the next several chapters, you'll change and format your data, row by row. Your expertise and confidence should grow chapter by chapter. By the end of Part II of this book, you should be able to produce very sophisticated reports in short order, to the considerable benefit of your company and yourself.

SQL*Plus is not the only way to interact with the Oracle database, but it is common to all Oracle environments. The concepts shown in this chapter—formatting the SQL SELECT command results with SQL*Plus directives—are common concepts in all development environments for Oracle databases. In fact, many of the SQL*Plus commands you've seen here will work in Oracle SQL Developer and produce the same results.

CHAPTER
7

Getting Text Information
and Changing It

T his chapter introduces *string functions,* which are software tools that allow you to manipulate a string of letters or other characters. To reference individual functions quickly, look them up by name in the Alphabetical Reference section of this book. This chapter focuses on the manipulation of text strings; to perform word searches (including word stem expansions and fuzzy matches) you should use Oracle Text, as described in Chapter 27.

Functions in Oracle work in one of two ways. Some functions create new objects from old ones; they produce a result that is a modification of the original information, such as turning lowercase characters into uppercase. Other functions produce a result that tells you something about the information, such as how many characters are in a word or sentence.

NOTE
If you use PL/SQL, you can create your own functions with the CREATE FUNCTION statement.

Datatypes

Just as people can be classified into different types based on certain characteristics (shy, outgoing, smart, silly, and so forth), different kinds of data can be classified into *datatypes* based on certain characteristics.

Datatypes in Oracle include NUMBER, CHAR (short for CHARACTER), DATE, TIMESTAMP, VARCHAR2 (variable length CHAR), LONG, RAW, LONG RAW, BLOB, CLOB, and BFILE. The first several are probably obvious. The rest are special datatypes that you'll encounter later. A full explanation of each of these can be found by name or under "Datatypes" in the Alphabetical Reference section of this book. Each datatype is covered in detail in the chapters ahead. As with people, some of the "types" overlap, and some are fairly rare. Some of them, specifically LONG, RAW, and LONG RAW are deprecated and should not be used in any new SQL development. Using either BLOB or CLOB eliminates the need to use these legacy datatypes, and it helps you avoid the limitations of using these older datatypes, as you will see later in this chapter.

If the information is of the character (VARCHAR2 or CHAR) type—a mixture of letters, punctuation marks, numbers, and spaces (also called *alphanumeric*)—you'll need string functions to modify or inform you of its characteristics. Oracle's SQL provides quite a few such tools.

What Is a String?

A *string* is a simple concept: a bunch of things in a line, such as houses, popcorn, pearls, numbers, or characters in a sentence.

Strings are frequently encountered in managing information. Names are strings of characters, as in Juan L'Heureaux. Phone numbers are strings of numbers, dashes, and sometimes parentheses, as in (415) 555-2676. Even a pure number, such as 5443702, can be considered as either a number or a string of characters.

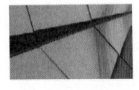

NOTE
Datatypes that are restricted to pure numbers (plus a decimal point, exponent, and sign, if needed) are called NUMBER, and they are not usually referred to as strings. A number can be used in certain ways that a string cannot, and vice versa.

Strings that can include any mixture of letters, numbers, spaces, and other symbols (such as punctuation marks and special characters) are called *character strings,* or just *character* for short.

Oracle has two main string datatypes. CHAR strings are always a fixed length. If you set a value to a string with a length less than that of a CHAR column, Oracle automatically pads the string with blanks. When you compare CHAR strings, Oracle compares the strings by padding each of them out to equal lengths with blanks. This means that if you compare "character   " with "character " in CHAR columns, Oracle considers the strings to be the same. The VARCHAR2 datatype is a variable-length string. The VARCHAR datatype is synonymous with VARCHAR2, but this may change in future versions of Oracle, so you should avoid using VARCHAR. Use CHAR for fixed-length character string fields and VARCHAR2 for all other character string fields.

The simple Oracle string functions, explained in this chapter, are shown in Table 7-1.

Function Name	Use
||	Glues or concatenates two strings together. The | symbol is called a *vertical bar* or *pipe*.
ASCII	Returns the decimal representation in the database character set of the first character of the string.
CHR	Returns the character having the binary equivalent to the string in either the database character set or the national character set.
CONCAT	Concatenates two strings together (same as ||).
INITCAP	Initial capital. Capitalizes the first letter of a word or series of words.
INSTR	Finds the location of a character in a string.
LENGTH	Tells the length of a string.
LOWER	Converts every letter in a string to lowercase.
LPAD	Left pad. Makes a string a certain length by adding a certain set of characters to the left.
LTRIM	Left trim. Trims all the occurrences of any one of a set of characters off the left side of a string.
NLS_INITCAP	INITCAP based on the National Language Support (NLS) value. Capitalizes the first letter of a word or series of words based on NLS value.
NLS_LOWER	LOWER based on the NLS value. Converts every letter in a string to lowercase based on the NLS setting.
NLS_UPPER	UPPER based on the NLS value. Converts every letter in a string into uppercase based on the NLS setting.
NLSSORT	Sorts based on the national language selected.
REGEXP_COUNT, REGEXP_INSTR, REGEXP_LIKE, REGEXP_REPLACE, and REGEXP_SUBSTR	Act like COUNT, INSTR, LIKE, REPLACE, and SUBSTR for Unix-like regular expressions.

TABLE 7-1.   *Oracle String Functions*

Function Name	Use
RPAD	Right pad. Makes a string a certain length by adding a certain set of characters to the right.
RTRIM	Right trim. Trims all the occurrences of any one of a set of characters off the right side of a string.
SOUNDEX	Finds words that sound like the example specified.
SUBSTR	Substring. Clips out a piece of a string.
TREAT	Changes the declared type of an expression.
TRIM	Trims all occurrences of any one of a set of characters off either or both sides of a string.
UPPER	Converts every letter in a string into uppercase.

TABLE 7-1. *Oracle String Functions* (continued)

Notation

Functions are shown with this kind of notation throughout the book:

```
FUNCTION(string [,option])
```

For the function definition, the function itself will be in uppercase. The thing it affects (usually a string) will be shown in lowercase italics. Any time the word *string* appears, it represents either a literal string of characters, the name of a character column in a table, or an expression consisting of any combination of literal strings or character columns or non-character columns converted to strings. When you actually use a string function, any literal must be in single quotes; any column name must appear without single quotes.

Every function has only one pair of parentheses. The value that function works on, as well as additional information you can pass to the function, goes between the parentheses.

Some functions have *options,* parts that are not always required that you can use to make the function work as you want. Options are always shown in square brackets: [ ]. See the discussion on LPAD and RPAD in the following section for an example of how options are used.

A simple example of how the LOWER function syntax is printed is as follows:

```
LOWER(string)
```

The word "LOWER" with the two parentheses is the function itself (an Oracle keyword), so it is shown here in uppercase; *string* stands for the actual string of characters to be converted to lowercase, and it's shown in lowercase italics. Therefore, when the user references a function like this:

```
lower('CAMP DOUGLAS')
```

it returns:

```
camp douglas
```

The string "CAMP DOUGLAS" is a literal, meaning that it is literally the string of characters that the function LOWER is to work on. Oracle uses single quotation marks to denote the beginning and end of any literal string. The string in LOWER also could have been the name of a column from a table, in which case the function would have operated on the contents of the column for every row brought back by a SELECT statement. For example,

```
select city, lower(city), lower('CITY') from weather;
```

would produce this result:

```
CITY        LOWER(CITY) LOWE
----------- ----------- ----
Lima        lima        city
Paris       paris       city
Manchester  manchester  city
Athens      athens      city
Chicago     chicago     city
Sydney      sydney      city
Sparta      sparta      city
```

At the top of the second column, in the LOWER function, CITY is not inside single quotation marks. This tells Oracle that it is a column name, not a literal.

In the third column's LOWER function, "CITY" is inside single quotation marks. This means you literally want the function LOWER to work on the word "CITY" (that is, the string of letters *C-I-T-Y*), not the column by the same name.

Concatenation (||)

The following notation tells Oracle to *concatenate,* or stick together, two strings:

```
string || string
```

The strings, of course, can be either column names or literals. Here's an example:

```
select city||country from location;
```

```
CITY||COUNTRY
--------------------------------------------------
AthensGreece
ChicagoUnited States
ConakryGuinea
LimaPeru
MadrasIndia
ManchesterEngland
MoscowRussia
ParisFrance
ShenyangChina
RomeItaly
TokyoJapan
SydneyAustralia
SpartaGreece
MadridSpain
```

Here, the cities vary in width from 4 to 12 characters. The countries push right up against them. This is just how the concatenate operator is supposed to work: It glues columns or strings together with no spaces in between.

This isn't very easy to read, of course. To make this a little more readable, you could list cities and countries with a comma and a space between them. You'd simply concatenate the CITY and COUNTRY columns with a literal string of a comma and a space, like this:

```
select city ||', '||country from location;

CITY||', '||COUNTRY
------------------------------------------------
Athens, Greece
Chicago, United States
Conakry, Guinea
Lima, Peru
Madras, India
Manchester, England
Moscow, Russia
Paris, France
Shenyang, China
Rome, Italy
Tokyo, Japan
Sydney, Australia
Sparta, Greece
Madrid, Spain
```

Notice the column title. See Chapter 6 for a review of column titles.

You could also use the CONCAT function to concatenate strings. For example, the query

```
select concat(city, country) from location;
```

is equivalent to

```
select city||country from location;
```

The CONCAT function follows the ANSI standard for SQL and, therefore, is more portable between different database vendors. The concatenation operator (||) is specific to Oracle SQL but definitely takes a lot less typing!

How to Cut and Paste Strings

In this section, you learn about a series of functions that often confuse users: LPAD, RPAD, LTRIM, RTRIM, TRIM, LENGTH, SUBSTR, and INSTR. These all serve a common purpose: they allow you to *cut* or *paste.*

Each of these functions does some part of cutting or pasting. For example, LENGTH tells you how many characters are in a string. SUBSTR lets you clip out and use a *substring*—a portion of a string—starting at one position in the string and continuing for a given length. INSTR lets you find the location of a group of characters within another string. LPAD and RPAD allow you to easily concatenate spaces or other characters on the left or right side of a string. LTRIM and RTRIM clip characters off the ends of strings, and TRIM can clip characters from both ends at once. Most interesting is that all of these functions can be used in combination with each other, as you'll soon see.

RPAD and LPAD

RPAD and LPAD are very similar functions. RPAD allows you to "pad" the right side of a column with any set of characters. The character set can be almost anything: spaces, periods, commas, letters or numbers, caret signs (^), or even exclamation marks (!). LPAD does the same thing as RPAD, but to the left side.

Here are the formats for RPAD and LPAD:

```
RPAD(string,length[,'set'])
```

```
LPAD(string,length[,'set'])
```

Here, *string* is the name of a CHAR or VARCHAR2 column from the database (or a literal string), *length* is the total number of characters that the result should be (in other words, its width), and *set* is the set of characters that do the padding. The set must be enclosed in single quotation marks. The square brackets mean that the set (and the comma that precedes it) is optional. If you leave this off, the function automatically pads with spaces. This is sometimes called the *default*; that is, if you don't tell the function which set of characters to use, it uses spaces by default.

Many users produce tables with dots to help guide the eye from one side of the page to the other. Here's how RPAD does this. In this example, the values are padded to a length of 35:

```
select rpad(city,35,'.'), temperature from weather;
```

```
RPAD(CITY,35,'.')                    TEMPERATURE
-----------------------------------  -----------
Lima...............................           45
Paris..............................           81
Manchester.........................           66
Athens.............................           97
Chicago............................           66
Sydney.............................           69
Sparta.............................           74
```

Notice what happened here. RPAD took each city, from Lima through Sparta, and concatenated dots on the right of it, adding just enough for each city so that the result (City plus dots) is exactly 35 characters long. The concatenate function (||) could not have done this. It would have added the same number of dots to every city, leaving a ragged edge on the right.

LPAD does the same sort of thing, but on the left. Suppose you want to reformat cities and temperatures so the cities are right-justified (that is, they all align on the right). For this example, the padded length is 11:

```
select lpad(city,11), temperature from weather;
```

```
LPAD(CITY,1 TEMPERATURE
----------- -----------
       Lima          45
      Paris          81
 Manchester          66
     Athens          97
    Chicago          66
     Sydney          69
     Sparta          74
```

LTRIM, RTRIM, and TRIM

LTRIM and RTRIM are like hedge trimmers. They trim off unwanted characters from the left and right ends of strings. For example, suppose you have a MAGAZINE table with a column in it that contains the titles of magazine articles, but the titles were entered by different people. Some people always put the titles in quotes, whereas others simply entered the words; some used periods, others didn't; some started titles with "The," whereas others did not. How do you trim these?

```
select title from magazine;

TITLE
-----------------------------------
The Barbers Who Shave Themselves.
"Hunting Thoreau In New Hampshire"
The Ethnic Neighborhood
Relational Design And Enthalpy
"Intercontinental Relations."
```

Here are the formats for RTRIM and LTRIM:

```
RTRIM(string[,'set'])

LTRIM(string[,'set'])
```

Here, *string* is the name of the column from the database (or a literal string), and *set* is the collection of characters you want to trim off. If no set of characters is specified, the functions trim off spaces.

You can trim off more than one character at a time; to do so, simply make a list (a string) of the characters you want removed. First, let's get rid of the quotes and periods on the right, as shown here:

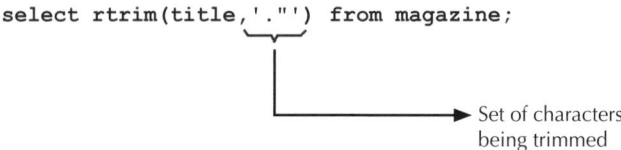

```
select rtrim(title,'."') from magazine;
```

Set of characters being trimmed

The preceding produces this:

```
RTRIM(TITLE,'."')
-----------------------------------
The Barbers Who Shave Themselves
"Hunting Thoreau In New Hampshire
The Ethnic Neighborhood
Relational Design And Enthalpy
"Intercontinental Relations
```

RTRIM removed both the double quotation marks and the periods from the right side of each of these titles. The *set* of characters you want to remove can be as long as you want. Oracle checks and rechecks the right side of each title until every character in your string has been removed—that is, until it runs into the first character in the string that is *not* in your set.

Combining Two Functions

Now what? You can use the LTRIM function to get rid of the quotes on the left. The TITLE column is buried in the middle of the RTRIM function. In this section, you learn how to combine functions.

You know that when you ran the SELECT statement

```
select title from magazine;
```

the result you got back was the content of the TITLE column, as shown next:

```
The Barbers Who Shave Themselves.
"Hunting Thoreau In New Hampshire"
The Ethnic Neighborhood
Relational Design And Enthalpy
"Intercontinental Relations."
```

Remember that the purpose of

```
rtrim(title,'."')
```

is to take each of these strings and remove the quotes on the right side, effectively producing a result that is a *new* column whose contents are shown here:

```
The Barbers Who Shave Themselves
"Hunting Thoreau In New Hampshire
The Ethnic Neighborhood
Relational Design And Enthalpy
"Intercontinental Relations
```

Therefore, if you pretend that RTRIM(TITLE,'."') is simply a column name itself, you can substitute it for *string* in the following:

```
LTRIM(string,'set')
```

So you simply type your SELECT statement to look like this:

```
select ltrim(rtrim(title,'."'),'"') from magazine;
```

This is called *nesting* the functions. Taking this apart for clarity, you see the following:

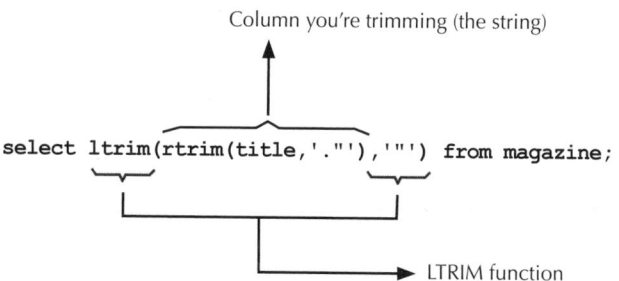

Is this how you want it? And what is the result of this combined function?

```
LTRIM(RTRIM(TITLE,'."'),'"')
---------------------------------
The Barbers Who Shave Themselves
Hunting Thoreau In New Hampshire
The Ethnic Neighborhood
Relational Design And Enthalpy
Intercontinental Relations
```

Your titles are now cleaned up.

Looking at a combination of functions the first (or the thousandth) time can be confusing, even for an experienced query user. It's difficult to assess which commas and parentheses go with which functions, particularly when a query you've written isn't working correctly; discovering where a comma is missing, or which parenthesis isn't properly matched with another, can be a real adventure.

One simple solution to this is to break functions onto separate lines, at least until they're all working the way you want. SQL*Plus (and the Oracle SQL engine that processes the SQL statement from any application) doesn't care at all where you break a SQL statement, as long as it's not in the middle of a word or a literal string. To better visualize how this RTRIM and LTRIM combination works, you could type it like this:

```
select ltrim(
            rtrim(title,'."')
                            ,'"')
from magazine;
```

This makes what you are trying to do obvious, and it will work even if it is typed on four separate lines with lots of spaces. SQL*Plus simply ignores extra spaces and lines.

Suppose now you decide to trim off the "The" (upper- or lowercase) from the front of two of the titles, as well as the space that follows it (and, of course, the double quote you removed before). You might do this:

```
select ltrim(rtrim(title,'."'),'"theTHE ')
from magazine;
```

which produces the following:

```
LTRIM(RTRIM(TITLE,'."'),'"THETHE')
---------------------------------
Barbers Who Shave Themselves
unting Thoreau In New Hampshire
nic Neighborhood
Relational Design And Enthalpy
Intercontinental Relations
```

What happened? The second and third row got trimmed more than expected. Why? Because LTRIM was busy looking for and trimming off anything that was a double quote, a *T/t*, an *H/h*, an *E/e*, or a space. It was not looking for the word *THE* or *the*. It was looking for the letters in the word, and LTRIM didn't quit the first time it saw any of the letters it was looking for. It quit when it saw a character that wasn't in its set.

What it trimmed:	What is left behind:
The	Barbers Who Shave Themselves
"H	unting Thoreau In New Hampshire
The Eth	nic Neighborhhood
	Relational Design And Enthalpy
"	Intercontinental Relations

In other words, all of the following and many other combinations of the letters will have the same effect when used as the set of an LTRIM or RTRIM:

```
'"TtHhEe'
'HETteh"'
'thE"THe'
'H"TtheE'
'ET"Hhte'
```

The order of the letters in the set has no effect on how this function works. Note, however, that the *case* of the letters is important. Oracle checks the case of both the letters in the set and in the string. It removes only those with an exact match.

LTRIM and RTRIM are designed to remove any characters in a set from the left or right of a string. They're not intended to remove words. To do that requires clever use of INSTR, SUBSTR, and even DECODE, which you will learn about in Chapter 16.

The previous example makes one point clear: It's better to make certain that data gets cleaned up or edited before it is stored in the database. It would have been a lot less trouble if the individuals typing these magazine article titles had simply avoided the use of quotes, periods, and the word "The".

Using the TRIM Function

The preceding example showed how to combine two functions—a useful skill when dealing with string manipulation. If you are trimming the exact same data from both the beginning and the end of the string, you can use the TRIM function in place of an LTRIM/RTRIM combination.

TRIM uses a unique syntax. The following example shows the use of the TRIM function with its associated FROM clause within the function. In this example, the double quotes are removed from the beginning and the end of the magazine article titles. Because the double quote is a character string, it is placed inside two single quotes:

```
select trim('"' from title) from magazine;

TRIM('"'FROMTITLE)
-----------------------------------
The Barbers Who Shave Themselves.
Hunting Thoreau In New Hampshire
The Ethnic Neighborhood
Relational Design And Enthalpy
Intercontinental Relations.
```

The quotes have been removed from the beginning and ending of the strings. If you just want to trim one end of the strings, you could use the LEADING or TRAILING clause, as shown in the following listing:

```
select trim(leading '"' from title) from magazine;
select trim(trailing '"' from title) from magazine;
```

Using the keyword LEADING makes TRIM act like LTRIM; TRAILING makes it act like RTRIM. The most powerful use of TRIM is its ability to act on both ends of the string at once, thus simplifying the code you have to write—provided the same characters are being removed from both ends of the string.

Adding One More Function

Suppose that you decide to RPAD your trimmed-up titles with dashes and carets, perhaps also asking for a magazine name and page number. Your query would look like this:

```
select name, rpad(ltrim(rtrim(title,'."'),'"'),47,'-^'), page
from magazine;
```

```
NAME              RPAD(LTRIM(RTRIM(TITLE,'."'),'"'),47,'-^')   PAGE
----------------  ------------------------------------------   -----
Bertrand Monthly  The Barbers Who Shave Themselves-^-^-^-^-^     70
Live Free Or Die  Hunting Thoreau In New Hampshire-^-^-^-^-^    320
Psychologica      The Ethnic Neighborhood-^-^-^-^-^-^-^-^-^-    246
Faded Issues      Relational Design And Enthalpy-^-^-^-^-^-^    279
Entropy Wit       Intercontinental Relations-^-^-^-^-^-^-^-^     20
```

Each function has parentheses that enclose the column it is going to transform into another value, so the real trick in understanding combined functions in SELECT statements is to read from the outside to the inside on both the left and right, watching (and even counting) the pairs of parentheses.

LOWER, UPPER, and INITCAP

These three related and very simple functions often are used together. LOWER takes any string or column and converts any letters in it to lowercase. UPPER does the opposite, converting any letters to uppercase. INITCAP takes the initial letter of every word in a string or column and converts just those letters to uppercase.

Here are the formats for these functions:

```
LOWER(string)
UPPER(string)
INITCAP(string)
```

Returning to the WEATHER table, recall that each city is stored in title case, like this:

```
Lima
Paris
Athens
Chicago
```

```
Manchester
Sydney
Sparta
```

Therefore,

```
select city, upper(city), lower(city), initcap(lower(city))
from weather;
```

produces this:

```
City          UPPER(CITY) LOWER(CITY) INITCAP(LOW
-----------   ----------- ----------- -----------
Lima          LIMA        lima        Lima
Paris         PARIS       paris       Paris
Manchester    MANCHESTER  manchester  Manchester
Athens        ATHENS      athens      Athens
Chicago       CHICAGO     chicago     Chicago
Sydney        SYDNEY      sydney      Sydney
Sparta        SPARTA      sparta      Sparta
```

Look carefully at what is produced in each column, and at the functions that produced it in the SQL statement. The INITCAP function doesn't do much in this query, but it is handy for converting any text in mixed case to title case.

LENGTH

This one is easy. LENGTH tells you how long a string is—how many characters it has in it, including letters, spaces, and anything else. Here is the format for LENGTH:

```
LENGTH(string)
```

And here's an example:

```
select name, length(name) from magazine;
```

```
NAME              LENGTH(NAME)
----------------  ------------
Bertrand Monthly            16
Live Free Or Die            16
Psychologica                12
Faded Issues                12
Entropy Wit                 11
```

LENGTH isn't normally useful by itself, but it can be used as part of another function, for calculating how much space you'll need on a report or as part of a WHERE or an ORDER by clause.

NOTE
You cannot perform functions such as LENGTH on a column that uses a LONG datatype. LONG datatypes are deprecated, and you shouldn't be using them anyway. Use LOB datatypes instead!

SUBSTR

You can use the SUBSTR function to clip out a piece of a string. Here is the format for SUBSTR:

```
SUBSTR(string,start[,count])
```

This tells SQL to clip out a subsection of *string,* beginning at position *start* and continuing for *count* characters. If you don't specify *count,* SUBSTR clips beginning at *start* and continuing to the end of the string. For example,

```
select substr(name,6,4) from magazine;
```

gives you this:

```
SUBS
----
and
Free
olog
 Iss
py W
```

You can see how the function works. It clipped out the piece of the magazine name starting in position 6 (counting from the left) and including a total of four characters.

A more practical use might be in separating out phone numbers from a personal address book. For example, assume that you have an ADDRESS table that contains, among other things, last names, first names, and phone numbers, as shown here:

```
select lastname, firstname, phone from address;
```

LASTNAME	FIRSTNAME	PHONE
Bailey	William	213-555-0223
Adams	Jack	415-555-7530
Soda	Angelina	214-555-8383
De Medeci	Lefty	312-555-1166
Demiurge	Frank	707-555-8900
Casey	Willis	312-555-1414
Zack	Jack	415-555-6842
Yarrow	Mary	415-555-2178
Werschky	Arny	415-555-7387
Brant	Glen	415-555-7512
Edgar	Theodore	415-555-6252
Hardin	Huggy	617-555-0125
Hild	Phil	603-555-2242
Loebel	Frank	202-555-1414
Moore	Mary	718-555-1638
Szep	Felicia	214-555-8383
Ziffel	Barney	503-555-7491

Suppose you want just those phone numbers in the 415 area code. One solution would be to have a separate column called AREACODE. Thoughtful planning about tables and columns will eliminate a good deal of reformatting effort later. However, in this instance, area codes and phone numbers are combined in a single column, so you must find a way to separate out the numbers in the 415 area code:

```
select lastname, firstname, phone from address
where phone like '415-%';
```

LASTNAME	FIRSTNAME	PHONE
Adams	Jack	415-555-7530
Zack	Jack	415-555-6842
Yarrow	Mary	415-555-2178
Werschky	Arny	415-555-7387
Brant	Glen	415-555-7512
Edgar	Theodore	415-555-6252

Next, because you do not want to dial your own area code when calling friends in the 415 area code, you can eliminate this from the result by using another SUBSTR:

```
select lastname, firstname, substr(phone,5) from address
where phone like '415-%';
```

LASTNAME	FIRSTNAME	SUBSTR(P
Adams	Jack	555-7530
Zack	Jack	555-6842
Yarrow	Mary	555-2178
Werschky	Arny	555-7387
Brant	Glen	555-7512
Edgar	Theodore	555-6252

Notice that the default version of SUBSTR was used here. SUBSTR(PHONE,5) tells SQL to clip out the substring of the phone number, starting at position 5 and going to the end of the string. Doing this eliminates the area code.

Of course,

```
substr(phone,5)
```

has exactly the same effect as the following:

```
substr(phone,5,8)
```

You can combine this with the column-renaming techniques discussed in Chapter 6 to produce a quick listing of local friends' phone numbers, as shown here:

```
select lastname ||', '||firstname as name,
       substr(phone,5) as phone
from address
where phone like '415-%';
```

NAME	PHONE
Adams, Jack	555-7530
Zack, Jack	555-6842
Yarrow, Mary	555-2178
Werschky, Arny	555-7387
Brant, Glen	555-7512
Edgar, Theodore	555-6252

To produce a dotted line following the name, add the RPAD function:

```
select rpad(lastname ||', '||firstname,25,'.') as name,
       substr(phone,5) as phone
from address
where phone like '415-%';
```

```
NAME                       PHONE
------------------------   --------
Adams, Jack.............   555-7530
Zack, Jack..............   555-6842
Yarrow, Mary............   555-2178
Werschky, Arny..........   555-7387
Brant, Glen.............   555-7512
Edgar, Theodore.........   555-6252
```

The use of negative numbers in the SUBSTR function is allowed too. Normally, the position value you specify for the starting position is relative to the *start* of the string. When you use a negative number for the position value, it is relative to the *end* of the string. For example,

```
substr(phone,-4)
```

would use the fourth position from the end of the Phone column's value as its starting point. Because no length parameter is specified in this example, the remainder of the string will be returned.

NOTE
Use this feature only for VARCHAR2 datatype columns. If you use it with columns that use the CHAR datatype, be careful. CHAR columns are fixed-length columns, so their values are padded with spaces to extend them to the full length of the column. Using a negative number for the SUBSTR position value in a CHAR column will determine the starting position relative to the end of the column (and, therefore, the length of the CHAR column), not the end of the string.

The following example shows the result of a negative number in the SUBSTR function when it is used on a VARCHAR2 column:

```
select substr(phone,-4)
from address
where phone like '415-5%';
```

```
SUBS
----
7530
6842
2178
7387
7512
6252
```

The *count* value of the SUBSTR function must always be positive or unspecified. Using a negative *count* will return a NULL result.

INSTR

The INSTR function allows for simple or sophisticated searching through a string for a set of characters, not unlike LTRIM and RTRIM, except that INSTR doesn't clip anything off. It simply tells you where in the string it found what you were searching for. This is similar to the LIKE logical operator described in Chapter 5, except that LIKE can only be used in a WHERE or HAVING clause, and INSTR can be used anywhere except in the FROM clause. Of course, LIKE can be used for complex pattern searches that would be quite difficult, if even possible, using INSTR. Here is the format for INSTR:

```
INSTR(string,set[,start[,occurrence]])
```

INSTR searches in the string for a certain *set* of characters. It has two options, one within the other. The first option is the default: It will look for the set starting at position 1. If you specify the location to *start,* it will skip over all the characters up to that point and begin its search there.

The second option is *occurrence.* A set of characters may occur more than once in a string, and you may really be interested only in whether something occurs more than once. By default, INSTR will look for the first *occurrence* of the set. By adding the option *occurrence* and making it equal to 3, for example, you can force INSTR to skip over the first two occurrences of the set and give the location of the third.

Some examples will make all this simpler to grasp. Recall the table of magazine articles. Here is a list of their authors:

```
select author from magazine;

AUTHOR
------------------------
Bonhoeffer, Dietrich
Chesterton, G.K.
Ruth, George Herman
Whitehead, Alfred
Crookes, William
```

To find the location of the first occurrence of the letter "O", INSTR is used without its options and with *set* as 'O' (note the single quotation marks since this is a literal), as shown in the following listing:

```
select author, instr(author,'o') from magazine;

AUTHOR                   INSTR(AUTHOR,'O')
------------------------ -----------------
Bonhoeffer, Dietrich                     2
Chesterton, G.K.                         9
Ruth, George Herman                      9
Whitehead, Alfred                        0
Crookes, William                         3
```

This is, of course, the same as the following:

```
select author, instr(author,'o',1,1) from magazine;
```

If INSTR had looked for the second occurrence of the letter "O", it would have found:

```
select author, instr(author,'o',1,2) from magazine;
```

```
AUTHOR                    INSTR(AUTHOR,'O',1,2)
------------------------  ---------------------
Bonhoeffer, Dietrich                          5
Chesterton, G.K.                              0
Ruth, George Herman                           0
Whitehead, Alfred                             0
Crookes, William                              4
```

INSTR found the second "O" in Bonhoeffer's name, at position 5, and in Crookes' name, at position 4. Chesterton has only one "O", so for him, Ruth, and Whitehead, the result is 0, meaning no success—no second "O" was found.

To tell INSTR to look for the second occurrence, you also must tell it where to start looking (in this case, position 1). The default value of *start* is 1, which means that's what it uses if you don't specify anything, but the *occurrence* option requires a *start,* so you have to specify both.

If *set* is not just one character but several, INSTR gives the location of the first letter of the set, as shown here:

```
select author, instr(author,'William') from magazine;
```

```
AUTHOR                    INSTR(AUTHOR,'WILLIAM')
------------------------  -----------------------
Bonhoeffer, Dietrich                            0
Chesterton, G.K.                                0
Ruth, George Herman                             0
Whitehead, Alfred                               0
Crookes, William                               10
```

This has many useful applications, such as in the MAGAZINE table, for instance:

```
select author, instr(author,',') from magazine;
```

```
AUTHOR                    INSTR(AUTHOR,',')
------------------------  -----------------
Bonhoeffer, Dietrich                     11
Chesterton, G.K.                         11
Ruth, George Herman                       5
Whitehead, Alfred                        10
Crookes, William                          8
```

Here, INSTR searched the strings of author names for a comma and then reported back the position in each string where it found one.

Suppose you want to reformat the names of the authors from the formal "last name, comma, first name" approach, and present them as they are normally spoken, as shown here:

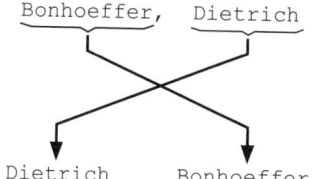

To do this using INSTR and SUBSTR, find the location of the comma, and use this location to tell SUBSTR where to clip. Taking this step by step, you must first find the comma as we did in the preceding listing.

Two SUBSTRs will be needed—one that clips out the author's last name up to the position before the comma, and one that clips out the author's first name from two positions after the comma through to the end.

First, look at the one that clips from position 1 to just before the comma:

```
select author, substr(author,1,instr(author,',')-1)
from magazine;
```

```
AUTHOR                           SUBSTR(AUTHOR,1,INSTR(AUT
------------------------         -------------------------
Bonhoeffer, Dietrich             Bonhoeffer
Chesterton, G.K.                 Chesterton
Ruth, George Herman              Ruth
Whitehead, Alfred                Whitehead
Crookes, William                 Crookes
```

Next, look at the one that clips from two positions past the comma to the end of the string:

```
select author, substr(author,instr(author,',')+2) from magazine;
```

```
AUTHOR                           SUBSTR(AUTHOR,INSTR(AUTHO
------------------------         -------------------------
Bonhoeffer, Dietrich             Dietrich
Chesterton, G.K.                 G.K.
Ruth, George Herman              George Herman
Whitehead, Alfred                Alfred
Crookes, William                 William
```

Look at the combination of these two, with the concatenation operator putting a space between them and a quick renaming of the column to BYFIRSTNAME:

```
column byfirstname heading "By First Name"

select author, substr(author,instr(author,',')+2)
               ||' '||
               substr(author,1,instr(author,',')-1)
               as byfirstname
from magazine;
```

```
AUTHOR                       By First Name
------------------------     --------------------
Bonhoeffer, Dietrich         Dietrich Bonhoeffer
Chesterton, G.K.             G.K. Chesterton
Ruth, George Herman          George Herman Ruth
Whitehead, Alfred            Alfred Whitehead
Crookes, William             William Crookes
```

It is daunting to look at a SQL statement like this one, but it was built using simple logic, and it can be broken down the same way. Bonhoeffer can provide the example. The first part looks like this:

```
substr(author,instr(author,',')+2)
```

This tells SQL to get the SUBSTR of AUTHOR starting two positions to the right of the comma and going to the end. This clips out DIETRICH—the author's first name.

The beginning of the author's first name is found by locating the comma at the end of his last name (INSTR does this) and then sliding over two steps to the right (where his first name begins).

The following illustration shows how the result of the INSTR function (plus 2) serves as the start for the SUBSTR function:

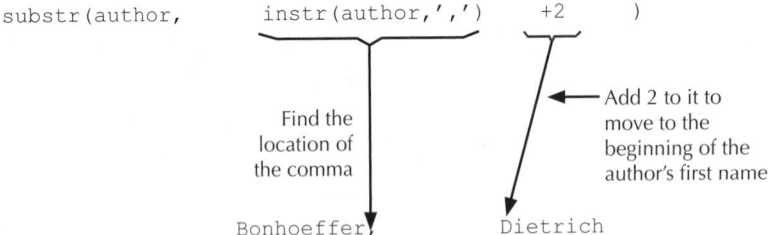

Here is the second part of the combined statement:

```
||' '||
```

This, of course, simply tells SQL to concatenate a space in the middle.

Here is the third part of the combined statement:

```
substr(author,1,instr(author,',')-1)
```

This tells SQL to clip out the portion of the author's name starting at position 1 and ending one position before the comma, which results in the author's last name:

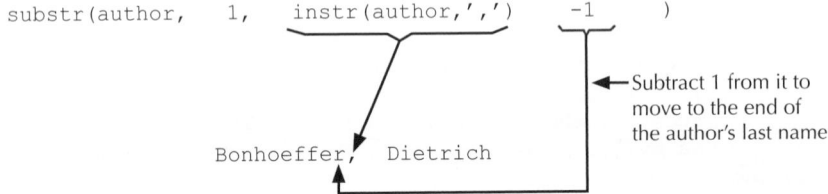

The fourth part simply assigns a column alias:

```
as byfirstname
```

This transposition was only possible to accomplish because each AUTHOR record in the MAGAZINE table followed the same formatting conventions. In each record, the last name was always the first word in the string and was immediately followed by a comma. This allowed you to use the INSTR function to search for the comma. Once the comma's position was known, you could determine which part of the string was the last name, and the rest of the string was treated as the first name.

Often this is not the case. Names are difficult to force into standard formats. Last names may include prefixes (such as *von* in von Hagel) or suffixes (such as Jr., Sr., and III). Using the previous example's SQL, the name Richards, Jr., Bob would have been transformed into Jr., Bob Richards.

Because of the lack of a standard formatting for names, many applications store the first and last names separately. Titles (such as MD) are usually stored in yet another column. A second option when storing such data is to force it into a single format and use SUBSTR and INSTR to manipulate that data when needed.

ASCII and CHR

The ASCII and CHR functions are seldom used during ad hoc queries. CHR converts numeric values to their ASCII character string equivalents:

```
select chr(70)||chr(83)||chr(79)||chr(85)||chr(71)
as chrvalues
from dual;

CHRVA
-----
FSOUG
```

Oracle translated CHR(70) to an "F", CHR(83) to an "S", and so on, based on the database's character set.

The ASCII function performs the reverse operation—but if you pass it a string, only the first character of the string is acted upon:

```
select ascii('FSOUG') from dual;

ASCII('FSOUG')
--------------
            70
```

To see each ASCII value, you can use the DUMP function.

```
select dump('FSOUG') from dual;

DUMP('FSOUG')
---------------------------
Typ=96 Len=5: 70,83,79,85,71
```

Using ORDER BY and WHERE with String Functions

String functions can be used in a WHERE clause, as shown here:

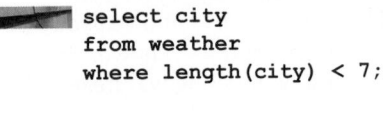

```
select city
from weather
where length(city) < 7;

CITY
-----------
Lima
Paris
Athens
Sydney
Sparta
```

They can also be used in an ORDER BY clause, as shown here:

```
select city
from weather
order by length(city);

CITY
-----------
Lima
Paris
Athens
Sydney
Sparta
Chicago
Manchester
```

These are simple examples; much more complex clauses could be used. For example, you could find all the authors with more than one "O" in their name by using INSTR in the WHERE clause:

```
select author from magazine
where instr(author,'o',1,2) > 0;

AUTHOR
-------------------------
Bonhoeffer, Dietrich
Crookes, William
```

This works by finding a second occurrence of the letter *O* in the author names. The use of "> 0" is a logical technique: Recall that functions generally produce two different kinds of results— one that creates new objects, and the other that tells you something about existing objects.

The INSTR function tells you something about a string, specifically the position of the set it has been asked to find. Here, it is asked to locate the second "O" in the AUTHOR string. Its result will be a number that's greater than zero for those names with at least two "O"s, and zero for those with one or less (when INSTR doesn't find something, its result is a zero). So a simple test for a result greater than zero checks for the success of the INSTR search for a second "O".

The WHERE clause using INSTR produces the same result as this:

```
where author like '%o%o%'
```

Remember that the percent sign (%) is a wildcard, meaning it takes the place of anything, so the LIKE clause here tells SQL to look for two "O"s with anything (or nothing) before, between, or after them. This is probably easier to understand than the previous example of INSTR.

There are often several ways to produce the same result in Oracle. Some are easier to understand, some work more quickly, some are more appropriate in certain situations, and some simply are a matter of personal style.

SOUNDEX

One string function is used almost exclusively in a WHERE clause: SOUNDEX. It has the unusual ability to find words that sound like other words, virtually regardless of how either is spelled. This is especially useful when you're not certain how a word or name is really spelled. Here is the format for SOUNDEX:

```
SOUNDEX(string)
```

And here are a few examples of its use:

```
select city,temperature,condition
from weather
where soundex(city)=soundex('menncestr');
```

```
CITY          TEMPERATURE CONDITION
----------- ----------- ---------
Manchester            66 Fog
```

```
select author from magazine
where soundex(author) = soundex('banheffer');
```

```
AUTHOR
------------------------
Bonhoeffer, Dietrich
```

SOUNDEX compares the sound of the entry in the selected column with the sound of the word in single quotation marks, and it looks for a close match. SOUNDEX makes certain assumptions about how letters and combinations of letters are usually pronounced in English, and the two words being compared must begin with the same letter. SOUNDEX will not always find the word you're searching for or have misspelled, but it can help.

It is not necessary that one of the two SOUNDEXs in the WHERE clause have a literal in it. SOUNDEX could be used to compare the data in two columns to find those that sound alike.

One useful purpose for this function is cleaning up mailing lists. Many lists have duplicate entries with slight differences in the spelling or format of the customers' names. By using SOUNDEX to list all the names that sound alike, you can discover and eliminate many of these duplicates.

Let's apply this to the ADDRESS table:

```
select lastname, firstname, phone
from address;
```

LASTNAME	FIRSTNAME	PHONE
Bailey	William	213-555-0223
Adams	Jack	415-555-7530
Sep	Felicia	214-555-8383
De Medici	Lefty	312-555-1166
Demiurge	Frank	707-555-8900
Casey	Willis	312-555-1414
Zack	Jack	415-555-6842
Yarrow	Mary	415-555-2178
Werschky	Arny	415-555-7387
Brant	Glen	415-555-7512
Edgar	Theodore	415-555-6252
Hardin	Huggy	617-555-0125
Hild	Phil	603-555-2242
Loebel	Frank	202-555-1414
Moore	Mary	718-555-1638
Szep	Felicia	214-555-8383
Zimmerman	Fred	503-555-7491

To find duplicates, you must force Oracle to compare each last name in the table to all the others in the same table.

Join the ADDRESS table to itself by creating an alias for the table, calling it first *A* and then *B*. Now it is as if there are two tables, A and B, with the common column LASTNAME.

In the WHERE clause, eliminate any row in which the last name in the result set from table A matches the last name in the result set from table B. This prevents a last name from matching to itself.

Those that sound alike are then selected:

```
select a.lastname, a.firstname, a.phone
from address a, address b
where soundex(a.lastname)=soundex(b.lastname);
```

LASTNAME	FIRSTNAME	PHONE
Szep	Felicia	214-555-8383
Sep	Felicia	214-555-8383

You can also perform SOUNDEX searches on individual words within a text entry. For examples of this and other complex text searches, see Chapter 27.

National Language Support

Oracle doesn't have to use English characters; it can represent data in any language through its implementation of *National Language Support* and its NCHAR and NVARCHAR2 datatypes. By using characters made up of longer pieces of information than ordinary characters, Oracle can represent Japanese and other such strings. See NLSSORT, NLS_INITCAP, NLS_LOWER, and NLS_UPPER in the Alphabetical Reference section of this book. In addition to the SUBSTR function, Oracle supports SUBSTRB (using bytes instead of characters), SUBSTRC (using Unicode complete characters), SUBSTR2 (using UCS2 codepoints), and SUBSTR4 (using UCS4 codepoints).

Regular Expression Support

The string functions INSTR, REPLACE, and SUBSTR have been extended to support regular expressions. Chapter 8 is devoted to the coverage of these advanced text-search features.

Review

Data comes in several types, primarily DATE, NUMBER, and character. Character data is basically a string of letters, numbers, or other symbols, and is often called a *character string*, or just a string. These strings can be changed or described by string functions. Oracle features two types of character datatypes: variable-length strings (the VARCHAR2 datatype) and fixed-length strings (the CHAR datatype). Values in CHAR columns are padded with spaces to the full column length if they are shorter than the defined length of the column.

Functions such as RPAD, LPAD, LTRIM, RTRIM, TRIM, LOWER, UPPER, INITCAP, and SUBSTR actually change the contents of a string before displaying it to you.

Functions such as LENGTH, INSTR, and SOUNDEX describe the characteristics of a string, such as how long it is, where in the string a certain character is located, or what the string sounds like.

All these functions can be used alone or in combination to select and present information from an Oracle database. This is a straightforward process, built up from simple logical steps that can be combined to accomplish very sophisticated tasks.

CHAPTER
8

Searching for
Regular Expressions

The SUBSTR, INSTR, LIKE, REPLACE, and COUNT functions have been enhanced and extended to support searches for Unix-like regular expressions. Regular expressions support a wide array of standardized controls and checks—for example, matching values a specific number of times, searches for punctuation characters, or searches for digits. You can use these new functions to perform advanced searches against strings. These functions, introduced in Oracle Database 10*g*, are named REGEXP_SUBSTR, REGEXP_INSTR, REGEXP_LIKE, REGEXP_REPLACE, and REGEXP_COUNT.

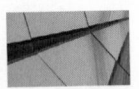

NOTE
*Users who have previously used the Unix **grep** command to search for regular expressions in text files may already be familiar with the concepts and search techniques involved.*

Search Strings

Let's start with an example. Phone numbers in the ADDRESS table are in the format 123-456-7890. To select all the exchanges (the middle set of numbers), you can select an expression that returns any string within the phone number that starts and ends with a hyphen (-) character.

Within the REGEXP_SUBSTR function, we need to tell Oracle where to start the string. In this case, we are looking for "-". The regular expression to search for begins thus:

```
select regexp_substr('123-456-7890', '-
```

We now need to tell Oracle to continue until it finds another "-" character in the string. To do this, use the "[^" operator, a bracket expression that says the acceptable values match any character except for the expressions represented in the list. The command now looks like this:

```
select regexp_substr('123-456-7890', '-[^-]+' ) regexp_substr
from dual;

REGE
----
-456
```

This command tells Oracle to look for "-", followed by one or more characters that are not "-", followed by "-". Note that if you add an extra "-" at the end of the regular expression, you get the trailing "-" as part of the returned string:

```
select regexp_substr('123-456-7890', '-[^-]+-' ) regexp_substr
from dual;

REGEX
-----
-456-
```

Most users (and developers) are not going to be comfortable typing in strings such as

```
'-[^-]+'
```

without training and practice. But as you use the REGEXP_ functions, you can quickly see how much more functionality they give you. Consider that to generate the same result as the preceding using only the functions SUBSTR and INSTR, and assuming that the length of the string between the "-" characters is not known, you would need to execute this query:

```
select substr('123-456-7890',
       instr('123-456-7890', '-',1,1),
       (instr('123-456-7890', '-',1,2)-
       instr('123-456-7890', '-',1,1))+1)
from dual;

SUBST
-----
-456-
```

By comparison, the REGEXP_SUBSTR function is much more concise. As you will see in the examples later in this chapter, the regular expression searches enable you to encode complex search patterns within a single function call.

Table 8-1 shows the regular expression operators and their descriptions. Understanding the operators involved is critical for effective use of the regular expression search capabilities.

Operator	Description
\ [a]	The backslash character can have four different meanings, depending on the context. It can stand for itself, quote the next character, introduce an operator, or do nothing.
*	Matches zero or more occurrences.
+	Matches one or more occurrences.
?	Matches zero or one occurrence.
|	Alternation operator for specifying alternative matches.
^ [b]	Matches the beginning-of-line character.
$ [b]	Matches the end-of-line character.
. [c]	Matches any character in the supported character set except for a NULL.
[ ] [d]	Bracket expression for specifying a matching list that should match any one of the expressions represented in the list. A nonmatching list expression begins with a caret (^) and specifies a list that matches any character except for the expressions represented in the list.
( )	Grouping expression, treated as a single subexpression.
{m}	Matches exactly m times.
{m, }	Matches at least m times.
{m, n}	Matches at least m times but no more than n times.
\n [e]	The backreference expression (n is a digit between 1 and 9) matches the nth subexpression enclosed between parentheses and the preceding \n.

TABLE 8-1. *Regular Expression Operators*

Operator	Description
[..] f	Specifies one collation element and can be a multicharacter element (for example, **[.ch.]** in Spanish).
[: :] g	Specifies character classes (for example, **[:alpha:]**). It matches any character within the character class.
[==] h	Specifies equivalence classes (for example, **[=a=]** matches all characters having base letter "a").

Notes on the POSIX operators and Oracle enhancements:

a. The backslash operator can be used to make the character following it normal if it is an operator. For example, '*' is interpreted as the asterisk string literal.

b. The characters ^ and $ are the POSIX anchoring operators. By default, they match only the beginning or end of an entire string. Oracle lets you specify ^ and $ to match the start or end of any line anywhere within the source string. This, in turn, lets you treat the source string as multiple lines.

c. In the POSIX standard, the "match any character" operator (.) is defined to match any English character except NULL and the newline character. In the Oracle implementation, the ' . ' operator can match any character in the database character set, including the newline character.

d. In the POSIX standard, a range in a regular expression includes all collation elements between the start and end points of the range in the linguistic definition of the current locale. Therefore, ranges in regular expressions are linguistic ranges rather than byte values ranges, and the semantics of the range expression are independent of character set. Oracle implements this independence by interpreting range expressions according to the linguistic definition determined by the NLS_SORT initialization parameter.

e. The backreference expression "\n" matches the same string of characters as was matched by the *n*th subexpression. The character *n* must be a digit from 1 to 9, designating the *n*th subexpression, numbered from left to right. The expression is invalid if the source string contains fewer than *n* subexpressions preceding the \n. For example, the regular expression ^(.*)\1$ matches a line consisting of two adjacent appearances of the same string. Oracle supports the backreference expression in the regular expression pattern and the replacement string of the REGEXP_REPLACE function.

f. A collating element is a unit of collation and is equal to one character in most cases, but may comprise two or more characters in some languages. Historically, regular expression syntax does not support ranges containing multicharacter collation elements, such as the range **'a'** through **'ch'**. The POSIX standard introduces the collation element delimiter **'[..]'**, which lets you delimit multicharacter collection elements such as **'[a-[.ch.]]'**. The collation elements supported by Oracle are determined by the setting of the NLS_SORT initialization parameter. The collation element is valid only inside the bracketed expression.

g. In English regular expressions, range expressions often indicate a character class. For example, **'[a-z]'** indicates any lowercase character. This convention is not useful in multilingual environments where the first and last character of a given character class may not be the same in all languages. The POSIX standard introduces the portable character class syntax **'[::]'**.

In addition to the operators, Oracle supports the following character classes based on character class definitions in NLS classification data:

TABLE 8-1. *Regular Expression Operators* (continued)

Character Class Syntax	Meaning
[:alnum:]	All alphanumeric characters
[:alpha:]	All alphabetic characters
[:blank:]	All blank space characters
[:cntrl:]	All control characters (nonprinting)
[:digit:]	All numeric digits
[:graph:]	All **[:punct:]**, **[:upper:]**, **[:lower:]**, and **[:digit:]** characters
[:lower:]	All lowercase alphabetic characters
[:print:]	All printable characters
[:punct:]	All punctuation characters
[:space:]	All space characters (nonprinting)
[:upper:]	All uppercase alphabetic characters
[:xdigit:]	All valid hexadecimal characters

This character class syntax lets you make better use of NLS character definitions to write flexible regular expressions. These character classes are valid only inside the bracketed expression.

h. Oracle supports the equivalence classes through the POSIX '[==]' syntax. A base letter and all of its accented versions constitute an equivalence class. For example, the equivalence class **'[=a=]'** matches "‰" and ",". The equivalence classes are valid only inside the bracketed expression.

Note this restriction on equivalence classes: Composed and decomposed versions of the same equivalence class do not match. For example, '‰' does not match "a" followed by an umlaut.

TABLE 8-1.   *Regular Expression Operators* (continued)

Let's apply some of these operators and character classes, starting with a simple search. First, search for a colon:

```
select regexp_substr
       ('MY LEDGER: Debits, Credits, and Invoices 1940',
        ':' ) regexp_substr
from dual;

R
-
:
```

Now, replace that search with a search for a punctuation character, using the [:punct:] regular expression character class:

```
select regexp_substr
       ('MY LEDGER: Debits, Credits, and Invoices 1940',
        '[:punct:]' ) regexp_substr
from dual;

R
-
:
```

Beginning from that point in the string, search from there to the next comma encountered:

```
select regexp_substr
        ('MY LEDGER: Debits, Credits, and Invoices 1940',
        '[:punct:][^,]+,' )   regexp_substr
from dual;

REGEXP_SU
---------
: Debits,
```

You can use the [:digit:] character class to find the numbers in the string:

```
select regexp_substr
        ('MY LEDGER: Debits, Credits, and Invoices 1940',
        '[[:digit:]]+' )   regexp_substr
from dual;

REGE
----
1940
```

As shown in this example, you can use the character classes to consolidate searches for multiple values. When you're working with search strings—particularly if you do not have prior experience with regular expressions—begin with the simplest version possible and then increase in complexity.

REGEXP_SUBSTR

The REGEXP_SUBSTR function, as shown in the preceding examples, uses regular expressions to specify the beginning and ending points of the returned string. The syntax for REGEXP_SUBSTR is shown in the following listing. REGEXP_SUBSTR returns the string as a VARCHAR2 or CLOB in the same character set as the *source_string*.

```
REGEXP_SUBSTR(source_string, pattern
                [, position
                    [, occurrence
                        [, match_parameter ]
                    ]
                ]
            )
```

The examples thus far in this chapter have focused on the *pattern* variable—the regular expression. The regular expression can contain up to 512 bytes. As shown in the syntax, you can also specify parameters related to the *position, occurrence,* and *match_parameter* conditions.

The *position* variable tells REGEXP_SUBSTR where to start searching within the *source_string*. The default *position* value is 1 (the first character). The *occurrence* variable is an integer indicating which occurrence of *pattern* in *source_string* Oracle should search for. The default *occurrence* value is 1. The *position* and *occurrence* variables are not available in the standard SUBSTR function. These represent significant extensions to the standard SUBSTR functionality.

You can use the *match_parameter* variable to further customize the search. *match_parameter* is a text literal that lets you change the default matching behavior of the function. Its possible values are as follows:

- **'i'** Used for case-insensitive matching.
- **'c'** Used for case-sensitive matching.
- **'n'** Allows the period (.), which is a wildcard (see Table 8-1), to match the newline character. If you omit this parameter, the period does not match the newline character.
- **'m'** Treats the source string as multiple lines. Oracle interprets ^ and $ as the start and end, respectively, of any line anywhere in the source string, rather than only at the start or end of the entire source string. If you omit this parameter, Oracle treats the source string as a single line.

If you specify multiple contradictory values for *match_parameter,* Oracle uses the last value. For example, if you specify "ic", Oracle will use case-sensitive matching. If you specify a character other than those shown here, Oracle will return an error.

If you omit *match_parameter,* the following will happen:

- The default case sensitivity is determined by the value of the NLS_SORT parameter.
- A period (.) does not match the newline character.
- The source string is treated as a single line.

Here is the REGEXP_SUBSTR search performed with case-insensitive matching:

```
select regexp_substr
       ('MY LEDGER: Debits, Credits, and Invoices 1940',
        'my',1,1,'i')    regexp_substr
from dual;

RE
--
MY
```

Now, change that to perform a case-sensitive search:

```
select regexp_substr
       ('MY LEDGER: Debits, Credits, and Invoices 1940',
        'my',1,1,'c')    regexp_substr
from dual;

RE
--
```

Nothing is returned due to the case mismatch. By default, searches are case sensitive.

You can use the *pattern* and *occurrence* parameters the same as you use them in INSTR. In the following example, the second digit is returned:

```
select regexp_substr
       ('MY LEDGER: Debits, Credits, and Invoices 1940',
```

```
                '[[:digit:]]' ,1,2)    regexp_substr
from dual;

R
-
9
```

Writing the same query using SUBSTR and INSTR (and assuming the two digits may not be consecutive) would be much more complex.

REGEXP_INSTR

The REGEXP_INSTR function uses regular expressions to return the beginning or ending point of the search pattern. The syntax for REGEXP_INSTR is shown in the following listing. REGEXP_INSTR returns an integer indicating the position of the beginning or ending of the search pattern, or a 0 if no match is found.

```
REGEXP_INSTR (source_string, pattern
                  [, position
                      [, occurrence
                          [, return_option
                              [, match_parameter ]
                          ]
                      ]
                  ]
              )
```

The REGEXP_SUBSTR function, shown in the preceding section, performs some of the capabilities normally associated with INSTR. REGEXP_INSTR adds a unique feature that makes it an important addition to your SQL toolset. Like REGEXP_SUBSTR, it has the variables *pattern*, *position* (starting position), *occurrence*, and *match_parameter*; see the prior section for a description of those variables. The new capability introduced here, *return_option*, allows you to tell Oracle what to return in relation to the occurrence of the pattern:

- If *return_option* is 0, Oracle returns the position of the first character of the occurrence. This is the default, and it's the same as the behavior of INSTR.

- If *return_option* is 1, Oracle returns the position of the character following the occurrence.

For example, the following query returns the location of the first digit found in the string:

```
select regexp_instr
        ('MY LEDGER: Debits, Credits, and Invoices 1940',
         '[[:digit:]]')   regexp_instr
from dual;

REGEXP_INSTR
------------
          42
```

What is the next position after the first digit of that string?

```
select regexp_instr
        ('MY LEDGER: Debits, Credits, and Invoices 1940',
         '[[:digit:]]',1,1,1)   regexp_instr
from dual;


REGEXP_INSTR
------------
          43
```

Even for searches that do not have complex patterns, you may decide to use REGEXP_INSTR in place of INSTR in order to simplify the math and logic involved in your queries that combine INSTR and SUBSTR capabilities. Be sure to carefully consider the case-sensitivity settings you specify via the *match_parameter* setting.

Here is a case that would otherwise require a procedural language such as Java or PL/SQL to accomplish the task. The following query returns employee IDs and names for any employee whose last name begins with the letters *E* through *T*, has at least two nonconsecutive lowercase *a* characters, with or without any blanks and ends with either an *a* or a *y*:

```
select employee_id, last_name
from employees
where regexp_instr(last_name,
               '^[E-T][[:alpha:] ]*a[^a]+a[[:alpha:] ]*[ay]$') > 0
order by last_name;


EMPLOYEE_ID LAST_NAME
----------- ------------------------
        106 Pataballa
        114 Raphaely
```

REGEXP_LIKE

In addition to the regular expression functions shown in previous listings, you can use the REGEXP_LIKE function. REGEXP_LIKE supports the use of regular expressions within where clauses. For example, which phone numbers start with "415"?

```
select lastname
from address
where regexp_like (Phone,'415+');


LASTNAME
-----------------------------
Adams
Zack
Yarrow
Werschky
Brant
Edgar
```

The format for REGEXP_LIKE is

```
REGEXP_LIKE(source_string, pattern
                [match_parameter ]
            )
```

Within the pattern, you can use all the search features shown earlier in this chapter—including the character class definitions—as part of a REGEXP_LIKE search. This capability makes performing very complex searches simple.

For example, how can you tell if a column value contains a numeric digit?

```
select lastname
from address
where regexp_like (phone, '[[:digit:]]');
```

If a TO_NUMBER function fails because a punctuation mark is found in the value, you can display the rows that caused it to fail:

```
select lastname
from address
where regexp_like (phone, '[[:punct:]]');
```

REPLACE and REGEXP_REPLACE

The REPLACE function replaces one value in a string with another. For example, you can replace each occurrence of a letter with a matching number. The format for REPLACE is

```
REPLACE ( char, search_string [,replace_string])
```

If you do not specify a value for the *replace_string* variable, the *search_string* value, when found, is removed. The input can be any of the character datatypes—CHAR, VARCHAR2, NCHAR, NVARCHAR2, CLOB, or NCLOB. Here's an example:

```
REPLACE('GEORGE', 'GE', 'EG') returns EGOREG
REPLACE('GEORGE', 'GE', NULL) returns OR
```

If the length of the search string is nonzero, you can tell how many times a string was found in the search string. First, you calculate the original string length:

```
LENGTH('GEORGE')
```

Then you calculate the length of the string after the search string values are removed:

```
LENGTH(REPLACE('GEORGE', 'GE', NULL))
```

Then you divide the difference by the length of the search string to find out how many occurrences of the search string were replaced:

```
select (length('GEORGE')
        - length(replace('GEORGE', 'GE', null)) ) /
        length('GE') counter
from dual;
```

```
COUNTER
-------
      2
```

The REGEXP_REPLACE function extends the capabilities of the REPLACE function in several ways. It supports the use of regular expressions in the search pattern, and it also supports the variables described earlier in this chapter—*position, occurrence,* and *match_parameter.* You can thus choose to replace only certain matched values, or make the matching case insensitive. The syntax for the REGEXP_REPLACE function is shown in the following listing:

```
REGEXP_REPLACE(source_string, pattern
              [, replace_string
                 [, position
                    [, occurrence
                       [, match_parameter ]
                    ]
                 ]
              ]
              )
```

With the exception of *replace_string,* all these variables have been described in the earlier parts of this chapter. The *replace_string* variable tells Oracle what to use to replace the part of the *source_string* that matched the *pattern.* The *occurrence* variable is a nonnegative integer that specifies the occurrence of the operation: If it is 0, all occurrences of the match are replaced; if you specify a positive integer, Oracle replaces the *n*th occurrence.

Let's consider the PHONE column of the ADDRESS table. First, we will look for numbers that are in the format "###-###-####". In that format, there are three digits followed by another set of three digits and then a set of four digits, separated by "-" characters. We can find the rows that match those criteria by looking for those sets of digits within a REGEXP_SUBSTR function call:

```
select regexp_substr (phone,
       '([[:digit:]]{3})-([[:digit:]]{3})-([[:digit:]]{4})'
       ) regexp_substr
from address;

REGEXP_SUBST
------------
213-555-0223
415-555-7530
214-555-8383
312-555-1166
707-555-8900
312-555-1414
415-555-6842
415-555-2178
415-555-7387
415-555-7512
415-555-6252
617-555-0125
603-555-2242
202-555-1414
```

```
718-555-1638
214-555-8383
503-555-7491
```

Now, use REGEXP_REPLACE to put parentheses around the first three digits while leaving out the first "-" character found. To do this, we will refer to that first set of data as \1, the second as \2, and the third as \3.

```
select regexp_replace (phone,
       '([[:digit:]]{3})-([[:digit:]]{3})-([[:digit:]]{4})'
     , '(\1) \2-\3'
     ) regexp_replace
from address;

REGEXP_REPLACE
----------------------------------------
(213) 555-0223
(415) 555-7530
(214) 555-8383
(312) 555-1166
(707) 555-8900
(312) 555-1414
(415) 555-6842
(415) 555-2178
(415) 555-7387
(415) 555-7512
(415) 555-6252
(617) 555-0125
(603) 555-2242
(202) 555-1414
(718) 555-1638
(214) 555-8383
(503) 555-7491
```

The output shows the result of the REGEXP_REPLACE function call—the area codes are enclosed within parentheses and the first "-" has been eliminated.

To show how the *occurrence* variable works, the following REGEXP_REPLACE function call replaces the second "5" found in a phone number with a period:

```
select regexp_replace (phone,
       '5', '.',
       1, 2
     ) regexp_replace
from address;

REGEXP_REPLACE
----------------------------------------
213-5.5-0223
415-.55-7530
214-5.5-8383
312-5.5-1166
707-5.5-8900
```

```
312-5.5-1414
415-.55-6842
415-.55-2178
415-.55-7387
415-.55-7512
415-.55-6252
617-5.5-0125
603-5.5-2242
202-5.5-1414
718-5.5-1638
214-5.5-8383
503-.55-7491
```

You can modify that query further to exclude the first three digits as possible matches (set the starting position to 4) and replace the fourth occurrence instead:

```
select regexp_replace (phone,
       '5', '.',
       4, 4
       ) regexp_replace
from address;

REGEXP_REPLACE
-----------------------------------------
213-555-0223
415-555-7.30
214-555-8383
312-555-1166
707-555-8900
312-555-1414
415-555-6842
415-555-2178
415-555-7387
415-555-7.12
415-555-62.2
617-555-012.
603-555-2242
202-555-1414
718-555-1638
214-555-8383
503-555-7491
```

You can limit the rows returned by using REGEXP_INSTR in a WHERE clause. In this case, only those rows that have at least four instances of "5" in them (beginning at the fourth character) will be displayed:

```
select regexp_replace (phone,
       '5', '.',
       4, 4
       ) regexp_replace
from address
where regexp_instr(phone,'5',4,4) > 0;
```

```
REGEXP_REPLACE
----------------------------------------
415-555-7.30
415-555-7.12
415-555-62.2
617-555-012.
```

Because this search pattern is not complex, you could use INSTR in the WHERE clause instead, but you'd still need REGEXP_REPLACE to return the desired result easily:

```
select regexp_replace (phone,
       '5', '.',
       4, 4
       ) regexp_replace
from address
where INSTR(phone,'5',4,4) > 0;
```

```
REGEXP_REPLACE
----------------------------------------
415-555-7.30
415-555-7.12
415-555-62.2
617-555-012.
```

You can use the ability to search for alternate values to combine multiple search criteria in a single query. The following replaces *either* a "5" or a "2"; occurrences of both "5" and "2" count toward the *occurrence* count:

```
select regexp_replace (Phone,
       '(5|2)', '.',
       4, 4
       ) regexp_replace
from ADDRESS
where regexp_instr(Phone, '(5|2)',4,4) > 0;
```

```
REGEXP_REPLACE
----------------------------------------
213-555-0.23
415-555-7.30
415-555-684.
415-555-.178
415-555-7.12
415-555-6.52
617-555-01.5
603-555-.242
```

The | character shown in this example is an alternation operator, so matches of either of the values specified will return a row. See Table 8-1 for additional operators supported within your regular expressions.

REGEXP_COUNT

As of Oracle Database 11*g*, you can use the REGEXP_COUNT function. REGEXP_COUNT returns the number of occurrences of a pattern found in the source string, complementing REGEXP_INSTR. Note that whereas COUNT is a set function that operates on groups of rows, REGEXP_COUNT is a single-row function that returns a result for the specified expression in each row.

The syntax for REGEXP_COUNT is

```
REGEXP_COUNT (source_char, pattern [, position [, match_param]])
```

REGEXP_COUNT returns the number of occurrences of *pattern* in the *source_char* string. If no match is found, the function returns 0. The *position* variable tells Oracle where within the source string to start the search. Each occurrence of the pattern following the starting position increments the count.

The *match_param* variable supports the following values:

- **'i'** Specifies case-insensitive matching.

- **'c'** Specifies case-sensitive matching.

- **'n'** Allows the period (.), which is the match-any-character character, to match the newline character. If you omit this parameter, the period does not match the newline character.

- **'m'** Treats the source string as multiple lines. Oracle interprets the caret (^) and dollar sign ($) as the start and end, respectively, of any line anywhere in the source string, rather than only at the start or end of the entire source string. If you omit this parameter, Oracle treats the source string as a single line.

- **'x'** Ignores whitespace characters. By default, whitespace characters match themselves.

If you specify multiple contradictory values, Oracle uses the last value.

The LENGTH example from earlier in this chapter can be modified to use REGEXP_COUNT. Instead of the syntax

```
select (length('GEORGE')
        - length(replace('GEORGE', 'GE', NULL)) ) /
        length('GE')   counter
from dual;
COUNTER
-------
      2
```

you could use the following syntax and get the same result:

```
select regexp_count('GEORGE','GE',1,'i')
from dual;
```

As a side benefit, you would be able to take advantage of case-insensitive searches, so that query could also be written as follows:

```
select regexp_count('GEORGE','ge',1,'i')
from dual;
```

Your use of the REGEXP_SUBSTR, REGEXP_INSTR, REGEXP_LIKE, REGEXP_REPLACE, and REGEXP_COUNT functions is limited only by your ability to develop regular expressions that reflect your needs. As shown in the examples in this chapter, you can use these functions to modify the display of existing data, to find complex patterns, and to return strings and counts of strings within patterns.

CHAPTER
9

Playing the Numbers

Virtually everything we do, particularly in business, is measured, explained, and often guided by numbers. Although Oracle cannot correct our obsession with numbers and the illusion of control they often give us, it will facilitate capable and thorough analysis of the information in a database. Good mathematical analysis of familiar numbers will often show trends and facts that were initially not apparent.

The Three Classes of Number Functions

Oracle functions deal with three classes of numbers: single values, groups of values, and lists of values. As with string functions (discussed in Chapters 7 and 8), some of these functions change the values they are applied to, whereas others merely report information about the values. The classes are distinguished as detailed in the following paragraphs.

A *single value* is one number, such as these:

- A literal number, such as 544.3702
- A numeric variable in SQL*Plus or PL/SQL
- One number from one column and one row of the database

Oracle single-value functions usually change these values through a calculation.

A *group of values* is all the numbers in one column from a series of rows, such as the closing stock price for all the rows of stocks in the stock market table from Chapter 4. Oracle group-value functions tell you something about the whole group, such as average stock price, but not about the individual members of the group.

A *list of values* is a series of numbers that can include the following:

- Literal numbers, such as 1, 7.3, 22, and 86
- Variables in SQL*Plus or PL/SQL
- Columns, such as OPENING_PRICE, CLOSING_PRICE, BID, and ASK

Oracle list functions choose one member of a list of values.

In the Alphabetical Reference section of this book, you will see these functions listed by class (numeric functions, list functions, aggregate functions, and analytic functions), with a description of each function and its usage

Notation

Functions will be shown with this kind of notation:

```
FUNCTION(value [,option])
```

The function itself will be uppercase. Values and options will be shown in lowercase italics. Whenever the word *value* appears this way, it represents one of the following: a literal number, the name of a number column in a table, the result of a calculation, a conversion to a numeric value, or a variable. Because Oracle does not allow numbers to be used as column names, a literal number should not appear in single quotation marks (as a literal string would be in a string function) because no string to numeric conversion is required. Column names also must not have single quotation marks.

Every function has only one pair of parentheses. The value that function works on, as well as additional information you can pass to the function, goes between the parentheses.

Some functions have *options*—parts that are not required to make the function work but that can give you more control if you choose to use them. Options are always shown in square brackets: [ ]. The required parts of a function always come before the optional parts.

Single-Value Functions

Most single-value functions are pretty straightforward. This section gives short examples of the major functions, and it shows both the results of the functions and how they correspond to columns, rows, and lists. After the examples, you'll learn how to combine these functions. The syntax for all the functions is found in the Alphabetical Reference of this book.

A table named MATH was created to show the calculation effects of the many math functions. It has only four rows and four columns, as shown here:

```
select name, above, below, empty from math;

NAME            ABOVE    BELOW  EMPTY
-------------   -------- ------- ------
Whole Number        11      -22
Low Decimal      33.33   -44.44
Mid Decimal       55.5    -55.5
High Decimal    66.666  -77.777
```

This table is useful because it has values with a variety of characteristics, which are spelled out by the names of the rows. WHOLE NUMBER contains no decimal parts. LOW DECIMAL has decimals that are less than 0.5, MID DECIMAL has decimals equal to 0.5, and HIGH DECIMAL has decimals greater than 0.5. This range is particularly important when using the ROUND (rounding) and TRUNC (truncate) functions and in understanding how they affect the value of a number.

To the right of the NAME column are three other columns: ABOVE, which contains only numbers above, or greater than, zero (positive numbers); BELOW, which contains only numbers below, or less than, zero; and EMPTY, which is NULL.

NOTE
In Oracle, a number column may have no value in it at all. When the column's value is NULL, it is not zero; it is simply empty. This has important implications in making computations, as you will see.

Not all the rows in this MATH table are needed to demonstrate how most math functions work, so the examples primarily use the last row, HIGH DECIMAL. In addition, the SQL*Plus column command has been used to show explicitly the precision of the calculation so the results of functions that affect a number's precision can be clearly seen. To review the SQL and SQL*Plus commands that produced the results that follow, see the script that accompanies the create table commands for the sample tables.

Addition (+), Subtraction (–), Multiplication (*), and Division (/)

The following query shows each of the four basic arithmetic functions, using the columns ABOVE and BELOW:

```
select name, above, below, empty,
       above + below  as plus,
       above - below  as subtr,
       above * below  as times,
       above / below  as divided
from math
where name = 'High Decimal';
```

NAME	ABOVE	BELOW	EMPTY	PLUS	SUBTR	TIMES	DIVIDED
High Decimal	66.666	-77.777		-11.111	144.443	-5185.0815	-.85714286

NULL

In the following example, the same four arithmetic operations are now done again, except instead of using ABOVE and BELOW, ABOVE and EMPTY are used. Note that any arithmetic operation that includes a NULL value has NULL as a result. The calculated columns (columns whose values are the result of a calculation) PLUS, SUBTR, TIMES, and DIVIDED are all empty.

```
select name, above, below, empty,
       above + empty  as plus,
       above - empty  as subtr,
       above * empty  as times,
       above / empty  as divided
from math
where name = 'High Decimal';
```

NAME	ABOVE	BELOW	EMPTY	PLUS	SUBTR	TIMES	DIVIDED
High Decimal	66.666	-77.777					

What you see here is evidence that a NULL value cannot be used in a calculation. NULL isn't the same as zero; think of NULL as a value that is unknown. For example, suppose you have a table with the names of your friends and their ages, but the AGE column for Pat Smith is empty because you don't know it. What's the difference in your ages? It's clearly not your age minus zero. Your age minus an unknown age is also unknown, or NULL. You can't fill in an answer because you don't have an answer. Because you can't make the computation, the answer is NULL.

This is also the reason you cannot use NULL with an equal sign in a WHERE clause (see Chapter 5). It makes no sense to say *x* is unknown and *y* is unknown; therefore, *x* and *y* are equal. If Mrs. Wilkins's and Mr. Adams's ages are unknown, it doesn't mean they're the same age.

There also will be instances where NULL means a value is irrelevant, such as an apartment number for a house. In some cases, the apartment number might be NULL because it is unknown (even though it really exists), whereas in other cases, it is NULL because there simply isn't an apartment number. NULLs are explored in more detail later in this chapter, under "NULLs in Group-Value Functions."

NVL: NULL-Value Substitution

The preceding section states the general case about NULLs—that NULL represents an unknown or irrelevant value. In particular cases, however, although a value is unknown, you may be able to make a reasonable guess. If you're a package carrier, for instance, and 30 percent of the shippers who call you for pickups can't tell you the weight or volume of their packages, will you declare it completely impossible to estimate how many cargo planes you'll need tonight? Of course not. You know from experience the average weight and volume of your packages, so you'd plug in these numbers for those customers who didn't supply you with the information. Here's the information as supplied by your clients:

```
select client, weight from shipping;
```

```
CLIENT          WEIGHT
-------------   ------
Johnson Tool        59
Dagg Software       27
Tully Andover
```

This is what the NULL-value substitution (NVL) function does:

```
select client, nvl(weight,43) from shipping;
```

```
CLIENT          NVL(WEIGHT,43)
-------------   --------------
Johnson Tool                59
Dagg Software               27
Tully Andover               43
```

Here, you know that the average package weight is 43 pounds, so you use the NVL function to plug in 43 anytime a client's package has an unknown weight—that is, where the value in the column is NULL. In this case, Tully Andover didn't know the weight of her package when she called it in, but you can still total these package weights and have a fair estimate.

Here is the format for NVL:

```
NVL(value,substitute)
```

If *value* is NULL, this function returns *substitute*. If *value* is not NULL, this function returns *value*. Note that *substitute* can be a literal number, another column, or a computation. If you really were a package carrier with this problem, you could even have a table join in your SELECT statement where *substitute* was from a view that actually averaged the weight of all non-NULL packages.

NVL is not restricted to numbers. It can be used with CHAR, VARCHAR2, DATE, and other datatypes as well, but *value* and *substitute* must be the same datatype. Also, NVL is really useful only in cases where the data is unknown, not where it's irrelevant.

A companion function, NVL2, is slightly more complex. Its format is

```
NVL2 (expr1,expr2,expr3)
```

In NVL2, *expr1* can never be returned; either *expr2* or *expr3* will be returned. If *expr1* is not NULL, NVL2 returns *expr2*. If *expr1* is NULL, NVL2 returns *expr3*. The argument *expr1* can have any datatype. The arguments *expr2* and *expr3* can have any datatypes except LONG.

You can use the NANVL function for the BINARY_FLOAT and BINARY_DOUBLE datatypes. NANVL takes two variables and returns the second if the first is not a number.

ABS: Absolute Value

Absolute value is the measure of the magnitude of something. For instance, in a temperature change or a stock index change, the magnitude of the change has meaning in itself, regardless of the direction of the change (which is important in its own right). Absolute value is always a positive number.

Here is the format for ABS:

```
ABS(value)
```

Note these examples:

```
ABS(-87.55) = 87.55
ABS(146) = 146
ABS(-30) =  30
```

CEIL

CEIL (for *ceiling*) simply produces the smallest integer (or whole number) that is greater than or equal to a specific value. Pay special attention to its effect on negative numbers.

The following shows the format for CEIL and some examples:

```
CEIL(value)
```

```
CEIL(2)    =  2
CEIL(1.3)  =  2
CEIL(-2)   = -2
CEIL(-2.3) = -2
```

FLOOR

FLOOR returns the largest integer equal to or less than a specific value. Here is the format for FLOOR and some examples:

```
FLOOR(value)
```

```
FLOOR(2)   =  2
FLOOR(1.3) =  1
```

```
FLOOR(-2)    = -2
FLOOR(-2.3) = -3
```

MOD

MOD (*modulus*) is a function primarily used in data processing for esoteric tasks such as "check digits," which help ensure the accurate transmission of a string of numbers. MOD divides a value by a divisor and tells you the remainder. For example, MOD(23,6) = 5 means divide 23 by 6. The answer is 3 with 5 left over, so 5 is the result of the modulus.

Here is the format for MOD:

```
MOD(value,divisor)
```

Both *value* and *divisor* can be any real number. The value of MOD is zero if *divisor* is zero or negative. Note the following examples:

```
MOD(100,10)    =  0
MOD(22,23)     = 22
MOD(10,3)      =  1
MOD(-30.23,7)  = -2.23
MOD(4.1,0.3)   =  0.2
```

The second example shows what MOD does whenever the divisor is greater than the dividend (the number being divided). It produces the dividend as a result. Also note this important case where *value* is not an integer:

```
MOD(value,1)    = 0
```

The preceding is a good test to see if a number is an integer.

You can use the REMAINDER function in a similar way. The MOD function is similar to REMAINDER, but it uses FLOOR in its formula, whereas REMAINDER uses ROUND. Several examples will show when the REMAINDER function differs from the MOD function:

```
select remainder(6,3),mod(6,3) from dual;
select remainder(7,3),mod(7,3) from dual;
select remainder(7.5,3),mod(7.5,3) from dual;
select remainder(4.5,3),mod(4.5,3) from dual;
select remainder(4.8,3),mod(4.8,3) from dual;
select remainder(4.3,3),mod(4.3,3) from dual;
```

```
REMAINDER(6,3) MOD(6,3)
-------------- --------
             0        0


REMAINDER(7,3) MOD(7,3)
-------------- --------
             1        1


REMAINDER(7.5,3) MOD(7.5,3)
---------------- ----------
             1.5        1.5
```

```
REMAINDER(4.5,3)  MOD(4.5,3)
----------------  ----------
            -1.5         1.5


REMAINDER(4.8,3)  MOD(4.8,3)
----------------  ----------
            -1.2         1.8


REMAINDER(4.3,3)  MOD(4.3,3)
----------------  ----------
             1.3         1.3
```

POWER

POWER simply provides the ability to raise a value to a given positive exponent, as shown here:

POWER(*value*,*exponent*)

```
POWER(3,2)        =      9
POWER(3,3)        =     27
POWER(-77.777,2)  = 6049.26173
POWER(3,1.086)    =      3.29726371
POWER(64,0.5)     =      8
```

The *exponent* can be any real number.

SQRT: Square Root

Oracle has a separate square root function that gives results equivalent to POWER(*value*,0.5):

SQRT(*value*)

```
SQRT(64)      = 8
SQRT(66.666)  = 8.16492498
SQRT(4)       = 2
```

The square root of a negative number is an imaginary number. Oracle doesn't support imaginary numbers, so it returns an error if you attempt to find the square root of a negative number.

EXP, LN, and LOG

The EXP, LN, and LOG functions are rarely used in business calculations but are quite common in scientific and technical work. EXP is e (2.71828183) raised to the specified power; LN is the "natural," or base e, logarithm of a value. The first two functions are reciprocals of one another: LN(EXP(*i*)) = *value*. The LOG function takes a base and a positive value. LN(*value*) is the same as LOG(2.71828183,*value*).

EXP(*value*)

```
EXP(3)        =  20.0855369
EXP(5)        = 148.413159
```

```
LN(value)

LN(3)          = 1.09861229
LN(20.0855369) = 3


LOG(value)

LOG(EXP(1),3) = 1.09861229
LOG(10,100)   = 2
```

ROUND and TRUNC

ROUND and TRUNC are two related single-value functions. TRUNC truncates, or chops off, digits of precision from a number; ROUND rounds numbers to a given number of digits of precision.

Here are the formats for ROUND and TRUNC:

```
ROUND(value,precision)
TRUNC(value,precision)
```

There are some properties worth paying close attention to here. First, look at this simple example of a SELECT from the MATH table. Two digits of precision are called for (counting toward the right from the decimal point).

```
select name, above, below,
       round(above,2),
       round(below,2),
       trunc(above,2),
       trunc(below,2)
from math;
```

NAME	ABOVE	BELOW	ROUND (ABOVE,2)	ROUND (BELOW,2)	TRUNC (ABOVE,2)	TRUNC (BELOW,2)
Whole Number	11	-22	11	-22	11	-22
Low Decimal	33.33	-44.44	33.33	-44.44	33.33	-44.44
Mid Decimal	55.5	-55.5	55.5	-55.5	55.5	-55.5
High Decimal	66.666	-77.777	66.67	-77.78	66.66	-77.77

Only the bottom row is affected, because only it has three digits beyond the decimal point. Both the positive and negative numbers in the bottom row were rounded or truncated: 66.666 was rounded to a higher number (66.67), but –77.777 was rounded to a lower (more negative) number (–77.78). When rounding is done to zero digits, this is the result:

```
select name, above, below,
       round(above,0),
       round(below,0),
       trunc(above,0),
       trunc(below,0)
from math;
```

NAME	ABOVE	BELOW	ROUND (ABOVE,0)	ROUND (BELOW,0)	TRUNC (ABOVE,0)	TRUNC (BELOW,0)
Whole Number	11	-22	11	-22	11	-22
Low Decimal	33.33	-44.44	33	-44	33	-44
Mid Decimal	55.5	-55.5	56	-56	55	-55
High Decimal	66.666	-77.777	67	-78	66	-77

Note that the decimal value of 0.5 was rounded up when 55.5 went to 56. This follows the most common American rounding convention (some rounding conventions round up only if a number is greater than 0.5). Compare these results with CEIL and FLOOR. They have significant differences:

```
ROUND(55.5)  = 56     ROUND(-55.5)  = -56
TRUNC(55.5)  = 55     TRUNC(-55.5)  = -55
CEIL(55.5)   = 56     CEIL(-55.5)   = -55
FLOOR(55.5)  = 55     FLOOR(-55.5)  = -56
```

Finally, note that both ROUND and TRUNC can work with negative precision, moving to the left of the decimal point:

```
select name, above, below,
       round(above,-1),
       round(below,-1),
       trunc(above,-1),
       trunc(below,-1)
from math;
```

NAME	ABOVE	BELOW	ROUND (ABOVE,-1)	ROUND (BELOW,-1)	TRUNC (ABOVE,-1)	TRUNC (BELOW,-1)
Whole Number	11	-22	10	-20	10	-20
Low Decimal	33.33	-44.44	30	-40	30	-40
Mid Decimal	55.5	-55.5	60	-60	50	-50
High Decimal	66.666	-77.777	70	-80	60	-70

Rounding with a negative number can be useful when producing such things as economic reports, where populations or dollar sums need to be rounded up to the millions, billions, or trillions.

SIGN

SIGN is the flip side of absolute value. Whereas ABS tells you the magnitude of a value but not its sign, SIGN tells you the sign of a value but not its magnitude.

Here is the format for SIGN:

```
SIGN(value)
```

```
Examples: SIGN(146) =  1   Compare to: ABS(146) = 146
          SIGN(-30) = -1               ABS(-30) =  30
```

The SIGN of 0 is 0:

```
SIGN(0)=0
```

The SIGN function is often used in conjunction with the DECODE function. DECODE is described in Chapter 16.

SIN, SINH, COS, COSH, TAN, TANH, ACOS, ATAN, ATAN2, and ASIN

The trigonometric functions sine, cosine, and tangent are scientific and technical functions not used much in business. SIN, COS, and TAN give you the standard trigonometric function values for an angle expressed in radians (degrees multiplied by *pi* divided by 180). SINH, COSH, and TANH give you the hyperbolic functions for an angle.

```
SIN(value)
```

```
SIN(30*3.141592655/180) = .5
```

```
COSH(value)
```

```
COSH(0)             = 1
```

The ASIN, ACOS, and ATAN functions return the arc sine, arc cosine, and arc tangent values (in radians) of the values provided. ATAN2 returns the arc tangent of two values. Input values are unbounded; outputs are expressed in radians.

Aggregate Functions

Aggregate or "group-value" functions are those statistical functions such as SUM, AVG, COUNT, and the like, that tell you something about a group of values taken as a whole: the average age of all the friends in the table, for instance, or the oldest member of the group, or the youngest, or the number of members in the group, and more. Even when one of these functions is supplying information about a single row—such as the oldest person—it is still information that is defined by the row's relation to the group.

You can use a wide array of advanced statistical functions against your data—including regression testing and sampling. In the following discussions, you will see descriptions of the most commonly used group-value functions; for the others, see the Alphabetical Reference.

NULLs in Group-Value Functions

Group-value functions treat NULL values differently than single-value functions do. Group functions (other than COUNT(*)) ignore NULL values and calculate a result without considering them.

Take AVG as an example. Suppose you have a list of 100 friends and their ages. If you picked 20 of them at random and averaged their ages, how different would the result be than if you picked a different list of 20, also at random, and averaged it, or if you averaged all 100? In fact, the averages of these three groups would be very close. What this means is that AVG is somewhat insensitive to missing rows, even when the missing data represents a high percentage of the total number of records available.

NOTE
AVG is not immune to missing data, and there can be cases where it will be significantly off (such as when missing data is not randomly distributed), but these cases are less common.

The relative insensitivity of AVG to missing data needs to be contrasted with, for instance, SUM. How close to correct is the SUM of the ages of only 20 friends to the SUM of all 100 friends? Not close at all. So if you had a table of friends, but only 20 out of 100 supplied their ages, and 80 out of 100 had NULL for their age, which one would be a more reliable statistic about the whole group and less sensitive to the absence of data—the AVG age of those 20 friends, or the SUM of them? Note that this is an entirely different issue than whether it is possible to estimate the sum of all 100 based on only 20 (in fact, it is precisely the AVG of the 20, times 100). The point is, if you don't know how many rows are NULL, you can use the following to provide a fairly reasonable result:

```
select avg(age) from birthday;
```

You cannot get a reasonable result from this, however:

```
select sum(age) from birthday;
```

This same test of whether or not results are reasonable defines how the other group functions respond to NULLs. STDDEV and VARIANCE are measures of central tendency; they, too, are relatively insensitive to missing data. (These are shown in "STDDEV and VARIANCE," later in this chapter.)

MAX and MIN measure the extremes of your data. They can fluctuate wildly while AVG stays relatively constant: If you add a 100-year-old man to a group of 99 people who are 50 years old, the average age only goes up to 50.5—but the maximum age has doubled. Add a newborn baby, and the average goes back to 50, but the minimum age is now 0. It's clear that missing or unknown NULL values can profoundly affect MAX, MIN, and SUM, so be cautious when using them, particularly if a significant percentage of the data is NULL.

Is it possible to create functions that also take into account how sparse the data is and how many values are NULL, compared to how many have real values, and make good guesses about MAX, MIN, and SUM? Yes, but such functions would be statistical projections, which must make explicit their assumptions about a particular set of data. This is not an appropriate task for a general-purpose group function. Some statisticians would argue that these functions should return NULL if they encounter any NULLs because returning any value can be misleading. Oracle returns something rather than nothing, but leaves it up to you to decide whether the result is reasonable.

COUNT is a special case. It can go either way with NULL values, but it always returns a number; it never evaluates to NULL. The format and usage for COUNT are shown shortly, but to simply contrast it with the other group functions, it counts all the non-NULL rows of a column, or it counts all the rows. In other words, if asked to count the ages of 100 friends, COUNT returns a value of 20 (because only 20 of the 100 gave their ages). If asked to count the rows in the table of friends without specifying a column, it returns 100. An example of these differences is given in "DISTINCT in Group Functions," later in this chapter.

Examples of Single- and Group-Value Functions

Neither the group-value functions nor the single-value functions are particularly difficult to understand, but a practical overview of how each function works is helpful in fleshing out some of the options and consequences of their use.

The COMFORT table in these examples contains basic temperature data, by city, at noon and midnight on each of four sample days in one year: the equinoxes (about March 21 and September 23) and the solstices (about June 22 and December 22). You ought to be able to characterize cities based on their temperatures on these days in one year.

For the sake of these examples, this table has only eight rows: the data from the four dates in 2003 for San Francisco, California, and Keene, New Hampshire. You can use Oracle's number functions to analyze these cities, their average temperature, the volatility of the temperature, and so on, for 2011. With more years and data on more cities, an analysis of temperature patterns and variability throughout the century could be made.

The table looks like this:

```
describe comfort
```

Name	Null?	Type
CITY	NOT NULL	VARCHAR2(13)
SAMPLE_DATE	NOT NULL	DATE
NOON		NUMBER(3,1)
MIDNIGHT		NUMBER(3,1)
PRECIPITATION		NUMBER

It contains this temperature data:

```
select city, sample_date, noon, midnight from comfort;
```

CITY	SAMPLE_DA	NOON	MIDNIGHT
San Francisco	21-MAR-11	62.5	42.3
San Francisco	22-JUN-11	51.1	71.9
San Francisco	23-SEP-11		61.5
San Francisco	22-DEC-11	52.6	39.8
Keene	21-MAR-11	39.9	-1.2
Keene	22-JUN-11	85.1	66.7
Keene	23-SEP-11	99.8	82.6
Keene	22-DEC-11	-7.2	-1.2

Remember that, by default, SQL*Plus truncates the column headers to fit the width of the data in the column. If you want to see the entire column name in the header, you can use the SQL*Plus COLUMN ... FORMAT ... directive to specify the column format to be wide enough to show the full column name.

AVG, COUNT, MAX, MIN, and SUM

Due to a power failure, the noon temperature in San Francisco on September 23 did not get recorded. The consequences of this can be seen in the following query:

```
select avg(noon), count(noon), max(noon), min(noon), sum(noon)
from comfort
where City = 'San Francisco';
```

```
AVG(NOON) COUNT(NOON) MAX(NOON) MIN(NOON) SUM(NOON)
--------- ----------- --------- --------- ---------
    55.4            3      62.5      51.1     166.2
```

AVG(NOON) is the average of the three temperatures that are known. COUNT(NOON) is the count of how many rows there are in the NOON column that are not NULL. MAX and MIN are self-evident. SUM(NOON) is the sum of only three dates because of the NULL for September 23. Note that

```
SUM(NOON)
---------
    166.2
```

is by no coincidence exactly three times AVG(NOON).

Combining Group-Value and Single-Value Functions

Suppose you would like to know how much the temperature changes in the course of a day. This is a measure of *volatility*. Your first attempt to answer the question might be to subtract the temperature at midnight from the temperature at noon:

```
select city, sample_date, noon-midnight
from comfort
where City = 'Keene';
```

```
CITY          SAMPLE_DA NOON-MIDNIGHT
------------- --------- -------------
Keene         21-MAR-11          41.1
Keene         22-JUN-11          18.4
Keene         23-SEP-11          17.2
Keene         22-DEC-11            -6
```

With only four rows to consider in this table, you can quickly convert (or ignore) the pesky minus sign. Volatility in temperature is really a magnitude—which means it asks by how much the temperature changed. It doesn't include a sign, so −6 isn't really correct. If this goes uncorrected and is included in a further calculation, such as the average change in a year, the answer you get will be absolutely wrong, as shown here:

```
select avg(noon-midnight)
from comfort
where city = 'Keene';
```

```
AVG(NOON-MIDNIGHT)
------------------
            17.675
```

The correct answer requires an absolute value, as shown next.

```
select avg(abs(noon-midnight))
from comfort
where city = 'Keene';
```

```
AVG(ABS(NOON-MIDNIGHT))
-----------------------
               20.675
```

Combining functions this way follows the same technique given in Chapter 7 in the section on string functions. An entire function such as

```
abs(noon-midnight)
```

is simply plugged into another function as its value, like this:

```
AVG(value)
```

which produces

```
avg(abs(noon-midnight))
```

This shows both single-value and group-value functions at work. You see that you can place single-value functions inside group-value functions. The single-value functions will calculate a result for every row, and the group-value functions will view that result as if it were the actual value for the row. Single-value functions can be combined (*nested* inside each other) almost without limit. Group-value functions can contain single-value functions in place of their value. They can, in fact, contain many single-value functions in place of their value.

What about combining group functions? First of all, it doesn't make any sense to nest them this way:

```
select sum(avg(noon)) from comfort;
```

The preceding will produce this error:

```
ERROR at line 1:
ORA-00978: nested group function without GROUP BY
```

Besides, if it actually worked, it would produce exactly the same result as

```
avg(noon)
```

because the result of AVG(NOON) is just a single value. The SUM of a single value is just the single value, so it is not meaningful to nest group functions. The exception to this rule is in the use of GROUP BY in the SELECT statement, the absence of which is why Oracle produced the error message here. This is covered in Chapter 12.

It *can* be meaningful to add, subtract, multiply, or divide the results of two or more group functions. For example,

```
select max(noon) - min(noon)
from comfort
where city = 'San Francisco';

MAX(NOON)-MIN(NOON)
-------------------
               11.4
```

gives the range of the temperatures in a year. In fact, a quick comparison of San Francisco and Keene could be done with just a bit more effort:

```
select city, avg(noon), max(noon), min(noon),
       max(noon) - min(noon) as swing
from comfort
group by city;
```

CITY	AVG(NOON)	MAX(NOON)	MIN(NOON)	SWING
Keene	54.4	99.8	-7.2	107
San Francisco	55.4	62.5	51.1	11.4

This query is a good example of discovering information in your data: The average temperatures in the two cities are nearly identical, but the huge temperature swing in Keene, compared to San Francisco, says a lot about the yearly temperature volatility of the two cities, and the relative effort required to dress (or to heat and cool a home) in one city compared to the other. The GROUP BY clause will be explained in detail in Chapter 12. Briefly, in this example, it forced the group functions to work not on the total table, but on the subgroups of temperatures by city.

STDDEV and VARIANCE

Standard deviation and variance have their common statistical meanings, and they use the same format as all group functions:

```
select max(noon), avg(noon), min(noon), stddev(noon),
       variance(noon)
from comfort
where city = 'Keene';
```

MAX(NOON)	AVG(NOON)	MIN(NOON)	STDDEV(NOON)	VARIANCE(NOON)
99.8	54.4	-7.2	48.3337701	2336.15333

See the Alphabetical Reference for the syntax for the statistical functions.

DISTINCT in Group Functions

All group-value functions have a DISTINCT versus ALL option. COUNT provides a good example of how this works.

Here is the format for COUNT (note that | means "or"):

```
COUNT([DISTINCT | ALL] value)
```

Here is an example:

```
select count(distinct city), count(city), count(*)
from comfort;
```

```
COUNT(DISTINCTCITY) COUNT(CITY) COUNT(*)
------------------- ----------- --------
                  2           8        8
```

This query shows a couple of interesting results. First, DISTINCT forces COUNT to count only the number of unique city names. If asked to count the DISTINCT midnight temperatures, it would return 7, because two of the eight temperatures were the same. When COUNT is used on CITY but not forced to look at DISTINCT cities, it finds 8.

This also shows that COUNT can work on a character column. It's not making a computation on the values in the column, as SUM or AVG must; it is merely counting how many rows have a value in the specified column.

COUNT has another unique property: *value* can be an asterisk, meaning that COUNT tells you how many rows are in the table, regardless of whether any specific columns are NULL. It will count a row even if all its fields are NULL.

The other group functions do not share COUNT's ability to use an asterisk, nor its ability to use a character column for *value* (although MAX and MIN can). They do all share its use of DISTINCT, which forces each of them to operate only on unique values. A table with values such as

```
select first_name, age from birthday;
```

```
FIRST_NAME        AGE
---------------   ----
GEORGE             42
ROBERT             52
NANCY              42
VICTORIA           42
FRANK              42
```

would produce this result:

```
select avg(distinct age) as average,
       sum(distinct age) as total
from birthday;
```

```
AVERAGE  TOTAL
-------  ------
     47      94
```

which, if you wanted to know the average age of your friends, is not the right answer. The use of DISTINCT other than in COUNT is likely to be extremely rare, except perhaps in some statistical calculations. MAX and MIN produce the same result with or without DISTINCT.

The alternative option to DISTINCT is ALL, which is the default. ALL tells SQL to check every row, even if the value is a duplicate of the value in another row. You do not need to type ALL; if you don't type DISTINCT, ALL is used automatically.

List Functions

Unlike the group-value functions, which work on a group of rows, the list functions work on a group of columns, either actual or calculated values, within a single row. In other words, list functions compare the values of each of several columns and pick either the greatest or least of the list. Consider the COMFORT table, shown here:

```
select city, sample_date, noon, midnight from comfort;
```

```
CITY          SAMPLE_DA NOON  MIDNIGHT
------------- --------- ----  --------
San Francisco 21-MAR-11 62.5     42.3
San Francisco 22-JUN-11 51.1     71.9
San Francisco 23-SEP-11          61.5
San Francisco 22-DEC-11 52.6     39.8
Keene         21-MAR-11 39.9     -1.2
Keene         22-JUN-11 85.1     66.7
Keene         23-SEP-11 99.8     82.6
Keene         22-DEC-11 -7.2     -1.2
```

Now compare this query result with the following one. Note especially June and September in San Francisco and December in Keene:

```
select city, sample_date, greatest(midnight,noon) as high,
       least(midnight,noon) as low
from comfort;
```

```
CITY          SAMPLE_DA HIGH  LOW
------------- --------- ----  ----
San Francisco 21-MAR-11 62.5  42.3
San Francisco 22-JUN-11 71.9  51.1
San Francisco 23-SEP-11
San Francisco 22-DEC-11 52.6  39.8
Keene         21-MAR-11 39.9  -1.2
Keene         22-JUN-11 85.1  66.7
Keene         23-SEP-11 99.8  82.6
Keene         22-DEC-11 -1.2  -7.2
```

September in San Francisco has a NULL result because GREATEST and LEAST couldn't legitimately compare an actual midnight temperature with an unknown noon temperature. In the other two instances, the midnight temperature was actually higher than the noon temperature.

Here are the formats for GREATEST and LEAST:

```
GREATEST(value1,value2,value3. . .)
LEAST(value1,value2,value3. . .)
```

Both GREATEST and LEAST can be used with many values, and the values can be columns, literal numbers, calculations, or combinations of other columns. GREATEST and LEAST can also be used with character columns. For example, they can choose the names that fall last (GREATEST) or first (LEAST) in alphabetical order:

```
least('Bob','George','Andrew','Isaiah') = Andrew
```

You can use the COALESCE function to evaluate multiple values for non-NULL values. Given a string of values, COALESCE will return the first non-NULL value encountered; if all are NULL, then a NULL result will be returned.

In the COMFORT table, there is a NULL value for NOON for one of the San Francisco measurements. The following query returns

```
select coalesce(noon, midnight)
from comfort
where city = 'San Francisco';

COALESCE(NOON,MIDNIGHT)
----------------------
                  62.5
                  51.1
                  61.5
                  52.6
```

In the first two records of the output, the value displayed is the NOON value. In the third record, NOON is NULL, so MIDNIGHT is returned instead. Oracle's DECODE and CASE functions provide similar functionality, as described in Chapter 16.

Finding Rows with MAX or MIN

Which city had the highest temperature ever recorded and on what date? The answer is easy with just eight rows to look at, but what if you have data from every city in the country and for every day of every year for the last 50 years? Assume, for now, that the highest temperature for the year occurred closer to noon than midnight. The following won't work:

```
select city, sample_date, max(noon)
from comfort;
```

Oracle flags the CITY column and gives this error message:

```
select city, sample_date, max(noon)
       *
ERROR at line 1:
ORA-00937: not a single-group group function
```

This error message is a bit opaque. It means that Oracle has detected a flaw in the logic of the question. Asking for columns means you want individual rows to appear; asking for MAX, a group function, means you want a group result for all rows. These are two different kinds of requests.

The first asks for a set of rows, but the second requests just one computed row, so there is a conflict. Here is how to construct the query:

```
select city, sample_date, noon
from comfort
where noon = (select max(noon) from comfort);

CITY          SAMPLE DA  NOON
------------  ---------- -----
Keene          23-SEP-11  99.8
```

This only produces one row. You might think, therefore, that the combination of a request for the CITY and SAMPLE_DATE columns, along with the MAX of NOON, is not so contradictory as was just implied. But what if you'd asked for the minimum temperature instead?

```
select city, sample_date, midnight
from comfort
where midnight = (select min(midnight) from comfort);

CITY          SAMPLE_DA MIDNIGHT
------------  --------- --------
Keene          21-MAR-11     -1.2
Keene          22-DEC-11     -1.2
```

Two rows! More than one satisfied the MIN request, so there is a conflict in trying to combine a regular column request with a group function.

It is also possible to use two subqueries, each with a group-value function in it (or two subqueries, where one does and the other doesn't have a group function). Suppose you want to know the highest and lowest noon temperatures for the year:

```
select city, sample_date, noon
from comfort
where noon = (select max(noon) from comfort)
or noon = (select min(noon) from comfort);

CITY          SAMPLE DA  NOON
------------  ---------- -----
Keene          23-SEP-11  99.8
Keene          22-DEC-11  -7.2
```

Precedence and Parentheses

When more than one arithmetic or logical operator is used in a single calculation, which one is executed first, and does it matter what order they are in? Consider the following query of the DUAL table (a one-column, one-row table provided by Oracle):

```
select 2/2/4 from dual;

2/2/4
-----
  .25
```

When parentheses are introduced, although the numbers and the operation (division) stay the same, the answer changes considerably:

```
select 2/(2/4) from dual;
```

```
2/(2/4)
-------
      4
```

The reason for this is *operator precedence*. Precedence defines the order in which mathematical computations are made, not just in Oracle but in mathematics in general. The rules are simple: Operations within parentheses have the highest precedence, then multiplication and division, then addition and subtraction. When an equation is computed, any calculations inside parentheses are made first. Multiplication and division are next. Finally, any addition and subtraction are completed. When operations of equal precedence appear in an expression, they are executed from left to right. Here are a few examples:

```
2*4/2*3 = 12                (the same as ( (2*4)/2 )*3)
(2*4)/(2*3) = 1.333
4-2*5 = -6                  (the same as 4 - (2*5))
(4-2)*5 = 10
```

AND and OR also obey precedence rules, with AND having the higher precedence. Observe the effect of the AND as well as the left-to-right order in these two queries:

```
select * from newspaper
where section = 'B' and page = 1 or page = 2;
```

```
FEATURE          S  PAGE
---------------  -  -----
Weather          C    2
Modern Life      B    1
Bridge           B    2
```

```
3 rows selected.
```

```
select * from newspaper
where page = 1 or page = 2 and section = 'B';
```

```
FEATURE          S  PAGE
---------------  -  -----
National News    A    1
Sports           D    1
Business         E    1
Modern Life      B    1
Bridge           B    2
```

```
5 rows selected.
```

If what you really want is page 1 or 2 in Section B, then parentheses are needed to overcome the precedence of the AND. Parentheses override any other operations.

```
select * from newspaper
where section = 'B' and (page = 1 or page = 2);


FEATURE          S  PAGE
---------------  -  -----
Modern Life      B    1
Bridge           B    2


2 rows selected.
```

The truth is that even experienced programmers and mathematicians have trouble remembering what will execute first when they write a query or an equation. It is always wise to make explicit the order you want Oracle to follow. Use parentheses whenever there could be the slightest risk of confusion.

Review

Single-value functions work on values in a row-by-row fashion. List functions compare columns and choose just one, again in a row-by-row fashion. Single-value functions almost always change the value of the column they are applied to. This doesn't mean, of course, that they have modified the database from which the value was drawn, but they do make a calculation with that value, and the result is different from the original value.

List functions don't change values in this way, but rather they simply choose (or report) the GREATEST or LEAST of a series of values in a row. Both single-value and list functions will not produce a result if they encounter a value that is NULL.

Both single-value and list functions can be used anywhere an expression can be used, such as in the SELECT and WHERE clauses.

The group-value functions tell something about a whole group of numbers—all of the rows in a set. The group-value functions tell you the average of those numbers, or the largest of them, or how many there are, or the standard deviation of the values, and so on. Group functions ignore NULL values, and this fact must be kept firmly in mind when reporting about groups of values; otherwise, there is considerable risk of misunderstanding the data.

Group-value functions also can report information on subgroups within a table, or they can be used to create a summary view of information from one or more tables. Chapter 12 gives details on these additional features.

Finally, mathematical and logical precedence affect the order in which queries are evaluated, and this can have a dramatic effect on query results. Get into the habit of using parentheses to make the order you want both explicit and easy to understand.

CHAPTER
10

Dates: Then, Now, and the Difference

One of Oracle's strengths is its ability to store and calculate dates, and the number of seconds, minutes, hours, days, months, and years between dates. In addition to basic date functions, Oracle supports a wide array of time zone–conversion functions. It also has the ability to format dates in virtually any manner you can conceive of, from the simple 01-MAY-12, to May 1st in the 782nd Year of the Reign of Louis IX. You probably won't use many of these date formatting and computing functions, but the most basic ones will prove to be very important.

Date Arithmetic

DATE is an Oracle datatype, just as VARCHAR2 and NUMBER are, and it has its own unique properties. The DATE datatype is stored in a special internal Oracle format that includes not just the month, day, and year, but also the hour, minute, and second. The benefit of all this detail should be obvious. If you have, for instance, a customer help desk, for each call that is logged, Oracle can automatically store the date and time of the call in a single DATE column. You can format the DATE column on a report to show just the date; or the date and the hour; or the century, date, hour, and minute; or the date, hour, minute, and second. You can use the TIMESTAMP datatype to store fractional seconds. See the "Using the TIMESTAMP Datatypes" section later in this chapter for details.

SQL*Plus and SQL recognize columns that are of the DATE datatype, and they understand that instructions to do arithmetic with them call for *date arithmetic,* not regular math. Adding 1 to a date, for instance, will give you another *date*—exactly one day later. Subtracting one date from another will give you a *number*—the count of days between the two dates.

However, because Oracle dates can include hours, minutes, and seconds, doing date arithmetic can prove to be tricky because Oracle could tell you, for example, that the difference between today and tomorrow is 0.516 days! (This is explained later in this chapter.)

SYSDATE, CURRENT_DATE, and SYSTIMESTAMP

Oracle taps into the computer's operating system for the current date and time. It makes these available to you through a special function called SYSDATE. Think of SYSDATE as a function whose result is always the current date and time, and it can be used anywhere any other Oracle function can be used. You also can regard it as a hidden column or pseudo-column that is in every table. Here, SYSDATE shows today's date:

```
select sysdate from dual;

SYSDATE
---------
28-FEB-12
```

NOTE
DUAL is a small but useful Oracle table created for testing functions or doing quick calculations. Later in this chapter, the sidebar "The DUAL Table for Quick Tests and Calculations" describes DUAL.

A second function, CURRENT_DATE, reports the system date in the session's time zone (you can set the time zone within your local session, which may differ from the database's time zone).

```
select current_date from dual;
```

```
CURRENT_D
---------
28-FEB-12
```

Another function, SYSTIMESTAMP, reports the system date in the TIMESTAMP datatype format:

```
select systimestamp from dual;
```

```
SYSTIMESTAMP
---------------------------------------------
28-FEB-12 04.49.31.718000 PM -05:00
```

See the "Using the TIMESTAMP Datatypes" section later in this chapter for details on the TIMESTAMP datatype and the time zone format and functions. The following sections focus on the use of the DATE datatype, because DATE will satisfy most date-processing requirements.

The Difference Between Two Dates

HOLIDAY is a table of some secular holidays in the United States during 2012:

```
select holiday, actual_date, celebrated_date from holiday;
```

```
HOLIDAY                  ACTUAL_DATE CELEBRATED_DATE
------------------------ ----------- ---------------
New Year's Day           01-JAN-12   02-JAN-12
Martin Luther King, Jr.  16-JAN-12   16-JAN-12
Lincoln's Birthday       12-FEB-12   20-FEB-12
Washington's Birthday    22-FEB-12   20-FEB-12
President's Day           20-FEB-12   20-FEB-12
Memorial Day             28-MAY-12   28-MAY-12
Independence Day         04-JUL-12   04-JUL-12
Labor Day                03-SEP-12   03-SEP-12
Columbus Day             08-OCT-12   08-OCT-12
Thanksgiving             25-NOV-12   25-NOV-12
```

Which holidays are not celebrated on the actual date of their anniversary during 2012? This can be easily answered by subtracting CELEBRATED_DATE from ACTUAL_DATE. If the answer is not zero, there is a difference between the two dates:

```
select holiday, actual_date, celebrated_date
from holiday
where celebrated_date-actual_date != 0;
```

```
HOLIDAY                  ACTUAL_DATE CELEBRATED_DATE
------------------------ ----------- ---------------
New Year's Day           01-JAN-12   02-JAN-12
Lincoln's Birthday       12-FEB-12   20-FEB-12
Washington's Birthday    22-FEB-12   20-FEB-12
```

The DUAL Table for Quick Tests and Calculations

DUAL is a tiny table Oracle provides with only one row and one column in it:

```
describe dual

Name                                        Null?       Type
------------------------------------------- ----------- -------------
DUMMY                                                   VARCHAR(1)
```

Because Oracle's many functions work on both columns and literals, using DUAL lets you see some functioning using just literals. In these examples, the SELECT statement doesn't care which columns are in the table, and a single row is sufficient to demonstrate a point. For example, suppose you want to quickly calculate POWER(4,3)—that is, four "cubed":

```
select power(4,3) from dual;

POWER(4,3)
----------
        64
```

The actual column in DUAL is irrelevant. This means you can experiment with date formatting and arithmetic using the DUAL table and the date functions in order to understand how they work. Then, those functions can be applied to actual dates in real tables.

Adding Months

If January 2 is "New Year's Day" in the country, perhaps six months later could be celebrated as "Half Way Over Day." If so, what would the date be? Simply use the ADD_MONTHS function, adding a *count* of six months, as shown here:

```
select add_months(celebrated_date,6) AS "Half Way Over"
from holiday
where holiday like >'New Y%';

Half Way Over
-------------
02-JUL-12
```

Subtracting Months

If picnic area reservations have to be made at least six months before Columbus Day, what's the last day you can make them? Take the CELEBRATED_DATE for Columbus Day and use ADD_MONTHS, adding a *negative count* of six months (this is the same as subtracting months). This will tell you the date six months before Columbus Day. Then subtract one day.

```
select add_months(celebrated_date,-6) - 1 "Last Day"
from holiday
where holiday = 'Columbus Day';
```

```
Last Day
---------
07-APR-12
```

GREATEST and LEAST

Which comes first for each of the holidays that were moved to fall on Mondays, the actual or the celebrated date? The LEAST function chooses the earliest date from a list of dates, whether columns or literals; GREATEST, on the other hand, chooses the latest date. These GREATEST and LEAST functions are exactly the same ones used with numbers and character strings:

```
select holiday, least(actual_date, celebrated_date) as first,
       actual_date, celebrated_date
from holiday
where actual_date - celebrated_date != 0;
```

```
HOLIDAY                  FIRST     ACTUAL_DATE CELEBRATED_DATE
------------------------ --------- ----------- ---------------
New Year's Day           01-JAN-12 01-JAN-12   02-JAN-12
Lincoln's Birthday       12-FEB-12 12-FEB-12   20-FEB-12
Washington's Birthday    20-FEB-12 22-FEB-12   20-FEB-12
```

Here, LEAST worked just fine, because it operated on DATE columns from a table. What about literals?

```
select least('20-JAN-12','20-DEC-12') from dual;
```

```
LEAST('20-JAN-12','20-DEC-12')
------------------------------
20-DEC-12
```

In this case, the first three characters (20-) are the same; the fourth character of each string is used as the basis for the comparison, and *D* comes before *J* in the alphabet.

It did not know to treat them as dates because they are just character strings without any specific indicators that they were date values. The TO_DATE function converts these literals into an internal DATE format Oracle can use for its date-oriented functions:

```
select least( to_date('20-JAN-12'), to_date('20-DEC-12') )
from dual;
```

```
LEAST(TO_DATE('20-JAN-12'),TO_DATE('20-DEC-12'))
------------------------------------------------
20-JAN-12
```

A Warning about GREATEST and LEAST

Unlike many other Oracle functions and logical operators, the GREATEST and LEAST functions will not evaluate literal strings that are in date format as dates. The dates are treated as strings:

```
select holiday, celebrated_date
from holiday
where celebrated_date =  least('16-JAN-12', '03-SEP-12');


HOLIDAY                     CELEBRATED_DATE
------------------------    ---------------
Labor Day                   03-SEP-12
```

This is quite wrong, almost as if you'd said GREATEST instead of LEAST. December 20, 2012, is not earlier than January 20, 2012. Why did this happen? Because LEAST treated these literals as *strings*.

In order for LEAST and GREATEST to work properly, the function TO_DATE must be applied to the literal strings:

```
select holiday, celebrated_date
from holiday
where celebrated_date =
  least( to_date('16-JAN-12'), to_date('03-SEP-12') );


HOLIDAY                     CELEBRATED_DATE
------------------------    ---------------
Martin Luther King, Jr.     16-JAN-12
```

NEXT_DAY

NEXT_DAY computes the date of the next named day of the week (that is, Sunday, Monday, Tuesday, Wednesday, Thursday, Friday, or Saturday) after the given date. For example, suppose payday is always the first Friday after the 15th of the month. The table PAYDAY contains only the pay-cycle dates, each one being the 15th of the month, with one row for each month of the year 2012:

```
select cycle_date from payday;

CYCLE_DATE
----------
15-JAN-12
15-FEB-12
15-MAR-12
15-APR-12
15-MAY-12
15-JUN-12
15-JUL-12
15-AUG-12
```

```
15-SEP-12
15-OCT-12
15-NOV-12
15-DEC-12
```

What are the actual payment dates?

```
select next_day(cycle_date,'FRIDAY') "Pay Day"
from payday;
```

```
Pay Day
---------
20-JAN-12
17-FEB-12
16-MAR-12
20-APR-12
18-MAY-12
22-JUN-12
20-JUL-12
17-AUG-12
21-SEP-12
19-OCT-12
16-NOV-12
21-DEC-12
```

This is nearly correct, except for June, because NEXT_DAY is the date of the *next* Friday after the cycle date. Because June 15, 2012, is a Friday, the previous query (wrongly) gives the following Friday instead. The correct version is as follows:

```
select next_day(cycle_date-1,'FRIDAY') "Pay Day"
from payday;
```

```
Pay Day
---------
20-JAN-12
17-FEB-12
16-MAR-12
20-APR-12
18-MAY-12
15-JUN-12
20-JUL-12
17-AUG-12
21-SEP-12
19-OCT-12
16-NOV-12
21-DEC-12
```

NEXT_DAY is really a "greater than" kind of function. It asks for the next date *greater than* the given date that falls on a specific day of the week. To catch those cycle dates that are already on Friday, subtract one from the cycle date. This makes every cycle date appear one day earlier to NEXT_DAY. The paydays are then always the correct Friday.

LAST_DAY

LAST_DAY produces the date of the last day of the month. Suppose that commissions and bonuses are always paid on the last day of the month. What were those dates in 2012?

```
select last_day(cycle_date) "End Month"
from payday;

End Month
---------
31-JAN-12
29-FEB-12
31-MAR-12
30-APR-12
31-MAY-12
30-JUN-12
31-JUL-12
31-AUG-12
30-SEP-12
31-OCT-12
30-NOV-12
31-DEC-12
```

MONTHS_BETWEEN Two Dates

You recently came across a file containing the birthdates of a group of friends. You load the information into a table called BIRTHDAY and display it:

```
select first_name, last_name, birthdate from birthday;

FIRST_NAME       LAST_NAME        BIRTHDATE
---------------  ---------------  ---------
George           Sand             12-MAY-76
Robert           James            23-AUG-67
Nancy            Lee              02-FEB-77
Victoria         Lynn             20-MAY-79
Frank            Pilot            11-NOV-72
```

To calculate each person's age, compute the months between today's date and their birth dates, and divide by 12 to get the years. The division will print the age with a decimal component. Because most people over the age of 7 don't report their age using portions of years, apply a FLOOR function to the computation.

```
select first_name, last_name, birthdate,
       floor(
             months_between(sysdate,birthdate)/12
             ) as age
from birthday;
```

```
FIRST_NAME       LAST_NAME        BIRTHDATE AGE
--------------- ---------------- --------- ---
George           Sand             12-MAY-76 36
Robert           James            23-AUG-67 45
Nancy            Lee              02-FEB-77 35
Victoria         Lynn             20-MAY-79 33
Frank            Pilot            11-NOV-72 40
```

Combining Date Functions

You are hired on February 29, 2012, at a great new job, with a starting salary that is lower than you had hoped, but with a promise of a review the first of the month after six months have passed. If the current date is February 29, 2012, when is your review date?

```
select sysdate as today,
       last_day(add_months(sysdate,6)) + 1 review
from dual;


TODAY     REVIEW
--------- ---------
29-FEB-12 01-SEP-12
```

ADD_MONTHS takes SYSDATE and adds six months to it. LAST_DAY takes this result and figures the last day of that month. You then add 1 to the date to get the first day of the next month. How many days until that review? You simply subtract today's date from it. Note the use of parentheses to ensure the proper order of the calculation:

```
select (last_day(add_months(sysdate,6))+ 1)-sysdate  wait
from dual;


 WAIT
-----
  189
```

ROUND and TRUNC in Date Calculations

Assume that this is today's SYSDATE:

```
SYSDATE
---------
29-FEB-12
```

In the beginning of the chapter, it was noted that Oracle could subtract one date from another, such as tomorrow minus today, and come up with an answer other than a whole number. Let's look at it:

```
select to_date('29-FEB-12') - sysdate from dual;


TO_DATE('29-FEB-12')-SYSDATE
---------------------------
                       .516
```

The reason for the fractional number of days between today and tomorrow is that Oracle keeps hours, minutes, and seconds with its dates, and SYSDATE is always current, up to the second. It is obviously less than a full day until tomorrow.

To simplify some of the difficulties you might encounter using fractions of days, Oracle makes a couple of assumptions about dates:

- A date entered as a literal, such as '29-FEB-12', is given a default time of 12 A.M. (midnight) at the beginning of that day.

- A date entered through SQL*Plus, unless a time is specifically assigned to it, is set to 12 A.M. (midnight) at the beginning of that day.

- SYSDATE always includes both the date and the time, unless you intentionally round it off. Using the ROUND function on any date sets it to 12 A.M. for that day if the time is before exactly noon and to 12 A.M. the next day if it is after noon. The TRUNC function acts similarly, except that it sets the time to 12 A.M. for any time up to and including one second before midnight.

To get the rounded number of days between today and tomorrow, use this:

```
select to_date('29-FEB-12') - round(sysdate) from dual;
```

```
TO_DATE('29-FEB-12')-ROUND(SYSDATE)
-----------------------------------
                                  1
```

If the current time is after noon, the rounded difference will be 0 days.

ROUND, without a '*format*' (see "Date Functions" in the Alphabetical Reference), always rounds a date to 12 A.M. of the closest day. If dates that you will be working with contain times other than noon, either use ROUND or accept possible fractional results in your calculations. TRUNC works similarly, but it sets the time to 12 A.M. of the current day.

TO_DATE and TO_CHAR Formatting

TO_DATE and TO_CHAR are alike insofar as they both have powerful formatting capabilities. They are opposite insofar as TO_DATE converts a character string or a number into an Oracle date, whereas TO_CHAR converts an Oracle date into a character string. The formats for these two functions are as follows:

```
TO_CHAR(date[,'format'[,'NLSparameters']])
```

```
TO_DATE(string[,'format'[,'NLSparameters']])
```

The *date* parameter must be a column defined as a DATE datatype in Oracle. It cannot be a string, even if it is in the most common date format of DD-MON-YY. The only way to use a string where *date* appears in the TO_CHAR function is to enclose it within a TO_DATE function.

The *string* parameter is a literal string, a literal number, or a database column containing a string or a number. In every case but one, the format of *string* must correspond to that described by *format*. Only if a string is in the default format can *format* be left out. The default starts out as DD-MON-YY, but you can change this with

```
alter session set NLS_DATE_FORMAT = 'DD/MON/YYYY';
```

for a given SQL session or with the NLS_DATE_FORMAT **init.ora** parameter.

The *format* parameter is a collection of many options that can be combined in quite a few different ways. (See the "Date Formats" entry in the Alphabetical Reference.) Once you understand the basic method of using the options, putting them into practice is simple.

NLSparameters is a string that sets the NLS_DATE_LANGUAGE option to a specific language, as opposed to using the language for the current SQL session. You shouldn't need to use this option often. Oracle will return day and month names in the language set for the session with ALTER SESSION.

NOTE
In many cases, you can use the EXTRACT function in place of TO_ CHAR. See the "Using the EXTRACT Function" section later in this chapter for examples.

TO_CHAR will be used as an example of how the options work. The first task is to define a column format for the TO_CHAR function results, because without a column format, TO_CHAR will produce a column heading in SQL*Plus nearly 100 characters wide. By renaming the column (so its heading is intelligible) and setting its format to 30 characters, a practical display is produced:

```
column Formatted format a30 word_wrapped
select birthdate,
       to_char(birthdate,'MM/DD/YY') as formatted
from birthday
where first_name = 'Victoria';


BIRTHDATE FORMATTED
--------- ------------------------------
20-MAY-79 05/20/79
```

BIRTHDATE shows the default Oracle date format: DD-MON-YY (day of the month, dash, three-letter abbreviation for the month, dash, the last two digits of the year). The TO_CHAR function in the SELECT statement is nearly self-evident. MM, DD, and YY in the TO_CHAR statement are key symbols to Oracle in formatting the date. The slashes (/) are just punctuation, and Oracle will accept a wide variety of punctuation.

```
select birthdate,
       to_char(birthdate,'YYMM>DD') as formatted
from birthday
where first_name = 'Victoria';


BIRTHDATE FORMATTED
--------- ------------------------------
20-MAY-79 7905>20
```

In addition to standard punctuation, Oracle allows you to insert text into the *format*. This is done by enclosing the desired text in *double* quotation marks:

```
select birthdate,
       to_char(birthdate,'Month, DDth "in, um,"
              YyyY') as formatted
from birthday;
```

```
BIRTHDATE FORMATTED
--------- -----------------------------
12-MAY-76 May     , 12TH in,
          um,
                        1976

23-AUG-67 August  , 23RD in,
          um,
                        1967

02-FEB-77 February , 02ND in,
          um,
                        1977

20-MAY-79 May     , 20TH in,
          um,
                        1979

11-NOV-72 November , 11TH in,
          um,
                        1972
```

Several consequences of the *format* are worth observing here. The full word "Month" told Oracle to use the full name of the month in the display. Because it was typed with the first letter in uppercase and the remainder in lowercase, each month in the result was formatted the same way. The options for month are as follows:

Format	Result
Month	August
month	august
Mon	Aug
mon	aug

The day of the month is produced by the DD in the *format*. A suffix of TH on DD tells Oracle to use *ordinal* suffixes, such as "TH," "RD," and "ND" with the number. In this instance, the suffixes are also case sensitive, but their case is set by the DD, not the TH:

Format	Result
DDth or DDTH	11TH
Ddth or DdTH	11Th
Ddth or ddTH	11th

This same approach holds true for all numbers in the *format,* including century, year, quarter, month, week, day of the month (DD), Julian day, hours, minutes, and seconds.

The words between double quotation marks are simply inserted where they are found. Spaces between any of these format requests are reproduced in the result (look at the three spaces before the word "in" in the preceding example). YyyY is included simply to show that case is irrelevant unless a suffix such as TH is being used. For simplicity's sake, consider this format request:

```
select birthdate, to_char(birthdate,'Month, ddth, YyyY')
        as formatted
from birthday;
```

```
BIRTHDATE FORMATTED
--------- ------------------------------
12-MAY-76 May       , 12th, 1976
23-AUG-67 August    , 23rd, 1967
02-FEB-77 February  , 02nd, 1977
20-MAY-79 May       , 20th, 1979
11-NOV-72 November  , 11th, 1972
```

This is a reasonably normal format. The days are all aligned, which makes comparing the rows easy. This is the default alignment, and Oracle accomplishes it by padding the month names on the right with spaces up to a width of nine spaces. There will be circumstances when it is more important for a date to be formatted normally, such as at the top of a letter. The spaces between the month and the comma would look odd. To eliminate the spaces, FM is used as a prefix for the words "month" and "day":

Format	Result
Month, ddth	August , 20th
fmMonth, ddth	August, 20th
Day, ddth	Monday , 20th
fmDay, ddth	Monday, 20th

This is illustrated in the following example:

```
select birthdate, to_char(birthdate,'fmMonth, ddth, YyyY')
        as formatted
from birthday;
```

```
BIRTHDATE FORMATTED
--------- ------------------------------
12-MAY-76 May, 12th, 1976
23-AUG-67 August, 23rd, 1967
02-FEB-77 February, 2nd, 1977
20-MAY-79 May, 20th, 1979
11-NOV-72 November, 11th, 1972
```

By combining all these format controls and adding hours and minutes, you can produce a birth announcement:

```
select first_name, birthdate, to_char(birthdate,
'"Baby Girl on" fmMonth ddth, YYYY, "at" HH:MI "in the Morning"')
        AS formatted
from birthday
where first_name = 'Victoria';
```

```
FIRST_NAME      BIRTHDATE FORMATTED
--------------- --------- ------------------------------
Victoria        20-MAY-79 Baby Girl on May 20th, 1979,
                          at 3:27 in the Morning
```

Suppose that after looking at this, you decide you'd rather spell out the date. Do this with the SP control:

```
select first_name, birthdate, to_char(birthdate,
'"Baby Girl on the" Ddsp "of" fmMonth, YYYY, "at" HH:MI')
      AS formatted
from birthday
where first_name = 'Victoria';
FIRST_NAME      BIRTHDATE FORMATTED
--------------- --------- ------------------------------
Victoria        20-MAY-79 Baby Girl on the Twenty of
                          May, 1979, at 3:27
```

Well, 20 was spelled out, but it still doesn't look right. Add the TH suffix to SP:

```
select first_name, birthdate, to_char(birthdate,
'"Baby Girl on the" Ddspth "of" fmMonth, YYYY, "at" HH:MI')
      AS formatted
from birthday
where first_name = 'Victoria';

FIRST_NAME      BIRTHDATE FORMATTED
--------------- --------- ------------------------------
Victoria        20-MAY-79 Baby Girl on the Twentieth of
                          May, 1979, at 3:27
```

But was it 3:27 A.M. or 3:27 P.M.? These could be added inside double quotation marks, but then the result would always say "A.M." or "P.M.," regardless of the actual time of day (because double quotation marks enclose a literal). Instead, Oracle lets you add *either* "A.M." or "P.M." after the time, but not in double quotation marks. Oracle then interprets this as a request to display whether it is A.M. or P.M. Note how the SELECT has this formatting control entered as P.M., but the result shows A.M., because the birth occurred in the morning:

```
select first_name, birthdate, to_char(birthdate,
'"Baby Girl on the" Ddspth "of" fmMonth, YYYY, "at" HH:MI P.M.')
      AS formatted
from birthday
where first_name = 'Victoria';

FIRST_NAME      BIRTHDATE FORMATTED
--------------- --------- ------------------------------
Victoria        20-MAY-79 Baby Girl on the Twentieth of
                          May, 1979, at 3:27 A.M.
```

Consult the entry "Date Formats" in the Alphabetical Reference for a list of all the possible date options. How would you construct a date format for the 782nd Year of the Reign of Louis IX? Use date arithmetic to alter the year from A.D. to A.L. (Louis's reign began in 1226, so subtract 1226 years from the current year), and then simply format the result using TO_CHAR.

The Most Common TO_CHAR Error

Always check the date formats when using the TO_CHAR function. The most common error is to interchange the "MM" (Month) format and the "MI" (Minutes) format when formatting the time portion of a date.

For example, to view the current time, use the TO_CHAR function to query the time portion of SYSDATE:

```
select to_char(sysdate,'HH:MI:SS') now
from dual;


NOW
--------
05:11:48
```

This example is correct because it uses "MI" to show the minutes. However, users often select "MM" instead—partly because they are also selecting two other pairs of double letters, "HH" and "SS." Selecting "MM" will return the month, not the minutes:

```
select to_char(sysdate,'HH:MM:SS') nowwrong
from dual;


NOWWRONG
--------
05:02:48
```

This time is incorrect, because the month was selected in the minutes place. Because Oracle is so flexible and has so many different supported date formats, it does not prevent you from making this error.

NEW_TIME: Switching Time Zones

The NEW_TIME function tells you the time and date of a date column or literal date in other time zones. Here is the format for NEW_TIME:

```
NEW_TIME(date,'this','other')
```

The *date* parameter is the date (and time) in *this* time zone. The *this* parameter will be replaced by a three-letter abbreviation for the current time zone. Finally, *other* will be replaced by a three-letter abbreviation of the other time zone for which you'd like to know the time and date. (See the "Date Functions" entry in the Alphabetical Reference.) To compare just the date, without showing the time, of Victoria's birth between Eastern standard time and Hawaiian standard time, use this:

```
select birthdate, new_time(birthdate,'EST','HST')
from birthday
where first_name = 'Victoria';


BIRTHDATE NEW_TIME(BIRTHDATE,'EST','HST')
--------- ------------------------------
20-MAY-79 19-MAY-79
```

But how could Victoria have been born on two different days? Because every date stored in Oracle also contains a time, it is simple enough using TO_CHAR and NEW_TIME to discover both the date and the time differences between the two zones. This will answer the question:

```
select to_char(birthdate,'fmMonth Ddth, YYYY "at" HH:MI AM') as birth,
       to_char(new_time(birthdate,'EST','HST'),
       'fmMonth ddth, YYYY "at" HH:MI AM') as birth
from birthday
where first_name = 'Victoria';

BIRTH                              BIRTH
-------------------------------    -------------------------------
May 20th, 1979 at 3:27 AM          May 19th, 1979 at 10:27 PM
```

TO_DATE Calculations

TO_DATE follows the same formatting conventions as TO_CHAR, with some restrictions. The purpose of TO_DATE is to turn a literal string, such as MAY 20, 1999, into an Oracle date format. This allows the date to be used in date calculations.

Here is the format for TO_DATE:

```
TO_DATE(string[,'format'])
```

To put the string 28-FEB-12 into Oracle date format, use this:

```
select to_date('28-FEB-12','DD-MON-YY') from dual;

TO_DATE('
---------
28-FEB-12
```

Note, however, that the 28-FEB-12 format is already in the default format in which Oracle displays and accepts dates. When a literal string has a date in this format, the *format* in TO_DATE can be left out, with exactly the same result:

```
select to_date('28-FEB-12') from dual;

TO_DATE('
---------
28-FEB-12
```

Note that the punctuation is ignored. Even if your default date format is 28/FEB/12, the query will still work, but it will return data in the format 28/FEB/12.

But what century is the date in? Is it 1912 or 2012? If you do not specify the full four-digit value for the year, then you are relying on the database to default to the proper century value.

If the string is in a familiar format, but not the default Oracle format of DD-MON-YY, TO_DATE fails:

```
select to_date('02/28/12') from dual;

select to_date('02/28/12') from dual;
                    *
```

```
ERROR at line 1:
ORA-01843: not a valid month
```

When the format matches the literal string, the string is successfully converted to a date and is then displayed in the default date format:

```
select to_date('02/28/12','MM/DD/YY') from dual;

TO_DATE('
---------
28-FEB-12
```

Suppose you need to know the day of the week of March 17. The TO_CHAR function will not work, even with the literal string in the proper format, because TO_CHAR requires a date or a valid numeric value (see its format at the very beginning of the "TO_DATE and TO_CHAR Formatting" section):

```
select to_char('17-MAR-08','Day') from dual;

ERROR at line 1:
ORA-01722: invalid number
```

The message is somewhat misleading, but the point is that the query fails. You could use the EXTRACT function, but this query will also work if you first convert the string to a date. Do this by combining the two functions TO_CHAR and TO_DATE:

```
select to_char( to_date('17-MAR-08'), 'Day') from dual;

TO_CHAR(T
---------
Monday
```

TO_DATE can also accept numbers, without single quotation marks, instead of strings, as long as they are formatted consistently. Here is an example:

```
select to_date(11051996,'MMDDYYYY') from dual;

TO_DATE(1
---------
05-NOV-96
```

The punctuation in the *format* is ignored, but the number must follow the order of the format controls. The number itself must not have punctuation.

How complex can the format control be in TO_DATE? Suppose you simply reversed the TO_CHAR SELECT statement shown earlier, put its result into the *string* portion of TO_DATE, and kept its format the same as TO_CHAR:

```
select to_date('Baby Girl on the Twentieth of May, 1979,
       at 3:27 A.M.',
       '"Baby Girl on the" Ddspth "of" fmMonth, YYYY,
       "at" HH:MI P.M.')
       AS formatted
```

```
from birthday
where first_name = 'Victoria';

ERROR at line 1:
ORA-01858: a non-numeric character was found
where a numeric was expected
```

This failed. As it turns out, only a limited number of the format controls can be used. Here are the restrictions on *format* that govern TO_DATE:

- No literal strings are allowed, such as "Baby Girl on the".
- Days cannot be spelled out. They must be numbers.
- Punctuation is permitted.
- FM is not necessary. If used, it is ignored.
- If Month is used, the month in the string must be spelled out. If Mon is used, the month must be a three-letter abbreviation. Uppercase and lowercase are ignored.

Dates in WHERE Clauses

Early in this chapter, you saw an example of date arithmetic used in a WHERE clause:

```
select holiday, actual_date, celebrated_date
from holiday
where celebrated_date - actual_date != 0;

HOLIDAY                  ACTUAL_DATE CELEBRATED_DATE
------------------------ ----------- ---------------
New Year's Day           01-JAN-12   02-JAN-12
Lincoln's Birthday       12-FEB-12   20-FEB-12
Washington's Birthday    22-FEB-12   20-FEB-12
```

Dates can be used with other Oracle logical operators as well, with some warnings and restrictions. The BETWEEN operator will do date arithmetic if the column preceding it is a date, even if the test dates are literal strings:

```
select holiday, celebrated_date
from holiday
where celebrated_date between
      '01-JAN-12' and '22-FEB-12';

HOLIDAY                  CELEBRATED_DATE
------------------------ ---------------
New Year's Day           02-JAN-12
Martin Luther King, Jr.  16-JAN-12
Lincoln's Birthday       20-FEB-12
Washington's Birthday    20-FEB-12
President's Day          20-FEB-12
```

The logical operator IN works as well with literal strings:

```
select holiday, celebrated_date
from holiday
where celebrated_date in ('02-JAN-12', '20-FEB-12');
```

```
HOLIDAY                       CELEBRATED_DATE
-----------------------       ---------------
New Year's Day                02-JAN-12
Lincoln's Birthday            20-FEB-12
Washington's Birthday         20-FEB-12
President's Day               20-FEB-12
```

If you do not want 2000 to be the default century value, you can use the TO_DATE function to specify the century values for the dates within the IN operator:

```
select holiday, celebrated_date
from holiday
where celebrated_date in
        (to_date('02-JAN-2012','DD-MON-YYYY'),
         to_date('20-FEB-2012','DD-MON-YYYY'));
```

```
HOLIDAY                       CELEBRATED_DATE
-----------------------       ---------------
New Year's Day                02-JAN-12
Lincoln's Birthday            20-FEB-12
Washington's Birthday         20-FEB-12
President's Day               20-FEB-12
```

LEAST and GREATEST do not work, because they assume the literal strings are *strings,* not *dates.* Refer to the sidebar "A Warning about GREATEST and LEAST," earlier in this chapter, for an explanation of LEAST and GREATEST.

Dealing with Multiple Centuries

If your applications use only two-digit values for years, you may encounter problems related to years around 2000. If you only specify two digits of a year (such as "98" for "1998"), you are relying on the database to specify the century value (the "19") when the record is inserted. If you are putting in dates prior to the year 2000 (for example, birth dates), you may encounter problems with the century values assigned to your data.

In Oracle, all date values have century values. If you only specify the last two digits of the year value, Oracle will, by default, use the current century as the century value when it inserts a record. For example, the following listing shows an INSERT into the BIRTHDAY table:

```
insert into birthday
(first_name, last_name, birthdate)
values
('Alicia', 'Ann', '21-NOV-49');
```

In the preceding example, no century value is specified for the BIRTHDATE column, and no age is specified. If you use the TO_CHAR function on the BIRTHDATE column, you can see the full birth date Oracle inserted—it defaulted to the current century:

```
select to_char(birthdate,'DD-MON-YYYY') AS bday
from birthday
```

```
where first_name = 'Alicia'
  and last_name = 'Ann';

BDAY
-----------
21-NOV-2049
```

For dates that can properly default to the current century, using the default does not present a problem. Alicia's BIRTHDATE value is 21-NOV-2049—wrong by 100 years! Wherever you insert date values, you should specify the full four-digit year value. That way, there is no ambiguity and you don't need to rely on a specific NLS setting being in place when your SQL statements run on another database.

If you are going to support dates from multiple centuries, consider using the "RR" date format instead of "YY." The "RR" format for years will pick the century value based on the year. Therefore, years in the first half of the century will have "20" for a century whereas year values in the last half of the century will have "19" for a century value. The use of the "RR" date format can be specified at the database level or the SQL statement level (such as during insert operations).

Using the EXTRACT Function

You can use the EXTRACT function in place of the TO_CHAR function when you are selecting portions of date values—such as just the month or day from a date. The EXTRACT function's syntax is

```
EXTRACT
( { { YEAR
    | MONTH
    | DAY
    | HOUR
    | MINUTE
    | SECOND
    }
  | { TIMEZONE_HOUR
    | TIMEZONE_MINUTE
    }
  | { TIMEZONE_REGION
    | TIMEZONE_ABBR
    }
  }
  FROM { datetime_value_expression | interval_value_expression }
)
```

For instance, to extract the month in which Victoria was born, you could execute the following:

```
select birthdate,
       extract(month from birthdate) as month
from birthday
where first_name = 'Victoria';
```

```
BIRTHDATE      MONTH
---------  ----------
20-MAY-79          5
```

For more complex extractions, you will need to use TO_CHAR, but EXTRACT can support many common date-value queries.

Using the TIMESTAMP Datatypes

The DATE datatype stores the date and time to the second; TIMESTAMP datatypes store the date to the billionth of a second.

The base datatype for timestamp values is called TIMESTAMP. Like DATE, it stores the year, month, day, hour, minute, and second. It also includes a *fractional_seconds_precision* setting that determines the number of digits in the fractional part of the seconds field. By default, the precision is 6; valid values are 0 to 9.

In the following example, a table is created with the TIMESTAMP datatype, and it's populated via the SYSTIMESTAMP function:

```
create table x1
    (tscol   timestamp(5));

insert into x1 values (systimestamp);
```

Now select that value from the table:

```
select * from x1;

TSCOL
----------------------------------
27-JUL-12 03.58.36.67918 AM
```

The output shows the second the row was inserted, down to five places after the decimal point.

The SYSTIMESTAMP function returns data in the form of the TIMESTAMP (*fractional_seconds_precision*) WITH TIME ZONE datatype. The exact same row, inserted into a column that is defined with the TIMESTAMP(5) WITH TIME ZONE datatype, returns the data in the following format:

```
create table x2
(tscol   timestamp(5) with time zone);

insert into x2 values (systimestamp);

select * from x2;

TSCOL
----------------------------------
27-JUL-12 03.59.53.75613 AM -05:00
```

In this output, the time zone is displayed as an offset of Coordinated Universal Time (UTC). The database is presently set to a time zone that is five hours prior to UTC.

Oracle also supports the TIMESTAMP (*fractional_seconds_precision*) WITH LOCAL TIME ZONE datatype, which is similar to TIMESTAMP WITH TIME ZONE. It differs in that the data is normalized to the database time zone when it is stored in the database, and during retrievals the users see data in the session time zone.

In addition to the TIMESTAMP datatypes, Oracle also supports two interval datatypes: INTERVAL YEAR (*year_precision*) TO MONTH and INTERVAL DAY (*day_precision*) TO SECOND (*fractional_seconds_precision*). INTERVAL YEAR TO MONTH stores a period of time in years and months, where the precision is the number of digits in the YEAR field (ranging from 0 to 9, with the default being 2). The INTERVAL DAY TO SECOND datatype stores a period of time in days, hours, minutes, and seconds; the precision for the day and seconds accepts values from 0 to 9. The INTERVAL datatypes are mostly used during statistical analysis and data mining.

CHAPTER
11

Conversion and
Transformation Functions

Τ his chapter looks at functions that convert, or *transform,* one datatype into another. Four major datatypes and their associated functions have been covered thus far:

- CHAR (fixed-length character strings) and VARCHAR2 (variable-length character strings) include any letter of the alphabet, any number, and any of the symbols on the keyboard. Character string literals must be enclosed in single quotation marks:

  `'Sault Ste. Marie!'`

- NUMBER includes just the digits 0 through 9, a decimal point, and a minus sign, if necessary. NUMBER literals are not enclosed in quotation marks:

  `246.320`

- Numbers can also be displayed in floating-point format, using an E to indicate a power of 10:

  `2.4632E+2`

- DATE is a special type that includes information about the date and time. It has a default format of DD-MON-YY (dependent on the setting of the NLS_DATE_FORMAT parameter), but can be displayed in many ways using the TO_CHAR function, as you saw in Chapter 10. DATE literals must be enclosed in single quotation marks as if they were strings:

  `'26-AUG-81'`

Each of these datatypes has a group of functions designed especially to manipulate data of its own type, as shown in Chapters 7, 8, 9, and 10. String functions are used with character columns, literals, or an expression containing any combination of both character columns and literals; arithmetic functions are used with any combination of NUMBER columns or literals; and DATE functions are used with DATE columns, DATE expressions, or literals. Most group and miscellaneous functions work with any of these types. Some of these functions change the object they affect to another datatype (whether CHAR, VARCHAR2, NUMBER, or DATE), whereas others report information about the object.

In one sense, most of the functions studied so far have been *transformation functions,* meaning they changed their objects. However, the functions covered in this chapter change their objects in an unusual way: They transform them from one datatype into another, or they make a profound transformation of the data in them. Table 11-1 describes these functions.

Function Name	Definition
ASCIISTR	Translates a string in any character set and returns an ASCII string in the database character set.
BIN_TO_NUM	Converts a binary value to its numerical equivalent.
CAST	CASTs one built-in or collection type to another; commonly used with nested tables and varying arrays.
CHARTOROWID	Changes a character string to act like an internal Oracle row identifier, or ROWID.

TABLE 11-1. *Conversion Functions*

Function Name	Definition
COMPOSE	Translates a string in any datatype to a Unicode string in its fully normalized form in the same character set as the input.
CONVERT	CONVERTs a character string from one National Language character set to another. The returned format is VARCHAR2.
DECOMPOSE	Translates a string in any datatype to a Unicode string after canonical decomposition in the same character set as the input.
HEXTORAW	Changes a character string of hex numbers into binary.
NUMTODSINTERVAL	Converts a NUMBER to an INTERVAL DAY TO SECOND literal.
NUMTOYMINTERVAL	Converts a NUMBER to an INTERVAL YEAR TO MONTH literal.
RAWTOHEX	Changes a string of binary numbers to a character string of hex numbers.
RAWTONHEX	Converts RAW to an NVARCHAR2 character value containing its hexadecimal equivalent.
ROWIDTOCHAR	Changes an internal Oracle row identifier, or ROWID, to a character string.
ROWIDTONCHAR	Converts a ROWID value to an NVARCHAR2 datatype.
SCN_TO_TIMESTAMP	Converts a system change number to an approximate timestamp.
TIMESTAMP_TO_SCN	Converts a timestamp to an approximate system change number.
TO_BINARY_DOUBLE	Returns a double-precision floating-point number.
TO_BINARY_FLOAT	Returns a single-precision floating-point number.
TO_CHAR	Converts a NUMBER or DATE to a character string.
TO_CLOB	Converts NCLOB values in a LOB column or other character strings to CLOB values.
TO_DATE	Converts a NUMBER, CHAR, or VARCHAR2 to a DATE (an Oracle datatype).
TO_DSINTERVAL	Converts a character string of CHAR, VARCHAR2, NCHAR, or NVARCHAR2 datatype to an INTERVAL DAY TO SECOND type.
TO_LOB	Converts a LONG to a LOB as part of an INSERT . . . AS SELECT.
TO_MULTI_BYTE	Converts the single-byte characters in a character string to multi-byte characters.
TO_NCHAR	Converts a character string, NUMBER, or DATE from the database character set to the national character set.
TO_NCLOB	Converts CLOB values in a LOB column or other character strings to NCLOB values.
TO_NUMBER	Converts a CHAR or VARCHAR2 to a number.
TO_SINGLE_BYTE	Converts the multi-byte characters in a CHAR or VARCHAR2 to single bytes.
TO_TIMESTAMP	Converts a character string to a value of TIMESTAMP datatype.
TO_TIMESTAMP_TZ	Converts a character string to a value of TIMESTAMP WITH TIME ZONE datatype.
TO_YMINTERVAL	Converts a character string of CHAR, VARCHAR2, NCHAR, or NVARCHAR2 datatype to an INTERVAL YEAR TO MONTH type.
TRANSLATE·USING	TRANSLATEs characters in a string into different characters.
UNISTR	Converts a string into Unicode in the database Unicode character set.

TABLE 11-1.   *Conversion Functions* (continued)

Elementary Conversion Functions

Although Table 11-1 lists many conversion functions, the most commonly used are the following three, whose purpose is to convert one datatype into another:

- **TO_CHAR**   Transforms a DATE or NUMBER expression into a character string.
- **TO_DATE**   Transforms a NUMBER, CHAR, or VARCHAR2 into a DATE. For working with timestamps, you can use TO_TIMESTAMP or TO_TIMESTAMP_TZ.
- **TO_NUMBER**   Transforms a CHAR or VARCHAR2 into a NUMBER.

Why are these transformations important? TO_DATE is obviously necessary to accomplish date arithmetic. TO_CHAR allows you to manipulate a number as if it were a string, using string functions. TO_NUMBER allows you to use a string that happens to contain only numbers as if it were a number; by using it, you can add, subtract, multiply, divide, and so on. Using a string value in a numeric expression implicitly converts the string to a numeric value, but Oracle best practices dictate that you use explicit conversion functions when the elements of an expression are not the same datatype.

This means that if you stored a nine-digit ZIP code as a number, you could transform it into a string and then use SUBSTR and concatenation || to add a dash (such as when printing addresses on envelopes):

```
select substr(to_char(948033515),1,5)||'-'||
       substr(to_char(948033515),6)  as zip
from dual;


zip
----------------------------------------
94803-3515
```

Here, the TO_CHAR function transforms the pure number 948033515 (notice that it has no single quotation marks around it, as a CHAR or VARCHAR2 string must) into a character string. SUBSTR then clips out positions 1 to 5 of this string, producing 94803. A dash is concatenated on the right end of this string, and then another TO_CHAR creates another string, which another SUBSTR clips out from position 6 to the end. The second string, 3515, is concatenated after the dash. The whole rebuilt string is relabeled ZIP, and Oracle displays it: 94803-3515. This TO_CHAR function lets you use string-manipulation functions on numbers (and dates) as if they were actually strings. Handy? Yes. But watch this:

```
select substr(948033515,1,5)||'-'||
       substr(948033515,6) as zip
from dual;


zip
----------------------------------------
94803-3515
```

This shouldn't work because 948033515 is a NUMBER, not a character string. Yet, the string function SUBSTR clearly worked anyway. Would it work with an actual NUMBER database column? Here's a table with ZIP as a NUMBER:

```
describe address
```

```
Name                                        Null?     Type
------------------------------------------  --------  ------------
LASTNAME                                               VARCHAR2(25)
FIRSTNAME                                              VARCHAR2(25)
STREET                                                 VARCHAR2(50)
CITY                                                   VARCHAR2(25)
STATE                                                  CHAR(2)
ZIP                                                    NUMBER
PHONE                                                  VARCHAR2(12)
EXT                                                    VARCHAR2(5)
```

Select just the ZIP code for all the Marys in the table:

```
select substr(zip,1,5)||'-'||
       substr(zip,6)  as zip
from address
where firstname = 'Mary';


ZIP
----------------------------------------
94941-4302
60126-2460
```

SUBSTR works here just as well as it does with strings, even though ZIP is a NUMBER column from the ADDRESS table. Will other string functions also work?

```
select zip, rtrim(zip,20)
from address
where firstname = 'Mary';

      ZIP RTRIM(ZIP,20)
--------- ---------------------------------------
949414302 9494143
601262460 60126246
```

The column on the left demonstrates that ZIP is a NUMBER; it is even right-justified, as numbers are by default. But the column using the RTRIM function is left-justified, just as strings are, and it has removed zeros and twos from the right side of the ZIP codes. Something else is peculiar here. Recall from Chapter 7 the format for RTRIM, shown here:

```
RTRIM(string [,'set'])
```

The *set* to be removed from the string is enclosed within single quotation marks, yet in this next example, there are no quotation marks:

```
rtrim(zip,20)
```

So what is going on?

Automatic Conversion of Datatypes

Oracle is automatically converting these numbers, both ZIP and 20, into strings, almost as if they both had TO_CHAR functions in front of them. In fact, with a few clear exceptions, Oracle will automatically transform any datatype into any other datatype, based on the function that is going to affect it and the precedence rules for datatype conversion. If it's a string function, Oracle will convert a NUMBER or a DATE instantly into a string, and the string function will work. If it's a DATE function and the column or literal is a string in the format DD-MON-YY, Oracle will convert it into a DATE. If the function is arithmetic and the column or literal is a character string, Oracle will convert it into a NUMBER and do the calculation.

Will this always work? No. For Oracle to convert one datatype into another automatically, the first datatype must already "look" like the datatype it is being converted to. The basic guidelines are as follows:

- Any NUMBER or DATE can be converted to a character string. Any string function can be used on a NUMBER or DATE column. Literal NUMBERs do not have to be enclosed in single quotation marks when used in a string function; literal DATEs do.

- A CHAR or VARCHAR2 value will be converted to a NUMBER if it contains only NUMBERs, a decimal point, or a minus sign on the left.

- A CHAR or VARCHAR2 value will be converted to a DATE only if it is in the default date format (usually DD-MON-YY). This is true for all functions except GREATEST and LEAST, which will treat the value as a string, and it's true for BETWEEN only if the column to the left after the word BETWEEN is a DATE. Otherwise, TO_DATE must be used, with the proper format.

These guidelines may be confusing, so favor the use of TO_DATE and other conversion functions to make sure the values are treated exactly the way you intend. The following examples should help to clarify the guidelines. The following are the effects of several randomly chosen string functions on NUMBERs and DATEs:

```
select initcap(lower(sysdate)) from dual;

INITCAP(LOWER(SYSDATE))
-----------------------
28-Feb-12
```

Note that the INITCAP function put the first letter of "Feb" into uppercase even though "Feb" was buried in the middle of the string "28-FEB-08". This is a feature of INITCAP that is not confined to dates, although it is illustrated here for the first time. It works because the following works:

```
select initcap('this-is_a.test,of:punctuation;for+initcap')
from dual;

INITCAP('THIS-IS_A.TEST,OF:PUNCTUATION;FO
-----------------------------------------
This-Is_A.Test,Of:Punctuation;For+Initcap
```

INITCAP puts the first letter of every word into uppercase. It determines the beginning of a word based on its being preceded by any character other than a letter. You can also cut and paste dates using string functions, just as if they were strings:

 `select substr(sysdate,4,3) from dual;`

```
SUB
---
FEB
```

NOTE
You can also use the TO_CHAR or EXTRACT function to return the month value from a date.

Here, a DATE is left-padded with 9s for a total length of 20:

`select lpad(sysdate,20,'9') from dual;`

```
LPAD(SYSDATE,20,'9')
--------------------
9999999999928-FEB-08
```

LPAD, or any other string function, also can be used on NUMBER columns, whether literal (as shown here) or as a column:

`select lpad(9,20,0) from dual;`

```
LPAD(9,20,0)
--------------------
00000000000000000009
```

These examples show how string functions treat both NUMBERs and DATEs as if they were character strings. The result of the function (what you see displayed) is itself a character string. In this next example, a string (note the single quotation marks) is treated as a NUMBER by the NUMBER function FLOOR:

`select floor('-323.78') from dual;`

```
FLOOR('-323.78')
----------------
            -324
```

Here, two literal character strings are converted to DATEs for the DATE function MONTHS_ BETWEEN. This works only because the literal strings are in the default NLS date format for the session, DD-MON-YY:

`select months_between('16-MAY-10','01-NOV-10') from dual;`

```
MONTHS_BETWEEN('16-MAY-10','01-NOV-10')
---------------------------------------
-5.51612903225806451612903225806451612903
```

One of the guidelines says that a DATE will not be converted to a NUMBER. Yet, here is an example of addition and subtraction with a DATE. Does this violate the guideline?

```
select sysdate, sysdate + 1, sysdate - 1 from dual;

SYSDATE   SYSDATE+1 SYSDATE-1
--------- --------- ---------
28-FEB-12 29-FEB-12 27-FEB-12
```

It does not, because the addition and subtraction is date arithmetic, not regular arithmetic. Date arithmetic (covered in Chapter 10) works only with addition and subtraction and only with DATEs. Most functions will automatically convert a character string in default date format into a DATE. An exception is this attempt at date addition with a literal:

```
select '28-feb-12' + 1 from dual;

ERROR: ORA-01722: invalid number
```

Date arithmetic, even with actual DATE datatypes, works only with addition and subtraction. Any other arithmetic function attempted with a date will fail. Dates are not converted to numbers, as this attempt to divide a date by 2 illustrates:

```
select sysdate / 2 from dual;
       *
ERROR at line 1:
ORA-00932: inconsistent datatypes: expected NUMBER got DATE
```

Finally, a NUMBER will never be automatically converted to a DATE, because a pure number cannot be in the default format for a DATE, which is DD-MON-YY:

```
select next_day(022808,'FRIDAY') from dual;
               *
ERROR at line 1:
ORA-00932: inconsistent datatypes: expected DATE got NUMBER
```

To use a NUMBER in a DATE function, TO_DATE is required.

A Warning About Automatic Conversion

The issue of whether allowing SQL to do automatic conversion of datatypes is a good practice or not has arguments on either side. On one hand, this practice considerably simplifies and reduces the functions necessary to make a SELECT statement work. On the other hand, if your assumption about what will be in the column is wrong (for example, you assume a particular character column will always have a number in it, meaning you can use it in a calculation), then, at some point, a query will stop working, Oracle will produce an error, and time will have to be spent trying to find the problem. Further, another person reading your SELECT statement may be confused by what appear to be inappropriate functions at work on characters or numbers. Using TO_NUMBER makes it clear that a numeric value is always expected, even if the column uses the VARCHAR2 datatype. You will still get an error if the TO_NUMBER function encounters a non-numeric value in the column.

The biggest problem with implicit conversions is that an index on the column will not be used if conversion takes place. If you have a column such as ID or ORDER_NUM as a VARCHAR2 column and you then create a PL/SQL procedure to access the data and pass a number in the procedure, the underlying index on ID or ORDER_NUM does not get used. Thus, performance suffers.

A simple rule of thumb might be that it is best to use functions where the risk is low, such as string-manipulation functions on numbers, rather than arithmetic functions on strings. For your benefit and that of others using your work, always put a note near the SELECT statement signaling the use of automatic type conversion.

Specialized Conversion Functions

As shown earlier in Table 11-1, Oracle includes several specialized conversion functions. If you expect to use SQL*Plus and Oracle simply to produce reports, you probably won't ever need any of these functions. On the other hand, if you plan to use SQL*Plus to use the UPDATE command to change the database, if you expect to build Oracle applications, or if you are using National Language Support (NLS), this information will eventually prove valuable. The functions can be found, by name, in the Alphabetical Reference section of this book.

NOTE
The CAST function is used with nested tables and varying arrays; see Chapter 39 for details. The DECODE function is covered in Chapter 16.

The conversion functions generally take a single value as input and return a single converted value as output. For example, the BIN_TO_NUM function converts binary values to decimal numeric values. Its input value is a list of the digits of a binary value, separated by commas and treated as a single input string:

```
select bin_to_num(1,1,0,1) from dual;

BIN_TO_NUM(1,1,0,1)
-------------------
                 13

select bin_to_num(1,1,1,0) from dual;

BIN_TO_NUM(1,1,1,0)
-------------------
                 14
```

NOTE
You can use the TO_BINARY_DOUBLE and TO_BINARY_FLOAT functions to convert values into double- and single-precision floating-point numbers, respectively.

When working with flashback operations (see Chapters 29 and 30), you can convert system change numbers (SCNs) to timestamp values via the SCN_TO_TIMESTAMP function; TIMESTAMP_TO_SCN returns the SCN for a particular timestamp.

Transformation Functions

Although in one sense any function that changes its object could be called a transformation function, there are two unusual functions that you can use in many interesting ways to control your output based on your input, instead of simply transforming it. These functions are TRANSLATE and DECODE.

TRANSLATE

TRANSLATE is a simple function that does an orderly character-by-character substitution in a string. This is the format for TRANSLATE:

```
translate(string,if,then)
```

TRANSLATE looks at each character in *string* and then checks *if* to see whether that character is there. If it is, it notes the position in *if* where it found the character and then looks at the same position in *then*. TRANSLATE substitutes whichever character it finds there for the character in *string*. Normally, the function is written on a single line, like this:

```
select translate(7671234,234567890,'BCDEFGHIJ')
from dual;


TRANSLA
-------
GFG1BCD
```

But it might be easier to understand if it's simply broken onto two lines (SQL doesn't care, of course):

```
select translate(7671234,234567890,
                       'BCDEFGHIJ')
from dual;


TRANSLA
-------
GFG1BCD
```

When TRANSLATE sees a 7 in *string,* it looks for a 7 in *if* and translates it to the character in the same position in *then* (in this case, an uppercase *G*). If the character is not in *if,* it is not translated (observe what TRANSLATE did with the 1).

TRANSLATE is technically a string function since it returns a string, but, as you can see, it will do automatic data conversion and work with a mix of strings and numbers. The following is an example of a simple code cipher, where every letter in the alphabet is shifted one position. Many years ago, spies used such character-substitution methods to encode messages before sending them. The recipient simply reversed the process. Do you remember the smooth-talking computer, HAL, in the movie *2001: A Space Odyssey*? If you TRANSLATE HAL's name with a one-character shift in the alphabet, you get this:

```
select translate('HAL','ABCDEFGHIJKLMNOPQRSTUVWXYZ',
                       'BCDEFGHIJKLMNOPQRSTUVWXYZA') as who
from dual;
```

```
WHO
---
IBM
```

See the discussion of the REGEXP_REPLACE function in Chapter 8 for details on the string manipulation possible with regular expressions.

DECODE

If TRANSLATE is a character-by-character substitution, DECODE can be considered a value-by-value substitution. For every value it sees in a field, DECODE checks for a match in a series of *if-then* tests. DECODE is an incredibly powerful function, with a broad range of areas where it can be useful. Chapter 16 is devoted entirely to the advanced use of DECODE and CASE.

This is the format for DECODE:

```
decode(value,if1,then1,if2,then2,if3,then3, . . . ,else)
```

Only three *if-then* combinations are illustrated here, but there is no practical limit. To see how this function works, recall the NEWSPAPER table you saw in earlier chapters:

```
select * from newspaper;
```

```
FEATURE           S       PAGE
--------------- - ----------
National News    A          1
Sports           D          1
Editorials       A         12
Business         E          1
Weather          C          2
Television       B          7
Births           F          7
Classified       F          8
Modern Life      B          1
Comics           C          4
Movies           B          4
Bridge           B          2
Obituaries       F          6
Doctor Is In     F          6
```

In the next example, the page number is decoded. If the page number is 1, then the words "Front Page" are substituted. If the page number is anything else, the words "Turn to" are concatenated with the page number. This illustrates that *else* can be a function, a literal, or another column.

```
select feature, section,
       decode(Page,'1','Front Page','Turn to '||Page)
from newspaper;
```

```
FEATURE          S DECODE(PAGE,'1','FRONTPAGE','TURNTO'||PAGE)
--------------- - ------------------------------------------------
National News    A Front Page
Sports           D Front Page
```

```
Editorials      A Turn to 12
Business        E Front Page
Weather         C Turn to 2
Television      B Turn to 7
Births          F Turn to 7
Classified      F Turn to 8
Modern Life     B Front Page
Comics          C Turn to 4
Movies          B Turn to 4
Bridge          B Turn to 2
Obituaries      F Turn to 6
Doctor Is In    F Turn to 6
```

There are some restrictions on the datatypes in the list of *if* and *then* clauses, which will be covered in Chapter 16.

Review

Most functions in Oracle, although they are intended for a specific datatype such as CHAR, VARCHAR2, NUMBER, or DATE, will actually work with other datatypes as well. They do this by performing an automatic type conversion. With a few logical exceptions, and the hope of future compatibility, they will do this as long as the data to be converted "looks" like the datatype required by the function.

Character functions will convert any NUMBER or DATE. NUMBER functions will convert a CHAR or VARCHAR2 if it contains the digits 0 through 9, a decimal point, or a minus sign on the left. NUMBER functions will not convert DATEs. DATE functions will convert character strings if they are in the format DD-MON-YY. However, they will not convert NUMBERs.

Two functions, TRANSLATE and DECODE, will fundamentally change the data they act on. TRANSLATE will do a character substitution according to any pattern you specify, and DECODE will do a value substitution for any pattern you specify.

CHAPTER

12

Grouping Things Together

U p to this point, you've seen how SQL can SELECT rows of information from database tables, how the WHERE clause can limit the number of rows being returned to only those that meet certain rules that you define, and how the rows returned can be sorted in ascending or descending sequence using ORDER BY. You've also seen how the values in columns can be modified by character, NUMBER, and DATE functions, and how group functions can tell you something about the whole set of rows.

Beyond the group functions you've seen, there are also two group clauses: HAVING and GROUP BY. These are parallel to the WHERE and ORDER BY clauses, except that they act on groups, not on individual rows. These clauses can provide very powerful insights into your data.

Using GROUP BY and HAVING

If you want to generate a count of titles on the bookshelf, categorized by the type of book, you would write a query like this:

```
select category_name, count(*)
from bookshelf
group by category_name;
```

and Oracle would respond with the following:

```
CATEGORY_NAME          COUNT(*)
--------------------   --------
ADULTFIC                      6
CHILDRENFIC                   5
ADULTNF                      10
ADULTREF                      6
CHILDRENPIC                   3
CHILDRENNF                    1
```

Notice the mix of a column name, CATEGORY_NAME, and the group function COUNT in the SELECT clause. This mix is possible only because CATEGORY_NAME is referenced in the GROUP BY clause. If it were not there, the opaque message first encountered in Chapter 9 would have resulted in this:

```
select category_name, count(*) from bookshelf;
```

```
select category_name, count(*) from bookshelf
Error at Command Line:9 Column:7
Error report:
SQL Error: ORA-00937: not a single-group group function
```

This result occurs because the group functions, such as SUM and COUNT, are designed to tell you something about a group of rows, not the individual rows of the table. The error is avoided by using CATEGORY_NAME in the GROUP BY clause, which forces the COUNT function to count all the rows grouped within each CATEGORY_NAME.

The HAVING clause works very much like a WHERE clause, except that its logic is only related to the results of group functions, as opposed to columns or expressions for individual rows, which can still be selected by a WHERE clause. Here, the rows in the previous example are further restricted to just those where there are more than five books in a category:

```
select category_name, count(*)
from bookshelf
group by category_name
having count(*) > 5;
```

```
CATEGORY_NAME          COUNT(*)
-------------------- ----------
ADULTFIC                      6
ADULTNF                      10
ADULTREF                      6
```

To determine the average rating by category, you can use the AVG function, as shown in the following listing:

```
select category_name, count(*), avg(rating)
from bookshelf
group by category_name;
```

```
CATEGORY_NAME        COUNT(*) AVG(RATING)
-------------------- -------- -----------
ADULTFIC                    6 3.666666667
CHILDRENFIC                 5         2.8
ADULTNF                    10         4.2
ADULTREF                    6 3.166666667
CHILDRENPIC                 3           1
CHILDRENNF                  1           3
```

RATING is a character column, defined as a VARCHAR2, but it contains numeric values, so Oracle can perform numeric functions on it (see Chapter 11). What is the overall average rating?

```
select avg(rating) from bookshelf;
```

```
AVG(RATING)
-----------
3.322580645
```

In this case, there is no GROUP BY clause because the entire set of rows in the BOOKSHELF table is treated as the group. Now you can use this result as part of a larger query: What categories have average ratings that are greater than the average rating of all books?

```
select category_name, count(*), avg(rating)
from bookshelf
group by category_name
having avg(rating) >
    (select avg(rating) from bookshelf);
```

```
CATEGORY_NAME        COUNT(*) AVG(RATING)
-------------------- -------- -----------
ADULTFIC                    6 3.666666667
ADULTNF                    10         4.2
```

Looking back at the earlier listings, this result is correct—only two of the groups have average rating values greater than the overall average.

Although the results are sorted by the CATEGORY_NAME column, the purpose of GROUP BY is not to produce a desired sequence but rather to collect "like" things together. The order they appear in is a byproduct of how GROUP BY works; GROUP BY is not meant to be used to change the sorting order.

Adding an ORDER BY

The solution for creating an alternative order for display is the addition of an ORDER BY clause following the HAVING clause. For example, you could add the following:

```
order by category_name desc
```

This reverses the order of the list:

```
select category_name, count(*)
from bookshelf
group by category_name
order by category_name desc;
```

```
CATEGORY_NAME        COUNT(*)
-------------------- --------
CHILDRENPIC                 3
CHILDRENNF                  1
CHILDRENFIC                 5
ADULTREF                    6
ADULTNF                    10
ADULTFIC                    6
```

Or, you could use this instead:

```
order by count(*) desc
```

Here's the result:

```
CATEGORY_NAME        COUNT(*)
-------------------- ----------
ADULTNF                    10
ADULTFIC                    6
ADULTREF                    6
CHILDRENFIC                 5
CHILDRENPIC                 3
CHILDRENNF                  1
```

Although you can use the column alias as part of the ORDER BY clause, you can't use it as part of the HAVING clause. Giving COUNT(*) an alias of "COUNTER" and attempting to use HAVING COUNTER > 1 as a clause in this query will result in an "invalid column name" error:

```
select category_name, count(*) as counter
from bookshelf
group by category_name
having counter > 1
order by count(*) desc;
```

```
having counter > 1
order by count(*) desc
Error at Command Line:41 Column:7
Error report:
SQL Error: ORA-00904: "COUNTER": invalid identifier
```

Order of Execution

The previous query has quite a collection of competing clauses! Here are the rules Oracle uses to execute each of them, and the order in which execution takes place:

1. Choose rows based on the WHERE clause.

2. Group those rows together based on the GROUP BY clause.

3. Calculate the results of the group functions for each group.

4. Choose and eliminate groups based on the HAVING clause.

5. Order the groups based on the results of the group functions in the ORDER BY clause. The ORDER BY clause must use either a group function or a column specified in the GROUP BY clause.

The order of execution is important because it has a direct impact on the performance of your queries. In general, the more records that can be eliminated via the WHERE clause, the faster the query will execute. This performance benefit is because of the reduction in the number of rows that must be processed during the GROUP BY operation.

If a query is written to use a HAVING clause to eliminate groups, you should check to see if the HAVING condition can be rewritten as a WHERE clause. In many cases, this rewrite won't be possible. It is usually only available when the HAVING clause is used to eliminate groups based on the grouping columns.

For example, suppose you have this query:

```
select category_name, count(*), avg(rating)
from bookshelf
where rating > 1
group by category_name
having category_name like 'A%'
order by count(*) desc;
```

```
CATEGORY_NAME          COUNT(*) AVG(RATING)
-------------------- ---------- -----------
ADULTNF                      10         4.2
ADULTFIC                      6  3.66666667
ADULTREF                      6  3.16666667
```

The order of execution would be as follows:

1. Eliminate rows based on

    ```
    where rating > 1
    ```

2. Group the remaining rows based on

    ```
    group by category_name
    ```

3. For each CATEGORY_NAME, calculate the

```
count(*)
```

4. Eliminate groups based on

```
having category_name like 'A%'
```

5. Order the remaining groups.

This query will run faster if the *groups* eliminated in Step 4 can be eliminated as *rows* in Step 1. If they are eliminated at Step 1, fewer rows will be grouped (Step 2), fewer calculations will be performed (Step 3), and no groups will be eliminated (Step 4). Thus, each of these steps in the execution will run faster.

Because the HAVING condition in this example is not based on a calculated column, it is easily changed into a WHERE condition:

```
select category_name, count(*), avg(rating)
from bookshelf
where rating > 1
  and category_name like 'A%'
group by category_name
order by count(*) desc;
```

```
CATEGORY_NAME          COUNT(*) AVG(RATING)
-------------------- ---------- -----------
ADULTNF                      10         4.2
ADULTREF                      6  3.16666667
ADULTFIC                      6  3.66666667
```

In the modified version, fewer rows are grouped, resulting in a performance savings. As the number of rows in your tables increases, the performance savings from eliminating rows early in the process can grow dramatically.

This example may seem trivial because the table has few rows in it. But even such a small query can have a significant impact in a production application. There are many examples of production applications whose performance is severely impacted by high volumes of executions of seemingly small queries. When those small queries are executed thousands or millions of times per day, they become the most resource-intensive queries in the database. When planning the SQL access paths for your application, tune even the small queries.

Views of Groups

In Chapter 5, a view called INVASION, which joined together the WEATHER and LOCATION tables, was created for the oracle at Delphi. This view appeared to be a table in its own right, with columns and rows, but each of its rows contained columns that actually came from two separate tables.

The same process of creating a view can be used with groups. The difference is that each row will contain information about a group of rows—a kind of subtotal table. For example, consider this group query:

```
select category_name, count(*)
from bookshelf
group by category_name;
```

You can create a view based on this query, and you can then query the view:

```
create or replace view category_count as
select category_name, count(*) as counter
from bookshelf
group by category_name;

desc category_count
```

```
Name            Null Type
------------    ---- ------------
CATEGORY_NAME        VARCHAR2(20)
COUNTER              NUMBER
```

```
select * from category_count;
```

```
CATEGORY_NAME            COUNTER
--------------------     -------
ADULTFIC                       6
CHILDRENFIC                    5
ADULTNF                       10
ADULTREF                       6
CHILDRENPIC                    3
CHILDRENNF                     1
```

NOTE
Because the COUNT(*) column is a function, you have to give it a column alias (in this case, COUNTER) when using the query as the basis for a view.

Renaming Columns with Aliases

Notice the name COUNTER in the SELECT clause. The AS COUNTER clause *renames* the column it follows. The new names are called *aliases* because they are used to disguise the real names of the underlying columns (which are complicated because they often are expressions containing functions).

When you query the view, you can (and must) now use the new column names:

```
select category_name, counter from category_count;
```

"COUNTER" is referred to as a *column alias*—another name to use when referring to a column. In the description of the view, and in the query, there is no evidence of the grouping function performed—just the COUNTER column name. It is as if the view CATEGORY_COUNT were a real table with rows of monthly sums. Why?

Oracle automatically takes a single word, without quotes, and uses it to rename the column the word follows. When it does this, Oracle forces the word—the alias—into uppercase, regardless of how it was typed. You can see evidence of this by comparing the column names in the CREATE VIEW and the DESCRIBE commands. When creating a view, *never* put double quotes around your column aliases. Always leave aliases in CREATE VIEW statements without quotes. This stores them in uppercase, which is required for Oracle to find them. See the sidebar "Aliases in View Creation" for a warning on aliases.

Aliases in View Creation

Internally, Oracle works with all column and table names in upper case. This is how they are stored in its data dictionary, and this is how it always expects them to be. When aliases are typed to create a view, they should always be naked—without quotation marks around them. Putting double quotation marks around an alias can force the column name stored internally by Oracle to be in mixed case. If you do this, Oracle will not be able to find the column when you execute a SELECT unless you enclose the column name within quotes for all references to the column.

Never use double quotation marks in creating aliases for a view.

You now have category counts collected in a view. A total for the entire bookshelf could also be created, using BOOK_COUNT as both the view name and the column alias for COUNT(*):

```
create or replace view book_count as
select count(*) book_count from bookshelf;
```

```
view BOOK_COUNT created.
```

If you query the view, you'll discover it has only one row:

```
select book_count
from book_count;
```

```
BOOK_COUNT
----------
        31
```

As new rows are added and committed to the BOOKSHELF table, the BOOK_COUNT and CATEGORY_COUNT views will automatically recalculate the counts when those views are accessed.

The Power of Views of Groups

Now you'll see the real power of a relational database. You've created a view with the count by category and a second view displaying the count for the entire table. These views can now be *joined* together, just as the tables were in Chapter 5, to reveal information never before apparent. For instance, what percentage of the books are in each category?

```
select category_name, counter, (counter/book_count)*100 as percent
from category_count, book_count
order by category_name;
```

```
CATEGORY_NAME            COUNTER    PERCENT
--------------------  ----------  ----------
ADULTFIC                      6  19.3548387
ADULTNF                      10  32.2580645
```

```
ADULTREF                          6 19.3548387
CHILDRENFIC                       5 16.1290323
CHILDRENNF                        1 3.22580645
CHILDRENPIC                       3 9.67741935
```

In this query, two views are listed in the FROM clause, but they are not joined in a WHERE clause. Why not? In this particular case, no WHERE clause is necessary because one of the views, BOOK_COUNT, will only return one row (as shown in the previous listing). The one row in BOOK_COUNT is joined to each row in CATEGORY_COUNT, yielding one row of output for each row in CATEGORY_COUNT. The same results could have been obtained by directly joining the BOOKSHELF *table* with the BOOK_COUNT *view*, but as you can see, the query is more complicated and difficult to understand—and as the number of groups expands, the query will grow even more cumbersome:

```
select category_name, count(*),
    (count(*)/max(book_count))*100 as percent
from bookshelf, book_count
group by category_name
order by category_name;
```

Notice the percentage calculation:

```
    (count(*)/max(book_count))*100 as percent
```

Because this result is part of a grouping function, each of the values must be grouped. Therefore, an initial attempt such as this would fail because BOOK_COUNT is not grouped:

```
    (count(*)/book_count)*100 as percent
```

Because there is only one row in the BOOK_COUNT view, you can perform a MAX function on it to return that single row, grouped by itself.

To create queries that compare one grouping of rows with another grouping of rows, at least one of the groupings must be a view or an "inline view" created in the FROM clause of the query. Beyond this technical restriction, however, it is just simpler and easier to understand doing the queries with views. Compare the last two examples, and the difference in clarity is apparent. Views hide complexity.

To use the inline view method, put the view's text within the FROM clause and give its columns aliases there:

```
select category_name, counter, (counter/book_count)*100 as percent
from category_count,
    (select count(*) as book_count from bookshelf)
order by category_name;
```

In this example, the BOOK_COUNT view has been removed from the FROM clause and replaced by its base query. In that query, the BOOK_COUNT alias is given to the result of a COUNT(*) performed against the BOOKSHELF table. In the main query, that BOOK_COUNT alias is then used as part of a calculation. Using this coding method, there is no need to create the BOOK_COUNT view. Be careful when working with multiple grouping levels within the same query—creating views commonly helps to simplify the creation and maintenance of the code.

Using ORDER BY in Views

From a strictly theoretical perspective, there is no reason to have an ORDER BY clause stored in a view—you can issue an ORDER BY clause when you query the view. Oracle supports the ORDER BY clause within views, as shown here:

```
create view bookshelf_sorted
as select * from bookshelf
order by title;
```

Having the data sorted in the view may simplify your application development. For example, if your code steps through a set of records, having those records presorted may make your processing and error checking simpler. In your application development, you will know that the data will always be returned to you in an ordered fashion. The following query selects the TITLE values, using the ROWNUM pseudo-column to limit the output to nine records:

```
select title from bookshelf_sorted
where rownum < 10;

TITLE
---------------------------------------------
Anne Of Green Gables
Box Socials
Charlotte's Web
Complete Poems Of John Keats
Either/Or
Emma Who Saved My Life
Good Dog, Carl
Gospel
Harry Potter And The Goblet Of Fire
```

The BOOKSHELF_SORTED view is doing more work than just querying from the BOOKSHELF table—it is performing a sorting operation to return the rows in a particular order. If you do not need the rows returned in that order, you are asking the database to do work that does not benefit your application.

The views also give you more power to use the many different character, NUMBER, and DATE datatypes at will, without worrying about things such as months appearing in alphabetical order.

Logic in the HAVING Clause

In the HAVING clause, the choice of the group function and the column on which it operates might bear no relation to the columns or group functions in the SELECT clause:

```
select category_name, count(*),
    (count(*)/max(book_count))*100 as percent
from bookshelf,book_count
group by category_name
having avg(rating) > 4
order by category_name;

CATEGORY_NAME          COUNT(*)    PERCENT
-------------------- ---------- ----------
ADULTNF                      10 32.2580645
```

Here, the HAVING clause selected only those categories (the GROUP BY collected all the rows into groups by CATEGORY_NAME) with an average rating greater than 4. All other groups are eliminated. For the group that met that criterion, the percentage of the total count was calculated.

The HAVING clause is effective for determining which rows in a table have duplicate values in specific columns. For example, if you are trying to establish a new unique index on a column (or set of columns) in a table, and the index creation fails due to uniqueness problems with the data, you can easily determine which rows caused the problem.

First, select the columns you want to be unique, followed by a COUNT(*) column. GROUP BY the columns you want to be unique, and use the HAVING clause to return only those groups having COUNT(*)>1. The only records returned will be duplicates. The following query shows this check being performed for the AUTHOR_NAME column of the AUTHOR table:

```
select author_name, count(*)
from author
group by author_name
having count(*) > 1
order by author_name;
```

```
no rows selected
```

Which books have more than one author? Select the titles from BOOKSHELF_AUTHOR for which the group (by TITLE) has more than one member:

```
column title format a40

select title, count(*)
from bookshelf_author
group by title
having count(*) > 1;
```

```
TITLE                                     COUNT(*)
---------------------------------------- --------
Kierkegaard Anthology                          2
Runaway Bunny                                  2
Complete Poems Of John Keats                   2
Journals Of Lewis And Clark                    4
```

Who are those ten authors? You could create a view based on this query, or try it as an inline view:

```
column title format a40
column author_name format a30

select title, author_name
from bookshelf_author,
    (select title as grouped_title, count(*) as title_counter
     from bookshelf_author
     group by title
     having count(*) > 1)
where title=grouped_title
order by title, author_name;
```

TITLE	AUTHOR_NAME
Complete Poems Of John Keats	John Barnard
Complete Poems Of John Keats	John Keats
Journals Of Lewis And Clark	Bernard De Voto
Journals Of Lewis And Clark	Meriwether Lewis
Journals Of Lewis And Clark	Stephen Ambrose
Journals Of Lewis And Clark	William Clark
Kierkegaard Anthology	Robert Bretall
Kierkegaard Anthology	Soren Kierkegaard
Runaway Bunny	Clement Hurd
Runaway Bunny	Margaret Wise Brown

This query may look complicated (and using a view would make it simpler to read), but it is based on the concepts covered in this chapter: An inline view performs a GROUP BY function and uses a HAVING clause to return only those titles with multiple authors. Those titles are then used as the basis of a query against the BOOKSHELF_AUTHOR table. In a single query, the BOOKSHELF_AUTHOR table is queried for grouped data and individual row data.

Using ORDER BY with Columns and Group Functions

The ORDER BY clause is executed after the WHERE, GROUP BY, and HAVING clauses. It can employ group functions, or columns from the GROUP BY, or a combination. If it uses a group function, that function operates on the groups and then the ORDER BY sorts the *results* of the function in order. If the ORDER BY uses a column from the GROUP BY, it sorts the rows that are returned based on that column. Group functions and single columns (so long as the column is in the GROUP BY) can be combined in the ORDER BY.

In the ORDER BY clause, you can specify a group function and the column it affects even though they have nothing at all to do with the group functions or columns in the SELECT, GROUP BY, or HAVING clause. On the other hand, if you specify a column in the ORDER BY clause that is not part of a group function, it must be in the GROUP BY clause. Let's take the last example and modify the ORDER BY clause:

```
order by title_counter desc, title, author_name
```

The titles and authors will now be ordered based on the number of authors (with the greatest number first) and then by TITLE and AUTHOR_NAME:

TITLE	AUTHOR_NAME
Journals Of Lewis And Clark	Bernard De Voto
Journals Of Lewis And Clark	Meriwether Lewis
Journals Of Lewis And Clark	Stephen Ambrose
Journals Of Lewis And Clark	William Clark
Complete Poems Of John Keats	John Barnard
Complete Poems Of John Keats	John Keats
Kierkegaard Anthology	Robert Bretall
Kierkegaard Anthology	Soren Kierkegaard
Runaway Bunny	Clement Hurd
Runaway Bunny	Margaret Wise Brown

Joining Columns

As explained in Chapter 5, joining two tables together requires that they have a relationship defined by a common column. This is also true in joining views or tables and views. The only exception is when one of the tables or views has just a single row, as the BOOK_COUNT table does. In this case, SQL joins the single row to every row in the other table or view, and no reference to the joining columns needs to be made in the query's WHERE clause.

Any attempt to join two tables that both have more than one row without specifying the joined columns in the WHERE clause produces what's known as a *Cartesian product,* usually a giant result where every row in one table is joined with every row in the other table. A small 80-row table joined to a small 100-row table in this way would produce 8000 rows in your display, and few of them would be at all meaningful.

More Grouping Possibilities

In addition to the operations shown in this chapter, you can perform complex groupings of rows—creating crosstab reports, following hierarchies within the data, and more. Those groupings, and the related functions and clauses (such as CONNECT BY, ROLLUP, GROUPING, and CUBE), are described in Chapter 14.

As you work with groupings within your application-development environment, you will generally find that using views makes the writing of complex queries simpler. You can use views to represent logical groupings of rows that are helpful to end users writing reports, while leaving the underlying table structures unchanged. This benefits the users—the data is presented in a format they understand—while allowing you to preserve the integrity of your database design.

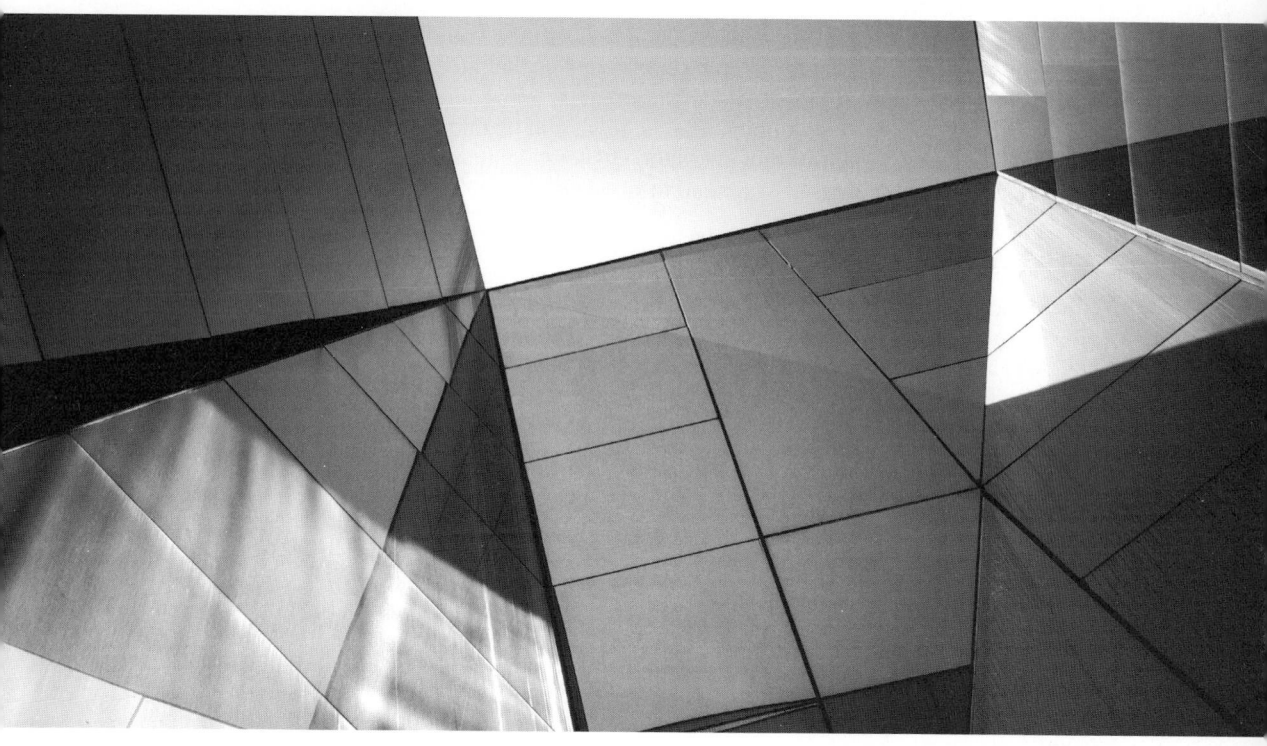

CHAPTER
13

When One Query
Depends on Another

This chapter and Chapter 14 introduce concepts that are more difficult than we've previously seen. Although many of these concepts are rarely used in the normal course of running queries or producing reports, there will be occasions that call for the techniques presented in these chapters. If they seem too challenging as you study them, read on anyway. The odds are good that by the time you need these methods, you'll be able to use them.

Advanced Subqueries

You've encountered *subqueries*—those SELECT statements that are part of a WHERE clause in a preceding SELECT statement—in earlier chapters. Subqueries also can be used in INSERT, UPDATE, and DELETE statements; this will be covered in Chapter 15.

Often, a subquery provides an alternative approach to a query. For example, suppose you want to know what categories of books have been checked out. The following three-way join provides this information:

```
select distinct c.parent_category, c.sub_category
from category c, bookshelf b, bookshelf_checkout bc
where c.category_name = b.category_name
  and b.title = bc.title;


PARENT_CATEGORY SUB_CATEGORY
--------------- --------------------
CHILDREN        PICTURE BOOK
ADULT           FICTION
ADULT           REFERENCE
CHILDREN        FICTION
ADULT           NONFICTION
```

Three tables are joined in the same way that two tables are. The common columns are set equal to each other in the WHERE clause, as shown in the preceding listing. To join three tables together, you must join two of them to a third. In this example, the CATEGORY table is joined to the BOOKSHELF table, and the result of that join is joined to the BOOKSHELF_CHECKOUT table. The DISTINCT keyword tells Oracle to return only the distinct combinations of PARENT_CATEGORY and SUB_CATEGORY.

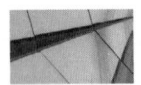

NOTE
Not every table is joined to every other table. In fact, the number of links between the tables is usually one less than the number of tables being joined. You may on occasion even have no links between the tables, but this is not common and is usually the result of an incorrectly constructed query.

Once the tables are joined, as shown in the first two lines of the WHERE clause, you can determine the count of checkouts by parent category and subcategory.

Correlated Subqueries

Is there another way to perform multitable joins? Recall that a WHERE clause can contain a subquery with a SELECT. Subquery SELECTs can be nested—that is, a WHERE clause in a subquery also can contain a WHERE clause with a subquery, which can contain a WHERE clause with a subquery—on down for more levels than you are ever likely to need. The following shows three SELECTs, each connected to another through a WHERE clause:

```
select distinct c.parent_category, c.sub_category
from category c
where category_name in
    (select category_name from bookshelf
     where title in
        (select title from bookshelf_checkout)
    );
```

```
PARENT_CATEGORY SUB_CATEGORY
--------------- --------------------
CHILDREN        PICTURE BOOK
ADULT           FICTION
ADULT           REFERENCE
CHILDREN        FICTION
ADULT           NONFICTION
```

This query selects any categories containing books that have been checked out. It does this simply by requesting a book whose title is in the BOOKSHELF table and whose checkout record is in the BOOKSHELF_CHECKOUT table. In a subquery, Oracle assumes the columns to be from the first SELECT statement, the one that contains the subquery in its WHERE clause. This is called a *nested* subquery, because for every CATEGORY_NAME in the main (outer) query, the CATEGORY_NAME may be correlated in the second WHERE clause.

Said differently, a subquery may refer to a column in a table used in its main query (the query that has the subquery in its WHERE clause). Consider the following query:

```
select title from bookshelf_author
where title in
    (select title from bookshelf
     where author_name = 'Stephen Jay Gould');
```

```
TITLE
------------------------
Wonderful Life
The Mismeasure Of Man
```

Why does this query work? Taken on its own, the subquery would fail:

```
select title from bookshelf
where author_name = 'Stephen Jay Gould';
```

```
Error starting at line 163 in command:
select title from bookshelf
where author_name = 'Stephen Jay Gould'
Error at Command Line:164 Column:6
Error report:
SQL Error: ORA-00904: "AUTHOR_NAME": invalid identifier
00904. 00000 -  "%s: invalid identifier"
```

When executed as a subquery, it is correlated to the parent query—you can reference columns of the first SELECT in the subquery. You don't even need an alias as long as the column does not exist in the tables joined in the subquery. For queries like this, however, coding the query with an alias might be advantageous just so it's clear you're referencing a column in the parent query:

```
select title from bookshelf_author ba
where title in
    (select title from bookshelf
     where ba.author_name = 'Stephen Jay Gould');
```

You'll see additional examples of correlated subqueries in this chapter and the chapters that follow.

Coordinating Logical Tests

If a reader is looking for more books in a particular category, what authors should he or she read? Suppose that Fred Fuller, who has checked out two biographies, asks for recommendations. Who else should you recommend?

```
select distinct author_name from bookshelf_author
where title in
    (select title from bookshelf
     where category_name in
         (select distinct category_name from bookshelf
          where title in
              (select title
               from bookshelf_checkout bc
               where bc.name = 'Fred Fuller')));
```

This statement may look a bit daunting at first, but it's easy to follow if you walk through the code from the inside out! Start at the innermost query: Get a list of the titles that Fred Fuller has checked out. For those titles, go to the BOOKSHELF table and get a list of the distinct CATEGORY_NAME values those books are assigned to. Now go to BOOKSHELF a second time and get all the titles in those categories. For those titles, go to the BOOKSHELF_ AUTHOR table and generate the list of authors. Here are the results:

```
AUTHORNAME
--------------------
Stephen Ambrose
Daniel Boorstin
Stephen Jay Gould
G. B. Talbot
Dietrich Bonhoeffer
David Mccullough
Bernard De Voto
Meriwether Lewis
William Clark
Beryl Markham
John Allen Paulos
```

Fred is asking for recommendations for new authors, so let's exclude the ones he's already read. To see who Fred has read, simply query the BOOKSHELF_CHECKOUT and BOOKSHELF_AUTHOR tables:

```
select distinct author_name
from bookshelf_author ba, bookshelf_checkout bc
where ba.title = bc.title
  and bc.name = 'Fred Fuller';


AUTHOR_NAME
-----------------------
David Mccullough
```

Now let's exclude that author from the list we're going to provide. We'll do that by adding an extra AND clause to the query:

```
select distinct author_name from bookshelf_author
where title in
    (select title from bookshelf
     where category_name in
        (select distinct category_name from bookshelf
         where title in
            (select title
             from bookshelf_checkout bc
             where bc.name = 'Fred Fuller')))
    and author_name not in
        (select author_name
         from bookshelf_author ba, bookshelf_checkout bc
         where ba.title = bc.title
            and bc.name = 'Fred Fuller');


AUTHOR_NAME
--------------------
Stephen Ambrose
Daniel Boorstin
Stephen Jay Gould
G. B. Talbot
Dietrich Bonhoeffer
Bernard De Voto
William Clark
Meriwether Lewis
John Allen Paulos
Beryl Markham
```

This AND is a part of the main query, even though it follows the subquery. Also note that some of the tables are queried at multiple points within the script; each of those queries is treated as a separate access of the table.

Using EXISTS and Its Correlated Subquery

EXISTS is a test for existence. It is placed the way IN might be placed with a subquery, but it differs in that it is a logical test for the return of rows from a query, not for the rows themselves.

How many authors have written more than one book on the bookshelf?

```
select author_name, count(*)
from bookshelf_author
group by author_name
having count(*) > 1;
```

```
AUTHOR_NAME                    COUNT(*)
------------------------       --------
W. P. Kinsella                      2
E. B. White                         2
Stephen Jay Gould                   2
Soren Kierkegaard                   2
Dietrich Bonhoeffer                 2
Wilton Barnhardt                    2
David Mccullough                    2
```

Attempting to find both AUTHOR_NAME and TITLE fails, however, because the GROUP BY made necessary by the COUNT(*) is on the primary key of the BOOKSHELF_AUTHOR table (AUTHOR_NAME, TITLE). Because each primary key, by definition, uniquely identifies only one row, the count of titles for that one row can never be greater than 1, so the HAVING clause always tests false—it doesn't find any rows:

```
select author_name, title, count(*)
from bookshelf_author
group by author_name, title
having count(*) > 1;
```

```
no rows selected.
```

The EXISTS clause provides a solution. The following subquery asks for each AUTHOR_NAME selected in the outer query, if an AUTHOR_NAME exists in the BOOKSHELF_AUTHOR table with a count of TITLEs greater than one. If the answer for a given name is yes, the EXISTS test is true, and the outer query SELECTs an AUTHOR and TITLE. The author names are correlated by the BA alias given to the first BOOKSHELF_AUTHOR table.

```
column AuthorName format a25
column Title format a30

select author_name, title
from bookshelf_author ba
where exists
     (select 'x'
      from bookshelf_author ba2
      where ba.author_name = ba2.author_name
      group by ba2.author_name
      having count(ba2.title) > 1);
order by author_name, title;
```

```
AUTHOR_NAME                     TITLE
------------------------        -------------------------------
David Mccullough                John Adams
David Mccullough                Truman
Dietrich Bonhoeffer             Letters And Papers From Prison
Dietrich Bonhoeffer             The Cost Of Discipleship
E. B. White                     Charlotte's Web
E. B. White                     Trumpet Of The Swan
Soren Kierkegaard               Either/Or
Soren Kierkegaard               Kierkegaard Anthology
Stephen Jay Gould               The Mismeasure Of Man
Stephen Jay Gould               Wonderful Life
W. P. Kinsella                  Box Socials
W. P. Kinsella                  Shoeless Joe
Wilton Barnhardt                Emma Who Saved My Life
Wilton Barnhardt                Gospel
```

The two queries are *correlated*—note that the subquery references the BA.AUTHOR_NAME column even though that column is in the outer query, not the subquery. Within the subquery, the BA2 alias is not required but helps make the code easier to maintain.

This same query could have been built using IN and a test on the column name. No correlated subquery is necessary here:

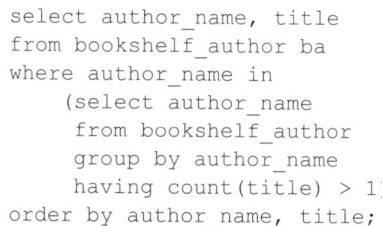

```
select author_name, title
from bookshelf_author ba
where author_name in
    (select author_name
     from bookshelf_author
     group by author_name
     having count(title) > 1)
order by author_name, title;
```

Outer Joins

Starting with Oracle9*i*, the syntax for outer joins has changed considerably. In the following examples, you will see both the Oracle12*c* syntax and the pre-Oracle9*i* syntax. The pre-Oracle9*i* syntax is still supported in Oracle12*c*, but its use should be discontinued. New development should use the new syntax. The newer syntax complies with ANSI SQL standards, whereas the old syntax does not. The old syntax is discussed here because many third-party tools (and lots of old code) continue to use it.

Pre-Oracle9*i* Syntax for Outer Joins

What books were checked out during the time period tracked in the BOOKSHELF_CHECKOUT table?

```
column Title format a40

select distinct title
from bookshelf_checkout;
```

```
TITLE
-----------------------------------------
The Shipping News
Midnight Magic
The Mismeasure Of Man
John Adams
Polar Express
The Discoverers
Innumeracy
Wonderful Life
West With The Night
Truman
My Ledger
Good Dog, Carl
To Kill A Mockingbird
Either/Or
Anne Of Green Gables
Harry Potter And The Goblet Of Fire
```

That's a correct report, but it doesn't show the 0 counts—the books that were not checked out. If you need to see the inventory of all books along with the checkout list, you'll need to join BOOKSHELF_CHECKOUT to BOOKSHELF:

```
select distinct b.title
from bookshelf_checkout bc, bookshelf b
where bc.title = b.title;
```

But that query will return the exact same records—the only rows in BOOKSHELF that can meet the join criteria are those that have been checked out. To list the rest of the books, you need to use an outer join, telling Oracle to return a row even if the join does not produce a match. Two versions of the outer join syntax are fully supported in Oracle. Pre-Oracle9*i,* the syntax for an outer join uses (+) on the side of the join that will return the additional rows. In this case, that's BOOKSHELF_CHECKOUT. The following query shows the maximum number of days each book was checked out:

```
select b.title, max(bc.returned_date - bc.checkout_date)
      "Most Days Out"
from bookshelf_checkout bc, bookshelf b
where bc.title(+) = b.title
group by b.title;
```

```
TITLE                                     Most Days Out
---------------------------------------- -------------
Anne Of Green Gables                               18
Box Socials
Charlotte's Web
Complete Poems Of John Keats
Either/Or                                           8
Emma Who Saved My Life
Good Dog, Carl                                     14
Gospel
Harry Potter And The Goblet Of Fire                11
Innumeracy                                         21
```

John Adams	29
Journals Of Lewis And Clark	
Kierkegaard Anthology	
Letters And Papers From Prison	
Midnight Magic	14
My Ledger	17
Polar Express	14
Preaching To Head And Heart	
Runaway Bunny	
Shoeless Joe	
The Cost Of Discipleship	
The Discoverers	49
The Good Book	
The Mismeasure Of Man	31
The Shipping News	60
To Kill A Mockingbird	15
Truman	19
Trumpet Of The Swan	
Under The Eye Of The Clock	
West With The Night	49
Wonderful Life	31

All the titles in BOOKSHELF are returned, even those that do not meet the join criteria. If you display the BOOKSHELF_CHECKOUT table's TITLE values instead, you'll see that those values are NULL. Think of (+), which must immediately follow the join column of the shorter table, as saying "add an extra (NULL) row of BC.TITLE anytime there's no match for B.TITLE."

Current Syntax for Outer Joins

You can use the ANSI SQL standard syntax as a better alternative for outer joins. In the FROM clause, you can tell Oracle to perform a LEFT, RIGHT, or FULL OUTER join. Let's start with the example from the last section:

```
select b.title, max(bc.returned_date - bc.checkout_date)
       "Most Days Out"
from bookshelf_checkout bc, bookshelf b
where bc.title(+) = b.title
group by b.title;
```

In this case, the BOOKSHELF_CHECKOUT table is having rows returned from it during the join, even if no matches are found. This can be rewritten as follows:

```
select b.title, max(bc.returned_date - bc.checkout_date)
       "Most Days Out"
from bookshelf_checkout bc
   right outer join bookshelf b
      on bc.title = b.title
group by b.title;
```

Note the use of the ON clause as part of the outer join syntax. Note that

```
from bookshelf_checkout bc
   right outer join bookshelf b
```

is equivalent to

```
from bookshelf b
    left outer join bookshelf_checkout bc
```

You can replace the ON clause with a USING clause along with the name of the column the tables have in common—do not qualify the column name with a table name or table alias.

```
select title, max(bc.returned_date - bc.checkout_date)
        "Most Days Out"
from bookshelf_checkout bc
    right outer join bookshelf b
        using (title)
group by title;
```

Note that you cannot specify a table alias for the columns listed in the USING clause—even in the GROUP BY and SELECT clauses.

As with the older syntax, the side used as the driving table for the outer join makes a difference; doing a LEFT OUTER JOIN will not return all the titles.

```
select b.title, max(bc.returned_date - bc.checkout_date)
        "Most Days Out"
from bookshelf_checkout bc
    left outer join bookshelf b
        on bc.title = b.title
group by b.title;
```

```
TITLE                                    Most Days Out
---------------------------------------- -------------
The Shipping News                                   60
Midnight Magic                                      14
The Mismeasure Of Man                               31
John Adams                                          29
Polar Express                                       14
The Discoverers                                     49
Innumeracy                                          21
Wonderful Life                                      31
West With The Night                                 49
Truman                                              19
My Ledger                                           17
Good Dog, Carl                                      14
To Kill A Mockingbird                               15
Either/Or                                            8
Anne Of Green Gables                                18
Harry Potter And The Goblet Of Fire                 11

16 rows selected.
```

A third option, FULL OUTER JOIN, returns all rows from both tables. Rows that do not satisfy the ON condition return NULL values. In this example, there are no rows to satisfy this condition, so the query returns the same 31 rows as the RIGHT OUTER JOIN.

```
select b.title, max(bc.returned_date - bc.checkout_date)
       "Most Days Out"
from bookshelf_checkout bc
   full outer join bookshelf b
      on bc.title = b.title
group by b.title;
```

Replacing NOT IN with an Outer Join

What books were not checked out? You could write a query like this:

```
select title
from bookshelf
where title not in
   (select title from bookshelf_checkout)
order by title;


TITLE
----------------------------------------
Box Socials
Charlotte's Web
Complete Poems Of John Keats
Emma Who Saved My Life
Gospel
Journals Of Lewis And Clark
Kierkegaard Anthology
Letters And Papers From Prison
Preaching To Head And Heart
Runaway Bunny
Shoeless Joe
The Cost Of Discipleship
The Good Book
Trumpet Of The Swan
Under The Eye Of The Clock

15 rows selected
```

This is typically the way such a query would be written. For performance reasons, the optimizer may internally transform that NOT IN to one of the following functionally identical approaches. The next query uses an outer join and produces the same result.

```
select distinct b.title
from bookshelf_checkout bc
   right outer join bookshelf b
      on bc.title = b.title
where bc.title is null
order by b.title;


TITLE
----------------------------------------
Box Socials
Charlotte's Web
```

```
Complete Poems Of John Keats
Emma Who Saved My Life
Gospel
Journals Of Lewis And Clark
Kierkegaard Anthology
Letters And Papers From Prison
Preaching To Head And Heart
Runaway Bunny
Shoeless Joe
The Cost Of Discipleship
The Good Book
Trumpet Of The Swan
Under The Eye Of The Clock
```

Why does it work and give the same results as the NOT IN? The outer join between the two tables ensures that all rows are available for the test, including those titles for which no checkout records are listed in the BOOKSHELF_CHECKOUT table. The line

```
where bc.title is null
```

produces only those titles that don't appear in the BOOKSHELF_CHECKOUT table (and are, therefore, returned as NULL titles by Oracle). The logic here is obscure, but it works. The best way to use this technique is simply to follow the model.

Replacing NOT IN with NOT EXISTS

A more common way to perform this type of query requires using the NOT EXISTS clause. NOT EXISTS is typically used to determine which values in one table do not have matching values in another table. In usage, it is identical to the EXISTS clause; in the following example, you'll see the difference in the query logic and the rows returned.

The NOT EXISTS clause allows you to use a correlated subquery to eliminate from a table all rows that may successfully be joined to another table. For this example, that means you can eliminate from the BOOKSHELF table all titles that are present in the TITLE column of the BOOKSHELF_CHECKOUT table. The following query shows how this is done:

```
select b.title
from bookshelf b
where not exists
   (select 'x'
    from bookshelf_checkout bc
    where bc.title = b.title)
order by b.title;

TITLE
---------------------------------------
Box Socials
Charlotte's Web
Complete Poems Of John Keats
Emma Who Saved My Life
Gospel
Journals Of Lewis And Clark
Kierkegaard Anthology
```

```
Letters And Papers From Prison
Preaching To Head And Heart
Runaway Bunny
Shoeless Joe
The Cost Of Discipleship
The Good Book
Trumpet Of The Swan
Under The Eye Of The Clock
```

This query shows the books that have not been checked out, as previously shown via the NOT IN and outer join methods. How does this query work?

For each record in the BOOKSHELF table, the NOT EXISTS subquery is checked. If the join of that record to the BOOKSHELF_CHECKOUT table returns a row, then the results of the subquery EXISTS. NOT EXISTS tells the query to reverse that return code; therefore, any row in BOOKSHELF that can be successfully joined to BOOKSHELF_CHECKOUT will not be returned by the outer query. The only rows left are the BOOKSHELF rows that do not have a matching row in BOOKSHELF_CHECKOUT.

NOT EXISTS is a very efficient way to perform this type of query, especially when multiple columns are used for the join and the join columns are indexed.

Natural and Inner Joins

You can use the NATURAL keyword to indicate that a join should be performed based on all columns that have the same name in the two tables being joined. For example, what titles in BOOK_ORDER match those already in BOOKSHELF?

```
select title
from book_order
   natural join bookshelf;


TITLE
-----------------------------------------
Gospel
Shoeless Joe
```

The natural join returned the results as if you had typed in the following:

```
select bo.title
from book_order bo, bookshelf
where bo.title = bookshelf.title
  and bo.publisher = bookshelf.publisher
  and bo.category_name = bookshelf.category_name;
```

The join was performed based on the columns the two tables had in common.

Inner joins are the default—they return the rows the two tables have in common—and are the alternative to outer joins. Note that inner joins support the ON and USING clauses, so you can specify your join criteria as shown in the following listing:

```
select bo.title
from book_order bo
   inner join bookshelf b
```

```
on bo.title = b.title;
```

```
TITLE
----------------------------------------
Gospel
Shoeless Joe
```

UNION, INTERSECT, and MINUS

Sometimes you need to combine information of a similar type from more than one table. A classic example of this is merging two or more mailing lists prior to a mailing campaign. Depending on the purpose of a particular mailing, you might want to send letters to any of these combinations of people:

- Everyone in both lists (while avoiding sending two letters to someone who happens to be in both lists)
- Only those people who are in both lists
- Those people in only one of the lists

These three combinations of lists are known in Oracle as UNION, INTERSECT, and MINUS. In the following examples, you will see how to use these three clauses to manage the results of multiple queries. The examples compare the books on hand (BOOKSHELF) with those on order (BOOK_ORDER).

To see all the books, use the UNION operator on the two tables. To reduce the size of the output, only the BOOKSHELF entries from the first half of the alphabet are selected. The following SELECT returns 14 rows:

```
select title
from bookshelf
where title < 'M';
```

And this SELECT returns six rows:

```
select title from book_order;
```

If we UNION them together, how many rows are returned?

```
select title from bookshelf
where title < 'M'
union
select title from book_order;
```

```
TITLE
----------------------------------------
Anne Of Green Gables
Box Socials
Charlotte's Web
Complete Poems Of John Keats
Either/Or
Emma Who Saved My Life
```

```
Galileo's Daughter
Good Dog, Carl
Gospel
Harry Potter And The Goblet Of Fire
Innumeracy
John Adams
Journals Of Lewis And Clark
Kierkegaard Anthology
Letters And Papers From Prison
Longitude
Once Removed
Shoeless Joe
Something So Strong

19 rows selected.
```

Where did the extra record go? The problem is that one of the TITLE values in BOOK_ORDER is already in the BOOKSHELF table. To show the duplicates, use UNION ALL instead of UNION:

```
select title from bookshelf
where title < 'M'
union all
select title from book_order
order by title;

TITLE
----------------------------------------
Anne Of Green Gables
Box Socials
Charlotte's Web
Complete Poems Of John Keats
Either/Or
Emma Who Saved My Life
Galileo's Daughter
Good Dog, Carl
Gospel
Gospel
Harry Potter And The Goblet Of Fire
Innumeracy
John Adams
Journals Of Lewis And Clark
Kierkegaard Anthology
Letters And Papers From Prison
Longitude
Once Removed
Shoeless Joe
Something So Strong

20 rows selected.
```

The duplicate title is now listed twice.

In the following, the two lists of books are *intersected*. This list contains only those names that are in both underlying tables (note that the restriction on TITLE < 'M' has been eliminated for this example):

```
select title from bookshelf
intersect
select title from book_order
order by title;


TITLE
---------------------------------------
Gospel
Shoeless Joe
```

Next, generate the list of new books (in BOOK_ORDER but not already in BOOKSHELF) with the MINUS operator:

```
select title from book_order
minus
select title from bookshelf
order by title;


TITLE
---------------------------------------
Galileo's Daughter
Longitude
Once Removed
Something So Strong
```

You could have also used MINUS to show which books had not been checked out:

```
select title from bookshelf
minus
select title from bookshelf_checkout;


TITLE
-----------------------------
Box Socials
Charlotte's Web
Complete Poems Of John Keats
Emma Who Saved My Life
Gospel
Journals Of Lewis And Clark
Kierkegaard Anthology
Letters And Papers From Prison
Preaching To Head And Heart
Runaway Bunny
Shoeless Joe
The Cost Of Discipleship
```

```
The Good Book
Trumpet Of The Swan
Under The Eye Of The Clock

 15 rows selected
```

You've just learned the basics of UNION, INTERSECT, and MINUS. Now let's go into detail. In combining two tables, Oracle does not concern itself with column names on either side of the combination operator—that is, Oracle requires each SELECT statement to be valid and to have valid columns for its own table(s), but the column names in the first SELECT statement do not have to be the same as those in the second. Oracle does have these stipulations, though:

- The SELECT statements must have the same number of columns. If the two tables being queried have differing numbers of columns selected, you can select strings in place of columns to make the two queries' column lists match.

- The corresponding columns in the SELECT statements must be the same datatype (but they needn't be the same length).

When ordering the output, Oracle uses the column names from the first SELECT statement in giving the query results. Consequently, only column names from the first SELECT statement can be used in the ORDER BY.

You can use combination operators with two or more tables, but when you do, precedence becomes an issue, especially if INTERSECT and MINUS appear. Use parentheses to force the order you want. Otherwise, Oracle evaluates these set operators from left to right (or more intuitively, from top to bottom!).

IN Subqueries

Combination operators can be used in subqueries, but you must be careful with precedence. A query of the form

```
select cola from table_a
where cola in
   (select col1 from table_1)
union
   (select col2 from table_2);
```

is poorly written and ambiguous. Which will be performed first, the UNION of the two queries as part of a single WHERE clause, or the IN clause based on the query of TABLE_1, followed by a UNION of that result with TABLE_2? Use parentheses to clarify your meaning and enforce the proper precedence of operations. The IN clause is always given a higher precedence than UNION, unless you use parentheses to alter the way the query is executed. If you want the UNION to have higher precedence, use parentheses:

```
select cola from table_a
where cola in
   (select col1 from table_1
   union
    select col2 from table_2);
```

Restrictions on UNION, INTERSECT, and MINUS

Queries that use UNION, INTERSECT, or MINUS in their WHERE clause must have the same number and type of columns in their SELECT list. Note that the equivalent IN construction does not have that limitation.

The use of combination operators in place of IN, AND, and OR is a matter of personal style. Most SQL users regard IN, AND, and OR as being clearer and easier to understand than combination operators.

CHAPTER
14

Some Complex
Possibilities

his chapter continues the study of the more complex Oracle functions and features. Of particular interest here is the creation of simple and group queries that can be turned into views, the use of totals in calculations, and the creation of reports showing a tree structure from one or more tables. Like the techniques covered in Chapter 13, these techniques are not essential for most reporting needs. If they look overly difficult, don't be frightened off. If you are new to Oracle and the use of its query capabilities, it is enough to know that these capabilities exist and you can turn to them if needed.

Complex Groupings

Views can build on each other. In Chapter 12, you saw the concept of creating a view of a grouping of rows from a table. As shown in Chapter 12, you can easily join views to other views and tables to produce additional views to simplify the tasks of querying and reporting.

As your groupings grow more complex, you will find that views are invaluable to your coding efforts; they simplify the representation of data at different grouping levels within your application. They also make it easier to use the more advanced analytic functions available.

Consider the CATEGORY_COUNT view, first encountered in Chapter 12:

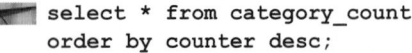

```
create or replace view category_count as
select category_name, COUNT(*) as counter
from bookshelf
group by category_name;
select *
from category_count
order by category_name;
```

```
CATEGORY_NAME             COUNTER
--------------------- ----------
ADULTFIC                        6
ADULTNF                        10
ADULTREF                        6
CHILDRENFIC                     5
CHILDRENNF                      1
CHILDRENPIC                     3
```

Let's order the results by their COUNTER column values, with the highest first:

```
select * from category_count
order by counter desc;
```

```
CATEGORY_NAME             COUNTER
--------------------- ----------
ADULTNF                        10
ADULTFIC                        6
ADULTREF                        6
CHILDRENFIC                     5
CHILDRENPIC                     3
CHILDRENNF                      1
```

The output shows the ranking of the categories; the ADULTNF category ranks first in terms of the number of books. Without displaying this list, you could determine where a different

COUNTER value would be in the rankings. To do this, we'll use the RANK built-in function. As shown in the following listing, the RANK function takes a value as its input and has additional clauses—the WITHIN GROUP and ORDER BY clauses—that tell Oracle how to do the ranking. Where would a COUNTER value of 3 rank?

```
select rank(3)
    within group
        (order by counter desc)
from category_count;
```

```
RANK(3)WITHINGROUP(ORDERBYCOUNTERDESC)
--------------------------------------
                                     5
```

A COUNTER value of 3 would be the fifth-highest COUNTER value. How about a COUNTER value of 8?

```
select rank(8)
    within group
        (order by counter desc)
from category_count;
```

```
RANK(8)WITHINGROUP(ORDERBYCOUNTERDESC)
--------------------------------------
                                     2
```

Adding those five books to the category would move it up to second place. From a percentile perspective, what would the ranking be for that category?

```
select percent_rank(8)
    within group
        (order by counter desc)
from category_count;
```

```
PERCENT_RANK(8)WITHINGROUP(ORDERBYCOUNTERDESC)
----------------------------------------------
                                    .166666667
```

As expected, it would be in the top one-sixth of the categories.

With this technique of using both summary views and analytic functions, you can create views and reports that include weighted average, effective yield, percentage of total, percentage of subtotal, and many similar calculations. There is no effective limit to how many views can be built on top of each other, although even the most complex calculations seldom require more than three or four levels of views built on views. Note that you can also create inline views in the FROM clause, as shown in Chapter 12.

Using Temporary Tables

You can create a table that exists solely for your session or whose data persists for the duration of your transaction. You can use temporary tables to support specialized rollups or specific application-processing requirements whose results will not persist beyond the session or even past a COMMIT statement.

To create a temporary table, use the CREATE GLOBAL TEMPORARY TABLE command. When you create a temporary table, you can specify whether it should last for the duration of your session (via the ON COMMIT PRESERVE ROWS clause) or whether its rows should be deleted when the transaction completes (via the ON COMMIT DELETE ROWS clause).

Unlike a permanent table, a temporary table does not automatically allocate space when it is created. Space will be dynamically allocated for the table as rows are inserted:

```
create global temporary table year_rollup (
    year      number(4),
    month     varchar2(9),
    counter   number)
on commit preserve rows;
```

You can see the duration of your data in YEAR_ROLLUP by querying the DURATION column of USER_TABLES for this table. In this case, the value of DURATION is SYS$SESSION. If ON COMMIT DELETE ROWS had been specified instead, the DURATION value would be SYS$TRANSACTION.

Now that the YEAR_ROLLUP table exists, you can populate it, for instance, via an INSERT AS SELECT command with a complex query. You can then query the YEAR_ROLLUP table as part of a join with other tables. You may find this method simpler to implement than the methods shown in Chapter 12 for creating views.

Using ROLLUP, GROUPING, and CUBE

How can you perform grouping operations, such as totals, within a single SQL statement rather than via SQL*Plus commands? You can use the ROLLUP and CUBE functions to enhance the grouping actions performed within your queries. Let's see how this enables us to manage the data related to book returns. The book loaner program has become more popular, so the loan time is now limited to 14 days, with a $0.20 fee per extra day. The following report shows the late charges by person:

```
set headsep !
column name format a20
column title format a20 word_wrapped
column daysout format 999.99 heading 'Days!Out'
column dayslate format 999.99 heading 'Days!Late'

break on name skip 1 on report
compute sum of latefee on name
set linesize 80
set pagesize 60
set newpage 0

select name, title, returned_date,
    returned_date-checkout_date as daysout /*count days*/,
    returned_date-checkout_date -14  dayslate,
```

```
    (returned_date-checkout_date -14)*0.20  latefee
from bookshelf_checkout
where returned_date-checkout_date > 14
order by name, checkout_date;
```

NAME	TITLE	RETURNED_	Days Out	Days Late	LATEFEE
--------------------	--------------------	---------	-------	-------	----------
Dorah Talbot	My Ledger	03-MAR-12	17.00	3.00	.6
********************					----------
sum					.6
Emily Talbot	Anne Of Green Gables	20-JAN-12	18.00	4.00	.8
********************					----------
sum					.8
Fred Fuller	John Adams	01-MAR-12	29.00	15.00	3
	Truman	20-MAR-12	19.00	5.00	1
********************					----------
sum					4
Gerhardt Kentgen	Wonderful Life	02-FEB-12	31.00	17.00	3.4
	The Mismeasure Of Man	05-MAR-12	21.00	7.00	1.4
********************					----------
sum					4.8
Jed Hopkins	Innumeracy	22-JAN-12	21.00	7.00	1.4
	To Kill A Mockingbird	01-MAR-12	15.00	1.00	.2
********************					----------
sum					1.6
Pat Lavay	The Mismeasure Of Man	12-FEB-12	31.00	17.00	3.4
********************					----------
sum					3.4
Roland Brandt	The Discoverers	01-MAR-12	49.00	35.00	7
	The Shipping News	12-MAR-12	60.00	46.00	9.2
	West With The Night	01-MAR-12	49.00	35.00	7
********************					----------
sum					23.2

12 rows selected.
```
```

We can eliminate the DAYSOUT derived column display and focus on the late fees, showing the fees due on each of the return dates:

```
clear compute
clear break
select returned_date, name,
    sum((returned_date-checkout_date -14)*0.20)   latefee
from bookshelf_checkout
where returned_date-checkout_date > 14
group by returned_date, name
order by returned_date, name;


RETURNED_ NAME                         LATEFEE
--------- -------------------- ----------
20-JAN-12 Emily Talbot                     .8
22-JAN-12 Jed Hopkins                     1.4
02-FEB-12 Gerhardt Kentgen                3.4
12-FEB-12 Pat Lavay                       3.4
01-MAR-12 Fred Fuller                       3
01-MAR-12 Jed Hopkins                      .2
01-MAR-12 Roland Brandt                    14
03-MAR-12 Dorah Talbot                     .6
05-MAR-12 Gerhardt Kentgen                1.4
12-MAR-12 Roland Brandt                   9.2
20-MAR-12 Fred Fuller                       1
```

Then we can modify it further to group the late fees by month:

```
select to_char(returned_date,'MONTH') month, name,
    sum((returned_date-checkout_date -14)*0.20)   latefee
from bookshelf_checkout
where returned_date-checkout_date > 14
group by to_char(returned_date,'MONTH'), name;


MONTH     NAME                       LATEFEE
--------- ------------------------ -------
FEBRUARY  Pat Lavay                    3.4
JANUARY   Jed Hopkins                  1.4
MARCH     Roland Brandt               23.2
MARCH     Fred Fuller                    4
JANUARY   Emily Talbot                 0.8
MARCH     Jed Hopkins                  0.2
FEBRUARY  Gerhardt Kentgen             3.4
MARCH     Dorah Talbot                 0.6
MARCH     Gerhardt Kentgen             1.4
```

Instead of simply grouping by MONTH and NAME, you can use the ROLLUP function to generate subtotals and totals. In the following example, the GROUP BY clause is modified to include a ROLLUP function call. Notice the additional rows generated at the end of the result set and after each month:

```
select to_char(returned_date,'MONTH') month, name,
    sum((returned_date-checkout_date -14)*0.20)   latefee
```

```
from bookshelf_checkout
where returned_date-checkout_date > 14
group by rollup(to_char(returned_date,'MONTH'), name);
```

MONTH	NAME	LATEFEE
FEBRUARY	Pat Lavay	3.4
FEBRUARY	Gerhardt Kentgen	3.4
FEBRUARY		6.8
JANUARY	Jed Hopkins	1.4
JANUARY	Emily Talbot	0.8
JANUARY		2.2
MARCH	Fred Fuller	4
MARCH	Jed Hopkins	0.2
MARCH	Dorah Talbot	0.6
MARCH	Roland Brandt	23.2
MARCH	Gerhardt Kentgen	1.4
MARCH		29.4
		38.4

For each month, Oracle has calculated the total late fee and shows it with a NULL value for NAME. The output shows two separate charges of $3.40 in February and a monthly total of $6.80. For the quarter, the total of the late charges is $38.40. You could have calculated these via SQL*Plus commands (see Chapter 6), but this method allows you to generate these sums via a single SQL command regardless of the tool used to query the database.

Let's refine the appearance of the report. You can use the GROUPING function to determine whether the row is a total or subtotal (generated by ROLLUP) or corresponds to a NULL value in the database itself. In the SELECT clause, the NAME column is selected as follows:

```
select decode(grouping(name),1, 'All names',name),
```

The GROUPING function returns a value of 1 if the column's value is generated by a ROLLUP action. This query uses DECODE (discussed at length in Chapter 16) to evaluate the result of the GROUPING function. If the GROUPING output is 1, the value was generated by the ROLLUP function, and Oracle prints the phrase 'All names'; otherwise, it prints the value of the NAME column. We'll apply similar logic to the MONTH column. The full query is shown in the following listing, along with its output:

```
select decode(grouping(to_char(returned_date,'MONTH')),1,
    'All months',to_char(returned_date,'MONTH')) month,
  decode(grouping(name),1, 'All names',name) name,
   sum((returned_date-checkout_date -14)*0.20)  latefee
from bookshelf_checkout
where returned_date-checkout_date > 14
group by rollup(to_char(returned_date, 'MONTH'), name);
```

MONTH	NAME	LATEFEE
FEBRUARY	Pat Lavay	3.4
FEBRUARY	Gerhardt Kentgen	3.4
FEBRUARY	All names	6.8
JANUARY	Jed Hopkins	1.4

```
JANUARY      Emily Talbot                      0.8
JANUARY      All names                         2.2
MARCH        Fred Fuller                         4
MARCH        Jed Hopkins                       0.2
MARCH        Dorah Talbot                      0.6
MARCH        Roland Brandt                    23.2
MARCH        Gerhardt Kentgen                  1.4
MARCH        All names                        29.4
All months   All names                        38.4
```

You can use the CUBE function to generate subtotals for *all* combinations of the values in the GROUP BY clause. The following query uses the CUBE function to generate these combinations:

```
select decode(grouping(to_char(returned_date,'MONTH')),1,
    'All months',to_char(returned_date,'MONTH')) month,
    decode(grouping(name),1, 'all names',name) name,
    sum((returned_date-checkout_date -14)*0.20) latefee
from bookshelf_checkout
where returned_date-checkout_date > 14
group by cube(to_char(returned_date,'MONTH'), name);
```

```
MONTH        NAME                          LATEFEE
----------   ------------------------      -------
All months   all names                        38.4
All months   Pat Lavay                         3.4
All months   Fred Fuller                         4
All months   Jed Hopkins                       1.6
All months   Dorah Talbot                      0.6
All months   Emily Talbot                      0.8
All months   Roland Brandt                    23.2
All months   Gerhardt Kentgen                  4.8
FEBRUARY     All names                         6.8
FEBRUARY     Pat Lavay                         3.4
FEBRUARY     Gerhardt Kentgen                  3.4
JANUARY      All names                         2.2
JANUARY      Jed Hopkins                       1.4
JANUARY      Emily Talbot                      0.8
MARCH        All names                        29.4
MARCH        Fred Fuller                         4
MARCH        Jed Hopkins                       0.2
MARCH        Dorah Talbot                      0.6
MARCH        Roland Brandt                    23.2
MARCH        Gerhardt Kentgen                  1.4
```

The CUBE function provided the summaries generated by the ROLLUP option, plus it shows the sums by NAME for the "All months" category. Being able to perform these summaries in standard SQL code greatly enhances your ability to pick the best reporting tool for your users.

Family Trees and CONNECT BY

One of Oracle's more interesting but little used or understood facilities is its CONNECT BY clause. Put simply, this method is used to report, in order, the branches of a *family tree.* Such trees are encountered often—the genealogy of human families, livestock, horses; corporate management, company divisions, manufacturing; literature, ideas, evolution, scientific research, theory; and even views built on views.

The CONNECT BY clause provides a means to report on all of the family members in any of these many trees. It lets you exclude branches or individual members of a family tree, and it allows you to travel through the tree either up or down, reporting on the family members encountered during the trip.

The earliest ancestor in the tree is technically called the *root node.* In everyday English, this is called the *trunk.* Extending from the trunk are *branches,* which have other branches, which have still other branches. The forks where one or more branches split away from a larger branch are called *nodes,* and the very end of a branch is called a *leaf,* or a *leaf node.* Figure 14-1 shows a picture of such a tree.

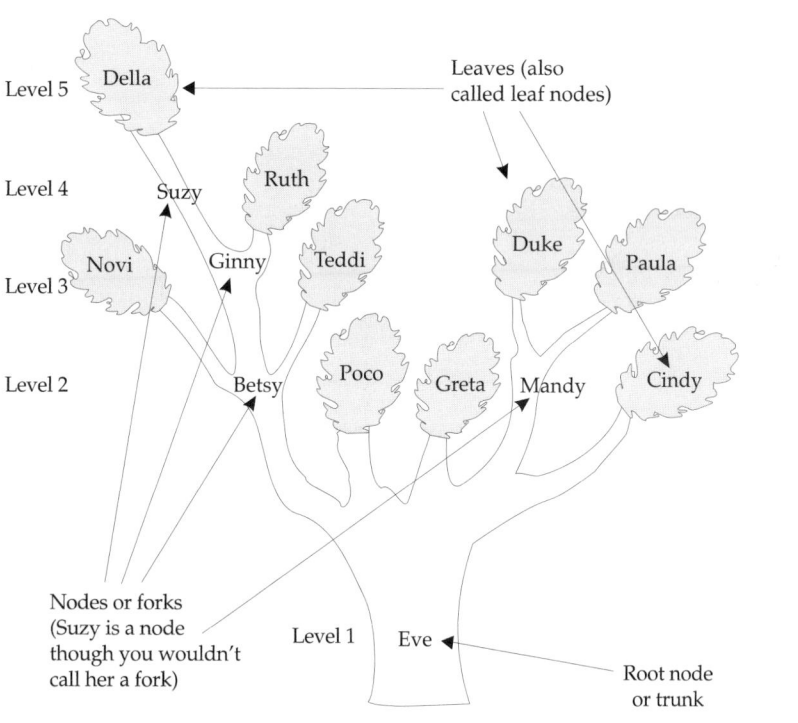

FIGURE 14-1.   *Eve's descendants*

The following is a table of cows and bulls born between January 1900 and October 1908. As each offspring is born, it is entered as a row in the table, along with its sex, parents (the cow and bull), and birth date. If you compare the cows and offspring in this table with Figure 14-1, you'll find they correspond. Eve has no recorded cow or bull parent because she was born on a different farm, and Adam and Bandit are bulls brought in for breeding, again with no parents in the table.

```
column Cow format a6
column Bull format a6
column Offspring format a10
column Sex format a3

select *
from breeding
order by birth_date;


OFFSPRING  SEX COW        BULL       BIRTH_DATE
---------- --- ---------- ---------- ----------
Betsy      F   Eve        Adam       02-JAN-00
Poco       M   Eve        Adam       15-JUL-00
Greta      F   Eve        Bandit     12-MAR-01
Mandy      F   Eve        Poco       22-AUG-02
Cindy      F   Eve        Poco       09-FEB-03
Novi       F   Betsy      Adam       30-MAR-03
Ginny      F   Betsy      Bandit     04-DEC-03
Duke       M   Mandy      Bandit     24-JUL-04
Teddi      F   Betsy      Bandit     12-AUG-05
Suzy       F   Ginny      Duke       03-APR-06
Paula      F   Mandy      Poco       21-DEC-06
Ruth       F   Ginny      Duke       25-DEC-06
Della      F   Suzy       Bandit     11-OCT-08
Adam       M
Eve        F
Bandit     M
```

Next, a query is written to illustrate the family relationships visually. You do this using LPAD and a special column, known as a *pseudo-column*, called LEVEL, that you use with CONNECT BY. LEVEL is a number, from 1 for Eve to 5 for Della, that is really the *generation*. If Eve is the first generation of cattle, then Della is the fifth generation. Whenever the CONNECT BY clause is used, the LEVEL column can be used in the SELECT statement to discover the generation of each row. LEVEL is a pseudo-column like SYSDATE and USER. It's not really a part of the table, but it is available under specific circumstances. The next listing shows an example of using LEVEL.

The results of this query are apparent in the following table, but why did the SELECT statement produce this? How does it work?

```
column Offspring format a30

select cow, bull, lpad(' ',6*(level-1))||offspring as offspring,
   sex, birth_date
from breeding
start with offspring = 'Eve'
connect by cow = prior offspring;
```

```
COW         BULL        OFFSPRING                          S BIRTH_DAT
----------  ----------  --------------------------------   - ---------
                        Eve                                F
Eve         Adam            Betsy                          F 02-JAN-00
Betsy       Bandit              Ginny                      F 04-DEC-03
Ginny       Duke                    Ruth                   F 25-DEC-06
Ginny       Duke                    Suzy                   F 03-APR-06
Suzy        Bandit                      Della              F 11-OCT-08
Betsy       Adam                Novi                       F 30-MAR-03
Betsy       Bandit              Teddi                      F 12-AUG-05
Eve         Poco        Cindy                              F 09-FEB-03
Eve         Bandit      Greta                              F 12-MAR-01
Eve         Poco        Mandy                              F 22-AUG-02
Mandy       Bandit          Duke                           M 24-JUL-04
Mandy       Poco            Paula                          F 21-DEC-06
Eve         Adam        Poco                               M 15-JUL-00
```

Note that this is really Figure 14-1 turned clockwise onto its side. Eve isn't centered, but she is the root node (trunk) of this tree. Her children are Betsy, Cindy, Greta, Mandy, and Poco. Betsy's children are Ginny, Novi, and Teddi. Ginny's children are Ruth and Suzy. And Suzy's child is Della. Mandy also has two children, Duke and Paula.

This tree started with Eve as the first "offspring." If the SQL statement had said start with Mandy, only Mandy, Duke, and Paula would have been in the output. START WITH defines the beginning of that portion of the tree that will be displayed, and it includes only branches stretching out from the individual that START WITH specifies. START WITH acts just as its name implies.

The LPAD in the SELECT statement is probably somewhat confusing. Recall from Chapter 7 the format for LPAD:

```
LPAD(string,length[,'set'])
```

That is, take the specified *string* and left-pad it for the specified *length* with the specified *set* of characters. If no *set* is specified, left-pad the string with blanks.

Compare this syntax to the LPAD in the SELECT statement shown earlier:

```
lpad(' ',6*(level-1))
```

In this case, the *string* is a single character (a space, indicated by the literal space enclosed in single quotation marks). Also, 6*(LEVEL−1) is the *length*, and because the *set* is not specified, spaces are used. In other words, this tells Oracle to take this string of one space and left-pad it to the number of spaces determined by 6*(LEVEL−1), a calculation made by first subtracting 1 from the LEVEL and then multiplying this result by 6. For Eve, the LEVEL is 1, so 6*(1−1), or 0 spaces, is used. For Betsy, the LEVEL (her generation) is 2, so an LPAD of 6 is used. Thus, for each generation after the first, six additional spaces are concatenated to the left of the OFFSPRING column. The effect is obvious in the result just shown. The name of each OFFSPRING is indented by left-padding with the number of spaces corresponding to its LEVEL or generation.

Why is this done, instead of simply applying the LPAD directly to OFFSPRING? There are two reasons. First, a direct LPAD on OFFSPRING would cause the names of the offspring to be right-justified. The names at each level would end up having their last letters lined up vertically. Second, if LEVEL−1 is equal to 0, as it is for Eve, the resulting LPAD of Eve will be 0 characters wide, causing Eve to vanish:

```
select cow, bull, lpad(offspring,6*(level-1),' ') as offspring,
    sex, birth_date
from breeding
start with offspring = 'Eve'
connect by cow = prior offspring;
```

```
COW        BULL       OFFSPRING                             S BIRTH_DAT
---------- ---------- ----------------------------------- - ---------
                                                            F
Eve        Adam       Betsy                                 F 02-JAN-00
Betsy      Bandit         Ginny                             F 04-DEC-03
Ginny      Duke               Ruth                          F 25-DEC-06
Ginny      Duke               Suzy                          F 03-APR-06
Suzy       Bandit                 Della                      F 11-OCT-08
Betsy      Adam           Novi                              F 30-MAR-03
Betsy      Bandit         Teddi                             F 12-AUG-05
Eve        Poco       Cindy                                 F 09-FEB-03
Eve        Bandit     Greta                                 F 12-MAR-01
Eve        Poco       Mandy                                 F 22-AUG-02
Mandy      Bandit         Duke                              M 24-JUL-04
Mandy      Poco           Paula                             F 21-DEC-06
Eve        Adam       Poco                                  M 15-JUL-00
```

Therefore, to get the proper spacing for each LEVEL, to ensure that EVE appears, and to make the names line up vertically on the left, use LPAD with the concatenation operator or function not directly on the OFFSPRING column.

Now, how does CONNECT BY work? Look again at Figure 14-1. Starting with Novi and traveling downward, which cows are the offspring prior to Novi? The first is Betsy, and the offspring just prior to Betsy is Eve. Even though it is not instantly readable, the clause

```
connect by cow = prior offspring
```

tells Oracle to find the next row in which the value in the COW column is equal to the value in the OFFSPRING column in the prior row. Look at the contents of the BREEDING table and you'll see that this is true.

Excluding Individuals and Branches

There are two methods of excluding cows from a report. One uses the normal WHERE clause technique, and the other uses the CONNECT BY clause itself. The difference is that the exclusion using the CONNECT BY clause excludes not just the cow mentioned, but all of its children as well. If you use CONNECT BY to exclude Betsy, then Novi, Ginny, Teddi, Suzy, Ruth, and Della all vanish. The CONNECT BY clause really tracks the tree structure. If Betsy had never been born, none of her offspring would have been either. In this example, the AND clause modifies the CONNECT BY clause:

```
select cow, bull, lpad(' ',6*(level-1))||offspring as offspring,
    sex, birth_date
from breeding
start with offspring = 'Eve'
connect by cow = prior offspring and offspring != 'Betsy';
```

```
COW        BULL        OFFSPRING                                 S BIRTH_DAT
---------- ---------- ------------------------------------------ - ---------
                       Eve                                       F
Eve        Poco              Cindy                               F 09-FEB-03
Eve        Bandit            Greta                               F 12-MAR-01
Eve        Poco              Mandy                               F 22-AUG-02
Mandy      Bandit                  Duke                          M 24-JUL-04
Mandy      Poco                    Paula                         F 21-DEC-06
Eve        Adam              Poco                                M 15-JUL-00
```

The WHERE clause removes only the cow or cows it mentions. If Betsy dies, she is removed from the chart, but her offspring are not. In fact, notice that Betsy is still there under the COW column as the mother of her children, Novi, Ginny, and Teddi:

```
select cow, bull, lpad(' ',6*(level-1))||offspring as offspring,
    sex, birth_date
from breeding
where offspring != 'Betsy'
start with offspring = 'Eve'
connect by cow = prior offspring;
```

```
COW        BULL        OFFSPRING                                 S BIRTH_DAT
---------- ---------- ------------------------------------------ - ---------
                       Eve                                       F
Betsy      Bandit            Ginny                               F 04-DEC-03
Ginny      Duke                    Ruth                          F 25-DEC-06
Ginny      Duke                    Suzy                          F 03-APR-06
Suzy       Bandit                        Della                   F 11-OCT-08
Betsy      Adam              Novi                                F 30-MAR-03
Betsy      Bandit            Teddi                               F 12-AUG-05
Eve        Poco              Cindy                               F 09-FEB-03
Eve        Bandit            Greta                               F 12-MAR-01
Eve        Poco              Mandy                               F 22-AUG-02
Mandy      Bandit                  Duke                          M 24-JUL-04
Mandy      Poco                    Paula                         F 21-DEC-06
Eve        Adam              Poco                                M 15-JUL-00
```

The order in which the family tree is displayed when using CONNECT BY is basically level by level, left to right, as shown in Figure 14-1, starting with the lowest level, Level 1.

Traveling Toward the Roots

Thus far, the direction of travel in reporting on the family tree has been from parents toward children. Is it possible to start with a child and move backward to parent, grandparent, great-grandparent, and so on? To do so, the word PRIOR is simply moved to the other side of the equal sign. In the following examples, the OFFSPRING is set equal to the PRIOR COW value; in the earlier examples, the COW was set equal to the PRIOR OFFSPRING value. The following traces Della's ancestry:

```
select cow, bull, lpad(' ',6*(level-1))||offspring as offspring,
    sex, birth_date
from breeding
```

```
start with offspring = 'Della'
connect by offspring = prior cow;
```

COW	BULL	OFFSPRING	S	BIRTH_DAT
Suzy	Bandit	Della	F	11-OCT-08
Ginny	Duke	Suzy	F	03-APR-06
Betsy	Bandit	Ginny	F	04-DEC-03
Eve	Adam	Betsy	F	02-JAN-00
		Eve	F	

This shows Della's own roots, but it's a bit confusing if compared to the previous displays. It looks as if Della is the ancestor and Eve the great-great-granddaughter. Adding an ORDER BY for BIRTH_DATE helps, but Eve is still further to the right:

```
select cow, bull, lpad(' ',6*(level-1))||offspring as offspring,
    sex, birth_date
from breeding
start with offspring = 'Della'
connect by offspring = prior cow
order by birth_date;
```

COW	BULL	OFFSPRING	S	BIRTH_DAT
Eve	Adam	Betsy	F	02-JAN-00
Betsy	Bandit	Ginny	F	04-DEC-03
Ginny	Duke	Suzy	F	03-APR-06
Suzy	Bandit	Della	F	11-OCT-08
		Eve	F	

The solution is simply to change the calculation in the LPAD function call:

```
select cow, bull, lpad(' ',6*(5-level))||offspring offspring,
    sex, birth_date
from breeding
start with offspring = 'Della'
connect by offspring = prior cow
order by birth_date;
```

COW	BULL	OFFSPRING	S	BIRTH_DAT
Eve	Adam	Betsy		F	02-JAN-00
Betsy	Bandit	Ginny		F	04-DEC-03
Ginny	Duke	Suzy		F	03-APR-06
Suzy	Bandit	Della	F	11-OCT-08
		Eve		F	

Finally, look how different this report is when the CONNECT BY tracks the parentage of the bull. Here are Adam's offspring:

```
select cow, bull, lpad(' ',6*(level-1))||offspring as offspring,
    sex, birth_date
from breeding
```

```
start with offspring = 'Adam'
connect by prior offspring = bull;
```

```
COW          BULL         OFFSPRING                          S  BIRTH_DAT
----------   ----------   ------------------------------     -  ---------
                          Adam                               M
Eve          Adam              Betsy                         F  02-JAN-00
Betsy        Adam              Novi                          F  30-MAR-03
Eve          Adam              Poco                          M  15-JUL-00
Eve          Poco                    Cindy                   F  09-FEB-03
Eve          Poco                    Mandy                   F  22-AUG-02
Mandy        Poco                    Paula                   F  21-DEC-06
```

Adam and Bandit were the original bulls at the initiation of the herd. To create a single tree that reports both Adam's and Bandit's offspring, you would have to invent a "father" for the two of them, which would be the root of the tree. One of the advantages that these alternative trees have over the type of tree shown earlier is that many inheritance groups—from families to projects to divisions within companies—can be accurately portrayed in more than one way:

```
select cow, bull, lpad(' ',6*(level-1))||offspring as offspring,
    sex, birth_date
from breeding
start with offspring = 'Bandit'
connect by prior offspring = bull;
```

```
COW          BULL         OFFSPRING                          S  BIRTH_DAT
----------   ----------   ------------------------------     -  ---------
                          Bandit                             M
Suzy         Bandit            Della                         F  11-OCT-08
Mandy        Bandit            Duke                          M  24-JUL-04
Ginny        Duke                    Ruth                    F  25-DEC-06
Ginny        Duke                    Suzy                    F  03-APR-06
Betsy        Bandit            Ginny                         F  04-DEC-03
Eve          Bandit            Greta                         F  12-MAR-01
Betsy        Bandit            Teddi                         F  12-AUG-05
```

Finding the Leaves

Occasionally it can be useful to identify those offspring who have themselves not produced any offspring, in other words, identifying only the leaves of the tree. Another pseudo-column, new to Oracle Database 11g, is CONNECT_BY_ISLEAF. It has a value of 1 if this row is a leaf node in the family tree.

Thus, we can take one of the earlier queries that shows the entire family tree and filter it to include only rows with CONNECT_BY_ISLEAF=1:

```
select offspring as leaf_offspring,
    cow, bull, sex, birth_date
from breeding
where connect_by_isleaf = 1
start with offspring = 'Eve'
connect by cow = prior offspring;
```

```
LEAF_OFFSPRING COW         BULL        SEX BIRTH_DATE
-------------- ----------  ----------  --- ----------
Ruth           Ginny       Duke        F   25-DEC-06
Della          Suzy        Bandit      F   11-OCT-08
Novi           Betsy       Adam        F   30-MAR-03
Teddi          Betsy       Bandit      F   12-AUG-05
Cindy          Eve         Poco        F   09-FEB-03
Greta          Eve         Bandit      F   12-MAR-01
Duke           Mandy       Bandit      M   24-JUL-04
Paula          Mandy       Poco        F   21-DEC-06
Poco           Eve         Adam        M   15-JUL-00
```

Therefore, nine offspring in the herd have not yet been parents.

The Basic Rules

Using CONNECT BY and START WITH to create tree-like reports is not difficult, but you must follow certain basic rules:

- The order of the clauses when using CONNECT BY is as follows:
    1. SELECT
    2. FROM
    3. WHERE
    4. START WITH
    5. CONNECT BY
    6. ORDER BY
- PRIOR forces reporting to be from the root out toward the leaves (if the PRIOR column is the parent) or from a leaf toward the root (if the PRIOR column is the child).
- A WHERE clause eliminates individual rows from the tree, but not their descendants (or ancestors, if PRIOR is on the right side of the equal sign).
- A qualification in the CONNECT BY (particularly a not equal) eliminates both an individual row and all of its descendants (or ancestors, depending on how you trace the tree).
- CONNECT BY cannot be used with a table join in the WHERE clause in versions previous to Oracle 11g.
- Pseudo-columns such as LEVEL and CONNECT_BY_ISLEAF can help to prune the tree when only certain rows need to be in the query result.

This particular set of commands is one that few people are likely to remember correctly. However, with a basic understanding of trees and inheritance, you should be able to construct a proper SELECT statement to report on a tree just by referring to this chapter for correct syntax and examples.

CHAPTER

15

Changing Data:
INSERT, DELETE,
UPDATE, and MERGE

U
ntil now, virtually everything you've learned about Oracle, SQL, and SQL*Plus has related to selecting data from tables in the database. This chapter shows how to *change* the data in a table—how to insert new rows, update the values of columns in rows, and delete rows entirely. Although these topics have not been covered explicitly, nearly everything you already know about SQL, including datatypes, calculations, string formatting, WHERE clauses, and the like, can be used here, so there really isn't much new to learn. Oracle gives you a transparent, distributed database capability that inserts, updates, and deletes data in remote databases as well (see Chapter 25). As you'll see in this chapter, Oracle allows you to combine these commands via multitable inserts and the MERGE command (to perform inserts and updates, and sometimes deletes, in a single command).

INSERT

The SQL command INSERT lets you place a row of information directly into a table (or indirectly, through a view). The COMFORT table tracks temperatures at noon and midnight as well as daily precipitation, city by city, for four sample dates throughout the year:

```
describe COMFORT
```

```
Name            Null      Type
------------    --------  ------------
CITY            NOT NULL  VARCHAR2(13)
SAMPLE_DATE     NOT NULL  DATE
NOON                      NUMBER(3,1)
MIDNIGHT                  NUMBER(3,1)
PRECIPITATION             NUMBER
```

To add a new row to this table, use this:

```
insert into comfort
values ('Walpole', '21-MAR-11',
       56.7, 43.8, 0);
```

```
1 rows inserted.
```

The word VALUES must precede the list of data to be inserted. A character string must be in single quotation marks. Numbers can stand by themselves. Each field is separated by commas, and the fields must be in the same order as the columns are when the table is described.

A date must be in single quotation marks and in the default Oracle date format. To insert a date not in your default format, use the TO_DATE function, with a formatting mask, as shown in the following example:

```
insert into comfort
values ('Walpole', to_date('06/22/2011','MM/DD/YYYY'),
       56.7, 43.8, 0);
```

```
1 rows inserted.
```

Inserting a Time

Inserting dates without time values produces a default time of midnight, the very beginning of the day. If you want to insert a date with a time other than midnight, simply use the TO_DATE function and include a time:

```
insert into comfort
values ('Walpole', to_date('06/22/2011 1:35',
       'MM/DD/YYYY HH24:MI'), 56.7, 43.8, 0);
```

```
1 rows inserted.
```

NOTE
To store fractional seconds, you can use the TIMESTAMP and TIMESTAMP WITH TIME ZONE datatypes, as described in Chapter 10.

Columns also can be inserted out of the order in which they appear when described, if you first (before the word VALUES) list the order the data is in. This doesn't change the fundamental order of the columns in the table; it simply allows you to list the data fields in a different order. (See Part V for information on inserting data into user-defined datatypes.)

You also can "insert" a NULL. This simply means the column will be left empty for this row, as shown in the following example:

```
insert into comfort (sample_date, precipitation, city, noon, midnight)
    values ('23-SEP-11', NULL,'Walpole', 86.3, 72.1);
```

```
1 rows inserted.
```

INSERT with SELECT

You also can insert information that has been selected from a table. Here, a mix of columns selected from the COMFORT table, together with literal values for SAMPLE_DATE (22-DEC-11) and CITY (Walpole), are inserted. Note the WHERE clause in the SELECT statement, which will retrieve only one row. Had the SELECT retrieved five rows, five new ones would have been inserted; if ten rows had been retrieved, then ten new rows would have been inserted, and so on.

```
insert into comfort(sample_date,precipitation,city,noon,midnight)
select '22-dec-11', precipitation,'Walpole', noon, midnight
from comfort
where city = 'Keene'
  and sample_date = '22-dec-11';
```

```
1 rows inserted.
```

NOTE
You cannot use the INSERT INTO . . . SELECT FROM syntax with LONG datatypes unless you are using the TO_LOB function to insert the LONG data into a LOB column. You shouldn't be using LONG datatypes any more anyway! LOBs have much more functionality than LONGs ever had, without the limitations.

Of course, you don't need to simply insert the value in a selected column. You can modify the column using any of the appropriate string, date, or number functions within the SELECT statement. The results of those functions are what will be inserted. You can attempt to insert a value in a column that exceeds its width (for character datatypes) or its magnitude (for number datatypes). You have to fit the value within the constraints you defined on your columns. These attempts will produce a "value too large for column" or "mismatched datatype" error message. If you now query the COMFORT table for the city of Walpole, the results you get will be the records you inserted:

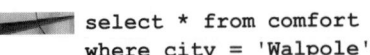

```
select * from comfort
where city = 'Walpole';


CITY            SAMPLE_DATE NOON MIDNIGHT PRECIPITATION
-------------   ----------- ---- -------- -------------
Walpole         21-MAR-11   56.7     43.8             0
Walpole         22-JUN-11   56.7     43.8             0
Walpole         22-JUN-11   56.7     43.8             0
Walpole         23-SEP-11   86.3     72.1
Walpole         22-DEC-11   -7.2     -1.2           3.9
```

Two records are shown for 22-JUN-11 because one of them has a time component. Use the TO_CHAR function to see the time:

```
select city, sample_date,
    to_char(sample_date,'hh24:mi:ss') as timeofday, noon
from comfort
where city = 'Walpole';


CITY            SAMPLE_DATE TIMEOFDAY NOON
-------------   ----------- --------- ----
Walpole         21-MAR-11   00:00:00  56.7
Walpole         22-JUN-11   00:00:00  56.7
Walpole         22-JUN-11   01:35:00  56.7
Walpole         23-SEP-11   00:00:00  86.3
Walpole         22-DEC-11   00:00:00  -7.2
```

Using the APPEND Hint to Improve INSERT Performance

As you will see in Chapter 46, Oracle uses an optimizer to determine the most efficient way to perform each SQL command. For INSERT statements, Oracle tries to insert each new record into an existing block of data already allocated to the table. This execution plan optimizes the use of space required to store the data. However, it may not provide adequate performance for an INSERT with a SELECT command that inserts multiple rows. You can improve the execution plan by using the APPEND hint to improve the performance of large inserts. The APPEND hint tells the database to find the last block into which the table's data has ever been inserted. The new records are then inserted starting in the first block of the new extent allocated above the table's high watermark (HWM), which will be explained shortly. Furthermore, the inserted data is written directly to the datafiles, bypassing the data block buffer cache. As a result, there is much less space management work for the database to do during the INSERT, which means the INSERT may complete faster when the APPEND hint is used.

You specify the APPEND hint within the INSERT command. A hint looks like a comment—it starts with /* and ends with */. The only difference is that the starting set of characters includes a plus sign (+) before the name of the hint (but no spaces between the asterisk and the plus sign, otherwise the hint is ignored). The following example shows an INSERT command whose data is appended to the table (above the HWM):

```
insert /*+ append */ into bookshelf (title)
   select title from book_order
   where title not in (select title from bookshelf);
```

The records from the BOOK_ORDER table will be inserted into the BOOKSHELF table. Instead of attempting to reuse space within the BOOKSHELF table, the new records will be placed at the end of the table's physical storage space.

Because the new records will not attempt to reuse available space that the table has already used, the space requirements for the BOOKSHELF table may increase. In general, you should use the APPEND hint only when inserting large volumes of data into tables with little reusable space. The point at which appended records are inserted is called the table's *high watermark*, or HWM—and the only way to reset the high watermark is to TRUNCATE the table. Because TRUNCATE deletes all records and cannot be rolled back, you should make sure you have a backup of the table's data prior to performing the TRUNCATE. See TRUNCATE in the Alphabetical Reference for further details.

ROLLBACK, COMMIT, and AUTOCOMMIT

When you insert, update, or delete data from the database, you can reverse, or *roll back,* the work you've done. This capability can be very important when an error is discovered. The process of committing or rolling back work is controlled by two SQL*Plus commands: COMMIT and ROLLBACK. Additionally, SQL*Plus has the facility to commit your work automatically without your explicitly telling it to do so. This is controlled by the AUTOCOMMIT feature of SET. Like other SET features, you can SHOW it like this:

```
show autocommit
```

```
autocommit OFF
```

OFF is the default, and in almost all cases, it's the preferred mode. You can also specify a number for the AUTOCOMMIT value; this value determines the number of commands after which Oracle issues a COMMIT. Having AUTOCOMMIT OFF means INSERT, UPDATE, and DELETE operations are not made final until you COMMIT them:

```
commit;
```

```
commit complete
```

Until you COMMIT, only you can see how your work affects the tables. Anyone else with access to these tables continues to get the old information. You will see *new* information whenever you SELECT from the table. Your work is, in effect, in a "staging" area, which you interact with until you COMMIT. You can perform quite a large number of INSERT, UPDATE, and DELETE operations and still undo the work (return the tables to the way they used to be) by issuing this command:

```
rollback;
```

```
rollback complete
```

However, the message "rollback complete" can be misleading. It means only that Oracle has rolled back any work that hasn't been committed. If you COMMIT a series of transactions, either explicitly with the word COMMIT or implicitly by another action, the "rollback complete" message won't really mean anything.

Using SAVEPOINTs

You can use *SAVEPOINTs* to roll back portions of your current set of transactions. Consider the following commands:

```
insert into comfort
values ('Walpole', '22-apr-11',50.1, 24.8, 0);
```

```
savepoint a;
```

```
insert into comfort
values ('Walpole', '27-may-11',63.7, 33.8, 0);
```

```
savepoint b;
```

```
insert into comfort
values ('Walpole', '07-aug-11',83.0, 43.8, 0);
```

Now, SELECT the data from COMFORT for Walpole:

```
select * from comfort
where city = 'Walpole';
```

CITY	SAMPLE_DATE	NOON	MIDNIGHT	PRECIPITATION
Walpole	21-MAR-11	56.7	43.8	0
Walpole	22-JUN-11	56.7	43.8	0
Walpole	22-JUN-11	56.7	43.8	0
Walpole	23-SEP-11	86.3	72.1	
Walpole	22-DEC-11	-7.2	-1.2	3.9
Walpole	22-APR-11	50.1	24.8	0
Walpole	27-MAY-11	63.7	33.8	0
Walpole	07-AUG-11	83	43.8	0

The output shows the five former records plus the three new rows we've added. Now roll back just the last INSERT:

```
rollback to savepoint b;
```

```
rollback complete.
```

If you now query COMFORT, you'll see that the last INSERT has been rolled back, but the others are still there:

```
select * from comfort
where city = 'Walpole';
```

CITY	SAMPLE_DATE	NOON	MIDNIGHT	PRECIPITATION
Walpole	21-MAR-11	56.7	43.8	0
Walpole	22-JUN-11	56.7	43.8	0
Walpole	22-JUN-11	56.7	43.8	0
Walpole	23-SEP-11	86.3	72.1	
Walpole	22-DEC-11	-7.2	-1.2	3.9
Walpole	22-APR-11	50.1	24.8	0
Walpole	27-MAY-11	63.7	33.8	0

The last two records are still not committed; you need to execute a COMMIT command or another command to force a commit to occur. You can still roll back the second INSERT (to SAVEPOINT A) or roll back all the INSERTs (via a ROLLBACK command).

Implicit COMMIT

The actions that will force a COMMIT to occur, even without your instructing it to, are QUIT, EXIT (the equivalent of QUIT), and any Data Definition Language (DDL) command, such as CREATE TABLE or ALTER INDEX. Using any of these commands forces a COMMIT.

Auto ROLLBACK

If you've completed a series of INSERT, UPDATE, or DELETE operations but have not yet explicitly or implicitly committed them, and you experience serious difficulties, such as a computer failure, Oracle automatically roll backs any uncommitted work. If the machine or database goes down, Oracle does the rollback as cleanup work the next time the database is brought back up.

Multitable INSERTs

You can perform multiple inserts in a single command. You can perform all the inserts unconditionally or you can specify conditions—using a WHEN clause to tell Oracle how to manage the multiple inserts. If you specify ALL, then all the WHEN clauses are evaluated; specifying FIRST tells Oracle to skip subsequent WHEN clauses after it finds one that is true for the row being evaluated. You can also use an ELSE clause to tell Oracle what to do if none of the WHEN clauses evaluates to true.

To illustrate this functionality, let's create a new table with a slightly different structure than COMFORT:

```
create table comfort_test (
   city          varchar2(13) not null,
   sample_date   date not null,
   measure       varchar2(10),
   value         number(3,1)
);
```

We'll insert multiple rows into COMFORT_TEST for each record in COMFORT—its MEASURE column will have values such as 'Midnight', 'Noon', and 'Precip', allowing us to store a greater number of measures for each city on each sample date.

Now populate COMFORT_TEST with data from COMFORT, unconditionally:

```
insert all
        into comfort_test (city, sample_date, measure, value)
      values (city, sample_date, 'Noon', noon)
        into comfort_test (city, sample_date, measure, value)
      values (city, sample_date, 'Midnight', midnight)
        into comfort_test (city, sample_date, measure, value)
      values (city, sample_date, 'Precip', precipitation)
select city, sample_date, noon, midnight, precipitation
from comfort
where city = 'Keene';

12 rows inserted.
```

This INSERT tells Oracle to insert multiple rows for each row returned from the COMFORT table. The query of COMFORT returns four rows. The first INTO clause inserts the 'Noon' value, along with a text string of 'Noon' into the MEASURE column. The second INTO clause inserts the 'Midnight' value, and the third inserts the 'Precip' value, as shown in the query of COMFORT_TEST following the INSERT:

```
select * from comfort_test;

CITY           SAMPLE_DATE MEASURE      VALUE
-------------  ----------- ----------   -----
Keene          21-MAR-11   Noon          39.9
Keene          22-JUN-11   Noon          85.1
Keene          23-SEP-11   Noon          99.8
Keene          22-DEC-11   Noon          -7.2
Keene          21-MAR-11   Midnight      -1.2
Keene          22-JUN-11   Midnight      66.7
Keene          23-SEP-11   Midnight      82.6
Keene          22-DEC-11   Midnight      -1.2
Keene          21-MAR-11   Precip         4.4
Keene          22-JUN-11   Precip         1.3
Keene          23-SEP-11   Precip
Keene          22-DEC-11   Precip         3.9

12 rows selected
```

What if you had used the FIRST keyword instead of the ALL keyword? Unless you use WHEN clauses, you can't use the FIRST keyword. The following example shows the use of the WHEN clause to restrict which INSERTs are performed within the multi-INSERT command. For this example, the ALL keyword is used:

```
insert all
        when noon > 80 then
          into comfort_test (city, sample_date, measure, value)
        values (city, sample_date, 'Noon', noon)
```

```
   when midnight > 70 then
     into comfort_test (city, sample_date, measure, value)
   values (city, sample_date, 'Midnight', midnight)
   when precipitation is not null then
     into comfort_test (city, sample_date, measure, value)
   values (city, sample_date, 'Precip', precipitation)
select city, sample_date, noon, midnight, precipitation
from comfort
where city = 'Keene';
```

```
6 rows inserted.
```

What six rows were inserted? The two Noon values met this condition:

```
   when noon > 80 then
```

The one Midnight value met this condition:

```
   when midnight > 70 then
```

And the three Precipitation values met this condition:

```
   when precipitation is not null then
```

You can see the results in COMFORT_TEST:

```
select * from comfort_test;
```

CITY	SAMPLE_DATE	MEASURE	VALUE
Keene	22-JUN-11	Noon	85.1
Keene	23-SEP-11	Noon	99.8
Keene	23-SEP-11	Midnight	82.6
Keene	21-MAR-11	Precip	4.4
Keene	22-JUN-11	Precip	1.3
Keene	22-DEC-11	Precip	3.9

What if you had used FIRST instead?

```
insert first
     when noon > 80 then
       into comfort_test (city, sample_date, measure, value)
     values (city, sample_date, 'noon', noon)
     when midnight > 70 then
       into comfort_test (city, sample_date, measure, value)
     values (city, sample_date, 'midnight', midnight)
     when precipitation is not null then
       into comfort_test (city, sample_date, measure, value)
     values (city, sample_date, 'precip', precipitation)
select city, sample_date, noon, midnight, precipitation
from comfort
where city = 'Keene';
```

```
4 rows inserted.
```

In this case, four rows are inserted:

```
select * from comfort_test;

CITY          SAMPLE_DATE MEASURE     VALUE
------------- ----------- ----------  -----
Keene         21-MAR-11   precip       4.4
Keene         22-DEC-11   precip       3.9
Keene         22-JUN-11   noon        85.1
Keene         23-SEP-11   noon        99.8
```

What happened to the Midnight value? Only one record passed the Midnight WHEN clause:

```
        when midnight > 70 then
```

This record also passed the Noon WHEN clause:

```
        when noon > 80 then
```

Therefore, its Noon value (99.8) was inserted. Because the FIRST keyword was used, and the condition that was evaluated first (Noon) was true, Oracle did not check the rest of the conditions for that row. The same process happened to the Precip measures—the other non-NULL Precipitation value was on the same record as the Noon reading of 85.1.

What if none of the conditions had been met? To show that option, let's create a third table, COMFORT2, with the same structure as COMFORT:

```
drop table comfort2;
create table comfort2 (
city             varchar2(13) not null,
sample_date      date not null,
noon             number(3,1),
midnight         number(3,1),
precipitation    number
);
```

Now, we'll execute an INSERT for all cities (using the FIRST clause) along with an ELSE clause specifying that any rows that fail the conditions will be placed into the COMFORT2 table. For this example, the WHEN conditions are changed to limit the number of rows that pass the conditions:

```
delete from comfort_test;
delete from comfort2;
commit;
insert first
        when noon > 80 then
          into comfort_test (city, sample_date, measure, value)
        values (city, sample_date, 'Noon', noon)
        when midnight > 100 then
          into comfort_test (city, sample_date, measure, value)
        values (city, sample_date, 'Midnight', midnight)
        when precipitation > 100 then
          into comfort_test (city, sample_date, measure, value)
        values (city, sample_date, 'precip', precipitation)
     else
```

```
         into comfort2
select city, sample_date, noon, midnight, precipitation
  from comfort
where city = 'Keene';
```

```
4 rows inserted.
```

The feedback tells you how many rows were created, but not which table they were created in. The total reported is for all INSERTs combined. In this case, two records were inserted into COMFORT_TEST and two were inserted into COMFORT2 because of the ELSE condition:

```
select * from comfort_test;
```

```
CITY            SAMPLE_DATE MEASURE    VALUE
-------------   ----------- ---------- -----
Keene           22-JUN-11   Noon       85.1
Keene           23-SEP-11   Noon       99.8
```

```
select * from comfort2;
```

```
CITY            SAMPLE_DATE NOON MIDNIGHT PRECIPITATION
-------------   ----------- ---- -------- -------------
Keene           21-MAR-11   39.9    -1.2          4.4
Keene           22-DEC-11   -7.2    -1.2          3.9
```

DELETE

Removing a row or rows from a table requires the DELETE command, as seen in the examples in the last section. The WHERE clause is essential to removing only the rows you intend. DELETE without a WHERE clause empties the table completely. The following command deletes the Walpole entries from the COMFORT table:

```
delete from comfort where city = 'Walpole';
```

Of course, a WHERE clause in a DELETE, just as in an UPDATE or a SELECT that is part of an INSERT, can contain as much logic as any SELECT statement, and may include subqueries, unions, intersects, and so on. You can always roll back a bad INSERT, UPDATE, or DELETE, but to make sure you are doing the right thing, you really should experiment with SELECT before actually making the change to the database.

Now that you've just deleted the rows where CITY = 'Walpole', you can test the effect of that DELETE with a simple query:

```
select * from comfort
where city = 'Walpole';
```

Now roll back the DELETE and run the same query:

```
rollback;
rollback complete.
```

```
select * from comfort
where city = 'Walpole';
```

```
CITY          SAMPLE_DATE NOON MIDNIGHT PRECIPITATION
------------- ----------- ---- -------- -------------
Walpole       21-MAR-11   56.7    43.8               0
Walpole       22-JUN-11   56.7    43.8               0
Walpole       22-JUN-11   56.7    43.8               0
Walpole       23-SEP-11   86.3    72.1
Walpole       22-DEC-11   -7.2    -1.2             3.9
Walpole       22-APR-11   50.1    24.8               0
Walpole       27-MAY-11   63.7    33.8               0

7 rows selected.
```

This illustrates that recovery is possible, so long as a COMMIT hasn't occurred. If the changes have been committed, you may be able to use flashback queries (see Chapter 29) to retrieve the data.

An additional command for deleting records, TRUNCATE, does not behave the same as DELETE. Whereas DELETE allows you to commit or roll back the deletion, TRUNCATE automatically deletes all records from the table. The action of the TRUNCATE command cannot be rolled back or committed; the truncated records are unrecoverable. You cannot perform a flashback query to see data that has been truncated. See the TRUNCATE command in the Alphabetical Reference for further details.

UPDATE

UPDATE requires setting specific values for each column you want to change, and specifying which row or rows you want to affect by using a carefully constructed WHERE clause:

```
update comfort set precipitation = .5, midnight = 73.1
where city = 'Keene'
  and sample_date = '22-dec-11';
```

Here is the effect, shown in the 22-DEC-11 record:

```
select * from comfort
  where city = 'Keene';
```

```
CITY          SAMPLE_DATE NOON MIDNIGHT PRECIPITATION
------------- ----------- ---- -------- -------------
Keene         21-MAR-11   39.9    -1.2             4.4
Keene         22-JUN-11   85.1    66.7             1.3
Keene         23-SEP-11   99.8    82.6
Keene         22-DEC-11   -7.2    73.1             0.5

4 rows selected.
```

What if you later discover that the thermometer used in Keene consistently reports its temperatures too high by one degree? You also can do calculations, string functions, and almost any other legitimate function in setting a value for the UPDATE (just as you can for an INSERT or in the WHERE clause of a DELETE). Here, each temperature in Keene is decreased by one degree:

```
update comfort set midnight = midnight - 1, noon = noon - 1
where city = 'Keene';
```

```
4 rows updated.
```

Here is the effect of the UPDATE:

```
select * from comfort
where city = 'Keene';
```

```
CITY           SAMPLE_DATE NOON MIDNIGHT PRECIPITATION
-------------  ----------- ---- -------- -------------
Keene          21-MAR-11   38.9    -2.2            4.4
Keene          22-JUN-11   84.1    65.7            1.3
Keene          23-SEP-11   98.8    81.6
Keene          22-DEC-11   -8.2    72.1            0.5
```

NOTE
If your UPDATE statement violates the column definitions or constraints, it will fail. In this case, setting NOON or MIDNIGHT to values of 100 or greater violates the numeric scale of the columns.

As with DELETE, the WHERE clause is critical for UPDATE operations. Without one, every row in the table will be updated. With an improperly constructed WHERE clause, the wrong rows will be updated, often in ways that are hard to discover or fix, especially if your work has been committed. Always SET FEEDBACK ON when doing UPDATEs, and look at the feedback to be sure the number of rows updated is what you expected it to be. Query the rows after you UPDATE to see if the expected change took place.

UPDATE with Embedded SELECT

It is possible to set values in an UPDATE by embedding a SELECT statement right in the middle of it. Note that this SELECT has its own WHERE clause, picking out the temperature for the city of Manchester from the WEATHER table, and the UPDATE has its own WHERE clause to affect just the city of Keene on a certain day:

```
update comfort set midnight =
        (select temperature
          from weather
          where city = 'Manchester')
where city = 'Keene'
  and sample_date = '22-dec-11';
```

```
1 rows updated.
```

Here is the effect of the UPDATE:

```
select * from comfort
where city = 'Keene';
```

CITY	SAMPLE_DATE	NOON	MIDNIGHT	PRECIPITATION
Keene	21-MAR-11	38.9	-2.2	4.4
Keene	22-JUN-11	84.1	65.7	1.3
Keene	23-SEP-11	98.8	81.6	
Keene	22-DEC-11	-8.2	66	0.5

4 rows selected.

When using a subquery with an UPDATE, you must be certain that the subquery will return no more than one row for each of the rows to be updated; otherwise, the UPDATE will fail. See Chapter 13 for details on correlated subqueries.

You also can use an embedded SELECT to UPDATE multiple columns at once. The columns must be in parentheses and separated by a comma, as shown here:

```
update comfort set (noon, midnight) =
       (select humidity, temperature
        from weather
        where city = 'Manchester')
where city = 'Keene'
  and sample_date = '22-dec-11';
```

1 rows updated.

Here is the result of the UPDATE:

```
select * from comfort
where city = 'Keene';
```

CITY	SAMPLE_DATE	NOON	MIDNIGHT	PRECIPITATION
Keene	21-MAR-11	38.9	-2.2	4.4
Keene	22-JUN-11	84.1	65.7	1.3
Keene	23-SEP-11	98.8	81.6	
Keene	22-DEC-11	98	66	0.5

The row for 22-DEC-11 was updated with the values from Manchester for NOON and MIDNIGHT.

UPDATE with NULL

You also can update a table and set a column equal to NULL. This is the sole instance of using the equal sign with NULL instead of the keyword IS. For example,

```
update comfort set noon = null
where city = 'Keene'
  and sample_date = '22-dec-11';
```

1 row updated.

will set the NOON temperature to NULL for Keene on December 22, 2011.

NOTE
The primary issues with INSERT, UPDATE, and DELETE are careful construction of WHERE clauses to affect (or INSERT) only the rows you really want and the normal use of SQL functions within these INSERT, UPDATE, and DELETE operations. It is extremely important that you exercise caution about committing work before you are certain it is correct. These commands extend the power of Oracle well beyond simple queries, and they allow you to directly manipulate data.

MERGE

You can use the MERGE command to perform INSERT and UPDATE operations in a single table using a single command. Based on the conditions you specify, Oracle takes the source data—either a table, view, or query—and updates existing values if the conditions are met. If the conditions are not met, the row is inserted.

For example, we can change the rows in the COMFORT2 table created earlier in this chapter:

```
delete from comfort2;
insert into comfort2
   values ('Keene', '21-mar-11',55, -2.2, 4.4);
insert into comfort2
   values ('Keene', '22-dec-11',55, 66, 0.5);
insert into comfort2
   values ('Keene', '16-may-11', 55, 55, 1);
commit;
```

The data in COMFORT2 should now look like this:

```
select * from comfort2;
```

CITY	SAMPLE_DATE	NOON	MIDNIGHT	PRECIPITATION
Keene	21-MAR-11	55	-2.2	4.4
Keene	22-DEC-11	55	66	0.5
Keene	16-MAY-11	55	55	1

The Keene data in COMFORT is

```
select * from comfort where city = 'Keene';
```

CITY	SAMPLE_DATE	NOON	MIDNIGHT	PRECIPITATION
Keene	21-MAR-11	38.9	-2.2	4.4
Keene	22-JUN-11	84.1	65.7	1.3
Keene	23-SEP-11	98.8	81.6	
Keene	22-DEC-11		66	0.5

With COMFORT2 as the data source, we can now perform a MERGE on the COMFORT table. For the rows that match (the 21-MAR-11 and 22-DEC-11 entries), we'll update the Noon values in

COMFORT. The rows that exist only in COMFORT2 (the 16-MAY-11 row) are inserted into COMFORT. The following listing shows the command to use:

```
merge into comfort c1
using (select city, sample_date,noon,midnight,precipitation
       from comfort2)   c2
   on (c1.city = c2.city and c1.sample_date=c2.sample_date)
when matched then
      update set noon = c2.noon
when not matched then
      insert (c1.city, c1.sample_date, c1.noon,
              c1.midnight, c1.precipitation)
      values (c2.city, c2.sample_date, c2.noon,
              c2.midnight, c2.precipitation);
```

```
3 rows merged.
```

The output tells you the number of rows processed from the source table, but does not tell you how many rows were inserted or updated. You can see the changes by querying COMFORT (note the NOON=55 rows):

```
select * from comfort where city = 'Keene';
```

```
CITY           SAMPLE_DATE NOON MIDNIGHT PRECIPITATION
-------------- ----------- ---- -------- -------------
Keene          21-MAR-11     55    -2.2            4.4
Keene          22-JUN-11   84.1    65.7            1.3
Keene          23-SEP-11   98.8    81.6
Keene          22-DEC-11     55      66            0.5
Keene          16-MAY-11     55      55              1
```

Take a look at the command to see how this was accomplished. In the first line, the target table is named and given an alias of C1:

```
merge into comfort c1
```

In the next two lines, the USING clause provides the source data for the MERGE, and the source is given the alias C2:

```
using (select city, sample_date,noon,midnight,precipitation
       from comfort2)   c2
```

The condition for the MERGE is then specified in the ON clause. If the source data's CITY and SAMPLE_DATE values match those in the target table, the data is updated. The WHEN MATCHED THEN clause, followed by an UPDATE command, tells Oracle what columns to update in the source table:

```
   on (c1.city = c2.city and c1.sample_date=c2.sample_date)
when matched then
      update set noon = c2.noon
```

If there is no match, then the row should be inserted, as specified in the WHEN NOT MATCHED clause:

```
when not matched then
      insert (c1.city, c1.sample_date, c1.noon,
            c1.midnight, c1.precipitation)
      values (c2.city, c2.sample_date, c2.noon,
            c2.midnight, c2.precipitation);
```

You can use the MERGE command to simplify operations in which many rows are inserted and updated from a single source. As with all UPDATE operations, you should be careful to use the appropriate WHERE clauses in the USING clause of your MERGE commands.

NOTE
You cannot UPDATE a column that is referenced in the ON condition clause.

In the MERGE command, you can specify either an UPDATE clause, an INSERT clause, or both. A DELETE option is also available in the WHEN MATCHED section.

To insert all the source rows into the table, you can use a *constant filter predicate* in the ON clause condition. An example of a constant filter predicate is ON (0=1). Oracle recognizes such a predicate and makes an unconditional insert of all source rows into the table. No join is performed during the MERGE command if a constant filter predicate is provided.

You can include a DELETE clause within the UPDATE portion of the MERGE command. The DELETE clause (with its own WHERE clause) can delete rows in the destination table that are updated by the MERGE. The DELETE WHERE clause evaluates the *updated* value, not the *original* value in the destination table. If a row of the destination table meets the DELETE WHERE condition but is not included in the set of rows acted on by the MERGE (as defined by the ON condition), then it is not deleted. Here's an example:

```
merge into comfort c1
using (select city, sample_date, noon, midnight,
         precipitation from comfort2)   c2
   on (c1.city = c2.city and c1.sample_date=c2.sample_date)
when matched then
   update set noon = c2.noon
   delete where ( precipitation is null )
when not matched then
   insert (c1.city, c1.sample_date, c1.noon,
         c1.midnight,c1.precipitation)
   values (c2.city, c2.sample_date, c2.noon,
         c2.midnight,c2.precipitation) ;
```

Clearly, these commands can become very complex very quickly. In this example, we are performing a conditional UPDATE and a conditional DELETE on the rows that are updated, along with a conditional INSERT of other rows. You can incorporate very complex business logic into a single command, substantially enhancing the capability of the standard INSERT, UPDATE, and DELETE commands.

Handling Errors

By default, all rows in a single transaction either succeed or fail. If you insert a large volume of rows in a single INSERT AS SELECT, an error in one row forces the whole INSERT to fail. You can override this behavior via the use of an *error log* table, along with special syntax within your commands to tell the database how to process the errors. Oracle then automatically logs the entries that failed and the reasons why each row failed while the transaction itself succeeds. In a sense this is a multitable insert—the rows that can be inserted are added to the targeted table, whereas the rows that fail are inserted into the error log table.

To use this approach, you must first create an error log table whose structure is based on the table you are updating. Oracle provides a procedure named CREATE_ERROR_LOG within the DBMS_ERRLOG package that creates an error log for each table you specify. The format for the CREATE_ERROR_LOG procedure is

```
DBMS_ERRLOG.CREATE_ERROR_LOG (
    dml_table_name          IN VARCHAR2,
    err_log_table_name      IN VARCHAR2 := NULL,
    err_log_table_owner     IN VARCHAR2 := NULL,
    err_log_table_space     IN VARCHAR2 := NULL,
    skip_unsupported        IN BOOLEAN := FALSE);
```

The parameters for CREATE_ERROR_LOG are

Parameter	Description
dml_table_name	The name of the table on which to base the error logging table. The name can be fully qualified (for example, BOOKSHELF or PRACTICE. BOOKSHELF). If a name component is enclosed in double quotes, it is be uppercased.
err_log_table_name	The name of the error logging table you will create. The default is the first 25 characters in the name of the DML table prefixed with "ERR$_" (such as ERR$_BOOKSHELF).
err_log_table_owner	The name of the owner of the error logging table. You can specify the owner in the dml_table_name parameter. Otherwise, the schema of the current connected user is used.
err_log_table_space	The tablespace the error logging table is created in. If this parameter is not specified, the default tablespace for the user owning the error logging table is used.
skip_unsupported	When this parameter is set to TRUE, column types that are not supported by error logging are skipped over and not added to the error logging table. When it is set to FALSE (the default), an unsupported column type causes the procedure to terminate.

For the BOOKSHELF table, you can create an error log table via the following command:

```
execute dbms_errlog.create_error_log('bookshelf','errlog');
```

When you insert rows into the BOOKSHELF table, you can use the LOG ERRORS clause to redirect errors:

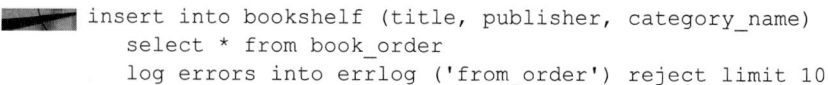

```
insert into bookshelf (title, publisher, category_name)
   select * from book_order
   log errors into errlog ('from_order') reject limit 10;
```

You can use the REJECT LIMIT clause to specify an upper limit for the number of errors that can be logged before the INSERT command fails. The default REJECT LIMIT is 0; you can set it to UNLIMITED.

If errors are encountered during the INSERT, they are written to the ERRLOG table. They are tagged with the value 'from_order' as specified in the LOG ERRORS clause shown in the listing. In addition to the BOOKSHELF table columns, the ERRLOG table has two additional columns:

- ORA_ERR_MESG$ contains the Oracle error message number and message text for the error encountered.

- ORA_ERR_TAG$ includes the tag specified in the INTO clause, as shown in the prior listing.

There is one entry in the ERRLOG table for each errant row, and the full row values are stored in the ERRLOG table.

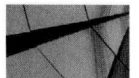

NOTE
The tag for the command can be a literal, a number, a bind variable, or a function expression, such as TO_CHAR(SYSDATE).

If there are errors and the INSERT completes, Oracle will not return any error code. You will need to check the error log table to determine whether any rows failed during the intended INSERT.

Commands will fail without invoking the error log capability for the following conditions:

- Violated deferred constraints

- Any direct-path INSERT or MERGE operation that raises a unique constraint or index violation

- Any UPDATE or MERGE operation that raises a unique constraint or index violation

You cannot track errors in the error logging table for LONG, LOB, or object type columns. However, the table that is the target of the DML operation can contain these types of columns.

CHAPTER
16

DECODE and CASE: IF, THEN, and ELSE in SQL

The DECODE function is without doubt one of the most powerful in Oracle's SQL. It is one of several extensions Oracle added to the standard SQL language. This chapter explores a number of ways that DECODE can be used, including the generation of "crosstab" reports. You can also use the CASE function and the COALESCE function to execute complex logical tests within your SQL statements.

DECODE and CASE are often used to pivot data—that is, to turn rows of data into columns of a report. In this chapter, you will see how to use DECODE, CASE, and the PIVOT operator (introduced in Oracle 11g) to generate crosstab reports.

IF, THEN, ELSE

In programming and logic, a common construction for evaluating conditions and performing certain actions based on those conditions is in the pattern *if, then, else*. For example, *if* this day is a Saturday, *then* Adah will play at home; *if* this day is a Sunday, *then* Adah will go to her grandparents' home; *if* this day is a holiday, *then* Adah will go over to Aunt Dora's; *else* Adah will go to school. In each case, "this day" is tested, and if it is one of a list of certain days, then a certain result follows, or else (if it is none of those days), another result follows. DECODE follows this kind of logic. Chapter 11 demonstrated the basic structure and usage of DECODE.

Here is DECODE's format:

```
DECODE(value,if1,then1,if2,then2,if3,then3,. . . ,else)
```

Here, *value* represents any column in a table (regardless of datatype) or any result of a computation (an *expression*), such as one date minus another, a SUBSTR of a character column, one number times another, and so on. *value* is tested for each row. If *value* equals *if1*, then the result of the DECODE is *then1*; if *value* equals *if2*, then the result of the DECODE is *then2*. This continues for virtually as many if-then pairs as you can construct. If *value* equals none of the *ifs*, then the result of the DECODE is *else*. Each of the *ifs* and *thens* as well as the *else* also can be a column or the result of a function or computation. You can have up to 255 elements within the parentheses.

Let's consider the checkout history for the bookshelf, as recorded in the BOOKSHELF_CHECKOUT table:

```
column name format a16
column title format a24 word_wrapped
set pagesize 60

select * from bookshelf_checkout;
```

NAME	TITLE	CHECKOUT_	RETURNED_
Jed Hopkins	Innumeracy	01-JAN-12	22-JAN-12
Gerhardt Kentgen	Wonderful Life	02-JAN-12	02-FEB-12
Dorah Talbot	Either/Or	02-JAN-12	10-JAN-12
Emily Talbot	Anne Of Green Gables	02-JAN-12	20-JAN-12
Pat Lavay	The Shipping News	02-JAN-12	12-JAN-12
Roland Brandt	The Shipping News	12-JAN-12	12-MAR-12
Roland Brandt	The Discoverers	12-JAN-12	01-MAR-12

Roland Brandt	West With The Night	12-JAN-12	01-MAR-12
Emily Talbot	Midnight Magic	20-JAN-12	03-FEB-12
Emily Talbot	Harry Potter And The Goblet Of Fire	03-FEB-12	14-FEB-12
Pat Lavay	The Mismeasure Of Man	12-JAN-12	12-FEB-12
Dorah Talbot	Polar Express	01-FEB-12	15-FEB-12
Dorah Talbot	Good Dog, Carl	01-FEB-12	15-FEB-12
Gerhardt Kentgen	The Mismeasure Of Man	13-FEB-12	05-MAR-12
Fred Fuller	John Adams	01-FEB-12	01-MAR-12
Fred Fuller	Truman	01-MAR-12	20-MAR-12
Jed Hopkins	To Kill A Mockingbird	15-FEB-12	01-MAR-12
Dorah Talbot	My Ledger	15-FEB-12	03-MAR-12
Gerhardt Kentgen	Midnight Magic	05-FEB-12	10-FEB-12

NOTE
Your output may contain an extra blank line due to word wrapping.
Extra blank lines are not shown here for readability.

As you look through the checkout list, you realize that some of the books were checked out for a rather long time. To highlight the readers who keep books for the longest time, you can order this list by the number of days checked out:

```
select name, title, returned_date-checkout_date daysout
from bookshelf_checkout
order by daysout desc;
```

NAME	TITLE	DAYSOUT
Roland Brandt	The Shipping News	60
Roland Brandt	West With The Night	49
Roland Brandt	The Discoverers	49
Gerhardt Kentgen	Wonderful Life	31
Pat Lavay	The Mismeasure Of Man	31
Fred Fuller	John Adams	29
Jed Hopkins	Innumeracy	21
Gerhardt Kentgen	The Mismeasure Of Man	21
Fred Fuller	Truman	19
Emily Talbot	Anne Of Green Gables	18
Dorah Talbot	My Ledger	17
Jed Hopkins	To Kill A Mockingbird	15
Dorah Talbot	Polar Express	14
Dorah Talbot	Good Dog, Carl	14
Emily Talbot	Midnight Magic	14
Emily Talbot	Harry Potter And The Goblet Of Fire	11
Pat Lavay	The Shipping News	10
Dorah Talbot	Either/Or	8
Gerhardt Kentgen	Midnight Magic	5

But is it specific readers who are the issue, or is it that there are certain categories of books that take longer to read? Multiple variables are involved, and looking at them in isolation may lead to incorrect decisions. What is the average number of days out for the books in each category?

```
select b.category_name,
       min(bc.returned_date-bc.checkout_date) minout,
       max(bc.returned_date-bc.checkout_date) maxout,
       avg(bc.returned_date-bc.checkout_date) avgout
from bookshelf_checkout bc, bookshelf b
where bc.title = b.title
group by b.category_name
order by b.category_name;
```

CATEGORY_NAME	MINOUT	MAXOUT	AVGOUT
ADULTFIC	10	60	28.3333333
ADULTNF	17	49	29.6666667
ADULTREF	8	8	8
CHILDRENFIC	5	18	12
CHILDRENPIC	14	14	14

This is more useful, but it doesn't factor in the impact of the different people checking out books in these categories. To accomplish that, you could use an additional level of grouping, but the results will be easier to use if you create a *crosstab* report. The following listing generates a report that shows the minimum, maximum, and average days out by person, by category. This query uses the DECODE function to perform the calculations. Three borrowers are used for the purposes of this example.

```
select b.category_name,
       max(decode(bc.name, 'Fred Fuller',
                  bc.returned_date-bc.checkout_date,null)) maxff,
       avg(decode(bc.name, 'Fred Fuller',
                  bc.returned_date-bc.checkout_date,null)) avgff,
       max(decode(bc.name, 'Dorah Talbot',
                  bc.returned_date-bc.checkout_date,null)) maxdt,
       avg(decode(bc.name, 'Dorah Talbot',
                  bc.returned_date-bc.checkout_date,null)) avgdt,
       max(decode(bc.name, 'Gerhardt Kentgen',
                  bc.returned_date-bc.checkout_date,null)) maxgk,
       avg(decode(bc.name, 'Gerhardt Kentgen',
                  bc.returned_date-bc.checkout_date,null)) avggk
from bookshelf_checkout bc, bookshelf b
where bc.title = b.title
group by b.category_name
order by b.category_name;
```

CATEGORY_NA	MAXFF	AVGFF	MAXDT	AVGDT	MAXGK	AVGGK
ADULTFIC						
ADULTNF	29	24	17	17	31	26
ADULTREF			8	8		
CHILDRENFIC					5	5
CHILDRENPIC			14	14		

The output now shows the borrowers across the top—Fred Fuller's maximum checkout time is the MAXFF column; Dorah Talbot's is the MAXDT column; and Gerhardt Kentgen's is the MAXGK column. The output shows that the ADULTNF category has the longest average checkout time for each of the borrowers shown, and that in Gerhardt Kentgen's case, it is significantly longer than the average checkout time in the other category he checked out.

How was this report generated? In the query, the grouping is by CATEGORY_NAME. The MAXFF column query is shown here:

```
select b.category_name,
       max(decode(bc.name, 'Fred Fuller',
               bc.returned_date-bc.checkout_date,null)) maxff,
```

DECODE is performing an *if-then* check on the data: If the BC.NAME column value in a row is 'Fred Fuller', then calculate the difference between the RETURNED_DATE and CHECKOUT_DATE; else, return a NULL. That list of values is then evaluated and the maximum value is returned. A similar set of operations returns the average checkout time for Fred Fuller:

```
       avg(decode(bc.name, 'Fred Fuller',
           bc.returned_date-bc.checkout_date,null)) avgff,
```

Replacing Values via DECODE

In the last example, DECODE was used to return values conditionally, depending on the name of the person who checked out a book. You can also use DECODE to replace values in a list. For example, selecting the category names from BOOKSHELF yields the following:

```
select distinct category_name from bookshelf
order by category_name;

CATEGORY_NA
-----------
ADULTFIC
ADULTNF
ADULTREF
CHILDRENFIC
CHILDRENNF
CHILDRENPIC
```

To replace these names, you could join BOOKSHELF to CATEGORY and select PARENT_CATEGORY and SUB_CATEGORY from the CATEGORY table. If the list of categories is static, you could avoid the join to the CATEGORY table and perform the replacement via a DECODE function, as shown in the following listing (note how DECODE supports multiple *if-then* combinations within a single call).

```
select distinct
       DECODE(Category_name,'ADULTFIC','Adult Fiction',
                            'ADULTNF','Adult Nonfiction',
                            'ADULTREF','Adult Reference',
                            'CHILDRENFIC','Children Fiction',
                            'CHILDRENNF','Children Nonfiction',
                            'CHILDRENPIC','Children Picturebook',
                            Category_name)
```

```
from BOOKSHELF
order by 1;

DECODE(CATEGORY_NAME
--------------------
Adult Fiction
Adult Nonfiction
Adult Reference
Children Fiction
Children Nonfiction
Children Picturebook
```

In this case, the data is static; for volatile data, hard-coding the translations into the application code would not be an acceptable programming practice. The technique shown here is useful for transaction-processing systems in which you are trying to minimize the number of database calls performed. In this example, there is no database access required to change 'ADULTNF' to 'Adult Nonfiction'; the change occurs within the DECODE function call. Note that if any other categories are found, the *else* condition in the DECODE function returns the original CATEGORY_NAME column value.

DECODE Within DECODE

You can place DECODE function calls within other DECODE function calls. Let's say you want to charge late fees, with different late-fee rates for different categories of books. Adult category books may be kept later, but the penalty for late days will be higher.

Start with a basic flat rate charge of $0.20 per day for books checked out for more than 14 days:

```
column name format a16
column title format a20 word_wrapped
column daysout format 999.99 heading 'days out'
column dayslate format 999.99 heading 'days late'
set pagesize 60
break on name

select name, title, returned_date,
       returned_date-checkout_date as daysout /* count days */,
       returned_date-checkout_date -14  dayslate,
       (returned_date-checkout_date -14)*0.20  latefee
from bookshelf_checkout
where returned_date-checkout_date > 14
order by name, checkout_date;
```

NAME	TITLE	RETURNED_	days out	days late	LATEFEE
Dorah Talbot	My Ledger	03-MAR-12	17.00	3.00	.6
Emily Talbot	Anne Of Green Gables	20-JAN-12	18.00	4.00	.8
Fred Fuller	John Adams	01-MAR-12	29.00	15.00	3
	Truman	20-MAR-12	19.00	5.00	1
Gerhardt Kentgen	Wonderful Life	02-FEB-12	31.00	17.00	3.4
	The Mismeasure Of Man	05-MAR-12	21.00	7.00	1.4

Jed Hopkins	Innumeracy	22-JAN-12	21.00	7.00	1.4
	To Kill A Mockingbird	01-MAR-12	15.00	1.00	.2
Pat Lavay	The Mismeasure Of Man	12-FEB-12	31.00	17.00	3.4
Roland Brandt	The Discoverers	01-MAR-12	49.00	35.00	7
	The Shipping News	12-MAR-12	60.00	46.00	9.2
	West With The Night	01-MAR-12	49.00	35.00	7

For books in the Adult categories, increase the allowed days late to 21 days. This won't change the number of days out, but it will change the DAYSLATE column calculation. Because CATEGORY_NAME is not a column in BOOKSHELF_CHECKOUT, this modification also requires the addition of the BOOKSHELF table to the FROM clause:

```
select bc.name, bc.title, bc.returned_date,
     bc.returned_date-bc.checkout_date as daysout /*count days*/,
     decode(substr(category_name,1,5), 'ADULT',
          bc.returned_date-bc.checkout_date -21,
          bc.returned_date-bc.checkout_date -14 ) dayslate,
     decode(substr(category_name,1,5), 'ADULT',
          (bc.returned_date-bc.checkout_date -21)*0.30,
          (bc.returned_date-bc.checkout_date -14)*0.20 ) latefee
from bookshelf_checkout bc, bookshelf b
where bc.title = b.title
  and bc.returned_date-bc.checkout_date >
        decode(substr(category_name,1,5), 'ADULT',21,14)
order by bc.name, bc.checkout_date;
```

NAME	TITLE	RETURNED_	days out	days late	LATEFEE
Emily Talbot	Anne Of Green Gables	20-JAN-12	18.00	4.00	.8
Fred Fuller	John Adams	01-MAR-12	29.00	8.00	2.4
Gerhardt Kentgen	Wonderful Life	02-FEB-12	31.00	10.00	3
Pat Lavay	The Mismeasure Of Man	12-FEB-12	31.00	10.00	3
Roland Brandt	The Shipping News	12-MAR-12	60.00	39.00	11.7
	West With The Night	01-MAR-12	49.00	28.00	8.4
	The Discoverers	01-MAR-12	49.00	28.00	8.4

In the SELECT clause, the query logic for the DAYSLATE column is

```
     decode(substr(category_name,1,5), 'ADULT',
          bc.returned_date-bc.checkout_date -21,
          bc.returned_date-bc.checkout_date -14 ) dayslate
```

In DECODE's *if-then-else* format, this says, "If the first five characters of the CATEGORY_NAME column match the string 'ADULT', then subtract 21 from the number of days late; otherwise, subtract 14 days." The LATEFEE calculation uses similar logic. The WHERE clause uses DECODE to determine the limiting value for the rows returned—for ADULT category books, allow 21 days; otherwise, allow 14:

```
  and bc.returned_date-bc.checkout_date >
        decode(substr(category_name,1,5), 'ADULT',21,14)
```

Now add an additional rule: for adult fiction category books, the late fee will be double the late fee for other adult books. From the last query, the calculation for LATEFEE is

```
decode(substr(category_name,1,5), 'ADULT',
       (bc.returned_date-bc.checkout_date -21)*0.30,
       (bc.returned_date-bc.checkout_date -14)*0.20 ) latefee
```

The new rule requires an additional category check within the DECODE function already performed. The new LATEFEE calculation is shown here:

```
decode(substr(category_name,1,5), 'ADULT',
       decode(substr(category_name,6,3),'FIC',
       (bc.returned_date-bc.checkout_date -21)*0.60,
       (bc.returned_date-bc.checkout_date -21)*0.30),
       (bc.returned_date-bc.checkout_date -14)*0.20 ) latefee
```

Reading through the preceding listing, the first DECODE function tells Oracle that if the first five letters of the CATEGORY_NAME are 'ADULT', then perform the second DECODE function. The second DECODE tells Oracle that if letters 6, 7, and 8 of the CATEGORY_NAME are 'FIC', then the late fee is $0.60 per day after the 21st day; otherwise, it is $0.30 per day after the 21st day. At that point, the inner DECODE function completes. For the first DECODE function, the *else* clause (for non-ADULT category books) then specifies the late-fee calculation. The query and result are shown in the following listing; you can see the impact by comparing the LATEFEE column for "The Shipping News" in this report and the last report:

```
select bc.name, bc.title, bc.returned_date,
       bc.returned_date-bc.checkout_date as daysout /*count days*/,
       decode(substr(category_name,1,5), 'ADULT',
              bc.returned_date-bc.checkout_date -21,
              bc.returned_date-bc.checkout_date -14 ) dayslate,
       decode(substr(category_name,1,5), 'ADULT',
              decode(substr(category_name,6,3),'FIC',
              (bc.returned_date-bc.checkout_date -21)*0.60,
              (bc.returned_date-bc.checkout_date -21)*0.30),
              (bc.returned_date-bc.checkout_date -14)*0.20 ) latefee
from bookshelf_checkout bc, bookshelf b
where bc.title = b.title
  and bc.returned_date-bc.checkout_date >
      decode(substr(category_name,1,5), 'ADULT',21,14)
order by bc.name, bc.checkout_date;
```

NAME	TITLE	RETURNED_	days out	days late	LATEFEE
Emily Talbot	Anne Of Green Gables	20-JAN-12	18.00	4.00	.8
Fred Fuller	John Adams	01-MAR-12	29.00	8.00	2.4
Gerhardt Kentgen	Wonderful Life	02-FEB-12	31.00	10.00	3
Pat Lavay	The Mismeasure Of Man	12-FEB-12	31.00	10.00	3
Roland Brandt	The Shipping News	12-MAR-12	60.00	39.00	23.4
	West With The Night	01-MAR-12	49.00	28.00	8.4
	The Discoverers	01-MAR-12	49.00	28.00	8.4

You can nest DECODEs within other DECODEs to support complex logic within your data processing. For example, you may choose to print one column if it has a non-NULL value and a second column if the first is NULL. With DECODE, that is a simple function call:

```
DECODE(column1, NULL, column2, column1)
```

If *column1* is NULL, *column2* will be returned; otherwise, *column1*'s non-NULL value will be returned. You could also use NVL or the COALESCE and NULLIF functions to perform similar logic.

COALESCE returns the first non-NULL value encountered in a list of values. The preceding DECODE example could be rewritten as

```
COALESCE(column1, column2)
```

NOTE
COALESCE can take more than two arguments, but NVL cannot.

Because COALESCE's name does not clearly convey its usage, be sure to provide comments within your code to explain the logical tests performed. In this example, you want to do an analysis on the ADDRESS table using the best information available for selected last names. If an ADDRESS entry has a zip code, return that. If there is no zip code, return the city and state. If there is no city or state, return the first name. This example shows the columns referenced in the COALESCE statement to see how it works on each row.

```
select lastname, city, state, zip,
    coalesce(to_char(zip),city||nvl2(state,' ',null)||state,firstname)
    best_location
from address
where lastname in ('Zack','Yarrow','Adams');
```

LASTNAME	CITY	STATE	ZIP	BEST_LOCATION
Adams				Jack
Zack	Baltimore	MD		Baltimore MD
Yarrow			949414302	949414302

Greater Than and Less Than in DECODE

DECODE supports logic checks, but how do you do numeric comparisons in this format? The simplest solution is often to use the SIGN function. SIGN returns a 1 if the number is positive, 0 if the number is 0, and –1 if the number is negative. Because SIGN operates on numbers, you can evaluate any function that returns a number, including date arithmetic.

Let's modify the LATEFEE business rule again. Using the same base calculation, we'll modify the outcome so we won't collect late fees that are less than or equal to $4.00. Here is the original LATEFEE calculation:

```
decode(substr(category_name,1,5), 'ADULT',
    decode(substr(category_name,6,3),'FIC',
    (bc.returned_date-bc.checkout_date -21)*0.60,
    (bc.returned_date-bc.checkout_date -21)*0.30),
    (bc.returned_date-bc.checkout_date -14)*0.20 ) latefee
```

If that value is less than 4, we return a 0; otherwise, we return the calculated value. To implement this requirement, subtract 4 from the LATEFEE value; if the result is positive (its SIGN value is 1), return that result; otherwise, return a 0.

```
decode(sign(
        decode(substr(category_name,1,5), 'ADULT',
            decode(substr(category_name,6,3),'FIC',
            (bc.returned_date-bc.checkout_date -21)*0.60,
            (bc.returned_date-bc.checkout_date -21)*0.30),
            (bc.returned_date-bc.checkout_date -14)*0.20 ) -4),
        1,
        decode(substr(category_name,1,5), 'ADULT',
            decode(substr(category_name,6,3),'FIC',
            (bc.returned_date-bc.checkout_date -21)*0.60,
            (bc.returned_date-bc.checkout_date -21)*0.30),
            (bc.returned_date-bc.checkout_date -14)*0.20 ),
        0) latefee
```

Building from a simple foundation, this series of DECODE function calls allows you to perform very complex logic on the LATEFEE calculations. The first DECODE evaluates the SIGN of the next DECODE function result when 4 is subtracted from it. If that number is positive, the calculated late fee is returned; otherwise, a 0 is returned. The following listing shows this calculation and the output that results:

```
select bc.name, bc.title, bc.returned_date,
        bc.returned_date-bc.checkout_date as daysout /*count days*/,
        decode(substr(category_name,1,5), 'ADULT',
            bc.returned_date-bc.checkout_date -21,
            bc.returned_date-bc.checkout_date -14 ) dayslate,
decode(sign(
        decode(substr(category_name,1,5), 'ADULT',
            decode(substr(category_name,6,3),'FIC',
            (bc.returned_date-bc.checkout_date -21)*0.60,
            (bc.returned_date-bc.checkout_date -21)*0.30),
            (bc.returned_date-bc.checkout_date -14)*0.20 ) -4),
        1,
        decode(substr(category_name,1,5), 'ADULT',
            decode(substr(category_name,6,3),'FIC',
            (bc.returned_date-bc.checkout_date -21)*0.60,
            (bc.returned_date-bc.checkout_date -21)*0.30),
            (bc.returned_date-bc.checkout_date -14)*0.20 ),
        0) latefee
from bookshelf_checkout bc, bookshelf b
where bc.title = b.title
  and bc.returned_date-bc.checkout_date >
        decode(substr(category_name,1,5), 'ADULT',21,14)
order by bc.name, bc.checkout_date;
```

```
NAME                TITLE                 RETURNED_ days out days late   LATEFEE
------------------- --------------------- --------- -------- --------- ----------
Emily Talbot        Anne Of Green Gables  20-JAN-12    18.00      4.00          0
Fred Fuller         John Adams            01-MAR-12    29.00      8.00          0
```

```
Gerhardt Kentgen Wonderful Life      02-FEB-12   31.00    10.00        0
Pat Lavay        The Mismeasure Of   12-FEB-12   31.00    10.00        0
                 Man
Roland Brandt    The Shipping News   12-MAR-12   60.00    39.00     23.4
                 West With The Night 01-MAR-12   49.00    28.00      8.4
                 The Discoverers     01-MAR-12   49.00    28.00      8.4
```

You can eliminate the display of the first four rows (with $0 late fees) by making a similar modification to the WHERE clause.

Using CASE

You can use the CASE function in place of DECODE. The CASE function uses the keywords WHEN, THEN, ELSE, and END to indicate the logic path followed. In general, SQL using the CASE function is wordier than the equivalent DECODE but may be easier to read and maintain.

Consider this simple DECODE example from earlier in this chapter:

```
select distinct
       decode(category_name,'ADULTFIC','Adult Fiction',
                            'ADULTNF','Adult Nonfiction',
                            'ADULTREF','Adult Reference',
                            'CHILDRENFIC','Children Fiction',
                            'CHILDRENNF','Children Nonfiction',
                            'CHILDRENPIC','Children Picturebook',
                            category_name)
    from bookshelf;
```

The equivalent CASE function is

```
select distinct
       case category_name
          when  'ADULTFIC' then 'Adult Fiction'
          when  'ADULTNF' then 'Adult Nonfiction'
          when  'ADULTREF' then 'Adult Reference'
          when  'CHILDRENFIC' then 'Children Fiction'
          when  'CHILDRENNF' then 'Children Nonfiction'
          when  'CHILDRENPIC' then 'Children Picturebook'
          else category_name
       end
from bookshelf
order by 1;

CASECATEGORY_NAMEWHE
--------------------
Adult Fiction
Adult Nonfiction
Adult Reference
Children Fiction
Children Nonfiction
Children Picturebook
```

CASE evaluates the first WHEN clause and returns a match if the limiting condition is met. As with DECODE, you can nest CASE function calls. How would you perform the LATEFEE column calculations using CASE?

The DECODE function began by calculating a higher rate for ADULT category books:

```
decode(substr(category_name,1,5), 'ADULT',
    (bc.returned_date-bc.checkout_date -21)*0.30,
    (bc.returned_date-bc.checkout_date -14)*0.20 ) latefee
```

The CASE equivalent is

```
case substr(category_name,1,5)
    when 'ADULT' then (bc.returned_date-bc.checkout_date -21)*0.30
    else (bc.returned_date-bc.checkout_date -14)*0.20
end
```

The second rule (ADULTFIC books have doubled late fees) requires a nested CASE command:

```
case substr(category_name,1,5)
    when 'ADULT' then
        case substr(category_name,6,3)
            when 'FIC' then (bc.returned_date-bc.checkout_date -21)*0.60
            else (bc.returned_date-bc.checkout_date -21)*0.30
        end
    else (bc.returned_date-bc.checkout_date -14)*0.20
end
```

This is more complex, but the logic is very easy to follow and is usually simpler to maintain than the equivalent DECODE clause. Now consider the final condition: If the calculated late fee is less than or equal to $4, return a 0. Because we are using the CASE function, we do not need to use a SIGN function—we can just use a "<" comparison as part of the command processing. The following example shows how to add this check: An additional CASE function is added, and the inner CASE function call is enclosed in parentheses. The result is compared to $4:

```
case when
    (case substr(category_name,1,5)
      when 'ADULT' then
          case substr(category_name,6,3)
              when 'FIC' then (bc.returned_date-bc.checkout_date -21)*0.60
              else (bc.returned_date-bc.checkout_date -21)*0.30
              end
      else (bc.returned_date-bc.checkout_date -14)*0.20
    end)
    < 4 then 0
```

The ELSE clause for this CASE function call is the same as the inner CASE execution—it calculates the late fee:

```
else
    case substr(category_name,1,5)
      when 'ADULT' then
          case substr(category_name,6,3)
```

```
            when 'FIC' then (bc.returned_date-bc.checkout_date -21)*0.60
            else (bc.returned_date-bc.checkout_date -21)*0.30
        end
    else (bc.returned_date-bc.checkout_date -14)*0.20
  end
end
```

The full query is shown in the following listing, along with its output:

```
column latefee format 999.99

select bc.name, bc.title, bc.returned_date,
    bc.returned_date-bc.checkout_date as daysout /*count days*/,
    decode(substr(category_name,1,5), 'ADULT',
        bc.returned_date-bc.checkout_date -21,
        bc.returned_date-bc.checkout_date -14 ) dayslate,
case when
   (case substr(category_name,1,5)
     when 'ADULT' then
        case substr(category_name,6,3)
            when 'FIC' then (bc.returned_date-bc.checkout_date -21)*0.60
            else (bc.returned_date-bc.checkout_date -21)*0.30
        end
     else (bc.returned_date-bc.checkout_date -14)*0.20
   end)
   < 4 then 0 else
   case substr(category_name,1,5)
     when 'ADULT' then
        case substr(category_name,6,3)
            when 'FIC' then (bc.returned_date-bc.checkout_date -21)*0.60
            else (bc.returned_date-bc.checkout_date -21)*0.30
            end
     else (bc.returned_date-bc.checkout_date -14)*0.20
   end
end  as latefee
 from bookshelf_checkout bc, bookshelf b
 where bc.title = b.title
   and bc.returned_date-bc.checkout_date >
       decode(substr(category_name,1,5), 'ADULT',21,14)
 order by bc.name, bc.checkout_date;
```

NAME	TITLE	RETURNED_	days out	days late	LATEFEE
Emily Talbot	Anne Of Green Gables	20-JAN-12	18.00	4.00	.00
Fred Fuller	John Adams	01-MAR-12	29.00	8.00	.00
Gerhardt Kentgen	Wonderful Life	02-FEB-12	31.00	10.00	.00
Pat Lavay	The Mismeasure Of Man	12-FEB-12	31.00	10.00	.00
Roland Brandt	The Shipping News	12-MAR-12	60.00	39.00	23.40
	West With The Night	01-MAR-12	49.00	28.00	8.40
	The Discoverers	01-MAR-12	49.00	28.00	8.40

Comparing the CASE version to the DECODE version earlier in this chapter, you can see that the CASE command is six lines longer, but it's simpler to read and maintain. CASE offers a powerful alternative to DECODE—and both CASE and DECODE provide solid solutions when you need to perform logic within your queries.

Using PIVOT

As of Oracle Database 11g, you can use the PIVOT and UNPIVOT operators to work with "crosstab" data. In a *crosstab* report, rows of data are displayed in separate columns. For example, earlier in this chapter values in rows of data (names) were used to populate columns of a report. In this query, the second and third columns are the Fred Fuller columns, the fourth and fifth are the Dorah Talbot columns, and so on. In the second column, the DECODE function checks to see if the NAME column value is 'Fred Fuller'. If it is, the calculation is performed; otherwise, a NULL is returned.

```
column category_name format a11

select b.category_name,
       max(decode(bc.name, 'Fred Fuller',
                  bc.returned_date-bc.checkout_date,null)) maxff,
       avg(decode(bc.name, 'Fred Fuller',
                  bc.returned_date-bc.checkout_date,null)) avgff,
       max(decode(bc.name, 'Dorah Talbot',
                  bc.returned_date-bc.checkout_date,null)) maxdt,
       avg(decode(bc.name, 'Dorah Talbot',
                  bc.returned_date-bc.checkout_date,null)) avgdt,
       max(decode(bc.name, 'Gerhardt Kentgen',
                  bc.returned_date-bc.checkout_date,null)) maxgk,
       avg(decode(bc.name, 'Gerhardt Kentgen',
                  bc.returned_date-bc.checkout_date,null)) avggk
  from bookshelf_checkout bc, bookshelf b
  where bc.title = b.title
  group by b.category_name
  order by b.category_name;
```

CATEGORY_NA	MAXFF	AVGFF	MAXDT	AVGDT	MAXGK	AVGGK
ADULTFIC						
ADULTNF	29	24	17	17	31	26
ADULTREF			8	8		
CHILDRENFIC					5	5
CHILDRENPIC			14	14		

In the output, the data has been *pivoted*—rows of entries (such as those that contain 'Fred Fuller' in the NAME column) have been transformed by the DECODE function so separate rows (for separate names) are now displayed as separate columns. The following example further illustrates the pivoting by eliminating the join to the BOOKSHELF table:

```
column category_name format a11
```

```
select max(decode(bc.name, 'Fred Fuller',
         bc.returned_date-bc.checkout_date,null)) maxfred,
     max(decode(bc.name, 'Dorah Talbot',
         bc.returned_date-bc.checkout_date,null)) maxdorah
from bookshelf_checkout bc;
```

```
  MAXFRED    MAXDORAH
---------- ----------
       29          17
```

The PIVOT operator simplifies the generation of this type of report.

```
select * from (
   select name, returned_date, checkout_date
   from bookshelf_checkout bc
)
pivot
(
     max(returned_date-checkout_date)
     for name in ('Fred Fuller','Dorah Talbot')
);
```

```
'Fred Fuller' 'Dorah Talbot'
------------- --------------
         29            17
```

The PIVOT query selects the data from the BOOKSHELF_CHECKOUT table and then pivots it, using the limiting conditions in the FOR clause to determine which rows to evaluate. In this case, it takes the rows for which the NAME is 'Fred Fuller' and calculates the maximum difference between the RETURNED_DATE and CHECKOUT_DATE for the first column, and uses the 'Dorah Talbot' rows for the second column.

The two queries produce the identical results—the maximum time a book was checked out for two different people, presented as separate columns in the report. The code for the PIVOT operator is simpler to read and simpler to manage. If, for example, you wanted to look at additional people's records, modifying the PIVOT code is simple—just add the names to the IN clause and new columns will appear in the output; in the DECODE version, you need to add the code for each new column separately.

Along with a PIVOT operator, Oracle Database 11*g* also provides an UNPIVOT operator. As you would expect, UNPIVOT performs the opposite function, turning columns into rows. Note that UNPIVOT cannot always undo a PIVOT operation; for example, if the PIVOT operation performs an aggregate function, you cannot use UNPIVOT to generate the detail rows that were aggregated.

The following example illustrates the use of the UNPIVOT operator. In this example, five separate values are selected from the DUAL table—one for each vowel in the alphabet. Each of those selections would normally be displayed as a separate column (in this case, named V1, V2, V3, V4, and V5). The UNPIVOT operator then transforms those columns into rows for the output.

```
select value
from
(
    (
        select
            'a' v1,
            'e' v2,
            'i' v3,
            'o' v4,
            'u' v5
        from DUAL
    )
    unpivot
    (
        value
        for value_type in
            (v1,v2,v3,v4,v5)
    )
)
;
```

The output for this query is shown in the following listing:

```
V
-
a
e
i
o
u
```

You can use the PIVOT and UNPIVOT operators to transform columns into rows and back again, as shown in these examples. In combination with DECODE and CASE, these operators provide powerful tools for the display and manipulation of data.

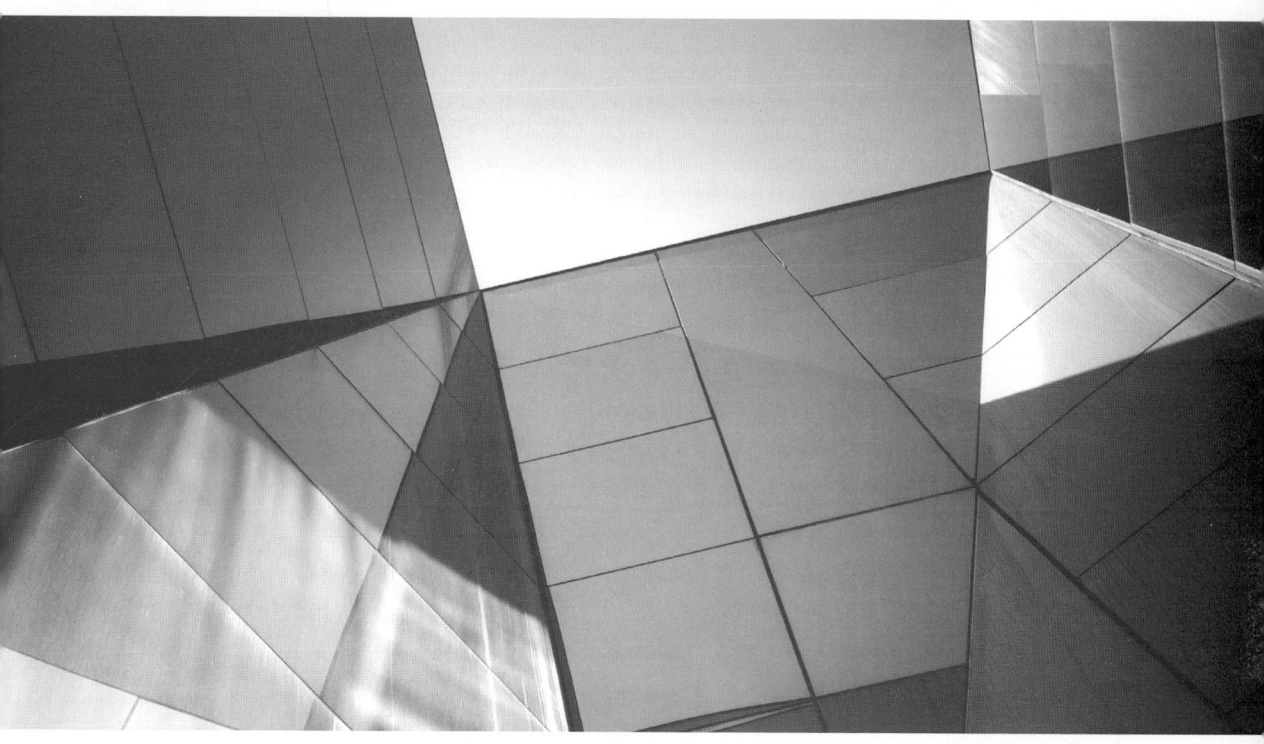

CHAPTER
17

Creating and Managing Tables, Views, Indexes, Clusters, and Sequences

U ntil now, the emphasis of this book has been on using tables. This chapter looks at creating, dropping, and changing tables, creating views, and using options such as index-organized tables. You've seen numerous CREATE TABLE commands up to this point; this chapter will reinforce those examples and show how to use the latest options. You will also see the commands for creating and managing views, indexes, clusters, and sequences.

Creating a Table

Consider the TROUBLE table. This is similar to the COMFORT table discussed earlier in the book, but it is used to track cities with unusual weather patterns.

```
describe trouble
```

```
Name                              Null?     Type
-----------------------------     --------  ------------
CITY                              NOT NULL  VARCHAR2(13)
SAMPLE_DATE                       NOT NULL  DATE
NOON                                        NUMBER(3,1)
MIDNIGHT                                    NUMBER(3,1)
PRECIPITATION                               NUMBER
```

The columns in the TROUBLE table represent three major datatypes in Oracle—VARCHAR2, DATE, and NUMBER. Here is the SQL that created this Oracle table:

```
create table trouble (
city          varchar2(13) not null,
sample_date   date not null,
noon          number(3,1),
midnight      number(3,1),
precipitation number
);
```

These are the basic elements of this command:

- The keywords CREATE TABLE
- The name of the table
- An opening parenthesis
- Column definitions
- A closing parenthesis
- A SQL terminator

The individual column definitions are separated by commas. There is no comma after the last column definition. The table and column names must start with a letter of the alphabet, but may include letters, numbers, and underscores. Names may be 1 to 30 characters in length, must be unique within the table, and cannot be an Oracle reserved word (see "Reserved Words" in the Alphabetical Reference of this book).

If the names are not within double quotes, case does not matter in naming a table. There are no options for DATE datatypes. Varying-length character datatypes must have their maximum length specified. NUMBERs may be either high precision (up to 38 digits) or specified precision, based on the maximum number of digits and the number of places allowed to the right of the decimal (an AMOUNT field for U.S. currency, for instance, would have only two decimal places). Specifying no precision for a NUMBER column allows for any precision up to 38 digits, with any number of digits to the right of the decimal up to 38 digits.

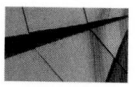

NOTE
Do not enclose table and column names within double quotes; otherwise, case will matter. This can be disastrous for your users or developers.

See Part V of this book for additional CREATE TABLE options for object-relational features.

Character Width and NUMBER Precision

Specifying the maximum length for character (CHAR and VARCHAR2) columns and the precision for NUMBER columns has consequences that you must consider when designing the table. You can correct improper decisions later using the ALTER TABLE command, but the process can be difficult.

Deciding on a Proper Width

A character column that is not wide enough for the data you want to put in it will cause an INSERT to fail and result in an error message:

```
ERROR at line 1:
ORA-12899: value too large for column "HR"."TROUBLE"."CITY"
(actual: 16, maximum: 13)
```

The maximum width for CHAR (fixed-length) columns is 2,000 characters. VARCHAR2 (varying-length character) columns can have up to 32,000 characters (to match the maximum width of a PL/SQL VARCHAR2 variable). In assigning width to a column, allot enough space to allow for all future possibilities. A VARCHAR2(15) for a city name, for instance, is just going to get you in trouble later on. You'll have to either alter the table or truncate or distort the names of some cities.

NOTE
There is no penalty in Oracle for defining a wide VARCHAR2 column. Oracle is clever enough not to store blank spaces at the end of VARCHAR2 columns. The city name "San Francisco", for example, is stored in 13 spaces, even if you've defined the column as VARCHAR2(50). And if a column has nothing in it (NULL), Oracle stores nothing in the column, not even a blank space (it does store a couple of bytes of internal database control information, but this is unaffected by the size you specify for the column). The only effect that choosing a higher number has is in the default SQL*Plus column formatting. SQL*Plus will create a default heading the same width as the VARCHAR2 definition.

Choosing NUMBER Precision

A NUMBER column with incorrect precision has one of two consequences. Oracle will either reject the attempt to INSERT the row of data or will drop some of the data's precision. Here are four INSERT statements and their results:

```
insert into trouble values
    ('Pleasant Lake','21-MAR-11',
    39.99,  -1.31, 3.6);

1 row created.

insert into trouble values
    ('Pleasant Lake','22-jun-11',
    101.44,  86.2, 1.63);
    *
ERROR at line 3:
ORA-01438: value larger than specified precision allows for this column

insert into trouble values
    ('Pleasant Lake','23-sep-11',
    92.85,  79.6, 1.00003);

1 row created.

insert into trouble values
    ('Pleasant Lake','22-dec-11',
    -17.445, -10.4, 2.4);

1 row created.
```

The first, third, and fourth rows were inserted, but the second INSERT failed because 101.44 exceeded the precision set in the CREATE TABLE statement, where NOON was defined as NUMBER(3,1). The 3 here indicates the maximum number of digits Oracle will store. The 1 means that one of those three digits is reserved for a position to the right of the decimal point. Therefore, 12.3 would be a legitimate number, but 123.4 would not be.

Note that the error here is caused by the 101, not the .44, because NUMBER(3,1) defines only two positions available to the left of the decimal point. The .44 will not cause the "value larger than specified precision" error. It is simply rounded to one decimal place. This will be demonstrated shortly, but first, let's look at the results of a query of the four rows we've attempted to INSERT:

```
select * from trouble;

CITY          SAMPLE_DA    NOON MIDNIGHT PRECIPITATION
------------- --------- -------- -------- -------------
Pleasant Lake 21-MAR-11       40     -1.3           3.6
Pleasant Lake 23-SEP-11     92.9     79.6       1.00003
Pleasant Lake 22-DEC-11    -17.4    -10.4           2.4
```

The three rows were successfully inserted; only the problematic row is missing. Oracle never inserted the single row for the INSERT statement that failed.

Rounding During Insertion

Suppose you correct the CREATE TABLE statement and increase the number of digits available for NOON and MIDNIGHT, as shown here:

```
drop table trouble;
create table trouble (
city           varchar2(13) not null,
sample_date    date not null,
noon           number(4,1),
midnight       number(4,1),
precipitation number
);
```

Now the four INSERT statements will all be successful. A query reveals this:

```
insert into trouble values
    ('Pleasant Lake','21-mar-11',
    39.99,  -1.31, 3.6);

insert into trouble values
    ('Pleasant Lake','22-jun-11',
    101.44,  86.2, 1.63);

insert into trouble values
    ('Pleasant Lake','23-sep-11',
    92.85,  79.6, 1.00003);

insert into trouble values
    ('Pleasant Lake','22-dec-11',
    -17.445, -10.4, 2.4);


select * from trouble;

CITY          SAMPLE_DA    NOON MIDNIGHT PRECIPITATION
------------- ---------  -------- -------- -------------
Pleasant Lake 21-MAR-11        40     -1.3          3.6
Pleasant Lake 22-JUN-11     101.4     86.2         1.63
Pleasant Lake 23-SEP-11      92.9     79.6      1.00003
Pleasant Lake 22-DEC-11     -17.4    -10.4          2.4
```

Look at the first INSERT statement. The value for NOON is 39.99. In the query, it is rounded to 40. MIDNIGHT in the INSERT is –1.31. In the query, it is –1.3. Oracle rounds the number based on the digit just to the right of the allowed precision. Table 17-1 shows the effects of precision in several examples. See Chapter 9 for examples of the ROUND function.

Value in INSERT Statement	Actual Value in Table
For precision of NUMBER(4,1)	
123.4	123.4
123.44	123.4
123.45	123.5
123.445	123.4
1234.5	INSERT fails
For precision of NUMBER(4)	
123.4	123
123.44	123
123.45	123
123.445	123
1234.5	1235
12345	INSERT fails
For precision of NUMBER(4,−1)	
123.4	120
123.44	120
123.45	120
123.445	120
125	130
1234.5	1230
12345	INSERT fails
For precision of NUMBER	
123.4	123.4
123.44	123.44
123.45	123.45
123.445	123.445
125	125
1234.5	1234.5
12345.6789012345678	12345.6789012345678

TABLE 17-1. *Effect of Precision on INSERTs*

Defining Constraints within CREATE TABLE

You can use the CREATE TABLE statement to enforce several different kinds of constraints on a table: candidate keys, primary keys, foreign keys, and check conditions. A CONSTRAINT clause can constrain a single column or group of columns in a table. The point of these constraints is to get

Oracle to do most of the work in maintaining the integrity of your database. The more constraints you add to a table definition, the less work you have to do in applications to maintain the data. On the other hand, the more constraints there are in a table, the longer it takes to update the data.

You can specify constraints in one of two ways: as part of the column definition (known as a *column* constraint) or at the end of the CREATE TABLE statement (known as a *table* constraint). Clauses that constrain several columns must be table constraints.

The Candidate Key

A *candidate key* is a combination of one or more columns, the values of which uniquely identify each row of a table. The following listing shows the creation of a UNIQUE constraint for the TROUBLE table:

```
drop table trouble;

create table trouble (
city           varchar2(13) not null,
sample_date    date not null,
noon           number(4,1),
midnight       number(4,1),
precipitation number,
constraint trouble_uq unique (city, sample_date)
);
```

The key for this table is the combination of CITY and SAMPLE_DATE. Notice that both columns are also declared to be NOT NULL. This feature requires you to specify values for certain columns in order for rows to be inserted. Clearly, temperature and precipitation information is not useful without knowing where or when it was collected. This technique is common for columns that are the table's primary key, but it's also useful if certain columns are critical for the row of data to be meaningful. If NOT NULL isn't specified, the column can have NULL values.

When you create a UNIQUE constraint, Oracle creates a unique index to enforce the uniqueness of the values. Within a primary key constraint, at least one of the columns in the primary key for each row must be NOT NULL.

The Primary Key

The *primary key* of a table is one of the candidate keys that you give some special characteristics. You can have only one primary key, and a primary key column cannot contain NULLs.

The following CREATE TABLE statement has the same effect as the previous one, except that you can have several UNIQUE constraints but only one PRIMARY KEY constraint:

```
drop table trouble;
create table trouble (
city           varchar2(13),
sample_date    date,
noon           number(4,1),
midnight       number(4,1),
precipitation number,
constraint trouble_pk primary key (city, sample_date)
);
```

For single-column primary or candidate keys, you can define the key on the column with a column constraint instead of a table constraint:

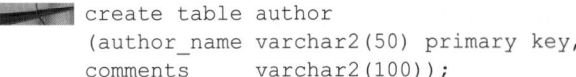

```
create table author
(author_name varchar2(50) primary key,
comments     varchar2(100));
```

In this case, the AUTHOR_NAME column is the primary key, and Oracle will generate a name for the PRIMARY KEY constraint. This is not recommended if you want to enforce a common naming standard for keys, as discussed later in "Naming Constraints."

Designating Index Tablespaces

UNIQUE and PRIMARY KEY constraints create indexes. Unless you tell Oracle differently, those indexes are placed in your default tablespace (tablespaces are described fully in Chapter 22). To specify a different tablespace, use the USING INDEX TABLESPACE clause of the CREATE TABLE command, as shown in the following listing:

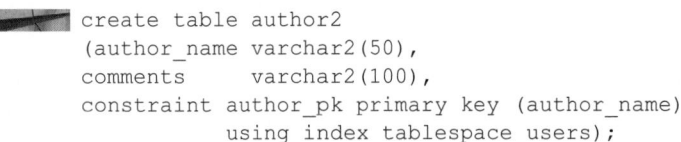

```
create table author2
(author_name varchar2(50),
comments     varchar2(100),
constraint author_pk primary key (author_name)
        using index tablespace users);
```

The index associated with the AUTHOR_PK primary key constraint will be placed in the USERS tablespace. See Chapter 22 for details on managing tablespaces.

NOTE
In most default installations, the USERS tablespace is created and is the default tablespace.

The Foreign Key

A *foreign key* is a combination of columns with values based on the primary key values from another table. A foreign key constraint, also known as a *referential integrity constraint,* specifies that the values of the foreign key correspond to actual values of the primary key in the other table. In the BOOKSHELF table, for example, the CATEGORY_NAME column refers to values for the CATEGORY_NAME column in the CATEGORY table:

```
create table bookshelf
(title          varchar2(100) primary key,
publisher       varchar2(20),
category_name varchar2(20),
rating          varchar2(2),
constraint catfk foreign key (category_name)
references category(category_name));
```

You can refer to a primary or unique key, even in the same table. However, you can't refer to a table in a remote database in the REFERENCES clause. You can use the table form (which is used earlier to create a PRIMARY KEY on the TROUBLE table) instead of the column form to specify foreign keys with multiple columns.

Sometimes you may want to delete these dependent rows when you delete the row they depend on. In the case of BOOKSHELF and CATEGORY, if you delete a CATEGORY_NAME from CATEGORY, you may want to make the matching BOOKSHELF CATEGORY_NAME column values NULL. In another case, you might want to delete the whole row. The clause ON DELETE CASCADE added to the REFERENCES clause tells Oracle to delete the dependent row when you delete the corresponding row in the parent table. This action automatically maintains referential integrity. For more information on the clauses ON DELETE CASCADE and REFERENCES, consult "Integrity Constraint" in the Alphabetical Reference of this book.

The CHECK Constraint

Many columns must have values that are within a certain range or that satisfy certain conditions. With a *CHECK constraint,* you can specify an expression that must always be true for every row in the table. For example, the RATING table stores valid ratings; to limit the available values beyond the limits enforced by the column definition, you can use a CHECK constraint, as shown in the following listing:

```
create table rating_with_check
(rating   number(1) check (rating <= 8),
rating_description varchar2(50));
```

A column-level CHECK constraint can't refer to values in other rows; it can't use the pseudo-columns such as SYSDATE, USER, CURRVAL, NEXTVAL, LEVEL, and ROWNUM. You can use the table constraint form (as opposed to the column constraint form) to refer to multiple columns in a CHECK constraint.

Naming Constraints

You can name your constraints. If you use an effective naming scheme for your constraint names, you will be better able to identify and manage the constraints. The name of a constraint should identify the table it acts on and the type of constraint it represents. For example, the primary key on the TROUBLE table could be named TROUBLE_PK.

You can specify a name for a constraint when you create the constraint. If you do not specify a name for the constraint, Oracle generates a name. Most of Oracle's generated constraint names are of the form SYS_C###### (for example, SYS_C000145). Because the system-generated constraint name does not tell you anything about the table or the constraint, you should name your constraints.

In the following example, the PRIMARY KEY constraint is created and named, as part of the CREATE TABLE command for the TROUBLE table (notice the CONSTRAINT clause):

```
create table trouble (
city            varchar2(13),
sample_date     date,
noon            number(4,1),
midnight        number(4,1),
precipitation number,
constraint trouble_pk primary key (city, sample_date)
);
```

The CONSTRAINT clause of the CREATE TABLE command names the constraint (in this case, TROUBLE_PK). You may use this constraint name later when enabling or disabling constraints.

Dropping Tables

Dropping tables is very simple. You use the words DROP TABLE and the table name, as shown here:

```
drop table trouble;
```

You drop a table only when you no longer need it. In Oracle, the TRUNCATE command lets you remove all the rows in the table and reclaim the space for other uses without removing the table definition from the database.

As of Oracle Database 10g, dropped tables retain their space—they are accessed via the "recycle bin." The dropped object can be recovered until space pressure forces the object to be purged permanently. But if you want to drop a table and remove it from the recycle bin at the same time, use the PURGE clause of the DROP TABLE command:

```
drop table trouble purge;
```

If the table has already been dropped, you can purge it from the recycle bin:

```
purge table trouble;
```

You can also purge all contents of your recycle bin:

```
purge recyclebin;
```

Truncating is also very simple:

```
truncate table trouble;
```

```
Table truncated.
```

Truncating can't be rolled back. If there are triggers that delete rows that depend on rows in the table, truncating does not execute those triggers. You should be *sure* you really want to TRUNCATE before doing it. You can choose to release the table's storage (via the DROP STORAGE clause, the default) or to retain it (via REUSE STORAGE).

Altering Tables

Table definitions can be altered in several ways: by adding a column to an existing table, by changing a column's definition, or by dropping a column. DBAs commonly alter tables in other ways to manage space and memory usage. Adding a column is straightforward, and this process is similar to creating a table. Suppose you decide to add two new columns to the TROUBLE table: CONDITION, which you believe should be NOT NULL, and WIND, for the wind speed. The first attempt starts by creating the table and populating it with a few records:

```
drop table trouble;

create table trouble (
city          varchar2(13),
sample_date   date,
noon          number(4,1),
midnight      number(4,1),
```

```
precipitation number);

insert into trouble values
    ('Pleasant Lake','21-mar-11',
    39.99,  -1.31, 3.6);

insert into trouble values
    ('Pleasant Lake','22-jun-11',
    101.44,  86.2, 1.63);

insert into trouble values
    ('Pleasant Lake','23-sep-11',
    92.85,  79.6, 1.00003);

insert into trouble values
    ('Pleasant Lake','22-dec-11',
    -17.445, -10.4, 2.4);
```

The first attempt at adding the new columns looks like this:

```
alter table trouble add (
condition    varchar2(9) not null,
wind         number(3)
);

alter table trouble add (
             *
ERROR at line 1: ORA-01758: table must be empty to add
mandatory (NOT NULL) column
```

You get an error message because you cannot add a column defined as NOT NULL—when you try to add it, the column won't have anything in it. Each row in the table would have a new empty column defined as NOT NULL.

Prior to Oracle 11g, the ALTER TABLE command's ADD clause works with a NOT NULL column if the table is empty, but usually it is impractical to empty a table of all its rows just to add a NOT NULL column.

The alternative is to first alter the table by adding the column without the NOT NULL restriction:

```
alter table trouble add (
condition    varchar2(9),
wind         number(3)
);

Table altered.
```

Then, you fill the column with data for every row (either with legitimate data or a placeholder until legitimate data can be obtained):

```
update trouble set condition = 'Sunny';
```

Finally, you alter the table again and modify the column definition to NOT NULL:

```
alter table trouble modify (
condition    varchar2(9) not null,
city         varchar2(17)
);
```

```
Table altered.
```

You can add NOT NULL columns to tables that already contain rows. To do so, you must specify a default value for the new column. For very large tables, doing this can present a problem because millions of rows may need to be updated to contain the new column value. Oracle 11g automatically handles this in a way that avoids significant impact on users.

Let's consider again an attempt to add just the CONDITION column to the TROUBLE table:

```
alter table trouble add (condition    varchar2(9) not null);
```

If TROUBLE already has rows, the CONDITION column can't be added because the existing rows would have NULL values for it. The solution is to add a DEFAULT constraint for the CONDITION column:

```
alter table trouble add (condition    varchar2(9)
   default 'Sunny' not null);
```

Oracle now creates the new column, but it will *not* update the existing rows. If a user selects a row that has a NULL value in the CONDITION column, the default value is returned. Oracle's approach solves two problems: It lets you add a NOT NULL column, and it avoids having to update every existing row. In large tables, that can represent a significant savings in terms of the space required to support the transaction size.

Note that the CITY column was also modified to enlarge it to 17 characters (just to show how this is done). When the table is described, it shows this:

```
describe trouble
```

```
Name                              Null?     Type
--------------------------------- --------- ------------
CITY                                        VARCHAR2(17)
SAMPLE_DATE                                 DATE
NOON                                        NUMBER(4,1)
MIDNIGHT                                    NUMBER(4,1)
PRECIPITATION                               NUMBER
CONDITION                         NOT NULL  VARCHAR2(9)
WIND                                        NUMBER(3)
```

The table contains the following:

```
select * from trouble;
```

```
CITY            SAMPLE DA    NOON MIDNIGHT PRECIPITATION CONDITION WIND
--------------- --------- ------- -------- ------------- --------- ----
Pleasant Lake   21-MAR-11      40     -1.3           3.6 Sunny
Pleasant Lake   22-JUN-11   101.4     86.2          1.63 Sunny
```

```
Pleasant Lake   23-SEP-11   92.9     79.6     1.00003 Sunny
Pleasant Lake   22-DEC-11  -17.4    -10.4         2.4 Sunny
```

Here, you see the effect of the changes. CITY is now 17 characters wide instead of 13. CONDITION has been added to the table as NOT NULL and is "Sunny" (temporarily). WIND has been added and is NULL.

To make a NOT NULL column nullable, use the ALTER TABLE command with the NULL clause, as follows:

```
alter table trouble modify
(condition null);
```

The Rules for Adding or Modifying a Column

These are the rules for modifying a column:

- You can increase a character column's width at any time.
- You can increase the number of digits in a NUMBER column at any time.
- You can increase the number of decimal places in a NUMBER column at any time; you can decrease the number of decimal places if the table is empty.

In addition, if a column is NULL for every row of the table, you can make any of these changes:

- You can change the column's datatype.
- You can decrease a character column's width.
- You can decrease the number of digits in a NUMBER column.

You can only change the datatype of a column if the column is empty (NULL) in all rows of the table.

There is one notable exception to the restrictions on datatype changes. Oracle supports the migration of LONG datatype columns to the LOB datatype, even if there is data already in the LONG column. The following listing illustrates this functionality:

```
create table longtest
(col1    number,
longcol  long);

table created.

insert into longtest values (1,'This is a LONG value');

1 row created.

alter table longtest modify (longcol clob);

table altered.

desc longtest
```

```
Name                                     Null?     Type
---------------------------------------- --------  --------
COL1                                               NUMBER
LONGCOL                                            CLOB
```

select longcol from longtest;

```
LONGCOL
----------------------------------
This is a LONG value
```

Creating Read-Only Tables

As of Oracle 11g, you can alter tables to be in read-only or read-write state. This allows you to prevent INSERT, UPDATE, and DELETE operations at the table level (in prior releases, this capability exists at the tablespace level, or it requires the use of views).

To make a table read-only, use the ALTER TABLE command:

```
alter table longtest read only;
```

Attempts to change the records within LONGTEST will then result in an error. To return the table to its prior state, use the READ WRITE clause of the ALTER TABLE command, as shown here:

```
alter table longtest read write;
```

To see the state of a table, query the READ_ONLY column of the USER_TABLES data dictionary view.

While a table is in read-only mode, you can continue to perform SELECT operations against it.

Altering Actively Used Tables

When you issue the ALTER TABLE command, Oracle attempts to acquire a DDL lock on the table. If anyone else is accessing the table at that time, your command will fail—you need to have exclusive access to the table while you are changing its structure. You may need to try to execute your command repeatedly to acquire the lock you need.

As of Oracle 11g, you can use the DDL lock timeout options to work around this problem. You can execute the ALTER SESSION command to set a value for the DDL_LOCK_TIMEOUT parameter, specifying the number of seconds during which Oracle should continually retry your command. The retry attempts continue until the command is successful or the timeout limit is reached, whichever comes first.

To try your command for 60 seconds, issue the following command:

```
alter session set ddl_lock_timeout=60;
```

DBAs can enable this DDL lock at the database level via the ALTER SYSTEM command, as shown next:

```
alter system set ddl_lock_timeout=60;
```

Creating Virtual Columns

As of Oracle 11g, you can create virtual columns in tables rather than storing derived data. You may have a virtual column that is based on other values in the same row (adding two columns together, for instance). In prior versions, you would create a view that performs the function necessary to create the column values. In Oracle 11*g* and 12*c,* you can specify the function as part of the table definition, which allows you to index the virtual column and partition the table by it.

Consider the AUTHOR table:

```
create table author
(author_name  varchar2(50) primary key,
comments      varchar2(100));
```

When values are inserted into AUTHOR, they are inserted in mixed case:

```
insert into author values
('Dietrich Bonhoeffer', 'German Theologian, Killed In A War Camp');

insert into author values
('Robert Bretall','Kierkegaard Anthologist');
```

You can create an additional uppercase column using the GENERATED ALWAYS clause to tell Oracle to create the virtual column:

```
create table author2
(author_name  varchar2(50) primary key,
 comments      varchar2(100),
 mixed_name    varchar2(50)
 generated always as
 (upper(author_name) ) virtual
);
```

The code used to create the virtual column can be complex, including CASE statements and other functions. Note that you do not have to create triggers or other mechanisms to populate the column; Oracle maintains it as a virtual value for each row in the table. The value is not physically stored with the table; it is generated when needed.

NOTE
Attempts to provide a value for the virtual column during INSERTs results in an error.

You can create an index on the virtual column as if it were a standard column in the table. Additionally, you can partition the table based on this column (as described in the next chapter).

Dropping a Column

You can drop a column from a table. Dropping a column is more complicated than adding or modifying a column because of the additional work that Oracle has to do. Just removing the column from the list of columns in the table—so it doesn't show up when you SELECT * from the table—is easy. It's recovering the space that was actually taken up by the column values that is more complex, and potentially very time-consuming for the database. For this reason, you can drop a column immediately, or you can mark it as "unused" and to be dropped at a later time. If the column is dropped immediately, the action may impact performance. If the column is marked as unused, there is no impact on performance. The column can actually be dropped at a later time when the database is less heavily used.

To drop a column, use either the SET UNUSED CLAUSE or the DROP clause of the ALTER TABLE command. You cannot drop a pseudo-column, a column of a nested table, or a partition key column.

In the following example, column WIND is dropped from the TROUBLE table:

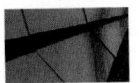

```
alter table trouble drop column wind;
```

Alternatively, you can mark the WIND column as unused:

```
alter table trouble set unused column wind;
```

Marking a column as "unused" does not release the space previously used by the column, until you drop the unused columns:

```
alter table trouble drop unused columns;
```

You can query USER_UNUSED_COL_TABS, ALL_UNUSED_COL_TABS, and DBA_UNUSED_COL_TABS to see all tables with columns marked as unused.

> **NOTE**
> *Once you have marked a column as "unused," you cannot access that column.*

You can drop multiple columns in a single command, as shown in the following listing:

```
alter table trouble drop (condition, wind);
```

> **NOTE**
> *When dropping multiple columns, you should not use the COLUMN keyword of the ALTER TABLE command, as it causes a syntax error. The multiple column names must be enclosed in parentheses, as shown in the preceding listing.*

If the dropped columns are part of primary keys or unique constraints, you need to also use the CASCADE CONSTRAINTS clause as part of your ALTER TABLE command. If you drop a column that belongs to a primary key, Oracle drops both the column and the primary key index.

Creating a Table from a Table

Oracle lets you create a new table on the fly, based on a SELECT statement on an existing table:

```
create table rain_table as
select city, precipitation
  from trouble;
```

```
Table created.
```

> **NOTE**
> *The CREATE TABLE ... AS SELECT ... command (CTAS) will not work if one of the selected columns uses the LONG datatype.*

When the new table is described, it reveals that it has "inherited" its column definitions from the TROUBLE table. A table created in this fashion can include all columns, using an asterisk if you like or a subset of columns from another table. It also can include "invented" columns, which are the product of functions or the combination of other columns, just as in a view. The character column definitions adjust to the size necessary to contain the data in the invented columns. NUMBER columns that specify precision in the source table, but undergo computation in inventing a new column, will simply be NUMBER columns, with no specified precision in the new table.

NOTE
The constraints on the source table, including NOT NULL constraints, are automatically created for the new table.

When the table RAIN_TABLE is described, it shows its column definitions:

```
describe rain_table
```

Name	Null?	Type
CITY		VARCHAR2(17)
PRECIPITATION		NUMBER

When RAIN_TABLE is queried, it contains just the columns and data selected from the TROUBLE table as it existed when RAIN_TABLE was created:

```
select * from rain_table;
```

CITY	PRECIPITATION
Pleasant Lake	3.6
Pleasant Lake	1.63
Pleasant Lake	1.00003
Pleasant Lake	2.4

NOTE
If one of the columns in the query is generated via a formula, you must specify a column alias that Oracle will use as the column name during table creation.

You also can use this technique to create a table with column definitions like those of the source table, but with no rows in it, by building a WHERE clause that selects no rows from the old table:

```
create table rain_empty as
select city, precipitation
from trouble
where 1=2;

Table created.
```

Querying this table shows there is nothing in it:

```
select * from rain_empty;
```

```
no rows selected.
```

You can create a table based on a query without generating *redo log entries* (chronological records of database actions used during database recoveries). Avoiding the generation of these entries is accomplished by using the NOLOGGING keyword in the CREATE TABLE command. When the redo log entries are circumvented in this way, CREATE TABLE command's performance will improve because less work is being done; the larger the table, the greater the impact. However, because the new table's creation is not being written to the *redo log files* (which record the redo log entries), the table will not be re-created if, following a database failure, those redo log files are used to recover the database. Therefore, you should consider performing a backup of the database soon after using the NOLOGGING option if you want to be able to recover the new table.

The following example shows how to use the NOLOGGING keyword during table creations based on queries (by default, table creations based on queries generate redo log entries):

```
create table rain_nolog
nologging
as
select * from trouble;
```

```
Table created.
```

Note that you can specify NOLOGGING at the partition level and at the LOB level (see Chapters 18 and 40). Using NOLOGGING improves the performance of the operations that load the data in the table as long as you're using direct path loading (above the high watermark) with the APPEND or APPEND_VALUES hint.

Creating an Index-Organized Table

An *index-organized table* keeps its data sorted according to the primary key column values for the table. An index-organized table stores its data as if the entire table was stored in an index. Indexes serve two main purposes:

- **To enforce uniqueness**   When a PRIMARY KEY or UNIQUE constraint is created, Oracle creates an index to enforce the uniqueness of the indexed columns.

- **To improve performance**   When a query can use an index, query performance may dramatically improve. See Chapter 46 for details on the conditions under which a query may use an index.

An index-organized table allows you to store its entire data in an index. A normal index only stores the indexed columns; an index-organized table stores all its columns in the index.

To create an index-organized table, use the ORGANIZATION INDEX clause of the CREATE TABLE command, as shown in the following example:

```
create table trouble_iot (
city          varchar2(13),
sample_date   date,
```

```
noon             number(4,1),
midnight         number(4,1),
precipitation number,
constraint trouble_iot_pk primary key (city, sample_date))
organization index;
```

To create TROUBLE as an index-organized table, you must create a PRIMARY KEY constraint on it.

An index-organized table is appropriate if you will always be accessing the TROUBLE data by the CITY and SAMPLE_DATE columns (in the WHERE clauses of your queries). To minimize the amount of active management required for the index, you should use an index-organized table only if the table's data is very static. If the table's data changes frequently, you should use a regular table with indexes as appropriate.

In general, an index-organized table is most effective when the primary key constitutes a large part of the table's columns. If the table contains many frequently accessed columns that are not part of the primary key, the index-organized table will need to access its overflow area repeatedly. Despite this drawback, you may choose to use index-organized tables to take advantage of a key feature that is not available with standard tables: the ability to use the MOVE ONLINE option of the ALTER TABLE command. You can use that option to move a table from one tablespace to another while it is being accessed by INSERT, UPDATE, and DELETE operations. The only other option for moving tables while allowing DML is to use the DBMS_REDEFINITION package, but that is not as easy to use and incurs a lot of overhead to maintain the table changes while moving the rest of the table to another tablespace. You cannot use the MOVE ONLINE option for partitioned index-organized tables. Partitioning is described in the next chapter.

Creating a View

Since you've already seen the techniques for creating a view in prior chapters, they are not reviewed extensively here. However, this section gives several additional points about views that will prove useful.

View stability maintains the accessibility of a view even if the view is re-created or new columns are added to an underlying table. Existing code that references the view does not have to change right away unless the existing code needs the new columns.

If a view is based on a single underlying table, you can INSERT, UPDATE, or DELETE rows in the view. This will actually INSERT, UPDATE, or DELETE rows in the underlying table. There are restrictions on your ability to do this, although the restrictions are quite sensible:

- You cannot INSERT if the underlying table has any NOT NULL columns that don't appear in the view.

- You cannot INSERT or UPDATE if any one of the view's columns referenced in the INSERT or UPDATE contains functions or calculations.

- You cannot INSERT, UPDATE, or DELETE if the view contains GROUP BY, DISTINCT, or a reference to the pseudo-column ROWNUM.

You can INSERT into a view based on multiple tables if Oracle can determine the proper rows to insert into the correct table. In a multi-table view, Oracle determines which of the tables are *key-preserved*. If a view contains enough columns from a table to identify the primary key for that table, the key is preserved, and Oracle may be able to insert rows into the table via the view.

View Stability

Remember that the results of querying a view are built instantly from a table (or tables) when you execute the query. Until that moment, the view has no data of its own, as a table does. It is merely a description (a SQL statement) of what information to pull out of other tables and how to organize it. As a consequence, if a table is dropped, the validity of a view is destroyed. Attempting to query a view where the underlying table has been dropped produces an error message about the view.

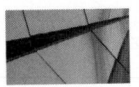

NOTE
The sole exception to this rule is the use of materialized views. In fact, a materialized view is actually a table that stores data you would normally query via a view. Materialized views are described in detail in Chapter 26.

In the following sequence, a view is created on an existing table, the table is dropped, and the view then is queried.

First, the view is created:

```
create view rain_view as
select city, precipitation
from trouble;

View created.
```

The underlying table is dropped:

```
drop table trouble;

Table dropped.
```

The view is queried:

```
select * from rain_view;
              *
ERROR at line 1:
ORA-04063: view "HR.RAIN_VIEW" has errors
```

Similarly, a view is created using the asterisk in the view creation:

```
create or replace view rain_view as
select * from trouble;

View created.
```

But then the underlying table is altered:

```
alter table trouble add (
warning        varchar2(20)
);

Table altered.
```

Despite the change to the view's base table, the view is still valid, but the WARNING column is not visible through it. After altering the table, replace the view so the WARNING column is visible. To re-create a view while keeping in place all the privileges that have been granted for it, use the CREATE OR REPLACE VIEW command, as shown in the following listing. This command replaces the view text of an existing view with the new view text, leaving the old grants on the view unaffected.

```
create or replace view rain_view as
select * from trouble;
```

Using ORDER BY in Views

You can use an ORDER BY in a CREATE VIEW statement, as shown in the following listing based on the re-created TROUBLE table (note that queries against this view may incur a performance penalty because of the additional sort activity they perform):

```
create view trouble_sorted
    as select * from trouble
order by city, sample_date;

View created.

select * from trouble_sorted;
```

CITY	SAMPLE_DA	NOON	MIDNIGHT	PRECIPITATION
Pleasant Lake	21-MAR-11	40	-1.3	3.6
Pleasant Lake	22-JUN-11	101.4	86.2	1.63
Pleasant Lake	23-SEP-11	92.9	79.6	1.00003
Pleasant Lake	22-DEC-11	-17.4	-10.4	2.4

Creating a Read-Only View

You can use the WITH READ ONLY clause of the CREATE VIEW command to prevent users from manipulating records via the view. Consider the RAIN_VIEW view created in the previous section:

```
create or replace view rain_view as
select * from trouble;
```

If a user has the ability to DELETE records from the TROUBLE table, the user could DELETE the TROUBLE records via the RAIN_VIEW view:

```
delete from rain_view;
```

The user could also INSERT or UPDATE the records in the TROUBLE table by performing those operations against the RAIN_VIEW view. If the view is based on a join of multiple tables, the user's ability to UPDATE the view's records is limited; a view's base tables cannot be updated unless only one table is involved in the UPDATE and the updated table's full primary key is included in the view's columns.

To prevent modifications to the base tables via a view, you can use the WITH READ ONLY clause of the CREATE VIEW command. If you use the WITH READ ONLY clause when creating a view, users will *only* be able to SELECT records from the view. Users will be unable to manipulate the records obtained from the view even if the view is based on a single table:

```
create or replace view rain_read_only as
select * from trouble
with read only;
```

You can also use INSTEAD OF triggers to manage the data-manipulation commands executed against views. See Chapter 38 for details on INSTEAD OF triggers.

Indexes

An *index* is a simple concept. It is typically a listing of *keywords* accompanied by the *location* of information on a subject. To find information on indexes, for instance, you look up the word "indexes" in the index at the back of this book. It will give the number of the page you are reading now. The word "indexes" is the key, and the page numbers given point you to the location of discussions about indexes in this book.

Although you could find the information on indexes simply by reading through this book until you encountered the page with the information on it, this method would be slow and time-consuming. Because the index at the back of the book is in alphabetical order, you can quickly go to the appropriate spot in the index (without reading every entry) where "index" is found. If the word is not common, this is quicker than reading through the book from front to back. These same principles apply to Oracle indexes. For example, if you are searching for a particular book, you can query with a limiting condition on the TITLE column:

```
select * from bookshelf
where publisher = 'Scholastic';
```

If BOOKSHELF does not have an index on the PUBLISHER column, Oracle has to read every row in the table until it finds all publishers that match the WHERE clause of your query. If the table is small, that may not cause a performance problem. As the table grows in size, the time required to return all the matching rows to the user may impact the application's performance and the business process it supports.

To speed data retrieval, you can create an index on the PUBLISHER column. Then, when you execute the same query, Oracle first looks in the index, which is sorted, thus finding the publisher named "Scholastic" very quickly (Oracle doesn't read every entry, but jumps directly within close vicinity of the name, much as you would in looking through the index of a book). The index entry then gives Oracle the exact location in the table (and on disk) of the row(s) for that publisher. The standard type of index in Oracle is called a B*-tree index, matching column values to their related ROWIDs.

Indexing an important column (one that's likely to appear in a WHERE clause) generally speeds up Oracle's response to a query. Indexing likewise speeds up queries where two tables are joined, if the columns that are related (by the WHERE clause) are indexed. These are the basics of indexing; the rest of this section shows a number of additional features and issues related to indexing that affect how quickly it works. For the impact of indexes on the optimization of your queries, see Chapter 46.

Creating an Index

You create an index via the CREATE INDEX command. When you designate a primary key or a unique column during table creation or maintenance, Oracle automatically creates a unique index to support that constraint. The full command syntax for CREATE INDEX is shown in the Alphabetical Reference. Its most commonly used format is as follows:

```
CREATE [BITMAP | UNIQUE] INDEX index
ON table(column [,column]. . .) [REVERSE];
```

index must be a unique name and follow the naming conventions of Oracle columns. *table* is simply the name of the table on which the index will be established, and *column* is the name of the column being indexed.

Bitmap indexes allow you to create useful indexes on columns with very few distinct values; see "Creating a Bitmap Index," later in this chapter. The REVERSE keyword tells Oracle to reverse the bytes of the indexed value, which may improve the I/O distribution during the insert of many sequential data values.

You can establish a single index on multiple columns by listing the columns one after the other, separated by commas. For the following examples, the BOOKSHELF_AUTHOR table was created without a primary key:

```
create table bookshelf_author
(title        varchar2(100),
author_name varchar2(50),
constraint titlefk foreign key (title) references bookshelf(title),
constraint author_name_fk foreign key (author_name)
references author(author_name));
```

Enforcing Uniqueness

Recall from Part I that a set of tables is said to be in Third Normal Form if all the columns in each table's rows are dependent only on the primary key. In the BOOKSHELF_AUTHOR table, the primary key is the combination of the columns TITLE and AUTHOR_NAME. In other tables, a primary key might be an employee ID, a client ID, an account number, or, in a bank, a combination of branch number and account number.

In each of these cases, the uniqueness of the primary key is critical. A bank with duplicate account numbers, or a billing system with duplicate client IDs, would wreak havoc as transactions were posted to accounts belonging to different people but having the same primary key (this is why names generally are not commonly used as primary keys—there are too many duplicates). To avoid this danger, have your database help prevent the creation of duplicate primary keys. Oracle offers two facilities that help:

■ You can guarantee the uniqueness of a key through either indexing or constraints.

■ You can use the sequence generators (discussed later in this chapter).

Creating a Unique Index

You can create a unique index on the combination of TITLE and AUTHOR_NAME in the BOOKSHELF_AUTHOR table in one of three ways: by creating a primary key constraint, by creating a unique constraint, or by creating a unique index. If you create a constraint, you will be able to create foreign keys that refer to it. If you create the unique index first, you will still be able to create a primary key on the table—Oracle will use the existing index as the primary key index.

The following listing shows the CREATE INDEX command for this multicolumn index:

```
create unique index ba$title_author
     on bookshelf_author(title, author_name);
```

The primary key method is shown here:

```
alter table bookshelf_author
   add constraint ba_pk primary key (title, author_name);
```

To create a unique constraint, just replace the PRIMARY KEY clause with UNIQUE. When you attempt to create a unique index on a table that already has data in it, the command will fail if any duplicates exist. If the CREATE UNIQUE INDEX statement succeeds, any future attempt to INSERT (or UPDATE) a row that would create a duplicate key will fail and result in this error message:

```
ERROR at line 1:
ORA-00001: unique constraint (BOOKSHELF_AUTHOR.BA_PK) violated
```

When you create an index, it requires storage space. See "Placing an Index in the Database," later in this chapter, for details concerning the location of the created indexes.

Creating a Bitmap Index

To help tune queries that use nonselective columns in their limiting conditions, you can use *bitmap indexes*. Bitmap indexes should only be used if the data is infrequently updated because they add to the cost of all data-manipulation transactions against the tables they index.

NOTE
Bitmap indexes should not be used for tables involved in online transaction-processing applications because of the internal mechanisms Oracle uses to maintain them. Restrict their usage to tables involved in batch transactions.

Bitmap indexes are appropriate when nonselective columns are used as limiting conditions in a query. For example, if there are very few distinct RATING values in a very large BOOKSHELF table, you would not usually create a traditional B*-tree index on RATING, even if it is commonly used in WHERE clauses. However, RATING may be able to take advantage of a bitmap index.

Internally, a bitmap index maps the distinct values for the columns to each record. For this example, assume there are five RATING values (1, 2, 3, 4, and 5) in a very large BOOKSHELF table. Because there are five RATING values, there are five separate bitmap entries for the RATING bitmap index. If the first five rows in the table have a RATING value of 1, and the next five have a RATING value of 2, then the RATING bitmap entries would resemble those shown in the following listing:

```
Rating bitmaps:
    1:  1 1 1 1 1 0 0 0 0 0
    2:  0 0 0 0 0 1 1 1 1 1
    3:  0 0 0 0 0 0 0 0 0 0
    4:  0 0 0 0 0 0 0 0 0 0
    5:  0 0 0 0 0 0 0 0 0 0
```

In the preceding listing, each column of 0s and 1s represents a row in the BOOKSHELF table. Because ten rows are considered, ten bitmap values are shown. Reading the bitmap for RATING, the first five records have a RATING value of 1 (the "1" values), and the next five do not (the "0" values). There is a separate bitmap entry for each possible value.

The Oracle Optimizer can dynamically convert bitmap index entries to ROWIDs during query processing. This conversion capability allows the optimizer to use indexes on columns that have many distinct values (via B*-tree indexes) and on those that have few distinct values (via bitmap indexes).

To create a bitmap index, use the BITMAP clause of the CREATE INDEX command, as shown in the following listing. You should indicate its nature as a bitmap index within the index name so it will be easy to detect during tuning operations.

```
create bitmap index bookshelf$bitmap_rating
    on bookshelf(rating);
```

If you choose to use bitmap indexes, you need to weigh the performance benefit during queries against the performance cost during data-manipulation commands. The more bitmap indexes there are on a table, the greater the cost will be during each transaction. You should not use bitmap indexes on a column that frequently has new values added to it. Each addition of a new value to the RATING column requires that a corresponding new bitmap be created.

When to Create an Index

Indexes are most useful on larger tables, on columns that are likely to appear in WHERE clauses either as a simple equality, such as

```
where author_name = 'Stephen Jay Gould'
    and rating = '5'
```

or in joins, such as this:

```
where bookshelf.title = bookshelf_author.title
```

In addition to supporting WHERE clauses and joins, indexes also support ORDER BY clauses and the MAX and MIN functions. In some circumstances, Oracle may choose to scan an index instead of performing a full scan on the table. See Chapter 46 for details on the Oracle Optimizer's use of indexes.

Creating Invisible Indexes

The presence of a new index may alter how an existing application works. In most cases, this is the intended behavior: You are creating the index to change the execution path chosen by a query. The new index should be designed to support the known query execution paths, and it will slow the performance of INSERTs and other DML operations. As of Oracle 11g, you can introduce an index to your environment in stages, first creating it and then making it visible to the optimizer.

After creating an index, you can tell the optimizer to not consider it when generating execution plans via the ALTER INDEX command:

```
alter index ba$title_author invisible;
```

With the index in an "invisible" state, you can now test your commands to determine exactly how the index will impact your operations. The invisible index will only be used if you use an INDEX hint (see Chapter 46) that explicitly names the index. The index will not be considered by the optimizer for general usage while it is invisible. Select the VISIBILITY column from the USER_INDEXES data dictionary view to determine if an index has been set to be invisible to the optimizer. Regardless of its visibility status, the index continues to use space and impact DML operations.

Variety in Indexed Columns

Traditional (B*-tree) indexes are most useful on columns with a significant amount of variety in their data. For instance, a column that indicates whether a company is a current client with a Y or N value would be a poor choice for a traditional index and could actually slow down a query; a bitmap index would be a much better choice for that example. A telephone number column would be a good candidate for a B*-tree index. An area code column would be marginal, depending on the distribution of unique area code values in the table.

In a multicolumn index, put the column likely to be accessed most often first. You can use the optimizer's skip-scan feature to use multicolumn indexes even if the leading column is not mentioned in the query. See Chapter 46 for examples of index usage.

Small tables may be better left unindexed, except to enforce uniqueness in the primary key. A small table is one that takes so few database blocks that Oracle can read all its data with one physical read; beyond that, indexing will nearly always be productive. The number of blocks read during a physical read is set via the DB_FILE_MULTIBLOCK_READ_COUNT initialization parameter.

Bitmap indexes present a viable indexing alternative for columns that have very few distinct values. Bitmap indexes are commonly used for "flag" columns that are restricted to values such as Y and N. Bitmap indexes are particularly effective when multiple bitmap indexes are used in a query; the optimizer can quickly evaluate the bitmaps and determine which rows meet all the criteria for which bitmap indexes are available.

How Many Indexes to Use on a Table

You can create many indexes on a single table, with many columns in each index. The tradeoff for indexing too many columns is the lessened speed of inserting new rows: Every index must be updated whenever an INSERT, UPDATE, or DELETE occurs. If your table is used primarily for queries, the only cost of indexing as many columns as you can (that have variety and are used in WHERE clauses, of course) is the extra disk space used. Strictly from a data-loading performance perspective, it is better to have a small number of indexes with many columns than to have many indexes with a small number of columns in each.

Except in cluster indexes (discussed later in this chapter), column values that are NULL do not appear in an index. Indexes based on more than one column have an entry if any of the columns are not NULL. If all indexed columns are NULL for a given row, no entry appears for this row in the index.

Placing an Index in the Database

You can specify where the index to a table is placed by assigning it to a specific tablespace. As will be described in detail in Chapter 22, a *tablespace* is a logical division of the database, corresponding to one or more datafiles. Datafiles provide the physical storage for the database—

sections of disk where tables and indexes are stored. Databases have several tablespaces, each with its own name. To enhance manageability and sometimes performance (if you're not using ASM), an index for a table can be placed in a tablespace that is on a physically separate disk drive from its corresponding table.

To specify the tablespace in which to locate an index, the normal CREATE INDEX statement is simply followed by the word TABLESPACE and the tablespace name, as shown here:

```
create unique index ba$title_author
    on bookshelf_author(title, author_name)
tablespace ba_indexes;
```

In this example, BA_INDEXES is the name given to a tablespace previously created by the database administrator. The use of the TABLESPACE option in a CREATE INDEX statement lets you physically separate your tables from their associated indexes.

When you create a primary key or unique constraint, Oracle automatically creates an index to enforce uniqueness. Unless you specify otherwise, that index is created in the same tablespace as the table that the constraint modifies, and it uses the default storage parameters for that tablespace. Because that storage location is often not ideal, you should take advantage of the USING INDEX clause when creating primary key and unique constraints.

The USING INDEX clause allows you to specify the storage parameters and tablespace location for an index created by a constraint. In the following example, a primary key is created on the BOOKSHELF_AUTHOR table and is placed in the BA_INDEXES tablespace. This example assumes that there is not an existing index on the specified columns.

```
alter table bookshelf_author
    add constraint ba_pk primary key (title, author_name)
using index tablespace ba_indexes;
```

See "Integrity Constraint" in the Alphabetical Reference for further options for the USING INDEX clause, and see CREATE INDEX in the Alphabetical Reference for performance-related index-creation options.

Rebuilding an Index

Oracle provides a *fast index rebuild* capability that allows you to re-create an index without having to drop the existing index. The currently available index is used as the data source for the index, instead of the table's being used as the data source. During the index rebuild, you can change its STORAGE parameters and TABLESPACE assignment.

In the following example, the BA_PK index is rebuilt (via the REBUILD clause). Its storage parameters are changed to use an initial extent size of 8MB and a next extent size of 4MB in the BA_INDEXES tablespace.

```
alter index ba_pk rebuild
storage (initial 8m next 4m pctincrease 0)
tablespace ba_indexes;
```

NOTE
When the BA_PK index is rebuilt, there must be enough space for both the old index and the new index to exist simultaneously. After the new index has been created, the old index will be dropped.

When you create an index that is based on previously indexed columns, Oracle may be able to use the existing indexes as data sources for the new index. The Oracle Optimizer may use parts of existing composite indexes as needed for queries, so you may not need to create many indexes to support the most common queries.

You can rebuild indexes while they are being accessed via the REBUILD ONLINE clause of the ALTER INDEX command.

```
alter index ba_pk rebuild tablespace ba_indexes online;
```

Function-Based Indexes

You can create *function-based indexes*. Any query that performs a function on a column generally does not use that column's index. Therefore, this query could not use an index on the TITLE column:

```
select * from bookshelf
where upper(title) = 'MY LEDGER';
```

However, this query could because it does not perform the UPPER function on the TITLE column:

```
select * from bookshelf
where title = 'My Ledger';
```

You can create indexes that allow function-based accesses to be supported by index accesses. Instead of creating an index on the column TITLE, you can create an index on the column expression UPPER(TITLE), as shown in the following listing:

```
create index bookshelf$upper_title on
bookshelf(upper(title));
```

Although function-based indexes can be useful, be sure to consider the following questions when creating them:

- Can you restrict the functions that will be used on the column? If so, can you restrict all functions from being performed on the column?
- Do you have adequate storage space for the additional indexes?
- When you drop the table, will you be dropping more indexes (and, therefore, more extents) than before? How will that impact the time required to drop the table?

Function-based indexes are useful, but you should implement them sparingly. The more indexes you create on a table, the longer all INSERT, UPDATE, and DELETE operations take. Typically, each index adds three times the overhead of maintaining a row without an index.

Clusters

Clustering is a method of storing tables that are intimately related and often joined together into the same area on disk. For example, instead of the BOOKSHELF table being in one section of the disk and the BOOKSHELF_AUTHOR table being somewhere else, their rows could be interleaved together in a single area, called a *cluster*. The *cluster key* is the column or columns by which the tables are usually joined in a query (for example, TITLE for the BOOKSHELF and BOOKSHELF_ AUTHOR tables). To cluster tables, you must own the tables you are going to cluster together.

The following is the basic format of the CREATE CLUSTER command:

```
CREATE CLUSTER clustername
(column datatype [,column datatype]. . .) [other options];
```

The *clustername* follows table-naming conventions, and *column datatype* is the name and datatype you will use as the cluster key. The *column* name may be the same as one of the columns of a table you will put in this cluster, or it may be any other valid name. Here's an example:

```
create cluster bookandauthor (col1 varchar2(100));

Cluster created.
```

This creates a cluster (disk space is set aside, as it would be for a table) with nothing in it. The use of COL1 for the cluster key is irrelevant; you'll never use it again. However, its definition should match the primary key of the table to be added. Next, tables are created to be included in this cluster:

```
create table bookshelf2
(title          varchar2(100) primary key,
publisher       varchar2(20),
category_name varchar2(20),
rating          varchar2(2),
constraint catfk foreign key (category_name)
references category(category_name)
)
cluster bookandauthor (title);
```

Prior to inserting rows into BOOKSHELF, you must create a cluster index:

```
create index bookandauthorndx
on cluster bookandauthor;
```

Recall that the presence of a CLUSTER clause here precludes the use of a TABLESPACE or STORAGE clause. Note how this structure differs from a standard CREATE TABLE statement:

```
create table bookshelf
(title          varchar2(100) primary key,
publisher       varchar2(20),
category_name varchar2(20),
rating          varchar2(2),
constraint catfk foreign key (category_name)
references category(category_name)
);
```

In the first CREATE TABLE statement, the cluster BOOKANDAUTHOR (TITLE) clause *follows* the closing parenthesis of the list of columns being created in the table. BOOKANDAUTHOR is the name of the cluster previously created. TITLE is the column in this table that will be stored in the cluster key COL1. It is possible to have multiple cluster keys in the CREATE CLUSTER statement and to have multiple columns stored in those keys in the CREATE TABLE statement. Notice that nowhere does either statement say explicitly that the TITLE column goes into the

COL1 cluster key. The match-up is done by position only: COL1 and TITLE were both the first objects mentioned in their respective cluster statements. Multiple columns and cluster keys are matched first to first, second to second, third to third, and so on. Now a second table is added to the cluster:

```
create table bookshelf_author
(title        varchar2(100),
author_name varchar2(50),
constraint titlefk foreign key (title) references bookshelf(title),
constraint authornamefk foreign key (author_name)
references author(author_name)
)
cluster bookandauthor (title);
```

When these two tables are clustered, each unique title is actually stored only once, in the cluster key. The columns from both of these tables are attached to each title. The data from both of these tables is actually stored in a single location, almost as if the cluster were a big table containing data drawn from both of the tables that make it up.

An additional cluster option, a *hash cluster,* uses the cluster column values to determine the physical location in which the row is stored. See the entry for the CREATE CLUSTER command in the Alphabetical Reference.

Sequences

You can assign unique numbers, such as customer IDs, to columns in your database by using a sequence; you don't need to create a special table and code to keep track of the unique numbers in use. You do this by using the CREATE SEQUENCE command, as shown here:

```
create sequence customer_id increment by 1 start with 1000;
```

This creates a sequence that can be accessed during INSERT and UPDATE commands (also SELECT, although this is rare). Typically, the unique sequence value is created with a statement like the following:

```
insert into customer_demo  /* pseudocode example */
       (name, contact, id)
values
       ('Cole Construction','Veronica',customer_id.nextval);
```

The NEXTVAL attached to CUSTOMER_ID tells Oracle you want the next available sequence number from the CUSTOMER_ID sequence. This is guaranteed to be unique; Oracle will not give it to anyone else. To use the same number more than once (such as in a series of INSERTs into related tables), CURRVAL is used instead of NEXTVAL, *after the first use.* That is, using NEXTVAL ensures that the sequence table gets incremented and that you get a unique number, so you have to use NEXTVAL first. Once you've used NEXTVAL, that number is stored in CURRVAL for your use anywhere—until you use NEXTVAL again, at which point both NEXTVAL and CURRVAL change to the new sequence number.

If you use both NEXTVAL and CURRVAL in a single SQL statement, both will contain the value retrieved by NEXTVAL. Neither of these can be used in subqueries, as columns in the SELECT clause of a view, with DISTINCT, UNION, INTERSECT, or MINUS, or in the ORDER BY, GROUP BY, or HAVING clause of a SELECT statement.

You can also cache sequence values in memory for faster access, and you can make the sequence cycle back to its starting value once a maximum value is reached. In RAC environments, Oracle recommends caching 20,000 sequence values per instance to avoid contention during writes. For non-RAC environments, you should cache at least 1,000 values. Note that if you flush the shared pool portion of the instance or you shut down and restart the database, any cached sequence values will be lost and there will be gaps in the sequence numbers stored in the database. See CREATE SEQUENCE in the Alphabetical Reference.

CHAPTER
18

Partitioning

As the number of rows in your tables grows, the impact on management and performance will increase. Backups will take longer, recoveries will take longer, and queries that span an entire table will take longer. You can mitigate the administrative and performance issues for large tables by separating the rows of a single table into multiple parts. Dividing a table's data in this manner is called *partitioning* the table; the table that is partitioned is called a *partitioned table,* and the parts are called *partitions*.

Partitioning is useful for very large tables. By splitting a large table's rows across multiple smaller partitions, you accomplish several important goals:

- The performance of queries against the tables may improve because Oracle may have to search only one partition (one part of the table) instead of the entire table to resolve a query.

- The table may be easier to manage. Because the partitioned table's data is stored in multiple parts, loading and deleting data in the partitions may be easier than in a single large table.

- Backup and recovery operations may perform better. Because the partitions are smaller than the partitioned table, you may have more options for backing up and recovering the partitions than you would have for a single large table.

The Oracle optimizer will know that the table has been partitioned; and, as shown later in this chapter, you can also specify the partition to use as part of the FROM clause of your queries.

Creating a Partitioned Table

To create a partitioned table, you specify how to set up the partitions of the table's data as part of the CREATE TABLE command. Typically, tables are partitioned by ranges of values (known as *range partitioning*).

Consider the BOOKSHELF table:

```
create table bookshelf
(title         varchar2(100) primary key,
publisher      varchar2(20),
category_name  varchar2(20),
rating         varchar2(2),
constraint catfk foreign key (category_name)
references category(category_name));
```

If you are storing a large number of records in the BOOKSHELF table, you may want to separate the rows across multiple partitions. To partition the table's records, use the PARTITION BY RANGE clause of the CREATE TABLE command, as shown next. The ranges determine the values stored in each partition.

```
create table bookshelf_range_part
(title         varchar2(100) primary key,
publisher      varchar2(20),
category_name  varchar2(20),
rating         varchar2(2),
constraint catfk3 foreign key (category_name)
references category(category_name)
)
```

```
partition by range (category_name)
  (partition part1   values less than ('B')
     tablespace part1_ts,
   partition part2   values less than (maxvalue)
     tablespace part2_ts);
```

The BOOKSHELF table will be partitioned based on the values in the CATEGORY_NAME column:

```
partition by range (category_name)
```

For any category values less than 'B' (the ADULT categories), the records will be stored in the partition named PART1. The PART1 partition will be stored in the PART1_TS tablespace (see Chapter 22 for details on tablespaces). Any other categories will be stored in the PART2 partition. Note that in the PART2 partition definition, the range clause is

```
partition part2   values less than (maxvalue)
```

You do not need to specify a maximum value for the last partition; the MAXVALUE keyword tells Oracle to use the partition to store any data that could not be stored in the earlier partitions.

You can create multiple partitions, each with its own upper value defined. For each partition, you only specify the maximum value for the range (less than, but not equal to, the maximum values specified—rows with the maximum value end up in the next partition). The minimum value for the range is implicitly determined by Oracle from the definition of the preceding partition.

In addition to range partitions, Oracle supports *hash partitions*. A hash partition determines the physical placement of data by performing a hash function on the values of the partition key. In *range partitioning*, consecutive values of the partition key are usually stored in the same partition. In *hash partitioning*, consecutive values of the partition key are not generally stored in the same partition. Hash partitioning distributes a set of records over a greater set of partitions than range partitioning does, potentially decreasing the likelihood for I/O contention.

To create a hash partition, use the PARTITION BY HASH clause in place of the PARTITION BY RANGE clause, as shown in the following listing:

```
create table bookshelf_hash_part
(title          varchar2(100) primary key,
publisher       varchar2(20),
category_name   varchar2(20),
rating          varchar2(2),
constraint catfk_hash foreign key (category_name)
references category(category_name)
)
partition by hash (category_name)
partitions 16;
```

NOTE
Because of the way that partition mapping is implemented in Oracle, it is recommended that the number of partitions in the table be set to a power of 2 (2, 4, 8, 16, for example) to get an even distribution of data.

You can name each partition and specify its tablespace, just as you would for range partitioning, as shown here:

```
create table bookshelf_hash_part
(title          varchar2(100) primary key,
publisher       varchar2(20),
category_name   varchar2(20),
rating          varchar2(2),
constraint catfk_hash foreign key (category_name)
references category(category_name)
)
partition by hash (category_name)
partitions 2
store in (part1_ts, part2_ts);
```

Following the PARTITION BY HASH (CATEGORY_NAME) line, you have two choices for the format:

- As shown in the preceding listing, you can specify the number of partitions and the tablespaces to use:

   ```
   partitions 2
   store in (part1_ts, part2_ts);
   ```

   This method creates partitions with system-generated names in the format SYS_P*nnn*. The number of tablespaces specified in the STORE IN clause does not have to equal the number of partitions. If more partitions than tablespaces are specified, the partitions are assigned to the tablespaces in a round-robin fashion.

- You can specify named partitions:

   ```
   partition by hash (category_name)
   (partition part1 tablespace part1_ts,
    partition part2 tablespace part2_ts);
   ```

   In this method, each partition is given a name and a tablespace, with the option of using an additional LOB or VARRAY storage clause (see Chapters 39 and 40). This method gives you more control over the location of the partitions, with the added benefit of letting you specify meaningful names for the partitions.

List Partitioning

You can use *list partitions* in place of range and hash partitioning. In list partitioning, you tell Oracle all the possible values and designate the partitions into which the corresponding rows should be inserted. The following example shows the BOOKSHELF entries list-partitioned by CATEGORY_NAME:

```
create table bookshelf_list_part
(title          varchar2(100) primary key,
publisher       varchar2(20),
```

```
category_name  varchar2(20),
rating          varchar2(2),
constraint catfk4 foreign key (category_name)
references category(category_name)
)
partition by list (category_name)
  (partition part1    values ('ADULTFIC', 'ADULTNF', 'ADULTREF')
      tablespace part1_ts,
   partition part2    values
        ('CHILDRENFIC', 'CHILDRENNF', 'CHILDRENPIC')
      tablespace part2_ts);
```

Additionally, you can use the DEFAULT keyword to create a list partition to handle category names that are not listed. Add a partition using the following clause:

```
partition category_other values (default)
```

and the values that do not match the CATEGORY_NAME values specified in your other partition definitions will be stored in this partition.

Creating Subpartitions

You can create *subpartitions*—that is, partitions of partitions. You can use subpartitions to combine all types of partitions: range partitions, list partitions, and hash partitions. For example, you can use hash partitions in combination with range partitions, creating hash partitions of the range partitions. For very large tables, this composite partitioning may be an effective way of separating the data into manageable and tunable divisions.

The following example range-partitions the BOOKSHELF table by the TITLE column, and it hash-partitions the TITLE partitions by CATEGORY_NAME values:

```
create table bookshelf_range_hash_part
(title        varchar2(100) primary key,
publisher     varchar2(20),
category_name  varchar2(20),
rating         varchar2(2),
constraint catfk5 foreign key (category_name)
references category(category_name)
)
partition by range (title)
subpartition by hash (category_name)
subpartitions 8
  (partition part1    values less than ('M')
     tablespace part1_ts,
   partition part2    values less than (maxvalue)
     tablespace part2_ts);
```

The BOOKSHELF table will be range-partitioned into two partitions, using the TITLE value ranges specified for the named partitions. Each of those partitions will then be hash-partitioned on the CATEGORY_NAME column.

Creating Reference and Interval Partitions

Two significant enhancements to partitioning introduced in Oracle 11g are reference partitioning and interval partitioning. *Reference partitioning* allows you to create a partition based on a column that is not in the table being partitioned, but rather is a foreign key reference to a different table. This can be useful for partitioning related tables in related ways, even if they do not share the same columns. *Interval partitioning* frees the DBA from having to manage the size of partitions that are defined with MAXVALUE; instead, new partitions are created automatically based on the appearance of new numeric or date values for a partition key.

Reference Partitioning

For example, an INVOICE_HEADERS table may include an INVOICE_DATE column, tracking the date on which an invoice was issued. The line items for invoices may be stored in an INVOICE_ LINE_ITEMS table—and from a normalization perspective, it would not be appropriate to store the INVOICE_DATE at the line-item level. However, if the INVOICE_DATE column is not in the INVOICE_LINE_ITEMS table, how can you partition INVOICE_LINE_ITEMS by the invoice date?

You can range-partition INVOICE_HEADERS by the INVOICE_DATE column on a monthly basis. Suppose the INVOICE_LINE_ITEMS table does not have a DATE datatype column—but it has a foreign key on the INVOICE_NUMBER column back to the INVOICE_HEADERS table. How can you partition it?

As of Oracle 11g, you can use a *reference partition* to solve this dilemma. The table creation for the INVOICE_LINE_ITEMS table (assuming the INVOICE_HEADERS table already exists and is partitioned) using a reference partition is shown in the following listing:

```
create table invoice_line_items
(
    invoicenum     number not null,
    line_id        number not null,
    sales_amt      number,
    constraint  fk_inv_01
     foreign key (invoicenum)
     references invoice_headers
)
partition by reference (fk_inv_01);
```

When you create the INVOICE_LINE_ITEMS table, it will be partitioned by the same column as is used to partition the INVOICE_HEADERS table, even if that column (INVOICE_DATE) is not in the INVOICE_LINE_ITEMS table. The two will be partitioned in sync.

This may seem to be a minor advance, but it is highly significant for effective management of data as it ages. As time goes by, you will need to be able to archive and delete related data from multiple tables in a consistent fashion. You will need to be able to remove data without worrying that there are dangling references that will invalidate referential integrity along the way. By using reference partitions, you are unifying the ways in which the data is divided across multiple tables, and that significantly eases the maintenance burden.

Interval Partitioning

The other new partition type available starting with Oracle 11g is the *interval partition*. In interval partitioning, you do not specify the specific range values for each partition; instead, you specify the duration of the interval. That is, instead of specifying that partition 1 ends on January 31 and partition 2 ends on February 29, you specify that each partition is one month long. When a new row is inserted, Oracle determines which partition to place the row in based on the interval definition. If you have not created a partition for that month, the database automatically creates a new one.

Use interval partitions with caution. You need to perform the data-value constraint checks yourself prior to inserting the row—if you do not, you may end up with unwanted partitions that were created simply because a data-entry person mistakenly entered "2098" for a year instead of "2008." The interval partitioned version of the INVOICE_HEADERS table is shown in the following listing:

```
create table invoice_headers
(
    invoice_num     number,
    customer_num    number,
    invoice_date    date
)
partition by range (invoice_date)
interval (numtoyminterval(1,'month'))
(
    partition p1101 values
      less than (to_date('2011-02-01','yyyy-mm-dd'))
);
```

Note that if you rely on interval partitioning automatically creating your partitions for you, your application developers cannot rely on consistent partition names because Oracle will create a system-generated name for each new partition it automatically creates.

Indexing Partitions

When you create a partitioned table, you should create an index on the table. The index may be partitioned according to the same range values used to partition the table. In the following listing, the CREATE INDEX command for the BOOKSHELF_LIST_PART (list-partitioned) table is shown. The index partitions are placed in the PART1_NDX_TS and PART2_NDX_TS tablespaces.

```
create index bookshelf__list_category
  on bookshelf_list_part(category_name)
    local
    (partition part1
      tablespace part1_ndx_ts,
     partition part2
      tablespace part2_ndx_ts);
```

Notice the LOCAL keyword. In this CREATE INDEX command, no ranges are specified. Instead, the LOCAL keyword tells Oracle to create a separate index for each partition of the BOOKSHELF_LIST_PART table. Two partitions are created on BOOKSHELF_LIST_PART. This index will create two separate index partitions—one for each table partition. Because there is one index per partition, the index partitions are "local" to the table partitions.

You can also create "global" indexes, as shown next. A *global index* contains values from all partitions.

```
create index bookshelf_list_category_g
on bookshelf_list_part(publisher)
 global;
```

The GLOBAL clause in this CREATE INDEX command allows you to create a nonpartitioned index (as shown here) or to specify ranges for the index values that are different from the ranges for the table partitions. Local indexes may be easier to manage than global indexes; however, global indexes may perform uniqueness checks faster than local (partitioned) indexes perform them.

Managing Partitioned Tables

You can use the ALTER TABLE command to ADD, DROP, EXCHANGE, MOVE, MODIFY, RENAME, SPLIT, and TRUNCATE partitions. These ALTER TABLE command options allow you to alter the existing partition structure, as may be required after a partitioned table has been used heavily. For example, the distribution of the CATEGORY_NAME values within the partitioned table may have changed, or the maximum value may have increased. See the ALTER TABLE entry in the Alphabetical Reference for information on these options.

During an INSERT into the partitioned table, Oracle uses the partitions' definitions to determine which partition the record should be inserted into. Thus, you can use a partitioned table as if it were a single table and rely on Oracle to manage the internal separation of the data.

One common use of partitions allows you to minimize downtime in applications. Assume you have a table that is batch-loaded and partitioned by day. When a new day's worth of data comes in, you create a new table to store that data. Structure the new table to look like a partition of the existing partitioned table. Load the data into the new table, then index it. This avoids the performance penalties associated with having the index in place during the data load.

Next, analyze the new table. In the partitioned table, create a new partition for today's data, then use the ALTER TABLE EXCHANGE PARTITION command to exchange that empty partition for the newly loaded table. By following this process, you can prevent the data load from adversely impacting user access to the partitioned table while you load, index, and analyze it.

Another benefit of partitions is that you can apply different compression settings to each partition. Older partitions can have a higher level of compression and save storage space; this is a good tradeoff for the higher cost of decompressing the older compressions if the older partitions are rarely accessed.

CHAPTER
19

Basic Oracle Security

I nformation is vital to success, but when damaged or in the wrong hands, it can threaten success. Oracle provides extensive security features to safeguard your information from both unauthorized viewing and intentional or inadvertent damage. This security is provided by granting or revoking privileges on a person-by-person and privilege-by-privilege basis, and is in addition to (and independent of) any security your computer system already has. Oracle uses the CREATE USER, CREATE ROLE, and GRANT commands to control data access.

In this chapter, you will see the basic security features available in Oracle. See Chapter 20 for coverage of advanced Oracle security features such as virtual private databases.

Users, Roles, and Privileges

Every Oracle user has a name and password and owns any tables, views, and other resources that he or she creates. An Oracle *role* is a set of *privileges* (or the type of access that each user needs, depending on his or her status and responsibilities). You can grant or bestow specific privileges to roles and then assign roles to the appropriate users. Users can also grant privileges directly to other users.

Database system privileges let you execute specific sets of commands. The CREATE TABLE privilege, for example, lets you create tables. The privilege GRANT ANY PRIVILEGE allows you to grant any system privilege.

Database object privileges let you perform some operations on various objects. The DELETE privilege, for example, lets you delete rows from tables and views. The SELECT privilege allows you to query with a SELECT from tables, views, sequences, and snapshots (materialized views).

See "Privilege" in the Alphabetical Reference at the end of this book for a complete list of system and object privileges.

Creating a User

The Oracle system comes with many users already created, including SYSTEM and SYS. The SYS user owns the core internal tables that Oracle uses to manage the database; SYSTEM owns additional tables and views. You can log onto the SYSTEM user to create other users because SYSTEM has that privilege.

When installing Oracle, you (or a system administrator) first create a user for yourself. This is the simplest format for the CREATE USER command:

```
CREATE USER user IDENTIFIED
    {BY password | EXTERNALLY | GLOBALLY AS 'extnm'};
```

Many other account characteristics can be set via this command; see the CREATE USER command in the Alphabetical Reference for details.

To connect your computer system's user id and password into Oracle's security so only one logon is required for host-based users, use EXTERNALLY instead of giving a password. A system administrator (who has a great many privileges) may want the extra security of having a separate password. Let's call the system administrator Dora in the following examples:

```
create user dora identified by avo40cadoS;
```

Dora's account now exists and is secured by a password.

You also can set up the user with specific tablespaces and *quotas* (limits) for space and resource usage. See CREATE USER in the Alphabetical Reference and Chapters 17 and 22 for a discussion of tablespaces and resources.

To change a password, use the ALTER USER command:

```
alter user dora identified by psYcHo90210;
```

Now Dora has the password "psYcHo90210" instead of "avo40cadoS." Dora cannot log into her account, however, until she first has the CREATE SESSION system privilege:

```
grant create session to dora;
```

You'll see additional examples of system privilege grants later in this chapter.

Password Management

Passwords can expire, and accounts may be locked due to repeated failed attempts to connect. A password history can be maintained to prevent reuse of previous passwords when you change your password.

The expiration characteristics of your account's password are determined by the profile assigned to your account. Profiles, which are created by the CREATE PROFILE command, are managed by the DBA (database administrator, discussed later in the chapter). See the CREATE PROFILE entry in the Alphabetical Reference for full details on the CREATE PROFILE command.

Relative to passwords and account access, profiles can enforce the following:

- The "lifetime" of your password, which determines how frequently you must change it
- The grace period following your password's "expiration date" during which you can change the password
- The number of consecutive failed connect attempts allowed before the account is automatically "locked"
- The number of days the account will remain locked
- The number of days that must pass before you can reuse a password
- The number of password changes that must take place before you can reuse a password

Additional password management features allow the minimum length and complexity of passwords to be enforced.

In addition to the ALTER USER command, you can use the PASSWORD command in SQL*Plus to change your password. If you use the PASSWORD command, your new password will not be displayed on the screen as you type. Database administrators can change any user's password via the PASSWORD command; other users can change only their own password.

When you enter the PASSWORD command, you are prompted for the old and new passwords, as shown in the following listing:

```
connect dora/ psYcHo90210
password
Changing password for dora
Old password:
New password:
Retype new password:
```

When the password has been successfully changed, you receive the feedback:

```
Password changed
```

You can set another user's password from an account with the DBA role. Simply append the username to the PASSWORD command. You are not asked for the old password:

```
password dora
Changing password for dora
New password:
Retype new password:
```

Enforcing Password Expiration

You can use profiles to manage the expiration, reuse, and complexity of passwords. You can limit the lifetime of a password and lock an account whose password is too old. You can also force a password to be at least moderately complex and lock any account that experiences repeated failed login attempts.

For example, if you set the FAILED_LOGIN_ATTEMPTS resource of the user's profile to 5, then 4 consecutive failed login attempts will be allowed for the account; the fifth will cause the account to be locked.

NOTE
If the correct password is supplied on the fifth attempt, the "failed login attempt count" is reset to 0, allowing for five more consecutive unsuccessful login attempts before the account is locked.

In the following listing, the LIMITED_PROFILE profile is created by the user JANE:

```
create profile limited_profile limit
failed_login_attempts 5;

create user jane identified by eyre707
profile limited_profile;

grant create session to jane;
```

If there are five consecutive failed connection attempts to the JANE account, the account is automatically locked by Oracle. When you then use the correct password for the JANE account, you receive an error.

```
connect jane/eyre707
ERROR:
ORA-28000: the account is locked
```

To unlock the account, use the ACCOUNT UNLOCK clause of the ALTER USER command (from a DBA account), as shown in the following listing:

```
alter user jane account unlock;
```

Following the unlocking of the account, connections to the JANE account will once again be allowed. You can manually lock an account via the ACCOUNT LOCK clause of the ALTER USER command.

```
alter user jane account lock;
```

NOTE
You can specify ACCOUNT LOCK as part of the CREATE USER command.

If an account is locked owing to repeated connection failures, it automatically becomes unlocked when its profile's PASSWORD_LOCK_TIME value is exceeded. For example, if PASSWORD_LOCK_TIME is set to 1, the JANE account in the previous example would be locked for one day, after which the account would be unlocked again.

You can establish a maximum lifetime for a password via the PASSWORD_LIFE_TIME resource within profiles. For example, you could force users of the LIMITED_PROFILE profile to change their passwords every 30 days:

```
alter profile limited_profile limit
    password_life_time 30;
```

In this example, the ALTER PROFILE command is used to modify the LIMITED_PROFILE profile. The PASSWORD_LIFE_TIME value is set to 30, so for each account that uses that profile, its password will expire after 30 days. If your password has expired, you must change it the next time you log in, unless the profile has a specified grace period for expired passwords. The grace period parameter is called PASSWORD_GRACE_TIME. If the password is not changed within the grace period, the account expires.

NOTE
If you are going to use the PASSWORD_LIFE_TIME parameter, you need to give the users a way to change their passwords easily.

An *expired* account is different from a *locked* account. A locked account, as discussed earlier in this section, may be automatically unlocked by the passage of time. An expired account, however, requires manual intervention by the DBA to be re-enabled.

NOTE
If you use the password expiration features, make sure the accounts that own your applications have different profile settings; otherwise, the accounts may become locked and the application may become unusable.

To re-enable an expired account, execute the ALTER USER command. In this example, the DBA manually expires JANE's password:

```
alter user jane password expire;
```
```
User altered.
```

Next, JANE attempts to connect to her account. When she provides her password, she is immediately prompted for a new password for the account.

```
connect jane/eyre707
ERROR:
ORA-28001: the password has expired
```

```
Changing password for jane
New password:
Retype new password:
Password changed
Connected.
```

You can also force users to change their passwords when they first access their accounts, via the PASSWORD EXPIRE clause of the CREATE USER command. The CREATE USER command does not, however, allow you to set an expiration date for the new password set by the user; to do that, you must use the PASSWORD_LIFE_TIME profile parameter shown in the previous examples.

To see the password expiration date of any account, query the EXPIRY_DATE column of the DBA_USERS' data dictionary view. Users who want to see the password expiration date for their accounts can query the EXPIRY_DATE column of the USER_USERS' data dictionary view (via either SQL*Plus or a client-based query tool).

Enforcing Password Reuse Limitations

To prevent a password from being reused, you can use one of two profile parameters: PASSWORD_REUSE_MAX or PASSWORD_REUSE_TIME. These two parameters are mutually exclusive; if you set a value for one of them, the other must be set to UNLIMITED.

The PASSWORD_REUSE_TIME parameter specifies the number of days that must pass before a password can be reused. For example, if you set PASSWORD_REUSE_TIME to 60, you cannot reuse the same password within 60 days.

The PASSWORD_REUSE_MAX parameter specifies the number of password changes that must occur before a password can be reused. If you attempt to reuse the password before the limit is reached, Oracle will reject your password change.

For example, you can set PASSWORD_REUSE_MAX for the LIMITED_PROFILE profile created earlier in this chapter:

```
alter profile limited_profile limit
password_reuse_max 3
password_reuse_time unlimited;
```

If the user JANE now attempts to reuse a recent password, the password change attempt will fail. For example, suppose she changes her password, as in the following line:

```
alter user jane identified by austen101;
```

And then she changes it again:

```
alter user jane identified by whitley217;
```

During her next password change, she attempts to reuse a recent password, and the attempt fails:

```
alter user jane identified by austen101;
alter user jane identified by austen101
*
ERROR at line 1:
ORA-28007: the password cannot be reused
```

She cannot reuse any of her recent passwords; she needs to come up with a new password.

Standard Roles

At the beginning of this chapter, we created a user named Dora. Now that Dora has an account, what can she do in Oracle? At this point, nothing—Dora has no system privileges other than CREATE SESSION. In many cases, application users receive privileges via roles. You can group system privileges and object accesses into roles specific to your application users' needs. You can create your own roles for application access, and you can use Oracle's default roles for some system access requirements. The most important standard roles created during database creation are

Role	Description
CONNECT	This role allows a user to connect to a database (the CREATE SESSION privilege).
RESOURCE	This role allows a user to create, modify, and delete various objects in his or her own schema such as tables, views, indexes, and sequences.
DBA	Most database administrative functions are available in this role except for the SYSDBA role. This role is granted by default to the SYS and SYSTEM users.
DELETE_CATALOG_ROLE, EXECUTE_CATALOG_ROLE, SELECT_CATALOG_ROLE	These roles are provided for accessing data dictionary views and packages.
EXP_FULL_DATABASE, IMP_FULL_DATABASE	These roles are provided for convenience when using the Import and Export utilities.
AQ_USER_ROLE, AQ_ADMINISTRATOR_ROLE	These roles are needed for Oracle Advanced Queuing.
SNMPAGENT	This role is used by the Enterprise Manager Intelligent Agent.
RECOVERY_CATALOG_OWNER	This role is required for the creation of a recovery catalog schema owner.
HS_ADMIN_ROLE	This role is needed for support of Heterogeneous Services.
SCHEDULER_ADMIN	This role allows the grantee to execute the DBMS_SCHEDULER package's procedures, and it should be restricted to DBAs.

The DBA role may have more privileges than you care to grant; therefore, it is recommended that you create custom roles if the user does not require all privileges in the DBA role in his or her job function. The CONNECT role gives users the ability to log in and perform basic functions. As of Oracle 11g, users with CONNECT may no longer create tables, views, sequences, clusters, synonyms, and database links. Users with RESOURCE can create their own tables, sequences, procedures, triggers, datatypes, operators, indextypes, indexes, and clusters. Users with the RESOURCE role also receive the UNLIMITED TABLESPACE system privilege, allowing them to bypass quotas on all tablespaces. Users with the DBA role can perform database administration functions, including creating and altering users, their tablespaces, and other objects.

In place of CONNECT, RESOURCE, and DBA, you should create your own roles that have the capability to execute specific system privileges. In the following sections, you learn how to grant privileges to users and roles.

Format for the GRANT Command

Here is the general format for the GRANT command for system privileges (see the Alphabetical Reference for the full syntax diagram):

```
GRANT {system privilege | role | ALL [PRIVILEGES] }
      [, {system privilege | role | ALL [PRIVILEGES] }. . .]
      TO {user | role} [, {user | role}]. . .
      [IDENTIFIED BY password ]
      [WITH ADMIN OPTION]
```

You can grant any system privilege or role to another user, to another role, or to PUBLIC. The WITH ADMIN OPTION clause permits the grantee to bestow the privilege or role on other users or roles. The ALL clause grants the user or role all privileges except the SELECT ANY DICTIONARY system privilege.

The grantor can revoke a role from a user as well.

Revoking Privileges

Privileges granted can be taken away. The REVOKE command is similar to the GRANT command:

```
REVOKE {system privilege | role | ALL [PRIVILEGES] }
       [, {system privilege | role | ALL [PRIVILEGES] }. . .]
       FROM {user | role} [, {user | role}]. . .
```

An individual with the DBA role can revoke CONNECT, RESOURCE, DBA, or any other privilege or role from anyone, including another DBA. This, of course, is dangerous, and is why DBA privileges should be given neither lightly nor to more than a tiny minority who really need them.

> **NOTE**
> *Revoking everything from a given user neither eliminates that user from Oracle, nor does it destroy any tables that the user created; it simply prohibits that user's access to them. Other users with access to the tables will still have exactly the same access they've always had.*

To remove a user and all the resources owned by that user, use the DROP USER command:

```
DROP USER username [CASCADE];
```

The CASCADE option drops the user along with all the objects owned by the user, including referential integrity constraints. The CASCADE option invalidates views, synonyms, stored procedures, functions, or packages that refer to objects in the dropped user's schema. If you don't use the CASCADE option and there are still objects owned by the user, Oracle does not drop the user and instead returns an error message.

> **NOTE**
> *See the "Privilege" entry in the Alphabetical Reference for the options for the GRANT command.*

What Users Can Grant

A user can grant privileges on any object he or she owns. The database administrator can grant any system privilege.

Suppose that user Dora owns the COMFORT table and is a database administrator. She creates two new users, Bob and Judy, with these privileges:

```
create user judy identified by sarah;
```

```
User created.
```

```
grant create session to judy;
```

```
Grant succeeded.
```

```
create user bob identified by carolyn;
```

```
User created.
```

```
grant create session, create table, create view,
create synonym to bob;
```

```
Grant succeeded.
```

```
alter user bob
default tablespace users
quota 5m on users;
```

```
User altered.
```

This sequence of commands gives both Judy and Bob the ability to connect to Oracle, and gives Bob some extra capabilities. But can either do anything with Dora's tables? Not without explicit access.

To give others access to your tables, use a second form of the GRANT command:

```
GRANT { object privilege | ALL [PRIVILEGES] }
    [(column [, column] . . .)]
    [, { object privilege | ALL [PRIVILEGES] }
    [(column [, column] . . .)] ] . . .
    ON object TO {user | role}
    [WITH GRANT OPTION]
    [WITH HIERARCHY OPTION];
```

The privileges a user can grant include these:

- On the user's tables, views, and materialized views, a user can grant
  - FLASHBACK
  - INSERT
  - UPDATE (all or specific columns)

- DELETE

- SELECT

NOTE
The INSERT, UPDATE, and DELETE privileges can only be granted on materialized views if they are updatable. See Chapter 26 for details on the creation of materialized views.

- On tables, a user can also grant

  - ALTER (table-all or specific columns)

  - DEBUG

  - REFERENCES

  - INDEX (columns in a table)

  - ON COMMIT REFRESH

  - QUERY REWRITE

  - ALL (of the items previously listed)

- On procedures, functions, packages, abstract datatypes, libraries, indextypes, and operators, a user can grant

  - EXECUTE

  - DEBUG

- On sequences, a user can grant

  - SELECT

  - ALTER

- On directories (for BFILE LOB datatypes and external tables), a user can grant

  - READ

  - WRITE

- On object types and views, a user can grant

  - UNDER (for the ability to create subviews under a view, or subtypes under a type)

When you execute another user's procedure or function, it is typically executed using the privileges of its owner. This means you don't need explicit access to the data the procedure or function uses; you see only the result of the execution, not the underlying data. You can also create stored procedures that execute under the privileges of the invoking user instead of the procedure owner.

Dora gives Bob SELECT access to the COMFORT table after creating her own copy of it:

```
create table comfort (
city          varchar2(13) not null,
sample_date   date not null,
noon          number(3,1),
midnight      number(3,1),
precipitation number
);
```

```
Table created.
```

```
grant select on comfort to bob;
```

```
Grant succeeded.
```

The WITH GRANT OPTION clause of the GRANT command allows the recipient of that grant to pass along the privileges he or she has received to other users. If the user Dora grants privileges on her tables to the user Bob using WITH GRANT OPTION, Bob can make grants on Dora's tables to other users (Bob can only pass along those privileges—such as SELECT—that he has been granted). If you intend to create views based on another user's tables and grant access to those views to other users, you first must be granted access WITH GRANT OPTION to the base tables.

Moving to Another User with CONNECT

To test the success of her grant, Dora connects to Bob's username with the CONNECT command. This command may be used via one of the following methods:

- By entering both the username and password on the same line as the command
- By entering the command alone and then responding to prompts
- By entering the command and username and responding to the prompt for the password

The latter two methods suppress the display of the password and are, therefore, inherently more secure. The following listing shows a sample connection to the database:

```
connect bob/car01yn
```

```
Connected.
```

Once connected, Dora selects from the table to which Bob has been given SELECT access.

NOTE
Unless a synonym is used, the table name must be preceded by the table owner's username. Without this, Oracle will say the table does not exist.

```
select * from dora.comfort;
```

```
CITY          SAMPLE_DA NOON  MIDNIGHT PRECIPITATION
------------- --------- ----- -------- -------------
San Francisco 21-Mar-03 62.5    42.3             .5
San Francisco 22-Jun-03 51.1    71.9             .1
San Francisco 23-Sep-03         61.5             .1
San Francisco 22-Dec-03 52.6    39.8            2.3
```

```
Keene           21-Mar-03  39.9    -1.2          4.4
Keene           22-Jun-03  85.1    66.7          1.3
Keene           23-Sep-03  99.8    82.6
Keene           22-Dec-03  -7.2    -1.2          3.9
```

A view named COMFORT is created, which is simply a straight SELECT from the table DORA. COMFORT:

```
create view comfort as select * from dora.comfort;
```

View created.

Selecting from this view produces exactly the same results as selecting from DORA.COMFORT:

```
select * from comfort;
```

```
CITY           SAMPLE_DA NOON MIDNIGHT PRECIPITATION
-------------- --------- ---- -------- -------------
San Francisco  21-Mar-03 62.5    42.3           .5
San Francisco  22-Jun-03 51.1    71.9           .1
San Francisco  23-Sep-03         61.5           .1
San Francisco  22-Dec-03 52.6    39.8          2.3
Keene          21-Mar-03 39.9    -1.2          4.4
Keene          22-Jun-03 85.1    66.7          1.3
Keene          23-Sep-03 99.8    82.6
Keene          22-Dec-03 -7.2    -1.2          3.9
```

Now Dora returns to her own username and creates a view that selects only a part of the COMFORT table:

```
connect dora/psych0w
Connected.

create view somecomfort as
select * from comfort
where city = 'Keene';
```

View created.

She then grants both SELECT and UPDATE privileges to Bob *on this view* and revokes all privileges from Bob (via the REVOKE command) for the whole COMFORT table:

```
grant select, update on somecomfort to bob;
```

Grant succeeded.

```
revoke all on comfort from bob;
```

Revoke succeeded.

Dora then reconnects to Bob's username to test the effects of this change:

```
connect bob/car01yn
Connected.
```

```
select * from comfort;
                *
ERROR at line 1:
ORA-04063: view "BOB.COMFORT" has errors
```

Attempting to select from his COMFORT view fails because the underlying table named in Bob's view was the DORA.COMFORT table. Not surprisingly, attempting to select from DORA. COMFORT would produce exactly the same message. Next, he makes an attempt to select from DORA.SOMECOMFORT:

```
select * from dora.somecomfort;

CITY          SAMPLE_DA  NOON MIDNIGHT PRECIPITATION
------------- ---------- ----- -------- -------------
Keene         21-Mar-03  39.9     -1.2           4.4
Keene         22-Jun-03  85.1     66.7           1.3
Keene         23-Sep-03  99.8     82.6
Keene         22-Dec-03  -7.2     -1.2           3.9
```

This works perfectly well, even though direct access to the COMFORT table had been revoked, because Dora gave Bob access to a portion of COMFORT through the SOMECOMFORT view. Bob has access to just that portion of the table related to Keene.

This example shows a powerful Oracle security feature: You can create a view using virtually any restrictions you like or any computations in the columns and then give access to the view, rather than to the underlying tables, to other users. They will see only the information the view presents. You can even extend this to be user specific. The "Defining Security by User" section, later in this chapter, gives complete details on this feature.

Now, the view LITTLECOMFORT is created under Bob's username, on top of the view SOMECOMFORT:

```
create view littlecomfort as select * from dora.somecomfort;

View created.
```

And the row for September 23, 2013, is updated:

```
update littlecomfort set noon = 88
where sample_date = '23-SEP-13';

1 row updated.
```

When the view LITTLECOMFORT is queried, it shows the effect of the UPDATE:

```
select * from littlecomfort;

CITY          SAMPLE_DA  NOON MIDNIGHT PRECIPITATION
------------- ---------- ----- -------- -------------
Keene         21-Mar-03  39.9     -1.2           4.4
Keene         22-Jun-03  85.1     66.7           1.3
Keene         23-Sep-03    88     82.6
Keene         22-Dec-03  -7.2     -1.2           3.9
```

A query of DORA.SOMECOMFORT would give the same results, as would a query of COMFORT itself if Dora queried it under her own username. The UPDATE was successful against the underlying table, even though it went through two views (LITTLECOMFORT and SOMECOMFORT) to reach it.

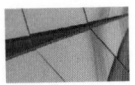

NOTE
You need to grant users SELECT access to any table in which they can update or delete records. This is in keeping with the evolving ANSI standard and reflects the fact that a user who only has the UPDATE or DELETE privilege on a table could use the database's feedback comments to discover information about the underlying data.

CREATE SYNONYM

An alternative method to creating a view that includes an entire table or view from another user is to create a synonym:

```
create synonym bobcomfort for dora.somecomfort;
```

This synonym can be queried exactly like a view. See the CREATE SYNONYM command in the Alphabetical Reference.

Using Ungranted Privileges

Let's say an attempt is made to delete the row just updated:

```
delete from littlecomfort where sample_date = '23-SEP-13';
                        *
ERROR at line 1:
ORA-01031: insufficient privileges
```

Dora has not given Bob DELETE privileges, so the attempt fails.

Passing Privileges

Bob can grant authority for other users to access his tables, but he cannot bestow on other users access to tables that don't belong to him. Here, he attempts to give INSERT authority to Judy:

```
grant insert on dora.somecomfort to judy;
            *
ERROR at line 1:
ORA-01031: insufficient privileges
```

Because Bob does not have this authority, he fails to give it to Judy. Next, Bob tries to pass on a privilege he does have, SELECT:

```
grant select on dora.somecomfort to judy;
            *
ERROR at line 1:
ORA-01031: insufficient privileges
```

He cannot grant this privilege either because the view SOMECOMFORT does not belong to him. If he had been granted access to SOMECOMFORT WITH GRANT OPTION, then the preceding GRANT command would have succeeded. The view LITTLECOMFORT does belong to him, though, so he can try to pass authority to that view on to Judy:

```
grant select on littlecomfort to judy;
```

```
ERROR at line 1:
ORA-01720: grant option does not exist for 'DORA.SOMECOMFORT'
```

Because the LITTLECOMFORT view relies on one of Dora's views, and Bob was not granted SELECT WITH GRANT OPTION on that view, Bob's grant fails.

In addition, a new table, owned by Bob, is created and loaded with the current information from his view LITTLECOMFORT:

```
create table nocomfort as
select * from littlecomfort;
```

```
Table created.
```

The SELECT privilege on the NOCOMFORT table is then granted to Judy:

```
grant select on nocomfort to judy;
```

```
Grant succeeded.
```

Queries are made from Judy's account against the table for which Bob granted Judy the SELECT privilege:

```
connect judy/sa4ah4
select * from bob.nocomfort;
```

```
CITY          SAMPLE_DA  NOON MIDNIGHT PRECIPITATION
------------- ---------- ----- -------- -------------
Keene         21-Mar-03  39.9     -1.2           4.4
Keene         22-Jun-03  85.1     66.7           1.3
Keene         23-Sep-03  88       82.6
Keene         22-Dec-03  -7.2     -1.2           3.9
```

This grant was successful. The NOCOMFORT table was created and is owned by Bob's username. He was able to give Judy access to this table successfully.

If Dora wants Bob to be able to pass on his privileges to others, she can add another clause to the GRANT statement:

```
connect dora/psyche
grant select, update on somecomfort to bob with grant option;
```

```
Grant succeeded.
```

The WITH GRANT OPTION clause enables Bob to pass on access to SOMECOMFORT to Judy through his LITTLECOMFORT view. Note that attempts to access a table to which a user does not have the SELECT privilege always result in the following message:

```
ERROR at line 1:
ORA-00942: table or view does not exist
```

This message appears (rather than a message about not having access privilege) so that a person without permission to query a table doesn't know that it even exists.

Creating a Role

In addition to the default roles shown earlier in this chapter, you can create your own roles within Oracle. The roles you create can comprise table or system privileges or a combination of both. In the following sections, you see how to create and administer roles.

To create a role, you need to have the CREATE ROLE system privilege. The syntax for role creation is shown in the following listing:

```
CREATE ROLE role_name
[NOT IDENTIFIED
|IDENTIFIED {BY password | USING [schema.]package
|EXTERNALLY | GLOBALLY }];
```

When a role is first created, it has no privileges associated with it. Password options for roles are discussed in "Adding a Password to a Role," later in this chapter.

Two sample CREATE ROLE commands are shown in the following example:

```
create role clerk;
create role manager;
```

The first command creates a role called CLERK, which will be used in the examples in the following sections of this chapter. The second command creates a role called MANAGER, which will also be featured in those examples.

Granting Privileges to a Role

Once a role has been created, you may GRANT privileges to it. The syntax for the GRANT command is the same for roles as it is for users. When granting privileges to roles, you use the role name in the TO clause of the GRANT command, as shown in the following listing:

```
grant select on comfort to clerk;
```

As shown in this example, the role name takes the place of the username in the GRANT command. The privilege to select from the COMFORT table is now available to any user of the CLERK role.

If you are a DBA, or have been granted the GRANT ANY PRIVILEGE system role, you may grant system privileges—such as CREATE SESSION, CREATE SYNONYM, and CREATE VIEW—to roles. These privileges are then available to any user of your role.

The ability to log into the database is given via the CREATE SESSION system privilege. In the following example, this privilege is granted to the CLERK role. This privilege is also granted to the MANAGER role, along with the CREATE VIEW system privilege.

```
grant create session to clerk;
grant create session, create view to manager;
```

Granting a Role to Another Role

Roles can be granted to other roles. You can do this via the GRANT command, as shown in the following example:

```
grant clerk to manager;
```

NOTE
You can't have circular grants, so you cannot now grant MANAGER to CLERK.

In this example, the CLERK role is granted to the MANAGER role. Even though you have not directly granted any table privileges to the MANAGER role, it will now inherit any privileges that have been granted to the CLERK role. Organizing roles in this way is a common design for hierarchical organizations.

When granting a role to another role (or to a user, as in the following section), you may grant the role using the WITH ADMIN OPTION clause, as shown in the following listing:

```
grant clerk to manager with admin option;
```

If the WITH ADMIN OPTION clause is used, the grantee has the authority to grant the role to other users or roles. The grantee can also alter or drop the role.

Granting a Role to Users

Roles can be granted to users. When granted to users, roles can be thought of as named sets of privileges. Instead of granting each privilege to each user, you grant the privileges to the role and then grant the role to each user. This greatly simplifies the administrative tasks involved in the management of privileges.

NOTE
Privileges that are granted to users via roles cannot be used as the basis for views, procedures, functions, packages, or foreign keys. When creating these types of database objects, you must rely on direct grants of the necessary privileges.

You can grant a role to a user via the GRANT command, as shown in the following example:

```
grant clerk to bob;
```

In this example, the user Bob will have all the privileges that were granted to the CLERK role (CREATE SESSION and SELECT privileges on COMFORT).

When granting a role to a user, you may grant the role using the WITH ADMIN OPTION clause, as shown in the following listing:

```
grant manager to dora with admin option;
```

Dora now has the authority to grant the MANAGER role to other users or roles, or to alter or drop the role.

Adding a Password to a Role

You can use the ALTER ROLE command for only one purpose: to change the authority needed to enable it. By default, roles do not have passwords associated with them. To enable security for a role, use the IDENTIFIED keyword in the ALTER ROLE command. There are two ways to implement this security.

First, you can use the IDENTIFIED BY clause of the ALTER ROLE command to specify a password, as shown in the following listing:

```
alter role manager identified by sinnusxi;
```

Anytime a user tries to activate that role, the password is required. If, however, that role is set up as a default role for the user, no password is required for that role when the user logs in. See the upcoming "Enabling and Disabling Roles" section of this chapter for more details on these topics.

Roles can be tied to operating system privileges as well. If this capability is available on your operating system, you use the IDENTIFIED EXTERNALLY clause of the ALTER ROLE command. When the role is enabled, Oracle checks the operating system to verify your access. Altering a role to use this security feature is shown in the following example:

```
alter role manager identified externally;
```

In most UNIX systems, the verification process uses the /etc/group file. To use this file for any operating system, you must set the OS_ROLES database startup parameter in the init.ora file to TRUE.

The following example of this verification process is for a database instance called LOCAL on a Unix system. The server's /etc/group file may contain the following entry:

```
ora_local_manager_d:NONE:1:dora
```

This entry grants the MANAGER role to the account named DORA. The _D suffix indicates that this role is to be granted, by default, when Dora logs in. A suffix of _A would indicate that this role is to be enabled with WITH ADMIN OPTION. If this role were also the user's default role, the suffix would be _ad. If more than one user were granted this role, the additional usernames would be appended to the /etc/group entry, as shown in the following listing:

```
ora_local_manager_d:NONE:1:dora,judy
```

If you use this option, database roles are enabled via the operating system.

Removing a Password from a Role

To remove a password from a role, use the NOT IDENTIFIED clause of the ALTER ROLE command, as shown in the following listing. By default, roles do not have passwords.

```
alter role manager not identified;
```

Enabling and Disabling Roles

When a user's account is altered, a list of default roles for that user can be created via the DEFAULT ROLE clause of the ALTER USER command. The default action of this command sets all of a user's roles as default roles, enabling all of them every time the user logs in.

NOTE
The maximum number of roles a user can have enabled at any time is set via the MAX_ENABLED_ROLES database initialization parameter.

The syntax for this portion of the ALTER USER command is as follows:

```
ALTER USER username
DEFAULT ROLE {[role1, role2]
[ALL | ALL EXCEPT role1, role2][NONE]};
```

As shown by this syntax, a user can be altered to have, by default, specific roles enabled, all roles enabled, all except specific roles enabled, or no roles enabled. For example, the following ALTER USER command enables the CLERK role whenever Bob logs in:

```
alter user bob
default role clerk;
```

To enable a nondefault role, use the SET ROLE command, as shown in this example:

```
set role clerk;
```

To see what roles are enabled within your current session, select from the SESSION_ROLES data dictionary view. Query SESSION_PRIVS to see the currently enabled system privileges.

You may also use the ALL and ALL EXCEPT clauses that were available in the ALTER USER command:

```
set role all;
set role all except clerk;
```

If a role has a password associated with it, that password must be specified via an IDENTIFIED BY clause:

```
set role manager identified by sinusxi;
```

To disable a role in your session, use the SET ROLE NONE command, as shown in the following listing. SET ROLE NONE disables all roles in your current session. Once all the roles have been disabled, re-enable the ones you want.

```
set role none;
```

Because you may find it necessary to execute a SET ROLE NONE command from time to time, you may want to grant the CREATE SESSION privilege to users directly rather than via roles.

Revoking Privileges from a Role

To revoke a privilege from a role, use the REVOKE command, described earlier in this chapter. Specify the privilege, object name (if it is an object privilege), and role name, as shown in the following example:

```
revoke select on comfort from clerk;
```

Users of the CLERK role are then unable to query the COMFORT table.

Dropping a Role

To drop a role, use the DROP ROLE command, as shown in the following example:

```
drop role manager;
drop role clerk;
```

The roles you specify, and their associated privileges, are then removed from the database entirely. GRANTs and REVOKEs of system and object privileges take effect immediately. GRANTs and REVOKEs of roles are only observed when a current user issues a SET ROLE command or a new user session is started.

Granting UPDATE to Specific Columns

You may want to grant users the SELECT privilege on more columns than you want to grant them the UPDATE privilege. Because SELECT columns can be restricted through a view, to further restrict the columns that can be updated requires a special form of the user's GRANT command. Here is an example for two columns in the COMFORT table:

```
grant update (noon, midnight) on comfort to judy;
```

Revoking Object Privileges

If object privileges can be granted, they can also be taken away. This is similar to the GRANT command:

```
REVOKE { object privilege | ALL [PRIVILEGES]}
        [(column [, column]. . . )]
[, { object privilege | ALL [PRIVILEGES]}
        [(column [, column]. . . )]]. . .]
ON object
FROM {user | role} [,{user | role}]
[CASCADE CONSTRAINTS] [FORCE];
```

REVOKE ALL removes any of the privileges listed previously, from SELECT through INDEX; revoking individual privileges leaves intact others that had also been granted. The WITH GRANT OPTION is revoked along with the privilege to which it was attached; the REVOKE then cascades so users who received their access via the WITH GRANT OPTION user also have their privileges revoked.

If a user defines referential integrity constraints on the object, Oracle drops these constraints if you revoke privileges on the object using the CASCADE CONSTRAINTS option. The FORCE option applies to object types. The FORCE option revokes the EXECUTE privilege on object types with table or type dependencies; all dependent objects are marked as invalid and the data in dependent tables becomes inaccessible until the necessary privilege is regranted.

Defining Security by User

Access to tables can be granted specifically, table by table and view by view, to each user or role. There is, however, an additional technique that simplifies this process in some cases. Recall the BOOKSHELF_CHECKOUT records:

```
select name, substr(title,1,30) from bookshelf_checkout;
```

```
NAME                           SUBSTR(TITLE,1,30)
------------------------       ------------------------------
Jed Hopkins                    Innumeracy
Gerhardt Kentgen               Wonderful Life
Dorah Talbot                   Either/Or
Emily Talbot                   Anne Of Green Gables
Pat Lavay                      The Shipping News
Roland Brandt                  The Shipping News
Roland Brandt                  The Discoverers
Roland Brandt                  West With The Night
Emily Talbot                   Midnight Magic
Emily Talbot                   Harry Potter And The Goblet Of
Pat Lavay                      The Mismeasure Of Man
Dorah Talbot                   Polar Express
Dorah Talbot                   Good Dog, Carl
Gerhardt Kentgen               The Mismeasure Of Man
Fred Fuller                    John Adams
Fred Fuller                    Truman
Jed Hopkins                    To Kill A Mockingbird
Dorah Talbot                   My Ledger
Gerhardt Kentgen               Midnight Magic
```

To enable each borrower to access this table, but restrict the access given to a view of only each borrower's own single row, you could create 19 separate views, each with a different name in the WHERE clause, and you could make separate grants to each of these views for each borrower. Alternatively, you could create a view whose WHERE clause contains USER, the pseudo-column, like this:

```
create or replace view my_checkout as
select * from bookshelf_checkout
where substr(name,1,instr(name,' ')-1) = user;
```

The owner of the BOOKSHELF_CHECKOUT table can create this view and grant SELECT on it to users. A user can then query the BOOKSHELF_CHECKOUT table through the MY_CHECKOUT view. The WHERE clause will find his or her username in the NAME column (see the WHERE clause) and return just that user's records.

In the following example, a username Jed is created and granted access to the MY_CHECKOUT view. Selecting from that view yields just those books checked out by Jed. This example assumes that the schema owning the BOOKSHELF_CHECKOUT table is named PRACTICE and is a database administrator:

```
create user jed identified by h00p3r;

User created.

grant create session to jed;

Grant succeeded.

grant select on my_checkout to jed;

Grant succeeded.

connect jed/hop

Connected.

select * from practice.my_checkout;

NAME
------------------------
TITLE
-------------------------------------------------------
CHECKOUTD RETURNEDD
--------- ---------
Jed Hopkins
Innumeracy
01-JAN-02 22-JAN-02

Jed Hopkins
To Kill A Mockingbird
15-FEB-02 01-MAR-02
```

Whenever MY_CHECKOUT is queried, it returns records depending on the pseudo-column user—the user of SQL*Plus at the moment the view is queried.

Granting Access to the Public

Rather than grant access to every worker, the GRANT command can be generalized to the public:

```
grant select on my_checkout to public;
```

This gives everyone access, including users created after this GRANT was made. However, each user still has to access the table using the owner's username as a prefix. To avoid this, a DBA may create a *public synonym* (which creates a name accessible to all users that stands for PRACTICE. MY_CHECKOUT):

```
create public synonym my_checkout for practice.my_checkout;
```

From this point forward, anyone can access MY_CHECKOUT without prefixing it with the schema owner (PRACTICE in this case). This approach gives tremendous flexibility for security. Workers can see only their own salaries, for instance, in a table that contains salaries for everyone. If, however, a user creates a table or view with the same name as a public synonym, any future SQL statements by this user will act on this new table or view, not on the one by the same name to which the public has access.

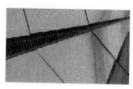

NOTE

All these accesses—and all attempts at system-level operations, such as logins—may be audited. See AUDIT in the Alphabetical Reference for an introduction to Oracle's security-auditing capabilities.

Granting Access to Limited Resources

When granting resource quotas in an Oracle database, you use the QUOTA parameter of the CREATE USER or ALTER USER command, as shown in the following listing. In this example, Bob is granted a quota of 100GB in the USERS tablespace:

```
alter user bob
quota 100g on users;
```

A user's space quota may be set when the user is created, via the CREATE USER command. If you want to remove limits on a user's space quota, you can grant that user the UNLIMITED TABLESPACE system privilege. See the CREATE USER and ALTER USER commands in the Alphabetical Reference for further details on these commands.

Profiles can also be used to enforce other resource limits, such as the amount of CPU time or idle time a user's requests to Oracle can take. A profile detailing these resource limits is created and then assigned to one or more users. See the CREATE PROFILE and ALTER USER command entries in the Alphabetical Reference for full details.

PART

III

Beyond the Basics

CHAPTER
20

Advanced Security—
Virtual Private Databases

I n prior chapters, you have seen how to use views to enhance security by displaying only the rows that meet specified criteria. In this chapter, you will see how to use a Virtual Private Database (VPD) to provide that type of record-level security across your application tables. In VPD, you attach security policies directly to tables, views, and synonyms so there is no way for users to bypass your security settings.

In a VPD, any SQL used to access a table, view, or synonym protected by a VPD policy is dynamically modified to include a limiting condition—a WHERE clause or an AND clause. The modification occurs transparently, and the user sees only the data that passes the limiting condition in the WHERE clause. This fine-grained access allows a great deal of control over all accesses of your application tables. VPD policies can be applied to SELECT, INSERT, UPDATE, INDEX, and DELETE commands. You can create different security policies for each type of access—one for SELECTs, another for INSERTs, and so on.

A VPD includes column-level policies, in which security policies are applied only when a particular column (or columns) is accessed. Oracle also supports *column masking,* in which protected columns may be displayed with NULL values if their rows are returned. Additionally, auditing has been enhanced so DBAs can perform fine-grained auditing of SELECT, INSERT, UPDATE, and DELETE commands.

NOTE
Implementing VPD requires the use of some advanced features—procedures, triggers, and PL/SQL. These features are covered in Part IV of this book. If you are not already familiar with those features, you may wish to review Part IV before proceeding with the advanced material in this chapter.

Initial Configuration

VPD allows you to customize the ways different users see the same table. To walk through the full example shown in this chapter, you need access to a SYSDBA-privileged account.

VPD requires a package named DBMS_RLS. From a SYSDBA-privileged account, grant the EXECUTE privilege on the DBMS_RLS package to all users. Also, create the users for the examples: PRACTICE (which owns the tables), ADAMS, and BURLINGTON, as shown in the following listing:

```
connect / as sysdba

grant create session to adams identified by john7;
grant create session to burlington identified by newj2;
```

NOTE
Using GRANT with IDENTIFIED BY along with any permissions is a great shortcut for simultaneously executing the CREATE USER and GRANT commands when creating a new user.

From the SYSDBA-privileged account, create the PRACTICE user (if it does not already exist) and give it the RESOURCE role along with the CREATE ANY CONTEXT and CREATE PUBLIC SYNONYM system privileges:

```
grant create session to practice identified by practice;
grant resource to practice;
grant create any context, create public synonym to practice;
grant create any procedure to practice;
grant unlimited tablespace to practice;
grant execute on dbms_rls to practice;
```

Within the PRACTICE user, you should now create two tables: the STOCK_ACCOUNT table and the STOCK_TRX table. The STOCK_ACCOUNT table contains one row for each account that can perform stock trades. The STOCK_TRX table contains one row for each stock bought or sold by that account holder.

```
connect practice/practice

create table stock_account
(account            number(10),
account_longname  varchar2(50));

insert into stock_account values (
   1234, 'ADAMS');
insert into stock_account values (
   7777, 'BURLINGTON');

create table stock_trx (
account    number(10),
symbol     varchar2(20),
price      number(6,2),
quantity   number(6),
trx_flag   varchar2(1));

insert into stock_trx values (
   1234, 'ADSP', 31.75, 100, 'b');
insert into stock_trx values (
   7777, 'ADSP', 31.50, 300, 's');
insert into stock_trx values (
   1234, 'ADSP', 31.55, 100, 'b');
insert into stock_trx values (
   7777, 'OCKS', 21.75, 1000, 'b');
commit;
```

Once you've created those tables, grant the ADAMS and BURLINGTON users access to them:

```
grant select, insert on stock_trx to adams, burlington;
grant select on stock_account to adams, burlington;
```

You now have the application configuration set—the PRACTICE schema owns the data table (STOCK_TRX) and has a table that you can use to map usernames to account numbers (STOCK_ACCOUNT). With this configuration in place, you can create an *application context,* as described in the next section.

Create an Application Context

The next step in the VPD configuration is to create an application context. The purpose of the context is to define the rules you will use to separate users. The context will be part of each session's characteristics.

First, use the CREATE CONTEXT command to specify the name of the package you will use to set the rules:

```
connect practice/practice

create context practice using practice.context_package;
```

Next, create the package with that same name (CONTEXT_PACKAGE). See Chapter 35 for details on using packages. The package consists of a single procedure call:

```
create or replace package context_package as
  procedure set_context;
end;
/
```

Now that you've created the package header, you can create the package body. The following listing shows the package body that sets the context for each session:

```
create or replace package body context_package is
  procedure set_context is
    v_user  varchar2(30);
    v_id    number;
  begin
    dbms_session.set_context('PRACTICE','SETUP','TRUE');
    v_user := sys_context('USERENV','SESSION_USER');
    begin
      select account
        into v_id
        from stock_account
       where account_longname = v_user;
      dbms_session.set_context('PRACTICE','USER_ID', v_id);
    exception
      when no_data_found then
        dbms_session.set_context('PRACTICE','USER_ID', 0);
    end;
    dbms_session.set_context('PRACTICE','SETUP','FALSE');
  end set_context;
end context_package;
/
```

The core of this package body is a single query:

```
select account
  into v_id
  from stock_account
 where account_longname = v_user;
```

The STOCK_ACCOUNT table contains a row for each user (Adams, Burlington, and so on). This query takes the name of the user who logged in and compares it to the ACCOUNT_LONGNAME values in the STOCK_ACCOUNT table. If there is a match, then the Account value is returned. If there is no match, then another part of the package returns a 0 as the account number. The Account value is set as the USER_ID variable for the session:

```
dbms_session.set_context('PRACTICE','USER_ID', v_id);
```

You can reference this context value in your programs, and VPD restrictions will be based on the context setting.

Now that you've created the package, grant public access to it:

```
grant execute on practice.context_package to public;
create public synonym context_package for practice.context_package;
```

You are now ready to activate the rules for establishing the context for sessions, as described in the next section.

Create a Logon Trigger

For the context to be set within each user's session, you must create a trigger that will execute each time a user logs into the database (see Chapter 34 for full details on triggers).

```
-- NOTE: connect to a SYSDBA account before running this
--
create or replace trigger practice.set_security_context
after logon on database
begin
  practice.context_package.set_context;
end;
/
```

Each time a user logs in, Oracle executes the SET_CONTEXT procedure within the PRACTICE user's CONTEXT_PACKAGE package. That procedure queries the STOCK_ACCOUNT table to see if there is a matching account name; if there is a match, then the session's context is altered to reflect the ACCOUNT value.

You should test the context setting before moving past this point in the implementation of a VPD. You can use the SYS_CONTEXT function to determine whether the configuration is working properly, as shown in the following listing:

```
connect adams/john7

select sys_context('USERENV', 'SESSION_USER') username,
       sys_context('PRACTICE', 'USER_ID') id
```

```
from dual;

USERNAME
------------------------------------------------------------
ID
------------------------------------------------------------
ADAMS
1234
```

The SYS_CONTEXT function output shows the power of the VPD configuration. For each user who logs in, Oracle checks the STOCK_ACCOUNT table and uses the matching ACCOUNT value to set a value for the session's USER_ID. In this case, Oracle looked up the ADAMS user in the STOCK_ACCOUNT table, found its account number (1234), and set its session's USER_ID variable to that value. If you have that information, you can restrict access to rows in other tables based on the account number in the STOCK_ACCOUNT table. VPD allows you to restrict that access automatically with no need to create views. Every time a user attempts to access a table, access can be restricted regardless of the tool used.

If you log in as a user not listed in the STOCK_ACCOUNT table (triggering a NO_DATA_FOUND exception), your USER_ID value will be 0, as the procedure dictates:

```
      when no_data_found then
         dbms_session.set_context('PRACTICE','USER_ID', 0);
```

Create a Security Policy

At this point, you've created the context and the logon triggers. For the context package to have an effect on the users' interaction with the database, you need to create a security package that acts on the output of the context package.

First, define the package header. In this example, there are two types of actions supported against the STOCK_TRX table (INSERTs and SELECTs), so two functions are created within the package:

```
connect practice/practice

create or replace package security_package as
  function stock_trx_insert_security(owner varchar2, objname varchar2)
    return varchar2;
  function stock_trx_select_security(owner varchar2, objname varchar2)
    return varchar2;
end security_package;
/
```

Next, create the package body. Both functions follow the same pattern, geared toward generating a predicate that will be applied every time a user queries the STOCK_TRX table. If the session username is the owner of the table, then the predicate is NULL. For all other users, the USER_ID context variable is evaluated and is passed as a limiting condition to any query. The object of these functions is to generate a predicate such as WHERE ACCOUNT=1234 to be applied each time a user queries the table.

```
create or replace package body security_package is
  function stock_trx_select_security(owner varchar2, objname varchar2)
```

```
    return varchar2 is
      predicate varchar2(2000);
    begin
      predicate := '1=2';
      if (sys_context('USERENV','SESSION_USER') = 'PRACTICE') then
        predicate := null;
      else
        predicate := 'account = sys_context(''PRACTICE'',''USER_ID'')';
      end if;
      return predicate;
    end stock_trx_select_security;

    function stock_trx_insert_security(owner varchar2, objname varchar2)
     return varchar2 is
      predicate varchar2(2000);
    begin
      predicate := '1=2';
      if (sys_context('USERENV','SESSION_USER') = 'PRACTICE') then
        predicate := null;
      else
        predicate := 'account = sys_context(''PRACTICE'',''USER_ID'')';
      end if;
      return predicate;
    end stock_trx_insert_security;
  end security_package;
  /
```

Because this package will be executed by all users who access the STOCK_TRX table, grant users the privilege to execute it and create a public synonym:

```
grant execute on practice.security_package to public;
create public synonym security_package for practice.security_package;
```

Apply the Security Policy to Tables

Now that the security package exists, you can relate it to tables. To add a policy to a table, use the ADD_POLICY procedure of the DBMS_RLS package, as shown in the following listing:

```
begin
  dbms_rls.add_policy('PRACTICE', 'STOCK_TRX', 'STOCK_TRX_INSERT_POLICY',
                      'PRACTICE', 'SECURITY_PACKAGE.STOCK_TRX_INSERT_SECURITY',
                      'INSERT', TRUE);
  dbms_rls.add_policy('PRACTICE', 'STOCK_TRX', 'STOCK_TRX_SELECT_POLICY',
                      'PRACTICE', 'SECURITY_PACKAGE.STOCK_TRX_SELECT_SECURITY',
                      'SELECT');
end;
/
```

The ADD_POLICY procedure is executed two times. The first time, the STOCK_TRX_INSERT_SECURITY function is specified for execution during attempts to insert rows into the STOCK_TRX table. The second time, the STOCK_TRX_SELECT_SECURITY function is applied to queries of the STOCK_TRX tables. You can have distinct security rules for different operations against the table. The variables passed to the ADD_POLICY procedure are the schema name, table name, and policy name; the schema name and function name for the security function; and the operation affected.

Test the VPD Security Policy

To see the results of the security policy, query the table. The STOCK_TRX table has four rows, two from the ADAMS account (1234) and two from the BURLINGTON account (7777). Log in as one of those users and query the table:

```
connect adams/john7

select * from practice.stock_trx;

    ACCOUNT SYMBOL                     PRICE   QUANTITY T
 ---------- -------------------- ---------- ---------- -
       1234 ADSP                      31.75        100 B
       1234 ADSP                      31.55        100 B
```

Although the ADAMS user did not provide a WHERE clause in his query, Oracle applied a predicate to his query, limiting the results to rows with the ACCOUNT value of 1234. What if the BURLINGTON user attempts the same query?

```
connect burlington/newj2

select * from practice.stock_trx;

    ACCOUNT SYMBOL                     PRICE   QUANTITY T
 ---------- -------------------- ---------- ---------- -
       7777 ADSP                       31.5        300 S
       7777 OCKS                      21.75       1000 B
```

The BURLINGTON user only sees the rows with the ACCOUNT value of 7777, based on his row in the STOCK_ACCOUNT table.

NOTE
Because the STOCK_ACCOUNT table is queried for each logon, make sure the query to retrieve the user context data is properly tuned.

What about other users? If they are not in the STOCK_ACCOUNT table, they cannot retrieve rows from the STOCK_TRX table:

```
connect sun/flower96

select * from PRACTICE.STOCK_TRX;

no rows selected
```

NOTE
Users who log in with the AS SYSDBA clause are still able to see all the table rows.

In addition to SELECTs, INSERTs are limited by the security policy; a user can only insert rows into STOCK_TRX if the ACCOUNT value matches the user's context settings. Attempts to insert other rows fail:

```
connect practice/practice
grant insert on stock_trx to adams;

connect adams/john7

insert into practice.stock_trx
values
(7777, 'ADSP',31.5,100, 'B');

ERROR at line 1:
ORAC-28115: policy with check option violation
```

The ORA-28115 error indicates that the user attempted to insert a row that the user would not be able to select owing to the VPD settings.

NOTE
You can establish several policies for the same table, view, or synonym. All policies applied to a table are enforced with AND syntax. If you have three policies applied to the STOCK_TRX table, each one is applied to the table.

How to Implement Column-Level VPD

You can implement VPD at the column level. If a column with secure data is referenced by a query, you can use column-level VPD to apply a security policy or display the column with NULL values. This approach is different from the row-based VPD shown in the prior examples; in column-level VPD all rows may be displayed, but the columns may be shielded from the user. You can apply column-level VPD to a table or a view.

To use column-level VPD, specify a value for the SEC_RELEVANT_COLS input parameters for the ADD_POLICY procedure of DBMS_RLS. When creating a second policy, STOCK_TRX_ SELECT_POLICY2, you can use the following command:

```
connect practice/practice

begin
  dbms_rls.add_policy
          (object_schema=>'PRACTICE',
           object_name=>'STOCK_TRX',
           policy_name=>'STOCK_TRX_SELECT_POLICY2',
        function_schema=>'PRACTICE',
        policy_function=>'SECURITY_PACKAGE.STOCK_TRX_SELECT_SECURITY',
```

```
                    sec_relevant_cols=>'Price');
  end;
  /
```

By default, the rows are returned based on the security policy function when the PRICE column is referenced by a query. To use the column-masking option, tell Oracle to return all rows by setting the SEC_RELEVANT_COLS_OPT parameter to DBMS_RLS.ALL_ROWS, following the SEC_RELEVANT_COLS parameter setting.

When this version of the policy is used, the query returns all rows. For the rows that the user would not normally be able to see, the secure column (PRICE) displays NULL values. The PRICE values are displayed for rows that the user can normally see.

Column masking applies only to queries, not to DML operations. Note that your applications must support the display of NULL values if you use column masking.

How to Disable VPD

To remove VPD functionality, reverse the steps shown in this chapter: Remove the policy from the table (via the DROP_POLICY procedure of the DBMS_RLS package), drop the logon trigger, and optionally drop the other packages.

Table 20-1 lists the procedures within the DBMS_RLS package.

To drop a policy, execute the DROP_POLICY procedure. Its three input variables are the schema name, the object name, and the policy. The following example drops the STOCK_TRX_INSERT_POLICY:

```
exec dbms_rls.drop_policy('PRACTICE', 'STOCK_TRX', 'STOCK_TRX_INSERT_POLICY');
```

Similarly, you can drop the STOCK_TRX_SELECT_POLICY:

```
exec dbms_rls.drop_policy('PRACTICE', 'STOCK_TRX', 'STOCK_TRX_SELECT_POLICY');
```

At this point, the policy is dropped, but the login trigger will execute during each login. Remember to drop the trigger (in this case, PRACTICE.SET_SECURITY_CONTEXT), so the database does not perform unnecessary work.

You can drop the security context trigger as shown in the following listing:

```
connect / as sysdba

select owner, trigger_name from dba_triggers
where triggering_event LIKE 'LOGON%';

OWNER               TRIGGER_NAME
----------------    ------------------------------
PRACTICE            SET_SECURITY_CONTEXT

drop trigger practice.set_security_context;

Trigger dropped.
```

Procedure	Purpose
ADD_POLICY	Adds a policy to a table, view, or synonym
DROP_POLICY	Drops a policy from a table, view, or synonym
REFRESH_POLICY	Invalidates cursors associated with nonstatic policies
ENABLE_POLICY	Enables (or disables) a policy you previously added to a table, view, or synonym
CREATE_POLICY_GROUP	Creates a policy group
ADD_GROUPED_POLICY	Adds a policy to the specified policy group
ADD_POLICY_CONTEXT	Adds the context for the active application
DELETE_POLICY_GROUP	Drops a policy group
DROP_GROUPED_POLICY	Drops a policy that is a member of the specified group
DROP_POLICY_CONTEXT	Drops the context for the application
ENABLE_GROUPED_POLICY	Enables a policy within a group
DISABLE_GROUPED_POLICY	Disables a policy within a group
REFRESH_GROUPED_POLICY	Reparses the SQL statements associated with a refreshed policy

TABLE 20-1.   *DBMS_RLS Procedures*

If the VPD restrictions are no longer needed, you can then drop the packages that set the application context.

How to Use Policy Groups

As shown in Table 20-1, a number of the available procedures within DBMS_RLS deal with *policy groups*. You can create policy groups, add policies to a policy group, and enable policies within a group.

You can create groups that integrate policies affecting the same tables. If multiple applications use the same tables, you can use groups to manage the table-level policies that should be enabled during application usage. All policies in a policy group can be applied at application run time.

By default, all policies belong to the SYS_DEFAULT policy group. Policies in the SYS_DEFAULT policy group are always executed along with the policy group specified by the driving context. You cannot drop the SYS_DEFAULT policy group.

To add a new policy group, use the CREATE_POLICY_GROUP procedure. The syntax is

```
DBMS_RLS.CREATE_POLICY_GROUP (
    object_schema    VARCHAR2,
    object_name      VARCHAR2,
    policy_group     VARCHAR2);
```

You can then add a policy to the group via the ADD_GROUPED_POLICY procedure. Its syntax is

```
DBMS_RLS.ADD_GROUPED_POLICY(
    object_schema   VARCHAR2,
    object_name     VARCHAR2,
    policy_group    VARCHAR2,
    policy_name     VARCHAR2,
    function_schema VARCHAR2,
    policy_function VARCHAR2,
    statement_types VARCHAR2,
    update_check    BOOLEAN,
    enabled         BOOLEAN,
    static_policy   IN BOOLEAN   FALSE,
    policy_type     IN BINARY_INTEGER NULL,
    long_predicate  IN BOOLEAN   FALSE,
    sec_relevant_cols IN VARCHAR2);
```

For example, you can create a policy group named TRXAUDIT and add the STOCK_TRX_SELECT_POLICY to it:

```
begin
dbms_rls.create_policy_group('PRACTICE','STOCK_TRX','TRXAUDIT');
dbms_rls.add_grouped_policy('PRACTICE','STOCK_TRX','TRXAUDIT',
'STOCK_TRX_SELECT_POLICY','PRACTICE', 'SECURITY_PACKAGE.STOCK_TRX_SELECT_SECURITY');
end;
/
```

When the database is accessed, the application initializes the driving context to specify the policy group to use. In the CREATE CONTEXT command, specify the name of the procedure to use (in the examples in this chapter, the context is set via PRACTICE.CONTEXT_PACKAGE).

```
create context practice2 using practice.context_package;
```

PRACTICE.CONTEXT_PACKAGE executes the SET_CONTEXT procedure to set the application context:

```
dbms_session.set_context('PRACTICE2','SETUP','TRUE');
```

For policy groups, the third parameter passed to SET_CONTEXT is the policy group name. For the application to invoke a specific context group, rewrite CONTEXT_PACKAGE to support a third input variable (policy group) and add that to the SET_CONTEXT execution using this template:

```
exec dbms_session.set_context('PRACTICE','SETUP','policy_group');
```

Within your application, execute CONTEXT_PACKAGE and set the *policy_group* value to TRXAUDIT. When the user queries the STOCK_TRX table, the VPD restrictions in SYS_DEFAULT and the TRXAUDIT policy group are then applied.

You can remove a policy from a policy group via DROP_GROUPED_POLICY, disable it via DISABLE_GROUPED_POLICY, or re-enable it via ENABLE_GROUPED_POLICY. Use DELETE_POLICY_GROUP to drop the policy group entirely. See the *Security Guide* for additional information on the procedures available within the DBMS_RLS package.

CHAPTER
21

Advanced Security—
Transparent Data
Encryption

O racle offers many advanced security features. Although some of them (such as VPD) require modifications of database tables and triggers, others can be implemented without changing any application code. This chapter introduces two of the advanced security features: column encryption and tablespace encryption.

Transparent Data Encryption for Columns

As discussed in earlier chapters, Oracle offers a number of mechanisms for securing the data within a database. You can use Transparent Data Encryption (TDE) to further ensure the integrity of your data. TDE encrypts the data in the datafiles, undo logs, redo logs, and the buffer cache of the system global area (SGA) in memory. You can select which columns of which tables will be encrypted.

Using TDE provides an enhanced level of security for sensitive data without you having to change anything about the application that uses the data. End users and application developers will continue to access and store rows the same as they always have; the only change will be the way those rows are physically stored at the operating system level. TDE is well suited for database applications in which sensitive data elements must be encrypted due to regulatory or business requirements.

TDE is a key-based encryption system. To use TDE, you need to configure a *wallet* for the database to use when it is first opened. The wallet file will require a password for the encrypted columns to be accessed. Thus, anyone who attempts to copy your datafiles in an effort to duplicate your database will need the datafiles, the wallet file, and the wallet password to access those columns. The wallet file should be stored on a server apart from the database server (to further enhance security). If a user attempts to access an encrypted column with the wallet closed, the database responds with the following error:

```
ORA-28365: wallet is not open
```

Once the database is opened with the wallet password, anything stored in the designated secured columns is encrypted when it is written to the datafiles. Other columns are not affected.

Setting Up TDE for Columns

To configure TDE, you need full DBA access, which means you need an account with the DBA role and access to the **oracle** account on the database server. The steps in this section assume you have full access to the account and all related configuration files.

When logged into the **oracle** user account, make sure your TNS_ADMIN environment variable is set and points to the directory containing the local **sqlnet.ora** file. Here's an example:

```
export TNS_ADMIN=/var/opt/oracle
```

If a **sqlnet.ora** file does not exist in that location, create it. If a **sqlnet.ora** file does exist in that location, add an entry for the ENCRYPTION_WALLET_LOCATION parameter value. Assuming the instance is named CC1, the parameter value resembles the following:

```
ENCRYPTION_WALLET_LOCATION=
  (SOURCE=
    (METHOD=file)
```

```
         (METHOD_DATA=
  (DIRECTORY=/opt/oracle/admin/CC1/wallet)))
```

Note that you should use the actual value for the directory name, not an environment variable such as $ORACLE_BASE or $ORACLE_SID.

If you have not already done so, create the directory specified by the ENCRYPTION_WALLET_LOCATION parameter value and make it available for read and write by the **oracle** user.

Now that the wallet directory is ready, you need to select the wallet password. The wallet and its password are critical; you must have them to open the database and access the encrypted column values.

NOTE
Be sure to keep careful records of the wallet passwords you use. In the event of a disaster, you will need to have the wallet passwords available at the disaster recovery site.

If you are configuring a Real Application Clusters (RAC) database system, check which instance runs on the server you are logged into. Be sure your ORACLE_SID environment variable points to the instance on your local server. Log into the instance:

```
sqlplus "sys@CC1 as sysdba"
```

To create a wallet file for the instance, issue the following command, putting in your wallet password where shown:

```
alter system set encryption key
   authenticated by "password";
```

When you execute the ALTER SYSTEM command, Oracle creates a wallet file in the directory specified by the ENCRYPTION_WALLET_LOCATION parameter value in your **sqlnet.ora** file.

Additional Setup for RAC Databases

If the instance is part of a RAC configuration (in which multiple instances access a single database), you now need to log into the other servers and repeat the first several steps: setting TNS_ADMIN, putting the ENCRYPTION_WALLET_LOCATION entry in the **sqlnet.ora** file, and creating the wallet directory. Instead of creating a new wallet file for the second server, you should copy the wallet file from the first server to the second server (enter the following command as one line):

```
scp node1:/opt/oracle/admin/CC1/wallet/ewallet.p12
       node2:/opt/oracle/admin/CC1/wallet
```

Now log into the instance that is local to the second server:

```
sqlplus "sys@CC2 as sysdba"
```

Then issue the following command, inserting your password where shown:

```
alter system set encryption wallet open
authenticated by "password";
```

The configuration of the wallet file for the RAC instances is now complete.

NOTE
The wallet file should be backed up as part of your regular backup procedures. In a RAC environment, you will have a separate copy of the wallet file on each of the clustered servers, providing added protection for the wallet.

Opening and Closing the Wallet

When you use TDE, you need to open the wallet when you open the database. When you shut down the database, the wallet is automatically closed, but there may be situations where you want to close the wallet temporarily while the database is still open.

During startup, you must open the wallet—and if you are using a RAC configuration, you must open the wallet on all instances of the RAC cluster.

To open the wallet, issue the following command with the open:

```
alter system set encryption wallet open
    authenticated by "password";
```

Before shutting down the database, you can close the wallet on both instances. Use the ALTER SYSTEM command to close the wallet in each instance, however:

```
alter system set encryption wallet close;
```

NOTE
If the database crashes for any reason, the wallet will be closed and will have to be reopened on all instances of the database.

It is critical to remember that the WALLET OPEN and WALLET CLOSE commands apply to an instance, not a database. It is possible to have the wallet open on one instance while the wallet is closed on other instances for the same database.

Encrypting and Decrypting Columns

To encrypt an existing column, use the ENCRYPT option within the ALTER TABLE command. In the following listing, the PHONE column of the ADDRESS table is encrypted:

```
alter table address modify
    (phone encrypt no salt);
```

For an existing table, Oracle dynamically encrypts the rows that already exist. Having an index on the column slows the encryption process. Note that encrypting a column substantially increases the size of the data stored in the table and in the index.

Updating the size of a column will cause row movement within the data blocks, and if every row in a block is updated, row migration will occur, which, in turn, will cause very poor performance. Tables will generally need to be reorganized using the ALTER TABLE MOVE command to remove the row migration.

By default, TDE adds *salt* (a random string) to *cleartext* (unencrypted text strings) before encrypting it, making the encryption more difficult to break. If you plan to index the encrypted column, you must use NO SALT, as shown in the preceding listing. You can use the ALTER TABLE command to modify an existing encryption from SALT to NO SALT, or from NO SALT to SALT.

You can specify the ENCRYPT option when creating a table, as shown in the following listing:

```
create table address (
 lastname    varchar2(25),
 firstname   varchar2(25),
 street      varchar2(50),
 city        varchar2(25),
 state       char(2),
 zip         number,
 phone       varchar2(12)   encrypt no salt,
 ext         varchar2(5)
);
```

Because the specified column's values are encrypted, index range scans will no longer be effective ways to retrieve that column's data from the table. In general, the Oracle Optimizer uses indexes on the encrypted columns for exact matches, but range scans would be negatively impacted by the encryption. For example, suppose you were to execute the following query:

```
select * from address
where phone like '415%';
```

If the PHONE column is encrypted, you should expect the optimizer to bypass any index on the PHONE column during the execution of the query.

NOTE
The CREATE INDEX command for encrypted columns is the same as the CREATE INDEX command for unencrypted columns.

You can encrypt a new column that is added via the ALTER TABLE command, as shown in the following listing:

```
alter table address add
   (mobilephone varchar2(20) encrypt no salt);
```

To decrypt a column, use the DECRYPT option within the ALTER TABLE command, as shown in the following listing:

```
alter table address modify
   (phone decrypt);
```

NOTE
Each encrypted column adds between 32 and 48 bytes to the length of each row in the table.

Transparent Data Encryption for Tablespaces

Instead of encrypting selected columns, you can encrypt an entire tablespace. Any object created in the tablespace will be encrypted. Tablespace-level encryption is useful if you cannot perform detailed analysis of the columns requiring encryption or if a majority of the columns require encryption.

As noted in the previous section, column-level encryption prevents Oracle from using index range scans during data retrieval. Tablespace-level encryption allows for index range scans on the encrypted data, providing consistent performance for queries of ranges of values.

As with column-level TDE, the data in the designated tablespace is stored in encrypted format on disk, whether in datafiles, undo logs, redo logs, or temporary tablespaces. To access the data (or re-create the database), you need the datafiles, the wallet file, and the wallet password.

Setting Up TDE on Tablespaces

To encrypt a tablespace, you must first set a tablespace master encryption key. The steps for creating the tablespace master encryption key mirror the setup steps described earlier in this chapter for encrypting columns. Tablespace encryption uses the same wallet used by column-level TDE.

NOTE
The examples in this section assume that you do not have any other encryption configured on your database.

As with column-level TDE, you use your **sqlnet.ora** file to point to a location for the wallet file. If a **sqlnet.ora** file does not exist in the TNS_ADMIN directory, create it. If a **sqlnet.ora** file does exist in that location, add an entry for the ENCRYPTION_WALLET_LOCATION parameter value. Assuming the instance is named CC1, the parameter value resembles the following:

```
ENCRYPTION_WALLET_LOCATION=
    (SOURCE=
        (METHOD=file)
            (METHOD_DATA=
    (DIRECTORY=/opt/oracle/admin/CC1/wallet)))
```

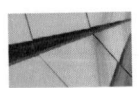

NOTE
If you want to use tablespace encryption alongside features such as hardware security modules (HSMs), you must set the tablespace master encryption key before configuring the HSM.

You can then connect to the database as the SYS user and execute the command:

```
alter system set encryption key
    authenticated by "password";
```

When you create a master encryption key for TDE, a master encryption key for tablespace encryption also gets created. When you issue the ALTER SYSTEM SET ENCRYPTION KEY command, it re-creates the standard TDE master key if one already exists and creates a new tablespace master encryption key. If the tablespace master encryption key already exists, a new key is not created.

Once the tablespace encryption key has been created, you must open the wallet. To open the wallet, issue the following command with the database open, the same as for column-level encryption:

```
alter system set encryption wallet open
    authenticated by "password";
```

Creating an Encrypted Tablespace

Once you have created a tablespace master encryption key and have opened the wallet and the database, you can create an encrypted tablespace. When using the CREATE TABLESPACE command, you can specify the encryption algorithm and key length for the encryption. The ENCRYPT keyword in the DEFAULT STORAGE clause tells Oracle to encrypt the tablespace.

The following listing shows the creation of an encrypted tablespace:

```
create tablespace encr_tspace
    datafile '+DATA'
    size 24g
    encryption using 'aes128'
    default storage(encrypt);
```

In this example, the tablespace is encrypted using the AES algorithm with a key length of 128 bits. See the CREATE TABLESPACE command entry in the Alphabetical Reference for the options. The default encryption algorithm is AES128.

Any table you now create in the ENCR_TSPACE tablespace will be encrypted. Aside from specifying the tablespace, you do not need to modify any of your application code to take advantage of this feature. To see if your tablespaces are encrypted, query the ENCRYPTED column of the DBA_TABLESPACES data dictionary view.

You cannot encrypt an existing tablespace. If the objects you need to encrypt are already stored within the database, use the MOVE clause of the ALTER TABLE command to move them to the encrypted tablespace. If enough space is available, you may be able to use the CREATE TABLE AS SELECT command to create a new encrypted table based on an existing unencrypted table. Using the Oracle utilities **expdp** and **impdp** is helpful for exporting and importing the logical version of the table data as an alternative to performing the move inside the database.

Regardless of the approach you choose, wallet-based security provides an important tool for securing your data without changing your application code. Additional security features available for Oracle DBAs include encrypted backups and secure files. See the *Oracle 12c DBA Handbook* for further details on these and other DBA-focused security options.

CHAPTER
22

Working with Tablespaces

T his chapter gives you an overview of using *tablespaces,* along with the commands needed to create and alter tablespaces. The commands needed to create and maintain tablespaces require that you have database administrator privileges. Chapter 51 will describe the creation and maintenance of tablespaces in greater detail. The goals of this chapter are to introduce the concepts, review new features, and provide developers with the information needed to make informed design decisions relative to their usage of tablespaces.

Tablespaces and the Structure of the Database

People who have worked with computers for any period of time are familiar with the concept of a file; it's a place on disk where information is stored, and it has a name. Its size is usually not fixed: If you add information to the file, it grows larger and takes up more disk space, up to the maximum available. This process is managed by the operating system and often involves distributing the information in the file over several smaller sections of the disk that are not physically near each other. The operating system handles the logical connection of these smaller sections without your being aware of it at all. To you, the file looks like a single whole.

Oracle uses files as a part of its organizational scheme, but its logical structure goes beyond the concept of a file. A *datafile* is an operating system file (or file within an Automatic Storage Management disk group) used to store Oracle data. Each datafile is assigned to a *tablespace*—a logical division within the database. Tablespaces commonly include SYSTEM (for Oracle's internal data dictionary), SYSAUX (for auxiliary internal objects), USERS (for user objects), and others for application tables, indexes, and additional database structures.

Datafiles can have a fixed size or they can be allowed to extend themselves automatically when they are filled, up to a defined limit. To add more space to a tablespace, you can manually extend your datafiles or add new datafiles. New rows can then be added to existing tables, and those tables may then have rows in multiple datafiles.

Each table has a single area of disk space, called a *segment,* set aside for it in the tablespace. Each segment, in turn, has an initial area of disk space, called the *initial extent,* set aside for it in the tablespace. Once the segment has used this space, the *next extent,* another single area of disk space, is set aside for it. When it has used this up as well, yet another extent is set aside. This process continues with every table until the whole tablespace is full. At that point, someone has to add a new datafile to the tablespace or extend the existing tablespace's files before tables can get any bigger.

Every database also contains a SYSTEM tablespace, which contains the data dictionary as well as the names and locations of all the tablespaces, tables, indexes, and clusters for this database. The objects within the SYSTEM tablespace are owned by the SYS and SYSTEM users; no other users should own objects in this tablespace because those objects could have an adverse performance impact on the database.

NOTE
You can rename a tablespace via the ALTER TABLESPACE command.

Tablespace Contents

You can query the USER_TABLESPACES data dictionary view to see the tablespaces available in the database. Tablespaces are created by privileged users, via the CREATE TABLESPACE command. The simplest syntax is

```
CREATE TABLESPACE tablespace_name
    DATAFILE datafile_name SIZE filesize;
```

Database administrators specify the tablespace space-allocation method when creating the tablespace. The following example creates a tablespace whose initial space allocation is a single 100MB file, but that file can automatically extend itself as needed:

```
create tablespace users_2
    datafile '/u01/oradata/users_2_01.dbf'
      size 100M autoextend on;
```

NOTE
In this chapter, the focus is on the developer's use of tablespaces. Database administrators should see Chapter 51 and the Alphabetical Reference for the detailed commands and options involved in creating tablespaces.

The CONTENTS column of USER_TABLESPACES shows the type of objects supported in each tablespace. The following shows a sample listing from a typical Oracle installation:

```
select tablespace_name, contents from user_tablespaces;
```

TABLESPACE_NAME	CONTENTS
SYSTEM	PERMANENT
UNDOTBS1	UNDO
SYSAUX	PERMANENT
TEMP	TEMPORARY
USERS	PERMANENT

The SYSTEM, SYSAUX, and USERS tablespaces support permanent objects—tables, indexes, and other user objects. The TEMP tablespace supports only temporary segments—segments created and managed by Oracle to support sorting operations. The UNDOTBS1 tablespace supports undo segment management (see Chapters 29 and 30).

When you create a table without specifying a tablespace, the table will be stored in your default tablespace. You can see that setting via the USER_USERS data dictionary view:

```
select default_tablespace, temporary_tablespace
from user_users;
```

DEFAULT_TABLESPACE	TEMPORARY_TABLESPACE
USERS	TEMP

In this example, the default tablespace is USERS and the temporary tablespace is TEMP. You can change those settings via the ALTER USER command.

Although USERS is your default tablespace, you don't automatically have any *quota*, or available space, in the tablespace. To see how much space you are allowed to use in a tablespace, query USER_TS_QUOTAS, as shown in the following listing:

```
select * from user_ts_quotas;
```

TABLESPACE_NAME	BYTES	MAX_BYTES	BLOCKS	MAX_BLOCKS
USERS	131072	-1	16	-1

In this case, the MAX_BYTES and MAX_BLOCKS values—the maximum space you can use—are both –1. If the value is negative, you have an unlimited quota in that tablespace. In this example, the user has only used 16 database blocks in 131,072 bytes. Because there are 1,024 bytes in a kilobyte, the user has 128KB allocated in the USERS tablespace.

The space in tablespaces can be *locally managed*. As an alternative, space management can be *dictionary managed* (the space management records are maintained in the data dictionary). In general, locally managed tablespaces are simpler to administer and should be used for all new tablespaces. You can display the extent management setting via the EXTENT_MANAGEMENT column of USER_TABLESPACES:

```
select tablespace_name, extent_management from user_tablespaces;
```

TABLESPACE_NAME	EXTENT_MAN
SYSTEM	LOCAL
UNDOTBS1	LOCAL
SYSAUX	LOCAL
TEMP	LOCAL
USERS	LOCAL

In a locally managed tablespace, the space map for the tablespace is maintained in the headers of the tablespace's datafiles. To see the datafiles allocated to a tablespace, database administrators can query the DBA_DATA_FILES data dictionary view; there is no equivalent view for nonprivileged users.

The default values for storage are operating system specific. You can query USER_TABLESPACES to see the block size and the defaults for the initial extent size, next extent size, minimum number of extents, maximum number of extents, and PCTINCREASE settings for objects:

```
select tablespace_name,
       block_size,
       initial_extent,
       next_extent,
       min_extents,
       max_extents,
       pct_increase
  from user_tablespaces;
```

To override the default settings, you can use the STORAGE clause when creating a table or index. See the entry for the STORAGE clause in the Alphabetical Reference for the full syntax. In general, you should work with the database administrators to establish appropriate defaults for the locally managed tablespaces and then rely on that sizing for your objects. Unless there are objects with extraordinary space requirements, you should avoid setting custom sizes for each of your tables and indexes. If you do not specify a STORAGE clause when you create an object, it will use the default for its tablespace. If you do not specify a TABLESPACE clause, the object will be stored in your default tablespace.

You can query the free space in a tablespace via the USER_FREE_SPACE data dictionary view. USER_FREE_SPACE displays one row for each contiguous free extent within a tablespace, as well as its exact location and length.

RECYCLEBIN Space in Tablespaces

Dropped objects do not release their allocated space unless you specify the PURGE clause when dropping them. By default, the objects maintain their space, allowing you to later recover them via the FLASHBACK TABLE TO BEFORE DROP command (see Chapter 30).

The space currently used by dropped objects is recorded in each user's RECYCLEBIN view (or, for the DBA, the DBA_RECYCLEBIN view). You can see how many bytes you are presently using in each tablespace, and you can use the PURGE command to purge old entries from the RECYCLEBIN. Here's an example:

```
select space --number of blocks still allocated
from recyclebin
where ts_name = 'USERS';
```

Dropped objects will automatically be purged if space is needed in the tablespace for new objects or for extending existing objects. See the PURGE command in the Alphabetical Reference and Chapter 30 for further details.

Read-Only Tablespaces

DBAs can alter a tablespace via the ALTER TABLESPACE command. Tablespaces may be altered to be read-only:

```
alter tablespace users read only;
```

Or they can be changed from read-only to writable:

```
alter tablespace users read write;
```

The data in a read-only tablespace cannot be altered. Although nonprivileged users cannot execute these commands, you should be aware of these commands because they may alter how you physically store your data. If you can move the unchanging data to its own tablespace, you may be able to designate the entire tablespace as read-only. Using read-only tablespaces may simplify backup and recovery efforts.

NOTE
You can *drop objects from read-only tablespaces.*

The read-only status for tablespaces is displayed via the STATUS column of the USER_TABLESPACES data dictionary view, as shown in the following example:

```
alter tablespace users read only;

Tablespace altered.

select status from user_tablespaces
where tablespace_name = 'USERS';

STATUS
---------
READ ONLY


alter tablespace users read write;

Tablespace altered.

select status from user_tablespaces
where tablespace_name = 'USERS';

STATUS
---------
ONLINE
```

NOLOGGING Tablespaces

You can disable the creation of redo log entries for specific objects. By default, Oracle generates log entries for all transactions. If you wish to bypass that functionality—for instance, if you are loading data and you can completely re-create all the transactions—you can specify that the loaded object or the tablespace be maintained in NOLOGGING mode.

You can see the current logging status for tablespaces by querying the LOGGING column of USER_TABLESPACES.

NOTE
The NOLOGGING mode only affects the initial creation of an index or table, or when you use the APPEND hint. Otherwise, normal DML activity is always logged.

Temporary Tablespaces

When you execute a command that performs a sorting or grouping operation, Oracle may create a temporary segment to manage the data. The temporary segment is created in a *temporary tablespace*, and the user executing the command does not have to manage that data. Oracle dynamically creates the temporary segment and releases its space when the instance is shut down and restarted. If there is not enough temporary space available and the temporary tablespace datafiles cannot auto-extend, the command fails. Each user in the database has an associated temporary tablespace—there may be just one such tablespace for all users to share. A *default temporary tablespace* is set at the database level so all new users will have the same temporary tablespace unless a different one is specified during the CREATE USER or ALTER USER command.

You can create and group multiple temporary tablespaces. You assign the temporary tablespaces to *tablespace groups* via the TABLESPACE GROUP clause of the CREATE TEMPORARY TABLESPACE or ALTER TABLESPACE command. You can then specify the group as a user's default tablespace. Tablespace groups can help to support parallel operations involving sorts.

Tablespaces for System-Managed Undo

You can use *Automatic Undo Management (AUM)* to place all undo data in a single tablespace and have it automatically managed by Oracle. When you create an undo tablespace, Oracle manages the storage, retention, and space utilization for your rollback data via *system-managed undo* (SMU). When a retention time is set (in the database's initialization parameter file), Oracle makes a best effort to retain all committed undo data in the database for the specified number of seconds. With that setting, any query taking less than the retention time should not result in an error as long as the undo tablespace has been sized properly. While the database is running, DBAs can change the UNDO_RETENTION parameter value via the ALTER SYSTEM command.

You can guarantee undo data is retained, even at the expense of current transactions in the database. When you create the undo tablespace, specify RETENTION GUARANTEE as part of your CREATE DATABASE or CREATE UNDO TABLESPACE command. Use care with this setting, because it may force transactions to fail in order to guarantee the retention of old undo data in the undo tablespace.

BIGFILE Tablespaces

You can use *BIGFILE tablespaces* to create a tablespace composed of one very large file instead of many smaller files. The traditional type of tablespace is referred to as a *SMALLFILE tablespace*. The use of BIGFILE tablespaces (supported only for locally managed tablespaces) significantly increases the storage capacity of an Oracle database. BIGFILEs can be 1024 times larger than SMALLFILEs; given a 32KB database block size, BIGFILEs can expand the database to 8 exabytes.

BIGFILE tablespaces are intended for use with volume managers that stripe files across pools of available storage devices. You can use Automatic Storage Management (ASM) (see Chapter 51) to manage the distribution of BIGFILE data across multiple devices.

The following shows the creation of a BIGFILE tablespace:

```
create bigfile tablespace bigfiletbs
datafile '/u01/oracle/data/bigtbs01.dbf' size 500g;
```

Most of the other CREATE TABLESPACE clauses, such as AUTOEXTEND and NEXT, work as you would expect with a BIGFILE tablespace:

```
create bigfile tablespace bigfiletbs_autoext
   datafile '+DATA' size 100g
   autoextend on next 50g
   maxsize 2t;

Tablespace created.
```

NOTE
You can specify the size in kilobytes, megabytes, gigabytes, or terabytes.

Encrypted Tablespaces

You can specify an encryption attribute for permanent tablespaces so the data is stored encrypted at rest. Data from an encrypted tablespace is automatically encrypted when written elsewhere in the database during transactions (such as in the undo tablespace and the redo logs).

To encrypt a tablespace, you must be using the Oracle's Transparent Data Encryption (TDE) feature, available as part of the advanced security options. TDE requires the use of a *wallet* for security (so anyone attempting to open a copy of your database would need the database, the wallet, and the password used to open the wallet). The wallet must be opened before you can use the encrypted tablespace. See Chapter 21 for a discussion of encryption using TDE.

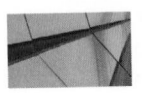

NOTE
You cannot encrypt an existing tablespace.

Supporting the FLASHBACK DATABASE Command

You can use the FLASHBACK DATABASE command to revert an entire database to a prior point in time. DBAs can configure tablespaces to be excluded from this option—the ALTER TABLESPACE FLASHBACK OFF command tells Oracle to exclude that tablespace's transaction from the data written to the flashback database area. See Chapter 30 for details on FLASHBACK DATABASE command usage.

Transporting Tablespaces

A *transportable tablespace* is a tablespace that can be "unplugged" from one database and "plugged into" another. To be transportable, a tablespace—or a set of tablespaces—must be *self-contained*. In other words, the tablespace or tablespace set cannot contain any objects that refer to objects in other tablespaces. Therefore, if you transport a tablespace containing indexes, you must move the tablespace containing the indexes' base tables as part of the same transportable tablespace set. The better you have organized and distributed your objects among tablespaces, the easier it is to generate a self-contained set of tablespaces to transport.

To transport tablespaces, you need to generate a tablespace set, copy or move that tablespace set to the new database, and plug the set into the new database. Because these are privileged operations, you must have database administration privileges to execute them. As a developer, you should be aware of this capability because it can significantly reduce the time required to migrate self-contained data among databases. For instance, you may create and populate a read-only tablespace of historical data in a test environment and then transport it to a production database, even across different hardware and OS platforms. See Chapter 51 for details on transporting tablespaces.

Planning Your Tablespace Usage

With all these options, Oracle can support very complex environments. You can maintain a read-only set of historical data tables alongside active transaction tables. You can place the most actively used tables in datafiles that are located on the fastest disks. You can partition tables (see Chapter 18) and store each partition in a separate tablespace. You can store related partitions together—for example, you can store the current month's partitions of multiple tables in the same tablespace. With all these options available, you should establish a basic set of guidelines for your tablespace architecture. This plan should be part of your early design efforts so you can take the best advantage of the available features. The following guidelines should be a starting point for your plan.

Separate Active and Static Tables

Tables actively used by transactions have space considerations that differ significantly from static lookup tables. The static tables may never need to be altered or moved; the active tables may need to be actively managed, moved, or reorganized. To simplify the management of the static tables, isolate them in a dedicated tablespace. Within the most active tables, there may be further divisions—some of them may be extremely critical to the application's performance, and you may decide to move them to yet another tablespace.

Taking this approach a step further, separate the active and static partitions of tables and indexes. Ideally, this separation will allow you to focus your tuning efforts on the objects that have the most direct impact on performance while eliminating the impact of other objects on the immediate environment.

Separate Indexes and Tables

Indexes may be managed separately from tables—you may create or drop indexes while the base table stays unchanged. Because their space is managed separately, indexes should be stored in dedicated tablespaces if you're using standard file system datafiles. You will then be able to create and rebuild indexes without worrying about that operation's impact on the space available to your tables.

If you're using ASM, however, load balancing is automatic and performance is not as big of an issue as manageability is. Therefore, with ASM, you can start by creating tablespaces for a particular application and keep the tables and their associated indexes in the same tablespace.

Separate Large and Small Objects

In general, small tables tend to be fairly static lookup tables—such as a list of countries, for example. Oracle provides tuning options for small tables (such as caching) that are not appropriate for large tables (which have their own set of tuning options). Because the administration of these types of tables may be dissimilar, you should try to keep them separate. In general, separating active and static tables will take care of this objective as well.

Separate Application Tables from Core Objects

The two sets of core objects to be aware of are the Oracle core objects and the enterprise objects. Oracle's core objects are stored in its default tablespaces—SYSTEM, SYSAUX, the temporary tablespace, and the undo tablespace. Do not create any application objects in these tablespaces or under any of the schemas provided by Oracle.

Within your application, you may have some objects that are core to the enterprise and could be reused by multiple applications. Because these objects may need to be indexed and managed to account for the needs of multiple applications, they should be maintained apart from the other objects your application needs.

Grouping the objects in the database according to the categories described here may seem fairly simplistic, but it is a critical part of successfully deploying an enterprise-scale database application. The better you plan the distribution of I/O and space, the easier it will be to implement, tune, and manage the application's database structures. Furthermore, database administrators can manage the tablespace separately—taking it offline, backing it up, or isolating its I/O activity. Therefore, separating object types facilitates ease of management if not just performance. In later chapters, you will see further details of other types of objects (such as materialized views) as well as additional examples of the commands used to create and alter tablespaces.

CHAPTER
23

Using SQL*Loader
to Load Data

In the scripts provided for the practice tables, a large number of INSERT commands are executed. In place of those INSERTS, you could create a file containing the data to be loaded and then use Oracle's SQL*Loader utility to load the data. This chapter provides you with an overview of SQL*Loader and its major capabilities. Two additional data-movement utilities, Data Pump Export and Data Pump Import, are covered in Chapter 24. SQL*Loader, Data Pump Export, and Data Pump Import are described in great detail in the *Oracle Database Utilities* documentation provided with the standard Oracle documentation set.

SQL*Loader loads data from external files into tables in the Oracle database. SQL*Loader uses two primary files: the datafile, which contains the information to be loaded, and the control file, which contains information on the format of the data, the records and fields within the file, the order in which the records are to be loaded, and even, when needed, the names of the multiple files that will be used for data. You can combine the control file information into the datafile itself, although the two are usually separated to make reusing the control file easier.

When executed, SQL*Loader automatically creates a log file and a "bad" file. The log file records the status of the load, such as the number of rows processed and the number of rows committed. The "bad" file contains all the rows that were rejected during the load due to data errors, such as non-unique values in primary key columns.

Within the control file, you can specify additional commands to govern the load criteria. If these criteria are not met by a row, the row is written to a "discard" file. The log, bad, and discard files will, by default, have the extensions **.log**, **.bad**, and **.dsc**, respectively. Control files are typically given the extension **.ctl**.

SQL*Loader is a powerful utility for loading data, for several reasons:

- It is highly flexible, allowing you to manipulate the data as it is being loaded.

- You can use SQL*Loader to break a single large data set into multiple sets of data during commit processing, significantly reducing the size of the transactions processed by the load.

- You can use its Direct Path loading option to perform loads very quickly.

To start using SQL*Loader, you should first become familiar with the control file, as described in the next section.

The Control File

The control file tells Oracle how to read and load the data. The control file tells SQL*Loader where to find the source data for the load and the tables into which to load the data, along with any other rules that must be applied during the load processing. These rules can include restrictions for discards (similar to WHERE clauses for queries) and instructions for combining multiple physical rows in an input file into a single row during an INSERT. SQL*Loader uses the control file to create the INSERT commands executed for the data load.

The control file is created at the operating system level, using any text editor that enables you to save plain text files. Within the control file, commands do not have to obey any rigid formatting requirements, but standardizing your command syntax will make later maintenance of the control file simpler.

The following listing shows a sample control file for loading data into the BOOKSHELF table:

```
load data
infile 'bookshelf.dat'
into table bookshelf
(title            position(01:100)     char,
 publisher        position(101:120)    char,
 category_name    position(121:140)    char,
 rating           position(141:142)    char)
```

In this example, data will be loaded from the file **bookshelf.dat** into the BOOKSHELF table. The **bookshelf.dat** file will contain the data for all four of the BOOKSHELF columns, with whitespace padding out the unused characters in those fields. Thus, the PUBLISHER column value always begins at position 101 in each line of the file, even if the TITLE value is less than 100 characters. Although this formatting makes the input file larger, it may simplify the loading process. No length needs to be given for the fields since the starting and ending positions within the input data stream effectively give the field length.

The INFILE clause names the input file, and the INTO TABLE clause specifies the table into which the data will be loaded. Each of the columns is listed, along with the position where its data resides in each physical record in the file. This format allows you to load data even if the source data's column order does not match the order of columns in your table.

To perform this load, the user executing the load must have INSERT privilege on the BOOKSHELF table.

Loading Variable-Length Data

If the columns in your input file have variable lengths, you can use SQL*Loader commands to tell Oracle how to determine when a value ends. In the following example, commas separate the input values:

```
load data
infile 'bookshelf.dat'
badfile '/u04/oradata/sqlldr/bookshelf.bad'
truncate
into table bookshelf
fields terminated by ","
(title, publisher, category_name, rating)
```

NOTE
Be sure to select a delimiter that is not present within the values being loaded. In this example, a comma is the delimiter, so any comma present within any text string being loaded will be interpreted as an end-of-field character.

The FIELDS TERMINATED BY "," clause tells SQL*Loader that during the load, each column value will be terminated by a comma. Thus, the input file does not have to be 142 characters wide for each row, as was the case in the first load example. The lengths of the columns are not specified in the control file because they will be determined during the load.

In this example, the name of the bad file is specified by the BADFILE clause. In general, the name of the bad file is only given when you want to redirect the file to a different directory.

This example also shows the use of the TRUNCATE clause within a control file. When this control file is executed by SQL*Loader, the BOOKSHELF table will be *truncated* before the start of the load. Because TRUNCATE commands cannot be rolled back, you should use care when using this option. In addition to TRUNCATE, you can use the following options:

- **APPEND** Adds rows to the table.
- **INSERT** Adds rows to an empty table. If the table is not empty, the load aborts with an error.
- **REPLACE** Empties the table and then adds the new rows. The user must have DELETE privilege on the table.

Starting the Load

To execute the commands in the control file, you need to run SQL*Loader with the appropriate parameters. SQL*Loader is started via the **sqlldr** command at the operating system prompt.

NOTE
*The SQL*Loader executable may consist of the name **sqlldr** followed by a version number. Consult your platform-specific Oracle documentation for the exact name.*

When you execute **sqlldr**, you need to specify the control file, username/password, and other critical load information, as shown in Table 23-1.

SQL*Loader Keyword	Description
USERID	Username and password for the load, separated by a slash.
CONTROL	Name of the control file.
DATA (or DATAFILE)	Name of the datafile. The default is the name of the control file with the extension **.dat**.
LOG	Name of the log file.
BAD	Name of the bad file.
DISCARD	Name of the discard file.
DISCARDMAX	Maximum number of rows to discard before stopping the load. The default is to allow all discards.
SKIP	Number of logical rows in the input file to skip before starting to load data. Generally used during reloads from the same input file following a partial load. The default is 0.
LOAD	Number of logical rows to load. The default is all.
ERRORS	Number of errors to allow. The default is 50.

TABLE 23-1. *SQL*Loader Options*

SQL*Loader Keyword	Description
ROWS	Number of rows to commit at a time. Use this parameter to break up the transaction size during the load. The default for conventional path loads is 64; the default for Direct Path loads is all rows.
BINDSIZE	Size of conventional path bind array, in bytes. The default is operating system–dependent.
SILENT	Suppress messages during the load.
DIRECT	Use Direct Path loading. The default is FALSE.
PARFILE	Name of the parameter file that contains additional load parameter specifications.
PARALLEL	Perform parallel loading. The default is FALSE.
FILE	File to allocate extents from (for parallel loading).
SKIP_UNUSABLE_ INDEXES	Allow loads into tables that have indexes in unusable states. The default is FALSE.
SKIP_INDEX_ MAINTENANCE	Stop index maintenance for Direct Path loads, leaving them in unusable states. The default is FALSE.
READSIZE	Size of the read buffer; default is 1MB.
EXTERNAL_TABLE	Use external table for load. Default is NOT_USED; other valid values are GENERATE_ONLY and EXECUTE.
COLUMNARRAYROWS	Number of rows for Direct Path column array; default is 5,000.
STREAMSIZE	Size in bytes of the Direct Path stream buffer; default is 256,000.
MULTITHREADING	A flag to indicate if multithreading should be used during a Direct Path load.
RESUMABLE	A TRUE/FALSE flag to enable or disable resumable operations for the current session; default is FALSE.
RESUMABLE_NAME	Text identifier for the resumable operation.
RESUMABLE_TIMEOUT	Wait time for the resumable operation; default is 7200 seconds.
DATE_CACHE	For Direct Path loads, DATE_CACHE enables the storing of the results from text strings to DATE datatype format. Default is enabled (for 1000 elements).

TABLE 23-1.   *SQL*Loader Options* (continued)

Each load must have a control file because none of the input parameters specify critical information for the load—the input file and the table being loaded.

You can separate the arguments to **sqlldr** with commas. Enter them with the keywords (such as USERID or LOG), followed by the parameter value. Keywords are always followed by an equal sign (=) and the appropriate argument.

If the USERID keyword is omitted and no username/password is provided as the first argument, you will be prompted for it. If a slash is given after the equal sign, an externally identified account will be used. You also can use an Oracle Net database specification string to log into a remote database and load the data into it. For example, your command may start

```
sqlldr userid=usernm/mypass@dev
```

NOTE
The DIRECT keyword, which invokes the Direct Path load option, is described in "Direct Path Loading" later in this chapter.

The SILENT keyword tells **sqlldr** to suppress certain informative data:

■ HEADER suppresses the SQL*Loader header.

■ FEEDBACK suppresses the feedback at each commit point.

■ ERRORS suppresses the logging (in the log file) of each record that caused an Oracle error, although the count is still logged.

■ DISCARDS suppresses the logging (in the log file) of each record that was discarded, although the count is still logged.

■ PARTITIONS disables the writing of the per-partition statistics to the log file.

■ ALL suppresses all of the preceding.

If more than one of these is entered, separate each with a comma and enclose the list in parentheses. For example, you can suppress the HEADER and ERRORS information via the following keyword setting:

```
silent=(HEADER,ERRORS)
```

NOTE
Commands in the control file override any in the calling command line.

Let's load a sample set of data into the BOOKSHELF table, which has four columns (TITLE, PUBLISHER, CATEGORY_NAME, and RATING). Create a plain text file named **bookshelf.txt**. The data to be loaded should be the only two lines in the file:

```
Good Record,Some Publisher,ADULTNF,3
Another Title,Some Publisher,ADULTPIC,4
```

NOTE
Each line ends with a carriage return. Even though the first line's last value is not as long as the column it is being loaded into, the row stops at the carriage return.

The data is separated by commas, and we don't want to delete the data previously loaded into BOOKSHELF, so the control file looks like this:

```
load data
infile 'bookshelf.txt'
append
into table bookshelf
fields terminated by ","
(title, publisher, category_name, rating)
```

Save that file as **bookshelf.ctl**, in the same directory as the input data file. Next, run **sqlldr** and tell it to use the control file. This example assumes that the BOOKSHELF table exists under the PRACTICE schema:

```
sqlldr practice/practice control=bookshelf.ctl log=bookshelf.log
```

When the load completes, you should have one successfully loaded record and one failure. The successfully loaded record is in the BOOKSHELF table:

```
select title
from bookshelf
where publisher like '%Publisher';

TITLE
-----------------------------------------
Good Record
```

A file named **bookshelf.bad** is then created and contains one record:

```
Another Title,Some Publisher,ADULTPIC,4
```

Why was that record rejected? Check the log file, **bookshelf.log**, which says, in part:

```
Record 2: Rejected - Error on table BOOKSHELF.
ORA-02291: integrity constraint (PRACTICE.CATFK) violated -
parent key not found

Table BOOKSHELF:
  1 Row successfully loaded.
  1 Row not loaded due to data errors.
```

Row 2, the "Another Title" row, was rejected because the value for the CATEGORY_NAME column violated the foreign key constraint—ADULTPIC is not listed as a category in the CATEGORY table.

Because the rows that failed are isolated in the bad file, you can use that file as the input for a later load once the data has been corrected.

Logical and Physical Records

In Table 23-1, several of the keywords refer to "logical" rows. A *logical row* is a row that is inserted into the database. Depending on the input file's structure, you can combine multiple physical records to make a single logical row.

For example, the input file may look like this:

```
Good Record,Some Publisher,ADULTNF,3
```

in which case there would be a one-to-one relationship between that physical record and the logical row (database row) it inserts. But the datafile may look like this instead:

```
Good Record,
Some Publisher,
ADULTNF,
3
```

To combine the data, you need to specify *continuation rules*. In this case, the column values are split one to a line, so there is a set number of physical records for each logical record. To combine them, use the CONCATENATE clause within the control file. In this case, you would specify CONCATENATE 4 to create a single logical row from the four physical records.

The logic for creating a single logical record from multiple physical records can be much more complex than a simple concatenation. You can use the CONTINUEIF clause to specify the conditions that cause logical records to be continued. You can further manipulate the input data to create multiple logical records from a single physical record (via the use of multiple INTO TABLE clauses). See the control file syntax for the SQLLDR entry in the Alphabetical Reference, and the notes in the next section of this chapter.

You can use SQL*Loader to generate multiple inserts from a single physical record (similar to the multitable insert capability described in Chapter 15). For example, suppose the input data is denormalized, with fields CITY and RAINFALL, whereas the input data is in the format CITY, RAINFALL1, RAINFALL2, RAINFALL3. The control file would resemble the following (depending on the actual physical stop and start positions of the data in the file):

```
into table rainfall
 when city != '      '
 (city          position(1:5)     char,
  rainfall      position(6:10)    integer external)   -- 1st row
 --
 into table rainfall
 when city != '      '
 (city          position(1:5)     char,
  rainfall      position(11:16)   integer external)   -- 2nd row
 --
 into table rainfall
 when city != '      '
 (city          position(1:5)     char,
  rainfall      position(16:21)   integer external)   -- 3rd row
```

Note that separate INTO TABLE clauses operate on each physical row. In this example, they generate separate rows in the RAINFALL table; they could also be used to insert rows into multiple tables.

Control File Syntax Notes

The full syntax for SQL*Loader control files is shown in the SQLLDR entry in the Alphabetical Reference, so it is not repeated here.

Within the LOAD clause, you can specify that the load is RECOVERABLE or UNRECOVERABLE. The UNRECOVERABLE clause only applies to Direct Path loading and is described in "Tuning Data Loads" later in this chapter.

In addition to using the CONCATENATE clause, you can use the CONTINUEIF clause to control the manner in which physical records are assembled into logical records. The THIS clause refers to the current physical record, whereas the NEXT clause refers to the next physical record. For example, you could create a two-character continuation character at the start of each physical record. If that record should be concatenated to the preceding record, set that value equal to '**'. You could then use the CONTINUEIF NEXT (1:2) = '**' clause to create a single logical record from the multiple physical records. The '**' continuation character will not be part of the merged record.

The syntax for the INTO TABLE clause includes a WHEN clause. The WHEN clause, shown in the following listing, serves as a filter applied to rows prior to their insertion into the table. For example, you can specify

```
when rating >'3'
```

to load only books with ratings greater than 3 into the table. Any row that does not pass the WHEN condition is written to the discard file. Thus, the discard file contains rows that can be used for later loads, but that did not pass the current set of WHEN conditions. You can use multiple WHEN conditions connected with AND clauses.

Use the TRAILING NULLCOLS clause if you are loading variable-length records for which the last column does not always have a value. With this clause in effect, SQL*Loader will generate NULL values for those columns.

As shown earlier in this chapter, you can use the FIELDS TERMINATED BY clause to load variable-length data. Rather than being terminated by a character, the fields can be TERMINATED BY WHITESPACE or ENCLOSED BY characters or OPTIONALLY ENCLOSED BY other characters.

For example, the following entry loads AUTHOR_NAME values and sets the values to uppercase during the insert. If the value is blank, a NULL is inserted:

```
author_name position(10:34)  char  terminated by whitespace
      nullif author_name=blanks  "upper(:author_name)"
```

When you load DATE datatype values, you can specify a date mask. For example, if you had a column named RETURN_DATE and the incoming data is in the format "Mon-DD-YYYY" in the first 11 places of the record, you could specify the RETURN_DATE portion of the load as follows:

```
returndate position (1:11) date "Mon-DD-YYYY"
```

Within the INTO TABLE clause, you can use the RECNUM keyword to assign a record number to each logical record as it is read from the datafile, and that value will be inserted into the assigned column of the table. The CONSTANT keyword allows you to assign a constant value to a column during the load. For character columns, enclose the constant value within single quotes. If you use the SYSDATE keyword, the selected column is populated with the current system date and time.

```
checkoutdate sysdate
```

If you use the SEQUENCE option, SQL*Loader maintains a sequence of values during the load. As records are processed, the sequence value is increased by the increment you specify. If the rows fail during INSERT (and are sent to the bad file), those sequence values are not reused. If you use the MAX keyword within the sequence option, the sequence values use the current maximum value of the column as the starting point for the sequence. The following listing shows the use of the SEQUENCE option:

```
seqnum_col  sequence(max,1)
```

You can also specify the starting value and increment for a sequence to use when inserting. The following example inserts values starting with a value of 100, incrementing by 2. If a row is rejected during the INSERT, its sequence value is skipped.

```
seqnum_col  sequence(100,2)
```

If you store numbers in VARCHAR2 columns, avoid using the SEQUENCE option for those columns. For example, if your table already contains the values 1 through 10 in a VARCHAR2 column, then the maximum value within that column is 9—the greatest character string. Using that as the basis for a SEQUENCE option causes SQL*Loader to attempt to INSERT a record using 10 as the newly created value—and that may conflict with the existing record. This behavior illustrates why storing numbers in character columns is a poor practice in general.

    SQL*Loader control files can support complex logic and business rules. For example, your input data for a column holding monetary values may have an implied decimal; 9990 would be inserted as 99.90. In SQL*Loader, you could insert this by performing the calculation during the data load:

```
money_amount   position (20:28) external decimal(9) ":tax_amount/100"
```

See "SQL*Loader Case Studies" in the *Oracle Database Utilities* book for additional SQL*Loader examples and sample control files.

Managing Data Loads

Loading large data volumes is a batch operation. Batch operations should not be performed concurrently with the small transactions prevalent in many database applications. If you have many concurrent users executing small transactions against a table, you should schedule your batch operations against that table to occur at a time when very few users are accessing the table.

    Oracle maintains *read consistency* for users' queries. If you execute the SQL*Loader job against the table at the same time that other users are querying the table, Oracle internally maintains undo entries to enable those users to see their data as it existed when they first queried the data. To minimize the amount of work Oracle must perform to maintain read consistency (and to minimize the associated performance degradation caused by this overhead), schedule your long-running data load jobs to be performed when few other actions are occurring in the database. In particular, avoid contention with other accesses of the same table.

    Design your data load processing to be easy to maintain and reuse. Establish guidelines for the structure and format of the input datafiles. The more standardized the input data formats are, the simpler it will be to reuse old control files for the data loads. For repeated scheduled loads into the same table, your goal should be to reuse the same control file each time. Following each load, you need to review and move the log, bad, data, and discard files so they do not accidentally get overwritten.

Within the control file, use comments to indicate any special processing functions being performed. To create a comment within the control file, begin the line with two dashes, as shown in the following example:

```
-- Limit the load to LA employees:
when location='LA'
```

If you have properly commented your control file, you increase the chance that it can be reused during future loads. You also simplify the maintenance of the data load process itself, as described in the next section.

Repeating Data Loads

Data loads do not always work exactly as planned. Many variables are involved in a data load, and not all of them will always be under your control. For example, the owner of the source data may change its data formatting, invalidating part of your control file. Business rules may change, forcing additional changes. Database structures and space availability may change, further affecting your ability to load the data.

In an ideal case, a data load either fully succeeds or fully fails. In many cases, however, a data load partially succeeds, making the recovery process more difficult. If some of the records have been inserted into the table, then attempting to reinsert those records should result in a primary key violation. If you are generating the primary key value during the INSERT (via the SEQUENCE option), then those rows may not fail the second time—and will be inserted twice.

To determine where a load failed, use the log file. The log file records the commit points as well as the errors encountered. All of the rejected records should be in either the bad file or the discard file. You can minimize the recovery effort by forcing the load to fail if many errors are encountered. To force the load to abort before a large number of errors is encountered, use the ERRORS keyword of the **sqlldr** command. You can also use the DISCARDMAX keyword to limit the number of discarded records permitted before the load aborts.

If you set ERRORS to 0, the first error will cause the load to fail. What if that load fails after 100 records have been inserted? You have two options: Identify and delete the inserted records and reapply the whole load, or skip the successfully inserted records. You can use the SKIP keyword in the SQL*Loader control file to skip the first 100 records during its load processing. The load will then continue with record 101 (which, we hope, has been fixed prior to the reload attempt). If you cannot identify the rows that have just been loaded into the table, you need to use the SKIP option during the restart process.

The proper settings for ERRORS and DISCARDMAX depend on the load. If you have full control over the data load process and the data is properly "cleaned" before being extracted to a load file, you may have very little tolerance for errors and discards. On the other hand, if you do not have control over the input datafile source, you need to set ERRORS and DISCARDMAX high enough to allow the load to complete. After the load has completed, review the log file, correct the data in the bad file, and reload the data using the original bad file as the new input file. If rows have been incorrectly discarded, perform an additional load using the original discard file as the new input file.

After modifying the errant CATEGORY_NAME value, you can rerun the BOOKSHELF table load example using the original **bookshelf.dat** file. During the reload, you have two options when using the original input datafile.

- Skip the first row by specifying SKIP=1 on the **sqlldr** command line.
- Attempt to load both rows, whereby the first row fails because it has already been loaded (and thus causes a primary key violation).

Alternatively, you can use the bad file as the new input datafile and not worry about errors and skipped rows.

Tuning Data Loads

In addition to running the data load processes at off-peak hours, you can take other steps to improve the load performance. The following steps all impact your overall database environment and must be coordinated with the database administrator. The tuning of a data load should not be allowed to have a negative impact on the database or on the business processes it supports.

First, batch data loads may be timed to occur while the database is in NOARCHIVELOG mode. While in NOARCHIVELOG mode, the database does not keep an archive of its online redo log files prior to overwriting them. Eliminating the archiving process improves the transaction performance. Because the data is being loaded from a file, you can re-create the loaded data at a later time by reloading the datafile rather than recovering it from an archived redo log file.

However, there are significant potential issues with disabling ARCHIVELOG mode. You will not be able to perform a point-in-time recovery of the database unless archiving is enabled. If nonbatch transactions are performed in the database, you will probably need to run the database in ARCHIVELOG mode all the time, including during your loads. Furthermore, switching between ARCHIVELOG and NOARCHIVELOG modes requires that you shut down the instance (all instances if you have a RAC database). If you switch the instance to NOARCHIVELOG mode, perform your data load, and then switch the instance back to ARCHIVELOG mode, you should back up the database (see Chapter 51) immediately following the restart.

Instead of running the entire database in NOARCHIVELOG mode, you can disable archiving for your data load process by using the UNRECOVERABLE keyword within SQL*Loader. The UNRECOVERABLE option disables the writing of redo log entries for the transactions within the data load. You should only use this option if you can re-create the transactions from the input files during a recovery. If you follow this strategy, you must have adequate space to store old input files in case they are needed for future recoveries. The UNRECOVERABLE option is only available for Direct Path loads, as described in the next section.

Rather than control the redo log activity at the load process level, you can control it at the table or partition level. If you define an object as NOLOGGING, then block-level inserts performed by SQL*Loader Direct Path loading and the INSERT /*+ APPEND */ command will not generate redo log entries. The block-level inserts will require additional space, however, as they will not reuse existing blocks below the table's high-water mark.

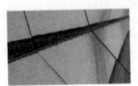

NOTE
Many critical databases have a standby database and are, therefore, set up with FORCED LOGGING set to TRUE to keep the two databases in sync. Setting NOLOGGING for any database object will not override this since that would defeat the purpose of having a standby database.

If your operating environment has multiple processors, you can take advantage of the CPUs by parallelizing the data load. The PARALLEL option of the **sqlldr** command, as described in the next section, uses multiple concurrent data load processes to reduce the overall time required to load the data.

In addition to these approaches, you should work with your database administrator to make sure the database environment and structures are properly tuned for data loads. Tuning efforts should include the following:

- Preallocate space for the table to minimize dynamic extensions during the loads.

- Allocate sufficient memory resources to the shared memory areas.

- Streamline the data-writing process by ensuring there are enough database writer (DBWR) processes for the database. Oracle best practices suggest allowing Oracle to determine the number of DBWR processes by default. Therefore, you should normally not change the number of DBWR processes unless directed by Oracle Support or if an Automatic Database Diagnostic Monitor (ADDM) report suggests that you set it manually at a higher value.

- Remove any unnecessary triggers during the data loads. If possible, disable or remove the triggers prior to the load, and perform the trigger operations on the loaded data manually after it has been loaded.

- Remove or disable any unnecessary constraints on the table. You can use SQL*Loader to dynamically disable and re-enable constraints.

- Remove any indexes on the tables. If the data has been properly cleaned prior to the data load, then performing uniqueness checks and foreign key validations are unnecessary during the data loads. Dropping indexes prior to data loads significantly improves performance.

- Pre-sort the data prior to loading. Sort the data based on the indexed columns to minimize the time needed to create and update the indexes.

Direct Path Loading

SQL*Loader generates a large number of INSERT statements. To avoid the overhead associated with using a large number of INSERTs, you may use the Direct Path option in SQL*Loader. The Direct Path option creates preformatted data blocks and inserts those blocks into the table. As a result, the performance of your load can dramatically improve. To use the Direct Path option, you must not be performing any functions on the values being read from the input file.

NOTE
As of Oracle Database 12c, direct path loads can be audited with the existing built-in Oracle auditing mechanisms.

Any indexes on the table being loaded are placed into a temporary DIRECT LOAD state (you can query the index status from USER_INDEXES). Oracle moves the old index values to a temporary index it creates and manages. Once the load has completed, the old index values are merged with the new values to create the new index, and Oracle drops the temporary index it created. When the index is once again valid, its status changes to VALID. To minimize the amount of space necessary for the temporary index, presort the data by the indexed columns. The name of the index for which the data is presorted should be specified via a SORTED INDEXES clause in the control file.

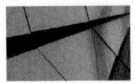

NOTE
Triggers will not fire during direct path loads even if the triggers are enabled.

To use the Direct Path option, specify

```
direct=true
```

as a keyword on the **sqlldr** command line or include this option in the control file.

If you use the Direct Path option, you can use the UNRECOVERABLE keyword to improve your data load performance. This instructs Oracle not to generate redo log entries for the load. If you need to recover the database at a later point, you will need to re-execute the data load to recover the table's data. All conventional path loads are recoverable, and all Direct Path loads are recoverable by default.

Direct Path loads are faster than conventional loads, and UNRECOVERABLE Direct Path loads are faster still. Since performing UNRECOVERABLE loads impacts your recovery operations, you need to weigh the costs of that impact against the performance benefit you will realize. If your hardware environment has additional resources available during the load, you can use the PARALLEL Direct Path load option to divide the data load work among multiple processes. The parallel Direct Path operations will usually complete the load job faster than a single-threaded Direct Path load (no parallelism).

Instead of using the PARALLEL option, you could partition the table being loaded (see Chapter 18). Since SQL*Loader allows you to load a single partition, you could execute multiple concurrent SQL*Loader jobs to populate the separate partitions of a partitioned table. This method requires more database administration work (to configure and manage the partitions), but it gives you more flexibility in the parallelization and scheduling of the load jobs.

You can take advantage of multithreaded loading functionality for Direct Path loads to convert column arrays to stream buffers and perform stream buffer loading in parallel. Use the STREAMSIZE parameter and MULTITHREADING flag to enable this feature.

Direct Path loading may impact the space required for the table's data. Because Direct Path loading inserts blocks of data, it does not follow the usual methods for allocating space within a table. The blocks are inserted at the end of the table, after its *high water mark,* which is the highest block into which the table's data has ever been written. If you INSERT 100 blocks worth of data into a table and then DELETE all of the rows, the high-water mark for the table will still be set at 100. If you then perform a conventional SQL*Loader data load, the rows will be inserted into the already allocated blocks. If you instead perform a Direct Path load, Oracle will insert new blocks of data following block 100, potentially increasing the table's space allocation. The only way to lower the high-water mark for a table is to TRUNCATE it (which deletes all rows and cannot be rolled back) or to drop and re-create it. You should work with your database administrator to identify space issues prior to starting your load.

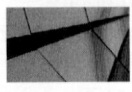

NOTE
As shown earlier in this chapter, you can issue a TRUNCATE command as part of the control file syntax. The table is then truncated prior to the data's being loaded.

SQL*Loader Express Mode

New to Oracle Database 12*c* is SQL*Loader Express Mode. If the table columns in your datafile are all in character, numeric, or date format and have only delimited fields, then SQL*Loader Express Mode lets you specify just the target table and uses default values for other parameters. In addition, one of the output files is a control file for the load, which you can use for an external table definition or to document the load.

Using the **bookshelf.txt** datafile from earlier in the chapter, this example uses Express Mode to load the BOOKSHELF table. To use Express Mode, you have to rename **bookshelf.txt** to **bookshelf .dat** for SQL*Loader to identify the datafile associated with the table.

```
[oracle@oel63 loader]$ sqlldr hr table=bookshelf
Password:
SQL*Loader: Release 12.1.0.1.0 - Production on Tue Jun 4 14:27:08 2013
Copyright (c) 1982, 2013, Oracle and/or its affiliates.  All rights reserved.
Express Mode Load, Table: BOOKSHELF
Path used:       External Table, DEGREE_OF_PARALLELISM=AUTO
SQL*Loader-579: switching to direct path for the load
SQL*Loader-583: ignoring trim setting with direct path,
   using value of LDRTRIM
SQL*Loader-584: ignoring DEGREE_OF_PARALLELISM setting with direct path,
   using value of NONE
Express Mode Load, Table: BOOKSHELF
Path used:       Direct
Load completed - logical record count 2.
Table BOOKSHELF:
 2 Rows successfully loaded.
Check the log file: bookshelf.log
for more information about the load.
[oracle@oel63 loader]$
```

That's it! The log file **bookshelf.log** contains the typical status and logging information plus the generated control file:

```
Generated control file for possible reuse:
OPTIONS (DIRECT=TRUE)
LOAD DATA
INFILE 'bookshelf'
APPEND
INTO TABLE BOOKSHELF
FIELDS TERMINATED BY ","
(
  TITLE,
  PUBLISHER,
  CATEGORY_NAME,
  RATING
)
End of generated control file for possible reuse.
```

Additional Features

In addition to features noted earlier in this chapter, SQL*Loader features support for Unicode and expanded datatypes. SQL*Loader can load integer and zoned/packed decimal datatypes across platforms with different byte ordering and accept EBCDIC-based (legacy mainframe) zoned or packed decimal data encoded in IBM format. SQL*Loader also offers support for loading XML columns, object types with subtypes, and Unicode (UTF16 character set). SQL*Loader also provides native support for the date, time, and interval-related datatypes (see Chapter 10).

If a SQL*Loader job fails, you may be able to resume it where it failed using the RESUMABLE, RESUMABLE_NAME, and RESUMABLE_TIMEOUT options. For example, if the segment to which the loader job was writing could not extend, you can disable the load job, fix the space allocation problem, and resume the job. Your ability to perform these actions depends on the database's configuration; work with your DBA to make sure the resumable features are enabled and that adequate undo history is maintained for your purposes.

You can access external files as if they are tables inside the database. This *external table* feature, described in Chapter 28, allows you potentially to avoid loading large volumes of data into the database. See Chapter 28 for implementation details.

CHAPTER
24

Using Data Pump
Export and Import

D ata Pump is a server-based data-extraction and import utility. Its features include significant architectural and functional enhancements over the original Import and Export utilities. Data Pump allows you to stop and restart jobs, see the status of running jobs, and restrict the data that is exported and imported. As of Oracle 11g, you can compress and encrypt the output data as it is being written, change it as it is being written (via the REMAP_DATA option), and have partitions imported as stand-alone tables.

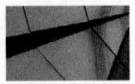

> **NOTE**
> *Data Pump can use files generated via the original Export utility, but the original Import utility cannot use the files generated from Data Pump Export.*

Data Pump runs as a server process, benefiting users in multiple ways. The client process that starts the job can disconnect and later reattach to the job. Performance is enhanced (as compared to Export/Import) because the data no longer has to be processed by a client program. Data Pump extractions and loads can be parallelized, further enhancing performance.

In this chapter, you will learn how to use Data Pump. The chapter includes descriptions and examples of Data Pump's major options.

Creating a Directory

Data Pump requires you to create directories for the datafiles and log files it will create and read. Use the CREATE DIRECTORY command to create the directory pointer within Oracle to the external directory you will use. To access the Data Pump files, users must have the READ and WRITE privileges on the directory.

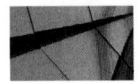

> **NOTE**
> *Before you start, verify that the external directory exists and that the user who will be issuing the CREATE DIRECTORY command has the CREATE ANY DIRECTORY system privilege.*

The following example creates a directory named DTPUMP and grants READ and WRITE access to the PRACTICE schema:

```
create directory dtpump as 'e:\dtpump';
grant read, write on directory dtpump to practice, bobby;
```

The PRACTICE and BOBBY schemas can now use the DTPUMP directory for Data Pump jobs.

Data Pump Export Options

Oracle provides a utility, **expdp**, that serves as the interface to Data Pump. If you have previous experience with the Export utility, some of the options will be familiar. However, significant features are available only via Data Pump. Table 24-1 shows the command-line input parameters for **expdp** when a job is created.

Parameter	Description
ATTACH	Connects a client session to a currently running Data Pump Export job.
COMPRESSION	Specifies which data to compress before writing the dump file set. Accepted values are ALL, DATA_ONLY, METADATA_ONLY, or NONE.
CONTENT	Filters what is exported: DATA_ONLY, METADATA_ONLY, or ALL.
DATA_OPTIONS	Provides options for handling data during exports and imports. For exports, the only valid value is XML_CLOBS, indicating XMLType columns are to be exported in uncompressed CLOB format.
DIRECTORY	Specifies the destination directory for the log file and the dump file set.
DUMPFILE	Specifies the names and directories for dump files.
ENCRYPTION	Specifies whether to encrypt data before writing it to the dump file set. ALL enables encryption for all data and metadata in the export operation. DATA_ONLY, ENCRYPTED_COLUMNS_ONLY, METADATA_ONLY, and NONE are the other valid values.
ENCRYPTION_ ALGORITHM	Specifies which cryptographic algorithm should be used to perform the encryption. Valid values are AES128, AES192, and AES256.
ENCRYPTION_ MODE	Specifies the type of security to use when encryption and decryption are performed.
ENCRYPTION_ PASSWORD	Specifies a password for encrypting encrypted column data, metadata, or table data in the export dump file. Note that all data in the dump file is encrypted.
ESTIMATE	Determines the method used to estimate the dump file size (BLOCKS or STATISTICS).
ESTIMATE_ONLY	Instructs Data Pump using a Y/N flag on whether the data should be exported or just estimated.
EXCLUDE	Specifies the criteria for excluding objects and data from being exported.
FILESIZE	Specifies the maximum file size of each export dump file.
FLASHBACK_SCN	Sets SCN for the database to flash back to during the export (see Chapter 30).
FLASHBACK_ TIME	Sets timestamp for the database to flash back to during the export (see Chapter 30).
FULL	Tells Data Pump to export all data and metadata in a Full mode export.
HELP	Displays a list of available commands and options.
INCLUDE	Specifies the criteria for which objects and data will be exported.
JOB_NAME	Specifies a name for the job; the default is system generated.
LOGFILE	Name and optional directory name for the export log.

TABLE 24-1. *Command-Line Input Parameters for* **expdp**

Parameter	Description
NETWORK_LINK	Specifies the source database link for a Data Pump job exporting a remote database.
NOLOGFILE	Uses a Y/N flag to suppress log file creation.
PARALLEL	Sets the number of workers for the Data Pump Export job.
PARFILE	Names the parameter file to use, if any.
QUERY	Filters rows from tables during the export.
REMAP_DATA	Names a remap function that is applied as the data is exported. The transformed data is stored in the dump file. This approach is commonly used for changing or masking sensitive personal information when creating a dump file that will be imported into a nonproduction database.
REUSE_DUMPFILES	Specifies if existing dump files should be overwritten. Default is N.
SAMPLE	Specifies a percentage of the data blocks to be sampled and unloaded from the source database.
SCHEMAS	Names the schemas to be exported for a Schema mode export.
STATUS	Displays detailed status of the Data Pump job.
TABLES	Lists the tables and partitions to be exported for a Table mode export.
TABLESPACES	Lists the tablespaces to be exported.
TRANSPORT_FULL_CHECK	Specifies whether the tablespaces being exported should first be verified as a self-contained set.
TRANSPORT_TABLESPACES	Specifies a Transportable Tablespace mode export.
TRANSPORTABLE	Specifies whether the Transportable option should be used during a Table mode export (specified with the TABLES parameter) to export metadata for specific tables, partitions, and subpartitions. NEVER is the default; ALWAYS tells Data Pump to use the Transportable option.
VERSION	Specifies the version of database objects to be created so the dump file set is compatible with earlier releases of Oracle. Options are COMPATIBLE, LATEST, and database version numbers (but not less than 10.0.0).

TABLE 24-1.   *Command-Line Input Parameters for* **expdp** *(continued)*

As shown in Table 24-1, five modes of Data Pump exports are supported. *Full* exports extract all the database's data and metadata. *Schema* exports extract the data and metadata for specific user schemas. *Tablespace* exports extract the data and metadata for tablespaces, and *Table* exports extract data and metadata for tables and their partitions. *Transportable Tablespace* exports extract metadata for specific tablespaces.

NOTE
You must have the EXP_FULL_DATABASE system privilege to perform a Full export or a Transportable Tablespace export.

When you submit a job, Oracle gives the job a system-generated name. If you specify a name for the job via the JOB_NAME parameter, you must be certain the job name will not conflict with the name of any table or view in your schema. During Data Pump jobs, Oracle creates and maintains a master table for the duration of the job. The master table has the same name as the Data Pump job, so its name cannot conflict with existing objects.

While a job is running, you can execute the commands listed in Table 24-2 via Data Pump's command-line interface.

As the entries in Table 24-2 imply, you can change many features of a running Data Pump Export job via the interactive command mode. If the dump area runs out of space, you can attach to the job, add files, and restart the job at that point; there is no need to kill the job or re-execute it from the beginning. You can display the job status at any time, either via the STATUS parameter or via the USER_DATAPUMP_JOBS and DBA_DATAPUMP_JOBS data dictionary views or the V$SESSION_LONGOPS view.

Starting a Data Pump Export Job

You can store your job parameters in a parameter file, referenced via the **expdp**'s PARFILE parameter. For example, you can create a file named **dp1.par** with the following entries:

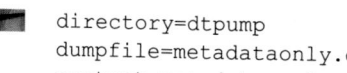

```
directory=dtpump
dumpfile=metadataonly.dmp
content=metadata_only
```

Parameter	Description
ADD_FILE	Adds dump files
CONTINUE_CLIENT	Exits the interactive mode and enters logging mode
EXIT_CLIENT	Exits the client session, but leaves the server Data Pump Export job running
FILESIZE	Redefines the default size to be used for any subsequent dump files
HELP	Displays online help for the import
KILL_JOB	Kills the current job and detaches related client sessions
PARALLEL	Alters the number of workers for the Data Pump Export job
START_JOB	Restarts the attached job
STATUS	Displays a detailed status of the Data Pump job
STOP_JOB	Stops the job for later restart

TABLE 24-2. *Parameters for Interactive Mode Data Pump Export*

You can then start the Data Pump Export job:

```
expdp practice/practice parfile=dp1.par
```

Oracle then passes the **dp1.par** entries to the Data Pump Export job. A Schema-type Data Pump Export (the default type) is executed, and the output (the metadata listings, but no data) is written to a file in the DTPUMP directory previously defined. When you execute the **expdp** command, the output is in the following format (there will be separate lines for each major object type—tables, grants, indexes, and so on):

```
Starting "PRACTICE"."SYS_EXPORT_SCHEMA_01":  practice/******** parfile=dp1.par
Processing object type SCHEMA_EXPORT/SE_PRE_SCHEMA_PROCOBJACT/PROCACT_SCHEMA
Processing object type SCHEMA_EXPORT/TYPE/TYPE_SPEC
Processing object type SCHEMA_EXPORT/TABLE/TABLE
Processing object type SCHEMA_EXPORT/TABLE/GRANT/OBJECT_GRANT
Processing object type SCHEMA_EXPORT/TABLE/INDEX/INDEX
Processing object type SCHEMA_EXPORT/TABLE/CONSTRAINT/CONSTRAINT
Processing object type SCHEMA_EXPORT/TABLE/COMMENT
Processing object type SCHEMA_EXPORT/VIEW/VIEW
Processing object type SCHEMA_EXPORT/PACKAGE/PACKAGE_SPEC
Processing object type SCHEMA_EXPORT/PACKAGE/PACKAGE_BODY
Processing object type SCHEMA_EXPORT/PACKAGE/GRANT/OBJECT_GRANT
Processing object type SCHEMA_EXPORT/TABLE/CONSTRAINT/REF_CONSTRAINT
Processing object type SCHEMA_EXPORT/SE_EV_TRIGGER/TRIGGER
Master table "PRACTICE"."SYS_EXPORT_SCHEMA_01" successfully loaded/unloaded
******************************************************************************
Dump file set for PRACTICE.SYS_EXPORT_SCHEMA_01 is:
  E:\DTPUMP\METADATAONLY.DMP
Job "PRACTICE"."SYS_EXPORT_SCHEMA_01" successfully completed at 17:30
```

The output file, as shown in the listing, is named **metadataonly.dmp**. The output dump file contains XML entries for re-creating the structures for the PRACTICE schema. During the export, Data Pump created and used a metadata table named SYS_EXPORT_SCHEMA_01.

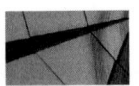

NOTE
Dump files will not overwrite previously existing dump files in the same directory.

You can use multiple directories and dump files for a single Data Pump Export. Within the DUMPFILE parameter setting, list the directory along with the filename, in this format:

```
dumpfile=directory1:file1.dmp,
         directory2:file2.dmp
```

Stopping and Restarting Running Jobs

After you have started a Data Pump Export job, you can close the client window you used to start the job. Because it is server based, the export continues to run. You can then attach to the job, check its status, and alter it. For example, you can start the job via **expdp**:

```
$ expdp practice/practice parfile=dp1.par
```

Press CTRL-C to exit the ongoing log and status display, and Data Pump returns you to the Export prompt:

```
Export>
```

Exit to the operating system via the EXIT_CLIENT command:

```
Export> exit_client
```

You can then restart the client and attach to the currently running job under your schema:

```
$ expdp practice/practice attach
```

NOTE
This sample export finishes quickly, so the job may finish before you reattach to it.

If you gave a name to your Data Pump Export job, specify the name as part of the ATTACH parameter call. For example, if you had named the job PRACTICE_JOB, attach to the job by name:

```
$ expdp practice/practice attach=practice_job
```

When you attach to a running job, Data Pump displays the status of the job—its basic configuration parameters and its current status. You can then issue the CONTINUE_CLIENT command to see the log entries as they are generated, or you can alter the running job:

```
Export> continue_client
```

You can stop a job via the STOP_JOB option:

```
Export> stop_job
```

With the job stopped, you can then add additional dump files in new directories, via the ADD_FILE option. You can then restart the job:

```
Export> start_job
```

You can specify a log file location for the export log via the LOGFILE parameter. If you do not specify a LOGFILE value, the log file is written to the same directory as the dump file.

Exporting from Another Database

You can use the NETWORK_LINK parameter to export data from a different database. If you are logged into the HQ database and you have a database link to a separate database, Data Pump can use that link to connect to the database and extract its data.

NOTE
If the source database is read-only, the user on the source database must have a locally managed tablespace assigned as the temporary tablespace; otherwise, the job will fail.

In your parameter file (or on the **expdp** command line), set the NETWORK_LINK parameter equal to the name of your database link. The Data Pump Export writes the data from the remote database to the directory defined in your local database.

Using EXCLUDE, INCLUDE, and QUERY

You can exclude or include sets of tables from the Data Pump Export via the EXCLUDE and INCLUDE options. You can exclude objects by type and by name. If an object is excluded, all its dependent objects are also excluded. The format for the EXCLUDE option is

```
EXCLUDE=object_type[:name_clause] [, ...]
```

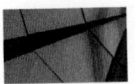

NOTE
You cannot specify EXCLUDE if you specify CONTENT=DATA_ONLY.

For example, to exclude the PRACTICE schema from a Full export, the format for the EXCLUDE option would be

```
exclude=schema:"='PRACTICE'"
```

NOTE
You can specify more than one EXCLUDE option within the same Data Pump Export job.

The EXCLUDE option in the preceding listing contains a limiting condition (='PRACTICE') within a set of double quotation marks. The *object_type* variable can be any Oracle object type, including grant, index, and table. The *name_clause* variable restricts the values returned. For example, to exclude from the export all tables whose names begin with "TEMP", you could specify the following:

```
EXCLUDE=TABLE:"LIKE 'TEMP%'"
```

When you enter this at the command line, you may need to use escape characters so the quotation marks and other special characters are properly passed to Oracle. Your **expdp** command will be in the format

```
$ expdp practice/practice exclude=table:\"LIKE \'TEMP%\'\"
```

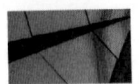

NOTE
This example shows part of the syntax, not the full syntax for the command.

If no *name_clause* value is provided, all objects of the specified type are excluded. To exclude all indexes, for example, you would specify the following:

```
$ expdp practice/practice exclude=index
```

For a listing of the objects you can filter, query the DATABASE_EXPORT_OBJECTS, SCHEMA_ EXPORT_OBJECTS, and TABLE_EXPORT_OBJECTS data dictionary views. If the *object_type* value is CONSTRAINT, NOT NULL constraints are excluded. Additionally, constraints needed for a table to be created successfully (such as primary key constraints for index-organized tables) cannot be excluded. If the *object_type* value is USER, the user definitions are excluded, but the objects within the user schemas are still exported. Use the SCHEMA *object_type*, as shown in the previous example, to exclude a user and all of the user's objects. If the *object_type* value is GRANT, all object grants and system privilege grants are excluded.

A second option, INCLUDE, is also available. When you use INCLUDE, only those objects that pass the criteria are exported; all others are excluded. INCLUDE and EXCLUDE are mutually exclusive. The format for INCLUDE is

```
INCLUDE = object_type[:name_clause] [, ...]
```

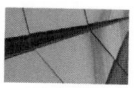

NOTE
You cannot specify INCLUDE if you specify CONTENT=DATA_ONLY.

For example, to export two tables and all procedures, your parameter file may include these two lines:

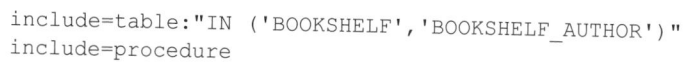

```
include=table:"IN ('BOOKSHELF','BOOKSHELF_AUTHOR')"
include=procedure
```

What rows will be exported for the objects that meet the EXCLUDE or INCLUDE criteria? By default, all rows are exported for each table. You can use the QUERY option to limit the rows that are returned. The format for the QUERY option is

```
QUERY = [schema.][table_name:]query_clause
```

If you do not specify values for the *schema* and *table_name* variables, the *query_clause* is applied to all the exported tables. Because *query_clause* usually includes specific column names, you should be very careful when selecting the tables to include in the export.

You can specify a QUERY value for a single table, as shown in the following listing:

```
query=bookshelf:'"where rating > 2"'
```

As a result, the dump file will only contain rows that meet the QUERY criteria as well as the INCLUDE or EXCLUDE criteria. You can also apply these restrictions during the subsequent Data Pump Import, as described in the next section of this chapter.

Data Pump Import Options

To import a dump file exported via Data Pump Export, use Data Pump Import. As with the export process, the import process runs as a server-based job you can manage as it executes. You can interact with Data Pump Import via the command-line interface, a parameter file, and an interactive interface. Table 24-3 lists the parameters for the command-line interface.

NOTE
The directory for the dump file and log file must already exist; see the beginning of the chapter for using the CREATE DIRECTORY command.

Parameter	Description
ATTACH	Attaches the client to a server session and places you in Interactive mode.
CONTENT	Filters what is imported: ALL, DATA_ONLY, or METADATA_ONLY.
DATA_OPTIONS	Provides options for how to handle certain types of data during exports and imports. For import operations, the only valid option for the DATA_OPTIONS parameter is SKIP_CONSTRAINT_ERRORS.
DIRECTORY	Specifies the location of the dump file set and the destination directory for the log and SQL files.
DUMPFILE	Specifies the names and, optionally, the directories for the dump file set.
ENCRYPTION_PASSWORD	Specifies a password for accessing encrypted column data in the dump file set.
ESTIMATE	Determines the method used to estimate the dump file size (BLOCKS or STATISTICS).
EXCLUDE	Excludes objects and data from being imported.
FLASHBACK_SCN	Sets SCN for the database to flash back to during the import (see Chapter 30).
FLASHBACK_TIME	Sets timestamp for the database to flash back to during the import (see Chapter 30).
FULL	Specifies using a Y/N flag that you want to import the full dump file.
HELP	Displays online help for the import.
INCLUDE	Specifies the criteria for objects to be imported.
JOB_NAME	Specifies a name for the job; the default is system generated.
LOGFILE	Specifies name and optional directory name for the import log.
NETWORK_LINK	Specifies the source database link for a Data Pump job importing a remote database.
NOLOGFILE	Uses a Y/N flag to suppress log file creation.
PARALLEL	Sets the number of workers for the Data Pump Import job.
PARFILE	Names the parameter file to use, if any.
PARTITION_OPTIONS	Specifies how table partitions should be created during an import operation. A value of DEPARTITION promotes each partition or subpartition to a new table. A value of MERGE combines all partitions and subpartitions into a new table.
QUERY	Filters rows from tables during the import.

TABLE 24-3. *Data Pump Import Command-Line Parameters*

Parameter	Description
REMAP_DATA	Allows you to remap data as it is being inserted into a new database. A common use is to regenerate primary keys to avoid conflict when importing a table into a preexisting table on the target database. The same function can be applied to multiple columns being dumped. This parameter is useful when you want to guarantee consistency in remapping both the child and parent column in a referential constraint.
REMAP_DATAFILE	Changes the name of the source datafile to the target datafile in CREATE LIBRARY, CREATE TABLESPACE, and CREATE DIRECTORY commands during the import.
REMAP_SCHEMA	Imports data exported from the source schema into the target schema.
REMAP_TABLESPACE	Imports data exported from the source tablespace into the target tablespace.
REUSE_DATAFILES	Specifies whether existing datafiles should be reused by CREATE TABLESPACE commands during Full mode imports.
SCHEMAS	Names the schemas to be imported for a Schema mode import.
SKIP_UNUSABLE_INDEXES	Uses a Y/N flag to specify whether the import loads data into tables whose indexes are set to the Index Unusable state. If set to Y, the import does not load the data into those tables.
SQLFILE	Names the file to which the DDL for the import is written. The data and metadata are not loaded into the target database.
STATUS	Displays detailed status of the Data Pump job.
STREAMS_CONFIGURATION	Specifies using a Y/N flag whether Streams configuration information should be imported.
TABLE_EXISTS_ACTION	Instructs Data Pump Import on how to proceed if the table being imported already exists. Values include SKIP, APPEND, TRUNCATE, and REPLACE. The default is APPEND if CONTENT=DATA_ONLY; otherwise, the default is SKIP.
TABLES	Lists tables for a Table mode import.
TABLESPACES	Lists tablespaces for a Tablespace mode import.
TRANSFORM	Directs changes to the segment attributes or storage during import.
TRANSPORT_DATAFILES	Lists the datafiles to be imported during a Transportable Tablespace mode import.
TRANSPORT_FULL_CHECK	Specifies whether the tablespaces being imported should first be verified as a self-contained set.
TRANSPORT_TABLESPACES	Lists the tablespaces to be imported during a Transportable Tablespace mode import.

TABLE 24-3. *Data Pump Import Command-Line Parameters* (continued)

Parameter	Description
TRANSPORTABLE	Specifies whether the transportable option should be used when a Table mode import (specified with the TABLES parameter) is performed.
VERSION	Specifies the version of database objects to be created so the dump file set is compatible with earlier releases of Oracle. Options are COMPATIBLE, LATEST, and database version numbers (not lower than 10.0.0). Only valid for NETWORK_LINK and SQLFILE.

TABLE 24-3. *Data Pump Import Command-Line Parameters* (continued)

As with Data Pump Export, five modes are supported: Full, Schema, Table, Tablespace, and Transportable Tablespace. If no mode is specified, Oracle attempts to load the entire dump file.

Table 24-4 lists the parameters that are valid in the interactive mode of Data Pump Import. Many of the Data Pump Import parameters are the same as those available for Data Pump Export. In the following sections, you will see how to start an import job, along with learning the major options unique to Data Pump Import.

NOTE
Oracle Database 12c Data Pump Export and Import fully support Oracle multitenant databases. Not only can you move a pluggable database (PDB) to another multitenant container database (CDB), but you can also transport a PDB into a non-CDB.

Parameter	Description
CONTINUE_CLIENT	Exits the interactive mode and enters logging mode. The job will be restarted if idle.
EXIT_CLIENT	Exits the client session, but leaves the server Data Pump Import job running.
HELP	Displays online help for the import.
KILL_JOB	Kills the current job and detaches related client sessions.
PARALLEL	Alters the number of workers for the Data Pump Import job.
START_JOB	Restarts the attached job.
STATUS	Displays detailed status of the Data Pump job.
STOP_JOB	Stops the job for later restart.

TABLE 24-4. *Interactive Parameters for Data Pump Import*

Starting a Data Pump Import Job

You can start a Data Pump Import job via the **impdp** executable provided with an installation of Oracle Database 12*c*. Use the command-line parameters to specify the import mode and the locations for all the files. You can store the parameter values in a parameter file and then reference the file via the PARFILE option.

In the first export example in this chapter, the parameter file named **dp1.par** contained the following entries:

```
directory=dtpump
dumpfile=metadataonly.dmp
content=metadata_only
```

The import can create the PRACTICE schema's objects in a different schema. The REMAP_SCHEMA option allows you to import objects into a different schema than was used for the export. If you want to change the tablespace assignments for the objects at the same time, use the REMAP_TABLESPACE option. The format for REMAP_SCHEMA is

```
REMAP_SCHEMA=source_schema:target_schema
```

Create a new user account to hold the objects:

```
create user newpractice identified by newp;
grant create session, resource to newpractice;
```

You can now add the REMAP_SCHEMA line to the **dp1.par** parameter file:

```
directory=dtpump
dumpfile=metadataonly.dmp
content=metadata_only
remap_schema=practice:newpractice
```

You can now start the import job. Because you are changing the owning schema for the data, you must have the IMP_FULL_DATABASE system privilege. Data Pump Import jobs are started via the **impdp** executable. The following listing shows the creation of a Data Pump Import job using the **dp1.par** parameter file:

```
$ impdp bobby/bryla parfile=dp1.par
```

NOTE
For Data Pump Import, you must specify all dump files at the time the job is started.

Oracle then performs the import and displays its progress. Because the NOLOGFILE option was not specified, the log file for the import is placed in the same directory as the dump file and is given the name **import.log**. You can verify the import's success by logging into the NEWPRACTICE schema. The NEWPRACTICE schema should have a copy of all the valid objects that have previously been created in the PRACTICE schema.

What if a table being imported already exists? In this example, with the CONTENT option set to METADATA_ONLY, the table would be skipped by default. If the CONTENT option was set to DATA_ONLY, the new data would be appended to the existing table data. To alter this behavior, use the TABLE_EXISTS_ACTION option. Valid values for TABLE_EXISTS_OPTION are SKIP, APPEND, TRUNCATE, and REPLACE.

Stopping and Restarting Running Jobs

After you have started a Data Pump Import job, you can close the client window you used to start the job. Because it is server based, the import continues to run. You can then attach to the job, check its status, and alter it:

```
$ impdp system/passwd parfile=dp1.par
```

Press CTRL-C to exit the ongoing log and status display, and Data Pump returns you to the Import prompt:

```
Import>
```

Exit to the operating system via the EXIT_CLIENT command:

```
Import> exit_client
```

You can then restart the client and attach to the currently running job under your schema:

```
$ impdp bobby/bryla attach
```

If you gave a name to your Data Pump Import job, specify the name as part of the ATTACH parameter call. When you attach to a running job, Data Pump displays the job's status—its basic configuration parameters and its current status. You can then issue the CONTINUE_CLIENT command to see the log entries as they are generated, or you can alter the running job:

```
Import> continue_client
```

You can stop a job via the STOP_JOB option:

```
Import> stop_job
```

While the job is stopped, you can increase its parallelism via the PARALLEL option. You can then restart the job:

```
Import> parallel=12
Import> start_job
```

EXCLUDE, INCLUDE, and QUERY

Data Pump Import, like Data Pump Export, allows you to restrict the data processed via the use of the EXCLUDE, INCLUDE, and QUERY options, as described earlier in this chapter. Because you can use these options on both the export and the import, your imports can be flexible. For example, you may choose to export an entire table but only import part of it—the rows that match your QUERY criteria. You could choose to export an entire schema but when recovering the database via import include only the most necessary tables so the application downtime can be minimized. EXCLUDE, INCLUDE, and QUERY provide powerful capabilities to developers and database administrators during both export and import jobs.

Generating SQL

Instead of importing the data and objects, you can generate the SQL for the objects (not the data) and store it in a file on your operating system. The file is written to the directory and file specified via the SQLFILE option. The SQLFILE option format is

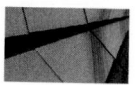

```
SQLFILE=[directory_object:]file_name
```

NOTE
If you do not specify a value for the DIRECTORY_OBJECT variable, the file is created in the dump file directory.

The following listing shows a sample parameter file for an import using the SQLFILE option. Note that the CONTENT option is not specified. The output is written to the DTPUMP directory.

```
directory=dtpump
dumpfile=metadataonly.dmp
sqlfile=sql.txt
```

You can then run the import to populate the **sql.txt** file:

```
$ impdp practice/practice parfile=dp1.par
```

In the **sql.txt** file the import creates, you see entries for each of the object types within the schema. The format for the output file is similar to the following listing, although the object IDs and SCNs will be specific to your environment. For brevity, not all entries in the file are shown here.

```
-- CONNECT PRACTICE
-- new object type path is: SCHEMA_EXPORT/SE_PRE_SCHEMA_PROCOBJACT/PROCACT_
SCHEMA

BEGIN
SYS.DBMS_LOGREP_IMP.INSTANTIATE_SCHEMA(SCHEMA_NAME=>'PRACTICE',
EXPORT_DB_NAME=>'ORCL', INST_SCN=>'3377908');
COMMIT;
END;
/


-- new object type path is: SCHEMA_EXPORT/TYPE/TYPE_SPEC
CREATE TYPE "PRACTICE"."ADDRESS_TY"
   OID '48D49FA5EB6D447C8D4C1417D849D63A' as object
(Street   VARCHAR2(50),
 City     VARCHAR2(25),
 State    CHAR(2),
 Zip      NUMBER);
/


CREATE TYPE "PRACTICE"."CUSTOMER_TY"
   OID '8C429A2DD41042228170643EF24BE75A' as object
(Customer_ID NUMBER,
 Name         VARCHAR2(25),
```

```
  Street        VARCHAR2(50),
  City          VARCHAR2(25),
  State         CHAR(2),
  Zip           NUMBER);
/
CREATE TYPE "PRACTICE"."PERSON_TY"
  OID '76270312D764478FAFDD47BF4533A5F8' as object
(Name          VARCHAR2(25),
 Address       ADDRESS_TY);
/

-- new object type path is: SCHEMA_EXPORT/TABLE/TABLE
CREATE TABLE "PRACTICE"."CUSTOMER"
   (  "CUSTOMER_ID" NUMBER,
      "NAME" VARCHAR2(25),
      "STREET" VARCHAR2(50),
      "CITY" VARCHAR2(25),
      "STATE" CHAR(2),
      "ZIP" NUMBER
  ) PCTFREE 10 PCTUSED 40 INITRANS 1 MAXTRANS 255 NOCOMPRESS LOGGING
STORAGE(INITIAL 65536 NEXT 1048576 MINEXTENTS 1 MAXEXTENTS 2147483645
PCTINCREASE 0 FREELISTS 1 FREELIST GROUPS 1 BUFFER_POOL DEFAULT)
  TABLESPACE "USERS" ;

CREATE TABLE "PRACTICE"."CUSTOMER_CALL"
   (  "CUSTOMER_ID" NUMBER,
      "CALL_NUMBER" NUMBER,
      "CALL_DATE" DATE
  ) PCTFREE 10 PCTUSED 40 INITRANS 1 MAXTRANS 255 NOCOMPRESS LOGGING
STORAGE(INITIAL 65536 NEXT 1048576 MINEXTENTS 1 MAXEXTENTS 2147483645
PCTINCREASE 0 FREELISTS 1 FREELIST GROUPS 1 BUFFER_POOL DEFAULT)
  TABLESPACE "USERS" ;

CREATE TABLE "PRACTICE"."STOCK_TRX"
   (  "ACCOUNT" NUMBER(10,0),
      "SYMBOL" VARCHAR2(20),
      "PRICE" NUMBER(6,2),
      "QUANTITY" NUMBER(6,0),
      "TRX_FLAG" VARCHAR2(1)
  ) PCTFREE 10 PCTUSED 40 INITRANS 1 MAXTRANS 255 NOCOMPRESS LOGGING
STORAGE(INITIAL 65536 NEXT 1048576 MINEXTENTS 1 MAXEXTENTS 2147483645
PCTINCREASE 0 FREELISTS 1 FREELIST GROUPS 1 BUFFER_POOL DEFAULT)
  TABLESPACE "USERS" ;

CREATE TABLE "PRACTICE"."STOCK_ACCOUNT"
   (  "ACCOUNT" NUMBER(10,0),
      "ACCOUNTLONGNAME" VARCHAR2(50)
  ) PCTFREE 10 PCTUSED 40 INITRANS 1 MAXTRANS 255 NOCOMPRESS LOGGING
STORAGE(INITIAL 65536 NEXT 1048576 MINEXTENTS 1 MAXEXTENTS 2147483645
PCTINCREASE 0 FREELISTS 1 FREELIST GROUPS 1 BUFFER_POOL DEFAULT)
```

```
    TABLESPACE "USERS" ;

-- new object type path is: SCHEMA_EXPORT/TABLE/GRANT/OBJECT_GRANT
GRANT SELECT ON "PRACTICE"."STOCK_TRX" TO "ADAMS";
GRANT SELECT ON "PRACTICE"."STOCK_TRX" TO "BURLINGTON";
GRANT SELECT ON "PRACTICE"."STOCK_ACCOUNT" TO "ADAMS";
GRANT SELECT ON "PRACTICE"."STOCK_ACCOUNT" TO "BURLINGTON";
GRANT INSERT ON "PRACTICE"."STOCK_TRX" TO "ADAMS";

-- new object type path is: SCHEMA_EXPORT/TABLE/INDEX/INDEX
CREATE UNIQUE INDEX "PRACTICE"."CUSTOMER_PK" ON "PRACTICE"."CUSTOMER"
("CUSTOMER_ID")
  PCTFREE 10 INITRANS 2 MAXTRANS 255
STORAGE(INITIAL 65536 NEXT 1048576 MINEXTENTS 1 MAXEXTENTS 2147483645
PCTINCREASE 0 FREELISTS 1 FREELIST GROUPS 1 BUFFER_POOL DEFAULT)
  TABLESPACE "USERS" PARALLEL 1 ;

ALTER INDEX "PRACTICE"."CUSTOMER_PK" NOPARALLEL;
```

The SQLFILE output is a plain text file, so you can edit the file, use it within SQL*Plus, or keep it as documentation of your application's database structures.

CHAPTER
25

Accessing Remote Data

A s your databases grow in size and number, you will very likely need to share data among them. Sharing data requires a method of locating and accessing the data. In Oracle, remote data accesses such as queries and updates are enabled through the use of database links. As described in this chapter, database links allow users to treat a group of distributed databases as if they were a single, integrated database. In this chapter, you will also find information about direct connections to remote databases, such as those used in client-server applications.

Database Links

Database links tell Oracle how to get from one database to another. If you frequently use the same connection to a remote database, a database link is appropriate.

How a Database Link Works

A database link requires Oracle Net Services (previously known as SQL*Net and Net8) to be running on each of the machines (hosts) involved in the remote database access. Oracle Net Services is usually started by the database administrator (DBA) or the system manager. A sample architecture for remote access using a database link is shown in Figure 25-1. This figure shows two hosts, each running Oracle Net Services. There is a database on each of the hosts. A database link defines a connection from the first database (named LOCAL, on the Branch host) to the second database (named REMOTE, on the Headquarters host). The database link shown in Figure 25-1 is located in the LOCAL database.

To support communication between the two databases, the Oracle Net Services configuration must include listener processes for the databases and service names for the databases. Oracle Net Services configuration files include **tnsnames.ora** (for translating database service names to databases, hosts, and ports) and **listener.ora** (for specifying the connection information for databases on the local host).

Database links specify the following connection information:

■ The communications protocol (such as TCP/IP) to use during the connection

■ The host on which the remote database resides

■ The name of the database on the remote host

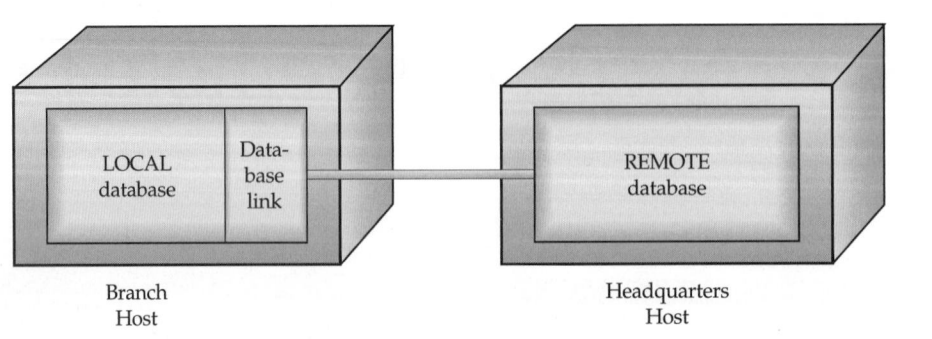

FIGURE 25-1. *Sample architecture for database link*

- The name of a valid account in the remote database (optional)
- The password for that account (optional)

When used, a database link actually logs in as a user in the remote database and the database link remains open for your session until you either log out of your session or execute the ALTER SESSION CLOSE DATABASE LINK command. A database link can be *private,* owned by a single user, or *public,* in which case all users in the LOCAL database can use the link.

Using a Database Link for Remote Queries

If you are a user in the LOCAL database shown in Figure 25-1, you can access objects in the REMOTE database via a database link. To do this, simply append the database link name to the name of any table or view that is accessible to the remote account. When appending the database link name to a table or view name, you must precede the database link name with an @ sign.

For local tables, you reference the table name in the FROM clause:

```
select *
from bookshelf;
```

For remote tables, use a database link named REMOTE_CONNECT. In the FROM clause, reference the table name followed by @REMOTE_CONNECT:

```
select *
from bookshelf@remote_connect;
```

NOTE
*If your database initialization parameters include GLOBAL_
NAMES=TRUE, then the database link name must be the same as the
name of the remote instance you are connecting to.*

When the database link in the preceding query is used, Oracle will log into the database specified by the database link, using the username and password provided by the link. It then queries the BOOKSHELF table in that account and returns the data to the user who initiated the query. This is shown graphically in Figure 25-2. The REMOTE_CONNECT database link shown in Figure 25-2 is located in the LOCAL database.

FIGURE 25-2. *Using a database link for a remote query*

As shown in Figure 25-2, logging into the LOCAL database and using the REMOTE_ CONNECT database link in the FROM clause returns the same results as logging in directly to the remote database and executing the query without the database link. It makes the remote database seem local.

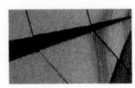

NOTE
The maximum number of database links that can be used in a single session is set via the OPEN_LINKS parameter in the database's initialization parameter file.

Queries executed using database links do have some restrictions. You should avoid using database links in queries that use the CONNECT BY, START WITH, and PRIOR keywords. Some queries using these keywords will work (for example, if PRIOR is not used outside of the CONNECT BY clause and START WITH does not use a subquery), but most tree-structured queries will fail when using database links.

Using a Database Link for Synonyms and Views

You may create local synonyms and views that reference remote objects. To do this, reference the database link name, preceded by an @ sign, wherever you refer to a remote table. The following example shows how to do this for synonyms. The CREATE SYNONYM command in this example is executed from an account in the LOCAL database.

```
create synonym bookshelf_syn
    for bookshelf@remote_connect;
```

In this example, a synonym called BOOKSHELF_SYN is created for the BOOKSHELF table accessed via the REMOTE_CONNECT database link. Every time this synonym is used in the FROM clause of a query, the remote database is queried. This is similar to the remote queries shown earlier; the only real change is that the database link is now defined as part of a local object (in this case, a synonym).

What if the remote account that is accessed by the database link does not own the table being referenced? In that event, any synonyms available to the remote account (either private or public) can be used. If no such synonyms exist for a table that the remote account has been granted access to, you must specify the table owner's name in the query, as shown in the following example:

```
create synonym bookshelf_syn
    for practice.bookshelf@remote_connect;
```

In this example, the remote account used by the database link neither owns the BOOKSHELF table, nor does the remote account have a synonym called BOOKSHELF. It does, however, have privileges on the BOOKSHELF table owned by the remote user PRACTICE in the REMOTE database. Therefore, the owner and table name are specified; both are interpreted in the REMOTE database. The syntax for these queries and synonyms is almost the same as if everything were in the local database; the only addition is the database link name.

To use a database link in a view, simply add it as a suffix to table names in the CREATE VIEW command. The following example creates a view in the local database of a remote table using the REMOTE_CONNECT database link:

```
create view local_bookshelf_view
as
select * from bookshelf@remote_connect
where title > 'M';
```

The FROM clause in this example refers to BOOKSHELF@REMOTE_CONNECT. Therefore, the base table for this view is not in the same database as the view. Also note that a WHERE clause is placed on the query to limit the number of records returned by it for the view.

This view may now be treated the same as any other view in the local database. Access to this view can be granted to other users, provided those users also have access to the REMOTE_ CONNECT database link.

Using a Database Link for Remote Updates

The database link syntax for remote updates is the same as that for remote queries. Append the name of the database link to the name of the table being updated. For example, to change the RATING values for books in a remote BOOKSHELF table, you would execute the UPDATE command shown in the following listing:

```
update bookshelf@remote_connect
set rating = '5'
where title = 'Innumeracy';
```

This UPDATE command uses the REMOTE_CONNECT database link to log into the remote database. It then updates the BOOKSHELF table in that database, based on the SET and WHERE conditions specified.

You can use subqueries in the SET portion of the UPDATE command (refer to Chapter 15). The FROM clause of such subqueries can reference either the local database or a remote database. To refer to the remote database in a subquery, append the database link name to the table names in the FROM clause of the subquery. An example of this is shown in the following listing:

```
update bookshelf@remote_connect          /*in remote database*/
   set rating =
       (select rating
        from bookshelf@remote_connect  /*in remote database*/
         where title = 'Wonderful Life')
where title = 'Innumeracy';
```

NOTE
If you do not append the database link name to the table names in the FROM clause of UPDATE subqueries, tables in the local database will be used. This is true even if the table being updated is in a remote database.

In this example, the remote BOOKSHELF table is updated based on the RATING value on the remote BOOKSHELF table. If the database link is not used in the subquery, as in the following example, then the BOOKSHELF table in the local database is used instead. If this is unintended, it will cause local data to be mixed into the remote database table. If you're doing this on purpose, be *very* careful.

```
update bookshelf@remote_connect          /*in remote database*/
   set rating =
       (select rating
          from bookshelf                  /*in local database*/
          where title = 'Wonderful Life')
where title = 'Innumeracy';
```

Syntax for Database Links

You can create a database link with the following command:

```
CREATE [SHARED] [PUBLIC] DATABASE LINK remote_database_name_link
CONNECT TO {CURRENT_USER | username
IDENTIFIED BY PASSWORD [authentication_clause]}
USING 'connect_string';
```

The specific syntax to use when creating a database link depends on two criteria:

- The "public" or "private" status of the database link (If the link does not have the PUBLIC and SHARED attributes, it is a private link.)
- The use of default or explicit logins for the remote database

These criteria and their associated syntax are described, in turn, in the following sections.

NOTE
To create a database link, you must have the CREATE DATABASE LINK system privilege. The account to which you connect in the remote database must have the CREATE SESSION system privilege.

If the value of the GLOBAL_NAMES initialization parameter is TRUE, the database link must have the same name as the database to which it connects. If the value of GLOBAL_NAMES is FALSE, you can specify any meaningful name for the link.

Public vs. Private Database Links

As mentioned earlier, a *public* database link is available to all users in a database. By contrast, a *private* database link is only available to the user who created it. It is not possible for one user to grant access on a private database link to another user. The database link must be either public (available to all users) or private.

To specify a database link as public, use the PUBLIC keyword in the CREATE DATABASE LINK command, as shown in the following example:

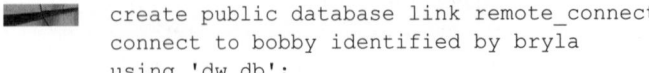

```
create public database link remote_connect
connect to bobby identified by bryla
using 'dw_db';
```

NOTE
To create a public database link, you must have the CREATE PUBLIC DATABASE LINK system privilege. This privilege is included in the DBA role in Oracle Database 12c.

Default vs. Explicit Logins

In place of the CONNECT TO . . . IDENTIFIED BY clause, you can use CONNECT TO CURRENT_ USER when creating a database link. If you use the CURRENT_USER option, then when that link is used, it will attempt to open a session in the remote database that has the same username and password as the local database account. This is called a *default login* because the username/ password combination defaults to the combination in use in the local database.

The following listing shows an example of a public database link created with a default login (the use of default logins is described further in "Using the USER Pseudo-Column in Views," later in this chapter):

```
create public database link remote_connect
connect to current_user
using 'HQ';
```

When this database link is used, it will attempt to log into the remote database identified by the HQ service name using the current user's username and password. If the current username is not valid in the remote database, or if the password is different, the login attempt fails. This failure will cause the SQL statement using the link to fail. Using default logins provides added security because the password for the remote account is not stored in the local database, but it makes account maintenance more complex. If you change an account's password in the local database, you also need to change it to the same password in remote databases accessed via database links, or the links may fail.

An *explicit* login specifies a username and password that the database link uses when connecting to the remote database. No matter which local account uses the link, the same remote account is used. The following listing shows the creation of a database link with an explicit login:

```
create public database link remote_connect
connect to warehouse_user identified by ACCESS339
using 'HQ';
```

This example shows a common usage of explicit logins in database links. In the remote database, a user named WAREHOUSE was created and was given the password ACCESS339. The WAREHOUSE account can then be granted SELECT access to specific tables, solely for use by database links. The REMOTE_CONNECT database link then provides access to the remote WAREHOUSE account for all local users.

Connect String Syntax

Oracle Net Services uses *net service names* to identify remote connections. The connection details for these service names are contained in files that are distributed to each host in the network. When a service name is encountered, Oracle checks the local Oracle Net Services configuration file (called **tnsnames.ora**) to determine which protocol, host name, and database name to use during the connection. All the connection information is found in external files.

When using Oracle Net Services, you must know the name of the service that points to the remote database. For example, if the service name HQ specifies the connection parameters for the database you need, then HQ should be used as the connect string in the CREATE DATABASE LINK command. The following example shows a private database link, using a default login and an Oracle Net Services service name:

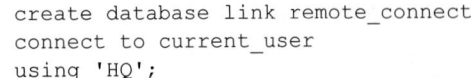

```
create database link remote_connect
connect to current_user
using 'HQ';
```

When this link is used, Oracle checks the **tnsnames.ora** file on the local host to determine which database to connect to. When it attempts to log into that database, it uses the current user's username and password.

The **tnsnames.ora** files for a network of databases should be coordinated by the DBAs for those databases (if you don't have an LDAP server available). A simplified version of an entry in the **tnsnames.ora** file (for a network using the TCP/IP protocol) is shown in the following listing:

```
HQ =(DESCRIPTION=
      (ADDRESS_LIST =
            (ADDRESS = (PROTOCOL=TCP)
            (HOST = bi_dw.localdomain.com)
            (PORT =1521))
        )
      (CONNECT DATA =
            (SERVICE_NAME = obi)
        )
    )
```

In this listing, the HQ service name is mapped to a connect descriptor that tells the database which protocol to use (TCP/IP) and which host (**bi_dw**) and database (OBI) to connect to. The "port" information refers to the port on the host that will be used for the connection; that data is environment specific. Different protocols have different keywords, but they all must convey the same content.

Using Shared Database Links

If you use the Shared Server option for your database connections (many clients using the same connection) and your application employs many concurrent database link connections, you may benefit from using *shared database links*. A shared database link uses shared server connections to support the database link connections. If you have multiple concurrent database link accesses into a remote database, you can use shared database links to reduce the number of server connections required.

NOTE
The Shared Server option should not be confused with the SHARED_SERVERS initialization parameter that specifies the maximum number of shared servers to be configured.

To create a shared database link, use the SHARED keyword of the CREATE DATABASE LINK command. As shown in the following listing, you also need to specify a schema and password for the remote database:

```
create shared database link hr_link_shared
connect to current_user
authenticated by hr identified by puffin55556d
using 'HQ';
```

The HR_LINK_SHARED database link uses the connected user's username and password when accessing the HQ database, as specified via the CONNECT TO CURRENT_USER clause. To prevent unauthorized attempts to use the shared link, shared links require the AUTHENTICATED BY clause. In this example, the account used for authentication is an application account, but you can also use an empty schema for authentication. The authentication account must have the CREATE SESSION system privilege. When using the HR_LINK_SHARED link, connection attempts will include authentication against the HR link account.

If you change the password on the authentication account, you need to drop and re-create each database link that references it. To simplify maintenance, create an account that is only used for the authentication of shared database link connections. The account should have only the CREATE SESSION system privilege and should not have any privileges on any of the application tables.

If your application uses database links infrequently, you should use traditional database links without the SHARED clause. Without the SHARED clause, each database link connection requires a separate connection to the remote database.

Using Synonyms for Location Transparency

Over an application's lifespan, its data very likely will move from one database to another or from one host to another. Therefore, it will simplify application maintenance if the exact physical location of a database object is shielded from the user (and the application).

The best way to implement such location transparency is through the use of synonyms. Instead of writing applications (or SQL*Plus reports) that contain queries that specify a table's owner, such as

```
select *
from practice.bookshelf;
```

you should create a synonym for that table and then reference the synonym in the query, as shown here:

```
create synonym bookshelf
for practice.bookshelf;

select *
from bookshelf;
```

The logic required to find the data has thus been moved out of your application and into the database. Moving the table location logic to the database benefits you anytime you move the table from one schema to another.

In addition to hiding table ownership from an application, you can hide the data's physical location through the use of database links and synonyms. By using local synonyms for remote tables, you move another layer of logic out of the application and into the database. For example, the local synonym BOOKSHELF, as defined in the following listing, refers to a table that is located in a different database on a different host. If that table ever moves, only the link has to be changed; the application code, which uses the synonym, will not change.

```
create synonym bookshelf
for bookshelf@remote_connect;
```

If the remote account used by the database link is not the owner of the object being referenced, you have two options. First, you can reference an available synonym in the remote database:

```
create synonym bookshelf
for bookshelf@remote_connect;
```

Here, BOOKSHELF, in the remote account used by the database link, is a synonym for another user's BOOKSHELF table.

Second, you can include the remote owner's name when creating the local synonym, as shown in the following listing:

```
create synonym bookshelf
for practice.bookshelf@remote_connect;
```

These two examples result in the same functionality for your queries, but there are differences between them. The second example, which includes the owner's name, is potentially more difficult to maintain because you are not using a synonym in the remote database and the remote object may be moved at a later time, thus invalidating your local synonym.

Using the USER Pseudo-Column in Views

The USER pseudo-column is quite useful when you are using remote data access methods. For example, you may not want all remote users to see all rows in a table. To solve this problem, you must think of remote users as special users within your database. To enforce the data restriction, you need to create a view that the remote accounts will access. But what can you use in the WHERE clause to properly restrict the records? The USER pseudo-column, combined with properly selected usernames, allows you to enforce this restriction.

As you may recall from Chapter 17, queries used to define views may also reference *pseudo-columns*. A pseudo-column is a "column" that returns a value when it is selected, but it is not an actual column in a table. The USER pseudo-column, when selected, always returns the Oracle username that executed the query. So, if a column in the table contains usernames, those values can be compared against the USER pseudo-column to restrict its records, as shown in the following example. In this example, the NAME table is queried. If the value of the first part of the Name column is the same as the name of the user entering the query, the records are returned.

```
create view my_checkout as
select * from bookshelf_checkout
where substr(name,1,instr(name,' ')-1) = user;
```

NOTE
We need to shift our point of view for this discussion. Because the discussion concerns operations on the database that owns the table being queried, we'll refer to that database as the "local" database and the users from other databases as "remote" users.

When restricting remote access to your table rows, you should first consider which columns would be the best used for the restriction. The data within a table has logical divisions, such as department or region. For each distinct division, create a separate user account in your local database. For this example, let's add a REGION column to the BOOKSHELF table. You should now be able to record the list of books from multiple distributed locations in a single table:

```
alter table bookshelf
add
(region varchar2(10));
```

Suppose you have four major regions represented in your BOOKSHELF table, and you have created an Oracle account for each region. You could then set up each remote user's database link to use his or her specific user account in your local database. For this example, assume the regions are called NORTH, EAST, SOUTH, and WEST. For each of the regions, a specific database link is created. For example, the members of the SOUTH department would use the database link shown in the following listing:

```
create database link south_link
connect to south identified by paw
using 'HQ';
```

The database link shown in this example is a private database link with an explicit login to the SOUTH account in the remote database.

When remote users query via their database links (such as SOUTH_LINK from the previous example), they will be logged into the HQ database, with their department name (such as SOUTH) as their username. Therefore, the value of the USER column for any table that the user queries will be SOUTH.

Now create a view of your base table, comparing the USER pseudo-column to the value of the DEPARTMENT column in the view's WHERE clause:

```
create or replace view restricted_bookshelf as
select *
from bookshelf
where region = user;
```

A user who connects via the SOUTH_LINK database link—and thus is logged in as the SOUTH user—would only be able to see the BOOKSHELF records that have a REGION value equal to 'SOUTH'. If users are accessing your table from a remote database, their logins are occurring via database links—and you know the local accounts they are using because you set them up.

This type of restriction can also be performed in the remote database rather than in the database where the table resides. Users in the remote database may create views within their databases of the following form:

```
create or replace view south_bookshelf as
select *
from bookshelf@remote_connect
where region = 'SOUTH';
```

In this case, the REGION restriction is still in force, but it is administered locally, and the REGION restriction is coded into the view's query. Choosing between the two restriction options (local or remote) is based on the number of accounts required for the desired restriction to be enforced.

To secure your production database, you should limit the privileges granted to the accounts used by database links. Grant those privileges via roles, and use views (with the WITH READ ONLY or WITH CHECK OPTION clause) to further limit the ability of those accounts to make unauthorized changes to the data.

As these examples show, the Branch host has few hardware requirements. All it has to support is the front-end tool and Oracle Net Services. A client machine, such as the Branch host, is used primarily for presentation of the data via the database access tools. The server side, such as the Headquarters host, is used to maintain the data and process the data access requests from users.

Regardless of the configuration you use and the configuration tools available, you need to tell Oracle Net Services how to find the remote database. Work with your DBA to make sure the remote server is properly configured to listen for new connection requests and to make sure the client machines are properly configured to issue those requests.

CHAPTER
26

Using Materialized Views

T o improve the performance of an application, you can make local copies of remote tables that use distributed data or create summary tables based on GROUP BY operations. Oracle provides *materialized views* to store copies of data or aggregations. Materialized views can be used to replicate all or part of a single table or to replicate the result of a query against multiple tables; the database can automatically refresh the replicated data at time intervals that you specify. In this chapter, you will learn about the general usage of materialized views, including their refresh strategies; this is followed by a discussion of the optimization strategies available.

Functionality

Materialized views are copies (also known as *replicas* or *snapshots*) of data based on queries. In its simplest form, a *materialized view* is similar to a table created by a command such as the following:

```
create table local_bookshelf
as
select * from bookshelf@remote_connect;
```

In this example, a regular table named LOCAL_BOOKSHELF is created in the local database and is populated with data from a remote database (defined by the database link named REMOTE_CONNECT). Once the LOCAL_BOOKSHELF table is created, though, its data may immediately become out of sync with the master table (BOOKSHELF@REMOTE_CONNECT). Also, LOCAL_BOOKSHELF may be updated by local users, further complicating its synchronization with the master table.

Despite these synchronization problems, there are benefits to replicating data in this way. Creating local copies of remote data may improve the performance of distributed queries, particularly if the master table's data does not change frequently. You may also use the local table creation process to restrict the rows returned, restrict the columns returned, or generate new columns (such as by applying functions to selected values). This strategy is common in decision-support environments, in which complex queries are used to periodically "roll up" data into summary tables for use during analyses.

Materialized views automate the data replication and refresh processes. When materialized views are created, a *refresh interval* is established to schedule refreshes of replicated data. Local updates can be prevented, and transaction-based refreshes can be used. Transaction-based refreshes, available for many types of materialized views, send from the master database only those rows that have changed for the materialized view. This capability, described later in this chapter, may significantly improve the performance of your refreshes.

Required System Privileges

To create a materialized view, you must have the privileges needed to create or access the underlying objects it will use. You must have the CREATE MATERIALIZED VIEW privilege, as well as the CREATE TABLE or CREATE ANY TABLE system privilege. In addition, you must have either the UNLIMITED TABLESPACE system privilege or a sufficient specified space quota in a local tablespace. To create a *refresh-on-commit* materialized view, you must also have the ON

COMMIT REFRESH system privilege on any tables you do not own or the ON COMMIT REFRESH system privilege.

Materialized views of remote tables require queries of remote tables; therefore, you must have privileges to use a database link that accesses the remote database. The link you use can be either public or private. If the database link is private, you need to have the CREATE DATABASE LINK system privilege to create the database link. See Chapter 25 for further information on database links.

If you are creating materialized views to take advantage of the *query rewrite* feature (in which the optimizer dynamically chooses to select data from the materialized view instead of the underlying table), you must have the QUERY REWRITE privilege. If the tables are in another user's schema, you must have the GLOBAL QUERY REWRITE privilege. If the materialized view is created with ON COMMIT REFRESH specified, you must have the ON COMMIT REFRESH system privilege or the ON COMMIT REFRESH object privilege on each table outside your schema.

NOTE
As of Oracle Database 11g, queries that reference remote tables can support query rewrite.

In Oracle Database 11g, query rewrite has been enhanced to support queries containing inline views. Prior to this release, queries containing inline views could rewrite only if there was an exact text match with the inline views in the materialized views.

For materialized views in Oracle Database 12c, availability has been improved. By leveraging partitioning and the known dependencies between base tables and related materialized views, the materialized view can be refreshed simultaneously with the base table(s). As a result, the amount of time that a materialized view is stale is significantly reduced.

Required Table Privileges

When creating a materialized view, you can reference tables in a remote database via a database link. The account that the database link uses in the remote database must have access to the tables and views used by the database link. You cannot create a materialized view based on objects owned by the user SYS.

Within the local database, you can grant the SELECT privilege on a materialized view to other local users. Because most materialized views are read-only (although they can be updatable), no additional GRANTs are necessary. If you create an updatable materialized view, you must grant users the UPDATE privilege on both the materialized view and the underlying local table it accesses.

Read-Only vs. Updatable

A *read-only* materialized view cannot pass data changes from itself back to its master table. An *updatable* materialized view can send changes back to its master table.

Although that may seem to be a simple distinction, the underlying differences between these two types of materialized views are not simple. A read-only materialized view is implemented as a CREATE TABLE AS SELECT command. When transactions occur, they occur only within the master table; the transactions are optionally sent to the read-only materialized view. Thus, the method by which the rows in the materialized view change is controlled—the materialized view's rows only change following a change to the materialized view's master table.

In an updatable materialized view, you have less control over the method by which rows in the materialized view are changed. Rows may be changed based on changes in the master table, or rows may be changed directly by users of the materialized view. As a result, you need to send records from the master table to the materialized view, *and* vice versa. Because multiple sources of changes exist, multiple masters exist (referred to as a *multimaster configuration*).

During the transfer of records from the materialized view to master, you need to decide how you will reconcile conflicts. For example, what if the record with ID=1 is deleted at the materialized view site, while at the master site, a record is created in a separate table that references (via a foreign key) the ID=1 record? You cannot delete the ID=1 record from the master site because that record has a "child" record that relates to it. You cannot insert the child record at the materialized view site because the parent (ID=1) record has been deleted. How do you plan to resolve such conflicts?

Read-only materialized views let you avoid conflict resolution by forcing all transactions to occur in the controlled master table. This may limit your functionality, but it is an appropriate solution for the vast majority of replication needs. If you need multimaster replication, see the *Advanced Replication Guide* for guidelines and detailed implementation instructions.

CREATE MATERIALIZED VIEW Syntax

The basic syntax for creating a materialized view is shown in the following listing. See the Alphabetical Reference for the full command syntax. Following the command description, examples are given that illustrate the creation of local replicas of remote data.

```
CREATE MATERIALIZED VIEW [user.]name
[ ORGANIZATION INDEX iot_clause]
[  { { segment attributes clauses }
   | CLUSTER cluster (column [, column] ...) }
   [ {partitioning clause | parallel clause | build clause } ]
   | ON PREBUILT TABLE [ {WITH | WITHOUT} REDUCED PRECISION ] ]
[ USING INDEX
  [ { physical attributes clauses| tablespace clause }
    [ physical attributes clauses| tablespace clause ]
    | USING NO INDEX ]
[ refresh clause ]
[ FOR UPDATE ] [{DISABLE | ENABLE} QUERY REWRITE]
  AS subquery;
```

The CREATE MATERIALIZED VIEW command has four major sections. The first section is the header, in which the materialized view is named (the first line in the listing):

```
CREATE MATERIALIZED VIEW [user.]name
```

The materialized view will be created in your user account (schema) unless a different schema name is specified in the header. In the second section, the storage parameters are set:

```
[ ORGANIZATION INDEX iot_clause]
[  { { segment attributes clauses }
```

```
  | CLUSTER cluster (column [, column] ...) }
  [ {partitioning clause | parallel clause | build clause } ]
  | ON PREBUILT TABLE [ {WITH | WITHOUT} REDUCED PRECISION ] ]
[ USING INDEX
  [ { physical attributes clauses | tablespace clause }
    [ physical attributes clauses | tablespace clause ]
    | USING NO INDEX ]
```

The storage parameters will be applied to a table that will be created in the local database. For information about the available storage parameters, see the STORAGE entry in the Alphabetical Reference. If the data has already been replicated to a local table, you can use the ON PREBUILT TABLE clause to tell Oracle to use that table as a materialized view.

NOTE
You can specify the storage parameters to be used for the index that is automatically created on the materialized view.

In the third section, the refresh options are set:

```
[ refresh clause ]
```

The syntax for the *refresh clause* is

```
{ REFRESH
  { { FAST | COMPLETE | FORCE }
  | ON { DEMAND | COMMIT }
  | { START WITH | NEXT } date
  | WITH { PRIMARY KEY | ROWID }
  | USING
    { DEFAULT [ MASTER | LOCAL ] ROLLBACK SEGMENT
    | [ MASTER | LOCAL ] ROLLBACK SEGMENT rollback_segment
    }
    [ DEFAULT [ MASTER | LOCAL ] ROLLBACK SEGMENT
    | [ MASTER | LOCAL ] ROLLBACK SEGMENT rollback_segment
    ]...
  }
  [ { FAST | COMPLETE | FORCE }
  | ON { DEMAND | COMMIT }
  | { START WITH | NEXT } date
  | WITH { PRIMARY KEY | ROWID }
  | USING
    { DEFAULT [ MASTER | LOCAL ] ROLLBACK SEGMENT
    | [ MASTER | LOCAL ] ROLLBACK SEGMENT rollback_segment
    }
    [ DEFAULT [ MASTER | LOCAL ] ROLLBACK SEGMENT
    | [ MASTER | LOCAL ] ROLLBACK SEGMENT rollback_segment
    ]...
  ]...
  | NEVER REFRESH
}
```

The REFRESH option specifies the mechanism Oracle should use when refreshing the materialized view. The three options available are FAST, COMPLETE, and FORCE. FAST refreshes are only available if Oracle can match rows in the materialized view directly to rows in the base table(s); the materialized view refresh process uses tables called *materialized view logs* to send specific rows from the master table to the materialized view. COMPLETE refreshes truncate the data and re-execute the materialized view's base query to repopulate it. FORCE refreshes tell Oracle to use a FAST refresh if it is available; otherwise, a COMPLETE refresh is used. If you have created a simple materialized view but want to use complete refreshes, specify REFRESH COMPLETE in your CREATE MATERIALIZED VIEW command. The refresh options are further described in "Refreshing Materialized Views," later in this chapter.

Within this section of the CREATE MATERIALIZED VIEW command, you also specify the mechanism used to relate values in the materialized view to the master table—whether ROWIDs or primary key values should be used. By default, primary keys are used.

If the master query for the materialized view references a join or a single-table aggregate, you can use the ON COMMIT option to control the replication of changes. If you use ON COMMIT, changes are sent from the master to the replica when the changes are committed on the master table. If you specify ON DEMAND, the refresh occurs when you manually execute a refresh command.

The fourth section of the CREATE MATERIALIZED VIEW command is the query that the materialized view uses:

```
[ FOR UPDATE ] [{DISABLE | ENABLE} QUERY REWRITE]
  AS subquery
```

If you specify FOR UPDATE, the materialized view is updatable; otherwise, it is read-only. Most materialized views are read-only replicas of the master data. If you use updatable materialized views, you need to be concerned with issues such as two-way replication of changes and the reconciliation of conflicting data changes. Updatable materialized views are an example of multimaster replication; for full details on implementing a multimaster replication environment, see the *Advanced Replication Guide*.

NOTE
The query that forms the basis of the materialized view should not use the USER or SYSDATE pseudo-columns.

The following example creates a read-only materialized view called LOCAL_BOOKSHELF in a local database, based on a remote table named BOOKSHELF that is accessible via the REMOTE_CONNECT database link. The materialized view is placed in the USERS tablespace.

```
create materialized view local_bookshelf_mv
tablespace users
refresh force
start with sysdate next sysdate+7
with primary key
as
select * from bookshelf@remote_connect;
```

Oracle responds with

```
Materialized view created.
```

The command shown in the preceding example creates a read-only materialized view called LOCAL_BOOKSHELF_MV. Its underlying table is created in a tablespace named USERS. You can place materialized view logs in tablespaces apart from the materialized views they support. The FORCE refresh option is specified because no materialized view log exists on the base table for the materialized view; Oracle tries to use a FAST refresh but will use a COMPLETE refresh until the materialized view log is created. The materialized view's query specifies that the entire BOOKSHELF table, with no modifications, is to be copied to the local database. As soon as the LOCAL_BOOKSHELF_MV materialized view is created, its underlying table is populated with the BOOKSHELF data. Thereafter, the materialized view will be refreshed every seven days. The storage parameters that are not specified will use the default values for those parameters for the USERS tablespace.

The following example creates a materialized view named LOCAL_CATEGORY_COUNT_MV in a local database, based on a remote table named BOOKSHELF in a database accessed via the REMOTE_CONNECT database link:

```
create materialized view local_category_count_mv
tablespace users
refresh force
start with sysdate next sysdate+7
 as
select category_name, count(*) countpercat
from bookshelf@remote_connect
group by category_name;
```

The query in the LOCAL_CATEGORY_COUNT_MV materialized view counts the number of books in each category in the remote BOOKSHELF table.

Here are a few important points about the two examples shown in this section:

- The GROUP BY query used in the LOCAL_CATEGORY_COUNT_MV materialized view could be performed in SQL*Plus against the LOCAL_BOOKSHELF materialized view. That is, the GROUP BY operation can be performed outside of the materialized view.

- Since LOCAL_CATEGORY_COUNT_MV uses a GROUP BY clause, it is a complex materialized view and may only be able to use COMPLETE refreshes. LOCAL_BOOKSHELF_MV, as a simple materialized view, can use FAST refreshes.

The two materialized views shown in the preceding examples reference the same table. Because one of the materialized views is a simple materialized view that replicates all columns and all rows of the master table, the second materialized view may, at first, appear to be redundant. However, sometimes the second, complex materialized view is the more useful of the two.

How can this be? First, remember that these materialized views are being used to service the query needs of *local* users. If those users always perform GROUP BY operations in their queries, and their grouping columns are fixed, then LOCAL_CATEGORY_COUNT_MV may be more useful to them. Second, if the transaction volume on the master BOOKSHELF table is very high, or the master BOOKSHELF table is very small, there may not be a significant difference in the refresh times of the FAST and COMPLETE refreshes. The most appropriate materialized view is the one that is most productive for your users.

Types of Materialized Views

The materialized views shown in the previous examples illustrated two types of materialized views. In the first, the materialized view created a local copy of remote data, with no aggregations. In the second, an aggregation was performed. Both of the base queries could be extended to include joins of multiple tables. The key distinguishing factor is the use of aggregations in the second example. A third type of materialized view is a *nested* materialized view—a materialized view whose definition is based on another materialized view.

If a materialized view contains an aggregate, a FAST refresh is still possible if the SELECT list contains all of the GROUP BY columns. There must also be a COUNT(*) or COUNT(COLUMN_NAME) on any aggregated columns.

If a materialized view contains only joins but no aggregates, a FAST refresh is available after any INSERT, UPDATE, or DELETE to the base tables. The ROWID columns from each table must be present in the SELECT list for the materialized view's base query, and all of the referenced tables must have materialized view logs.

Because they send the incremental changes from the referenced tables to the materialized view, FAST refreshes usually represent the fastest way to update the data in your materialized views.

ROWID vs. Primary Key–Based Materialized Views

You can base materialized views on the master table's primary key values instead of basing them on the master table's ROWIDs. You should decide between these options depending on several factors:

- **System stability** If the master site is not stable, then you may need to perform database recoveries involving the master table. When you use Oracle's Data Pump Export and Import utilities to perform recoveries, the ROWID values of rows will change. If the system requires frequent exports and imports, you should use primary key–based materialized views.

- **Size of materialized view log table** Oracle allows you to store the changes to master tables in separate tables called *materialized view logs* (described later in this chapter). If the primary key consists of many columns, the materialized view log table for a primary key–based materialized view may be considerably larger than the materialized view log for a comparable ROWID-based materialized view.

- **Referential integrity** To use primary key–based materialized views, you must have defined a primary key on the master table. If you cannot define a primary key on the master table, then you must use ROWID-based materialized views.

Using Prebuilt Tables

When you create a materialized view, you can specify BUILD IMMEDIATE to populate the materialized view immediately or BUILD DEFERRED to populate the materialized view later (via a complete refresh). If you need to carefully manage the transactions that initially populate the materialized view, you can create a table that has the same structure as the materialized view and populate it. When the table is fully loaded and properly indexed, use the ON PREBUILT TABLE clause of the CREATE MATERIALIZED VIEW command. The table and the materialized view must have the same name, and the table must have the same columns and datatypes as the materialized view (you can SPECIFY WITH REDUCED PRECISION to accommodate differences in precision). The table can contain additional, unmanaged columns.

Once the table has been registered as a materialized view, you can maintain it via refreshes, and the optimizer can use it in query rewrite operations. For query rewrite to work properly on a prebuilt table, you must set the QUERY_REWRITE_INTEGRITY initialization parameter to STALE_TOLERATED or TRUSTED.

Indexing Materialized View Tables

When you create a materialized view, Oracle creates a local base table containing the data that satisfies the base query. Because that data has been replicated with a goal in mind (usually to improve performance in the database or the network), it is important to follow through on that goal after the materialized view has been created. As with regular tables, use indexes on materialized view columns to improve performance. Index columns that are frequently used in the WHERE clauses of queries; if a set of columns is frequently accessed in queries, create a concatenated index on that set of columns. (See Chapter 46 for more information on the Oracle Optimizer.)

Oracle does not automatically create indexes for complex materialized views on columns other than the primary key. You need to create these indexes manually. To create indexes on your local base table, use the CREATE INDEX command (see the Alphabetical Reference). Do *not* create any constraints on the materialized view's local base table; Oracle will maintain the constraint-based relationships on the master tables.

Because no indexes are created on the columns that users are likely to query from the materialized view, you should create indexes on the materialized view's local base table.

Using Materialized Views to Alter Query Execution Paths

For a large database, a materialized view may offer several performance benefits. You can use materialized views to influence the optimizer to change the execution paths for queries. This feature, called *query rewrite,* enables the optimizer to use a materialized view in place of the table queried by the materialized view, even if the materialized view is not named in the query. For example, if you have a large SALES table, you may create a materialized view that sums the SALES data by region. If a user queries the SALES table for the sum of the SALES data for a region, Oracle can redirect that query to use your materialized view in place of the SALES table. As a result, you can reduce the number of accesses against your largest tables, improving system performance. Further, because the data in the materialized view is already grouped by region, any summarization is already complete by the time the query is issued.

NOTE
You must specify ENABLE QUERY REWRITE in the materialized view definition for the view to be used as part of a query rewrite operation.

To use the query rewrite capability effectively, you should create a dimension that defines the hierarchies within the table's data. To execute the CREATE DIMENSION command, you need to have been granted the CREATE DIMENSION system privilege. For instance, you can create a dimension that supports the hierarchy between the COUNTRY and CONTINENT sample tables:

```
create dimension geography
   level country_id      is country.country
   level continent_id    is continent.continent
   hierarchy country_rollup (
      country_id          child of
      continent_id
   join key country.continent references continent_id);
```

To enable a materialized view for query rewrite, all of the master tables for the materialized view must be in the materialized view's schema, and you must have the QUERY REWRITE system privilege. If the view and the tables are in separate schemas, you must have the GLOBAL QUERY REWRITE system privilege. In general, you should create materialized views in the same schema as the tables on which they are based; otherwise, you will need to manage the permissions and grants required to create and maintain the materialized view.

You can enable or disable query rewrite at the SQL statement level via the REWRITE and NOREWRITE hints. When using the REWRITE hint, you can specify materialized views for the optimizer to consider.

NOTE
Query rewrite decisions are based on the costs of the different execution paths, so your statistics should be kept up to date.

For query rewrite to be possible, you must set the following initialization parameters:

- OPTIMIZER_MODE = ALL_ROWS or FIRST_ROWS
- QUERY_REWRITE_ENABLED = TRUE
- QUERY_REWRITE_INTEGRITY = STALE_TOLERATED, TRUSTED, or ENFORCED

By default, QUERY_REWRITE_INTEGRITY is set to ENFORCED; in this mode, all constraints must be validated. The optimizer only uses fresh data from the materialized views and only uses those relationships that are based on ENABLED VALIDATED primary, unique, or foreign key constraints. In TRUSTED mode, the optimizer trusts that the data in the materialized view is fresh and the relationships declared in dimensions and constraints are correct. In STALE_TOLERATED mode, the optimizer uses materialized views that are valid but contain stale data, as well as those that contain fresh data.

If you set QUERY_REWRITE_ENABLED to FORCE, the optimizer rewrites queries to use materialized views even when the estimated query cost of the original query is lower.

If query rewrite occurs, the explain plan for the query (see Chapter 46) will list the materialized view as one of the objects accessed, along with an operation listed as "MAT_VIEW REWRITE ACCESS." You can use the DBMS_MVIEW.EXPLAIN_REWRITE procedure to see if rewrite is possible for a query, and which materialized views would be involved. If the query cannot be rewritten, the procedure will document the reasons.

EXPLAIN_REWRITE takes three input parameters—the query, a materialized view name, and a statement identifier—and can store its output in a table. Oracle provides the CREATE TABLE command for the output table in a script named **utlxrw.sql** in the **./rdbms/admin** directory under the Oracle software home directory. The **utlxrw.sql** script creates a table named REWRITE_TABLE.

You can query the REWRITE_TABLE for the original cost, rewritten cost, and the optimizer's decision. The MESSAGE column displays the reasons for the optimizer's decision.

See the *Data Warehousing Guide* for further details and constraints related to query rewrite.

Using DBMS_ADVISOR

You can use the SQL Access Advisor to generate recommendations for the creation and indexing of materialized views. The SQL Access Advisor may recommend specific indexes (and types of indexes) to improve the performance of joins and other queries. The SQL Access Advisor may also generate recommendations for altering a materialized view so it supports query rewrite or FAST refreshes. You can execute the SQL Access Advisor from within Oracle Enterprise Manager or via executions of the DBMS_ADVISOR package.

NOTE
For best results from the DBMS_ADVISOR package, you should gather statistics about all tables, indexes, and join columns prior to generating recommendations.

To use the SQL Access Advisor, either from Oracle Enterprise Manager or via DBMS_ADVISOR, follow these four steps:

1.   Create a task.
2.   Define the workload.
3.   Generate recommendations.
4.   View and implement recommendations.

You can create a task in one of two ways: by executing the DBMS_ADVISOR.CREATE_TASK procedure or by using the DBMS_ADVISOR.QUICK_TUNE procedure (as shown in the next section).

The workload consists of one or more SQL statements plus the statistics and attributes that relate to the statement. The workload may include all SQL statements for an application. The SQL Access Advisor ranks the entries in the workload according to statistics and business importance. The workload is created using the DBMS_ADVISOR.CREATE_SQLWKLD procedure. To associate a workload with a parent SQL Access Advisor task, use the DBMS_ADVISOR.ADD_SQLWKLD_REF procedure. If a workload is not provided, the SQL Access Advisor can generate and use a hypothetical workload based on the dimensions defined in your schema.

Once a task exists and a workload is associated with the task, you can generate recommendations via the DBMS_ADVISOR.EXECUTE_TASK procedure. The SQL Access Advisor considers the workload and the system statistics and attempts to generate recommendations for tuning the application. You can see the recommendations by executing the DBMS_ADVISOR. GET_TASK_SCRIPT function or via data dictionary views. Each recommendation can be viewed via USER_ADVISOR_RECOMMENDATIONS (there are "ALL" and "DBA" versions of this view available, as well). To relate recommendations to a SQL statement, you need to use the USER_ADVISOR_SQLA_WK_STMTS view and USER_ADVISOR_ACTIONS.

When you execute the GET_TASK_SCRIPT procedure, Oracle generates an executable SQL file that contains the commands needed to create, alter, or drop the recommended objects. You should review the generated script prior to executing it, particularly noting the tablespace specifications. In the following section, you will see how to use the QUICK_TUNE procedure to simplify the tuning advisor process for a single command.

To tune a single SQL statement, use the QUICK_TUNE procedure of the DBMS_ADVISOR package. QUICK_TUNE has two input parameters—a task name and a SQL statement. Using QUICK_TUNE shields the user from the steps involved in creating workloads and tasks via DBMS_ADVISOR.

For example, the following procedure call evaluates a query:

```
begin
    dbms_advisor.quick_tune(dbms_advisor.sqlaccess_advisor,
        'mv_tune','select publisher from bookshelf');
end;
```

NOTE
The user executing this command needs the ADVISOR system privilege.

You can view the recommendation generated by QUICK_TUNE via USER_ADVISOR_ACTIONS, but it is easier to read if you use the DBMS_ADVISOR procedures to generate a script file. The recommendation is that a materialized view be created to support the query. Because only one SQL statement was provided, this recommendation is given in isolation and does not consider any other aspects of the database or application.

You can use the CREATE_FILE procedure to automate the generation of a file containing the scripts needed to implement the recommendations. First, create a directory object to hold the file:

```
create directory scripts as '/u01/orascripts';
grant read, write on directory scripts to public;
```

Next, execute the CREATE_FILE procedure. It has three input variables: the script (generated via GET_TASK_SCRIPT, to which you pass the name of the task), the output directory, and the name of the file to be created:

```
begin
    dbms_advisor.create_file(dbms_advisor.get_task_script('mv_tune'),
        'SCRIPTS','mv_tune.sql');
end;
```

The **mv_tune.sql** file created by the CREATE_FILE procedure will contain commands similar to those shown in the following listing. Depending on the specific version of Oracle, the recommendations may differ.

```
Rem  Username:       PRACTICE
Rem  Task:           MV_TUNE
Rem
```

```
set feedback 1
set linesize 80
set trimspool on
set tab off
set pagesize 60

whenever sqlerror CONTINUE

CREATE MATERIALIZED VIEW "PRACTICE"."MV$$_021F0001"
    REFRESH FORCE WITH ROWID
    ENABLE QUERY REWRITE
    AS SELECT PRACTICE.BOOKSHELF.ROWID C1,
"PRACTICE"."BOOKSHELF"."PUBLISHER" M1
FROM PRACTICE.BOOKSHELF;

begin
  dbms_stats.gather_table_stats('"PRACTICE"',
'"MV$$_021F0001"',NULL,dbms_stats.auto_sample_size);
end;
/

whenever sqlerror EXIT SQL.SQLCODE

begin
dbms_advisor.mark_recommendation('MV_TUNE',1,'IMPLEMENTED');
end;
/
```

The MARK_RECOMMENDATION procedure allows you to annotate the recommendation so it can be skipped during subsequent script generations. Valid actions for MARK_RECOMMENDATION include ACCEPT, IGNORE, IMPLEMENTED, and REJECT.

You can use the TUNE_MVIEW procedure of the DBMS_ADVISOR package to generate recommendations for reconfiguring your materialized views. TUNE_MVIEW generates two sets of output results—for the creation of new materialized views and for the removal of previously created materialized views. The end result should be a set of materialized views that can be FAST refreshed, replacing materialized views that cannot be FAST refreshed.

You can view the TUNE_MVIEW output via the USER_TUNE_MVIEW data dictionary view, or you can generate its scripts via the GET_TASK_SCRIPT and CREATE_FILE procedures shown in the previous listings.

Refreshing Materialized Views

The data in a materialized view may be replicated either once (when the view is created) or at intervals. The CREATE MATERIALIZED VIEW command allows you to set the refresh interval, delegating the responsibility for scheduling and performing the refreshes to the database. In the following sections, you will see how to perform both manual and automatic refreshes.

What Kind of Refreshes Can Be Performed?

To see what kind of refresh and rewrite capabilities are possible for your materialized views, you can query the MV_CAPABILITIES_TABLE table. The capabilities may change between versions, so you should reevaluate your refresh capabilities following Oracle software upgrades. To create this table, execute the **utlxmv.sql** script located in the **./rdbms/admin** directory under the Oracle software home directory.

The columns of MV_CAPABILITIES_TABLE are

```
desc mv_capabilities_table
```

Name	Null?	Type
STATEMENT_ID		VARCHAR2(30)
MVOWNER		VARCHAR2(30)
MVNAME		VARCHAR2(30)
CAPABILITY_NAME		VARCHAR2(30)
POSSIBLE		CHAR(1)
RELATED_TEXT		VARCHAR2(2000)
RELATED_NUM		NUMBER
MSGNO		NUMBER(38)
MSGTXT		VARCHAR2(2000)
SEQ		NUMBER

To populate the MV_CAPABILITIES_TABLE table, execute the DBMS_MVIEW.EXPLAIN_MVIEW procedure, using the name of the materialized view as the input value as shown in the following listing:

```
begin
    dbms_mview.explain_mview('LOCAL_BOOKSHELF_MV');
end;
```

The **utlxmv.sql** script provides guidance on interpreting the column values, as shown in the following listing:

```
CREATE TABLE MV_CAPABILITIES_TABLE
  (STATEMENT_ID     VARCHAR(30),  -- Client-supplied unique statement identifier
   MVOWNER          VARCHAR(30),  -- NULL for SELECT based EXPLAIN_MVIEW
   MVNAME           VARCHAR(30),  -- NULL for SELECT based EXPLAIN_MVIEW
   CAPABILITY_NAME  VARCHAR(30),  -- A descriptive name of the particular
                                  -- capability:
                                  -- REWRITE
                                  --    Can do at least full text match
                                  --    rewrite
                                  -- REWRITE_PARTIAL_TEXT_MATCH
                                  --    Can do at least full and partial
                                  --    text match rewrite
                                  -- REWRITE_GENERAL
                                  --    Can do all forms of rewrite
```

```
                                    -- REFRESH
                                    --    Can do at least complete refresh
                                    -- REFRESH_FROM_LOG_AFTER_INSERT
                                    --    Can do fast refresh from an mv log
                                    --    or change capture table at least
                                    --    when update operations are
                                    --    restricted to INSERT
                                    -- REFRESH_FROM_LOG_AFTER_ANY
                                    --    can do fast refresh from an mv log
                                    --    or change capture table after any
                                    --    combination of updates
                                    -- PCT
                                    --    Can do Enhanced Update Tracking on
                                    --    the table named in the RELATED_NAME
                                    --    column.  EUT is needed for fast
                                    --    refresh after partitioned
                                    --    maintenance operations on the table
                                    --    named in the RELATED_NAME column
                                    --    and to do non-stale tolerated
                                    --    rewrite when the mv is partially
                                    --    stale with respect to the table
                                    --    named in the RELATED_NAME column.
                                    --    EUT can also sometimes enable fast
                                    --    refresh of updates to the table
                                    --    named in the RELATED_NAME column
                                    --    when fast refresh from an mv log
                                    --    or change capture table is not
                                    --    possible.
  POSSIBLE          CHARACTER(1),   -- T = capability is possible
                                    -- F = capability is not possible
  RELATED_TEXT      VARCHAR(2000),  -- Owner.table.column, alias name, etc.
                                    -- related to this message.  The
                                    -- specific meaning of this column
                                    -- depends on the MSGNO column.  See
                                    -- the documentation for
                                    -- DBMS_MVIEW.EXPLAIN_MVIEW() for details
  RELATED_NUM       NUMBER,         -- When there is a numeric value
                                    -- associated with a row, it goes here.
                                    -- The specific meaning of this column
                                    -- depends on the MSGNO column.  See
                                    -- the documentation for
                                    -- DBMS_MVIEW.EXPLAIN_MVIEW() for details
  MSGNO             INTEGER,        -- When available, QSM message #
                                    -- explaining why not possible or more
                                    -- details when enabled.
  MSGTXT            VARCHAR(2000),  -- Text associated with MSGNO.
  SEQ               NUMBER);        -- Useful in ORDER BY clause when
                                    -- selecting from this table.
```

Once the EXPLAIN_MVIEW procedure has been executed, you can query MV_CAPABILITIES_TABLE to determine your options.

```
select capability_name, msgtxt
from mv_capabilities_table
where msgtxt is not null;
```

For the LOCAL_BOOKSHELF_MV materialized view, the query returns the following:

```
CAPABILITY_NAME
-----------------------------
MSGTXT
-------------------------------------------------------------
PCT_TABLE
relation is not a partitioned table

REFRESH_FAST_AFTER_INSERT
the detail table does not have a materialized view log

REFRESH_FAST_AFTER_ONETAB_DML
see the reason why REFRESH_FAST_AFTER_INSERT is disabled

REFRESH_FAST_AFTER_ANY_DML
see the reason why REFRESH_FAST_AFTER_ONETAB_DML is disabled

REFRESH_FAST_PCT
PCT is not possible on any of the detail tables in the
materialized view

REWRITE_FULL_TEXT_MATCH
query rewrite is disabled on the materialized view

REWRITE_PARTIAL_TEXT_MATCH
query rewrite is disabled on the materialized view

REWRITE_GENERAL
query rewrite is disabled on the materialized view

REWRITE_PCT
general rewrite is not possible or PCT is not possible on
any of the detail tables

PCT_TABLE_REWRITE
relation is not a partitioned table

10 rows selected.
```

Because the QUERY REWRITE clause was not specified when creating the materialized view, the query rewrite capabilities are disabled for LOCAL_BOOKSHELF_MV. FAST refresh capabilities are not supported because the base table does not have a materialized view log. If you change

your materialized view or its base table, you should regenerate the data in MV_CAPABILITIES_
TABLE to see the new capabilities.

As shown in the preceding listing, the LOCAL_BOOKSHELF_MV materialized view cannot
use a FAST refresh because its base table does not have a materialized view log. There are other
constraints that will limit your ability to use FAST refreshes:

- The materialized view must not contain references to nonrepeating expressions such as
  SYSDATE and ROWNUM.

- The materialized view must not contain references to RAW or LONG RAW datatypes.

- For materialized views based on joins, ROWIDs from all tables in the FROM list must be
  part of the SELECT list.

- If there are outer joins, all the joins must be connected by ANDs, the WHERE clause
  must have no selections, and unique constraints must exist on the join columns of the
  inner join table.

- For materialized views based on aggregates, the materialized view logs must contain all
  columns from the referenced tables, must specify the ROWID and INCLUDING NEW
  VALUES clauses, and must specify the SEQUENCE clause.

See the *Data Warehousing Guide* for additional restrictions related to FAST refreshes of
complex aggregates.

NOTE
*You can specify an ORDER BY clause in the CREATE MATERIALIZED
VIEW command. The ORDER BY clause only affects the initial creation
of the materialized view; it will not affect any refresh.*

FAST Refresh with CONSIDER FRESH

You may need to accumulate historical information in a materialized view, even though the
detailed information is no longer in the base tables. As of Oracle 11g, you can use the CONSIDER
FRESH clause of the ALTER MATERIALIZED VIEW command to instruct the database that the
contents of the materialized view correctly reflect the base tables even if that is not the case.

For example, you may have a materialized view that summarizes data from a detail
transactional table. If you remove historical data from the transactional table, the materialized
view should be refreshed, because Oracle will know its data is stale. You can use the
CONSIDER FRESH clause to change the status of the materialized view, enabling the
materialized view to be used for query rewrites. You can then continue to take advantage of
query rewrite capabilities while scheduling a refresh of the materialized view so it will
accurately reflect the underlying data.

Automatic Refreshes

Consider the LOCAL_BOOKSHELF_MV materialized view described earlier. Its refresh schedule
settings, defined by its CREATE MATERIALIZED VIEW command, are shown in bold in the
following listing:

```
create materialized view local_bookshelf_mv
   tablespace users
```

```
refresh force
start with sysdate next sysdate+7
with primary key
as
select * from bookshelf@remote_connect;
```

The refresh schedule has three components. First, the type of refresh (FAST, COMPLETE, NEVER, or FORCE) is specified. FAST refreshes use *materialized view logs* (described later in this chapter) to send changed rows from the master table to the materialized view. COMPLETE refreshes delete all rows from the materialized view and repopulate it. The FORCE option for refreshes tells Oracle to use a FAST refresh if it is available; otherwise, use a COMPLETE refresh.

The START WITH clause tells the database when to perform the first replication from the master table to the local base table. It must evaluate to a future point in time. If you do not specify a START WITH time but specify a NEXT value, Oracle will use the NEXT clause to determine the start time. To maintain control over your replication schedule, you should specify a value for the START WITH clause.

The NEXT clause tells Oracle how long to wait between refreshes. Because this clause's value is applied to a different base time each time the materialized view is refreshed, the NEXT clause specifies a date expression instead of a fixed date. In the preceding example, the expression is

```
next sysdate+7
```

Every time the materialized view is refreshed, the next refresh is scheduled for seven days later. Although the refresh schedule in this example is fairly simple, you can use many of Oracle's date functions to customize a refresh schedule. For example, if you want to refresh every Monday at noon, regardless of the current date, you can set the NEXT clause to

```
next_day(trunc(sysdate),'MONDAY')+12/24
```

This example finds the next Monday after the current system date; the time portion of that date is truncated, and 12 hours is added to the date. (For information on date functions in Oracle, see Chapter 10.)

For automatic materialized view refreshes to occur, you must have at least one background snapshot refresh process running in your database. The refresh process periodically "wakes up" and checks whether any materialized views in the database need to be refreshed. The number of processes running in your database is determined by an initialization parameter called JOB_QUEUE_PROCESSES. That parameter must be set (in your initialization parameter file) to a value greater than 0; for most cases, a value of 1 should be sufficient. A coordinator process starts job queue processes as needed.

If the database is not running the job queue processes, you need to use manual refresh methods, described in the next section.

Manual Refreshes

In addition to the database's automatic refreshes, you can perform manual refreshes of materialized views. These override the normally scheduled refreshes; the new START WITH value will be based on the time of your manual refresh.

To refresh a single materialized view, use DBMS_MVIEW.REFRESH. Its two main parameters are the name of the materialized view to be refreshed and the method to use. For this method, you can specify "c" for a COMPLETE refresh, "f" for FAST refresh, "p" for a FAST refresh using Partition Change Tracking (PCT), and "?" for FORCE. For example:

```
execute dbms_mview.refresh('local_bookshelf_mv','c');
```

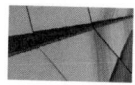

NOTE
Partition Change Tracking (PCT) occurs when partition maintenance operations have been performed on the tables referenced by the materialized view. In PCT, Oracle performs the refresh by recomputing the rows in the materialized view affected by the changed partitions in the detail tables, avoiding the need for a complete refresh.

If you are refreshing multiple materialized views via a single execution of DBMS_MVIEW. REFRESH, list the names of all the materialized views in the first parameter, and their matching refresh methods in the second parameter, as shown here:

```
execute dbms_mview.refresh('local_bookshelf_mv,local_category_count_mv','?c');
```

In this example, the materialized view named LOCAL_BOOKSHELF_MV will be refreshed via a FORCE refresh, whereas the second materialized view will use a COMPLETE refresh.

You can use a separate procedure in the DBMS_MVIEW package to refresh all of the materialized views that are scheduled to be automatically refreshed. This procedure, named REFRESH_ALL_MVIEWS, refreshes each materialized view separately. It does not accept any parameters other than an output variable that returns the number of materialized view refresh failures. The following listing shows an example of its execution:

```
set serveroutput on
declare
   num_failures       number;
begin
   dbms_mview.refresh_all_mviews(num_failures);
   dbms_output.put_line('# failures = ' || num_failures);
end;
/

# failures = 0

PL/SQL procedure successfully completed.
```

Because the materialized views are refreshed via REFRESH_ALL consecutively, they are not all refreshed at the same time. Therefore, a database or server failure during the execution of this procedure may cause the local materialized views to be out of sync with each other. If that happens, simply rerun this procedure after the database has been recovered. As an alternative, you can create refresh groups, as described in the next section.

REFRESH_ALL_MVIEWSnebo refreshes all materialized views that have the following properties:

- The materialized view has not been refreshed since the most recent change to a master table or master materialized view on which the materialized view depends.

- The materialized view and all of the master tables or master materialized views on which the materialized view depends are local.
- The materialized view is in the view DBA_MVIEWS.

If you create nested materialized views, you can use the DBMS_MVIEW.REFRESH_DEPENDENT procedure to ensure all materialized views within a tree are refreshed.

CREATE MATERIALIZED VIEW Log Syntax

A materialized view log is a table that records changes to the rows in the master table and the materialized views' replication history. The record of changed rows can then be used during refreshes to send to the materialized views only those rows that have changed in the master table. Multiple materialized views based on the same table can use the same materialized view log.

The full syntax for the CREATE MATERIALIZED VIEW LOG command is shown in the Alphabetical Reference. The following listing shows part of the syntax; as you may note from its syntax, it has all of the parameters normally associated with tables:

```
CREATE MATERIALIZED VIEW LOG ON [schema.] table
[{ physical_attributes_clause
 | TABLESPACE tablespace
 | { LOGGING | NOLOGGING }
 | { CACHE | NOCACHE }
 }
 [ physical_attributes_clause
 | TABLESPACE tablespace
 | { LOGGING | NOLOGGING }
 | { CACHE | NOCACHE }
 ]...
]
[parallel_clause] [partitioning_clauses]
[WITH
 { OBJECT ID | PRIMARY KEY | ROWID | SEQUENCE | ( column [, column]... ) }
 [, { OBJECT ID | PRIMARY KEY | ROWID | SEQUENCE | ( column [, column]... )
}]
   ...]
 [{ INCLUDING | EXCLUDING } NEW VALUES];
```

The CREATE MATERIALIZED VIEW LOG command is executed in the master table's database, usually by the master table's owner. Do not create materialized view logs for tables that are only involved in complex materialized views (since they wouldn't be used anyway). No name is specified for the materialized view log.

You can create a materialized view log for the BOOKSHELF table via the following command, executed from within the account that owns the table:

```
create materialized view log on bookshelf
with sequence, rowid
(title, publisher, category_name, rating)
including new values;
```

The WITH SEQUENCE clause is needed to support the replication of mixed-DML operations against multiple base tables.

Because materialized view logs may grow unpredictably over time in production databases, you should consider storing their associated objects in tablespaces that are dedicated to materialized view logs.

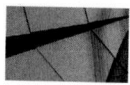

NOTE
As of Oracle 11g, the capture of changes in materialized view logs can be disabled for an individual session while logging continues for changes made by other sessions.

To create the materialized view log, you must have CREATE TABLE and CREATE TRIGGER system privileges. If you are creating the materialized view log from a user account that does not own the master table, you need to have CREATE ANY TABLE, COMMENT ANY TABLE, and CREATE ANY TRIGGER system privileges as well as the SELECT privilege on the materialized view master table.

Altering Materialized Views and Logs

You may alter the storage parameters, refresh option, and refresh schedule for existing materialized views. If you are unsure of the current settings for a snapshot, check the USER_ MVIEWS data dictionary view.

The syntax for the ALTER MATERIALIZED VIEW command is shown in the Alphabetical Reference. The command in the following listing alters the refresh option used by the LOCAL_ BOOKSHELF_MV materialized view:

```
alter materialized view local_bookshelf_mv
refresh complete;
```

All future refreshes of LOCAL_BOOKSHELF_MV will refresh the entire local base table.

To alter a materialized view, you must

- Own the materialized view, or
- Have the ALTER ANY MATERIALIZED VIEW system privilege

In contrast, to alter a materialized view log, you must

- Own the table, or
- Have the ALTER privilege on the table, or
- Have the ALTER ANY TABLE system privilege

If you create the materialized view log without the ROWID or the SEQUENCE clauses, you can add them after the fact via the ALTER MATERIALIZED VIEW command.

Dropping Materialized Views and Logs

To drop a materialized view, you must have the system privileges required to drop both the materialized view and all of its related objects. You need to have the DROP MATERIALIZED VIEW system privilege if the object is in your schema or the DROP ANY MATERIALIZED VIEW system privilege if the materialized view is not in your schema.

The following command drops the LOCAL_CATEGORY_COUNT_MV materialized view created earlier in this chapter:

```
drop materialized view local_category_count_mv;
```

NOTE
When you drop a materialized view that was created on a prebuilt table, the table still exists but the materialized view is dropped.

You can drop materialized view logs via the DROP MATERIALIZED VIEW LOG command. Once the materialized view log is dropped from a master table, FAST refreshes cannot be performed for simple materialized views based on that table. Therefore, you should drop a materialized view log when no simple materialized views are based on the master table. The following command drops the materialized view log that was created on the BOOKSHELF table earlier in this chapter:

```
drop materialized view log on bookshelf;
```

To drop a materialized view log, you must have the ability to drop both the materialized view log and its related objects. If you own the materialized view log, you must have the DROP TABLE and DROP TRIGGER system privileges. If you do not own the materialized view log, you need the DROP ANY TABLE and DROP ANY TRIGGER system privileges to execute this command.

CHAPTER
27

Using Oracle Text
for Text Searches

A s the amount of text in your database increases, so does the complexity of the text queries performed against the database. Instead of simply performing string matches, you'll need new text-search features—such as weighting the terms in a search of multiple terms or ranking the results of a text search.

You can use Oracle Text to perform text-based searches. Text-searching capabilities include wildcard searching, "fuzzy matches," relevance ranking, proximity searching, term weighting, and word expansions. In this chapter, you'll see how to configure and use Oracle Text.

Adding Text to the Database

You can add text to a database either by physically storing the text in a table or by storing pointers to external files in the database. That is, for the books on the bookshelf (the actual books on your bookshelf, which are referenced in the BOOKSHELF table), you can store reviews either in the database or in external files. If you store the reviews in external files, then you store only the filenames in the database.

To store the reviews in the database, create the BOOK_REVIEW_* tables. In this chapter, you'll see examples of two types of indexes: CONTEXT and CTXCAT. To support these examples, we'll create two separate tables: BOOK_REVIEW_CONTEXT and BOOK_REVIEW_CTXCAT, both loaded with the same data.

```
create table book_review_context
(title        varchar2(100) primary key,
 reviewer     varchar2(25),
 review_date  date,
 review_text  varchar2(4000));

insert into book_review_context values
('My Ledger', 'Emily Talbot', '01-MAY-12',
'A fascinating look into the transactions and finances of G. B. Talbot
and Dora Talbot as they managed a property in New Hampshire around 1900.
The stories come through the purchases - for medicine, doctor visits and
gravesites - for workers during harvests - for gifts at the general store
at Christmas.  A great read. ');

create table book_review_ctxcat
(title        varchar2(100) primary key,
 reviewer     varchar2(25),
 review_date  date,
 review_text  varchar2(4000));

insert into book_review_ctxcat values
('My Ledger', 'Emily Talbot', '01-MAY-12',
'A fascinating look into the transactions and finances of G. B. Talbot
and Dora Talbot as they managed a property in New Hampshire around 1900.
The stories come through the purchases - for medicine, doctor visits and
gravesites - for workers during harvests - for gifts at the general store
at Christmas.  A great read. ');
```

The REVIEW_TEXT column of the BOOK_REVIEW_* tables is defined as having a VARCHAR2(4000) datatype. For text values longer than 32767 (the maximum VARCHAR2 size in Oracle 12c), consider the use of CLOB datatypes. See Chapter 40 for details on CLOB datatypes.

You can select the review text from the database:

```
set linesize 74

select review_text
from book_review_context
where title = 'My Ledger';

REVIEW_TEXT
--------------------------------------------------------------------------
A fascinating look into the transactions and finances of G. B. Talbot
and Dora Talbot as they managed a property in New Hampshire around 1900.
The stories come through the purchases - for medicine, doctor visits and
gravesites - for workers during harvests - for gifts at the general store
at Christmas.  A great read.
```

Text Queries and Text Indexes

Querying text is different from querying data because words have shades of meaning, relationships to other words, and opposites. You may want to search for words that are near each other or for words that are related to others. These queries would be extremely difficult if all you had available were the standard relational operators. By extending SQL to include text indexes, Oracle Text permits you to ask very complex questions about the text.

To use Oracle Text, you need to create a text index on the column in which the text is stored. *Text index* is a slightly confusing term—it is actually a collection of tables and indexes that store information about the text stored in the column. In other words, a text index does perform an index-like function for text queries, but its structure is significantly more complex than a standard B*-tree index on a table column.

In this chapter, you'll see examples of both CONTEXT and CTXCAT text indexes. You can also use a third type of type index, CTXRULE, to build a content-based document classification application. See the *Oracle Text Application Developer's Guide* for details on the use of CTXRULE indexes.

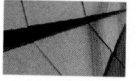

NOTE
Before creating a text index on a table, you must create a primary key for the table if one does not already exist.

You can create a text index via a special version of the CREATE INDEX command. For a CONTEXT index, specify the CTXSYS.CONTEXT index type in the INDEXTYPE clause, as shown in the following listing:

```
create index review_context_index
    on book_review_context(review_text)
indextype is ctxsys.context;
```

NOTE
Be sure to include the TEXT option when installing your database; otherwise, the DML statements in this chapter will fail. You can also add the TEXT option after the fact using the Database Creation Assistant (DBCA).

When the text index is created, Oracle creates a number of indexes and tables in your schema to support your text queries. You can rebuild your text index via the ALTER INDEX command just as you would for any other index.

You can use a CTXCAT index type in place of the CONTEXT index type:

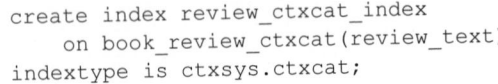

```
create index review_ctxcat_index
    on book_review_ctxcat(review_text)
indextype is ctxsys.ctxcat;
```

The CTXCAT index type supports the transactional synchronization of data between the base table (BOOK_REVIEW_CTXCAT) and its text index. With CONTEXT indexes, you need to manually tell Oracle to update the values in the text index after data changes in the base table. CTXCAT index types do not generate "score" values during text queries (as CONTEXT indexes do), but the query syntax is largely the same for the two types. The following sections illustrate the types of text queries you can perform via Oracle Text.

Text Queries

Once a text index is created on the REVIEW_TEXT column of the BOOK_REVIEW_CONTEXT table, text-searching capabilities increase dramatically. You can now look for any book review that contains the word "property":

```
select title
from book_review_context
where contains(review_text, 'property') >0;
```

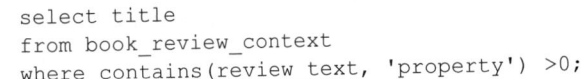

NOTE
The matching row is returned regardless of the case of the word "property" within the text-indexed column.

The CONTAINS function takes two parameters—the column name and the search string—and checks the text index for the REVIEW_TEXT column. If the word "property" is found in the REVIEW_TEXT column's text index, then a *score* greater than 0 is returned by the database, and the matching TITLE value is returned. The score is an evaluation of how well the record being returned matches the criteria specified in the CONTAINS function.

If you create a CTXCAT index, use the CATSEARCH function in place of CONTAINS. CATSEARCH takes three parameters: the column name, the search string, and the name of the index set. *Index sets* are described in the "Index Sets" section, later in this chapter. For this example, there is no index set, so that parameter is set to NULL:

```
select title
from book_review_ctxcat
where catsearch(review_text, 'property', null) >0;
```

CATSEARCH does not compute a score but uses the >0 syntax, therefore, simplifying your migration from CONTEXT indexes to CTXCAT indexes. CTXCAT indexes support the use of index sets, described later in this chapter.

When a function such as CONTAINS or CATSEARCH is used in a query, the text portion of the query is processed by Oracle Text. The remainder of the query is processed just like a regular query within the database. The results of the text query processing and the regular query processing results are merged to return a single set of records to the user.

Available Text Query Expressions

Oracle Text would be rather limited if it allowed you to search only for exact matches of words. Therefore, it offers a broad array of text-searching capabilities you can use to customize your queries. Most of the text-searching capabilities are enabled via the CONTAINS and CATSEARCH functions, which can appear only in the WHERE clause of a SELECT statement or subquery, never in the WHERE clauses of INSERTs, UPDATEs, or DELETEs.

The operators within CONTAINS allow you to perform the following text searches:

- Exact matches of a word or phrase
- Exact matches of multiple words, using Boolean logic to combine searches
- Searches based on how close words are to each other in the text
- Searches for words that share the same word "stem"
- "Fuzzy" matches of words
- Searches for words that sound like other words

CATSEARCH supports the exact-match search functions as well as the creation of index sets, described later in this chapter. In the following sections, you'll see examples of these types of text searches, along with information about the operators you can use to customize text searches.

Searching for an Exact Match of a Word

To reiterate, here are the CONTEXT and CTXCAT methods to query the BOOK_REVIEW table and return the title for all reviews that include the word "property":

```
--  CONTAINS method for CONTEXT indexes:
select title
from book_review_context
where contains(review_text, 'property')>0;

--  CATSEARCH method for CTXCAT indexes:
select title
from book_review_ctxcat
where catsearch(review_text, 'property', null)>0;
```

Within the function calls, the > sign is called a *threshold* operator. The preceding text search can be translated to the following pseudo-code:

```
select all the TITLE column values
from the BOOK_REVIEW_CONTEXT table
where the score for the text search of the REVIEW_TEXT column
```

```
for an exact match of the word 'property'
exceeds a threshold value of 0.
```

The threshold analysis compares the score—the internal score Oracle calculated when the text search was performed—to the specified threshold value. Score values for individual searches range from 0 to 10 for each occurrence of the search string within the text. For CONTEXT indexes, you can display the score as part of your query.

To show the text-search score, use the SCORE function, which has a single parameter—a label you assign to the score within the text search:

```
column title format a30

select title, score(10)
from book_review_context
where contains(review_text, 'property', 10)>0;


TITLE                             SCORE(10)
------------------------------   ----------
MY LEDGER                                3
```

In this listing, the CONTAINS function's parameters are modified to include a label (10) for the text-search operation performed. The SCORE function displays the score of the text search associated with that label. The score is an internal calculation based on how well the indexed text matches the search criteria.

For CONTEXT indexes, you can use the SCORE function in the SELECT list (as shown in the preceding query) or in a GROUP BY clause or an ORDER BY clause.

Searching for an Exact Match of Multiple Words

What if you want to search the text for multiple words? You can use Boolean logic (ANDs and ORs) to combine the results of multiple text searches in a single query. You can also search for multiple terms within the same function calls and let Oracle resolve the search results.

For example, if you want to search for reviews that have the words "property" and "harvests" in the review text, you enter the following query:

```
--   CONTAINS method for CONTEXT indexes:
select title
from book_review_context
where contains(review_text, 'property and harvests')>0;

--   CATSEARCH method for CTXCAT indexes:
select title
from book_review_ctxcat
where catsearch(review_text, 'property and harvests', null)>0;
```

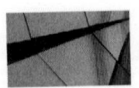

NOTE
This search does not look for the phrase "property and harvests" but rather for two individual words anywhere in the searched text. The syntax for phrase searches is in the next section.

Instead of using AND in the CONTEXT index query, you could use an ampersand (&). Before using this method in SQL*Plus, you should SET DEFINE OFF so the & character is not seen as part of a variable name:

```
set define off

--   CONTAINS method for CONTEXT indexes:
select title
from book_review_context
where contains(review_text, 'property & harvests')>0;
```

For the CTXCAT index, the word AND can be left out entirely:

```
--   CATSEARCH method for CTXCAT indexes:
select title
from book_review_ctxcat
where catsearch(review_text, 'property harvests', null)>0;
```

Using either the & character or the word AND denotes an AND operation—so the CONTAINS function returns a row only if the review text includes *both* the words "property" and "harvests." Each search must pass the threshold criteria defined for the search scores. If you want to search for more than two terms, just add them to the CONTAINS or CATSEARCH clause, as shown in the following listing:

```
--   CONTAINS method for CONTEXT indexes:
select title
from book_review_context
where contains(review_text, 'property and harvests and workers')>0;

--   CATSEARCH method for CTXCAT indexes:
select title
from book_review_ctxcat
where catsearch(review_text, 'property harvests workers', null)>0;
```

The query in this listing returns a row only if its search scores for "property," "harvests," and "workers" are all greater than 0.

In addition to AND, you can use the OR operator—in which case a record is returned if either of the search conditions meets the defined threshold. The symbol for OR in Oracle Text is a vertical line (|), so the following two queries are processed identically:

```
--   CONTAINS method for CONTEXT indexes:
select title
from book_review_context
where contains(review_text, 'property or harvests')>0;

select title
from book_review_context
where contains(review_text, 'property | harvests')>0;
```

When these queries are executed, a record is returned if either of the two separate searches (for "property" and "harvests") returns a score greater than 0. The CATSEARCH method is similar:

```
-- CATSEARCH method for CTXCAT indexes:

select title
from book_review_ctxcat
where catsearch(review_text, 'property or harvests', null)>0;

select title
from book_review_ctxcat
where catsearch(review_text, 'property | harvests', null)>0;
```

The ACCUM (accumulate) operator provides another method for combining searches. ACCUM sums the scores of the individual searches and compares the accumulated score to the threshold value. The symbol for ACCUM is a comma (,). Therefore, the two queries shown in the following listing are equivalent:

```
-- CONTAINS method for CONTEXT indexes:
select title
from book_review_context
where contains(review_text, 'property accum harvests')>0;

select title
from book_review_context
where contains(review_text, 'property , harvests')>0;
```

The ACCUM syntax is supported in CATSEARCH function calls but should not be used because CATSEARCH does not calculate a score to compare to the threshold value.

You can also use Oracle Text to subtract the scores from multiple searches before comparing the result to the threshold score. The MINUS operator in CONTAINS subtracts the score of the second term's search from the score of the first term's search. The queries in the following listing determine the search score for "property" and subtract from it the search score for "house" and then compare the difference to the threshold score:

```
-- CONTAINS method for CONTEXT indexes:
select title
from book_review_context
where contains(review_text, 'property minus house')>0;

select title
from book_review_context
where contains(review_text, 'property - house')>0;
```

Also, you can use the minus symbol (–) in place of the MINUS operator, as shown in the preceding listing.

For CONTEXT indexes, the – operator reduces the score when comparing the overall search score to the threshold value, but it does not eliminate the row from consideration. To eliminate rows based on search terms in CONTEXT indexes, use the ~ character as the NOT operator.

For CTXCAT indexes, the symbol – has a different meaning than it does with CONTEXT indexes. For CTXCAT indexes, – tells Oracle Text not to return the row if the search term after the – is found (similar to ~ in CONTEXT indexes). If the second term is found, CATSEARCH does not return the row. For CATSEARCH queries, you can replace – with the word NOT.

```
--  CATSEARCH method for CTXCAT indexes:

select title
from book_review_ctxcat
where catsearch(review_text, 'property - harvests', null)>0;

select title
from book_review_ctxcat
where catsearch(review_text, 'property not harvests', null)>0;
```

You can use parentheses to clarify the logic within your search criteria. If your search uses both ANDs and ORs, you should use parentheses to clarify the way in which the rows are processed. For example, the following query returns a row if the searched text contains either the word "house" or both the words "workers" and "harvests":

```
--  CONTAINS method for CONTEXT indexes:
select title
from book_review_context
where contains(review_text, 'house or (workers and harvests)')>0;
```

CATSEARCH, however, does not require the word AND between "workers" and "harvests":

```
--  CATSEARCH method for CTXCAT indexes:
select title
from book_review_ctxcat
where catsearch(review_text, 'house | (workers harvests)', null)>0;
```

If you change the location of the parentheses, you change the logic of the text search. The following query returns a row if the searched text contains either "house" or "workers" and also contains the word "harvests":

```
select title
from book_review_context
where contains(review_text, '(house or workers) and harvests')>0;
```

When evaluating the scores of multiple searches against CONTEXT indexes, you can tell Oracle Text to weigh the scores of some searches more heavily than others. For example, if you want the search score for "harvests" to be doubled when compared to the threshold score, you can use the asterisk symbol (*) to indicate the factor by which the search score should be multiplied.

The following query doubles the search score for "harvests" when it is evaluated in an OR condition:

```
select title, score(10)
from book_review_context
where contains(review_text, 'harvests*2 or property*1',10)>5;
```

Through the use of the AND, OR, ACCUM, and MINUS operators, you should be able to search for any combination of word matches.

> **NOTE**
> *The EQUIV operator treats two search terms as the same during search scoring. EQUIV, which can be replaced with the equal sign (=), may be useful in combination with the operators that compare search scores.*

In the next section, you'll see how to search for phrases.

Searching for an Exact Match of a Phrase

When searching for an exact match for a phrase, you specify the whole phrase as part of the search string. If your phrase includes a reserved word (such as "and," "or," or "minus"), you need to use the *escape* characters shown in this section so the search is executed properly. If the search phrase includes a reserved word within Oracle Text, then you must use curly braces ({ }) to enclose the text.

The following query searches for any title whose review entry includes the phrase "doctor visits":

```
-- CONTAINS method for CONTEXT indexes:
select title
from book_review_context
where contains(review_text, 'doctor visits')>0;
```

```
-- CATSEARCH method for CTXCAT indexes:
select title
from book_review_ctxcat
where catsearch(review_text, 'doctor visits',null)>0;
```

The following query searches for the phrase "transactions and finances." The word "and" is enclosed in braces.

```
-- CONTAINS method for CONTEXT indexes:
select title
from book_review_context
where contains(review_text, 'transactions {and} finances')>0;
```

```
-- CATSEARCH method for CTXCAT indexes:
select title
from book_review_ctxcat
where catsearch(review_text, 'transactions {and} finances',null)>0;
```

The query of 'transactions {and} finances' is different from a query of 'transactions and finances'. The query of 'transactions {and} finances' returns a record only if the *phrase* "transactions and finances" exists in the searched text. The query of 'transactions and finances' returns a record if the search score for the *word* "transactions" and the search score for the *word* "finances" are both greater than the threshold score (or in a CTXCAT index, if both are found).

You can also enclose the entire phrase within curly braces, in which case any reserved words within the phrase are treated as part of the search criteria, as shown in the following example:

```
--  CONTAINS method for CONTEXT indexes:
select title
from book_review_context
where contains(review_text, '{transactions and finances}')>0;
```

Searching for Words That Are Near Each Other

You can use the *proximity search* capability to perform a text search based on how close terms are to each other within the searched document. A proximity search returns a high score for words that are next to each other, and it returns a low score for words that are far apart. If the words are next to each other, the proximity search returns a score of 100.

To use proximity searching against CONTEXT indexes, use the keyword NEAR, as shown in the following example:

```
--  CONTAINS method for CONTEXT indexes:
select title
from book_review_context
where contains(review_text, 'workers near harvests')>0;
```

You can replace the NEAR operator with its equivalent symbol, the semicolon (;). The revised query is shown in the following listing:

```
--  CONTAINS method for CONTEXT indexes:
select title
from book_review_context
where contains(review_text, 'workers ; harvests')>0;
```

In CONTEXT index queries, you can specify the maximum number of words between the search terms. For example, for words within ten words of each other, you may use a search string of

```
'near((workers, harvests),10)'
```

You can use the phrase- and word-searching methods shown in this chapter to search for exact matches of words and phrases, as well as to perform proximity searches of exact words and phrases. Thus far, all the searches have used exact matches of the search terms as the basis for the search. In the next four sections, you'll see how to expand the search terms via four methods: wildcards, word stems, fuzzy matches, and SOUNDEX searches.

Using Wildcards During Searches

In the previous examples in this chapter, the queries selected text values that exactly matched the criteria specified. For example, the search terms included "workers" but not "worker." To expand the list of valid search terms used during your query, you can use wildcards.

Just as in regular text-string wildcard processing, two wildcards are available:

Character	Description
%	Percent sign; multiple-character wildcard
_	Underscore; single-character wildcard

The following query searches for all text matches for all words that start with the string "worker":

```
--  CONTAINS method for CONTEXT indexes:
select title
from book_review_context
where contains(review_text, 'worker%')>0;
```

The following query limits the expansion of the text string to exactly three characters. In place of the % sign in the preceding query, three underscores " _ _ _ " are used. Because the underscore is a single-character wildcard, the text string cannot expand beyond a three-character limit specified in the search. For example, the word "workers" could be returned by the text search, but the word "workplace" would be too long to be returned.

```
--  CONTAINS method for CONTEXT indexes:
select title
from book_review_context
where contains(review_text, 'work___')>0;
```

You should use wildcards when you are certain about some of the characters within the search string. If you are uncertain of the search string, you should use one of the methods described in the following sections—word stems, fuzzy matches, or SOUNDEX matches.

Searching for Words That Share the Same Stem

Rather than using wildcards, you can use *stem-expansion* capabilities to expand the list of text strings. Given the "stem" of a word, Oracle expands the list of words to search for, to include all words having the same stem. Sample expansions are shown here:

Stem	Sample Expansions
play	plays, played, playing, playful
works	working, work, worked, workman, workplace
have	had, has, haven't, hasn't
story	stories

Because "works" and "work" have the same stem, a stem-expansion search using the word "works" returns text containing the word "work."

To use stem expansion within a query, you need to use the dollar sign ($) symbol. Within the search string, the $ should immediately precede the word to be expanded.

The following listing shows the result of a query against BOOK_REVIEW_CONTEXT for all reviews that contain a word sharing the stem of the word "manage":

```
-- CONTAINS method for CONTEXT indexes:
select title
from book_review_context
where contains(review_text, '$manage')>0;
```

When this query is executed, Oracle expands the pattern "$manage" to include all words with the same stem and then performs the search. If a review contains one of the words with a stem of "manage," the record is returned to the user.

The expansion of terms via word stems simplifies the querying process for the user. You no longer need to know what form of a verb or noun was used when the text was entered—all forms are used as the basis for the search. You do not need to specify specific text strings, as you do when querying for exact matches or using wildcards. Instead, you specify a word, and Oracle Text dynamically determines all the words that should be searched for, based on the word you specified.

Searching for Fuzzy Matches

A *fuzzy match* expands the specified search term to include words that are spelled similarly but that do not necessarily have the same word stem. Fuzzy matches are most helpful when the text contains misspellings. The misspellings can be either in the searched text or in the search string specified by the user during the query.

For example, "My Ledger" is be returned by this query because its review does not contain the word "hardest":

```
-- CONTAINS method for CONTEXT indexes:
select title
from book_review_context
where contains(review_text, 'hardest')>0;
```

It does, however, contain the word "harvest." A fuzzy match returns reviews containing the word "harvest," even though "harvest" has a different word stem than the word used as the search term.

To use a fuzzy match, precede the search term with a question mark (?), with no space between the question mark and the beginning of the search term. The following example illustrates the use of the fuzzy match capability:

```
-- CONTAINS method for CONTEXT indexes:
select title
from book_review_context
where contains(review_text, '?hardest')>0;
```

As an alternative, you can use the FUZZY operator, as shown here:

```
select title
from book_review_context
where contains(review_text,'{fuzzy(hardest,60,100,w}')>0;
```

For the FUZZY operator, the parameters are (in order) the term, the score, the number of results, and the weight. These parameters are described in the following list:

- **TERM**   Used to specify the word on which to perform the FUZZY expansion. Oracle Text expands the term to include words only in the index. The word needs to be at least three characters for the FUZZY operator to process it.

- **SCORE**   Used to specify a similarity score. Terms in the expansion whose score is less than this number are discarded. Use a number between 1 and 80. The default is 60.

- **NUMRESULTS**   Used to specify the maximum number of terms to use in the expansion of a term. Use a number between 1 and 5000. The default is 100.

- **WEIGHT**   Specify WEIGHT (or W) for the results to be weighted according to their similarity scores. Specify NOWEIGHT (or N) for no weighting of results.

Searching for Words That Sound Like Other Words

Stem-expansion searches expand a search term to multiple terms based on the stem of the word. Fuzzy matches expand a search term based on similar words in the text index. A third kind of search-term expansion, SOUNDEX, expands search terms based on how the word sounds. The SOUNDEX expansion method uses the same text-matching logic available via the SOUNDEX function in SQL.

To use the SOUNDEX option, you must precede the search term with an exclamation mark (!). During the search, Oracle evaluates the SOUNDEX values of the terms in the text index and searches for all words that have the same SOUNDEX value.

As shown in the following query, you can search for all reviews that include the word "great," using a SOUNDEX match technique:

```
-- CONTAINS method for CONTEXT indexes:
select title
from book_review_context
where contains(review_text, '!grate')>0;
```

The "My Ledger" review is returned because the words "grate" and "great" have the same SOUNDEX value.

Nesting Search Operators

You can also *nest* operators, allowing you to perform stem expansions on the terms returned by a fuzzy match. In the following example, a fuzzy match is performed on the word "stir," and the terms returned from the fuzzy match are expanded using stem expansion:

```
-- CONTAINS method for CONTEXT indexes:
select title
from book_review_context
where contains(review_text, '$?stir')>0;
```

Summarizing the Search Options

The major search options for CONTAINS are summarized in Table 27-1. For a list of all supported syntax (including thesaurus use, synonym expansion, and XML support), see the *Oracle Text Reference* guide.

The search options for CATSEARCH are summarized in Table 27-2. Table 27-2 does not list the deprecated CONTAINS features, such as ACCUM, that are not documented as supported features for CATSEARCH.

Operator	Description
OR	Returns a record if either search term has a score that exceeds the threshold.
|	Same as OR.
AND	Returns a record if both search terms have a score that exceeds the threshold.
&	Same as AND.
ACCUM	Returns a record if the sum of the search terms' scores exceeds the threshold.
,	Same as ACCUM.
MINUS	Returns a record if the score of the first search minus the score of the second search exceeds the threshold.
−	Same as MINUS.
*	Assigns different weights to the score of the searches.
NEAR	The score is based on how near the search terms are to each other in the searched text.
;	Same as NEAR.
NOT	Excludes the row if the term after the NOT is found.
~	Same as NOT.
EQUIV	Treats two terms (term1 is equivalent to term2) as the same during search scoring.
=	Same as EQUIV.
{ }	Encloses reserved words such as AND if they are part of the search term.
%	Multiple-character wildcard.
_	Single-character wildcard.
$	Performs stem expansion of the search term prior to performing the search.
?	Performs a fuzzy match of the search term prior to performing the search.
!	Performs a SOUNDEX search.
( )	Specifies the order in which search criteria are evaluated.

TABLE 27-1. *Major CONTAINS Options*

Operator	Description
|	Returns a record if either search term is found.
AND	Returns a record if both search terms are found. This is the default action, so (a b) is treated as (a AND b).
–	If there are spaces around the hyphen, returns rows that contain the term preceding the hyphen (–) and do not contain the term following it. A hyphen with no space is treated as a regular character.
NOT	Same as –.
' '	Encloses phrases.
( )	Specifies the order in which search criteria are evaluated.
*	Specifies wildcard character to match multiple characters. Can be at the end of the term or in the middle of characters.

TABLE 27-2.   *CATSEARCH Options*

Using the ABOUT Operator

In Oracle Text, you can search on themes of documents. Thematic searching is integrated with text-term searching. You can use the ABOUT operator to search for terms that have to do with the theme of the document rather than the specific terms within the document. Here's an example:

```
--  CONTAINS method for CONTEXT indexes:
select title
from book_review_context
where contains(review_text, 'about(medicine)')>0;

--  CATSEARCH method for CTXCAT indexes:
select title
from book_review_ctxcat
where catsearch(review_text, 'about(medicine)', null)>0;
```

Index Synchronization

By default, when using CONTEXT indexes, you have to manage the text index contents; the text indexes are not updated when the base table is updated. As soon as a REVIEW_TEXT value is updated, its text index is out of sync with the base table. To sync the index, execute the SYNC_INDEX procedure of the CTX_DDL package, as shown in the following listing.

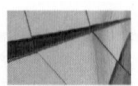

> **NOTE**
> *Grant the PRACTICE user EXECUTE privilege on the CTX_DDL package to support these maintenance activities.*

```
execute ctx_ddl.sync_index('review_context_index');
```

CONTEXT indexes can be maintained automatically, at commit time, or at specified intervals. As part of the CREATE INDEX command for a CONTEXT index, you can use the SYNC clause:

```
[[METADATA] SYNC (MANUAL | EVERY "interval" | ON COMMIT)]
```

Here's an example:

```
drop index review_context_index;

create index review_context_index
    on book_review_context(review_text)
indextype is ctxsys.context
parameters ('sync (on commit)');
```

Index Sets

Historically, problems with text index queries have occurred when other criteria are used alongside text searches as part of the WHERE clause. For example, are WHERE clauses on nontext columns applied before or after the text searches are completed, and how are the results properly ordered? To improve the "mixed" query capability, you can use *index sets*. The indexes within the index set may be on structured relational columns or on text columns.

To create an index set, use the CTX_DDL package to create the index set and add indexes to it. When you create a text index, you can then specify the index set it belongs to. To execute this example, you should first drop the REVIEW_CTXCAT_INDEX text index (created earlier in this chapter) on the BOOK_REVIEW_CTXCAT table:

```
drop index review_ctxcat_index;
```

To create an index set named REVIEWS, use the CREATE_INDEX_SET procedure:

```
execute ctx_ddl.create_index_set('reviews');
```

You can now add indexes to the index set via the ADD_INDEX procedure. First, add a standard, nontext index:

```
execute ctx_ddl.add_index('reviews', 'reviewer');
execute ctx_ddl.add_index('reviews', 'review_date');
```

Now create a CTXCAT text index. Specify CTXSYS.CTXCAT as the index type, and list the index set in the PARAMETERS clause:

```
create index review_ctxcat_index
    on book_review_ctxcat(review_text)
indextype is ctxsys.ctxcat
parameters ('index set reviews');
```

You can now order your results by the result of the combined index set search:

```
select * from book_review_ctxcat
where catsearch(review_text, 'great',
                 'reviewer=''Emily Talbot''
                  order by review_date desc')>0;
```

To resolve this query, Oracle Text uses the index set, allowing you to order the results properly. Note that there are two quotes around the string "Emily Talbot" because this is a text string search—it is converted to a set of single quotes when the query is executed.

Index sets can contain up to 99 indexes on NUMBER, DATE, CHAR, and VARCHAR2 datatypes. No column in an index set index can exceed 30 bytes (so, in this example, the TITLE column cannot be indexed as part of an index set). The indexed columns must not contain NULL values.

Oracle Text includes a tracing facility to help identify bottlenecks in indexing and querying. Use the ADD_TRACE procedure of the CTX_OUTPUT package to enable the trace. The available traces include the time spent on the different search components, the number of bytes read, and the number of rows processed.

For more details on index sets, text index management, text application development, and tracing, see *Oracle Text Application Developer's Guide* and *Oracle Text Reference,* both provided as part of the standard Oracle documentation set.

CHAPTER
28

Using External Tables

Y
ou can use the external table feature to access external files as if they were tables inside the database. When you create an external table, you define its structure and location within Oracle. When you query the table, Oracle reads the external table and returns the results just as if the data had been stored within the database. But because the data is outside the database, you do not have to be concerned about the process for loading it into the database—a potentially significant benefit for data warehouses and large databases.

External tables have limits—you cannot UPDATE or DELETE their rows from within Oracle, and you cannot index them. Because they are part of the database application, however, you will have to account for them as part of your backup and recovery processes. Despite these complications, external tables can be a powerful addition to your database architecture plans. Additionally, you can use external tables to unload data from tables to external files via the ORACLE_DATAPUMP access driver.

Accessing the External Files

To access external files from within Oracle, you must first use the CREATE DIRECTORY command to define a directory object pointing to the external files' location. Users who will access the external files must have the READ privilege on the directory.

NOTE
Before you start, verify that the external directory exists and that the user who will be issuing the CREATE DIRECTORY command has the CREATE ANY DIRECTORY system privilege.

The following example creates a directory named BOOK_DIR and grants READ and WRITE access to the PRACTICE schema:

```
create directory book_dir as '/u01/external';
grant read,write on directory book_dir to hr;
```

The HR user can now read files in the **/u01/external** directory as if he or she were inside the database. Because HR has also been granted WRITE privilege on that directory, the HR user can create log, discard, and bad files within the directory—just as if that user were executing the SQL*Loader utility (see Chapter 23).

The following listing generates two files for sample data—one from BOOKSHELF and one from BOOKSHELF_AUTHOR. Note the SPOOL command cannot use the directory name created via CREATE DIRECTORY; you need to specify the full operating-system directory name.

```
connect hr/hr

set pagesize 0 newpage 0 feedback off
select title||'~'||publisher||'~'||category_name||'~'||rating||'~'
from bookshelf
order by title

spool /u01/external/bookshelf_dump.lst
/
```

```
spool off

select title||'~'||author_name||'~'
from bookshelf_author
order by title

spool /u01/external/book_auth_dump.lst
/
spool off
```

In addition to the data, the output files will contain a single line at the top with SQL>/ and a final line that reads SQL> spool off. To simplify the examples, you should manually edit the file at the operating system level to delete these extra lines before proceeding.

If another user is to access the data in the **bookshelf_dump.lst** and **book_auth_dump.lst** files, you must grant that user READ privilege on the BOOK_DIR directory:

```
grant read on directory book_dir to another_user;
```

Also, the files themselves must be readable by the oracle user at the operating-system level.

Creating an External Table

Now that the external data is available and accessible, you can create a table structure that accesses it. To do so, you need to use the ORGANIZATION EXTERNAL clause of the CREATE TABLE command. Within that clause, you can specify the data structure much as you would for a SQL*Loader control file. The following listing shows the creation of the BOOKSHELF_EXT table, based on the data in the **bookshelf.lst** spool file created in the prior section:

```
create table bookshelf_ext
(title          varchar2(100),
publisher       varchar2(20),
category_name   varchar2(20),
rating          varchar2(2)
)
organization external
(type oracle_loader
 default directory book_dir
 access parameters (records delimited by newline
 fields terminated by "~"
                    (title          char(100),
                     publisher      char(20),
                     category_name  char(20),
                     rating         char(2)
                    ))
 location ('bookshelf_dump.lst')
);

Table BOOKSHELF_EXT created.
```

The table definition now exists in the data dictionary, although no data has been stored inside the Oracle database.

Similarly, you can create a table based on the **book_auth_dump.lst** spool file:

```
create table bookshelf_author_ext
(title        varchar2(100),
author_name  varchar2(50)
)
organization external
(type oracle_loader
 default directory book_dir
 access parameters (records delimited by newline
                    fields terminated by "~"
                    (title        char(100),
                     author_name  char(50)
                   ))
 location ('book_auth_dump.lst')
);
```

NOTE
Oracle performs only cursory validation when the external table is created. You will not see most errors until you attempt to query the table. The syntax for the access parameters is very specific, and minor errors in the access definition—including the order of the clauses— may prevent all the rows from being accessed.

You can verify the contents of the external tables by querying from them and comparing them to the source tables, as shown in the following listing:

```
select title from bookshelf
where category_name = 'CHILDRENPIC';

TITLE
-----------------------------------------
Good Dog, Carl
Polar Express
Runaway Bunny

3 rows selected.


select title from bookshelf_ext
where category_name = 'CHILDRENPIC';

TITLE
-----------------------------------------
Good Dog, Carl
Polar Express
Runaway Bunny
```

```
3 rows selected.
```

```
select count(*) from bookshelf_author;
```

```
  COUNT(*)
----------
        37
```

```
select count(*) from bookshelf_author_ext;
```

```
  COUNT(*)
----------
        37
```

You can join the "internal" table BOOKSHELF_AUTHOR to its external counterpart, BOOKSHELF_AUTHOR_EXT, to verify that no rows are missing or added:

```
select * from bookshelf_author ba
where not exists
(select null from bookshelf_author_ext bae
 where ba.title = bae.title
 and ba.author_name = bae.author_name);
```

```
no rows selected
```

The BOOKSHELF_AUTHOR_EXT table points to the **book_auth_dump.lst** file. If you alter the data in the file, the data in BOOKSHELF_AUTHOR_EXT changes. As illustrated here, you can query external tables the same way you query standard tables—in joins, as part of views, and so on. You can perform functions on the external table columns during queries just as you would for standard tables.

You can query the USER_EXTERNAL_TABLES data dictionary view for information about your external tables, including the default directory and access definitions:

```
desc user_external_tables
```

Name	Null?	Type
TABLE_NAME	NOT NULL	VARCHAR2(30)
TYPE_OWNER		CHAR(3)
TYPE_NAME	NOT NULL	VARCHAR2(30)
DEFAULT_DIRECTORY_OWNER		CHAR(3)
DEFAULT_DIRECTORY_NAME	NOT NULL	VARCHAR2(30)
REJECT_LIMIT		VARCHAR2(40)
ACCESS_TYPE		VARCHAR2(7)
ACCESS_PARAMETERS		VARCHAR2(4000)
PROPERTY		VARCHAR2(10)

For example, the BOOKSHELF_AUTHOR_EXT table uses BOOK_DIR as its default directory, as shown in the following listing:

```
set long 500

select default_directory_name,
       access_parameters
from user_external_tables
where table_name = 'BOOKSHELF_AUTHOR_EXT';

DEFAULT_DIRECTORY_NAME
------------------------------
ACCESS_PARAMETERS
--------------------------------------------------
BOOK_DIR
records delimited by newline
                    fields terminated by "~"
                    (Title        CHAR(100),
                     AuthorName    CHAR(50)
                    )
```

USER_EXTERNAL_TABLES does not show the name of the external file (or files) that the table references. To see that information, query USER_EXTERNAL_LOCATIONS:

```
select * from user_external_locations;

TABLE_NAME
------------------------------
LOCATION
-------------------------------------------
DIR DIRECTORY_NAME
--- ------------------------------
BOOKSHELF_EXT
bookshelf_dump.lst
SYS BOOK_DIR

BOOKSHELF_AUTHOR_EXT
book_auth_dump.lst
SYS BOOK_DIR
```

External Table Creation Options

Within the ORGANIZATION EXTERNAL clause are four main subclauses: TYPE, DEFAULT DIRECTORY, ACCESS PARAMETERS, and LOCATION. When you create an external table, you can use these clauses to customize the way Oracle views the external data.

Type and Default Directory

The syntax for the TYPE component is

```
( [TYPE access_driver_type] external_data_properties )
[REJECT LIMIT { integer | UNLIMITED }]
```

For external tables, the access driver is the API used to transform the external data. Use TYPE ORACLE_LOADER for your external tables—as shown in the examples earlier in this chapter—or TYPE ORACLE_DATAPUMP if you are using Data Pump (see Chapter 24) or if you are loading the external table when you create it. You must specify the ORACLE_DATAPUMP access driver if you use the AS subquery clause to unload data from one database and then reload it. The TYPE ORACLE_LOADER access driver is the default.

> **NOTE**
> *Because the access driver is part of the Oracle software, only files accessible by the database can be accessed as external tables. Files the Oracle user cannot access cannot be used as external tables.*

Following the TYPE declaration, you can set a "reject limit" value. By default, no rows can be rejected—any problem with any row will cause the SELECT statement to return an error. Let's generate another copy of the BOOKSHELF data to a separate file, and this time leave in the extra lines SQL*Plus inserts during the SPOOL operation:

```
set pagesize 0 newpage 0 feedback off
select title||'~'||publisher||'~'||category_name||'~'||rating||'~'
from bookshelf
order by title

spool /u01/external/bookshelf_dump_2.lst
/
spool off
```

Now let's create a new table that references this spool file, telling Oracle to skip the first record (SKIP 1) and to allow one other error (REJECT LIMIT 1). That will account for the / character in the first line and SQL> spool off in the last line:

```
create table bookshelf_ext_2
(title          varchar2(100),
publisher       varchar2(20),
category_name varchar2(20),
rating          varchar2(2)
)
organization external
(type oracle_loader
 default directory book_dir
```

```
access parameters (records delimited by newline
                    skip 1
                    fields terminated by
                    "~"
                    (title           char(100),
                     publisher       char(20),
                     category_name char(20),
                     rating          char(2)
                    ) )
 location ('bookshelf_dump_2.lst')
)
reject limit 1
;
```

You can now verify the number of rows in the table:

```
select count(*) from bookshelf_ext_2;

  COUNT(*)
----------
        31
```

The DEFAULT DIRECTORY clause specifies the directory object to be used for all datafiles that do not specify another directory. If you use multiple external files located in multiple directories, you can name one of them as the default directory and specify the others by directory name in the LOCATION clause. You must use directory object names (such as BOOK_DIR) in the LOCATION clause, not the full directory path name.

Access Parameters

The ACCESS PARAMETERS clause tells Oracle how to map the rows in the file to rows in the table. Its syntax is shown in the following illustration:

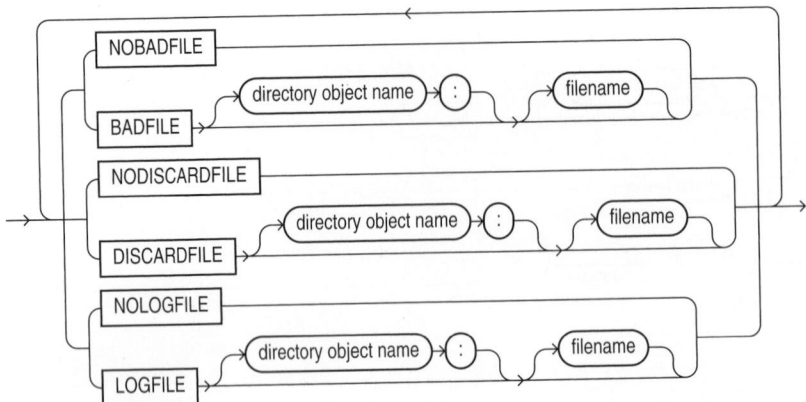

Within the ACCESS PARAMETERS clause, you first tell Oracle how to create a record—whether its length is fixed or variable, and how rows are delimited. In the case of the BOOKSHELF_EXT example, the records are delimited by newlines. If there were multiple rows on a single line, you could use a character string as a separator between rows. Because the external data may come from a non-Oracle database, Oracle supports multiple character sets and string sizes.

As with SQL*Loader, you can specify a WHEN clause to limit which rows are selected. In the following listing, the BOOKSHELF_EXT_3 table is created, with a WHEN clause (shown in bold) to limit it to only books in the CHILDRENPIC category.

```
create table bookshelf_ext_3
(title         varchar2(100),
publisher      varchar2(20),
category_name  varchar2(20),
rating         varchar2(2)
)
organization external
(type oracle_loader
 default directory book_dir
 access parameters (records delimited by newline
                    load when category_name = 'CHILDRENPIC'
                                          skip 1
                    fields terminated by "~"
                    (title         char(100),
                     publisher     char(20),
                     category_name char(20),
                     rating        char(2)
                    ) )
 location ('bookshelf_dump_2.lst')
)
reject limit 1
;
```

You can see the result here:

```
select substr(title, 1,30), category_name
from bookshelf_ext_3;
```

```
SUBSTR(TITLE,1,30)                 CATEGORY_NAME
------------------------------     --------------------
Good Dog, Carl                     CHILDRENPIC
Polar Express                      CHILDRENPIC
Runaway Bunny                      CHILDRENPIC

3 rows selected.
```

BOOKSHELF_EXT_3 accesses the same file as BOOKSHELF_EXT_2, but it only shows the records for the CHILDRENPIC category because of its LOAD WHEN clause.

As with SQL*Loader, you can create a log file, a bad file, and a discard file. Rows that fail the LOAD WHEN condition are written to the discard file. Rows that fail the ACCESS PARAMETERS conditions are written to the bad file, and the load details are written to the log file. For all three types of files, you can specify a directory object along with the filename, so you can write the output to a directory other than your input datafile directory. You can specify NODISCARDFILE, NOBADFILE, and NOLOGFILE to prevent these files from being created. Use directory object names (such as BOOK_DIR in this chapter's examples) when specifying locations for discard files, bad files, and log files. If you don't specify locations for log files, bad files, and discard files, Oracle creates them in the default directory with system-generated names.

Within the ACCESS PARAMETERS clause, you also specify the field definitions and delimiters, such as

```
fields terminated by "~"
(title           char(100),
 publisher       char(20),
 category_name   char(20),
 rating          char(2))
```

You can use the MISSING FIELD VALUES ARE NULL clause to set values for NULL column values, but you must exercise caution when using this option. For example, the AUTHOR table has NULL values in its COMMENTS column. Creating the external table for AUTHOR_EXT is shown in the following listing:

```
set pagesize 0 newpage 0 feedback off
select author_name||'~'||comments||'~'
from author
order by author_name

spool /u01/external/author_dump.lst
/
spool off

set feedback on heading on newpage 1 pagesize 60
create table author_ext
(author_name    varchar2(50),
```

```
 comments        varchar2(100)
)
organization external
(type oracle_loader
 default directory book_dir
 access parameters (records delimited by newline
                    skip 1
                    fields terminated by "~"
                    missing field values are null
                    (author_name    char(50),
                      comments       char(100)
                    ) )
 location ('author_dump.lst')
)reject limit 1
;
```

But this is not correct—if you select the AUTHOR_NAME values from AUTHOR_EXT, you will see that the values include the following:

```
select author_name from author_ext
where author_name like 'S%';

AUTHOR_NAME
--------------------------------------------------
Soren Kierkegaard
Stephen Ambrose
Stephen Jay Gould
SQL> spool off

4 rows selected.
```

Because of the MISSING FIELD VALUES ARE NULL clause, the `SQL> spool off` line at the end of the listing was read as an AUTHOR_NAME value, with a NULL COMMENTS value. This highlights the problem with coding exceptions into your loader definitions—you need to ensure you fully understand the source data and the way the loader will treat it. In most cases, your data integrity is better served by forcing rows to fail (into bad files or discard files) and evaluating the failed rows apart from your general loads.

See the SQL*Loader entry in the Alphabetical Reference for the full syntax available for the ACCESS PARAMETERS clause.

Location

In the LOCATION clause, you specify the datafiles to use as the source data for the table. You can name multiple files in the LOCATION clause if they all exist in directory objects the user has READ privilege on. The following example combines two separate BOOKSHELF spool files to illustrate the ability to combine multiple files into a single external table:

```
create table bookshelf_ext_4
 (title         varchar2(100),
  publisher     varchar2(20),
  category_name varchar2(20),
```

```
rating          varchar2(2)
)
organization external
(type oracle_loader
 default directory book_dir
 access parameters (records delimited by newline
                    skip 1
                    fields terminated by "~"
                    (title          char(100),
                     publisher      char(20),
                     category_name  char(20),
                     rating         char(2)
                    ) )
 location ('bookshelf_dump_2.lst', 'bookshelf_dump.lst')
)
reject limit 1
;
```

The order of the files is important—SKIP 1 applies to the first file, not to the second file. The second file, **bookshelf_dump.lst**, is the file that was previously edited to eliminate the non-data rows in its first and last rows. The result, reflecting the rows in both, is shown in the following listing:

```
select count(*) from bookshelf_ext_4;

  COUNT(*)
----------
        62
```

Loading External Tables on Creation

You can create an external table that is populated via a CREATE TABLE AS SELECT command. When you create the table, Oracle performs the specified query and creates an external file with the query results formatted based on the query. To load an external file, you need to use the ORACLE_DATAPUMP driver in place of ORACLE_LOADER.

When you use the ORACLE_DATAPUMP driver, Oracle creates a dump file that contains the table data. You can use that file as the basis for additional external tables. You cannot perform additional inserts or updates on the external data via SQL once the table has been populated.

As of Oracle Database 11g, you can direct the data stored in the external file to be compressed and encrypted during the table creation process. By default, both compression and encryption are disabled.

The following listing shows the use of the ORACLE_DATAPUMP driver to populate a dump file:

```
create table bookshelf_xt
organization external
  (
   type oracle_datapump
   default directory book_dir
   location ('bk_xt.dmp')
```

```
      )
   as select * from bookshelf;
```

You can now use the **bk_xt.dmp** file as the source for another external table, or you can query the BOOKSHELF_XT table directly.

To enable compression, modify the ACCESS PARAMETERS setting, as shown in the following listing:

```
create table bookshelf_xt_compr
organization external
   (
    type oracle_datapump
    default directory book_dir
    access parameters (compression enabled)
    location ('bk_xt_compr.dmp')
    )
as select * from bookshelf;
```

To encrypt the dump file as it is written, use the ENCRYPTION option of the ACCESS PARAMETERS clause, as shown in the following listing:

```
create table bookshelf_xt_encr
organization external
   (
    type oracle_datapump
    default directory book_dir
    access parameters (encryption enabled)
    location ('bk_xt_encr.dmp')
    )
as select * from bookshelf;
```

Altering External Tables

You can alter external table definitions to change the way Oracle interprets the flat file. The available options are detailed in the following subsections.

ACCESS PARAMETERS

You can change the access parameters without dropping and re-creating the external table definition, thereby preserving GRANTs, file definitions, and so on. For example, here's how to increase the number of records to skip in the BOOKSHELF_EXT_4 table:

```
alter table bookshelf_ext_4
access parameters (records delimited by newline
                   skip 10
                   fields terminated by "~"
                   (title          char(100),
                    publisher      char(20),
                    category_name char(20),
                    rating         char(2)
                ) );
```

```
select count(*) from bookshelf_ext_4;

  COUNT(*)
----------
        53
```

ADD COLUMN

You can use the ADD COLUMN clause of the ALTER TABLE command to add a column to the external table, using the same syntax used for standard tables.

DEFAULT DIRECTORY

You can use the DEFAULT DIRECTORY clause of the ALTER TABLE command to change the default directory for the external files accessed by the table. The directory must be created via the CREATE DIRECTORY command.

DROP COLUMN

You can use the DROP COLUMN clause of the ALTER TABLE command to drop a column from the external table, using the same syntax used for standard tables. The data in the file remains unchanged.

LOCATION

You can change the files accessed by the external table via the LOCATION clause of the ALTER TABLE command. You may use this option to add new files to the list or to change the order in which the external table accesses the files.

MODIFY COLUMN

You can use the MODIFY COLUMN clause of the ALTER TABLE command to modify a column in the external table, using the same syntax used for standard tables.

PARALLEL

You can use the PARALLEL clause of the ALTER TABLE command to change the degree of parallelism for the external table, using the same syntax used for standard tables.

PROJECT COLUMN

The PROJECT COLUMN clause of the ALTER TABLE command tells the access driver how to validate rows in subsequent queries. If you use the PROJECT COLUMN REFERENCED option, the access driver only processes the columns selected by the query. If you then query a different set of columns from the external table, the results may be inconsistent with the first query's results. If you use the PROJECT COLUMN ALL option, the access driver processes all columns defined on the external table, resulting in a consistent set of query results. The PROJECT COLUMN REFERENCED option is the default.

REJECT LIMIT

You can use the REJECT LIMIT clause of the ALTER TABLE command to change the allowable number of rejected rows for the external table. Here's an example:

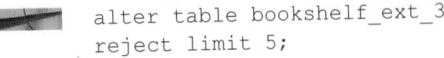

```
alter table bookshelf_ext_3
reject limit 5;
```

RENAME TO

You can use the RENAME TO clause of the ALTER TABLE command to change the name of the external table, using the same syntax used for standard tables. Here's an example:

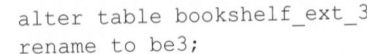

```
alter table bookshelf_ext_3
rename to be3;
```

Limitations, Benefits, and Potential Uses of External Tables

External tables have limitations that may make them inappropriate for some online transaction-processing applications. You cannot perform any UPDATE or DELETE operations on external tables. The more dynamic the table is, the less appropriate external tables may be. As shown in the examples earlier in this chapter, you can change the files dynamically at the operating-system level. If your application generates INSERTs only, you may be able to write those inserted records into an external file instead of a database table.

You cannot index external tables. The lack of indexes on external tables does not have to be a negative factor in application performance. Queries of external tables complete very quickly, even though a full table scan is required with each access. There is I/O involved, but modern I/O systems use caching and RAID techniques to significantly reduce the performance penalty associated with repeated full scans of the same file.

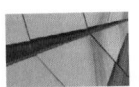

> **NOTE**
> *To analyze external tables, use the DBMS_STATS package. You cannot analyze external tables via the ANALYZE command. The ANALYZE command will be deprecated in future releases of Oracle Database.*

You cannot specify constraints on an external table. Even creating a NOT NULL or foreign key constraint fails:

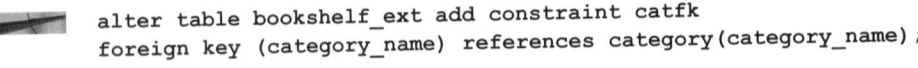

```
alter table bookshelf_ext add constraint catfk
foreign key (category_name) references category(category_name);

foreign key (CATEGORY_NAME) references CATEGORY(CATEGORY_NAME)
*
ERROR at line 2:
ORA-30657: operation not supported on external organized table
```

Despite these limitations, external tables offer many useful features. You can join external tables (to each other or to standard tables). You can use hints to force the optimizer to choose different join paths, and you can see the results in the query execution paths (see Chapter 46 for details on hints and the Oracle Optimizer).

As an alternative to data loading, external tables offer DBAs and application developers the possibility of accessing data without supporting long-running load programs. Because the files can be edited at the operating-system level, you can quickly replace a table's data without worrying about outstanding transactions modifying the table. For example, you could use this capability to create multiple external tables and create a UNION ALL view across them, creating a partition view across multiple files. You can then manage each table's data separately at the file-system level, replacing its contents as needed.

Because the external table can be queried, you can use the external table as the data source for an INSERT AS SELECT command. During that operation, Oracle attempts to load the external files in parallel, potentially improving performance. To further improve performance of the INSERT AS SELECT operation, you should use the APPEND optimizer hint to force block-level INSERTs above the high watermark (HWM) of the table. When you specify the degree of parallelism for the INSERT AS SELECT operation, Oracle starts multiple ORACLE_LOADER access drivers to process the data in parallel. To further enhance load performance, avoid using variable-length fields, delimited fields, character set conversion, NULLIF, DEFAULTIF, and datatype conversion operations. Turning off BADFILE (with NOBADFILE) eliminates the costs associated with the file creation and the maintenance of the original row's context.

During the INSERT AS SELECT, you can perform functions on the data as it is processed. You can perform the functions either in the INSERT AS SELECT command syntax or in the external table definition. This capability highlights an important benefit of external tables—you can centralize the representation and processing requirements for your data, building translation routines into your table definitions. There is no processing data stored in SQL*Loader control files or PL/SQL routines; all the logic is built into the table definition, accessible via USER_EXTERNAL_TABLES.

During queries, external tables allow you to select specific data sets (via the LOAD WHEN clause, as illustrated in this chapter). If you have multiple data sources for a data warehouse load, you can choose which data will be made available even while the data is outside the database. You can use this feature to maintain application availability during data loads. These loads can occur in parallel if the external file has a FIXED file format.

The limited-access feature also allows you to enforce complex security rules concerning data access. For example, you may keep sensitive data outside the database, in a secure directory. Users with READ access to that directory are then able to use the external table and join it to other tables; users without that access are limited to the data inserted into the publicly accessible tables. Highly secure data, or lightly accessed dynamic data, need not be inserted into the database until it is needed, if at all.

If you use external tables in your database architecture, you must make sure your backup and recovery plans account for those files as well as the rest of your database. If the external files change more rapidly than the database files, you may need to back them up more frequently in order to take advantage of Oracle's full recovery capabilities.

CHAPTER
29

Using Flashback Queries

As part of its read consistency model, Oracle displays data that has been committed to the database. You can query data as it existed prior to a transaction being committed. If you accidentally COMMIT an errant UPDATE or DELETE, you can use this capability—called a *flashback query*—to see the data as it existed prior to the COMMIT. You can then use the results of the flashback query to restore the data.

To support flashback queries, your database must have Automatic Undo Management enabled, which is the default on Oracle Database 12*c*. Flashback queries can also be executed against remote databases.

Oracle attempts to maintain enough undo information in the undo tablespace to support flashback queries during the retention time period. The retention time setting and the amount of space available in the undo tablespace can significantly impact your ability to execute a flashback query successfully.

NOTE
Oracle uses undo to roll back transactions, provide read consistency, and support flashback queries. Oracle uses redo (captured in the online redo log files) to apply transactions during database recoveries.

Flashback queries are important tools during partial recovery efforts. In general, you should not rely on flashback queries as part of your application design because they depend on system elements outside of the application developer's control (such as the number of transactions during a time period and the size of the undo tablespace). Rather, you should treat them as an option during critical periods of testing, support, and data recovery. For example, you could use them to create copies of tables at multiple past points in time for use when reconstructing changed data.

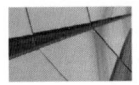

NOTE
To use some features of flashback queries, you must have the EXECUTE privilege on the DBMS_FLASHBACK package. Most users will not need privileges on this package.

Time-Based Flashback Example

The BOOK_ORDER table has six records, as shown in the following listing:

```
column title format a30
select * from book_order;
```

TITLE	PUBLISHER	CATEGORY_NAME
Shoeless Joe	Mariner	ADULTFIC
Gospel	Picador	ADULTFIC
Something So Strong	Pandoras	ADULTNF
Galileo's Daughter	Penguin	ADULTNF
Longitude	Penguin	ADULTNF
Once Removed	Sanctuary Pub	ADULTNF

```
6 rows selected
```

A shipment has arrived, and the old BOOK_ORDER records are deleted and then the DELETE is committed. Unfortunately, not all the books were in the shipment, so the DELETE is inappropriate:

```
delete from book_order;
commit;
```

How can you reconstruct the unreceived book records from the BOOK_ORDER table with only the received books in hand? You could perform a database recovery by using Data Pump Import (see Chapter 24) to restore the table, or you could perform a physical database recovery to recover the database to a point in time prior to the DELETE. Data Pump Import only helps, however, if you have an existing export dump file, and doing a physical database recovery is much like using a sledgehammer on a mosquito. In other words, you'll get your deleted rows back but you'll have to shut down the database and lose any other DML that occurred after the BOOK_ORDER rows were deleted. But with flashback queries, you can avoid having to perform these recovery operations.

First, let's query the old data from the database. You can use the AS OF TIMESTAMP and AS OF SCN clauses of the SELECT command to specify how far Oracle should flash back the data.

```
select count(*) from book_order;

  COUNT(*)
----------
         0

select count(*) from book_order
   as of timestamp (sysdate - 5/1440); -- 5 minutes ago

  COUNT(*)
----------
         6
```

When you execute a flashback query, only the state of the data is changed. The current system time is used (as you can see by querying the SYSDATE value), and the current data dictionary is used. If the structure of the table has changed, the query will fail.

Saving the Data

As shown in the BOOK_ORDER example, flashback queries are simple to implement, provided the undo management of the database is properly configured and the undo information is available. But how can you work with the flashback data to get it back into the table itself?

The simplest method involves saving the data to a separate table. There are 1440 minutes in a day, so "SYSDATE – 5/1440" directs the database to a point in time five minutes ago. Note that the query may return no rows if more than five minutes have passed since the COMMIT.

```
create table book_order_old
as select * from book_order
as of timestamp (sysdate - 5/1440);

Table created.
```

```
select count(*) from book_order_old;

  COUNT(*)
----------
         6
```

You can verify that the data is correct:

```
column title format a30

select * from book_order_old;

TITLE                           PUBLISHER            CATEGORY_NAME
------------------------------  -------------------  --------------
Shoeless Joe                    Mariner              ADULTFIC
Gospel                          Picador              ADULTFIC
Something So Strong             Pandoras             ADULTNF
Galileo's Daughter              Penguin              ADULTNF
Longitude                       Penguin              ADULTNF
Once Removed                    Sanctuary Pub        ADULTNF

6 rows selected.
```

You can then work with that data to restore the missing data, perform selective updates, insert only incorrectly deleted rows, or whatever other operation is needed.

The new table, BOOK_ORDER_OLD, has no indexes on it and no referential integrity constraints. If you need to join it to other tables, you may need to create flashback copies of multiple tables in order to maintain the referential integrity of the data in all related tables. Also, note that each query is executed at a different point in time—and the relative times used in the AS OF TIMESTAMP clause can, therefore, lead to confusing or inconsistent results.

You can work directly with the old data—however, you are relying on the old data being available for your transaction. It is generally safer to create a table and store the old data temporarily as you work with it. If a lot of other database activity is occurring and your UNDO tablespace is relatively small or your undo retention time is short, the rows you want may be gone if you wait too long.

SCN-Based Flashback Example

When you perform time-based flashbacks, you are really doing SCN-based flashbacks; you're just relying on Oracle to find an System Change Number (SCN) near the time you specified. If you know the exact SCN, you can perform a flashback with a great degree of precision.

To begin an SCN-based flashback, you must first know your transaction's SCN. To get the latest change number, issue a COMMIT and then use the AS OF SCN clause of the SELECT command. You can find the current SCN by executing the GET_SYSTEM_CHANGE_NUMBER function of the DBMS_FLASHBACK package prior to executing your transaction.

NOTE
Prior to executing the following example, you must have the EXECUTE privilege on the DBMS_FLASHBACK package.

The following example shows this process as part of a transaction against the BOOK_ORDER_OLD table, which we created and populated in the first part in this chapter. First, the current SCN is assigned to a variable named SCN_FLASH and displayed via the SQL*Plus PRINT command:

```
commit;

variable scn_flash number;
execute :scn_flash := dbms_flashback.get_system_change_number;

PL/SQL procedure successfully completed.

print scn_flash

 SCN_FLASH
----------
   2034307
```

Next, the DELETE command is issued and the result is committed:

```
delete from book_order_old;
6 rows deleted.

commit;
```

You can now query the flashback data. Although the SCN value is known, you can continue to use the SCN_FLASH variable value if you are within the same session:

```
select count(*) from book_order_old;

  COUNT(*)
----------
         0

select count(*) from book_order_old
  as of scn (:scn_flash);

  COUNT(*)
----------
         6
```

You can now use the flashback data in BOOK_ORDER_OLD, accessed by the AS OF SCN clause, to populate it with its old values:

```
insert into book_order_old
select * from book_order_old
  as of scn (:scn_flash);

6 rows inserted.

commit;

committed.
```

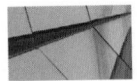

NOTE
DDL operations that alter the structure of a table invalidate the old undo data for the table, and flashback capabilities are limited to the time since the DDL was executed. Space-related changes (such as changing PCTFREE) do not invalidate the old undo data. See Chapter 30 for details on the FLASHBACK TABLE and FLASHBACK DATABASE commands.

What If the Flashback Query Fails?

If there is not enough space in the undo tablespace to maintain all the data needed for the flashback query, the query will fail. Even if the DBA created a large undo tablespace, a series of large transactions can use all the space available. A portion of each failed query will be written to the database's alert log.

From the perspective of a user attempting to recover old data, you should attempt to recover data that is as correct and timely as possible. Often, you may need to execute multiple flashback queries to determine how far back you can successfully query the data and then save the oldest data you can access and the data closest to the point at which the problem occurred. Once the oldest data is gone from the undo tablespace, you can no longer use flashback queries to retrieve it.

If it is not possible to flash back to data that is old enough for your needs, you need to perform some sort of database recovery—either flashing back the entire database or recovering specific tables and tablespaces via traditional database recovery methods. If this problem happens routinely, increase the undo retention time and the space allotted for the undo tablespace and examine the application usage to determine why questionable transactions are occurring on a persistent basis.

Other recovery methods require additional setup by the DBA but can be effective in recovering your data promptly with minimal downtime. Flashback Data Archive keeps a private UNDO area for one or more tables and is useful when your tables are large and you can't rely on the original version of changed or deleted rows being in the global UNDO tablespace. Block change tracking keeps the original copies of changed database blocks in the flash recovery area and makes it easy to roll back the entire database to a previous point in time without requiring a full database restore and recover. The syntax for Flashback Data Archive is in the Alphabetical Reference and both methodologies are covered in detail in the *Oracle Database 12c DBA Handbook*.

What SCN Is Associated with Each Row?

You can see the most recent SCN associated with each row in the database.

Let's start by repopulating our BOOK_ORDER table with the data that was restored to the BOOK_ORDER_OLD table:

```
delete from book_order;

0 rows deleted.

insert into book_order
select * from book_order_old;
```

```
6 rows created.
```

commit;

Now, use the ORA_ROWSCN to see the SCN associated with each row:

select title, ora_rowscn from book_order;

```
TITLE                            ORA_ROWSCN
-------------------------------- ----------
Shoeless Joe                        2033380
Gospel                              2033380
Something So Strong                 2033380
Galileo's Daughter                  2033380
Longitude                           2033380
Once Removed                        2033380
```

All the rows were part of the same transaction, occurring at SCN 2033380 (the SCN in your database will differ from the one in this example). Now, wait for other transactions to occur in the database and then insert a new row:

insert into book_order
values ('Innumeracy','Vintage Books','ADULTNF');

```
1 row created.
```

commit;

Now that a new change has been committed, you can see the SCN associated with it:

select title, ora_rowscn from book_order;

```
TITLE                            ORA_ROWSCN
-------------------------------- ----------
Shoeless Joe                        2033380
Gospel                              2033380
Something So Strong                 2033380
Galileo's Daughter                  2033380
Longitude                           2033380
Once Removed                        2033380
Innumeracy                          2035159
```

NOTE
The ORA_ROWSCN pseudo-column value is not absolutely precise, because Oracle tracks SCNs by the transaction committed for the block in which the row resides. A new transaction in the block may update the ORA_ROWSCN values for all rows in the block.

What time does that SCN map to? You can use the SCN_TO_TIMESTAMP function to display the date at which the change was made:

```
select scn_to_timestamp(2035159) from dual;

SCN_TO_TIMESTAMP(2035159)
-------------------------------
29-APR-13 12.23.15.000000000 PM
```

You can also integrate the two queries to see the latest transaction times for each row:

```
select title, scn_to_timestamp(ora_rowscn)
from book_order;
```

Flashback Version Queries

You can display the different versions of rows that existed during specified intervals. As with the examples shown previously in this chapter, the changes are SCN dependent, so only those that are committed are displayed.

> **NOTE**
> *Flashback version queries require that the DBA has set a nonzero value for the UNDO_RETENTION initialization parameter. If the UNDO_RETENTION value is too low, you may get an ORA-30052 error.*

To prepare for these examples, delete the old rows from BOOK_ORDER:

```
delete from book_order;
```

Next, repopulate BOOK_ORDER:

```
select systimestamp from dual;

SYSTIMESTAMP
-------------------------------------
29-APR-13 12.49.42.523891000 PM -05:00

insert into book_order
select * from book_order_old;

6 rows inserted.

select systimestamp from dual;

SYSTIMESTAMP
-------------------------------------
29-APR-13 12.50.49.345205000 PM -05:00
```

Then, wait for a few minutes and update all rows:

```
select systimestamp from dual;

SYSTIMESTAMP
-------------------------------------
29-APR-13 01.00.26.616973000 PM -05:00

update book_order set category_name = 'ADULTF';

6 rows updated.

select systimestamp from dual;

SYSTIMESTAMP
-------------------------------------
29-APR-13 01.01.07.973431000 PM -05:00
```

To execute a flashback version query, use the VERSIONS between clause of the SELECT statement. You can specify either the timestamp or the SCN. In this example, the format for the timestamp clause is based on Oracle's standard format (SELECT SYSTIMESTAMP FROM DUAL for the current value):

```
select *
from book_order
versions between timestamp
   to_timestamp('29-APR-13 12.30.00','dd-mon-yy hh24.mi.ss')
   and
   to_timestamp('29-APR-13 13.01.08','dd-mon-yy hh24.mi.ss');

TITLE                            PUBLISHER              CATEGORY_NAME
-------------------------------- ---------------------- --------------------
Once Removed                     Sanctuary Pub          ADULTF
Longitude                        Penguin                ADULTF
Galileo's Daughter               Penguin                ADULTF
Something So Strong              Pandoras               ADULTF
Gospel                           Picador                ADULTF
Shoeless Joe                     Mariner                ADULTF
Something So Strong              Pandoras               ADULTNF
Shoeless Joe                     Mariner                ADULTFIC
Once Removed                     Sanctuary Pub          ADULTNF
Longitude                        Penguin                ADULTNF
Innumeracy                       Vintage Books          ADULTNF
Gospel                           Picador                ADULTFIC
Galileo's Daughter               Penguin                ADULTNF
Shoeless Joe                     Mariner                ADULTFIC
Gospel                           Picador                ADULTFIC
Something So Strong              Pandoras               ADULTNF
Galileo's Daughter               Penguin                ADULTNF
Longitude                        Penguin                ADULTNF
Once Removed                     Sanctuary Pub          ADULTNF
Innumeracy                       Vintage Books          ADULTNF

20 rows selected
```

When you execute the query, Oracle returns one row for each version of each row that occurred between the start and end points you specify in the VERSIONS BETWEEN clause. For the rows that are returned, you can query additional pseudo-columns:

Pseudo-Column	Description
VERSIONS_STARTSCN	The SCN when the data first had the values reflected. If NULL, then the row was created before the lower bound for the query.
VERSIONS_STARTTIME	The timestamp when the data first had the values reflected. If NULL, then the row was created before the lower bound for the query.
VERSIONS_ENDSCN	The SCN when the row version expired. If NULL, then the row is current or has been deleted.
VERSIONS_ENDTIME	The timestamp when the row version expired. If NULL, then the row is current or has been deleted.
VERSIONS_XID	The identifier of the transaction that created the row version.
VERSIONS_OPERATION	The operation that performed the transaction (I for insert, U for update, D for delete).

The following example shows the use of the flashback version query. The VERSIONS_ STARTSCN values are NULL for the current rows; the old rows have been updated. The timestamps will be different on your platform.

```
select title, versions_startscn, versions_operation
from book_order
versions between timestamp
    to_timestamp('29-APR-13 13.06.00','dd-mon-yy hh24.mi.ss')
    and
    to_timestamp('29-APR-13 13.10.08','dd-mon-yy hh24.mi.ss');


TITLE                            VERSIONS_STARTSCN V
-------------------------------- ----------------- -
Once Removed                               2033665 U
Longitude                                  2033665 U
Galileo's Daughter                         2033665 U
Something So Strong                        2033665 U
Gospel                                     2033665 U
Shoeless Joe                               2033665 U
Shoeless Joe
Gospel
Something So Strong
Galileo's Daughter
Longitude
Once Removed
```

The VERSIONS BETWEEN clause can also be used in subqueries of DML and DDL commands.

You can use the FLASHBACK_TRANSACTION_QUERY data dictionary view to track changes made by a particular transaction. For a given transaction, FLASHBACK_TRANSACTION_QUERY shows the name of the user who executed it, the operation performed, the table to which the transaction was applied, the start and end SCNs and timestamps, and the SQL needed to undo the transaction.

Planning for Flashbacks

For DBAs, flashback queries may offer a means of performing partial recovery operations quickly. If the data can be reconstructed via flashback queries, and if the data volume is not overwhelming, you may be able to save the results of multiple flashback queries in separate tables. You could then compare the data in the tables via the SQL options shown in prior chapters—correlated subqueries, EXISTS, NOT EXISTS, MINUS, and so on. If you cannot avoid the need for a recovery operation, you should be able to pinpoint the time period to be used for a time-based recovery operation.

As you will see in the next chapter, Oracle supports additional options—the FLASHBACK DATABASE and FLASHBACK TABLE commands.

For application developers and application administrators, flashback queries provide an important tool for reconstructing data. Flashback queries may be particularly critical during testing and support operations. Rather than making flashback queries part of your production application design, you should use them as a fallback option for those support cases that cannot be resolved before data is affected.

CHAPTER
30

Flashback—
Tables and Databases

You can use the FLASHBACK TABLE and FLASHBACK DATABASE commands to simplify and enhance your data-recovery efforts. The FLASHBACK TABLE command automates the process of restoring a full table to its prior state. The FLASHBACK DATABASE command flashes back an entire database, and it requires modifications to the database status and its logs. The following sections describe the details on implementing these options.

The FLASHBACK TABLE Command

The FLASHBACK TABLE command restores an earlier state of a table in the event of human or application error. Oracle cannot restore a table to an earlier state across any DDL operations that change the table's structure.

NOTE
The database should be using Automatic Undo Management (AUM) for FLASHBACK TABLE to work. The ability to flash back to old data is limited by the amount of undo retained in the UNDO tablespace and the UNDO_RETENTION initialization parameter setting.

You cannot roll back a FLASHBACK TABLE statement. You can issue another FLASHBACK TABLE statement, however, and specify a time just prior to the current time.

NOTE
Record the current SCN before issuing a FLASHBACK TABLE command.

Privileges Required

You must have either the FLASHBACK object privilege on the table or the FLASHBACK ANY TABLE system privilege. You must also have SELECT, INSERT, DELETE, and ALTER object privileges on the table. Row movement must be enabled for all tables in the flashback list. To flash back a table to before a DROP TABLE operation, you only need the privileges necessary to drop the table.

Recovering Dropped Tables

Consider the AUTHOR table:

```
describe author
```

```
Name                Null?     Type
------------------- --------- ---------------------------
AUTHORNAME          NOT NULL  VARCHAR2(50)
COMMENTS                      VARCHAR2(100)
```

Now, let's drop the table:

```
drop table author cascade constraints;
```

```
Table dropped.
```

How can we recover the table? By default, a dropped table does not fully disappear. Its blocks are still maintained in its tablespace, and it still counts against your space quota. You can see the dropped objects by querying the RECYCLEBIN data dictionary view. Note that the format for the OBJECT_NAME column may differ between versions.

```
select * from recyclebin;
```

```
OBJECT_NAME                            ORIGINAL_NAME                      OPERATION
----------------------------------     ---------------------------------  ---------
TYPE                    TS_NAME                        CREATETIME
----------------------  -----------------------------  -------------------
DROPTIME                DROPSCN PARTITION_NAME                           CAN CAN
------------------  ----------  ---------------------------------  --- ---
   RELATED BASE_OBJECT PURGE_OBJECT     SPACE
---------- ----------- ----------- ----------
BIN$yrMK1ZaVMhfgNAgAIYowZA==$0 AUTHOR                                    DROP
TABLE                   USERS                          2013-02-23:16:10:58
2013-02-25:14:30:23     720519                                      YES YES
    48448        48448          48448            8

BIN$DBo9UChtZSbgQFeMiThArA==$0 SYS_C004828                               DROP
INDEX                   USERS                          2013-02-23:16:10:58
2013-02-25:14:30:23     720516                                      NO  YES
    48448        48448          48449            8
```

RECYCLEBIN is a public synonym for the USER_RECYCLEBIN data dictionary view, showing the recycle bin entries for the current user. DBAs can see all dropped objects via the DBA_RECYCLEBIN data dictionary view.

As shown in the preceding listing, Oracle has dropped the AUTHOR table and its associated primary key index. Although they have been dropped, they are still available for flashback. Note that the recycle bin listings show the SCN for the DROP command used to drop the base object.

For the objects in the recycle bin, the naming convention is BIN$*unique_id*$*version,* where *unique_id* is a 26-character globally unique identifier for this object (which makes the recycle bin name unique across all databases) and *version* is a version number assigned by the database.

You can use the FLASHBACK TABLE to before drop command to recover the table from the recycle bin:

```
flashback table author to before drop;
```

```
Flashback complete.
```

The table has been restored, along with its rows, indexes, and statistics, as shown here:

```
select count(*) from author;
```

```
COUNT(*)
----------
     31
```

What happens if you drop the AUTHOR table, re-create it, and then drop it again? The recycle bin will contain both tables. Each entry in the recycle bin will be identified via its SCN and the timestamp for the drop.

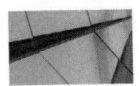

NOTE
The FLASHBACK TABLE TO BEFORE DROP command does not recover referential integrity constraints.

To purge old entries from the recycle bin, use the PURGE command. You can purge all your dropped objects, all dropped objects in the database (if you are a DBA), all objects in a specific tablespace, or all objects for a particular user in a specific tablespace. See the PURGE command in the Alphabetical Reference for the full syntax and command options.

You can use the RENAME TO clause of the FLASHBACK TABLE command to rename the table as you flash it back.

Enabling and Disabling the Recycle Bin

You can enable and disable the recycle bin with the RECYCLEBIN initialization parameter. By default, this parameter is set to ON. When the recycle bin is disabled, dropped tables and their dependent objects are not placed in the recycle bin; they are just dropped, and you must use other means to recover them (such as recovering from backup).

You can disable the recycle bin at the system level (with a database restart):

```
alter system set recyclebin=off scope=spfile;
```

You can also do this at the session level (this can be changed dynamically without a database restart):

```
alter session set recyclebin=off;
```

You can re-enable it by setting those values to ON:

```
alter system set recyclebin=on scope=spfile;
```

Here's how to do this at the session level:

```
alter session set recyclebin=on;
```

NOTE
Disabling the recycle bin does not purge or otherwise affect objects already in the recycle bin.

Flashing Back to SCN or Timestamp

As shown in Chapter 29, you can save the results of a flashback query in a separate table while the main table stays unaffected. You can also update the rows of a table based on the results of a flashback query. You can use the FLASHBACK TABLE command to transform a table into its prior version—wiping out the changes that were made since the specified flashback point.

During a FLASHBACK TABLE operation, Oracle acquires exclusive DML locks on all the tables specified. The command is executed in a single transaction across all tables; if any of them fails, the entire statement fails. You can flash back a table to a specific SCN or timestamp.

NOTE
FLASHBACK TABLE TO SCN or TO TIMESTAMP does not preserve ROWIDs.

The following UPDATE command attempts to update the comment for the entry for Clement Hurd. However, the WHERE clause is not specified; all rows are updated with the same comment, and the change is committed.

```
update author
    set Comments = 'Illustrator of books for children';

31 rows updated.
```

```
commit;
```

In this case, we know that almost the entire table has incorrect data, and we know the transaction that was executed incorrectly. To recover the correct data, we can flash back the database to a prior time and then apply any new commands needed to bring the data up to date.

First, let's make sure we know the current SCN in case we need to return to this point:

```
commit;
```

```
variable scn_flash number;
execute :scn_flash :=dbms_flashback.get_system_change_number;

PL/SQL procedure successfully completed.
```

```
print scn_flash

SCN_FLASH
----------
183365895
```

Now, let's flash back the table to a time just prior to the update. First, we must enable row movement for the table:

```
alter table author enable row movement;

Table altered.
```

We can then flash back the table (to how it was more five minutes ago):

```
flashback table author to timestamp (systimestamp - 5/1440);
```

You can use the TO SCN clause, if you wish, to specify an SCN instead of a timestamp.

Indexes and Statistics

When a table is flashed back, its statistics are not flashed back. Indexes that exist on the table are reverted and reflect the state of the table at the flashback point. Indexes dropped since the flashback point are not restored. Indexes created since the flashback point continue to exist and are updated to reflect the older data.

When recovered from the recycle bin, indexes retain the names they had in the recycle bin. You can return those indexes to their original names via the ALTER INDEX … RENAME TO … command.

The FLASHBACK DATABASE Command

The FLASHBACK DATABASE command returns the database to a past time or SCN, providing a fast alternative to performing incomplete database recovery. Following a FLASHBACK DATABASE operation, in order to have write access to the flashed back database you must reopen it with an ALTER DATABASE OPEN RESETLOGS command. You must have the SYSDBA system privilege to use the FLASHBACK DATABASE command.

NOTE
The database must have been put in flashback mode with an ALTER DATABASE FLASHBACK ON command. The database must also be mounted in EXCLUSIVE mode but not be open when that command is executed.

The syntax for the FLASHBACK database command is as follows:

```
FLASHBACK [STANDBY] DATABASE [database]
{ TO {scn | timestamp} expr
| TO BEFORE  {scn | timestamp } expr
}
```

You can use either the TO SCN or TO TIMESTAMP clause to set the point to which the entire database should be flashed back. You can flash back TO BEFORE a critical point (such as a transaction that produced an unintended consequence for multiple tables). Use the ORA_ROWSCN pseudo-column to see the SCNs of transactions that most recently acted on rows.

To use FLASHBACK database, you must first alter the database while it is mounted but not open. If you have not already done so, you need to shut down your database and enable flashback during the startup process:

```
startup mount exclusive;
alter database archivelog;
alter database flashback on;
alter database open;
```

NOTE
You must have enabled media recovery via the ALTER DATABASE ARCHIVELOG command prior to executing the ALTER DATABASE FLASHBACK ON command.

Two initialization parameter settings control how much flashback data is retained in the database. The DB_FLASHBACK_RETENTION_TARGET initialization parameter sets the upper limit (in minutes) for how far in time the database can be flashed back. The DB_RECOVERY_FILE_ DEST initialization parameter sets the size of the flash recovery area. Note that the FLASHBACK TABLE command uses the UNDO tablespace, whereas the FLASHBACK DATABASE command relies on *flashback logs* stored in a flash recovery area.

The flash recovery area can contain control files, online redo logs, archived redo logs, flashback logs, and RMAN backups. Files in the recovery area are either permanent or transient. Permanent files are active files used by the database instance. All files that are not permanent are transient. In general, Oracle Database eventually deletes transient files after they become obsolete under the backup retention policy or have been backed up to tape.

Table 30-1 describes the files in the recovery area, the classification of each file as permanent or temporary, and how database availability is affected.

Files	Type	Database Behavior When Flash Recovery Area Is Inaccessible
Multiplexed copies of the current control file	Permanent	The instance fails if the database cannot write to a multiplexed copy of the control file stored in the flash recovery area. Failure occurs even if accessible multiplexed copies are located outside the recovery area.
Online redo log files	Permanent	Instance availability is not affected if a mirrored copy of the online redo log exists in an accessible location outside the flash recovery area. Otherwise, the instance fails.
Archived redo log files	Transient	Instance availability is not affected if the log is archived to an accessible location outside the flash recovery area. Otherwise, the database eventually halts because it cannot archive the online redo logs.
Foreign archived redo log files	Transient	Instance availability is not affected.
Image copies of datafiles and control files	Transient	Instance availability is not affected.
Backup pieces	Transient	Instance availability is not affected.
Flashback logs	Transient	Instance availability is not affected because the database automatically disables the flashback database, writes a message to the alert log, and continues with database processing.

TABLE 30-1.   *Types of Files in the Flash Recovery Area*

You can determine how far back you can flash back the database by querying the V$FLASHBACK_DATABASE_LOG view. The amount of flashback data retained in the database is controlled by the initialization parameter and the size of the flash recovery area. The following listing shows the available columns in V$FLASHBACK_DATABASE_LOG and sample contents:

```
desc v$flashback_database_log

Name                                      Null?     Type
-------------------------------------     --------  -------
OLDEST_FLASHBACK_SCN                                NUMBER
OLDEST_FLASHBACK_TIME                               DATE
RETENTION_TARGET                                    NUMBER
FLASHBACK_SIZE                                      NUMBER
ESTIMATED_FLASHBACK_SIZE                            NUMBER
```

```
select * from v$flashback_database_log;

OLDEST_FLASHBACK_SCN OLDEST_FL RETENTION_TARGET FLASHBACK_SIZE
-------------------- --------- ---------------- --------------
ESTIMATED_FLASHBACK_SIZE
------------------------
             722689 25-FEB-13             1440       16384000
                  0
```

You can verify the database's flashback status by querying V$DATABASE; the FLASHBACK_ON column will have a value of YES if the flashback has been enabled for the database.

```
select current_scn, flashback_on from v$database;

CURRENT_SCN      FLA
---------------- ---
      183365895 YES
```

With the database open for over an hour, verify that the flashback data is available and then flash it back—you will lose all transactions that occurred during that time:

```
shutdown immediate;
startup mount exclusive;
flashback database to timestamp sysdate-(1/24);
```

Note that the FLASHBACK DATABASE command requires that the database be mounted in EXCLUSIVE mode, which will affect its participation in any RAC clusters (see Chapter 50).

When you execute the FLASHBACK DATABASE command, Oracle checks to ensure all required flashback logs, archived redo log files, and online redo log files are available. If the logs are available, the online datafiles are reverted to the time or SCN specified.

If there is not enough data online in the archive logs and the flashback area, you will need to use traditional database recovery methods to recover the data. For example, you may need to use a file system recovery method or an RMAN RESTORE and RECOVER operation followed by rolling the data forward with your archived redo log files.

NOTE
Some database operations, such as dropping a tablespace or shrinking a datafile, cannot be reversed with FLASHBACK DATABASE. In these cases, the flashback database window begins at the time immediately following that operation.

Once the flashback has completed, you must open the database using the RESETLOGS option in order to have write access to the database:

```
alter database open resetlogs;
```

To turn off the flashback database option, execute the ALTER DATABASE FLASHBACK OFF command when the database is mounted but not open:

```
startup mount exclusive;
alter database flashback off;
alter database open;
```

As shown in this and the preceding chapter, you can use the flashback options to perform an array of actions—recovering old data, reverting a table to its earlier data, maintaining a history of changes on a row basis, and quickly restoring an entire database. All of these actions are greatly simplified if the database has been configured to support Automatic Undo Management. Also, note that the FLASHBACK DATABASE command requires modification of the database status. Although these requirements can present additional burdens to DBAs, the benefits involved in terms of the number of recoveries required and the speed with which those recoveries can be completed may be dramatic.

CHAPTER
31

SQL Replay

A s of Oracle 11g, you can use "replay" features to capture the commands executed in a database and then replay them elsewhere. Operations can be captured from one database and replayed on another. You can use the capture and replay features to perform diagnostic operations or to test applications under production conditions.

Replay capabilities are particularly useful when evaluating the impacts of changes on multiuser packaged applications for which you do not have direct access to all the code. Oracle will capture the commands executed within the database regardless of their origin; the captured behavior is independent of the originating program.

High-level Configuration

Replay consists of the following processes and components.
On the source database:

■   The workload-capture process logs the SQL executed within the database.

On the target database:

■   The workload-preprocessing step prepares the logs for execution.

■   Replay clients establish sessions in the database.

■   The workload-replay process executes the SQL in the new database via the replay clients.

As the workload is being replayed on the target database, you can analyze the database and generate performance-tuning recommendations. In the following sections, you'll see how to execute the workload capture and replay processes. First, though, you need to make sure your systems are properly configured to support them, as described in the next section.

Isolation and Links

Before you start, you should configure the target database (where the captured replay will be executed) to minimize its interaction with external files and objects. In the source database, you should carefully examine the use of database links and external files prior to beginning the capture. During the replay, Oracle executes the captured commands from the source database in the target database. If the target database has the same links and access as the source database, remote objects may be manipulated based on the repeat of transactions in the target database.

If the remote databases are only used for data lookups (that is, mainly read-only), this may not present a problem. If the remote databases are updated by the source database, the repeat of those transactions during the replay in the target database may generate unwanted transactions in the remote database. For example, if the source database contains a materialized view that performs a refresh during the testing period and the same command is executed from a cloned testing database during the replay execution, the results will most likely be undesirable. For the best control over the replay environment, isolate it. Where possible, avoid the use of directory objects, URLs, UTF_FILE package, and programs that generate e-mail.

NOTE
For best results during the replay, you may also need to alter the system time on the target system. Replay is, therefore, best suited for situations in which the target system is a testing environment, rather than generating the replay in a testing environment and then executing it in a production database.

Before starting the capture on the source database, make sure there are no active transactions within the database. If you have DBA privileges, you can accomplish this by terminating any open and active sessions; alternatively, you can shut down and restart the database. You should then capture the data as it exists in the source system (via a backup method such as Data Pump Export/Import or RMAN). When the workload is replayed on the target system, you want the data environment to be virtually identical to the source database environment.

To further control the transactions allowed within the source system, you may elect to start it in RESTRICTED mode. Because this limits the sessions that can connect to the database during your workload capture, you need to determine if such restricted behavior is an accurate depiction of standard usage for the application.

Creating a Workload Directory

The log file for the SQL workload is written to a directory on the source server. To specify the physical location for that directory, you must create a directory object within the database (a logical pointer to the physical directory). Use the CREATE DIRECTORY command, as shown here, to create a directory object:

```
create directory workload_dir as '/u03/workload';
```

You can now use the WORKLOAD_DIR directory as the destination for the SQL log files. Make sure the file system you are pointing to has space available and is actively monitored for space usage.

Capturing the Workload

You can execute all the commands needed to create a directory and capture the workload via the Oracle Enterprise Manager (OEM) console or stored procedure calls. In the examples in this chapter, you'll see the command-line entries needed to execute the commands because not all users will have access to OEM.

The workload-capture process is controlled via the DBMS_WORKLOAD_CAPTURE package. You can use DBMS_WORKLOAD_CAPTURE to control the filters used for the workload, start a capture, stop a capture, and export Automated Workload Repository (AWR) snapshot data for the capture.

The functions and procedures within DBMS_WORKLOAD_CAPTURE are shown in Table 31-1.

Subprogram	Description
ADD_FILTER	Adds a filter
DELETE_CAPTURE_INFO	Deletes rows in the DBA_WORKLOAD_CAPTURES and DBA_WORKLOAD_FILTERS views
DELETE_FILTER	Deletes a specified filter
EXPORT_AWR	Exports the AWR snapshots associated with a given capture ID
FINISH_CAPTURE	Either finalizes the workload capture or returns the database to normal operating mode
GET_CAPTURE_INFO	Retrieves all the information regarding a workload capture, imports the information into the DBA_WORKLOAD_CAPTURES and DBA_WORKLOAD_FILTERS views, and returns the appropriate DBA_WORKLOAD_CAPTURES.ID
IMPORT_AWR	Imports the AWR snapshots associated with a given capture ID
REPORT	Generates a report based on the workload capture
START_CAPTURE	Initiates the capture process

TABLE 31-1. *Functions and Procedures within DBMS_WORKLOAD_CAPTURE*

Defining Filters

By default, the capture process captures all activity in the database. Filters allow you to capture a specified subset of the workload. To add a filter, use the ADD_FILTER procedure.

The syntax for ADD_FILTER is shown in the following listing:

```
DBMS_WORKLOAD_CAPTURE.ADD_FILTER (
    FNAME           IN    VARCHAR2 NOT NULL,
    FATTRIBUTE      IN    VARCHAR2 NOT NULL,
    FVALUE          IN    VARCHAR2 NOT NULL);
```

The *fname* variable is the name for the filter. The *fattribute* variable specifies the attribute to which the filter needs to be applied. The possible values for *fattribute* are INSTANCE_NUMBER, USER, MODULE, ACTION, PROGRAM, and SERVICE. You can then pass in the value for the attribute via the *fvalue* variable, as shown next:

```
begin
    dbms_workload_capture.add_filter (
                fname => 'USER_PRACTICE',
                fattribute => 'USER',
                fvalue => 'PRACTICE');
end;
/
```

You can delete a filter by passing the filter name to the DELETE_FILTER procedure. The syntax for the DELETE_FILTER procedure is shown in the following listing:

```
DBMS_WORKLOAD_CAPTURE.DELETE_FILTER (
    FILTER_NAME            IN    VARCHAR2(40) NOT NULL);
```

When you start the capture, you tell Oracle how to use the filter; it can either restrict the capture to just values that meet the filter criteria or capture everything that does not meet the filter criteria.

Starting the Capture

To start a capture, execute the START_CAPTURE procedure. If you have not specified a filter, the capture will apply to all commands executed in the database.

The syntax for START_CAPTURE is shown in the following listing:

```
DBMS_WORKLOAD_CAPTURE.START_CAPTURE (
    NAME              IN   VARCHAR2,
    DIR               IN   VARCHAR2,
    DURATION          IN   NUMBER   DEFAULT NULL,
    DEFAULT_ACTION    IN   VARCHAR2 DEFAULT 'INCLUDE',
    AUTO_UNRESTRICT   IN   BOOLEAN  DEFAULT TRUE);
```

The input parameters for START_CAPTURE are as follows:

- The *name* parameter is the name you assign to the workload capture.

- *dir* is the name of the directory object you created to store the workload-capture files.

- The optional *duration* parameter allows you to specify the duration, in seconds, of the capture. By default, the *duration* value is set to NULL, and the capture continues until it is explicitly ended via a FINISH_CAPTURE procedure call.

- The *default_action* parameter tells the capture process how to use the filters. If it's set to INCLUDE (the default), all commands are captured except those specified in the filters. If it's set to EXCLUDE, only the commands that pass the filters are captured.

- The *auto_restrict* parameter, when set to TRUE (the default), tells Oracle to start the database in unrestricted mode upon the successful start of the capture.

```
begin
  dbms_workload_capture.start_capture
        (name => 'PRACTICE_CAPTURE',
         dir => 'WORKLOAD_DIR',
         default_action => 'EXCLUDE');
end;
/
```

Oracle then begins to capture the workload data executed in the database.

You can determine the capture ID assigned to the capture by executing the GET_CAPTURE_INFO function, as shown next:

```
select dbms_workload_capture.get_capture_info
    (dir => 'WORKLOAD_DIR')
from dual;
```

You need to know the capture ID in order to export the AWR statistics at the end of the capture.

Stopping the Capture

If you have not specified a duration, you must stop the capture manually. To stop the capture, execute the FINISH_CAPTURE procedure, as shown here:

```
begin
    dbms_workload_capture.finish_capture ();
end;
/
```

Exporting AWR Data

To export the AWR data for the capture (for use in later analysis), execute the EXPORT_AWR procedure. Here is the syntax:

```
DBMS_WORKLOAD_CAPTURE.EXPORT_AWR (
    CAPTURE_ID      IN NUMBER);
```

Processing the Workload

Now that the workload has been captured, you need to move all the captured workload logs to the target system. As noted earlier, the target database should be separate from the production database and should be as isolated as possible from the external structures accessed by the production database. The target database should run the same version of Oracle as the source system.

The preprocessing step, in which the workload logs are transformed into replay files and metadata is created, must be performed for every captured workload before it can be replayed. If the target database is a RAC cluster, you can use one instance of the cluster for the replay preprocessing.

You can initiate the preprocessing via OEM or via the DBMS_WORKLOAD_REPLAY package, as shown in the following listing:

```
begin
    dbms_workload_replay.process_capture
    (capture_dir => 'WORKLOAD_DIR');
end;
/
```

The *capture_dir* variable value must be the name of a directory object within the database that points to the physical directory where the workload logs are stored. Once the preprocessing step has completed, you can replay the workload on the test database as described in the following section.

Replaying the Workload

The workload files that have been preprocessed can be replayed against a target database. As noted earlier in this chapter, the target database should contain a copy of the source database objects and the source data. Where possible, the target database should be a clone of the production system as it existed immediately prior to the start of the capture. The target database should be isolated, with no access to the external objects used by the production database (such as external files, database links, or the source tables for remote materialized views). You need to be careful that the replay of transactions in the target database does not create invalid data in other databases.

NOTE
Because some aspects of the workload replay may be time dependent (such as the execution of time-based scheduled jobs or the use of the SYSDATE function), it is recommended that you reset the system time on the test server prior to starting the replay.

The target database must have a directory object that points to the physical directory where the workload files are stored. If the target database was used for the preprocessing step, that same directory can be used for the replay. If such a directory does not exist, use the CREATE DIRECTORY command to create one.

When the replay is executed, attempts to connect to the production database will be executed. On the target server, these connections must be redirected to the target database. For example, if the production server is accessed by the PROD service name, on the target server the PROD service name must point to the target database.

Controlling and Starting the Replay Clients

The replay is executed by replay clients. A *replay client* is a multithreaded program named **wrc**; each of the program's threads submits a workload from a captured session. The replay clients must connect to the target database before the replay can begin; you must provide the username and password for a DBA-privileged account (other than SYS) in the target database. The replay clients must have access to the directory where the processed workload files are stored.

The replay client executable for Windows, **wrc.exe**, is in the **bin** subdirectory in your Oracle software home directory, or in $**ORACLE_HOME/bin** on Unix. The **wrc** syntax is

```
wrc [user/password[@server]] mode=[value] [keyword=[value]]
```

NOTE
*If you enter **wrc** with no parameters, Oracle displays a full list of the available options for each parameter.*

The *user* and *password* parameters tell the workload client how to connect to the target database where the workload will be replayed. The *server* parameter specifies the name of the server where the replay client is run. The *mode* parameter tells Oracle how to run the workload; valid values are **replay** (the default), **calibrate**, and **list_hosts**. The *keyword* parameter tells Oracle how to configure the clients.

Because a single replay client can initiate multiple database sessions, you do not need to start one client per session. If you use the **calibrate** option for the *mode* parameter, as shown next, Oracle provides a recommendation for the number of clients to start:

```
wrc mode=calibrate replaydir=/u03/workload
```

The *replaydir* parameter specifies the physical directory where the processed replay files are located. The **wrc** output recommends the number of clients to start, along with the maximum number of concurrent sessions involved.

To start the replay client, use the **mode=replay** option, as shown here:

```
wrc dbacct/pass@target mode=replay replaydir=/u03/workload
```

The replay client remains active while the workload is replayed and terminates itself when the replay has completed.

Initializing and Running the Replay

With the workload data processed and the replay clients configured, you can now begin to work with the replay, via either OEM or the DBMS_WORKLOAD_REPLAY package. The available procedures and functions for DBMS_WORKLOAD_REPLAY are shown in Table 31-2.

Subprogram	Description
CALIBRATE	Operates on a processed workload capture directory to estimate the number of hosts and workload replay clients needed for the replay
CANCEL_REPLAY	Cancels the replay in progress
DELETE_REPLAY_INFO	Deletes the rows in DBA_WORKLOAD_REPLAY that correspond to the given workload replay ID
EXPORT_AWR	Export the AWR snapshots associated with a given replay ID
GET_REPLAY_INFO	Retrieves information about the workload capture and replay history
IMPORT_AWR	Imports the AWR snapshots associated with a given replay ID
INITIALIZE_REPLAY	Initializes replay
PREPARE_REPLAY	Puts the RDBMS in a special "Prepare" mode
PROCESS_CAPTURE	Processes the workload capture
REMAP_CONNECTION	Remaps the captured connection to a new one so the user sessions can connect to the database in a desired way during workload replay.
REPORT	Generates a report on the replay.
START_REPLAY	Starts the replay.

TABLE 31-2. *DBMS_WORKLOAD_REPLAY Procedures and Functions*

The initialization step loads the metadata into the test system and prepares the database for the replay to start. The syntax for INITIALIZE_REPLAY is shown here:

```
DBMS_WORKLOAD_REPLAY.INITIALIZE_REPLAY (
    REPLAY_NAME     IN  VARCHAR2,
    REPLAY_DIR      IN  VARCHAR2);
```

The *replay_dir* parameter is the name of the directory object within the target database that points to the physical directory where the processed workload files are stored.

Connection strings used within the captured workload may need to be remapped. When the workload SQL attempts to connect to external databases (via connection strings within the captured workload), you either need to have those remote databases available, let the sessions connect to the default host, or use the REMAP_CONNECTION procedure to specify how the connections should be redirected. As noted earlier, you should ideally be working in an isolated environment, and the default approach is to have those connections default to the target host.

With the workload initialized and the replay clients ready, you can now prepare and start the replay. To prepare the replay, use the PREPARE_REPLAY procedure:

```
DBMS_WORKLOAD_REPLAY.PREPARE_REPLAY (
    SYNCHRONIZATION          IN BOOLEAN   DEFAULT TRUE,
    CONNECT_TIME_SCALE       IN NUMBER    DEFAULT 100,
    THINK_TIME_SCALE         IN NUMBER    DEFAULT 100,
    THINK_TIME_AUTO_CORRECT  IN BOOLEAN   DEFAULT TRUE);
```

The *synchronization* parameter preserves the COMMIT order within the replay when set to TRUE. The *connect_time_scale* and *think_time_scale* parameters are percentages used to increase or decrease the number of concurrent users during the workload replay. The *think_time_auto_correct* parameter autocorrects the "think time" between calls when user calls take longer to complete during the replay than during the initial capture. The autocorrection is necessary when the target system performance does not match that of the source system.

If the *connect_time_scale* value is 10, the intervals between session connections during the replay are reduced to 10 percent of their original values. If the *think_time_scale* parameter is set to 20, the "think time" between operations during the replay is reduced to 20 percent of its original value. If the *think_time_scale* parameter is set to 200 percent, the "think time" between operations is doubled during the replay.

To start the replay, use the START_REPLAY procedure, as shown in the following listing:

```
begin
    dbms_workload_replay.start_replay ();
end;
/
```

To stop the replay, use the CANCEL_REPLAY procedure, as shown in the following listing:

```
begin
    dbms_workload_replay.cancel_replay ();
end;
/
```

Exporting AWR Data

You can export the AWR data for the replay via the EXPORT_AWR procedure. Its sole parameter is the *replay_id*, as shown in the following listing:

```
begin
    dbms_workload_replay.export_awr (replay_id => 1);
end;
/
```

Any AWR snapshots corresponding to "replay_id => 1" are exported. You can then compare the AWR report for the replay execution to the AWR reports for the same workload in the production environment to evaluate the performance differences and execution behavior changes across the databases.

The replay can be executed multiple times, provided you first re-create the objects in the test database and reset the system time each time. You can, therefore, use the replay tools to determine the impact of parameter changes in the test environment prior to introducing them into the production environment.

PART
IV
PL/SQL

CHAPTER
32

An Introduction to PL/SQL

P L/SQL is Oracle's procedural language (PL) superset of the Structured Query Language (SQL). You can use PL/SQL to do such things as codify your business rules through the creation of stored procedures and packages, trigger database events to occur, and add programming logic to the execution of SQL commands.

The steps involved in the creation of triggers, stored procedures, and packages are described in the following chapters in this part of the book. In this chapter, you will learn about the basic structures and syntax used in PL/SQL.

PL/SQL Overview

PL/SQL code is grouped into structures called *blocks*. If you create a stored procedure or package, you give the block of PL/SQL code a name; if the block of PL/SQL code is not given a name, it is called an *anonymous block*. The examples in this chapter feature anonymous blocks of PL/SQL code; the following chapters in Part IV illustrate the creation of named blocks.

A block of PL/SQL code contains three sections:

Section	Description
Declarations	Defines and initializes the variables and cursors used in the block
Executable Commands	Uses flow-control commands (such as **if** statements and loops) to execute the commands and assign values to the declared variables
Exception Handling	Provides customized handling of error conditions

Within a PL/SQL block, the first section is the Declarations section. Within the Declarations section, you define the variables and cursors that the block will use. The Declarations section starts with the keyword **declare** and ends when the Executable Commands section starts (as indicated by the keyword **begin**). The Executable Commands section is followed by the Exception Handling section; the **exception** keyword signals the start of the Exception Handling section. The PL/SQL block is terminated by the **end** keyword.

The structure of a typical PL/SQL anonymous block is shown in the following listing:

```
declare
  <declarations section>
begin
  <executable commands>
exception
  <exception handling>
end;
```

The following sections describe each section of the PL/SQL block.

Declarations Section

The Declarations section begins a PL/SQL block. The Declarations section starts with the **declare** keyword, followed by a list of variable and cursor definitions. You can define variables to have constant values, and variables can inherit datatypes from existing columns and query results, as shown in the following examples.

In the following listing, the area of a circle is calculated. The result is stored in a table named AREAS. The AREAS table has two columns to store radius and area values. The area of the circle is calculated by squaring the value for the circle's radius and multiplying that value by the constant **pi**:

```
declare
   pi       constant number(9,7) := 3.1415927;
   radius integer(5);
   area     number(14,2);
begin
   radius := 3;
   area := pi*power(radius,2);
   insert into areas values (radius, area);
end;
/
```

The **end;** line signals the end of the PL/SQL block; depending on the tool you use, you may need to add a slash (/) to execute the PL/SQL block. When the PL/SQL block is executed, you will receive the following response from Oracle:

```
PL/SQL procedure successfully completed.
```

To verify that the PL/SQL block completed correctly, you can select from the database the rows that were inserted by the PL/SQL code. The query and results in the following listing show the row the PL/SQL block created in the AREAS table:

```
select * from areas;

    RADIUS        AREA
---------- ----------
         3      28.27
```

The output shows that a single row was inserted into the AREAS table by the PL/SQL block. Only one row was created because only one RADIUS value was specified.

In the first section of the PL/SQL block, shown in the following listing, three variables are declared. You must declare the variables that will be used in the Executable Commands section of the PL/SQL block.

```
declare
   pi       constant number(9,7) := 3.1415927;
   radius integer(5);
   area     number(14,2);
```

The first variable declared is **pi**, which is set to a constant value via the **constant** keyword. Because it is declared as a **constant**, the value of the variable **pi** cannot be changed in the Executable Commands section. The value is assigned via the := operator:

```
pi       constant number(9,7) := 3.1415927;
```

You can also assign constant values via the **default** keyword:

```
pi       number(9,7) default 3.1415927;
```

The next two variables are defined but are not given default values:

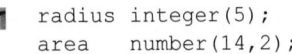

```
radius integer(5);
area   number(14,2);
```

You can assign an initial value to a variable in the Declarations section. To set an initial value for a variable, simply follow its datatype specification with the value assignment, as shown in the following listing:

```
radius integer(5)  := 3;
```

In the example, the datatypes include NUMBER and INTEGER. PL/SQL datatypes include all the valid SQL datatypes as well as complex datatypes based on query structures. Table 32-1 lists the supported PL/SQL datatypes.

NOTE
As of Oracle Database 12c, the maximum size of a VARCHAR2 or NVARCHAR2 column in Oracle SQL has been increased to 32,767 bytes to match the same datatypes in PL/SQL.

Scalar Datatypes

BINARY_DOUBLE	FLOAT	NUMBER	SMALLINT
BINARY_FLOAT	INT	NUMERIC	STRING
BINARY_INTEGER	INTEGER	NVARCHAR2	TIMESTAMP
BOOLEAN	INTERVAL DAY TO SECOND	PLS_INTEGER	TIMESTAMP WITH LOCAL TIME ZONE
CHAR	INTERVAL YEAR TO MONTH	POSITIVE	TIMESTAMP WITH TIME ZONE
CHARACTER	LONG	POSITIVEN	UROWID
DATE	LONG RAW	RAW	VARCHAR
DEC	NATURAL	REAL	VARCHAR2
DECIMAL	NATURALN	ROWID	
DOUBLE PRECISION	NCHAR	SIGNTYPE	

Composite Types

RECORD	TABLE	VARRAY	

Reference Types

REF CURSOR	REF *object_type*		

LOB Types

BFILE	BLOB	CLOB	NCLOB

TABLE 32-1. *PL/SQL Datatypes*

In the following example, a cursor is declared to retrieve a record from the RADIUS_VALS table. RADIUS_VALS is a table with one column, named RADIUS, that holds radius values to be used in these examples. The cursor is declared in the Declarations section, and a variable named **rad_val** is declared with a datatype based on the cursor's results.

NOTE
For this example, the table RADIUS_VALS contains a single row with a **radius** *value of 3.*

```
declare
    pi       constant number(9,7) := 3.1415927;
    area     number(14,2);
    cursor rad_cursor is
        select * from radius_vals;
    rad_val rad_cursor%rowtype;
begin
  open rad_cursor;
  fetch rad_cursor into rad_val;
    area := pi*power(rad_val.radius,2);
    insert into areas values (rad_val.radius, area);
  close rad_cursor;
end;
/
```

In the first part of the Declarations section, the **pi** and **area** variables are defined, as they were in the examples earlier in this chapter. The **radius** variable is not defined; instead, a cursor named **rad_cursor** is defined. The cursor definition consists of a cursor name (**rad_cursor**) and a query (**select * from radius_vals;**). A cursor holds the results of a query for processing by other commands within the PL/SQL block:

```
declare
    pi       constant number(9,7) := 3.1415927;
    area     number(14,2);
    cursor rad_cursor is
        select * from radius_vals;
```

A final declaration creates a variable whose structure is anchored by the cursor's result set:

```
    rad_val rad_cursor%rowtype;
```

The **rad_val** variable can reference each column of the query's result set. In this example, the query only returns a single column, but if the table contained multiple columns, you could reference all of them via the **rad_val** variable.

In addition to the %ROWTYPE declaration, you can use the %TYPE declaration to inherit datatype information. If you use the %ROWTYPE declaration, the variable inherits the column and datatype information for all the columns in the cursor's result set. If you use the %TYPE declaration, the variable only inherits the definition of the column used to define it. You can even base %TYPE definitions on cursors, as shown in the following example:

```
    cursor rad_cursor is
        select * from radius_vals;
```

```
rad_val rad_cursor%rowtype;
rad_val_radius  rad_val.radius%type;
```

In the preceding listing, the **rad_val** variable inherits the datatypes of the result set of the **rad_cursor** cursor. The **rad_val_radius** variable inherits the datatype of the RADIUS column within the **rad_val** variable.

The advantage of datatype anchoring using %ROWTYPE and %TYPE definitions is that it makes the datatype definitions in your PL/SQL code independent of the underlying data structures. If the RADIUS_VALS RADIUS column is changed from a NUMBER(5) datatype to a NUMBER(4,2) datatype, you do not need to modify your PL/SQL code; the datatype assigned to the associated variables will be determined dynamically at runtime.

Executable Commands Section

In the Executable Commands section, you manipulate the variables and cursors declared in the Declarations section of your PL/SQL block. The Executable Commands section always starts with the keyword **begin**. The following listing repeats the first PL/SQL block example from the Declarations section: The area of a circle is calculated, and the results are inserted into the AREAS table:

```
declare
   pi      constant number(9,7) := 3.1415927;
   radius integer(5);
   area    number(14,2);
begin
   radius := 3;
   area := pi*power(radius,2);
   insert into areas values (radius, area);
end;
/
```

In the preceding listing, the Executable Commands section is

```
begin
   radius := 3;
   area := pi*power(radius,2);
   insert into areas values (radius, area);
end;
```

Following the **begin** keyword, the PL/SQL block's work begins. First, a value is assigned to the **radius** variable, and the **radius** variable and the **pi** constant value are used to determine the value of the **area** variable. The **radius** and **area** values are then inserted into the AREAS table.

The Executable Commands section of the PL/SQL block may contain commands that execute the cursors declared in the Declarations section. In the following example (from the "Declarations Section" section of this chapter), the Executable Commands section features several commands that reference the **rad_cursor** cursor:

```
declare
   pi      constant number(9,7) := 3.1415927;
   area    number(14,2);
```

```
   cursor rad_cursor is
       select * from radius_vals;
   rad_val rad_cursor%rowtype;
begin
  open rad_cursor;
  fetch rad_cursor into rad_val;
    area := pi*power(rad_val.radius,2);
    insert into areas values (rad_val.radius, area);
  close rad_cursor;
end;
/
```

The first command involving the cursor is the **open** command:

```
open rad_cursor;
```

When the **rad_cursor** cursor is **open**ed, the query declared for that cursor is executed and the records to be returned are identified. Next, records are **fetch**ed from the cursor:

```
fetch rad_cursor into rad_val;
```

In the Declarations section, the **rad_val** variable is declared to anchor its datatypes to the **rad_cursor** cursor:

```
cursor rad_cursor is
        select * from radius_vals;
   rad_val rad_cursor%rowtype;
```

When you **fetch** a record from the cursor into the **rad_val** variable, you can still address each column value selected via the cursor's query. When the cursor's data is no longer needed, you can **close** the cursor, as shown in the following listing:

```
close rad_cursor;
```

The Executable Commands section may contain conditional logic, such as **if** commands and loops. In the following sections, you will see examples of each of the major types of flow-control operations permitted in PL/SQL. You can use the flow-control operations to alter the manner in which the fetched records and executable commands are managed.

Conditional Logic

Within PL/SQL, you can use **if**, **else**, **elsif**, **continue**, and **case** commands to control the flow of commands within the Executable Commands section. The formats of the **if** clauses are shown in the following listing:

```
if   <some condition>
  then  <some command>
elsif  <some condition>
  then  <some command>
else  <some command>
end if;
```

You can nest **if** conditions within each other, as shown in the following listing:

```
if    <some condition>
  then
    if   <some condition>
      then   <some command>
    end if;
  else   <some command>
  end if;
```

By nesting **if** conditions, you can quickly develop complex logic flows within your Executable Commands section. When nesting **if** conditions, make sure you are not making the flow control more complex than it needs to be; always check to see whether logical conditions can be combined into simpler expressions.

Let's modify the "area of a circle" example used in the previous section to include conditional logic. In the following listing, the Executable Commands section of the PL/SQL block has been modified to include **if** and **then** commands:

```
declare
  pi       constant number(9,7) := 3.1415927;
  area     number(14,2);
  cursor rad_cursor is
      select * from radius_vals;
  rad_val rad_cursor%rowtype;
begin
  open rad_cursor;
  fetch rad_cursor into rad_val;
    area := pi*power(rad_val.radius,2);
    if   area > 30
      then
        insert into areas values (rad_val.radius, area);
    end if;
  close rad_cursor;
end;
/
```

In the preceding listing, an **if** condition controls the flow of commands within the Executable Commands section of the PL/SQL block. The flow-control commands are shown in the following listing:

```
    if   area > 30
      then
        insert into areas values (rad_val.radius, area);
    end if;
```

The flow-control commands in this example begin after the **area** variable's value has been determined. If the value is greater than 30, then a record is inserted into the AREAS table; if the value is less than 30, then no record is inserted into the table. You can use this sort of flow control to direct which of several SQL statements are to be executed, based on the conditions in your **if** clause.

The following listing shows the syntax for flow control involving SQL commands:

```
if  area>30
  then   <some command>
elsif  area<10
  then   <some command>
else   <some command>
end if;
```

The following are examples of the supported types of loops; then we'll look at using **case** commands for flow control.

Loops

You can use loops to process multiple records within a single PL/SQL block. PL/SQL supports three types of loops:

Simple loops	A loop that keeps repeating until an **exit** or **exit when** statement is reached within the loop
for loops	A loop that repeats a specified number of times
while loops	A loop that repeats while a condition is met

The following sections give examples of each type of loop. The loop examples use as their starting point the PL/SQL blocks seen previously in this chapter. You can use loops to process multiple records from a cursor.

Simple Loops

In the following listing, a simple loop generates multiple rows in the AREAS table. The loop is started by the **loop** keyword, and the **exit when** clause determines when the loop should be exited. An **end loop** clause identifies the end of the loop.

```
declare
  pi       constant number(9,7)  := 3.1415927;
  radius integer(5);
  area     number(14,2);
begin
  radius := 3;
  loop
    area := pi*power(radius,2);
      insert into areas values (radius, area);
    radius := radius+1;
    exit when area >100;
  end loop;
end;
/
```

The loop section of this example establishes the flow control for the commands in the Executable Commands section of the PL/SQL block. The steps within the loop are described in the following commented version of the **loop** commands:

```
loop
      /* Calculate the area, based on the radius value.    */
    area := pi*power(radius,2);
       /* Insert the current values into the AREAS table.   */
       insert into AREAS values (radius, area);
       /* Increment the radius value by 1.                  */
    radius := radius+1;
       /* Evaluate the last calculated area.  If the value  */
       /* exceeds 100, then exit.  Otherwise, repeat the    */
       /* loop using the new radius value.                  */
    exit when area >100;
       /* Signal the end of the loop.                       */
  end loop;
```

The loop should generate multiple entries in the AREAS table. The first record will be the record generated by a **radius** value of 3. Once an **area** value exceeds 100, no more records will be inserted into the AREAS table.

Sample output following the execution of the PL/SQL block is shown in the following listing:

```
select * from areas
order by radius;
```

RADIUS	AREA
3	28.27
4	50.27
5	78.54
6	113.1

Because the **area** value for a **radius** value of 6 exceeds 100, no further **radius** values are processed and the PL/SQL block completes.

Simple Cursor Loops

You can use the attributes of a cursor—such as whether any rows are left to be fetched—as the exit criteria for a loop. In the following example, a cursor is executed until no more rows are returned by the query. To determine the cursor's status, the cursor's attributes are checked. Cursors have four attributes you can use in your program:

%FOUND	A record can be fetched from the cursor.
%NOTFOUND	No more records can be fetched from the cursor.
%ISOPEN	The cursor has been opened.
%ROWCOUNT	The number of rows fetched from the cursor so far.

The %FOUND, %NOTFOUND, and %ISOPEN cursor attributes are Booleans; they are set to either TRUE or FALSE. Because they are Boolean attributes, you can evaluate their settings without explicitly matching them to values of TRUE or FALSE. For example, the following command causes an exit to occur when **rad_cursor%NOTFOUND** is TRUE:

```
exit when rad_cursor%notfound;
```

In the following listing, a simple loop is used to process multiple rows from a cursor:

```
declare
  pi       constant number(9,7)  := 3.1415927;
  area     number(14,2);
  cursor rad_cursor is
      select * from radius_vals;
  rad_val rad_cursor%rowtype;
begin
  open rad_cursor;
  loop
    fetch rad_cursor into rad_val;
    exit when rad_cursor%notfound;
    area := pi*power(rad_val.radius,2);
    insert into areas values (rad_val.radius, area);
  end loop;
  close rad_cursor;
end;
/
```

The loop section of the PL/SQL block uses values from the RADIUS_VALS table as its input. Instead of basing the exit criteria on the **area** value, the cursor's %NOTFOUND attribute is checked. If no more rows are found in the cursor, then %NOTFOUND is TRUE—and, therefore, you'll exit the loop. The commented version of the loop is shown in the following listing:

```
loop
      /*  Within the loop, fetch a record.         */
    fetch rad_cursor into rad_val;
      /*  If the fetch attempt reveals no more      */
      /*  records in the cursor, then exit the loop. */
    exit when rad_cursor%notfound;
      /*  If the fetch attempt returns a record,     */
      /*  then process the radius value and insert   */
      /*  a record into the AREAS table.             */
    area := pi*power(rad_val.radius,2);
    insert into areas values (rad_val.radius, area);
      /*  Signal the end of the loop.               */
  end loop;
```

When the preceding PL/SQL block is executed, the loop processes every record in the RADIUS_VALS table. So far, the RADIUS_VALS table only contains one record—a **radius** value of 3.

NOTE
*Prior to executing the PL/SQL block for this section, add two new **radius** values—4 and 10—to the RADIUS_VALS table.*

The following listing shows the addition of the new records to the RADIUS_VALS table:

```
insert into radius_vals values (4);
insert into radius_vals values (10);
commit;

select * from radius_vals
order by radius;

    RADIUS
----------
         3
         4
        10
```

Once the new records have been added to the RADIUS_VALS table, execute the PL/SQL block shown earlier in this section. The output of the PL/SQL block is shown in the following listing:

```
select * from areas
order by radius;

    RADIUS       AREA
---------- ----------
         3      28.27
         4      50.27
        10     314.16
```

The query of the AREAS table shows that every record in the RADIUS_VALS table was fetched from the cursor and processed. When there were no more records to process in the cursor, the query exited the loop and the PL/SQL block completed.

FOR Loops

A simple loop executes until an **exit** condition is met, whereas a **for** loop executes a specified number of times. An example of a **for** loop is shown in the following listing. The **for** loop's start is indicated by the keyword **for**, followed by the criteria used to determine when the processing is complete and the loop can be exited. Because the number of times the loop is executed is set when the loop is begun, an **exit** command isn't needed within the loop.

In the following example, the areas of circles are calculated based on **radius** values ranging from 1 through 7, inclusive.

```
delete from areas;

declare
   pi      constant number(9,7) := 3.1415927;
   radius integer(5);
   area    number(14,2);
begin
   for radius in 1..7 loop
      area := pi*power(radius,2);
```

```
      insert into areas values (radius, area);
   end loop;
end;
/
```

The steps involved in processing the loop are shown in the following commented listing:

```
   /*  Specify the criteria for the number of loop     */
   /*  executions.                                      */
for radius in 1..7 loop
   /*  Calculate the area using the current radius      */
   /*  value.                                           */
   area := pi*power(radius,2);
   /*  Insert the area and radius values into the AREAS */
   /*  table.                                           */
   insert into areas values (radius, area);
   /*  Signal the end of the loop.                      */
end loop;
```

Note that there is no line that says

```
radius := radius+1;
```

in the **for** loop. Because the specification of the loop specifies

```
for radius in 1..7 loop
```

the **radius** values are already specified. For each value, all the commands within the loop are executed (these commands can include other conditional logic, such as **if** conditions). Once the loop has completed processing a **radius** value, the limits on the **for** clause are checked, and either the next **radius** value is used or the loop execution is complete.

Sample output from the **for** loop execution is shown in the following listing:

```
select * from areas
order by radius;

    RADIUS        AREA
---------- ----------
         1        3.14
         2       12.57
         3       28.27
         4       50.27
         5       78.54
         6       113.1
         7      153.94

7 rows selected.
```

Cursor FOR Loops

Whereas a **for** loop executes a specified number of times, a Cursor **for** loop uses the results of a query to dynamically determine the number of times the loop is executed. In a Cursor **for** loop, the opening, fetching, and closing of cursors is performed implicitly; you do not need to explicitly specify these actions.

The following listing shows a Cursor **for** loop that queries the RADIUS_VALS table and inserts records into the AREAS table:

```
delete from areas;

declare
   pi      constant number(9,7) := 3.1415927;
   area    number(14,2);
   cursor rad_cursor is
       select * from radius_vals;
begin
   for rad_val in rad_cursor
     loop
        area := pi*power(rad_val.radius,2);
        insert into areas values (rad_val.radius, area);
     end loop;
end;
/
```

In a Cursor **for** loop, there is no **open** or **fetch** command. The command

```
for rad_val in rad_cursor
```

implicitly opens the **rad_cursor** cursor and fetches a value into the **rad_val** variable. When no more records are in the cursor, the query exits the loop and the cursor is closed. In a cursor **for** loop, you do not need a **close** command. Note that **rad_val** is not explicitly declared in the block.

The loop portion of the PL/SQL block is shown in the following listing, with comments to indicate the flow control. The loop is controlled by the existence of a fetchable record in the **rad_cursor** cursor. There is no need to check the cursor's %NOTFOUND attribute—that is automated via the Cursor **for** loop.

```
      /*  If a record can be fetched from the cursor,   */
      /*  then fetch it into the rad_val variable.  If   */
      /*  no rows can be fetched, then skip the loop.    */
   for rad_val in rad_cursor
      /*  Begin the loop commands.                       */
      loop
         /*  Calculate the area based on the radius value */
         /*  and insert a record into the AREAS table.    */
        area := pi*power(rad_val.radius,2);
         insert into areas values (rad_val.radius, area);
      /*  Signal the end of the loop commands.           */
      end loop;
```

Sample output is shown in the following listing; for this example, the RADIUS_VALS table has three records, with **radius** values of 3, 4, and 10:

```
select * from radius_vals
order by radius;
```

```
    RADIUS
----------
         3
         4
        10
```

The execution of the PL/SQL block with the Cursor **for** loop generates the following records in the AREAS table:

```
select * from areas
order by radius;
```

```
    RADIUS       AREA
---------- ----------
         3      28.27
         4      50.27
        10     314.16
```

WHILE Loops

A **while** loop is processed until an exit condition is met. Instead of the exit condition being specified via an **exit** command within the loop, the exit condition is specified in the **while** command that initiates the loop.

In the following listing, a **while** loop is created so multiple RADIUS values will be processed. If the current value of the **radius** variable meets the **while** condition in the loop's specification, then the loop's commands are processed. Once a RADIUS value fails the **while** condition in the loop's specification, the loop's execution is terminated:

```
delete from areas;

declare
  pi      constant number(9,7) := 3.1415927;
  radius integer(5);
  area    number(14,2);
begin
  radius := 3;
  while radius<=7
    loop
      area := pi*power(radius,2);
      insert into areas values (radius, area);
    radius := radius+1;
  end loop;
end;
/
```

The **while** loop is similar in structure to the simple loop because it terminates based on a variable's value. The following listing shows the steps involved in the loop, with embedded comments:

```
    /*  Set an initial value for the radius variable.    */
  radius := 3;
```

```
   /*  Establish the criteria for the termination of    */
   /*  the loop.  If the condition is met, execute the  */
   /*  commands within the loop.  If the condition is    */
   /*  not met, then terminate the loop.                 */
while radius<=7
    /*  Begin the commands to be executed.               */
   loop
      /*  Calculate the area based on the current       */
      /*  radius value and insert a record in the       */
      /*  AREAS table.                                   */
    area := pi*power(radius,2);
    insert into areas values (radius, area);
    /*  Set a new value for the radius variable.  The   */
    /*  new value of radius will be evaluated against   */
    /*  the termination criteria and the loop commands  */
    /*  will be executed for the new radius value or    */
    /*  the loop will terminate.                        */
    radius := radius+1;
    /*  Signal the end of the commands within the loop. */
   end loop;
```

When executed, the PL/SQL block in the previous listing generates records in the AREAS table. The output of the PL/SQL block is shown in the following listing:

```
select * from areas
order by radius;

    RADIUS        AREA
---------- ----------
         3       28.27
         4       50.27
         5       78.54
         6       113.1
         7      153.94
```

Because of the value assigned to the **radius** variable prior to the loop, the loop is forced to execute at least once. You should verify that your variable assignments meet the conditions used to limit the loop executions.

Using CONTINUE and CONTINUE WHEN Statements

You can use the **continue** statement within loops to exit the current iteration of the loop and transfer control to the next iteration. For example, if you iterate through a set of counter values, you can skip specific values without exiting the loop entirely. The two forms of the **continue** statement are **continue** and **continue when**.

The following listing shows how to use the **continue** statement. In this example, the loop starts with a value of 1 for the first iteration. When the **if** clause is evaluated, any value less than 5 triggers the **continue** statement, and the next iteration of the loop begins.

```
declare
  pi       constant number(9,7)  := 3.1415927;
```

```
   radius integer(5);
   area    number(14,2);
 begin
   radius := 1;
   loop
    if radius < 5 then
     continue;
    end if;
     area := pi*power(radius,2);
       insert into areas values (radius, area);
     radius := radius+1;
     exit when area >100;
   end loop;
 end;
 /
 select * from areas
 order by radius;

     RADIUS        AREA
 ----------   ----------
         5       78.54
         6       113.1
```

You can use the **continue when** statement within loops. The **when** portion provides the condition to be evaluated. If the condition is true, the current iteration of the loop will complete and control will pass to the next iteration. The following listing shows the **continue when** statement.

```
 declare
   pi       constant number(9,7) := 3.1415927;
   radius integer(5);
   area    number(14,2);
 begin
   radius := 1;
   loop
    continue when radius < 5;
     area := pi*power(radius,2);
       insert into areas values (radius, area);
     radius := radius+1;
     exit when area >100;
   end loop;
 end;
 /
```

You can use the **continue** statement to force the loop to process only even-numbered iterations (for which **mod(radius,2)=0**) or any custom condition you want to apply.

CASE Statements

You can use **case** statements to control the branching logic within your PL/SQL blocks. For example, you can use **case** statements to assign values conditionally or to transform values prior to inserting them. In the following example, **case** expressions use the **radius** values to determine which rows to insert into the AREAS table:

```
declare
   pi      constant number(9,7) := 3.1415927;
   area    number(14,2);
   cursor rad_cursor is
       select * from radius_vals;
   rad_val rad_cursor%rowtype;
begin
   open rad_cursor;
   loop
     fetch rad_cursor into rad_val;
     exit when rad_cursor%notfound;
     area := pi*power(rad_val.radius,2);
     case
       when rad_val.radius = 3
         then
           insert into areas values (rad_val.radius, area);
       when rad_val.radius = 4
         then
           insert into areas values (rad_val.radius, area);
       when rad_val.radius = 10
         then
           insert into areas values (0, 0);
       else raise case_not_found;
     end case;
   end loop;
   close rad_cursor;
end;
/
```

This block generates the following output. When the **radius** value is 10, the **case** clause inserts a row with the **radius** and **area** values both set to 0:

```
select * from areas;

    RADIUS       AREA
---------- ----------
         3      28.27
         4      50.27
         0          0
```

The keyword **case** begins the clause:

```
    case
      when rad_val.radius = 3
        then
          insert into areas values (rad_val.radius, area);
```

The **when** clauses are evaluated sequentially. The **else** keyword within the **case** clause works similarly to the **else** keyword within an **if-then** clause. If you omit the **else** keyword, PL/SQL adds the following implicit **else** clause:

```
else raise case_not_found;
```

The **end case** clause ends the **case** clause. The **case** clause is commonly used to translate lists of values to their descriptions, as in the case of the bookshelf category names. The following listing shows how CATEGORY_NAME values can be translated to other values as part of SQL commands:

```
case category_name
   when  'ADULTFIC' then 'Adult Fiction'
   when  'ADULTNF' then 'Adult Nonfiction'
   when  'ADULTREF' then 'Adult Reference'
   when  'CHILDRENFIC' then 'Children Fiction'
   when  'CHILDRENNF' then 'Children Nonfiction'
   when  'CHILDRENPIC' then 'Children Picturebook'
   else category_name
end
```

See Chapter 16 for examples of the **case**'s complex uses.

Exception Handling Section

When user-defined or system-related exceptions (errors) are encountered, the control of the PL/SQL block shifts to the Exception Handling section. Within the Exception Handling section, the **when** clause is used to evaluate which exception is to be "raised"—that is, executed.

If an exception is raised within the Executable Commands section of your PL/SQL block, the flow of commands immediately leaves the Executable Commands section and searches the Exception Handling section for an exception matching the error encountered. PL/SQL provides a set of system-defined exceptions and allows you to add your own exceptions. Examples of user-defined exceptions are shown in Chapters 34 and 35.

The Exception Handling section always begins with the keyword **exception**, and it precedes the **end** command that terminates the Executable Commands section of the PL/SQL block. The placement of the Exception Handling section within the PL/SQL block is shown in the following listing:

```
declare
   <declarations section>
begin
   <executable commands>
exception
   <exception handling>
end;
```

The Exception Handling section of a PL/SQL block is optional—none of the PL/SQL blocks shown previously in this chapter included an Exception Handling section. However, the examples shown in this chapter have been based on a very small set of known input values with very limited processing performed.

In the following listing, the simple loop for calculating the area of a circle is shown, with two modifications. A new variable named **some_variable** is declared in the Declarations section, and a calculation to determine the variable's value is created in the Executable Commands section.

```
declare
    pi       constant number(9,7) := 3.1415927;
    radius integer(5);
    area    number(14,2);
    some_variable    number(14,2);
begin
    radius := 3;
    loop
      some_variable := 1/(radius-4);
      area := pi*power(radius,2);
        insert into areas values (radius, area);
      radius := radius+1;
      exit when area >100;
    end loop;
end;
/
```

Because the calculation for **some_variable** involves division, you may encounter a situation in which the calculation attempts to divide by zero—an error condition. The first time through the loop, the **radius** variable (with an initial value of 3) is processed and a record is inserted into the AREAS table. The second time through the loop, the **radius** variable has a value of 4—and the calculation for **some_variable** encounters an error:

```
declare
*
ERROR at line 1:
ORA-01476: divisor is equal to zero
ORA-06512: at line 9
```

Because an error was encountered, the first row inserted into AREAS is rolled back, and the PL/SQL block terminates.

You can modify the processing of the error condition by adding an Exception Handling section to the PL/SQL block, as shown in the following listing:

```
delete from areas;

declare
    pi       constant number(9,7) := 3.1415927;
    radius integer(5);
    area    number(14,2);
    some_variable    number(14,2);
```

```
begin
  radius := 3;
  loop
    some_variable := 1/(radius-4);
    area := pi*power(radius,2);
      insert into areas values (radius, area);
    radius := radius+1;
    exit when area >100;
  end loop;
exception
  when zero_divide
    then insert into areas values (0,0);
end;
/
```

The Exception Handling section of the PL/SQL block is repeated in the following listing:

```
exception
  when zero_divide
    then insert into areas values (0,0);
```

When the PL/SQL block encounters an error, it scans the Exception Handling section for the defined exceptions. In this case, it finds the ZERO_DIVIDE exception, which is one of the system-defined exceptions available in PL/SQL. In addition to the system-defined exceptions and user-defined exceptions, you can use the **when others** clause to address all exceptions not defined within your Exception Handling section. The command within the Exception Handling section for the matching exception is executed and a row is inserted into the AREAS table. The output of the PL/SQL block is shown in the following listing:

```
select * from areas;

    RADIUS        AREA
---------- ----------
         3       28.27
         0           0
```

The output shows that the first RADIUS value (3) was processed and that the exception was encountered on the second pass through the loop.

> **NOTE**
> *Once an exception is encountered, you cannot return to your normal command-processing flow within the Executable Commands section. If you need to maintain control within the Executable Commands section, you should use **if** conditions to test for possible exceptions before they are encountered by the program, or create a nested block with its own local exception handling.*

The available system-defined exceptions are listed in the "Exception" entry in the Alphabetical Reference. Examples of user-defined exceptions are shown in Chapters 34 and 35.

See Chapter 36 for details on using dynamic PL/SQL, which allows for the dynamic creation of the commands executed within the PL/SQL block.

PL/SQL supports complex queries that use the most recent features in Oracle's SQL. For example, flashback version queries (see Chapter 29) and regular expression functions (see Chapter 8) are both supported within PL/SQL as of their introduction in Oracle Database 10g. See those chapters for details on the new features; they can be introduced into your PL/SQL and may simplify and enhance your processing capabilities.

CHAPTER
33

Online Application
Upgrades

A s business needs change, the applications that support them need to change as well. Oracle provides many ways to modify existing applications; you can use new and enhanced features introduced with Oracle 12*c* to modify your applications while maintaining the high availability demanded by application users.

In this chapter, you learn how to minimize the impact to your applications while supporting the need for changes. A number of these approaches are described in other chapters as well.

Highly Available Databases

If an application depends on the database being available, the database architecture must support high availability throughout its design. At the database level, this involves choosing from among many configuration options:

- *RAC databases,* where multiple instances access a single shared database, can provide transparent application failover in the event a node fails.

- *Replicated databases,* where separate databases serve as the "master" site for the data, provide full failover capability for both the database and the instance. Replicated databases may add complexity to your design as you decide how to resolve data-level conflicts among the separate databases.

- *Standby databases,* where one database is the primary database and a separate database serves as a secondary database, are available in case the primary fails.

These options all support high-availability requirements; the right choice for your environment depends on your specific application requirements. When you're evaluating high-availability options, the evaluation criteria are usually based on disaster scenarios, the amount of lost data, and the time required to recover. You should also consider the more mundane and more common scenario, however: the need to make a change to an existing database table.

In the RAC solution, there is only one table to be changed because the separate instances share the same database. Any action that creates a DDL lock on a table affects all instances.

In a replicated environment, the objects are usually kept closely in sync; any change to one environment must be matched by the same change in the replica. Outages for DDL changes in one database are typically accompanied by outages in the replica.

In a standby solution, the standby database can be an exact physical replica or it can be a logical standby database, with different objects than the primary database. Because of this architecture, you can use a standby database to implement rolling upgrades of your application objects—first changing them in one environment and then in the second, without taking a significant outage for your application. You need to work closely with your DBAs to configure and manage the standby environment to support this approach, but for applications that require high availability while undergoing maintenance, this architecture provides a significant benefit.

Standby databases are supported via a technology called Oracle Data Guard. Although the creation and configuration of Data Guard databases is a DBA task, developers should be aware of the architecture and features involved. For example, standby databases can be started in read-only mode to support users and then returned to standby mode. Changes to the primary database can be automatically relayed from the primary database to the standby databases with a guarantee of no data lost in the process. The standby database servers can be physically separate from the primary server.

In the following sections, you see how to configure an Oracle Data Guard environment, followed by several Oracle features that minimize downtime during object changes.

Oracle Data Guard Architecture

In a Data Guard implementation, a database running in ARCHIVELOG mode is designated as the primary database for an application. One or more standby databases, accessible via Oracle Net, provide for failover capabilities. Data Guard automatically transmits redo information to the standby databases, where it is applied. As a result, the standby databases are transactionally consistent. Depending on how you configure the redo application process, the standby databases may be in sync with the primary database or may lag behind it.

The redo log data is transferred to the standby databases automatically as defined via your initialization parameter settings. On the standby server, the redo log data is received and applied.

Physical vs. Logical Standby Databases

Two types of standby databases are supported: physical standbys and logical standbys. A *physical standby* database has the same structures as the primary database. A *logical standby* database may have different internal structures (such as additional indexes used for reporting). You synchronize a logical standby database with the primary by transforming the redo data into SQL statements that are executed against the standby database.

Physical and logical standby databases serve different purposes. A physical standby database is a block-for-block copy of the primary database, so it can be used for database backups in place of the primary database. During disaster recovery, the physical standby looks exactly like the primary database it replaces.

A logical standby database, because it supports additional database structures, can more easily be used to support specific reporting requirements that would otherwise burden the primary database. Additionally, rolling upgrades of primary and standby databases can be performed with minimal downtime when logical standbys are used. The type of standby to use depends on your needs; many environments start out using physical standby databases for disaster recovery and then add in other logical standby databases to support specific reporting and business requirements.

NOTE
The operating system and platform architecture on the primary and standby locations must be identical. The directory structures and operating system patch levels may differ, but you should minimize the differences to simplify administration and failover processes. If the standby is located on the same server as the primary, you must use a different directory structure for the two databases, and they cannot share an archive log directory.

Data Protection Modes

When you configure the primary and standby databases, you need to determine the level of data loss that is acceptable to the business. In the primary database, you define the archive log destination areas, at least one of which will refer to the remote site used by the standby database. The ASYNC, SYNC, ARCH, LGWR, NOAFFIRM, and AFFIRM attributes of the LOG_ARCHIVE_DEST_*n* parameter setting for the standby database will direct Oracle Data Guard to select among several operation modes, described next.

- In *maximum protection* (or "no data loss") mode, at least one standby location must be written to before a transaction commits in the primary database. The primary database shuts down if the standby database's log location is unavailable.

- In *maximum availability* mode, at least one standby location must be written to before a transaction commits in the primary database. If the standby location is not available, the primary database does not shut down. When the fault is corrected, the redo generated since the fault is transported and applied to the standby databases.

- In *maximum performance* mode (the default), transactions can commit before their redo information is sent to the standby locations. Commits in the primary database occur as soon as writes to the local online redo logs complete.

Once you have decided on the type of standby and data protection mode for your configuration, you can create your standby database.

Creating the Standby Database Configuration

You can use SQL*Plus, Oracle Enterprise Manager (OEM), or Data Guard–specific tools to configure and administer Data Guard configurations. The parameters you set depend on the configuration you choose.

If the primary and standby databases are on the same server, you need to set a value for the DB_UNIQUE_NAME initialization parameter. Because the directory structures for the two databases are different, you must either manually rename files or define values for the DB_FILE_NAME_CONVERT and LOG_FILE_NAME_CONVERT parameters in the standby database. You must set up unique service names for the primary and standby databases via the SERVICE_NAMES initialization parameter.

If the primary and standby databases are on separate servers, you can use the same directory structures for each, avoiding the need for filename conversion parameters. If you use a different directory structure for the database files, you need to define the values for the DB_FILE_NAME_CONVERT and LOG_FILE_NAME_CONVERT parameters in the standby database.

In physical standby databases, all the redo comes from the primary database. When physical standby databases are opened in read-only mode, no redo is generated. Oracle Data Guard does, however, use archived redo log files to support the replication of the data and SQL commands used to update the standby databases.

NOTE
For each standby database, you should create a standby redo log file to store redo data received from the primary database.

Creating Logical Standby Databases

Logical standby databases follow many of the same steps used to create physical standby databases. Because they rely on the reexecution of SQL commands, logical standby databases have greater restrictions on their use. If any of your tables in the primary database use the following datatypes, they will be skipped during the redo application process:

- BFILE
- ROWID
- UROWID

- User-defined datatypes
- Object types
- REFs
- Varying arrays
- Nested tables
- XMLtype

NOTE
Encrypted columns are not supported in a logical standby database.

Additionally, tables that use table compression and the schemas that are installed with the Oracle software are skipped during redo applications. The DBA_LOGSTDBY_UNSUPPORTED view lists the objects that are not supported for logical standby databases. The DBA_LOGSTDBY_SKIP view lists the schemas that will be skipped.

A logical standby database is not identical to the primary database. Each transaction that is executed in the logical standby database must be the logical equivalent of the transaction that was executed in the primary database. Therefore, you should ensure your tables have the proper constraints on them—primary keys, unique constraints, check constraints, and foreign keys—so the proper rows can be targeted for update in the logical standby database. You can query DBA_LOGSTDBY_NOT_UNIQUE to list tables that lack primary keys or unique constraints in the primary database.

Using Real-Time Apply

By default, redo data is not applied to a standby database until the standby redo log file is archived. When you use the real-time apply feature, redo data is applied to the standby database as it is received, thus reducing the time lag between the databases and potentially shortening the time required to fail over to the standby database.

To enable real-time apply in a physical standby database, execute the following command in the standby database:

```
alter database recover managed standby database
    using current logfile;
```

For a logical standby database, the command to use is

```
alter database start logical standby apply immediate;
```

The RECOVERY_MODE column of the V$ARCHIVE_DEST_STATUS view will have a value of MANAGED REAL-TIME APPLY if real-time apply has been enabled.

As shown earlier in this chapter, you can enable the redo application on a physical standby database via this command:

```
alter database recover managed standby database
    disconnect from session;
```

The DISCONNECT FROM SESSION clause allows the command to run in the background after you disconnect from your Oracle session. When you start a foreground session and issue the same command without the DISCONNECT FROM SESSION clause, control is not returned to the command prompt until the recovery is cancelled by another session. To stop the redo application in a physical standby database—whether in a background session or a foreground session—use the following command:

```
alter database recover managed standby database cancel;
```

For a logical standby database, the command to stop the log apply services is

```
alter database stop logical standby apply;
```

Managing Roles—Switchovers and Failovers

Each database that participates in a Data Guard configuration has a role—it is either a primary database or a standby database. At some point, those roles may need to change. For example, if a hardware failure occurs on the primary database's server, the primary database may fail over to the standby database. Depending on your configuration choices, you may experience some data loss during a failover.

A second type of role change is called a *switchover*. This occurs when the primary database switches roles with a standby database, and the standby becomes the new primary database. During a switchover, no data should be lost. Switchovers and failovers require manual intervention by a database administrator.

Switchovers

Switchovers are planned role changes, usually so maintenance activities can be performed on the primary database server. A standby database is chosen to act as the new primary database, the switchover occurs, and applications now write their data to the new primary database. At some later point in time, you can switch the databases back to their original roles.

NOTE
You can perform switchovers with either a logical standby database or a physical standby database; the physical standby database is the preferred option.

What if you have defined multiple standby databases? When one of the physical standby databases becomes the new primary database, the other standby databases must be able to receive their redo log data from the new primary database. In that configuration, you must define the LOG_ARCHIVE_DEST_*n* parameters so those standby sites receive data from the new primary database location.

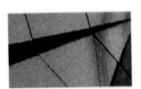

NOTE
Verify that the database that will become the new primary database is running in ARCHIVELOG mode.

The following sections detail the steps required to perform a switchover to a standby database. The standby database should be actively applying redo log data prior to the switchover because this will minimize the time required to complete the task.

Switchovers to Physical Standby Databases

Switchovers are initiated on the primary database and completed on the standby database. In this section, you learn the steps for performing a switchover to a physical standby database.

Begin by verifying that the primary database is capable of performing a switchover. Query V$DATABASE for the value of the SWITCHOVER_STATUS column:

```
select switchover_status from v$database;
```

If the SWITCHOVER_STATUS column's value is anything other than TO STANDBY, you cannot perform the switchover (usually due to a configuration or hardware issue). If the column's value is SESSIONS ACTIVE, you should terminate active user sessions. Valid values for the SWITCHOVER_STATUS column are shown in Table 33-1.

From within the primary database, you can initiate its transition to the physical standby database role with the following command:

```
alter database commit to switchover to physical standby;
```

As part of executing this command, Oracle backs up the current primary database's control file to a trace file. At this point, you should shut down the primary database and mount it:

```
shutdown immediate;
startup mount;
```

The primary database is prepared for the switchover; you should now go to the physical standby database that will serve as the new primary database.

In the physical standby database, check the switchover status in the V$DATABASE view; its status should be TO PRIMARY (see Table 33-1). You can now switch the physical standby database to the primary via the following command:

```
alter database commit to switchover to primary;
```

Shut down and start up the database, and it will complete its transition to the primary database role. After the database starts, force a log switch via the ALTER SYSTEM SWITCH LOGFILE command and then start the redo apply services on the standby databases if they were not already running in the background.

Switchovers to Logical Standby Databases

Switchovers are initiated on the primary database and completed on the standby database. This section describes the steps for performing a switchover to a logical standby database.

Begin by verifying that the primary database is capable of performing a switchover. Query V$DATABASE for the value of the SWITCHOVER_STATUS column:

```
select switchover_status from v$database;
```

For the switchover to complete, the status must be either TO STANDBY, TO LOGICAL STANDBY, or SESSIONS ACTIVE.

In the primary database, issue the following command to prepare the primary database for the switchover:

```
alter database prepare to switchover to logical standby;
```

SWITCHOVER_STATUS Value	Description
NOT ALLOWED	The current database is not a primary database with standby databases.
PREPARING DICTIONARY	This logical standby database is sending its redo data to a primary database and other standby databases to prepare for the switchover.
PREPARING SWITCHOVER	Used by logical standby configurations while redo data is being accepted for the switchover.
RECOVERY NEEDED	This standby database has not received the switchover request.
SESSIONS ACTIVE	There are active SQL sessions in the primary database; they must be disconnected before continuing.
SWITCHOVER PENDING	Valid for standby databases in which the primary database switchover request has been received but not processed.
SWITCHOVER LATENT	The switchover did not complete and went back to the primary database.
TO LOGICAL STANDBY	This primary database has received a complete dictionary from a logical standby database.
TO PRIMARY	This standby database can switch over to a primary database.
TO STANDBY	This primary database can switch over to a standby database.

TABLE 33-1. *SWITCHOVER_STATUS Values*

In the logical standby database, issue the following command:

```
alter database prepare to switchover to primary;
```

At this point, the logical standby database begins to transmit its redo data to the current primary database and to the other standby databases in the configuration. The redo data from the logical standby database is sent but is not applied at this point.

In the primary database, you must now verify that the dictionary data was received from the logical standby database. The SWITCHOVER_STATUS column value in V$DATABASE must read TO LOGICAL STANDBY in the primary database before you can continue to the next step. When that status value is shown in the primary database, switch the primary database to the logical standby role:

```
alter database commit to switchover to logical standby;
```

You do not need to shut down and restart the old primary database. You should now go back to the original logical standby database and verify its SWITCHOVER_STATUS value in

V$DATABASE (it should be TO PRIMARY). You can then complete the switchover; in the original logical standby database, issue the following command:

```
alter database commit to switchover to primary;
```

The original logical standby database is now the primary database. In the new primary database, perform a log switch:

```
alter system archive log current;
```

In the new logical standby database (the old primary database), start the redo apply process:

```
alter database start logical standby apply;
```

The switchover is now complete.

Making Low-Impact DDL Changes

If you only have one database available, you need to be careful when making changes to your tables and indexes. When you create or modify an object, you must first acquire a DDL lock on the object to prevent other types of access against the object. Because of this locking issue, avoid changing objects while users are accessing them. Furthermore, changing an object invalidates the stored procedures that reference the object.

Although you should ideally make changes to objects at times when users are not accessing them, your maintenance time windows may not be sufficiently large enough to support that requirement. Always plan for enough time to make the change, test the change, and recompile any objects that the change impacts. In the following sections, you'll learn methods for making changes in ways that minimize the size of the maintenance window needed.

Creating Virtual Columns

As of Oracle 11g, you can create virtual columns in tables rather than storing derived data. You may have a virtual column that is based on other values in the same row (adding two columns together, for instance). In Oracle 11g, you can also specify the function as part of the table definition, which allows you to index the virtual column and partition the table by it.

From a change perspective, the benefit to this feature is that you can avoid creating physical columns in the database. Rather than trying to add a column of derived data to a very large table, you can create a virtual column—and the data will be available to the users even though you have not executed a very time-consuming DDL command.

Consider the AUTHOR table:

```
create table author
(author_name  varchar2(50) primary key,
comments  varchar2(100));
```

When values are inserted into AUTHOR, they are inserted in uppercase:

```
insert into author values
('DIETRICH BONHOEFFER', 'German theologian, killed in a war camp');

insert into author values
('ROBERT BRETALL','Kierkegaard anthologist');
```

You can create an additional mixed-case column using the GENERATED ALWAYS clause to tell Oracle to create the virtual column:

```
create table author2
(author_name  varchar2(50) primary key,
comments  varchar2(100),
mixed_name varchar2(50)
generated always as
(initcap(author_name) ) virtual
);
```

The code used to create the virtual column can be complex, including CASE statements and other functions. Note that you do not have to create triggers or other mechanisms to populate the column; Oracle maintains it as a virtual value for each row in the table. The value is not physically stored with the table; it is generated when needed.

> **NOTE**
> *Attempts to provide a value for the virtual column during inserts will result in an error.*

You can create an index on the virtual column as if it were a standard column in the table. Additionally, you can partition the table based on this column (as described later in this chapter).

Altering Actively Used Tables

When you issue the ALTER TABLE command, Oracle attempts to acquire a DDL lock on the table. If anyone else is accessing the table at that time, your command will fail—you need to have exclusive access to the table while you are changing its structure. You may need to try repeatedly to execute your command to acquire the lock you need.

As of Oracle 11g, you can use the DDL lock timeout options to work around this problem. You can execute the ALTER SESSION command to set a value for the DDL_LOCK_TIMEOUT parameter, specifying the number of seconds during which Oracle should continually retry your command. The retry attempts will continue until the command is successful or the timeout limit is reached, whichever comes first.

To try your command for 60 seconds, issue the following command:

```
alter session set ddl_lock_timeout=60;
```

DBAs can enable this at the database level via the ALTER SYSTEM command, as shown here:

```
alter system set ddl_lock_timeout=60;
```

Adding NOT NULL Columns

In all recent versions of Oracle, you can add NOT NULL columns to tables that already contain rows. To do so, you must specify a default value for the new column. For very large tables, this can present a problem because millions of rows may need to be updated to contain the new column value. Oracle 11g automatically handles this in a way that avoids significant impacts to the users.

Let's consider again an attempt to add just the CONDITION column to the TROUBLE table:

```
alter table trouble add (condition    varchar2(9) not null);
```

If TROUBLE already has rows, the CONDITION column can't be added because the existing rows would have NULL values for it. The solution is to add a DEFAULT constraint for the CONDITION column:

```
alter table trouble add (condition    varchar2(9)
    default 'Sunny' not null);
```

Oracle now creates the new column, but it will *not* update the existing rows. If a user selects a row that has a NULL value in the CONDITION column, the default value is returned. Oracle's approach solves two problems: It lets you add a NOT NULL column, and it avoids having to update every existing row. In large tables, that can represent a significant savings in terms of the space required to support the transaction size.

Online Object Reorganizations

Several online options are available when moving an object online. For indexes, you can use the ALTER INDEX REBUILD ONLINE clause to modify an index while its base table is being accessed. You can use the ALTER INDEX REBUILD ONLINE command to move the partitions of an existing index.

For index-organized tables, you can use the MOVE ONLINE option of the ALTER TABLE command.

For partitioned tables, you can move partitions via the PARTITION clauses of the ALTER TABLE command.

You can perform online reorganizations of most types of tables via the DBMS_REDEFINITION package. The DBMS_REDEFINITION approach creates a replica of your table and creates triggers and logs to keep the replica in sync with the original table (as if it were a materialized view). The movement of the table data can take place any time you want; you can execute manual refreshes of the data in the replica. When you are ready to apply the change to your system, the FINISH_ REDEF_TABLE completes the redefinition process and the replica takes the place of the original table. Note that the original table still exists and still has all its original data until you manually drop it.

The redefinition process has five steps:

1. Verify the table can be rebuilt online.
2. Create an interim table and its indexes, grants, constraints, and triggers.
3. Start the redefinition.
4. Optionally sync the source/destination tables.
5. Abort or finish the redefinition.

The following sections show the redefinition of the PRACTICE.EMP table from the USERS to the USERS_DEST tablespace. In the process, we'll also partition the EMP table on the fly.

Verify the Table Can Be Rebuilt Online

To verify the table can be rebuilt online, execute the CAN_REDEF_TABLE procedure, providing the schema owner and table name as input:

```
execute dbms_redefinition.can_redef_table('PRACTICE','EMP');
```

If an error stack is reported, the first error listed will tell you what the problem is; later errors concerning the DBMS_REDEFINITION package can be ignored.

Create the Interim Table

What do you want EMP to look like in the new tablespace? Create an interim table to use during the redefinition process. To simplify matters, keep the column names and order the same as the source EMP table.

```
create table emp_dest
(empno     number(4) primary key,
 ename     varchar2(10),
 job       varchar2(9),
 mgr       number(4),
 hiredate  date,
 sal       number(7,2),
 comm      number(7,2),
 deptno    number(2))
partition by range (deptno)
(partition part1
      values less than ('30'),
 partition part2
      values less than (maxvalue))
tablespace users_dest;
```

In this example, the EMP_DEST table serves as the interim table during the redefinition. Once the process is complete, EMP_DEST replaces the old EMP table—and the only indexes, constraints, triggers, and grants available for EMP then will be those you create on EMP_DEST now. You can optionally create the indexes, triggers, grants, and constraints after the redefinition process completes, but creating them now avoids the need for DDL locks on active tables later.

You can execute the COPY_TABLE_DEPENDENTS procedure to create on the target (EMP_DEST) all the indexes, triggers, constraints, privileges, and statistics that exist on the source. The format for COPY_TABLE_DEPENDENTS is shown in the following listing:

```
DBMS_REDEFINITION.COPY_TABLE_DEPENDENTS(
    uname               IN  VARCHAR2,
    orig_table          IN  VARCHAR2,
    int_table           IN  VARCHAR2,
    copy_indexes        IN  PLS_INTEGER := 1,
    copy_triggers       IN  BOOLEAN     := TRUE,
    copy_constraints    IN  BOOLEAN     := TRUE,
    copy_privileges     IN  BOOLEAN     := TRUE,
    ignore_errors       IN  BOOLEAN     := FALSE,
    num_errors          OUT PLS_INTEGER,
    copy_statistics     IN  BOOLEAN     := FALSE,
    copy_mvlog          IN  BOOLEAN     := FALSE);
```

Start the Redefinition

The START_REDEF_TABLE procedure begins the redefinition. The EMP_DEST table will now be populated with the committed data in the EMP table, so the time and undo requirements for this step depend on the size of the EMP table. Pass the schema owner, old table name, and the interim table name as parameters:

```
execute dbms_redefinition.start_redef_table -
  ('PRACTICE','EMP','EMP_DEST');
```

If EMP_DEST had a different column list than EMP, that column list is passed as the fourth parameter to the START_REDEF_TABLE procedure. Once this procedure has completed, you can query EMP_DEST to verify its data contents.

Abort the Process (Optional)

If you need to abort the redefinition process at this point, use the ABORT_REDEF_TABLE procedure, with the schema owner, source table, and interim table as input parameters:

```
execute dbms_redefinition.abort_redef_table -
  ('PRACTICE','EMP','EMP_DEST');
```

After aborting the redefinition, you should consider truncating the interim (EMP_DEST) table as well.

Sync the Tables (Optional)

To conclude the redefinition process, Oracle syncs the data between the source and interim tables. To shorten the time required by that part of the process, you can sync the tables prior to the final step. This optional step allows you to instantiate the latest production data in the interim table, minimizing later impact on your online users.

To sync the source and interim tables, use the SYNC_INTERIM_TABLE procedure, with the schema owner, source table, and interim table as input parameters:

```
execute dbms_redefinition.sync_interim_table -
  ('PRACTICE','EMP','EMP_DEST');
```

Finish the Redefinition Process

To complete the redefinition process, execute the FINISH_REDEF_TABLE procedure, as shown in the following example. The input parameters are the owner, source table, and interim table names.

```
execute dbms_redefinition.finish_redef_table -
  ('PRACTICE','EMP','EMP_DEST');
```

Verify the Redefinition

Because the EMP table should now be partitioned and moved to USERS_DEST, you can verify its redefinition by querying DBA_TAB_PARTITIONS:

```
select table_name, tablespace_name, high_value
from dba_tab_partitions
```

```
where owner = 'PRACTICE';

TABLE_NAME      TABLESPACE_NAME HIGH_VALUE
------------    --------------- ----------
EMP             USERS_DEST      MAXVALUE
EMP             USERS_DEST      '30'
```

As shown in the preceding listing, the EMP table partitions both reside in the USERS_DEST tablespace. At this point, you should verify that the foreign keys on EMP are enabled, that all necessary grants are in place, that the indexes are all in place, and that all triggers are enabled.

Dropping a Column

You can use the table reorganization options to drop columns (because the source and target can have different column definitions). As an alternative, you can mark columns to have an "unused" state during regular usage, and then drop them when a longer maintenance window is available.

For example, you can mark the WIND column as unused:

```
alter table trouble set unused column wind;
```

Marking a column as "unused" does not release the space previously used by the column until you drop the unused columns:

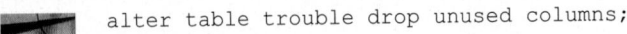

```
alter table trouble drop unused columns;
```

You can query USER_UNUSED_COL_TABS, ALL_UNUSED_COL_TABS, and DBA_UNUSED_COL_TABS to see all tables with columns marked as unused.

NOTE
Once you have marked a column as "unused," you cannot access that column.

You can drop multiple columns in a single command, as shown in the following listing:

```
alter table trouble drop (condition, wind);
```

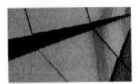

NOTE
When dropping multiple columns, you should not use the COLUMN keyword of the ALTER TABLE command; it causes a syntax error. The multiple column names must be enclosed in parentheses, as shown in the preceding listing.

If the dropped columns are part of primary keys or unique constraints, you will need to also use the CASCADE CONSTRAINTS clause as part of your ALTER TABLE command. If you drop a column that belongs to a primary key, Oracle will drop both the column and the primary key index.

CHAPTER
34

Triggers

A *trigger* defines an action the database should take when some database-related event occurs. Triggers may be used to supplement declarative referential integrity, enforce complex business rules, or audit changes to data. The code within a trigger, called the *trigger body,* is made up of PL/SQL blocks (see Chapter 32).

The execution of triggers is transparent to the user. Triggers are executed by the database when specific types of data manipulation commands are performed on specific tables. Such commands may include INSERTs, UPDATEs, and DELETEs. Updates of specific columns may also be used as triggering events. Triggering events may also include DDL commands and database events such as shutdowns and logins.

Because of their flexibility, triggers may supplement referential integrity; however, they should not be used to replace it. When enforcing the business rules in an application, you should first rely on the declarative referential integrity available with Oracle; use triggers to enforce rules that cannot be coded through referential integrity.

Required System Privileges

To create a trigger on a table, you must be able to alter that table. Therefore, you must either own the table, have the ALTER privilege for the table, or have the ALTER ANY TABLE system privilege. In addition, you must have the CREATE TRIGGER system privilege; to create triggers in another user's schema, you must have the CREATE ANY TRIGGER system privilege.

To alter a trigger, you must either own the trigger or have the ALTER ANY TRIGGER system privilege. You may also enable or disable triggers by altering the tables they are based on, which requires that you have either the ALTER privilege for that table or the ALTER ANY TABLE system privilege. For information on altering triggers, see "Enabling and Disabling Triggers," later in this chapter.

To create a trigger on a database-level event, you must have the ADMINISTER DATABASE TRIGGER system privilege.

Required Table Privileges

Triggers may reference tables other than the one that initiated the triggering event. For example, if you use triggers to audit changes to data in the BOOKSHELF table, then you may insert a row into a different table (say, BOOKSHELF_AUDIT) every time a row is changed in BOOKSHELF. To do this, you need to have privileges to insert into BOOKSHELF_AUDIT (to perform the triggered transaction).

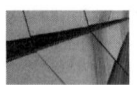

NOTE
The privileges needed for triggered transactions cannot come from roles; they must be granted directly to the trigger's creator.

Types of Triggers

A trigger's type is defined by the type of triggering transaction and by the level at which the trigger is executed. The following sections describe these classifications, along with relevant restrictions.

Row-Level Triggers

Row-level triggers execute once for each row affected by a DML statement. For the BOOKSHELF table auditing example described earlier, each row that is changed in the BOOKSHELF table may be processed by the trigger. Row-level triggers are the most common type of trigger; they are often used in data auditing applications. Row-level triggers are also useful for keeping distributed data in sync. Materialized views, which use internal row-level triggers for this purpose, are described in Chapter 26.

Row-level triggers are created using the FOR EACH ROW clause in the CREATE TRIGGER command. The syntax for triggers is shown in "Trigger Syntax," later in this chapter.

Statement-Level Triggers

Statement-level triggers execute once for each DML statement. For example, if a single INSERT statement inserts 500 rows into the BOOKSHELF table, a statement-level trigger on that table would be executed only once. Statement-level triggers, therefore, are not often used for data-related activities; they are normally used to enforce additional security measures on the types of actions that may be performed on a table.

Statement-level triggers are the default type of trigger created via the CREATE TRIGGER command. The syntax for triggers is shown in "Trigger Syntax," later in this chapter.

BEFORE and AFTER Triggers

Because triggers are executed by events, they may be set to occur immediately before or after those events. Because the events that execute triggers include database DML statements, triggers can be executed immediately before or after INSERTs, UPDATEs, and DELETEs. For database-level events, additional restrictions apply; you cannot trigger an event to occur before a login or startup takes place.

Within the trigger, you can reference the old and new values involved in the DML statement. The access required for the old and new data may determine which type of trigger you need. "Old" refers to the data as it existed prior to the DML statement; UPDATEs and DELETEs usually reference old values. "New" values are the data values that the DML statement creates (such as the columns in an inserted row).

If you need to set a column value in an inserted row via your trigger, then you need to use a BEFORE INSERT trigger to access the "new" values. Using an AFTER INSERT trigger would not allow you to set the inserted value since the row will already have been inserted into the table.

Row-level AFTER INSERT triggers are frequently used in auditing applications since they do not fire until the row has been modified. The row's successful modification implies that it has passed the referential integrity constraints defined for that table.

INSTEAD OF Triggers

You can use INSTEAD OF triggers to tell Oracle what to do *instead of* performing the actions that invoked the trigger. For example, you could use an INSTEAD OF trigger on a view to redirect INSERTs into a table or to UPDATE multiple tables that are part of a view. You can use INSTEAD OF triggers on either object views (see Chapter 38) or relational views.

For example, if a view involves a join of two tables, your ability to use the UPDATE command on rows in the view is limited. If you use an INSTEAD OF trigger, however, you can tell Oracle how to UPDATE, DELETE, or INSERT rows in the view's underlying tables when a user attempts to change values via the view. The code in the INSTEAD OF trigger is executed *in place of* the INSERT, UPDATE, or DELETE command you enter.

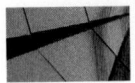

NOTE
You can access or change LOB data within BEFORE and INSTEAD OF triggers.

In this chapter, you will learn how to implement basic triggers. INSTEAD OF triggers, which were initially introduced to support object views, are described in Chapter 38.

Schema Triggers

You can create triggers on schema-level operations such as CREATE TABLE, ALTER TABLE, DROP TABLE, AUDIT, RENAME, TRUNCATE, and REVOKE. You can even create a BEFORE DDL trigger. For the most part, schema-level triggers provide two capabilities: preventing DDL operations and providing additional security monitoring when DDL operations occur.

Database-Level Triggers

You can create triggers to be fired on database events, including errors, logins, logoffs, shutdowns, and startups. You can use this type of trigger to automate database maintenance or auditing actions. Virtual Private Databases, as described in Chapter 20, rely on database-level triggers to establish session-context variable values.

Compound Triggers

As of Oracle 11g, you can combine multiple types of triggers in a single *compound* trigger. You can use a compound trigger to perform calculations and processing that would not be possible if the triggers were executed separately. For example, you may have an INSERT trigger that requires a calculation of an average value from the table you are inserting rows into. Ordinarily that would generate a "mutating table" error—the inserted row changes the table and, therefore, would change the average value. You can use compound triggers to share variable values among various triggered commands and avoid mutating table errors.

Trigger Syntax

The full syntax for the CREATE TRIGGER command is shown in the Alphabetical Reference section of this book. The following listing contains an abbreviated version of the command syntax:

```
CREATE [OR REPLACE] TRIGGER [schema .] trigger
{ BEFORE | AFTER | INSTEAD OF }
{ dml_event_clause
| { ddl_event [OR ddl_event]...
  | database_event [OR database_event]...
  }
  ON { [schema .] schema | DATABASE }
}
[WHEN ( condition ) ]
{ pl/sql_block | call_procedure_statement }
```

The syntax options available depend on the type of trigger you're using. For example, a trigger on a DML event uses the *dml_event_clause*, which follows this syntax:

```
{ DELETE | INSERT | UPDATE [OF column [, column]...] }
[OR { DELETE | INSERT | UPDATE [OF column [, column]...] }]...
ON { [schema .] table | [NESTED TABLE nested_table_column OF]
[schema .] view }
[referencing_clause] [FOR EACH ROW]
```

Clearly, trigger designs have a great deal of flexibility. The BEFORE and AFTER keywords indicate whether the trigger should be executed before or after the triggering event. If the INSTEAD OF clause is used, the trigger's code is executed instead of the event that caused the trigger to be invoked. The DELETE, INSERT, and UPDATE keywords (the last of which may include a column list) indicate the type of data manipulation that will constitute a triggering event. When referring to the old and new column values, you can use the defaults ("old" and "new"), or you can use the REFERENCING clause to specify other names.

When you use the FOR EACH ROW clause, the trigger will be a row-level trigger; otherwise, it will be a statement-level trigger. Use the WHEN clause to further restrict when the trigger is executed. The restrictions enforced in the WHEN clause may include checks of old and new data values.

For example, suppose we want to track any changes to the RATING value in the BOOKSHELF table whenever RATING values are lowered. First, we create a table that will store the audit rows:

```
drop table bookshelf_audit;
create table bookshelf_audit
(title          varchar2(100),
publisher       varchar2(20),
category_name   varchar2(20),
old_rating      varchar2(2),
new_rating      varchar2(2),
audit_date      date);
```

The following row-level BEFORE UPDATE trigger will be executed only if the RATING value is lowered. This example also illustrates the use of the NEW keyword, which refers to the new value of the column, and the OLD keyword, which refers to the old value of the column.

```
create or replace trigger bookshelf_bef_upd_row
before update on bookshelf
for each row
when (new.rating < old.rating)
begin
  insert into bookshelf_audit
    (title, publisher, category_name,
     old_rating, new_rating, audit_date)
  values
    (:old.title, :old.publisher, :old.category_name,
     :old.rating, :new.rating, sysdate);
end;
/
```

Breaking this CREATE TRIGGER command into its components makes it easier to understand. First, the trigger is named:

```
create or replace trigger bookshelf_bef_upd_row
```

The name of the trigger contains the name of the table it acts on and the type of trigger it is. (See "Naming Triggers," later in this chapter, for information on naming conventions.)

This trigger applies to the BOOKSHELF table; it will be executed before UPDATE transactions have been committed to the database:

```
before update on bookshelf
```

Because the FOR EACH ROW clause is used, the trigger applies to each row changed by the UPDATE statement. If this clause is not used, then the trigger executes at the statement level:

```
for each row
```

The WHEN clause adds further criteria to the triggering condition. The triggering event not only must be an UPDATE of the BOOKSHELF table, but also must reflect a lowering of the RATING value:

```
when (new.rating < old.rating)
```

The PL/SQL code shown in the following listing is the trigger body. The commands shown here are to be executed for every UPDATE of the BOOKSHELF table that passes the WHEN condition. For this to succeed, the BOOKSHELF_AUDIT table must exist, and the owner of the trigger must have been granted privileges (directly, not via roles) on that table. This example INSERTs the old values from the BOOKSHELF row into the BOOKSHELF_AUDIT table before the BOOKSHELF row is updated.

```
begin
   insert into bookshelf_audit
     (title, publisher, category_name,
      old_rating, new_rating, audit_date)
   values
     (:old.title, :old.publisher, :old.category_name,
      :old.rating, :new.rating, sysdate);
end;
```

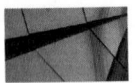

NOTE
When the NEW and OLD keywords are referenced in the PL/SQL block, they are preceded by colons (:).

This example is typical of auditing triggers. The auditing activity is completely transparent to the user who performs the UPDATE of the BOOKSHELF table. However, the transaction against the BOOKSHELF table is dependent on the successful execution of the trigger.

Combining DML Trigger Types

Triggers for multiple INSERT, UPDATE, and DELETE commands on a table can be combined into a single trigger, provided they are all at the same level (row level or statement level). The following example shows a trigger that is executed whenever an INSERT or an UPDATE occurs. Several points (shown in bold) should stand out in this example:

- The UPDATE portion of the trigger occurs only when the RATING column's value is updated.

- An **if** clause is used within the PL/SQL block to determine which of the two commands invoked the trigger.

- The column to be changed is specified in the *dml_event_clause* instead of in the WHEN clause, as in prior examples.

```
drop trigger bookshelf_bef_upd_row;

create or replace trigger bookshelf_bef_upd_ins_row
before insert or update of rating on bookshelf
for each row
begin
 if inserting then
  insert into bookshelf_audit
   (title, publisher, category_name,
    new_rating, audit_date)
  values
   (:new.title, :new.publisher, :new.category_name,
    :new.rating, sysdate);
 else -- if not inserting then we are updating the rating
  insert into bookshelf_audit
   (title, publisher, category_name,
    old_rating, new_rating, audit_date)
  values
   (:old.title, :old.publisher, :old.category_name,
    :old.rating, :new.rating, sysdate);
 end if;
end;
/
```

Again, look at the trigger's component parts. First, it is named and identified as a BEFORE INSERT and BEFORE UPDATE (of RATING) trigger, executing FOR EACH ROW:

```
create or replace trigger bookshelf_bef_upd_ins_row
before insert or update of rating on bookshelf
for each row
```

The trigger body then follows. In the first part of the trigger body, shown in the following listing, the type of transaction is checked via an **if** clause. Valid transaction types are **inserting**, **deleting**, and **updating**. In this case, the trigger checks to see if the row is being inserted into the BOOKSHELF table. If it is, then the first part of the trigger body is executed. The **inserting** portion of the trigger body inserts the new values of the row into the BOOKSHELF_AUDIT table.

```
begin
 if inserting then
  insert into bookshelf_audit
```

```
    (title, publisher, category_name,
     new_rating, audit_date)
  values
    (:new.title, :new.publisher, :new.category_name,
     :new.rating, sysdate);
```

Other transaction types can then be checked. In this example, because the trigger executes, the transaction is either an INSERT or an UPDATE of the RATING column's value. Because the **if** clause in the first half of the trigger body checks for INSERTs, and the trigger is only executed for INSERTs and UPDATEs, the only conditions that should execute the second half of the trigger body are UPDATEs of the RATING column. Therefore, no additional **if** clauses are necessary to determine the DML event type. This portion of the trigger body is the same as in the previous example: Prior to being updated, the old values in the row are written to the BOOKSHELF_AUDIT table.

```
  else -- if not inserting then we are updating the rating
    insert into bookshelf_audit
      (title, publisher, category_name,
       old_rating, new_rating, audit_date)
    values
      (:old.title, :old.publisher, :old.category_name,
       :old.rating, :new.rating, sysdate);
```

Combining trigger types in this manner may help you to coordinate trigger development among multiple developers because it consolidates all the database events that depend on a single table.

Setting Inserted Values

You may use triggers to set column values during INSERTs and UPDATEs. The previous examples in this chapter set the BOOKSHELF_AUDIT.AUDIT_DATE value to the result of the SYSDATE function. You may also use UPDATEs to support different application needs, such as storing an uppercase version of a value along with the mixed-case version entered by users. In that case, you may have partially denormalized your table to include a column for the derived data. Storing this data in an uppercase format (for this example, in the column UPPER_NAME) allows you to display data to the users in its natural format while using the uppercase column during queries.

Because the uppercase version of the value is derived data, it may become out of sync with the user-entered column. Unless your application supplies a value for the uppercase version during INSERTs, that column's value will be NULL when a new row is entered.

To avoid this synchronization problem, you can use a table-level trigger. Put a BEFORE INSERT and a BEFORE UPDATE trigger on the table; they will act at the row level. As shown in the following listing, this approach can set a new value for UPPER_NAME every time the NAME column's value is changed in BOOKSHELF_CHECKOUT:

```
alter table bookshelf_checkout add (upper_name varchar2(25));

create or replace trigger bookshelf_checkout_bui_row
before insert or update of name on bookshelf_checkout
for each row
begin
```

```
  :new.upper_name := upper(:new.name);
end;
/
```

In this example, the trigger body determines the value for UPPER_NAME by using the UPPER function on the NAME column. This trigger is executed every time a row is inserted into BOOKSHELF_CHECKOUT and every time the NAME column is updated. The NAME and UPPER_NAME columns are thus kept in sync.

Maintaining Duplicated Data

The method of setting values via triggers, shown in the preceding section, can be combined with the remote data access methods described in Chapter 25. As with materialized views, you may replicate all or some of the rows in a table.

For example, you may want to create and maintain a second copy of your application's audit log. By doing so, you safeguard against a single application's erasing the audit log rows created by multiple applications. Duplicate audit logs are frequently used in security monitoring.

Consider the BOOKSHELF_AUDIT table used in the examples in this chapter. A second table, BOOKSHELF_AUDIT_DUP, could be created, possibly in a remote database. For this example, assume you can use a database link called AUDIT_LINK to connect the user to the database in which BOOKSHELF_AUDIT_DUP resides (refer to Chapter 25 for details on database links).

```
drop table bookshelf_audit_dup;
create table bookshelf_audit_dup
(title        varchar2(100),
publisher     varchar2(20),
category_name varchar2(20),
old_rating    varchar2(2),
new_rating    varchar2(2),
audit_date    date);
```

To automate populating the BOOKSHELF_AUDIT_DUP table, place the following trigger on the BOOKSHELF_AUDIT table:

```
create or replace trigger bookshelf_audit_aft_ins_row
after insert on bookshelf_audit
for each row
begin
  insert into bookshelf_audit_dup@audit_link
    (title, publisher, category_name,
     new_rating, audit_date)
    values (:new.title, :new.publisher, :new.category_name,
      :new.new_rating, :new.audit_date);
end;
/
```

As the trigger header shows, this trigger executes for each row that is inserted into the BOOKSHELF_AUDIT table. It inserts a single row into the BOOKSHELF_AUDIT_DUP table in the database defined by the AUDIT_LINK database link. AUDIT_LINK may point to a database located on a remote server. If there is any problem with the remote INSERT initiated via the trigger, the local INSERT will fail.

TIP
*For asynchronous replication requirements, consider using
materialized views instead (see Chapter 26).*

You can see the actions of these triggers by inserting a row into BOOKSHELF:

```
insert into bookshelf
(title, publisher, category_name, rating) values
('Harry Potter And The Chamber Of Secrets',
'Scholastic','CHILDRENFIC','4');
```

```
1 row created.
```

```
select title from bookshelf_audit;
```

```
TITLE
--------------------------------------------------
Harry Potter And The Chamber Of Secrets
```

```
select title from bookshelf_audit_dup;
```

```
TITLE
--------------------------------------------------
Harry Potter And The Chamber Of Secrets
```

Customizing Error Conditions

Within a single trigger, you may establish different error conditions. For each of the error
conditions you define, you may select an error message that appears when the error occurs. The
error numbers and messages that are displayed to the user are set via the RAISE_APPLICATION_
ERROR procedure, which may be called from within any trigger.

The following example shows a statement-level BEFORE DELETE trigger on the BOOKSHELF
table. When a user attempts to DELETE a row from the BOOKSHELF table, this trigger is executed
and checks two system conditions: that the day of the week is neither Saturday nor Sunday, and
that the Oracle username of the account performing the DELETE begins with the letters "LIB." The
trigger's components are described following the listing.

```
create or replace trigger bookshelf_bef_del
before delete on bookshelf
declare
    weekend_error exception;
    not_library_user exception;
begin
if to_char(sysdate,'DY') = 'SAT' or
    to_char(sysdate,'DY') = 'SUN' then
    raise weekend_error;
```

```
end if;
if substr(user,1,3) <> 'LIB' then
   raise not_library_user;
end if;
exception
  when weekend_error then
     raise_application_error (-20001,
      'Deletions not allowed on weekends');
  when not_library_user then
     RAISE_APPLICATION_ERROR (-20002,
      'Deletions only allowed by Library users');
end;
/
```

The header of the trigger defines it as a statement-level BEFORE DELETE trigger:

```
create or replace trigger bookshelf_bef_del
before delete on bookshelf
```

This trigger contains no WHEN clauses, so the trigger body is executed for all DELETEs.

The next portion of the trigger declares the names of the two exceptions that are defined within this trigger:

```
declare
   weekend_error exception;
   not_library_user exception;
```

The first part of the trigger body contains an **if** clause that uses the TO_CHAR function on the SYSDATE function. If the current day is either Saturday or Sunday, then the WEEKEND_ERROR error condition is raised. This error condition, called an *exception,* must be defined within the trigger body.

```
begin
if to_char(sysdate,'DY') = 'SAT' or 'SAT' or
   to_char(sysdate,'DY') = 'SUN' then
   raise weekend_error;
end if;
```

A second **if** clause checks the USER pseudo-column to see if its first three letters are "LIB." If the username does not begin with "LIB," then the NOT_LIBRARY_USER exception is raised. In this example, the <> operator is used; this is equivalent to ! = (meaning "not equals").

```
if substr(user,1,3) <> 'LIB' then
   raise not_library_user;
end if;
```

The final portion of the trigger body tells the trigger how to handle the exceptions. It begins with the keyword EXCEPTION, followed by a WHEN clause for each of the exceptions. Each of the exceptions in this trigger calls the RAISE_APPLICATION_ERROR procedure, which takes two input parameters: the error number (which must be between –20001 and –20999) and the error message to display. In this example, two different error messages are defined, one for each of the defined exceptions:

```
exception
   when weekend_error then
      raise_application_error (-20001,
       'Deletions not allowed on weekends');
   when not_library_user then
      raise_application_error (-20002,
       'Deletions only allowed by Library users');
```

The use of the RAISE_APPLICATION_ERROR procedure gives you great flexibility in managing the error conditions that may be encountered within your trigger. For a further description of procedures, see Chapter 35.

NOTE
The exceptions are still raised even if the DELETE operations find no rows to delete.

When a non-"LIB" user attempts to delete a row from BOOKSHELF on a weekday, here is the result:

```
delete from bookshelf
where title = 'My Ledger';

delete from BOOKSHELF
             *
ERROR at line 1:
ORA-20002: Deletions only allowed by Library users
ORA-06512: at "PRACTICE.BOOKSHELF_BEF_DEL", line 17
ORA-04088: error during execution of trigger 'PRACTICE.BOOKSHELF_BEF_DEL'
```

If you attempt to delete a row on a Saturday or Sunday, the ORA-20001 error is returned instead. As soon as an exception is encountered, Oracle leaves the main executable commands section of the trigger and processes the exception. You will only see the first exception encountered.

Calling Procedures Within Triggers

Rather than creating a large block of code within a trigger body, you can save the code as a stored procedure and call the procedure from within the trigger, by using the **call** command. For example, if you create an INSERT_BOOKSHELF_AUDIT_DUP procedure that inserts rows into BOOKSHELF_AUDIT_DUP, you can call it from a trigger on the BOOKSHELF_AUDIT table, as shown in the following listing:

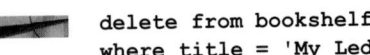

```
create or replace trigger bookshelf_aft_ins_row
after insert on bookshelf_audit
for each row
begin
   call insert_bookshelf_audit_dup(:new.title, :new.publisher,
```

```
      :new.category_name, :new.old_rating, :new.new_rating,
      :new.audit_date);
end;
/
```

Naming Triggers

The name of a trigger should clearly indicate the table it applies to, the DML commands that trigger it, its before/after status, and whether it is a row-level or statement-level trigger. Because a trigger name cannot exceed 30 characters in length, you need to use a standard set of abbreviations when naming. In general, the trigger name should include as much of the table name as possible. Thus, when creating a BEFORE UPDATE, row-level trigger on a table named BOOKSHELF_CHECKOUT, you should not name the trigger BEFORE_UPDATE_ROW_LEVEL_BC. A better name would be BOOKSHELF_CHECKOUT_BEF_UPD_ROW.

Creating DDL Event Triggers

You can create triggers that are executed when a DDL event occurs. If you are planning to use this feature solely for security purposes, you should investigate using the AUDIT command instead. For example, you can use a DDL event trigger to execute the trigger code for CREATE, ALTER, and DROP commands performed on a cluster, function, index, package, procedure, role, sequence, synonym, table, tablespace, trigger, type, user, or view. If you use the ON SCHEMA clause, the trigger executes for any new data dictionary objects created in your schema. The following example executes a procedure named INSERT_AUDIT_ROW whenever objects are created within your schema:

```
create or replace trigger create_db_object_audit
after create on schema
begin
   call insert_audit_row (ora_dict_obj_name);
end;
/
```

As shown in this example, you can reference system attributes such as the object name. The available attributes are listed in Table 34-1.

To protect the objects within a schema, you may want to create a trigger that is executed for each attempted DROP TABLE command. That trigger has to be a BEFORE DROP trigger:

```
create or replace trigger prevent_drop
   before drop on practice.schema
begin
   if ora_dict_obj_owner = 'PRACTICE'
      and ora_dict_obj_name like 'BOO%'
      and ora_dict_obj_type = 'TABLE'
   then
      raise_application_error (
         -20002, 'Operation not permitted.');
   end if;
end;
/
```

Attribute	Type	Description	Example
ora_client_ip_ address	VARCHAR2	Returns the IP address of the client in a LOGON event when the underlying protocol is TCP/IP.	```if (ora_sysevent = 'LOGON') then addr := ora_client_ip_address; end if;```
ora_database_ name	VARCHAR2(50)	Provides the database name.	```declare db_name varchar2(50); begin db_name := ora_database_name; end;```
ora_des_ encrypted_ password	VARCHAR2	Provides the DES encrypted password of the user being created or altered.	```if (ora_dict_obj_type = 'USER') then insert into event_table (ora_des_encrypted_password); end if;```
ora_dict_obj_ name	VARCHAR(30)	Sets name of the dictionary object on which the DDL operation occurred.	```insert into event_table ('Changed object is ' || ora_dict_obj_name');```
ora_dict_ obj_name_ list(name_list OUT ora_ name_list_t)	BINARY_ INTEGER	Returns the list of object names of objects being modified in the event.	```if (ora_sysevent = 'ASSOCIATE STATISTICS') then number_modified := ora_dict_obj_name_list (name_list); end if;```
ora_dict_obj_ owner	VARCHAR(30)	Sets owner of the dictionary object on which the DDL operation occurred.	```insert into event_table ('object owner is' || ora_dict_obj_owner');```
ora_dict_ obj_owner_ list(owner_list OUT ora_ name_list_t)	BINARY_ INTEGER	Returns the list of object owners of objects being modified in the event.	```if (ora_sysevent = 'ASSOCIATE STATISTICS') then number_of_modified_ objects := ora_dict_obj_owner_list(owner_list); end if;```
ora_dict_obj_ type	VARCHAR(20)	Sets type of dictionary object on which the DDL operation occurred.	```insert into event_table ('This object is a ' || ora_dict_obj_type);```
ora_grantee(user_list OUT ora_ name_list_t)	BINARY_ INTEGER	Returns the grantees of a grant event in the OUT parameter; returns the number of grantees in the return value.	```if (ora_sysevent = 'GRANT') then number_of_users := ora_grantee(user_list); end if;```

TABLE 34-1. *System-Defined Event Attributes*

Attribute	Type	Description	Example

ora_instance_ num	NUMBER	Provides instance number.	```if (ora_instance_num = 1)```
			``` then insert into event_table```
			```('1');```
			```end if;```

ora_is_alter_ column(column_ name IN VARCHAR2)	BOOLEAN	Returns TRUE if the specified column is altered.	```if (ora_sysevent = 'ALTER' and```
			``` ora_dict_obj_type = 'TABLE')```
			```then alter_column :=```
			``` ora_is_alter_column('FOO');```
			```end if;```

ora_is_ creating_ nested_table	BOOLEAN	Returns TRUE if the current event is creating a nested table.	```if (ora_sysevent = 'CREATE' and```
			``` ora_dict_obj_type = 'TABLE' and```
			``` ora_is_creating_nested_table)```
			```then insert into event_tab```
			```values ('A nested table is```
			```created');```
			```end if;```

ora_is_drop_ column(column_ name IN VARCHAR2)	BOOLEAN	Returns TRUE if the specified column is dropped.	```if (ora_sysevent = 'ALTER' and```
			``` ora_dict_obj_type = 'TABLE')```
			```then drop_column :=```
			``` ora_is_drop_column('FOO');```
			```end if;```

ora_is_ servererror	BOOLEAN	Returns TRUE if given error is on error stack, FALSE otherwise.	```if (ora_is_servererror(error_```
			``` number))```
			``` then insert into event_table```
			```('Server error!!');```
			```end if;```

ora_login_user	VARCHAR2(30)	Gives login username.	```select ora_login_user``` ```from dual;```

ora_partition_ pos	BINARY_ INTEGER	In an INSTEAD OF trigger for CREATE TABLE, provides the position within the SQL text where you could insert a PARTITION clause.	```-- Retrieve ora_sql_txt into```
			```-- sql_text variable first.```
			
			```n := ora_partition_pos;```
			```new_stmt :=```
			```substr(sql_text, 1, n-1) ||```
			```' ' || my_partition_clause ||```
			```' ' || substr(sql_text, n));```

ora_privilege_ list(privilege_ list OUT ora_ name_list_t)	BINARY_ INTEGER	Returns the list of privileges being granted by the grantee or the list of privileges revoked from the revokees in the OUT parameter; returns the number of privileges in the return value.	```if (ora_sysevent = 'GRANT' or```
			``` ora_sysevent = 'REVOKE')```
			```then number_of_privileges :=```
			``` ora_privilege_list(priv_list);```
			```end if;```

TABLE 34-1. *System-Defined Event Attributes* (continued)

Attribute	Type	Description	Example
ora_revokee (user_list OUT ora_name_ list_t)	BINARY_ INTEGER	Returns the revokees of a revoke event in the OUT parameter; returns the number of revokees in the return value.	```if (ora_sysevent = 'REVOKE') then number_of_users := ora_revokee(user_list);```
ora_server_ error	NUMBER	Given a position (1 for top of stack), returns the error number at that position on error stack.	```insert into event_table ('top stack error ' || ora_server_error(1));```
ora_server_ error_depth	BINARY_ INTEGER	Returns the total number of error messages on the error stack.	```n := ora_server_error_depth; -- This value is used with -- other functions such as -- ora_server_error```
ora_server_ error_msg (position in binary_ integer)	VARCHAR2	Given a position (1 for top of stack), returns the error message at that position on error stack.	```insert into event_table ('top stack error message' || ora_server_error_msg(1));```
ora_server_ error_num_ params (position in binary_ integer)	BINARY_ INTEGER	Given a position (1 for top of stack), returns the number of strings that have been substituted into the error message using a format like "%s".	```n := ora_server_error_num_params(1);```
ora_server_ error_param (position in binary_ integer, param in binary_ integer)	VARCHAR2	Given a position (1 for top of stack) and a parameter number, returns the matching "%s", "%d", and so on, substitution value in the error message.	```-- e.g. the 2nd %s in a message -- like "Expected %s, found %s" param := ora_server_error_param(1,2);```

TABLE 34-1. *System-Defined Event Attributes* (continued)

Attribute	Type	Description	Example

ora_sql_txt (sql_text outora_name_ list_t)	BINARY_ INTEGER	Returns the SQL text of the triggering statement in the OUT parameter. If the statement is long, it is broken up into multiple PL/SQL table elements. The function return value specifies how many elements are in the PL/SQL table.	`--...`
			`-- create table event_table`
			`create table event_table (col`
			`  varchar2(2030));`
			`--...`
			`declare`
			`sql_text dbms_standard.ora_name_list_t;`
			`n pls_integer;`
			`v_stmt varchar2(2000);`
			`begin`
			`n := ora_sql_txt(sql_text);`
			
			`for i in 1..n loop`
			`v_stmt := v_stmt || sql_text(i);`
			`end loop;`
			
			`insert into event_table values ('text of triggering statement: ' || v_stmt);`
			`end;`

ora_sysevent	VARCHAR2(20)	Provides system event firing the trigger: event name is same as that in the syntax.	`Insert into event_table` `(ora_sysevent);`

ora_with_ grant_option	BOOLEAN	Returns TRUE if the privileges are granted with grant option.	`if (ora_sysevent = 'GRANT' and`
			`    ora_with_grant_option = true)`
			`  then insert into event_table`
			`  ('with grant option');`
			`end if;`

space_error_ info(error_number OUT NUMBER, error_type OUT VARCHAR2, object_owner OUT VARCHAR2, table_space_ name OUT VARCHAR2, object_name OUT VARCHAR2, sub_object_ name OUT VARCHAR2)	BOOLEAN	Returns TRUE if the error is related to an out-of-space condition, and fills in the OUT parameters with information about the object that caused the error.	`if (space_error_info(eno,typ,owner,ts,obj,`
			`    subobj) =true)`
			`  then.put_line('The`
			`object ' || run out of space.');`
			`dbms_outputobj || ' owned by '`
			`|| owner || ' has`
			`end if;`

TABLE 34-1.   *System-Defined Event Attributes* (continued)

Note that the trigger references the event attributes within its **if** clauses. Attempting to drop a table in the PRACTICE schema whose name starts with "BOO" results in the following:

```
drop table bookshelf_audit_dup;
```

```
drop table bookshelf_audit_dup
*
ERROR at line 1:
ORA-00604: error occurred at recursive SQL level 1
ORA-20002: Operation not permitted.
ORA-06512: at line 6
```

You should verify if the intended DROP operation completed successfully.

You can use the RAISE_APPLICATION_ERROR procedure to further customize the error message displayed to the user.

Creating Database Event Triggers

Like DML events, database events can execute triggers. When a *database event* occurs (a shutdown, startup, or error), you can execute a trigger that references the attributes of the event (as with DDL events). You could use a database event trigger to perform system maintenance functions immediately after each database startup.

For example, the following trigger pins packages on each database startup. *Pinning packages* is an effective way to keep large PL/SQL objects in the shared memory pool, improve performance, and enhance database stability. This trigger, PIN_ON_STARTUP, runs each time the database is started. You should create this trigger while connected as a user with the ADMINISTER DATABASE TRIGGER privilege.

```
--  while connected as a user with the
--  ADMINISTER DATABASE TRIGGER system privilege:

create or replace trigger pin_on_startup
after startup on database
begin
   dbms_shared_pool.keep (
      'SYS.STANDARD', 'P');
end;
/
```

This example shows a simple trigger that will be executed immediately after a database startup. You can modify the list of packages in the trigger body to include those most used by your applications.

Startup and shutdown triggers can access the ORA_INSTANCE_NUM, ORA_DATABASE_NAME, ORA_LOGIN_USER, and ORA_SYSEVENT attributes listed in Table 34-1. See the Alphabetical Reference for the FULL CREATE TRIGGER command syntax.

Creating Compound Triggers

As of Oracle 11g, you can create a trigger that has a section for each of the following timing points: BEFORE statement, BEFORE each row, AFTER each row, and AFTER statement. The ability to combine statement-level and row-level trigger commands allows you to perform complex commands that share data at the statement and row level when performing processing. As a result, you can avoid mutating table errors and can improve performance.

A compound trigger has a section for each of its component areas (before and after statements and rows). All of those sections can access shared PL/SQL state information, such as variable values. When the triggering statement completes, that state information is no longer available.

To create a compound trigger, use the COMPOUND TRIGGER clause of the CREATE TRIGGER command, as shown in the following listing:

```
create or replace trigger bookshelf_audit_compound
for insert on bookshelf_audit
compound trigger
--declare and set variable values here
before statement is
-- statement level commands
end before statement;
after each row is
begin
 insert into bookshelf_audit_dup@audit_link
   (title, publisher, category_name,
    new_rating, audit_date)
   values (:new.title, :new.publisher, :new.category_name,
    :new.new_rating, :new.audit_date);
end;
/
```

You can declare variables that will be shared across all components of the compound trigger. For example, the BEFORE STATEMENT trigger could perform a query that calculates the average value for a column. You could then pass that value (via the shared variables) to an AFTER EACH ROW section of the same trigger.

NOTE
Compound triggers can only be triggered by DML statements.

To use a compound trigger, you must abide by the following restrictions:

■ The body of a compound trigger must be a compound trigger block.

■ A compound trigger must be a DML trigger.

■ A compound trigger must be defined on either a table or a view.

■ The declaration section cannot include **pragma autonomous_transaction**.

■ A compound trigger body cannot have an initialization block; therefore, it cannot have an exception section. This is not a problem, however, because the BEFORE STATEMENT section always executes exactly once before any other timing point section executes.

■ An exception that occurs in one section must be handled in that section. It cannot transfer control to another section.

■ If a section includes a **goto** statement, the target of the **goto** statement must be in the same section.

- **:old**, **:new**, and **:parent** cannot appear in the declaration section, the BEFORE STATEMENT section, or the AFTER STATEMENT section.
- Only the BEFORE EACH ROW section can change the value of **:new**.
- If, after the compound trigger fires, the triggering statement rolls back due to a DML exception
  - Local variables declared in the compound trigger sections are reinitialized, and any values computed thus far are lost.
  - Side effects from firing the compound trigger are not rolled back.
- The firing order of compound triggers is not guaranteed. Their firing can be interleaved with the firing of simple triggers.
- If compound triggers are ordered using the FOLLOWS option, and if the target of FOLLOWS does not contain the corresponding section as source code, the ordering is ignored.

Enabling and Disabling Triggers

Unlike declarative integrity constraints (such as NOT NULL and PRIMARY KEY), triggers do not necessarily affect all rows in a table. They only affect operations of the specified type and then only while the trigger is enabled. Any data created prior to a trigger's creation will not be affected by the trigger.

By default, a trigger is enabled when it is created. In certain situations, however, you may want to disable a trigger. The two most common reasons involve data loads. During large data loads, you may want to disable triggers that would execute during the load. Disabling the triggers during data loads may dramatically improve the load's performance. After the data has been loaded, you need to perform the data manipulation manually that the trigger would have performed had it been enabled during the data load.

The second data load–related reason for disabling a trigger occurs when a data load fails and has to be performed a second time. In such a case, the data load likely partially succeeded—and thus the trigger was executed for a portion of the rows loaded. During a subsequent load, the same rows would be inserted. Thus, the same trigger may be executed twice for the same INSERT operation (when that INSERT operation occurs during both loads). Depending on the nature of the operations and the triggers, this may not be desirable. If the trigger was enabled during the failed load, then you may need to disable it prior to the start of a second data-load process. After the data has been loaded, you need to perform the data manipulation manually that the trigger would have performed had it been enabled during the data load.

To enable a trigger, use the ALTER TRIGGER command with the ENABLE keyword. To use this command, you must either own the table or have the ALTER ANY TRIGGER system privilege. The following is a sample ALTER TRIGGER command :

```
alter trigger bookshelf_bef_upd_ins_row enable;
```

A second method of enabling triggers uses the ALTER TABLE command, with the ENABLE ALL TRIGGERS clause. You may not enable specific triggers with this command; you must use the ALTER TRIGGER command to do that. The following example shows the ALTER TABLE command:

```
alter table bookshelf enable all triggers;
```

To use the ALTER TABLE command, you must either own the table or have the ALTER ANY TABLE system privilege.

You can disable triggers using the same basic commands (requiring the same privileges) with modifications to their clauses. For the ALTER TRIGGER command, use the DISABLE clause:

```
alter trigger bookshelf_bef_upd_ins_row disable;
```

For the ALTER TABLE command, use the DISABLE ALL TRIGGERS clause:

```
alter table bookshelf disable all triggers;
```

You can manually compile triggers. Use the ALTER TRIGGER COMPILE command to manually compile existing triggers that have become invalid. Because triggers have dependencies, they can become invalid if an object the trigger depends on changes. The ALTER TRIGGER DEBUG command adds debugging breakpoints to the trigger code during trigger recompilation.

Replacing Triggers

The status of a trigger is the only portion that can be altered. To alter a trigger's body, the trigger must be re-created or replaced. When replacing a trigger, use the CREATE OR REPLACE TRIGGER command (refer to "Trigger Syntax" and the examples earlier in the chapter and in the Alphabetical Reference).

Dropping Triggers

Triggers may be dropped via the DROP TRIGGER command. To drop a trigger, you must either own the trigger or have the DROP ANY TRIGGER system privilege. An example of this command is shown here:

```
drop trigger bookshelf_bef_upd_ins_row;
```

CHAPTER
35

Procedures, Functions,
and Packages

S ophisticated business rules and application logic can be stored as *procedures* within Oracle. *Stored procedures*—groups of SQL, PL/SQL, and Java statements—enable you to move code that enforces business rules from your application to the database. As a result, the code will be stored once for use by multiple applications. Because Oracle supports stored procedures, the code within your applications can become more consistent and easier to maintain.

NOTE
For details on Java and its use in stored procedures, see Chapters 42, 43, and 44. This chapter focuses on PL/SQL procedures.

You may group procedures and other PL/SQL commands into *packages*. The following sections describe the implementation details and recommendations for packages, procedures, and *functions* (procedures that can return values to the user).

You may experience performance gains when using procedures for two reasons:

- The processing of complex business rules may be performed within the database—and therefore by the server. In client-server or three-tier applications, shifting complex processing from the application (on the client) to the database (on the server) may dramatically improve performance.

- Because the procedural code is stored within the database and is fairly static, you may also benefit from reusing the same queries within the database. The Shared SQL Area in the System Global Area (SGA) stores the parsed versions of the executed commands. Thus, the second time a procedure is executed, it can take advantage of the parsing that was previously performed, improving the performance of the procedure's execution.

In addition to these advantages, your application development efforts may also benefit. Business rules that are consolidated within the database no longer need to be written into each application, saving you time during application creation and simplifying the maintenance process.

Required System Privileges

To create a procedural object, you must have the CREATE PROCEDURE system privilege. If the procedural object is in another user's schema, then you must have the CREATE ANY PROCEDURE system privilege.

Once a procedural object has been created, it may be executed. When a procedural object is executed, it may rely on the table privileges of its owner or may rely on the privileges of the user who is executing it. When the procedure is created using the *definer's* rights, a user executing the procedure does not need to be granted access to the tables that the procedure accesses. If a procedure relies on the *invoker's* rights, the user must have access to all of the database objects accessed by the procedure. Unless stated otherwise, the examples in this chapter assume users are executing procedures under the owner's privileges.

To allow other users to execute your procedural object, GRANT them the EXECUTE privilege on that object, as shown in the following example:

```
grant execute on my_procedure to dora;
```

The user DORA can now execute the procedure named MY_PROCEDURE. If you do not GRANT the EXECUTE privilege to users, they must have the EXECUTE ANY PROCEDURE system privilege in order to execute the procedure.

When executed, procedures usually have variables passed to them. For example, a procedure that interacts with the BOOKSHELF table may accept as input a value for the TITLE column. In this example, we'll assume the procedure creates a new record in the BOOKSHELF table when a new book is received (from the list of books in the BOOK_ORDER table). This procedure can be called from any application within the database (provided the user calling the procedure has been granted the EXECUTE privilege for it).

The syntax used to execute a procedure depends on the environment from which the procedure is called. From within SQL*Plus, a procedure can be executed by using the EXECUTE command, followed by the procedure name. Any arguments to be passed to the procedure must be enclosed in parentheses following the procedure name, as shown in the following example (which uses a procedure called NEW_BOOK):

```
execute new_book('Once Removed');
```

The command executes the NEW_BOOK procedure, passing to it the value "Once Removed".

From within another procedure, function, package, or trigger, the procedure can be called without the EXECUTE command. If the NEW_BOOK procedure was called from a trigger on the BOOK_ORDER table, the body of that trigger may include the following command:

```
new_book(:new.title);
```

The NEW_BOOK procedure is executed using the new value of the TITLE column as its input. (See Chapter 34 for further information on the use of old and new values within triggers.)

To execute a procedure owned by another user, you must either create a synonym for that procedure or reference the owner's name during the execution, as shown in the following listing:

```
execute practice.new_book('Once Removed');
```

This command executes the NEW_BOOK procedure in the PRACTICE schema.

Alternatively, you could create a synonym for the procedure by using the following command:

```
create synonym new_book for practice.new_book;
```

The owner of that synonym would then no longer need to refer to the procedure's owner to execute the procedure. You could simply enter the command

```
execute new_book('Once Removed');
```

and the synonym would point to the proper procedure.

When you execute remote procedures, the name of a database link must be specified (see Chapter 25 for information on database links). The name of the database link must immediately follow the procedure's name and precede the variables, as shown in the following example:

```
execute new_book@remote_connect('Once Removed');
```

The command uses the REMOTE_CONNECT database link to access a procedure called NEW_BOOK in a remote database.

To make the location of the procedure transparent to the user, you may create a synonym for the remote procedure, as shown in the following example:

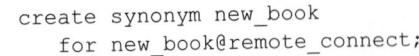

```
create synonym new_book
    for new_book@remote_connect;
```

Once this synonym has been created, the user may refer to the remote procedure by using the name of the synonym. Oracle assumes that all remote procedure calls involve updates in the remote database.

Required Table Privileges

Procedural objects may reference tables. For the objects to execute properly, the owner of the procedure, package, or function being executed must have privileges on the tables it uses. Unless you are using invoker rights, the user who is executing the procedural object does not need privileges on its underlying tables.

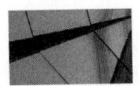

NOTE
The privileges needed for procedures, packages, and functions cannot come from roles; they must be granted directly to the owner of the procedure, package, or function.

Procedures vs. Functions

Procedures do not have to return a value to the caller. Functions can return a value to the caller, and functions can be directly referenced in queries. This value is returned through the use of the **return** keyword within the function. Examples of functions are shown in "CREATE FUNCTION Syntax," later in this chapter.

Procedures vs. Packages

Packages are groups of procedures, functions, variables, and SQL statements grouped together into a single unit. To execute a procedure within a package, you must first list the package name and then list the procedure name, as shown in the following example:

```
execute book_inventory.new_book('Once Removed');
```

Here, the NEW_BOOK procedure within the BOOK_INVENTORY package is executed.

Packages allow multiple procedures to use the same variables, constants, and cursors. Procedures within packages may be either available to the public (as is the NEW_BOOK procedure in the prior example) or private, in which case they are only accessible via commands from within the package (such as calls from other procedures). Examples of packages are shown in "CREATE PACKAGE Syntax," later in this chapter.

Packages may also include commands that are to be executed each time the package is called, regardless of the procedure or function called within the package. Thus, packages not only group procedures but also give you the ability to execute commands that are not procedure specific. See "CREATE PACKAGE Syntax," later in this chapter, for an example of code that is executed each time a package is called.

CREATE PROCEDURE Syntax

The full syntax for the CREATE PROCEDURE command is shown in the Alphabetical Reference. The brief syntax is

```
CREATE [OR REPLACE] PROCEDURE [schema.] procedure
[( argument [ IN | OUT | IN OUT ] [NOCOPY] datatype
  [, argument [ IN | OUT | IN OUT ] [NOCOPY] datatype]...
)]
[AUTHID { CURRENT_USER | DEFINER }]
{ IS | AS } { pl/sql_subprogram_body |
  LANGUAGE { JAVA NAME 'string'| C [NAME name] LIBRARY lib_name
}};
```

Both the header and the body of the procedure are created by this command.
The NEW_BOOK procedure is created by the command shown in the following listing:

```
create or replace procedure new_book (aTitle in varchar2,
    aPublisher in varchar2, aCategoryName in varchar2)
as
begin
    insert into bookshelf (title, publisher, category_name, rating)
      values (aTitle, aPublisher, aCategoryName, null);
    delete from book_order
      where title = aTitle;
end;
/
```

The NEW_BOOK procedure accepts a book's title, publisher, and category as its input. It can be called from any application. It inserts a record into the BOOKSHELF table, with a NULL value for the RATING column, and deletes the matching TITLE from the BOOK_ORDER table.

If a procedure already exists, you may replace it via the CREATE OR REPLACE PROCEDURE command. The benefit of using this command (instead of dropping and re-creating the old procedure) is that the EXECUTE privilege grants previously made on the procedure remain in place.

The IN qualifier is used for arguments for which values must be specified when calling the procedure. In the NEW_BOOK example, the **aTitle**, **aPublisher**, and **aCategoryName** arguments are declared as IN. The OUT qualifier signifies that the procedure passes a value back to the caller through this argument. The IN OUT qualifier signifies that the argument is both an IN and an OUT: A value must be specified for this argument when the procedure is called, and the procedure will return a value to the caller via this argument. If no qualifier type is specified, then the default value is IN.

In the CREATE PROCEDURE syntax, AUTHID refers to the type of authentication: definer rights (the default) or invoker rights (the CURRENT_USER). The NOCOPY keyword tells Oracle to pass the variable value back to the user as quickly as possible.

By default, a procedure consists of a block of code written in PL/SQL (*block* refers to the code that the procedure executes when called). In the NEW_BOOK example, the block is as follows:

```
begin
    insert into bookshelf (title, publisher, category_name, rating)
```

```
      values (aTitle, aPublisher, aCategoryName, null);
   delete from book_order
      where title = aTitle;
end;
```

The PL/SQL block shown is fairly simple, consisting of a single SQL statement. PL/SQL blocks within procedures can include any DML statement; they cannot be used for DDL statements (such as CREATE VIEW).

Alternatively, LANGUAGE refers to the language in which the code is written. For Java examples, see Chapter 44.

The following listing shows the execution of the NEW_BOOK procedure and the resulting changes to the BOOK_ORDER and BOOKSHELF tables.

```
select title from book_order;

TITLE
-------------------------------------------------------------
Galileo's Daughter
Gospel
Longitude
Once Removed
Shoeless Joe
Something So Strong

execute new_book('Once Removed','Sanctuary Pub','ADULTNF');

PL/SQL procedure successfully completed.


select title from book_order;

TITLE
-------------------------------------------------------------
Galileo's Daughter
Gospel
Longitude
Shoeless Joe
Something So Strong


select * from bookshelf
where title = 'Once Removed';

TITLE
-------------------------------------------------------------
PUBLISHER             CATEGORY_NAME         RA
--------------------  --------------------  --
Once Removed
Sanctuary Pub         ADULTNF
```

NOTE
You can make external C procedures and Java libraries available within PL/SQL by creating external procedures. To do so, you need to set up an agent (named EXTPROC by default) in the network configuration files. If you need to reference external libraries, work with your database administrator to configure the network environment, the agents that are needed, and the creation of directories and libraries within the database.

CREATE FUNCTION Syntax

The syntax for the CREATE FUNCTION command is more complicated than the syntax for the CREATE PROCEDURE command. At a high level, the syntax is

```
CREATE [OR REPLACE] FUNCTION [schema.] function
[( argument [ IN | OUT | IN OUT ] [NOCOPY] datatype
   [, argument [ IN | OUT | IN OUT ] [NOCOPY] datatype]...
 )]
RETURN datatype
[{ invoker_rights_clause | DETERMINISTIC | parallel_enable_clause }
 [ invoker_rights_clause | DETERMINISTIC | parallel_enable_clause ]...
]
{ { AGGREGATE | PIPELINED } USING [schema.] implementation_type
 | [PIPELINED] { IS | AS } { pl/sql_function_body | call_spec }};
```

Both the header and the body of the function are created by this command.

The RETURN keyword specifies the datatype of the function's return value. This can be any valid PL/SQL datatype (see Chapter 32). Every function must have a RETURN clause because the function must, by definition, return a value to the calling environment.

The following example shows a function named OVERDUE_CHARGES, which returns the overdue book charges by person, based on calculations against the BOOKSHELF_CHECKOUT table. The input is the person's name, while the output is the balance for that person.

```
create or replace function overdue_charges (aName in varchar2)
   return number
   is
   owed_amount number(10,2);
begin
    select sum(((returned_date-checkout_date) -14)*0.20)
    into owed_amount
     from bookshelf_checkout
     where name = aName;
   return(owed_amount);
end;
/
```

First, the function is named and the input is specified:

```
create or replace function overdue_charges (aName in varchar2)
```

Next, you define the characteristics of the value to be returned. The definition of the variable whose value will be returned has three parts: its datatype, its name, and its length. The datatype in this example is set via the RETURN NUMBER clause. The variable is then named **owed_amount** and is defined as a NUMBER(10,2). Thus, all three parts of the variable—its datatype, its name, and its length—have been defined.

```
return number
is
owed_amount number(10,2);
```

The PL/SQL block follows. In the SQL statement, the sum of all late charges ($0.20 per day over 14 days) is calculated. The sum is selected into a variable called **owed_amount** (which we previously defined). The **return(owed_amount)** line then returns the value in the **owed_amount** variable to the calling program.

```
begin
    select sum(((returned_date-checkout_date)-14)*0.20)
    into owed_amount
      from bookshelf_checkout
    where name = aName;
    return(owed_amount);
end;
```

If a function already exists, you may replace it via the CREATE OR REPLACE FUNCTION command. If you use the OR REPLACE clause, any EXECUTE grants previously made on the function remain in place.

If the function is to be created in a different schema, you must have the CREATE ANY PROCEDURE system privilege. If no schema is specified, the function is created in your schema. To create a function in your schema, you must have been granted the CREATE PROCEDURE system privilege (which is part of the RESOURCE role). Having the privilege to create procedures gives you the privilege to create functions and packages as well.

You can check the function by creating a variable and setting its value equal to the function's returned value:

```
variable owed number;
execute :owed := overdue_charges('Fred Fuller');
```

```
PL/SQL procedure successfully completed.
```

You can verify the results by printing the variable's value:

```
print owed
```

```
     OWED
----------
       3.8
```

Referencing Remote Tables in Procedures

Remote tables can be accessed by the SQL statements in procedures. A remote table can be queried via a database link in the procedure, as shown in the following example. In this example, the NEW_BOOK procedure inserts a record into the BOOKSHELF table in the database defined by the REMOTE_CONNECT database link while deleting from a local copy of BOOK_ORDER.

> **NOTE**
> *The following example requires the existence of the REMOTE_ CONNECT database link and a remote database containing the referenced objects.*

```
create or replace procedure new_book (aTitle in varchar2,
   aPublisher in varchar2, aCategoryName in varchar2)
as
begin
   insert into bookshelf@remote_connect
     (title, publisher, category_name, rating)
     values (aTitle, aPublisher, aCategoryName, null);
   delete from book_order
     where title = aTitle;
end;
/
```

Procedures may also use local synonyms. For example, you may create a local synonym for a remote table, as follows here:

```
create synonym bookshelf_remote for bookshelf@remote_connect;
```

You can then rewrite your procedure to remove the database link specifications:

```
create or replace procedure new_book (aTitle in varchar2,
   aPublisher in varchar2, aCategoryName in varchar2)
as
begin
   insert into bookshelf_remote
     (title, publisher, category_name, rating)
     values (aTitle, aPublisher, aCategoryName, null);
   delete from book_order
     where title = aTitle;
end;
/
```

Removing database link names from procedures allows you to remove the details of the table's physical location from the procedure. If the table changes location, only the synonym changes; the procedure will still be valid.

Debugging Procedures

The SQL*Plus SHOW ERRORS command displays all the errors associated with the most recently created procedural object. This command checks the USER_ERRORS data dictionary view for the errors associated with the most recent compilation attempt for that object. SHOW ERRORS displays the line and column number for each error, as well as the text of the error message.

To view errors associated with previously created procedural objects, you may query USER_ ERRORS directly, as shown in the following listing. This example queries USER_ERRORS for error messages encountered during the creation of the OVERDUE_CHARGES function shown earlier in this chapter. If any errors were encountered, the lines in the code that resulted in the error conditions would be returned by the query.

```
select line,      /*Line number of the error. */
       position,  /*Column number of the error.*/
       text       /*Text of the error message.*/
from user_errors
where name = 'OVERDUE_CHARGES'
   and TYPE = 'FUNCTION'
order by sequence;
```

Valid values for the TYPE column are VIEW, PROCEDURE, PACKAGE, FUNCTION, and PACKAGE BODY.

Two other data dictionary view levels—ALL and DBA—may also be used to retrieve information about errors involving procedural objects. For information on these views, see Chapter 45.

NOTE
As of Oracle 11g, you can use the PL/SQL Hierarchical Profiler to report the dynamic execution time by subprogram calls. Its output displays the time for the PL/SQL steps apart from the SQL execution time. The profile package, DBMS_HPROF, generates output for each function call. See the package documentation for details on the generation and interpretation of its output. See Chapter 37 for guidance on the performance tuning of PL/SQL procedures.

In addition to the debugging information provided by the SHOW ERRORS command, you may use the DBMS_OUTPUT package, one of a set of packages that is automatically installed when you create an Oracle database.

To use DBMS_OUTPUT, you must issue the SET SERVEROUTPUT ON command before executing the procedural object you are debugging.

DBMS_OUTPUT allows you to use three debugging functions within your package:

DBMS_OUTPUT Debugging Function	Description
PUT	Puts multiple outputs on the same line
PUT_LINE	Puts each output on a separate line
NEW_LINE	Used with PUT—signals the end of the current output line

PUT and PUT_LINE are used to generate the debugging information you want to display. For example, if you are debugging a procedure that includes a loop (refer to Chapter 32), you may want to track the changes in a variable with each pass through the loop. To track the variable's value, you may use a command similar to the one shown in the following listing. In this example, the value of the OWED_AMOUNT column is printed, prefixed by the literal string "Owed:".

```
dbms_output.put_line('Owed:'||owed_amount);
```

To use DBMS_OUTPUT, you should first issue the SET SERVEROUTPUT ON command within your session. You may also use PUT and PUT_LINE outside of loops, but such uses may be better accomplished via the **return** command in functions (refer to "CREATE FUNCTION Syntax," earlier in this chapter).

NOTE
For additional debugging capabilities, you can use the DBMS_ DEBUG procedure if you have the DEBUG CONNECT SESSION system privilege. The DEBUG ANY PROCEDURE system privilege is equivalent to having the DEBUG privilege for all objects in the database.

Creating Your Own Functions

Rather than just calling custom functions via EXECUTE commands, you may use them within SQL expressions. Doing this enables you to extend the functionality of SQL, customizing it to your needs. Such functions can be used in the same manner as Oracle-provided functions such as SUBSTR and TO_CHAR. Custom functions cannot be used in CHECK or DEFAULT constraints and cannot manipulate any database values.

You can call either stand-alone functions (created via the CREATE FUNCTION command shown in the previous sections) or functions declared in package specifications (to be covered in "CREATE PACKAGE Syntax," later in this chapter). Procedures are not directly callable from SQL, but may be called by the functions you create.

For example, consider the OVERDUE_CHARGES function shown earlier in this chapter, which calculated the total owed for overdue books. It had a single input variable—the person's name. To see the OVERDUE_CHARGES results for all of the book borrowers, however, you would normally need to execute this procedure once for each record in the BOOKSHELF_CHECKOUT table.

You can improve the overdue charges calculation process. Consider the following query:

```
create view book_borrowers
as select distinct name from bookshelf_checkout;

select name,
    overdue_charges(name)
from book_borrowers;
```

Oracle returns the following output:

```
NAME                          OVERDUE_CHARGES(NAME)
----------------------------  ---------------------
Dorah Talbot                                    -.8
Emily Talbot                                     .2
Fred Fuller                                      3.8
Gerhardt Kentgen                                 2.8
```

```
Jed Hopkins                                    1.4
Pat Lavay                                      2.6
Roland Brandt                                 22.6
```

```
7 rows selected.
```

This single query uses the custom OVERDUE_CHARGES function to calculate the overdue charges for all book borrowers. It's not quite correct—people are getting credit for books they returned early. You can use the CREATE OR REPLACE FUNCTION command to add a WHERE clause to the function's query:

```
create or replace function overdue_charges (aName in varchar2)
   return number
   is
   owed_amount number(10,2);
begin
     select sum(((returned_date-checkout_date)-14)*0.20)
     into owed_amount
       from bookshelf_checkout
      where name = aName
        and returned_date-checkout_date > 14;
     return(owed_amount);
end;
/
```

The corrected output is shown in the following listing:

```
select name,
    overdue_charges(name)
from book_borrowers;
```

```
NAME                         OVERDUE_CHARGES(NAME)
-------------------------    ---------------------
DORAH TALBOT                                    .4
EMILY TALBOT                                    .8
FRED FULLER                                    3.8
GERHARDT KENTGEN                               4.6
JED HOPKINS                                    1.4
PAT LAVAY                                      3.4
ROLAND BRANDT                                 22.6
```

The query selected each name from BOOK_BORROWERS; for each name, it executed the OVERDUE_CHARGES function, which selected data from BOOKSHELF_CHECKOUT.

To take advantage of this feature, your functions must follow the same guidelines as Oracle's functions. Most notably, they must not update the database and must contain only IN parameters.

Customizing Error Conditions

You may establish different error conditions within procedural objects (refer to Chapter 34 for examples of customized error conditions within triggers). For each of the error conditions you define, you may select an error message that will appear when the error occurs. The error numbers and messages that are displayed to the user are set by you via the RAISE_APPLICATION_ ERROR procedure, which may be called from within any procedural object.

You can call RAISE_APPLICATION_ERROR from within procedures, packages, and functions. It requires two inputs: the message number and the message text. You get to assign both the message number and the text that will be displayed to the user. This is a powerful addition to the standard exceptions that are available in PL/SQL (see "Exception" in the Alphabetical Reference).

The following example shows the OVERDUE_CHARGES function defined earlier in this chapter. Now, however, it has an additional section (shown in bold). Titled **exception**, this section tells Oracle how to handle nonstandard processing. In this example, the NO_DATA_FOUND exception's standard message is overridden via the RAISE_APPLICATION_ERROR procedure.

```
create or replace function overdue_charges (aName in varchar2)
   return number
   is
   owed_amount number(10,2);
begin
     select sum(((returned_date-checkout_date) -14)*0.20)
     into owed_amount
       from bookshelf_checkout
       where name = aName
        and (returned_date-checkout_date) > 14;
     return(owed_amount);
   exception
    when no_data_found then
      raise_application_error(-20100,
      'No books borrowed.');
end;
/
```

In the preceding example, the NO_DATA_FOUND exception was used. If you want to define custom exceptions, you need to name the exception in a Declarations section of the procedure, which immediately precedes the **begin** section. As shown in the following listing, this section should include entries for each of the custom exceptions you have defined, listed as type **exception**:

```
declare
some_custom_error exception;
```

NOTE
If you are using the exceptions already defined (that is, built in) within PL/SQL, you do not need to list them in the Declarations section of the procedural object. See "Exception" in the Alphabetical Reference for a list of the predefined exceptions.

In the **exception** portion of the procedural object's code, you tell the database how to handle the exceptions. It begins with the keyword **exception**, followed by a **when** clause for each exception. Each exception may call the RAISE_ APPLICATION_ERROR procedure, which takes two input parameters: the error number (which must be between –20001 and –20999) and the error message to be displayed. In the preceding example, only one exception was defined.

Multiple exceptions can be defined, as shown in the following listing; you may use the **when others** clause to handle all nonspecified exceptions:

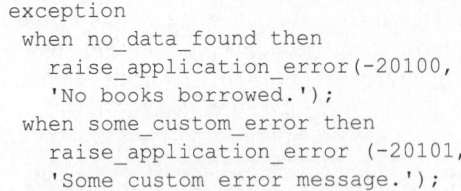

```
exception
  when no_data_found then
    raise_application_error(-20100,
    'No books borrowed.');
  when some_custom_error then
    raise_application_error (-20101,
    'Some custom error message.');
```

The use of the RAISE_APPLICATION_ERROR procedure gives you great flexibility in managing the error conditions that may be encountered within procedural objects.

Naming Procedures and Functions

Procedures and functions should be named according to the business function they perform or business rule they enforce. There should be no ambiguity about their purpose.

The NEW_BOOK procedure shown earlier should be renamed. NEW_BOOK performs a business function—inserting records into BOOKSHELF and deleting them from BOOK_ORDER—so its name should reflect that function. A better choice for the name would be RECEIVE_BOOK_ORDER. Because it performs a function, a verb (in this case, "receive") should describe what it does. The name of the procedure should also include the name of the major table(s) it impacts. If the tables are properly named, then the name of the table should be the direct object on which the verb acts (in this case, BOOK_ORDER or BOOKSHELF). For the sake of consistency, I'll continue to refer to the procedure as NEW_BOOK for the remainder of this chapter.

CREATE PACKAGE Syntax

When creating packages, the package specification and the package body are created separately. Thus, there are two commands to use: CREATE PACKAGE for the package specification and CREATE PACKAGE BODY for the package body. Both of these commands require that you have the CREATE PROCEDURE system privilege. If the package is to be created in a schema other than your own, then you must have the CREATE ANY PROCEDURE system privilege.

Here is the syntax for creating package specifications:

```
CREATE [OR REPLACE] PACKAGE [user.] package
[AUTHID {DEFINER | CURRENT_USER} ]
{IS | AS}
 package specification;
```

A *package specification* consists of the list of functions, procedures, variables, constants, cursors, and exceptions that are available to users of the package.

A sample CREATE PACKAGE command is shown in the following listing. In this example, the BOOK_MANAGEMENT package is created. The OVERDUE_CHARGES function and NEW_BOOK procedure seen earlier in this chapter are included in the package.

```
create or replace package book_management
as
   function overdue_charges(aName in varchar2) return number;
```

```
procedure new_book (aTitle in varchar2,
    aPublisher in varchar2, aCategoryName in varchar2);
end book_management;
/
```

NOTE
*You may append the name of the procedural object to the **end** clause
to make coordinating the logic within your code easier.*

A *package body* contains the blocks and specifications for all of the public objects listed in
the package specification. The package body may include objects that are not listed in the package
specification; such objects are said to be *private* and are not available to users of the package.
Private objects may only be called by other objects within the same package body. A package body
may also include code that is run every time the package is invoked, regardless of the part of the
package that is executed.

The syntax for creating package bodies is

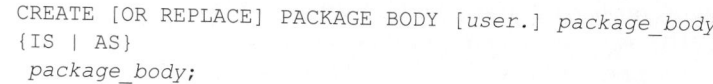

```
CREATE [OR REPLACE] PACKAGE BODY [user.] package_body
{IS | AS}
 package_body;
```

The name of the package body should be the same as the name of the package specification.

Continuing the BOOK_MANAGEMENT example, its package body can be created via the
CREATE PACKAGE BODY command shown in the following example:

```
create or replace package body book_management
as
function overdue_charges (aName in varchar2)
  return number
  is
  owed_amount number(10,2);
begin
    select sum(((returned_date-checkout_date) -14)*0.20)
    into owed_amount
      from bookshelf_checkout
      where name = aName
        and (returned_date-checkout_date) > 14;
  return(owed_amount);
  exception
  when no_data_found then
    raise_application_error(-20100,
    'No books borrowed.');
end overdue_charges;
procedure new_book (aTitle in varchar2,
   aPublisher in varchar2, aCategoryName in varchar2)
is
begin
   insert into bookshelf
     (title, publisher, category_name, rating)
     values (aTitle, aPublisher, aCategoryName, NULL);
```

```
       delete from book_order
       where title = aTitle;
  end new_book;
  end book_management;
  /
```

The CREATE OR REPLACE PACKAGE BODY command shown in the preceding example combines the CREATE FUNCTION command for the OVERDUE_CHARGES function with the CREATE PROCEDURE command for the NEW_BOOK procedure. The **end** clauses all have the names of their associated objects appended to them (shown in bold in the prior listing).

Additional functions, procedures, exceptions, variables, cursors, and constants may be defined within the package body, but they are not available to the public unless they have been declared within the package specification (via the CREATE PACKAGE command). If a user has been granted the EXECUTE privilege on a package, then that user can access any of the public objects that are declared in the package specification.

NOTE
*You can hide the internals of your application code by using the PL/ SQL wrapper. The WRAP executable (found in the **./bin** directory under the Oracle software home directory) takes an input filename as its input and generates an output file containing the object code. You cannot unwrap a package that has been wrapped.*

Packages may include code that is to be run the first time a user executes a function or procedure in the package within each session. In the following example, the BOOK_ MANAGEMENT package body is modified to include a SQL statement that records the current user's username and the timestamp for the first time a package component is executed within the session. Two new variables must also be declared in the package body to record these values.

Because the two new variables are declared within the package body, they are not available to the public. Within the package body, they are separated from the procedures and functions. The package initialization code is shown in bold in the following listing:

```
create or replace package body book_management
as
user_name varchar2(30);
entry_date date;
function overdue_charges (aName in varchar2)
  return number
  is
  owed_amount number(10,2);
begin
    select sum(((returned_date-checkout_date) -14)*0.20)
    into owed_amount
    from bookshelf_checkout
    where name = aName
        and (returned_date-checkout_date) > 14;
   return(owed_amount);
  exception
   when no_data_found then
```

```
      raise_application_error(-20100,
        'No books borrowed.');
end overdue_charges;
procedure new_book (aTitle in varchar2,
   aPublisher in varchar2, aCategoryName in varchar2)
is
begin
   insert into bookshelf
     (title, publisher, category_name, rating)
      values (aTitle, aPublisher, aCategoryName, null);
   delete from book_order
   where title = aTitle;
end new_book;
begin
  select user, sysdate
    into user_name, entry_date
    from dual;
end book_management;
/
```

NOTE
*The code that is to be run the first time that a component of the package is executed is stored in its own PL/SQL block at the bottom of the package body. It does not have its own **end** clause; it uses the package body's **end** clause.*

The first time a BOOK_MANAGEMENT package component is executed in the user's session, the **user_name** and **entry_date** variables are populated by the query shown in the previous listing. These two variables can then be used by the functions and procedures within the package, although in the interest of brevity this example does not use them.

To EXECUTE a procedure or function that is within a package, specify both the package name and the name of the procedure or function in the EXECUTE command, as follows:

```
execute book_management.new_book('Something So Strong','Pandoras','ADULTNF');
```

Viewing Source Code for Procedural Objects

The source code for existing procedures, functions, packages, and package bodies can be queried from the following data dictionary views:

Procedural View Name	View Description
USER_SOURCE	For procedural objects owned by the user
ALL_SOURCE	For procedural objects owned by the user or to which the user has been granted access
DBA_SOURCE	For all procedural objects in the database

Select information from the USER_SOURCE view via a query similar to the one shown in the following listing. In this example, the TEXT column is selected, ordered by the LINE number. The NAME of the object and the object TYPE are used to define which object's source code is to be displayed. The following example uses the NEW_BOOK procedure shown earlier in this chapter:

```
select text
from user_source
where name = 'NEW_BOOK'
  and type = 'PROCEDURE'
order by line;

TEXT
----------------------------------------------------------------
procedure new_book (aTitle in varchar2,
   aPublisher in varchar2, aCategoryName in varchar2)
as
begin
   insert into bookshelf (title, publisher, category_name, rating)
     values (aTitle, aPublisher, aCategoryName, null);
   delete from book_order
   where title = aTitle;
end;
```

As shown in this example, the USER_SOURCE view contains one record for each line of the NEW_BOOK procedure. The sequence of the lines is maintained by the LINE column; therefore, the LINE column should be used in the ORDER BY clause.

Valid values for the TYPE column are PROCEDURE, FUNCTION, PACKAGE, PACKAGE BODY, JAVA SOURCE, TYPE, and TYPE BODY.

Compiling Procedures, Functions, and Packages

Oracle compiles procedural objects when they are created. Procedural objects may become invalid, however, if the database objects they reference change. The next time the procedural objects are executed, they will be recompiled by the database.

You can avoid this run-time compiling—and the performance degradation it may cause—by explicitly recompiling the procedures, functions, and packages. To recompile a procedure, use the ALTER PROCEDURE command, as shown in the following listing. The COMPILE clause is the only valid option for this command.

```
alter procedure new_book compile;
```

To recompile a procedure, you must either own the procedure or have the ALTER ANY PROCEDURE system privilege.

To recompile a function, use the ALTER FUNCTION command, with the COMPILE clause:

```
alter function overdue_charges compile;
```

To recompile a function, you must either own the function or have the ALTER ANY PROCEDURE system privilege.

When recompiling packages, you may either recompile both the package specification and the body or just recompile the package body. By default, both the package specification and the package body are recompiled. You cannot use the ALTER FUNCTION or ALTER PROCEDURE command to recompile functions and procedures stored within a package.

If the source code for the procedures or functions within the package body has changed but the package specification has not, you may want to recompile only the package body. In most cases, it is appropriate to recompile both the specification and the package body.

The following is the syntax for the ALTER PACKAGE command:

```
ALTER PACKAGE [user.]package_name
COMPILE [DEBUG] [PACKAGE | BODY | SPECIFICATION];
```

To recompile a package, use the preceding ALTER PACKAGE command with the COMPILE clause, as follows:

```
alter package book_management compile;
```

To recompile a package, you must either own the package or have the ALTER ANY PROCEDURE system privilege. Because neither PACKAGE nor BODY was specified in the preceding example, the default of PACKAGE was used, resulting in both the package specification and the package body being recompiled.

Replacing Procedures, Functions, and Packages

Procedures, functions, and packages may be replaced via their respective CREATE OR REPLACE command. Using the OR REPLACE clause keeps in place any existing grants that have been made for those objects. If you choose to drop and re-create procedural objects, you have to re-GRANT any EXECUTE privileges that were previously granted.

Dropping Procedures, Functions, and Packages

To drop a procedure, use the DROP PROCEDURE command, as follows:

```
drop procedure new_book;
```

To drop a procedure, you must either own the procedure or have the DROP ANY PROCEDURE system privilege.

To drop a function, use the DROP FUNCTION command, as follows:

```
drop function overdue_charges;
```

To drop a function, you must either own the function or have the DROP ANY PROCEDURE system privilege.

To drop a package body, use the DROP PACKAGE command with the BODY clause, as follows:

```
drop package body book_management;
```

To drop a package body, you must either own the package or have the DROP ANY PROCEDURE system privilege.

To drop a package (both the specification and the body), use the DROP PACKAGE command, as follows:

```
drop package book_management;
```

To drop a package, you must either own the package or have the DROP ANY PROCEDURE system privilege.

CHAPTER
36

Using Native Dynamic
SQL and DBMS_SQL

You can use *native dynamic SQL* to create general-purpose procedures and to execute DDL commands within PL/SQL. You can use dynamic SQL to execute SQL commands that are built at run time rather than at program-creation time within stored procedural objects (such as packages) and in anonymous PL/SQL blocks. For example, you can create procedures that create tables, that take table names as input parameters, or that take WHERE clauses as input parameters.

Using EXECUTE IMMEDIATE

The script in the following example creates a procedure called ANYSTRING. The ANYSTRING procedure has a single input variable: a SQL command. When you execute the ANYSTRING procedure, you pass it the SQL command to execute; the SQL command may be either a DML command (such as SELECT or INSERT) or a DDL command (such as CREATE TABLE).

```
create or replace procedure anystring(string in varchar2) as
begin
    execute immediate (string);
end;
/
```

You can execute the ANYSTRING procedure via the EXECUTE command in SQL*Plus or SQL Developer, as shown in the upcoming examples of DDL and DML commands. Note that the strings are not terminated with semicolons and that EXECUTE is a SQL*Plus command whereas **execute immediate** is a PL/SQL command.

If you are going to run DDL commands through dynamic SQL, you must have been granted the necessary system privileges explicitly—not via roles. If you do not have the CREATE TABLE system privilege explicitly granted to you, the following command will fail with an "ORA-01031: insufficient privileges" error:

```
execute anystring('create table cd (artist varchar2(25), -
    title varchar2(25)) ');

execute anystring('insert into cd values(''Neil Finn'', -
    ''Try Whistling This'') ');
```

The first command in the preceding listing executes the following SQL command:

```
create table cd
(artist varchar2(25),
 title  varchar2(25));
```

The second command in the listing inserts a record into the CD table:

```
insert into cd values ('Neil Finn', 'Try Whistling This');
```

If the SQL statements passed to ANYSTRING contain single quotation marks, each quotation mark should be replaced with a set of two quotation marks, as shown in the preceding execution of ANYSTRING for the INSERT command. After each command, you receive the following response:

```
PL/SQL procedure successfully completed.
```

You can verify that the commands succeeded by querying the new table:

```
select * from cd;

ARTIST                    TITLE
------------------------ ------------------------
Neil Finn                 Try Whistling This
```

You can write native dynamic SQL for which the input parameters are passed to the SQL commands:

```
declare
   symbol varchar2(6) := 'EPIC';
begin
     execute immediate 'delete from stock where symbol = :symbol'
     using symbol;
end;
/
```

The *symbol* variable is set equal to the value "EPIC", and that value is then passed to the DELETE command via the **using** clause.

In the following listing, a procedure named DELETE_ROWS deletes all rows from the table passed in as a variable. If a **where_clause** value is entered when the procedure is executed, it is dynamically appended to the DELETE command; otherwise, all rows are deleted.

```
create or replace procedure delete_rows (
   table_name in varchar2,
   condition in varchar2 default null) as
   where_clause varchar2(100) := ' where ' || condition;
begin
   if condition is null then where_clause := null; end if;
   execute immediate 'delete from ' || table_name || where_clause;
end;
/
```

You can call the DELETE_ROWS procedure anytime you want to delete rows from a table. You could call it within another procedure or within an application without having to grant anyone access to perform DELETE commands directly within SQL*Plus. The following command deletes all the rows in the STOCK table:

```
execute delete_rows('STOCK');
```

In addition to calling SQL statements, you can execute procedures and PL/SQL blocks via native dynamic SQL.

Using Bind Variables

One of the benefits of native dynamic SQL is the ability to use bind variables in your code. For example, consider this example from earlier in this chapter:

```
declare
    symbol varchar2(6) := 'EPIC';
begin
    execute immediate 'delete from stock where symbol = :symbol'
    using symbol;
end;
/
```

In the preceding listing, *:symbol* is a bind variable. Successive values of *symbol* can be passed in to the **execute immediate** command. Because a bind variable is used, the command will not have to be parsed repeatedly. If you monitor the database as the application is used, you'll see in V$SQL one entry for the command. If you had not used bind variables, you would see a separate entry in V$SQL for each separate execution of the command. That is, instead of seeing

```
delete from stock where symbol = :symbol
```

in the library cache, you would see one entry for each unique deletion, such as

```
delete from stock where symbol = 'EPIC'
```

and so on.

Each of these commands would be separately parsed, and each would be taking space in memory. Failing to use bind variables may thus fill your shared pool with a large number of very similar commands—a waste of the resources that the database is supposed to be exploiting and a potential cause of performance problems. Database administrators can resolve a portion of this problem by setting the CURSOR_SHARING initialization parameter to SIMILAR, but at its heart, this is a problem that should be solved by using a proper development approach.

When the query is run, bind arguments replace their corresponding placeholders in the string. Each of the placeholders must be associated with a bind variable in the **using** clause or a **returning into** clause. Bind variables can be numeric, character, or string literals.

The following example illustrates the use of bind variables within a dynamic UPDATE statement:

```
declare
    sql_stmt    varchar2(200);
    symbol      varchar2(6) := 'EPIC';
    close_today number(6,2);
begin
sql_stmt := 'update stock set close_today = 32 where symbol = :1
    returning close_today into :2';
    execute immediate sql_stmt using symbol returning into close_today;
end;
/
```

The **returning into** clause is only used in INSERT, UPDATE, and DELETE commands that have a **returning** clause. For each value returned by the command, there must be a corresponding variable in the **returning into** clause.

Using DBMS_SQL

In older versions of Oracle Database, dynamic SQL required the DBMS_SQL package. You can still use the DBMS_SQL method, as shown in this section. Using DBMS_SQL may give you greater control over the processing flow within the dynamic SQL, but it is generally more complicated to write than the native dynamic SQL shown earlier in this chapter.

The script in the following example creates the DBMS_SQL version of the ANYSTRING procedure shown earlier. The ANYSTRING procedure has a single input variable: a SQL command. When you execute the ANYSTRING procedure, you pass it the SQL command to execute; the SQL command may be either a DML command (such as SELECT or INSERT) or a DDL command (such as CREATE TABLE).

```
create or replace procedure anystring(string in varchar2) as
    cursor_name integer;
    ret integer;
begin
    cursor_name := dbms_sql.open_cursor;
    dbms_sql.parse(cursor_name, string, dbms_sql.native);
    ret := dbms_sql.execute(cursor_name);
    dbms_sql.close_cursor(cursor_name);
end;
/
```

As with the earlier version, you can execute the ANYSTRING procedure via the EXECUTE command, as shown in the following examples of DDL and DML commands:

```
execute anystring('drop table cd');
execute anystring('create table cd (artist varchar2(25), -
  title varchar2(25))');
execute anystring('insert into cd values(''Neil Finn'', -
  ''Try Whistling This'')');
```

If the SQL statements passed to ANYSTRING contain quotation marks, each quotation mark should be replaced with a set of two quotation marks, as shown in the preceding execution of ANYSTRING for the INSERT command. After each command, you receive the following response:

```
PL/SQL procedure successfully completed.
```

You can verify the commands succeeded by querying the new table, as shown in the next example:

```
select * from CD;


ARTIST                          TITLE
------------------------        ------------------------
Neil Finn                       Try Whistling This
```

In the following sections, you learn about the major functions and procedures used within dynamic SQL statements.

OPEN_CURSOR

The OPEN_CURSOR function of the DBMS_SQL package opens a cursor and returns to your program a cursor ID number. Thus, within the ANYSTRING procedure, the **cursor_name** variable is defined as an INTEGER datatype:

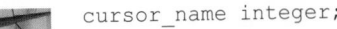

```
cursor_name integer;
```

Within the main **begin** block of the procedure, the **cursor_name** variable is set to the output of the OPEN_CURSOR execution:

```
cursor_name := dbms_sql.open_cursor;
```

PARSE

Parsing a statement checks its syntax and associates the statement with the cursor. To parse a statement, use the PARSE procedure of the DBMS_SQL package. For example, in the ANYSTRING procedure, the following command parses the SQL command. PARSE takes three parameters: the cursor ID, the command being parsed, and a language flag.

```
dbms_sql.parse(cursor_name, string, dbms_sql.native);
```

The language flag specifies the behavior for the statement. The DBMS_SQL.NATIVE setting shown in this example specifies behavior according to the current version of the database.

NOTE
DDL commands (such as CREATE TABLE) are executed when they are parsed.

BIND_VARIABLE and BIND_ARRAY

If your dynamic SQL procedure performs data manipulation, you need to use bind variables. Any dynamic SQL command that INSERTs, UPDATEs, or DELETEs records needs to use either the BIND_VARIABLE or BIND_ARRAY procedure within DBMS_SQL as part of its processing. You must call one of these procedures to supply the value of a variable in your program to the placeholder. When the SQL statement is then executed, Oracle uses the data that your program has placed in the output and input, or *bind,* variables.

For example, the PARSE execution in the following listing parses a SQL command in which one of the values is unknown—the value of the bind variable used in the procedure:

```
dbms_sql.parse(cursor_name, 'delete from cd where artist > :artist',
               dbms_sql.native);
```

Following the PARSE execution, you must bind the **:artist** bind variable to the **artist_name** variable passed to the procedure. When a user executes the procedure, a value is specified for the **artist_name** variable. The BIND_VARIABLE procedure shown in the following listing binds the **artist_name** value to the **:artist** bind variable used by the command string being parsed:

```
dbms_sql.bind_variable(cursor_name, ':artist', artist_name);
```

You can use dynamic SQL to execute a DML statement multiple times—each time with a different bind variable. You can use the BIND_ARRAY procedure to bind an array of values, each of which is used as an input variable once per EXECUTE.

EXECUTE

To execute your dynamically created SQL statement, use the EXECUTE function of the DBMS_SQL package. The following listing, from the ANYSTRING procedure, shows the use of the EXECUTE function:

```
ret := dbms_sql.execute(cursor_name);
```

When you use the EXECUTE function, you pass the cursor ID value (in this example, the **cursor_name** variable) as input. The *ret* variable holds the output of the EXECUTE function, which is the number of rows processed (if the executed statement performs DML).

DEFINE_COLUMN

If your cursor performs a query, you must execute the DEFINE_COLUMN function once for each column being selected. If the column is defined with a LONG datatype, you must use the DEFINE_COLUMN_LONG function in place of DEFINE_COLUMN. If you are selecting values into a PL/SQL array, you must use DEFINE_ARRAY in place of DEFINE_COLUMN.

For example, consider the query parsed in the following command:

```
dbms_sql.parse(cursor_name,'select artist, title from cd',
                    dbms_sql.native);
```

Prior to executing the cursor, you must define the columns by their position in the query, as shown in the following listing:

```
dbms_sql.define_column(cursor_name, 1, artist, 25);
dbms_sql.define_column(cursor_name, 2, title, 25);
```

Once you have defined the columns, you can use the EXECUTE function to execute the cursor.

FETCH_ROWS, EXECUTE_AND_FETCH, and COLUMN_VALUE

If your dynamic SQL command performs a query, you can call the FETCH_ROWS function to retrieve the query's rows. The EXECUTE_AND_FETCH function both executes and fetches rows.

For example, suppose you have a table called CD_COPY, with the same column definitions as the CD table created earlier in this chapter. You can use dynamic SQL to SELECT records from the CD table and INSERT them into the CD_COPY table. For this example, the GET_CD_CURSOR statement retrieves rows from the CD table, and the INSERT_CD_COPY_CURSOR statement inserts the retrieved values into the CD_COPY table.

In this example, the GET_CD_CURSOR cursor has already been parsed. The sample code executes the FETCH_ROWS function. If the number of rows fetched is greater than zero, the record is processed.

```
if dbms_sql.fetch_rows(get_cd_cursor)>0 then
```

For the fetched record, the COLUMN_VALUE procedure is executed once for each column selected:

```
dbms_sql.column_value(get_cd_cursor, 1, artist);
dbms_sql.column_value(get_cd_cursor, 2, title);
```

Now that the queried values have been bound to variables, you can bind those values into the cursor that INSERTs records into the CD_COPY table:

```
dbms_sql.bind_variable(insert_cd_copy_cursor, 'artist', artist);
dbms_sql.bind_variable(insert_cd_copy_cursor, 'title', title);
```

You can now execute the cursor that INSERTs values into the CD_COPY table:

```
ret := dbms_sql.execute(insert_cd_copy_cursor);
```

The **ret** variable holds the number of rows INSERTed into the CD_COPY table. If you called a procedure from within an anonymous PL/SQL block, execute the VARIABLE_VALUE function to retrieve the values assigned to its output variables.

CLOSE_CURSOR

You can close an open cursor by executing the CLOSE_CURSOR procedure of the DBMS_SQL package. The example in the following listing, from the ANYSTRING procedure, shows that the CLOSE_CURSOR procedure uses the cursor ID value as its sole input parameter:

```
dbms_sql.close_cursor(cursor_name);
```

Closing a cursor frees the memory used by the cursor and reduces the number of concurrently open cursors in your session.

Unless you need very detailed control over the steps involved in executing dynamic SQL, you should use the **execute immediate** approach shown earlier in this chapter. If you must use the DBMS_SQL package approach, see the "PL/SQL Packages and Types Reference" in the Oracle documentation for detailed descriptions of all of the DBMS_SQL package's procedures and functions.

CHAPTER
37

PL/SQL Tuning

T uning PL/SQL code involves several steps: tuning the SQL, tuning the procedural steps within the code, and taking advantage of features. In this chapter, you'll see how to approach tuning PL/SQL, how to use the profiling facilities available within PL/SQL to isolate the causes of performance problems, and how to use PL/SQL features such as the FORALL operator.

Tune the SQL

Given a poorly performing PL/SQL procedure, the first step is to look at the SQL within the package. The time spent executing SQL usually accounts for the bulk of the execution time for a procedure, so any improvements made to the SQL can have a significant impact on the procedure's performance. See Chapter 46 for details on tuning SQL statements.

Depending on the structure of your procedures, you may be unable to extract SQL that exactly matches the queries executed. For example, the SQL commands may be assembled via dynamic SQL or may use bind variables in the WHERE clauses. In those cases, you need to monitor the programs to see exactly what SQL is being executed. You can monitor the programs via trace utilities or via the dynamic performance views (including V$SQL) that show the SQL commands executed by each session. SQL that performs a large number of physical reads (usually due to missing indexes) or a large number of logical reads (due to inefficient processing or poor index selections) can negatively impact the performance of any PL/SQL block that calls it.

If you can exactly replicate the SQL being executed, use the EXPLAIN PLAN or SET AUTOTRACE commands described in Chapter 46 to determine the execution path chosen by the optimizer, along with the anticipated cost.

Steps for Tuning the PL/SQL

Even if the SQL in your PL/SQL code is written efficiently, you may still be able to improve your code. In writing PL/SQL code, you should follow these best practices:

1. Use the functions and procedures provided.
Avoid writing your own version of functions provided by Oracle. Use Oracle's searching and sorting routines instead of writing your own.

2. Take the shortcuts available.
Take advantage of the ways Oracle performs control logic evaluation. If you have multiple conditions that control branching, Oracle evaluates them in the order you provide. It will not evaluate all of the conditions unless it needs to, so you may be able to order your conditions in a manner that allows Oracle to take shortcuts. If there are multiple conditions evaluated, such as

```
if salary > 1000 or bonus > 1000
```

put the most restrictive condition first; if the SALARY value is greater than 1000, then the BONUS value is not evaluated. If one of the conditions performs a user-defined function call, such as

```
if salary > 1000 or range_balance(bonus) > 1000
```

then placing that condition second will limit the number of times it is called. Changing the order of the conditions, as shown next, makes Oracle evaluate that function call every time the **if** clause is executed:

```
if range_balance(bonus) > 1000 or salary > 1000
```

3. Avoid dynamic datatype conversions.
Avoid comparing variables that have different datatypes. The time spent on the datatype conversions during each execution could be reclaimed if the datatypes were converted to a consistent set prior to comparisons.

4. Size VARCHAR2 variables appropriately.
Developers have a tendency to size VARCHAR2 variables to be significantly larger than their expected values. For example, you may have a standard that mandates creating variables as VARCHAR2(200), even if the maximum length of the variable is less than 200. Oracle's memory allocation within PL/SQL contains a sizing algorithm that you should take into account when creating large VARCHAR2 variables.

Oracle allocates memory differently depending on the size of the VARCHAR2 variable:

- If the size is greater than or equal to 2000, PL/SQL dynamically allocates only enough memory to handle the actual value.

- If the size is less than 2000, PL/SQL allocates enough memory to hold the declared length of the variable.

If you store a 500-byte value in two separate VARCHAR2 variables, what is the impact on memory usage? If the value is stored in a VARCHAR2(1000) variable, PL/SQL allocates memory for 1000 bytes. If the value is stored in a VARCHAR2(2000) variable, PL/SQL allocates memory for only the actual value, 500 bytes. Using the larger size for the variable reduces the allocated size from 1000 to 500 bytes.

NOTE
As of Oracle Database 12c, the SQL VARCHAR2 datatype has a maximum length of 32,767 to match the maximum length of VARCHAR2 datatypes in PL/SQL. To enable this capability, the new initialization parameter MAX_STRING_SIZE must be set to EXTENDED.

In the next sections of this chapter, you'll learn how to identify the lines in your code that are incurring the highest execution times and how to use PL/SQL options to tune bulk operations.

Use PL/SQL Within SQL Statements
Any PL/SQL code (functions, procedures, or packages) used repeatedly by multiple applications and users should probably be stored in a common location for documentation and ease of maintenance. However, in Oracle Database 12c, you can use PL/SQL blocks within the WITH clause of a SELECT statement. While this seems somewhat counterintuitive, you can realize potential performance gains by including a PL/SQL function as part of a query.

For example, the fictional company RJB Closeout Warehouse tracks the order number and the URL visited by the customer to place the order in the HR.ORDER_SOURCE table:

```
SQL> select order_num, order_url from hr.order_source;

ORDER_NUM ORDER_URL
--------- -----------------------------------------------------
  3890782 http://www.EpikOutfitters.com/kiosk_mdse
  4909893 https://www.rjbMedSuppliesOnline.com/EpiGear
  7903442 http://www.WorldWearhouseDeals.com/SpringFashion
  4910875 https://www.rjbMedSuppliesOnline.com/EpiPen
```

For loading into the data warehouse, the list of distinct web domains (without the "www." prefix and any other pages within the domain) needs to be extracted from the ORDER_URL table. Although you could write a complex expression to retrieve the domain in a traditional SELECT statement, a PL/SQL function would be easier to read, maintain, and potentially more efficient from an execution perspective, considering the Oracle result cache could be used for the results of the function. The final SELECT statement looks like this:

```
with
function get_domain(url varchar2) return varchar2 is
   surl        varchar2(200);
   www_pos     pls_integer;
   page_loc    pls_integer;
begin
   surl := url;
   www_pos := instr(url,'www.');
   if www_pos > 0 then
      surl := substr(surl,www_pos+4);
   end if;
   page_loc := instr(surl,'/');
   if page_loc > 0 then
      surl := substr(surl,1,page_loc-1);
   end if;
   return surl;
end;
select distinct get_domain(order_url)
from order_source;

GET_DOMAIN(ORDER_URL)
----------------------------------------
WorldWearhouseDeals.com
EpikOutfitters.com
rjbMedSuppliesOnline.com
```

The SELECT statement is easy to read and maintain. Even with improved performance, the proliferation of dozens of variants of the embedded function definition in this SELECT statement may justify creating the function as part of a common package.

Use DBMS_PROFILER to Identify Problems

You can use the DBMS_PROFILER package to identify the lines in your code that take the most time when executed. DBMS_PROFILER is available in earlier releases of Oracle, but was not always installed by default. In Oracle Database 12*c*, the DBMS_PROFILER package is automatically installed.

Oracle provides an additional script called: **proftab.sql**. Each person using the profiler needs a set of tables in his or her schema to capture the profiling statistics; the profiling tables are created by executing **$ORACLE_HOME/rdbms/admin/proftab.sql** script in that user's schema.

When using the profiler, you need to know the line numbers in your code. Let's start with the simple loop example, which calculates areas and inserts rows into the AREAS table:

```
declare
    pi constant number(9,7) := 3.141593;
    radius integer(5);
    area number(14,2);
begin
    radius :=3;
    loop
        area:=pi*power(radius,2);
        insert into areas values (radius, area);
        radius := radius+1;
        exit when area>100;
    end loop;
end;
/

PL/SQL procedure successfully completed.
```

To verify that the SQL executed correctly, query the AREAS table:

```
SQL> select * from areas;

    RADIUS        AREA
---------- ----------
         3       28.27
         4       50.27
         5       78.54
         6       113.1
```

Both of these commands—the PL/SQL block and the query of the AREAS table—have now been parsed and stored in the shared pool. The time required to parse the commands will, therefore, not be a factor in the performance profiling done in the next steps.

Delete the rows from the AREAS table so the table is ready for the test:

```
SQL> delete from areas;

4 rows deleted.

SQL> commit;

Commit complete.
```

Next, execute the START_PROFILER procedure of the DBMS_PROFILER package. Oracle collects the statistics for the commands that are run following the execution of START_PROFILER.

```
SQL> exec dbms_profiler.start_profiler;

PL/SQL procedure successfully completed.
```

Now run the PL/SQL block again:

```
declare
    pi constant number(9,7) := 3.141593;
    radius integer(5);
    area number(14,2);
begin
    radius :=3;
    loop
       area:=pi*power(radius,2);
       insert into areas values (radius, area);
       radius := radius+1;
       exit when area>100;
    end loop;
end;
/

PL/SQL procedure successfully completed.
```

Stop the profiler, as shown in the following lines of code:

```
SQL> exec dbms_profiler.stop_profiler;

PL/SQL procedure successfully completed.
```

If you have executed the **profrep.sql** script in your schema, you can now query the profiler statistics from the views provided. PLSQL_PROFILER_RUNS displays the schema name and the date the code was executed, as shown in the following listing:

```
SQL> set pagesize 1000

SQL> select * from plsql_profiler_runs;

     RUNID RELATED_RUN RUN_OWNER                                 RUN_DATE
---------- ----------- --------------------------------- ---------
RUN_COMMENT
-----------------------------------------------------------------
RUN_TOTAL_TIME
--------------
RUN_SYSTEM_INFO
-----------------------------------------------------------------
RUN_COMMENT1
-----------------------------------------------------------------
SPARE1
```

```
-------------------------------------------------------------------
      1            0 PRACTICE                        08-NOV-12
08-NOV-12
     1.7515E+10
```

The PLSQL_PROFILER_DATA view shows the time, in nanoseconds, for each line. If the same code is executed multiple times, it will display the total time, the maximum time, and the minimum time per line, as shown here:

```
SQL> select * from plsql_profiler_data;

     RUNID UNIT_NUMBER      LINE# TOTAL_OCCUR TOTAL_TIME   MIN_TIME   MAX_TIME
---------- ----------- ---------- ----------- ---------- ---------- ----------
    SPARE1      SPARE2     SPARE3      SPARE4
---------- ----------- ---------- ----------
         1           1          1           1       1400       1400       1400

         1           2          1           0       8900       8900       8900

         1           2          2           1       3000       3000       3000

         1           2          6           1        700        700        700

         1           2          8           4      19200       2000      11800

         1           2          9           4     444700      26400     357500

         1           2         10           4       5200        700       2900

         1           2         11           4       3100        400       1900

         1           2         13           1       3100       3100       3100

         1           3          1           2      37600       1800      30100

10 rows selected.
```

As shown in the preceding listing, the most time-intensive step, at 444,700 nanoseconds, is line 9. You can now go back to the code and see that line 9 is

```
    9    insert into areas values (radius, area);
```

By comparison, line 8 (which does the area calculation) took less than 5 percent of the time line 9 took. Any effort spent tuning the PL/SQL block should start with tuning the step that is by far the most expensive one—the SQL command that inserts the rows into the table one at a time.

How scalable is the code? What happens if you insert many more rows? Let's use the profiler to see how each step's performance changes. To make sure there is no confusion with prior statistics, execute the **proftab.sql** script to drop and re-create the statistics tables in the schema:

```
SQL> @proftab

Table dropped.

Table dropped.

Table dropped.

Sequence dropped.

Table created.

Comment created.

Table created.

Comment created.

Table created.

Comment created.

Sequence created.
```

Next, start the profiler:

```
SQL> exec dbms_profiler.start_profiler;

PL/SQL procedure successfully completed.
```

Execute the AREAS PL/SQL block again, but this time change line 11 so the exit criteria is AREA > 1000:

```
declare
    pi constant number(9,7) := 3.141593;
    radius integer(5);
    area number(14,2);
begin
    radius :=3;
    loop
       area:=pi*power(radius,2);
       insert into areas values (radius, area);
       radius := radius+1;
       exit when area > 1000;
```

```
      end loop;
end;
/
```

PL/SQL procedure successfully completed.

Next, stop the profiler:

```
SQL> exec dbms_profiler.stop_profiler;
```

PL/SQL procedure successfully completed.

Then, check the reporting views to see the statistics:

```
SQL> select * from plsql_profiler_units
  2  order by total_time;
```

UNIT_OWNER	UNIT_NAME				
UNIT_TYPE		LINE#	TOTAL_OCCUR	TOTAL_TIME	MIN_TIME
MAX_TIME					
<anonymous>	<anonymous>				
ANONYMOUS BLOCK		6	1	300	300
300					
<anonymous>	<anonymous>				
ANONYMOUS BLOCK		2	1	2500	2500
2500					
<anonymous>	<anonymous>				
ANONYMOUS BLOCK		13	1	3100	3100
3100					
<anonymous>	<anonymous>				
ANONYMOUS BLOCK		11	16	6900	300
1800					
<anonymous>	<anonymous>				
ANONYMOUS BLOCK		10	16	13600	700
2800					
<anonymous>	<anonymous>				
ANONYMOUS BLOCK		8	16	45700	2000
12600					
<anonymous>	<anonymous>				
ANONYMOUS BLOCK		1	3	48300	1200
31100					

```
<anonymous>                    <anonymous>
ANONYMOUS BLOCK                          9        16      1787400        26200
   1380900
```

```
8 rows selected.
```

As shown in the TOTAL_OCCUR column in the listing, the different lines of the PL/SQL block are executed various numbers of times. The lines within the loop are executed multiple times, and for those lines the total time shown is the cumulative execution time for all of the times those lines are executed. How did the number of executions change the average time per execution?

Line 9, the INSERT, took a total of 444,700 nanoseconds during the first test. That test required inserting four rows, so the inserts averaged 111,175 nanoseconds each. During the second test, 16 rows were inserted in 1,787,400 nanoseconds—an average of 111,702 nanoseconds per row. The INSERT operation performance is linear; on average, every INSERT takes almost exactly the same amount of time regardless of the number of INSERTs. Although its performance is predictable, that kind of performance will not scale well; ideally, you want each new execution of a step to take no additional time.

If you are tuning PL/SQL code that performs many separate transactions, you should look into the use of bulk INSERT and bulk SELECT operations, as described in the next sections of this chapter.

Use PL/SQL Features for Bulk Operations

PL/SQL provides many features for enhancing the performance of code that performs many separate queries or many separate transactions. By combining multiple small operations, you may be able to realize performance gains, particularly in their CPU usage. By combining multiple commands into one, you can decrease the number of parsing operations and the related processing costs. These savings will be small when the number of transactions is small, but as the number of transactions increases, the savings can be considerable. The following sections provide brief overviews and examples of two such methods: **forall** and **bulk collect**.

FORALL

The **forall** operator issues a series of dynamic or static DML commands, replacing **for** loops. You can specify upper and lower bounds for the values the **forall** command iterates through during its processing. The **forall** operator uses bulk binding, allowing you to pass collection of data to the database in a single command. Queries can pass back multiple results without requiring a separate fetch for each row.

Consider the following example. First, let's create a new table to use during this testing:

```
create table bookshelf_temp
as select * from bookshelf;
```

Now, delete all the rows in BOOKSHELF_TEMP that have RATING values of 1, 2, or 3. You can use PL/SQL to iterate through and issue separate DELETE commands for each RATING (within a **for** loop). The following listing shows the use of **forall** to perform the deletes in a bulk fashion:

```
declare
   type numlist is varray(20) of number;
```

```
      ratings numlist := numlist(1, 2, 3);
   begin
      forall i in ratings.first..ratings.last
        delete from bookshelf_temp
        where rating = ratings(i);
      commit;
   end;
   /
```

The line

```
      ratings numlist := numlist(1, 2, 3);
```

defines the RATINGS collection; it uses the NUMLIST datatype (a varying array with up to 20 values). You can then use the RATINGS collection values in controlling the commands to be executed. In this case, you go from the first entry to the last:

```
      forall i in ratings.first..ratings.last
```

For each of those ratings, you perform the same DELETE:

```
        delete from bookshelf_temp
        where rating = ratings(i);
```

The following example, from Oracle, provides a quick comparison of the performance of **forall** commands during INSERTs. To see the output of the DBMS_OUTPUT calls, you should first enable the output from those calls:

```
   set serveroutput on
```

With the output display enabled, the following commands will show the performance improvements **forall** provides:

```
   create table parts1 (pnum integer, pname varchar2(15));
   create table parts2 (pnum integer, pname varchar2(15));
   declare
     type numtab is table of parts1.pnum%type index by pls_integer;
     type nametab is table of parts1.pname%type index by pls_integer;
     pnums   numtab;
     pnames nametab;
     iterations constant pls_integer := 500;
     t1 integer;
     t2 integer;
     t3 integer;
   begin
     for j in 1..iterations loop  -- load index-by tables
       pnums(j) := j;
       pnames(j) := 'Part No. ' || to_char(j);
     end loop;
     t1 := dbms_utility.get_time;
     for i in 1..iterations loop  -- use for loop
       insert into parts1 values (pnums(i), pnames(i));
```

```
      end loop;
      t2 := dbms_utility.get_time;
      forall i in 1..iterations   -- use forall statement
          insert into parts2 values (pnums(i), pnames(i));
      t3 := dbms_utility.get_time;
      dbms_output.put_line('Execution Time (secs)');
      dbms_output.put_line('--------------------');
      dbms_output.put_line('FOR loop: ' || to_char((t2 - t1)/100));
      dbms_output.put_line('FORALL:   ' || to_char((t3 - t2)/100));
      commit;
   end;
   /
```

The sample code inserts data via two separate loops. The first inserts data into the PARTS1 table via a traditional **for** loop:

```
      for i in 1..iterations loop   -- use for loop
          insert into parts1 values (pnums(i), pnames(i));
      end loop;
```

The second loop uses the **forall** approach:

```
      forall i in 1..iterations   -- use FORALL statement
          insert into parts2 values (pnums(i), pnames(i));
```

The example only does 500 rows, so the performance difference will be limited:

```
      iterations constant pls_integer := 500;
```

With that small of a data set, any difference in the performance is significant; the difference indicates how the performance will trend as the number of iterations increases. Running on a fairly robust server, the following results were achieved:

```
   FOR loop: 0.03 sec
   FORALL:   0.01 sec
```

As the number of rows increases, the times savings increases.

When using **forall**, you should take considerable care with the values it will iterate through. You can set up distinct lists of values (as in the preceding DELETE example) or tell Oracle to iterate through a specific number of values. See the *Oracle PL/SQL Language Reference* for the complete list of options available for **forall**.

BULK COLLECT

Like **forall**, **bulk collect** operates on sets of records in an efficient manner. Whereas **forall** supports data manipulation, **bulk collect** supports queries. Instead of looping through each row of a cursor, you can use **bulk collect** to store the query results in collections in a single operation. The **bulk collect** operator supports the use of **select into**, **fetch into**, and **returning into**, as shown in the following examples.

In a **bulk collect** query, all of the variables you are selecting data into must be collections (nested tables or varying arrays). The basic format for a **bulk collect** operation is shown in the following example from Oracle (this example presumes the existence of an EMPLOYEES table in your schema):

```
declare
    type numtab is table of employees.employee_id%type;
    type nametab is table of employees.last_name%type;
    enums numtab;   -- no need to initialize the collections.
    names nametab;  -- values will be filled in by the select into.
    procedure print_results is
    begin
      if enums.count = 0 then
        dbms_output.put_line('No results!');
      else
        dbms_output.put_line('Results:');
        for i in enums.first .. enums.last
        loop
          dbms_output.put_line('  Employee #' || enums(i) || ': ' ||
names(i));
        end loop;
      end if;
    end;
begin
 -- Retrieve data for employees with Ids greater than 1000
    select employee_id, last_name
      bulk collect into enums, names from employees where employee_id > 1000;
-- The data has all been brought into memory by BULK COLLECT
-- No need to FETCH each row from the result set
    print_results();
 -- Retrieve approximately 20% of all rows
    SELECT employee_id, last_name
       bulk collect into enums, names from employees sample (20);
    print_results();
END;
/
```

NOTE
The collections are initialized automatically. If you use a varying array, all the return values must fit in the varying array's declared size.

As in the **forall** example, the first step involves declaring the variables:

```
declare
    type numtab is table of employees.employee_id%type;
    type nametab is table of employees.last_name%type;
    enums numtab;   -- no need to initialize the collections.
    names nametab;  -- Values will be filled in by the SELECT INTO.
```

Within the executable commands block, the number of results is first evaluated via the use of the COUNT attribute for the nested table:

```
begin
  if enums.count = 0 then
    dbms_output.put_line('No results!');
  else
    dbms_output.put_line('Results:');
    for i in enums.first .. enums.last
    loop
      dbms_output.put_line('  Employee #' || enums(i) || ': ' ||
names(i));
    end loop;
  end if;
end;
```

You can use the **bulk collect** operator to select the data into the nested tables declared in the prior section of the listing:

```
-- Retrieve data for employees with Ids greater than 1000
  select employee_id, last_name
    bulk collect into enums, names from employees where employee_id > 1000;
-- The data has all been brought into memory by BULK COLLECT
-- No need to FETCH each row from the result set
  print_results();
```

See the *Oracle PL/SQL Language Reference* for a full description of the capabilities for **bulk collect** and **forall** operations. From a planning perspective, you should consider the bulk operations when designing code that will routinely process large volumes of data. Avoid row-by-row operations that will have difficulty scaling (as shown in the profiler example earlier in this chapter).

Sound design for PL/SQL procedures involves understanding the SQL, the control paths, and the data volumes. Your tuning efforts should follow those same steps—evaluating the SQL, profiling the costs of the control paths, and modifying coding approaches to support the data volumes properly. As the application and database mature, you will need to revisit the code periodically to make sure it can continue to meet the business's performance capacity needs.

PART V

Object-Relational Databases

CHAPTER
38

Implementing Object Types,
Object Views, and Methods

In this chapter, you'll learn about using object types. This chapter covers several related topics, including security administration for object types and the indexing of object type attributes. You'll also read about creating methods for object types, along with using object views and INSTEAD OF triggers.

To benefit from the information provided in this chapter, you should be familiar with datatypes (see Chapter 5), views (see Chapter 17), the GRANT command (see Chapter 20), indexes (see Chapter 17), and PL/SQL procedures and triggers (see Chapters 32, 34, and 35). Elements of each of these topics play a part in the implementation of an object-relational database.

Working with Object Types

You can use object types to group related columns into objects. For example, columns that are part of address information can be grouped into an ADDRESS_TY datatype via the CREATE TYPE command. For this example, use an account named HR with CONNECT and RESOURCE roles:

```
-- connected as HR
create type address_ty as object
(street  varchar2(50),
 city    varchar2(25),
 state   char(2),
 zip     number);
/
```

The CREATE TYPE command in the preceding listing creates an ADDRESS_TY object type. You can use ADDRESS_TY when creating additional database objects. For example, the following CREATE TYPE command creates the PERSON_TY datatype, using the ADDRESS_TY datatype as the datatype for its ADDRESS column:

```
create type person_ty as object
(name       varchar2(25),
 address    address_ty);
/
```

Because the ADDRESS column of the PERSON_TY datatype uses the ADDRESS_TY datatype, it holds not one value but four—the four columns that constitute the ADDRESS_TY datatype.

Security for Object Types

The preceding example assumes that the same user owns both the ADDRESS_TY datatype and the PERSON_TY datatype. What if the owner of the PERSON_TY datatype were different from the ADDRESS_TY datatype's owner?

For example, what if the account named HR owns the ADDRESS_TY datatype, and the user of the account named GEORGE tries to create the PERSON_TY datatype? GEORGE executes the following command:

```
-- while connected as GEORGE:

create type person_ty as object
```

```
(name       varchar2(25),
 address    address_ty);
 /
```

If GEORGE does not own the ADDRESS_TY object type, Oracle responds to this CREATE TYPE command with the following message:

```
Warning: Type created with compilation errors.
```

The compilation errors are caused by problems creating the *constructor method*—a special method created by Oracle when the datatype is created. Oracle cannot resolve the reference to the ADDRESS_TY datatype because GEORGE does not own a datatype with that name. GEORGE could issue the CREATE TYPE command again (using the OR REPLACE clause) to reference HR's ADDRESS_TY datatype specifically:

```
create or replace type person_ty as object
(name       varchar2(25),
 address    hr.address_ty);
 /
```

```
Warning: Type created with compilation errors.
```

To see the errors associated with the datatype creation, use the SHOW ERRORS command:

```
show errors
Errors for TYPE PERSON_TY:

LINE/COL ERROR
-------- -----------------------------------------------------------
0/0      PL/SQL: Compilation unit analysis terminated
3/11     PLS-00201: identifier 'HR.ADDRESS_TY' must be declared
```

GEORGE will not be able to create the PERSON_TY datatype (which includes the ADDRESS_TY datatype) unless HR first grants him the EXECUTE privilege on her type. The following listing shows this grant:

```
--   while connected as HR:
```

```
grant execute on address_ty to george;
```

Now that the proper grants are in place, GEORGE can create a datatype that is based on HR's ADDRESS_TY datatype, as shown in the following listing.

```
--   while connected as GEORGE:
```

```
create or replace type person_ty as object
(name       varchar2(25),
 address    hr.address_ty);
 /
```

Using another user's object types is not trivial. For example, during INSERT operations, you must specify the owner of each type or use a synonym. GEORGE can create a table based on his PERSON_TY datatype (which includes HR's ADDRESS_TY object type), as shown in the following listing:

```
create table customer
(customer_id  number,
 person        person_ty);
```

If GEORGE owned the PERSON_TY and ADDRESS_TY datatypes, an INSERT into CUSTOMER would use the following format:

```
insert into customer values
(1,person_ty('SomeName',
   address_ty('StreetValue','CityValue','ST',11111)));
```

Because GEORGE does not own the ADDRESS_TY datatype, this command will fail. During the INSERT, the ADDRESS_TY constructor method is used—and HR owns it. Therefore, the INSERT command must be modified to specify HR as the owner of ADDRESS_TY. The following example shows the corrected INSERT statement, with the reference to HR shown in bold:

```
insert into customer values
(1,person_ty('SomeName',
   hr.address_ty('StreetValue','CityValue','ST',11111)));
```

GEORGE can simplify the SQL by creating a synonym named ADDRESS_TY:

```
create synonym address_ty for hr.address_ty;
```

This synonym can be used in queries, in DML (Data Manipulation Language), and in DDL (Data Definition Language).

You can use a synonym for another user's object type during queries and inserts. For example, GEORGE's insert works now that the ADDRESS_TY synonym exists:

```
insert into customer values
(1,person_ty('SomeName',
   address_ty('StreetValue','CityValue','ST',11111)));
```

NOTE
When you create a synonym, Oracle does not check the validity of the object for which you are creating a synonym. When you CREATE SYNONYM X FOR Y, Oracle does not check to make sure that Y is a valid object name or valid object type. The validity of that object is only checked when the object is accessed via the synonym.

In a relational-only implementation of Oracle, you grant the EXECUTE privilege on procedural objects such as procedures and packages. Within the object-relational implementation of Oracle, the EXECUTE privilege is extended to cover object types as well. The EXECUTE privilege is appropriate because object types can include *methods*—PL/SQL functions and procedures that operate on the datatype. If you grant someone the privilege to use your object type, you are granting that user the privilege to execute the methods you have defined on the object type. Although HR did not yet define any methods on the ADDRESS_TY object type, Oracle automatically creates constructor methods to access the data. Any object (such as PERSON_TY) that uses the ADDRESS_TY object type uses the constructor method associated with ADDRESS_TY. Even if you haven't created any methods for your object type, it still has procedures associated with it.

You can describe CUSTOMER:

```
describe customer
```

Name	Null?	Type
CUSTOMER_ID		NUMBER
PERSON		PERSON_TY

You can use the SET DESCRIBE DEPTH command in SQL*Plus to show the datatype attributes for tables that use object-relational features. You can specify depth values from 1 to 50:

```
set describe depth 2

desc customer
```

Name	Null?	Type
CUSTOMER_ID		NUMBER
PERSON		PERSON_TY
NAME		VARCHAR2(25)
ADDRESS		HR.ADDRESS_TY

```
set describe depth 3

desc customer
```

Name	Null?	Type
CUSTOMER_ID		NUMBER
PERSON		PERSON_TY
NAME		VARCHAR2(25)
ADDRESS		HR.ADDRESS_TY
STREET		VARCHAR2(50)
CITY		VARCHAR2(25)
STATE		CHAR(2)
ZIP		NUMBER

Indexing Object Type Attributes

As shown in the previous listings, the CUSTOMER table contains a normal column (CUSTOMER_ID) and a PERSON column that is defined by the PERSON_TY object type.

From the datatype definitions shown in the preceding section of this chapter, you can see that PERSON_TY has one column (NAME) followed by an ADDRESS column defined by the ADDRESS_TY datatype.

During queries, you fully qualify the datatype attributes when referencing columns within the object types by prefacing the attribute name with the column name and by prefacing the column name with a *correlation* variable. For example, the following query returns the CUSTOMER_ID column along with the NAME column. The NAME column is an attribute of the datatype that defines the PERSON column, so you refer to the attribute as PERSON.NAME:

```
select customer_id, c.person.name
from customer c;
```

NOTE
When querying the attributes of an object type, you must use a correlation variable for the table, as shown in this example.

To set the display attributes for an object type's attributes in SQL*Plus, use the COLUMN command, specifying the name of the datatype and the attribute:

```
column customer_id format 9999999
column person.name format a25
```

You can refer to attributes within the ADDRESS_TY object type by specifying the full path through the related columns. For example, the STREET column is referred to as PERSON. ADDRESS.STREET, fully describing its location within the structure of the table. In the following example, the CITY column is referenced twice—once in the list of columns to select and once within the WHERE clause. In each reference, a correlation variable (in this example, *c*) is required.

```
select c.person.name,
       c.person.address.city
from customer c
where c.person.address.city like 'C%';
```

Because the CITY column is used with a range search in the WHERE clause, the Oracle Optimizer may be able to use an index when resolving the query. If an index is available on the CITY column, Oracle can quickly find all the rows that have CITY values starting with the letter *C*, as requested by the query.

NOTE
See Chapter 46 for guidelines regarding the columns to index.

To create an index on a column that is part of an object type, you need to specify the full path to the column as part of the CREATE INDEX command. To create an index on the CITY column (which is part of the ADDRESS column), you can execute the following command:

```
create index i_customer$city
    on customer(person.address.city);
```

This command creates an index named I_CUSTOMER$CITY on the PERSON.ADDRESS.CITY column. Whenever the CITY column is accessed, the Oracle optimizer will evaluate the SQL used to access the data and determine if the new index can improve the query's performance.

NOTE
In the CREATE INDEX command, you do not use correlation variables when referencing the attributes of object types.

When creating tables based on object types, you should consider how the columns within the object types will be accessed. If, like the CITY column in the preceding example, certain columns will commonly be used as part of limiting conditions in queries, they should be indexed. In this regard, the representation of multiple columns in a single object type may hinder your application performance because it may obscure the need to index specific columns within the datatype. When using object types, you become accustomed to treating a group of columns as a single entity, such as the ADDRESS columns or the PERSON columns. It is important to remember that the optimizer, when evaluating query access paths, will consider the columns individually. In addition, remember that indexing the CITY column in one table that uses the ADDRESS_TY object type does not affect the CITY column in a second table that uses the ADDRESS_TY object type. For example, if there is a second table named BRANCH that uses the ADDRESS_TY object type, *its* CITY column will not be indexed unless you create an index for it. The fact that there is an index on the CITY column in the CUSTOMER table will have no impact on the CITY column in the BRANCH table.

Therefore, one of the advantages of object types—the ability to improve adherence to standards for logical data representation—does not extend to the physical data representation. You need to address each physical implementation separately.

Implementing Object Views

The CUSTOMER table created in the previous section of this chapter assumed that a PERSON_TY datatype already existed. When implementing object-relational database applications, you should first use the relational database design methods described in the first part of this book. After the database design is properly normalized, you should look for groups of columns (or individual columns) that constitute the representation of an object type. You can then create your tables based on the object types, as shown earlier in this chapter.

But what if your tables already exist? What if you have previously created a relational database application and now want to implement object-relational concepts in your application without rebuilding and re-creating the entire application? To do this, you need the ability to overlay object-oriented (OO) structures, such as object types, on existing relational tables. Oracle provides *object views* as a means for defining objects used by existing relational tables.

NOTE
Throughout the examples in this book, the names of object views will always end with the suffix OV.

In the examples earlier in this chapter, the order of operations was as follows:

1. Create the ADDRESS_TY datatype.
2. Create the PERSON_TY datatype, using the ADDRESS_TY datatype.
3. Create the CUSTOMER table, using the PERSON_TY datatype.

If the CUSTOMER table already existed, you could create the ADDRESS_TY and PERSON_TY datatypes and use object views to relate them to the CUSTOMER table. In the following listing, the CUSTOMER table is created as a relational table, using only the built-in datatypes. To keep the examples separated, create these objects under a new schema.

```
--    connect as a new user:

create table customer
(customer_id number    primary key,
 name           varchar2(25),
 street         varchar2(50),
 city           varchar2(25),
 state          char(2),
 zip            number);
/
```

If you want to create another table or application that stores information about people and addresses, you may choose to create the ADDRESS_TY and PERSON_TY object types. However, for consistency, they should be applied to the CUSTOMER table as well.

With the CUSTOMER table already created (and possibly containing data), you should create the object types. First, create ADDRESS_TY:

```
drop type person_ty;
drop type address_ty;
drop synonym address_ty;

create or replace type address_ty as object
(street  varchar2(50),
 city    varchar2(25),
 state   char(2),
 zip     number);
/
```

Next, create PERSON_TY, which uses ADDRESS_TY:

```
create or replace type person_ty as object
(name        varchar2(25),
 address     address_ty);
/
```

Now, create an object view based on the CUSTOMER table using the object types you have defined. An object view starts with the CREATE VIEW command. Within the CREATE VIEW command, you specify the query that will form the basis of the view. Use the object types you just created. The code for creating the CUSTOMER_OV object view is shown in the following listing:

```
create view customer_ov (customer_id, person) as
select customer_id,
       person_ty(name,
       address_ty(street, city, state, zip))
  from customer;
```

Let's look at this command closely. In the first line, the object view is named:

```
create view customer_ov (customer_id, person) as
```

The CUSTOMER_OV view will have two columns: the CUSTOMER_ID column and the PERSON column (the latter is defined by the PERSON_TY object type). Note that you cannot specify "object" as an option within the CREATE VIEW command.

In the next section of the CREATE VIEW command, you create the query that will form the basis for the view:

```
select customer_id,
       person_ty(name,
       address_ty(street, city, state, zip))
from customer;
```

This example presents several important syntax issues. When a table is built on existing object types, you select column values from the table by referring to the names of the columns (such as PERSON and ADDRESS in earlier examples) instead of their constructor methods. When creating the object view, however, you refer to the names of the constructor methods (PERSON_TY and ADDRESS_TY) instead.

You can use a WHERE clause in the query that forms the basis of the object view. In the following example, CUSTOMER_OV is modified to include a WHERE clause that limits it to showing the CUSTOMER values for which the STATE column has a value of "DE":

```
create or replace view customer_ov (customer_id, person) as
select customer_id,
       person_ty(name,
       address_ty(street, city, state, zip))
from customer
where state = 'DE';
```

Note that when you create the object view CUSTOMER_OV, the WHERE clause of the view's base query does not refer to the object type. Instead, it refers directly to the CUSTOMER table. The WHERE clause refers directly to the STATE column because the query refers directly to the CUSTOMER table—a relational table that is not based on any object types.

To create object views based on relational tables, the order of operations is as follows:

1. Create the CUSTOMER table if it does not already exist.
2. Create the ADDRESS_TY object type.
3. Create the PERSON_TY object type, using the ADDRESS_TY object type.
4. Create the CUSTOMER_OV object view, using the defined object types.

There are two main benefits to using object views. First, they allow you to create object types that operate against tables that already exist. Because you can use the same object types in multiple tables within your application, you can improve your application's adherence to standard representation of data and your ability to reuse existing objects. Because you can define methods for the object types, the methods will apply to the data within any new tables you create as well as to your existing tables.

Second, object views provide two different ways to enter data into the base table. The flexibility of data manipulation for object views—being able to treat the base table as either a relational table or an object table—is a significant benefit for application developers. In the next section, you'll see the data-manipulation options available for object views.

Manipulating Data via Object Views

You can update the data in the CUSTOMER table via the CUSTOMER_OV object view, or you can update the CUSTOMER table directly. By treating CUSTOMER as just a table, you can insert data into it via a normal SQL INSERT command, as shown in the following example:

```
insert into customer values
    (123,'Sigmund','47 Haffner Rd','Lewiston','NJ',22222);
```

This INSERT command inserts a single record into the CUSTOMER table. Even though you have created an object view on the table, you can still treat the CUSTOMER table as a regular relational table.

Because the object view has been created on the CUSTOMER table, you can INSERT into CUSTOMER via the constructor methods used by the view. As previously shown in this chapter, when you insert data into an object that uses object types, you specify the names of the constructor methods within the INSERT command. The example shown in the following listing inserts a single record into the CUSTOMER_OV object view using the CUSTOMER_TY, PERSON_TY, and ADDRESS_TY constructor methods:

```
insert into customer_ov values
    (234,
    person_ty('Evelyn',
    address_ty('555 High St','Lowlands Park','NE',33333)));
```

Because you can use either technique to insert values into the CUSTOMER_OV object view, you can standardize the manner in which your application performs data manipulation. If your INSERTs are all based on object types, you can use the same kind of code for INSERTs regardless of whether the object types were created before or after the table was.

You can query the rows just entered from either CUSTOMER or CUSTOMER_OV; but because the view has a WHERE clause, CUSTOMER_OV will only show the rows that pass that limiting condition.

Using INSTEAD OF Triggers

If you create an object view, you can use an INSTEAD OF trigger to tell Oracle how to update the underlying tables that are part of the view. You can use INSTEAD OF triggers on either object views or standard relational views.

For example, if a view involves a join of two tables, your ability to UPDATE records in the view is limited. However, if you use an INSTEAD OF trigger, you can tell Oracle how to update, delete, or insert records in tables when a user attempts to change values via the view. The code in the INSTEAD OF trigger is executed *in place of* the INSERT, UPDATE, or DELETE command you enter.

For example, you may have a view that joins the BOOKSHELF table to BOOKSHELF_AUTHOR:

```
create or replace view author_publisher as
   select ba.author_name, title, b.publisher
   from bookshelf_author ba inner join bookshelf b
   using (title);
```

You can select values from this view—and if you use INSTEAD OF triggers, you can also perform data manipulation via this view. Consider these records:

```
select author_name, publisher from author_publisher
where author_name = 'W. P. Kinsella';
```

```
AUTHORNAME                                              PUBLISHER
-------------------------------------------------- ----------
W. P. Kinsella
W. P. Kinsella                                         Mariner
                                                      Ballantine
```

If you attempt to update the PUBLISHER value, the update fails:

```
update author_publisher
set publisher = 'Mariner'
where author_name = 'W. P. Kinsella';
```

```
set Publisher = 'Mariner'
    *
ERROR at line 2:
ORA-01779: cannot modify a column which maps to a
           non key-preserved table
```

The problem is that Oracle cannot determine which publisher in which record to update in BOOKSHELF. To perform the UPDATE via the view, you need to use an INSTEAD OF trigger.

In the following listing, an INSTEAD OF trigger for the AUTHOR_PUBLISHER view is created:

```
create or replace trigger author_publisher_update
instead of update on author_publisher
for each row
begin
  if :old.publisher <> :new.publisher
  then
    update bookshelf
       set publisher = :new.publisher
     where title = :old.title;
  end if;
  if :old.author_name <> :new.author_name
  then
    update bookshelf_author
       set author_name = :new.author_name
     where title = :old.title;
  end if;
end;
/
```

In the first part of this trigger, the trigger is named and its purpose is described via the INSTEAD OF clause. The trigger has been named to make its function clear: It is used to support UPDATE commands executed against the AUTHOR_PUBLISHER view. It is a row-level trigger; each changed row will be processed, as shown next:

```
create trigger author_publisher_update
instead of update on author_publisher
for each row
```

The next section of the trigger tells Oracle how to process the UPDATE. In the first check within the trigger body, the PUBLISHER value is checked. If the old PUBLISHER value is equal to the new PUBLISHER value, no changes are made. If the values are not the same, the BOOKSHELF table is updated with the new PUBLISHER value:

```
vbegin
   if :old.publisher <> :new.publisher
   then
     update bookshelf
        set publisher = :new.publisher
      where title = :old.title;
   end if;
```

In the next section of the trigger, the AUTHOR_NAME value is evaluated. If the AUTHOR_NAME value has changed, the BOOKSHELF table is updated to reflect the new AUTHOR_NAME value:

```
   if :old.author_name <> :new.author_name
   then
     update bookshelf_author
        set author_name = :new.author_name
      where title = :old.title;
   end if;
```

Thus, the view relies on two tables—BOOKSHELF and BOOKSHELF_AUTHOR—and an UPDATE of the view can update *either* or *both* of the tables. The INSTEAD OF trigger, introduced to support object views, is a powerful tool for application development.

You can now update the AUTHOR_PUBLISHER view directly and have the trigger update the proper underlying table. For example, the following command updates the BOOKSHELF table:

```
update author_publisher
set publisher = 'Mariner'
where author_name = 'W. P. Kinsella';
```

```
2 rows updated.
```

Verify the UPDATE by querying the BOOKSHELF table:

```
select publisher from bookshelf
where title in
   (select title from bookshelf_author
    where author_name = 'W. P. Kinsella');
```

```
PUBLISHER
-------------------
Mariner
Mariner
```

INSTEAD OF triggers are very powerful. As shown in this example, you can use them to perform operations against different database tables, using the flow-control logic available within PL/SQL. In dealing with object views, you can use INSTEAD OF triggers to redirect DML against the object views to the base tables for the views.

Methods

When you created an object view on the CUSTOMER table, you defined object types that the table used. Those datatypes help to standardize the representation of data, but they serve another purpose as well. You can define methods that apply to datatypes, and by applying those datatypes to existing tables, you can apply those methods to the data in those tables.

Consider the CUSTOMER_OV object view:

```
create or replace view customer_ov (customer_id, person) as
select customer_id,
       person_ty(name,
       address_ty(street, city, state, zip))
from customer;
```

This view applies the PERSON_TY and ADDRESS_TY object types to the data in the CUSTOMER table. If any methods are associated with those object types, they will apply to the data in the table. When you create an object type, you use the CREATE TYPE command. When you create a method, you use the CREATE TYPE BODY command.

Syntax for Creating Methods

Before creating the body for a method, you must name the method within the datatype declaration. For example, let's create a new datatype, ANIMAL_TY. The datatype definition for ANIMAL_TY is shown in the following listing:

```
create or replace type animal_ty as object
(breed        varchar2(25),
 name         varchar2(25),
 birth_date date,
 member function age (birth_date in date) return number);
/
```

The ANIMAL_TY datatype could be used as part of an object view on the BREEDING table used in Chapter 14. In the BREEDING table, the name of an offspring, its sex, its parents, and its birthdate are recorded.

Within the CREATE TYPE command, the line

```
member function age (birth_date in date) return number)
```

names the function that is a "member" of the ANIMAL_TY datatype. Because AGE returns a value, it is a function (see Chapter 35). To define the AGE function, use the CREATE TYPE BODY command, whose full syntax is shown in the Alphabetical Reference.

Let's create the AGE function as a member function within the ANIMAL_TY datatype. The AGE function returns the age, in days, of the animals:

```
create or replace type body animal_ty as
member function age (birth_date date) return number is
   begin
      return round(sysdate - birth_date);
   end;
end;
/
```

If you had additional functions or procedures to code, you specify them within the same CREATE TYPE BODY command, before the final END clause.

Now that the AGE function has been created, it is associated with the ANIMAL_TY object type. If a table uses this object type, it can use the AGE function.

NOTE
You cannot drop or re-create a type that is in use by an existing table.

You can use the AGE function within a query. If ANIMAL_TY is used as the object type for a column named ANIMAL in the table named ANIMAL, the table structure could be as follows:

```
create table animal
(id        number,
 animal    animal_ty);

insert into animal values
(11,animal_ty('Cow','Mimi',to_date('01-JAN-2007','DD-MON-YYYY')));
```

You can now invoke the AGE function, which is part of the ANIMAL_TY object type. Like the attributes of an object type, the member methods are referenced using the column names that use the object types (in this case, ANIMAL.AGE). Your result reflects the current system date when you execute the query:

```
select a.animal.age(a.animal.birth_date)
from animal a;

A.ANIMAL.AGE(A.ANIMAL.BIRTHDATE)
--------------------------------
                            2694
```

The A.ANIMAL.AGE(A.ANIMAL.BIRTH_DATE) call executes the AGE method within the ANIMAL_TY datatype. Therefore, you do not have to store variable data such as AGE within your database. Instead, you can store static data—such as BIRTH_DATE—in your database and use function and procedure calls to derive the variable data.

NOTE
In this example, you need to use correlation variables in two places—when calling the AGE method and when passing the name of the BIRTH_DATE column to that method.

Managing Methods

You can add new methods to an object type by altering the object type (via the ALTER TYPE command). When altering an object type, list all its methods, both the old and the new. After altering the object type, alter the object type's body, listing all the object type's methods in a single command.

You do not need to grant EXECUTE privilege on the member functions and procedures of object types. If you grant another user EXECUTE privilege on the ANIMAL_TY object type, that user automatically has EXECUTE privilege on the methods that are part of the object type. Thus, the GRANT of access to the object type includes both the data representation and its data access methods, in accordance with OO concepts.

When creating member functions, you can specify them as being map methods or order methods (or neither, as in the case of the ANIMAL_TY.AGE member function). A *map method* returns the relative position of a given record in the ordering of all records within the object. A type body can contain only one map method, which must be a function.

An *order method* is a member function that takes a record in the object as an explicit argument and returns an integer value. If the returned value is negative, zero, or positive, the implicit "self" argument of the function is less than, equal to, or greater than, respectively, that of the explicitly specified record. When multiple rows within an object are compared in an ORDER BY clause, the order method is automatically executed to order the rows returned. An object type specification can contain only one order method, which must be a function with the return type INTEGER.

The notion of ordering within the rows of an object type may have more relevance when you consider the implementation of *collectors*—datatypes that hold multiple values per row. Oracle offers two types of collectors, called *nested tables* and *varying arrays*. In the next chapter, you'll see how to implement these collector types.

CHAPTER
39

Collectors (Nested Tables and Varying Arrays)

C ollectors make use of object types. You should be familiar with the creation and implementation of object types (see Chapter 38) before attempting to use varying arrays and nested tables.

Varying Arrays

A *varying array* allows you to store repeating attributes of a record in a single row. For example, suppose you want to track which of your tools were borrowed by which of your neighbors. You could model this in a relational database by creating a BORROWER table:

```
create table borrower
(name           varchar2(25),
 tool           varchar2(25),
 constraint borrower_pk primary key (name, tool));
```

Even though the borrower's NAME value does not change, it is repeated in each row because it is part of the primary key. Collectors such as varying arrays allow you to repeat *only* those column values that change, potentially saving storage space. You can use collectors to represent relationships between object types accurately in your database objects. In the following sections, you'll learn how to create and use collectors.

Creating a Varying Array

You can create a varying array based on either an object type or one of Oracle's standard datatypes (such as NUMBER). For example, you could create a new object type, TOOL_TY, as shown in the following listing, that has only one column; you should limit varying arrays to one column. If you need to use multiple columns in an array, consider using nested tables (described later in this chapter).

```
create type tool_ty as object
(toolname  varchar2(25));
/
```

You do not have to create the base type—in this case, TOOL_TY—before you can create a varying array (to be named TOOLS_VA). Because the varying array is based on only one column, you can create the TOOLS_VA type in a single step. To create the varying array, use the AS VARRAY() clause of the CREATE TYPE command:

```
create or replace type tools_va as varray(5) of varchar2(25);
/
```

When this CREATE TYPE command is executed, a type named TOOLS_VA is created. The AS VARRAY(5) clause tells Oracle that a varying array is being created, and it will hold a maximum of five entries per table row. The name of the varying array is the pluralized TOOLS (instead of TOOL) to show that this type will be used to hold multiple values. The suffix VA makes it clear that the type is a varying array. You can now use this type as the basis for a column definition, as shown in the following listing:

```
drop table borrower;

create table borrower
(name           varchar2(25),
 tools          tools_va,
 constraint borrower_pk primary key (name));
```

Describing the Varying Array

The BORROWER table contains one row for each borrower, even if that borrower has multiple tools. The multiple tools are stored in the TOOLS column, using the TOOLS_VA varying array. You can describe the BORROWER table as follows:

```
desc borrower
```

```
Name                                Null?      Type
----------------------------------- --------   ------------
NAME                                NOT NULL   VARCHAR2(25)
TOOLS                                          TOOLS_VA
```

NOTE
The SET DESCRIBE DEPTH command shown in Chapter 38 will not affect this output in these examples.

You can query similar information from USER_TAB_COLUMNS:

```
column data_type format a12

select column_name,
       data_type
from user_tab_columns
where table_name = 'BORROWER';
```

```
COLUMN_NAME                         DATA_TYPE
----------------------------------- ------------
NAME                                VARCHAR2
TOOLS                               TOOLS_VA
```

USER_TYPES shows TOOLS_VA is a collection, with no attributes:

```
select typecode,
       attributes
from user_types
where type_name = 'TOOLS_VA';
```

```
TYPECODE                            ATTRIBUTES
----------------------------------- ----------
COLLECTION                                   0
```

For more details on TOOLS_VA, query the USER_COLL_TYPES data dictionary view, as shown in the following listing:

```
select coll_type,
       elem_type_owner,
       elem_type_name,
       upper_bound,
       length
from user_coll_types
where type_name = 'TOOLS_VA';


COLL_TYPE                            ELEM_TYPE_OWNER
----------------------------         ---------------------------
ELEM_TYPE_NAME                       UPPER_BOUND    LENGTH
----------------------------         -----------    ----------
VARYING ARRAY
VARCHAR2                                       5            25
```

If you base a varying array on an existing object type, the object type's owner is displayed in the ELEM_TYPE_OWNER column, and the object type's name is displayed in the ELEM_TYPE_NAME column. Because TOOLS_VA uses VARCHAR2 instead of an object type, the ELEM_TYPE_OWNER column's value is NULL.

Inserting Rows into the Varying Array

Because a varying array is an object type, you need to use constructor methods to insert rows into tables that use varying arrays. Furthermore, because the varying array is itself an object type, you may need to nest calls to multiple constructor methods to insert a row into a table that uses a varying array.

The following command inserts a single row into the BORROWER table. In this example, the row will have a single NAME column value and three TOOLS values.

```
insert into borrower values
('Jed Hopkins',
  tools_va('hammer','sledge','ax'));
```

This INSERT command first specifies the value for the NAME column. Because the NAME column is not part of any object type, it is populated in the same way you would insert values into any relational column:

```
insert into borrower values
('Jed Hopkins',
```

The next part of the INSERT command inserts records into the TOOLS column. Because the TOOLS column uses the TOOLS_VA varying array, you need to use the TOOLS_VA constructor method:

```
tools_va('hammer','sledge','ax'));
```

Because this is a varying array, you can pass multiple values to the TOOLS_VA constructor method. As the preceding listing shows, three tools are listed in a single INSERT for the single borrower name. If the varying array had been based on the TOOL_TY object type, you would have instead nested calls to TOOL_TY within the TOOLS_VA calls, as shown here:

```
insert into borrower values
('Jed Hopkins',
   tools_va(
      tool_ty('hammer'),
      tool_ty('sledge'),
      tool_ty('ax')));
```

Basing the varying array on an Oracle-supplied datatype (and using only a single column) instead of a user-defined object type simplifies the INSERT command by eliminating the nested calls to additional constructor methods.

The TOOLS_VA varying array was defined to have up to five values. In this INSERT command, only three values were entered for the row; the other two are uninitialized. If you want to set the uninitialized values to NULL, you can specify that in the INSERT command:

```
insert into borrower values
('Jed Hopkins',
   tools_va('hammer','sledge','ax',null,null));
```

If you specify too many values to insert into the varying array, Oracle responds with the following:

```
ORA-22909: exceeded maximum VARRAY limit
```

You cannot insert rows into a table that contains a varying array unless you know the structure and datatypes within the array. This example assumes that all the datatypes used by the BORROWER table were within the schema used to create the BORROWER table. If the object types are owned by a separate schema, the creator of the BORROWER table needs EXECUTE privilege on those datatypes. See Chapter 38 for examples of using object types created under other schemas.

Selecting Data from Varying Arrays

You can query the varying array data directly from the table:

```
select tools from borrower;

TOOLS
-----------------------------------------
TOOLS_VA('hammer', 'sledge', 'ax')
```

You can use the TABLE function in the FROM clause to display the data from varying arrays on separate lines. Consider the following query and its output:

```
select b.name, n.*
from borrower b, table(b.tools) n;

NAME                     COLUMN_VALUE
------------------------  ------------------------
Jed Hopkins              hammer
```

```
Jed Hopkins                    sledge
Jed Hopkins                    ax
Jed Hopkins
Jed Hopkins
```

How did that work? The TABLE function took as its input the name of the varying array, and its output is given the alias N. The values within N are selected, generating the second column of the output. All five entries in the varying array are shown, including the two NULL values that were not specified during the INSERT.

To display the varying array data on separate lines, you can also use PL/SQL. You can query the varying array to determine its maximum number of entries per row, called its LIMIT, and the current number of entries per row, called its COUNT. To retrieve the COUNT, LIMIT, and data from a varying array, you can use a set of nested Cursor FOR loops, as shown in the following listing:

NOTE
For an overview of PL/SQL and Cursor FOR loops, see Chapter 32.

```
set serveroutput on
declare
   cursor borrower_cursor is
     select * from borrower;
begin
   for borrower_rec in borrower_cursor
   loop
     dbms_output.put_line('Contact Name: '||borrower_rec.Name);
     for i in 1..borrower_rec.Tools.Count
     loop
       dbms_output.put_line(borrower_rec.Tools(i));
     end loop;
   end loop;
end;
/
```

The following is the output of this PL/SQL script:

```
Contact Name: Jed Hopkins
hammer
sledge
ax

PL/SQL procedure successfully completed.
```

The script uses several PL/SQL features to retrieve data from the varying array. The data is displayed via the PUT_LINE procedure of the DBMS_OUTPUT package (see Chapter 35), so you must first enable PL/SQL output to be displayed:

```
set serveroutput on
```

In the Declarations section of the PL/SQL block, a cursor is declared; the cursor's query selects all the values from the BORROWER table:

```
declare
    cursor borrower_cursor is
        select * from borrower;
```

The Executable Commands section of the PL/SQL block contains two nested FOR loops. In the first loop, each row from the cursor is evaluated and the NAME value is printed via PUT_LINE:

```
begin
    for borrower_rec in borrower_cursor
    loop
        dbms_output.put_line('Contact Name: '||borrower_rec.Name);
```

In the next section of the PL/SQL block, the rows are evaluated further to retrieve the data stored in the varying array. A second FOR loop, nested within the first loop, is executed. The inner FOR loop is limited by the number of values in the array, as defined by the COUNT method (the maximum number of values in the array is available via the LIMIT method).

The values in the TOOLS array will be printed, one by one, by this loop:

```
        for i in 1..borrower_rec.Tools.Count
        loop
            dbms_output.put_line(borrower_rec.Tools(i));
```

The notation

```
Tools(i)
```

tells Oracle to print the array value that corresponds to the value of *i*. Thus, the first time through the loop, the first value in the array is printed; then the value of *i* is incremented, and the second value in the array is printed.

The last part of the PL/SQL block closes the two nested loops and ends the block:

```
        end loop;
    end loop;
end;
```

Because this method involves nested loops within PL/SQL, selecting data from varying arrays is not trivial.

Note that we may get a different number of tools for each borrower—anywhere from zero to five. For example, the following row inserts a row with just one entry in the varying array:

```
insert into borrower values
('Fred Fuller',
  tools_va('hammer'));
```

You can select that data via PL/SQL, via the TABLE function, or via SQL:

```
select b.name, n.*
from borrower b, table(b.tools) n;
```

```
NAME                          COLUMN_VALUE
------------------------      ------------------------
Fred Fuller                   hammer
Jed Hopkins                   hammer
Jed Hopkins                   sledge
Jed Hopkins                   ax
```

For greater flexibility in selecting data from collectors, you should consider using *nested tables*, as described in the next section.

NOTE
You can use the MODIFY LIMIT clause of the ALTER TYPE command to change the maximum number of entries allowed in a varying array.

Following the nested table examples, you'll learn about additional functions that you can use against varying arrays and nested tables.

Nested Tables

Whereas varying arrays have a limited number of entries, a second type of collector, called a *nested table,* has no limit on the number of entries per row. A nested table is, as its name implies, a table within a table. In this case, it is a table that is represented as a column within another table. You can have multiple rows in the nested table for each row in the main table.

For example, if you have a table of animal breeders, you may also have data about their animals. Using a nested table, you could store the information about breeders and all of their animals within the same table. Consider the ANIMAL_TY datatype introduced in Chapter 38:

```
create or replace type animal_ty as object
(breed       varchar2(25),
 name        varchar2(25),
 birthdate   date);
/
```

NOTE
To keep this example simple, this version of the ANIMAL_TY datatype does not include any methods. For this example, you should drop the ANIMAL table if it exists in your practice schema.

The ANIMAL_TY datatype contains a row for each animal—its breed, name, and birth date. To use this datatype as the basis for a nested table, you need to create a new datatype:

```
create type animals_nt as table of animal_ty;
/
```

The AS TABLE OF clause of this CREATE TYPE command tells Oracle that you will use this type as the basis for a nested table. The name of the type, ANIMALS_NT, has a pluralized root to indicate that it stores multiple rows, and it has the suffix NT to indicate that it is a nested table.

You can now create a table of breeders, using the ANIMALS_TY datatype:

```
create table breeder
(breeder_name       varchar2(25),
 animals            animals_nt)
 nested table animals store as animals_nt_tab;
```

In this CREATE TABLE command, the BREEDER table is created. The first column of the BREEDER table is a BREEDER_NAME column. The second column is a column named ANIMALS, whose definition is the nested table ANIMALS_NT.

When creating a table that includes a nested table, you must specify the name of the table that will be used to store the nested table's data. That is, the data for the nested table is not stored "inline" with the rest of the table's data. Instead, it is stored apart from the main table. The data in the ANIMALS column is stored in one table, and the data in the BREEDER_NAME column is stored in a separate table. Oracle maintains pointers between the tables. In this example, the "out-of-line" data for the nested table is stored in a table named ANIMALS_NT_TAB:

```
nested table animals store as animals_nt_tab;
```

This example highlights the importance of naming standards for collectors. If you pluralize the column names ("ANIMALS" instead of "ANIMAL") and consistently use suffixes (TY, NT, and so forth), you can tell what an object is just by its name. Furthermore, because nested tables and varying arrays may be based directly on previously defined datatypes, their names may mirror the names of the datatypes on which they are based. Therefore, a datatype named ANIMAL_TY could be used as the basis for a varying array named ANIMALS_VA or a nested table named ANIMALS_NT. The nested table would have an associated out-of-line table named ANIMALS_NT_TAB. If you know that a table named ANIMALS_NT_TAB exists and you are consistent in your object naming, you automatically know that it stores data based on a datatype named ANIMAL_TY.

Specifying Tablespaces for Nested Tables

When you create the BREEDER table with the ANIMALS nested table, the nested table's storage is created in the same table as the parent table. If you create a nested table within a nested table, the child table is created in the same tablespace as its parent table unless you specify a different tablespace.

You can use the CREATE TABLE command to specify a tablespace for the nested table, as shown in the following listing. In this example, the BREEDER table is stored in the user's default tablespace, whereas the ANIMALS nested table is stored in the USERS tablespace:

```
drop table breeder;

create table breeder
(breeder_name       varchar2(25),
 animals            animals_nt)
 nested table animals store as animals_nt_tab (tablespace users);
```

You can move the nested table via the MOVE clause of the ALTER TABLE command. If you execute the ALTER TABLE MOVE command on the BREEDER table, its nested table will not be moved. To move the nested table, use the name of the storage table listed in the CREATE TABLE command:

```
alter table animals_nt_tab move tablespace users2;
```

Inserting Rows into a Nested Table

You can insert rows into a nested table by using the constructor methods for its datatype. For the ANIMALS column, the datatype is ANIMALS_NT; therefore, you'll use the ANIMALS_NT constructor method. The ANIMALS_NT type, in turn, uses the ANIMAL_TY datatype. As shown in the following example, inserting a row into the BREEDER table requires that you use both the ANIMALS_NT and ANIMAL_TY constructor methods. In the example, three animals are listed for the breeder named Jane James.

```
insert into breeder values
('Jane James',
   animals_nt(
         animal_ty('dog', 'Butch', '31-mar-11'),
         animal_ty('dog', 'Rover', '05-jun-11'),
         animal_ty('dog', 'Julio', '10-jun-11')
));
```

This INSERT command first specifies the name of the breeder:

```
insert into breeder values
('Jane James',
```

Next, the value for the ANIMALS column is entered. Because the ANIMALS column uses the ANIMALS_NT nested table, the ANIMALS_NT constructor method is called:

```
animals_nt(
```

The ANIMALS_NT nested table uses the ANIMAL_TY datatype, so the ANIMAL_TY constructor method is called for each value inserted:

```
         animal_ty('dog', 'Butch', '31-mar-11'),
         animal_ty('dog', 'Rover', '05-jun-11'),
         animal_ty('dog', 'Julio', '10-jun-11')
));
```

You can see the datatypes that constitute the table and its nested table via the DESCRIBE command. Use the SET DESCRIBE DEPTH SQL*Plus command to enable the display of the datatype attributes:

```
set describe depth 2

desc breeder
```

Name	Null?	Type
BREEDER_NAME		VARCHAR2(25)

```
ANIMALS                              ANIMALS_NT
    BREED                                VARCHAR2(25)
    NAME                                 VARCHAR2(25)
    BIRTHDATE                            DATE
```

You can query this metadata from USER_TAB_COLUMNS, USER_TYPES, USER_COLL_TYPES, and USER_TYPE_ATTRS data dictionary views, as in the examples earlier in this chapter.

Working with Nested Tables

Nested tables support a great variety of queries. A nested table is a column within a table. To support queries of the columns and rows of a nested table, use the TABLE function introduced earlier in this chapter.

To see how the TABLE function is used, first consider the nested table by itself. If it were a normal column of a relational table, you would be able to query it via a normal SELECT command:

```
select birth_date   /* This won't work. */
from animals_nt
where name = 'Julio';
```

ANIMALS_NT is not a normal table; it's a datatype (an object table). To select columns (such as BIRTH_DATE) from the nested table, you first need to "flatten" the table so it can be queried. First, apply the TABLE function to the nested table column (BREEDER.ANIMALS), as shown in the following listing:

```
select breeder_name, n.name, n.birthdate
from breeder, table(breeder.animals) n;
```

BREEDER_NAME	NAME	BIRTHDATE
Jane James	Butch	31-MAR-11
Jane James	Rover	05-JUN-11
Jane James	Julio	10-JUN-11

With the data in this format, retrieving the proper row is simple:

```
select breeder_name, n.name, n.birthdate
from breeder, table(breeder.animals) n
where n.name = 'Julio';
```

BREEDER_NAME	NAME	BIRTHDATE
Jane James	Julio	10-JUN-11

You can use the TABLE function whenever you need to perform INSERTs or UPDATEs directly against the nested table. For example, a breeder probably has more animals as time goes by, so you need the ability to add new rows to the ANIMALS_NT nested table within the BREEDER table. To do this, you have to insert rows into the nested table without adding new rows into the BREEDER table, and you need to relate the new ANIMAL rows to breeders who are already in the BREEDER table.

The following INSERT statement adds a new row to the nested table in Jane James's BREEDER row:

```
insert into table(select animals
                  from breeder
                  where breeder_name = 'Jane James')
values (animal_ty('dog','Marcus','01-aug-11'));
```

The INSERT does not provide a value for the BREEDER_NAME column; we are only inserting into the nested table of a breeder's row. The TABLE function is again used to "flatten" the nested table in the ANIMALS column (for Jane's row), and the new values are inserted. Note the use of the WHERE clause within the TABLE function call to specify the rows to be acted on.

You can also update the dog's birth date. Julio's birth date was originally entered as 10-JUN-11 but has since been discovered to be 01-SEP-11. The following UPDATE changes the nested table's BIRTH_DATE value for Julio. Its syntax and structure are very close to the query examples shown earlier in this chapter.

```
update table(select animals
             from breeder
             where breeder_name = 'Jane James') n
   set n.birthdate = '01-sep-11'
where n.name = 'Julio';
```

You can verify this change by querying the nested table data:

```
select breeder_name, n.name, n.birthdate
from breeder, table(breeder.animals) n;
```

BREEDER_NAME	NAME	BIRTHDATE
Jane James	Butch	31-MAR-11
Jane James	Rover	05-JUN-11
Jane James	Julio	01-SEP-11
Jane James	Marcus	01-AUG-11

You can delete nested table entries as well:

```
delete table(select animals
             from breeder
             where breeder_name = 'Jane James') N
where n.name = 'Julio';

1 row deleted.

select breeder_name, n.name, n.birthdate
from breeder, table(breeder.animals) n;
```

BREEDER_NAME	NAME	BIRTHDATE
Jane James	Butch	31-MAR-11

```
Jane James              Rover               05-JUN-11
Jane James              Marcus              01-AUG-11
```

Additional Functions for Nested Tables and Varying Arrays

In addition to the functions already shown in this chapter, Oracle provides a number of functions specifically intended for use with collectors.

The CARDINALITY function returns the number of elements in a nested table or varying array:

```
select cardinality(animals) from breeder;

CARDINALITY(ANIMALS)
--------------------
                   3
```

The MULTISET EXCEPT function takes two nested tables as input and returns the set of rows that are in the first nested table but not in the second nested table (similar to a MINUS operator). MULTISET INTERSECT returns the rows two nested tables have in common. MULTISET UNION performs a union of two nested tables; you can specify MULTISET UNION ALL (the default) or MULTISET UNION DISTINCT.

The SET function converts a nested table into a set while eliminating duplicates, returning a nested table of distinct values:

```
set linesize 60
select set(animals) from breeder;

SET(ANIMALS)(BREED, NAME, BIRTHDATE)
------------------------------------------------------------
ANIMALS_NT(ANIMAL_TY('DOG', 'BUTCH', '31-MAR-01'), ANIMAL_TY
('DOG', 'ROVER', '05-JUN-01'), ANIMAL_TY('DOG', 'MARCUS', '0
1-AUG-01'))
```

See the Alphabetical Reference for the syntax for these functions, along with the COLLECT, POWERMULTISET, and POWERMULTISET_BY_CARDINALITY functions.

Management Issues for Nested Tables and Varying Arrays

When storing data that is related to a table, you can choose one of three methods: a varying array, a nested table, or a separate table. If you have a limited number of rows, a varying array may be appropriate. As the number of rows increases, however, you may begin to encounter performance problems while accessing the varying array. These problems may be caused by a characteristic of varying arrays: They cannot be indexed. Nested tables and standard relational tables, however, can be indexed. As a result, the performance of a VARRAY collector may worsen as it grows in size.

Varying arrays are further burdened by the difficulty in querying data from them. If varying arrays are not a good solution for your application, which alternative should you use—a nested table or a separate relational table? Nested tables and relational tables serve different purposes, so your answer depends on what you are trying to do with the data. Here are the key differences:

■ Nested tables are object types, created via the CREATE TYPE command. Therefore, they can have methods associated with them. If you plan to attach methods to the data, you should use nested tables instead of relational tables. Alternatively, you could consider using object views with methods, as described in Chapter 38.

■ Relational tables are easily related to other relational tables. If the data may be related to many other tables, it may be best not to nest the data within one table. Storing it in its own table gives you the greatest flexibility in managing the data relationships.

Variability in Collectors

You can use object types to enforce standards within your database. However, you may not be able to realize the same standardization benefits when you are using collectors. Consider the TOOLS_VA varying array shown earlier in this chapter. If another application or table wants to use a TOOLS_VA varying array, that application must use the same definition for the array, including the same maximum number of values. However, the new application may have a different value for the maximum number of tools. Therefore, the array must be altered to support the greatest possible number of values it may contain in any of its implementations. As a result, the usefulness of the array's limiting powers may diminish. To support multiple array limits, you would need to create multiple arrays, thus eliminating any object reuse benefits you may have received from creating the varying arrays. You would then need to manage the different array limits and know what the limit is in each array.

You may also find that multiple nested tables are similar, with a difference in only one or two columns. You may be tempted to create a single, all-inclusive nested table type that is used in multiple tables, but that table would also encounter management problems. You would need to know which columns of the nested table were valid for which implementations. If you cannot use the same column structure, with the same meaning and relevance of the columns in each instance, you should not use a shared nested-table object type. If you want to use nested tables in that environment, you should create a separate nested-table object type for each instance in which you will use the nested table and manage them all separately. Having multiple nested-table object types complicates database management.

Location of the Data

In a varying array, the data in the array is stored with the rest of the data in the table. In nested tables, however, the data may be stored "out of line" (and, as shown earlier in this chapter, the data may be stored in a separate tablespace). As a result, the amount of data scanned during queries that do not involve the collector data may be less for a nested table than for a varying array. That is, during a query, the database may not need to read through the data in the nested table; if a varying array is used, the database may need to read through the varying array's data to find the data it needs. Out-of-line data, as used by nested tables, can improve the query performance.

Out-of-line collector data mimics the way the data would be stored in a normal relational database application. For example, in a relational application, you would store related data (such as books and authors) in separate tables, and the tables would be physically stored apart. Out-of-line nested tables store their data apart from the main table but maintain a relationship with the main table. Out-of-line data may improve the query performance by distributing the I/O performed against the main table across multiple tables.

Out-of-line data is also used to store large objects (LOBs) that are stored internally (as opposed to BFILEs, which are pointers to LOBs external to the database). In the next chapter, you'll see how to create and manipulate LOB values. The combination of object types, object views, collectors, and LOBs provides a strong foundation for the implementation of an object-relational database application.

CHAPTER
40

Using Large Objects

In place of LONG and LONG RAW, you should use the LOB datatypes (BLOB, CLOB, NCLOB, and BFILE) for storage of long data. Although Oracle still allows you to create LONG and LONG RAW columns, Oracle recommends that you create new columns using the LOB datatypes and that you convert existing LONG and LONG RAW columns to CLOB or BLOB columns, respectively. If you use one of these datatypes to store large objects (LOBs), you can take advantage of new capabilities for viewing and manipulating the data. You can also use Oracle Text (see Chapter 27) to perform text searches on CLOB data.

In this chapter, you will learn how to use the LOB datatypes and manipulate the data—which does not even have to be stored within the database!

Available Datatypes
Four types of LOBs are supported:

LOB Datatype	Description
BLOB	Binary LOB—binary data stored in the database
CLOB	Character LOB—character data stored in the database
BFILE	Binary file—read-only binary data stored outside the database, the length of which is limited by the operating system
NCLOB	A CLOB column that supports a multibyte character set

You can create multiple LOBs per table. For example, suppose you want to create a PROPOSAL table to track formal proposals you submit. Your proposal records may consist of a series of word-processing files and spreadsheets used to document and price the proposed work. The PROPOSAL table will contain VARCHAR2 datatypes (for columns such as the name of the proposal recipient) plus LOB datatypes (containing the word-processing and spreadsheet files).

CAUTION
You cannot create multiple LONG or LONG RAW columns in a single table. And you should not be creating any more columns with these datatypes! They will be deprecated in a future release. BLOB and CLOB datatypes have all the functionality of LONG and LONG RAW datatypes (and more).

The CREATE TABLE command in the following listing creates the PROPOSAL table:

```
create table proposal
(proposal_id         number(10),
 recipient_name      varchar2(25),
 proposal_name       varchar2(25),
 short_description    varchar2(1000),
 proposal_text       clob,
 budget              blob,
 cover_letter        bfile,
constraint proposal_pk primary key (proposal_id));
```

Because you may submit multiple proposals to the same recipient, assign each proposal a PROPOSAL_ID number. The PROPOSAL table stores the recipient of the proposal, the name of the proposal, and a short description. Then, taking advantage of the LOB datatypes available in Oracle, the PROPOSAL table includes three columns:

PROPOSAL_TEXT   A CLOB containing the text of the proposal

BUDGET   A BLOB containing a spreadsheet showing calculations of the cost and profit for the proposed work

COVER_LETTER   A binary file (BFILE) stored outside the database that contains your cover letter that accompanies the proposal

Each row in the PROPOSAL table will have up to three LOB values stored. Oracle will use the normal database capabilities to support data integrity and concurrency for the PROPOSAL and BUDGET entries, but not for the COVER_LETTER values. Because the COVER_LETTER column uses the BFILE datatype, its data is stored outside the database. Internally, the database stores only a locator value that allows it to find the external file, thus reducing the space and management requirements for the database. Oracle does not guarantee the data integrity of BFILE files stored outside the database. Also, Oracle does not validate that these files exist when you insert a record using a BFILE datatype. Data concurrency and integrity are maintained only for internally stored LOBs.

The data for the LOB columns may be physically apart from the PROPOSAL table. Within the PROPOSAL table, Oracle stores locator values that point to data locations. For BFILE datatypes, the locator points to an external file; for BLOB and CLOB datatypes, the locator points to a separate data location that the database creates to hold the LOB data. The data location for the LOB data may be inline with the rest of the PROPOSAL row or stored out of line. By default, the LOB data is stored inline if its length is less than approximately 4000 bytes.

Storing the data *out of line* allows the database to avoid having to scan the LOB data each time it reads multiple rows from the database. The LOB data is only read when it is required; otherwise, only its locator values are read. You can specify the storage parameters (tablespace and sizing) for the area used to hold the LOB data, as described in the next section.

Specifying Storage for LOB Data

When you create a table that includes a LOB column, you can specify the storage parameters for the area used for the LOB data. Thus, for a table that has no LOB columns, you may have a STORAGE clause in the CREATE TABLE command (see Chapter 17). If the table has at least one LOB column, you also need an additional LOB clause within your CREATE TABLE command.

Consider the PROPOSAL table, this time with a TABLESPACE clause:

```
create table proposal
 (proposal_id          number(10),
  recipient_name       varchar2(25),
  proposal_name        varchar2(25),
  short_description    varchar2(1000),
  proposal_text        clob,
  budget               blob,
  cover_letter         bfile,
 constraint proposal_pk primary key (proposal_id))
 tablespace proposals;
```

Because there are three LOB columns, the CREATE TABLE command should be modified to include the storage specifications for the out-of-line LOB data (if you plan to store the LOB data out of line). Two of the LOB columns—PROPOSAL_TEXT and BUDGET—will store data within the database. The revised version of the CREATE TABLE command, with the LOB storage clause specified, is shown in the following listing:

```
create table proposal
 (proposal_id        number(10),
  recipient_name     varchar2(25),
  proposal_name      varchar2(25),
  short_description  varchar2(1000),
  proposal_text      clob,
  budget             blob,
  cover_letter       bfile,
 constraint proposal_pk primary key (proposal_id))
  tablespace proposals
lob (proposal_text, budget) store as
(tablespace proposal_lobs
    storage (initial 100m next 100m pctincrease 0)
            chunk 16k pctversion 10 nocache logging);
```

The last four lines of the CREATE TABLE command tell Oracle how to store the out-of-line LOB data. The instructions are as follows:

```
lob (proposal_text, budget) store as
(tablespace proposal_lobs
    storage (initial 100m next 100m pctincrease 0)
            chunk 16k pctversion 10 nocache logging);
```

The LOB clause tells Oracle that the next set of commands deals with the out-of-line storage specifications for the table's LOB columns. The two LOB columns (PROPOSAL_TEXT and BUDGET) are explicitly listed. When the two columns' values are stored out of line, they are stored in a segment as specified via the LOB clause:

```
lob (proposal_text, budget) store as
```

NOTE
If there were only one LOB column, you could specify a name for the LOB segment. You would name the segment immediately after the STORE AS clause in the preceding command.

The next two lines specify the tablespace and storage parameters for the out-of-line LOB storage. The TABLESPACE clause assigns the out-of-line data to the PROPOSAL_LOBS tablespace, as shown next, and an optional STORAGE clause can be used to specify the INITIAL, NEXT, and PCTINCREASE values that the out-of-line data storage will use. See the entry for the STORAGE clause in the Alphabetical Reference for an explanation of the available storage parameters for segments.

```
(tablespace proposal_lobs
```

Because the segments are for storing LOB data, several additional parameters are available, and they are specified within the LOB clause:

```
chunk 16k pctversion 10
```

The CHUNK LOB storage parameter tells Oracle how much space to allocate during each LOB value manipulation. The default CHUNK size is the same as the default database block size (typically 8KB), going up to a maximum value of 32KB.

The PCTVERSION parameter is the maximum percentage of overall LOB storage space used for creating new versions of the LOB. By default, older versions of the LOB data will not be overwritten until 10 percent of the available LOB storage space is used.

The last two parameters of the LOB storage space tell Oracle how to handle the LOB data during reads and writes:

```
nocache logging);
```

The NOCACHE parameter in the LOB storage clause specifies that the LOB values are not stored in memory for faster access during queries. The default LOB storage setting is NOCACHE; its opposite is CACHE.

The LOGGING parameter specifies that all operations against the LOB data will be recorded in the database's redo log files. The opposite of LOGGING, NOLOGGING keeps operations from being recorded in the redo log files, thereby improving the performance of table-creation operations. You can also specify the TABLESPACE and STORAGE parameters for a LOB index. See the CREATE TABLE command entry in the Alphabetical Reference for the full syntax related to LOB indexes.

If you specify CACHE and omit the NOLOGGING/LOGGING clause, logging is automatically implemented because you cannot specify CACHE NOLOGGING. If CACHE is not specified and the NOLOGGING/LOGGING clause is omitted, the logging value is obtained from the tablespace in which the LOB value is stored.

Now that the table has been created, you can begin to enter records into it. In the next section, you'll see how to insert LOB values into the PROPOSAL table and how to use the DBMS_LOB package to manipulate the values.

You can have as many LOB STORE AS columns as you have LOB columns. Simply specify the LOB column name (or names) as part of the LOB clause, as shown here:

```
lob (proposal_text, budget) store as
(tablespace proposal_lobs
    storage (initial 100m next 100m pctincrease 0)
            chunk 16k pctversion 10 nocache logging)
```

Manipulating and Selecting LOB Values

You can select or manipulate LOB data in several ways. You can use the character string functions you would use on VARCHAR2 columns against LOB datatypes. For large LOB values (32KB or more in length), or for more complex operations against the data, you should manipulate LOB data via the DBMS_LOB package. Other methods for manipulating LOB data include using application programming interface (API) and Oracle Call Interface (OCI) programs. This section describes the string functions plus gives an overview of the DBMS_LOB package. As these examples demonstrate, LOBs are much more flexible than LONG datatypes in terms of data-manipulation possibilities.

Table 40-1 lists the procedures and functions available via the DBMS_LOB package.

Subprogram	Description
APPEND procedure	Appends the contents of the source LOB to the destination LOB
CLOSE procedure	Closes a previously opened internal or external LOB
COMPARE function	Compares two entire LOBs or parts of two LOBs
COPY procedure	Copies all, or part, of the source LOB to the destination LOB
CONVERTTOBLOB procedure	Reads character data from a source CLOB or NCLOB instance, converts the character data to the specified character, writes the converted data to a destination BLOB instance in binary format, and returns the new offsets
CONVERTOCLOB procedure	Reads character data from a source CLOB or NCLOB instance, converts the character data to the specified character, writes the converted data to a destination BLOB instance in binary format, and returns the new offsets
CREATETEMPORARY procedure	Creates a temporary BLOB or CLOB and its corresponding index in the user's default temporary tablespace
ERASE procedure	Erases all or part of a LOB
FILECLOSE procedure	Closes the file
FILECLOSEALL procedure	Closes all previously opened files
FILEEXISTS function	Checks whether the file exists on the server
FILEGETNAME procedure	Gets the directory alias and filename
FILEISOPEN function	Checks whether the file was opened using the input BFILE locators
FILEOPEN procedure	Opens a file
FRAGMENT_DELETE procedure	Deletes the data at the given offset for the given length within the LOB
FRAGMENT_INSERT procedure	Inserts the data at the given offset (limit 32KB) within the LOB
FRAGMENT_MOVE procedure	Moves the amount of bytes (BLOB) or characters (CLOB/NCLOB) from the given offset to the new offset specified
FRAGMENT_REPLACE procedure	Replaces the data at the given offset with the given data (not to exceed 32KB)
FREETEMPORARY procedure	Frees the temporary BLOB or CLOB in the user's default temporary tablespace
GETCHUNKSIZE function	Returns the amount of space used in the LOB chunk to store the LOB value

TABLE 40-1. *DBMS_LOB Functions and Procedures*

Subprogram	Description
GETLENGTH function	Gets the length of the LOB value
GET_OPTIONS function	Obtains settings corresponding to the *option_types* field for a particular LOB
GET_STORAGE_LIMIT function	Returns the storage limit for LOBs in your database configuration
INSTR function	Returns the matching position of the *n*th occurrence of the pattern in the LOB
ISOPEN function	Checks to see whether the LOB was already opened using the input locator
ISTEMPORARY function	Checks whether the locator is pointing to a temporary LOB
LOADFROMFILE procedure	Loads BFILE data into an internal LOB
LOADBLOBFROMFILE procedure	Loads BFILE data into an internal BLOB
LOADCLOBFROMFILE procedure	Loads BFILE data into an internal CLOB
OPEN procedure	Opens a LOB (internal, external, or temporary) in the indicated mode
READ procedure	Reads data from the LOB starting at the specified offset
SETOPTIONS procedure	Enables CSCE features on a per-LOB basis, overriding the default LOB column settings
SUBSTR function	Returns part of the LOB value starting at the specified offset
TRIM procedure	Trims the LOB value to the specified shorter length
WRITE procedure	Writes data to the LOB from a specified offset
WRITEAPPEND procedure	Writes a buffer to the end of a LOB

TABLE 40-1. *DBMS_LOB Functions and Procedures* (continued)

Initializing Values

Consider the PROPOSAL table again. The PROPOSAL_ID column is the primary key column for the PROPOSAL table. The PROPOSAL table contains three LOB columns—one BLOB, one CLOB, and one BFILE. For each of the LOB columns, Oracle will store a *locator value* that tells it where to find any out-of-line data stored for the record.

When you insert a record into a table that contains LOBs, you use functions to tell Oracle to create an empty locator value for the internally stored LOB columns. An empty locator value is different from a NULL value. If an internally stored LOB column's value is NULL, you have to set it to an empty locator value before updating it to a non-NULL value.

Suppose you begin to work on a proposal and enter a record in the PROPOSAL table. At this point, you have neither a budget spreadsheet nor a cover letter. The INSERT command is shown in the following listing:

```
insert into proposal
(proposal_id, recipient_name, proposal_name, short_description,
 proposal_text, budget, cover_letter)
values
(1, 'Dot Rodale', 'Maintain organic garden', NULL,
 'This is the text of a proposal to maintain an organic garden.',
 EMPTY_BLOB(),NULL);
```

The inserted record has a PROPOSAL_ID value of 1 and a RECIPIENT_NAME value of "Dot Rodale". The PROPOSAL_NAME value is "Maintain organic garden", and the SHORT_DESCRIPTION column is left NULL for now. The PROPOSAL_TEXT column is set equal to a short character string for now. To set the BUDGET column to an empty locator value, you use the EMPTY_BLOB function. If you had wanted to set a CLOB datatype column equal to an empty locator value, you would have used the EMPTY_CLOB function. The COVER_LETTER column, because it is an externally stored BFILE value, is set to NULL.

To set a LOB column to an empty locator value, you have to know its datatype:

Datatype	Initialization Method
BLOB	Use EMPTY_BLOB().
CLOB	Use EMPTY_CLOB().
NCLOB	Use EMPTY_CLOB().
BFILE	Use BFILENAME.

You use the BFILENAME procedure to point to a directory and filename combination. Before entering a value for the directory in the BFILENAME function, a user with the DBA role or the CREATE ANY DIRECTORY system privilege must create the directory. To create a directory, use the CREATE DIRECTORY command, as shown in the following example:

```
create directory proposal_dir as '/u01/proposal/letters';
```

When inserting BFILE entries, you refer to the logical directory name—such as PROPOSAL_DIR—instead of the physical directory name on the operating system. Users with DBA authority can grant READ access to the directory names to users. See the entry for the CREATE DIRECTORY command in the Alphabetical Reference for further details.

You can now enter a second PROPOSAL record; this record will have a COVER_LETTER value:

```
insert into proposal
(proposal_id, recipient_name, proposal_name, short_description,
 proposal_text, budget, cover_letter)
values
```

```
(2, 'Brad Ohmont', 'Rebuild fence', NULL,
 EMPTY_CLOB(), EMPTY_BLOB(),
 BFILENAME('proposal_dir','p2.docx'));
```

In this listing, a second proposal—rebuilding a fence—is inserted into the PROPOSAL table. The EMPTY_CLOB() and EMPTY_BLOB() functions are optionally used to insert empty locator values in the table. The BFILENAME function tells Oracle exactly where to find the cover letter—it's in the PROPOSAL_DIR directory and its name is **p2.docx**. Within the BFILENAME function, the first parameter is always the directory name, and the second parameter is the name of the file within that directory.

NOTE
*The **p2.docx** file does not have to exist for this record to be inserted successfully.*

When you select the value from a LOB column, Oracle uses the locator value to find the data that is associated with the LOB data. You never need to know or specify the locator values. And, as you'll see in the following sections, you can do things with LOB values that are impossible to do with LONG datatypes.

Using INSERT with Subqueries

What if you want to duplicate a proposal record? For example, suppose you begin to work on a third proposal, and it is very similar to the first proposal:

```
insert into proposal
 (proposal_id, recipient_name, proposal_name, short_description,
  proposal_text, budget, cover_letter)
select 3, 'Skip Gates', 'Clear gates field', null,
          proposal_text, budget, cover_letter
 from proposal
where proposal_id = 1;
```

This INSERT command tells Oracle to find the PROPOSAL record with a PROPOSAL_ID value of 1. Take the PROPOSAL_TEXT, BUDGET, and COVER_LETTER column values and the literal values specified ("3", "Skip Gates", and so forth) and insert a new record in the PROPOSAL table. Note that the inserted LOB columns will be set to empty locator values. The ability to perform INSERTs based on queries is a significant advantage of using LOB datatypes—you cannot perform this type of INSERT if a LONG column is part of the query.

NOTE
If you use INSERT AS SELECT to populate LOB values, you may have multiple BFILE values pointing to the same external file. You may need to update the new values to point to the correct external files. Oracle does not maintain referential integrity for the external files.

Updating LOB Values

In the third record that was created, the PROPOSAL_TEXT value was copied from the first record. To update the PROPOSAL_TEXT value of the record that has a PROPOSAL_ID of 3, execute the following command:

```
update proposal
    set proposal_text = 'This is the new proposal text.'
where proposal_id = 3;
```

You can also update the COVER_LETTER column to point to the correct cover letter. Use the BFILENAME function to point to the correct file:

```
update proposal
    set cover_letter = bfilename('proposal_dir', 'p3.docx')
where proposal_id = 3;
```

You can update NULL values of BFILE columns without first setting them to empty locator values.

Using String Functions to Manipulate LOB Values

You can use the Oracle-provided string functions against CLOB values. For example, you can use SUBSTR, INSTR, LTRIM, and INITCAP to modify the strings. See Chapter 7 for descriptions of the built-in string functions.

In the PROPOSAL table, the PROPOSAL_TEXT column is defined as a CLOB datatype. Here are the three PROPOSAL_TEXT values (the second is NULL):

```
select proposal_text from proposal;
```

```
PROPOSAL_TEXT
------------------------------------------------------------------
This is the text of a proposal to maintain an organic garden.

This is the new proposal text.
```

Applying INITCAP to the third record yields this result:

```
select initcap(proposal_text) from proposal
where proposal_id = 3;
```

```
INITCAP(PROPOSAL_TEXT)
--------------------------------------------------
This Is The New Proposal Text.
```

Applying INSTR to all three rows returns the expected result:

```
select instr(proposal_text,'new',1,1) from proposal;
```

```
INSTR(PROPOSAL_TEXT,'NEW',1,1)
------------------------------
                             0
                             0
                            13
```

You can use SUBSTR to return the first ten characters of the text:

```
select substr(proposal_text,1,10) from proposal
where proposal_id = 3;
```

```
SUBSTR(PROPOSAL_TEXT,1,10)
------------------------------------
This is th
```

For complex manipulations, you should use the DBMS_LOB package, as described in the following sections.

NOTE
The regular expression functions (see Chapter 8) may also be used against LOB datatypes.

Using DBMS_LOB to Manipulate LOB Values

You can use the DBMS_LOB package to change or select LOB values. In the following sections, you'll see how to perform SQL functions such as SUBSTR and INSTR on LOB values, as well as how to append to LOB values, compare LOB values, and read LOB values.

The string comparison and manipulation procedures and functions available within the DBMS_LOB package are listed in Table 40-1.

The major procedures and functions available within the DBMS_LOB package are described in the following sections. When using BFILEs, the maximum number of files you can concurrently have open is limited by the setting of the SESSION_MAX_OPEN_FILES parameter in the database's system parameter file. The default maximum number of concurrently open BFILE files is 10; the maximum is either 50 or the value of the MAX_OPEN_FILES parameter at the operating-system level, whichever is lower.

NOTE
For the full listing of all DBMS_LOB subprograms, see the Oracle documentation set. The functions and procedures described in this chapter are the ones expected to be most frequently used by developers.

In the following examples, the PROPOSAL_TEXT CLOB column is used to show the impact of the major procedures and functions.

READ

The READ procedure reads a piece of a LOB value. In the PROPOSAL table example, the PROPOSAL_TEXT for the first row is

```
select proposal_text
from proposal
where proposal_id = 1;
```

```
PROPOSAL_TEXT
------------------------------------------------------------
This is the text of a proposal to maintain an organic garden.
```

This description is fairly short, so it could have been stored in a VARCHAR2 datatype column. Because it is stored in a CLOB column, though, its maximum length is much greater than it would have been if it had been stored in a VARCHAR2 column. The maximum size for both BLOBs and CLOBs is defined via the formula (4GB – 1) * database block size, yielding values between 8TB and 128TB. For these examples, we'll use this short string for purposes of demonstration; you can use the same functions and operations against longer CLOB strings as well.

The READ procedure has four parameters, which must be specified in this order:

1. The LOB locator (for either a BLOB, CLOB, or BFILE)

2. The number of bytes or characters to be read

3. The offset (starting point of the read) from the beginning of the LOB value

4. The output data from the READ procedure

If the end of the LOB value is reached before the specified number of bytes is read, the READ procedure returns an error.

Because the READ procedure requires the LOB locator as input, the READ procedure is executed within PL/SQL blocks. You will need to select the LOB locator value, provide that as input to the READ procedure, and then display the text read via the DBMS_OUTPUT package.

A Word About the DBMS_OUTPUT Package   As noted in Chapter 35, you can use the DBMS_OUTPUT package to display the values of variables within a PL/SQL block. The PUT_LINE procedure within DBMS_OUTPUT displays the specified output on a line. Before using the DBMS_OUTPUT package, you should first execute the SET SERVEROUTPUT ON command. In the next section, you'll see how to create the PL/SQL block that will read the data from a LOB.

A READ Example   To use the READ procedure, you need to know the locator value of the LOB you want to read. The locator value must be selected from the table that contains the LOB. Because the locator value must be supplied as input to the READ procedure, you should use PL/SQL variables to hold the locator value. The READ procedure, in turn, will place its output in a PL/SQL variable. You can use the DBMS_OUTPUT package to display the output value. The structure of the PL/SQL block (in pseudo-code) for this example is as follows:

```
declare
    variable to hold locator value
    variable to hold the amount (the number of characters/bytes to read)
    variable to hold the offset
    variable to hold the output
begin
    set value for amount_var;
    set value for offset_var;
    select locator value into locator var from table;
    DBMS_LOB.READ(locator var, amount var, offset var, output var);
    DBMS_OUTPUT.PUT_LINE('Output:' || output var);
end;
```

NOTE
See Chapter 32 for an overview of PL/SQL blocks and their components.

For the PROPOSAL table, selecting the first ten characters from the PROPOSAL_TEXT column looks like this:

```
declare
    locator_var    clob;
    amount_var     integer;
    offset_var     integer;
    output_var     varchar2(10);
begin
  amount_var := 10;
  offset_var := 1;
  select proposal_text into locator_var
  from proposal
  where proposal_id = 1;
  dbms_lob.read(locator_var, amount_var, offset_var, output_var);
  dbms_output.put_line('Start of proposal text: ' || output_var);
end;
/
```

When you execute the preceding PL/SQL block, the output matches the SQL SUBSTR example shown earlier:

```
Start of proposal text: This is th

PL/SQL procedure successfully completed.
```

The output shows the first ten characters of the PROPOSAL_TEXT value, starting at the first character of the LOB value.

The PL/SQL block in the preceding example first declares the variables to use:

```
declare
    locator_var    clob;
    amount_var     integer;
    offset_var     integer;
    output_var     varchar2(10);
```

Next, values are assigned to the variables:

```
begin
    amount_var := 10;
    offset_var := 1;
```

Then the locator value is selected from the table and stored in a variable named *locator_var:*

```
select proposal_text into locator_var
    from proposal
    where proposal_id = 1;
```

Next, the READ procedure is called, using the values that have been assigned so far:

```
dbms_lob.read(locator_var, amount_var, offset_var, output_var);
```

As a result of executing the READ procedure, the *output_var* variable is populated with the data that was read. The PUT_LINE procedure displays that data:

```
dbms_output.put_line('Start of proposal text: ' || output_var);
```

This format for PL/SQL blocks will be used throughout the rest of this chapter. You can optionally set the variable values when they are declared.

If you want to select a different portion of the PROPOSAL_TEXT CLOB, just change the *amount* and *offset* variables. If you change the number of characters read, you need to change the size of the output variable, too. In the following example, 12 characters are read from PROPOSAL_TEXT, starting from the tenth character:

```
declare
    locator_var    clob;
    amount_var     integer;
    offset_var     integer;
    output_var     varchar2(12);
begin
    amount_var := 12;
    offset_var := 10;
    select proposal_text into locator_var
    from proposal
     where proposal_id = 1;
    dbms_lob.read(locator_var, amount_var, offset_var, output_var);
    dbms_output.put_line('Part of proposal text: ' || output_var);
end;
/
```

Output from this PL/SQL block is shown in the following listing:

```
Part of proposal text: he text of a

PL/SQL procedure successfully completed.
```

If PROPOSAL_TEXT had been created as a VARCHAR2 column, you could have selected this data using the SUBSTR function. However, you would have been limited to a maximum column length of 32,767 (4,000 in Oracle Database 11g) characters. Also, note that the LOB column can contain binary data (BLOB datatypes), and you can use the READ procedure to select data from BLOBs in the same way you select from CLOBs. For BLOBs, you should declare the output buffer to use the RAW datatype. In PL/SQL, RAW and VARCHAR2 datatypes (used for the output variables for CLOB and BLOB reads) have a maximum length of 32,767 characters.

For the READ procedure, possible exceptions are VALUE_ERROR, INVALID_ARGVAL, NO_DATA_FOUND, UNOPENED_FILE, NOEXIST_DIRECTORY, NOPRIV_DIRECTORY, INVALID_DIRECTORY, INVALID_OPERATION, and BUFFERING_ENABLED.

SUBSTR
The SUBSTR function within the DBMS_LOB package performs the SQL SUBSTR function on a LOB value. This function has three input parameters, which must be specified in this order:

1. The LOB locator
2. The number of bytes or characters to be read

CHAPTER 40: Using Large Objects

3. The offset (starting point of the read) from the beginning of the LOB value

Because SUBSTR is a function, there is no output variable value returned directly from SUBSTR as there was with READ. For the READ procedure, you declared an output variable and then populated it within the READ procedure call. The PL/SQL block used for the READ procedure is shown in the following listing, with the lines related to the output variable shown in bold:

```
declare
    locator_var    clob;
    amount_var     integer;
    offset_var     integer;
    output_var     varchar2(12);
begin
    amount_var := 12;
    offset_var := 10;
    select proposal_text into locator_var
    from proposal
    where proposal_id = 1;
    dbms_lob.read(locator_var, amount_var, offset_var, output_var);
    dbms_output.put_line('Section of proposal text: ' || output_var);
end;
/
```

Because SUBSTR is a function, you populate the output variable differently. The format is

```
output_var := dbms_lob.substr(locator_var, amount_var, offset_var);
```

The preceding PL/SQL statement uses the SUBSTR function of the DBMS_LOB package to select 12 characters from the PROPOSAL_TEXT LOB column, starting at the 10th character. The full PL/SQL block is

```
declare
    locator_var    clob;
    amount_var     integer;
    offset_var     integer;
    output_var     varchar2(12);
begin
    amount_var := 12;
    offset_var := 10;
    select proposal_text into locator_var
    from proposal
    where proposal_id = 1;
    output_var := dbms_lob.substr(locator_var, amount_var, offset_var);
    dbms_output.put_line('Section of proposal text: ' || output_var);
end;
/
```

The output is shown in the following listing:

```
Section of proposal text: he text of a
PL/SQL procedure successfully completed.
```

The equivalent SQL function call is

```
select substr(proposal_text,10,12)
from proposal
where proposal_id = 1;
```

The SUBSTR example differs from the READ example in only two ways: the name of the function call and the manner of assigning a value to the output variable. As with the READ procedure example, the PUT_LINE procedure of the DBMS_OUTPUT package is used to display the results.

In general, you should use the SUBSTR function whenever you are interested in selecting only a specific section of the LOB value. The READ function can be used to select only a portion of a text string (as in the previous examples), but it is more often used within a loop. For example, suppose the LOB value is larger than the largest allowed RAW or VARCHAR2 variable in PL/SQL (32,767 bytes). In that case, you can use the READ procedure within a loop to read all the data from the LOB value. Refer to Chapter 32 for details on the different loop options available in PL/SQL.

For the SUBSTR function, possible exceptions are UNOPENED_FILE, NOEXIST_DIRECTORY, NOPRIV_DIRECTORY, INVALID_DIRECTORY, INVALID_OPERATION, and BUFFERING_ENABLED.

INSTR

The INSTR function within the DBMS_LOB package performs the SQL INSTR function on a LOB value.

The INSTR function has four input parameters, which must be specified in this order:

1. The LOB locator
2. The pattern to be tested for (RAW bytes for BLOBs, character strings for CLOBs)
3. The offset (starting point of the read) from the beginning of the LOB value
4. The occurrence of the pattern within the LOB value

The INSTR function within DBMS_LOB searches the LOB for a specific pattern of bytes or characters. The occurrence variable allows you to specify which occurrence of the pattern within the searched value should be returned. The output of the INSTR function is the position of the start of the pattern within the searched string. For example, in SQL,

```
1
```

means that within the string "ABCABC", the pattern A is searched for, starting at the first position of the string, and looking for the first occurrence. The A is found in the first position of the searched string. If you start the search at the second position of the string, the answer is different:

```
4
```

Because this INSTR starts at the second position, the first A is not part of the value that is searched. Instead, the first A found is the one in the fourth position.

If you change the last parameter in the SQL INSTR to look for the second occurrence of the string A, starting at the second position, the pattern is not found:

```
0
```

If the SQL INSTR function cannot find the matching occurrence of the pattern, 0 is returned. The INSTR function of the DBMS_LOB package operates in the same manner.

Because INSTR is a function, you need to assign its output variable in the same manner as the SUBSTR function's output variable was assigned. In the following listing, the PROPOSAL_TEXT CLOB value is searched for the string "pr". The *position_var* variable is declared to hold the output of the INSTR function.

```
declare
    locator_var    clob;
    pattern_var    varchar2(2);
    offset_var     integer;
    occur_var      integer;
    position_var   integer;
begin
    pattern_var := 'pr';
    offset_var := 1;
    occur_var := 1;
    select proposal_text into locator_var
    from proposal
    where proposal_id = 1;
    position_var := dbms_lob.instr(locator_var, pattern_var,
      offset_var, occur_var);
    dbms_output.put_line('Found string at position: ' || position_var);
end;
/
```

The output would be

```
Found string at position: 23

PL/SQL procedure successfully completed.
```

The output shows that the search string "pr" is found within the PROPOSAL_TEXT column, starting at the 23rd character of the LOB value. Because Oracle supports SQL string functions against CLOB columns, this function call is equivalent to the following query:

```
select instr(proposal_text ,'pr',1,1)
from proposal
where proposal_id = 1;
```

For the INSTR function, possible exceptions are UNOPENED_FILE, NOEXIST_DIRECTORY, NOPRIV_DIRECTORY, INVALID_DIRECTORY, INVALID_OPERATION, and BUFFERING_ENABLED.

GETLENGTH

The GETLENGTH function of the DBMS_LOB package returns the length of the LOB value. The DBMS_LOB.GETLENGTH function is similar in function to the SQL LENGTH function, but it's used only for LOB values.

The GETLENGTH function of the DBMS_LOB package has only one input parameter: the locator value for the LOB. In the following listing, variables are declared to hold the locator value and the output value. The GETLENGTH function is then executed, and the result is reported via the PUT_LINE procedure:

```
declare
   locator_var    clob;
   length_var     integer;
begin
   select proposal_text into locator_var
   from proposal
   where proposal_id = 1;
   length_var := dbms_lob.getlength(locator_var);
   dbms_output.put_line('Length of LOB: ' || length_var);
end;
/
```

The following is the GETLENGTH output:

```
Length of LOB: 61

PL/SQL procedure successfully completed.
```

If the LOB value is NULL, the GETLENGTH function returns a value of NULL.
The equivalent SQL function for CLOB values is

```
select length(proposal_text)
from proposal
where proposal_id = 1;
```

COMPARE

The COMPARE function of the DBMS_LOB package compares two LOB values. If the two LOB values are the same, the COMPARE function returns 0; otherwise, it returns a nonzero integer value (usually 1 or –1). To execute the COMPARE function, the DBMS_LOB package essentially performs two READ functions and compares the results. Thus, for each of the LOB values to be compared, you need to supply a locator value and an offset value; the number of characters or bytes to be compared is the same for both LOB values. You can only compare LOBs of the same datatype.

The COMPARE function has five input parameters, which must be specified in this order:

1. The LOB locator for the first LOB
2. The LOB locator for the second LOB
3. The amount variable (the number of bytes or characters to compare)
4. The offset (starting point of the read) from the beginning of the first LOB value
5. The offset (starting point of the read) from the beginning of the second LOB value

Because the two LOBs being compared can have different offset values, you can compare the first part of one LOB value with the second part of a different LOB value. The example in the following listing compares the first 25 characters of the PROPOSAL_TEXT column values from two entries—the PROPOSAL_ID #1 row and the PROPOSAL_ID #3 row:

```
declare
   first_locator_var      clob;
   second_locator_var     clob;
   amount_var             integer;
   first_offset_var       integer;
   second_offset_var      integer;
   output_var             integer;
begin
   amount_var        := 25;
   first_offset_var  := 1;
   second_offset_var := 1;
   select proposal_text into first_locator_var
   from proposal
   where proposal_id = 1;
   select proposal_text into second_locator_var
   from proposal
   where proposal_id = 3;
   output_var :=dbms_lob.compare(first_locator_var, second_locator_var,
          amount_var, first_offset_var, second_offset_var);
   dbms_output.put_line('Comparison value (0 if the same): '||
     output_var);
end;
/
```

The following is the output:

```
Comparison value (0 if the same): 1

PL/SQL procedure successfully completed.
```

If the two strings are the same, the COMPARE function returns 0.

In the following listing, the same two LOBs are compared, but this time only their first five characters are used for the comparison. Because both start with the string "This ", the COMPARE returns 0:

```
declare
   first_locator_var      clob;
   second_locator_var     clob;
   amount_var             integer;
   first_offset_var       integer;
   second_offset_var      integer;
   output_var             integer;
begin
   amount_var        := 5;
   first_offset_var  := 1;
   second_offset_var := 1;
   select proposal_text into first_locator_var
   from proposal
   where proposal_id = 1;
   select proposal_text into second_locator_var
   from proposal
```

```
   where proposal_id = 3;
   output_var :=dbms_lob.compare(first_locator_var, second_locator_var,
          amount_var, first_offset_var, second_offset_var);
   dbms_output.put_line('Comparison value (0 if the same): ' ||
     output_var);
end;
/
```

```
Comparison value (0 if the same): 0

PL/SQL procedure successfully completed.
```

The COMPARE function allows you to compare character strings to character strings and binary data to binary data. If you are using the COMPARE function on BLOB columns, you should define the locator variables as RAW datatypes.

For the COMPARE function, possible exceptions are UNOPENED_FILE, NOEXIST_DIRECTORY, NOPRIV_DIRECTORY, INVALID_DIRECTORY, INVALID_OPERATION, and BUFFERING_ENABLED.

WRITE

The WRITE procedure of the DBMS_LOB package allows you to write data in specific locations of the LOB. For example, you can write binary data into a section of a BLOB, overwriting the existing data there. You can write character data into CLOB fields using the WRITE procedure. This procedure has four input parameters, which must be specified in this order:

1. The LOB locator for the LOB
2. The amount variable (the number of bytes or characters to write)
3. The offset (starting point of the write) from the beginning of the LOB value
4. The buffer variable assigned to the character string or binary data being added

Because the WRITE procedure updates the LOB value, you should first lock the row via a SELECT FOR UPDATE, as shown in bold in the following listing. In this example, a record is selected and locked. The text ADD NEW TEXT is then written to the LOB value, overwriting the data starting in position 10 (as defined by the *offset* variable).

```
declare
   locator_var    clob;
   amount_var     integer;
   offset_var     integer;
   buffer_var     varchar2(12);
begin
   amount_var := 12;
   offset_var := 10;
   buffer_var := 'ADD NEW TEXT';
   select proposal_text into locator_var
   from proposal
   where proposal_id = 3
   for update;
   dbms_lob.write(locator_var, amount_var, offset_var, buffer_var);
```

```
commit;
end;
/
```

Because the WRITE procedure changes the data, a COMMIT command is added before the END clause of the PL/SQL block to make the changes permanent and release the lock on the row.

NOTE
Test without a COMMIT first so you can see the impact of your procedure call before committing the change to the database.

For the WRITE procedure, no output is provided. To see the changed data, you need to either call the READ procedure (within the same PL/SQL block, if you want) or select the LOB value from the table again:

```
select proposal_text
from proposal
where proposal_id = 3;

PROPOSAL_TEXT
-----------------------------------------------------------
This is tADD NEW TEXTsal text.
```

The WRITE procedure overwrote 12 characters, starting at the 10th character of PROPOSAL_TEXT. You can use the WRITEAPPEND procedure to append new data to the end of an existing LOB value.

For CLOB data, you can rewrite this using an UPDATE statement combined with SUBSTR and concatenation functions.

For the WRITE function, possible exceptions are VALUE_ERROR, INVALID_ARGVAL, QUERY_WRITE, BUFFERING_ENABLED, and SECUREFILE_OUTOFBOUNDS.

APPEND

The APPEND procedure of the DBMS_LOB package appends data from one LOB to a second LOB. Because this amounts to an update of a LOB value, the record being updated should be locked prior to executing the APPEND procedure.

The APPEND procedure takes only two parameters: the locator value for the destination LOB and the locator value for the source LOB. If either parameter is NULL, the APPEND procedure returns an error.

In the following example, two locator variables are defined. The first locator variable is named *dest_locator_var*; this is the locator value for the LOB into which the data is to be appended. The second locator variable, *source_locator_var,* is the locator value for the source data that is to be appended to the destination LOB. The destination LOB, because it is being updated, is locked via a SELECT FOR UPDATE command. In this example, the PROPOSAL_TEXT value for the PROPOSAL_ID #1 row is appended to the PROPOSAL_TEXT value for the PROPOSAL_ID #3 row:

```
declare
    dest_locator_var      clob;
    source_locator_var    clob;
begin
```

```
      select proposal_text into dest_locator_var
      from proposal
      where proposal_id = 3
      for update;
      select proposal_text into source_locator_var
      from proposal
      where proposal_id = 1;
      dbms_lob.append(dest_locator_var, source_locator_var);
   commit;
   end;
   /
```

To see the changed data, you can select the record from the PROPOSAL table:

```
select proposal_text
from proposal
where proposal_id = 3;


PROPOSAL_TEXT
---------------------------------------------------------------
This is tADD NEW TEXTsal text.This is the text of a proposal to
maintain an orga
```

What happened to the rest of the text? By default, only 80 characters of LONG and LOB values are displayed during queries. To see the rest of the text, use the SET LONG command:

```
set long 1000

select proposal_text
from proposal
where proposal_id = 3;


PROPOSAL_TEXT
---------------------------------------------------------------
This is tADD NEW TEXTsal text.This is the text of a proposal to
maintain an organic garden.
```

In this example, the first 1000 characters of the LOB value were displayed. If you need to know how long the LOB is, use the GETLENGTH function, as described earlier in this chapter.

In addition to allowing you to append CLOB values, the APPEND procedure allows you to append BLOB values. When appending BLOB data, you need to be aware of the format of the BLOB data and the impact of appending new data on the end of the BLOB value. For BLOB values, the APPEND function may be most useful for applications in which the BLOB contains only raw data (such as digital data transmissions) rather than formatted binary data (such as spreadsheet files formatted by a program).

For CLOB data, you could rewrite this with an UPDATE statement, setting the PROPOSAL_TEXT column equal to the concatenation of multiple values.

For the APPEND procedure, VALUE_ERROR, QUERY_WRITE, and BUFFERING_ENABLED are the defined exceptions.

ERASE

You can use the ERASE procedure of the DBMS_LOB package to erase the characters or bytes in any part of a LOB. You can use ERASE to erase the entire LOB value, or you can specify which section of the LOB to erase. ERASE is similar in function to WRITE. If you erase data in a BLOB value, the data is replaced with zero-byte filler. If you erase data in a CLOB value, spaces are inserted into the CLOB.

Because you are updating a LOB value, you should follow the standard procedures for LOB updates: lock the row and commit when the procedure has completed.

In the following PL/SQL block, a portion of PROPOSAL_TEXT for the row with PROPOSAL_ ID #3 is erased. The erased characters will start at an offset of 10 and continue for 17 characters. The parameters for the ERASE procedure, in order, are

1. The LOB locator for the LOB
2. The amount variable (the number of bytes or characters to erase)
3. The offset (starting point of the erasure) from the beginning of the LOB value

```
declare
   locator_var   clob;
   amount_var    integer;
   offset_var    integer;
begin
   amount_var := 17;
   offset_var := 10;
   select proposal_text into locator_var
   from proposal
   where proposal_id = 3
   for update;
   dbms_lob.erase(locator_var, amount_var, offset_var);
commit;
end;
/
```

The change to the record can be seen by querying the PROPOSAL_TEXT column:

```
select proposal_text
from proposal
where proposal_id = 3;
```

```
PROPOSAL_TEXT
----------------------------------------------------------------
This is t               ext.This is the text of a proposal to
maintain an organic garden.
```

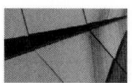

NOTE
The space previously held by the erased data is replaced by blanks; the rest of the data in the LOB does not change its position.

For CLOB data, you can rewrite this operation using an UPDATE statement, setting a new value for PROPOSAL_TEXT by concatenating SUBSTR results and a blank string.

For the ERASE procedure, possible exceptions are VALUE_ERROR, INVALID_ARGVAL, QUERY_WRITE, and BUFFERING_ENABLED.

TRIM

You can use the TRIM procedure of the DBMS_LOB package to reduce the size of a LOB value by trimming characters or bytes from the end of the value (like the SQL RTRIM function). When the TRIM procedure is executed, you specify the locator value for the LOB and the LOB's new length.

In the following listing, the PROPOSAL_TEXT for the PROPOSAL_ID #3 row is trimmed to its first ten characters. Because the TRIM procedure changes the data, a COMMIT command is added before the END clause of the PL/SQL block.

```
declare
    locator_var      clob;
    new_length_var   integer;
begin
    new_length_var    := 10;
    select proposal_text into locator_var
    from proposal
    where proposal_id = 3
    for update;
    dbms_lob.trim(locator_var, new_length_var);
commit;
end;
/
```

For the TRIM procedure, no output is provided. To see the changed data, you need to select the LOB value from the table again:

```
select proposal_text
from proposal
where proposal_id = 3;

PROPOSAL_TEXT
------------------------------------------------------------------
This is t
```

The sample output shows the results of the TRIM procedure following the ERASE procedure executed in the preceding section. For CLOB data, you could rewrite this as a simple UPDATE:

```
update proposal
set proposal_text = substr(proposal_text,1,10)
where proposal_id = 3;
```

For the TRIM procedure, possible exceptions are VALUE_ERROR, INVALID_ARGVAL, QUERY_WRITE, and BUFFERING_ENABLED.

COPY

You can use the COPY procedure of the DBMS_LOB package to copy data from a part of one LOB into a second LOB. Unlike the APPEND procedure, you do not have to copy the full text of one LOB value into another. During the COPY procedure, you can specify the offset to read from and the offset to write to. The five parameters of the COPY procedure in order, are

1. The destination LOB locator
2. The source LOB locator
3. The amount (the number of characters or bytes to copy)
4. The offset to start writing to within the destination LOB value
5. The offset to start reading from within the destination LOB value

COPY is a combination of the READ and WRITE capabilities. Like the WRITE operation, the COPY procedure modifies the LOB value. Therefore, the record should first be locked, and the PL/SQL block must contain a COMMIT command. In the following example, the first 61 characters of the PROPOSAL_ID #1 row are copied to the PROPOSAL_ID #3 row. Because the destination LOB uses an offset of 1, the copied data will *overwrite* data within the destination LOB.

```
declare
    dest_locator_var      clob;
    source_locator_var    clob;
    amount_var            integer;
    dest_offset_var       integer;
    source_offset_var     integer;
begin
    amount_var        := 61;
    dest_offset_var   := 1;
    source_offset_var := 1;
    select proposal_text into dest_locator_var
    from proposal
    where proposal_id = 3
    for update;
    select proposal_text into source_locator_var
    from proposal
    where proposal_id = 1;
    dbms_lob.copy(dest_locator_var, source_locator_var,
        amount_var, dest_offset_var, source_offset_var);
    commit;
end;
/
```

The COPY procedure displays no output. To see the changed data, you need to select the LOB value from the table again:

```
select proposal_text
from proposal
where proposal_id = 3;
```

```
PROPOSAL_TEXT
------------------------------------------------------------
This is the text of a proposal to maintain an organic garden.
```

For the COPY procedure, possible exceptions are VALUE_ERROR, INVALID_ARGVAL, QUERY_WRITE, and BUFFERING_ENABLED.

Using the BFILE Functions and Procedures

Because BFILE values are stored externally, several functions and procedures are used to manipulate the files prior to executing READ, SUBSTR, INSTR, GETLENGTH, or COMPARE operations on BFILE LOBs. The BFILE-related procedures and functions within DBMS_LOB, shown earlier in Table 40-1, allow you to open files, close files, get the filename, check whether a file exists, and check whether a file is open. The existence-check function is necessary because Oracle does not maintain the data stored in the external file; Oracle only maintains the pointer created via the BFILENAME procedure when the record is inserted or updated. You should use the procedures and functions in Table 40-1 to control the files used by your PL/SQL code. For example, to read the first ten bytes from the COVER_LETTER BFILE for the PROPOSAL_ID #2 row, you would open the file and then execute the READ procedure. The PUT_LINE procedure of the DBMS_OUTPUT package can then be called to show the data that was read.

See *SecureFiles and Large Objects Developer's Guide* for additional code samples and descriptions of the access methods provided.

```
/* Checking if a pattern exists in a BFILE using instr
/* Procedure compareBFILEs_proc is not part of DBMS_LOB package: */

create or replace procedure comparebfiles_proc is
   /* initialize the bfile locator: */
   file_loc1     bfile := bfilename('MEDIA_DIR', 'keyboard.jpg');
   file_loc2     bfile;
   retval        integer;
begin
   dbms_output.put_line('------------ LOB COMPARE EXAMPLE ------------');
   /* Select the LOB: */
   select ad_graphic into file_loc2 from print_media
   where product_id = 3060 and ad_id = 11001;
   /* Open the BFILEs: */
   dbms_lob.open(file_loc1, dbms_lob.lob_readonly);
   dbms_lob.open(file_loc2, dbms_lob.lob_readonly);
   retval :=
      dbms_lob.compare(file_loc2, file_loc1, dbms_lob.lobmaxsize, 1, 1);
   /* close the bfiles: */
   dbms_lob.close(file_loc1);
   dbms_lob.close(file_loc2);
end;
/
```

The approach shown in this example mimics that of the COMPARE example shown earlier. Because we are working with BFILEs, there are two additional sections: the DBMS_LOB.OPEN calls to open the files and the DBMS_LOB.CLOSE calls to close the files when the COMPARE has completed.

Reading data from BFILEs follows the steps shown earlier for the READ function, with the addition of the calls to open and close the file. The READ process is illustrated via another BFILE example:

```
/* Procedure readBFILE_proc is not part of DBMS_LOB package: */

create or replace procedure readbfile_proc is
    file_loc      bfile;
    amount        integer := 32767;
    position      integer := 1;
    buffer        raw(32767);
begin
    dbms_output.put_line('----------- BFILE READ EXAMPLE ------------');
    /* Select the LOB: */
    select ad_graphic into file_loc from print_media
        where product_id = 3060 and ad_id = 11001;
    /* open the bfile: */
    dbms_lob.open(file_loc, dbms_lob.lob_readonly);
    /* read data: */
    dbms_lob.read(file_loc, amount, position, buffer);
    /* close the bfile: */
    dbms_lob.close(file_loc);
end;
/
```

If you use an Exception Handling section in your PL/SQL block, you need to include FILECLOSE procedure calls within the declared exceptions. (Refer to Chapter 32 for further details on Exception Handling within PL/SQL blocks.)

To move data from an external file into a BLOB datatype, you can create a BFILE datatype in a table and use the BFILENAME function to create a LOB locator that points to the external file. The BFILENAME function takes two parameters: the directory name and the filename. Here's an example:

```
insert into proposal (proposal_id, cover_letter)
values (4, bfilename ('proposal_dir','extfile.docx'));
```

You can then open the file and use the LOADFROMFILE, LOADBLOBFROMFILE, or LOADCLOBFROMFILE procedure to load the BLOB datatype with the data from the external file.

If the data is presently in a LONG datatype, you can change it to a CLOB or NCLOB column via the ALTER TABLE command. You can also use ALTER TABLE to change a LONG RAW column to a BLOB datatype column. For INSERT AS SELECT operations, you can use the TO_LOB SQL function to move the data from the LONG column to a BLOB column.

Deleting LOBs

When you delete LOB values, the locator value is deleted. If the deleted value is an internal LOB (BLOB, CLOB, or NCLOB), both the locator and the LOB value are deleted. If the deleted value is an external LOB (BFILE), only the locator value is deleted; you will need to manually delete the file to which the locator points with an operating system command.

CHAPTER
41

Advanced
Object-Oriented
Concepts

I n the preceding chapters, all of Oracle's object-oriented programming (OOP) features shown
share two characteristics: they are embedded objects, and they are column objects. An
embedded object is one that is completely contained within another. For example, a nested
table is contained within a table, so it is an embedded object. Although a nested table's data is
stored apart from the main table, its data can only be accessed via the main table. A *column
object* is one that is represented as a column in a table. For example, a varying array is
represented as a column in a table, so it is a column object.

To take full advantage of OOP capabilities, a database must also support *row objects*—objects
that are represented as rows instead of columns. The row objects are not embedded objects;
instead, they are *referenced objects,* accessible via references from other objects. In this chapter,
you will see how row objects are created and referenced.

Object-oriented structures may not be appropriate for many applications—you may be limited
based on your toolset, interfaces, or existing relationships within the database. In this chapter,
you'll see how Oracle has implemented row objects and how to use object views to bridge the
object-oriented and relational architectures. In addition to row objects, this chapter covers the
application of objects to PL/SQL—creating *object PL/SQL.*

Row Objects vs. Column Objects

The distinction between row objects and column objects is critical. First, consider column
objects. Column objects are based on extensions of features already in the database. An object
type or a varying array can be embedded as a column within a table. A nested table or a large
object (LOB) can be stored in a single column of a table. In each case, the object is represented as
a column within a table.

Nested tables and LOBs, however, involve data that is stored out-of-line from the main table.
When you use a LOB (see Chapter 40), you specify the storage values for the table that will store
the LOB data, and Oracle creates LOB locators that point from the main table to the rows in the
LOB table if the LOB data is stored out-of-line. When you create a nested table, you specify the
name of the table in which the nested table's records will be stored—and Oracle creates pointers
from the main table to the records in the nested tables. Thus, the main table and its embedded
nested table are related.

In row objects, the objects are represented as rows, not columns. The data is not embedded
within the main table; instead, the main table contains a reference to another table. Nested tables,
because they are stored apart from the main table, provide a useful tool for understanding row
objects. What if the nested table's data is not embedded within the main table and each of its
rows is a row object? The main table will define references to the related data.

Oracle's object-relational features that are described in earlier chapters relied on column
objects. In this chapter, the focus is on the advanced OOP capabilities, which are based on row
objects. You use row objects to create references between the rows of different tables.

Object Tables and OIDs

In an *object table,* each row is a row object. An object table differs from a normal relational table
in several ways. First, each row within the object table has an *OID*—an *object identifier* value—
assigned by Oracle when the row is created. Second, the rows of an object table can be
referenced by other objects within the database.

You can create an object table via the CREATE TABLE command. Consider the ANIMAL_TY datatype shown in previous chapters. To avoid conflicts with objects created during earlier chapters, create this type in a new schema:

```
create or replace type animal_ty as object
(breed        varchar2(25),
 name         varchar2(25),
 birth_date date);
/
```

NOTE
To keep this example simple, the ANIMAL_TY datatype is created without any member functions.

To create an object table of the ANIMAL_TY datatype, issue the following CREATE TABLE command:

```
create table animal of animal_ty;
```

```
Table created.
```

Note that the command has an unusual syntax—creating the table of an object type. The resulting table may first appear to be a normal relational table:

```
describe animal
```

```
Name                            Null?    Type
------------------------------- -------- ------------
BREED                                    VARCHAR2(25)
NAME                                     VARCHAR2(25)
BIRTH_DATE                               DATE
```

The ANIMAL table's columns map to the attributes of the ANIMAL_TY object type. However, because it is an object table, there are significant differences in how you can use the table. As noted earlier in this section, each row within the object table has an OID value, and the rows can be referenced as objects.

Inserting Rows into Object Tables

Because ANIMAL is an object table, you can use its object type's constructor method when INSERTing data into the table. Because the ANIMAL table is based on the ANIMAL_TY object type, the ANIMAL_TY constructor method can be used when INSERTing values into ANIMAL.

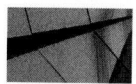

NOTE
Refer to Chapter 38 for details on constructor methods.

In the following listing, three rows are INSERTed into the ANIMAL object table. In each command, the ANIMAL_TY constructor method is called.

```
insert into animal values
        (animal_ty('Mule','Frances', '01-APR-12'));
```

```
insert into animal values
        (animal_ty('Dog','Annie', '03-SEP-11'));
insert into animal values
        (animal_ty('Crocodile','Lyle', '14-MAY-10'));
```

If the object type on which the object table is based is itself based on a second object type, you may need to nest calls to multiple constructor methods within your INSERT command. (Refer to Chapter 39 for examples of nested object types.)

NOTE
If an object table is based on a datatype that does not contain any nested datatypes, you can also insert records into the object table using the normal INSERT command syntax for relational tables.

When you INSERT a row into an object table, Oracle assigns an OID to the row. Having an OID allows you to use the row as a referenceable object. OID values are not reused.

Selecting Values from Object Tables

When the ANIMAL table was created, it was based entirely on the ANIMAL_TY datatype:

```
create table animal of animal_ty;
```

When you select from a table that contains an object type, you refer to the object type's columns as part of the table's columns. That is, if you used the ANIMAL_TY datatype as the basis for a *column* named ANIMAL, then you would select the animal names by selecting ANIMAL. NAME from the table.

An object table, though, is based on an object type—it has no other columns. Therefore, you do not need to reference the object type when accessing the columns. To select the names from the ANIMAL table, just query the attributes directly:

```
select name
from animal;

NAME
------------------------
Frances
Benji
Lyle
```

You can refer to the columns within the WHERE clause just as if ANIMAL were a relational table:

```
select name
from animal
where breed = 'Crocodile';

NAME
------------------------
Lyle
```

If the ANIMAL_TY object type used another object type for one of its columns, that object type's column would be referenced during all SELECTs, UPDATEs, and DELETEs.

Updating and Deleting from Object Tables

If the object table is based on an object type that uses no other object types, an UPDATE or DELETE of an object table uses the same format as you would use for relational tables. The ANIMAL_TY datatype does not use any other object type for one of its columns, so your UPDATEs and DELETEs from the ANIMAL object table behave the same as if ANIMAL were a relational table.

The following command UPDATEs one of the rows of the ANIMAL table:

```
update animal
set birth_date = '01-MAY-10'
where name = 'Lyle';
```

```
1 row updated.
```

Note that during the UPDATE, the columns of the object table are referred to as if ANIMAL were a relational table. During a DELETE, you use the same means to reference the object table's columns in the WHERE clause:

```
delete from animal
where Name = 'Lyle';
```

```
1 row deleted.
```

Keeping a crocodile alongside mules and dogs probably wasn't such a good idea anyway.

Using the REF Function

The REF function allows you to reference existing row objects. For example, the ANIMAL table has (after the deletion of one row, shown in the preceding section) two row objects, each of which has an OID value assigned to it. You can see the OID assigned to each row by using the REF function, as shown here:

```
select ref(a)
from animal   a
where name = 'Frances';
```

```
REF(A)
--------------------------------------------------
0000280209DCC6AFCDC6BD7755E04365F5A8C00072DCC6AFCDC
6BC7755E04365F5A8C000720180036E0000
```

NOTE
Your REF(A) value should be different from the one shown here. The REF(A) value is wrapped over multiple lines in this listing, but you could see it all on one line if you SET LINESIZE long enough.

In the preceding listing, the ANIMAL table was given the alias *A,* and that alias was used as input to the REF function. The output shows the OID for the row object that met the limiting condition of the query.

> **NOTE**
> *The REF function takes as its input the alias given to the object table.*
> *The other functions shown later in this chapter also take aliases as*
> *inputs, so you should become familiar with this syntax.*

Since the REF function can only reference row objects, you cannot use it to reference column objects. Column objects include object types, LOBs, and collectors.

As you can see, the REF function by itself does not give you any useful information. You need to use another function—DEREF—that translates the REF output into values. You can then use REF and DEREF to reference row-object values, as described in the next section.

Using the DEREF Function

The REF function takes a row object as its argument and returns a reference value. The DEREF function does the opposite—it takes a reference value (the OID generated for a reference) and returns the value of the row object.

Earlier in this chapter, the ANIMAL object table was created using the ANIMAL_TY object type:

```
create table animal of animal_ty;
```

To see how DEREF and REF work together, consider a table that is related to the ANIMAL table. The KEEPER table tracks the people who take care of the animals. It has a column for the name of the keeper (KEEPER_NAME) and a reference to the ANIMAL object table (ANIMAL_ KEPT), as shown in the following listing:

```
create table keeper
(keeper_name    varchar2(25),
 animal_kept    ref animal_ty);
```

The first part of the CREATE TABLE command looks normal:

```
create table keeper
(keeper_name    varchar2(25),
```

but the last line shows a new feature:

```
 animal_kept    ref animal_ty);
```

The ANIMAL_KEPT column references data that is stored elsewhere. The REF function points the ANIMAL_KEPT column to a row object of the ANIMAL_TY datatype. Because ANIMAL is an object table of the ANIMAL_TY datatype, the ANIMAL_KEPT column can point to the row objects within the ANIMAL object table. You can point the REF to any object table of that type. You can think of a REF type as a foreign key of sorts, except that it's just a pointer and it can point to an object in an object table.

When you DESCRIBE the KEEPER table, you can see that its ANIMAL_KEPT column relies on a REF:

```
describe keeper
```

```
Name                                Null?     Type
--------------------------------    --------  ----
KEEPER_NAME                                   VARCHAR2(25)
ANIMAL_KEPT                                   REF OF ANIMAL_TY
```

To see the full details, use a higher value for the DESCRIBE depth:

```
set describe depth 2
```

```
desc keeper
```

```
Name                                     Null?     Type
-------------------------------------    --------  ----------------
KEEPER_NAME                                        VARCHAR2(25)
ANIMAL_KEPT                                        REF OF ANIMAL_TY
   BREED                                           VARCHAR2(25)
   NAME                                            VARCHAR2(25)
   BIRTH_DATE                                      DATE
```

Now, INSERT a record into KEEPER. You need to use the REF function to store the ANIMAL references in the ANIMAL_KEPT column.

```
insert into keeper
select 'Catherine Weilz',
   ref(a)
from animal a
where name = 'Annie';
```

Let's look at this INSERT command closely. First, the KEEPER_NAME value is selected as a literal value:

```
insert into keeper
select 'Catherine Weilz',
```

Next, the value for the ANIMAL_KEPT column must be specified. But the datatype of ANIMAL_KEPT is REF of ANIMAL_TY, so you must select the reference from the ANIMAL object table to populate the ANIMAL_KEPT column:

```
   ref(a)
from animal a
where name = 'Annie';
```

What's going on here? First, the ANIMAL object table is queried, and the REF function returns the OID for the row object selected. The OID is then stored in the KEEPER table as a pointer to that row object in the ANIMAL object table.

Does the KEEPER table contain the animal information? No. KEEPER contains the name of the keeper and a reference to a row object in the ANIMAL table. You can see the reference OID by querying KEEPER:

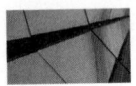

```
select * from keeper;

KEEPER_NAME
-----------------------
ANIMAL_KEPT
--------------------------------------------------

Catherine Weilz
00002202088817DC34109A4A929C632C0FAF1F78EF9A233BD5F
FD34A7E82D8C0C5CFB88FC0
```

NOTE
Your ANIMAL_KEPT value and text wrapping will differ from those shown here.

The ANIMAL_KEPT column, as shown in this listing, contains the reference to the row object, not the value of the data stored in the row object.

You can't see the referenced value unless you use the DEREF function. When you select from KEEPER, Oracle uses the OID to evaluate the reference (REF). The DEREF function takes the reference and returns a value.

In the following query, the value of the ANIMAL_KEPT column in KEEPER is the parameter passed to the DEREF function. DEREF takes the OID from ANIMAL_KEPT and finds the referenced object; the function then evaluates the reference and returns the values to the user.

```
select deref(k.animal_kept)
from keeper k
where keeper_name = 'Catherine Weilz';

DEREF(K.ANIMALKEPT)(BREED, NAME, BIRTH_DATE)
--------------------------------------------------
ANIMAL_TY('Dog', 'Annie', '03-SEP-11')
```

NOTE
The parameter for the DEREF function is the column name of the REF column, not the table name.

The result shows that the "Catherine Weilz" record in KEEPER references an ANIMAL record for the animal named "Annie". A few aspects of this query are noteworthy:

- The query used a reference to a row object to travel from one table (KEEPER) to a second (the ANIMAL object table). Thus, a join is performed in the background, without your specifying the join criteria.

- The object table itself is not mentioned in the query. The only table listed in the query is KEEPER. You do not need to know the name of the object table to DEREF its values.

- The entire referenced row object was returned, not just part of the row.

These are significant differences that separate object queries from relational queries. Thus, when querying your tables, you need to know the way in which their relationships are established. Are the relationships based on foreign keys and primary keys, or on object tables and REF datatypes? If you are planning to use Oracle's object-oriented features, you need to accommodate the changes in SQL and the ways relationships are enforced. To help smooth the transition between relational and object-oriented approaches, Oracle allows you to create object views that contain REFs superimposed on existing relational tables. See "Object Views with REFs" later in this chapter.

Using the VALUE Function

The DEREF function was applied to the relational table—the KEEPER table, in this case. The DEREF function returns the value of the reference that goes from the relational table to the object table.

What about querying from the object table? Can you select from ANIMAL?

```
select * from animal;
```

BREED	NAME	BIRTH_DATE
Mule	Frances	01-APR-12
Dog	Annie	03-SEP-11

Even though ANIMAL is an object table, you can select from it as if it were a relational table. This is consistent with the examples of INSERTs and SELECTs shown earlier in this chapter. However, that is not what was shown via the DEREF. The DEREF showed the full structure of the object type used by the ANIMAL object table:

```
select deref(k.animal_kept)
from keeper k
where keeper_name = 'Catherine Weilz';

DEREF(K.ANIMALKEPT)(BREED, NAME, BIRTH_DATE)
--------------------------------------------------
ANIMAL_TY('Dog', 'Annie', '03-SEP-11')
```

To see the same structures from a query of the ANIMAL object table, use the VALUE function. As shown in the following listing, VALUE shows you the data in the same format that DEREF uses. The parameter for the VALUE function is the table alias.

```
select value(a)
from animal a
where name = 'Annie';

VALUE(A)(BREED, NAME, BIRTH_DATE)
-----------------------------------------
ANIMAL_TY('Dog', 'Annie', '03-SEP-11')
```

The VALUE function is useful when debugging references and within PL/SQL, as shown in "Object PL/SQL," later in this chapter. Because the VALUE function allows you to query the formatted values directly from the object table, you can select those values without using the DEREF query of KEEPER's ANIMAL_KEPT column.

Invalid References

You can DELETE the object to which a reference points. For example, you can DELETE a row from the ANIMAL object table to which a KEEPER record points:

```
delete from animal
where name = 'Annie';
```

The record in KEEPER that references this ANIMAL record now has what is called a *dangling REF*. If you INSERT a new ANIMAL row for the animal named "Annie", it won't be recognized as being part of the same reference established earlier. The reason is that the first time you INSERTed a "Annie" row, Oracle generated an OID for the row object, and that is what the KEEPER column referenced. When you DELETEd the row object, the OID went away—and Oracle does not reuse OID numbers. Therefore, when the new "Annie" record is entered, it is given a *new* OID value—and the KEEPER record still points to the old value.

This is a critical difference between relational and OOP systems. In a relational system, the join between two tables depends only on the current data. In an OOP system, the join is between objects—and just the fact that two objects have the same data doesn't mean they are the same.

Object Views with REFs

You can use object views to superimpose OOP structures on existing relational tables (refer to Chapter 38). For example, you can create object types and use them within the object view of an existing table. Using object views allows you to access the table via either relational command syntax or object type syntax. As a result, object views provide an important technological bridge from existing relational applications to object-relational applications.

A Quick Review of Object Views

This example from Chapter 38 will serve as part of the basis for the advanced object views in this chapter. First, you create CUSTOMER table, with the CUSTOMER_ID column as its primary key:

```
create table customer
(customer_id number constraint customer_pk primary key,
  name       varchar2(25),
  street     varchar2(50),
  city       varchar2(25),
  state      char(2),
  zip        number);
```

Next, you create two object types. The first, ADDRESS_TY, contains attributes for addresses: STREET, CITY, STATE, and ZIP. The second, PERSON_TY, contains a NAME attribute plus an ADDRESS attribute that uses the ADDRESS_TY datatype, as shown in the following listing:

```
create or replace type address_ty as object
(street  varchar2(50),
  city    varchar2(25),
```

```
 state    char(2),
 zip      number);
/

create or replace type person_ty as object
(name        varchar2(25),
 address     address_ty);
/
```

Since the CUSTOMER table was created without using the ADDRESS_TY and PERSON_TY datatypes, you need to use object views to access CUSTOMER data via object-based accesses (such as methods). You can create an object view that specifies the object types that apply to the CUSTOMER table. In the following listing, the CUSTOMER_OV object view is created:

```
create view customer_ov (customer_id, person) as
select customer_id,
       person_ty(name,
       address_ty(street, city, state, zip))
from customer;
```

In the creation of the CUSTOMER_OV object view, the constructor methods for the two object types (ADDRESS_TY and PERSON_TY) are specified. You can now access the CUSTOMER table directly (as a relational table) or via the constructor methods for the object types.

The CUSTOMER table will be used in the next set of examples in this chapter.

Object Views Involving References

If the CUSTOMER table shown in the previous section is related to another table, you can use object views to create a reference between the tables. That is, Oracle will use the existing primary key/foreign key relationships to simulate OIDs for use by REFs between the tables. You can therefore access the tables either as relational tables or as objects. When you treat the tables as objects, you can use the REFs to perform joins of the tables automatically (refer to "Using the DEREF Function," earlier in this chapter, for examples).

The CUSTOMER table has a primary key of CUSTOMER_ID. Let's create a small table that contains a foreign key reference to the CUSTOMER_ID column. In the following listing, the CUSTOMER_CALL table is created. The primary key of the CUSTOMER_CALL table is the combination of CUSTOMER_ID and CALL_NUMBER. The CUSTOMER_ID column of CUSTOMER_CALL is a foreign key back to CUSTOMER—you cannot record a call for a customer who does not already have a record in CUSTOMER. A single nonkey attribute, CALL_DATE, is created within the CUSTOMER_CALL table.

```
create table customer_call
(customer_id    number,
 call_number    number,
 call_date      date,
 constraint customer_call_pk
     primary key (customer_id, call_number),
 constraint customer_call_fk foreign key (customer_id)
    references customer(customer_id));
```

For example, you could have the following CUSTOMER and CUSTOMER_CALL entries:

```
insert into customer values
(123,'Sigmund','47 Haffner Rd','Lewiston','NJ',22222);
insert into customer values
(234,'Evelyn','555 High St','Lowlands Park','NE',33333);

insert into customer_call values
(123,1,trunc(sysdate)-1);
insert into customer_call values
(123,2,trunc(sysdate));
```

The foreign key from CUSTOMER_CALL to CUSTOMER defines the relationship between the tables. From an OOP point of view, the records in CUSTOMER_CALL reference the records in CUSTOMER. Therefore, we must find a way to assign OID values to the records in CUSTOMER and generate references in CUSTOMER_CALL.

How to Generate OIDs

First, use an object view to assign OIDs to the records in CUSTOMER. Remember that OIDs are assigned to records in an object table—and an object table, in turn, is based on an object type. Therefore, you first need to create an object type that has the same structure as the CUSTOMER table:

```
create or replace type customer_ty as object
(customer_id number,
 name         varchar2(25),
 street       varchar2(50),
 city         varchar2(25),
 state        char(2),
 zip          number);
```

Now, create an object view based on the CUSTOMER_TY type, while assigning OID values to the records in CUSTOMER:

```
create or replace view customer_ov of customer_ty
with object identifier (customer_id) as
select customer_id, name, street, city, state, zip
from customer;
```

The first part of this CREATE VIEW command gives the view its name (CUSTOMER_OV) and tells Oracle that the view's structure is based on the CUSTOMER_TY datatype:

```
create or replace view customer_ov of customer_ty
```

The next part of the CREATE VIEW command tells the database how to construct OID values for the rows in CUSTOMER. The WITH OBJECT IDENTIFIER clause is followed by the column to use for the OID—in this case, the CUSTOMER_ID value. You can then address the rows within the CUSTOMER table as if they are referenceable row objects within an object table.

```
with object identifier (customer_id) as
```

The final part of the CREATE VIEW command gives the query on which the view's data access will be based. The columns in the query must match the columns in the view's base datatype.

```
select customer_id, name, street, city, state, zip
from customer;
```

The rows of CUSTOMER are now accessible as row objects via the CUSTOMER_OV view. The OID values generated for the CUSTOMER_OV rows are called *pkOIDs*, because they are based on CUSTOMER's primary key values. Relational tables can be accessed as row objects if you create object views for them.

How to Generate References

The rows of CUSTOMER_CALL reference rows in CUSTOMER. From a relational perspective, the relationship is determined by the foreign key pointing from the CUSTOMER_CALL.CUSTOMER_ID column to the CUSTOMER.CUSTOMER_ID column. Now that the CUSTOMER_OV object view has been created and the rows in CUSTOMER can be accessed via OIDs, you need to create reference values in CUSTOMER_CALL that reference CUSTOMER. Once the REFs are in place, you can use the DEREF function (shown earlier in this chapter) to access the CUSTOMER data from within CUSTOMER_CALL.

The CREATE VIEW command for the object view of CUSTOMER_CALL is shown in the following listing. It uses a new function, MAKE_REF, which is described following the listing.

```
create view customer_call_ov as
select make_ref(customer_ov, customer_id) customer_id,
       call_number,
       call_date
from customer_call;
```

With the exception of the MAKE_REF operation, this CREATE VIEW command looks like a normal CREATE VIEW command. The MAKE_REF operation is shown in this line:

```
select make_ref(customer_ov, customer_id) customer_id,
```

The MAKE_REF function takes as arguments the name of the object view being referenced and the name of the column (or columns) that form the foreign key in the local table. In this case, the CUSTOMER_ID column of the CUSTOMER_CALL table references the column that is used as the basis of OID generation in the CUSTOMER_OV object view. Therefore, two parameters are passed to MAKE_REF: CUSTOMER_OV and CUSTOMER_ID. The result of the MAKE_REF operation is given the column alias CUSTOMER_ID. Because this command creates a view, the result of an operation must be given a column alias.

What does MAKE_REF do? It creates references (called *pkREFs* because they are based on primary keys) from the CUSTOMER_CALL_OV view to the CUSTOMER_OV view. You can now query the two views as if CUSTOMER_OV were an object table and CUSTOMER_CALL_OV were a table that contains a REF datatype that references CUSTOMER_OV.

Querying the Object Views

The queries of the object views with REFs mirror the structure of the queries of table REFs. You use the DEREF function to select the value of the referenced data, as shown earlier in this chapter. Applied to the object views, the query will be

```
select deref(ccov.customer_id)
from customer_call_ov ccov
where call_date = trunc(sysdate);

DEREF(CCOV.CUSTOMER_ID)(CUSTOMER_ID, NAME, STREET, CITY, STATE,ZIP)
-----------------------------------------------------------------
CUSTOMER_TY(123, 'Sigmund', '47 Haffner Rd', 'Lewiston','NJ',22222)
```

The query finds the record in CUSTOMER_CALL for which the CALL_DATE value is the current system date. It then takes the CUSTOMER_ID value from that record and evaluates its reference. That CUSTOMER_ID value, from the MAKE_REF function, points to a pkOID value in the CUSTOMER_OV object view. The CUSTOMER_OV object view returns the record whose pkOID matches the referenced value. The DEREF function then returns the value of the referenced row. The query thus returns rows from CUSTOMER even though the user only queries CUSTOMER_CALL.

Object views of column objects enable you to work with tables as if they were both relational tables and object-relational tables. When extended to row objects, object views enable you to generate OID values based on established foreign key/primary key relationships. Object views allow you to continue to use the existing constraints and standard INSERT, UPDATE, DELETE, and SELECT commands. They also allow you to use OOP features such as references against the object tables. Object views thus provide an important technological bridge for migrating to an OOP database architecture.

As described earlier in this chapter, Oracle performs joins that resolve the references defined in the database. When the referenced data is retrieved, it brings back the entire row object that was referenced. To reference the data, you need to establish pkOIDs in the table that is the "primary key" table in the relationship and use MAKE_REF to generate references in the table that is the "foreign key" table in the relationship. You can then work with the data as if it were stored in object tables.

Object PL/SQL

PL/SQL programs can use the object types you have created. Whereas earlier versions of PL/SQL could only use the Oracle-provided datatypes (such as DATE, NUMBER, and VARCHAR2), you can now use your own object types as well. The result is the merging of SQL, procedural logic, and OOP extensions—a combination referred to as *object PL/SQL*.

The following anonymous PL/SQL block uses object PL/SQL concepts. The CUSTOMER_TY object type is used as the datatype for the **Cust1** variable, and its value is populated by a query of the CUSTOMER_OV object view.

```
set serveroutput on
declare
    Cust1        customer_ty;
begin
    select value(cov)  into Cust1
    from customer_ov cov
    where customer_id = 123;
    dbms_output.put_line(Cust1.name);
    dbms_output.put_line(Cust1.street);
end;
/
```

The output of this PL/SQL block is

```
Sigmund
47 Haffner Rd
```

In the first part of the PL/SQL block, a variable is declared using the CUSTOMER_TY datatype:

```
declare
     Cust1          customer_ty;
```

The **Cust1** variable value is selected from the CUSTOMER_OV object view (created in the preceding section of this chapter). The VALUE function is used to retrieve the data in the structure of the object type. Because the data is selected in the format of the object type, you need to use the CUSTOMER_OV object view created on the CUSTOMER table.

```
begin
     select value(cov)   into Cust1
     from customer_ov cov
     where customer_id = 123;
```

The CUST1.NAME and CUST1.STREET values are then retrieved from the attributes of the **Cust1** variable and displayed. You cannot pass the entire **Cust1** variable to the PUT_LINE procedure.

```
     dbms_output.put_line(Cust1.name);
     dbms_output.put_line(Cust1.street);
end;
```

This exercise is deliberately simple, but it shows the power of object PL/SQL. You can use object PL/SQL anywhere you use object types. Your PL/SQL is thus no longer bound to the Oracle-provided datatypes and may more accurately reflect the objects in your database. In this example, an object view was queried to illustrate that the queries can access either column objects or row objects. You can then select the attributes of the object type and manipulate or display them. If you have defined methods for the object type, you can apply them as well.

For example, you can call the object type's constructor methods within your PL/SQL blocks. In the following example, a variable named **NewCust** is defined using the CUSTOMER_TY datatype. The **NewCust** variable is then set equal to a set of values using the CUSTOMER_TY constructor method. The **NewCust** variable's set of values is then inserted via the CUSTOMER_OV object view.

```
declare
     NewCust      customer_ty;
begin
     NewCust :=
       customer_ty(345,'NewCust','StreetVal', 'City','ST',00000);
     insert into customer_ov
     values (NewCust);
end;
/
```

You can see the result of the INSERT by querying CUSTOMER_OV:

```
select customer_id, name from customer_ov;

CUSTOMER_ID NAME
----------- ------------------------
        123 Sigmund
        234 Evelyn
        345 NewCust
```

In addition to calling constructor methods, you can call the methods you have created on your object types. If you are comparing the values of variables that use the object types, you need to define map or order methods for the datatypes. This capability allows you to further extend object PL/SQL—you define the datatypes and the functions at the database level, and they are callable within any of your PL/SQL programs. Object PL/SQL represents a significant enhancement over traditional PL/SQL.

Objects in the Database

The features available in Oracle—column objects, row objects, and object extensions to PL/SQL—enable you to implement objects in your database without sacrificing the investment you have already made in analysis and design. You can continue to create systems based on relational design techniques and tune them based on relational access methods. The tools that Oracle provides allow you to create an OOP layer above your relational tables. Once you have that layer in place, you can access the relational data as if it were stored in a fully OOP database.

Having an OOP layer allows you to realize some of the benefits of an OOP system, such as abstraction and encapsulation. You can apply the methods for each object type across a set of consistently implemented objects, and benefit from object reuse and standards enforcement. At the same time, you can benefit from Oracle's relational features. The ability to use both relational and object technology within an application lets you apply the proper tool for the proper job within the database.

Note that implementing object-relational features may force you to change your approach to data relationships and the tools you use to access the data. If you use row objects, the relationships among tables are among row objects, not their data—possibly resulting in dangling REFs. Additionally, unless you use object views you will need to use new SQL syntax for queries and DML operations.

When implementing the object portion of an object-relational database, start by defining the object types that are the core components of your business. Every object-relational feature, whether it relates to column objects or row objects, is based on an object type. The better you have defined your object types and their methods, the better you can implement objects. If necessary, nest objects so you can have multiple variations of the same core object type. The result is a database that is properly designed to take advantage of both relational and object-oriented features.

PART
VI

Java in Oracle

CHAPTER
42

An Introduction to Java

his chapter gives you an overview of Java as it relates to Oracle database applications. Java has numerous uses beyond Oracle applications, and many features of the language will not be used by most Oracle developers. The goal of this chapter is to provide developers who have a background in SQL and PL/SQL with an understanding of the Java language structures. This is not an exhaustive review of Java (numerous books are available that accomplish that goal) but rather a short overview of the Java language components most commonly used by Oracle developers.

Although in many cases PL/SQL and Java correlate well to each other, they are significantly different in terminology and usage. That shouldn't be surprising because the two programming languages were developed independently. Furthermore, PL/SQL's object-oriented capabilities were not part of its initial implementation, whereas Java has been object oriented since its inception. To use Java effectively, you need to take a different approach than the one you may have taken in the past with PL/SQL.

Chapter 32 presented an introduction to the PL/SQL language structures and flow control. This chapter mirrors that approach: You'll learn about Java structures and the basic flow-control methods provided. Where applicable, I'll show you the matching PL/SQL structures. You should be familiar with PL/SQL (Chapter 32); packages, functions, and procedures (Chapter 35); and user-defined types and methods (Chapter 38) before reading this chapter.

Java vs. PL/SQL: An Overview

In comparing PL/SQL to Java, you get no further than the basic PL/SQL structure—a block—before you encounter a significant difference in terminology between the two languages. In PL/SQL, a *block* is a structured piece of code that has a Declarations section, an Executable Commands section, and an Exception Handling section. For a PL/SQL block, the structure may be represented as follows:

```
declare
  <declarations section>
begin
  <executable commands>
exception
  <exception handling>
end;
```

In Java, the term *block* refers to a much smaller subset of code. In Java, a block is a collection of statements enclosed by curly braces: { and }. For example, the following pseudo-code contains two Java blocks:

```
if (some condition) {
  block of code to process if condition is met
}
else {
  block of code to process if condition is not met
}
```

Within PL/SQL, that entire code section would be merely one part of a larger block; within Java, it contains two separate blocks. Throughout this chapter, all references to "blocks" refer to Java blocks unless otherwise specified.

A PL/SQL procedure is bound by a BEGIN and END, whereas a Java method is bound by opening and closing braces. These braces are also utilized to isolate individual blocks of scoped code or as indicators of the opening and closing of conditional segments.

A second major difference between PL/SQL and Java is in the declaration of variables. In a PL/SQL block, you define your variables before you begin the Executable Commands section. In a Java program, you can define variables where they are needed within the program. A Java program has no Declarations section comparable to the one used in PL/SQL blocks.

Throughout this chapter, you'll see a number of other differences between PL/SQL and Java. It's important to remember that Java does not replace PL/SQL within your applications—you can continue to use PL/SQL for Oracle applications. For data-retrieval operations, you should test the performance differences between PL/SQL and Java before deciding on a technical direction to follow.

Getting Started

To use the examples in this section, you need a copy of the Java Development Kit (JDK), which is available for free download from http://www.oracle.com/technetwork/java/index.html. You need to install the JDK on the server on which you'll be running the Java programs.

NOTE
The JDK is installed as part of the Oracle Database installation. Be sure to install both the database kernel software and the associated client software.

Declarations

Within Java, you can declare variables as needed. A variable has a name and a datatype, and it's used to store a data value during the program's execution. A variable also has a scope, allowing it to be publicly accessible or private—similar to the manner in which procedures within packages can have private variables.

Here are examples of Java variable declarations:

```
char     aCharVariable = 'J';
boolean aBooleanVariable = false;
```

By convention, Java variables always start with a lowercase letter, as shown in this example, where the datatypes are CHAR and BOOLEAN, and each variable is assigned an initial value. Note that the assignment character in Java is =, as opposed to : = or => in PL/SQL. Each declaration is terminated with a semicolon.

The available primitive datatypes in Java are listed in Table 42-1.

In addition to the primitive datatypes listed in Table 42-1, you can use reference datatypes, which are based on the contents of variables. You may note that there is no primitive datatype for variable-length character strings—Java provides a String class for that purpose. Classes are discussed later in this chapter.

Datatype	Description
Byte	Byte-length integer
Short	Short integer
Int	Integer
Long	Long integer
Float	Single-precision floating-point real number
Double	Double-precision floating-point real number
Char	A single Unicode character
Boolean	A Boolean value, true or false

TABLE 42-1. *Java Primitive Datatypes*

Executable Commands

You can assign values to variables by using expressions and statements. The arithmetic operators supported by Java include the following:

Operator	Description
*	Multiplication
/	Division
+	Addition
−	Subtraction
%	Modulus

In addition to these operators, you can use Java's *unary* operators to simplify your coding. For example, you can increment variables by using the ++ operator, as shown here:

```
aLoopCounter = aLoopCounter++;
```

Or you could simply write this:

```
aLoopCounter++
```

In PL/SQL, that would have been written as follows:

```
aLoopCounter := aLoopCounter +1;
```

NOTE
The ++ operator is called a unary operator because it has only one operand. If an operator requires two operands (such as *), it is called a binary operator.

If the ++ operator is placed in front of the variable name, it is a *pre-increment* operator rather than a *post-increment* operator:

```
int anotherCounter = ++aLoopCounter;
```

In this example, the variable *anotherCounter* is set to the incremented value of *aLoopCounter*. By contrast

```
int anotherCounter = aLoopCounter++;
```

sets *anotherCounter* to the value of *aLoopCounter* before it is incremented. You can decrement a variable's value via the -- unary operator:

```
aLoopCounter = aLoopCounter--;
```

You can also combine the assignment of values with an operation. For example, instead of writing

```
aNumberVariable = aNumberVariable * 2;
```

you can write

```
aNumberVariable *= 2;
```

You can perform similar combinations using /=, %=, +=, and -=.

If you perform multiple arithmetic operations, you should use parentheses to clearly indicate the order in which the operations should be evaluated, as shown in the following example:

```
aNumberVariable = (aNumberVariable*2) +2;
```

Terminating these operations with semicolons makes them *statements*—complete units of execution.

Conditional Logic

You can evaluate variables by using expressions and statements. To do so, you may use one or more of the fundamental classes provided as part of Java. A full listing of those methods is beyond the scope of this book; see one of the many Oracle Press Java books available for the functionality currently provided.

NOTE
The number of supplied classes may change significantly with each release of Java.

In the following listing, the Character.isUpperCase method is used to evaluate the *aCharVariable* variable declared earlier:

```
if (Character.isUpperCase(aCharVariable)) {
  some commands to execute
}
```

If the *aCharVariable* value is uppercase, the commands in the following block are executed; otherwise, flow continues to the next part of the program.

The following is the general syntax for **if** clauses:

```
if (expression) {
  statement
}
```

Notice the lack of a **then** clause. If the expression being evaluated is true, the following block is automatically executed. Also, note the lack of an **end if** clause. Java blocks are simply terminated by the statement's closing brace.

You can also have **else** clauses to evaluate different conditions, as shown in the following listing:

```
if (expression) {
  statement
}
else {
  statement
}
```

If you have multiple conditions to check, you can use the **else if** clause to evaluate each in turn, ending with an **else** clause. The following listing illustrates the use of **else if** clauses:

```
if (aCharVariable == 'V') {
  statement
}
else if (aCharVariable == 'J') {
  statement
}
else {
  statement
}
```

NOTE
PL/SQL supports the use of ELSIF clauses to choose between alternatives. A single IF clause can have multiple ELSIF clauses.

In addition to supporting **if** clauses for conditional logic, Java features a **switch** clause. Used in conjunction with its **break** clause and statement labels, the **switch** clause can approximate the functionality of **goto** clauses (which Java does not support). First, let's look at a simple **switch** example. Using the **case** statement, multiple values of the *aMonth* variable are evaluated. Depending on the *aMonth* value, the text name for the month is displayed, and the processing leaves the **switch** block by means of a **break**.

```
int aMonth=2;
switch (aMonth) {
  case 1:
      System.out.println("January");
      break;
  case 2:
      System.out.println("February");
      break;
```

```
    case 3:
        System.out.println("March");
        break;
    default:
        System.out.println("Out of range");
        break;
}
```

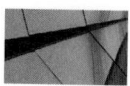

NOTE
*In Java, the arguments of a **case** statement must be integers.*

This kind of code is much more complex to write than a simple TO_CHAR, but it illustrates the **switch** usage. The **switch** operator takes the *aMonth* variable as its input and then evaluates its value. If the value matches a **case** value, the System.out.println method is called to print the month's name, and processing control leaves the **switch** block by means of a **break**. If the value does not match one of the **case** clauses, the **default** option is executed.

Where does control go? By default, it goes to the next section of the program. However, you have the option of creating labels for sections of your code and passing the names of those labels to the **break** clause. The following listing shows an example of a label and a **break** clause:

```
somelabel:
if (aCharVariable == 'V') {
  statement
}
else {
  statement
}
int aMonth=2;
switch (aMonth) {
  case 1:
      System.out.println("January");
      break somelabel;
  case 2:
      System.out.println("February");
      break someotherlabel;
  case 3:
      System.out.println("March");
      break somethirdlabel;
  default:
      System.out.println("Out of range");
      break;
}
```

In this example, the **if** clause is evaluated, followed by the **switch** clause. Note that the *aMonth* variable is not declared until just before it is needed. For this example, the *aMonth* variable is assigned a value of 2, so the program will display the word "February" and then branch over to the section of code identified by the *someotherlabel* label. If the *aMonth* value had been 1, the **if** clause at the beginning of the code listing would have been re-executed.

Java also supports a *ternary* operator—an operator that takes three operands and whose function is similar to that of PL/SQL's DECODE. Acting as an inline if-else combination, the ternary operator evaluates an expression. If the expression evaluates to true, the second operand is returned; otherwise, the third is returned. The syntax is as follows:

```
expression ? operand1 : operand2
```

The following listing shows a sample ternary operation:

```
aStatusVariable = (aCharVariable == 'V') ? "OK" :   "Invalid";
```

In this example, the expression

```
(aCharVariable == 'V')
```

is evaluated. If it is true, "OK" is returned; otherwise, "Invalid" is returned.

You can use the ternary operator to simulate the use of a **greatest** function:

```
double greatest = (a > b) ? a : b;
```

In this example, the expression `(a > b)` is evaluated, where *a* and *b* are the names of variables. If that expression is true, *a*'s value is returned; otherwise, *b*'s value is returned.

NOTE
*Java has a "greatest" method for numeric values—the **Max** method within the **java.lang.Math** class. The ternary example in the preceding listing can be rewritten as **double greatest = Math.Max(a, b);**.*

You can combine multiple logic checks in PL/SQL via the use of AND and OR operations. In Java, an AND operation is represented by the `&&` operator:

```
if (aCharVariable == 'V' && aMonth == 3) {
   statement
}
```

The OR operation is represented by `||`, as shown in the following listing:

```
if (aCharVariable == 'V' || aMonth == 3) {
   statement
}
```

For performance reasons, the `&&` and `||` operations are carried out only if required; the second expression is not evaluated if the first expression determines the result. In the case of the AND operator, if the first value is false, the evaluation ends at that point and the Boolean value false is returned. In the case of the OR operator, if the first expression is false, the second expression is still evaluated because only one of the test conditions needs to be true for the Boolean value true to be returned. If the first value of the OR operator were true, subsequent expressions would not need to be evaluated and true would be returned.

The `&` and `|` operators are bitwise AND and OR; they are not short-circuited as `&&` and `||` are. All expressions are always evaluated. This functionality can be important if you are testing the return values of method calls and you need to make sure the methods are executed.

Loops

Java supports three main types of loops: **while** loops, **do-while** loops, and **for** loops. This section contains examples of each type of loop. Because Java is not written as an extension of SQL, it does not support Cursor FOR loops as PL/SQL does.

WHILE Loops and DO-WHILE Loops

A **while** clause evaluates a condition; if the condition is true, the associated block of statements is executed. The syntax for a **while** loop follows this form:

```
while (expression) {
  statement
  statement
}
```

The **while** loop executes the block of statements (the section within the { and } braces) repeatedly until the *expression* is no longer true:

```
int aNumberVariable = 3;
while (aNumberVariable < 7)  {
  some_processing_statement
  aNumberVariable++;
}
```

In this example, a counter variable *(aNumberVariable)* is created and initialized. The variable's value is then evaluated via the **while** clause. If the value is less than 7, the associated statement block is executed. As part of that block, the variable is incremented. When the block completes, the variable is again evaluated and the loop continues.

NOTE
*For examples of **while** loop processing, see "Classes" later in this chapter.*

You could also write this as a **do-while** loop:

```
int aNumberVariable = 3;
do {
  some_processing_statement
  aNumberVariable++;
} while (aNumberVariable < 7);
```

In a **do-while** loop, the expression's value is not evaluated until the block has been processed at least one time.

FOR Loops

You can use a **for** loop to repeatedly execute a block of code. In a **for** loop, you specify an initial value, a termination value, and an increment for the loop counter. The loop counter is incremented each time through the loop, by the increment you specify, until the termination value is reached. The following is the syntax for a **for** loop:

```
for (initialization; termination; increment) {
  statement;
}
```

The prior section's **while** example can be rewritten with a **for** clause, as shown in the following listing:

```
for (int aNumberVariable=3; aNumberVariable<7; aNumberVariable++)  {
  some_processing_statement
}
```

The **for** loop version for this example is much shorter than the **while** version. In this example, the *aNumberVariable* variable is declared and initialized within the **for** loop. As long as the variable's value does not exceed 7, the block is executed. For each pass through the loop, the variable's value is incremented by 1 via the ++ unary operator.

Within a loop, you can use the **continue** clause to jump to another statement within the loop. If you just use the **continue** clause by itself, the process flow jumps to the end of the loop body and evaluates the loop's termination test. If you use **continue** with a label (as shown previously in "Conditional Logic"), processing continues at the next iteration of the labeled loop.

Cursors and Loops

Within PL/SQL, you can use Cursor FOR loops to iterate through the results of a query. You can use Java's **while** and **for** loops to simulate the functionality of a PL/SQL Cursor FOR loop.

Oracle provides sample files that accompany the Oracle software installation, with a large number of examples illustrating standard coding approaches. The client installation uses the Oracle Universal Installer to load software drivers and demonstration files, including those supporting JDBC development. Following installation of the client software, the JDBC examples are in the Java-related subdirectories under the Oracle software home directory. The exact files provided may change from version to version.

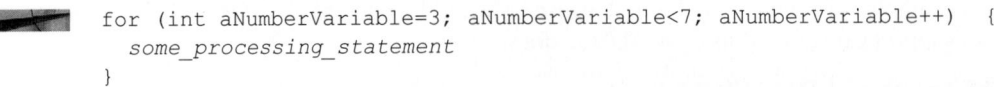

NOTE
The README file under the /jdbc subdirectory of the Oracle software home directory provides extensive information on the versions supported, environment variable settings by platform, and features supported. It is critical to read and follow those instructions to use Java effectively against Oracle Database 12c on your platform.

The following example shows a code fragment from an example provided with the Oracle client installation:

```
Statement stmt  conn.createStatement();
ResultSet rset = stmt.executeQuery ("select first_name, "
                                  + "last_name from employees");

    // Iterate through the result and print the employee names
    while (rset.next ())
       System.out.println (rset.getString (1) + " " + rset.getString (2));
```

This example assumes that a connection to the database has already been established. The first line of the example creates a variable called *stmt,* based on a connection variable called *conn* (not shown in this partial listing). The second line of the example creates a variable called *rset,* based on the result set that the query *stmt* will return. Following a comment (prefixed by //), a **while** clause fetches each row in the result set. If the fetch retrieves a row from the result set, the ENAME from that EMP row is printed; otherwise, the loop ends.

From a programming perspective, you should be specific in the data returned (as in the preceding example), specifying the column names to be returned.

The Java Database Connectivity (JDBC, see Chapter 43) demos provided by Oracle show examples of queries involving procedure calls, LOBs, and DML. In most cases, your Java code will perform in a similar manner to the previous example: Write the process flow-control language in Java and pass it a statement to execute. Based on the outcome of that statement, you can direct different actions to occur via the use of **while**, **for**, **if**, **break**, **continue**, and **switch** clauses, as shown earlier in this chapter.

Exception Handling

In a PL/SQL procedure, you have a single EXCEPTION block; in Java, you can have as many **try/ catch** blocks as you desire. Java provides a robust set of error-handling routines and enables you to create complex error-handling procedures. In PL/SQL, you *raise* an exception; in Java, you *throw* exceptions. If an exception is thrown, you need to use the Java **catch** clause to capture and properly process the exception.

Java's exception-handling syntax is based on three blocks: **try**, **catch**, and **finally**. The **try** block includes the statements that might throw an exception. The **catch** block immediately following the **try** block associates exception handlers with the exceptions that may be thrown by the **try** block. The **finally** block cleans up any system resources not properly cleaned up during the **catch** block processing. The general structure is as follows:

```
try {
   statements
}
catch () {
   statements
}
catch () {
   statements
}
finally {
   statements
}
```

For example, consider the following Java code:

```
try {
    Statement stmt = conn.createStatement ();
    stmt.execute ("drop table plsqltest");
}
catch (SQLException e) {
}
```

In this example, a variable named *stmt* is created to execute a DROP TABLE command. If the execution fails—for example, if the table does not exist—how will that error be processed? The **catch** clause tells Java to handle it via an exception object called SQLException, a standard part of Java's SQL implementation. As shown in the example, the **catch** clause takes two parameters (an exception object and a variable name) and is optionally followed by a block of statements to execute.

The **try** block can contain multiple statements, or you can create separate **try** blocks for each statement. In general, it is easier to manage exception handling if you consolidate your **catch** blocks, so consolidating your **try** blocks will help you manage your code as it changes and grows. The WHEN OTHERS clause in PL/SQL is essentially **catch (Throwable th)** in Java.

The **finally** block cleans up the state of the current code section before passing control to any subsequent parts of the program. At run time, the contents of the **finally** block are always executed, regardless of the outcome of the **try** block. For example, you could use the **finally** block to close a database connection.

Reserved Words

The reserved words in Java are listed in Table 42-2. You cannot use these words as the names of classes, methods, or variables.

Classes

In the prior sections of this chapter, you saw the basic syntax structures for Java. In this section, you'll see how to use that syntax to create and use objects. A simple program for printing the word "Oracle" is shown in the following listing:

```
public class HelloOracle {
   public static void main (String[] args) {
      System.out.println("Oracle");
   }
}
```

This example creates a *class* called **HelloOracle**. Within the **HelloOracle** class, a public method called **main** is created. The **main** method prints the word "Oracle." This is significantly more complex than

```
select 'Oracle' from dual;
```

abstract	else	interface	super
boolean	extends	long	switch
break	false	native	synchronized
byte	final	new	this
case	finally	null	throw
catch	float	package	throws
char	for	private	transient
class	goto	protected	true
const	if	public	try
continue	implements	return	void
default	import	short	volatile
do	instanceof	static	while
double	int	strictfp	

TABLE 42-2. *Java Reserved Words*

but the Java version has features lacking in the SQL version. **HelloOracle** is a class, and as such its methods can be called from within other classes. **HelloOracle** could have multiple methods; in this example, it has only the **main** method.

The main method's declaration (**public static void main**) has a number of keywords that you should become familiar with:

public	Defining the class as **public** allows all classes to call this method.
static	Declares that this is a class method; you use **static** to declare class methods. An additional option is the keyword **final** for methods and variables whose values cannot change (similar to PL/SQL's CONSTANT option).
void	Specifies the return value's datatype from the procedure. Because this procedure does not return values, its type is **void**.

In this example, the method is given the name **main** because that simplifies running the class's method. Now that the class has been created, you can compile and load it.

NOTE
*To compile and execute a Java class, you must have the JDK on your server. The following examples assume that the binaries that are part of that kit are located in a directory that is automatically searched via the PATH environment variable and that the directory containing your class files is included in the CLASSPATH environment variable (see the /jdc/README file for details on environment variable settings). The programs referenced here (**javac and java**) are located in the /bin subdirectory of the JDK software directory.*

First, save the program as a plain text file called **HelloOracle.java**. Next, compile it:

```
javac HelloOracle.java
```

A new file, called **HelloOracle.class**, is created on your server. You can then run the class:

```
java HelloOracle
```

Then the output is displayed:

```
Oracle
```

As shown in the HelloOracle example, the class is first given a name, along with other optional attributes related to its inheritance of other classes' attributes. In the class body, all the class variables and methods are defined. As with abstract datatypes in Oracle, Java classes have methods associated with them for manipulating their related data.

Let's consider a more complex example. The following listing is a Java program that computes the area of a circle, given a radius value as input (see Chapter 32 for the PL/SQL version):

```
//  AreaOfCircle.java
//
public class AreaOfCircle {
  public static void main(String[] args) {
```

```
    try {
        int input = Integer.parseInt(args[0]);
        double result=area(input);
        System.out.println(result);
    }
    catch (ArrayIndexOutOfBoundsException oob) {
        System.out.println("You did not provide the radius of the circle.");
        System.out.println("Usage: java AreaOfCircle 10");
    }
    catch (NumberFormatException nfe) {
        System.out.println("Enter a valid number for the radius.");
        System.out.println("Usage: java AreaOfCircle 10");
    }
} // main

public static double area (int rad) {
    double pi=3.1415927;
    double areacircle=pi*rad*rad;
    return areacircle;
} // area
} //AreaOfCircle
```

NOTE
*Be sure to include a closing brace (}) for each block. In the examples
shown in this chapter, the closing braces are always on lines by
themselves to simplify debugging and processing flow-control errors
that may arise.*

First, note that the class and the name of the file must be the same. In this case, the class is named AreaOfCircle, so this text is stored in a file called **AreaOfCircle.java**. The class has two methods, called **main** and **area**. When you execute the class, the **main** method is automatically executed. The **main** method takes the string provided as input and parses it as an integer into the *input* variable:

```
int input=Integer.parseInt(args[0]);
```

At least two possible exceptions could be thrown when running this code. The first exception handled, **ArrayIndexOutOfBoundsException**, occurs when you try to reference a position in an array that doesn't exist. Because the code explicitly references the first position of the array named **args** (**args[0]**), an exception is thrown if no data is passed to the program. The other possible error, **NumberFormatException**, occurs if a nonnumeric value is passed in. For example, if you run the program by entering **"java AreaOfCircle XYZ"** instead of **"java AreaOfCircle 123"**, the **NumberFormatException** will be thrown because **XYZ** isn't a valid number. Both of these exceptions are handled by the two **catch** statements that provide the user with useful feedback regarding the error's cause:

```
catch (ArrayIndexOutOfBoundsException oob) {
    System.out.println("You did not provide the radius of the circle.");
    System.out.println("Usage: java AreaOfCircle 10");
}
catch (NumberFormatException nfe) {
```

```
        System.out.println("Enter a valid number for the radius.");
        System.out.println("Usage: java AreaOfCircle 10");
    }
```

Next, a variable named *result* is declared and is set equal to the value returned by the call to **area(input)**:

```
    double result=area(input);
```

To process that directive, the **area** method is executed using the *input* variable's value as its input. That method is as follows:

```
    public static double area (int rad) {
        double pi=3.1415927;
        double areacircle=pi*rad*rad;
        return areacircle;
    }
```

In its definition, the **area** method specifies that it will accept one variable, an integer type named **rad**. That variable's value (passed from the input variable in the **main** method) is then processed, and a variable named *areacircle* is calculated and returned to **main**. In **main**, that value is then printed:

```
    double result=area(input);
    System.out.println(result);
```

Testing the program is straightforward:

```
javac AreaOfCircle.java
java AreaOfCircle 10
```

The following is the output:

```
314.15927
```

Let's extend this example to include **while** loop processing. In this example, the area method is called repeatedly until the resulting input value exceeds a given value:

```
//   AreaOfCircleWhile.java
//
public class AreaOfCircleWhile {
    public static void main(String[] args) {
        try {
            int input=Integer.parseInt(args[0]);
            while (input < 7) {
                double result=area(input);
                System.out.println(result);
                input++;
            }
        }
        catch (ArrayIndexOutOfBoundsException oob) {
            System.out.println("You did not provide the radius of the circle.");
```

```
        System.out.println("Usage: java AreaOfCircle 10");
    }
    catch (NumberFormatException nfe) {
        System.out.println("Enter a valid number for the radius.");
        System.out.println("Usage: java AreaOfCircle 10");
    }
  } // main
  public static double area (int rad) {
    double pi=3.1415927;
    double areacircle=pi*rad*rad;
    return areacircle;
  } // area
} // AreaOfCircleWhile
```

In this listing, the **area** method and the exception-handling blocks are unchanged from the prior example. The change is in the **main** method:

```
int input=Integer.parseInt(args[0]);
while (input < 7) {
    double result=area(input);
    System.out.println(result);
    input++;
}
```

When the input value is less than 7, the input value is processed. After the area for that radius value has been calculated and printed, the input value is incremented:

```
input++;
```

Then the loop is evaluated again. Sample output is shown in the following listing:

```
javac AreaOfCircleWhile.java
java AreaOfCircleWhile 4

50.2654832
78.5398175
113.0973372
```

The output shows the area calculations for input radius values of 4, 5, and 6.

This example is not as complete as a finished program—you may need additional exception handling to handle non-integers, for example—but the structure is the important lesson to learn from this example. In addition to the methods shown in this example, you could create a constructor for the **AreaOfCircleWhile** class. All Java classes have constructors (see Chapter 38) to initialize new objects based on the class. The constructor's name is the same as the name of the class. If you create a class with no constructor, Java creates a default constructor at run time. Like a method, the constructor body can contain local variable declarations, loops, and statement blocks. The constructor initializes these variables for the class.

In the following chapters, you'll see how to implement Java within Oracle—within stored procedures and via JDBC. Those chapters assume that you have the basic knowledge of Java provided in this chapter.

CHAPTER
43

JDBC Programming

ava Database Connectivity (JDBC) builds on the Java and programming basics described earlier in this book. The discussions and examples in this chapter assume you are familiar with the Java syntax and structures described in Chapter 42. This chapter does not cover every aspect of JDBC but focuses on its basic usage.

You can use JDBC to execute dynamic SQL statements in Java programs. Oracle provides sample files with the Oracle software installation. You can use the sample files as examples to follow when creating your own JDBC programs.

NOTE
Even though JDK 1.6 is included with the default installation of Oracle Database 12c, JDK 1.6 is no longer supported as of February 2013. Use JDK 1.7 with Oracle Database 12c.

As part of the Oracle 12*c* installation, the following libraries and files can be found in the **/jdbc/lib** directory under your Oracle software home directory:

- **ojdbc6.jar**   This file contains classes for use with JDK 1.6. It contains the JDBC driver classes, except classes for NLS support in Oracle Object and Collection types.

- **ojdbc6g.jar**   This file is the same as ojdbc6.jar, except that classes have been compiled with **javac -g** and contain tracing code.

- **ojdbc7.jar**   This file contains classes for use with JDK 1.7. It contains the JDBC driver classes, except classes for NLS support in Oracle Object and Collection types.

- **ojdbc7_g.jar**   This file is the same as ojdbc7.jar, except that classes have been compiled with **javac -g** and contain tracing code.

The JDBC JavaDoc for the public API of the public classes of Oracle JDBC is found in **$ORACLE_HOME/jdbc/doc/javadoc.tar**. Sample JDBC programs are provided **$ORACLE_HOME/jdbc/demo/demo.tar**. For National Language Support (NLS), the file **$ORACLE_HOME/jlib/orai18n.jar** provides the NLS classes for use with JDK 1.6 and 1.7.

When you execute a SQL statement via JDBC, the SQL statement is not checked for errors until it is run. The JDBC program that contains the SQL command will compile even if the SQL statement is invalid.

Using the JDBC Classes

JDBC is implemented in Oracle via a set of Oracle-provided classes whose names begin with **oracle.sql**, whereas the standard JDBC classes provided with the JDK begin with **java.sql**. The **JdbcCheckup.java** class, shown in the following listing, provides a good roadmap for beginning JDBC programmers. **The JdbcCheckup.java** class assumes you are using Oracle Net to connect to the database.

NOTE
The following code is provided by Oracle. Your programming standards may implement these commands differently, for instance, by calling System.out.println in place of System.out.print, or by placing the brackets in different places.

```
/*
 * This sample can be used to check the JDBC installation.
 * Just run it and provide the connect information.  It will select
 * "Hello World" from the database.
 *
 */

// You need to import the java.sql package to use JDBC
import java.sql.*;

// We import java.io to be able to read from the command line
import java.io.*;

import oracle.jdbc.pool.OracleDataSource;

class JdbcCheckup
{
  public static void main (String args [])
       throws SQLException, IOException
  {
    // Prompt the user for connect information
    System.out.println ("Please enter information to test connection to the
database");
    String user;
    String password;
    String database;

    user = readEntry ("user: ");
    int slash_index = user.indexOf ('/');
    if (slash_index != -1)
    {
      password = user.substring (slash_index + 1);
      user = user.substring (0, slash_index);
    }
    else
      password = readEntry ("password: ");
    database = readEntry ("database (a TNSNAME entry, name-value pairs): ");

    // Create an OracleDataSource and set URL
    OracleDataSource ods = new OracleDataSource();
    ods.setURL("jdbc:oracle:oci8:" + user + "/" + password + "@" + database);

    System.out.print ("Connecting to the database...");
    System.out.flush ();

    // Connect to the database
    // You can put a database name after the @ sign in the connection URL.

    System.out.println ("Connecting...");
    Connection conn = ods.getConnection();
```

```java
    System.out.println ("connected.");

    // Create a statement
    Statement stmt = conn.createStatement ();

    // Do the SQL "Hello World" thing
    ResultSet rset = stmt.executeQuery ("select 'Hello World' from dual");

    while (rset.next ())
      System.out.println (rset.getString (1));

    System.out.println ("Your JDBC installation is correct.");

    // close the resultSet
    rset.close();

    // Close the statement
    stmt.close();

    // Close the connection
    conn.close();
  }

  // Utility function to read a line from standard input
  static String readEntry (String prompt)
  {
    try
    {
      StringBuffer buffer = new StringBuffer ();
      System.out.print (prompt);
      System.out.flush ();
      int c = System.in.read ();
      while (c != '\n' && c != -1)
      {
        buffer.append ((char)c);
        c = System.in.read ();
      }
      return buffer.toString ().trim ();
    }
    catch (IOException e)
    {
      return "";
    }
  }
}
```

NOTE
Production applications would be expected to include many more exception-handling sections than shown in this brief example. See Chapter 42 for an example of exception handling.

Starting at the top, this script first imports the **java.sql** classes provided by Oracle:

```
import java.sql.*;
```

The Oracle-provided data source driver is then imported:

```
import oracle.jdbc.pool.OracleDataSource;
```

When you are prompted for information, the *user* variable is populated via a call to the readEntry function:

```
user = readEntry ("user: ");
```

The readEntry function is defined later in the class, in the section beginning

```
// Utility function to read a line from standard input
static String readEntry (String prompt)
```

Once the connection data has been input, a *connection object* is created to maintain the state of the database session, based on the OracleDataSource definition. The getConnection call in the following listing starts the connection:

```
Connection conn = ods.getConnection();
```

If you receive an error during the connection, this step is usually the cause. An incorrect username/password combination, a mismatched set of drivers, or failure to install and configure Oracle Net correctly will cause this step to fail.

By default, a connection object is created with AUTOCOMMIT turned on—every transaction is automatically committed. To change that setting, you can use the following command (assuming you name the connection object **conn**, as shown in the example):

```
conn.setAutoCommit(false);
```

The class then creates a statement, executes a hard-coded query, and prints the output:

```
// Create a statement
Statement stmt = conn.createStatement ();

// Do the SQL "Hello World" thing
ResultSet rset = stmt.executeQuery ("select 'Hello World' from dual");

while (rset.next ())
  System.out.println (rset.getString (1));
```

The result set, statement, and connection are then closed and the program completes. Note that there are two steps to execute the statement: First, it's created via the call to the createStatement method. Second, it's executed via the executeQuery method. In place of executeQuery, you can use execute, or, if you're running an INSERT, UPDATE, or DELETE SQL statement, executeUpdate. If you select a column value (instead of just a text string), you should specify that column value in the **println** command, as shown in the following listing:

```
ResultSet rset =stmt.executeQuery("select User from dual");
while (rset.next ()) {
  System.out.println (rset.getString ("USER"));
```

Using JDBC for Data Manipulation

Let's combine the pieces that have been described so far—the basic connection syntax from this chapter with the Java classes from Chapter 42. The example in this section queries the RADIUS_ VALS table, calculates an area for each value, and inserts those values into the AREAS table. Therefore, it requires the use of the Java equivalent of a Cursor FOR loop, along with support for executable commands and INSERTs.

For the example, put three records into the RADIUS_VALS table and delete any rows in the AREAS table:

```
delete from radius_vals;
insert into radius_vals(radius) values (3);
insert into radius_vals(radius) values (4);
insert into radius_vals(radius) values (10);
delete from areas;
commit;
```

The following listing, **JdbcCircle.java**, contains the connection components from **JdbcCheckup.java**. The executable commands for the circle area start in the section called RetrieveRadius, shown in bold in the listing.

```
// You need to import the java.sql package to use JDBC
import java.sql.*;
// We import java.io to be able to read from the command line
import java.io.*;

import oracle.jdbc.pool.OracleDataSource;

class JdbcCircle {

  public static void main (String args [])
       throws SQLException, IOException {

    // Prompt the user for connect information
    System.out.println ("Please enter information for connection");
    String user;
    String password;
    String database;

    user = readEntry ("user: ");
    int slash_index = user.indexOf ('/');
    if (slash_index != -1) {

      password = user.substring (slash_index + 1);
      user = user.substring (0, slash_index);
    }
    else {
      password = readEntry ("password: ");
    }
    database = readEntry ("database (a TNSNAME entry): ");
    System.out.println ("Connecting to the database...");
```

```
// Create an OracleDataSource and set URL
OracleDataSource ods = new OracleDataSource();
ods.setURL("jdbc:oracle:oci8:" + user + "/" + password + "@" + database);
System.out.flush ();

// Connect to the database
// You can put a database name after the @ sign in the connection URL.

Connection conn = ods.getConnection();

System.out.println ("connected.");

// Create a statement
Statement stmt = conn.createStatement ();

// RetrieveRadius
ResultSet rset =stmt.executeQuery("select radius from radius_vals");

while (rset.next ())  {
  // if you wish to print the values:
  // System.out.println (rset.getInt ("RADIUS"));
  int radInput =  rset.getInt ("RADIUS");

  // Retrieve Radius value, calculate area:
  double result = area(radInput);

  // insert the value into AREAS
  String sql = "insert into areas values ("+radInput+","+result+ ")";
  // If you want to print the SQL statement:
  // System.out.println(sql);

  // Create a statement for the insert:
  Statement insArea = conn.createStatement();
  // Execute the insert:
  boolean insertResult = insArea.execute(sql);
}

  // close the resultSet
  rset.close();
  // Close the statement
  stmt.close();
  // Close the connection
  conn.close();
}

// Utility function to calculate the area
public static double area (int rad) {
  double pi=3.1415927;
  double areacircle=pi*rad*rad;
  return areacircle;
}
```

```
  // Utility function to read a line from standard input
  static String readEntry (String prompt) {

    try {
      StringBuffer buffer = new StringBuffer ();
      System.out.print (prompt);
      System.out.flush ();
      int c = System.in.read ();
      while (c != '\n' && c != -1) {

        buffer.append ((char)c);
        c = System.in.read ();
      }
      return buffer.toString ().trim ();
    }
    catch (IOException e) {
      return "";
    }
  }
}
```

In the RetrieveRadius section, the query to be executed is passed to the executeQuery method. The result of the query is stored in a variable named *rset*.

```
// RetrieveRadius
  ResultSet rset =stmt.executeQuery("select Radius from RADIUS_VALS");
```

As noted in Chapter 42, you can use a **while** loop in Java to approximate the functionality of a PL/SQL Cursor FOR loop. The following part of the RetrieveRadius section uses the getInt method to retrieve the integer Radius value from the result set. If the value had been a string, we would have used the getString method instead.

```
  while (rset.next ())  {
  // if you wish to print the values:
  // System.out.println (rset.getInt ("RADIUS"));
  int radInput =  rset.getInt ("RADIUS");
```

The *radInput* variable, assigned in the preceding listing, can now be used as input to the area calculation. The area calculation is performed via a utility function (see the full JdbcCircle listing) based on the code examples presented in Chapter 42.

```
// Retrieve Radius value, calculate area:
  double result = area(radInput);
```

We now have the radius value (the *radInput* variable) and the area value (the *result* variable) to use when populating the AREAS table. Let's build the INSERT statement to perform the insert. First, use the string concatenation functions in Java to concatenate text with the variable values. Make sure not to include a semicolon at the end of the generated command string.

```
// insert the value into AREAS
  String sql = "insert into areas values ("+radInput+","+result+ ")";
```

```
// If you want to print the SQL statement:
// System.out.println(sql);
```

Next, create a statement and execute the INSERT command (via a call to the *sql* variable that contains the command text):

```
// Create a statement for the insert:
Statement insArea = conn.createStatement();
// Execute the insert:
boolean insertResult = insArea.execute(sql);
```

Did it work? Compile and execute the **JdbcCircle.java** file:

```
javac JdbcCircle.java
java JdbcCircle
```

When prompted, provide a username and password for the owner of the RADIUS_VALS and AREAS tables. After the program completes, check the AREAS table:

```
select * from areas
order by Radius;

    RADIUS      AREA
--------- ---------
        3     28.27
        4     50.27
       10    314.16
```

This example is based on a simple calculation—the area of a circle—but it illustrates the key concepts in JDBC development: connecting to the database, retrieving data, implementing a Cursor FOR loop, assigning variables, generating a dynamic SQL statement, and executing DML.

JDBC supports extensive programming features, including statement caching, connection caching, connection failover, distributed transactions, support for LOBs, and more. See the *JDBC Developer's Guide* for further details on the use of JDBC.

CHAPTER
44

Java Stored Procedures

Y ou can write stored procedures, triggers, object type methods, and functions that call Java classes. In this chapter, you learn about a sample set of Java procedures, along with the commands required to execute a procedure. To get the most from this chapter, you should already be familiar with Java structures (refer to Chapter 42) and Java classes and JDBC (Chapter 43). You should also be familiar with the basic syntax and usage of stored procedures (refer to Chapter 35).

To focus on the database access operations of the Java classes, the example in this chapter is brief. The following class, called BookshelfDML, contains methods to insert and delete records from the BOOKSHELF table. In this example, the calculation of the area is not performed; rather, all required values are supplied during the INSERT. The following listing shows the **BookshelfDML.java** class file:

```java
import java.sql.*;
import java.io.*;
import oracle.jdbc.*;

public class BookshelfDML {
  public static void insertBookshelf (String title, String publisher,
      String categoryname, String rating) throws SQLException {
        String sql = "INSERT INTO BOOKSHELF VALUES (?,?,?,?)";
        try {
          Connection conn =
            DriverManager.getConnection("jdbc:default:connection:");
          PreparedStatement pstmt = conn.prepareStatement(sql);
          pstmt.setString(1, title);
          pstmt.setString(2, publisher);
          pstmt.setString(3, categoryname);
          pstmt.setString(4, rating);
          pstmt.executeUpdate();
          pstmt.close();
        } catch (SQLException e) {System.err.println(e.getMessage());}
    }

    public static void updateBookshelf (String rating,
        String title) throws SQLException {
        String sql = "UPDATE BOOKSHELF SET Rating = ? " +
          "WHERE Title = ? ";
        try {
          Connection conn =
            DriverManager.getConnection("jdbc:default:connection:");
          PreparedStatement pstmt = conn.prepareStatement(sql);
          pstmt.setString(1, rating);
          pstmt.setString(2, title);
          pstmt.executeUpdate();
          pstmt.close();
        } catch (SQLException e) {System.err.println(e.getMessage());}
    }
```

```
public static void deleteBookshelf (String title) throws SQLException {
    String sql = "DELETE FROM BOOKSHELF WHERE TITLE = ?";
    try {
      Connection conn =
        DriverManager.getConnection("jdbc:default:connection:");
      PreparedStatement pstmt = conn.prepareStatement(sql);
      pstmt.setString(1, title);
      pstmt.executeUpdate();
      pstmt.close();
    } catch (SQLException e) {System.err.println(e.getMessage());}
  }
}
```

The **BookshelfDML.java** file defines the BookshelfDML class. Within the BookshelfDML class, there are separate methods for processing INSERTs, UPDATEs, and DELETEs. In each of the method specifications, the datatypes for the BOOKSHELF table's related columns are specified (in this example, they are all VARCHAR2 datatypes).

These parameters use the datatypes provided as part of Oracle's class libraries. If you use the standard Java datatypes, you may encounter datatype-related problems during the class execution.

The next part of the INSERT method inserts the values into the BOOKSHELF table:

```
string sql = "insert into bookshelf values (?,?,?,?)";
```

The four variables are defined via setString (setInt would be used for integers):

```
pstmt.setString(1, title);
pstmt.setString(2, publisher);
pstmt.setString(3, categoryname);
pstmt.setString(4, rating);
```

Note that the variable names are case sensitive—they must exactly match the names declared earlier.

The DELETE method is very similar in structure. Its SQL statement is

```
string sql = "delete from bookshelf where title = ?";
```

Note that no part of the class creates a connection to the database, in contrast with the examples in Chapter 43. The connection used to invoke this class will provide the connection context for the class's methods.

You can verify that the class compiles properly by processing it via the Java compiler. Note that this step will not validate your SQL:

```
javac BookshelfDML.java
```

This step should complete successfully. If you encounter errors during this compilation step, check your environment configuration (see the README file supplied with your Oracle software) and your class file.

Loading the Class into the Database

You can use the **loadjava** utility to load the class into the database. The syntax for the **loadjava** utility is as follows:

```
loadjava {-user | -u} username/password[@database]
    [-option_name -option_name ...] filename filename ...
```

The options available for the **loadjava** utility are shown in Table 44-1.

For example, to load the **BookshelfDML.java** file into the Practice schema in an instance named **orcl**, you can use the following command:

```
loadjava -user practice/practice@orcl -verbose BookshelfDML.java
```

NOTE
Depending on your specific configuration, you may need to use the
-encoding argument as well.

You should see a series of comments related to the loading of the class into the database. If any errors are reported, the load will not complete.

NOTE
The name of the class should not match the name of any of the
existing objects in your schema.

Argument	Description
-casesensitivepub	Publishing creates case-sensitive names. Unless the names are already all uppercase, you will usually have to quote the names in PL/SQL.
-cleargrants	The **-grant** option causes the **loadjava** tool to grant EXECUTE privileges to classes, sources, and resources. However, it does not cause it to revoke any privileges. If **-cleargrants** is specified, then the **loadjava** tool revokes any existing grants of execute privilege before it grants the EXECUTE privilege to the users and roles specified by the **-grant** operand. For example, if the intent is to have execute privilege granted to only SCOTT, then the proper options are `-grant scott -cleargrants`
-debug	This turns on SQL logging.
-definer	By default, class schema objects run with the privileges of their invoker. This option confers definer privileges on classes instead. This option is conceptually similar to the UNIX **setuid** facility.
-dirprefix prefix	For any files or JAR entries that start with prefix, this prefix is deleted from the name before the name of the schema object is determined. For classes and sources, the name of the schema object is determined by their contents. Therefore, this option only affects resources.

TABLE 44-1.   *Loadjava Utility Options*

Argument	Description
-encoding	This argument identifies the source file encoding for the compiler, overriding the matching value, if any, in JAVA$OPTIONS. Values are the same as for the **javac -encoding** option. If you do not specify an encoding on the command line or in JAVA$OPTIONS, then the encoding is assumed to be the value returned by: `System.getProperty("file.encoding");` This option is relevant only when loading a source file.
filenames	You can specify any number and combination of .java, .class, .sqlj, .ser, .jar, .zip, and resource filename arguments.
-fileout file	This displays all messages to the designated file.
-force	This argument forces files to be loaded, even if they match digest table entries.
-genmissing	This argument determines what classes and methods are referred to by the classes that the **loadjava** tool is asked to process. Any classes not found in the database or file arguments are called missing classes. This option generates dummy definitions for missing classes containing all the referred methods. It then loads the generated classes into the database. This processing happens before the class resolution. Because detecting references from source is more difficult than detecting references from class files, and because source is not generally used for distributing libraries, the **loadjava** tool will not attempt to do this processing for source files. The schema in which the missing classes are loaded will be the one specified by the **-user** option, even when referring classes are created in some other schema. The created classes will be flagged so tools can recognize them. In particular, flagging is needed so the verifier can recognize the generated classes.
-genmissingjar jar_file	This option performs the same actions as **-genmissing**. In addition, it creates a JAR file, **jar_file**, that contains the definitions of any generated classes.
-grant	This argument grants the EXECUTE privilege on loaded classes to the listed users. Any number and combination of usernames can be specified, separated by commas, but not spaces. Granting the EXECUTE privilege on an object in another schema requires that the original CREATE PROCEDURE privilege was granted via the WITH GRANT options. **Note:** **-grant** is a cumulative option. Users are added to the list of those with the EXECUTE privilege. To remove privileges, use the **-cleargrants** option. The schema name should be in uppercase.

TABLE 44-1. *Loadjava Utility Options* (continued)

Argument	Description
-help	This option displays a message on how to use the **loadjava** tool and its options.
-jarasresource	Instead of unpacking the JAR file and loading each class within it, this argument loads the whole JAR file into the schema as a resource.
-jarsasdbobjects	This argument indicates that JARs processed by the current **loadjava** tool command should be stored in the database as database resident JARs.
-noaction	This argument indicates that no action should be taken on the files. Actions include creating the schema objects, granting execute permissions, and so on. The normal use of this argument is within an option file to suppress creation of specific classes in a JAR. When used on the command line, unless overridden in the option file, it will cause the **loadjava** tool to ignore all files, except that JAR files will still be examined to determine if they contain a META-INF/loadjava-options entry. If so, then the option file is processed. The **-action** option in the option file overrides **the -noaction** option specified on the command line.
-norecursivejars	This argument treats JAR files contained in other JAR files as resources. This is the default behavior. This option is used to override the **-recursivejars** option.
-nosynonym	This default behavior does not create a public synonym for the classes. This option overrides the **-synonym** option.
-nousage	This option suppresses the usage message that is given if no option is specified or if the **-help** option is specified.
-noverify	This argument sets the classes to be loaded without bytecode verification. oracle.aurora.security.JServerPermission(Verifier) must be granted to use this option. To be effective, this option must be used in conjunction with **-resolve**.
-oci | -oci8	This option directs the **loadjava** tool to communicate with the database using the JDBC Oracle Call Interface (OCI) driver. **-oci** and **-thin** are mutually exclusive. If neither is specified, then **-oci** is used by default. Choosing **-oci** implies the syntax of the **-user** value. You do not need to provide the URL.
-prependjarnames	This option is used with the **-jarsasdbobjects** option. This option enables classes with the same names coming from different JARs to coexist in the same schema. It does this by prefixing a version of the name of the JAR to the class name to produce a unique name for the database object.

TABLE 44-1. *Loadjava Utility Options* (continued)

Argument	Description

-proxy *host:port*	If you do not have physical access to the server host or the **loadjava** client for loading classes, resources, and Java source, you can use an HTTP URL with the **loadjava** tool to specify the JAR, class file, or resource, and then load the class from a remote server. *host* is the host name or address, and *port* is the port the proxy server is using. The URL implementation must be such that the **loadjava** tool can determine the type of file to load—that is, JAR, class, resource, or Java source. For example:
	
	`loadjava -u scott -r -v -proxy proxy_server:1020`
	`http://my.server.com/this/is /the/path/my.jar`
	`Password: password`
	When the URL support is used inside the server, you should have proper Java permissions to access the remote source. The URL support also includes ftp: and file: URLs.

-publish *package*	The package is created or replaced by the **loadjava** tool. Wrappers for the eligible methods are defined in this package. Through the use of option files, a single invocation of the **loadjava** tool can be instructed to create more than one package. Each package undergoes the same name transformations as the methods.
-pubmain *number*	A special case applied to methods with a single argument, which is of type java.lang.String. Multiple variants of the SQL procedure or function are created, each of which takes a different number of arguments of type VARCHAR. In particular, variants are created taking all arguments up to and including number. The default value is 3. This option applies to **main**, as well as any method that has exactly one argument of type java .lang.String.
-recursivejars	Normally, if the **loadjava** tool encounters an entry in a JAR with a .jar extension, it loads the entry as a resource. If this option is specified, then the **loadjava** tool processes contained JAR files as if they were top-level JAR files. That is, it reads their entries and loads classes, sources, and resources.
-resolve	This option compiles, if necessary, and resolves external references in classes after all classes on the command line have been loaded. If you do not specify the **-resolve** option, the **loadjava** tool loads files, but does not compile or resolve them.
-resolveonly	This tells the **loadjava** tool to skip the initial creation step. It will still perform grants, resolves, create synonyms, and so on, however.

TABLE 44-1.   *Loadjava Utility Options* (continued)

Argument	Description
-resolver	This option specifies an explicit resolver specification, which is bound to the newly loaded classes. If **-resolver** is not specified, then the default resolver specification, which includes current user's schema and PUBLIC, is used.
-schema	This argument designates the schema where schema objects are created. If not specified, then the **-user** schema is used. To create a schema object in a schema that is not your own, you must have the CREATE PROCEDURE or CREATE ANY PROCEDURE privilege. You must have CREATE TABLE or CREATE ANY TABLE privilege. Finally, you must have the JServerPermission loadLibraryInClass for the class.
-stdout	This option directs the output to stdout, rather than to stderr.
-stoponerror	Normally, if an error occurs while the **loadjava** tool is processing files, it issues a message and continues to process other classes. This option makes it stop when an error occurs. In addition, it reports all errors that apply to Java objects and are contained in the USER_ERROR table of the schema in which classes are being loaded, except that it does not report ORA-29524 errors. These are errors that are generated when a class cannot be resolved because a referred class could not be resolved. Therefore, these errors are a secondary effect of whatever caused a referred class to be unresolved.
-synonym	This argument creates a PUBLIC synonym for loaded classes, making them accessible outside the schema into which they are loaded. To specify this option, you must have the CREATE PUBLIC SYNONYM privilege. If **-synonym** is specified for source files, then the classes compiled from the source files are treated as if they had been loaded with **-synonym**.
-tableschema schema	This option creates the **loadjava** tool internal tables within the specified schema, rather than in the Java file destination schema.
-thin	This option directs the **loadjava** tool to communicate with the database using the JDBC Thin driver. Choosing **-thin** implies the syntax of the **-user** value. You do need to specify the appropriate URL through the **-user** option.
-unresolvedok	When combined with **-resolve**, this argument ignores unresolved errors.
-user	This argument specifies a username, password, and database connection string. The files will be loaded into this database instance.
-verbose	This argument directs the **loadjava** tool to display detailed status messages while running. Use the **-verbose** option to learn when the **loadjava** tool does not load a file because it matches a digest table entry.

TABLE 44-1. *Loadjava Utility Options* (continued)

The AreasDML class is now loaded into the database. During loading, Oracle will create multiple tables and Java objects within your schema.

> **NOTE**
> *You can load Java files manually from local BFILE or LOB columns via the CREATE JAVA [source | class | resource] commands.*

If you are running your database on a stand-alone server and you have not defined a service name for the database, you need to specify a full connection specification for the **loadjava** program call. The format is

```
loadjava -user practice/practice@localhost:1521:orcl -v BookshelfDML.java
```

How to Access the Class

Now that the BookshelfDML class has been loaded into the database, you must create a procedure to call each of the methods. The CREATE PROCEDURE command in the following listing creates a procedure called InsertBookshelfViaJava:

```
create or replace procedure InsertBookshelfViaJava
(title varchar2, publisher varchar2,
 category_name varchar2, rating varchar2 )
as
language java
name 'BookshelfDML.insertBookshelf(java.lang.String, java.lang.String,
java.lang.String, java.lang.String)';
/
```

This brief procedure has four parameters—the four columns of the BOOKSHELF table. Its LANGUAGE JAVA clause tells Oracle that the procedure is calling a Java method. The name of the method is specified in the NAME clause (be consistent with your use of capital letters). The formats for the Java method call are then specified.

A separate procedure deletes the BOOKSHELF table's records via a method call:

```
create or replace procedure DeleteBookshelfViaJava
(Title varchar2 )
as
language java
name 'BookshelfDML.deleteBookshelf(java.lang.String)';
/
```

A third procedure update the RATING value based on TITLE:

```
create or replace procedure UpdateBookshelfViaJava
(rating varchar2, title varchar2 )
as
language java
name 'BookshelfDML.updateBookshelf(java.lang.String, java.lang.String)';
/
```

Now, go into SQL*Plus and use the CALL command to execute the Java classes:

```
call InsertBookshelfViaJava('TEST','TESTPub','ADULTNF','2');
```

You'll see this response:

```
Call completed.
```

Instead of using CALL, you can execute the procedure within a PL/SQL block:

```
begin
   InsertBookshelfViaJava('TEST','TESTPub','ADULTNF','2');
end;
/
```

The CALL command passes the column values as parameters to the InsertBookshelfViaJava stored procedure. It formats them according to the specifications in the NAME clause and passes them to the BookshelfDML.insertBookshelf method. That method uses your current connection to execute its commands, and the row is inserted. Most of these libraries and classes will not have been loaded yet within the database. That's a lot of steps to go through, so performance will be affected the first time you run the Java stored procedure, but subsequent executions will be much faster. You can verify its success by querying the BOOKSHELF table:

```
column Title format a10
select * from bookshelf where title like 'TEST';
```

```
TITLE      PUBLISHER            CATEGORYNAME          RA
---------- -------------------- -------------------- --
TEST       TESTPub              ADULTNF               2
```

You can update the rating via UpdateBookshelfViaJava:

```
begin
   UpdateBookshelfViaJava('3','TEST');
end;
/
```

```
select * from bookshelf where title like 'TEST';
```

```
TITLE      PUBLISHER            CATEGORYNAME          RA
---------- -------------------- -------------------- --
TEST       TESTPub              ADULTNF               3
```

And you can delete that record via a call to DeleteBookshelfViaJava:

```
begin
   DeleteBookshelfViaJava('TEST');
end;
/
```

```
select * from BOOKSHELF where Title like 'TEST';
```

```
no rows selected
```

The call to DeleteBookshelfViaJava will complete much faster than the call to InsertBookshelfViaJava because your Java libraries will have been loaded the first time you executed InsertBookshelfViaJava.

If your insert is not acceptable—for example, if you attempt to insert a character string into a NUMBER datatype column—Oracle will display an error. When debugging Java stored procedures, you can call System.err.println from within your Java code, as shown in the **BookshelfDML.java** listing earlier in this chapter. To display the output within your SQL*Plus session, you must first execute the following commands:

```
set serveroutput on
call dbms_java.set_output(10000);
```

Calling DBMS_JAVA.SET_OUTPUT redirects the output of System.out.println to DBMS_OUTPUT.PUT_LINE.

Calling Java Stored Procedures Directly

Oracle provides an application programming interface (API) to support direct invocation of static Java stored procedures. The classes for this method are found in the oracle.jpub.reflect package, so you must import this package into your client-side code. The Java interface for the API is

```
public class Client
{
    public static String getSignature(Class[]);
    public static Object invoke(Connection, String, String,
                                String, Object[]);
    public static Object invoke(Connection, String, String,
                                Class[], Object[]);
}
```

When accessed via this API, the procedures' arguments cannot be OUT or IN OUT. Returned values must all be part of the function result. Note that the method invocation uses invoker's rights. See the Java developer's guides that accompany the Oracle software installation for further details on the API.

Where to Perform Commands

The BookshelfDML example provides an overview of the process of implementing Java stored procedures. Suppose you now want to make the procedures more complex, involving additional tables and calculations. As shown in previous chapters, you can perform those calculations either in Java or in PL/SQL.

Your choice of a platform and language for your data processing impacts your performance. In general, you pay a performance penalty the first time you execute a Java stored procedure (as the classes are loaded), but subsequent executions will not pay the same penalty. If you repeatedly execute the same commands, the performance impact of the first execution is minimal.

Logging out and logging back in impacts your performance, but not nearly as much as executing a procedure the first time. When you use Java stored procedures, be aware of the way in which the application interacts with Oracle. If your users frequently log out and log back in, they will pay a performance penalty the first time they execute the procedure following each login. Furthermore, the first execution of the procedure following a database startup will pay the most severe performance penalty. The performance impact of these actions must be taken into account during the design stage of your application development.

Here are some tips to reduce the performance penalties associated with the Java stored procedure calls:

- Execute each Java stored procedure following database startup. In the case of the BookshelfDML example, this may involve inserting and deleting a test record following each startup.

- Reduce the number of short-term database connections (for example, by connection pooling).

- Perform most of your direct database manipulation via standard SQL and PL/SQL.

Java is an appropriate technology to use for many computational processes and for display manipulation. In general, SQL and PL/SQL are slightly more efficient than Java for database connections and data manipulation. However, the performance of Java within Oracle makes it a strong alternative to PL/SQL; the primary source of the performance penalty for Java stored procedures is the time required to go through the PL/SQL wrapper. When designing applications that integrate Java, SQL, and PL/SQL, focus on using each language for the functions that it performs best.

If your code involves many loops and manipulations of data, Java may outperform PL/SQL. The costs of using Java—for Java object creation and the PL/SQL header interaction—may be offset by the improved performance Java yields during the actual work. Note that the compiled native PL/SQL first available in Oracle Database 11g should provide a strong alternative to Java from a performance perspective.

In general, actions that involve selecting data from the database and manipulating it are best handled by PL/SQL and SQL. Computations on the selected data may be processed faster by Java. In your application design, be sure to use the proper tool for the proper function, and avoid unnecessary performance penalties.

PART
VII

Hitchhiker's Guides

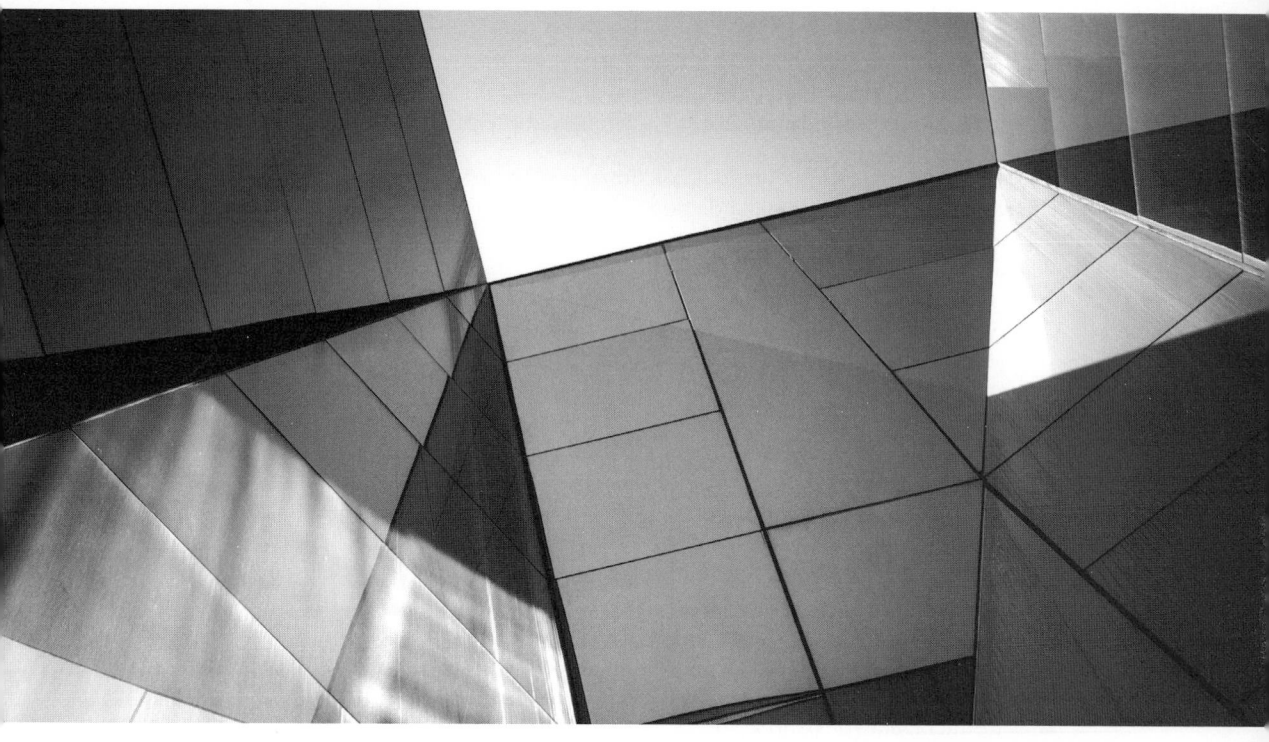

CHAPTER
45

The Hitchhiker's Guide to the Oracle Data Dictionary

O racle's data dictionary stores all the information that is used to manage the objects in the database. Although the data dictionary is usually the domain of database administrators (DBAs), it also is a source of valuable information for developers and end users.

In this chapter, you will see the data dictionary—Oracle's internal directory—from the perspective of an end user; the data dictionary tables and views are not listed alphabetically, but rather are grouped by function (tables, security, and so on). This organization is designed to let you quickly find your way to the information you need. The most-used data dictionary views are all shown here, along with examples of their usage.

Depending on which Oracle configuration options you are using, some of the groups will not apply to your database. The most commonly used views are discussed first. The groupings used in this chapter are, in order,

- New Views Introduced in Oracle Database 12c
- New Views Introduced in Oracle Database 11g
- The Road Maps: DICTIONARY (DICT) and DICT_COLUMNS
- Things You Select From: Tables (and Columns), Views, Synonyms, and Sequences
- Recycle Bin: USER_RECYCLEBIN and DBA_RECYCLEBIN
- Constraints and Comments
- Indexes and Clusters
- Abstract Datatypes and LOBs
- Database Links and Materialized Views
- Triggers, Procedures, Functions, and Packages
- Dimensions
- Space Allocation and Usage, Including Partitions and Subpartitions
- Users and Privileges
- Roles
- Auditing
- Miscellaneous
- Monitoring: The V$ Dynamic Performance Tables

NOTE
As new features are added, the data dictionary will most likely be modified with each future release of Oracle. This chapter is not intended to be an exhaustive discussion of all the data dictionary views. Those discussed here are the most commonly accessed by user queries.

A Note about Nomenclature

With some exceptions, the names of the objects in the Oracle data dictionary begin with one of three prefixes: "USER," "ALL," or "DBA." Records in the "USER" views usually show information about objects owned by the account performing the query. Records in the "ALL" views include the "USER" records plus information about objects on which privileges have been granted to PUBLIC or to the user. "DBA" views encompass all of the database objects, regardless of owner. For most database objects, "USER," "ALL," and "DBA" views are available.

In keeping with the user focus of this guide, the emphasis is on the "USER" views or those that are accessible to all users. The "ALL" and "DBA" views are described when they are applicable.

New Views Introduced in Oracle Database 12c

For users already familiar with the data dictionary in Oracle Database 10g and Oracle Database 11g, Table 45-1 lists the views that are introduced in Oracle Database 12c.

ALL_ Views	DBA_ Views	USER_ Views
ALL_APPLY_INSTANTIATED_GLOBAL	DBA_APPLY_INSTANTIATED_GLOBAL	
ALL_APPLY_INSTANTIATED_OBJECTS	DBA_APPLY_INSTANTIATED_OBJECTS	
ALL_APPLY_INSTANTIATED_SCHEMAS	DBA_APPLY_INSTANTIATED_SCHEMAS	
ALL_ATTRIBUTE_TRANSFORMATIONS	DBA_ATTRIBUTE_TRANSFORMATIONS	USER_ATTRIBUTE_TRANSFORMATIONS
ALL_CODE_ROLE_PRIVS	DBA_CODE_ROLE_PRIVS	USER_CODE_ROLE_PRIVS
ALL_CREDENTIALS	DBA_CREDENTIALS	USER_CREDENTIALS
ALL_CUBE_NAMED_BUILD_SPECS	DBA_CUBE_NAMED_BUILD_SPECS	USER_CUBE_NAMED_BUILD_SPECS
ALL_CUBE_SUB_PARTITION_LEVELS	DBA_CUBE_SUB_PARTITION_LEVELS	USER_CUBE_SUB_PARTITION_LEVELS
ALL_ERROR_TRANSLATIONS	DBA_ERROR_TRANSLATIONS	USER_ERROR_TRANSLATIONS
ALL_GG_INBOUND_PROGRESS	DBA_GG_INBOUND_PROGRESS	
ALL_GOLDENGATE_INBOUND	DBA_GOLDENGATE_INBOUND	
ALL_GOLDENGATE_PRIVILEGES	DBA_GOLDENGATE_PRIVILEGES	USER_GOLDENGATE_PRIVILEGES

TABLE 45-1.   *New Data Dictionary Views in Oracle Database 12c*

ALL_ Views	DBA_ Views	USER_ Views
ALL_GOLDENGATE_RULES	DBA_GOLDENGATE_RULES	
ALL_HEAT_MAP_SEG_HISTOGRAM	DBA_HEAT_MAP_SEG_HISTOGRAM	USER_HEAT_MAP_SEG_HISTOGRAM
ALL_HEAT_MAP_SEGMENT	DBA_HEAT_MAP_SEGMENT	USER_HEAT_MAP_SEGMENT
ALL_MEASURE_FOLDER_SUBFOLDERS	DBA_MEASURE_FOLDER_SUBFOLDERS	USER_MEASURE_FOLDER_SUBFOLDERS
ALL_METADATA_PROPERTIES	DBA_METADATA_PROPERTIES	USER_METADATA_PROPERTIES
ALL_PLSQL_COLL_TYPES	DBA_PLSQL_COLL_TYPES	USER_PLSQL_COLL_TYPES
ALL_PLSQL_TYPE_ATTRS	DBA_PLSQL_TYPE_ATTRS	USER_PLSQL_TYPE_ATTRS
ALL_PLSQL_TYPES	DBA_PLSQL_TYPES	USER_PLSQL_TYPES
ALL_POLICY_ATTRIBUTES	DBA_POLICY_ATTRIBUTES	USER_POLICY_ATTRIBUTES
ALL_SQL_TRANSLATION_PROFILES	DBA_SQL_TRANSLATION_PROFILES	USER_SQL_TRANSLATION_PROFILES
ALL_SQL_TRANSLATIONS	DBA_SQL_TRANSLATIONS	USER_SQL_TRANSLATIONS
ALL_TAB_IDENTITY_COLS	DBA_TAB_IDENTITY_COLS	USER_TAB_IDENTITY_COLS
ALL_TRANSFORMATIONS	DBA_TRANSFORMATIONS	USER_TRANSFORMATIONS
ALL_XML_NESTED_TABLES	DBA_XML_NESTED_TABLES	USER_XML_NESTED_TABLES
ALL_XML_OUT_OF_LINE_TABLES	DBA_XML_OUT_OF_LINE_TABLES	USER_XML_OUT_OF_LINE_TABLES
ALL_XML_SCHEMA_ATTRIBUTES	DBA_XML_SCHEMA_ATTRIBUTES	USER_XML_SCHEMA_ATTRIBUTES
ALL_XML_SCHEMA_COMPLEX_TYPES	DBA_XML_SCHEMA_COMPLEX_TYPES	USER_XML_SCHEMA_COMPLEX_TYPES
ALL_XML_SCHEMA_ELEMENTS	DBA_XML_SCHEMA_ELEMENTS	USER_XML_SCHEMA_ELEMENTS
ALL_XML_SCHEMA_NAMESPACES	DBA_XML_SCHEMA_NAMESPACES	USER_XML_SCHEMA_NAMESPACES
ALL_XML_SCHEMA_SIMPLE_TYPES	DBA_XML_SCHEMA_SIMPLE_TYPES	USER_XML_SCHEMA_SIMPLE_TYPES
ALL_XML_SCHEMA_SUBSTGRP_HEAD	DBA_XML_SCHEMA_SUBSTGRP_HEAD	USER_XML_SCHEMA_SUBSTGRP_HEAD
ALL_XML_SCHEMA_SUBSTGRP_MBRS	DBA_XML_SCHEMA_SUBSTGRP_MBRS	USER_XML_SCHEMA_SUBSTGRP_MBRS

TABLE 45-1. *New Data Dictionary Views in Oracle Database 12c* (continued)

ALL_ Views	DBA_ Views	USER_ Views
ALL_XSTREAM_ ADMINISTRATOR	DBA_XSTREAM_ADMINISTRATOR	
ALL_XSTREAM_OUT_ SUPPORT_MODE	DBA_XSTREAM_OUT_SUPPORT_ MODE	
ALL_XSTREAM_ TRANSFORMATIONS	DBA_XSTREAM_ TRANSFORMATIONS	
AUDIT_UNIFIED_ CONTEXTS		
AUDIT_UNIFIED_ ENABLED_POLICIES		
AUDIT_UNIFIED_ POLICIES		
AUDIT_UNIFIED_ POLICY_COMMENTS		
AUDITABLE_SYSTEM_ ACTIONS		
DATABASE_EXPORT_ OBJECTS		
	DBA_ACL_NAME_MAP	
	DBA_ALERT_HISTORY_DETAIL	
	DBA_CDB_RSRC_PLAN_DIRECTIVES	
	DBA_CDB_RSRC_PLANS	
	DBA_CONTAINER_DATA	
	DBA_DIGEST_VERIFIERS	
	DBA_DISCOVERY_SOURCE	
	DBA_EDITIONED_TYPES	USER_EDITIONED_TYPES
	DBA_GOLDENGATE_SUPPORT_ MODE	
	DBA_HEATMAP_TOP_OBJECTS	
	DBA_HEATMAP_TOP_TABLESPACES	
	DBA_HIST_APPLY_SUMMARY	
	DBA_HIST_ASH_SNAPSHOT	
	DBA_HIST_CAPTURE	
	DBA_HIST_PDB_INSTANCE	
	DBA_HIST_REPLICATION_TBL_STATS	
	DBA_HIST_REPLICATION_TXN_ STATS	

TABLE 45-1.   *New Data Dictionary Views in Oracle Database 12c* (continued)

ALL_ Views	DBA_ Views	USER_ Views
	DBA_HIST_REPORTS	
	DBA_HIST_REPORTS_CONTROL	
	DBA_HIST_REPORTS_DETAILS	
	DBA_HIST_REPORTS_TIMEBANDS	
	DBA_HIST_SESS_SGA_STATS	
	DBA_HIST_TABLESPACE	
	DBA_HOST_ACES	USER_HOST_ACES
	DBA_HOST_ACLS	
	DBA_ILMDATAMOVEMENTPOLICIES	USER_ILMDATAMOVEMENTPOLICIES
	DBA_ILMEVALUATIONDETAILS	USER_ILMEVALUATIONDETAILS
	DBA_ILMOBJECTS	USER_ILMOBJECTS
	DBA_ILMPARAMETERS	
	DBA_ILMPOLICIES	USER_ILMPOLICIES
	DBA_ILMRESULTS	USER_ILMRESULTS
	DBA_ILMTASKS	USER_ILMTASKS
	DBA_LOGSTDBY_EDS_SUPPORTED	
	DBA_LOGSTDBY_EDS_TABLES	
	DBA_LOGSTDBY_PLSQL_MAP	
	DBA_LOGSTDBY_PLSQL_SUPPORT	
	DBA_MINING_MODEL_TABLES	
	DBA_OBJECT_USAGE	USER_OBJECT_USAGE
	DBA_OPTSTAT_OPERATION_TASKS	
	DBA_PDB_HISTORY	
	DBA_PDBS	
	DBA_PRIV_CAPTURES	
	DBA_ROLLING_DATABASES	
	DBA_ROLLING_EVENTS	
	DBA_ROLLING_PARAMETERS	
	DBA_ROLLING_PLAN	
	DBA_ROLLING_STATISTICS	
	DBA_ROLLING_STATUS	
	DBA_SENSITIVE_COLUMN_TYPES	
	DBA_SENSITIVE_COLUMNS	

TABLE 45-1. *New Data Dictionary Views in Oracle Database 12c* (continued)

ALL_ Views	DBA_ Views	USER_ Views
	DBA_SQL_PLAN_DIR_OBJECTS	
	DBA_SQL_PLAN_DIRECTIVES	
	DBA_SR_GRP_STATUS	USER_SR_GRP_STATUS
	DBA_SR_GRP_STATUS_ALL	USER_SR_GRP_STATUS_ALL
	DBA_SR_OBJ	USER_SR_OBJ
	DBA_SR_OBJ_ALL	USER_SR_OBJ_ALL
	DBA_SR_OBJ_STATUS	USER_SR_OBJ_STATUS
	DBA_SR_OBJ_STATUS_ALL	USER_SR_OBJ_STATUS_ALL
	DBA_SR_PARTN_OPS	USER_SR_PARTN_OPS
	DBA_SR_STLOG_EXCEPTIONS	USER_SR_STLOG_EXCEPTIONS
	DBA_SR_STLOG_STATS	USER_SR_STLOG_STATS
	DBA_SUPPLEMENTAL_LOGGING	
	DBA_TSDP_IMPORT_ERRORS	
	DBA_TSDP_POLICY_CONDITION	
	DBA_TSDP_POLICY_FEATURE	
	DBA_TSDP_POLICY_PARAMETER	
	DBA_TSDP_POLICY_PROTECTION	
	DBA_TSDP_POLICY_TYPE	
	DBA_UNUSED_OBJPRIVS	
	DBA_UNUSED_OBJPRIVS_PATH	
	DBA_UNUSED_PRIVS	
	DBA_UNUSED_SYSPRIVS	
	DBA_UNUSED_SYSPRIVS_PATH	
	DBA_UNUSED_USERPRIVS	
	DBA_UNUSED_USERPRIVS_PATH	
	DBA_USED_OBJPRIVS	
	DBA_USED_OBJPRIVS_PATH	
	DBA_USED_PRIVS	
	DBA_USED_PUBPRIVS	
	DBA_USED_SYSPRIVS	
	DBA_USED_SYSPRIVS_PATH	
	DBA_USED_USERPRIVS	
	DBA_USED_USERPRIVS_PATH	
	DBA_WALLET_ACES	USER_WALLET_ACES

TABLE 45-1. *New Data Dictionary Views in Oracle Database 12c* (continued)

ALL_ Views	DBA_ Views	USER_ Views
	DBA_WI_CAPTURE_FILES	
	DBA_WI_JOBS	
	DBA_WI_OBJECTS	
	DBA_WI_PATTERN_ITEMS	
	DBA_WI_PATTERNS	
	DBA_WI_STATEMENTS	
	DBA_WI_TEMPLATE_EXECUTIONS	
	DBA_WI_TEMPLATES	
	DBA_WORKLOAD_ACTIVE_USER_MAP	
	DBA_WORKLOAD_REPLAY_SCHEDULES	
	DBA_WORKLOAD_SCHEDULE_CAPTURES	
	DBA_WORKLOAD_SCHEDULE_ORDERING	
	DBA_WORKLOAD_USER_MAP	
	DBA_XS_AUDIT_POLICY_OPTIONS	
	DBA_XS_AUDIT_TRAIL	
	DBA_XS_ENB_AUDIT_POLICIES	
	DBA_XSTREAM_SPLIT_MERGE	
	DBA_XSTREAM_SPLIT_MERGE_HIST	
	DBA_XSTREAM_STMT_HANDLERS	
	DBA_XSTREAM_STMTS	
PDB_PLUG_IN_VIOLATIONS		
REDACTION_COLUMNS		
REDACTION_POLICIES		
REDACTION_VALUES_FOR_TYPE_FULL		
SCHEMA_EXPORT_OBJECTS		
TABLE_EXPORT_OBJECTS		
UNIFIED_AUDIT_TRAIL		
		USER_PRIVILEGE_MAP

TABLE 45-1.   *New Data Dictionary Views in Oracle Database 12c (continued)*

New Views Introduced in Oracle Database 11*g*

For users familiar with the data dictionary in Oracle Database 10*g*, Table 45-2 lists the views that are introduced in Oracle Database 11*g*.

ALL_ Views	DBA_ Views	USER_ Views
	DBA_ADDM_FDG_BREAKDOWN	USER_ADDM_FDG_BREAKDOWN
	DBA_ADDM_FINDINGS	USER_ADDM_FINDINGS
	DBA_ADDM_INSTANCES	USER_ADDM_INSTANCES
	DBA_ADDM_SYSTEM_DIRECTIVES	
	DBA_ADDM_TASK_DIRECTIVES	USER_ADDM_TASK_DIRECTIVES
	DBA_ADDM_TASKS	USER_ADDM_TASKS
	DBA_ADVISOR_DIR_DEFINITIONS	
	DBA_ADVISOR_DIR_INSTANCES	
	DBA_ADVISOR_DIR_TASK_INST	USER_ADVISOR_DIR_TASK_INST
	DBA_ADVISOR_EXEC_PARAMETERS	USER_ADVISOR_EXEC_PARAMETERS
	DBA_ADVISOR_EXECUTION_TYPES	
	DBA_ADVISOR_EXECUTIONS	USER_ADVISOR_EXECUTIONS
	DBA_ADVISOR_FDG_BREAKDOWN	USER_ADVISOR_FDG_BREAKDOWN
	DBA_ADVISOR_FINDING_NAMES	
	DBA_ADVISOR_SQLA_COLVOL	USER_ADVISOR_SQLA_COLVOL
	DBA_ADVISOR_SQLA_TABLES	USER_ADVISOR_SQLA_TABLES
	DBA_ADVISOR_SQLA_TABVOL	USER_ADVISOR_SQLA_TABVOL
	DBA_ADVISOR_SQLA_WK_SUM	USER_ADVISOR_SQLA_WK_SUM
	DBA_ADVISOR_SQLPLANS	USER_ADVISOR_SQLPLANS
	DBA_ADVISOR_SQLSTATS	USER_ADVISOR_SQLSTATS
	DBA_ARGUMENTS	
ALL_ASSEMBLIES	DBA_ASSEMBLIES	USER_ASSEMBLIES
	DBA_AUTOTASK_CLIENT	
	DBA_AUTOTASK_CLIENT_HISTORY	

TABLE 45-2.   *New Data Dictionary Views in Oracle Database 11*g

ALL_ Views	DBA_ Views	USER_ Views
	DBA_AUTOTASK_CLIENT_JOB	
	DBA_AUTOTASK_OPERATION	
	DBA_AUTOTASK_SCHEDULE	
	DBA_AUTOTASK_TASK	
	DBA_AUTOTASK_WINDOW_CLIENTS	
	DBA_AUTOTASK_WINDOW_HISTORY	
ALL_CHANGE_PROPAGATION_SETS		
ALL_CHANGE_PROPAGATIONS		
ALL_CHANGE_SETS		
ALL_CHANGE_SOURCES		
ALL_CHANGE_TABLES		
ALL_COL_PENDING_STATS	DBA_COL_PENDING_STATS	USER_COL_PENDING_STATS
	DBA_COMPARISON	USER_COMPARISON
	DBA_COMPARISON_COLUMNS	USER_COMPARISON_COLUMNS
	DBA_COMPARISON_ROW_DIF	USER_COMPARISON_ROW_DIF
	DBA_COMPARISON_SCAN	USER_COMPARISON_SCAN
	DBA_COMPARISON_SCAN_SUMMARY	USER_COMPARISON_SCAN_SUMMARY
	DBA_COMPARISON_SCAN_VALUES	USER_COMPARISON_SCAN_VALUES
	DBA_CPOOL_INFO	
	DBA_CQ_NOTIFICATION_QUERIES	USER_CQ_NOTIFICATION_QUERIES
ALL_CUBE_ATTR_VISIBILITY	DBA_CUBE_ATTR_VISIBILITY	USER_CUBE_ATTR_VISIBILITY
ALL_CUBE_ATTRIBUTES	DBA_CUBE_ATTRIBUTES	USER_CUBE_ATTRIBUTES
ALL_CUBE_BUILD_PROCESSES	DBA_CUBE_BUILD_PROCESSES	USER_CUBE_BUILD_PROCESSES
ALL_CUBE_CALCULATED_MEMBERS	DBA_CUBE_CALCULATED_MEMBERS	USER_CUBE_CALCULATED_MEMBERS
ALL_CUBE_DIM_LEVELS	DBA_CUBE_DIM_LEVELS	USER_CUBE_DIM_LEVELS
ALL_CUBE_DIM_MODELS	DBA_CUBE_DIM_MODELS	USER_CUBE_DIM_MODELS
ALL_CUBE_DIM_VIEW_COLUMNS	DBA_CUBE_DIM_VIEW_COLUMNS	USER_CUBE_DIM_VIEW_COLUMNS
ALL_CUBE_DIM_VIEWS	DBA_CUBE_DIM_VIEWS	USER_CUBE_DIM_VIEWS

TABLE 45-2. *New Data Dictionary Views in Oracle Database 11g* (continued)

ALL_ Views	DBA_ Views	USER_ Views
ALL_CUBE_ DIMENSIONALITY	DBA_CUBE_DIMENSIONALITY	USER_CUBE_DIMENSIONALITY
ALL_CUBE_DIMENSIONS	DBA_CUBE_DIMENSIONS	USER_CUBE_DIMENSIONS
ALL_CUBE_HIER_LEVELS	DBA_CUBE_HIER_LEVELS	USER_CUBE_HIER_LEVELS
ALL_CUBE_HIER_VIEW_ COLUMNS	DBA_CUBE_HIER_VIEW_ COLUMNS	USER_CUBE_HIER_VIEW_COLUMNS
ALL_CUBE_HIER_VIEWS	DBA_CUBE_HIER_VIEWS	USER_CUBE_HIER_VIEWS
ALL_CUBE_HIERARCHIES	DBA_CUBE_HIERARCHIES	USER_CUBE_HIERARCHIES
ALL_CUBE_MEASURES	DBA_CUBE_MEASURES	USER_CUBE_MEASURES
ALL_CUBE_VIEW_COLUMNS	DBA_CUBE_VIEW_COLUMNS	USER_CUBE_VIEW_COLUMNS
ALL_CUBE_VIEWS	DBA_CUBE_VIEWS	USER_CUBE_VIEWS
ALL_CUBES	DBA_CUBES	USER_CUBES
	DBA_EPG_DAD_ AUTHORIZATION	USER_EPG_DAD_AUTHORIZATION
	DBA_FLASHBACK_ARCHIVE	USER_FLASHBACK_ARCHIVE
	DBA_FLASHBACK_ARCHIVE_ TABLES	USER_FLASHBACK_ARCHIVE_ TABLES
	DBA_FLASHBACK_ARCHIVE_TS	
	DBA_FLASHBACK_TXN_REPORT	USER_FLASHBACK_TXN_REPORT
	DBA_FLASHBACK_TXN_STATE	USER_FLASHBACK_TXN_STATE
	DBA_HIST_BASELINE_DETAILS	
	DBA_HIST_BASELINE_METADATA	
	DBA_HIST_BASELINE_TEMPLATE	
	DBA_HIST_CLUSTER_INTERCON	
	DBA_HIST_COLORED_SQL	
	DBA_HIST_EVENT_HISTOGRAM	
	DBA_HIST_IC_CLIENT_STATS	
	DBA_HIST_IC_DEVICE_STATS	
	DBA_HIST_INTERCONNECT_ PINGS	
	DBA_HIST_IOSTAT_FILETYPE	
	DBA_HIST_IOSTAT_FILETYPE_ NAME	
	DBA_HIST_IOSTAT_FUNCTION	
	DBA_HIST_IOSTAT_FUNCTION_ NAME	
	DBA_HIST_MEM_DYNAMIC_ COMP	

TABLE 45-2.   *New Data Dictionary Views in Oracle Database 11*g (continued)

ALL_ Views	DBA_ Views	USER_ Views
	DBA_HIST_MEMORY_RESIZE_OPS	
	DBA_HIST_MEMORY_TARGET_ADVICE	
	DBA_HIST_MUTEX_SLEEP	
	DBA_HIST_PERSISTENT_QUEUES	
	DBA_HIST_PERSISTENT_SUBS	
	DBA_HIST_RSRC_CONSUMER_GROUP	
	DBA_HIST_RSRC_PLAN	
ALL_IDENTIFIERS	DBA_IDENTIFIERS	USER_IDENTIFIERS
ALL_IND_PENDING_STATS	DBA_IND_PENDING_STATS	USER_IND_PENDING_STATS
	DBA_INVALID_OBJECTS	
ALL_JAVA_COMPILER_OPTIONS	DBA_JAVA_COMPILER_OPTIONS	USER_JAVA_COMPILER_OPTIONS
	DBA_LOGSTDBY_UNSUPPORTED_TABLE	
ALL_MEASURE_FOLDER_CONTENTS	DBA_MEASURE_FOLDER_CONTENTS	USER_MEASURE_FOLDER_CONTENTS
ALL_MEASURE_FOLDERS	DBA_MEASURE_FOLDERS	USER_MEASURE_FOLDERS
ALL_MINING_MODEL_ATTRIBUTES	DBA_MINING_MODEL_ATTRIBUTES	USER_MINING_MODEL_ATTRIBUTES
ALL_MINING_MODEL_SETTINGS	DBA_MINING_MODEL_SETTINGS	USER_MINING_MODEL_SETTINGS
ALL_MINING_MODELS	DBA_MINING_MODELS	USER_MINING_MODELS
ALL_MVIEW_DETAIL_PARTITION	DBA_MVIEW_DETAIL_PARTITION	USER_MVIEW_DETAIL_PARTITION
ALL_MVIEW_DETAIL_SUBPARTITION	DBA_MVIEW_DETAIL_SUBPARTITION	USER_MVIEW_DETAIL_SUBPARTITION
	DBA_NETWORK_ACL_PRIVILEGES	USER_NETWORK_ACL_PRIVILEGES
	DBA_NETWORK_ACLS	
	DBA_OLDIMAGE_COLUMNS	USER_OLDIMAGE_COLUMNS
	DBA_REGISTRY_DATABASE	
	DBA_REGISTRY_DEPENDENCIES	
	DBA_REGISTRY_PROGRESS	
	DBA_RSRC_CAPABILITY	
	DBA_RSRC_CATEGORIES	

TABLE 45-2. *New Data Dictionary Views in Oracle Database 11*g (continued)

ALL_ Views	DBA_ Views	USER_ Views
	DBA_RSRC_INSTANCE_CAPABILITY	
	DBA_RSRC_IO_CALIBRATE	
	DBA_RSRC_STORAGE_POOL_MAPPING	
ALL_SCHEDULER_CREDENTIALS	DBA_SCHEDULER_CREDENTIALS	USER_SCHEDULER_CREDENTIALS
	DBA_SCHEDULER_JOB_ROLES	
ALL_SCHEDULER_REMOTE_DATABASES	DBA_SCHEDULER_REMOTE_DATABASES	
ALL_SCHEDULER_REMOTE_JOBSTATE	DBA_SCHEDULER_REMOTE_JOBSTATE	USER_SCHEDULER_REMOTE_JOBSTATE
	DBA_SQL_MANAGEMENT_CONFIG	
	DBA_SQL_PATCHES	
	DBA_SQL_PLAN_BASELINES	
ALL_STAT_EXTENSIONS	DBA_STAT_EXTENSIONS	USER_STAT_EXTENSIONS
ALL_STREAMS_COLUMNS	DBA_STREAMS_COLUMNS	
	DBA_STREAMS_TP_COMPONENT	
	DBA_STREAMS_TP_COMPONENT_LINK	
	DBA_STREAMS_TP_COMPONENT_STAT	
	DBA_STREAMS_TP_DATABASE	
	DBA_STREAMS_TP_PATH_BOTTLENECK	
	DBA_STREAMS_TP_PATH_STAT	
	DBA_SUBSCR_REGISTRATIONS	USER_SUBSCR_REGISTRATIONS
ALL_SYNC_CAPTURE	DBA_SYNC_CAPTURE	
ALL_SYNC_CAPTURE_PREPARED_TABS	DBA_SYNC_CAPTURE_PREPARED_TABS	
ALL_SYNC_CAPTURE_TABLES	DBA_SYNC_CAPTURE_TABLES	
ALL_TAB_HISTGRM_PENDING_STATS	DBA_TAB_HISTGRM_PENDING_STATS	USER_TAB_HISTGRM_PENDING_STATS
ALL_TAB_PENDING_STATS	DBA_TAB_PENDING_STATS	USER_TAB_PENDING_STATS
ALL_TAB_STAT_PREFS	DBA_TAB_STAT_PREFS	USER_TAB_STAT_PREFS
	DBA_TEMP_FREE_SPACE	

TABLE 45-2. *New Data Dictionary Views in Oracle Database 11g (continued)*

ALL_ Views	DBA_ Views	USER_ Views
ALL_TRIGGER_ORDERING	DBA_TRIGGER_ORDERING	USER_TRIGGER_ORDERING
	DBA_USERS_WITH_DEFPWD	
	DBA_WORKLOAD_CAPTURES	
	DBA_WORKLOAD_CONNECTION_MAP	
	DBA_WORKLOAD_FILTERS	
	DBA_WORKLOAD_REPLAY_DIVERGENCE	
	DBA_WORKLOAD_REPLAYS	

TABLE 45-2. *New Data Dictionary Views in Oracle Database 11g* (continued)

The Road Maps: DICTIONARY (DICT) and DICT_COLUMNS

Descriptions for the objects that make up the Oracle data dictionary are accessible via a view named DICTIONARY. This view, also accessible via the public synonym DICT, queries the database to determine which data dictionary views you can see. It also searches for public synonyms for those views.

The following example queries DICT for the names of all data dictionary views whose names include the string "MVIEWS". Selecting from DICT via a non-DBA account, as shown in the following listing, returns the object name and comments for each data dictionary object that matches your search criteria. This view has only two columns: TABLE_NAME and the table's associated COMMENTS.

```
column comments format a35 word_wrapped
column table_name format a25

select table_name, comments
from dict
where table_name like '%MVIEWS%'
order by table_name;


TABLE_NAME                COMMENTS
------------------------- -----------------------------------
ALL_BASE_TABLE_MVIEWS     All materialized views with log(s)
                          in the database that the user can
                          see
ALL_MVIEWS                All materialized views in the
                          database
ALL_REGISTERED_MVIEWS     Remote materialized views of local
                          tables that the user can see
USER_BASE_TABLE_MVIEWS    All materialized views with log(s)
                          owned by the user in the database
```

| USER_MVIEWS | All materialized views in the database |
| USER_REGISTERED_MVIEWS | Remote materialized views of local tables currently using logs owned by the user |

```
6 rows selected.
```

You can query the columns of the dictionary views via the DICT_COLUMNS view. Like the DICTIONARY view, DICT_COLUMNS displays the comments that have been entered into the database for the data dictionary views. DICT_COLUMNS has three columns: TABLE_NAME, COLUMN_NAME, and COMMENTS. Querying DICT_COLUMNS lets you determine which data dictionary views would be most useful for your needs.

For example, if you want to view space allocation and usage information for your database objects but are not sure which data dictionary views store that information, you can query DICT_COLUMNS, as shown in the following example, which looks for all the dictionary tables that have a column named BLOCKS:

```
select table_name
from dict_columns
where column_name = 'BLOCKS'
  and table_name like 'USER%'
order by table_name;

TABLE_NAME
--------------------
USER_ALL_TABLES
USER_EXTENTS
USER_FREE_SPACE
USER_OBJECT_TABLES
USER_SEGMENTS
USER_TABLES
USER_TAB_PARTITIONS
USER_TAB_PENDING_STATS
USER_TAB_STATISTICS
USER_TAB_SUBPARTITIONS
USER_TS_QUOTAS
```

To list all of the available column names that you could have used in the last example, query DICT_COLUMNS:

```
select distinct column_name
from dict_columns
order by column_name;
```

Whenever you're unsure about where to find the data you want, just check DICTIONARY and DICT_COLUMNS. If it appears that a large number of views could be useful, query DICTIONARY (as in the first example) to see the comments on each view.

Things You Select From: Tables (and Columns), Views, Synonyms, and Sequences

A user's catalog lists all of those objects that the user can SELECT records from—that is, any object that can be listed in the FROM clause of a query. Although sequences are not referenced directly in FROM clauses, Oracle includes them in the catalog. In this section, you'll learn how to retrieve information about tables, columns, views, synonyms, sequences, and the user catalog.

Catalog: USER_CATALOG (CAT)

Querying USER_CATALOG displays all tables, views, synonyms, and sequences the user owns. The TABLE_NAME column shows the name of the object (even if it is not a table), and the TABLE_TYPE column shows the type of object:

```
select table_name, table_type
from user_catalog
where table_name like 'T%';
```

USER_CATALOG may also be referred to by the public synonym CAT.

Two additional catalogs are available. ALL_CATALOG lists everything in your USER_CATALOG view plus any objects that you or PUBLIC have been granted access to. DBA_CATALOG is a DBA-level version of the catalog showing all tables, views, sequences, and synonyms in the database. In addition to the TABLE_NAME and TABLE_TYPE columns shown in the USER_CATALOG query, ALL_CATALOG and DBA_CATALOG include an OWNER column.

Objects: USER_OBJECTS (OBJ)

USER_CATALOG only displays information for tables, views, sequences, and synonyms. To retrieve information on all types of objects, query USER_OBJECTS. You can use this view to find out about many types of objects, including clusters, database links, directories, functions, indexes, libraries, packages, package bodies, Java classes, abstract datatypes, resource plans, sequences, synonyms, tables, triggers, materialized views, LOBs, and views. USER_OBJECTS' columns are shown in the following listing:

```
COLUMN_NAME
-------------------------------
OBJECT_NAME
SUBOBJECT_NAME
OBJECT_ID
DATA_OBJECT_ID
OBJECT_TYPE
CREATED
LAST_DDL_TIME
TIMESTAMP
TEMPORARY
GENERATED
SECONDARY
NAMESPACE
EDITION_NAME
```

USER_OBJECTS (also known by its public synonym OBJ) contains several vital pieces of information that are not found in other data dictionary views. It records object creation dates (the CREATED column) and the last time an object was altered (the LAST_DDL_TIME column). These columns are very useful when trying to reconcile different sets of objects in the same application.

NOTE
*If you re-create objects in any way, such as via the **impdp** utility, their CREATED values will change to the last time they were created.*

Two additional object listings are available. ALL_OBJECTS lists everything in your USER_OBJECTS view plus any objects for which access has been granted to you or PUBLIC. DBA_OBJECTS is a DBA-level version of the object listing, showing all of the objects in the database. In addition to the columns shown in the USER_OBJECTS view, ALL_OBJECTS and DBA_OBJECTS include an OWNER column.

Tables: USER_TABLES (TABS)

Although all of a user's objects are shown in USER_OBJECTS, few attributes of those objects are shown there. To get more information about an object, you need to look at the view that is specific to that type of object. For tables, that view is USER_TABLES. It can also be referenced via the public synonym TABS.

NOTE
Earlier versions of Oracle included a view called TAB. That view, which is similar in function to TABS, is still supported because of Oracle products that reference it. However, TAB does not contain the columns that TABS contains. Use TABS in your data dictionary queries.

The columns in USER_TABLES can be divided into four major categories (identification, space-related, statistics-related, and other). The following listing shows the columns of the USER_TABLES view:

```
TABLE_NAME
TABLESPACE_NAME
CLUSTER_NAME
IOT_NAME
STATUS
PCT_FREE
PCT_USED
INI_TRANS
MAX_TRANS
INITIAL_EXTENT
NEXT_EXTENT
MIN_EXTENTS
MAX_EXTENTS
PCT_INCREASE
FREELISTS
FREELIST_GROUPS
```

```
LOGGING
BACKED_UP
NUM_ROWS
BLOCKS
EMPTY_BLOCKS
AVG_SPACE
CHAIN_CNT
AVG_ROW_LEN
AVG_SPACE_FREELIST_BLOCKS
NUM_FREELIST_BLOCKS
DEGREE
INSTANCES
CACHE
TABLE_LOCK
SAMPLE_SIZE
LAST_ANALYZED
PARTITIONED
IOT_TYPE
TEMPORARY
SECONDARY
NESTED
BUFFER_POOL
ROW_MOVEMENT
GLOBAL_STATS
USER_STATS
DURATION
SKIP_CORRUPT
MONITORING
CLUSTER_OWNER
DEPENDENCIES
COMPRESSION
COMPRESS_FOR
DROPPED
READ_ONLY
```

The table's name is shown in the TABLE_NAME column. The BACKED_UP column shows whether the table has been backed up since its last modification. The PARTITIONED column will have a value of "YES" if the table has been partitioned (data dictionary views related to partitions are described in the "Space Allocation and Usage, Including Partitions and Subpartitions" section of this chapter).

The space-related columns, such as PCT_FREE, INITIAL_EXTENT, MAX_EXTENTS, and PCT_INCREASE, are described in the STORAGE entry of the Alphabetical Reference. The statistics-related columns, such as NUM_ROWS, BLOCKS, EMPTY_BLOCKS, AVG_ROW_LEN, and LAST_ANALYZED, are populated when the table is analyzed with a DBMS_STATS procedure (preferred) or the ANALYZE command (deprecated).

NOTE
You can use the USER_TAB_STATISTICS view to access the statistics for your tables. You can use USER_TAB_PENDING_STATS for pending statistics.

Querying the TABLE_NAME column from USER_TABLES displays the names of all of the tables in the current account. The following query lists all of the tables whose names begin with the letter *L*:

```
select table_name from user_tables
where table_name like 'L%';
```

The ALL_TABLES view shows all of the tables owned by the user as well as any to which the user has been granted access (either directly or via grants to PUBLIC). Most third-party reporting tools that list available tables for queries obtain that list by querying ALL_TABLES. Because ALL_ TABLES can contain entries for multiple users, it contains an OWNER column in addition to the columns in USER_TABLES. DBA_TABLES, which lists all tables in the database, has the same column definitions as ALL_TABLES.

The DEGREE and INSTANCES columns in USER_TABLES relate to how the table is queried during parallel queries. For information on DEGREE, INSTANCES, and the other table parameters, see CREATE TABLE in the Alphabetical Reference.

NOTE
For external tables, see USER_EXTERNAL_TABLES and USER_ EXTERNAL_LOCATIONS in Chapter 28.

USER_TABLES and other data dictionary views contain a new column named DROPPED. That column has a value of "YES" or "NO"; see "Recycle Bin: USER_RECYCLEBIN and DBA RECYCLEBIN," for details on the views containing the names of dropped objects.

Columns: USER_TAB_COLUMNS (COLS)

Although users do not query from columns, the data dictionary view that shows columns is closely tied to the data dictionary view of tables. This view, called USER_TAB_COLUMNS, lists information specific to columns. USER_TAB_COLUMNS can also be queried via the public synonym COLS.

The columns you can query from USER_TAB_COLUMNS can be separated into three major categories:

- Identification, such as TABLE_NAME, COLUMN_NAME, and COLUMN_ID
- Definition related, such as DATA_TYPE, DATA_LENGTH, DATA_PRECISION, DATA_ SCALE, NULLABLE, and DEFAULT_LENGTH
- Statistics related, such as NUM_DISTINCT, LOW_VALUE, HIGH_VALUE, DENSITY, NUM_NULLS, and others

The TABLE_NAME and COLUMN_NAME columns contain the names of your tables and columns. Definition-related column usage is described in the "Datatypes" entry in the Alphabetical Reference. The statistics-related columns are populated when the table is analyzed. Statistics for columns are also provided in the USER_TAB_COL_STATISTICS view (described shortly).

To see the column definitions for a table, query USER_TAB_COLUMNS, specifying the *table_name* in the WHERE clause:

```
select column_name, data_type
from user_tab_columns
where table_name = 'NEWSPAPER';

COLUMN_NAME     DATA_TYPE
-------------   ---------
FEATURE         VARCHAR2
SECTION         CHAR
PAGE            NUMBER
```

The information in this example is also obtainable via the SQL*Plus DESCRIBE command; however, DESCRIBE does not give you the option of seeing the column defaults and statistics. The ALL_TAB_COLUMNS view shows the columns for all of the tables and views owned by the user as well as any to which the user has been granted access (either via direct grants or via grants to PUBLIC). Because ALL_TAB_COLUMNS can contain entries for multiple users, it contains an OWNER column in addition to the columns in USER_TAB_COLUMNS. DBA_TAB_COLUMNS, which lists the column definitions for all tables and views in the database, has the same column definitions as ALL_TAB_COLUMNS.

Column Statistics

Most of the column statistics are available in both USER_TAB_COLUMNS (their former home) and USER_TAB_COL_STATISTICS. The columns available in USER_TAB_COL_STATISTICS are the statistics-related columns of USER_TAB_COLUMNS plus the TABLE_NAME and COLUMN_NAME columns.

USER_TAB_COL_STATISTICS contains statistics columns that are also provided via USER_TAB_COLUMNS for backward compatibility. You should access them via USER_TAB_COL_STATISTICS.

Column Value Histograms

You can use histograms to improve the analysis used by the cost-based optimizer. The USER_TAB_HISTOGRAMS view contains information about each column's histogram: the TABLE_NAME, COLUMN_NAME, ENDPOINT_NUMBER, ENDPOINT_VALUE, and ENDPOINT_ACTUAL_VALUE. The optimizer uses the values in USER_TAB_HISTOGRAMS to determine the distribution of the column values within the table. "ALL" and "DBA" versions of USER_TAB_HISTOGRAMS are available.

Updatable Columns

You can update records in views that contain joins in their view queries, provided the join meets certain criteria. The USER_UPDATABLE_COLUMNS view lists all columns you can update. You can query the OWNER, TABLE_NAME, and COLUMN_NAME for the column; the UPDATABLE column has a value of "YES" if the column can be updated, and a value of "NO" if the column cannot be updated. You can also query to determine whether you can insert or delete records from the view via the INSERTABLE and DELETABLE columns.

Views: USER_VIEWS

The base query of a view is accessible via the USER_VIEWS data dictionary view, which contains ten columns; the three main columns are as follows:

VIEW_NAME	The name of the view
TEXT_LENGTH	The length of the view's base query, in characters
TEXT	The query that the view uses

The other columns, described later in this section, are primarily related to object views and editioning.

NOTE
This section only applies to traditional views. For materialized views, see "Database Links and Materialized Views" later in the chapter.

The TEXT column is a LONG datatype. This may cause a problem when querying USER_VIEWS via SQL*Plus, because SQL*Plus truncates LONGs. The point at which truncation occurs, however, can be changed via the SET LONG command. USER_VIEWS provides a mechanism for determining the proper setting for the LONG truncation point, as you'll see in the following example.

The TEXT_LENGTH column shows the length in characters of the view's query. Therefore, the SQL*Plus LONG truncation point must be set to a value equal to or greater than the view's TEXT_LENGTH value. For example, the following listing shows a view whose VIEW_NAME is AGING and whose TEXT_LENGTH is 355:

```
select view_name, text_length
from user_views
where view_name = 'AGING';
```

```
VIEW_NAME          TEXT_LENGTH
---------------    -------------
AGING              355
```

Because the length of the view's text is 355 characters, use the SET LONG command to increase the LONG truncation point to at least 355 (the default is 80) to see the full text of the view's query:

```
set long 355
```

You can then query USER_VIEWS for the view's TEXT, using the query shown in the following listing:

```
select text
from user_views
where view_name = 'AGING';
```

If you had not used the SET LONG command, then the output would have been truncated at 80 characters, with no message telling you why the truncation occurred. Before querying other views, you need to recheck their TEXT_LENGTH values.

NOTE
*You can query the column definitions for views from USER_TAB_*
COLUMNS, the same view you query for tables.

If you use column aliases in your views, and your column aliases are part of the view's query, then your data dictionary queries for information about views will be simplified. Because the entire text of the view's query is displayed in USER_VIEWS, the column aliases are displayed as well.

You can create views using this format:

```
create view newspaper_view (somefeature, somesection)
as select feature, section
from newspaper;
```

Listing the column names in the header of the CREATE VIEW command removes the column aliases from the query and thus prevents you from seeing them via USER_VIEWS. The only way to see the view's column names would be to query USER_TAB_COLUMNS. If the column names are in the query, then you only need to query one data dictionary view (USER_VIEWS) for both the query and the column names.

For example, given the NEWSPAPER_VIEW view created in the last example, if you were to query USER_VIEWS, you would see

```
select text
from user_views
where view_name ='NEWSPAPER_VIEW';
```

```
TEXT
----------------------------------------
select feature, section from NEWSPAPER
```

This query does *not* show you the new column names you assigned since you did not make those column names part of the view's query. To make those column names appear in USER_VIEWS, add them as column aliases in the view's query:

```
create or replace view newspaper_view
as select feature somefeature, section somesection
from newspaper;
```

Now when you query USER_VIEWS, the column aliases are displayed as part of the view's query text:

```
select text
from user_views
where view_name ='NEWSPAPER_VIEW';
```

```
TEXT
----------------------------------------------
select feature somefeature, section somesection
from newspaper
```

To support object views, USER_VIEWS contains the following columns:

TYPE_TEXT	Type clause of the typed view
TYPE_TEXT_LENGTH	Length of the type clause of the typed view
OID_TEXT	WITH OID clause of the typed view
OID_TEXT_LENGTH	Length of the WITH OID clause of the typed view
VIEW_TYPE_OWNER	Owner of the view's type for typed views
VIEW_TYPE	Type of the view

See Chapters 38 and 41 for information on object views and types.

The ALL_VIEWS view lists all of the views owned by the user as well as any views to which the user has been granted access, either via direct grants or via grants to PUBLIC. Since ALL_VIEWS can contain entries for multiple users, it contains an OWNER column in addition to the columns listed earlier in this section. DBA_VIEWS, which lists all views in the database, has the same column definitions as ALL_VIEWS.

Synonyms: USER_SYNONYMS (SYN)

USER_SYNONYMS lists all of the synonyms that a user owns. The columns are as follows:

SYNONYM_NAME	The name of the synonym
TABLE_OWNER	The owner of the table that the synonym refers to
TABLE_NAME	The name of the table that the synonym refers to
DB_LINK	The name of the database link used in the synonym

USER_SYNONYMS is useful when debugging programs or resolving problems with users' access to objects within applications. USER_SYNONYMS is also known by the public synonym SYN.

The DB_LINK column is NULL if the synonym does not use a database link. Therefore, if you want to see a list of the database links currently in use by the synonyms owned by your account, execute this query:

```
select distinct db_link
from user_synonyms
where db_link is not null;
```

The ALL_SYNONYMS view lists all of the user-owned synonyms, public synonyms, and all synonyms to which the user has been granted access. Because ALL_SYNONYMS can contain entries for multiple users, it contains an OWNER column in addition to the columns listed earlier in this section. DBA_SYNONYMS, which lists all synonyms in the database, has the same column definitions as ALL_SYNONYMS.

Sequences: USER_SEQUENCES (SEQ)

To display the attributes of sequences, you can query the USER_SEQUENCES data dictionary view. This view can also be queried using the public synonym SEQ. The columns of USER_SEQUENCES are as follows:

SEQUENCE_NAME	Name of the sequence
MIN_VALUE	Minimum value of the sequence
MAX_VALUE	Maximum value of the sequence
INCREMENT_BY	Increment between sequence values
CYCLE_FLAG	A flag to indicate whether the value should cycle back to the MIN_VALUE once the MAX_VALUE is reached
ORDER_FLAG	A flag to indicate whether sequence numbers are generated in order
CACHE_SIZE	The number of sequence entries cached in memory
LAST_NUMBER	The last sequence number used or cached, typically greater than the last value in cache

The LAST_NUMBER column is not updated during normal database operation; it is used during database restart/recovery operations.

ALL_SEQUENCES lists all of the sequences owned by the user or to which the user or PUBLIC has been granted access. Since ALL_SEQUENCES can contain entries for multiple users, it contains a SEQUENCE_OWNER column in addition to the columns listed. DBA_SEQUENCES, which lists all sequences in the database, has the same column definitions as ALL_SEQUENCES.

Recycle Bin: USER_RECYCLEBIN and DBA_RECYCLEBIN

You can use the FLASHBACK TABLE command to recover tables and dependent objects that have been dropped. To see the objects presently in your recycle bin, query USER_RECYCLEBIN. The public synonym RECYCLEBIN can be used in place of USER_RECYCLEBIN in your queries. You will see the original object name, whether it can be recovered (the CAN_UNDROP column), and whether it was dropped because it was related to a base object that was dropped (the BASE_OBJECT column value).

Objects stay in the recycle bin until they are purged. Objects can be removed from the recycle bin automatically if the tablespace they were dropped from no longer has any free space. DBAs can see all objects in all users' recycle bins via the DBA_RECYCLEBIN view. There is no "ALL" version of this view. See the PURGE command entry in the Alphabetical Reference for details on removing objects from the recycle bin.

Constraints and Comments

Constraints and comments help you to understand how tables and columns relate to each other. Comments are strictly informational; they do not enforce any conditions on the data stored in the objects they describe. Constraints, on the other hand, define the conditions under which that data is valid. Typical constraints include NOT NULL, UNIQUE, PRIMARY KEY, and FOREIGN KEY. In the following sections, you'll see how to retrieve data about constraints and comments from the data dictionary.

Constraints: USER_CONSTRAINTS

Constraint information is accessible via the USER_CONSTRAINTS view. This information is quite useful when trying to alter data constraints or resolve problems with an application's data. This view's columns are shown in the following listing:

```
COLUMN_NAME
------------------------------
OWNER
CONSTRAINT_NAME
CONSTRAINT_TYPE
TABLE_NAME
SEARCH_CONDITION
R_OWNER
R_CONSTRAINT_NAME
DELETE_RULE
STATUS
DEFERRABLE
DEFERRED
VALIDATED
GENERATED
BAD
RELY
LAST_CHANGE
INDEX_OWNER
INDEX_NAME
INVALID
VIEW_RELATED
```

Although this is a "USER" view, it contains an OWNER column. In this view, OWNER refers to the owner of the constraint, not the owner of the table (who is the user).

Valid values for the CONSTRAINT_TYPE column are as follows:

- **'C'**   CHECK constraint (includes NOT NULLs)
- **'P'**   PRIMARY KEY constraint
- **'R'**   FOREIGN KEY (reference) constraint
- **'U'**   UNIQUE constraint
- **'V'**   WITH CHECK OPTION constraint (for views)
- **'O'**   WITH READ ONLY constraint (for views)

Understanding the constraint types is crucial when you are trying to get useful information about your constraints.

FOREIGN KEY constraints always have values for the R_OWNER and R_CONSTRAINT_ NAME columns. These two columns tell you which constraint the FOREIGN KEY references.

A FOREIGN KEY references another *constraint,* not another column. NOT NULL constraints on columns are stored as CHECK constraints, so they have a CONSTRAINT_TYPE of "C".

Querying USER_CONSTRAINTS gives you the names of all the constraints on a table. This is important when trying to interpret error messages that only provide the name of the violated constraint.

Once you know the name and type of a constraint, you can check the columns associated with it via the USER_CONS_COLUMNS view, described in the next section.

If you do not assign constraint names when creating them, Oracle will generate unique constraint names. See "Integrity Constraint" in the Alphabetical Reference for further details. If a constraint name has been system-generated, that fact is indicated via the GENERATED column.

If you defer a constraint (as indicated by the DEFERRED column), the constraint will not be enforced for the duration of a transaction. For example, if you were performing bulk UPDATEs on related tables and could not guarantee the order of transactions, you may decide to defer constraint checking on the tables until all of the UPDATEs have completed.

ALL_CONSTRAINTS lists the constraints on all of the tables that the user or PUBLIC can access. DBA_CONSTRAINTS lists all of the constraints in the database. Each of these views has the same set of columns as USER_CONSTRAINTS (since they all include the OWNER column).

Constraint Columns: USER_CONS_COLUMNS

You can view the columns associated with constraints via the USER_CONS_COLUMNS data dictionary view. If you have already queried USER_CONSTRAINTS to obtain the types and names of the constraints involved, you can use USER_CONS_COLUMNS to determine which columns are involved in the constraint. The columns in this view are the following:

OWNER	The owner of the constraint
CONSTRAINT_NAME	The name of the constraint
TABLE_NAME	The name of the table associated with the constraint
COLUMN_NAME	The name of the column associated with the constraint
POSITION	The order of the column within the constraint definition

There are only two columns in USER_CONS_COLUMNS that are not in USER_ CONSTRAINTS: COLUMN_NAME and POSITION. A sample query of this table is shown in the following listing (your constraint names will differ because this constraint name was system-assigned):

```
select column_name, position
from user_cons_columns
where constraint_name = 'SYS_C0008791';

COLUMN_NAME   POSITION
-----------   --------
FIRSTNAME            1
LASTNAME             2
```

As shown in the preceding listing, the combination of FIRSTNAME and LASTNAME forms the constraint (in this case, a primary key).

The POSITION column is significant. When you create a UNIQUE or PRIMARY KEY constraint, Oracle automatically creates a unique index on the set of columns you specify. The index is created based on the column order you specify. The column order, in turn, affects index performance. An index comprising multiple columns may be used most efficiently if the leading column of that index (POSITION=1) is used in the query's WHERE clause. See Chapter 46 for further details on the optimizer.

The ALL_CONS_COLUMNS and DBA_CONS_COLUMNS views have the same column definitions as USER_CONS_COLUMNS. ALL_CONS_COLUMNS can be used to display column information about constraints on all tables that the user can access regardless of owner. DBA_CONS_COLUMNS lists the column-level constraint information for the entire database.

Constraint Exceptions: EXCEPTIONS

When enabling constraints on tables that already contain data, you may encounter constraint violations within the data. For example, you may attempt to create a PRIMARY KEY constraint on a column that contains the same value for multiple records, but such an attempt would fail due to uniqueness constraint violations.

You can capture information about the rows that cause constraint creations to fail. First, create a table called EXCEPTIONS in your schema; the SQL script that should be used to create this table is named **utlexcpt.sql** and is usually located in the **./rdbms/admin** directory under the Oracle home directory.

The EXCEPTIONS table contains four columns: ROW_ID (the ROWID of each row that violated the constraint), OWNER (the owner of the violated constraint), TABLE_NAME (the table on which the violated constraint was created), and CONSTRAINT (the constraint violated by the row). After creating the EXCEPTIONS table, attempt to enable a PRIMARY KEY constraint:

```
alter table newspaper enable primary key
exceptions into exceptions;

ORA-02437: cannot enable (NEWSPAPER.SYS_C00516) - primary key violated
```

The constraint creation fails, and a reference to all rows that violate the constraint is placed in the EXCEPTIONS table. For example, if the PRIMARY KEY constraint in the last example generated exceptions, then you could query the EXCEPTIONS table as shown in the following listing:

```
select owner, table_name, constraint from exceptions;

OWNER       TABLE_NAME  CONSTRAINT
----------  ----------  ----------
PRACTICE    NEWSPAPER   SYS_C00516
PRACTICE    NEWSPAPER   SYS_C00516
```

Two rows violated the constraint named SYS_C00516 (which, in this example, is the constraint name given to the PRIMARY KEY constraint for the NEWSPAPER table). You can determine which rows of the NEWSPAPER table correspond to these exceptions by joining the ROW_ID column of the EXCEPTIONS table to the ROWID pseudo-column of the table on which the constraint was being placed (in this example, the NEWSPAPER table):

```
select *
from newspaper
```

```
where rowid in
    (select row_id from exceptions);
```

The rows that caused the constraint violations will then be displayed.

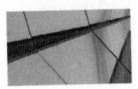

NOTE
*ROW_ID is an actual column in the EXCEPTIONS table, with a
datatype of ROWID. It is joined to the ROWID pseudo-column in the
table from which the exceptions were generated.*

Flashback and recovery operations may change the ROWIDs for rows previously inserted into tables.

Table Comments: USER_TAB_COMMENTS

You can add a comment to a table, view, or column after it has been created. Comments on the data dictionary views are the basis for the records displayed via the DICTIONARY and DICT_COLUMNS views. To display comments about your own tables, use the USER_TAB_ COMMENTS view.

USER_TAB_COMMENTS contains three columns:

TABLE_NAME	The name of the table or view
TABLE_TYPE	The object type (table, object table, or view)
COMMENTS	Comments that have been entered for the object

To add a comment to a table, use the COMMENT command, as shown in the following listing:

```
comment on table birthday is
    'Birthday list for Blacksburg employees';
```

Query USER_TAB_COMMENTS by specifying the TABLE_NAME you want to see the comments for, as shown in the following listing:

```
select comments
from user_tab_comments
where table_name = 'BIRTHDAY';

COMMENTS
------------------------------------
Birthday list for Blacksburg employees
```

To remove a comment, set the comment to two single quotes with no space between them:

```
comment on table birthday is '';
```

You can view the comments on all of the tables you can access via the ALL_TAB_ COMMENTS view. ALL_TAB_COMMENTS has an additional column, OWNER, which specifies the owner of the table. DBA_TAB_COMMENTS lists all of the tables in the database, and it has an OWNER column as well.

Column Comments: USER_COL_COMMENTS

USER_COL_COMMENTS displays the comments that have been entered for columns within your tables. These comments are added to the database via the COMMENT command. USER_COL_COMMENTS contains three columns:

TABLE_NAME	The name of the table or view
COLUMN_NAME	The name of the column
COMMENTS	Comments that have been entered for the column

To add a comment to a column, use the COMMENT command, as shown in the following listing:

```
comment on column birthday.age is 'Age in years';
```

Query USER_COL_COMMENTS by specifying the TABLE_NAME and COLUMN_NAME you want to see the comments for.

```
select comments
from user_col_comments
where table_name = 'BIRTHDAY'
  and column_name = 'AGE';
```

To remove a comment, set the comment to two single quotes with no space between them:

```
comment on column birthday.age is '';
```

You can view the column comments on all of the tables you can access via the ALL_COL_COMMENTS view. ALL_COL_COMMENTS has an additional column, OWNER, which specifies the owner of the table. DBA_COL_COMMENTS lists all of the columns in all of the tables in the database, and it has an OWNER column as well.

Indexes and Clusters

Indexes and clusters do not change the data that is stored in tables; however, they do change the way that data is accessed. The following sections cover data dictionary views that describe indexes and clusters. The data dictionary views related to partitioned indexes are described in "Space Allocation and Usage, Including Partitions and Subpartitions," later in this chapter.

Indexes: USER_INDEXES (IND)

In Oracle, indexes are closely related to constraints. The PRIMARY KEY and UNIQUE constraints always have associated indexes. As with constraints, two data dictionary views are used to query information about indexes: USER_INDEXES and USER_IND_COLUMNS. USER_INDEXES is also known by its public synonym, IND.

The columns in USER_INDEXES can be grouped into four categories (identification, space-related, statistics-related, and other). The columns of USER_INDEXES are shown in the following listing:

```
INDEX_NAME
INDEX_TYPE
TABLE_OWNER
```

```
TABLE_NAME
TABLE_TYPE
UNIQUENESS
COMPRESSION
PREFIX_LENGTH
TABLESPACE_NAME
INI_TRANS
MAX_TRANS
INITIAL_EXTENT
NEXT_EXTENT
MIN_EXTENTS
MAX_EXTENTS
PCT_INCREASE
PCT_THRESHOLD
INCLUDE_COLUMN
FREELISTS
FREELIST_GROUPS
PCT_FREE
LOGGING
BLEVEL
LEAF_BLOCKS
DISTINCT_KEYS
AVG_LEAF_BLOCKS_PER_KEY
AVG_DATA_BLOCKS_PER_KEY
CLUSTERING_FACTOR
STATUS
NUM_ROWS
SAMPLE_SIZE
LAST_ANALYZED
DEGREE
INSTANCES
PARTITIONED
TEMPORARY
GENERATED
SECONDARY
BUFFER_POOL
USER_STATS
DURATION
PCT_DIRECT_ACCESS
ITYP_OWNER
ITYP_NAME
PARAMETERS
GLOBAL_STATS
DOMIDX_STATUS
DOMIDX_OPSTATUS
FUNCIDX_STATUS
JOIN_INDEX
IOT_REDUNDANT_PKEY_ELIM
DROPPED
VISIBILITY
DOMIDX_MANAGEMENT
```

The name of the index is shown in the INDEX_NAME column. The owner and name for the table being indexed are in the TABLE_OWNER and TABLE_NAME columns. The UNIQUENESS column is set to UNIQUE for unique indexes and set to NONUNIQUE for nonunique indexes. TABLE_TYPE records whether the index is on a "TABLE" or a "CLUSTER". The DROPPED column identifies indexes that are in the recycle bin. The VISIBILITY column identifies indexes that are visible to the optimizer.

Space-related columns are described in the STORAGE entry in the Alphabetical Reference.

The statistics-related columns are populated when the table is analyzed (see the ANALYZE command in the Alphabetical Reference). The DEGREE and INSTANCES columns refer to the degree of parallelism used when the index is created.

NOTE
You can use the USER_IND_STATISTICS view to access the statistics for your indexes.

To see all of the indexes on a table, query USER_INDEXES using the TABLE_OWNER and TABLE_NAME columns in the WHERE clause, as shown in the following listing:

```
select index_name, uniqueness
from user_indexes
where table_owner = 'PRACTICE'
  and table_name = 'BIRTHDAY';


INDEX_NAME         UNIQUENES
----------------   ---------
PK_BIRTHDAY        UNIQUE
```

The CLUSTERING_FACTOR column is not directly related to clusters, but rather represents the degree to which the rows in the table are ordered. The more ordered those rows are, the more efficient range queries will be (*range queries* are those in which a range of values is given for a column, such as WHERE LASTNAME LIKE 'A%').

To discover which columns are part of the index and their order within the index, you need to query the USER_IND_COLUMNS view, which is described in the next section.

ALL_INDEXES shows all of the indexes owned by the user as well as any created on tables to which the user or PUBLIC has been granted access. Because ALL_INDEXES can contain entries for multiple users, it contains an OWNER column in addition to the columns in USER_INDEXES. DBA_INDEXES, which lists all indexes in the database, has the same column definitions as ALL_INDEXES.

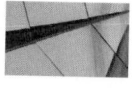

NOTE
For function-based indexes, see USER_IND_EXPRESSIONS.

Indexed Columns: USER_IND_COLUMNS

You can determine which columns are in an index by querying USER_IND_COLUMNS. The columns available via this view are as follows:

INDEX_NAME	The name of the index
TABLE_NAME	The name of the indexed table
COLUMN_NAME	The name of a column within the index
COLUMN_POSITION	The column's position within the index
COLUMN_LENGTH	The indexed length of the column
CHAR_LENGTH	Maximum code point length of the column (Unicode)
DESCEND	A Y/N flag to indicate whether the column is sorted in descending order

Five columns in this view are not in USER_INDEXES: COLUMN_NAME, COLUMN_POSITION, COLUMN_LENGTH, CHAR_LENGTH, and DESCEND. COLUMN_LENGTH, like the statistics-related columns in USER_INDEXES, is populated when the index's base table is analyzed. A sample query of this table, using the INDEX_NAME from the USER_INDEXES example, is shown in the following listing (in this example, the COLUMN_POSITION column is given the alias POS):

```
select column_name, column_position pos
from user_ind_columns
where index_name = 'PK_BIRTHDAY';
```

```
COLUMN_NAME   POS
-----------   ---
FIRSTNAME      1
LASTNAME       2
```

As you can see from this query, the PK_BIRTHDAY index consists of two columns: FIRSTNAME and LASTNAME, in that order. See Chapter 46 for details on how the optimizer uses multicolumn indexes.

ALL_IND_COLUMNS can be used to display column information about indexes on all tables that the user can access regardless of owner. DBA_IND_COLUMNS lists the column-level index information for the entire database.

If you create a bitmap join index, you can query USER_JOIN_IND_COLUMNS for the join details. USER_JOIN_IND_COLUMNS records the names of the tables involved in the join and the inner and outer join columns.

Clusters: USER_CLUSTERS (CLU)

The storage and statistics parameters associated with clusters are accessible via USER_CLUSTERS (also known by the public synonym CLU). The columns in this data dictionary view are shown in the following listing:

```
COLUMN_NAME
-----------------------------
CLUSTER_NAME
TABLESPACE_NAME
PCT_FREE
PCT_USED
KEY_SIZE
INI_TRANS
MAX_TRANS
INITIAL_EXTENT
NEXT_EXTENT
MIN_EXTENTS
MAX_EXTENTS
PCT_INCREASE
FREELISTS
FREELIST_GROUPS
AVG_BLOCKS_PER_KEY
CLUSTER_TYPE
FUNCTION
HASHKEYS
DEGREE
INSTANCES
CACHE
BUFFER_POOL
SINGLE_TABLE
DEPENDENCIES
```

The CLUSTER_NAME column contains the name of the cluster. CLUSTER_TYPE specifies whether the cluster uses a standard B*-tree index or a hashing function for the cluster.

The usage of the space-related columns is described in the STORAGE entry in the Alphabetical Reference. The statistics-related columns are populated when the table is analyzed.

ALL_CLUSTERS and DBA_CLUSTERS have an additional column, OWNER, since they list clusters in multiple schemas.

Cluster Columns: USER_CLU_COLUMNS

To see the mapping of table columns to cluster columns, query USER_CLU_COLUMNS, whose columns are the following:

CLUSTER_NAME	The name of the cluster
CLU_COLUMN_NAME	The name of the key column in the cluster
TABLE_NAME	The name of a table within the cluster
TAB_COLUMN_NAME	The name of the key column in the table

Because a single cluster can store data from multiple tables, USER_CLU_COLUMNS is useful for determining which columns of which tables map to the cluster's columns.

There is no "ALL" version of this view. There are only USER_CLU_COLUMNS for the user's cluster columns, and DBA_CLU_COLUMNS, which shows the column mappings for all clusters in the database.

Abstract Datatypes and LOBs

The following sections describe the data dictionary views associated with object-relational structures such as abstract datatypes, methods, and large objects (LOBs). "ALL" and "DBA" versions of all of these data dictionary views are available. Because they contain records for multiple owners, the "ALL" and "DBA" versions of these views contain OWNER columns as well as the columns listed in this section.

Abstract Datatypes: USER_TYPES

Abstract datatypes created within your schema are listed in USER_TYPES, which includes columns for the TYPE_NAME, number of attributes (ATTRIBUTES), and number of methods (METHODS) defined for the datatype.

For example, the ANIMAL_TY datatype has three attributes and one method (methods are defined via the CREATE TYPE BODY command), as shown in the following listing:

```
select type_name,
       attributes,
       methods
from user_types
where type_name = 'ANIMAL_TY';


TYPE_NAME                            ATTRIBUTES   METHODS
------------------------------------ ----------   ----------
ANIMAL_TY                                3           1
```

Datatype Attributes: USER_TYPE_ATTRS

To see the datatype's attributes, you need to query the USER_TYPE_ATTRS view. The columns in USER_TYPE_ATTRS are shown in the following listing:

```
COLUMN_NAME
------------------------------
TYPE_NAME
ATTR_NAME
ATTR_TYPE_MOD
ATTR_TYPE_OWNER
ATTR_TYPE_NAME
LENGTH
PRECISION
SCALE
CHARACTER_SET_NAME
ATTR_NO
INHERITED
```

You can query USER_TYPE_ATTRS to see the relationships between nested abstract datatypes. For example, the PERSON_TY datatype uses the ADDRESS_TY datatype, as shown in the following listing:

```
select attr_name,
       length,
```

```
          attr_type_name
from user_type_attrs
where type_name = 'PERSON_TY';
```

```
ATTR_NAME                                LENGTH ATTR_TYPE_NAME
------------------------------------ ---------- ------------------
NAME                                         25 VARCHAR2
ADDRESS                                         ADDRESS_TY
```

Datatype Methods: USER_TYPE_METHODS and USER_METHOD_PARAMS

If a type has methods defined for it, then you query USER_TYPE_METHODS to determine the methods' names. USER_TYPE_METHODS contains columns showing the type name (TYPE_NAME), method name (METHOD_NAME), method number (METHOD_NO, used for overloaded methods), and method type (METHOD_TYPE). USER_TYPE_METHODS also includes columns that show the number of parameters (PARAMETERS) and results (RESULTS) returned by the method.

For example, the ANIMAL_TY datatype has one method, a member function named AGE. The AGE method has one input parameter (BIRTHDATE) and one output result (the age, in days). Querying USER_TYPE_METHODS shows that *two* parameters are defined for AGE, not one as expected:

```
select parameters,
       results
from user_type_methods
where type_name = 'ANIMAL_TY'
  and method_name = 'AGE';
```

```
PARAMETERS    RESULTS
---------- ----------
        2          1
```

Why does AGE have two parameters if it only has one input parameter defined? To find out, you can query USER_METHOD_PARAMS, which describes the parameters for your methods:

```
select param_name, param_no, param_type_name
from user_method_params
order by param_no;
```

```
PARAM_NAME                             PARAM_NO PARAM_TYPE_NAME
------------------------------------ ---------- ------------------
SELF                                          1 ANIMAL_TY
BIRTHDATE                                     2 DATE
```

USER_METHOD_PARAMS shows that for each method, Oracle creates an implicit SELF parameter. The results of your methods are shown in USER_METHOD_RESULTS:

```
select method_name,
       result_type_name
from user_method_results
where type_name = 'ANIMAL_TY';
```

```
METHOD_NAME                        RESULT_TYPE_NAME
----------------------------       ----------------------------
AGE                                NUMBER
```

Other Datatypes: USER_REFS, USER_COLL_TYPES, and USER_NESTED_TABLES

If you use REFs (see Chapter 41), you can query the USER_REFS data dictionary view to display the REFs you have defined. USER_REFS shows the name of the table containing the REF column (TABLE_NAME) and the column name of the object column (COLUMN_NAME). The attributes of the REF—such as whether it is stored with the ROWID—are also accessible via USER_REFS.

Collector types (nested tables and varying arrays) are described via the USER_COLL_TYPES data dictionary view. The columns of USER_COLL_TYPES include TYPE_NAME, UPPER_BOUND (for varying arrays), and the LENGTH and PRECISION of the elements. You can use USER_COLL_TYPES in conjunction with the abstract datatype data dictionary views shown earlier in this section to determine the type structure of a collector. You can also query USER_NESTED_TABLES and USER_VARRAYS to see details for your collections.

LOBs: USER_LOBS

As described in Chapter 40, you can store large objects inside the database. The USER_LOBS view provides information on the LOBs defined in your tables; a sample listing is shown here:

```
column column_name format a30

select table_name,
       column_name
from user_lobs;
```

```
TABLE_NAME                         COLUMN_NAME
----------------------------       ----------------------------
PROPOSAL                           PROPOSAL_TEXT
PROPOSAL                           BUDGET
```

USER_LOBS also shows the names of the segments used to hold the LOB data when it grows large; however, it does not show the datatypes of the LOB columns. To see the LOB datatypes, you can either DESCRIBE the table that includes the LOBs or query USER_TAB_COLUMNS (as shown earlier in this chapter).

To use BFILE datatypes for LOBs, you have to create directories (see the entry for the CREATE DIRECTORY command in the Alphabetical Reference). The ALL_DIRECTORIES data dictionary view shows the OWNER, DIRECTORY_NAME, and DIRECTORY_PATH columns for each directory to which you have been granted access. A "DBA" version of this view is also available. No "USER" version of this view is available.

Database Links and Materialized Views

Database links and materialized views are used to manage access to remote data. Depending on the type of materialized view you use, you may be able to use materialized view logs. The following sections describe the data dictionary views you can use to display information about database links and materialized views. For further information on database links, see Chapter 25. For further information on materialized views, see Chapter 26.

Database Links: USER_DB_LINKS

To see the database links created under your account, query USER_DB_LINKS. The columns of this view, including the link name (DB_LINK), username to connect to (USERNAME), the account password (PASSWORD), and the connection string (HOST), show the information about the remote connection that the link will be used to establish. The USERNAME and PASSWORD values will be used to log into the remote database defined by the HOST value.

The HOST column stores the Oracle Net service names. This column stores the exact character string you specify during the CREATE DATABASE LINK command and does not alter its case. Therefore, you should be careful with the case you use when creating database links. Otherwise, your queries against USER_DB_LINKS have to take into account inconsistencies in the case of the HOST column. For example, looking for a database link that uses the 'HQ' service descriptor would require you to enter

```
select *
from user_db_links
where upper(host)='HQ';
```

since entries may have a HOST value of "hq" instead of "HQ".

NOTE
If you are using default logins to the remote database, then PASSWORD is NULL.

The ALL_DB_LINKS view lists all of the database links that either are owned by the user or are PUBLIC database links. DBA_DB_LINKS lists all database links in the database. ALL_DB_LINKS and DBA_DB_LINKS share most of the same column definitions as USER_DB_LINKS; they have an OWNER column rather than the PASSWORD column.

See Chapter 25 for further information on database links.

Materialized Views

You can query USER_MVIEWS to display information about the materialized views owned by your account. This view, whose columns appear in the following listing, shows the structural information about the materialized view as well as its refresh schedule.

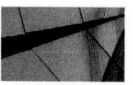

NOTE
See Chapter 26 for details on materialized views.

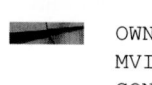

```
OWNER
MVIEW_NAME
CONTAINER_NAME
QUERY
QUERY_LEN
UPDATABLE
```

```
UPDATE_LOG
MASTER_ROLLBACK_SEG
MASTER_LINK
REWRITE_ENABLED
REWRITE_CAPABILITY
REFRESH_MODE
REFRESH_METHOD
BUILD_MODE
FAST_REFRESHABLE
LAST_REFRESH_TYPE
LAST_REFRESH_DATE
STALENESS
AFTER_FAST_REFRESH
UNKNOWN_PREBUILT
UNKNOWN_PLSQL_FUNC
UNKNOWN_EXTERNAL_TABLE
UNKNOWN_CONSIDER_FRESH
UNKNOWN_IMPORT
UNKNOWN_TRUSTED_FD
COMPILE_STATE
USE_NO_INDEX
STALE_SINCE
NUM_PCT_TABLES
NUM_FRESH_PCT_REGIONS
NUM_STALE_PCT_REGIONS
```

The name of the materialized view is found in the MVIEW_NAME column of USER_MVIEWS. The local base table for the view is the CONTAINER_NAME column. To determine which database links are being used by your materialized views, query the MASTER_LINK column, as shown in the following example:

```
select master_link
from user_mviews;
```

The names of the database links returned by this query can be used as input for queries against USER_DB_LINKS. This query will display all of the database link information available for database links used in your materialized views:

```
select *
from user_db_links
where db_link in
    (select master_link
     from user_mviews);
```

Additional queries that are useful for managing materialized views are provided in Chapter 26.

The ALL_MVIEWS and DBA_MVIEWS views have the same column definitions as USER_MVIEWS. You can use ALL_MVIEWS to display information about all materialized views that the user can access regardless of owner. DBA_MVIEWS lists materialized view information for all users in the database.

Two related views—USER_REFRESH and USER_REFRESH_CHILDREN—display information about refresh groups. USER_MVIEW_REFRESH_TIMES shows the last time each materialized view

was refreshed. You can access comments on the materialized views via USER_MVIEW_
COMMENTS and query rewrite details via USER_REWRITE_EQUIVALENCES.

You can query USER_MVIEW_ANALYSIS to see the materialized views that support query
rewrite. If a materialized view contains references to a remote table, it is not listed in this view.
You can query the owner of the materialized view, its name (MVIEW_NAME), and the owner of
the base table (MVIEW_TABLE_OWNER). Many of the columns in this view are flags, such as
SUMMARY ("Y" if the view contains an aggregation), KNOWN_STALE ("Y" if the view's data is
inconsistent with the base table), and CONTAINS_VIEWS ("Y" if the materialized view references
a view).

If the materialized view contains aggregations, you can query USER_MVIEW_AGGREGATES
for details on the aggregations. Columns in this view are as follows:

OWNER	Owner of the materialized view
MVIEW_NAME	Name of the materialized view
POSITION_IN_SELECT	Position within the query
CONTAINER_COLUMN	Name of the column
AGG_FUNCTION	Aggregate function
DISTINCTFLAG	"Y" if the aggregation uses the DISTINCT function
MEASURE	The SQL text of the measure, excluding the aggregate function

You can query details of the relations within materialized views from the USER_MVIEW_
DETAIL_RELATIONS and USER_MVIEW_KEYS data dictionary views. If the materialized view is
based on joins, see USER_MVIEW_JOINS for the join details. In general, USER_MVIEW_
ANALYSIS is the most commonly used data dictionary view related to materialized views.

Materialized View Logs: USER_MVIEW_LOGS

Materialized view logs can be used by many materialized views to determine which records in
the master table need to be refreshed in the materialized view of that table. You can query USER_
MVIEW_LOGS for information about a user's logs, including the name of the master table
(MASTER), the table holding the log records (LOG_TABLE), and whether the materialized view is
based on the primary key or the ROWID (the PRIMARY_KEY and ROWIDs columns). USER_
MVIEW_LOGS is usually queried for maintenance purposes, such as to determine the name of the
trigger used to create the materialized view log records.

DBA_MVIEW_LOGS has the same column definitions as USER_MVIEW_LOGS and shows all
materialized view logs in the database. You can query USER_BASE_TABLE_MVIEWS for a listing
of the materialized view master tables using materialized view logs.

Triggers, Procedures, Functions, and Packages

You can use procedures, functions, packages, and triggers—blocks of PL/SQL code stored in the
database—to enforce business rules or to perform complicated processing. Triggers are described
in Chapter 34. Procedures, functions, and packages are described in Chapter 35. In the following
sections, you'll learn how to query the data dictionary for information about triggers, procedures,
packages, and functions.

Triggers: USER_TRIGGERS

USER_TRIGGERS contains information about the triggers owned by your account. This view, whose columns appear in the following listing, shows the trigger type and body.

```
TRIGGER_NAME
TRIGGER_TYPE
TRIGGERING_EVENT
TABLE_OWNER
BASE_OBJECT_TYPE
TABLE_NAME
COLUMN_NAME
REFERENCING_NAMES
WHEN_CLAUSE
STATUS
DESCRIPTION
ACTION_TYPE
TRIGGER_BODY
CROSSEDITION
```

The ALL_TRIGGERS view lists the triggers for all tables to which you have access. DBA_TRIGGERS lists all of the triggers in the database. Both of these views contain an additional column, OWNER, which records the owner of the trigger.

A second trigger-related data dictionary view, USER_TRIGGER_COLS, shows how columns are used by a trigger. It lists the name of each column affected by a trigger, as well as how the trigger is used. Like USER_TRIGGERS, "ALL" and "DBA" versions of this data dictionary view are available.

As of Oracle 11g, you can query the USER_TRIGGER_ORDERING data dictionary view. The columns of USER_TRIGGER_ORDERING include the name of the trigger, the trigger that it references, and the ordering type (to follow or precede the referenced trigger).

Procedures, Functions, and Packages: USER_SOURCE

The source code for existing procedures, functions, packages, and package bodies can be queried from the USER_SOURCE data dictionary view. The TYPE column in USER_SOURCE identifies the procedural object as a "PROCEDURE", "FUNCTION", "PACKAGE", "PACKAGE BODY", "TRIGGER", "TYPE", "TYPE BODY", or "JAVA SOURCE". Each line of code is stored in a separate record in USER_SOURCE.

You can select information from USER_SOURCE via a query similar to the one shown in the following listing. In this example, the TEXT column is selected and ordered by LINE number. The NAME of the object and the object TYPE are used to specify which object's source code to display.

```
select text
from user_source
where name = '&procedure_name'
  and type = 'PROCEDURE'
order by line;
```

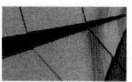

NOTE
The sequence of the lines is maintained by the LINE column; therefore, you should use the LINE column in the ORDER BY clause.

The ALL_SOURCE and DBA_SOURCE views have all of the columns found in USER_SOURCE plus an additional OWNER column (the owner of the object). ALL_SOURCE can be used to display the source code for all procedural objects that the user can access regardless of owner. DBA_SOURCE lists the source code for all users in the database.

NOTE
To see the persistent parameter settings for PL/SQL units, query USER_STORED_SETTINGS.

Code Errors: USER_ERRORS

The SHOW ERRORS command in SQL*Plus checks the USER_ERRORS data dictionary view for the errors associated with the most recent compilation attempt for a procedural object. SHOW ERRORS displays the line and column number for each error, as well as the text of the error message.

To view errors associated with previously created procedural objects, you may query USER_ERRORS directly. You may need to do this when viewing errors associated with package bodies because a package compilation that results in an error may not display the package body's error when you execute the SHOW ERROR command. You may also need to query USER_ERRORS when you encounter compilation errors with multiple procedural objects.

The following are the columns available in USER_ERRORS:

NAME	The name of the procedural object
TYPE	The object type (which can be one of these: PROCEDURE, FUNCTION, PACKAGE, PACKAGE BODY, TRIGGER, TYPE, TYPE BODY, VIEW, JAVA CLASS, or JAVA SOURCE)
SEQUENCE	The line sequence number, for use in the query's ORDER BY clause
LINE	The line number within the source code at which the error occurs
POSITION	The position within the line at which the error occurs
TEXT	The text of the error message
ATTRIBUTE	Flag to indicate whether the selected row is an error ('ERROR') or a warning ('WARNING')
MESSAGE_NUMBER	Numerical error number, without prefix

Queries against this view should always include the SEQUENCE column in the ORDER BY clause. "ALL" and "DBA" versions of this view are also available; they feature an additional column, OWNER, which records the owner of the object.

Code Size: USER_OBJECT_SIZE

You can query the amount of space used in the SYSTEM tablespace for a procedural object from the USER_OBJECT_SIZE data dictionary view. As shown in the following listing, the four separate size areas can be summed to determine the total space used in the SYSTEM data dictionary tables to store the object. The four SIZE columns, along with the NAME and TYPE columns, constitute all of the columns in this view.

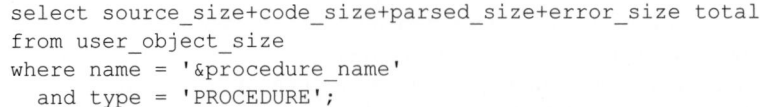

```
select source_size+code_size+parsed_size+error_size total
from user_object_size
where name = '&procedure_name'
  and type = 'PROCEDURE';
```

A "DBA" version of this view is also available: DBA_OBJECT_SIZE lists the sizes for all objects in the database.

Dimensions

You can query the DIMENSION_NAME column of the USER_DIMENSIONS view to see the names of your dimensions. USER_DIMENSIONS also contains columns for the dimension owner (OWNER), status (the INVALID column, set to "Y" or "N"), and revision level (the REVISION column). The attributes of a dimension are accessed via additional data dictionary views.

To see the hierarchies within a dimension, query USER_DIM_HIERARCHIES. This view has only three columns: OWNER, DIMENSION_NAME, and HIERARCHY_NAME. Querying USER_DIM_HIERARCHIES for the GEOGRAPHY dimension returns the name of its hierarchies:

```
select hierarchy_name
from user_dim_hierarchies;


HIERARCHY_NAME
------------------------------
COUNTRY_ROLLUP
```

You can see the hierarchy details for COUNTRY_ROLLUP by querying USER_DIM_CHILD_OF, as shown in the following listing. The first command creates a dimension named GEOGRAPHY that records the hierarchies of countries and continents.

```
create dimension geography
    level country_id     is country.country
    level continent_id   is continent.continent
    hierarchy country_rollup (
       country_id            child of
       continent_id
    join key country.continent references continent_id);

column join_key_id format a4

select child_level_name,
       parent_level_name,
       position, join_key_id
from user_dim_child_of
where hierarchy_name = 'COUNTRY_ROLLUP';
```

```
CHILD_LEVEL_NAME          PARENT_LEVEL_NAME                    POSITION JOIN
------------------------- ------------------------------------ --------- ----
COUNTRY_ID                CONTINENT_ID                               1 1
```

To see the join key for a hierarchy, query USER_DIM_JOIN_KEY:

```
select level_name, child_join_column
from user_dim_join_key
where dimension_name = 'GEOGRAPHY'
  and hierarchy_name = 'COUNTRY_ROLLUP';


LEVEL_NAME                         CHILD_JOIN_COLUMN
---------------------------------  -----------------------------
CONTINENT_ID                       CONTINENT
```

You can see the levels of a dimension by querying the USER_DIM_LEVELS data dictionary view and see the key columns for the levels via USER_DIM_LEVEL_KEY. Attribute information for dimensions is accessible via USER_DIM_ATTRIBUTES.

There are "ALL" and "DBA" views of all of the data dictionary views related to dimensions. Because the "USER" views for dimensions contain an OWNER column, there are no additional columns found in the corresponding "ALL" and "DBA" views.

Space Allocation and Usage, Including Partitions and Subpartitions

You can query the data dictionary to determine the space that is available and allocated for database objects. In the following sections, you'll learn how to determine the default storage parameters for objects, your space usage quota, available free space, and the way in which objects are physically stored. For information on Oracle's methods of storing data, see Chapters 22 and 51.

Tablespaces: USER_TABLESPACES

You can query the USER_TABLESPACES data dictionary view to determine which tablespaces you have been granted access to and the default storage parameters in each. A tablespace's default storage parameters are used for each object stored within that tablespace unless the CREATE or ALTER command for that object specifies its own storage parameters. The storage-related columns in USER_TABLESPACES, shown in the following listing, are very similar to the storage-related columns in USER_TABLES. See the STORAGE entry in the Alphabetical Reference for further details.

```
TABLESPACE_NAME
BLOCK_SIZE
INITIAL_EXTENT
NEXT_EXTENT
MIN_EXTENTS
MAX_EXTENTS
MAX_SIZE
PCT_INCREASE
MIN_EXTLEN
```

```
STATUS
CONTENTS
LOGGING
FORCE_LOGGING
EXTENT_MANAGEMENT
ALLOCATION_TYPE
SEGMENT_SPACE_MANAGEMENT
DEF_TAB_COMPRESSION
RETENTION
BIGFILE
PREDICATE_EVALUATION
ENCRYPTED
COMPRESS_FOR
```

There is no "ALL" version of this view. DBA_TABLESPACES shows the storage parameters for all tablespaces.

Space Quotas: USER_TS_QUOTAS

USER_TS_QUOTAS is a very useful view for determining the amount of space you have currently allocated and the maximum amount of space available to you by tablespace. A sample query of USER_TS_QUOTAS is shown in the following listing:

```
select * from user_ts_quotas;


TABLESPACE_NAME       BYTES  MAX_BYTES      BLOCKS MAX_BLOCKS
--------------- ---------- ---------- ---------- ----------
USERS                 67584          0         33          0
```

USER_TS_QUOTAS contains one record for each TABLESPACE_NAME. The BYTES column reflects the number of bytes allocated to objects owned by the user. MAX_BYTES is the maximum number of bytes the user can own in that tablespace; if there is no quota for that tablespace, then MAX_BYTES displays a value of 0. The BYTES and MAX_BYTES columns are translated into Oracle blocks in the BLOCKS and MAX_BLOCKS columns, respectively.

There is no "ALL" version of this view. DBA_TS_QUOTAS shows the storage quotas for all users for all tablespaces and is an effective way to list space usage across the entire database.

Segments and Extents: USER_SEGMENTS and USER_EXTENTS

As described in Chapter 22, space is allocated to objects (such as tables, clusters, and indexes) in *segments,* the physical counterparts to the logical objects created in the database. You can query USER_SEGMENTS to see the current storage parameters and space usage in effect for your segments. USER_SEGMENTS is extremely useful when you are in danger of exceeding one of the storage limits; its columns are shown in the following listing:

```
SEGMENT_NAME
PARTITION_NAME
SEGMENT_TYPE
SEGMENT_SUBTYPE
```

```
TABLESPACE_NAME
BYTES
BLOCKS
EXTENTS
INITIAL_EXTENT
NEXT_EXTENT
MIN_EXTENTS
MAX_EXTENTS
MAX_SIZE
RETENTION
MINRETENTION
PCT_INCREASE
FREELISTS
FREELIST_GROUPS
BUFFER_POOL
```

Segments consist of contiguous sections called *extents*. The extents that constitute segments are described in USER_EXTENTS. In USER_EXTENTS, you will see the actual size of each extent within the segment; this is handy for tracking the impact of changes to the NEXT and PCTINCREASE settings (in dictionary-managed tablespaces). In addition to the SEGMENT_NAME, SEGMENT_TYPE, and TABLESPACE_NAME columns, USER_EXTENTS has three new columns: EXTENT_ID (to identify the extent within the segment), BYTES (the size of the extent, in bytes), and BLOCKS (the size of the extent, in Oracle blocks).

Both USER_SEGMENTS and USER_EXTENTS have "DBA" versions, which are useful for listing the space usage of objects across owners. Both DBA_SEGMENTS and DBA_EXTENTS have an additional OWNER column. If you want to list all of the owners who own segments in a tablespace, you can query based on the TABLESPACE_NAME column in DBA_SEGMENTS and list all of the owners of segments in that tablespace. There are no "ALL" versions of these views.

Partitions and Subpartitions

A single table's data can be stored across multiple partitions. See Chapter 18 for examples of partitions and descriptions of the indexing options available. To see how a table is partitioned, you should query the USER_PART_TABLES data dictionary view, whose columns are shown in the following listing:

```
TABLE_NAME
PARTITIONING_TYPE
SUBPARTITIONING_TYPE
PARTITION_COUNT
DEF_SUBPARTITION_COUNT
PARTITIONING_KEY_COUNT
SUBPARTITIONING_KEY_COUNT
STATUS
DEF_TABLESPACE_NAME
DEF_PCT_FREE
DEF_PCT_USED
DEF_INI_TRANS
DEF_MAX_TRANS
DEF_INITIAL_EXTENT
```

```
DEF_NEXT_EXTENT
DEF_MIN_EXTENTS
DEF_MAX_EXTENTS
DEF_MAX_SIZE
DEF_PCT_INCREASE
DEF_FREELISTS
DEF_FREELIST_GROUPS
DEF_LOGGING
DEF_COMPRESSION
DEF_COMPRESS_FOR
DEF_BUFFER_POOL
REF_PTN_CONSTRAINT_NAME
INTERVAL
```

Most of the USER_PART_TABLES columns define the default storage parameters for the table partitions. When a partition is added to the table, it will, by default, use the storage parameters shown in USER_PART_TABLES. USER_PART_TABLES also shows the number of partitions in the table (PARTITION_COUNT), the number of columns in the partition key (PARTITIONING_KEY_COUNT), and the type of partitioning (PARTITIONING_TYPE).

USER_PART_TABLES stores a single row for each table that has been partitioned. To see information about each of the individual partitions that belong to the table, you can query USER_TAB_PARTITIONS. In USER_TAB_PARTITIONS, you will see one row for each of the table's partitions. The columns of USER_TAB_PARTITIONS are shown in the following listing:

```
TABLE_NAME
COMPOSITE
PARTITION_NAME
SUBPARTITION_COUNT
HIGH_VALUE
HIGH_VALUE_LENGTH
PARTITION_POSITION
TABLESPACE_NAME
PCT_FREE
PCT_USED
INI_TRANS
MAX_TRANS
INITIAL_EXTENT
NEXT_EXTENT
MIN_EXTENT
MAX_EXTENT
MAX_SIZE
PCT_INCREASE
FREELISTS
FREELIST_GROUPS
LOGGING
COMPRESSION
COMPRESS_FOR
NUM_ROWS
BLOCKS
EMPTY_BLOCK
```

```
AVG_SPACE
CHAIN_CNT
AVG_ROW_LEN
SAMPLE_SIZE
LAST_ANALYZED
BUFFER_POOL
GLOBAL_STATS
USER_STATS
```

USER_TAB_PARTITIONS contains columns that identify the table to which the partition belongs and shows the partition's storage parameters and the statistics for the partition. The statistics-related columns are populated when the table is analyzed. The identification columns show the high value for the range used to define the partition (HIGH_VALUE) and the position of the partition within the table (PARTITION_POSITION).

The columns used for the partition key are accessible via the USER_PART_KEY_COLUMNS data dictionary view. USER_PART_KEY_COLUMNS contains only four columns:

NAME	The name of the partitioned table or index
OBJECT_TYPE	Object type (TABLE or INDEX)
COLUMN_NAME	The name of the column that is part of the partition key
COLUMN_ POSITION	The position of the column within the partition key

Statistics for the partition columns are accessible via the USER_PART_COL_STATISTICS data dictionary view. The columns in USER_PART_COL_STATISTICS closely mirror those in USER_TAB_COL_STATISTICS.

Data histogram information for partitions is accessible via the USER_PART_HISTOGRAMS data dictionary view. The columns of this view display the endpoint values for each of the buckets in the histogram. The columns are TABLE_NAME, PARTITION_NAME, COLUMN_NAME, BUCKET_NUMBER, ENDPOINT_VALUE, and ENDPOINT_ACTUAL_VALUE.

Because indexes may be partitioned, a USER_IND_PARTITIONS data dictionary view is available. The columns in USER_IND_PARTITIONS parallel those in USER_INDEXES, with a few modifications to the identification columns. The identification columns for partitioned indexes include the name of the partition, the high value for the partition, and the position of the partition within the table. The statistics-related columns are populated when the partition is analyzed. The space-related columns describe the space allocation for the index; see the STORAGE entry in the Alphabetical Reference for information on storage parameters.

If a partition has subpartitions, you can see the details for the subpartitions via data dictionary views. USER_IND_SUBPARTITIONS contains the space-related and statistics-related columns of USER_IND_PARTITIONS, along with columns to identify the subpartition (SUBPARTITION_NAME and SUBPARTITION_POSITION). Similarly, USER_TAB_SUBPARTITIONS contains the space-related and statistics-related columns of USER_TAB_PARTITIONS, along with SUBPARTITION_ NAME and SUBPARTITION_POSITION columns. Thus, you can determine the space definitions of each of your partitions and subpartitions.

As shown earlier in this section, you can query the USER_PART_COL_STATISTICS and USER_ PART_HISTOGRAMS data dictionary views for statistical information regarding partitions. For subpartitions, you can query USER_SUBPART_COL_STATISTICS and USER_SUBPART_ HISTOGRAMS, whose structures mirror that of the partition statistics views. To see the subpartition key columns, you can query USER_SUBPART_KEY_COLUMNS, whose column structure is identical to that of USER_PART_KEY_COLUMNS.

Free Space: USER_FREE_SPACE

In addition to viewing the space you have used, you can also query the data dictionary to see how much space is currently marked as "free" space. USER_FREE_SPACE lists the free extents in all tablespaces accessible to the user. It lists by TABLESPACE_NAME the FILE_ID, BLOCK_ID, and relative file number of the starting point of the free extent. The size of the free extent is listed in both bytes and blocks. DBA_FREE_SPACE is frequently used by DBAs to monitor the amount of free space available and the degree to which it has become fragmented.

Users and Privileges

Users and their privileges are recorded within the data dictionary. In the following sections, you'll see how to query the data dictionary for information about user accounts, resource limits, and user privileges.

Users: USER_USERS

You can query USER_USERS to list information about your account. The USER_USERS view includes your USERNAME, USER_ID (a number assigned by the database), DEFAULT_ TABLESPACE, TEMPORARY_TABLESPACE, and CREATED date (when your account was created). The ACCOUNT_STATUS column in USER_USERS displays the status of your account, whether it is locked, unlocked ("OPEN"), or expired. If the account is locked, the LOCK_DATE column displays the date the account was locked and the EXPIRY_DATE column displays the expiration date. You can also query information about the resource consumer group (INITIAL_RSRC_ CONSUMER_GROUP) assigned to you by the DBA and your EXTERNAL_NAME value.

ALL_USERS contains only the USERNAME, User_ID, and CREATED columns from USER_ USERS, but it lists that information for all accounts in the database. ALL_USERS is helpful when you need to know the usernames that are available (for example, during GRANT commands). DBA_USERS contains all of the columns in USER_USERS, plus two additional columns: PASSWORD (the encrypted password for the account) and PROFILE (the user's resource profile). DBA_USERS lists this information for all users in the database.

Resource Limits: USER_RESOURCE_LIMITS

In Oracle, *profiles* can be used to place limits on the amount of system and database resources available to a user. If no profiles are created in a database, the default profile, which specifies unlimited resources for all users, is used. The resources that can be limited are described in the CREATE PROFILE entry of the Alphabetical Reference. Profiles enforce additional security measures, such as expiration dates on accounts and the minimum length of passwords.

To view the limits that are in place for your current session, you can query USER_ RESOURCE_LIMITS. It has the following columns:

RESOURCE_NAME	The name of the resource (for example, SESSIONS_PER_USER)
LIMIT	The limit placed on this resource

USER_PASSWORD_LIMITS describes the password profile parameters for the user. It has the same columns as USER_RESOURCE_LIMITS.

This view has no "ALL" or "DBA" version; it is limited to the user's current session. To see the cost associated with each available resource, you can query the RESOURCE_COST view. DBAs can access the DBA_PROFILES view to see the resource limits for all profiles. The RESOURCE_TYPE column of DBA_PROFILES indicates whether the resource profile is a PASSWORD or KERNEL profile.

Table Privileges: USER_TAB_PRIVS

To view grants for which you are the grantee, the grantor, or the object owner, query USER_TAB_PRIVS (user table privileges). In addition to its GRANTEE, GRANTOR, and OWNER columns, this view contains columns for the TABLE_NAME, HIERARCHY, PRIVILEGE, and a flag (set to "YES" or "NO") to indicate whether the privilege was granted WITH ADMIN OPTION (GRANTABLE).

USER_TAB_PRIVS_MADE displays the USER_TAB_PRIVS records for which the user is the owner (it, therefore, lacks an OWNER column). USER_TAB_PRIVS_RECD (user table privileges received) displays the USER_TAB_PRIVS records for which the user is the grantee (it, therefore, lacks a GRANTEE column). Because both USER_TAB_PRIVS_MADE and USER_TAB_PRIVS_RECD are simply subsets of USER_TAB_PRIVS, you can duplicate their functionality simply by querying against USER_TAB_PRIVS with an appropriate WHERE clause to view the subset you want.

"ALL" versions are available for USER_TAB_PRIVS, USER_TAB_PRIVS_MADE, and USER_TAB_PRIVS_RECD. The "ALL" versions list those objects for which either the user or PUBLIC is the grantee or grantor. There is a "DBA" version of USER_TAB_PRIVS named DBA_TAB_PRIVS that lists all object privileges granted to all users in the database. DBA_TAB_PRIVS has the same column definitions as USER_TAB_PRIVS. Instead of an OWNER column, ALL_TAB_PRIVS has a TABLE_SCHEMA column that displays the object schema.

Column Privileges: USER_COL_PRIVS

In addition to granting privileges on tables, you can also grant privileges at the column level. For example, you can grant users the ability to UPDATE only certain columns in a table. See Chapter 19 and the GRANT command in the Alphabetical Reference for further details.

The data dictionary views used to display column privileges are almost identical in design to the table privileges views described in the previous section. There is an additional COLUMN_NAME column in each of the COL views, and the HIERARCHY column is not found there. USER_COL_PRIVS is analogous to USER_TAB_PRIVS, USER_COL_PRIVS_MADE is analogous to USER_TAB_PRIVS_MADE, and USER_COL_PRIVS_RECD is analogous to USER_TAB_PRIVS_RECD.

"ALL" versions are available for all of the column privileges views. DBA_COL_PRIVS lists all column privileges that have been granted to users in the database (just as DBA_TAB_PRIVS lists all table privileges granted to users).

System Privileges: USER_SYS_PRIVS

USER_SYS_PRIVS lists the system privileges that have been granted to the user. Its columns are USERNAME, PRIVILEGE, and ADMIN_OPTION (a flag set to "YES" or "NO" to indicate whether the privilege was granted WITH ADMIN OPTION). All system privileges directly granted to a user are displayed via this view. System privileges granted to a user via a role are not displayed here. The following query shows sample output for the PRACTICE account:

```
select username, privilege * from user_sys_privs;

USERNAME                            PRIVILEGE
----------------------------        ----------------------
PRACTICE                            CREATE DIMENSION
PRACTICE                            UNLIMITED TABLESPACE
```

There is no "ALL" version of this view. To see the system privileges granted to all users in the database, query DBA_SYS_PRIVS, which has nearly the same column definitions as USER_SYS_PRIVS (the DBA version has a GRANTEE column, whereas the USER version has a USERNAME column).

Roles

In addition to privileges granted directly to users, sets of privileges may be grouped into roles. Roles may be granted to users or to other roles, and may consist of both object and system privileges. For information on using and managing roles, see Chapter 19.

To see which roles have been granted to you, query the USER_ROLE_PRIVS data dictionary view. Any roles that have been granted to PUBLIC will also be listed here. The available columns for USER_ROLE_PRIVS are as follows:

Column Name	Description
USERNAME	The username (may be PUBLIC)
GRANTED_ROLE	The name of the role granted to the user
ADMIN_OPTION	A flag to indicate whether the role was granted WITH ADMIN OPTION (YES or NO)
DEFAULT_ROLE	A flag to indicate whether the role is the user's default role ("YES" or "NO")
OS_GRANTED	A flag to indicate whether the operating system is being used to manage roles ("YES" or "NO")

To list all of the roles available in the database, you need to have DBA authority; you can then query DBA_ROLES to list all roles. DBA_ROLE_PRIVS lists the assignment of those roles to all of the users in the database.

Roles may receive three different types of permissions assigned, and each has a corresponding data dictionary view:

Permission Type	Data Dictionary Views
Table/column grants	ROLE_TAB_PRIVS. Similar to USER_TAB_PRIVS and USER_COL_PRIVS, except that it has a ROLE column instead of a GRANTEE column and does not have a GRANTOR column.
System privileges	ROLE_SYS_PRIVS. Similar to USER_SYS_PRIVS, except that it has a ROLE column instead of a USERNAME column.
Role grants	ROLE_ROLE_PRIVS. Lists all roles that have been granted to other roles.

NOTE
If you are not a DBA, these data dictionary views list only those roles that have been granted to you.

In addition to these views, there are two views, each with a single column, that list the privileges and roles enabled for the current session:

Dictionary View	Description
SESSION_PRIVS	The PRIVILEGE column lists all system privileges available to the session, whether granted directly or via roles.
SESSION_ROLES	The ROLE column lists all roles that are currently enabled for the session.

SESSION_PRIVS and SESSION_ROLES are available to all users.

NOTE
See Chapter 19 for information on enabling and disabling roles and setting default roles.

Auditing

As a non-DBA user within an Oracle database, you cannot enable the database's auditing features. If auditing has been enabled, there are data dictionary views that anyone can use to view the audit trail. As of Oracle Database 12c, monitoring index usage is easier and more robust.

Auditing Privileges, DML, and Authentication

Many different audit trail data dictionary views are available. Most of these views are based on a single audit trail table in the database (SYS.AUD$). The most generic of the audit trail views available is named USER_AUDIT_TRAIL. Because this view shows the audit records for many different types of actions, many of the columns may be inapplicable for any given row. The "DBA" version of this view, DBA_AUDIT_TRAIL, lists all entries from the audit trail table; USER_AUDIT_TRAIL lists only those that are relevant to the user.

A vast number of auditing capabilities is available (see the AUDIT command in the Alphabetical Reference for a complete listing). Each type of audit can be accessed via its own data dictionary view. The following are the available views:

USER_AUDIT_OBJECT	For statements concerning objects
USER_AUDIT_SESSION	For connections and disconnections
USER_AUDIT_STATEMENT	For GRANT, REVOKE, AUDIT, NOAUDIT, and ALTER SYSTEM commands issued by the user

There are "DBA" versions available for each of the "USER" views in the previous list; the "DBA" versions show all of the audit trail records that fit in the view's category.

You can view the auditing options that are currently in effect for your objects by querying USER_OBJ_AUDIT_OPTS. For each object listed in USER_OBJ_AUDIT_OPTS, the audit options for each command that may be performed on that object (identified by the OBJECT_NAME and

OBJECT_TYPE columns) are listed in USER_OBJ_AUDIT_OPTS. The column names of USER_OBJ_AUDIT_OPTS correspond to the first three letters of the command (for example, ALT for ALTER, UPD for UPDATE, and so on). Each column records whether that command is audited for that object when the command is successful ("S"), unsuccessful ("U"), or both. The default auditing options in effect for any new objects in the database can be displayed via the ALL_DEF_AUDIT_OPTS view, which has the same column naming conventions as USER_OBJ_AUDIT_OPTS. USER_OBJ_AUDIT_OPTS includes OBJECT_NAME and OBJECT_TYPE columns.

The commands that can be audited are stored in a reference table named AUDIT_ACTIONS, which has two columns: ACTION (the numeric code for the action) and NAME (the name of the action/command). ACTION and NAME correspond to the ACTION and ACTION_NAME columns of USER_AUDIT_TRAIL.

DBAs can use several additional auditing views that do not have "USER" counterparts, including DBA_AUDIT_EXISTS, DBA_PRIV_AUDIT_OPTS, DBA_STMT_AUDIT_OPTS, and STMT_AUDIT_OPTION_MAP. See the *Oracle Database Reference* for details on these DBA-only views.

Monitoring Object Usage

In previous releases of Oracle Database, you could use ALTER INDEX *indexname* MONITORING USAGE to see if a specific index was accessed during the time that the monitoring flag was set on the index. To see if an index had been accessed, the user would look at the dynamic performance view V$OBJECT_USAGE.

This method has one major drawback: V$OBJECT_USAGE has no OWNER column , so each user has to connect to the database to see if his or her indexes were accessed. As of Oracle Database 12c, DBA_OBJECT_USAGE makes monitoring usage across schemas easier. For a single user, USER_OBJECT_USAGE has the same columns as the existing dynamic performance view V$OBJECT_USAGE without the OWNER column. Here are the columns in DBA_OBJECT_USAGE:

OWNER	Index owner
INDEX_NAME	Index name in SYS.OBJ$.NAME
TABLE_NAME	Table name in SYS.OBJ$.NAME
MONITORING	A flag to indicate if the index is currently being monitored, ("YES" or "NO")
USED	A flag to indicate if the index has been accessed while being monitored ("YES" or "NO")
START_MONITORING	Date and time when monitoring was started on the index
END_MONITORING	Date and time when monitoring was ended on the index

DBA_OBJECT_USAGE makes it easier for a DBA or a user with the SELECT privilege on DBA_OBJECT_USAGE to check the monitoring status of indexes with one database connection and one SELECT query.

Miscellaneous

In addition to the data dictionary views described earlier in this chapter, several miscellaneous views and tables may be available within your data dictionary. These views and tables include DBA-only views and the table used when the EXPLAIN PLAN command is executed. The following sections contain brief descriptions for each of the miscellaneous view types.

Monitoring: The V$ Dynamic Performance Tables

The views that monitor the database environment performance are called the *dynamic performance views*. The dynamic performance views are commonly referred to as the *V$* (pronounced "Vee-Dollar") tables because they all begin with the letter *V* followed by the dollar sign ($).

The definitions and usage of columns within the monitoring views are subject to change with each version of the database that is released. Correctly interpreting the results of ad hoc queries against views usually requires referring to the *Oracle Database Administrator's Guide*. Normally, only the DBA uses the V$ tables. Consult the *Oracle Database Reference* and the *Oracle Database 12c DBA Handbook* for details on using the V$ views.

CHAINED_ROWS

The ANALYZE command can be used to generate a listing of the chained or migrated rows within a table. This listing of chained rows can be stored in a table called CHAINED_ROWS. To create the CHAINED_ROWS table in your schema, run the **utlchain.sql** script (usually found in the **./rdbms/admin** subdirectory under the Oracle home directory).

NOTE
The ANALYZE command will be deprecated in future releases. Use DBMS_STATS procedures instead.

To populate the CHAINED_ROWS table, use the LIST CHAINED ROWS INTO clause of the ANALYZE command, as shown in the following listing:

```
analyze table birthday list chained rows into chained_rows;
```

The CHAINED_ROWS table lists the OWNER_NAME, TABLE_NAME, CLUSTER_NAME (if the table is in a cluster), PARTITION_NAME (if the table is partitioned), SUBPARTITION_NAME (if the table contains subpartitions), HEAD_ROWID (the ROWID for the row), and an ANALYZE_TIMESTAMP column that shows the last time the table or cluster was analyzed. You can query the table based on the HEAD_ROWID values in CHAINED_ROWS, as shown in the following example:

```
select * from birthday
where rowid in
      (select head_rowid
       from chained_rows
       where table_name = 'BIRTHDAY');
```

If the chained row is short in length, then it may be possible to eliminate the chaining by deleting and reinserting the row.

PLAN_TABLE

When tuning SQL statements, you may want to determine the steps that the optimizer will take to execute your query. To view the query path, you must first create a table in your schema named PLAN_TABLE. The script used to create this table is called **utlxplan.sql** and is usually stored in the **./rdbms/admin** subdirectory of the Oracle software home directory.

After you have created the PLAN_TABLE table in your schema, you can use the EXPLAIN PLAN command, which will generate records in your PLAN_TABLE, tagged with the STATEMENT_ID value you specify for the query you want to have explained. See Chapter 46 for details on generating EXPLAIN PLAN listings.

The ID and PARENT_ID columns in PLAN_TABLE establish the hierarchy of steps (OPERATIONs) that the optimizer will follow when executing the query. See Chapter 46 for details on the Oracle Optimizer and the interpretation of PLAN_TABLE records.

Interdependencies: USER_DEPENDENCIES and IDEPTREE

Objects within Oracle databases can depend on each other. For example, a stored procedure may depend on a table, or a package may depend on a package body. When an object within the database changes, any procedural object that depends on it has to be recompiled. This recompilation can take place either automatically at run time (with a consequential performance penalty) or manually (see Chapter 35 for details on compiling procedural objects).

Two sets of data dictionary views are available to help you track dependencies. The first is USER_DEPENDENCIES, which lists all *direct* dependencies of objects. However, this view only goes one level down the dependency tree. To fully evaluate dependencies, you must create the recursive dependency-tracking objects in your schema. To create these objects, run the **utldtree .sql** script (usually located in the **./rdbms/admin** subdirectory of the Oracle home directory). This script creates two objects you can query: DEPTREE and IDEPTREE. They contain identical information (although their column definitions differ), but IDEPTREE is indented based on the pseudo-column LEVEL and is thus easier to read and interpret.

DBA-Only Views

Since this chapter is intended for use by developers and end users, the data dictionary views available only to DBAs are not covered here. The DBA-only views are used to provide information about distributed transactions, lock contention, rollback segments, and other internal database functions. For information on the DBA-only views, see the *Oracle Database Administrator's Guide.*

Oracle Label Security

Users of Oracle Label Security can view additional data dictionary views, including ALL_SA_GROUPS, ALL_SA_POLICIES, ALL_SA_USERS, and ALL_SA_USER_PRIVS. For details on these views, see the *Oracle Label Security Administrator's Guide.*

SQL*Loader Direct Load Views

To manage the direct load option within SQL*Loader, Oracle maintains a number of data dictionary views. These generally are only queried for debugging purposes, on request from Oracle Customer Support. The SQL*Loader direct load option is described under the SQLLDR entry in the Alphabetical Reference; its supporting data dictionary views are listed here:

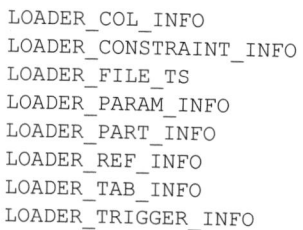

```
LOADER_COL_INFO
LOADER_CONSTRAINT_INFO
LOADER_FILE_TS
LOADER_PARAM_INFO
LOADER_PART_INFO
LOADER_REF_INFO
LOADER_TAB_INFO
LOADER_TRIGGER_INFO
```

For details on using these views, see the **catldr.sql** script, usually located in the **./rdbms/admin** subdirectory of the Oracle home directory.

Globalization Support Views

Three data dictionary views are used to display information about the Globalization Support parameters currently in effect in the database. Nonstandard values for the NLS parameters (such as NLS_DATE_FORMAT and NLS_SORT) can be set via the database's parameter file or via the ALTER SESSION command. (See the ALTER SESSION command in the Alphabetical Reference for further information on NLS settings.) To see the current NLS settings for your session, instance, and database, query NLS_SESSION_PARAMETERS, NLS_INSTANCE_PARAMETERS, and NLS_DATABASE_PARAMETERS, respectively.

Libraries

Your PL/SQL routines (see Chapter 35) can call external C programs. To see which external C program libraries that you own, you can query USER_LIBRARIES, which displays the name of the library (LIBRARY_NAME), the associated file (FILE_SPEC), whether the library is dynamically loadable (DYNAMIC), and the library's status (STATUS). ALL_LIBRARIES and DBA_LIBRARIES are also available; they include an additional OWNER column to indicate the library owner. For further information on libraries, see the entry for the CREATE LIBRARY command in the Alphabetical Reference.

Heterogeneous Services

To support the management of heterogeneous services, Oracle provides a number of data dictionary views. All of the views in this category begin with the letters "HS" instead of "DBA." In general, these views are used primarily by DBAs. For details on the "HS" views, see the *Oracle Database Reference*.

Indextypes and Operators

Operators and indextypes are closely related. You can use the CREATE OPERATOR command to create a new operator and define its bindings. You can reference operators in indextypes and in SQL statements. The operators, in turn, reference functions, packages, types, and other user-defined objects.

You can query the USER_OPERATORS view to see each operator's OWNER, OPERATOR_NAME, and NUMBER_OF_BINDS values. Ancillary information for operators is accessible via USER_OPANCILLARY, and you can query USER_OPARGUMENTS to see the operator arguments. You can query USER_OPBINDINGS to see the operator bindings.

USER_INDEXTYPE_OPERATORS lists the operators supported by indextypes. Indextypes, in turn, are displayed via USER_INDEXTYPES. There are "ALL" and "DBA" views of all the operator and indextype views. You can see the indextype arraytypes via the USER_INDEXTYPE_ARRAYTYPES view.

Outlines

When you use stored outlines, you can retrieve the names of, and details for, the outlines via the USER_OUTLINES data dictionary views. To see the hints that make up the outlines, query USER_OUTLINE_HINTS. "ALL" and "DBA" versions of USER_OUTLINES and USER_OUTLINE_HINTS are available.

Advisors

You can access data dictionary views related to tuning recommendations. These views begin with "USER_ADVISOR_", and there is a matching set of views at the "DBA_" level; DBA-only advisor views are available as well (such as DBA_ADVISOR_DEFINITIONS).

For example, USER_ADVISOR_ACTIONS contains data about the actions associated with all recommendations in the database. Each action is specified in the COMMAND column, with six related attribute columns. USER_ADVISOR_LOG displays information about the current state of all the tasks, as well as execution-specific data such as progress monitoring and completion status. Parameters for the advisors are accessible via USER_ADVISOR_PARAMETERS; you can see the rationale for recommendations via the USER_ADVISOR_RATIONALE view.

For the results of an analysis of all recommendations in the database, see the USER_ADVISOR_ RECOMMENDATIONS view. A recommendation can have multiple actions associated with it (see USER_ADVISOR_ACTIONS) based on the rationales used.

See Tables 45-1 and 45-2 for the full list of Advisor-related data dictionary views added in Oracle Database 11*g* and 12*c*. For the vast majority of users, those views will only be accessed via the Oracle Enterprise Manager or other graphical interfaces.

Schedulers

You can access a set of views related to Scheduler jobs in the database. These include USER_SCHEDULER_JOBS (all Scheduler jobs owned by the user), USER_SCHEDULER_PROGRAMS (the scheduler programs), and USER_SCHEDULER_PROGRAM_ARGS (the arguments for the scheduler programs). You can see the execution details for the jobs via the USER_SCHEDULER_JOB_LOG, USER_SCHEDULER_JOB_RUN_DETAILS, and USER_SCHEDULER_RUNNING_JOBS views. You can see the schedules via USER_SCHEDULER_SCHEDULES.

CHAPTER
46

The Hitchhiker's Guide
to Tuning Applications
and SQL

With each new release of its products, Oracle adds features to enhance the performance of your applications. These features may include new options that you must manually implement (such as partitioning) or under-the-cover changes that provide a performance benefit without your making any changes to your application.

Do not approach tuning as something done after an application goes into production or after a system test has been performed. As you will see, planning for application performance must be part of the design process.

This chapter describes the major new tuning changes introduced with Oracle Database 11g and 12c. It provides a set of guidelines and best practices related to tuning Oracle applications. The final section of the chapter is dedicated to integrating those features with the recommended best practices. You'll also learn about the guidelines for generating and interpreting explain plans and stored outlines.

An Overview of Oracle Database Tuning Features

Oracle Database 11g introduced a number of new features aimed at simplifying and automating the tuning process. With Oracle Database 12c, DBAs and developers who previously had to perform manual steps related to tuning will now find that the database performs some of these steps with no intervention. Note that the database cannot redesign your application; it can only make the commands it receives complete as quickly as possible. Please see the "Tuning—Best Practices" section for the principles of sound performance design. As this book is intended for all users, the DBA-specific tools are not the focus here; rather, the focus is on designing and developing systems whose performance can be easily administered.

The following performance-related features are new as of Oracle Database 11g or either added or enhanced in Oracle Database 12c. For further details on all tuning-related features, see the *Performance Tuning Guide* that comes as part of the Oracle documentation set.

- **Active session history (ASH) enhancements**   ASH statistics are enhanced to provide row-level activity information for each captured SQL statement. This information can be used to identify which part of the SQL execution contributed most significantly to the SQL elapsed time. The ASH views, accessible to DBAs, provide historical information about the active sessions in the database.

- **Automatic Database Diagnostic Monitor (ADDM) enhancements**   DBAs and developers can use ADDM to analyze the database and generate recommendations for performance tuning. In Oracle 11g, ADDM was enhanced to perform analysis on database clusters on various levels of granularity (such as database cluster, database instance, or specific targets) over any specified time period.

- **Automated SQL tuning**   DBAs can use the SQL Tuning Advisor to generate recommendations for tuning SQL commands. You can automate the scheduling of SQL Tuning Advisor tasks to run during maintenance windows using Automated Maintenance Task. In addition, Oracle Database 12c includes an array of automated tuning features called *Performance with Zero Effort* that literally tunes and retunes your queries in real-time. *Adaptive query optimization* allows an execution with a given plan to stop and be re-analyzed based on the initial part of the execution. If row count estimates are off by a magnitude or more, a NESTED LOOP query step may be restarted with a HASH JOIN instead. In addition, statistics gathered during the execution are made available to other queries.

- **AWR baselines**   The Automated Workload Repository (AWR) reports provide baseline statistics for the database and show the database performance during specified intervals. A baseline contains performance data from a specific time period that is preserved for comparison with other similar workload periods when performance problems occur. Several types of baselines are available in Oracle Database: fixed baselines, moving window baselines, and baseline templates.

- **Database Replay**   You can capture a database workload on a production system and replay it on a test system to ensure that system changes, such as database upgrades, will yield the desired results. (See Chapter 31.)

- **Enhanced I/O statistics**   I/O statistics are collected for all I/O calls made by Oracle Database in the following dimensions: consumer group, database file, and database function.

- **Enhanced optimizer statistics maintenance**   The collection and publication of statistics is now decoupled. You can collect optimizer statistics, store them as pending statistics, test them, and then publish them only if the statistics are valid.

- **Extended statistics**   The optimizer now gathers information on a group of columns in a table (multicolumn statistics) to analyze column dependencies in column groups. It also gathers information about expressions in columns.

- **I/O calibration**   The I/O calibration feature enables you to assess the performance of the storage subsystem and determine whether I/O performance problems are caused by the database or the storage subsystem.

- **Query result caches**   You can store results of frequently run SQL queries in server-side and client-side result caches. This ensures a faster response time when these queries are subsequently executed. (See Chapter 47.)

- **Concurrent UNION and UNION ALL executions**   Oracle automatically runs multiple queries joined by UNION and UNION ALL to further leverage parallelism without explicitly specifying a PARALLEL hint or setting the PARALLEL attribute at the table level.

- **Real-time SQL monitoring**   Real-time SQL monitoring enables you to monitor the execution of long-running SQL statements as they are being executed. Both cursor-level statistics (such as CPU time and I/O time) and execution plan statistics (such as cardinality of intermediate results, memory, and temporary space used by each operator in the plan) are updated in near real-time while the statement executes. These statistics are exposed by two new fixed views: V$SQL_MONITOR and V$SQL_PLAN_MONITOR.

- **SQL Performance Analyzer**   The SQL Performance Analyzer enables DBAs to forecast the impact of system changes on SQL performance by testing these changes using a SQL workload on a test system.

- **SQL plan baselines**   Changes to the execution plan for a SQL statement can cause severe performance degradation. Oracle Database can capture, select, and evolve SQL plan baselines, preventing the optimizer from using a new plan until it has been verified to be more efficient than the existing plan. This feature replaces the plan stability feature in previous versions of Oracle Database.

■   **SQL test case builder**   The SQL test case builder provides the ability to build a reproducible test case by gathering and packaging the necessary information related to a SQL incident so that it can be reproduced on another system.

Tuning—Best Practices

At least 50 percent of the time—conservatively—performance problems are designed into an application. During the design of the application and the related database structures, the application architects may not know all the ways in which the business will use the application data over time. As a result, there may always be some components whose performance is poor during the initial release, whereas other problems appear later as the business usage of the application changes.

In some cases, the fix is relatively straightforward—changing an initialization parameter, adding an index, or rescheduling large operations. In other cases, the problem cannot be fixed without altering the application architecture. For example, an application may be designed to heavily reuse functions for all data access—so that functions call other functions, which call additional functions even to perform the simplest database actions. As a result, a single database call may result in tens of thousands of function calls and database accesses. Such an application will usually not scale well; as more users are added to the system, the burden of the number of executions per user will slow the performance for the individual users. Tuning the individual SQL statements executed as part of that application may yield little performance benefit; the statements themselves may be well tuned already. Rather, it is the sheer number of executions that leads to the performance problem.

The following best practices may seem overly simplistic—but they are violated over and over in database applications, and those violations directly result in performance problems. There are always exceptions to the rules because the next change to your software or environment may allow you to violate the rules without affecting your performance. In general, though, following these rules will allow you to meet performance requirements as application usage increases.

Do as Little as Possible

End users do not care, in general, if the underlying database structures are fully normalized to Third Normal Form or if they are laid out in compliance with object-oriented standards. Users want to perform a business process, and the database application should be a tool that helps that business process complete as quickly as possible. The focus of your design should not be the achievement of theoretical design perfection; it should always be on the end user's ability to do his or her job. Simplify the processes involved at every step in the application.

In Your Application Design, Strive to Eliminate Logical Reads

In the past, there was a heavy focus on eliminating physical reads—and while this is still a good idea, no physical reads occur unless logical reads require them.

Let's take a simple example. Select the current time from DUAL. If you select down to the second level, the value will change 86,400 times per day. Yet there are application designers who repeatedly perform this query, executing it millions of times per day. Such a query likely performs few physical reads throughout the day—so if you are focused solely on tuning the physical I/O, you would likely disregard it. However, it can significantly impact application performance. How? By using the CPU resources available. Each execution of the query forces Oracle to perform work, using processing power to find and return the correct data. As more and more users execute the command repeatedly, you may find that the number of logical reads used by the query exceeds all other queries. In some cases, multiple processors on the server are dedicated to servicing repeated small queries of this sort. What business benefit do they generate? Little to none.

Consider the following real-world example. A programmer wants to implement a pause in a program, forcing it to wait 30 seconds between completing two steps. Since the performance of the environment will not be consistent over time, the programmer codes the routine in the following format (shown in pseudo-code):

```
perform Step 1
select SysDate from DUAL into a StartTime variable
begin loop
   select SysDate from DUAL in a CurrentTime variable;
   Compare CurrentTime with the StartTime variable value.
   If 30 seconds have passed, exit the loop;
Otherwise repeat the loop, calculating SysDate again.
end loop
perform Step 2.
```

Is this a reasonable approach? Absolutely not! It will do what the developer wants, but at a significant cost to the application and there is nothing a database administrator can do to improve its performance. In this case, the cost will not be due to I/O activity—the DUAL table will stay in the instance's memory area—but rather in CPU activity. Every time this program is run, by every user, the database will spend 30 seconds consuming as many CPU resources as the system can support. In this particular case, the SELECT SYSDATE FROM DUAL query accounts for over 40 percent of all of the CPU time used by the application. All of that CPU time is wasted. Tuning the individual SQL statement will not help; the application design must be revised to eliminate the needless execution of commands. A far better solution is to develop a way to track the completion of the first step and any subsequent processing and then start the second step with no embedded wait time calculation.

For those who favor tuning based on the buffer cache hit ratio, this database has a hit ratio of almost 100 percent due to the high number of completely unnecessary logical reads without related physical reads. The buffer cache hit ratio compares the number of logical reads to the number of physical reads; if 10 percent of the logical reads require physical reads, the buffer cache hit ratio is 100 less 10, or 90 percent. Low hit ratios identify databases that perform a high number of physical reads; extremely high hit ratios such as found in this example may identify databases that perform an excessive number of logical reads.

In Your Application Design, Strive to Avoid Trips to the Database

Remember that you are tuning an application, not a query. You may need to combine multiple queries into a single procedure so that the database can be visited once rather than multiple times for each screen. This bundled-query approach is particularly relevant for "thin-client" applications that rely on multiple application tiers. Look for queries that are interrelated based on the values they return, and see if there are opportunities to transform them into single blocks of code. The goal is not to make a monolithic query that will never complete; the goal is to avoid doing work that does not need to be done. In this case, the constant back-and-forth communication among the database server, the application server, and the end user's computer is targeted for tuning.

This problem is commonly seen on complex data-entry forms in which each field displayed on the screen is populated via a separate query. Each of those queries is a separate trip to the database. As with the example in the previous section, the database is forced to execute large numbers of related queries. Even if each of those queries is tuned, the burden of the number of commands—multiplied by the number of users—will consume the CPU resources available on the server. Such a design may also impact the network usage, but the network is seldom the problem—the issue is the number of times the database is accessed.

Within your packages and procedures, you should strive to eliminate unnecessary database accesses. Store commonly needed values in local variables instead of repeatedly querying the database. If you don't need to make a trip to the database for information, don't make it. That sounds simple, but you would be amazed at how often application developers fail to consider this advice.

There is no initialization parameter that can make this change take effect. It is a design issue and requires the active involvement of developers, designers, DBAs, and application users in the application performance planning and tuning process.

For Reporting Systems, Store the Data the Way the Users Will Query It

If you know the queries that will be executed—such as via parameterized reports—you should strive to store the data so Oracle does as little work as possible to transform the format of the data in your tables into the format presented to the user. Doing this may require the creation and maintenance of materialized views or reporting tables. That maintenance is, of course, extra work for the database to perform—but it is performed in batch mode and does not directly affect the end user. The end user, on the other hand, benefits from the ability to perform the query faster. The database as a whole will perform fewer logical and physical reads because the accesses to the base tables to populate and refresh the materialized views are performed infrequently when compared to the end-user queries against the views.

Avoid Repeated Connections to the Database

Opening a database connection may be a slow and largely avoidable operation. If you need to connect to the database, keep the connection open and reuse the connection. At the application level, you may be able to use connection pooling to support this need. Within the database, you may be able to use stored procedures, packages, and other methods to maintain connections while you are performing your processing.

Another real-life example: An application designer wants to verify that the database is running prior to executing a report. The solution is to open a session and execute the following query: SELECT COUNT(*) FROM DUAL. If the query comes back with the proper result (1), then the database is running, a new connection is opened, and the report query is executed. What is wrong with that approach? In small systems, you may be able to survive such a design decision. In OLTP systems with a high number of concurrent users, you will encounter significant performance problems as the database spends most of its time opening and closing connections. Within the database, the SELECT COUNT(*) FROM DUAL query will be executed millions of times per day—Oracle will spend the bulk of the resources available to the application opening and closing connections and returning the database status to the application. The query performs little I/O but its impact is seen in its CPU usage and the constant opening of connections.

Why is such a step even needed? If you properly handle the errors from the report queries themselves, it would be obvious that the database connection is not functioning properly in the event of a failure. The unnecessary database availability check is made worse by the failure to reuse the same connection. No DBA action can correct this; the application must be designed from the start to reuse connections properly.

Use the Right Indexes

In an effort to eliminate physical reads, some application developers create many indexes on every table. Aside from their impact on data load times (discussed in the "Test Correctly" section later in this chapter), it is possible that many of the indexes will never be needed. In OLTP applications, you should not use bitmap indexes; if a column has few distinct values, you should consider leaving it unindexed. The optimizer supports skip-scan index accesses, so you may use an index on a set of columns even if the leading column of the index is not a limiting condition for the query.

Do It as Simply as Possible

Now that you have eliminated the performance costs of unnecessary logical reads, unneeded database trips, unmanaged connections, and inappropriate indexes, take a look at the commands that remain.

Go Atomic

You can use SQL to combine many steps into one large query. In some cases, this may benefit your application—you can create stored procedures and reuse the code and reduce the number of database trips performed. You can take this too far, however, creating large queries that fail to complete quickly enough. These queries commonly include multiple sets of grouping operations, inline views, and complex multirow calculations against millions of rows.

If you are performing batch operations, you may be able to break such a query into its atomic components, creating temporary tables to store the data from each step. If you have an operation that takes hours to complete, you almost always can find a way to break it into smaller component parts. Divide and conquer the performance problem.

For example, a batch operation may combine data from multiple tables, perform joins and sorts, and then insert the result into a table. On a small scale, this may perform satisfactorily. On a large scale, you may have to divide this operation into multiple steps:

1. Create a work table using a Global Temporary Table (GTT). Insert rows into it from one of the source tables for the query, selecting only those rows and columns that you care about later in the process.

 NOTE
GTTs have the advantage of cleaning up after themselves and dropping all rows once the session is terminated.

2. Create a second work table for the columns and rows from the second table.

3. Create any needed indexes on the work tables. Note that all of the steps to this point can be parallelized—the inserts, the queries of the source tables, and the creation of the indexes.

4. Perform the join, again parallelized. The join output may go into another work table.

5. Perform any sorts needed. Sort as little data as possible.

6. Insert the data into the target table.

Why go through all of those steps? Because you can tune them individually, you may be able to tune them to complete much faster individually than Oracle can complete them as a single command. For batch operations, you should consider making the steps as simple as possible. You will need to manage the space allocated for the work tables, but this approach can generate significant benefits to your batch-processing performance.

Eliminate Unnecessary Sorts

As part of the example in the preceding section, the sort operation was performed last. In general, sort operations are inappropriate for OLTP applications. Sort operations do not return any rows to the user until the entire set of rows is sorted. Row operations, on the other hand, return rows to the user as soon as those rows are available.

Consider the following simple test: Perform a full table scan of a large table. As soon as the query starts to execute, the first rows are displayed. Now, perform the same full table scan but add an ORDER BY clause on an unindexed column. No rows are displayed until all of the rows have been sorted. Why does this happen? Because for the second query Oracle performs a SORT ORDER BY operation on the results of the full table scan. As it is a set operation, the set must be completed before the next operation is performed.

Now, imagine an application in which there are many queries executed within a procedure. Each of the queries has an ORDER BY clause. This turns into a series of nested sorts—no operation can start until the one before it completes.

Note that UNION operations perform sorts. If it is appropriate for the business logic, use a UNION ALL operation in place of a UNION, as a UNION ALL does not perform a sort (because it does not eliminate duplicates).

Eliminate the Need to Query Undo Segments

When performing DML operations, the UNDO tablespace stores the file, block, and ROWID of the previous column values until the transaction is committed. When another user runs a SELECT statement while the DML is still active, the database will need to retrieve the earlier version of the rows needed for the query from the undo segment to see the row as it existed at the time your query began. Even after the DML statement has committed its changes, any in-progress SELECT statements must still use the blocks from the UNDO tablespace to maintain the view of the tables as of the time the SELECT statement started. Application designs that call for queries to access data frequently that others may be changing at the same time force the database to do more work—it has to look in multiple locations for one piece of data. Again, this is a design issue. DBAs may be able to size the undo segment areas to reduce the possibility of queries encountering "snapshot too old" or failed DML statements, but correcting the fundamental problem requires a change to the application design.

Tell the Database What It Needs to Know

The Oracle Optimizer relies on statistics when it evaluates the thousands of possible paths to take during the execution of a query. How you manage those statistics can significantly impact the performance of your queries.

Keep Your Statistics Updated

How often should you gather statistics? With each major change to the data in your tables, you should reanalyze the tables. If you have partitioned the tables, you can analyze them on a partition-by-partition basis. You can use the Automatic Statistics Gathering feature to automate the collection of statistics. By default, that process gathers statistics during a maintenance window from 10 P.M. to 6 A.M. each night and all day on weekends.

Because the analysis job is usually a batch operation performed after hours, you can tune it by improving sort and full table scan performance at the session level. The result will be greatly enhanced performance for the sorts and full table scans that the analysis performs.

Hint Where Needed

In most cases, the optimizer selects the most efficient execution path for queries. However, you may have information about a better path. For example, you may be joining a local table to a table in a remote database, in which case you would want to avoid repeatedly querying individual rows from the remote table; you would most likely benefit from doing fewer retrievals of many rows from the remote database. You may give Oracle a hint to influence the join operations, the overall query goal, the specific indexes used, or the parallelism of the query. See the "Related Hints" sections later in this chapter for an overview of the major hints.

Maximize the Throughput in the Environment

In an ideal environment, you never need to query information outside the database; all of the data stays in memory all of the time. Unless you are working with a very small database, however, this is not a realistic approach. This section presents guidelines for maximizing the throughput of the environment.

Use Disk Caching

If Oracle cannot find the data it needs in the database, it performs a physical read. But how many of the physical reads actually reach the disk? If you use disk caching, you may be able to prevent 90 percent or more of the access requests for the most-needed blocks. If the database buffer cache hit ratio is 90 percent, you are accessing the disks 10 percent of the time—and if the disk cache prevents 90 percent of those requests from reaching the disk, your effective hit ratio is 99 percent. Oracle's internal statistics do not reflect this improvement; you will need to work with your disk administrators to configure and monitor the disk cache. Oracle's Query Result Cache lets you use part of the SGA as a cache for frequently executed queries as well, to avoid contention for buffer cache blocks and to reuse query results that have been generated previously and will not change because the rows in the base table(s) have not changed.

Use a Larger Database Block Size

The default and Oracle-recommended database block size is 8K. If your average row size is greater than 8K, however, use a block size that is at least big enough to hold one row. Otherwise, every query will require retrieving at least two blocks to retrieve a single row.

Store Data Efficiently at the Block Level

Oracle stores blocks of data in memory. It is in your best interest to make sure those blocks are as densely packed with data as possible. If your data storage is inefficient at the block level, you will not gain as much benefit as you can from the caches available in the database.

If the rows in your application are not going to be updated, set the PCTFREE as low as possible. For partitioned tables, set the PCTFREE value for each partition to maximize the row storage within blocks. By default, each partition uses the PCTFREE setting for the table. Set a low PCTFREE value for indexes as long as the source of the indexed column is a sequence or some other ascending value that places index entries in the rightmost blocks of the index. For indexes on columns with character strings, a low value for PCTFREE may cause block splits and make the number of blocks in the index larger instead of smaller!

If the PCTFREE setting is too low, updates may force Oracle to move the row (called a *migrated row*). In some cases, row chaining is inevitable, such as when your row length is greater than your database block size. When row chaining and migration occur, each access of a row requires accessing multiple blocks, impacting the number of logical reads required for each command. You can detect row chaining by analyzing the table and then checking its statistics via USER_TABLES; the CHAIN_CNT column will be populated with the number of chained rows when the table is analyzed.

Design to Throughput, Not Disk Space

Take an application that is running on eight 128GB disks and move it to a single 1TB disk. Will the application run faster or slower? In general, it will run slower because the throughput of the single disk is unlikely to be equal to the combined throughput of the eight separate disks. Rather than designing your disk layout based on the space available (a common method), design it based on the throughput of the disks available. You may decide to use only part of each disk. The remaining space on the disk will not be used by the production application unless the throughput available for that disk improves.

Avoid the Use of the Temporary Segments

Whenever possible, perform all sorts in memory. Any operation that writes to the temporary segments is potentially wasting resources. Oracle uses temporary segments when the sort area within the PGA does not allocate enough memory to support the sorting requirements of operations. Sorting operations include index creations, ORDER BY clauses, statistics gathering, GROUP BY operations, and some joins. As noted earlier in this chapter, you should strive to sort as few rows as possible. When performing the sorts that remain, perform them in memory.

NOTE
Oracle does not recommend using the SORT_AREA_SIZE parameter unless the instance is configured with the shared server option. Oracle recommends that you enable automatic sizing of SQL working areas by setting PGA_AGGREGATE_TARGET instead. SORT_AREA_SIZE is retained for backward compatibility.

Divide and Conquer Your Data

If you cannot avoid performing expensive operations on your database, you can attempt to split the work into more manageable chunks. Often you can severely limit the number of rows acted on by your operations, substantially improving performance.

Use Partitions

Partitions can benefit end users, DBAs, and application support personnel. For end users, there are two potential benefits: improved query performance and improved availability for the database. Query performance may improve because of *partition elimination*. The optimizer knows what partitions may contain the data requested by a query. As a result, the partitions that will not participate are eliminated from the query process. Since fewer logical and physical reads are needed, the query should complete faster.

Availability improves because of the benefits partitions generate for DBAs and application support personnel. Many administrative functions can be performed on single partitions, allowing the rest of the table to be unaffected. For example, you can TRUNCATE a single partition of a table. You can split a partition, move it to a different tablespace, or switch it with an existing table (so that the previously independent table is then considered a partition). You can gather statistics on one partition at a time. All of these capabilities narrow the scope of administrative functions, reducing their impact on the availability of the database as a whole.

Use Materialized Views

You can use materialized views to divide the types of operations users perform against your tables. When you create a materialized view, you can direct users to query the materialized view directly, or you can rely on Oracle's query rewrite capability to redirect queries to the materialized view. As a result, you will have two copies of the data—one that services the input of new transactional data, and a second, the materialized view, that services queries. As a result, you can take one of them offline for maintenance without affecting the availability of the other. Also note that you can index the base table and the materialized view differently, with each having the structures needed for the specific data access types it is intended for.

Use Parallelism

Almost every major operation can be parallelized—including queries, inserts, object creations, and data loads. The parallel options allow you to involve multiple processors in the execution of a single command, effectively dividing the command into multiple smaller coordinated commands. As a result, the command may perform better. You can specify a degree of parallelism at the object level and can override it via hints in your queries.

NOTE
Parallel operations work best when the operations involve large sets of data.

Test Correctly

In most development methodologies, application testing has multiple phases, including module testing, full system testing, and performance stress testing. Many times, the full system test and performance stress test are not performed adequately because of time constraints as the application nears its delivery deadline. The result is that applications are released into production without any way to guarantee that the functionality and performance of the application as a whole will meet the needs of the users. This is a serious and significant flaw and should not be tolerated by any user of the application. Users do not need just one component of the application to function properly; they need the entire application to work properly in support of a business process. If they cannot do a day's worth of business in a day, the application fails.

This is a key tenet regarding identifying the need for tuning: *If the application slows the speed of the business process, it should be tuned.* The tests you perform must be able to determine if the application will hinder the speed of the business process under the expected production load.

Test with Large Volumes of Data

As described earlier in this chapter, objects within the database function differently after they have been used for some time. For example, the PCTFREE setting may cause blocks to be only half-used or rows to be chained. Each of these causes performance problems that will only be seen after the application has been used for some time.

A further problem with data volume concerns indexes. As B*-tree indexes grow in size, they may split internally—the level of entries within the index increases. As a result, you can picture the new level as being an index within the index. The additional level in the index increases the effect of the index on data load rates. You will not see this impact until *after* the index is split. Applications that work acceptably for the first week or two in production, only to suddenly falter after the data volume reaches critical levels, do not support the business needs. In testing, there is no substitute for production data loaded at production rates while the tables already contain a substantial amount of data.

Test with Many Concurrent Users
Testing with a single user does not reflect the expected production usage of most database applications. You must be able to determine if concurrent users will encounter deadlocks, data consistency issues, or performance problems. For example, suppose an application module uses a work table during its processing. Rows are inserted into the table, manipulated, and then queried. A separate application module does similar processing—and uses the same table. When executed at the same time, the two processes attempt to use each other's data. Unless you are testing with multiple users executing multiple application functions simultaneously, you may not discover this problem and the business data errors it generates.

Testing with many concurrent users also helps to identify areas in the application in which users frequently use undo segments to complete their queries, impacting performance.

Test the Impact of Indexes on Your Load Times
Every additional index on a table adds about three times the overhead for DML against that table. There are some exceptions—sorted data has much less of an impact, for example—but the rule is generally true. If you can load 3,000 rows per second into an unindexed table in your environment, adding a single index to the table should slow your insert speed to around 1,000 rows per second. The impact depends on your operating environment, the data structures involved, and the degree to which the data is sorted.

How many rows per second can you insert in your environment? Perform a series of simple tests. Create a table with no indexes and insert a large number of rows into it. Repeat the tests to reduce the impact of physical reads on the timing results. Calculate the number of rows inserted per second. In most environments, you can insert tens of thousands of rows per second into the database. Perform the same test in your other database environments so you can identify any that are significantly different than the others.

Now consider your application. Are you able to insert rows into your tables via your application at anywhere near the rate you just calculated? Many applications run at less than 5 percent of the rate the environment supports. They are bogged down by unneeded indexes or the type of code design issues described earlier in this chapter. If their load rate decreases—say from 40 rows per second to 20 rows per second—the tuning focus should not be solely on how that decrease occurred but also on how the application managed to get only 40 rows per second inserted in an environment that supports thousands of rows inserted per second.

Make All Tests Repeatable
Most regulated industries have standards for tests. Their standards are so reasonable that *all* testing efforts should follow them. Among the standards is that all tests must be repeatable. To be

compliant with the standards, you must be able to re-create the data set used, the exact action performed, the exact result expected, and the exact result seen and recorded. Preproduction tests for validation of the application must be performed on the production hardware. Moving the application to different hardware requires retesting the application. The tester and the business users must sign off on all tests.

Most people, on hearing those restrictions, would agree that they are good steps to take in any testing process. Indeed, your business users may be expecting that the people developing the application are following such standards even if they are not required by the industry. But are they followed, and if not, then why not? There are two commonly cited reasons for not following such standards: time and cost. Such tests require planning, personnel resources, business user involvement, and time for execution and documentation. Testing on production-caliber hardware may require the purchase of additional servers. Those are the most evident costs—but what is the business cost of failing to perform such tests? The testing requirements for validated systems in the U.S. pharmaceutical industry were implemented because those systems directly impact the integrity of critical products such as the safety of the blood supply. If your business has critical components served by your application (and if it does not, then why are you building the application?), you must consider the costs of insufficient, rushed testing and communicate those potential costs to the business users. The evaluation of the risks of incorrect data or unacceptably slow performance must involve the business users. In turn, that may lead to an extended deadline to support proper testing.

In many cases, the rushed testing cycle occurs because there was not a testing standard in place at the start of the project. If there is a consistent, thorough, and well-documented testing standard in place at the enterprise level when the project starts, then the testing cycle will be shorter when it is finally executed. Testers will know long in advance that repeatable data sets will be needed. Templates for tests will be available. If there is an issue with any test result, or if the application needs to be retested following a change, the test can be repeated. And the application users will know that the testing is robust enough to simulate the production usage of the application. If the system fails the tests for performance reasons, the problem may be a design issue (as described in the previous sections) or a problem with an individual query. In the following sections, you'll see how to display the execution path for a SQL statement, the major operations involved, and the related hints you can employ when tuning SQL.

Generating and Reading Explain Plans

You can display the execution path in SQL*Plus for a query in these ways:

- The SET AUTOTRACE ONcommand
- The EXPLAIN PLANcommand

In the following sections, both commands are explained; for the remainder of the chapter, the SET AUTOTRACE ON command will be used to illustrate execution paths as reported by the optimizer.

Using SET AUTOTRACE ON

You can have the execution path automatically displayed for every transaction you execute within SQL*Plus. The SET AUTOTRACE ON command causes each query, after being executed, to display both its execution path and high-level trace information about the processing involved in resolving the query.

To use the SET AUTOTRACE ON command, you must first create a PLAN_TABLE table within your account. The PLAN_TABLE structure may change with each Oracle release, so you should drop and re-create your copy of PLAN_TABLE with each Oracle upgrade. The commands shown in the following listing drop any existing PLAN_TABLE and replace it with the current version.

The file that creates the PLAN_TABLE table is located in the **./rdbms/admin** subdirectory under the Oracle software home directory. This file is executed automatically during an installation of Oracle Database 11*g* or 12*c* using the Database Creation Assistant (DBCA).

```
drop table plan_table;
@$ORACLE_HOME/rdbms/admin/utlxplan.sql
```

When you use SET AUTOTRACE ON, records are inserted into your copy of the PLAN_TABLE to show the order of operations executed. After the query completes, the selected data is displayed. After the query's data is displayed, the order of operations is shown followed by statistical information about the query processing. The following explanation of SET AUTOTRACE ON focuses on the section of the output that displays the order of operations.

NOTE
To show the explain plan output without running the query, use the SET AUTOTRACE TRACE EXPLAIN command.

If you use the SET AUTOTRACE ON command with its default options, you will not see the explain plan for your queries until *after* they complete. The EXPLAIN PLAN command (described next) shows the execution paths without running the queries first. Therefore, if the performance of a query is unknown, you may choose to use the EXPLAIN PLAN command before running it. If you are fairly certain that the performance of a query is acceptable, use SET AUTOTRACE ON to verify its execution path.

NOTE
When you use the SET AUTOTRACE ON command, Oracle automatically deletes the records it inserts into PLAN_TABLE once the execution path has been displayed.

If you use the parallel query options or query remote databases, an additional section of the SET AUTOTRACE ON output will show the text of the queries executed by the parallel query server processes or the query executed within the remote database.

To disable the autotrace feature, use the SET AUTOTRACE OFF command.

To use SET AUTOTRACE, you must be able to access the database via SQL*Plus. If you have SQL access but not SQL*Plus access, you can use EXPLAIN PLAN instead, as described in the next section.

In the following example, a full table scan of the BOOKSHELF table is executed. The rows of output are not displayed for the sake of brevity. The order of operations is displayed after the query.

```
select *
from bookshelf;

Execution Plan
------------------------------------------------------------
   0      SELECT STATEMENT Optimizer=ALL_ROWS (Cost=1 Card=31 Bytes=12
          40)
   1   0    TABLE ACCESS (FULL) OF 'BOOKSHELF' (TABLE) (Cost=4 Card=31
          Bytes=1240)
```

The "Execution Plan" shows the steps the optimizer usese to execute the query. Each step is assigned an ID value (starting with 0). The second number shows the "parent" operation of the current operation. Thus, for the preceding example, the second operation—the TABLE ACCESS (FULL) OF 'BOOKSHELF'—has a parent operation (the SELECT statement itself). Each step displays a cumulative cost for that step plus all of its child steps.

You can generate the order of operations for DML commands, too. In the following example, a DELETE statement's execution path is shown:

```
delete
from bookshelf_author;

Execution Plan
------------------------------------------------------------
   0      DELETE STATEMENT Optimizer=ALL_ROWS (Cost=4 Card=37 Bytes=12
          58)
   1   0    DELETE OF 'BOOKSHELF_AUTHOR'
   2   1      TABLE ACCESS (FULL) OF 'BOOKSHELF_AUTHOR' (TABLE) (Cost=
          4 Card=37 Bytes=1258)
```

The DELETE command, as expected, involves a full table scan. If you have analyzed your tables, the EXECUTION PLAN's column's output shows the number of rows from each table, the relative cost of each step, and the overall cost of the operation. The costs shown at the steps are cumulative; they are the costs of that step plus all of its child steps. You could use that information to pinpoint the operations that are the most costly during the processing of the query.

In the following example, a slightly more complex query is executed. An index-based query is made against the BOOKSHELF table, using its primary key index.

```
select /*+ index(bookshelf) */ *
from bookshelf
where Title like 'M%';

Execution Plan
------------------------------------------------------------
   0      SELECT STATEMENT Optimizer=ALL_ROWS (Cost=3 Card=2 Bytes=80)
   1   0    TABLE ACCESS (BY INDEX ROWID) OF 'BOOKSHELF' (TABLE) (Cost
          =3 Card=2 Bytes=80)
   2   1      INDEX (RANGE SCAN) OF 'SYS_C004834' (INDEX (UNIQUE)) (Co
st=1 Card=2)
```

This listing includes three operations. Operation #2, the INDEX RANGE SCAN of the BOOKSHELF primary key index (its name was system-generated), provides data to operation #1, the TABLE ACCESS BY INDEX ROWID operation. The data returned from the TABLE ACCESS BY INDEX ROWID is used to satisfy the query (operation #0).

The preceding output also shows that the optimizer is automatically indenting each successive step within the execution plan. In general, you should read the list of operations from the inside out and from top to bottom. Thus, if two operations are listed, the one that is the most indented will usually be executed first. If the two operations are at the same level of indentation, then the one that is listed first (with the lowest operation number) will be executed first.

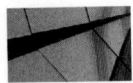

NOTE
Many factors influence the choices the optimizer makes when selecting an execution path for your query. When you execute the examples shown here in your database, the optimizer may choose a different path than is shown in the examples. That's okay; the optimizer is considering your database, environment, parameter settings, and options when determining which path to choose.

In the following example, BOOKSHELF and BOOKSHELF_AUTHOR are joined without the benefit of indexes. Oracle will use a join operation called a *merge join*, in which each table is separately sorted prior to the two sorted row sets being joined:

```
select /*+ use_merge (bookshelf, bookshelf_author)*/
bookshelf_author.authorname
from bookshelf, bookshelf_author
where bookshelf.title = bookshelf_author.title;


Execution Plan
----------------------------------------------------------
   0      SELECT STATEMENT Optimizer=ALL_ROWS (Cost=7 Card=5 Bytes=320)
   1    0   MERGE JOIN (Cost=7 Card=5 Bytes=320)
   2    1     INDEX (FULL SCAN) OF 'SYS_C004834' (INDEX (UNIQUE)) (Cos
          t=1 Card=31)
   3    1     SORT (JOIN) (Cost=5 Card=37 Bytes=1258)
   4    3       TABLE ACCESS (FULL) OF 'BOOKSHELF_AUTHOR' (TABLE) (Cos
          t=1 Card=37 Bytes=1258)
```

The indentation here may seem confusing at first, but the operational parentage information provided by the operation numbers clarifies the order of operations. The innermost operations are performed first—the TABLE ACCESS FULL and INDEX FULL SCAN operations. Next, the full table scan's data is processed via a SORT JOIN operation (in operation #4), whereas the output from the index scan (which is sorted already) is used as the basis for a TABLE ACCESS BY INDEX ROWID (step 2). Both step 2 and step 4 have operation #1, the MERGE JOIN, as their parent operations. The MERGE JOIN operation provides data back to the user via the SELECT statement.

If the same query were run as a NESTED LOOPS join, a different execution path would be generated. As shown in the following listing, the NESTED LOOPS join would be able to take advantage of the primary key index on the TITLE column of the BOOKSHELF table.

NOTE
Based on the size of the tables and the available statistics, Oracle may choose to perform a different type of join, called a hash join, instead of a NESTED LOOPS join.

```
select /*+ index(bookshelf) */
bookshelf_author.authorname
from bookshelf, bookshelf_author
where bookshelf.title = bookshelf_author.title;


Execution Plan
------------------------------------------------------------
   0       SELECT STATEMENT Optimizer=ALL_ROWS (Cost=4 Card=37 Bytes=19
           24)
   1    0    NESTED LOOPS (Cost=4 Card=37 Bytes=1924)
   2    1      TABLE ACCESS (FULL) OF 'BOOKSHELF_AUTHOR' (TABLE) (Cost=
           4 Card=37 Bytes=1258)
   3    1      INDEX (UNIQUE SCAN) OF 'SYS_C004834' (INDEX (UNIQUE))
 (Cost=1 Card=1 Bytes=18)
```

NESTED LOOPS joins are among the few execution paths that do not follow the "read from the inside out" rule of indented execution paths. To read the NESTED LOOPS execution path correctly, examine the order of the operations that directly provide data to the NESTED LOOPS operation (in this case, operations #2 and #3). Of those two operations, the operation with the lowest number (#2, in this example) is executed first. Thus, the TABLE ACCESS FULL of the BOOKSHELF_AUTHOR table is executed first (BOOKSHELF_AUTHOR is the driving table for the query).

Once you have established the driving table for the query, the rest of the execution path can be read from the inside out and from top to bottom. The second operation performed is the INDEX UNIQUE SCAN of the BOOKSHELF primary key index. The NESTED LOOPS operation is then able to return rows to the user.

If a hash join had been selected instead of a NESTED LOOPS join, the execution path would have been

```
select /*+ use_hash (bookshelf) */
bookshelf_author.authorname
from bookshelf, bookshelf_author
where bookshelf.title = bookshelf_author.title;


Execution Plan
------------------------------------------------------------
   0       SELECT STATEMENT Optimizer=ALL_ROWS (Cost=6 Card=37 Bytes=19
           24)
   1    0    HASH JOIN (Cost=6 Card=37 Bytes=1924)
   2    1      INDEX (FULL SCAN) OF 'SYS_C004834' (INDEX (UNIQUE))
 (Cost=2 Card=31 Bytes=558)
   3    1      TABLE ACCESS (FULL) OF 'BOOKSHELF_AUTHOR' (TABLE) (Cost=
           1 Card=37 Bytes=1258)
```

The hash join execution path shows that two separate scans are performed. Since the two operations are listed at the same level of indentation, the BOOKSHELF table's primary key index is scanned first (because it has the lower operation number).

Using EXPLAIN PLAN

You can use the EXPLAIN PLAN command to generate the execution path for a query without first running the query. To use the EXPLAIN PLAN command, you must first create a PLAN_TABLE table in your schema (see the previous instructions on creating the table). To determine the execution path of a query, prefix the query with the following SQL:

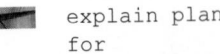

```
explain plan
for
```

An example of the execution of the EXPLAIN PLAN command is shown in the following listing:

```
explain plan
for
select /*+ use_hash (bookshelf) */
bookshelf_author.authorname
from bookshelf, bookshelf_author
where bookshelf.title = bookshelf_author.title;
```

When the EXPLAIN PLAN command is executed, records are inserted into PLAN_TABLE. You can query PLAN_TABLE directly, or you can use the DBMS_XPLAN package to format the results for you. The use of the DBMS_XPLAN package is shown in the following listing:

```
select * from table(dbms_xplan.display);
```

NOTE
*The **utlxplp.sql** script, located in the **$ORACLE_HOME/rdbms/admin** directory, displays the EXPLAIN PLAN for the most recently executed command by calling the DBMS_XPLAN.DISPLAY procedure.*

The result is a formatted explain plan listing:

```
PLAN_TABLE_OUTPUT
---------------------------------------------------------------------------
---------------------------------------------------------------------------
| Id | Operation          | Name             | Rows | Bytes | Cost (%CPU)| Time     |
---------------------------------------------------------------------------
|  0 | SELECT STATEMENT   |                  |   37 |  1924 |    4   (25)| 00:00:01 |
|* 1 | HASH JOIN          |                  |   37 |  1924 |    4   (25)| 00:00:01 |
|  2 | INDEX FULL SCAN    | SYS_C004834      |   32 |   608 |    1  (100)| 00:00:01 |
|  3 | TABLE ACCESS FULL  | BOOKSHELF_AUTHOR |   37 |  1258 |    4   (25)| 00:00:01 |


Predicate Information (identified by operation id):
---------------------------------------------------

   1 - access("BOOKSHELF"."TITLE"="BOOKSHELF_AUTHOR"."TITLE")
```

The output includes the COST column, which displays the relative "cost" of each step and its child steps. It also includes the ID values, indenting to show the relationships between steps, and an additional section listing the limiting conditions applied at each step.

When tuning a query, you should watch for steps that scan many rows but only return a small number of rows. For example, you should avoid performing a full table scan on a multimillion row table in order to return three rows. You can use the explain plan output to identify those steps that deal with the greatest number of rows.

Major Operations Within Explain Plans

As illustrated in the preceding listings, the explain plan for a query provides insight into the methods Oracle uses to retrieve and process rows. The following sections describe the most commonly used operations.

TABLE ACCESS FULL

A full table scan sequentially reads each row of a table. The optimizer calls the operation used during a full table scan a TABLE ACCESS FULL. To optimize the performance of a full table scan, Oracle reads multiple blocks during each database read.

A full table scan may be used whenever there is no WHERE clause on a query. For example, the following query selects all of the rows from the BOOKSHELF table:

```
select *
from BOOKSHELF;
```

To resolve the preceding query, Oracle performs a full table scan of the BOOKSHELF table. If the BOOKSHELF table is small, a full table scan of BOOKSHELF may be fairly quick, incurring little performance cost. As BOOKSHELF grows in size, however, the cost of performing a full table scan increases. If you have multiple users performing full table scans of BOOKSHELF, then the cost associated with the full table scan increases even more.

With proper planning, full table scans need not cause performance problems. You should work with your database administrators to ensure the database has been configured to take advantage of features such as Parallel Query and multi-block reads. Unless you have properly configured your environment for full table scans, you should carefully monitor their use.

NOTE
Depending on the data being selected, the optimizer may choose a full index scan in place of a full table scan.

TABLE ACCESS BY INDEX ROWID

To improve the performance of table accesses, you can use Oracle operations that access rows by their ROWID values. The ROWID records the physical location where the row is stored. Oracle uses indexes to correlate data values with ROWID values—and thus with the physical locations of the data. Given the ROWID of a row, Oracle can use the TABLE ACCESS BY INDEX ROWID operation to retrieve the row.

When you know the ROWID, you know exactly where the row is physically located. You can use indexes to access the ROWID information, as described in the next major section, "Operations That Use Indexes." Because indexes provide quick access to ROWID values, they help to improve the performance of queries that make use of indexed columns.

Related Hints

Within a query, you can specify hints that direct the optimizer in its processing of the query. To specify a hint, use the syntax shown in the following example. Immediately after the SELECT keyword, enter the following string:

```
/*+
```

Next, add the hint, such as

```
full(bookshelf)
```

Close the hint with the following string:

```
*/
```

Hints use Oracle's syntax for comments within queries, with the addition of the + sign at the start of the hint. Throughout this chapter, the hints relevant to each operation will be described. For table accesses, the FULL hint tells Oracle to perform a full table scan (the TABLE ACCESS FULL operation) on the listed table, as shown in the following listing:

```
select /*+ full(bookshelf) */ *
from bookshelf
where title like 'T%';
```

If you did not use the FULL hint, Oracle would normally plan to use the primary key index on the TTITLE column to resolve this query. Because the table is presently small, the full table scan is not costly. As the table grows, you would probably favor the use of a ROWID-based access for this query.

Operations That Use Indexes

Oracle has two major types of indexes: *unique indexes,* in which each row of the indexed table contains a unique value for the indexed column(s), and *non-unique indexes,* in which the rows' indexed values can repeat. The operations used to read data from the indexes depend on the type of index in use and the way in which you write the query that accesses the index.

Consider the BOOKSHELF table:

```
create table bookshelf
(title          varchar2(100) primary key,
 publisher      varchar2(20),
 category_name varchar2(20),
 rating         varchar2(2),
 constraint catfk foreign key (category_name)
 references category(category_name));
```

The TITLE column is the primary key for the BOOKSHELF table—that is, it uniquely identifies each row, and each attribute is dependent on the TITLE value.

Whenever a PRIMARY KEY or UNIQUE constraint is created, Oracle creates a unique index to enforce uniqueness of the values in the column. As defined by the CREATE TABLE command, a PRIMARY KEY constraint will be created on the BOOKSHELF table. The index that supports the primary key will be given a system-generated name because the constraint was not explicitly named.

You can create indexes on other columns of the BOOKSHELF table manually. For example, you could create a non-unique index on the CATEGORY_NAME column via the CREATE INDEX command:

```
create index i_bookshelf_category
    on bookshelf(category_name)
tablespace indexes;
```

The BOOKSHELF table now has two indexes on it: a unique index on the TITLE column and a non-unique index on the CATEGORY_NAME column. One or more of the indexes could be used during query resolution, depending on how the query is written and executed. As part of the index creation, its statistics are automatically built. Because the table is already populated with rows, you do not need to execute a separate command to analyze the index.

INDEX UNIQUE SCAN

To use an index during a query, your query must be written to allow the use of an index. In most cases, you allow the optimizer to use an index via the WHERE clause of the query. For example, the following query could use the unique index on the TITLE column:

```
select *
from bookshelf
where title = 'Innumeracy';
```

Internally, the execution of the preceding query is divided into two steps. First, the TITLE column index is accessed via an INDEX UNIQUE SCAN operation. The ROWID value that matches the title 'Innumeracy' is returned from the index; that ROWID value is then used to query BOOKSHELF via a TABLE ACCESS BY INDEX ROWID operation.

If all of the columns selected by the query had been contained within the index, then Oracle would not need to use the TABLE ACCESS BY INDEX ROWID operation; because the data would be in the index, the index would be all you need to satisfy the query. Because the query selected all columns from the BOOKSHELF table, and the index did not contain all of the columns of the BOOKSHELF table, the TABLE ACCESS BY INDEX ROWID operation was necessary.

INDEX RANGE SCAN

If you query the database based on a range of values, or if you query using a non-unique index, then you use an INDEX RANGE SCAN operation to query the index.

Consider the BOOKSHELF table again, with a unique index on its TITLE column. A query of the form

```
select title
from bookshelf
where title like 'M%';
```

would return all TITLE values beginning with "M". Since the WHERE clause uses the TITLE column, the primary key index on the TITLE column can be used while resolving the query. However, a unique value is not specified in the WHERE clause; a range of values is specified. Therefore, the unique primary key index will be accessed via an INDEX RANGE SCAN operation. Because INDEX RANGE SCAN operations require reading multiple values from the index, they are less efficient than INDEX UNIQUE SCAN operations.

In the preceding example, only the TITLE column was selected by the query. Because the values for the TITLE column are stored in the primary key index—which is being scanned—there is no need for the database to access the BOOKSHELF table directly during the query execution. The INDEX RANGE SCAN of the primary key index is the only operation required to resolve the query.

The CATEGORY_NAME column of the BOOKSHELF table has a non-unique index on its values. If you specify a limiting condition for CATEGORY_NAME values in your query's WHERE clause, an INDEX RANGE SCAN of the CATEGORY_NAME index may be performed. Because the BOOKSHELF$CATEGORY index is a non-unique index, the database cannot perform an INDEX UNIQUE SCAN on BOOKSHELF$CATEGORY, even if CATEGORY_NAME is equated to a single value in your query.

When Indexes Are Used

Since indexes have a great impact on query performance, you should be aware of the conditions under which an index will be used to resolve a query. The following sections describe the conditions in which an index is used while resolving a query.

If You Set an Indexed Column Equal to a Value

In the BOOKSHELF table, the CATEGORY_NAME column has a non-unique index named BOOKSHELF$CATEGORY. A query that compares the CATEGORY_NAME column to a value will be able to use the BOOKSHELF$CATEGORY index.

The following query compares the CATEGORY_NAME column to the value "ADULTNF":

```
select title
from bookshelf
where category_name= 'ADULTNF';
```

Because the BOOKSHELF$CATEGORY index is a non-unique index, this query may return multiple rows, and an INDEX RANGE SCAN operation may be used when reading data from it. Depending on the table's statistics, Oracle may choose to perform a full table scan instead.

If it uses the index, the execution of the preceding query may include two operations: an INDEX RANGE SCAN of BOOKSHELF$CATEGORY (to get the ROWID values for all of the rows with "ADULTNF" values in the CATEGORY_NAME column), followed by a TABLE ACCESS BY INDEX ROWID of the BOOKSHELF table (to retrieve the TITLE column values).

If a column has a unique index created on it, and the column is compared to a value with an = sign, then an INDEX UNIQUE SCAN will be used instead of an INDEX RANGE SCAN.

If You Specify a Range of Values for an Indexed Column

You do not need to specify explicit values for an index to be used. The INDEX RANGE SCAN operation can scan an index for ranges of values. In the following query, the TITLE column of the BOOKSHELF table is queried for a range of values (those that start with "M"):

```
select title
from bookshelf
where title like 'M%';
```

You can also perform a range scan when using the > or < operators:

```
select title
from bookshelf
where title > 'M';
```

When specifying a range of values for a column, an index will not be used to resolve the query if the first character specified is a wildcard. The following query will *not* perform an INDEX RANGE SCAN on the available indexes:

```
select publisher
from bookshelf
where title like '%M%';
```

Because the first character of the string used for value comparisons is a wildcard, the index cannot be used to find the associated data quickly. Therefore, a full table scan (TABLE ACCESS FULL operation) is performed instead. Depending on the statistics for the table and the index, Oracle may choose to perform a full scan of the index. In this example, if the selected column is the TITLE column, the optimizer may choose to perform a full scan of the primary key index rather than a full scan of the BOOKSHELF table.

If No Functions Are Performed on the Column in the WHERE Clause

Consider the following query, which uses the BOOKSHELF$CATEGORY index:

```
select count(*)
from bookshelf
where category_name= 'ADULTNF';
```

NOTE
Given the size of the BOOKSHELF table, the optimizer will usually elect to perform a full table scan rather than use an index for this lookup. For larger tables, the index-based approach should be chosen.

What if you did not know whether the values in the CATEGORY_NAME column were stored as uppercase, mixed case, or lowercase values? In that event, you may write the query as follows:

```
select count(*)
from bookshelf
where upper(category_name) = 'ADULTNF';
```

The UPPER function changes the MANAGER values to uppercase before comparing them to the value "ADULTNF". However, using the function on the column may prevent the optimizer from using an index on that column. The preceding query (using the UPPER function) will perform a TABLE ACCESS FULL on the BOOKSHELF table unless you have created a function-based index on UPPER(CATEGORY_NAME); see Chapter 17 for details on function-based indexes.

If you concatenate two columns together or a string to a column, then indexes on those columns will not be used. The index stores the real value for the column, and any change to that value will prevent the optimizer from using the index. A function-based index on the concatenated columns can also help in this scenario.

If No IS NULL or IS NOT NULL Checks Are Used for the Indexed Column

NULL values are not stored in indexes. Therefore, the following query will not use an index; there is no way the index could help to resolve the query:

```
select title
from bookshelf
where category_name is null;
```

Since CATEGORY_NAME is the only column with a limiting condition in the query, and the limiting condition is a NULL check, the BOOKSHELF$CATEGORY index will not be used and a TABLE ACCESS FULL operation will be used to resolve the query.

What if an IS NOT NULL check is performed on the column? All of the non-NULL values for the column are stored in the index; however, the index search would not be efficient. To resolve the query, the optimizer needs to read every value from the index and access the table for each row returned from the index. In most cases, perform a full table scan would be more efficient than performing an index scan (with associated TABLE ACCESS BY INDEX ROWID operations) for all of the values returned from the index. Therefore, the following query may not use an index:

```
select title
from bookshelf
where category_nameis not null;
```

If the selected columns are in an index, the optimizer may choose to perform a full index scan in place of the full table scan.

If Equivalence Conditions Are Used

In the examples in the prior sections, the TITLE value was compared to a value with an = sign, as in this query:

```
select *
from bookshelf
where title = 'Innumeracy';
```

What if you want to select all of the records that do not have a TITLE of "Innumeracy"? The = would be replaced with !=, and the query would now be

```
select *
from bookshelf
where title != 'Innumeracy';
```

When resolving the revised query, the optimizer may not use an index. Indexes are used when values are compared exactly to another value—when the limiting conditions are equalities, not inequalities. The optimizer only chooses an index in this example if it decides the full index scan (plus the TABLE ACCESS BY INDEX ROWID operations to get all the columns) would be faster than a full table scan.

Another example of an inequality is the NOT IN clause when used with a subquery. The following query selects values from the BOOKSHELF table for books that aren't written by Stephen Jay Gould:

```
select *
from bookshelf
where title not in
(select title
 from bookshelf_author
 where author_name = 'Stephen Jay Gould');
```

In some cases, the query in the preceding listing would not be able to use an index on the TITLE column of the BOOKSHELF table because it is not set equal to any value. Instead, the BOOKSHELF.TITLE value is used with a NOT IN clause to eliminate the rows that match those returned by the subquery. To use an index, you should set the indexed column equal to a value. In many cases, Oracle will internally rewrite the NOT IN as a NOT EXISTS clause, allowing the query to use an index. The following query, which uses an IN clause, could use an index on the BOOKSHELF.TITLE column or it could perform a non-indexed join between the tables; the optimizer will choose the path with the lowest cost based on the available statistics:

```
select *
from bookshelf
where title in
(select title
 from bookshelf_author
 where author_name= 'Stephen Jay Gould');
```

If the Leading Column of a Multicolumn Index Is Set Equal to a Value

An index can be created on a single column or on multiple columns. If the index is created on multiple columns, the index will be used if the leading column of the index is used in a limiting condition of the query.

If your query specifies values for only the non-leading columns of the index, the index can be used via the index skip-scan feature. Skip-scan index access enables the optimizer to potentially use a concatenated index even if its leading column is not listed in the WHERE clause. You may need to use the INDEX hint (described later in this section) to tell the optimizer to use the index for skip-scan access. You can use the INDEX_SS hint to suggest a skip-scan index access.

If the MAX or MIN Function Is Used

If you select the MAX or MIN value of an indexed column, the optimizer may use the index to quickly find the maximum or minimum value for the column.

If the Index Is Selective

All of the previous rules for determining whether an index will be used consider the syntax of the query being performed and the structure of the index available. The optimizer can use the selectivity of the index to judge whether using the index will lower the cost of executing the query.

In a highly selective index, a small number of records are associated with each distinct column value. For example, if a table has 100 records and a column in that table has 80 distinct values, the selectivity of an index on that column is 80 / 100 = 0.80. The higher the selectivity, the fewer the number of rows returned for each distinct value in the column.

The number of rows returned per distinct value is important during range scans. If an index has a low selectivity, then the many INDEX RANGE SCAN operations and TABLE ACCESS BY INDEX ROWID operations used to retrieve the data may involve more work than a TABLE ACCESS FULL of the table.

The selectivity of an index is not considered by the optimizer unless you have analyzed the index. The optimizer can use histograms to make judgments about the distribution of data within a table. For example, if the data values are heavily skewed so that most of the values are in a very small data range, the optimizer may avoid using the index for values in that range while using the index for values outside the range.

Related Hints

Several hints are available to direct the optimizer in its use of indexes. The INDEX hint is the most commonly used index-related hint. The INDEX hint tells the optimizer to use an index-based scan on the specified table. You do not need to mention the index name when using the INDEX hint, although you can list specific indexes if you choose.

For example, the following query uses the INDEX hint to suggest the use of an index on the BOOKSHELF table during the resolution of the query:

```
select /*+ index(bookshelf bookshelf$category) */ title
from bookshelf
where category_name= 'ADULTNF';
```

According to the rules provided earlier in this section, the preceding query should use the index without the hint being needed. If the index is nonselective or the table is small, however, the optimizer may choose to ignore the index. If you know that the index is selective for the data values given, you can use the INDEX hint to force an index-based data access path to be used.

In the hint syntax, name the table (or its alias, if you give the table an alias) and, optionally, the name of the suggested index. The optimizer may choose to disregard any hints you provide.

If you do not list a specific index in the INDEX hint, and multiple indexes are available for the table, the optimizer evaluates the available indexes and chooses the index whose scan is likely to have the lowest cost. The optimizer could also choose to scan several indexes and merge them via the AND-EQUAL operation.

A second hint, INDEX_ASC, functions the same as the INDEX hint: It suggests an ascending index scan for resolving queries against specific tables. A third index-based hint, INDEX_DESC, tells the optimizer to scan the index in descending order (from its highest value to its lowest). To suggest an index fast full scan, use the INDEX_FFS hint. The ROWID hint is similar to the INDEX hint, suggesting the use of the TABLE ACCESS BY INDEX ROWID method for the specified table. The AND_EQUAL hint suggests the optimizer merge the results of multiple index scans.

Additional Tuning Issues for Indexes

When you're creating indexes on a table, two issues commonly arise: Should you use multiple indexes or a single concatenated index, and if you use a concatenated index, which column should be the leading column of the index?

In general, it is faster for the optimizer to scan a single concatenated index than to scan and merge two separate indexes. The more rows returned from the scan, the more likely the concatenated index scan will outperform the merge of the two index scans. As you add more columns to the concatenated index, it becomes less efficient for range scans.

For the concatenated index, which column should be the leading column of the index? The leading column should frequently be used as a limiting condition against the table, and it should be highly selective. In a concatenated index, the optimizer bases its estimates of the index's selectivity (and thus its likelihood of being used) on the selectivity of the leading column of the index. Of these two criteria—being used in limiting conditions and being the most selective column—the first is more important.

A highly selective index based on a column that is never used in limiting conditions will never be used. A poorly selective index on a column that is frequently used in limiting conditions will not benefit your performance greatly. If you cannot achieve the goal of creating an index that is both highly selective and frequently used, then you should consider creating separate indexes for the columns to be indexed.

Many applications emphasize online transaction processing over batch processing; there may be many concurrent online users but a small number of concurrent batch users. In general, index-based scans allow online users to access data more quickly than if a full table scan had been performed. When creating your application, you should be aware of the kinds of queries executed within the application and the limiting conditions in those queries. If you are familiar with the queries executed against the database, you may be able to index the tables so the online users can quickly retrieve the data they need. When the database performance directly impacts the online business process, the application should perform as few database accesses as possible.

Operations That Manipulate Data Sets

Once the data has been returned from the table or index, it can be manipulated. You can group the records, sort them, count them, lock them, or merge the results of the query with the results of other queries (via the UNION, MINUS, and INTERSECT operators). In the following sections, you'll see how the data manipulation operations are used.

Most of the operations that manipulate sets of records do not return records to the users until the entire operation is completed. For example, sorting records while eliminating duplicates (known as a SORT UNIQUE NOSORT operation) cannot return records to the user until all of the records have been evaluated for uniqueness. On the other hand, index scan operations and table access operations can return records to the user as soon as a record is found.

When an INDEX RANGE SCAN operation is performed, the first row returned from the query passes the criteria of the limiting conditions set by the query—there is no need to evaluate the next record returned prior to displaying the first record. If a set operation—such as a sorting operation—is performed, then the records will not be immediately displayed. During set operations, the user has to wait for all rows to be processed by the operation. Therefore, you should limit the number of set operations performed by queries used by online users (to limit the application's perceived response time). Sorting and grouping operations are most common in large reports and batch transactions.

Ordering Rows

Three of Oracle's internal operations sort rows without grouping the rows. The first is the SORT ORDER BY operation, which is used when an ORDER BY clause is used in a query. For example, the BOOKSHELF table is queried and sorted by PUBLISHER:

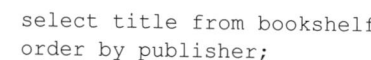

```
select title from bookshelf
order by publisher;
```

When the preceding query is executed, the optimizer retrieves the data from the BOOKSHELF table via a TABLE ACCESS FULL operation (since there are no limiting conditions for the query, all rows will be returned). The retrieved records are not immediately displayed to the user; a SORT ORDER BY operation sorts the records before the user sees any results.

Occasionally, a sorting operation may be required to eliminate duplicates as it sorts records. For example, what if you only want to see the distinct PUBLISHER values in the BOOKSHELF table? The query would be as follows:

```
select distinct publisher from bookshelf;
```

As with the prior query, this query has no limiting conditions, so a TABLE ACCESS FULL operation will be used to retrieve the records from the BOOKSHELF table. However, the DISTINCT keyword tells the optimizer to return only the distinct values for the PUBLISHER column.

To resolve the query, the optimizer takes the records returned by the TABLE ACCESS FULL operation and sorts them via a SORT UNIQUE NOSORT operation. No records are displayed to the user until all of the records have been processed.

In addition to being used by the DISTINCT keyword, the SORT UNIQUE NOSORT operation is invoked when the MINUS, INTERSECT, and UNION (but not UNION ALL) functions are used.

A third sorting operation, SORT JOIN, is always used as part of a MERGE JOIN operation and is never used on its own. The implications of SORT JOIN on the performance of joins are described in "Operations That Perform Joins," later in this chapter.

Grouping Rows

Two of Oracle's internal operations sort rows while grouping like records together. The two operations— SORT AGGREGATE and SORT GROUP BY—are used in conjunction with grouping functions (such as MIN, MAX, and COUNT). The syntax of the query determines which operation is used.

In the following query, the maximum PUBLISHER value, alphabetically, is selected from the BOOKSHELF table:

```
select max(publisher)
from bookshelf;
```

To resolve the query, the optimizer performs two separate operations. First, a TABLE ACCESS FULL operation selects the PUBLISHER values from the table. Second, the rows are analyzed via a SORT AGGREGATE operation, which returns the maximum PUBLISHER value to the user.

If the PUBLISHER column were indexed, the index could be used to resolve queries of the maximum or minimum value for the index (as described in "Operations That Use Indexes," earlier in this chapter). Because the PUBLISHER column is not indexed, a sorting operation is required. The maximum PUBLISHER value will not be returned by this query until all of the records have been read and the SORT AGGREGATE operation has completed.

The SORT AGGREGATE operation was used in the preceding example because there was no GROUP BY clause in the query. Queries that use the GROUP BY clause use an internal operation named SORT GROUP BY.

What if you want to know the number of titles from each publisher? The following query selects the count of each PUBLISHER value from the BOOKSHELF table using a GROUP BY clause:

```
select publisher, count(*)
from bookshelf
group by publisher;
```

This query returns one record for each distinct PUBLISHER value. For each PUBLISHER value, the number of its occurrences in the BOOKSHELF table are calculated and displayed in the COUNT(*) column.

To resolve this query, Oracle first performs a full table scan (there are no limiting conditions for the query). Since a GROUP BY clause is used, the rows returned from the TABLE ACCESS FULL operation are processed by a SORT GROUP BY operation. Once all the rows have been sorted into groups and the count for each group has been calculated, the records are returned to the user. As with the other sorting operations, no records are returned to the user until all of the records have been processed.

The operations to this point have involved simple examples—full table scans, index scans, and sorting operations. Most queries that access a single table use the operations described in the previous sections. When tuning a query for an online user, avoid using the sorting and grouping operations that force users to wait for records to be processed. When possible, write queries that allow application users to receive records quickly as the query is resolved. The fewer sorting and grouping operations you perform, the faster the first record will be returned to the user. In a batch transaction, the performance of the query is measured by its overall time to complete, not the time to return the first row. As a result, batch transactions may use sorting and grouping operations without impacting the application's perceived performance.

If your application does not require all of the rows to be sorted prior to presenting query output, consider using the FIRST_ROWS hint. FIRST_ROWS tells the optimizer to favor execution paths that do not perform set operations.

UNION, MINUS, and INTERSECT

The UNION, MINUS, and INTERSECT clauses allow the results of multiple queries to be processed and compared. Each of the functions has an associated operation—the names of the operations are UNION, MINUS, and INTERSECTION.

The following query selects all of the TITLE values from the BOOKSHELF table and from the BOOK_ORDER table:

```
select title
from bookshelf
union
select title
from book_order;
```

When the preceding query is executed, the optimizer executes each of the queries separately and then combines the results. The first query is

```
select title
from bookshelf
```

There are no limiting conditions in the query, and the TITLE column is indexed, so the primary key index on the BOOKSHELF table will be scanned.

The second query is

```
select title
from book_order
```

There are no limiting conditions in the query, and the TITLE column is indexed, so the primary key index on the BOOK_ORDER table will be scanned.

Because the query performs a UNION of the results of the two queries, the two result sets are then merged via a UNION-ALL operation. Using the UNION operator forces Oracle to eliminate duplicate records, so the result set is processed by a SORT UNIQUE NOSORT operation before the records are returned to the user. If the query had used a UNION ALL clause in place of UNION, the SORT UNIQUE NOSORT operation would not have been necessary. The query would be

```
select title
from bookshelf
union all
select title
from book_order;
```

When processing the revised query, the optimizer would perform the scans required by the two queries, followed by a UNION-ALL operation. No SORT UNIQUE NOSORT operation would be required because a UNION ALL clause does not eliminate duplicate records.

When processing the UNION query, the optimizer addresses each of the UNIONed queries separately. Although the examples shown in the preceding listings all involve simple queries with full table scans, the UNIONed queries can be very complex, with correspondingly complex execution paths. The results are not returned to the user until all of the records have been processed.

NOTE
UNION ALL is a row operation. UNION, which includes a SORT UNIQUE NOSORT, is a set operation.

When a MINUS clause is used, the query is processed in a manner very similar to the execution path used for the UNION example. In the following query, the TITLE values from the BOOKSHELF and BOOK_ORDER tables are compared. If a TITLE value exists in BOOK_ORDER but does not exist in BOOKSHELF, then that value will be returned by the query. In other words, we want to see all of the titles on order that we don't already have.

```
select title
from book_order
minus
select title
from bookshelf;
```

When the query is executed, the two MINUSed queries are executed separately. The first of the queries

```
select title
from book_order
```

requires an index scan based on the BOOK_ORDER primary key. The second query

```
select title
from bookshelf
```

requires a full index scan of the BOOKSHELF primary key index. Here is a typical EXPLAIN PLAN for that operation:

```
---------------------------------------------------------------------------
| Id | Operation           | Name         | Rows | Bytes | Cost (%CPU)| Time     |
---------------------------------------------------------------------------
|  0 | SELECT STATEMENT    |              |    4 |   772 |    4  (75)| 00:00:01 |
|  1 |  MINUS              |              |      |       |           |          |
|  2 |   SORT UNIQUE NOSORT|              |    4 |    52 |    2  (50)| 00:00:01 |
|  3 |    INDEX FULL SCAN  | SYS_C0010190 |    4 |    52 |    1   (0)| 00:00:01 |
|  4 |   SORT UNIQUE NOSORT|              |   36 |   720 |    2  (50)| 00:00:01 |
|  5 |    INDEX FULL SCAN  | SYS_C0010194 |   36 |   720 |    1   (0)| 00:00:01 |
---------------------------------------------------------------------------
```

To execute the MINUS clause, each of the sets of records returned by the full table scans is sorted via a SORT UNIQUE NOSORT operation (in which rows are sorted and duplicates are eliminated). The sorted sets of rows are then processed by the MINUS operation. The MINUS operation is not performed until each set of records returned by the queries is sorted. Neither of the sorting operations returns records until the sorting operation completes, so the MINUS operation cannot begin until both of the SORT UNIQUE NOSORT operations have completed. Like the UNION query example, the example query shown for the MINUS operation will perform poorly for online users who measure performance by the speed with which the first row is returned by the query.

The INTERSECT clause compares the results of two queries and determines the rows they have in common. The following query determines the TITLE values that are found in both the BOOKSHELF and BOOK_ORDER tables:

```
select title
from book_order
intersect
select title
from bookshelf;
```

To process the INTERSECT query, the optimizer starts by evaluating each of the queries separately. The first query

```
select title
from book_order
```

requires a full scan against the BOOK_ORDER primary key index. The second query

```
select title
from bookshelf
```

requires a full scan of the BOOKSHELF primary key index. The results of the two table scans are each processed separately by SORT UNIQUE NOSORT operations. That is, the rows from BOOK_ORDER are sorted, and the rows from BOOKSHELF are sorted. The results of the two sorts are compared by the INTERSECTION operation, and the TITLE values returned from both sorts are returned by the INTERSECT clause.

The execution path of a query that uses an INTERSECT clause requires SORT UNIQUE NOSORT operations to be used. Since SORT UNIQUE NOSORT operations do not return records to the user until the entire set of rows has been sorted, queries using the INTERSECT clause have to wait for both sorts to complete before the INTERSECTION operation can be performed. Because of the reliance on sort operations, queries using the INTERSECT clause will not return any records to the user until the sorts complete.

The UNION, MINUS, and INTERSECT clauses all involve processing sets of rows prior to returning any rows to the user. Online users of an application may perceive that queries using these functions perform poorly, even if the table accesses involved are tuned; the reliance on sorting operations will affect the speed with which the first row is returned to the user.

Selecting from Views

When you create a view, Oracle stores the query that the view is based on. For example, the following view is based on the BOOKSHELF table:

```
create or replace view adultfic as
select title, publisher
from bookshelf
where category_name= 'ADULTFIC';
```

When you select from the ADULTFIC view, the optimizer takes the criteria from your query and combines them with the query text of the view. If you specify limiting conditions in your query of the view, those limiting conditions will—if possible—be applied to the view's query text. For example, if you execute the query

```
select title, publisher
from adultfic
where title like 'T%';
```

the optimizer will combine your limiting condition

```
where title like 'T%';
```

with the view's query text, and it will execute the query:

```
select title, publisher
from bookshelf
where category_name= 'ADULTFIC'
and title like 'T%';
```

In this example, the view has no impact on the query's performance. When the view's text is merged with your query's limiting conditions, the options available to the optimizer increase; it can choose among more indexes and more data access paths.

The way that a view is processed depends on the query on which the view is based. If the view's query text cannot be merged with the query that uses the view, the view will be resolved first before the rest of the conditions are applied. Consider the following view:

```
create or replace view publisher_count as
select publisher, count(*) count_pub
from bookshelf
group by publisher;
```

The PUBLISHER_COUNT view displays one row for each distinct PUBLISHER value in the BOOKSHELF table along with the number of records that have that value. The COUNT_PUB column of the PUBLISHER_COUNT view records the count per distinct PUBLISHER value.

How will the optimizer process the following query of the PUBLISHER_COUNT view?

```
select *
from publisher_count
where count_pub > 1;
```

The query refers to the view's COUNT_PUB column. However, the query's WHERE clause cannot be combined with the view's query text because COUNT_PUB is created via a grouping operation. The WHERE clause cannot be applied until *after* the result set from the PUBLISHER_COUNT view has been completely resolved.

Views that contain grouping operations are resolved before the rest of the query's criteria are applied. Like the sorting operations, views with grouping operations do not return any records until the entire result set has been processed. If the view does not contain grouping operations, the query text may be merged with the limiting conditions of the query that selects from the view. As a result, views with grouping operations limit the number of choices available to the optimizer and do not return records until all of the rows are processed—and such views may perform poorly when queried by online users.

When the query is processed, the optimizer first resolves the view. Because the view's query is

```
select publisher, count(*) count_pub
from bookshelf
group by publisher;
```

the optimizer reads the data from the BOOKSHELF table via a TABLE ACCESS FULL operation. Since a GROUP BY clause is used, the rows from the TABLE ACCESS FULL operation are processed by a SORT GROUP BY operation. An additional operation—FILTER—then processes the data. The FILTER operation is used to eliminate rows based on the criteria in the query:

```
where count_pub > 1
```

If you use a view that has a GROUP BY clause, rows will not be returned from the view until all of the rows have been processed by the view. As a result, it may take a long time for the query to return the first row, and online users may perceive the view's performance as unacceptable. If you can remove the sorting and grouping operations from your views, you increase the likelihood that the view text can be merged with the text of the query that calls the view—and as a result, performance may improve (although the query may use other set operations that negatively impact performance).

When the query text is merged with the view text, the options available to the optimizer increase. For example, combining the query's limiting conditions with the view's limiting conditions may allow a previously unusable index to be used during query execution.

The automatic merging of the query text and view text can be disabled via the NO_MERGE hint. The PUSH_PRED hint forces a join predicate into a view; PUSH_SUBQ causes nonmerged subqueries to be evaluated as early as possible in the execution path.

Selecting from Subqueries

Whenever possible, the optimizer combines the text from a subquery with the rest of the query. For example, consider the following query:

```
select title
from bookshelf
where title in
(select title from book_order);
```

The optimizer, in evaluating the preceding query, determines that the query is functionally equivalent to the following join of the BOOKSHELF and BOOK_ORDER tables:

```
selectbookshelf.title
from bookshelf, book_order
where bookshelf.title = book_order.title;
```

With the query now written as a join, the optimizer has a number of operations available to process the data (as described in the following section, "Operations That Perform Joins").

If the subquery cannot be resolved as a join, it will be resolved before the rest of the query text is processed against the data—similar in function to the manner in which the FILTER operation is used for views. As a matter of fact, the FILTER operation is used for subqueries if the subqueries cannot be merged with the rest of the query!

Subqueries that rely on grouping operations have the same tuning issues as views that contain grouping operations. The rows from such subqueries must be fully processed before the rest of the query's limiting conditions can be applied.

Operations That Perform Joins

Often, a single query needs to select columns from multiple tables. To select the data from multiple tables, the tables are joined in the SQL statement—the tables are listed in the FROM clause, and the join conditions are listed in the WHERE clause. In the following example, the BOOKSHELF and BOOK_ORDER tables are joined, based on their common TITLE column values:

```
selectbookshelf.title
from bookshelf, book_order
where bookshelf.title = book_order.title;
```

which can be rewritten as

```
select title
from bookshelf inner join book_order
using (title);
```

or

```
select title
from bookshelf natural inner join book_order;
```

The join conditions can function as limiting conditions for the join. Because the BOOKSHELF .TITLE column is equated to a value in the WHERE clause in the first listing, the optimizer may be able to use an index on the BOOKSHELF.TITLE column during query execution. If an index is available on the BOOK_ORDER.TITLE column, that index would be considered for use by the optimizer as well.

Oracle has three main methods for processing joins: MERGE JOIN operations, NESTED LOOPS operations, and HASH JOIN operations. Based on the conditions in your query, the available indexes, and the available statistics, the optimizer chooses which join operation to use. Depending on the nature of your application and queries, you may want to force the optimizer to use a method different from its first choice of join methods. The following sections describe the characteristics of the different join methods and the conditions under which each is most useful.

How Oracle Handles Joins of More Than Two Tables

If a query joins more than two tables, the optimizer treats the query as a set of multiple joins. For example, if your query joins three tables, then the optimizer executes the joins by joining two of the tables together and then joining the result set of that join to the third table. The size of the result set from the initial join impacts the performance of the rest of the joins. If the size of the result set from the initial join is large, then many rows will be processed by the second join.

If your query joins three tables of varying size—such as a small table named SMALL, a medium-sized table named MEDIUM, and a large table named LARGE—you need to be aware of the order in which the tables will be joined. If the join of MEDIUM to LARGE returns many rows, then the join of the result set of that join with the SMALL table may perform a great deal of work. Alternatively, if SMALL and MEDIUM are joined first, then the join between the result set of the SMALL-MEDIUM join and the LARGE table may minimize the amount of work performed by the query.

MERGE JOIN

In a MERGE JOIN operation, the two inputs to the join are processed separately, sorted, and joined. MERGE JOIN operations are commonly used when there are no indexes available for the limiting conditions of the query.

In the following query, the BOOKSHELF and BOOKSHELF_AUTHOR tables are joined. If neither table has an index on its TITLE column, then there are no indexes that can be used during the query (since there are no other limiting conditions in the query). This example uses a hint to force the use of MERGE JOIN:

```
select /*+ use_merge (bookshelf, bookshelf_author)*/
bookshelf_author.authorname
from bookshelf, bookshelf_author
where bookshelf.title = bookshelf_author.title
  and bookshelf.publisher> 'T%';
```

or

```
select /*+ use_merge (bookshelf, bookshelf_author)*/
bookshelf_author.authorname
from bookshelf inner join bookshelf_author
   on bookshelf.title = bookshelf_author.title
where bookshelf.publisher> 'T%';
```

To resolve the query, the optimizer may choose to perform a MERGE JOIN of the tables. To perform the MERGE JOIN, each of the tables is read individually (usually by a TABLE ACCESS FULL operation or a full index scan). The set of rows returned from the table scan of the BOOKSHELF_AUTHOR table is sorted by a SORT JOIN operation. The set of rows returned from the INDEX FULL SCAN and TABLE ACCESS BY INDEX ROWID of the BOOKSHELF table is already sorted (in the index), so no additional SORT JOIN operation is needed for that part of the execution path. The data from the SORT JOIN operations is then merged via a MERGE JOIN operation.

When a MERGE JOIN operation is used to join two sets of records, each set of records is processed separately before being joined. The MERGE JOIN operation cannot begin until it has received data from both of the SORT JOIN operations that provide input to it. The SORT JOIN operations, in turn, will not provide data to the MERGE JOIN operation until all of the rows have been sorted. If indexes are used as data sources, the SORT JOIN operations may be bypassed.

If the MERGE JOIN operation has to wait for two separate SORT JOIN operations to complete, a join that uses the MERGE JOIN operation will typically perform poorly for online users. The perceived poor performance is due to the delay in returning the first row of the join to the users. As the tables increase in size, the time required for the sorts to be completed increases dramatically. If the tables are of greatly unequal size, then the sorting operation performed on the larger table will negatively impact the performance of the overall query.

Because MERGE JOIN operations involve full scanning and sorting of the tables involved, you should only use MERGE JOIN operations if both tables are very small or if both tables are very large. If both tables are very small, then the process of scanning and sorting the tables will complete quickly. If both tables are very large, then the sorting and scanning operations required by MERGE JOIN operations can take advantage of Oracle's parallel options.

Oracle can parallelize operations, allowing multiple processors to participate in the execution of a single command. Among the operations that can be parallelized are the TABLE ACCESS FULL and sorting operations. Since a MERGE JOIN uses the TABLE ACCESS FULL and sorting operations, it can take full advantage of Oracle's parallel options. Parallelizing queries involving MERGE JOIN operations frequently improves query performance (provided adequate system resources are available to support the parallel operations).

NESTED LOOPS

NESTED LOOPS operations join two tables via a looping method: The records from one table are retrieved, and for each record retrieved, an access is performed of the second table. The access of the second table is performed via an index-based access.

A form of the query from the preceding MERGE JOIN section is shown in the following listing. A hint is used to recommend an index-based access of the BOOKSHELF table:

```
select /*+ index(bookshelf) */
bookshelf.publisher,
bookshelf_author.authorname
from bookshelf, bookshelf_author
where bookshelf.title = bookshelf_author.title;
```

Since the TITLE column of the BOOKSHELF table is used as part of the join condition in the query, the primary key index can resolve the join. When the query is executed, a NESTED LOOPS operation can be used to execute the join.

To execute a NESTED LOOPS join, the optimizer must first select a *driving table* for the join, which is the table that will be read first (usually via a TABLE ACCESS FULL operation, although index scans are commonly seen). For each record in the driving table, the second table in the join will be queried. The example query joins BOOKSHELF and BOOKSHELF_AUTHOR, based on values of the TITLE column. During the NESTED LOOPS execution, an operation selects all of the records from the BOOKSHELF_AUTHOR table. The primary key index of the BOOKSHELF table is probed to determine whether it contains an entry for the value in the current record from the BOOKSHELF_AUTHOR table. If a match is found, then the TITLE value will be returned from the BOOKSHELF primary key index. If other columns were needed from BOOKSHELF, the row would be selected from the BOOKSHELF table via a TABLE ACCESS BY INDEX ROWID operation.

At least two data access operations are involved in the NESTED LOOPS join: an access of the driving table and an access, usually index-based, of the driven table. The data access methods most commonly used—TABLE ACCESS FULL, TABLE ACCESS BY INDEX ROWID, and index scans—return records to successive operations as soon as a record is found; they do not wait for the whole set of records to be selected. Because these operations can provide the first matching rows quickly to users, NESTED LOOPS joins are commonly used for joins that are frequently executed by online users.

When implementing NESTED LOOPS joins, you need to consider the size of the driving table. If the driving table is large and is read via a full table scan, then the TABLE ACCESS FULL operation performed on it may negatively affect the performance of the query. If indexes are available on both sides of the join, Oracle will select a driving table for the query. The optimizer checks the statistics for the tables' size and the indexes' selectivity and then chooses the path with the lowest overall cost.

When joining three tables together, Oracle performs two separate joins: a join of two tables to generate a set of records and then a join between that set of records and the third table. If NESTED LOOPS joins are used, then the order in which the tables are joined is critical. The output from the first join generates a set of records, and that set of records is used as the driving table for the second join.

The size of the set of records returned by the first join impacts the performance of the second join—and thus may have a significant impact on the performance of the overall query. You should attempt to join the most selective tables first so the impact of those joins on future joins will be negligible. If large tables are joined in the first join of a multi-join query, then the size of the tables will impact each successive join and will negatively impact the overall performance of the query. The optimizer should select the proper join path; you can confirm the costs and join path by generating the explain plan.

NESTED LOOPS joins are useful when the tables in the join are of unequal size—you can use the smaller table as the driving table and select from the larger table via an index-based access. The more selective the index is, the faster the query completes.

HASH JOIN

The optimizer may dynamically choose to perform joins using the HASH JOIN operation in place of either MERGE JOIN or NESTED LOOPS. The HASH JOIN operation compares two tables in memory. During a HASH JOIN, the first table is scanned and the database applies "hashing" functions to the data to prepare the table for the join. The values from the second table are then read (typically via a TABLE ACCESS FULL operation), and the hashing function compares the second table with the first table. The rows that result in matches are returned to the user.

The optimizer may choose to perform hash joins even if indexes are available. In the sample query shown in the following listing, the BOOKSHELF and BOOKSHELF_AUTHOR tables are joined on the TITLE column:

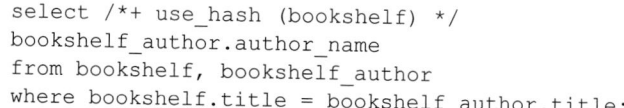

```
select /*+ use_hash (bookshelf) */
bookshelf_author.author_name
from bookshelf, bookshelf_author
where bookshelf.title = bookshelf_author.title;
```

The BOOKSHELF table has a unique index on its TITLE column. Since the index is available and can be used to evaluate the join conditions, the optimizer may choose to perform a NESTED LOOPS join of the two tables as shown in the previous section. If a HASH JOIN is performed, then each table will be read via a separate operation. The data from the table and index scans serve as input to a HASH JOIN operation. The HASH JOIN does not rely on operations that process sets of rows. The operations involved in HASH JOINs return records quickly to users. HASH JOINs are appropriate for queries executed by online users if the tables are small and can be scanned quickly.

Processing Outer Joins

When processing an outer join, the optimizer uses one of the three methods described in the previous sections. For example, if the sample query performs an outer join between BOOK_ ORDER and CATEGORY (to see which categories had no books on order), a NESTED LOOPS OUTER operation may be used instead of a NESTED LOOPS operation. In a NESTED LOOPS OUTER operation, the table that is the "outer" table for the outer join is typically used as the driving table for the query; as the records of the inner table are scanned for matching records, NULL values are returned for rows with no matches.

Related Hints

You can use hints to override the optimizer's selection of a join method. Hints allow you to specify the type of join method to use or the goal of the join method.

In addition to the hints described in this section, you can use the FULL and INDEX hints, described earlier, to influence the way in which joins are processed. For example, if you use a hint to force a NESTED LOOPS join to be used, then you may also use an INDEX hint to specify which index should be used during the NESTED LOOPS join and which table should be accessed via a full table scan.

Hints About Goals

You can specify a hint that directs the optimizer to execute a query with a specific goal in mind. The available goals related to joins are the following:

- **ALL_ROWS**   Execute the query so all of the rows are returned as quickly as possible.
- **FIRST_ROWS**   Execute the query so the first row is returned as quickly as possible.

By default, the optimizer executes a query using the execution path that is selected to minimize the total time needed to resolve the query. Thus, the default is to use ALL_ROWS as the goal. If the optimizer is only concerned about the total time needed to return all rows for the query, then set-based operations such as sorts and MERGE JOIN can be used. However, the ALL_ROWS goal may not always be appropriate. For example, online users tend to judge the performance of a system based on the time it takes for a query to return the first row of data. The users thus have FIRST_ROWS as their primary goal, with the time it takes to return all of the rows as a secondary goal.

The available hints mimic the goals: the ALL_ROWS hint allows the optimizer to choose from all available operations to minimize the query's overall processing time, and the FIRST_ROWS hint tells the optimizer to select an execution path that minimizes the time required to return the first row to the user.

If you use the FIRST_ROWS hint, the optimizer will be less likely to use MERGE JOIN and more likely to use NESTED LOOPS.

Hints About Methods

In addition to specifying the goals the optimizer should use when evaluating join method alternatives, you can list the specific operations to use and the tables to use them on. If a query involves only two tables, you do not need to specify the tables to join when providing a hint for a join method to use.

The USE_NL hint tells the optimizer to use a NESTED LOOPS operation to join tables. In the following example, the USE_NL hint is specified for the join query example. Within the hint, the BOOKSHELF table is listed as the inner table for the join.

```
select /*+ use_nl(bookshelf) */
bookshelf.publisher,
bookshelf_author.author_name
from bookshelf, bookshelf_author
where bookshelf.title = bookshelf_author.title;
```

If you want all of the joins in a many-table query to use NESTED LOOPS operations, you could just specify the USE_NL hint with no table references. In general, you should specify table names whenever you use a hint to specify a join method because you do not know how the query may be used in the future. You may not even know how the database objects are currently set up—for example, one of the objects in your FROM clause may be a view that has been tuned to use MERGE JOIN operations.

If you specify a table in a hint, you should refer to the table alias or the unqualified table name. That is, if your FROM clause refers to a table as

```
from fred.his_table, me.my_table
```

then you should *not* specify a hint such as

```
/*+ use_nl(me.my_table) */
```

Instead, you should refer to the table by its name, without the owner:

```
/*+ use_nl(my_table) */
```

If multiple tables have the same name, then you should assign table aliases to the tables and refer to the aliases in the hint. For example, if you join a table to itself, then the FROM clause may include the text shown here:

```
from bookshelf b1, bookshelf b2
```

A hint forcing the BOOKSHELF-BOOKSHELF join to use NESTED LOOPS would be written to use the table aliases, as shown here:

```
/*+ use_nl(b2) */
```

The optimizer ignores any hint that isn't written with the proper syntax. Any hint with improper syntax is treated as a comment (since it is enclosed within the /* and */ characters).

If you are using NESTED LOOPS joins, then you need to be concerned about the order in which the tables are joined. The ORDERED hint, when used with NESTED LOOPS joins, influences the order in which tables are joined.

When you use the ORDERED hint, the tables are joined in the order in which they are listed in the FROM clause of the query. If the FROM clause contains three tables, such as

```
from book_order, bookshelf, bookshelf_author
```

then the first two tables are joined by the first join, and the result of that join is joined to the third table.

Because the order of joins is critical to the performance of NESTED LOOPS joins, the ORDERED hint is often used in conjunction with the USE_NL hint. If you use hints to specify the join order, be certain that the relative distribution of values within the joined tables will not change dramatically over time; otherwise, the specified join order may cause performance problems in the future.

You can use the USE_MERGE hint to tell the optimizer to perform a MERGE JOIN between specified tables. In the following listing, the hint instructs the optimizer to perform a MERGE JOIN operation between BOOKSHELF and BOOKSHELF_AUTHOR:

```
select /*+ use_merge (bookshelf, bookshelf_author)*/
bookshelf_author.author_name
from bookshelf, bookshelf_author
where bookshelf.title = bookshelf_author.title
  and bookshelf.publisher> 'T%';
```

You can use the USE_HASH hint to tell the optimizer to consider using a HASH JOIN method. If no tables are specified, then the optimizer will select the first table to be scanned into memory based on the available statistics.

```
select /*+ use_hash (bookshelf) */
bookshelf.publisher,
bookshelf_author.author_name
from bookshelf, bookshelf_author
where bookshelf.title = bookshelf_author.title;
```

Additional Tuning Issues

As noted in the discussions of NESTED LOOPS and MERGE JOIN operations, operations differ in the time they take to return the first row from a query. Because MERGE JOIN relies on set-based operations, it will not return records to the user until all of the rows have been processed. NESTED LOOPS, on the other hand, can return rows to the user as soon as rows are available.

Because NESTED LOOPS joins are capable of returning rows to users quickly, they are often used for queries that are frequently executed by online users. Their efficiency at returning the first row, however, is often impacted by set-based operations applied to the rows that have been selected. For example, adding an ORDER BY clause to a query adds a SORT ORDER BY operation to the end of the query processing—and no rows will be displayed to the user until all of the rows have been sorted.

As described in "Operations That Use Indexes," earlier in this chapter, using functions on a column prevents the database from using an index on that column during data searches unless you have created a function-based index.

Some techniques that were used in previous versions of Oracle to disable indexes no longer are available. For example, some developers would append a null string to each column involved in a join in an effort to suppress index usage:

```
selectbookshelf_author.author_name
from bookshelf, bookshelf_author
where bookshelf.title||'' = bookshelf_author.title||'';
```

As of Oracle Database 10g, the optimizer does not allow the null strings to block the index usage—the query uses the index on the BOOKSHELF.TITLE column as part of a HASH JOIN execution.

As noted during the discussion of the NESTED LOOPS operation, the order of joins is as important as the join method selected. If a large or nonselective join is the first join in a series, the large data set returned will negatively impact the performance of the subsequent joins in the query as well as the performance of the query as a whole.

Depending on the hints, optimizer goal, and statistics, the optimizer may choose to use a variety of join methods within the same query. For example, the optimizer may evaluate a three-table query as a NESTED LOOPS join of two tables, followed by a MERGE JOIN of the NESTED LOOPS output with the third table. Such combinations of join types are usually found when the ALL_ROWS optimizer goal is in effect.

To see the order of operations, you can use the SET AUTOTRACE ON command to see the execution path, as described earlier in this chapter.

Parallelism and Cache Issues

In addition to the operations and hints listed in the previous sections, you can use two other sets of hints to influence the query processing. The additional hints allow you to control the parallelism of queries and the caching of data within the data buffer cache.

If your server has multiple processors, and the data being queried is distributed across multiple devices, then you may be able to improve query processing by parallelizing the data access and sorting operations. When a query is parallelized, multiple processes are run in parallel, each of which accesses or sorts data. A query coordinator process distributes the workload and assembles the query results for the user.

The *degree of parallelism*—the number of scanning or sorting processes started for a query—can be set at the table level (see the CREATE TABLE command in the Alphabetical Reference). The optimizer will detect the table-level settings for the degree of parallelism and will determine the number of query server processes to be used during the query. The optimizer will dynamically check the number of processors and devices involved in the query and will base its parallelism decisions on the available resources.

You can influence the parallelism of your queries via the PARALLEL hint. In the following example, a degree of parallelism of 4 is set for a query of the BOOKSHELF table:

```
select /*+ parallel (bookshelf,4) */ *
from bookshelf;
```

In the preceding query, a second operation—the SORT ORDER BY operation for the ORDER BY PUBLISHER clause—was added. Because the sorting operation can also be parallelized, the query may use nine query server processes instead of five (four for the table scan, four for the sort, and one for the query coordinator). The optimizer dynamically determines the degree of parallelism to use based on the table's settings, the database layout, and the available system resources.

If you want to disable parallelism for a query, you can use the NO_PARALLEL hint (called NOPARALLEL in versions prior to Oracle Database 10*g*). The NO_PARALLEL hint may be used if you want to serially execute a query against a table whose queries are typically executed in a parallelized fashion.

If a small, frequently accessed table is read via a full table scan, that table's data can be kept in the SGA for as long as possible. You can mark the table as belonging to the KEEP pool, using the BUFFER_POOL clause of the CREATE TABLE or ALTER TABLE command. If the table has been designated for storage in the KEEP pool, its blocks in memory are kept apart from the main cache. If the KEEP pool is sized adequately, the blocks will remain in memory until the database is shut down. The KEEP pool must be configured by the DBA, and it must be large enough to accommodate the tables that are to use it. Creating a KEEP pool that is too small generates the opposite of the intended effect—more physical reads will be required for the most active tables.

If a table is commonly used by many queries or users, and there is no appropriate indexing scheme available for the query, then you should use the KEEP pool to improve the performance of accesses to that table. This approach is most useful for static tables.

Review

The preceding sections have shown the methods used by the optimizer to access and manipulate data. When tuning queries, you need to keep in mind several factors:

- **The goal of the user**   Do you want rows to be quickly returned, or do you care more about the total throughput time for the query?

- **The application design**   How does this query fit within the overall design of the application? How is it executed? Are there external factors that affect its performance?

- **The type of joins used**   Are the tables properly indexed?

- **The size of the tables**   How large are the tables that are being queried? If there are multiple joins, how large is the set of data returned from each join?

- **The selectivity of the data**   How selective are the indexes in use?

- **The sorting operations**   How many sorting operations are performed? Are nested sorting operations being performed?

If you can carefully manage the issues related to performance, then the number of "problem" queries within your database should diminish. If a query appears to be taking more resources than it should, then you should use the SET AUTOTRACE ON or EXPLAIN PLAN command to determine the order of operations used for the query. You can use the tips and discussions provided throughout this chapter to then tune the operations or the set of operations.

CHAPTER
47

The Hitchhiker's Guide to SQL Result Cache and Client-Side Query Cache

The primary goal of designing database applications is to return the correct results as quickly as possible. Application developers spend countless hours trying to write efficient SQL code, and Oracle DBAs tune the database memory structures to provide efficient access to the data and index blocks needed to satisfy the queries.

Tuning an application normally involves finding the best path to touch the least amount of data and/or index blocks in the Oracle database buffer cache. Accessing data in memory is always much faster than accessing data from disk. Oracle uses algorithms to keep highly used data blocks in memory to reduce the number of physical disk reads. Oracle DBAs can increase the size of the default buffer cache or make use of the KEEP buffer pools to increase the number of blocks resident in memory for heavily used tables and indexes. Even if all the data and index blocks are in memory, the query still has to read them to obtain the result set.

As of Oracle Database 11g, a feature called the SQL Result Cache helps to leverage available memory to cache a read-consistent version of the query results of commonly executed queries. Static queries that are run time and time again, especially those that contain expensive DISTINCT, GROUP BY, and ORDER BY operations, no longer need to read the underlying data and index blocks but instead can read the results of queries from the new SQL Result Cache memory area within the shared pool of the SGA. A SQL statement is run once to read all the necessary index and data blocks that produce a query result, which can optionally be stored in the SQL Result Cache via a hint in the statement or by setting database initialization parameters.

The SQL Result Cache is stored within the SGA so all users connecting to the database instance have access to the query results stored there. Anyone executing the same SQL statement including the RESULT_CACHE hint will be able to make use of the SQL Result Cache and will not have to perform the physical and logical I/O to generate the results of the query.

Let's take a look at how the SQL Result Cache works. The following query performs a full table scan to generate its output. This query has to access all the same data blocks each time it is run by the same user or a different user.

```
set autotrace on
select state_code, prod_code, sum(amt) from sales
where state_code in ('IL','IN','MI')
group by state_code, prod_code order by 1,2;

ST   PROD_CODE     SUM(AMT)
--   ----------   ----------
IL      100860        16520
IL      100861       189180
...
MI      200380          208
55 rows selected.
Elapsed: 00:00:00.45
Execution Plan
----------------------------------------------------------
Plan hash value: 3229864837
```

Id	Operation	Name	Rows	Bytes	Cost (%CPU)	Time
0	SELECT STATEMENT		66	792	317 (9)	00:00:04
1	SORT GROUP BY		66	792	317 (9)	00:00:04

```
|*  2 |   TABLE ACCESS FULL| SALES | 21775 |   255K|   312  (7)| 00:00:04 |
-----------------------------------------------------------------------------
Predicate Information (identified by operation id):
---------------------------------------------------
   2 - filter("STATE_CODE"='IL' OR "STATE_CODE"='IN' OR
            "STATE_CODE"='MI')
Statistics
---------------------------------------------------------------
        0   recursive calls
        0   db block gets
     1071   consistent gets
        0   physical reads
        0   redo size
     1737   bytes sent via SQL*Net to client
      453   bytes received via SQL*Net from client
        5   SQL*Net roundtrips to/from client
        1   sorts (memory)
        0   sorts (disk)
       55   rows processed
```

From the preceding trace, you can see that the query performed 1,071 consistent gets while doing a full table scan of the sales table. Total time for the query was 0.45 seconds. That may seem fast for a table containing 225,000 records, but if database users have to perform this query over and over again, the elapsed time certainly adds up to a large number of seconds.

The easiest way to make use of the SQL Result Cache is to include a RESULT_CACHE hint in the SQL statement, as shown in the following example. The first time this query is run, it has to access all the same data blocks as the preceding query, but now the result of the query will be stored in the Result Cache area of the SGA for other queries to use.

```
select /*+ result_cache */  state_code, prod_code, sum(amt) from sales
where state_code in ('IL','IN','MI')
group by state_code, prod_code order by 1,2;

ST  PROD_CODE   SUM(AMT)
--  ----------  ----------
IL    100860       16520
IL    100861      189180
...
MI    200380         208
55 rows selected.
Elapsed: 00:00:00.45
Execution Plan
---------------------------------------------------------------
Plan hash value: 3229864837
---------------------------------------------------------------
```

Id	Operation	Name	Rows	Bytes	Cost (%CPU)	Time
0	SELECT STATEMENT		66	792	317	

```
(9)| 00:00:04 |
|   1 |  RESULT CACHE        | gx61vnrf7aqs046gr4r3m70kqs |        |        |       |
|
|   2 |    SORT GROUP BY      |                            |     66 |    792 |   317
(9)| 00:00:04 |
|*  3 |     TABLE ACCESS FULL| SALES                      |  21775 |   255K|   312
(7)| 00:00:04 |
---------------------------------------------------------------------------------
---------------
Predicate Information (identified by operation id):
-------------------------------------------------------
   3 - filter("STATE_CODE"='IL' OR "STATE_CODE"='IN' OR "STATE_CODE"='MI')
Result Cache Information (identified by operation id):
-------------------------------------------------------
   1 - column-count=3; dependencies=(DEMO.SALES); parameters=(nls);
name="select /*+ result_cache */  state_code, prod_code, sum(amt) from sales
where state_code in ('IL','IN','MI')
GROUP BY STATE_CODE,"
Statistics
-------------------------------------------------------
          1  recursive calls
          0  db block gets
       1071  consistent gets
          0  physical reads
          0  redo size
       1737  bytes sent via SQL*Net to client
        453  bytes received via SQL*Net from client
          5  SQL*Net roundtrips to/from client
          1  sorts (memory)
          0  sorts (disk)
         55  rows processed
```

The number of consistent gets (1,071) and the time to execute this query (0.45 seconds) are exactly the same as the first query. Note that the plan hash value (3229864837) is the same for both execution plans, but the explain plan is different. An additional line in the second explain plan lists the operation as the RESULT CACHE and gives it a hexadecimal name. Because this is the first execution of this statement with the RESULT_CACHE hint, Oracle stores the result in the SQL Result Cache of this database instance. Anyone executing this same SQL statement on this database instance will be able to make use of this query result in the cache. If this were a RAC database, each instance would have its own SQL Result Cache and the results would only be available on an instance if the preceding query (including the hint) is executed on that instance.

Now, let's execute the query again to see if it makes use of the SQL Result Cache:

```
select /*+ result_cache */  state_code, prod_code, sum(amt) from sales
where state_code in ('IL','IN','MI')
group by state_code, prod_code order by 1,2;

ST  PROD_CODE   SUM(AMT)
--  ----------  ----------
IL     100860       16520
```

```
IL      100861     189180
...
MI      200380        208
55 rows selected.
Elapsed: 00:00:00.12
Execution Plan
------------------------------------------------------------
Plan hash value: 3229864837
--------------------------------------------------------------------------------
| Id | Operation           | Name                 | Rows  | Bytes | Cost
 (%CPU)| Time      |
--------------------------------------------------------------------------------
----------------
|  0 | SELECT STATEMENT    |                      |    66 |   792 |   317
 (9)| 00:00:04 |
|  1 |  RESULT CACHE       | gx61vnrf7aqs046gr4r3m70kqs |       |       |
 |
|  2 |   SORT GROUP BY     |                      |    66 |   792 |   317
 (9)| 00:00:04 |
|* 3 |    TABLE ACCESS FULL| SALES                | 21775 |   255K|   312
 (7)| 00:00:04 |
--------------------------------------------------------------------------------
----------------
Predicate Information (identified by operation id):
---------------------------------------------------
   3 - filter("STATE_CODE"='IL' OR "STATE_CODE"='IN' OR "STATE_CODE"='MI')
Result Cache Information (identified by operation id):
-----------------------------------------------------
   1 - column-count=3; dependencies=(DEMO.SALES); parameters=(nls);
name="select /*+ result_cache */  state_code, prod_code, sum(amt) from sales
where state_code in ('IL','IN','MI') GROUP BY STATE_CODE,"
Statistics
-----------------------------------------------------
        0   recursive calls
        0   db block gets
        0   consistent gets
        0   physical reads
        0   redo size
     1737   bytes sent via SQL*Net to client
      453   bytes received via SQL*Net from client
        5   SQL*Net roundtrips to/from client
        0   sorts (memory)
        0   sorts (disk)
       55   rows processed
```

Looking at the trace, you can see that the execution plan is exactly the same as the query that loaded the data into the SQL Result Cache and that the plan hash value is exactly the same as the value for both preceding queries. What is different is the execution time. Instead of 0.45 seconds elapsed time, the query ran in 0.12 seconds. I ran the query several different times and from different sessions, and, in each case, the elapsed time was 0.12 seconds and the consistent gets (logical reads) was always 0.

What happens if the table is updated? Oracle continues to use the results for the query that are stored in the SQL Result Cache until the changes are committed. Other memory structures within the SQL Result Cache maintain a dependency list containing the objects used to generate the results of the query in the Result Cache.

To test this, update the SALES table in a second SQL*Plus session:

```
-- now do an update in another session
update sales set amt =amt + 1 where state_code = 'IL'
   and prod_code = 100860;
```

Now run the query again in the first session and note that the output is the same because the changes have not been committed:

```
select /*+ result_cache */  state_code, prod_code, sum(amt) from sales
where state_code in ('IL','IN','MI')
group by state_code, prod_code order by 1,2;

ST  PROD_CODE   SUM(AMT)
--  ----------  ----------
IL     100860       16520
IL     100861      189180
...
MI     200380         208
55 rows selected.
Elapsed: 00:00:00.15
Execution Plan
---------------------------------------------------------
Plan hash value: 3229864837
---------------------------------------------------------------------------------
| Id  | Operation          | Name                     | Rows  | Bytes | Cost(%CPU)| Time    |
---------------------------------------------------------------------------------
|   0 | SELECT STATEMENT   |                          |    66 |   792 |   317  (9)| 00:00:04 |
|   1 |  RESULT CACHE      | gx61vnrf7aqs046gr4r3m70kqs |     |       |           |          |
|   2 |   SORT GROUP BY    |                          |    66 |   792 |   317  (9)| 00:00:04 |
|*  3 |    TABLE ACCESS FULL| SALES                   | 21775 |  255K |   312  (7)| 00:00:04 |
---------------------------------------------------------------------------------

Predicate Information (identified by operation id):
---------------------------------------------------
   3 - filter("STATE_CODE"='IL' OR "STATE_CODE"='IN' OR "STATE_CODE"='MI')
Result Cache Information (identified by operation id):
---------------------------------------------------
   1 - column-count=3; dependencies=(DEMO.SALES); parameters=(nls);
```

```
name="select /*+ result_cache */  state_code, prod_code, sum(amt) from sales
where state_code in ('IL','IN','MI') GROUP BY STATE_CODE,"
Statistics
----------------------------------------------------------
          0  recursive calls
          0  db block gets
          0  consistent gets
          0  physical reads
          0  redo size
       1737  bytes sent via SQL*Net to client
        453  bytes received via SQL*Net from client
          5  SQL*Net roundtrips to/from client
          0  sorts (memory)
          0  sorts (disk)
         55  rows processed
```

Looking at this trace, you can see that the SQL Result Cache has been used as expected and that the output of the query provides read-consistent results that you would expect because the second session has not committed the changes yet.

Now let's see what happens when you run the query in the first session after you commit the changes in the second session:

```
-- now commit in second session
commit;
Commit complete
select /*+ result_cache */  state_code, prod_code, sum(amt) from sales
where state_code in ('IL','IN','MI')
group by state_code, prod_code order by 1,2;

ST  PROD_CODE   SUM(AMT)
--  ----------  ----------
IL    100860      16672
IL    100861     189180
...
MI    200380        208
55 rows selected.
Elapsed: 00:00:00.55
Execution Plan
-------------------------------------------------------
Plan hash value: 3229864837
--------------------------------------------------------------------------------
----------------
| Id  | Operation           | Name                         | Rows  | Bytes  |
Cost(%CPU)| Time   |
--------------------------------------------------------------------------------
----------------
|   0 | SELECT STATEMENT    |                              |    66 |   792 |   317
(9)| 00:00:04 |
|   1 |  RESULT CACHE       | gx61vnrf7aqs046gr4r3m70kqs   |       |       |      |
|   2 |   SORT GROUP BY     |                              |    66 |   792 |   317
(9)| 00:00:04 |
```

```
|*  3 |    TABLE ACCESS FULL| SALES                  | 21775 |    255K|    312
(7)| 00:00:04 |
-----------------------------------------------------------------------------
Predicate Information (identified by operation id):
-----------------------------------------------------------------------------
   3 - filter("STATE_CODE"='IL' OR "STATE_CODE"='IN' OR "STATE_CODE"='MI')
Result Cache Information (identified by operation id):
-----------------------------------------------------------------------------
   1 - column-count=3; dependencies=(DEMO.SALES); parameters=(nls);
name="select /*+ result_cache */  state_code, prod_code, sum(amt) from sales
where state_code in ('IL','IN','MI') GROUP BY STATE_CODE,"
Statistics
-----------------------------------------------------------------------------
          0  recursive calls
          0  db block gets
       1071  consistent gets
          0  physical reads
          0  redo size
       1737  bytes sent via SQL*Net to client
        453  bytes received via SQL*Net from client
          5  SQL*Net roundtrips to/from client
          1  sorts (memory)
          0  sorts (disk)
         55  rows processed
```

Oracle determined that the table being queried has been changed and that the changes were committed. It, therefore, forced the SQL*Plus session to requery the data and place it in the result set. The updated values now show up in the output of the query as expected. Notice that the consistent reads are back to 1,071, as they were when the query was first run, and that the time has increased from 0.12 to 0.55 seconds as a result of having to access all the data blocks once again.

Running the query again produces the same results, but the consistent reads are 0 because the SQL Result Cache is being used, once again, as shown here:

```
select /*+ result_cache */  state_code, prod_code, sum(amt) from sales
where state_code in ('IL','IN','MI')
group by state_code, prod_code order by 1,2;

ST  PROD_CODE   SUM(AMT)
--  ----------  ----------
IL     100860      16672
IL     100861     189180
...
MI     200380        208
55 rows selected.
Elapsed: 00:00:01.21
Execution Plan
-----------------------------------------------------------------------------
Plan hash value: 3229864837
-----------------------------------------------------------------------------
```

```
----------------
| Id  | Operation              | Name                         | Rows  | Bytes  |
Cost(%CPU)| Time   |
----------------------------------------------------------------------------------
|   0 | SELECT STATEMENT       |                              |    66 |   792  |   317
(9)| 00:00:04 |
|   1 |  RESULT CACHE          | gx61vnrf7aqs046gr4r3m70kqs | |        |        |    |
|
|   2 |   SORT GROUP BY        |                              |    66 |   792  |   317
(9)| 00:00:04 |
|*  3 |    TABLE ACCESS FULL| SALES                          | 21775 |   255K |   312
(7)| 00:00:04 |
----------------------------------------------------------------------------------
--------------
Predicate Information (identified by operation id):
---------------------------------------------------
   3 - filter("STATE_CODE"='IL' OR "STATE_CODE"='IN' OR "STATE_CODE"='MI')
Result Cache Information (identified by operation id):
-----------------------------------------------------
   1 - column-count=3; dependencies=(DEMO.SALES); parameters=(nls);
name="select /*+ result_cache */  state_code, prod_code, sum(amt) from sales
where state_code in ('IL','IN','MI') GROUP BY STATE_CODE,"

Statistics
----------------------------------------------------------
          0  recursive calls
          0  db block gets
          0  consistent gets
          0  physical reads
          0  redo size
       1737  bytes sent via SQL*Net to client
        453  bytes received via SQL*Net from client
          5  SQL*Net roundtrips to/from client
          0  sorts (memory)
          0  sorts (disk)
         55  rows processed
```

Database Parameter Settings for SQL Result Cache

The SQL Result Cache is part of the shared pool, and Oracle has provided a number of parameters related to this feature.

You can use the RESULT_CACHE_MODE parameter to turn the SQL Result Cache on or off at the database level. You can set it to the following values:

- **MANUAL** The RESULT_CACHE hint must be used in the SQL statement to have the result set of a query stored in the cache. This is the default.

- **FORCE** All query results that the Oracle Optimizer deems useful for the Result Cache are automatically stored in the Result Cache.

Use of the RESULT_CACHE or the NORESULT_CACHE hint in a SELECT statement takes precedence over the database RESULT_CACHE_MODE initialization parameter setting.

The RESULT_CACHE_MAX_SIZE parameter determines the size of the SQL Result Cache within the shared pool area of the SGA. Here are some points to keep in mind:

- If this parameter is set to zero, the SQL Result Cache is disabled.

- This parameter cannot be greater than 75 percent of the shared pool area size and is usually much, much less. Making the Result Cache too large means that more I/O has to occur in the standard buffer cache for other queries.

- The default depends on other memory settings, is platform specific, and is derived from the MEMORY_TARGET, the SGA TARGET, and the SHARED_POOL_SIZE parameters. In other words, computing an ideal size for the result cache using the dynamic performance views such as V$RESULT_CACHE_OBJECTS and V$RESULT_CACHE_STATISTICS is usually beneficial.

The RESULT_CACHE_MAX_RESULT parameter determines the maximum size of a result set in the SQL Result Cache. The default is 5 percent of the size specified by the RESULT_CACHE_MAX_SIZE parameter.

The RESULT_CACHE_REMOTE_EXPIRATION parameter is used to specify the number of minutes that a result set using a remote object is to be considered valid before it will be requeried by the next user to execute the corresponding SQL statement. Here are some points to keep in mind:

- Setting the RESULT_CACHE_REMOTE_EXPIRATION parameter to zero indicates that result sets using remote database objects should not be cached.

- Setting this parameter to a nonzero value can produce incorrect results if the remote table has changed.

- The default value is zero.

The DBMS_RESULT_CACHE Package

The DBMS_RESULT_CACHE package includes a number of procedures and functions that can be used to monitor and administer the SQL Result Cache within the shared pool.

The DBMS_RESULT_CACHE.MEMORY_REPORT procedure produces a detailed report of the SQL Result Cache's memory usage:

```
set serveroutput on
exec dbms_result_cache.memory_report;
Result Cache Memory Report
 [Parameters]
Block Size        = 1K bytes
Maximum Cache Size = 1568K bytes (1568 blocks)
Maximum Result Size = 78K bytes (78 blocks)
 [Memory]
Total Memory = 100300 bytes [0.057% of the Shared Pool]
... Fixed Memory = 5132 bytes [0.003% of the Shared Pool]
... Dynamic Memory = 95168 bytes [0.054% of the Shared Pool]
```

```
....... Overhead = 62400 bytes
....... Cache Memory = 32K bytes (32 blocks)
.......... Unused Memory = 27 blocks
.......... Used Memory = 5 blocks
.............. Dependencies = 1 blocks (1 count)
.............. Results = 4 blocks
................. SQL    = 2 blocks (1 count)
................. Invalid = 2 blocks (1 count)
PL/SQL procedure successfully completed.
```

The DBMS_RESULT_CACHE.FLUSH procedure can be used to flush the memory used by the result cache. You can include parameters to retain the current size of the result cache and to keep the current statistics. Both parameters are false by default. The following example shows that the dynamic memory usage is 0 after the flush procedure is executed:

```
execute dbms_result_cache.flush;
```

```
PL/SQL procedure successfully completed.
```

```
exec dbms_result_cache.memory_report;
```

```
R e s u l t   C a c h e   M e m o r y   R e p o r t
  [Parameters]
Block Size        = 1K bytes
Maximum Cache Size  = 1568K bytes (1568 blocks)
Maximum Result Size = 78K bytes (78 blocks)
  [Memory]
Total Memory = 5132 bytes [0.003% of the Shared Pool]
... Fixed Memory = 5132 bytes [0.003% of the Shared Pool]
... Dynamic Memory = 0 bytes [0.000% of the Shared Pool]
PL/SQL procedure successfully completed.
```

The DBMS_RESULT_CACHE.STATUS function can be used to determine the status of the result cache:

```
select dbms_result_cache.status from dual;
```

```
STATUS
-----------------------------------------------------------------------------
ENABLED
```

The DBMS_RESULT_CACHE.INVALIDATE function can be used to invalidate queries that depend on a specific table:

```
execute dbms_result_cache.invalidate ('HR','EMPLOYEES');
```

Dictionary Views for the SQL Result Cache

Several data dictionary views provide detailed information about the SQL Result Cache:

- V$RESULT_CACHE_DEPENDENCY displays the relationship between cached results and the objects used to derive those results.

- V$RESULT_CACHE_MEMORY displays all the result cache memory blocks and their status.
- V$RESULT_CACHE_OBJECTS displays all the objects (both cached results and dependencies) and their attributes.
- V$RESULT_CACHE_STATISTICS displays various result cache settings and usage statistics.

Additional Details for SQL Result Cache

The SQL Result Cache can also be used for the following:

- Subqueries and inline queries, even if the outer query changes.
- Functions that return values to a calling statement. Use the RESULT_CACHE clause in the function declaration and optionally specify any dependencies using the RELIES_ON clause to list underlying tables that should invalidate the result set. Note that the function must be deterministic to produce accurate results.
- Flashback queries. (These can also be cached.)

The SQL Result Cache is automatically disabled for the following:

- Temporary tables and dictionary tables
- CURRVAL and NEXTVAL sequences
- Queries containing CURRENT_DATE or SYSDATE

Memory is not automatically released from the result cache. You can use DBMS_RESULT_CACHE.INVALIDATE to release the memory used by SQL statements that depend on a specific table. You can also use the DBMS_RESULT_CACHE.FLUSH procedure to free up the entire result cache.

Oracle Call Interface (OCI) Client Query Cache

In addition to the SQL Result Cache, Oracle has implemented a client-side query cache that you can use to cache data in the memory of client systems for applications using OCI calls. Query results for commonly executed query sets are cached locally, thus eliminating the need to make the roundtrip to the database to retrieve commonly used application data. This, in turn, eliminates the CPU and process load on the database server and the corresponding network traffic.

The client query cache is best suited for static result sets and commonly executed queries that are used by the application. Benefits include enhanced performance of lookup tables and the ability to extend the server-side query cache to the client. The client-side query cache is automatically refreshed if the result cache changes in the database.

To make use of the client-side cache, the Oracle DBA has to set up an additional cache within the SGA of the database using the following parameters:

- **CLIENT_RESULT_CACHE_SIZE** All OCI client processes get this maximum size. This can be overridden by the **sqlnet.ora** configuration parameter OCI_RESULT_CACHE_MAX_SIZE. The default is zero; this is a static parameter.

- **CLIENT_RESULT_CACHE_LAG**   Specifies the maximum time (in milliseconds) since the last roundtrip to the server before which the OCI client query makes a roundtrip to get any database changes related to the queries cached on the client. The default is 5000 milliseconds; this parameter is not dynamic.

Oracle Call Interface (OCI) Client Query Cache Restrictions

Queries written in the OCI calls must include the RESULT_CACHE hint to indicate that results are to be stored in the query result cache. Applications must be relinked with Oracle 11g or 12c, and the clients must connect to an Oracle 11g or higher database.

The client-side query cache is best used for applications that reference read-only or read-mostly database objects. In addition, if the RESULT_CACHE hint is for queries that return large results sets, a large amount of client result cache memory will be used.

The following parameters can be used in a client configuration file or within a **sqlnet.ora** file to override the cache parameters set in the database parameter file:

- **OCI_RESULT_CACHE_MAX_SIZE**   Specifies the maximum size of the CLIENT_RESULT_ CACHE_SIZE for this client

- **OCI_RESULT_CACHE_MAX_RSET_SIZE**   Specifies the maximum size of an individual result set, in bytes

- **OCI_RESULT_CACHE_MAX_RSET_ROWS**   Specifies the maximum number of rows for an individual result

You can query the view CLIENT_RESULT_CACHE_STATS$ to display the client-side result cache usage statistics.

CHAPTER
48

Case Studies in Tuning

As described in Chapter 46, performance tuning begins with design. In many cases, the core performance problem in a database application has been designed into the system. You may be able to identify the most resource-intensive parts of the application, focusing future tuning efforts on specific database parameters or SQL statements. In this chapter, you will read case studies related to different performance problems and their resolutions. The case studies present three common problem areas—environmental issues, problem queries, and application architecture—from an application tuner's perspective.

Case Study 1: Waits, Waits, and More Waits

A large online transaction-processing system experienced significant performance problems as the number of concurrent users increased. At times of intense batch activity, such as month-end closing processes, the system performance was unacceptable for the online users. Is the problem with the environment, the application, or the implementation of the application in the environment? To identify the core problems and develop a path toward improved performance, the database statistics were reviewed. The system was complex, but the core problems from Oracle's perspective were similar to those described in Chapter 46—the database was being asked to execute a large number of slow SELECT and other DML statements.

The first step in tuning the database involved looking at the dynamic performance statistics during times when the application was performing acceptably and then again when the performance was unacceptable. The Automatic Workload Repository (AWR) framework tools were used to gather the statistics into *snapshots*. For these intervals, the following statistics were examined in detail:

- Number of executions per second
- Number of logical reads per second
- Number of waits for physical reads
- Number of waits during data writes
- Number of waits for undo segment headers and blocks
- Number of physical reads per second
- Number of sorts performed on disk and in memory

Capturing these statistics is important, both to identify problem areas and to measure the impact on performance as the database environment and application SQL are changed during the tuning process. Each of these statistics over time is reported via AWR (and its predecessor, Statspack). You can select the statistics for the database since it was last started from the dynamic performance views, such as V$SYSSTAT and V$WAITSTAT, but those statistics will be skewed by other activity in the database unassociated with your application. The following table shows the initial statistics gathered over a three-hour test. The results are shown here:

Statistic	Value
Test duration	10,800 seconds (3 hours)
Executions per second	1,700

Statistic	Value
Logical reads per second	67,000
Physical reads per second	6,300
Buffer busy waits	600,000
Undo header waits	300
Sorts in memory	800,000
Sorts on disk	200
Physical read waits that occurred:	
DB file sequential read (one-block reads)	32,700,000
DB file scattered read (multi-block reads)	4,500,000
Transactions per second	10
Physical writes per second	100

Given this information, what is the first area to focus on? The system was very active—1,700 executions per second and 67,000 logical reads per second were evidence of a large number of database requests executed constantly over a three-hour period. To analyze the statistics properly, you should start by transforming them into a consistent set of units. In this example, let's consider all the activity on a per-second basis. Divide the statistics that were previously presented at the interval level by 10,800 to see their per-second values:

Statistic	Value (per Second)
Executions	1,700
Logical reads	67,000
Physical reads	6,300
Buffer busy waits	55
Undo header waits	0.03
Sorts in memory	74
Sorts on disk	0.02
Physical read waits that occurred:	
DB file sequential read (one-block reads)	3,028
DB file scattered read (multi-block reads)	416
Transactions	10
Physical writes	100

With all the statistics presented in the same units, you can quickly develop an overview of what an average second looks like in the database. The total number of physical read waits occurring during a typical second was 3,028 + 416 = 3,444. Those waits were incurred when the database attempted to resolve a request for a physical read—and in a typical second, there were 6,300 such requests. Therefore, a physical read event had to wait, on average, almost 55 percent of the time (3,444/6,300). Only about 45 percent of the read requests were completed without a wait occurring.

At the same time, writes were also waiting. There were 55 data block waits per second as the database attempted to perform 100 physical writes—again, a 55 percent wait ratio. A review of the datafile I/O statistics (available via Statspack reports, AWR reports, or queries against V$FILESTAT) showed that the database I/O was distributed evenly across the most active tablespaces. If the I/O were not evenly distributed, it is likely that a single disk or set of disks encountering problems would be the main source of the I/O waits (using ASM can help to keep your I/O across disks or disk groups balanced—see Chapter 51).

How could you reduce the number of physical waits? If you only consider the queries that are performing full table scans as possible causes of performance problems, you would very likely have little impact on this application. Full table scans led to the scattered read waits shown in the prior table—and they accounted for only 12 percent (416/3,444) of the physical read waits that occurred. If you completely removed all the waits generated by full table scans, you probably would not have a significant impact on the performance of the application.

NOTE
If the full table scans are performed via parallel queries, they will always be read from disk into the PGA and not from the buffer cache.

Given this scenario, you can develop the following hypotheses:

- The application requirements exceeded the I/O capacity of the system as it is configured.
- The application generated a large number of SQL command executions.
- Most of the SQL commands executed did not generate physical reads. The data block buffer cache hit ratio was greater than 90 percent (1 − 6,300/67,000, in this case).
- The application may be consuming large amounts of CPU resources as well because it is executing many commands and actively managing the I/O queue.

Given those hypotheses, where should the tuning effort start? The application profile was of a read-intensive application (there are 6,300 physical reads per second to go with only 100 physical writes). The queries themselves appeared to be fairly well tuned (as judged by the overall hit ratio; it is likely that some individual queries were not properly tuned). Both reads and waits were reporting the same problem—they could not access the disks fast enough to avoid waits. As a result, the focus should first be on stabilizing the I/O environment. Is it performing well? If you find no problem with the I/O system and you can't change application SQL, you might have to upgrade or enhance the environment to support the loads generated by the application.

You should evaluate all aspects of the common I/O environment for their impact on performance—controllers, network interface cards, the disk array, and the network (for shared network storage). In many systems, the I/O is spread across many disks, and the performance is more impacted by the common elements used to access those disks than the disks themselves.

In most modern enterprise-scale configurations, a buffer area is available for the disk environment. As a result, most physical read requests do not reach the disk; the buffer services the read requests. In this study, around 10 percent of logical reads generated physical read requests. The I/O environment was intended to handle 90 percent of those physical read requests via its buffer. Because the buffer in this environment was not properly configured to support this volume of activity (as determined by the storage management personnel), most physical read requests were reaching the disk. Improving the use of the buffer improved all I/O in the environment and eliminated many of the disk accesses.

As a side effect of the I/O improvement, the application's CPU requirements may be reduced. The CPU requirements may be lowered because the system does not have to spend so much time managing I/O queues—and those resources are now available to user processes instead. It is possible that some other process on the system may now be free to take more of the available resources, illustrating the need to continue monitoring the system even after the tuning effort has been completed.

To further reduce the system load, operations that could be performed in batch mode were removed from the online processing portion of the application. For comparison, the following table shows the statistics following the tuning of the I/O environment and the modification of the application:

Statistic	Value (per Second)
Logical reads	67,000
Physical reads	3,830 (was 6,300)
Buffer busy waits	25 (was 55)
Physical read waits that occurred:	
DB file sequential read (one-block reads)	466 (was 3,028)
DB file scattered read (multi-block reads)	173 (was 416)
Transactions	10
Physical writes	115

In the revised environment, the number of physical reads was reduced by 40 percent, but the number of waits was reduced by over 80 percent. The database was able to support the same number of logical reads, transactions, and physical writes (with fewer waits during writes)—and the end-user performance is now acceptable. The batch processes will still require attention; rescheduling poorly written code may lessen contention for the online users, but that work will still need to be done later.

This is not the end of the story—there are still waits occurring, the database will grow over time, users will develop new queries, and application modules will be added over time. During those changes, you should track the critical statistics over time so you can isolate the impact of changes on the environment, identify problem areas, and forecast future performance.

Case Study 2: Application-Killing Queries

Almost every database eventually supports a query that consumes many more resources than it should. The query may be performing multiple full table scans (in the event that indexes are missing). The query may be generating Cartesian products (when multiple tables are listed in the FROM clause but their join syntax is not specified). The query may be performing multiple nested sorts of millions of rows.

In general, when tuning SQL, you should strive to work with as few rows as possible. If you only need ten rows out of a ten-million-row table, try to use an index that returns as few rows as possible for your WHERE clause criteria, and then filter through those rows for the ten rows you want.

Although this approach may seem straightforward, it is repeatedly violated. When developing an application, you should consider how each of the SQL statements you write will be executed—its frequency, its performance requirements for each execution, its dependencies on other commands, the indexes it will use, and so on. The goal is to support the business process as efficiently as possible. If you fail to consider how the code will be used, the application may suffer and the speed of the application may drive the speed of the business process—an unacceptable condition.

In a large online processing application, queries of the following format were the most frequently executed commands (based on the statistics in the EXECUTIONS column of V$SQL). Because the query performed a full table scan, the cumulative number of physical reads (the DISK_READS column) approached the cumulative number of logical reads (the BUFFER_GETS column) in its V$SQL entry:

```
select t35.c1
from t35
where (lower(t35.c4) like '%orchid sol%');
```

At least three things are wrong with this query if it is to be used in a production application. If you were to run this query one time, the performance might be acceptable—you'll be performing a full table scan of the T35 table because of the reasons listed in the next paragraph. But what happens when many users concurrently execute similar queries and the T35 table contains millions of rows? What if you make this kind of query available to a world of users via a web interface? The application performance suffers and adversely impacts the very process the application is supposed to support.

The problems with the query include the following:

- *There's no use of bind variables.* Every execution of the query is parsed separately unless the database administrator has set the CURSOR_SHARING initialization parameter to FORCE (the preferred setting). If CURSOR_SHARING is set to EXACT, the shared SQL area will be filled with thousands of almost identical commands, separately parsed and differing only in the literal value passed in as the search string.

- *No function-based index was defined on the C4 column, but the query is performing a LOWER function on the column.* If there is only a standard index available, Oracle will not be able to use the index to support this query.

- *The search string begins with a percent wildcard.* As a result, you would expect Oracle to perform a full table scan in order to find values that meet the criteria.

NOTE
You should generate the explain plan for any queries that are targeted for tuning, and for every significant query in the workload. Save each explain plan for comparison later when queries are running longer than expected.

Let's consider one possible solution to the third problem—the content of the search string. In this application, the user typed in the name ("orchid sol" in this case) and the application code put wildcards in front and behind the name, trying to maximize the number of potential matches that would be found. The application developer presented the user with all the potential values that could possibly match the exact search string.

From the database administration side, you can make sure CURSOR_SHARING is properly configured, and you can create a function-based index on the C4 column so index scans may be chosen instead of table scans. But the core problem remains—how can the query be rewritten to select as few rows as possible in order to generate its result set?

The answer lies in the use of Oracle Text. As described in Chapter 27, you can create text indexes on columns to support searches for strings, wildcards, text expansions, and more. In this case, you pass the name as the search string, and the text index searches its indexed values for matches—taking into account the wildcards. The application developer will have to change the query to use the Oracle Text syntax, and the database administrator will need to create and maintain the text index objects. However, the performance benefits are significant—the full text scans on the large table are eliminated. In this case, that benefit for commonly executed queries offsets the overhead costs involved in maintaining the text indexes.

NOTE
If you use indexes to index names, you need to create an empty Oracle Text stoplist. Otherwise, Oracle skips common words (such as "an") that may be real names.

In this particular case, the use of text indexes for this query dramatically reduced the search times for web-based users. The number of physical and logical reads against the search table was cut significantly and remained low as the application grew. The database administrator and application maintenance team had additional text index objects to manage as a trade-off for the performance benefit gained.

Text indexes are not the solution to every problem. In most situations, a standard index containing multiple columns will be the solution. The important step is to identify the most resource-intensive queries (by querying V$SQL or using Statspack or AWR reports) and reviewing them from an application architecture perspective. For each query, ask what it is used for and why it is doing what it is doing. Consider a simple query such as the following:

```
select count(*) from countries;
```

Individually, each execution of this query completes very quickly—there are only several hundred countries, and the table can be cached in the data block buffer cache. But if this query is executed several million times a day, it may perform more logical reads than any other query in the database. Those logical reads translate into CPU resources allocated for repeated queries of static data that could be spent on more useful queries of dynamic data. When looking for problem queries, be sure to check for queries that are executed many times in addition to those that are expensive for each execution.

Using the 10053 Trace Event

A query may not use the same explain plan in every environment. When a query is parsed, Oracle examines the possible ways to execute the query and assigns a cost to each of the alternatives. The costs are not arbitrary; Oracle considers the statistics on the tables (such as the number of rows), the indexes (including their selectivity), and the database parameter values.

Oracle provides a trace event you can use to see the calculations the optimizer performs when evaluating alternative paths. The output of the trace event is a trace file written to a subdirectory within the DIAGNOSTIC_DEST directory (as defined in the initialization parameter file) on the database server.

Within your session, you can enable tracing via the following command:

```
alter session set
events '10053 trace name context forever, level 1';
```

With tracing turned on for your session, you should now run the SQL you want to analyze. When the SQL command completes, you can turn off tracing via the following command:

```
alter session set
events '10053 trace name context off';
```

The trace information is only generated the first time a command is parsed. If the command has already been parsed within the instance, the trace file will show the command you executed but not the calculations performed by the optimizer.

The order of the sections of the trace file output vary between releases of Oracle, but, in general, they include the following:

- The initialization parameters for the database
- The object-level statistics
- The table access paths considered
- The join order and operations options considered
- The chosen path

The parameter settings and the object-level statistics are important to note when evaluating the query's execution path. The same query run in different databases may follow different execution paths, leading to significantly different performance for the application. Often these differences are due to variances in the statistics across databases; you can use this trace to see how those statistics influence the chosen path.

For each table involved in the query, the trace file shows the table statistics and the index statistics. Given the statistics and initialization parameters, tuning is not an art or a mystery; it is, therefore, a math problem. What is the cost of a full scan of each table? What is the cost of each type of join (NESTED LOOPS, SORT MERGEs, and HASH JOINs)? How large is the sort area size, and how likely is it that the query will need to use a temporary segment for storage? For each type of join, what happens if you switch the order in which the tables are accessed?

Each of these permutations is evaluated, with a cost generated for each approach. These costs are then compared, and the approach with the lowest cost is selected.

Changing parameter values at the database or session level influences how the costs are calculated and thus influences which join path is selected. For example, increasing the setting for DB_FILE_MULTIBLOCK_READ_COUNT makes full table scans "cost" less (more blocks are read for each disk access), and decreasing the OPTIMIZER_INDEX_COST_ADJ parameter setting makes index accesses "cost" less (favoring the use of an index instead of a full table scan).

Additionally, changing the object statistics influences the costs used during the optimizer's calculations. If you are concerned about the optimizer's choices in a coming production release, you can export the statistics from the production database and import them into the testing database. The next time the commands are parsed, they will use the new statistics and will generate explain plans that will reflect the calculations.

You can use the 10053 trace event to verify the optimizer calculations for critical queries during significant changes in the database lifecycle. For example, you can use the trace events to determine how the optimizer choices are impacted by the following:

- Changes in the database version
- Changes in the operating platform
- Changes in the initialization parameters
- Changes in the object statistics
- Changes in the hints provided to the query

In each case, the trace output provides the foundation for the calculations the optimizer is performing, thus eliminating the guesswork in query tuning.

Case Study 3: Long-Running Batch Jobs

A company was planning to move a large volume of data on a repeated basis from a transactional system to a reporting system. The transactional system was outside of their control, so there was no opportunity to use database links, materialized views, or other replication methods directly interacting with the source system. Instead, the data source was a single large file sent each day from the transactional system.

Attempting to load the large file into the reporting system repeatedly caused availability problems—the time needed to load the data through conventional inserts exceeded the available time window for the operation. Any failures during the loading process created even greater problems because the partially loaded data was deleted and reloaded. As a result, the performance of the load job affected the availability of the entire reporting application. Based on the current and anticipated data volumes, the amount of data loaded daily is expected to triple within 12 months.

Assuming the database is properly configured so there are no I/O or memory issues to resolve, several approaches are available to resolve this type of problem:

- Even though the source system provides the data in one set, you may not have to insert it all at once. Instead of loading data into the reporting system once each day, consider sending incremental loads throughout the day. If the loading process does not impact the queries (for example, by invalidating indexes during the load or causing irregularities in the reported data), these small loads may be able to work alongside user queries.

- Don't load the data into an intermediate Oracle table; use external tables instead. This approach is ideal for situations in which a small number of well-defined queries report against the data a small number of times.

- Parallelize large operations. Use all the available resources on the server. Although this may help the current performance problems, it may affect the application's ability to scale well with increased data volumes.

- Load the data into temporary work tables, then treat them as partitions of existing tables.

Each of these options involves at least a minor design change, and you cannot select the proper solution and make the change without understanding how the end users use the data. Is the data loaded into a single table or into multiple tables? Do the end users directly access the tables the data is loaded into? How stale can the data in the tables be?

Let's first consider the worst-case scenario: The users need all the data available at once, so no incremental feed is available. The loaded data is inserted into multiple related tables. Further, the load should have minimal impact on the availability of the rest of the data in the database. Lastly, the end users query the loaded tables directly.

In such a scenario, you should consider partitioning the table being loaded. For each day's data load, create a new table whose structure is the same as the table the users will be querying. Load the data into the table, index it, analyze it, and perform whatever transforms are necessary to format the data properly for the user. When the data is ready to be presented to the user, execute the ALTER TABLE EXCHANGE PARTITION command, telling Oracle to treat the table you have created as a partition of the table the users will query. Because you only touch the application's tables when you add the new partition, the downtime for the application is minimal—particularly if you are able to use only local indexes on the partitioned table.

The EXCHANGE PARTITION approach effectively divides the two operations being performed on the table—its loading by you and its querying by the users. Once you are able to separate those two operations, your design and maintenance capabilities increase dramatically.

Consider a slightly better scenario: The users need all the data available at once, but they do not directly query the table being loaded. The users query materialized views based on the table. You should tune the materialized views to make the materialized views fast-refreshable, allowing changes to the loaded table to be incrementally applied to the objects the users will be querying. Again, separating the bulk load operation from the queries of the same objects significantly enhances your maintenance options. See Chapter 26 for details on the configuration of materialized view refresh options.

If the users always query materialized views that aggregate the data, you should consider not loading the data at all. Instead, use external tables (see Chapter 28) to reference the data file during an INSERT AS SELECT operation into a summary table. External tables cannot be indexed and will, therefore, result in a full scan of the file—but because you are not loading the raw data, the INSERT AS SELECT of the summary may complete faster than if you had loaded the data and then aggregated it. As a side benefit, you only have to store the raw data once (at the file-system level) rather than twice.

Regardless of which of these options you choose, you should investigate the use of options that exploit the available system resources—including parallel query, parallel DML, parallel loading, partitioning, and bulk processing. In terms of improving the performance of the load itself, many features are available: using NOLOGGING during loads, using SQL*Loader Direct Path loads, and starting parallel Data Pump jobs. Note that many of these options can be applied on a partition-by-partition level.

Tuning batch loads requires you to make an educated judgment about the degree to which set processing will be used. You can configure the application to process one row at a time. For example, you can insert one row into a master table and then insert all its children rows into other tables before inserting a second row into the master table and repeating the process. That row-based approach will suffer as the volume of rows increases. The row-based approach guarantees read consistency across the loaded tables, but if the job is executed during off-hours (or the EXCHANGE PARTITION method is used), that benefit may not be realized by the users.

By comparison, you can create set operations that process huge volumes of rows at once. It is likely that at some point the number of rows processed in a set will impact the performance of the load, particularly if complex sorts are involved. In such a case, you may need to break the large batch process into smaller steps and process smaller groups. For example, the operation flow may be

1. Select 100,000 rows from the input tables.
2. Perform the aggregations and transforms on those rows.
3. Store the results of those aggregations and transforms in a temporary work table.
4. Select the next 100,000 rows from the input tables.
5. Repeat until all the rows have been processed and inserted into the temporary work table.
6. Properly index and analyze the temporary work table.
7. Perform additional operations on the data in the temporary work table (such as generating grand totals or new columns or performing joins with other tables).
8. Insert rows from the temporary work table into the production table.
9. Drop or truncate the temporary work table.

Such a sequence of operations attempts to gain the benefits of both approaches—a procedural approach that operates on sets of rows. How large should each set of rows be? That depends on your operating environment, the operations performed, and the data itself. You should properly test the process to make sure the more procedural approach completes faster than the single batch operation. You should take into consideration the greater number of potential points of failure in the procedural approach and handle exceptions accordingly.

In this example, the original daily load job took 12 hours to complete. By breaking it into smaller pieces, the total time was reduced to 3 hours—long enough to run the job multiple times within the load window if required.

Those design decisions require you to know your data, how it is used, and how it affects the business process. Regardless of your architecture, you need to be able to test the application while simulating a real-life workload under repeatable conditions. During the tests and during production usage, you must be able to monitor the environment and the application for performance problems as the data volumes grow.

During the tuning process, you may have to make trade-offs. For example, in the batch-process tuning effort, you may allocate more disk space to the database (for the temporary work table) in order to improve overall performance. Each part of the application should be considered as a critical part of the whole application, and developed and planned accordingly. When the application performance affects the business process performance, you should identify the problem areas—such as the environment, particular queries, or the data-flow architecture—and implement a design more in tune with the application's needs.

CHAPTER
49

The Hitchhiker's Guide to Pluggable Databases

sing a database appliance such as Oracle Exadata helps the database administrator to consolidate dozens, if not hundreds, of databases in one cabinet. Managing each of these databases separately, however, is still a challenge from a resource management perspective. Instances for each of those databases may use their memory and CPU resources inefficiently, preventing even more databases from being deployed to the server. With pluggable databases (PDB), introduced in Oracle Database 12c, you can leverage your database resources more efficiently because many different databases (each consisting of a collection of schemas) can coexist within a single container database (CDB). A CDB is also known as a *multitenant* container database.

Pluggable databases make database administration simpler for a DBA. Performance metrics are gathered for all PDBs as a whole. In addition, the DBA only needs to manage one SGA and not one for each PDB. Fewer database patches need to be applied as well: only one CDB needs to be patched instead of having to patch each PDB within the CDB. With pluggable databases, hardware is used more efficiently, and the DBA can manage many more databases in the same amount of time.

Developers, network administrators, storage administrators, or database application users will rarely interact with a pluggable database and know that they are using a pluggable database. One day the pluggable database may be plugged into container database CDB01 and the next day into container database CDB02, which is the point: a container database acts just like any other database except for the decreased maintenance effort for the DBA and generally higher availability for database users. For a more in-depth analysis and additional use cases for pluggable databases and container databases, see the *Oracle Database 12c DBA Handbook*.

Pluggable Database Concepts

The features of the pluggable database architecture look much like a replication, migration, and template environment, making the Oracle transportable tablespace feature simplistic in comparison. Figure 49-1 shows the architecture of a pluggable database environment.

Pluggable database users fall into two categories: common users and local users. This feature helps to ensure the separation of duties mandated in highly secure environments that give database administrators only the privileges they need to manage a specific subset of databases within a container. This functionality complements the Database Vault features first available in Oracle Database 11g.

Container Database Components

Any pluggable database must either be unplugged or plugged into a single CDB at any point in time. A CDB has the following components:

- **Root** There is one and only one root database in a CDB. A *root* is much like a template database with the metadata and other components used to manage PDBs within the CDB. The root in any CDB is called CDB$ROOT and contains metadata for each PDB within the CDB.

- **Seed** The *seed* PDB is called PDB$SEED and is a template for creating new PDBs. It is read-only and thus cannot be modified.

FIGURE 49-1.   *Pluggable database architecture*

■   **PDB**   Each PDB within a CDB looks like a traditional database to end users and is fully
compatible with databases created before Oracle Database 12*c*.

Each of these components is also called a *container;* the CDB is a container (multitenant
environment) that encapsulates the root, seed, and zero or more PDB containers. You can unplug
a PDB from a CDB with one command and plug it back in with another command. An unplugged
PDB consists of an XML file that describes the PDB along with its component files, much like a
transportable tablespace and the DDL for the objects in the transportable tablespace in Oracle
Database 11*g*.

CDB User Accounts
A CDB has two kinds of user accounts: common users and local users. A *common user* has the
same identity in the root and all PDBs—both current and those created in the future. Common
users may or may not have the same privileges in each container, however. Common users with
administrative privileges can plug in, unplug, or drop PDBs.
    Local users, in contrast, exist only in each PDB or in the CDB. They can have the same
username but will have different credentials in each container. Having local users facilitates
separation of duties across all containers within a CDB.

Prerequisites
To use pluggable databases, you must be using Oracle Database 12*c*. The operating system
requirements are essentially the same as for a single-instance database except that the memory,
disk, and CPU requirements are higher. The database compatibility level must be at least 12.1.0 to
use any CDB or PDB features.

Creating Container and Pluggable Databases

You create a single CDB to house one or more PDBs. Ideally, you use the Oracle Database Creation Assistant (DBCA) for most of your CDB and PDB creation activities, but just as with a traditional database, you can use the CREATE DATABASE (for creating CDBs) or CREATE PLUGGABLE DATABASE (for creating PDBs) commands if you need to perform some customization or automation that is not available with DBCA.

Creating the Container Database

Creating a CDB is almost trivial using DBCA. After launching DBCA with the **dbca** command, you specify database attributes much as you would for a non-CDB, except that you specify that the new database will be a CDB, as shown in Figure 49-2.

FIGURE 49-2. *Creating a container database*

In the next window, you can review the summary of the container database to be created. Note in Figure 49-3 that creating a container database creates a pluggable database as well.

The Progress Page, shown in Figure 49-4, shows the progress of creating the container database and the initial pluggable database.

Once the installation completes, you can see the container database listed in **/etc/oratab**:

```
#
# Multiple entries with the same $ORACLE_SID are not allowed.
#
#
+ASM:/u01/app/product/12.1.0/grid:N:          # line added by Agent
complref:/u01/app/product/12.1.0/database:N:  # line added by Agent
cdb58:/u01/app/product/12.1.0/database:N:     # line added by Agent
```

FIGURE 49-3. *Create Database – Summary page*

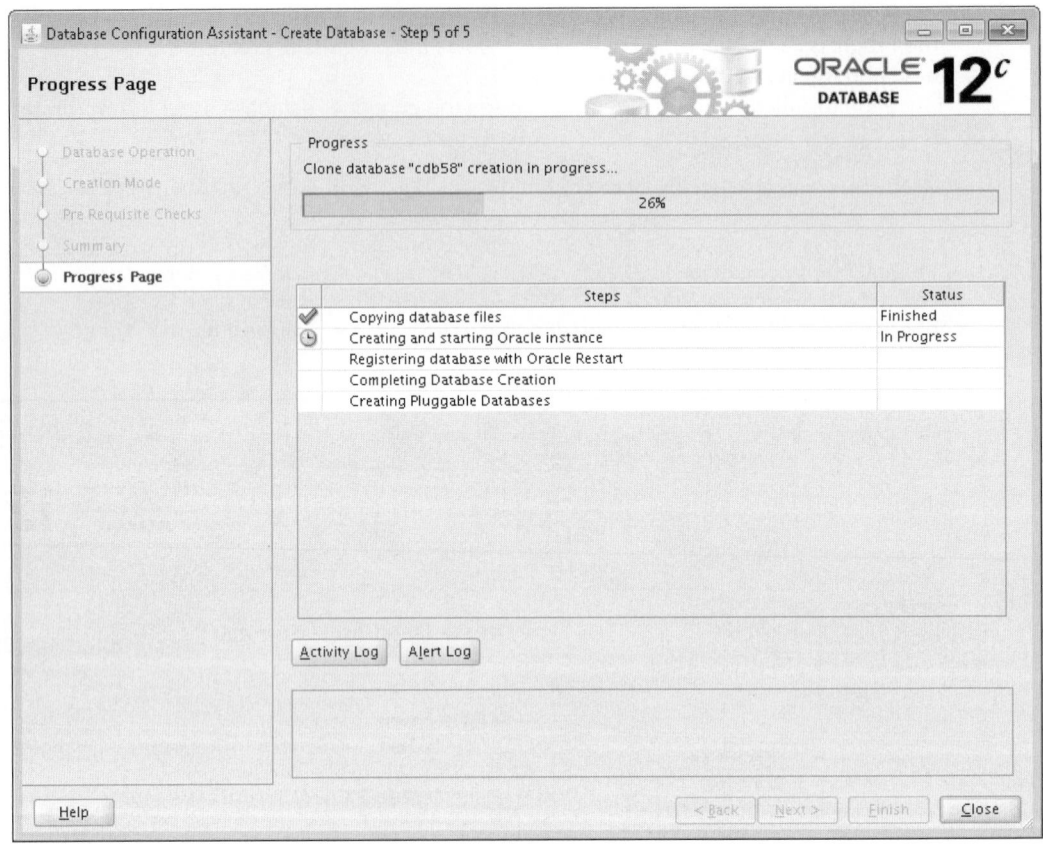

FIGURE 49-4. *Container database Progress Page*

But where is the initial pluggable database? For clues you can check the listener:

```
[oracle@oel63 ~]$ lsnrctl status
LSNRCTL for Linux: Version 12.1.0.1.0 - Production on 27-MAY-2013 20:47:02
. . .
Service "cdb58" has 1 instance(s).
  Instance "cdb58", status READY, has 1 handler(s) for this service...
. . .
Service "complrefXDB" has 1 instance(s).
  Instance "complref", status READY, has 1 handler(s) for this service...
Service "rptqa10" has 1 instance(s).
  Instance "cdb58", status READY, has 1 handler(s) for this service...
The command completed successfully
[oracle@oel63 ~]$
```

The listener hands off any requests for **rptqa10** to the pluggable database with the same name in the container database **cdb58**.

Creating a Pluggable Database

You can create a new pluggable database using DBCA. In the Database Operation window, select Manage Pluggable Databases. On the next page, shown in Figure 49-5, select Create a Pluggable Database.

In Figure 49-6, select the container database **cdb58**.

Specify the new pluggable database name, as shown in Figure 49-7, along with a username that will have administrative privileges in the new pluggable database.

FIGURE 49-5. *Creating a pluggable database*

FIGURE 49-6. *Specifying the container database*

After the pluggable database is created, you can see it listed in the DBA_PDBS data dictionary view:

```
SQL> select pdb_id,pdb_name,status from dba_pdbs;

    PDB_ID PDB_NAME          STATUS
---------- ---------------- -------------
         3 RPTQA10          NORMAL
         2 PDB$SEED         NORMAL
         4 RPTQA12          NORMAL
```

FIGURE 49-7. *Specifying pluggable database name and administrator*

The new pluggable database is immediately available via the listener:

```
Service "rptqa12" has 1 instance(s).
    Instance "cdb58", status READY, has 1 handler(s) for this service...
```

Managing Pluggable Databases

You can manage container and pluggable databases using either DBCA or the command line. Usually, you create new pluggable databases via DBCA because all of the other setup, including the dozens of SQL scripts run after instance creation, is done by DBCA. For almost all other operations, the SQL*Plus command line may be much faster.

Unplugging a Pluggable Database

To unplug a database from its container, you must first close it. After closing the pluggable database, it is in MOUNT mode, much like a non-pluggable database:

```
SQL> alter pluggable database rptqa10 close immediate;
Pluggable database altered.
SQL>
```

Once it is in MOUNT mode, you can unplug it from the container. Note that when you unplug a pluggable database, you must specify an XML file to contain the metadata for the structure of the database:

```
SQL> alter pluggable database rptqa10
  2  unplug into '/u01/app/pdb/rptqa10.xml';
Pluggable database altered.
SQL>
```

Dropping a Pluggable Database

To drop the pluggable database, you use the DROP PLUGGABLE DATABASE command. In this example, you decide to keep the datafiles just in case you didn't really want to drop that database:

```
SQL> drop pluggable database rptqa10 keep datafiles;
Pluggable database dropped.
SQL>
```

Plugging In a Pluggable Database

Realizing that you really didn't want to unplug that database, you can plug the **rptqa10** database back into the container using the retained datafiles plus the XML file you saved when you unplugged the database:

```
SQL> create pluggable database rptqa10
  2  using '/u01/app/pdb/rptqa10.xml' nocopy;
Pluggable database created.
SQL>
```

Monitoring Pluggable Databases

A number of data dictionary views help you monitor and maintain container and pluggable databases from the container database. Many dynamic performance views that you're already familiar with have additional columns related to CDBs and PDBs. You can look at V$SESSION to see sessions by PDB:

```
SQL> select username,status,server,con_id
  2  from v$session
  3  where username is not null;
```

```
USERNAME                             STATUS    SERVER    CON_ID
------------------------------       --------  --------- ----------
RJB                                  INACTIVE  DEDICATED 3
SYS                                  ACTIVE    DEDICATED 3
SYS                                  ACTIVE    DEDICATED 0
```

The CON_ID column in V$SESSION identifies the container ID, which can be cross-referenced (joined) to DBA_PDBS:

```
SQL> select pdb_id,pdb_name,status from dba_pdbs;

    PDB_ID PDB_NAME          STATUS
---------- ---------------- -------------
         2 PDB$SEED          NORMAL
         4 RPTQA12           NORMAL
         3 RPTQA10           NORMAL

SQL>
```

Container ID=0 is always the root container (the CDB).

CHAPTER
50

The Hitchhiker's Guide to Oracle Real Application Clusters

I n an Oracle Real Application Clusters (RAC) environment, multiple instances access a single database. The instances are commonly created on separate servers that are connected via a high-speed interconnect with access to a shared disk area. The database files reside on a shared set of disks, and each instance has its own control files and online redo log files that are also stored on the shared disks.

Every instance shares the same datafiles and the same control file. Online redo log files are assigned to a specific instance using the THREAD parameter, and only that instance with that thread number writes to them. Every instance has to be able to read all online redo log files so that any instance can archive the log files if the owning instance is shut down. A user can be directed to connect to the database through one of the instances attached to it; if an instance goes down, the connection may be dynamically reconnected to the database via another instance in the cluster. RAC thus provides a high-availability solution (accounting for server and instance failure) and a scalable high-performance solution (by increasing the memory and processors available to the connecting processes).

This chapter gives you an overview of the installation and management of RAC. Many of the details are operating system–specific, but the configuration process flow will be the same across platforms. See the *Oracle Database 12c DBA Handbook* for a more in-depth discussion of Oracle RAC, including the Oracle Exadata Machine, the ultimate engineered RAC system.

Oracle Database 12c takes the clustered environment to a new level. Prior to Oracle Database 12c, an ASM instance was required on each server that was running a database instance. Now, using Oracle Flex ASM, the ASM instances may run on separate physical servers from the Oracle Database 12c instances. In addition, multiple Oracle Flex ASM servers can themselves be clustered to support a large set of databases across an enterprise.

Preinstallation Steps

Before starting the Oracle RAC installation, you need to verify that your environment and cluster are properly configured to support it. The servers that will host the instances are referred to as *nodes* in the cluster. Each of the nodes should have external shared disks. Each node should have redundant switches to support failover requirements. Each node should have one private Internet Protocol (IP) address for private connections and one public IP address for client connections and connection failovers from other nodes. Each node must also support Transmission Control Protocol/Internet Protocol (TCP/IP) and a supported interconnect software protocol.

NOTE
You must choose an interconnect technology that is supported by Oracle. For example, see http://www.oracle.com/technetwork/ database/clustering/tech-generic-linux-new-086754.html for the Linux certification matrix.

Oracle provides clusterware (the Grid Infrastructure), simplifying the installation and configuration process. For the shared disk area, Oracle requires the use of its Automatic Storage Management feature (see Chapter 51).

NOTE
Be sure to install all required patches on the operating system prior to starting the installation process. As part of your standard Oracle software installation procedures, you should review all required operating system patch levels. The Oracle Universal Installer (OUI) will warn you (and offer to adjust) minimum OS-level settings required to run Oracle RAC.

DBAs and application developers typically do not get involved in network system design, but for RAC installations, the DBA needs to be actively involved in the network configuration. For example, the MTU network setting determines how large each packet is when data is sent from server to server. In RAC installations, many database blocks may be sent between the nodes, and it is critical that communication be as efficient as possible. If MTU is set to 1500 bytes (its historical value, and the default in some installations), then each 32K database block will require over 20 separate network packets. Even if those packets are transferred between nodes in 1 millisecond, which equates to a 20-millisecond read time for a single block, you can probably read the data off your disks faster than that. If the hardware supports increasing the MTU, you may be able to improve the transfer speeds for blocks across the cluster interconnect. If you are moving to a RAC environment, you need to understand how the network and hardware configuration impacts the performance and scalability of your applications. Your system administrators should ensure your configuration appropriately supports the anticipated transfer of blocks across the RAC nodes with as little overhead as possible.

Installing RAC

Installing RAC in Oracle Database 12c is a two-step process. The first step is to use the Oracle Universal Installer (OUI) to install Oracle Grid Infrastructure (which includes ASM). Grid Infrastructure provides an integrated set of solutions for cluster management. You can use Cluster Ready Services (CRS) to manage cluster membership, group services, group resource management, and high-availability configuration. You can also use CRS to define services that support distributing workload across servers. The Automatic Workload Repository (AWR) collects statistics on the services; see Chapter 46 for further details on AWR.

NOTE
RAC is available with both the Standard Edition and the Enterprise Edition of Oracle Database 11g and 12c.

Both steps of the installation process use the OUI; see Chapter 3 for details on OUI. After completing the first step (installing Grid Infrastructure), you can begin the second step of the installation process: installing the Oracle Database 12c software with RAC in a different Oracle home directory than you used in the first step. You should also use the installer to create and configure services for your RAC environment. After your software installation completes, OUI starts the Database Configuration Assistant to complete environment configuration and create the RAC database.

NOTE
If you have installed a previous Oracle clustered database version, the Database Upgrade Assistant (DBUA) will upgrade your database to the Release 12c version of Grid Infrastructure and RAC.

Storage

You should use Automatic Storage Management (ASM) to create disk groups and simplify their management. As described in Chapter 51, database administrators can add new disks to disk groups; Oracle will manage the contents and the distribution of the files among the disks involved.

Oracle ASM provides many benefits to your database environment. ASM provides redundancy from within Oracle if no hardware redundancy is available. When you define a disk group, you can specify a failure group; Oracle uses the failure group as a redundant version of the primary group of disks in the disk group. Oracle's installation programs refer to the software-based redundancy as "normal" redundancy. You can specify multiple failure groups for additional redundant protection (at the cost of additional space). If hardware mirroring is available, you can use external (file system–based) redundancy.

Many RAC environments use a combination of raw devices and logical volume management software. Logical volume management (LVM) provides a file-system management interface to raw devices.

You can use ASM disk groups to further reduce the management complexity of the RAC database—Oracle manages the files and the file systems. You can administer the files and disk groups manually or via Oracle Cloud Control 12c (known in previous releases as Grid Control).

Initialization Parameters

As part of configuring the instances, you must set values for the database initialization parameters maintained in the server parameter file. RAC installations should use the server parameter file to manage the set of parameters shared by the instances.

The following initialization parameters must have the same value for all instances in the RAC cluster:

- ACTIVE_INSTANCE_COUNT
- ARCHIVE_LAG_TARGET
- COMPATIBLE
- CLUSTER_DATABASE
- CLUSTER_DATABASE_INSTANCES
- CONTROL_FILES
- DB_BLOCK_SIZE
- DB_DOMAIN
- DB_FILES
- DB_NAME
- DB_RECOVERY_FILE_DEST
- DB_RECOVERY_FILE_DEST_SIZE

- DB_UNIQUE_NAME
- INSTANCE_TYPE (RDBMS or ASM)
- PARALLEL_MAX_SERVERS
- REMOTE_LOGIN_PASSWORD_FILE
- UNDO_MANAGEMENT

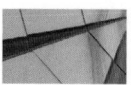

NOTE
If DML_LOCKS and RESULT_CACHE_MAX_SIZE are set to 0, their values in all instances must be identical.

The following initialization parameters must have unique values for each instance in the RAC cluster:

- ASM_PREFERRED_READ_FAILURE_GROUPS (for ASM instances only)
- INSTANCE_NAME
- INSTANCE_NUMBER
- UNDO_TABLESPACE

NOTE
Within an instance, set INSTANCE_NUMBER and THREAD to the same value.

In addition to these parameters, you should specify identical values for the following initialization parameters across the instances:

Parameter	Description
ARCHIVE_LAG_TARGET	Different values for instances in your Oracle RAC database are likely to increase overhead because of additional automatic synchronization performed by the database processing. When using Streams with your Oracle RAC database, the value should be greater than zero.
LICENSE_MAX_USERS	Because this parameter determines a database-wide limit on the number of users defined in the database, having the same value on all instances of your database is useful so you can see the current value no matter which instance you are using. Setting different values may cause Oracle to generate additional warning messages during instance startup or cause commands related to database user management to fail on some instances.
LOG_ARCHIVE_FORMAT	If you do not use the same value for all your instances, you unnecessarily complicate media recovery. The recovering instance expects the required archive log file names to have the format defined by its own value of LOG_ARCHIVE_FORMAT, regardless of which instance created the archive log files. Databases that support Data Guard, either to send or receive archived redo log files, must use the same value of LOG_ARCHIVE_FORMAT for all instances.

Parameter	Description
SPFILE	If this parameter does not identify the same file to all instances, then each instance may behave differently and unpredictably in failover, load-balancing, and during normal operations. Additionally, a change you make to the SPFILE with an ALTER SYSTEM SET or ALTER SYSTEM RESET command is saved only in the SPFILE used by the instance where you run the command. Your change will not be reflected in instances using different SPFILEs. If the SPFILE values are different in instances where the values were set by the server, you should restart the instances that are not using the default SPFILE.
TRACE_ENABLED	If you want diagnostic trace information to be always available for your Oracle RAC database, you must set TRACE_ENABLED to TRUE on all your database instances. If you trace on only some of your instances, diagnostic information might not be available when required should the only accessible instances be those with TRACE_ENABLED set to FALSE.
UNDO_RETENTION	By setting different values for UNDO_RETENTION in each instance, you are likely to reduce scalability and encounter unpredictable behavior following a failover. Therefore, you should carefully consider whether you will accrue any benefits before you assign different values for this parameter to the instances in your Oracle RAC database.

Avoid using the dynamic memory management features (such as Automatic Memory Management) in RAC instances. Dynamic memory management generates network traffic that can negatively impact the performance of the database as a whole without benefiting the applications it is supporting.

Starting and Stopping RAC Instances

You can use Cloud Control 12c to manage all of the instances associated with a RAC database. You can stop, start, and monitor databases, instances, and their listeners via Cloud Control 12c. As with any non-RAC database, you can use SQL*Plus to issue SHUTDOWN and STARTUP commands. For RAC databases, you can also use the **srvctl** utility, as shown in the examples in this section.

Regardless of the tool used to shut down or start the instance, the following rules apply to RAC clusters:

- Shutting down an instance does not affect the operation of other running instances.

- Shutting down a database mounted in shared mode (CLUSTER_DATABASE=TRUE) requires that you shut down every instance in the cluster before the database is considered closed.

- After a SHUTDOWN NORMAL or a SHUTDOWN IMMEDIATE, no instance recovery is needed. If you use SHUTDOWN ABORT on a RAC instance, a still-running instance performs instance recovery for the shutdown instance. If the aborted instance was the last one running, the next instance to start will perform the recovery.

■ If you use SHUTDOWN TRANSACTIONAL with the LOCAL option, all transactions in the instance will have to be either committed or rolled back prior to the shutdown. Transactions on other instances do not impact the local SHUTDOWN TRANSACTIONAL. If you do not specify the LOCAL clause, then the SHUTDOWN TRANSACTIONAL waits for all transactions on all instances that started prior to the SHUTDOWN command to complete.

You can use SQL*Plus commands to shut down and start RAC databases one at a time until the whole environment has been launched. See Chapter 51 for details on the STARTUP and SHUTDOWN commands. You can start up an instance in MOUNT mode on your local node via the STARTUP MOUNT command, just as you would for a single-instance database.

You can use the **srvctl** utility to manage multiple instances in a single command. The syntax to start instances is

```
srvctl start instance -d <db_name> -i <inst_name_list>
              [-o <start_options>] [-c <connect_str> | -q]
```

The keyword following **srvctl start** specifies the service being started—instances, database, services, or ASM. Note that multiple instances can be passed as part of the *inst_name_list* parameter value (via a comma-separated list). The *start_options* are **open**, **mount**, and **nomount**. The *connect_str* parameter allows you to pass a connect string when connecting to the database. The *q* parameter, if specified, tells **srvctl** to prompt for user connection information when **srvctl** is run; by default, **srvctl** connects to the local database as SYSDBA.

The following command starts and opens a local database named MYDB and starts all instances of the MYDB database:

```
srvctl start -database -d mydb -o open
```

The following command starts two instances for the MYDB database:

```
srvctl start instance -d mydb -i mydb1,mydb2
```

For ASM instances, specify the node name (**-n**), the instance name (**-i**), and the startup options (**-o**), as in the following example. The instance name is optional because only one instance of ASM can run on a single node.

```
srvctl start asm -n mynode1 -i asm1 -o open
```

NOTE
*To see the instances that are part of your cluster, you can use either OEM or SQL*Plus. From within SQL*Plus, query the V$ACTIVE_INSTANCES view. The view displays one row for each instance—showing the instance number, the host name, and the instance name.*

You can use the

```
srvctl stop {database | instance | service | nodeapps | asm }
```

command to stop databases, instances, and other services.

Other available **srvctl** commands are listed in Table 50-1.

srvctl Command	Description
srvctl add {database | instance | service |nodeapps | asm}	Adds a configuration to your cluster database configuration. **srvctl add service** adds services to a database and assigns them to instances. You can use the **srvctl add service** command to configure the Transparent Application Failover (TAF) policy for a service
srvctl config {database | service | nodeapps | asm}	Displays the configuration information stored in the Oracle Cluster Registry (OCR)
srvctl disable {database | instance | service | asm}	Disables the named object and prevents it from being started automatically
srvctl enable {database | instance | service | asm}	Enables the named object to be started automatically
srvctl getenv {database |instance |service | nodeapps}	Displays environment status
srvctl modify {database | instance |service | nodeapps}	Modifies the object configuration without removing and adding the CRS resources
srvctl relocate service	Relocates the named service names from one named instance to another named instance
srvctl remove {database |instance | service | nodeapps | asm}	Removes the named object from the cluster environment
srvctl setenv {database|instance|service |nodeapps}	Sets environment values in the configuration file
srvctl start {database | instance |service | nodeapps | asm}	Starts CRS-enabled, nonrunning applications for the database, all or named instances, all or named service names, or node-level applications
srvctl status {database |instance |service | nodeapps | asm}	Displays the current state of the named object
srvctl stop {database|instance|service |nodeapps|asm}	Stops the CRS applications for the database, all or named instances, all or named service names, or node-level applications
srvctl unsetenv {database | instance | service | nodeapps}	Unsets environment values in the configuration file

TABLE 50-1. *srvctl Command Options*

Transparent Application Failover

RAC provides support for transparent application failover (TAF) in the event of an instance failure. To guard against hardware failure, the database file storage must be failure tolerant (generally through the use of RAID arrays, mirroring, or ASM-enforced software mirroring). When a user connects to the database through an instance, any transactions executed by the user are recorded in the redo log thread for that instance.

If an instance fails (or is shut down via a SHUTDOWN ABORT), one of the surviving instances performs the needed recoveries. With TAF, the user's connection is reestablished via another instance in the same cluster, connecting to the same database.

When you install and configure the RAC environment, Oracle configures the network services for you. For example, if you create a service called **db.us.acme.com**, the service name entry in the **tnsnames.ora** file may resemble this:

```
db.us.acme.com=
(description= (load_balance=on) (failover=on)
(address_list=
  (address=(protocol=tcp)(host=db1-server)(port=1521))
  (address=(protocol=tcp)(host=db2-server)(port=1521)))
(connect_data= (service_name=db.us.acme.com)))
```

The user can connect to the instance via the **db.us.acme.com** service name (for example, via a remote SQL*Plus session) and execute queries. While the user is connected, you can shut down the **db1-server** host. If the user—still in the same session—attempts to execute another query, the session is transparently reestablished via the **db2-server** host and the query is executed.

The **listener.ora** file entry for the database contains entries similar to the following listing:

```
listeners_db.us.acme.com=
(address=(protocol=tcp)(host=db1-server)(port=1521))
(address=(protocol=tcp)(host=db2-server)(port=1521))
```

If the user has changed environment variables within the session (via ALTER SESSION), or has set session-specific variables, those values may need to be reestablished in the newly connected session.

As described earlier in this chapter, you can create and manage services within your RAC environment. You can assign services to run on one or more instances; services integrate cluster database resources to simplify cluster manageability.

You can also use **srvctl** to create and add services. You can assign services to instances for preferred (normal) and available (recovery) processing. You can identify other instances that are available to support the service levels change or for planned outages.

NOTE
You can use the DBCA to manage service assignments and service preferences, but Oracle best practices recommend that the **srvctl** *utility should be used to add or modify services.*

Assigning services to nodes is a critical part of the RAC design process. The goal is for the configuration to be a benefit rather than a hindrance. To achieve that goal, you should avoid creating a RAC configuration in which multiple sessions will be executing long-running updates of the same blocks at the same time on different cluster nodes. If you can isolate your users so they can share data rather than compete for it, you will dramatically improve your likelihood of success. You may need to force specific users to specific cluster nodes rather than relying on the round-robin assignment of users; the more you can control the use of locks against your tables, the more you can control cluster performance.

Adding Nodes and Instances to the Cluster

You can add nodes to an existing cluster, and you can add instances to an existing RAC environment. The nodes must meet the criteria listed earlier in this chapter—they must be configured with the proper networking protocol configurations, and they must support high-speed data transmissions with the other nodes in the cluster. It is generally simplest to make the operating system on the new node a copy of one of the existing nodes in the cluster. The nodes must be able to execute remote commands via equivalence files.

The specific installation steps for the new node vary by operating system. In general, a Unix cluster administrator adds the new node to the clusterware configuration (based on directions from its vendor). You can then start the Oracle Universal Installer (OUI) in **addNode** mode (in UNIX, via *<CRS_HOME>*/OUI/bin/addNode.sh, and in Windows, via *<CRS_HOME>\oui\bin\addNode.bat*). OUI then presents you with a series of prompts to add the new node to the cluster as it verifies the configuration.

Once the node has been added to the cluster, you can add an instance. Start the Database Configuration Assistant (see Chapter 2) and choose Real Application Clusters Database. You can then select Add Instance and the name of the database the instance will access. Enter the instance parameters where prompted and accept the summary information to initiate the instance creation. Oracle creates the instance and its network services.

To remove an existing instance from a RAC cluster, start the DBCA on a node other than the node hosting the instance that will be removed. The DBCA displays a list of the current instances in the configuration; select the one to be removed from the list. DBCA then displays a list of services assigned to that instance so you can relocate them to other instances in the cluster. The selected instance will be deregistered from the RAC cluster.

CHAPTER
51

The Hitchhiker's Guide to
Database Administration

I n this chapter, you will learn the basic steps involved in administering an Oracle Database 12*c* database. The database administrator (DBA) job has many components, and there are books written specifically for DBAs. This chapter gives you an overview of the tasks of a DBA, along with guidance on using standard DBA tools. This chapter does not provide a full, detailed description of every DBA task.

Earlier chapters described many of the functions of a DBA, such as creating tables, indexes, views, users, synonyms, database links, and packages. The DBA topics described in this chapter will, therefore, focus on the production-control functions of the DBA role, including

- Creating a database
- Starting and stopping the database
- Sizing and managing the memory areas for the database
- Allocating and managing space for the objects
- Creating and managing undo
- Performing backups

For each of these topics, many options are available to both developers and DBAs. The following sections of this chapter should provide you with enough information to get started and to learn what questions to ask of your DBAs and system administrators. See Chapter 49 for an overview of pluggable databases, one of the most exciting and versatile features of Oracle Database 12*c*. For further details on all of these topics, see the *Oracle Database 12c DBA Handbook*.

Creating a Database

The simplest way to generate a CREATE DATABASE script is via the Oracle Universal Installer (OUI). When you install Oracle, OUI gives you the option to create a database via the Database Configuration Assistant (DBCA). If you use that option, DBCA will create a database as part of the software installation process; you can invoke DBCA at any later time to create additional databases. You can even save the SQL generated by DBCA to create the database for future reference. See the CREATE DATABASE entry in the Alphabetical Reference for the full command syntax.

The CREATE DATABASE command is issued from within SQL*Plus, via an account with the SYSDBA system privilege:

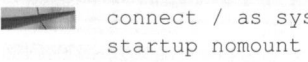

```
connect / as sysdba
startup nomount
create database...
```

To issue CONNECT as SYSDBA successfully, you must have the proper authorization at the operating system and database levels. See your operating system–specific Oracle documentation for information on the operating system rights needed.

Using the Oracle Enterprise Manager

Oracle Enterprise Manager (OEM), a graphical user interface (GUI) tool, is supplied as part of the standard Oracle toolset to enable DBAs to manage databases from a personal computer. The OEM toolset provides a robust interface for remote database administration. All DBAs can use the same central OEM repository (a set of tables created in a database) to perform their work. In addition to those changes, OEM includes task scheduling and assignment features to enable around-the-clock database coverage.

You must make several key decisions before installing and configuring OEM. You need to decide where the OEM repository is to be created and how and when you are going to perform backups to protect this repository. Since you can use OEM as an interface to Oracle Recovery Manager (RMAN), recovery information can be stored in the OEM repository. You may want to create a small, separate database in which to store the OEM repository. You should ensure that this database is backed up frequently so recovery of the repository itself is assured.

If you are the only DBA working with the OEM toolset, you do not have to consider who will handle administration of specific databases in your environment. If there are several DBAs at the site, you need to determine task definitions, database responsibilities, and schedules. With OEM, you can grant levels of access and privilege to each DBA in the group on a task-by-task basis. You can configure OEM to enable you to send e-mail requests and assignments to other DBAs or take control of a problem to speed resolution.

If you have a previous version of OEM installed, migrate that repository to the newest version to take advantage of the new features. If you have more than one repository on your system, you need to take precautions to ensure that you migrate each version of the repository without damaging currently stored information.

Although you do not have to use OEM, it provides a common GUI for managing your databases. As your enterprise grows in size (and in number of databases and DBAs), the consistency of the DBA interface will support consistent implementation of your change-control and production-control processes.

OEM enables you to manage Real Application Clusters (RAC) environments and Grid environments. By providing a graphical interface to administer the database, OEM simplifies the learning curve for new DBAs and allows you to perform complex functions easily.

Starting and Stopping the Database

To start a database, issue the STARTUP command from within SQL*Plus, as shown in the following listing. In the examples in this chapter, the name of the database is MYDB.

```
connect / as sysdba;
startup open mydb;
```

Alternatively, you can mount the database:

```
connect / as sysdba;
startup mount mydb;
```

When the database is mounted but not open, you can manage its files. For example, if you moved some of the database's files while the database was shut down, you need to let Oracle know where to find them before it will restart. To give the new locations of the files, you can mount the database (as shown in the preceding listing) and then use the ALTER DATABASE command to rename the old files to their new locations. Once you have finished telling Oracle the new locations for the files, you can open the database via the ALTER DATABASE open command.

Four primary options are available for shutting down the database. In a normal shutdown (the default), Oracle waits for all users to log out of the database before shutting down. In a transactional shutdown, Oracle waits for active transactions to complete before shutting down. In an immediate shutdown, Oracle rolls back all existing uncommitted transactions and logs out any users currently logged in. In an abort shutdown, the database immediately shuts down, and all uncommitted transactions are lost.

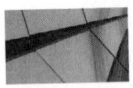

NOTE
While the database is in the process of shutting down or starting up, no new logins are permitted.

To perform a normal shutdown, use the SHUTDOWN command. For a transactional shutdown, use SHUTDOWN TRANSACTIONAL. An immediate shutdown, as shown in the following listing, uses the SHUTDOWN IMMEDIATE version of the SHUTDOWN command. To abort the database, use SHUTDOWN ABORT.

```
connect / as sysdba;
shutdown immediate
```

If you use SHUTDOWN ABORT, Oracle will automatically perform recovery operations during the next database startup. A SHUTDOWN ABORT may also be useful in situations where the database needs to be stopped in the shortest possible time, for example, for an impending power failure. During the subsequent startup, Oracle will perform any necessary recovery operations. In all cases, use SHUTDOWN ABORT as a last resort so your database is in a logically consistent state when it is shut down.

You may also use OEM to start up and shut down the instance, via the General tab on the Instance Manager/Configuration screen.

Sizing and Managing Memory Areas

When you start a database, Oracle allocates a memory area (the System Global Area, or SGA) shared by all the database users. The two largest areas of the SGA are usually the *database buffer cache* and the *shared pool*; their size directly impacts the memory requirements for the database and the performance of database operations. Their sizes are controlled by parameters in the database's initialization file.

The database buffer cache is an area in the SGA used to hold the data blocks that are read from the data segments in the database, such as tables and indexes. The size of the database buffer cache is determined by the DB_CACHE_SIZE parameter (expressed in terms of number of bytes) in the initialization parameter file for the database. The default size for the database blocks is set via the DB_BLOCK_SIZE parameter specified in the parameter file during database creation. Managing the size of the database buffer cache is an important part of managing and tuning the database.

The database has a default block size, but you can establish cache areas for different database block sizes and then create tablespaces to use those caches. For example, you can create a 4KB block–size database with some tablespaces set to 8KB. The size of the 8KB cache would be set via the DB_8K_CACHE_SIZE parameter. To create tablespaces to use that cache, specify BLOCKSIZE 8K as part of the CREATE TABLESPACE command. If the default block size for the database is 4KB, you would not set a value for DB_4K_CACHE_SIZE; the size specified for DB_CACHE_SIZE would be used for the 4KB cache.

NOTE
The cache for the block size must exist before you create a tablespace that uses that block size.

The different cache areas can be resized while the database is running. Caches can only be made larger if unallocated memory is available. The caches must be increased or decreased in *granules*. For a database with an SGA less than 128M, the granule size is 4M—so DB_8K_ CACHE_SIZE can be 4M, 8M, 12M, and so on. If you attempt to use any other setting, Oracle will round it up to the next granule size. The following line of code shows the setting of the DB_8K_ CACHE_SIZE parameter. To see if memory is available, query the V$SGA_DYNAMIC_FREE_ MEMORY view.

```
alter system set db_8k_cache_size = 8m;
```

If you create a tablespace that uses a nondefault database block size, be sure that the related cache size parameter (such as DB_8K_CACHE_SIZE) is updated in your database parameter file. If you are using an **init.ora** file, you must update it with the new value. If you are using a system parameter file (an SPFILE, the preferred method), it will be automatically updated when you execute the ALTER SYSTEM command with the SCOPE=BOTH clause.

NOTE
You cannot alter the SGA_MAX_SIZE or JAVA_POOL_SIZE parameter values while the database is open.

Oracle manages the space in the buffer caches by using an algorithm that keeps the most actively used blocks in memory for as long as possible. When free space is needed in the cache, the new data blocks use either the space occupied by infrequently accessed blocks or the space occupied by a modified block once it has been written out to disk.

If the SGA is not large enough to hold the most frequently used data, different objects will contend for space within the data block buffer cache. Contention is particularly likely when multiple applications use the same database and thus share the same SGA. In that case, the most recently used tables and indexes from each application constantly contend for space in the SGA with the most recently used objects from other applications. As a result, requests for data from the data block buffer cache will result in a lower ratio of "hits" to "misses." Data block buffer cache misses result in physical I/Os for data reads, causing performance degradation.

The shared pool stores the data dictionary cache (information about the database structures) and the *library cache* (information about statements that are run against the database). While the data block buffer and dictionary cache enable sharing of structural and data information among users in the database, the library cache allows the sharing of commonly used SQL statements.

The shared pool contains the execution plan and parse tree for SQL statements run against the database. The second time that an identical SQL statement is run (by any user), Oracle takes advantage of the parse information available in the shared pool to expedite the statement's execution. Like the data block buffer cache, the shared pool is managed via an LRU algorithm. As the shared pool fills, less recently used execution paths and parse trees are removed from the library cache to make room for new entries. If the shared pool is too small, statements will be continually reloaded into the library cache, affecting performance.

The size (in bytes) of the shared pool is set via the SHARED_POOL_SIZE initialization parameter. Like the other caches, the shared pool size can be altered while the database is open.

TIP
Monitor the dynamic performance view V$SGA_RESIZE_OPS to see which memory regions are adjusted and how often. Too many resize operations can have an adverse effect on performance.

You can use Automatic Shared Memory Management (ASMM) to manage the sizes of the memory areas dynamically. To activate ASMM, set a nonzero value for the SGA_TARGET database initialization parameter. After you set SGA_TARGET to the size of the SGA you want (that is, all of the caches added together), you then set the other cache-related parameters (DB_CACHE_SIZE, SHARED_POOL_SIZE, JAVA_POOL_SIZE, and LARGE_POOL_SIZE) each to 0. Shut down and restart the database for those changes to take effect; the database then begins actively managing the sizes of the different caches. You can monitor the sizes of the caches at any time via the V$SGASTAT dynamic performance view. While the database is running, you can alter the SGA_TARGET parameter value and Oracle will automatically alter the sizes of the related caches.

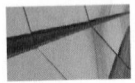

NOTE
To minimize inter-instance traffic, RAC instances should use fixed cache sizes instead of dynamic cache management.

As the workload in the database changes, the database alters the cache sizes to reflect the needs of the application. For example, if there is a heavy batch-processing load at night and a more intensive online transaction load during the day, the database may alter the cache sizes as the load changes. These changes occur automatically, without DBA intervention. If you specify a value for a pool in your initialization parameter file, then Oracle uses that as the minimum value for that pool.

NOTE
DBAs can create KEEP and RECYCLE pools in the buffer cache. KEEP and RECYCLE pools are not affected by the dynamic cache resizing.

From within OEM, you can see if dynamic memory management is enabled by clicking on the Memory Parameters option; the Automatic Shared Memory Management button can be set to Enabled or Disabled.

The Initialization Parameter File

The characteristics of the database instance—such as the size of the SGA and the number of background processes—are specified during startup. These parameters are stored in a file called the *system parameter file*. To generate the system parameter file for an open database, use the

CREATE SPFILE command. You can generate a readable version of the system parameter file via the CREATE PFILE from spfile command. See the Alphabetical Reference for the command syntax for these commands. The "pfile" version of the parameter file, formerly known as the **init.ora** file, usually contains the database name as part of the filename. For example, a database named MYDB may have a pfile file named **initmydb.ora**. In general, you should use the server parameter file (SPFILE) option for managing your parameter settings because it supports dynamic changes to the parameters while the database is running.

Allocating and Managing Space for the Objects

When a database is created, it is divided into multiple logical sections called *tablespaces*. The SYSTEM tablespace is the first tablespace created, and the SYSAUX tablespace is created as part of every Oracle Database 12*c* database. You can then create additional tablespaces to hold different types of data (such as tables, indexes, and undo segments). Tablespaces can be renamed via the RENAME TO clause of the ALTER TABLESPACE command.

NOTE
SYSAUX is created as part of every database starting with Oracle 10g. It is created automatically if you use the Database Upgrade Assistance provided by Oracle.

When a tablespace is created, *datafiles* are created to hold its data. These files immediately allocate the space specified during their creation. Each datafile can support only one tablespace. Datafiles can be set to extend automatically when they run out of space; you can set the increment by which they extend and their maximum size. Each user's schema is a collection of logical database objects, such as tables and indexes, that refer to physical data structures that are stored in tablespaces. Objects from a user's schema may be stored in multiple tablespaces, and a single tablespace can contain objects from multiple schemas.

When a database object (such as a table or index) is created, it is assigned to a tablespace via user defaults or specific instructions. A *segment* is created in that tablespace to hold the data associated with that object.

A segment is made up of sections called *extents*—contiguous sets of Oracle blocks. Once the existing extents can no longer hold new data, the segment obtains another extent. If a segment is composed of multiple extents, there is no guarantee that those extents will be contiguous.

Tablespaces can be created as locally managed (the default) or dictionary managed. Databases have one or more tablespaces, and tablespaces consist of one or more datafiles. Within those tablespaces, Oracle stores segments for database objects. Each segment can have multiple extents. Extent information for a specific object is stored in both the data dictionary and the segment headers. If a segment grows over a specific number of extents depending on the block size and platform, Oracle creates extent map blocks to keep track of the additional extents.

Managing the space used by tablespaces, datafiles, segments, and database objects is one of the basic functions of the DBA.

When you create a tablespace, specify the default storage parameters for the tablespace. Every object that is created in that tablespace will then use those storage parameters unless you explicitly override them. By establishing a consistent set of storage parameter values, you can simplify space allocation and management within your tablespaces, as shown in the following section of this chapter.

Implications of the STORAGE Clause

The amount of space used by a segment is determined by its storage parameters. These parameters are determined by the database at segment-creation time; if no specific storage parameters are given in the CREATE TABLE, CREATE INDEX, or CREATE CLUSTER command, then the database uses the default storage parameters for the tablespace in which the segment is to be stored.

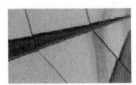

NOTE
You can assign default tablespaces to users, and you can assign space quotas within those tablespaces, via the CREATE USER, ALTER USER, and GRANT commands. See the Alphabetical Reference for the command syntax.

When you create a table, index, or other segment, you can use the default values for a locally managed tablespace (the recommended option) or specify a STORAGE clause as part of the CREATE command. You can also specify a TABLESPACE clause, enabling you to direct Oracle to store the data in a particular tablespace. For example, a CREATE TABLE command in a dictionary-managed tablespace may include the following clauses:

```
tablespace users
   storage (initial 1m next 1m pctincrease 0 minextents 1)
```

If no STORAGE clause is specified, the tablespace's default storage parameters will be used. For a locally managed USERS tablespace, the CREATE TABLE command would only need to include

```
tablespace users
```

The storage parameters specify the INITIAL extent size, the NEXT extent size, the PCTINCREASE (a factor by which each successive extent will geometrically grow), and the MINEXTENTS (minimum number of extents). After the segment has been created, the INITIAL and MINEXTENTS values cannot be altered unless you perform a reorganization of the object. The default values for the storage parameters for each tablespace are available in the DBA_TABLESPACES and USER_TABLESPACES views.

NOTE
The MAXEXTENTS clause is ignored for objects in a locally managed tablespace.

When you create a tablespace, you specify its default storage parameters. The following command creates a locally managed tablespace and specifies its default storage parameters. See the syntax for CREATE TABLESPACE in the Alphabetical Reference.

```
create tablespace codes_tables
   datafile '/u01/oracle/VLDB/codes_tables.dbf' size 20g
   extent management local uniform size 256K;
```

When a segment is created, it acquires at least one extent. The initial extent is used to store data until it no longer has any free space available (you can use the PCTFREE clause to reserve a percentage of space within each block in the segment to remain available for updates of existing rows). If you create a dictionary-managed tablespace, the extent sizes may not be uniform; the segment will extend by obtaining a second extent of the size specified by the NEXT parameter. By default, tablespaces are created with local extent management.

NOTE

Oracle best practices suggest a minimum extent size of 8MB for tables that will grow larger than 100MB.

Assuming that the block size for the database in which this tablespace is created is 4KB in this example, the tablespace is created with the extent management declared as LOCAL and with a uniform size of 256KB. Each bit in the bitmap describes 64 blocks (256/4). If the UNIFORM size clause is omitted, the default is AUTOALLOCATE. The default SIZE for UNIFORM is 1MB.

NOTE

If you specify LOCAL in a CREATE TABLESPACE command, you cannot specify a DEFAULT STORAGE clause, MINEXTENTS, or TEMPORARY.

Locally managed tablespaces can take over some of the space management tasks performed by DBAs in dictionary-managed tablespaces. Because of their architecture, they are less likely to be fragmented, and their objects are less likely to have space-related problems.

You can create a set of locally managed tablespaces with a small number of storage parameters and resolve most of the space requests in your database. For example, you could create three DATA tablespaces, as shown here:

```
create tablespace data_small
datafile '/u01/oracle/vldb/data_small.dbf'
size 100m
extent management local uniform size 1m;

create tablespace data_medium
datafile '/u01/oracle/vldb/data_medium.dbf'
size 1000m
extent management local uniform size 4m;

create tablespace data_large
datafile '/u01/oracle/vldb/data_large.dbf'
size 10000m
extent management local uniform size 16m;
```

In this example, the DATA_SMALL tablespace creates objects with extent sizes that are each 1MB; DATA_MEDIUM uses 4MB extent sizes, and DATA_LARGE uses 16MB extent sizes. If you have a small table, simply place it in the DATA_SMALL tablespace. If it grows significantly in size, you can move it to the DATA_MEDIUM or DATA_LARGE tablespace.

Within each of these example tablespaces, all objects have the same storage parameters, simplifying any future maintenance you perform. Using consistent extent sizes also improves space reuse once an object has been dropped from the tablespace or moved.

The following sections describe space management of each major object type. Note that if you use locally managed tablespaces, many of the STORAGE clause issues do not apply; you rely on the tablespace to manage the space based on the parameters defined at the tablespace level. Although this may result in some overallocation of space, it will greatly simplify the space management operations in your database.

Table Segments

Table segments, also called *data segments,* store the rows of data associated with tables or clusters. Each data segment contains a header block that serves as a space directory for the segment.

Once a data segment acquires an extent, it keeps that extent until the segment is dropped, truncated, or compressed. Deleting rows from a table via the DELETE command has no impact on the amount of space that has been allocated to that table. The number of extents will increase until either the user's quota in the tablespace is reached or the tablespace runs out of space (if the datafiles cannot autoextend).

To minimize the amount of wasted space in a data block, tune the PCTFREE parameter. The PCTFREE parameter specifies the amount of space that will be kept free within each datablock. The free space can then be used when NULL-VALUED columns are updated to have values or when updates to other values in the row force the total length of the row to increase. The proper setting of PCTFREE is application-specific because it depends on the nature of the updates that are being performed.

You can use the ALTER TABLE command to alter most storage parameters for an existing table. You can use the MOVE option of the ALTER TABLE command to change the tablespace assignment for a table.

Index Segments

Like table segments, *index segments* hold the space that has been allocated to them until they are dropped; however, they can also be indirectly dropped if the table or cluster they index is dropped. To minimize contention, indexes should be stored in a tablespace that is different from the tablespace that holds their associated tables.

You can use the REBUILD option of the ALTER INDEX command to alter the STORAGE and TABLESPACE settings for an index. In the following listing, the JOB_PK index is rebuilt in the INDEXES tablespace.

```
alter index job_pk rebuild
tablespace indexes;
```

During the index REBUILD process, both the old and the new indexes temporarily coexist in the database. Therefore, you must have enough space available to store both indexes prior to executing the ALTER INDEX REBUILD command.

NOTE
Add the ONLINE clause to the ALTER INDEX REBUILD command to allow DML to occur while the index is being rebuilt. There is some overhead for rebuilding objects online but may be worth the cost if high availability is critical.

While the index is being built, the optimizer will, by default, gather statistics about the index's contents.

System-Managed Undo

You can use *Automatic Undo Management (AUM)* to place all undo data in a single tablespace. When you create an undo tablespace, Oracle manages the storage, retention, and space utilization for your rollback data via system-managed undo.

To start using AUM, you must first create an undo tablespace using the following command:

```
create undo tablespace undo_tablespace datafile 'filespec' size n;
```

Next, set the UNDO_MANAGEMENT initialization parameter in your system parameter file or **init.ora** file to AUTO. Specify your undo tablespace via the UNDO_TABLESPACE initialization parameter. You do not need to create or manage any rollback segments within the undo tablespace.

Setting Undo Retention

You can explicitly manage how long Oracle retains undo data in the undo tablespace via the UNDO_RETENTION initialization parameter. Retaining undo serves two purposes: it supports the retention of inactive, in-use data for long-running queries, and it supports queries that show the prior state of current data (see Chapter 29).

For example, if you set

```
undo_retention=600
```

then Oracle will make a best effort to retain all committed undo data in the database for 600 seconds. With that setting, any query taking less than 10 minutes should not result in an ORA-1555 ("Snapshot too old") error. While the database is running, you can change the UNDO_RETENTION parameter value via the alter system command. You can use the CREATE TABLESPACE and ALTER TABLESPACE commands to force Oracle to guarantee that the requested undo retention is maintained even at the expense of current transactions.

Creating an Undo Tablespace

You can create an undo tablespace during the database creation process, as shown in the following listing:

```
create database undodb
undo tablespace undo_tbs1
...
```

In an existing database, you can use the CREATE TABLESPACE command to create an undo tablespace:

```
create undo tablespace undo_tbs
datafile '/u01/oracle/undodb/undo_tbs_1.dbf'
size 1500m;
```

See the Alphabetical Reference for the full syntax of the CREATE TABLESPACE command.

Once you have created an undo tablespace, you can manage it via the ALTER TABLESPACE command. For example, you can add datafiles to the undo tablespace or rename existing datafiles the same as you would for any other tablespace. To stop using a tablespace as your undo tablespace, use the ALTER SYSTEM command to set a new value for the UNDO_TABLESPACE initialization parameter, or change that parameter during a database shutdown/startup.

Temporary Segments

Temporary segments store temporary data during sorting operations (such as large queries, index creations, and UNIONs). Each user has a temporary tablespace specified when the account is created via CREATE USER, or altered via ALTER USER. The user's temporary tablespace must be a tablespace that has been designated as a temporary tablespace.

When you create a database, you can specify a default temporary tablespace for all users. For an existing database, you can change the default tablespace via the ALTER DATABASE command, as shown in the following listing:

```
alter database default temporary tablespace temp;
```

When you alter the database's default temporary tablespace assignment, users who had been assigned the old default temporary tablespace are redirected to the new default temporary tablespace. To see the current default temporary tablespace, execute the following query:

```
select property_value
from database_properties
where property_name = 'DEFAULT_TEMP_TABLESPACE';
```

You can specify a tablespace as a "temporary" tablespace via the CREATE TEMPORARY TABLESPACE command. A temporary tablespace cannot be used to hold any permanent segments, only temporary segments created during operations. The first sort to use the temporary tablespace allocates a temporary segment within the temporary tablespace; when the query completes, the space used by the temporary segment is not dropped. Instead, the space used by the temporary segment is available for use by other queries, allowing the sorting operation to avoid the costs of allocating and releasing space for temporary segments. If your application frequently uses temporary segments for sorting operations, the sorting process should perform better if a dedicated temporary tablespace is used.

You can create multiple temporary tablespaces and group them. Assign the temporary tablespaces to tablespace groups via the TABLESPACE group clause of the CREATE TEMPORARY TABLESPACE or ALTER TABLESPACE command. You can then specify the group as a user's default tablespace. Tablespace groups can help to support parallel operations involving sorts. To dedicate an existing tablespace for temporary segments, specify the TEMPORARY clause of the CREATE TABLESPACE or ALTER TABLESPACE command, as shown in the following listing:

```
alter tablespace temp temporary;
```

NOTE
If there are any permanent segments (tables or indexes, for example) stored in TEMP, the preceding command will fail.

To enable the TEMP tablespace to store permanent (nontemporary) objects, use the PERMANENT clause of the CREATE TABLESPACE or ALTER TABLESPACE command, as shown here:

```
alter tablespace temp permanent;
```

The CONTENTS column in the DBA_TABLESPACES data dictionary view displays the status of the tablespace as either "TEMPORARY" or "PERMANENT."

Free Space

A *free extent* in a tablespace is a collection of contiguous free blocks in the tablespace. A tablespace may contain multiple data extents and free extents. When a segment is dropped, its extents are not, by default, deallocated and marked as free. As of Oracle Database 10*g*, the default behavior is for the space to be retained while the object moves to the user's recycle bin. You can recover the object from the recycle bin via the FLASHBACK TABLE TO BEFORE DROP command (see Chapter 30). Space can be freed from the recycle bin via the PURGE command (see the Alphabetical Reference).

To force the tablespace to coalesce its free space, use the COALESCE clause of the ALTER TABLESPACE clause, as shown in the following listing:

```
alter tablespace data coalesce;
```

The preceding command forces the neighboring free extents in the DATA tablespace to be coalesced into larger free extents. The command coalesces up to eight separate areas, just like SMON.

NOTE
The ALTER TABLESPACE command will not coalesce free extents that are separated by data extents.

Locally managed tablespaces do not require the same degree of free space management. Because locally managed tablespaces can be configured to have consistent extent sizes for all segments, dropped extents are easily reused.

When allocating a new extent, Oracle will not merge contiguous free extents unless there is no alternative. In dictionary-managed tables, this can result in the large free extent at the rear of the tablespace being used while the smaller free extents toward the front of the tablespace are relatively unused. The small free extents become "speed bumps" in the tablespace because they are not, by themselves, of adequate size to be of use. As this usage pattern progresses, the amount of space wasted in the tablespace increases.

In an ideal database, all objects are created at their appropriate size, and all free space is always stored together, a resource pool waiting to be used. If you can avoid dynamic space allocation during application usage, you remove both an impact on performance and a source of potential application failure.

Sizing Database Objects

Choosing the proper space allocation parameters for database objects is critical. Developers should begin estimating space requirements before the first database objects are created.

Afterward, the space requirements can be refined based on actual usage statistics. The following sections discuss the space estimation methods for tables, indexes, and clusters.

Why Size Objects?

You should size your database objects for three reasons:

- To preallocate space in the database, thereby minimizing the amount of future work required to manage object space requirements
- To reduce the amount of space wasted due to overallocation of space
- To improve the likelihood of a dropped free extent being reused by another segment

You can accomplish all of these goals by following the sizing methodology shown in the following sections. This methodology is based on Oracle's internal methods for allocating space to database objects. Rather than rely on detailed calculations, the methodology relies on approximations that dramatically simplify the sizing process while simplifying the long-term maintainability of the database.

The Golden Rule for Space Calculations

Keep your space calculations simple, generic, and consistent across databases. You have far more productive ways to spend your work time than performing extremely detailed space calculations that Oracle may ignore anyway. Even if you follow the most rigorous sizing calculations, you cannot be sure how Oracle will load the data into the table or index.

Consider an index on a table with 100,000 rows. During tests, loading the data into the table in sorted order required 920 blocks for the index. The table and index were then truncated and the data was reloaded in a nonsorted order; the index now required 1,370 blocks. The 49 percent increase in space required by the index was due to Oracle's internal index management processes. If you can't reliably be within 49 percent of the correct answer, why spend a lot of time on sizing exercises?

In the following section, you'll see how to simplify the space estimation process, freeing you to perform much more useful DBA functions. These processes should be followed whether you are generating the default storage values for a dictionary-managed tablespace or the extent sizes for locally managed tablespaces.

The Ground Rules for Space Calculations

Oracle follows a set of internal rules when allocating space:

- Oracle only allocates whole blocks, not parts of blocks.
- Oracle allocates sets of blocks.
- Oracle may allocate larger or smaller sets of blocks depending on the available free space in the tablespace.

For locally managed tablespaces, the extents are always of a uniform size specified at creation or generated via the auto-allocate algorithm. Your goal should be to work with Oracle's space allocation methods instead of against them. If you use consistent extent sizes, you can largely delegate the space allocation to Oracle.

The Impact of Extent Size on Performance

No direct performance benefit is gained by reducing the number of extents in a table. In some situations (such as in parallel query environments), having multiple extents in a table can reduce I/O contention and enhance your performance. To simplify management, the extents need to be properly sized.

Oracle reads data from tables in two ways: by ROWID (usually immediately following an index access) and via full table scans. If the data is read via ROWID, then the number of extents in the table is not a factor in read performance. Oracle will read each row from its physical location (as specified in the ROWID) and retrieve the data.

To avoid paying any possible performance penalties for your extent sizes, you must choose between one of the following strategies:

- Create extents that are significantly larger than the I/O buffer size for your operating system. If the extents are very large, then few additional reads will be necessary even if the extent size is not a multiple of the I/O buffer size.

- Set DB_FILE_MULTIBLOCK_READ_COUNT to take full advantage of the I/O buffer size for your operating system. Note that setting it too high may make the optimizer think that full table scans are more efficient than they actually are, resulting in changes to existing execution plans. This parameter is also modifiable at the session level.

- If you must create small extents, choose extent sizes that are a multiple of the I/O buffer size for your operating system.

Sizing the Objects

To effectively manage your space, all you need to do is select a set of space values that meet the criteria described in the preceding sections. Once the space allocations are finalized, separate them by tablespace. For example:

```
create tablespace data_1m
datafile '/u01/oracle/vldb/data_1m.dbf'
size 100m
extent management local uniform size 1m;

create tablespace data_4m
datafile '/u02/oracle/vldb/data_4m.dbf'
size 400m
extent management local uniform size 4m;

create tablespace data_16m
datafile '/u03/oracle/vldb/data_16m.dbf'
size 16000m
extent management local uniform size 16m;
```

In this example, three separate DATA tablespaces are created, with extent sizes of 1MB, 4MB, and 16MB. If you need to create a table 3MB in size, you can create it either with three 1MB extents in DATA_1M or with one 4MB extent in DATA_4M. A table that will grow to 10MB can be placed in DATA_16M.

As your tables grow in size, your default storage clauses will grow in a consistent fashion, following the space rules and your standards for extent sizes. DATA_64M would be next, followed by DATA_256M and DATA_1G. Use the same extent sizes across your databases to ease space management of your entire database environment.

As the extent sizes grow, the distribution of extent sizes across tablespaces will usually result in a separation of table types—small static tables will be isolated in the tablespaces with small extent sizes. Large transaction processing tables (or their partitions) will be segregated to the large extent size tables, simplifying later management and tuning activities.

NOTE
The database block size may change at the tablespace level. Be sure the extent sizes you choose account for the largest block size in use in the database. Limiting the usage of nonstandard block sizes in the database simplifies cross-database maintenance and your sizing procedures.

Monitoring an Undo Tablespace

As described in Chapter 29, you can use Automatic Undo Management (AUM) to simplify transaction management. Specify values for the UNDO_TABLESPACE, UNDO_RETENTION, and UNDO_MANAGEMENT initialization parameters.

The primary view for gathering statistics on the undo tablespace usage is V$UNDOSTAT. The V$UNDOSTAT view provides a histogram of the retained data usage. In ten-minute intervals, Oracle records the total number of undo blocks consumed in the UNDOBLKS column of V$UNDOSTAT and the number of transactions supported in the TXNCOUNT column. You can use the data from V$UNDOSTAT to determine if the undo tablespace is properly sized for the transaction volume of the application. Oracle maintains 144 rows in V$UNDOSTAT, reflecting the past day's statistics.

Other columns of interest in V$UNDOSTAT include MAXQUERYLEN, which records the duration in seconds of the longest query executed; the undo retention must be greater than this value. If the NOSPACEERRCNT column of V$UNDOSTAT has a nonzero value, you should add space to the undo tablespace to avoid future space-related errors. Another column, SSOLDERRCNT, records the number of times an ORA-01555 ("snapshot too old") error occurs. Increasing the UNDO_RETENTION value can reduce this error's occurrence.

Automatic Storage Management

You can use Automatic Storage Management (ASM) to enhance and simplify your storage management efforts. ASM offers a number of significant advantages, including the following:

- You can easily add new disks to the set of disks available to the database; Oracle decides how to best use the disks to distribute the I/O workload.

- The I/O workload is dynamically distributed among the available disks, without DBA intervention.

- The I/O stripe width can be maintained at different levels for different types of files, all maintained by the database.

- Software mirroring can be enabled if hardware mirroring is not.

Configuring ASM

To use ASM, you must configure an ASM instance. See Chapters 2 and 3 on the use of the Oracle-provided tools for installing and configuring ASM and the database software.

You can then use the CREATE diskgroup command with the available disks. For example, you may have four disks available to you:

```
create diskgroup diskgroup1
external redundancy
disk '/u01', '/u02', '/u03', '/u04';
```

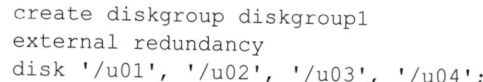

NOTE
You can use wildcards in the disk names.

The EXTERNAL REDUNDANCY clause means that the disk group is relying on hardware mirroring. To use software mirroring, use the NORMAL REDUNDANCY clause and specify the disks that comprise the mirror set via the FAILGROUP clause. In software mirroring, Oracle uses the mirror set as a set of disks, not as a one-to-one mirror of the diskgroup disks. To see the disks that constitute a disk group, query the V$ASM_DISK dynamic view.

Now that the disk group is available, create a tablespace that uses the disk group, as shown in the following example:

```
create tablespace users2 datafile '+diskgroup1/users2_01'
size 500m;
```

Oracle then creates the datafile for the USERS2 tablespace in the specified disk group and manages its I/O requirements across the available disks. If you need to add more disks to the disk group, use the ALTER DISKGROUP command:

```
alter diskgroup diskgroup1 add disk '/u05';
```

Diskgroups may be dropped via the DROP DISKGROUP command.

ASM instances are mounted but not opened. Once you create an ASM instance on a server, your database instances can use the ASM instance to manage the logical volumes for the database-related files.

In general, you should create separate diskgroups for separate types of files (datafiles, redo log files, archive log files, Data Pump Export files, and so on). You can then manage the physical layout for each type of file, allowing the write-intensive log files to be stored using a physical configuration that best supports writes, whereas the datafiles are stored in a layout that best supports reads.

Segment Space Management

In addition to automating the management of storage at the diskgroup level, Oracle has capabilities for managing the space within segments. You can use these options to reclaim unused space within segments, estimate future space needs, and reorganize tables online.

If your application frequently deletes rows from a table, that table's blocks may be only partially filled with rows. You can manually compress the space within the table via the ALTER TABLE command. First, enable row movement within the table:

```
alter table bookshelf_checkout enable row movement;
```

Next, have Oracle move rows within the table to compress the allocation of rows within blocks:

```
alter table bookshelf_checkout shrink space compact;
```

The SHRINK SPACE compact operation reorganizes the rows of the table so they are stored more compactly. However, the high-water mark for the table—the highest block number to which rows have ever been written—is unaffected. Because all full table scans read all blocks up to the high-water mark, you should adjust that value. You can adjust the high-water mark via the SHRINK SPACE clause of the ALTER TABLE command:

```
alter table bookshelf_checkout shrink space;
```

You can cascade the effects of this change to the table's indexes via the SHRINK SPACE cascade option.

To predict space usage, you can use the OBJECT_GROWTH_TREND function of the DBMS_ SPACE package. As parameters, pass the schema name, object name, and object type, as shown in the following listing. You should run this as a SYSDBA-privileged user.

```
select * from
table(dbms_space.object_growth_trend
('PRACTICE','BOOKSHELF_CHECKOUT','TABLE'));
```

The output shows the past space usage for the object along with projected space requirements for the object. The results are based on statistics gathered via the Automated Workload Repository (AWR). Using the MMON background process, AWR collects and stores database statistics that support administration and tuning on an hourly basis. The information gathered via AWR allows Oracle to project your future space usage as well as identify tuning opportunities.

Transporting Tablespaces

A *transportable* tablespace is a tablespace that can be "unplugged" from one database and "plugged into" another (see Chapter 49 for creating and using pluggable databases). To be transportable, a tablespace—or a set of tablespaces—must be self-contained. The tablespace set cannot contain any objects that refer to objects in other tablespaces. Thus, if you transport a tablespace containing indexes, you must move the tablespace containing the indexes' base tables as part of the same transportable tablespace set. The better you have organized and distributed your objects among tablespaces, the easier it is to generate a self-contained set of tablespaces to transport.

To transport tablespaces, you need to generate a tablespace set, copy or move that tablespace set to the new database, and plug the set into the new database. The databases must be on the same operating system, with the same version of Oracle and character set.

Generating a Transportable Tablespace Set

A transportable tablespace set contains all of the datafiles for the tablespaces being moved, along with an export of the metadata for those tablespaces. You can optionally choose whether to include referential integrity constraints as part of the transportable tablespace set. If you choose to use referential integrity constraints, the transportable tablespace set will increase to include the tables required to maintain the key relationships. Referential integrity is optional because you may have the same code tables in multiple databases. For example, you may be planning to move a tablespace from your test database to your production database. If you have a COUNTRY table in the test database, then you may already have an identical COUNTRY table in the production database. Because the code tables are identical in the two databases, you do not need to transport that portion of the referential integrity constraints. You could transport the tablespace containing the noncode tables and then reenable the referential integrity in the target database once the tablespace has been moved, simplifying the creation of the transportable tablespace set.

To determine if a tablespace set is self-contained, execute the TRANSPORT_SET_CHECK procedure of the DBMS_TTS package. This procedure takes two input parameters: the set of tablespaces and a Boolean flag set to TRUE if you want referential integrity constraints to be considered. In the following example, referential integrity constraints are not considered for the combination of the AGG_DATA and AGG_INDEXES tablespaces:

```
execute dbms_tts.transport_set_check('AGG_DATA,AGG_INDEXES',false);
```

NOTE
You cannot transport the SYSTEM, SYSAUX, or temporary tablespaces.

If there are any self-containment violations in the specified set, Oracle will populate the TRANSPORT_SET_VIOLATIONS data dictionary view. If there are no violations, the view will be empty.

Once you have selected a self-contained set of tablespaces, make the tablespaces read-only, as shown here:

```
alter tablespace agg_data read only;
alter tablespace agg_indexes read only;
```

Next, export the metadata for the tablespaces, using the TRANSPORT_TABLESPACES and TABLESPACES parameters for the Oracle Data Pump **expdp** command:

```
expdp transport_tablespaces=y tablespaces=(agg_data,agg_indexes)
   constraints=n  grants=y triggers=n
```

As shown in the example, you can specify whether triggers, constraints, and grants are exported along with the tablespace metadata. You should also note the names of the accounts that own objects in the transportable tablespace set. You can now copy the tablespaces' datafiles to a separate area. If needed, you can put the tablespaces back into read-write mode in their current database. After you have generated the transportable tablespace set, you can move its files (including the export) to an area that the target database can access.

Plugging in the Transportable Tablespace Set

Once the transportable tablespace set has been moved to an area accessible to the target database, you can plug the set into the target database. First, use the Oracle Data Pump **impdp** command to import the exported metadata:

```
impdp transport_tablespaces=y datafiles=(agg_data.dbf, agg_indexes.dbf)
```

In the import, you specify the datafiles that are part of the transportable tablespace set. You can optionally specify the tablespaces (via the TABLESPACES parameter) and the object owners (via the OWNERS parameter).

After the import completes, all tablespaces in the transportable tablespace set are left in read-only mode. You can issue the ALTER TABLESPACE read write command in the target database to place the new tablespaces in read-write mode:

```
alter tablespace agg_data read write;
alter tablespace agg_indexes read write;
```

Note that you cannot change the ownership of the objects being transported.

Transportable tablespaces support fast movement of large datasets. In a data warehouse, you could use transportable tablespaces to publish aggregations from core warehouse to datamart, or from the datamarts to a global data warehouse. Any read-only data can be quickly distributed to multiple databases—instead of sending SQL scripts, you can send datafiles and exported metadata. This modified data movement process may greatly simplify your procedures for managing remote databases, remote datamarts, and large data-movement operations.

As of Oracle 11g, you can transport one partition of a partitioned table. When the partition's metadata is imported on the target side, use the DEPARTITION option for Data Pump Import (**impdp**) to import the partition as a stand-alone table in the new environment. See Chapter 24 for details on Oracle Data Pump.

> **NOTE**
> *The source and target operating systems can be different; endian conversion is supported during this process. The datafiles must be converted via RMAN's CONVERT TABLESPACE TO PLATFORM command.*

Performing Backups

Like the rest of the material in this chapter, this section provides an overview rather than an in-depth review. Backup and recovery is a complex topic, and all backup and recovery methods should be thoroughly tested and practiced before being implemented in a production environment. The purpose of this section is to give developers an understanding of Oracle's capabilities, along with an understanding of the impact of backup decisions on recovery efforts and availability. Before using backup and recovery methods in a production environment, you should refer to books that are dedicated to that topic, including Oracle's documentation.

The backup methods provided by Oracle can be categorized as follows:

■ Logical backups using Data Pump Export and Import

- Physical file system backups: offline backups and online backups
- Incremental physical file system backups via Recovery Manager (RMAN)

The following sections describe each of these methods and their capabilities.

Data Pump Export and Import

Data Pump is a server-based data-extraction and import utility. Its features include significant architectural and functional enhancements over the original Import and Export utilities. Data Pump allows you to stop and restart jobs, see the status of running jobs, and restrict the data that is exported and imported. As of Oracle 11*g*, you can compress and encrypt the output data as it is being written, change it as it is being written (via the REMAP_DATA option), and have partitions imported as stand-alone tables.

NOTE
Data Pump can use files generated via the original Export utility, but the original Import utility cannot use the files generated from Data Pump Export.

Data Pump runs as a server process, thus benefiting users in multiple ways. The client process that starts the job can disconnect and later reattach to the job. Performance is enhanced (as compared to Export/Import) because the data no longer has to be processed by a client program. Data Pump extractions and loads can be parallelized, thus further enhancing performance.

Data Pump performs a logical backup of the data; it queries the data from the tables in a running database. During a recovery, Data Pump can be used to restore the database (or selected tables) to the point in time when the export was started. The data restored via Data Pump cannot then be rolled forward to later points in time—it is a fixed snapshot of the data as it existed when the backup was executed.

See Chapter 24 for a full description of Data Pump and its capabilities.

Offline Backups

An *offline backup* (sometimes called a *cold backup*) is a physical backup of the database files, made after the database has been shut down via either a SHUTDOWN NORMAL or a SHUTDOWN IMMEDIATE or a SHUTDOWN TRANSACTIONAL command. While the database is shut down, each of the files that is actively used by the database is backed up. These files provide a complete image of the database as it existed at the moment it was shut down.

The following files should be backed up during cold backups:

- All datafiles
- One copy of the control file
- Password file
- Initialization parameter file **init***DB*.**ora**

Having all of these files backed up *while the database is closed* provides a complete image of the database as it existed at the time it was closed. The full set of these files could be retrieved from the backups at a later date and the database would be able to function. It is *not* valid to perform a file system backup of the database while it is open unless an online backup is being performed (as discussed in the next section of this chapter).

NOTE
Oracle best practice suggests that your online redo log files do not need to be backed up.

Ideally, all of the datafiles are located in directories at the same level on each device. For example, all database files may be stored in an instance-specific subdirectory under an **/oracle** directory for each device (such as **/db01/oracle/MYDB**). Directories such as these should contain all of the datafiles, redo log files, and control files for a database. The only file you may optionally add to the offline backup that will not be in this location is the production initialization parameter file, which should be in either the **/u01/app/oracle/admin/*instance_name*/pfile** subdirectory under the Oracle software base directory or the **./dbs** directory under the Oracle software home directory.

If you use the directory structure in the prior example, your backup commands are greatly simplified because you can use wildcards in the filenames. After shutting down the database, back up the files to the backup destination area (either a tape or a separate disk area).

Because offline backups involve changes to the database's availability, they are usually scheduled to occur at night.

Offline backups are very reliable. To reduce their impact on the database's availability, you may use online backups. As described in the following section, online backups use Oracle's ARCHIVELOG mode to allow consistent file system backups during database usage.

Online Backups

You can use online backups for any database that is running in ARCHIVELOG mode. In this mode, the online redo logs are archived, creating a full log of all transactions within the database.

Oracle writes to the online redo log files in a cyclical fashion; after filling the first log file, it begins writing to the second log until that one fills, and then it begins writing to the third. Once the last online redo log file is filled, the Log Writer (LGWR) background process begins to overwrite the contents of the first redo log file.

When Oracle is run in ARCHIVELOG mode, the ARC0-ARCt (Archiver) background processes make a copy of each redo log file before overwriting it. These archived redo log files are usually written to a disk device. The archived redo log files may also be written directly to a tape device, but this tends to be quite operator-intensive.

You can perform file system backups of a database while that database is open, provided the database is running in ARCHIVELOG mode. An online backup involves setting each tablespace (or the entire database) into a backup state, backing up the related datafiles, and then restoring the tablespaces to their normal state.

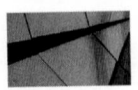

NOTE
When using the Oracle-supplied RMAN utility, you do not have to place each tablespace into a backup state.

The database can be fully recovered from an online backup, and can, via the archived redo logs, be rolled forward to any point in time. When the database is then opened, any committed transactions that were in the database at that time will have been restored and any uncommitted transactions will have been rolled back.

While the database is open, the following files can be backed up, depending on the RMAN command used:

- All datafiles
- All archived redo log files
- One control file, via the ALTER DATABASE command

Online backup procedures are powerful for two reasons. First, they provide full point-in-time recovery. Databases that are not running in ARCHIVELOG mode can only be recovered to the point in time when the backup occurred. Second, they allow the database to remain open during the file system backup. Thus, even databases that cannot be shut down owing to user requirements can still have file system backups.

Getting Started

To make use of the ARCHIVELOG capability, the database must first be placed in ARCHIVELOG mode. The following listing shows the steps needed to place a database in ARCHIVELOG mode. Run SQL*Plus and mount the database (providing its name in place of MYDB in these examples), and then alter it as shown here:

```
connect / as sysdba
startup mount mydb;
alter database archivelog;
alter database open;
```

The following command displays the current ARCHIVELOG status of the database from within SQL*Plus:

```
archive log list
```

NOTE
To see the currently active online redo log and its sequence number, query the V$LOG dynamic view.

To change a database back to NOARCHIVELOG mode, use the following set of commands after shutting down the database:

```
connect / as sysdba
startup mount mydb;
alter database noarchivelog;
alter database open;
```

A database that has been placed in ARCHIVELOG mode remains in that mode until it is placed in NOARCHIVELOG mode. The location of the archived redo log files is determined by the settings in the database's parameter file. The parameters to note are as follows (with sample values):

```
log_archive_dest_1          = /db01/oracle/arch/CC1
log_archive_dest_state_1    = ENABLE
log_archive_format = arch%s.arc
```

In this example, the archived redo log files are being written to the directory **/db01/oracle/arch/CC1**. The archived redo log files all begin with the letters *arch,* followed by a sequence number. For example, the archived redo log file directory may contain the following files:

```
arch_170.arc
arch_171.arc
arch_172.arc
```

Each of these files contains the data from a single online redo log. They are numbered sequentially, in the order in which they are created. The size of the archived redo log files varies, but does not exceed the size of the online redo log files. Within the LOG_ARCHIVE_FORMAT setting, the available variables are

Variable	Description
%s	Log sequence number
%S	Log sequence number, zero filled
%t	Thread number
%T	Thread number, zero filled
%a	Activation ID
%d	Database ID
%r	Reset logs ID that ensures unique names are constructed for the archived log files across multiple incarnations of the database

If the destination directory of the archived redo log files runs out of space, then ARCH stops processing the online redo log data and the database temporarily hangs. This situation can be resolved by adding more space to the archived redo log file destination disk or by backing up the archived redo log files and then removing them from this directory. You can also specify an alternate location via the LOG_ARCHIVE_DEST_*n* parameter; this location will only be used when the initial location is full.

NOTE
Never delete archived redo log files until you have backed them up and verified that you can restore them successfully.

The database will *not* be in ARCHIVELOG mode unless you have executed the ALTER DATABASE archivelog command shown earlier in this section. Once the database is in ARCHIVELOG mode, it remains in that mode through subsequent database shutdowns and startups until you explicitly place it in NOARCHIVELOG mode via the ALTER DATABASE

NOARCHIVELOG command. The LOG_ARCHIVE_MAX_PROCESSES parameter must be set to a value greater than 0 for archiving to start; its default value is 2.

NOTE
The archivelog destination area is different from the flash recovery area. The flash recovery area supports the FLASHBACK DATABASE command. See Chapter 30 for details of this command and its associated parameters.

Performing Online Database Backups Using O/S Utilities

Once a database is running in ARCHIVELOG mode, you can back it up while it is open and available to users. This capability allows round-the-clock database availability to be achieved while still guaranteeing the recoverability of the database.

Although online backups can be performed during normal working hours, they should be scheduled for the times of the least user activity for several reasons. First, the online backups use operating-system commands to back up the physical files, and these commands use the available I/O resources in the system (impacting the system performance for interactive users). Second, while the tablespaces are being backed up, the manner in which transactions are written to the archived redo log files changes. When you put a tablespace in "backup" mode, the DBWR process writes all of the blocks in the buffer cache that belong to any file that is part of the tablespace back to disk. When the blocks are read back into memory and then changed, they are copied to the log buffer the first time that a change is made to them. As long as they stay in the buffer cache, they are not recopied to the online redo log file. This uses a great deal more space in the archived redo log file destination directory.

The command file for a hot backup has three parts:

- A backup of the datafiles, which in turn consists of
  - Setting the tablespaces into backup state
  - Backing up the tablespace's datafiles
  - Restoring the tablespace to its normal state
- A backup of the archived redo log files, which consists of
  - Recording which files are in the archived redo log destination directory
  - Backing up the archived redo log files, then (optionally) deleting or compressing them
- A backup of the control file via the ALTER DATABASE BACKUP CONTROLFILE command

NOTE
The online backup process is automated via the RMAN utility.

You can create a script to perform the backups, but using RMAN is preferred.

When the datafiles are being backed up, you may back them up directly to tape or to disk. If you have enough disk space available, choose the latter option because it greatly reduces the time necessary for the backup procedures to complete.

Recovery Manager

A Recovery Manager utility called RMAN is provided with the Oracle database to enable you to back up and recover your databases in an automated manner using either a command-line mode or the Recovery Manager from within the Oracle Enterprise Manager. You can use either approach to back up, restore, and recover database files. One of the biggest benefits of RMAN is that it does not put the tablespaces into hot backup mode, so changed data blocks are not copied to the online redo log files, which impacts system I/O resources.

Recovery Manager keeps track of backups either through a Recovery Catalog or by placing the required information into the control file for the database being backed up. Recovery Manager adds new backup capabilities that are unavailable in the other Oracle backup utilities.

The Recovery Manager has four components: the RMAN executable, one or more target databases, the recovery catalog database (optional), and the media management software (if you're not using disk as a backup medium). The only components that you must have are the RMAN executable and a target database.

Recovery Manager allows you to perform incremental physical backups of datafiles. During a full (called a *level 0*) datafile backup, all of the blocks ever used in the datafile are backed up. During a cumulative (*level 1*) datafile backup, all of the blocks used since the last full datafile backup are backed up. An incremental (*level 2*) datafile backup backs up only those blocks that have changed since the most recent cumulative or full backup. You can define the levels used for incremental backups.

The ability to perform incremental and cumulative backups of datafiles may greatly improve the performance of backups. The greatest performance improvements will be realized by very large databases in which only a small subset of a large tablespace changes. Using the traditional backup methods, you would need to back up *all* of the datafiles in the tablespace. Using Recovery Manager, you only back up the blocks that have changed since the last backup.

During database recovery using Recovery Manager, you need to know which files are current, which are restored, and the backup method you plan to use. If you use the recovery catalog, Recovery Manager stores its catalog of information in an Oracle database—and you need to back up that database or else you may lose your entire backup and recovery catalog of information.

Recovery Manager is only used by DBAs who need to make the decisions regarding the Recovery Manager architecture for your environment (for example, deciding on the location of the recovery catalog). You should work with your DBA to understand the recovery options in use and their implications for database availability and recovery time.

Where to Go from Here

This chapter has given you a high-level overview of the topics that production DBAs deal with every day. In addition to the topics discussed here, DBAs monitor databases, tune databases, install software, maintain database connectivity, and many other tasks. If you are interested in learning more about those tasks, see your Oracle documentation set or the *Oracle Database 12*c *DBA Handbook*. The more developers understand about database administration, the more likely they are to build applications that take advantage of the database's inherent capabilities.

CHAPTER
52

The Hitchhiker's Guide to XML in Oracle

Xtensible Markup Language (XML) is a standardized syntax for describing hierarchical data. Rather than being a programming language, XML is a universal format for structured documents and data. Its tag-based syntax, which will be familiar to those familiar with HTML (Hypertext Markup Language), gives it the flexibility to handle complex data. Whereas HTML tells a web browser how to present data, XML tells applications what the data means.

XML is well suited to solving data-interchange problems among heterogeneous systems; database-resident data is easily accessed, converted, and stored. This chapter is an overview of the XML access methods available in Oracle. XML and its toolsets are always evolving; see www. w3.org for the most current information.

Document Type Definitions, Elements, and Attributes

In XML, application-specific tags or "elements" wrap around the data they describe. The syntax for these tags is defined in a special kind of XML document called a *Document Type Definition (DTD)*. The DTD defines the structure for a valid XML document. The structure is strictly hierarchical.

Each XML document is an instantiation of an *infoset*—the abstract data model consisting of a document and its information items. Information items are mostly elements, attributes, and content. For example, an XML infoset may contain the following:

```
<book>
   <title>My Ledger</title>
   <chapter num="1">
      <title>Beginning</title>
      <text>&chapter1;</text>
   </chapter>
</book>
```

In this example, the tags **<book>** and **</book>** define the starting and ending points of the infoset. The XML document describes a book named "My Ledger." That book has chapters, and the first chapter's title is "Beginning." The text of the chapter is not stored inside the XML document; instead, a pointer is created to an external file.

In addition to being a tag in the file, **title** is an element. It has content (in this example, "My Ledger"). As shown in this example, you can set the content of elements by providing values between tags (for the title) or within the tag (as in the chapter number setting). Elements can contain content, child elements, or both, or they may be empty. For data interchange, you should avoid creating elements that contain both content and child elements. To create an empty element, its tag would be in this format:

```
<name/>
```

NOTE
Element names are case sensitive.

Each element has exactly one parent, and a parent can have any number of children. The strict hierarchical nature of XML means that if an element starts within another element (such as **chapter** within **book**), its ending tag must precede the ending tag for the parent element.

As shown in the book example, elements have attributes. For example, the chapter element has an attribute named *num*. The attribute value is enclosed in double quotes:

```
<chapter num="1">
```

NOTE
Like element names, attribute names are case sensitive.

In general, applications use element attributes for specific items (such as the chapter number) and element content for the bulk of the data (in this case, the chapter text).

An XML document is said to be "well-formed" if the following conditions are met:

- Every start tag has a matching end tag.

- Elements do not overlap.

- There is one root element.

- Attribute values are always within quotes.

- An element does not have two attributes within the same name.

- Comments and processing instructions do not appear inside tags.

- There are no "unescaped" < or & signs in an element's or attribute's character data.

These are the basic syntax rules. Even if an XML document conforms to these rules, however, it may still not be valid. To be valid, the XML document must conform to the rules of a *Document Type Definition (DTD)*. The DTD is a formal way of describing what elements and entities-may appear in an XML document and what each element's contents and attributes are.

For example, consider the following XML document:

```
<?xml version="1.0" encoding="UTF-8"?>
<!DOCTYPE CustomerList SYSTEM "Example1.dtd">
<CustomerList>
    <Customer preferredCustomer="">
        <ID>123454321</ID>
        <Address>
            <Name>Epic</Name>
            <Street>1979 Milky Way Drive</Street>
            <City>Verona</City>
            <State>WI</State>
            <Country>USA</Country>
            <ZIP_CODE>53593</ZIP_CODE>
            <PHONE>608-271-9000</PHONE>
        </Address>
        <CreditRating>Excellent</CreditRating>
        <SalesRepID></SalesRepID>
        <RegionID>5</RegionID>
        <Comments>This is a test XML document</Comments>
```

```
    <ShippingMethod>M</ShippingMethod>
  </Customer>
</CustomerList>
```

The first line is an XML declaration, which starts with **<?** and ends with **?>**:

```
<?xml version="1.0" encoding="UTF-8"?>
```

The *version* attribute should be set to 1.0 for now. The *encoding* attribute is optional; its default value is UTF-8. You can also set a third attribute, *standalone*. In this case, the XML document is not a stand-alone document; it has a related DTD, as specified in the second line:

```
<!DOCTYPE CustomerList SYSTEM "Example1.dtd">
```

For this example, the related DTD file **Example1.dtd** is shown in the following listing:

```
<?xml version="1.0" encoding="UTF-8"?>
<!ELEMENT CustomerList (Customer*)>
<!ELEMENT Customer (ID, Address, CreditRating*, SalesRepID*,
                    RegionID, Comments*, ShippingMethod)>
<!ATTLIST Customer preferredCustomer CDATA #IMPLIED>
<!ELEMENT ID (#PCDATA)>
<!ELEMENT Address (Name, Street*, City, County,
                   State, Country, ZIP_CODE, PHONE)>
<!ELEMENT Name (#PCDATA)>
<!ELEMENT Street (#PCDATA)>
<!ELEMENT City (#PCDATA)>
<!ELEMENT County (#PCDATA)>
<!ELEMENT State (#PCDATA)>
<!ELEMENT Country (#PCDATA)>
<!ELEMENT ZIP_CODE (#PCDATA)>
<!ELEMENT PHONE (#PCDATA)>
<!ELEMENT CreditRating (#PCDATA)>
<!ELEMENT SalesRepID (#PCDATA)>
<!ELEMENT RegionID (#PCDATA)>
<!ELEMENT Comments (#PCDATA)>
<!ELEMENT ShippingMethod (#PCDATA)>
```

The DTD is analogous to the control file specifications for SQL*Loader and external tables. It tells applications what they will find in the XML document—the element names and the hierarchy of elements. An XML document can have only one DTD.

The syntax for the element declarations is

```
<!ELEMENT element_name (content_model)>
```

where *content_model* specifies what children an element can or must have and the order they are in. The simplest content model is #PCDATA, which says that the element can contain only parsed character data. Here's an example:

```
<!ELEMENT Name (#PCDATA)>
```

In this example, the **CustomerList** element contains zero or more **Customer** elements, as indicated by the * suffix:

```
<!ELEMENT CustomerList (Customer*)>
```

The allowable suffixes are as follows:

```
*     Permits zero or more occurrences
+     Permits one or more occurrences
?     Permits zero or one occurrences
```

As shown in the **Address** element specification, you can specify a sequence of multiple elements by separating them with commas:

```
<!ELEMENT Address (Name, Street*, City, County,
                   State, Country, ZIP_CODE, PHONE)>
```

You can provide multiple options within the specification, separated by the vertical bar (|) character. For example, a point on a two-dimensional graph may be specified via its horizontal and vertical measurements or its distance and angle from the center:

```
<!ELEMENT Point ((x,y) | (distance, angle))>
```

For real-world applications, DTDs can quickly become very complex. You can have attribute lists, external references, entity attributes, IDs, conditional inclusions, and other structures within your DTD. Refer to XML documentation for a thorough review of DTD structures and options.

XML Schema

The XML Schema specification is an alternative to DTDs. It includes datatyping, which is particularly helpful when working with relational databases. Whereas DTDs are not extensible (they're just control files), XML Schema is extensible in the following ways:

- Parts of schemas can be reused in other schemas.
- Complex structures can be reused in other schemas.
- Derived datatypes can be created based on existing datatypes.
- A single document instance can reference multiple schemas.

Within XML Schema, elements are declared using **xsd:element**, as shown in the following listing:

```
<xsd:element name="Date">
```

The element's datatype can be declared via the *type* attribute:

```
<xsd:element name="Date" type="date">
```

You can specify the minimum and maximum number of occurrences for the element via the *minOccurs* and *maxOccurs* attributes:

```
<xsd:element name="Date" type="date" minOccurs="0" maxOccurs="1">
```

Built-in XML Schema types include primitive types (such as **string**, **Boolean**, **number**, **float**, **date**, **time**, and **datetime**) and derived types (such as **normalizedString**, **integer**, **token**, and **language**). The full list of types can be found at www.w3.org/TR/xmlschema-2/.

You can create and name complex types, just as you can create abstract datatypes in Oracle. The following code creates the **Address** type:

```
<xsd:complexType name="Address">
  <xsd:sequence>
    <xsd:element name="Street1"/>
    <xsd:element name="Street2"/>
    <xsd:element name="City"/>
    <xsd:element name="State"/>
    <xsd:element name="Zip"/>
  </xsd:sequence>
</xsd:complexType>
```

You can then refer to the **Address** complex type when defining your elements:

```
<xsd:element name="mailingAddress" type="Address"/>
<xsd:element name="billingAddress" type="Address"/>
```

If you are declaring a content model for a single element, use an anonymous type, as shown in the following listing:

```
<xsd:element name="Name">
  <xsd:complexType>
    <xsd:sequence>
      <xsd:element name="First"/>
      <xsd:element name="MiddleInitial"/>
      <xsd:element name="Last"/>
    </xsd:sequence>
  </xsd:complexType>
</xsd:element>
```

Attributes are declared using **xsd:attribute**, as shown in the following example:

```
<xsd:attribute name="paid" type="boolean"/>
```

You can create attributes within a complex type:

```
<xsd:element name="Invoice">
  <xsd:complexType>
    <xsd:attribute name="paid" use="optional" default="True"/>
  </xsd:complexType>
</xsd:element>
```

In addition to creating attributes, you can create attribute groups and model groups. *Model groups* are groups or element definitions named for reuse. The **group** element must be a top-level schema component (a child of the **schema** element). For example, the following listing shows the creation of a **MealOptions** group, referenced by the **FlightDinner** element:

```
<xsd:element name="FlightDinner">
   <xsd:sequence>
      <xsd:element ref="Name"/>
      <xsd:group ref="MealOptions"/>
   </xsd:sequence>
</xsd:element>

<xsd:group name="MealOptions">
   <xsd:choice>
      <xsd:element name="Fish" type="Meal"/>
      <xsd:element name="Meat" type="Meal"/>
      <xsd:element name="Vegetarian" type="Meal"/>
   </xsd:choice>
</xsd:group>
```

Attributes are commonly grouped together if elements often use the same set of attributes. This approach is similar to the one described in Chapter 39, in which common attributes are combined to form new object types. For example, the following definition for a **Product** element uses an attribute group named *productDetails*. Other elements can reuse this same attribute group, improving your ability to enforce a standardized representation of this data.

```
<xsd:element name="Product">
   <xsd:complexType>
      <xsd:attributeGroup ref="productDetails"/>
   </xsd:complexType>
</xsd:element>

<xsd:attributeGroup name="productDetails">
   <xsd:attribute name="productID" use="required" type="xsd:ID"/>
   <xsd:attribute name="name" use="required" type="xsd:string"/>
   <xsd:attribute name="description" use="required" type="xsd:string"/>
   <xsd:attribute name="unit" type="xsd:positiveInteger"/>
   <xsd:attribute name="price" use="required" type="xsd:decimal"/>
   <xsd:attribute name="stock" type="xsd:integer"/>
</xsd:attributeGroup>
```

You can enforce uniqueness within a document instance by using **xsd:unique**:

```
<xsd:unique name="uniqueProductID">
   <xsd:selector xpath="tc:Product/"/>
   <xsd:field xpath="tc:@productID"/>
</xsd:unique>
```

Uniqueness is declared at the same level as the complex type definition for the **Product** element. The **tc:** namespace is for the schema you are creating and is declared in the **xsd:schema** element. The **xsd:selector** value specifies the elements to constrain (the **Product** elements), and **xsd:field** specifies the attribute to constrain (PRODUCTID).

You can use **xsd:key** and **xsd:keyref** to create references between elements. For example, you can create a **Customer** element and then reference it from multiple **Invoice** elements:

```
<xsd:key name="customerID">
   <xsd:selector xpath="tc:SalesData/"/>
   <xsd:field xpath="tc:Customer/@CustID"/>
</xsd:key>

<xsd:keyref name="item" refer="customerID">
   <xsd:selector xpath="tc:SalesData/"/>
   <xsd:field xpath="tc:Invoice/@CustID"/>
</xsd:keyref>
```

To allow an element to be **NULL**, use the *nillable* attribute:

```
<xsd:element name="FlightDinner" nillable="true"/>
```

Using XSU to Select, Insert, Update, and Delete XML Values

You can use Oracle's XML-SQL Utility (XSU) to convert the result of a SQL query to XML. XSU supports dynamic generation of DTDs and the insertion of XML into database tables. You can also use XSU to update or delete rows from database objects.

You can access XSU via Java and PL/SQL APIs (application programming interfaces). The XSU Java classes are part of the Oracle kernel software. The PL/SQL API is a wrapper that publishes the Java classes to PL/SQL. Because the XSU classes are stored in the database, you can write new stored procedures to access XSU's Java classes directly. Because a PL/SQL API is available, XSU's functionality can be accessed directly through SQL.

For example, you can generate the XML version of the RATING table via the XSU PL/SQL procedures. The following listing creates a procedure named PRINTCLOBOUT that will be called as part of the data-output process. The data will be read in as a CLOB.

```
create or replace procedure printclobout(result in out nocopy clob)
  is
xmlstr varchar2(32767);
line varchar2(2000);
begin
  xmlstr := dbms_lob.substr(result,32767);
  loop
    exit when xmlstr is null;
    line := substr(xmlstr,1,instr(xmlstr,chr(10))-1);
    dbms_output.put_line('| '||line);
    xmlstr := substr(xmlstr,instr(xmlstr,chr(10))+1);
  end loop;
end;
/
```

Now that the PRINTCLOBOUT procedure exists, run the following anonymous PL/SQL block. This block queries the RATING table, so that table must be accessible from your schema.

NOTE
You must SET SERVEROUTPUT ON prior to executing this PL/SQL block.

```
declare
   queryctx dbms_xmlquery.ctxtype;
   result clob;
begin
   -- set up the query context...
   queryctx := dbms_xmlquery.newcontext('select * from rating');
    -- get the result...
   result := dbms_xmlquery.getxml(queryctx);
   -- now you can use the result to put it in tables/send as messages...
   printclobout(result);
   dbms_xmlquery.closecontext(queryctx);  -- you must close the query...
end;
/
```

The result is the RATING table, formatted with XML tags:

```
| <?xml version = '1.0'?>
| <ROWSET>
|    <ROW num="1">
|       <RATING>1</RATING>
|       <RATINGDESCRIPTION>ENTERTAINMENT</RATINGDESCRIPTION>
|    </ROW>
|    <ROW num="2">
|       <RATING>2</RATING>
|       <RATINGDESCRIPTION>BACKGROUND INFORMATION</RATINGDESCRIPTION>
|    </ROW>
|    <ROW num="3">
|       <RATING>3</RATING>
|       <RATINGDESCRIPTION>RECOMMENDED</RATINGDESCRIPTION>
|    </ROW>
|    <ROW num="4">
|       <RATING>4</RATING>
|       <RATINGDESCRIPTION>STRONGLY RECOMMENDED</RATINGDESCRIPTION>
|    </ROW>
|    <ROW num="5">
|       <RATING>5</RATING>
|       <RATINGDESCRIPTION>REQUIRED READING</RATINGDESCRIPTION>
|    </ROW>
| </ROWSET>

PL/SQL procedure successfully completed.
```

Insert, Update, and Delete Processing with XSU

To insert a document into a table or view, use the DBMS_XMLSAVE package. XSU will parse the document and create an INSERT statement that inserts the values into all the columns of the table or view. An absent element is treated as a NULL value.

```
create or replace procedure insproc(xmldoc in clob,
tablename in varchar2) is
    insctx dbms_xmlsave.ctxtype;
    rows number;
  begin
    insctx := dbms_xmlsave.newcontext(tablename); -- get the context
    rows := dbms_xmlsave.insertxml(insctx,xmldoc); -- insert the doc
    dbms_xmlsave.closecontext(insctx);             -- close the handle
  end;
  /
```

You can now pass in XML documents as CLOB input values to the INSPROC procedure, along with the table name. INSPROC will take the XML document and insert its values into the table. Updates can be executed via calls to a separate procedure, UPDATEPROC, shown in the following listing:

```
create or replace procedure updateproc ( xmldoc in clob) is
    updctx dbms_xmlsave.ctxtype;
    rows number;
  begin
    updctx := dbms_xmlsave.newcontext('rating');  -- get context
    dbms_xmlsave.clearupdatecolumnlist(updctx); -- clear settings
    dbms_xmlsave.setkeycolumn(updctx,'rating'); -- set rating as key
    rows := dbms_xmlsave.updatexml(updctx,xmldoc);  -- update
    dbms_xmlsave.closecontext(updctx);              -- close context
  end;
  /
```

In this example, the RATING column is the key column used for the update's WHERE clause:

```
    dbms_xmlsave.setkeycolumn(updctx,'rating'); -- set rating as key
```

The new values are passed in as an XML document in CLOB format, and the RATING table values are updated based on the contents of the XML document.

Delete operations function in much the same way. The following procedure takes an XML document as its input, establishes the RATING column as the key for the RATING table, and performs the DELETE based on the key values in the input document. Note that **newContext** takes the table name RATING as its input value, whereas **setKeyColumn** takes the key column name (which in this case happens to also be RATING).

```
create or replace procedure deleteproc(xmldoc in clob) is
    delctx dbms_xmlsave.ctxtype;
    rows number;
  begin
    delctx  := dbms_xmlsave.newcontext('RATING');
```

```
      dbms_xmlsave.setkeycolumn(delctx,'RATING');
      rows := dbms_xmlsave.deletexml(delctx,xmldoc);
      dbms_xmlsave.closecontext(delctx);
   end;
   /
```

XSU and Java

If you prefer, you can perform the XSU DML operations via calls to Java classes instead of the PL/
SQL procedures. In place of the DBMS_XMLQUERY package, you should execute the **oracle.xml
.sql.query.OracleXMLQuery** class. In place of the DBMS_XMLSAVE package, use **oracle.xml.sql
.dml.OracleXMLSave**.

For example, the Oracle-provided sample Java program for XML queries is customized slightly
in the following listing. It relies on connection management in a fashion similar to that shown in
the JDBC examples. The program imports the **oracle.xml.sql.query.OracleXMLQuery** class,
enabling it to get the XML string; Java's **System.out.println** method is then called to display the
output.

```java
import oracle.xml.sql.query.OracleXMLQuery;
import java.lang.*;
import java.sql.*;

// class to test the String generation!
class testXMLSQL {

   public static void main(String[] argv)
   {

     try{
      // Create the connection.
      Connection conn  = getConnection("practice","practice");

      // Create the query class.
      OracleXMLQuery qry = new OracleXMLQuery(conn, "select * from rating");

      // Get the XML string.
      String str = qry.getXMLString();

      // Print the XML output.
      System.out.println(" The XML output is:\n"+str);
      // Always close the query to get rid of any resources...
      qry.close();
      }catch(SQLException e){
      System.out.println(e.toString());
      }
   }

   // Get the connection given the user name and password...!
   private static Connection getConnection(String username,
 String password)
     throws SQLException
```

```
    {
        // Register the JDBC driver...
DriverManager.registerDriver(new oracle.jdbc.OracleDriver());

        // Create the connection using the OCI8 driver.
        Connection conn =
DriverManager.getConnection("jdbc:oracle:oci8:@or90",username,password);

        return conn;
    }
}
```

For details on connection management and Java, see Part VI of this book.

Customizing the Query Process

You can create your own procedures to simplify the interaction with the DBMS_XMLQUERY and DBMS_XMLSAVE packages. For example, the following listing creates a function named GET_XML, which selects the rows from the table and displays them in XML format.

```
create function get_xml (in_sql varchar2)
    return clob
is queryctx dbms_xmlquery.ctxtype;
    result clob;
begin  queryctx := dbms_xmlquery.newcontext(in_sql);
    result := dbms_xmlquery.getxml(queryctx);
    dbms_xmlquery.closecontext(queryctx);
    return result;
end;
/
```

The data is returned in CLOB format, so you can use the SET LONG command to set the maximum display length (the default is 80 characters). You can call GET_XML from within SQL queries, as shown in the following listing:

```
set pagesize 100 long 2000

select get_xml('select * from category') from dual;

GET_XML('SELECT*FROMCATEGORY')
--------------------------------------------------
<?xml version = '1.0'?>
<ROWSET>
   <ROW num="1">
      <CATEGORYNAME>ADULTREF</CATEGORYNAME>
      <PARENTCATEGORY>ADULT</PARENTCATEGORY>
      <SUBCATEGORY>REFERENCE</SUBCATEGORY>
   </ROW>
   <ROW num="2">
      <CATEGORYNAME>ADULTFIC</CATEGORYNAME>
```

```
        <PARENTCATEGORY>ADULT</PARENTCATEGORY>
        <SUBCATEGORY>FICTION</SUBCATEGORY>
    </ROW>
    <ROW num="3">
        <CATEGORYNAME>ADULTNF</CATEGORYNAME>
        <PARENTCATEGORY>ADULT</PARENTCATEGORY>
        <SUBCATEGORY>NONFICTION</SUBCATEGORY>
    </ROW>
    <ROW num="4">
        <CATEGORYNAME>CHILDRENPIC</CATEGORYNAME>
        <PARENTCATEGORY>CHILDREN</PARENTCATEGORY>
        <SUBCATEGORY>PICTURE BOOK</SUBCATEGORY>
    </ROW>
    <ROW num="5">
        <CATEGORYNAME>CHILDRENFIC</CATEGORYNAME>
        <PARENTCATEGORY>CHILDREN</PARENTCATEGORY>
        <SUBCATEGORY>FICTION</SUBCATEGORY>
    </ROW>
    <ROW num="6">
        <CATEGORYNAME>CHILDRENNF</CATEGORYNAME>
        <PARENTCATEGORY>CHILDREN</PARENTCATEGORY>
        <SUBCATEGORY>NONFICTION</SUBCATEGORY>
    </ROW>
</ROWSET>
```

Using XMLType

You can use **XMLType** as a datatype in your tables. **XMLType** can be used to store and query XML data in the database. As a type, **XMLType** has member functions to access, extract, and query XML data using a class of operations known as **Xpath** expressions. The SYS_XMLGEN, SYS_XMLAGG, and DBMS_XMLGEN packages create **XMLType** values from existing object-relational data. When you designate a column as using the **XMLType** datatype, Oracle stores the data internally in a CLOB datatype.

The following listing shows the creation of a table using the **XMLType** datatype:

```
create table my_xml_table
(key1        number,
 xml_column  sys.xmltype);
```

If you describe the table, you will see its columns:

```
desc MY_XML_TABLE
```

Name	Null?	Type
KEY1		NUMBER
XML_COLUMN		SYS.XMLTYPE

If you increase the describe depth, you will see the member functions for the **XMLType** column as well. The following listing shows the first few of the many functions and methods available:

```
set describe depth 5
desc my_xml_table
```

```
 Name                                        Null?    Type
 ----------------------------------------- -------- --------------------
 KEY1                                                NUMBER
 XML_COLUMN                                          SYS.XMLTYPE


METHOD
------
 STATIC FUNCTION CREATEXML RETURNS XMLTYPE
 Argument Name                    Type                      In/Out Default?
 ------------------------------ ----------------------- ------ --------
 XMLDATA                          CLOB                      IN


METHOD
------
 MEMBER FUNCTION EXTRACT RETURNS XMLTYPE
 Argument Name                    Type                      In/Out Default?
 ------------------------------ ----------------------- ------ --------
 XPATH                            VARCHAR2                  IN


METHOD
------
 MEMBER FUNCTION EXISTSNODE RETURNS NUMBER
 Argument Name                    Type                      In/Out Default?
 ------------------------------ ----------------------- ------ --------
 XPATH                            VARCHAR2                  IN


METHOD
------
 MEMBER FUNCTION ISFRAGMENT RETURNS NUMBER


METHOD
------
 MEMBER FUNCTION GETCLOBVAL RETURNS CLOB


METHOD
------
 MEMBER FUNCTION GETSTRINGVAL RETURNS VARCHAR2


METHOD
------
 MEMBER FUNCTION GETNUMBERVAL RETURNS NUMBER
```

You can now insert values into MY_XML_TABLE by calling **XMLType**'s CREATEXML method:

```
insert into my_xml_table (key1, xml_column)
values (1, sys.xmltype.createxml
 ('<book>
  <title>My Ledger</title>
  <chapter num= "1">
     <title>Beginning</title>
     <text>This is the ledger of G.B. Talbot</text>
  </chapter>
</book>'));
```

You can query the data by calling the GETCLOBVAL method. For example, the query

```
select m.xml_column.getclobval() as xml_data
  from my_xml_table m
 where key1 = 1;
```

returns this data:

```
XML_DATA
------------------------------------------------------
<book>
  <title>My Ledger</title>
  <chapter num="1">
     <title>Beginning</title>
     <text>This is the ledger of G.B. Talbot</text>
  </chapter>
</book>
```

NOTE
You can create function-based indexes on columns created with the **XMLType** *datatype to improve the performance of queries.*

Other Features

This chapter has given you a very high-level view of XML data interacting with the Oracle database. There are many other possibilities, including using style sheets for data formatting and creating XSQL pages. You can even create text indexes on **XMLType** columns, provided you have installed the Oracle Context option:

```
create index xml_index on my_xml_table (xml_column)
  indextype is ctxsys.context;
```

Oracle provides a number of packages to interact with XML data, including DBMS_XMLDOM, DBMS_XMLGEN, DBMS_XMLINDEX, DBMS_XMLPARSER, DBMS_XMLQUERY, DBMS_XMLSAVE, DBMS_XMLSCHEMA, DBMS_XMLSTORE, and DBMS_XMLTRANSLATIONS.

Oracle provides utilities to support additional uses, such as **oraxml** (a command-line interface to parse an XML document) and **oraxsl** (a command-line interface used to apply a style sheet on multiple XML documents). A full discussion of every utility and data-access method is beyond the scope of this book; see the XML-related documentation provided with Oracle Database 12c for additional options and sample programs. See the Alphabetical Reference for descriptions of functions that act on **XMLType** instances, including EXTRACT, EXTRACTVALUE, SYS_XMLAGG, SYS_XMLGEN, UPDATEXML, XMLAGG, XMLCONCAT, and XMLELEMENT.

PART
VIII

Alphabetical Reference

This part contains references for most major Oracle commands, functions, and keywords with cross-referencing of topics. The reference is intended for use by both developers and users of Oracle, but assumes some familiarity with the products. Reading the introduction to this reference will help you make the most productive use of the entries.

What This Alphabetical Reference Includes

This alphabetical reference contains entries for virtually every Oracle command in SQL, PL/SQL, and SQL*Plus used in Oracle Database 12*c* as well as all of the SQL commands (SELECT, INSERT, MERGE, and so forth). Each command is listed with its correct format or syntax, an ex planation of its purpose and use, and important details, restrictions, and hints about it, along with examples to illustrate proper usage. Topics are in alphabetical order and are cross-referenced, both within the alphabetical reference and to preceding chapters in the book.

What This Alphabetical Reference Does Not Include

This is not a tutorial; it does not explain the screen-oriented development and administration tools. Additionally, there are a few areas where usage is likely to be so specialized or infrequent that inclusion here did not seem of much benefit. In these instances, the text refers you to the Oracle manual in which you can find the needed information.

General Format of Entries

Entries in this reference are typically either definitions of terms or descriptions of functions, commands, and keywords. These are usually structured in six sections: the keyword, its type, a SEE ALSO cross-reference, the format in which the keyword appears, a description of its components, and an example of its use. Depending on the type and complexity of the command, not every entry will include every section. A typical entry looks like the following:

RPAD
SEE ALSO CHARACTER FUNCTIONS, **LPAD**, **LTRIM**, **RTRIM**, **TRIM**, Chapter 7
FORMAT RPAD(*string,length* [,'*set*'])
DESCRIPTION Right **PAD**. **RPAD** makes a string a certain length by adding a certain set of characters to the right. If *set* is not specified, the default pad character is a space.
EXAMPLE

```
select RPAD('HELLO ',24,'WORLD') from DUAL;
```

produces this:

```
HELLO WORLDWORLDWORLDWOR
```

The Sections of Each Entry

The KEYWORD usually appears on a line by itself. In some cases, a brief definition follows. If a keyword has more than one definition, either in different Oracle tools or in different Oracle versions, the keyword is followed by a brief qualifier to indicate that more than one listing exists for this keyword.

SEE ALSO suggests other topics that are closely related to the keyword, or gives the chapter or chapters in the book that provide detailed descriptions of how the keyword is used in practice.

Occasionally you will be referred to an Oracle manual or other reference book that contains detail beyond the scope of this reference.

FORMAT generally follows the notation of Oracle manuals, with all SQL and other keywords in uppercase. In actual use, these must be entered exactly as they are shown (except that case is irrelevant). Variables and variable parameters are shown in lowercase *italic*. This indicates that some appropriate value should be substituted. When parentheses are shown, they must be entered where they appear, as must words shown in uppercase.

Standard Usages for Variables

Some standard usages for variables follow:

This Variable	Indicates
column	The name of a column
database	The name of a database
link	The name of a link in Oracle Net
password	A password
segment	The name of a segment (table, index, etc.)
table	The name of a table
tablespace	The name of a tablespace
user	The name of a user or owner
view	The name of a view

Other Formatting Guidelines

Some other guidelines for formatting follow:

- *character* means the value must be a single character.

- *string* typically represents a character column or an expression or column that can be treated like a CHAR or VARCHAR2 column after automatic data conversion.

- *value* usually represents a NUMBER column or an expression or column that can be treated like a NUMBER column after automatic data conversion.

- *date* usually represents a DATE column or an expression or column that can be treated like a DATE column after automatic data conversion.

- *datetime* usually represents a TIMESTAMP column or an expression or column that can be treated like a TIMESTAMP column after automatic data conversion.

- *integer* must be a whole number, such as –3, 0, or 12.

- *expression* means any form of a result that can be stored in a database column. This could be a literal, a variable, a mathematical computation, a function, or virtually any combination of functions and columns whose final result is a single value, such as a string, a number, or a date.

- Occasionally other notation is used as well, such as **condition** or **query**. This is explained or is apparent in context.

- Optional items are enclosed in square brackets, as in **[user.]**, meaning that "*user.*" is not necessarily required.

- Alternative items in a list are separated by a single broken vertical bar, as in OFF | ON, which should be read "OFF or ON." On some systems, this vertical bar is displayed as a solid vertical bar.

- Required options, where one item of a list of items is required, are surrounded by curly braces, as in {OFF | ON}.

- The default item in a list, if there is one, will be listed first.

- Three periods (an ellipsis) indicate that the preceding expression can be repeated any number of times, as in *column [,column]. . .*, which means that *,column* may be any number of additional columns separated by commas.

- In rare instances, normal notation is either insufficient or inappropriate for what is being shown. In these cases, the **DESCRIPTION** section spells out more fully what is intended in the **FORMAT** section.

Other Elements of a Listing

A few commands have a return type, which indicates the datatype of the value returned by a function.

DESCRIPTION is an explanation of the command and its parts. **Boldface** words within the description usually refer to either commands or variables shown in the FORMAT section.

EXAMPLE shows either the results of a function or how a keyword is used in a real command. The style of the examples is not the same as the style of the FORMAT section. Instead, it follows the style of the first part of this book (described in Chapter 5) because that style is more typical of real coding practice.

The Order of the Keywords

This reference is in alphabetical order, with all entries that begin with symbols coming before the first entry beginning with the letter *A*.

Words that are hyphenated or that have an underscore character in them are alphabetized as if the hyphen or underscore were a space.

Symbols

The symbols are listed in order of appearance with a short definition or name.

_	underline (also called *underscore* or *underbar*)
!	exclamation mark
"	double quotation mark
#	pound sign
$	dollar sign
?	question mark
%	percent sign
&	ampersand
&&	double ampersand
'	single quotation mark or apostrophe
()	parentheses
*	asterisk or multiplication
**	exponentiation in PL/SQL
+	plus
-	subtraction or hyphen
--	double hyphen, SQL comment minus or hyphen
.	period or dot, a name or variable separator
..	to
/	division or slash

/*	slash asterisk, start of a SQL comment
:	colon
:=	is set equal to in PL/SQL
;	semicolon
<< >\>	label name delimiter in PL/SQL
<	less than
<=	less than or equal to
< >	not equal
!=	not equal
=	equal
>	greater than
>=	greater than or equal to
@	at sign
@@	double at sign
[]	square brackets
^	caret
^=	not equal
{}	curly braces
|	broken vertical bar
||	concatenation

_ (Underscore)

The underscore represents a single position with the **LIKE** operator. *See* **LIKE**.

_EDITOR

See **EDIT**.

! (Exclamation Mark)

SEE ALSO   **$, =, CONTAINS, SOUNDEX**, Chapter 27
FORMAT   Within SQL, **!** is used as part of the "not equal" expression, **!=**. For example, you can select all the city values that are not in the continent of Asia:

```
select city
from location
where continent != 'Asia';
```

For CONTEXT text indexes, **!** signals the text engine to perform a **SOUNDEX** search. The terms to search for will be expanded to include terms that sound like the search term, using the text's **SOUNDEX** value to determine possible matches.

```
select title
from book_review_context
where contains(review_text, '!grate')>0;
```

" (Double Quotation Mark)

SEE ALSO   **ALIAS, TO_CHAR**, Chapters 7 and 10
DESCRIPTION   " surrounds a table or column alias that contains special characters or a space, or surrounds literal text in a date format clause of **TO_CHAR**.

EXAMPLE Here " is used as an alias:

```
select next_day(cycledate,'FRIDAY') "Pay Day!"
from payday;
```

And here it is used as a formatting portion of **TO_CHAR**:

```
select firstname, birthdate, to_char(birthdate,
       '"Baby Girl on" fmMonth ddth, YYYY, "at" HH:MI "in the Morning"')
       "Formatted"
from birthday
where FirstName = 'Victoria';
```

```
FIRSTNAME        BIRTHDATE Formatted
---------------  --------- ----------------------------
Victoria         20-MAY-49 Baby Girl on May 20th, 1949,
                           at 3:27 in the Morning
```

(Pound Sign)

SEE ALSO REMARK, /* */, Chapter 6
DESCRIPTION # completes a block of documentation in a SQL*Plus start file where the block begins with the word DOCUMENT. SQL*Plus ignores all lines from the line where it sees the word DOCUMENT until the line after the #.

$ (Dollar Sign)

SEE ALSO @, @@, **HOST**, **START**, **CONTAINS**, Chapter 27
FORMAT For SQL*Plus:

```
$ host_command
```

In Unix and Linux environments, the **$** symbol can be replaced with **!** when executing host commands.
For CONTEXT text indexes:

```
select column
from table
where contains(text_column, '$search_term') >0;
```

DESCRIPTION **$** passes any host command back to the operating system for execution without exiting SQL*Plus. **$** is shorthand for **HOST**. This doesn't work on all hardware or operating systems.
For a CONTEXT text index, **$** instructs the search engine to perform a stem expansion on the search term. A stem expansion includes in the search those words that have the same word stem. For example, a stem expansion of the word 'sing' would include 'singing', 'sang', and 'sung'.

? (Question Mark)

SEE ALSO CONTAINS, Chapter 27
FORMAT

```
select column
from table
where contains(text_column, '?term')>0;
```

DESCRIPTION For CONTEXT text indexes, **?** instructs the text engine to perform a fuzzy match search. The terms to search for will be expanded to include terms that are spelled similarly to the search term, using the text index as the source for possible matches.

% (Percent)

% is a wildcard used to represent any number of positions and characters with the **LIKE** operator. *See* **LIKE**.

%FOUND

SEE ALSO   %**ISOPEN**, %**NOTFOUND**, %**ROWCOUNT**, **CURSOR**, **SQL CURSOR**, Chapter 32
FORMAT

```
cursor%FOUND
```

or

```
SQL%FOUND
```

DESCRIPTION   %**FOUND** is a success flag for **SELECT**, **INSERT**, **UPDATE**, and **DELETE**. cursor is the name of an explicit cursor declared in a PL/SQL block or the implicit cursor named **SQL**. %**FOUND** can be attached to a cursor name as a suffix. The two together are a success flag for the execution of **SELECT**, **INSERT**, **UPDATE**, and **DELETE** statements in PL/SQL blocks.

PL/SQL temporarily sets aside a section of memory as a scratchpad for the execution of SQL statements and for storing certain kinds of information (or *attributes*) about the state of that execution. If the SQL statement is a **select**, this area will contain one row of data.

%**FOUND** is one of those attributes. %**FOUND** is typically tested (via **IF/THEN** logic) after an explicit **fetch** has been performed from the cursor. It will be TRUE if the **fetch** retrieved a row, and FALSE otherwise. It always evaluates to TRUE, FALSE, or **NULL**. %**NOTFOUND** is the logical opposite. It is FALSE when %**FOUND** is TRUE, TRUE when %**FOUND** is FALSE, and **NULL** when %**FOUND** is **NULL**.

Testing %**FOUND** for the condition of an explicit cursor before it is **OPEN**ed raises an EXCEPTION (error code ORA-01001, INVALID CURSOR).

%ISOPEN

SEE ALSO   SQL CURSOR, Chapter 32
FORMAT

```
cursor%ISOPEN
```

DESCRIPTION   *cursor* must be either the name of an explicitly declared cursor or the implicit cursor named **SQL**. %**ISOPEN** evaluates to TRUE if the named cursor is open, and to FALSE if it is not. **SQL%ISOPEN** will *always* evaluate to FALSE because the SQL cursor is opened and closed automatically when a SQL statement not explicitly declared is executed (*see* **SQL CURSOR**). %**ISOPEN** is used in PL/SQL logic; it cannot be a part of a SQL statement.

%NOTFOUND

See %**FOUND**.

%ROWCOUNT

SEE ALSO   **CLOSE**, **DECLARE CURSOR**, **DELETE**, **FETCH**, **INSERT**, **OPEN**, **SELECT**, **UPDATE**, Chapter 32
FORMAT

```
cursor%ROWCOUNT
```

DESCRIPTION   *cursor* must be either the name of an explicitly declared cursor or the implicit cursor named **SQL**. *cursor*%**ROWCOUNT** contains the cumulative total number of rows that have been **fetch**ed from the active set in this cursor. %**ROWCOUNT** can be used to intentionally process only a fixed number of rows, but is more commonly used as an exception handler for **select**s that are intended to return just one row (for example, **select. . .into**). In these cases, **%ROWCOUNT** is set to 0 if no rows are returned (**%NOTFOUND** can make this test as well), and to 2 if more than one row is returned, regardless of the actual number.

%ROWCOUNT is used in PL/SQL logic; it cannot be a part of a SQL statement. If **SQL%ROWCOUNT** is used, it can only refer to the most recently opened implicit cursor. If no implicit cursor has been opened, **SQL%ROWCOUNT** returns **NULL**.

%ROWTYPE

SEE ALSO   **FETCH**, Chapter 32
FORMAT

```
{[user.]table | cursor}%ROWTYPE
```

DESCRIPTION   **%ROWTYPE** declares a record variable to have the same structure as an entire row in a table (or view) or as a row retrieved by the named cursor. **%ROWTYPE** is used as part of a variable declaration and assures that the variable will contain the appropriate fields and datatypes to handle all of the columns being fetched. If [user.]*table* is used, the table (or view) must exist in the database.

To create a variable that will contain corresponding fields, use **declare**, a variable name, and **%ROWTYPE** with the table name, and then select a row into the record. Because the variable has the same structure as the table, you can reference the fields as *variable.field*, using notation similar to *table.column* used in SQL statements. **SELECT. . .INTO** and **FETCH. . .INTO** are the only methods for loading an entire record variable. Individual fields within the record can be loaded using :=, as shown here:

```
bookshelf_record.publisher := 'Pandoras';
```

If a cursor is used as the prefix for **%ROWTYPE**, then it can contain a **SELECT** statement with only as many columns as are needed. However, if a column that is **FETCH**ed from a named cursor is an expression, rather than a simple column name, the expression must be given an alias in the **SELECT** statement before it can be referenced using this technique.

%TYPE

SEE ALSO   **%ROWTYPE**, Chapter 32
FORMAT

```
{[user.]table.column | variable}%TYPE
```

DESCRIPTION   **%TYPE** is used to declare a variable to be of the same type as a previously declared variable, or as a particular column in a table that exists in the database you're connected to.
EXAMPLE   In this example a new variable, **writer**, is declared to be the same type as the AUTHOR_NAME column in the AUTHOR table. Since **writer** now exists, it can be used to declare yet another new variable, **coauthor**.

```
writer      author.authorname%type;
coauthor    writer%type;
```

& or && (Ampersand or Double Ampersand)

SEE ALSO   **:, ACCEPT, DEFINE, START, CONTAINS**, Chapter 27
FORMAT   For SQL*Plus:

```
&integer
&variable
&&variable
```

For CONTEXT indexes:

```
select title
from book_review_context
where CONTAINS(review_text, 'property & harvests')>0;
```

DESCRIPTION   **&** and **&&** can be used in several ways (**&&** applies only to the second definition):

- As a prefix for parameters in a SQL*Plus start file. Values are substituted for &1, &2, etc. *See* **START**.

- As a prefix for a substitution variable in a SQL command in SQL*Plus. SQL*Plus will prompt for a value if an undefined **&** or **&&** variable is found. **&&** will define the variable and thereby preserve its value; **&** will not define or preserve the value, but only substitute what is entered one time. *See* **ACCEPT** and **DEFINE**.

- When using CONTEXT indexes, **&** is used to signal an AND condition for text searches involving multiple search terms. If any of the search terms is not found, the text will not be returned by the search.

' (Single Quotation Mark)
SEE ALSO   " (Double Quotation Mark), Chapter 7
FORMAT

```
'string'
```

DESCRIPTION   ' surrounds a literal, such as a character string or date constant. To use one quotation mark or an apostrophe in a string constant, use two ' marks (not a double quotation mark). Avoid the use of apostrophes in data (and elsewhere) whenever possible unless you ensure that string constants use two apostrophes within the string itself and you account for apostrophes when running EXECUTE IMMEDIATE commands in PL/SQL.
EXAMPLE

```
select 'William' from dual;
```

produces this:

```
William
```

whereas

```
select 'William''s brother' from dual;
```

produces this:

```
William's brother
```

() (Parentheses)
SEE ALSO   PRECEDENCE, SUBQUERY, UPDATE, Chapters 13 and 15
DESCRIPTION   Parentheses enclose subqueries or lists of columns, or control precedence within expressions.

* (Multiplication)
SEE ALSO   +, –, /, Chapters 9 and 27
FORMAT

```
value1 * value2
```

DESCRIPTION   *value1* * *value2* means *value1* multiplied by *value2*. For CONTEXT indexes, * is used to weight the individual search terms differently.

** (Exponentiation)

SEE ALSO   POWER
FORMAT

```
x ** y
```

DESCRIPTION   *x* is raised to the power *y*. *x* and *y* may be constants, variables, columns, or expressions. Both must be numeric.
EXAMPLE   4**4 = 256

+ (Addition)

SEE ALSO   –, *, /, Chapter 9
FORMAT

```
value1 + value2
```

DESCRIPTION   *value1* + *value2* means *value1* plus *value2*.

– (Subtraction [Form 1])

SEE ALSO   +, *, /, Chapter 9, **CONTAINS**, **MINUS**, Chapter 27
FORMAT

```
value1 - value2
```

DESCRIPTION   *value1* – *value2* means *value1* minus *value2*. For CONTEXT indexes, a – tells the text search of two terms to subtract the score of the second term's search from the score of the first term's search before comparing the result to the threshold score. For CTXCAT indexes, a – tells the text search engine to exclude the row from the result set if the term following the – is found.

- (Hyphen [Form 2])

SEE ALSO   Chapter 6
FORMAT

```
command text -
         text -
         text
```

DESCRIPTION   SQL*Plus command continuation; a - continues a command on the following line.
EXAMPLE

```
ttitle left 'Current Portfolio' -
right 'November 1st, 1999'      skip 1 -
center 'Industry Listings    '  skip 4;
```

-- (Comment)

SEE ALSO   /* */, **REMARK**, Chapter 6
FORMAT

```
-- any text
```

DESCRIPTION   -- tells Oracle a comment has begun. Everything from that point to the end of the line is treated as a comment. These delimiters are used only within SQL itself or in PL/SQL and must appear before the **SQLTERMINATOR**.

EXAMPLE

```
select feature, section, page
-- this is just a comment
from newspaper    -- this is another comment
where section = 'F';
```

. (Period or Dot [Form 1]) (SQL*Plus)

FORMAT

```
&variable.suffix
```

DESCRIPTION   The . is a variable separator, which is used in SQL*Plus to separate the variable name from a suffix so that the suffix is not considered a part of the variable name.

EXAMPLE   Here, the suffix "st" is effectively concatenated to the contents of the variable &Avenue:

```
define Avenue = 21
select '100 &Avenue.st Street' from DUAL;
```

produces this:

```
100 21st Street
```

This same technique might also be used in a WHERE clause.

. (Period or Dot [Form 2])

SEE ALSO   SYNTAX OPERATORS, Chapter 38

FORMAT

```
[user.][table.]column
```

DESCRIPTION   The . is a name separator, used to specify the complete name of a column, including (optionally) its table or user. The . is also used to address columns within abstract datatypes during **SELECT**s, **UPDATE**s, and **DELETE**s.

EXAMPLE

```
select practice.bookshelf.title
from practice.bookshelf, practice.bookshelf_author
where practice.bookshelf.title = practice.bookshelf_author.title;
```

If the table contains columns based on an abstract datatype, the datatype's attributes may be accessed via the . notation.

```
select c.person.address.city
from company c
where c.person.address.state = 'FL';
```

See Chapter 38 for further examples.

.. (To)

See **LOOP**.

/ (Division [Form 1])

SEE ALSO +, –, *, Chapter 9
FORMAT

```
value1 / value2
```

DESCRIPTION *value1* / *value2* means *value1* divided by *value2*.

/ (Slash [Form 2]) (SQL*Plus)

SEE ALSO ;, **BUFFER, EDIT, GET, RUN, SQLTERMINATOR** under **SET**
DESCRIPTION / executes the SQL in the SQL buffer without displaying it, unlike **RUN**, which displays it first.

/* */ (Comment)

SEE ALSO **REMARK**, Chapter 6
FORMAT

```
/* any text */
```

DESCRIPTION /* tells Oracle a comment has begun. Everything Oracle sees from that point forward, even for many words and lines, it regards as a comment until it sees the ending */, which ends the comment. Comments cannot be embedded within comments; that is, a /* is terminated by the first following */, even if there is an intervening /*.
EXAMPLE

```
select feature, section, page
     /* this is a multi-line comment
         used to extensively document the code */
from newspaper
where section = 'F';
```

: (Colon, Host Variable Prefix)

SEE ALSO INDICATOR VARIABLE
FORMAT

```
:name
```

DESCRIPTION *name* is the name of a host variable. When PL/SQL is embedded in a host language through an Oracle precompiler, host variables can be referenced from within the PL/SQL blocks by prefixing their host language names with a colon. In effect, this is the host variable. If PL/SQL changes its value through an assignment (:=), the value of the host variable is changed. Host variables may be used anywhere a PL/SQL variable can be used. The one exception is in assigning the value **NULL** to a host variable, which is not supported directly, but requires the use of an indicator variable.
EXAMPLE

```
int   bookcount;
...
   select count(*) into :bookcount from bookshelf;
```

:= (Set Equal To)

SEE ALSO **DECLARE CURSOR, FETCH, SELECT INTO**, Chapter 32
FORMAT

```
variable := expression
```

DESCRIPTION   The PL/SQL *variable* is set equal to the *expression*, which may be a constant, NULL, or a calculation with other variables, literals, and PL/SQL functions.
EXAMPLE

```
extension := quantity * price;
title := 'Barbers Who Shave Themselves';
name := null;
```

; (Semicolon)
SEE ALSO   / (Slash), **EDIT**, **GET**, **RUN**, **SQLTERMINATOR** under **SET**, **CONTAINS**, **NEAR**, Chapter 27
DESCRIPTION   **;** executes the SQL or the command that precedes it. For CONTEXT indexes, **;** indicates that a proximity search should be executed for the specified text strings. If the search terms are 'summer' and 'lease', then a proximity search for the two terms could be

```
select text
from sonnet
where contains(text,'summer;lease') >0;
```

When evaluating the text search results, text with the words 'summer' and 'lease' near to each other in the text will have higher scores than text with the words 'summer' and 'lease' farther apart.

< < > > (PL/SQL Label Name Delimiter)
See **BEGIN**, BLOCK STRUCTURE, **END**, **GOTO**, **LOOP**, Chapter 32

@ ("At" Sign [Form 1]) (SQL*Plus)
SEE ALSO   **@@**, **START**
FORMAT

```
@file
```

DESCRIPTION   **@** starts the SQL*Plus start file named file. **@** is similar to **START**, but does not allow command-line arguments.

@ ("At" Sign [Form 2])
SEE ALSO   **CONNECT**, **COPY**, **CREATE DATABASE LINK**, Chapter 25
FORMAT

```
CON[NECT] user[/password] [@database];
COPY [FROM user/password@database]
     [TO user/password@database]
     {APPEND | CREATE | INSERT | REPLACE}
     table [ (column, [column]...) ]
     USING query;
SELECT... FROM [user.]table[link]  [, [user.]table[@link] ]...
```

DESCRIPTION   **@** prefixes a database name in a **CONNECT** or **COPY** command, or a link name in a **FROM** clause.

@@ (Double "At" Sign) (SQL*Plus)
SEE ALSO   **@** (Form 1), **START**
FORMAT

```
@@file
```

DESCRIPTION   @@ starts a nested SQL*Plus start *file* named file. @@ is similar to @, but differs in that @@, when used in a command file, will search for a start file in the same directory as the command file that called it (rather than in the directory you are in when you execute the command file).

{} (Curly Braces)

SEE ALSO   **CONTAINS**, Chapter 27, Chapter 42
FORMAT   For text searches, {} indicates that the enclosed text should be considered part of the search string even if it is a reserved word. For example, if the search term is 'in and out', and you want to search for the entire phrase, then you must enclose the word 'and' within braces:

```
REM  CONTAINS method for CONTEXT indexes:
select title
from book_review_context
where contains(review_text, 'transactions {and} finances')>0;
```

Within Java, {} indicates the beginning and ending of a block.

| (Vertical Bar)

SEE ALSO   **BTITLE**, **SET HEADSEP**, **TTITLE**, Chapter 6, Chapter 27
FORMAT

```
text|text
```

DESCRIPTION   When used in a SQL*Plus **COLUMN**, **TTITLE**, or **BTITLE** command, | is the default **HEADSEP** character, and is used to denote the splitting of a line onto a second line. (When used in listings in this Reference, | denotes a break between alternative choices: *variable* | *literal* would be read "variable or literal." On some machines this shows as a solid vertical bar.) Within text queries, | signals an OR condition for searches involving two search terms. If either of the search terms is found, and its search score exceeds the specified threshold value, the text will be returned by the search.
EXAMPLE   Here's how | is used as a **HEADSEP** character.

```
TTITLE 'This is the First Line|and This is the Second'
```

produces this:

```
This is the First Line
and This is the Second
```

Here's how | is used as an **OR** clause in a text search query:

```
REM  CONTAINS method for CONTEXT indexes:
select title
from book_review_context
where contains(review_text, 'property | harvests')>0;
REM  CATSEARCH method for CTXCAT indexes:
select title
from book_review_ctxcat
where catsearch(review_text, 'property | harvests', null)>0;
```

|| (Concatenation)

SEE ALSO   . (Period or Dot [Form 1]), CHARACTER FUNCTIONS, **SUBSTR**, Chapter 7
FORMAT

```
expression1 || expression2
```

DESCRIPTION || concatenates two strings together.
EXAMPLE
Use || to display a column of cities, followed by a comma, a space, and the country:

```
select city||', '||country from location;
```

ABS (Absolute Value)

SEE ALSO   NUMBER FUNCTIONS, Chapter 9
FORMAT

```
ABS(value)
```

value must be a number, whether a literal number, the name of a number column, a literal character string containing a valid number, or a character column containing only a valid number.
DESCRIPTION   Absolute value is the measure of the magnitude of something and is always a positive number.
EXAMPLES

```
146
abs(-30) =  30
abs('-27.88') = 27.88
```

ABSTRACT DATATYPES

Abstract datatypes are datatypes that consist of one or more attributes. Rather than being constrained to the standard datatypes of **NUMBER**, **DATE**, and **VARCHAR2**, abstract datatypes can consist of multiple attributes and/or other, previously defined abstract datatypes. Abstract datatypes are more commonly known as *object types*. *See* Chapter 38 for examples, and **CREATE TYPE** for creation syntax.

ACCEPT

SEE ALSO   &, &&, DEFINE
FORMAT

```
ACC[EPT] variable [NUM[BER]|CHAR|DATE|BINARY_FLOAT|BINARY_DOUBLE]
   [FOR[MAT] format]  [DEF[AULT] default] [PROMPT text | NOPR[OMPT]] [HIDE]
```

DESCRIPTION   **ACCEPT** takes input from a user's keyboard and puts it in the named variable with the specified datatype. If the variable has not been previously **DEFINEd**, it is created. *format* specifies the input format for the reply (such as A20). **DEFAULT** sets the default value if a reply is not given. **PROMPT** displays the text to the user before accepting the input. **NOPROMPT** skips a line and waits for input without displaying any prompt. Using neither **PROMPT** nor **NOPROMPT** causes **ACCEPT** to invent a prompt asking for the value of the variable. **HIDE** suppresses the user's entry and is valuable for passwords and the like.
EXAMPLE   The following prompts the user with "How hot?" and puts the user's entry in a number variable named Temperature:

```
accept temperature number prompt 'How hot? '
```

ACCUMULATE

See **CONTAINS**.

ACOS

SEE ALSO   ASIN, ATAN, ATAN2, COS, COSH, EXP, LN, LOG, SIN, SINH, TAN, TANH

FORMAT

```
ACOS(value)
```

DESCRIPTION **ACOS** returns the arc cosine of a value. Input values range from –1 to 1; outputs are expressed in radians.

ADD_MONTHS

SEE ALSO DATE FUNCTIONS, Chapter 10
FORMAT

```
ADD_MONTHS(date,integer)
```

DESCRIPTION **ADD_MONTHS** adds a number of months to *date*, and returns the date that is that many months in the future. *date* must be a legitimate Oracle date. *integer* must be an integer; a noninteger value will be truncated to the next smallest integer. A negative value for *integer* will return a date in the past.

EXAMPLE **ADD_MONTHS** adds 1 month and 0.3 month to April 22, 2011:

```
select add_months(to_date('22-APR-11'),1),
       add_months(to_date('22-APR-11'),.3) from dual;


ADD_MONTH ADD_MONTH
--------- ---------
22-MAY-11 22-APR-11
```

AGGREGATE FUNCTIONS

SEE ALSO Chapter 9
DESCRIPTION An aggregate function computes a single summary value (such as sum or average) from the individual number values in a group of values. This is an alphabetical list of all current group functions in the Oracle version of SQL. Each of these is listed elsewhere in this reference under its own name, with its proper format and use. Aggregate functions are useful in select lists and **ORDER BY** and **HAVING** clauses.

FUNCTION NAME AND USE

AVG gives the average of the values for a group of rows.

COLLECT takes the input *column* value and creates a nested table of the input type out of the rows selected.

CORR returns the coefficient of correlation of a set of number pairs.

CORR_* supports nonparametric or rank correlation (**CORR_K** and **CORR_S**).

COUNT gives the count of rows for a column or for a table (with *).

COVAR_POP returns the population covariance of a set of number pairs.

COVAR_SAMP returns the sample covariance of a set of number pairs.

CUME_DIST calculates the cumulative distribution of a value in a group of values.

DENSE_RANK computes the rank of a row in an ordered group of rows.

FIRST operates on a set of values from a set of rows that ranks as the first with respect to a given sorting specification.

GROUP_ID distinguishes duplicate groups resulting from a GROUP BY specification.

GROUPING distinguishes super-aggregate rows from regular grouped rows.

GROUPING_ID returns a number corresponding to the GROUPING bit vector associated with a row.

LAST operates on a set of values from a set of rows that ranks as the last with respect to a given sorting specification.

MAX gives the maximum of all values for a group of rows.

MEDIAN gives the median value for a group of rows, ignoring **NULL**s.

MIN gives the minimum of all values for a group of rows.

PERCENT_RANK performs a percent ranking calculation.

PERCENTILE_CONT is a percentile calculation function that assumes a continuous distribution model.

PERCENTILE_DISC is a percentile calculation function that assumes a discrete distribution model.

RANK calculates the rank of a value in a group of values.

REGR functions perform linear regression analysis on a group of values.

STATS_BINOMIAL_TEST tests the difference between a sample proportion and a given proportion.

STATS_CROSSTAB analyzes two nominal values.

STATS_F_TEST tests whether two variables are significantly different.

STATS_KS_TEST tests whether two variables are from the same population.

STATS_MODE returns the value that occurs with the greatest frequency in a group.

STATS_MW_TEST tests two independent samples against a null hypothesis.

STATS_ONE_WAY_ANOVA is a one-way analysis of variance.

STATS_T_TEST_* functions measure the significance of a difference of means.

STATS_WSR_TEST determines whether the differences between samples are significantly different from zero.

STDDEV gives the standard deviation of all values for a group of rows.

STDDEV_POP computes the population standard deviation and returns the square root of the population variance.

STDDEV_SAMP computes the cumulative sample standard deviation and returns the square root of the sample variance.

SUM gives the sum of all values for a group of rows.

VAR_POP returns the population variance of a set of numbers after discarding the **NULL**s in this set.

VAR_SAMP returns the sample variance of a set of numbers after discarding the **NULL**s in this set.

VARIANCE gives the variance of all values for a group of rows.

ALIAS

An alias is a temporary name assigned to a table or a column within a SQL statement and is used to refer to it elsewhere in the same statement (if a table) or in a SQL*Plus command (if a column). You can use the **AS** keyword to separate the column definition from its alias. *See* **"** (Double Quotation Mark), **AS**, and **SELECT**. When used for a table, the alias is referred to as a *correlation name*.

ALL

SEE ALSO ANY, **BETWEEN**, **EXISTS**, **IN**, LOGICAL OPERATORS, Chapter 13
FORMAT

```
operator ALL list
```

DESCRIPTION   **!= ALL** is the equivalent of **NOT IN**. *operator* can be any one of =, >, >=, <, <=, or !=, and *list* can be a series of literal strings (such as "Talbot", "Jones", "Hild"), a series of literal numbers (such as 2, 43, 76, 32.06, 444), or a column from a subquery, where each row of the subquery becomes a member of the list, such as this:

```
location.city != all (select city from weather)
```

The *list* value can be a series of columns in the **WHERE** clause of the main query, as shown here:

```
prospect != all (vendor, client)
```

RESTRICTIONS   *list* cannot be a series of columns in a subquery, such as this:

```
prospect != all (select vendor, client from . . .)
```

Many people find this operator and the **ANY** operator very difficult to remember because the logic for some of their cases is not immediately intuitive. As a result, some form of **EXISTS** is usually substituted. The combination of an operator with **ALL** and a list can be illustrated with the following explanations:

page = all (4,2,7)	PAGE is equal to every item in the list—no number qualifies. A subquery *could* return a list where all the items were identical, and a value of PAGE could be equal to every one of them, but this would be very rare.
page > all (4,2,7)	PAGE is greater than the greatest item in the list (4,2,7)—anything greater than 7 qualifies.
page >= all (4,2,7)	PAGE is greater than or equal to the greatest item in the list (4,2,7)—anything equal to or greater than 7 qualifies.
page < all (4,2,7)	PAGE is less than the lowest item in the list (4,2,7)—anything less than 2 qualifies.
page <= all (4,2,7)	PAGE is less than or equal to the lowest item in the list (4,2,7)—anything equal to or less than 2 qualifies.
page != all (4,2,7)	PAGE is not equal to any item in the list—any number qualifies except 4, 2, and 7.

ALTER CLUSTER

SEE ALSO   CREATE CLUSTER, CREATE TABLE, STORAGE, Chapter 17
FORMAT
   alter_cluster::=

   physical_attributes_clause::=

allocate_extent_clause::=

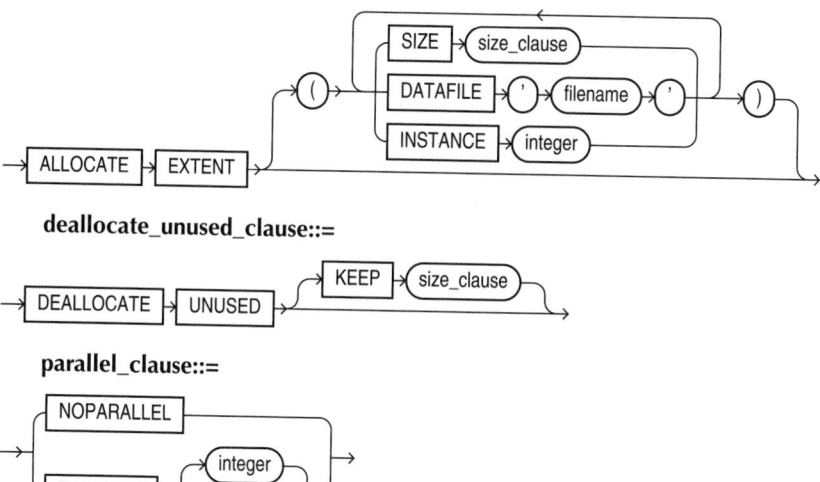

deallocate_unused_clause::=

parallel_clause::=

DESCRIPTION   Descriptions of the parameters can be found under **CREATE TABLE**. They have the same purpose and effect, except that here they are used to alter a cluster. Size is described under **CREATE CLUSTER**. In order to alter a cluster, you must either own the cluster or have **ALTER ANY CLUSTER** system privilege.

All tables in a cluster use the **STORAGE** values set by **CREATE CLUSTER**. **ALTER CLUSTER** changes these values for future cluster blocks, but does not affect those that already exist. **ALTER CLUSTER** does not allow changing the **extent** parameters in **STORAGE**. The **DEALLOCATE UNUSED** clause allows the cluster to shrink in size, freeing unused space.

EXAMPLE

```
alter cluster bookandauthor size 1024;
```

ALTER DATABASE

SEE ALSO   ALTER ROLLBACK SEGMENT, CREATE DATABASE, RECOVER, STARTUP, SHUTDOWN, Chapter 51

FORMAT
    alter_database::=

    startup_clauses::=

    recovery_clauses::=

general_recovery::=

full_database_recovery::=

partial_database_recovery::=

parallel_clause::=

managed_standby_recovery::=

database_file_clauses::=

create_datafile_clause::=

alter_datafile_clause::=

alter_tempfile_clause::=

move_datafile_clause::=

ASM_filename::=

autoextend_clause::=

maxsize_clause::=

logfile_clauses::=

add_logfile_clauses::=

drop_logfile_clauses::=

switch_logfile_clause::=

supplemental_db_logging::=

supplemental_id_key_clause::=

supplemental_plsql_clause::=

logfile_descriptor::=

controlfile_clauses::=

trace_file_clause::=

standby_database_clauses::=

activate_standy_db_clause::=

maximize_standby_db_clause::=

register_logfile_clause::=

switchover_clause::=

failover_clause::=

commit_switchover_clause::=

start_standby_clause::=

stop_standby_clause::=

convert_standby_clause::=

default_settings_clauses::=

set_time_zone_clause::=

flashback_mode_clause::=

instance_clauses::=

security_clause::=

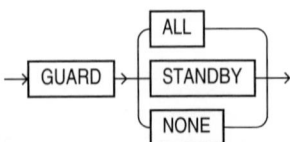

DESCRIPTION   To alter a database, you must have the ALTER DATABASE system privilege. *database* is the database name, and must be eight or fewer characters long.

When a database is first created, it is **MOUNT**ed in **EXCLUSIVE** mode, meaning no one but its creator has access to it. To allow multiple instances to access the database, use **MOUNT PARALLEL** if you have installed the Oracle Real Application Clusters option.

After mounting a database, you **OPEN** it. **RESETLOGS** resets the redo log, cleaning out any redo entries. You use this option to restore a database after a partial recovery from a media failure. The **NORESETLOGS** option leaves everything the same when you **OPEN** the database.

You can recover the database with a **RECOVER** clause. This command performs media recovery for a lost database. You can use multiple recovery processes to apply redo entries to datafiles for each instance. *See* **RECOVER**. You can **BACKUP** a **CONTROLFILE** to the specified file or to a trace file.

STANDBY databases provide a mechanism for automated failover in the event of a database failure. See the *Oracle Database 12c Administrator's Guide* for details on the creation and management of standby databases.

RENAME changes the name of an existing database or redo log file. DBAs can also **CREATE DATAFILE**s and **CREATE TEMPFILE**s and manage the increments by which datafiles autoextend. The **AUTOEXTEND** clause can be used to dynamically extend datafiles as needed, in increments of **NEXT** size, to a maximum of **MAXSIZE** (or **UNLIMITED**). You can use the **RESIZE** clause to increase or decrease the size of an existing datafile. You can bring a file **ONLINE** or take it **OFFLINE** with the **DATAFILE** clause. You can **CREATE** a new **DATAFILE** to replace an old one to re-create a datafile lost without backup.

ARCHIVELOG and **NOARCHIVELOG** define the way redo log files are used. **NOARCHIVELOG** is the default, and using it means that redo log files will be reused without saving their contents elsewhere. This provides instance recovery except from a media failure, such as a disk crash. **ARCHIVELOG** forces redo log files to be archived (usually to another disk or a tape), so that you can recover from a media failure. This mode also supports instance recovery.

ADD LOGFILE adds a redo log file or files to the database. *redo_logfile_spec* specifies the redo log file names and sizes. **SIZE** is the number of bytes set aside for this file. Suffixing this with **K** multiplies the value by 1024; using **M** multiplies it by 1048576. **REUSE** (without **SIZE**) means destroy the contents of any file by this name and give the name to this database. **SIZE** with **REUSE** creates the file if it doesn't exist, and checks its size if it does. **SIZE** alone creates the file if it doesn't exist, but returns an error if it does exist. The redo log file is assigned to a thread, either explicitly with the **THREAD** clause or to the thread assigned to the current instance of Oracle. A **GROUP** is a collection of redo log files. You can add a **GROUP** of redo log files by listing them, and you can name the group with an integer.

ADD LOGFILE MEMBER adds new files to an existing redo log file group, either by specifying the **GROUP** integer or by listing all the redo log files in the group.

DROP LOGFILE drops an existing redo log file group. **DROP LOGFILE MEMBER** drops one or more members of a redo log file group.

You can **RENAME GLOBAL_NAME** to change the name of the database. If you specify a domain, tell Oracle where the database is on the network. You must change references to the database from remote databases as well.

You can use the **RESET COMPATIBILITY** option, in conjunction with the **COMPATIBLE** parameter in the initialization parameter file, to revert from compatibility with one version of Oracle to a previous version.

You can **ENABLE** or **DISABLE** a **THREAD**. **PUBLIC** makes the thread available to any instance not requesting a specific thread.

As of Oracle Database 11*g*, the **ALTER DATABASE** command has been enhanced to simplify and expand the *managed_standby_recovery* and *standby_database_clauses* options. The *supplemental_db_ logging* clause contains new syntax for supplemental logging of PL/SQL calls.

ALTER DIMENSION

SEE ALSO   **CREATE DIMENSION**, **DROP DIMENSION**, Chapter 26
FORMAT
    alter_dimension::=

    level_clause::=

    hierarchy_clause::=

dimension_join_clause::=

attribute_clause::=

extended_attribute_clause::=

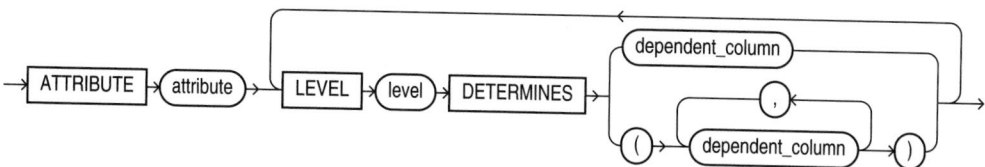

DESCRIPTION   **ALTER DIMENSION** modifies the attributes, hierarchy, and levels of an existing dimension. *See* **CREATE DIMENSION**.

EXAMPLE

```
alter dimension time drop hierarchy month_to_date;
```

ALTER DISKGROUP

SEE ALSO **CREATE DISKGROUP**, **DROP DISKGROUP**, Chapter 51

FORMAT

alter_diskgroup::=

add_disk_clause::=

qualified_disk_clause::=

drop_disk_clause::=

resize_disk_clause::=

replace_disk_clause::=

disk_online_clause::=

disk_offline_clause::=

timeout_clause::=

undrop_disk_clause::=

rebalance_diskgroup_clause::=

check_diskgroup_clause::=

diskgroup_template_clauses::=

qualified_template_clause::=

redundancy_clause::=

striping_clause::=

disk_region_clause::=

diskgroup_directory_clauses::=

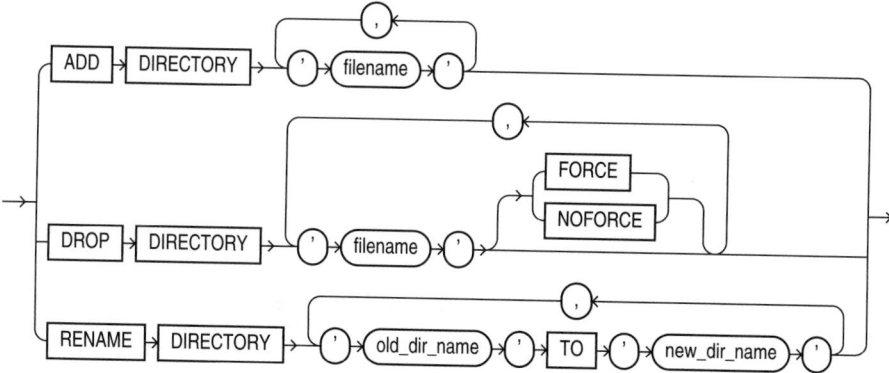

diskgroup_alias_clauses::=

diskgroup_volume_clauses::=

add_volume_clause::=

size_clause::=

modify_volume_clause::=

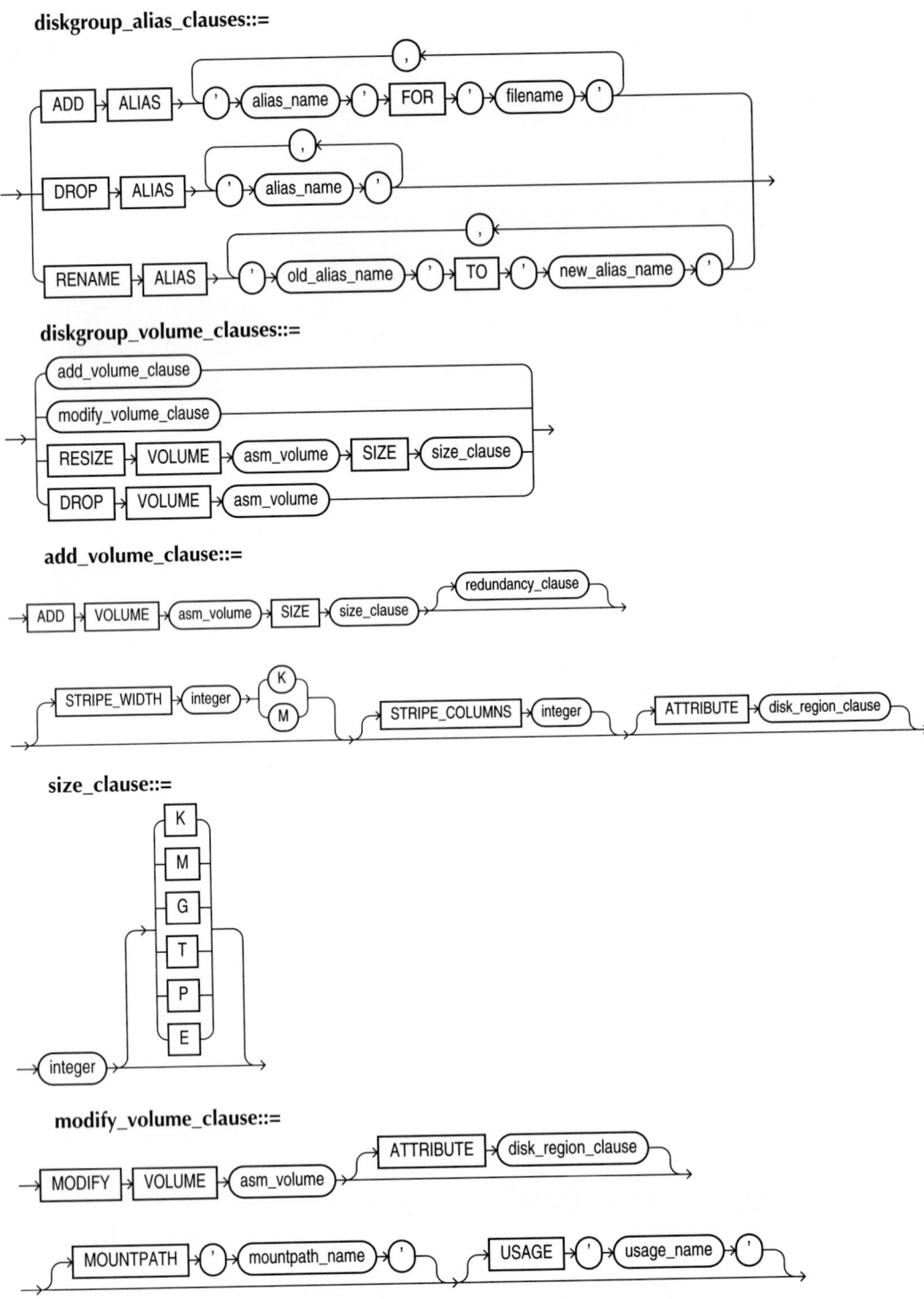

diskgroup_attributes::=

modify_diskgroup_file::=

drop_diskgroup_file_clause::=

usergroup_clauses::=

user_clauses::=

file_permissions_clause::=

file_owner_clause::=

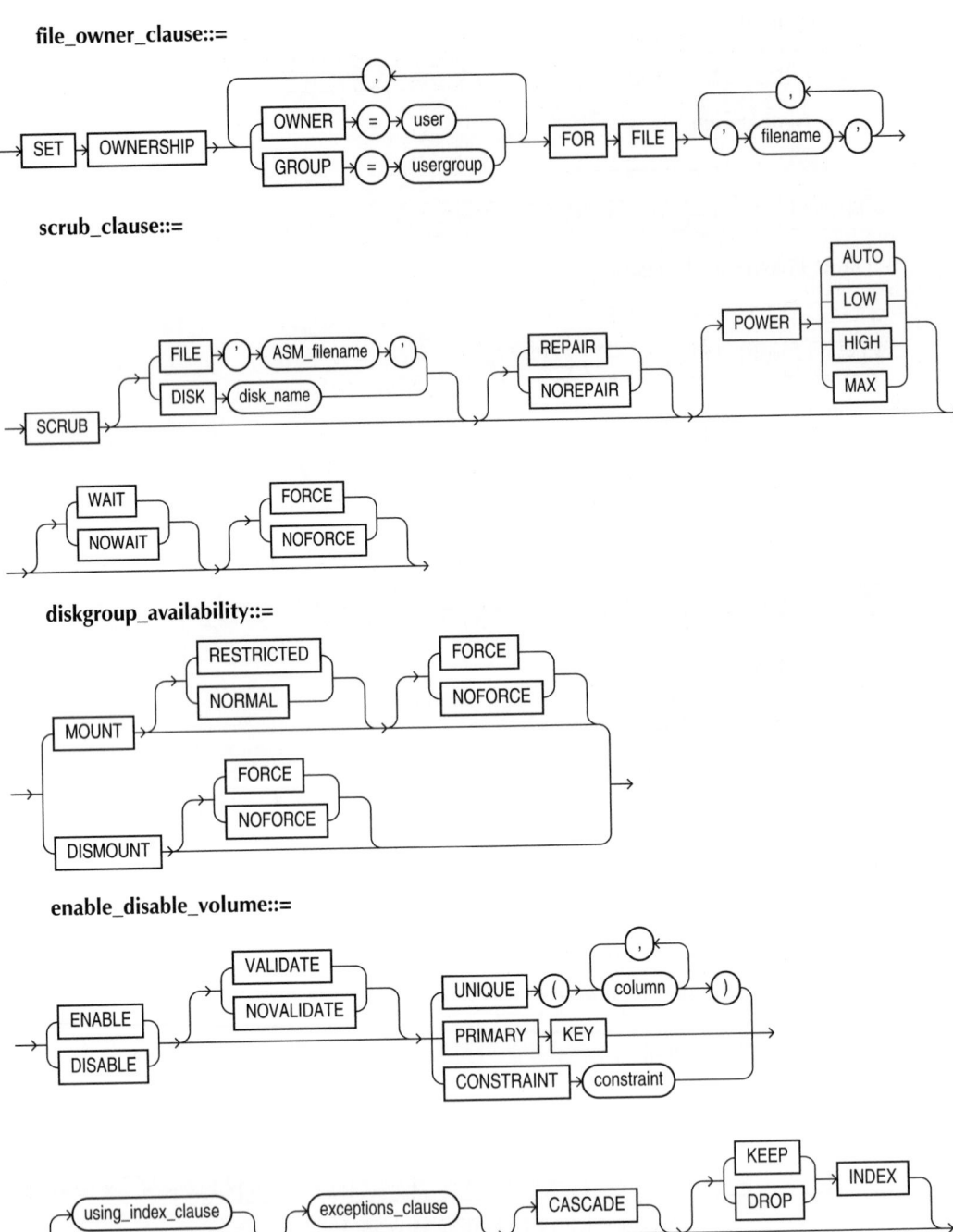

scrub_clause::=

diskgroup_availability::=

enable_disable_volume::=

DESCRIPTION **ALTER DISKGROUP** lets you perform a number of operations on a disk group or on the disks in a disk group.

The **DISK_CLAUSES** options include adding, dropping, and resizing disks within a group. Within the **DISKGROUP_CLAUSES** option, you can rebalance and check disk groups.

The **ALTER DISKGROUP** command is only valid if you have installed Automatic Storage Management (ASM) and have started an ASM instance.

For example, here's how to drop a disk from an existing disk group:

```
alter diskgroup dgroup_01 drop disk dgroup_01_0007;
```

As of Oracle Database 11*g*, the **ALTER DISKGROUP** command includes enhanced and simplified versions of the *check_diskgroup_clause* and *diskgroup_availability* options and adds the *disk_offline_clause* and *disk_online_clauses* options. For Oracle Database 12*c,* new options include *user_clauses, user_group_clauses, file_owner_clause, scrub_clause,* and *enable_disable_volume.*

ALTER FLASHBACK ARCHIVE

SEE ALSO   **CREATE FLASHBACK ARCHIVE**, **DROP FLASHBACK ARCHIVE**

FORMAT

alter_flashback_archive::=

flashback_archive_quota::=

flashback_archive_retention::=

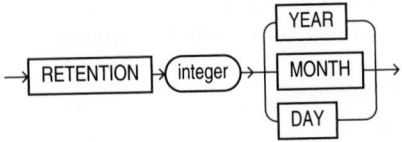

DESCRIPTION   Use **ALTER FLASHBACK ARCHIVE** to perform the following tasks:

- Designate a flashback data archive as the default flashback data archive for the system.
- Add a tablespace for use by the flashback data archive.
- Change the quota of a tablespace used by the flashback data archive.
- Remove a tablespace from use by the flashback data archive.
- Change the retention period of the flashback data archive.
- Purge the flashback data archive of old data that is no longer needed.

You must have the FLASHBACK ARCHIVE ADMINISTER system privilege to alter a flashback data archive in any way. You must also have appropriate privileges on the affected tablespaces to add, modify, or remove a flashback data archive tablespace.

The **OPTIMIZE DATA** clause, new to Oracle Database 12c, directs Oracle to optimize the storage of the data in the archive using one of several storage features relevant to the data being stored in the archive: Advanced Row Compression, Advanced LOB Compression, Advanced LOB deduplication, segment-level compression tiering, or row-level compression tiering. **NO OPTIMIZE DATA** is the default.

ALTER FUNCTION
SEE ALSO   **CREATE FUNCTION**, **DROP FUNCTION**, Chapter 35
FORMAT
    alter_function::=

    function_compile_clause::=

    compiler_parameters_clause::=

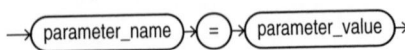

DESCRIPTION   Use the **ALTER FUNCTION** command to recompile an invalid stand-alone stored function. Explicit recompilation eliminates the need for implicit run-time recompilation. Use the **DEBUG** option to generate and store the code for use by the PL/SQL debugger.

EXAMPLE

```
alter function overdue_charges compile;
```

ALTER INDEX

SEE ALSO **CREATE INDEX**, **DROP INDEX**, **STORAGE**, Chapters 17 and 46
FORMAT
   alter_index::=

deallocate_unused_clause::=

allocate_extent_clause::=

shrink_clause::=

parallel_clause::=

physical_attributes_clause::=

logging_clause::=

partial_index_clause::=

rebuild_clause::=

key_compression::=

alter_index_partitioning::=

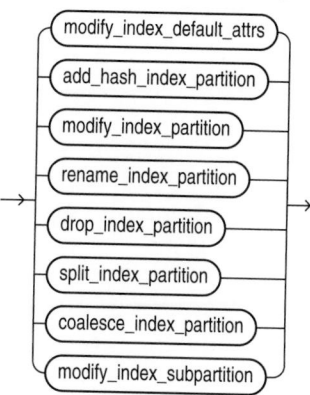

modify_index_default_attrs::=

add_hash_index_partition::=

coalesce_index_partition::=

modify_index_partition::=

rename_index_partition::=

drop_index_partition::=

split_index_partition::=

index_partition_description::=

segment_attributes_clause::=

modify_index_subpartition::=

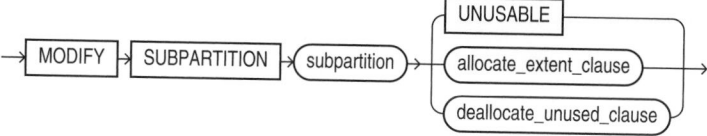

DESCRIPTION   *user* is the user who owns the index you wish to alter (if you are not that user, you must have DBA privileges). *index* is the name of an existing index. *See* **CREATE TABLE** for a description of **INITRANS**. The default for **INITRANS** for indexes is 2. **STORAGE** contains subclauses that are described under **STORAGE**. You must have the INDEX privilege on the table to create an index, and you must also either own the index or have the ALTER ANY INDEX system privilege.

You can use the **REBUILD** clause of the **ALTER INDEX** command to change the storage characteristics of an existing index. **REBUILD** uses the existing index as the basis for the new index. All index storage commands are supported, such as **STORAGE** (for extent allocation), **TABLESPACE** (to move the index to a new tablespace), and **INITRANS** (to change the initial number of entries).

You can modify, rename, drop, split, or rebuild index partitions.

COMPRESS enables key compression, eliminating repeated occurrence of key column values for non-unique indexes. *integer* specifies the prefix length (number of prefix columns to compress). By default, indexes are not compressed. You cannot compress a bitmapped index.

COMPUTE STATISTICS generates statistics for the cost-based optimizer at the time the index is rebuilt.

As of Oracle 11*g*, **ALTER INDEX** includes the following options:

- A *migrate* parameter that allows the migration of a domain index from user-managed storage tables to system-managed storage tables.
- An *invisible* parameter that lets you modify an index so it is invisible to the optimizer.
- A parameters clause that lets you rebuild an XMLIndex as well as a domain index.

As of Oracle 12*c*, **ALTER INDEX** includes the **PARTIAL_INDEX_CLAUSE** to index or re-index partitions of a partitioned table whose indexing property is set to ON. Partition indexes whose indexing property is set to OFF are marked as UNUSABLE.

ALTER INDEXTYPE
SEE ALSO **CREATE INDEXTYPE, DROP INDEXTYPE**
FORMAT
alter_indextype::=

using_type_clause::=

array_DML_clause::=

storage_table_clause::=

DESCRIPTION   Use **ALTER INDEXTYPE** to add or drop an operator of the indextype, to modify the implementation type, or to change the properties of the indextype.

As of Oracle Database 11g, you can specify that domain indexes be range-partitioned and have their storage tables and partition maintenance operations managed by the database.

ALTER JAVA

SEE ALSO   **CREATE JAVA**, **DROP JAVA**, Chapter 42
FORMAT
    alter_java::=

    invoker_rights_clause::=

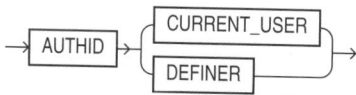

DESCRIPTION   **ALTER JAVA** recompiles a Java source schema object. You can also use this command to change the authorization enforced (definer or current user). To alter Java source schema objects, you must either own the source or class or have the ALTER ANY PROCEDURE system privilege.

ALTER MATERIALIZED VIEW

SEE ALSO   **CREATE MATERIALIZED VIEW**, **DROP MATERIALIZED VIEW**, Chapter 26

FORMAT
    alter_materialized_view::=

physical_attributes_clause::=

modify_mv_column_clause::=

table_compression::=

LOB_storage_clause::=

LOB_storage_parameters::=

LOB_parameters::=

modify_LOB_storage_clause::=

modify_LOB_parameters::=

parallel_clause::=

logging_clause::=

allocate_extent_clause::=

deallocate_unused_clause::=

shrink_clause::=

alter_iot_clauses::=

index_org_table_clause::=

index_org_overflow_clause::=

alter_overflow_clause::=

add_overflow_clause::=

scoped_table_ref_constraint::=

alter_mv_refresh::=

evaluation_edition_clause::=

alter_query_rewrite_clause::=

unusable_editions_clause::=

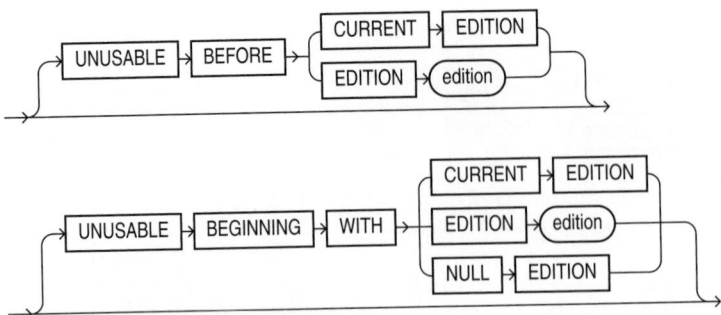

DESCRIPTION   The keyword **SNAPSHOT** is supported as a replacement for **MATERIALIZED VIEW** for backward compatibility.

ALTER MATERIALIZED VIEW lets you change the storage characteristics or refresh mode and times of a materialized view. You can also enable or disable query rewrite for the materialized view. To alter a materialized view, you must own the materialized view or have the ALTER ANY SNAPSHOT or ALTER ANY MATERIALIZED VIEW system privilege. *See* **CREATE MATERIALIZED VIEW** and Chapter 26 for details.

EXAMPLE

```
alter materialized view monthly_sales
    enable query rewrite;
```

ALTER MATERIALIZED VIEW LOG

SEE ALSO   **CREATE MATERIALIZED VIEW, CREATE MATERIALIZED VIEW LOG, DROP MATERIALIZED VIEW LOG**, Chapter 26

FORMAT

alter_materialized_view_log::=

physical_attributes_clause::=

add_mv_log_column_clause::=

allocate_extent_clause::=

shrink_clause::=

move_mv_log_clause::=

parallel_clause::=

mv_log_augmentation_clause::=

new_values_clause::=

mv_log_purge_clause::=

for_refresh_clause::=

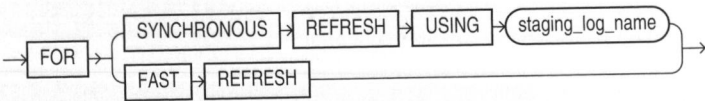

DESCRIPTION The keyword **SNAPSHOT** is supported as a replacement for **MATERIALIZED VIEW** for backward compatibility.

    ALTER MATERIALIZED VIEW LOG lets you change the storage characteristics of a materialized view log. To alter the log, you must either have the ALTER privilege on the log table or have the ALTER ANY TABLE system privilege. *See* **CREATE MATERIALIZED VIEW LOG** and Chapter 26.

    Oracle Database 12*c* includes the *for_refresh_clause* to change the refresh mode from fast to synchronous, complete to synchronous, synchronous to fast, or complete to fast.

ALTER OPERATOR

SEE ALSO **CREATE OPERATOR, DROP OPERATOR**
FORMAT

alter_operator::=

add_binding_clause::=

implementation_clause::=

context_clause::=

using_function_clause::=

drop_binding_clause::=

DESCRIPTION   You can use **ALTER OPERATOR** to add bindings to, drop bindings from, or compile an existing operator.

ALTER OUTLINE
SEE ALSO   **CREATE OUTLINE**, **DROP OUTLINE**, Chapter 46
FORMAT
    alter_outline::=

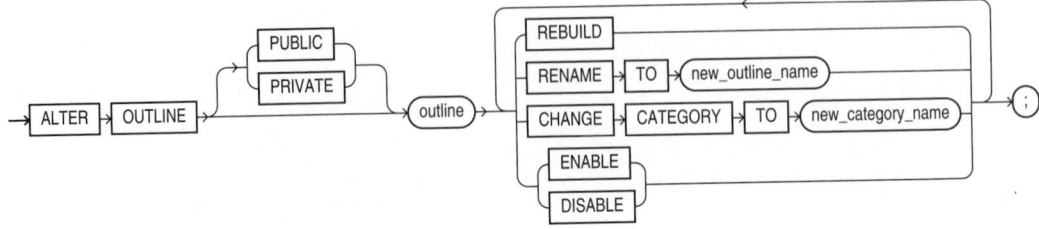

DESCRIPTION   You can use **ALTER OUTLINE** to rename a stored outline or to assign it to a different category. Stored outlines maintain sets of hints for previously executed queries.

ALTER PACKAGE
SEE ALSO   **CREATE PACKAGE**, **DROP PACKAGE**, Chapter 35
FORMAT
    alter_package::=

    package_compile_clause::=

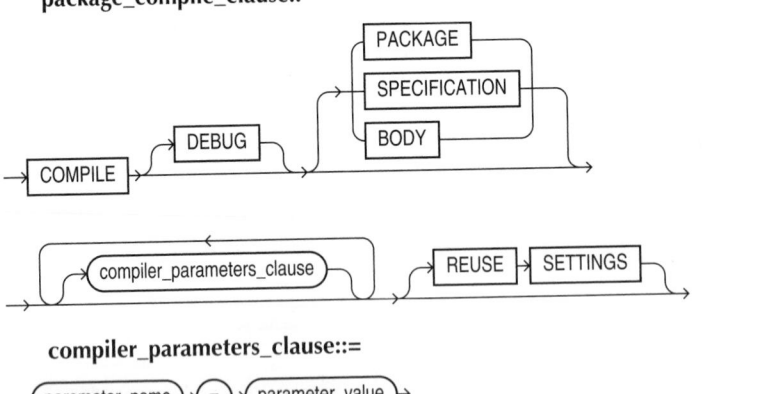

    compiler_parameters_clause::=

DESCRIPTION   **ALTER PACKAGE** recompiles a package specification and/or body. If you recompile the specification using **PACKAGE**, you recompile both the specification and the body. Recompiling the specification causes referencing procedures to be recompiled. You can recompile the **BODY** without affecting the specification. To alter a package, you must either be the owner of the package or have the ALTER ANY PROCEDURE system privilege.

ALTER PLUGGABLE DATABASE

SEE ALSO   **CREATE PLUGGABLE DATABASE, DROP PLUGGABLE DATABASE,** Chapters 49, 50, 51
FORMAT

alter_pluggable_database::=

pdb_unplug_clause::=

pdb_settings_clause::=

pds_storage_clause::=

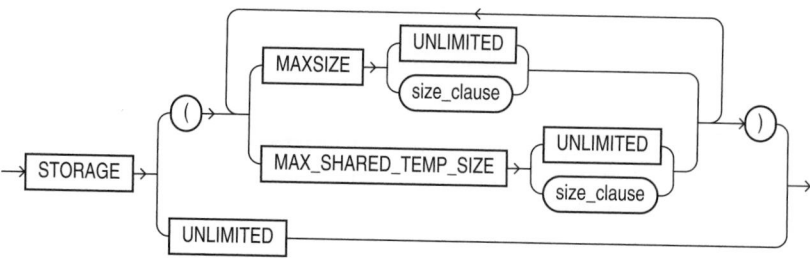

pdb_datafile_clause::=

pdb_recovery_clauses::=

pdb_general_recovery::=

pdb_change_state::=

pdb_open::=

instances_clause::=

pdb_close::=

relocate_clause::=

pdb_change_state_from_root::=

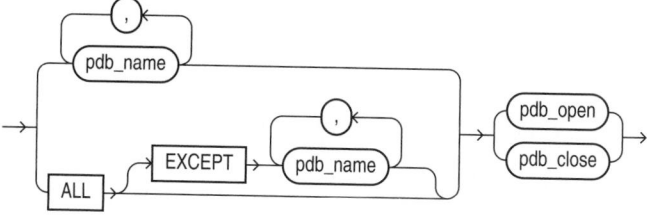

DESCRIPTION **ALTER PLUGGABLE DATABASE** modifies a pluggable database (PDB). These modifications include unplugging a PDB from a container database (CDB), bringing PDBs online or offline, backing up or recovering a PDB, and modifying the state of all PDBs within a CDB.

ALTER PROCEDURE
SEE ALSO **CREATE PROCEDURE**, **DROP PROCEDURE**, Chapter 35
FORMAT
    alter_procedure::=

procedure_compile_clause::=

compiler_parameters_clause::=

DESCRIPTION   ALTER PROCEDURE recompiles a PL/SQL procedure. You can avoid run-time overhead and error messages by explicitly compiling a procedure in advance. To alter a procedure, you must either own the procedure or have the ALTER ANY PROCEDURE system privilege.

ALTER PROFILE
SEE ALSO   CREATE PROFILE, DROP PROFILE, Chapter 19
FORMAT
   alter_profile::=

resource_parameters::=

password_parameters::=

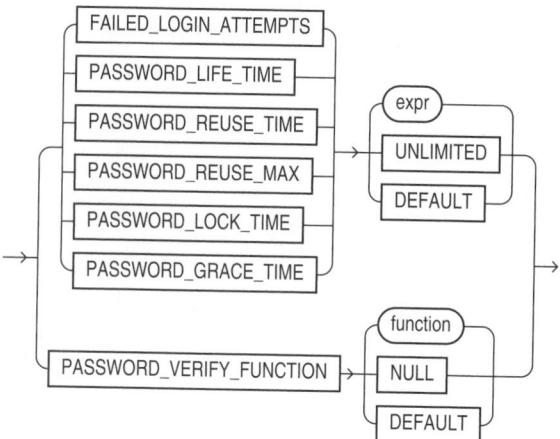

DESCRIPTION **ALTER PROFILE** lets you modify a particular profile setting. *See* **CREATE PROFILE** for details.

ALTER RESOURCE COST

SEE ALSO **CREATE PROFILE**

FORMAT

alter_resource_cost::=

DESCRIPTION The resource cost formula calculates the total cost of resources used in an Oracle session. **ALTER RESOURCE COST** lets you assign a weight to several resources. *cpu_per_session* is the amount of CPU used in a session in hundredths of a second. *connect_time* is the elapsed time of the session in minutes. *logical_reads_per_session* is the number of data blocks read from both memory and disk during a session. *private_sga* is the number of bytes in a private System Global Area (SGA), which is only relevant if you are using the shared server architecture. By assigning weights, you change the formula used to calculate the total resource cost.

ALTER ROLE

SEE ALSO   **CREATE ROLE**, **DROP ROLE**, Chapter 19
FORMAT
    alter_role::=

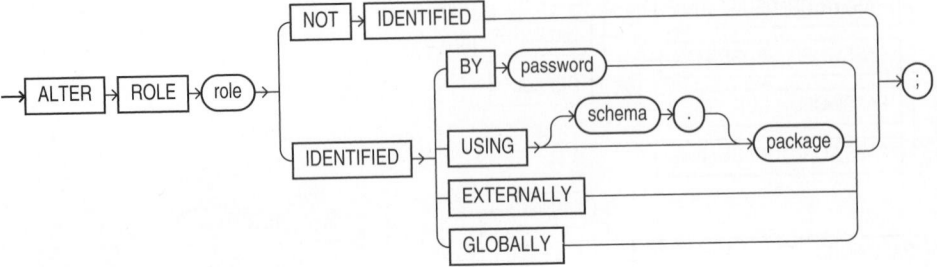

DESCRIPTION   **ALTER ROLE** lets you modify a role.

ALTER ROLLBACK SEGMENT

SEE ALSO   **CREATE DATABASE**, **CREATE ROLLBACK SEGMENT**, **CREATE TABLESPACE**, **DROP ROLLBACK SEGMENT**, **STORAGE**, Chapter 51
FORMAT
    alter_rollback_segment::=

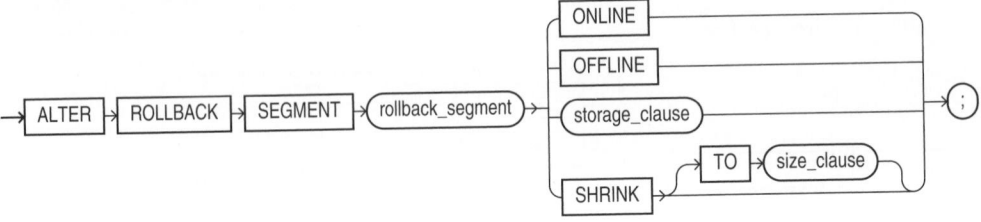

DESCRIPTION   *rollback_segment* is a name assigned to this rollback segment. **STORAGE** contains subclauses that are described under **STORAGE**. The **INITIAL** and **MINEXTENTS** options are not applicable. A rollback segment can be taken **ONLINE** or **OFFLINE** while the database is open. You can **SHRINK** it to a specified size (the default is its **OPTIMAL** size).

    You should use System-Managed Undo so the database will automatically create and drop rollback segments as needed.

ALTER SEQUENCE

SEE ALSO   AUDIT, **CREATE SEQUENCE**, **DROP SEQUENCE**, **GRANT**, **REVOKE**, **NEXTVAL** and **CURRVAL** under PSEUDO-COLUMNS, Chapter 17
FORMAT
  alter_sequence::=

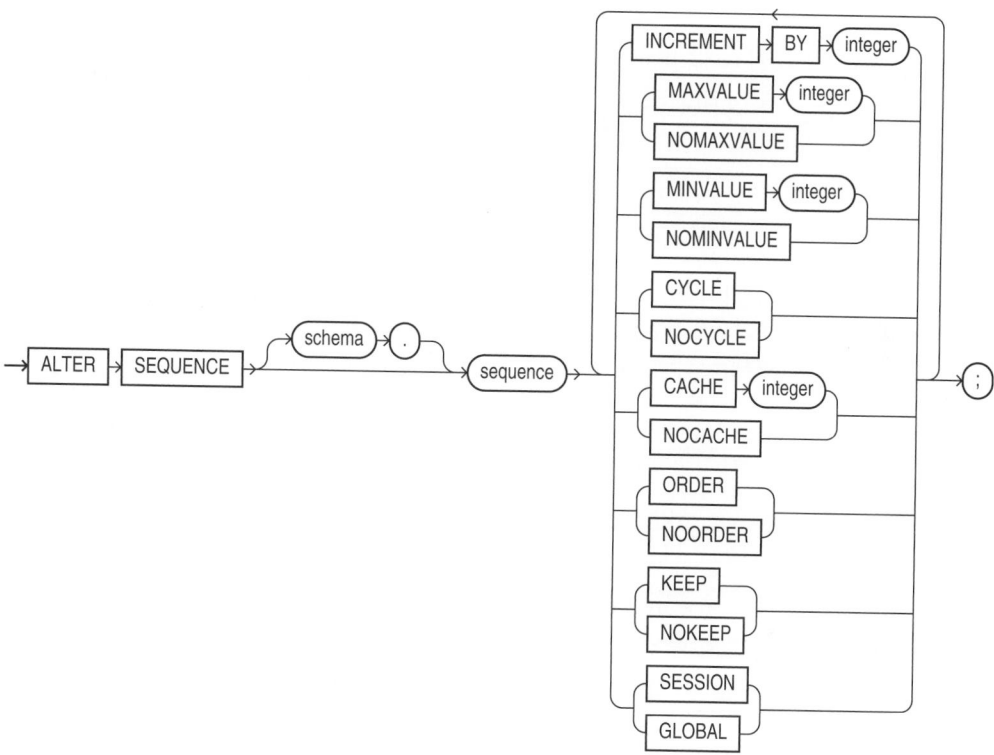

DESCRIPTION   All of these options affect the future use of an existing sequence with the name sequence. (Note that **START WITH** is not available. To change the value with which a sequence starts, you must **DROP** the sequence and **CREATE** it again.)

A new **MAXVALUE** cannot be specified that is lower than the existing **CURRVAL** on an ascending sequence (one that has a positive number as its **INCREMENT BY**). A similar rule applies for **MINVALUE** on a descending sequence (which has a negative **INCREMENT BY**).

To alter a sequence, you must either have the ALTER privilege on the sequence or have the ALTER ANY SEQUENCE system privilege.

All other features of **ALTER SEQUENCE** work as they do in **CREATE SEQUENCE**, except that they apply to an existing sequence. *See* **CREATE SEQUENCE** for details.

ALTER SESSION

SEE ALSO   **ALTER SYSTEM**

FORMAT
alter_session::=

alter_session_set_clause::=

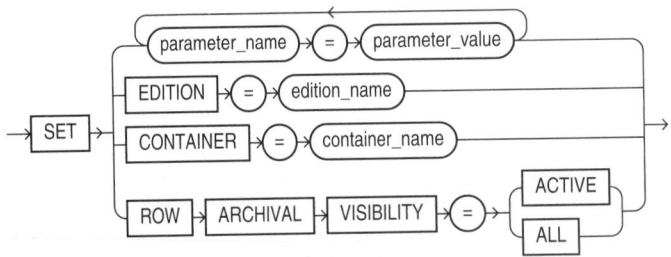

DESCRIPTION The **ALTER SESSION** command alters settings in effect for the current user session. You can specify whether procedures can **COMMIT** or not, the degree to which DML operations are parallelized, and whether resumable operations are enabled. If you enable parallel DML or DDL for your session, you still must specify the PARALLEL hint for the operations to be executed in parallel.

To enable or disable resumable space allocation, you must have the RESUMABLE system privilege.

ALTER SYNONYM
SEE ALSO **CREATE SYNONYM**

FORMAT
　　alter_synonym::=

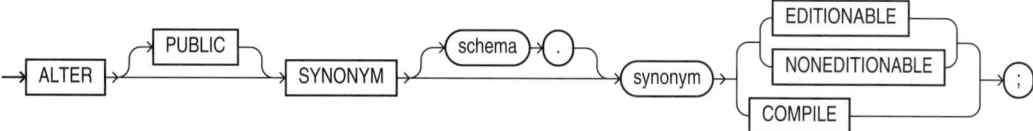

DESCRIPTION　The **ALTER SYNONYM** command changes the characteristics of existing public or private synonyms. **ALTER SYNONYM** is new in Oracle Database 12c.

　　You can specify the **COMPILE** keyword to verify that the target of the synonym still exists and is valid. You can modify PUBLIC synonyms or synonyms not owned by your schema if you have the CREATE PUBLIC SYNONYM or DROP PUBLIC SYNONYM privileges.

ALTER SYSTEM

SEE ALSO　**ALTER SESSION, CREATE PROFILE**
FORMAT
　　alter_system::=

archive_log_clause::=

checkpoint_clause::=

check_datafiles_clause::=

distributed_recov_clauses::=

end_session_clauses::=

quiesce_clauses::=

rolling_migration_clauses::=

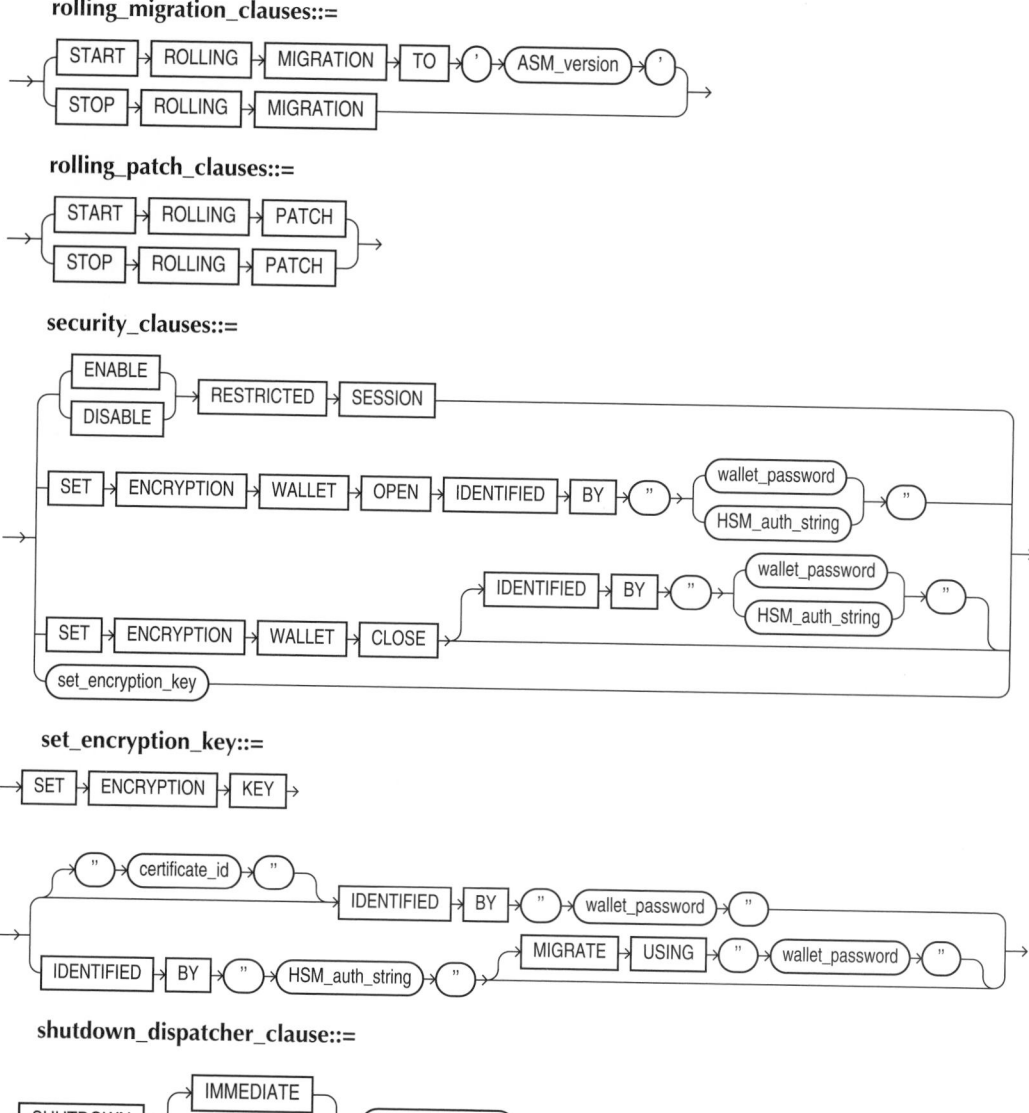

rolling_patch_clauses::=

security_clauses::=

set_encryption_key::=

shutdown_dispatcher_clause::=

alter_system_set_clause::=

set_parameter_clause::=

alter_system_reset_clause::=

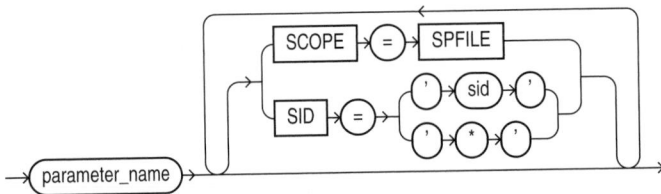

DESCRIPTION **ALTER SYSTEM** lets you configure your Oracle instance in many ways. Via the **SET** options, you can change many of the initialization parameter values while the database is running. If you are using a system parameter file, the changes are saved and will be in effect the next time the database is started.

You can also use the **ALTER SYSTEM** command to **SWITCH LOGFILE**, forcing Oracle to change redo log file groups.

CHECKPOINT performs a checkpoint for all instances (**GLOBAL**) or your instance (**LOCAL**) of Oracle. **CHECK DATAFILES** verifies that every instance (**GLOBAL**) or your instance (**LOCAL**) of Oracle can access all online datafiles.

ENABLE or **DISABLE RESTRICTED SESSION** turns on or off a restricted session, accessible only to users with that system privilege.

ENABLE or **DISABLE DISTRIBUTED RECOVERY** turns this option on or off, respectively.

FLUSH SHARED_POOL clears all data from the SGA shared pool.

FLUSH BUFFER_CACHE, available as of Oracle Database 10g, clears the buffer cache of the SGA.

SUSPEND suspends database activity; **RESUME** re-enables the database.

QUIESCE RESTRICTED places the database into a consistent state during which only SYS and SYSTEM, connected as SYSDBA, can perform operations. **UNQUIESCE** returns the database to its normal mode.

ARCHIVE LOG manually archives the redo log files or enables automatic archiving.

KILL SESSION ends a session with both the SID column and the SERIAL# column of the V$SESSION table identifying the session. **DISCONNECT SESSION**, unlike **KILL SESSION**, gives you the option of forcing the session's outstanding transactions to be posted prior to the termination of the session.

As of Oracle Database 11g, you can use **ALTER SYSTEM** to kill sessions in another instance of a RAC environment. Additionally, you can use the new *rolling_migration_clauses* to prepare an ASM cluster for migration and return it to normal operations after all nodes have migrated to the same software version. In Oracle Database 12c, you can use **ALTER SYSTEM** with the *rolling_patch_clauses* to start or stop a rolling patch in a RAC environment.

ALTER TABLE

SEE ALSO   **ALTER TRIGGER**, **CREATE TABLE**, **DROP TABLE**, **ENABLE**, Chapter 17
FORMAT
   alter_table::=

alter_table_properties::=

physical_attributes_clause::=

logging_clause::=

table_compression::=

ilm_clause::=

ilm_policy_clause::=

tiering_clause::=

supplemental_table_logging::=

supplemental_log_grp_clause::=

supplemental_id_key_clause::=

allocate_extent_clause::=

deallocate_unused_clause::=

shrink_clause::=

upgrade_table_clause::=

records_per_block_clause::=

parallel_clause::=

row_movement_clause::=

flashback_archive_clause::=

alter_iot_clauses::=

index_org_table_clause::=

mapping_table_clauses::=

key_compression::=

index_org_overflow_clause::=

partition_extended_name::=

subpartition_extended_name::=

segment_attributes_clause::=

alter_overflow_clause::=

add_overflow_clause::=

alter_mapping_table_clauses::=

column_clauses::=

add_column_clause::=

column_definition::=

identity_clause::=

identity_option::=

virtual_column_definition::=

evaluation_edition_clause::=

unusable_editions_clause::=

modify_column_clauses::=

modify_col_properties::=

encryption_spec::=

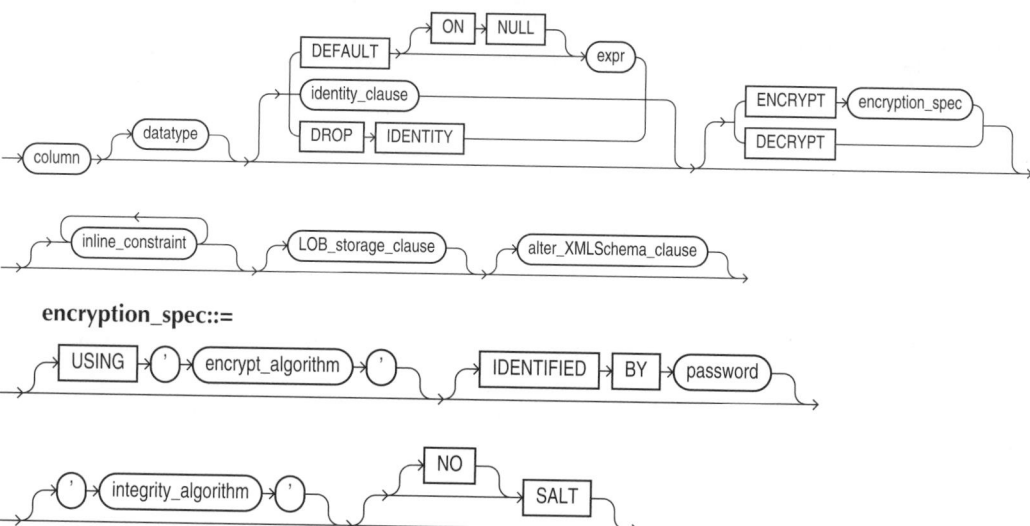

modify_virtcol_properties::=

modify_col_visibility::=

modify_col_substitutable::=

drop_column_clause::=

add_period_clause::=

period_definition::=

drop_period_clause::=

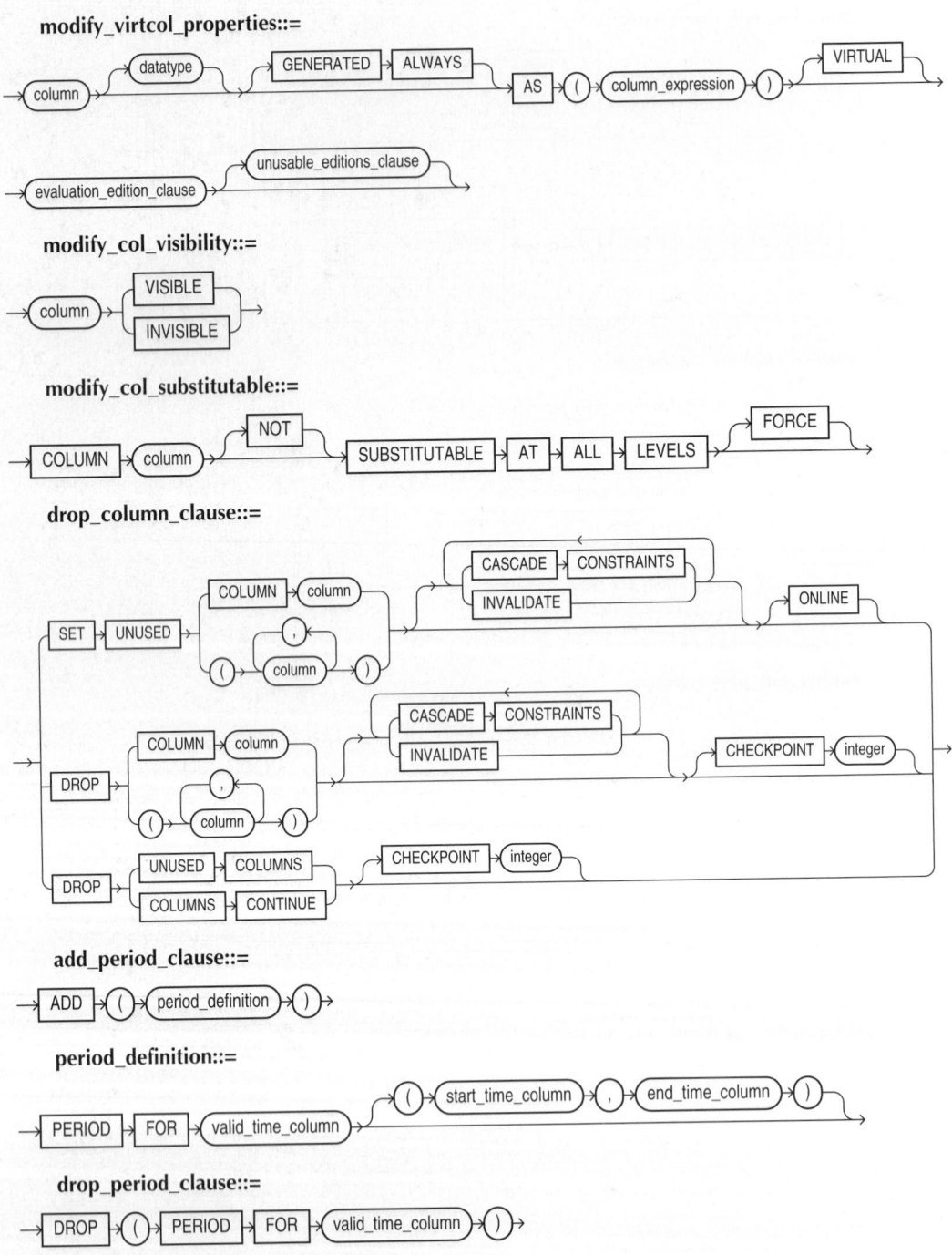

rename_column_clause::=

modify_collection_retrieval::=

constraint_clauses::=

drop_constraint_clause::=

column_properties::=

out_of_line_part_storage::=

object_type_col_properties::=

substitutable_column_clause::=

nested_table_col_properties::=

object_properties::=

supplemental_logging_props::=

physical_properties::=

deferred_segment_creation::=

varray_col_properties::=

varray_storage_clause::=

LOB_storage_clause::=

LOB_storage_parameters::=

LOB_parameters::=

modify_LOB_storage_clause::=

modify_LOB_parameters::=

LOB_retention_clause::=

LOB_deduplicate_clause::=

LOB_compression_clause::=

alter_varray_col_properties::=

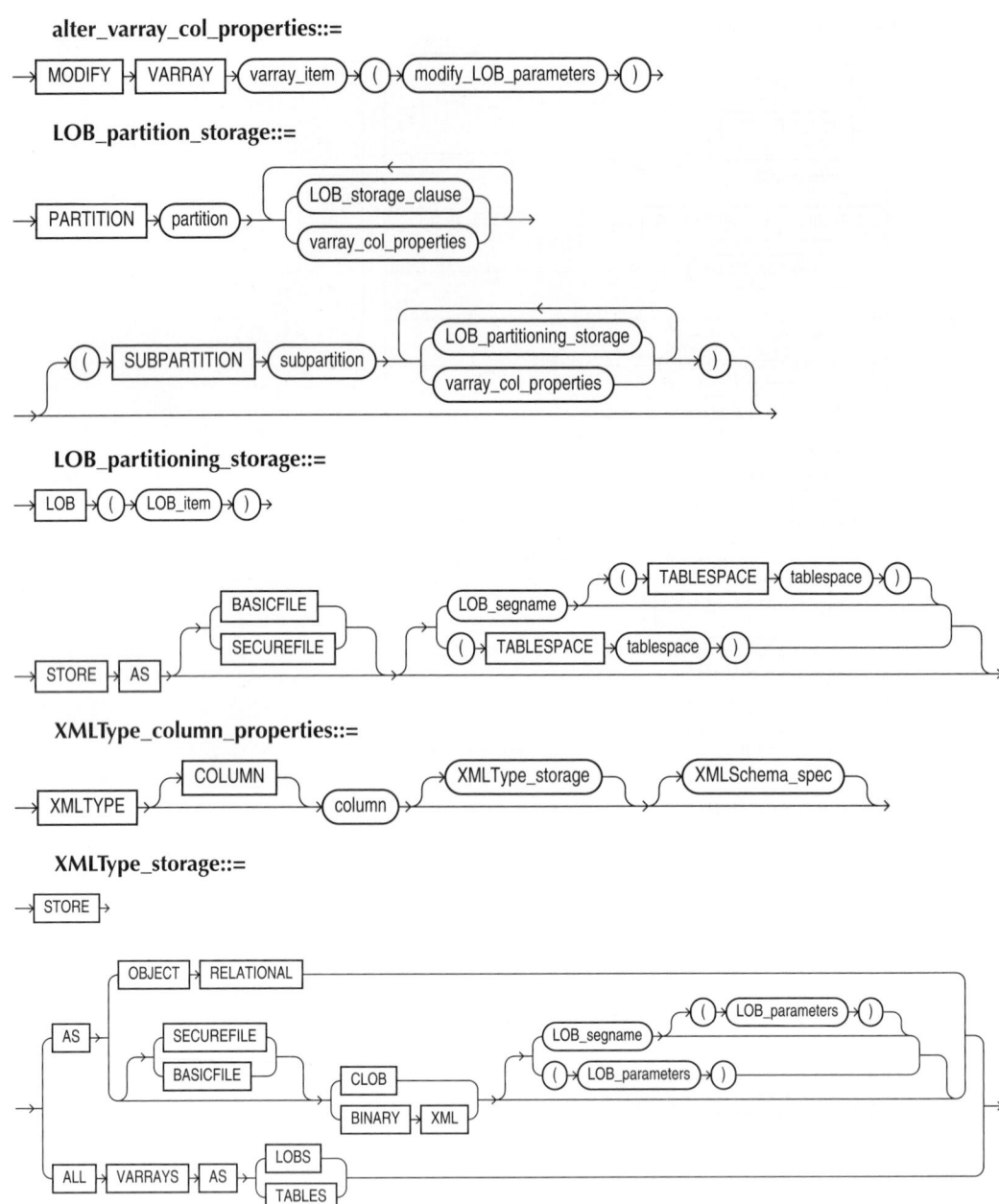

LOB_partition_storage::=

LOB_partitioning_storage::=

XMLType_column_properties::=

XMLType_storage::=

XMLSchema_spec::=

alter_XMLSchema_clause::=

alter_external_table::=

external_data_properties::=

alter_table_partitioning::=

modify_table_default_attrs::=

indexing_clause::=

alter_interval_partitioning::=

set_subpartition_template::=

modify_table_partition::=

modify_range_partition::=

modify_hash_partition::=

modify_list_partition::=

modify_table_subpartition::=

move_table_partition::=

move_table_subpartition::=

add_table_partition::=

add_range_partition_clause::=

add_hash_partition_clause::=

add_list_partition_clause::=

add_system_partition_clause::=

add_range_subpartition::=

add_hash_subpartition::=

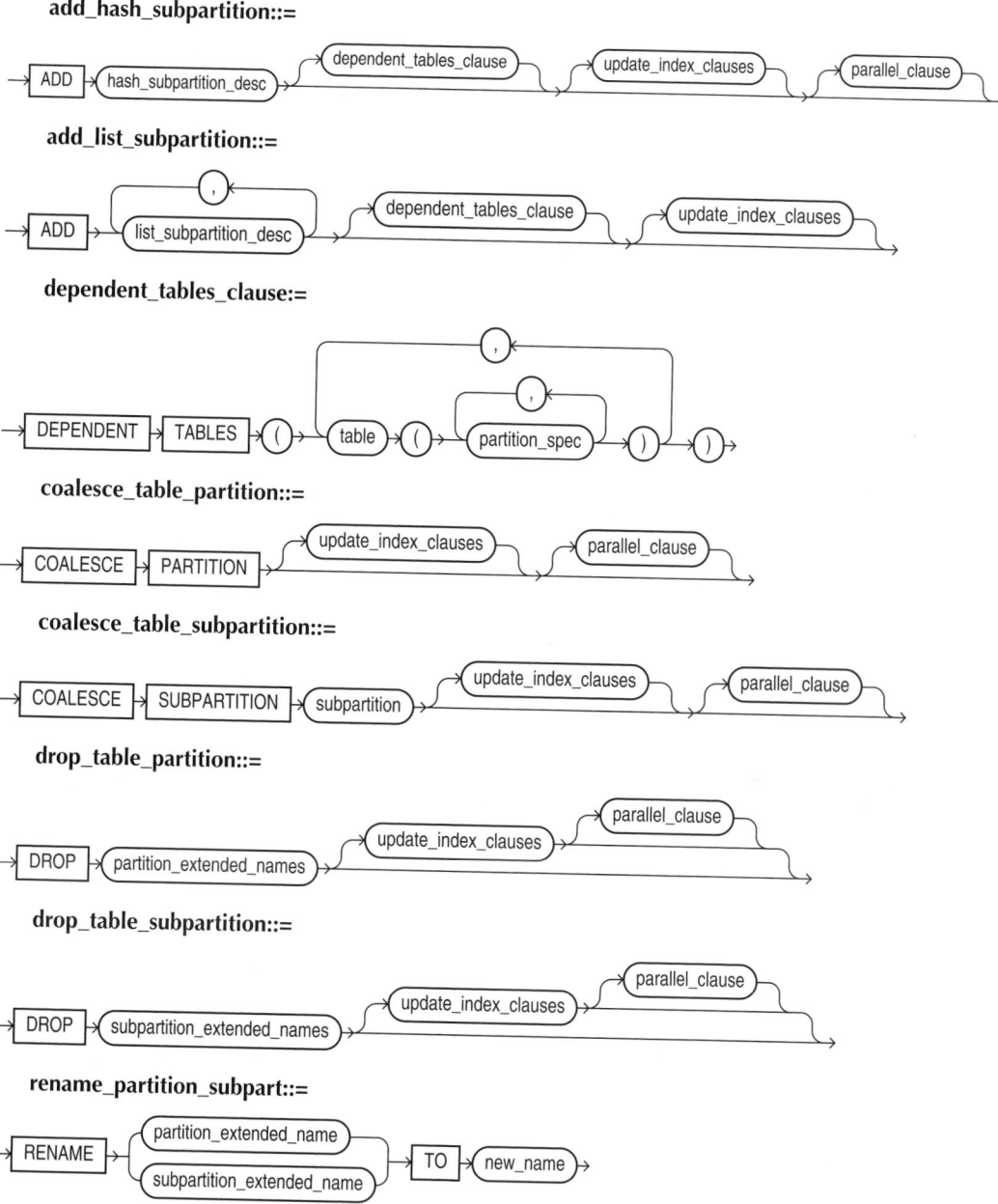

add_list_subpartition::=

dependent_tables_clause:=

coalesce_table_partition::=

coalesce_table_subpartition::=

drop_table_partition::=

drop_table_subpartition::=

rename_partition_subpart::=

truncate_partition_subpart::=

partition_extended_names::=

subpartition_extended_names::=

split_table_partition::=

split_nested_table_part::=

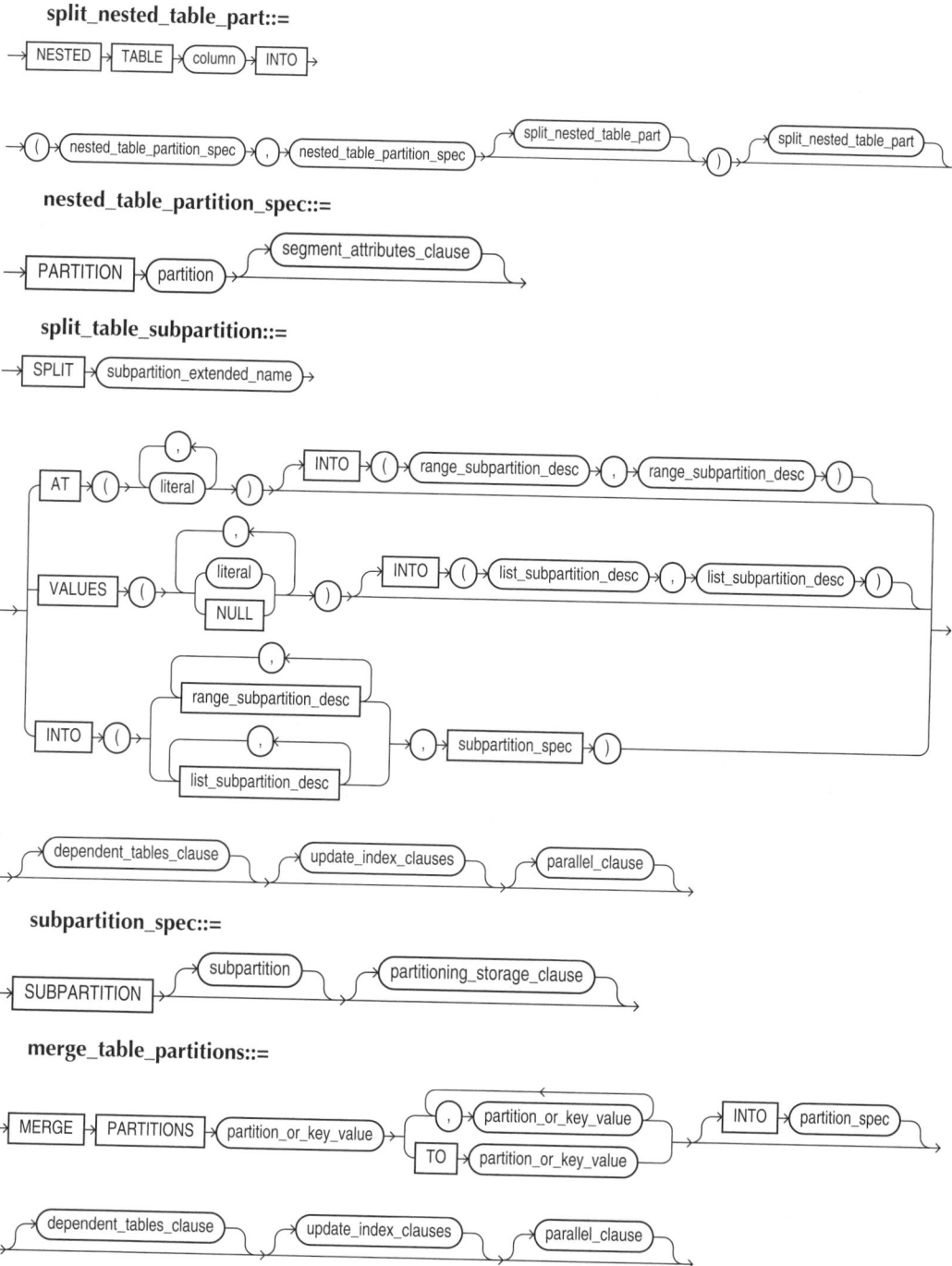

nested_table_partition_spec::=

split_table_subpartition::=

subpartition_spec::=

merge_table_partitions::=

partition_or_key_value::=

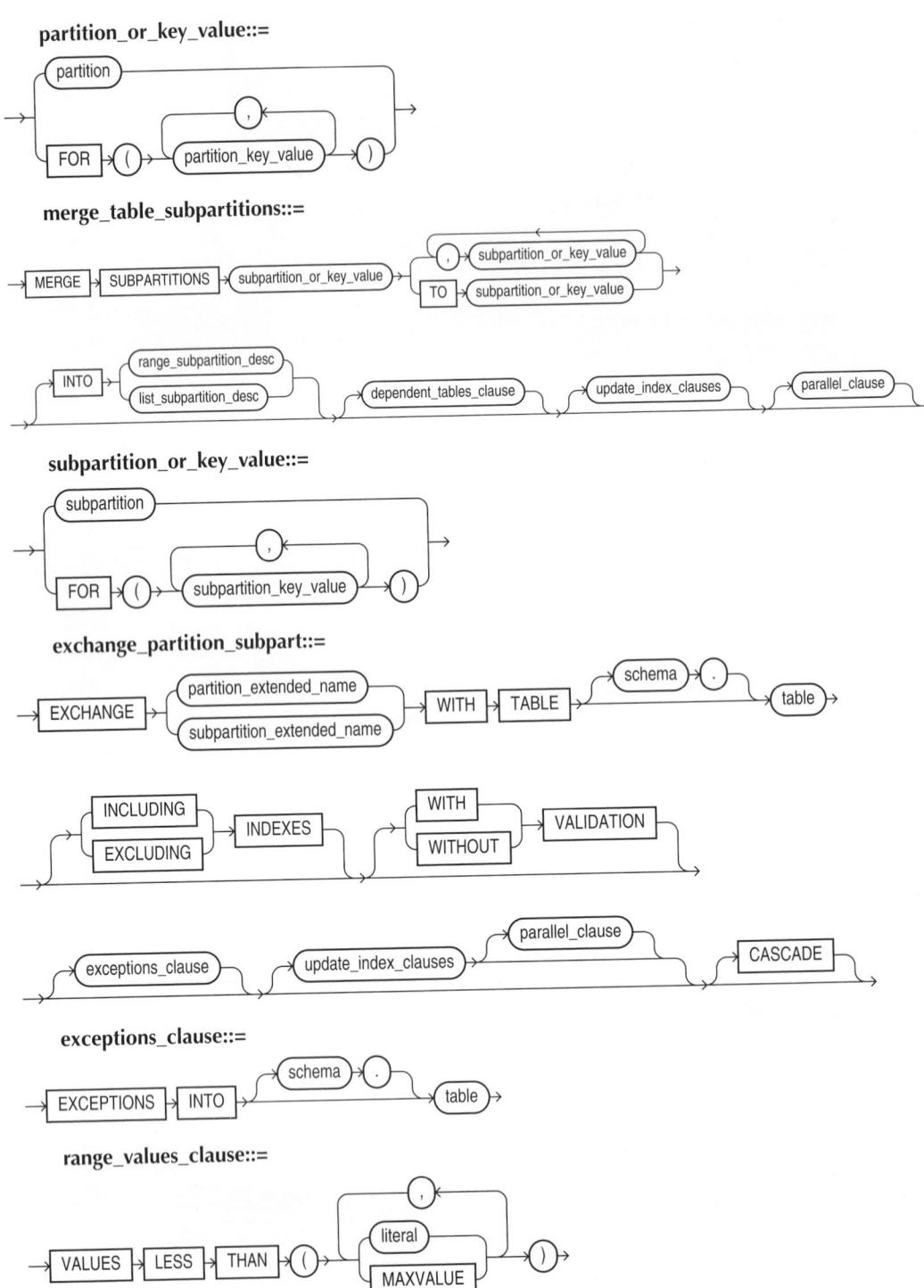

merge_table_subpartitions::=

subpartition_or_key_value::=

exchange_partition_subpart::=

exceptions_clause::=

range_values_clause::=

list_values_clause::=

table_partition_description::=

range_partition_desc::=

list_partition_desc::=

range_subpartition_desc::=

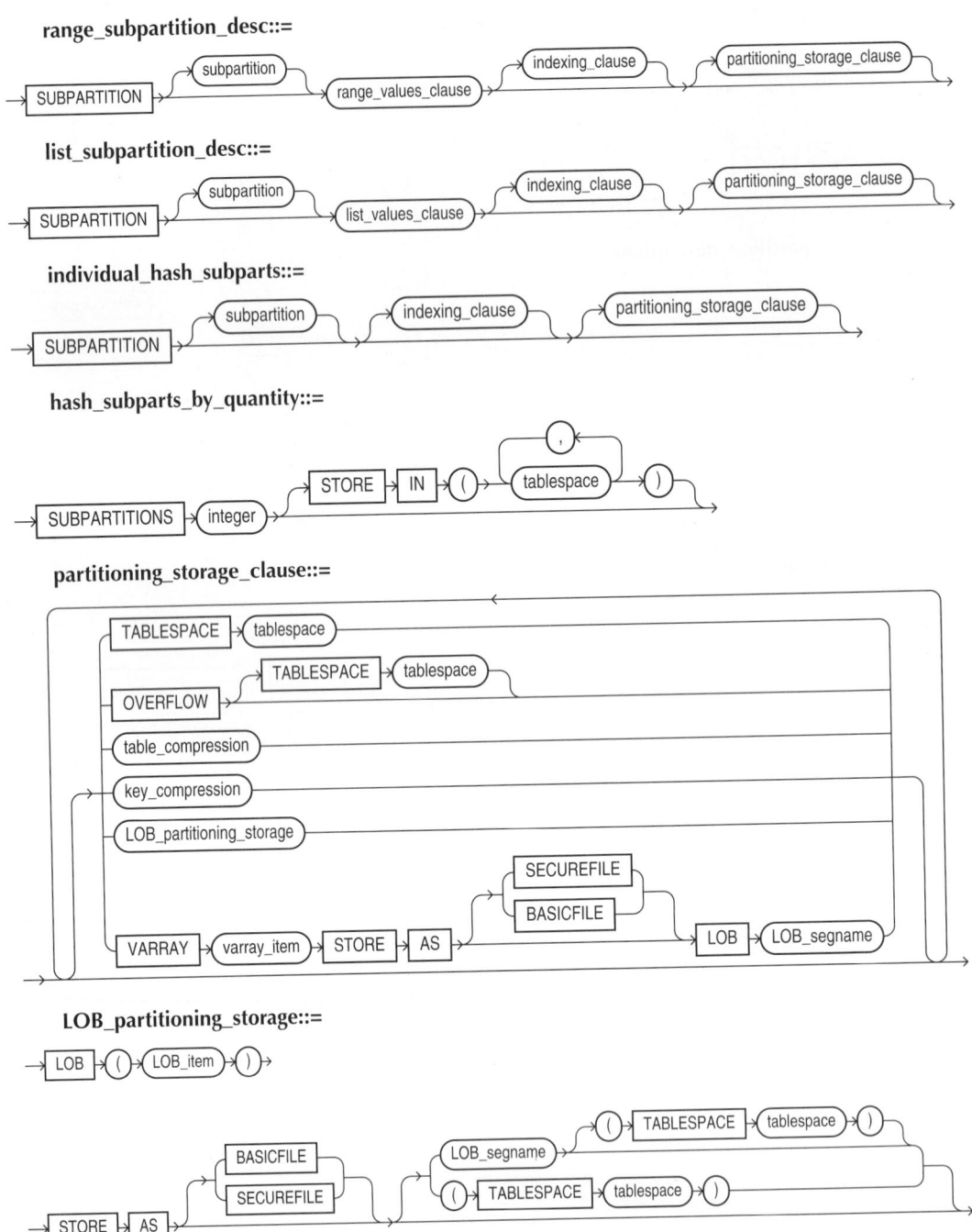

list_subpartition_desc::=

individual_hash_subparts::=

hash_subparts_by_quantity::=

partitioning_storage_clause::=

LOB_partitioning_storage::=

partition_attributes::=

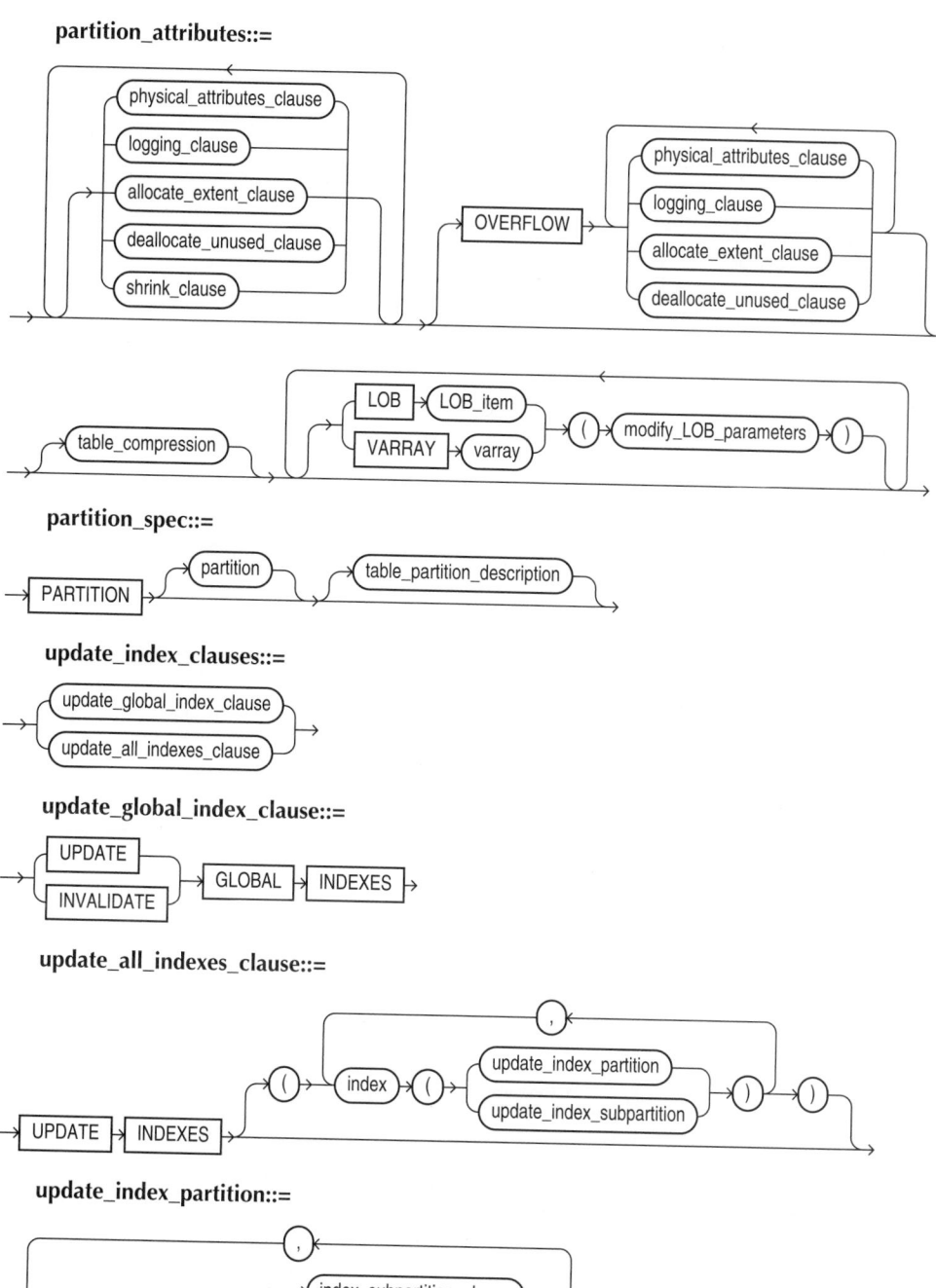

partition_spec::=

update_index_clauses::=

update_global_index_clause::=

update_all_indexes_clause::=

update_index_partition::=

update_index_subpartition::=

index_partition_description::=

index_subpartition_clause::=

parallel_clause::=

move_table_clause::=

enable_disable_clause::=

using_index_clause::=

index_properties::=

index_attributes::=

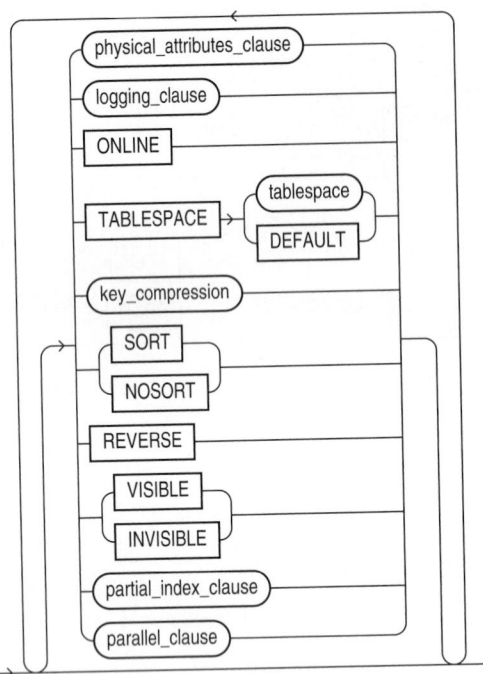

DESCRIPTION   **ALTER TABLE** changes the definition of an existing table. **ADD** allows you to add a new column to the end of an existing table, or add a constraint to the table's definition. These follow the same format used in **CREATE TABLE**.

MODIFY changes an existing column, with some restrictions:

- You may change the type of column or decrease its size only if the column is **NULL** in every row of the table.

- A **NOT NULL** column may be added only to a table with no rows.

- An existing column can be modified to **NOT NULL** only if it has a non-**NULL** value in every row or if a default value is specified during the alteration.

- Increasing the length of a **NOT NULL** column without specifying **NULL** will leave it **NOT NULL**.

You can use the **SET UNUSED** clause to mark columns as unused. When you use the **DROP UNUSED COLUMNS** clause, the table will be reorganized and all unused columns will be dropped.

ALLOCATE EXTENT lets you allocate a new extent explicitly. **ENABLE** and **DISABLE** enable and disable constraints. All other features of **ALTER TABLE** work as they do in **CREATE TABLE**, except that they apply to an existing table. *See* **CREATE TABLE** for details.

To alter a table, you must either have the ALTER privilege for that table or have the ALTER ANY TABLE system privilege.

CACHE specifies that the blocks for this table, when read, are to be marked as "most recently used" and kept in the data block buffer cache for as long as possible. This option is useful if the tables are small and fairly static. **NOCACHE** (the default) reverts the table back to the normal Last Recently Used (LRU) list behavior.

PARALLEL, along with **DEGREE** and **INSTANCES**, specifies the parallel characteristics of the table (for databases using the Real Application Clusters option). **DEGREE** specifies the number of query servers to use; **INSTANCES** specifies how the table is to be split among instances of Real Application Clusters for parallel query processing. An integer *n* specifies that the table is to be split among the specified number of available instances.

You can use **ALTER TABLE** to **ADD**, **DROP**, **EXCHANGE**, **MODIFY**, **MOVE**, **SPLIT**, or **TRUNCATE** partitions. *See* Chapter 17 and **CREATE TABLE**.

The LOB storage clauses specify the storage area to be used for LOB data that will not be stored in the table itself (out-of-line).

The **MOVE ONLINE** option allows you to access a table for DML operations during an online table reorganization. The **MOVE** and **MOVE ONLINE** options are only available for nonpartitioned index-organized tables. During a **MOVE ONLINE** operation, parallel DML operations against the table are not supported.

You can use the **COMPRESS** keyword to instruct Oracle to compress data segments to reduce disk and memory use for tables that are loaded with direct-path **INSERT**s.

As of Oracle Database 11*g,* **ALTER TABLE** has been enhanced in the following ways:

- The performance of the *add_column_clause* has been improved.

- The READ ONLY | READ WRITE clauses let you put a table into read-only mode, thus preventing DDL or DML changes to the table until you put the table back into read-write mode.

- The *add_table_partition* clause syntax has been expanded to support adding a system partition.

- The *flashback_archive_clause* lets you enable or disable historical tracking for a table.

- The *add_column_clause* supports the addition of virtual columns to tables.

- You can modify an XMLType table to add or remove one of more XMLSchemas.

- The *alter_interval_partitioning* clause lets you convert a range-partitioned table to an interval-partitioned table.

- The *dependent_tables_clause* lets you instruct the database to cascade various partition maintenance operations on a table to reference-partitioned child tables.

In Oracle Database 12*c,* there are new options to merge and split partitions as well as to selectively rebuild local indexes while deferring the rebuild of a global index.

ALTER TABLESPACE
SEE ALSO   **CREATE TABLESPACE**, **DROP TABLESPACE**, **STORAGE**, Chapters 22 and 51
FORMAT
   alter_tablespace::=

datafile_tempfile_clauses::=

tablespace_logging_clauses::=

tablespace_group_clause::=

tablespace_state_clauses::=

autoextend_clause::=

maxsize_clause::=

flashback_mode_clause::=

tablespace_retention_clause::=

DESCRIPTION   *tablespace* is the name of an existing tablespace. **ADD DATAFILE** adds to the tablespace a file or series of files described according to a *file_specification,* which defines the database filenames and sizes.

The filename format is operating-system specific. **SIZE** is the number of bytes set aside for this file. Suffixing this with **K** multiplies the value by 1024; using **M** multiplies it by 1048576. **REUSE** (without **SIZE**) means destroy the contents of any file by this name and assign it for use by this tablespace. **REUSE** with **SIZE** creates the file if it doesn't exist, and checks its size if it does. **SIZE** alone creates the file if it doesn't exist, but returns an error if it does exist.

You can use the **AUTOEXTEND** clause to dynamically resize your datafiles as needed, in increments of **NEXT** size, to a maximum of **MAXSIZE** (or **UNLIMITED**).

NOLOGGING specifies the default action for the writing of redo log entries for certain types of transactions in the tablespace. You can override this setting at the object level. **RENAME DATAFILE** changes the name of an existing tablespace file. The tablespace should be offline while the renaming takes place. Note that **RENAME** does not actually rename the files; it only associates their new names with this tablespace. Actually renaming operating system files must be done with the operating system itself. To rename files properly, first **ALTER TABLESPACE OFFLINE**, rename the files in the operating system, **RENAME** them with **ALTER TABLESPACE**, and then **ALTER TABLESPACE ONLINE**.

DEFAULT STORAGE defines the default storage for all future objects created in this tablespace, unless those defaults are overridden, such as by **CREATE TABLE**. **ONLINE** brings the tablespace back online. **OFFLINE** takes it offline, either without waiting for its users to log off (**IMMEDIATE**) or after they've all stopped using it (**NORMAL**).

MINIMUM EXTENT sets the minimum size for any extent created in the tablespace. **COALESCE** combines neighboring free extents in the tablespace into fewer, larger free extents.

READ ONLY tablespaces are never updated by Oracle and can be placed on read-only media. Read-only tablespaces do not need repeated backups. All tablespaces are created read-write. To change a read-only tablespace back to read-write status, use the **READ WRITE** clause.

BEGIN BACKUP can be executed at any time. It puts the tablespace in a state such that an online backup can occur while users are accessing the tablespace. **END BACKUP** indicates the system backup is finished. If the tablespace is online, any system backup must also back up archive redo logs. If it is offline, this is unnecessary.

TEMPORARY tablespaces cannot contain any permanent objects (such as tables or indexes); they can only hold the temporary segments used by Oracle during the processing of sorting operations and index creations. A **PERMANENT** tablespace can hold every type of Oracle segment.

NOTE

*For BIGFILE tablespaces, you can use **ALTER TABLESPACE** for commands (such as **RESIZE**) that would only work at the datafile level for smallfile tablespaces.*

You can rename a tablespace (the **RENAME** clause). You can also guarantee that unexpired undo data will be preserved, even at the expense of ongoing transactions that require undo space (via **RETENTION GUARANTEE**).

As of Oracle Database 11*g*, you can shrink the space used by a temporary tablespace and an individual tempfile.

ALTER TRIGGER

SEE ALSO   **CREATE TRIGGER**, **DROP TRIGGER**, Chapter 34
FORMAT
    alter_trigger::=

    trigger_compile_clause::=

    compiler_parameters_clause::=

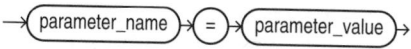

DESCRIPTION   **ALTER TRIGGER** enables, disables, renames, or recompiles a PL/SQL trigger. To use the **ALTER TRIGGER** command, you must either own the trigger or have ALTER ANY TRIGGER system privilege.

You can use the **COMPILE** clause to manually recompile an invalid trigger object. Because triggers have dependencies, they can become invalid if an object the trigger depends on changes. The **DEBUG** clause allows PL/SQL information to be generated during trigger recompilation.

ALTER TYPE

SEE ALSO **CREATE TYPE**, **CREATE TYPE BODY**, Chapter 38
FORMAT
  alter_type::=

  alter_type_clause::=

  type_compile _clause::=

  compiler_parameters_clause::=

type_replace_ clause::=

invoker_rights_clause::=

element_spec::=

inheritance_clauses::=

subprogram_spec::=

procedure_spec::=

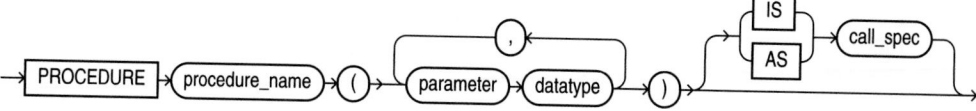

function_spec::=

FUNCTION → name → (→ parameter → datatype →) → return_clause →

constructor_spec::=

FINAL → INSTANTIABLE → CONSTRUCTOR → FUNCTION → datatype →

SELF → IN → OUT → datatype → , → parameter → datatype →) →

RETURN → SELF → AS → RESULT → IS / AS → call_spec →

map_order_function_spec::=

MAP / ORDER → MEMBER → function_spec →

pragma_clause::=

PRAGMA → RESTRICT_REFERENCES → (→ method_name / DEFAULT → , → RNDS / WNDS / RNPS / WNPS / TRUST →) →

alter_method_spec::=

ADD / DROP → map_order_function_spec / subprogram_spec

alter_attribute_definition::=

alter_collection_clauses::=

dependent_handling_clause::=

exceptions_clause::=

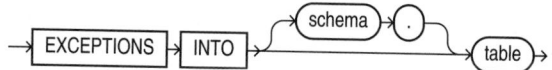

DESCRIPTION   **ALTER TYPE** allows you to modify existing abstract datatypes. When you create a method that acts on the abstract datatype, you use the **CREATE TYPE BODY** command (see entry in this appendix). Each method defined in the type body must first be listed in the type.

ALTER USER
SEE ALSO   **CREATE TABLESPACE**, **GRANT**, **CREATE PROFILE**, **CREATE USER**, Chapter 19

FORMAT
    alter_user::=

proxy_clause::=

db_user_proxy::=

container_data_clause::=

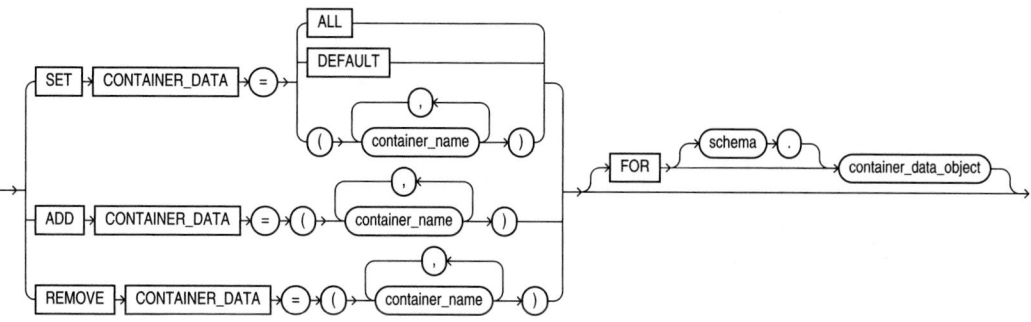

DESCRIPTION   You use **ALTER USER** to change a user's password or the **DEFAULT** tablespace (for objects the user owns) or the **TEMPORARY** tablespace (for temporary segments used by the user). Without **ALTER USER**, the defaults for both of these are set by the defaults of the first tablespace (both for objects and temporary segments) to which the user is **GRANT**ed resources and the default temporary tablespace defined at the database level. **ALTER USER** can also change the quota, the resource profile, or the default role (*see* **CREATE USER**). You can use the **PASSWORD EXPIRE** clause to force a user's password to expire, in which case the user must change his or her password during the next login. The **ACCOUNT UNLOCK** clause allows you to unlock an account that has exceeded its maximum number of consecutive failed login attempts. *See* **CREATE PROFILE** for details on password control. To alter a user, you must have the ALTER USER system privilege.

You can use the **PROXY** clause to connect as the specified user and to activate all, some, or none of the user's roles. **PROXY** is typically used in three-tier applications involving application servers.

ALTER USER includes the *container_data_clause* for manipulating user attributes within and across container databases (CDBs) in Oracle Database 12*c*.

ALTER VIEW
SEE ALSO   **CREATE VIEW**, **DROP VIEW**, Chapter 17
FORMAT
    alter_view::=

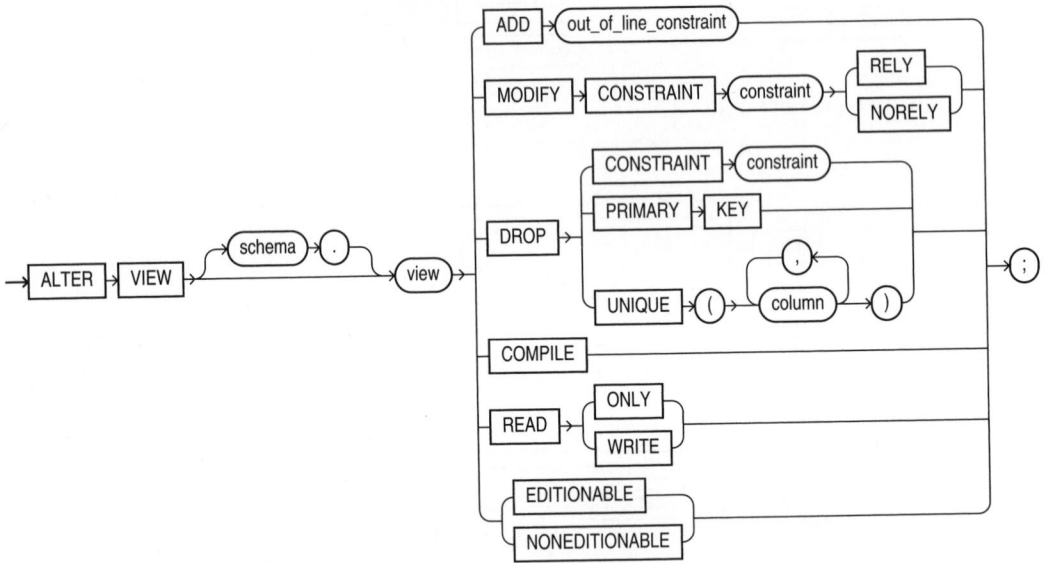

DESCRIPTION   **ALTER VIEW** recompiles a view or alters its constraints. To alter a view, you must either own the view or have ALTER ANY TABLE system privilege.

ANALYTIC FUNCTIONS
Analytic functions compute an aggregate value based on a group of rows; they return multiple rows for each group. Many of the analytic functions are listed under the AGGREGATE FUNCTIONS entry; when used as analytic functions, they can only be used within the **ORDER BY** clause.

    In the following alphabetical list of analytic functions (see the individual entries for syntax descriptions), the functions followed by an asterisk allow for the use of a windowing clause: **AVG***, **CORR***, **COUNT**, **COVAR_POP***, **COVAR_SAMP***, **CUME_DIST**, **DENSE_RANK**, **FIRST**, **FIRST_ VALUE***, **LAG**, **LAST**, **LAST_VALUE***, **LEAD**, **MAX***, **MIN***, **NTILE**, **PERCENT_RANK**, **PERCENTILE_ CONT**, **PERCENTILE_DISC**, **RANK**, **RATIO_TO_REPORT**, **REGR_***, **ROW_NUMBER**, **STDDEV***, **STDDEV_POP***, **STDDEV_SAMP***, **SUM***, **VAR_POP***, **VAR_SAMP***, **VARIANCE***.

ANALYZE
SEE ALSO   Chapter 46

FORMAT

    analyze::=

partition_extension_clause::=

validation_clauses::=

into_clause::=

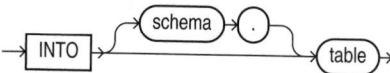

DESCRIPTION   Oracle recommends that you use the DBMS_STATS package in place of the **ANALYZE** command unless you need things that DBMS_STATS does not provide, such as identifying chained rows, validating index structure, or collecting information on freelist blocks. **ANALYZE** lets you collect statistics about a table, cluster, partition, or index for the optimizer, and stores them in the data dictionary; it lets you delete these statistics; it validates the structure of an object; and it identifies migrated and chained rows of a table or cluster with a listing in a local table. You use the **VALIDATE STRUCTURE** clause to test an object for possible data corruption. To analyze a table, you must either own the table or have the ANALYZE ANY system privilege.

The **LIST CHAINED ROWS** clause records information about row chaining in a table you specify.

AND
See LOGICAL OPERATORS, PRECEDENCE, **CONTAINS**

ANY
SEE ALSO   **ALL**, **BETWEEN**, **EXISTS**, **IN**, LOGICAL OPERATORS, Chapter 13
FORMAT

```
operator ANY list
```

DESCRIPTION   **= ANY** is the equivalent of **IN**. *operator* can be any one of **=, >, >=, <, <=,** or **!=**, and *list* can be a series of literal strings (such as 'Talbot', 'Jones', or 'Hild'), a series of literal numbers (such as 2, 43, 76, 32.06, or 444), or a column from a subquery, where each row of the subquery becomes a member of the list, as shown here:

```
location.city = any (select city from weather)
```

The *list* variable also can be a series of columns in the **WHERE** clause of the main query, as shown here:

```
prospect = any (vendor, client)
```

RESTRICTIONS   *list* cannot be a series of columns in a subquery, like this:

```
prospect = any (select vendor, client from . . .)
```

Many people find this operator and the **ALL** operator very difficult to remember, because the logic for some of their cases is not immediately intuitive. As a result, some form of **EXISTS** is usually substituted.

The combination of an operator with **ANY** and a list can be illustrated with these explanations:

`Page = ANY (4,2,7)`	Page is in the list (4,2,7)—2, 4, and 7 all qualify.
`Page > ANY (4,2,7)`	Page is greater than any single item in the list (4,2,7)—even 3 qualifies because it is greater than 2.
`Page >= ANY (4,2,7)`	Page is greater than or equal to any single item in the list (4,2,7)—even 2 qualifies because it is equal to 2.
`Page < ANY (4,2,7)`	Page is less than any single item in the list (4,2,7)—even 6 qualifies because it is less than 7.
`Page <= ANY (4,2,7)`	Page is less than or equal to any single item in the list (4,2,7)—even 7 qualifies.
`Page != ANY (4,2,7)`	Page is not equal to any single item in the list (4,2,7)—any number qualifies so long as the list has more than one value. With only one value, **!= ANY** is the equivalent of **!=**.

APPEND (SQL*Plus)
SEE ALSO CHANGE, DEL, EDIT, LIST, Chapter 6
FORMAT

```
A[PPEND] text
```

DESCRIPTION **APPEND** is a feature of the SQL*Plus command-line editor. **APPEND** places the text at the end of the current line in the current buffer, with no intervening spaces. If you want a space between the end of the current line and *text*, put two spaces between **APPEND** and *text*. If you want to append a semicolon at the end of a line, put two of them together (one of them will be regarded as a command terminator and discarded). **APPEND** is not available in iSQL*Plus.
EXAMPLE

```
append ;;
```

APPENDCHILDXML
FORMAT

```
APPENDCHILDXML
   ( XMLType_instance, XPath_string, value_expr [, namespace_string ] )
```

DESCRIPTION **APPENDCHILDXML** appends a user-supplied value onto the target XML as the child of the node indicated by an XPath expression.

ARCHIVE LOG
SEE ALSO ALTER DATABASE, RECOVER, Chapter 51
FORMAT

```
ARCHIVE LOG {LIST|STOP}|{START|NEXT|ALL|integer} [TO destination]
```

DESCRIPTION **ARCHIVE LOG** starts or stops automatic archiving of online redo log files, manually archives specific redo log files, or displays information about redo log files. **START** enables automatic archiving; **STOP** disables it. **LIST** shows the archive status for the online redo logs. **NEXT** manually archives the next online redo log file group that has been filled but not yet archived. **ALL** manually archives all filled but not yet archived redo log file groups. You can specify the online redo log group number and the destination area for the archived files.
EXAMPLE

```
archive log all
archive log list
```

AS
SEE ALSO ALIAS, TO_CHAR, Chapters 7 and 10
DESCRIPTION **AS** is used to separate column formulas from column aliases.
EXAMPLE Here **AS** separates the column alias PayDay from its column formula:

```
select next_day(CycleDate,'FRIDAY') AS PayDay
from payday;
```

ASCII
SEE ALSO ASCIISTR, CHARACTER FUNCTIONS, **CHR**
FORMAT

```
ASCII(string)
```

DESCRIPTION   ASCII is an acronym for *American Standard Code for Information Interchange*. It is a convention for using digital data to represent printable characters.

The **ASCII** function returns the ASCII value of the first (leftmost) character in the string. The ASCII value of a character is an integer between 0 and 255. Those between 0 and 127 are well defined. Those above 127 ("extended ASCII set") tend to differ by country, application, and computer manufacturer. The letter *A*, for instance, is equal to the ASCII number 65, *B* is 66, *C* is 67, and so on. The decimal point is 46. A minus sign is 45. The number 0 is 48, 1 is 49, 2 is 50, and so on.

EXAMPLE

```
select ascii('.'), ascii(.5),
       ascii('E'), ascii('Emily')
from dual;

ASCII('.') ASCII(.5) ASCII('E') ASCII('EMILY')
---------- --------- ---------- --------------
        46        46         69             69
```

ASCIISTR

SEE ALSO   ASCII, CHARACTER FUNCTIONS, **CHR**
FORMAT

```
ASCIISTR(string)
```

DESCRIPTION   The **ASCII** function takes a string and returns its ASCII equivalent in the database character set.

EXAMPLE

```
select asciistr('E'), asciistr('Emily')
from dual;

A ASCII
- -----
E Emily
```

ASIN

SEE ALSO   ACOS, ATAN, ATAN2, COS, COSH, EXP, LN, LOG, SIN, SINH, TAN, TANH
FORMAT

```
ASIN(value)
```

DESCRIPTION   **ASIN** returns the arc sine of a value. Input values range from –1 to 1; outputs are expressed in radians.

ASSOCIATE STATISTICS

SEE ALSO   ANALYZE
FORMAT
    associate_statistics::=

column_association::=

function_association::=

using_statistics_type::=

default_cost_clause::=

default_selectivity_clause::=

storage_table_clause::=

DESCRIPTION   ASSOCIATE STATISTICS associates a set of statistics functions with one or more columns, stand-alone functions, packages, types, or indexes. You must have the required privileges to **ALTER** the object being modified.

You can view associations in USER_USTATS after you analyze the object with which you are associating your statistics functions.

As of Oracle Database 11g, you can specify that the database should manage storage of statistics collected on a system-managed domain index.

ATAN
SEE ALSO   ACOS, ASIN, ATAN2, COS, COSH, EXP, LN, LOG, SIN, SINH, TAN, TANH
FORMAT

```
ATAN(value)
```

DESCRIPTION   ATAN returns the arc tangent of a value. Input values are unbounded; outputs are expressed in radians.

ATAN2
SEE ALSO   ACOS, ASIN, ATAN, COS, COSH, EXP, LN, LOG, SIN, SINH, TAN, TANH
FORMAT

```
ATAN2(value1, value2)
```

DESCRIPTION   ATAN2 returns the arc tangent of two values. Input values are unbounded; outputs are expressed in radians.

ATTRIBUTE (SQL*Plus)
SEE ALSO   COLUMN, Chapter 38
FORMAT

```
ATTRIBUTE [type_name.attribute_name [option ...]]
```

option can be one of the following:

```
ALI[AS] alias
CLE[AR]
FOR[MAT] format
LIKE {type_name.attribute_name|alias}
ON|OFF
```

DESCRIPTION   ATTRIBUTE sets the display attributes for attributes of a user-defined type column in SQL*Plus.
EXAMPLE

```
attribute address_ty.street format a50
```

AUDIT
SEE ALSO   CREATE DATABASE LINK, NOAUDIT, PRIVILEGE

FORMAT
  audit::=

  audit_operation_clause::=

  auditing_by_clause::=

  audit_schema_object_clause::=

auditing_on_clause::=

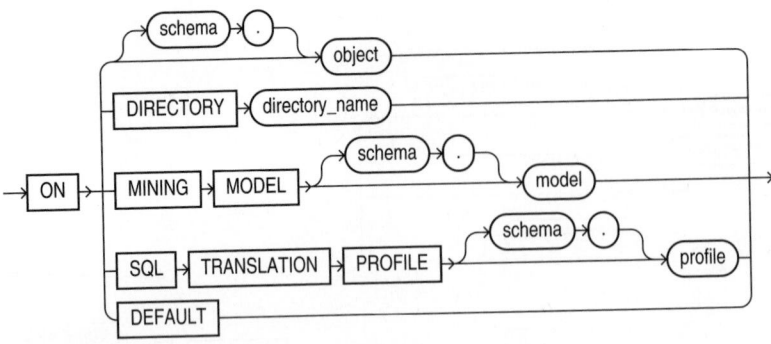

DESCRIPTION   You can **AUDIT** statements executed by users and statements that access specific objects.

The *statement options* are as follows:

Option	Audits
ALTER SYSTEM	Alter system
CLUSTER	Create, alter, drop, or truncate cluster
CONTEXT	Create or drop context
DATABASE LINK	Create or drop database link
DIMENSION	Create, alter, or drop dimension
DIRECTORY	Create or drop directory
INDEX	Create, alter, analyze, or drop index
MATERIALIZED VIEW	Create, alter, or drop materialized view
NOT EXISTS	SQL statements that fail because an object does not exist
PROCEDURE	Create or drop procedure, function, library, or package; create package body
PROFILE	Create, alter, or drop profile
PUBLIC DATABASE LINK	Create or drop public database link
PUBLIC SYNONYM	Create or drop public synonym
ROLE	Create, alter, drop, or set role
ROLLBACK SEGMENT	Create, alter, or drop rollback segment
SEQUENCE	Create or drop sequence
SESSION	Logon attempts
SYNONYM	Create or drop synonym
SYSTEM AUDIT	Audit or noaudit of SQL statements
SYSTEM GRANT	Grant or revoke system privileges and roles
TABLE	Create, drop, or truncate table
TABLESPACE	Create, alter, or drop tablespace
TRIGGER	Create, alter, or drop trigger; alter table with ENABLE|DISABLE ALL TRIGGERS
TYPE	Create, alter, or drop type or type body

Option	Audits
USER	Create, alter, or drop user
VIEW	Create or drop view

The following are additional statement-level options that are available:

Option	Commands Audited
ALTER SEQUENCE	ALTER SEQUENCE
ALTER TABLE	ALTER TABLE
COMMENT TABLE	COMMENT ON TABLE *table, view, materialized view* COMMENT ON COLUMN *table.column, view.column,* *materialized view.column*
DELETE TABLE	DELETE FROM *table, view*
EXECUTE PROCEDURE	CALL Execution of any procedure or function or access to any variable, library, or cursor inside a package
GRANT DIRECTORY	GRANT privilege ON directory REVOKE privilege ON directory
GRANT PROCEDURE	GRANT privilege ON procedure, function, package REVOKE privilege ON procedure, function, package
GRANT SEQUENCE	GRANT privilege ON sequence REVOKE privilege ON sequence
GRANT TABLE	GRANT privilege ON table, view, materialized view REVOKE privilege ON table, view, materialized view
GRANT TYPE	GRANT privilege ON TYPE REVOKE privilege ON TYPE
INSERT TABLE	INSERT INTO table, view
LOCK TABLE	LOCK TABLE table, view
SELECT SEQUENCE	Any statement containing sequence.CURRVAL or sequence.NEXTVAL
SELECT TABLE	SELECT FROM table, view, materialized view
UPDATE TABLE	UPDATE table, view

BY *user* audits only SQL statements issued by particular users. The default is to audit all users.

WHENEVER [NOT] SUCCESSFUL writes a row to an audit table only when an attempted access to an audited table or system facility is (or is **NOT**) successful. Omitting this optional clause causes a row to be written whether an access is successful or not.

Auditing information is written to a table named SYS.AUD$ and accessed via data dictionary views.

EXAMPLE   This audits all updates by a user named CLERK_USER:

```
audit update table by clerk_user;
```

AVG
SEE ALSO   **COMPUTE**, AGGREGATE FUNCTIONS, Chapter 9
FORMAT

```
AVG ( [ DISTINCT | ALL ] expr ) [OVER ( analytic_clause )]
```

DESCRIPTION **AVG** is the average of *expr* for a group of rows. **DISTINCT** forces only unique values to be averaged. **NULL** rows are ignored by this function, which may affect results.

BEGIN

SEE ALSO BLOCK STRUCTURE, **DECLARE CURSOR**, **END**, **EXCEPTION**, **SQLTERMINATOR** under **SET**, Chapter 32

FORMAT

```
[<<block label>>]
[DECLARE]
BEGIN
    ... block logic ...
END [block label];
```

DESCRIPTION **BEGIN** is the opening statement of a PL/SQL block's executable section. It can be followed with any legal PL/SQL logic and an exception handler, and is closed with the **END** statement. At least one executable statement is required between **BEGIN** and **END**. *See* BLOCK STRUCTURE.

block label is a name given to a PL/SQL block that starts with the word **BEGIN** and finishes with the word **END**. The word **END** is followed by a terminator, usually a semicolon (*see* **SQLTERMINATOR** under **SET** for exceptions). *block label* follows normal naming conventions for objects and must be bracketed by << and >>. These symbols tell PL/SQL that this is a label. **BEGIN** may optionally be preceded by a section called **DECLARE** (which follows the *block label*) and may optionally contain a section called **EXCEPTION**.

BETWEEN

See LOGICAL OPERATORS.

BFILE

BFILE is a datatype (*see* DATATYPES) used for binary LOB data stored outside the database. Oracle does not maintain read consistency or data integrity for the externally stored data. Within the database, a LOB locator value is stored to point to the external file. Before creating a BFILE entry, you must first create a directory. *See* **CREATE DIRECTORY**.

BFILENAME

SEE ALSO BFILE, **CREATE DIRECTORY**, Chapter 40

FORMAT

```
BFILENAME ( 'directory' , 'filename' )
```

DESCRIPTION **BFILENAME** returns a BFILE locator associated with the specified filename and directory object.

BINARY_DOUBLE

See DATATYPES.

BINARY_FLOAT

See DATATYPES.

BIN_TO_NUM

SEE ALSO NUMBER FUNCTIONS, Chapter 9

FORMAT

```
BIN_TO_NUM ( expr [, expr]... )
```

DESCRIPTION **BIN_TO_NUM** converts a bit vector to its equivalent number.

EXAMPLE

```
select BIN_TO_NUM(1,0,0,1) from DUAL;

BIN_TO_NUM(1,0,0,1)
-------------------
                  9
```

BITAND

SEE ALSO **DECODE**, Chapter 16

FORMAT

```
BITAND ( argument1, argument2 )
```

DESCRIPTION **BITAND** computes an **AND** operation on the bits of *argument1* and *argument2*, both of which must resolve to nonnegative integers, and returns an integer. This function is commonly used with the **DECODE** function.

BLOB

A BLOB is a binary large object stored inside the database. *See* Chapter 41.

BLOCK STRUCTURE

A block structure is a structure of block sections in PL/SQL.

SEE ALSO **BEGIN, DECLARE CURSOR, END, EXCEPTION, GOTO**, Chapter 32

DESCRIPTION PL/SQL blocks can be embedded in SQL*Plus and any of several programming languages, through the use of the Oracle precompilers. PL/SQL blocks are structured like this:

```
[<<block label>>]
[DECLARE
.. declarations (CURSOR, VARIABLE and EXCEPTION)...]

BEGIN

... block logic (executable code)...

[EXCEPTION

... exception handling logic (for fatal errors)...]

END [block label];
```

As the brackets show, both the **DECLARE** and **EXCEPTION** sections are optional. A block may optionally be labeled by a block name, which must be bracketed by << and >>.

The sections of a block must be in this order, although blocks may nest inside of other blocks in either the block logic or Exception Handling logic sections. *blocks* may be used for branching using a **GOTO** or as a prefix in referencing a variable in another block (*see* **DECLARE** for details on this). If a variable will be referenced in a cursor declaration, it must be declared before the cursor is declared.

EXAMPLE

```
<<calc_areas>>
DECLARE
    pi      constant NUMBER(9,7) := 3.14159;
    area    NUMBER(14,2);
    cursor rad_cursor is
            select * from radius_vals;
    rad_val rad_cursor%ROWTYPE;
BEGIN
    open rad_cursor;
     loop`
      fetch rad_cursor into rad_val;
        exit when rad_cursor%NOTFOUND;
        area := pi*power(rad_val.radius,2);
        insert into AREAS values (rad_val.radius, area);
     end loop;
    close rad_cursor;
END calc_areas;
```

BREAK (SQL*Plus)

SEE ALSO   **CLEAR**, **COMPUTE**, Chapter 6
FORMAT

```
BRE[AK]  [ON report_element [action [action]]] ...
```

where *report_element* is

```
{column|expr|ROW|REPORT}
```

and *action* is

```
[SKI[P]n|[SKI[P]] PAGE][NODUP[LICATES]|DUP[LICATES]]
```

DESCRIPTION   A break occurs when SQL*Plus detects a specified change, such as the end of a page or a change in the value of an expression. A break will cause SQL*Plus to perform some action you've specified in the **BREAK** command, such as **SKIP**, and to print some result from a **COMPUTE** command, such as averages or totals for a column. Only one **BREAK** command may be in effect at a time. A new **BREAK** command may specify changes, and their associated actions, that are to cause a break.

A **BREAK ON REPORT** causes a break at the end of a report or query.

A change in the value of an expression may occur at any time prior to the **REPORT** break, and there may be several **ON** expression clauses in a single **BREAK** statement; however, their order in the **BREAK** command should be the same as in the **ORDER BY** of the **SELECT** statement. That is, each expression that appears in the **BREAK** command also should be placed in the **ORDER BY** clause of **SELECT**, in identical sequence, or the result will be meaningless. In addition, their order should be from the largest grouping to the smallest (for example, ON Corporation, ON Division, ON Project).

ON ROW causes a break for every row selected.

ON PAGE causes a break at the end of each page and is independent of breaks caused by *expression*, **ON ROW**, or **ON REPORT**.

SKIP skips a number of lines, and **PAGE** or **SKIP PAGE** skips to a new page, before printing the result of the associated **COMPUTE** for the break.

NODUPLICATES suppresses the printing of the values in the expression or column in the **BREAK** for every row except the first one after the **BREAK** occurs.

BREAK by itself displays the current break settings.
CLEAR BREAKS removes any existing **BREAK**s.

BTITLE (SQL*Plus)

SEE ALSO **ACCEPT**, **DEFINE**, PARAMETERS, **REPFOOTER**, **REPHEADER**, **SET HEADSEP**, **TTITLE** **FORMAT**

```
BTI[TLE] [printspec [text|variable]... | OFF | ON]
```

DESCRIPTION **BTITLE** puts *text* (may be multiline) at the bottom of each page of a report. **OFF** and **ON** suppress and restore the display of the *text* without changing its contents. **BTITLE** by itself displays the current **BTITLE** options and text or variable. *text* is a bottom title that you wish to give this report, and *variable* is a user-defined variable or a system-maintained variable, including SQL.LNO, the current line number, SQL.PNO, the current page number, SQL.RELEASE, the current Oracle release number, SQL.SQLCODE, the current error code, and SQL.USER, the username.

printspec options are as follows:

- **COL *n*** skips directly to position *n* (from the left margin) of the current line.

- **S[KIP] *n*** prints *n* blank lines. If no *n* is specified, one blank line is printed. If *n* is 0, no blank lines are printed and the current position for printing becomes position 1 of the current line (leftmost on the page).

- **TAB *n*** skips forward *n* positions (backward if *n* is negative).

- **BOLD** prints the output data in bold print.

- **LE[FT]**, **CE[NTER]**, and **R[IGHT]** left-justify, center, and right-justify data, respectively, on the current line. Any text or variables following these commands are justified as a group, up to the end of the command, or a **LEFT**, **CENTER**, **RIGHT**, or **COL**. **CENTER** and **RIGHT** use the value set by the **SET LINESIZE** command to determine where to place the text or variable.

- **FORMAT *string*** specifies the format model that will control the format of the following text or variables, and follows the same syntax as **FORMAT** in a **COLUMN** command, such as **FORMAT** A12 or **FORMAT** $999,999.99. Each time a **FORMAT** appears, it supersedes the previous one that was in effect. If no **FORMAT** model has been specified, the one set by **SET NUMFORMAT** is used. If **NUMFORMAT** has not been set, the default for SQL*Plus is used.

Data values are printed according to the default format unless a variable has been loaded with a date reformatted by **TO_CHAR**.

Any number of options, text, and variables may be used in a single **BTITLE**. Each is printed in the order specified, and each is positioned and formatted as specified by the clauses that precede it.

CALL

SEE ALSO **EXECUTE**, Chapter 44

FORMAT
   call::=

   [CALL] → routine_clause / object_access_expression →

   INTO → : → host_variable → INDICATOR → : → indicator_variable → ;

   routine_clause::=

   schema . → type . / package . → function / procedure / method

   @ → dblink_name → (→ argument , →) →

   object_access_expression::=

   table_alias . column . / object_table_alias . / (expr) . → . attribute / . method (argument ,) / method (argument ,) →

DESCRIPTION   You can use **CALL** to execute a stored procedure or function from within SQL. You must have EXECUTE privilege on the procedure or function, or on the package in which the procedure or function exists.

As of Oracle Database 11g, you can use positional, named, and mixed notation in the argument to the routine being called, if the routine takes any arguments.

CARDINALITY
SEE ALSO   COLLECTION FUNCTIONS
FORMAT

```
CARDINALITY ( nested_table )
```

DESCRIPTION   CARDINALITY returns the number of elements in a nested table. If the nested table is empty, or is a null collection, then **CARDINALITY** returns **NULL**.

CASE

SEE ALSO   OTHER FUNCTIONS, **DECODE**, **TRANSLATE**, Chapter 16

SQL CASE Expressions FORMAT

case_expression::=

simple_case_expression::=

searched_case_expression::=

else_clause::=

PL/SQL CASE Statement FORMAT

simple_case_statement::=

searched_case_statement::=

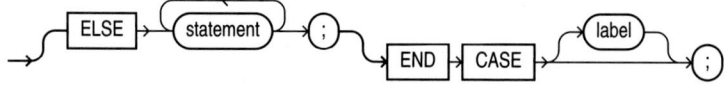

DESCRIPTION   CASE supports if-then-else logic within SQL statements. Use **WHEN/THEN** clauses to tell the database what to do for each condition. You can use an **ELSE** clause to handle exceptions to your **WHEN** clauses.

EXAMPLE

```
select distinct
      case category_name
```

```
        when  'ADULTFIC' then 'Adult Fiction'
        when  'ADULTNF' then 'Adult Nonfiction'
        when  'ADULTREF' then 'Adult Reference'
        when  'CHILDRENFIC' then 'Children Fiction'
        when  'CHILDRENNF' then 'Children Nonfiction'
        when  'CHILDRENPIC' then 'Children Picturebook'
        else category_name
     end
from bookshelf;
```

CAST

SEE ALSO   Chapter 39
FORMAT

```
CAST ( { expr | ( subquery ) | MULTISET ( subquery ) } AS type_name )
```

DESCRIPTION   You can use **CAST** to convert one datatype to another. **CAST** is most commonly used when working with collectors such as nested tables.

CATSEARCH

CATSEARCH is used for text searches against CTXCAT text indexes created within Oracle Text. *See* Chapter 27 for index creation and text search examples. Supported text search operators include the following:

Operator	Description
|	Returns a record if either search term has a score that exceeds the threshold.
AND	Returns a record if both search terms have a score that exceeds the threshold. This is the default action.
-	Returns rows that contain the term preceding the - that do not contain the term following it.
NOT	Same as -.
()	Specifies the order in which search criteria are evaluated.
" "	Encloses phrases.

CEIL

SEE ALSO   **FLOOR**, NUMBER FUNCTIONS
FORMAT

```
CEIL(value)
```

DESCRIPTION   **CEIL** is the smallest integer greater than or equal to *value*.
EXAMPLE

```
CEIL(1.3)  =   2
CEIL(-2.3) = -2
```

CHANGE (SQL*Plus)

SEE ALSO   **APPEND, DEL, EDIT, LIST**, Chapter 6
FORMAT

```
C[HANGE] /old text/new text/
```

DESCRIPTION **CHANGE** is a feature of the SQL*Plus command-line editor. It changes *old text* to *new text* in the current line of the current buffer (the line marked with an * in the LIST). **CHANGE** is not available in iSQL*Plus (which has been deprecated as of Oracle Database 10*g*).

CHANGE ignores case in searching for old text. Three dots are a wildcard. If *old text* is prefixed with '**. . .**', everything up to and including the first occurrence of *old text* is replaced by *new text*. If *old text* is suffixed with '**. . .**', everything including and after the first occurrence of *old text* is replaced by *new text*. If *old text* has **. . .** embedded in it, everything from the part of *old text* before the dots, through the part of *old text* after the dots, is replaced by *new text*.

The space between the **CHANGE** and the first / may be omitted; the final delimiter is unnecessary if no trailing spaces need to be inserted. A delimiter other than / may be used. Any character following the word **CHANGE** (other than a space) is assumed to be the delimiter.

EXAMPLES If this is the current line of the current buffer

```
where category_name = 'ADULTFN'
```

then

```
C /ADULTFN/ADULTNF
```

would change the line to this:

```
where category_name = 'ADULTNF'
```

CHAR DATATYPE

See DATATYPES.

CHARACTER FUNCTIONS

SEE ALSO CONVERSION FUNCTIONS, NUMBER FUNCTIONS, OTHER FUNCTIONS, Chapter 7
DESCRIPTION This is an alphabetical list of all current character functions in the Oracle version of SQL. Each of these is listed elsewhere in this reference under its own name, with its proper format and use.

Function Name and Use

```
string || string
```

|| concatenates two strings. The | symbol is called a broken vertical bar, although on some computers it may be a solid bar.

```
ASCII(string)
```

ASCII gives the ASCII value of the first character of a string.

```
CHR(integer)
```

CHR gives the character with an ASCII value equal to a given positive integer.

```
CONCAT(string1,string2)
```

CONCAT concatenates two strings. It is equivalent to ||.

```
INITCAP(string)
```

This stands for **INIT**ial **CAP**ital. It changes the first letter of a word or series of words into uppercase.

```
INSTR(string, set [, start [ ,occurrence ] ])
```

INSTR finds the location of the beginning of a set of characters **IN** a **STR**ing.

```
LENGTH(string)
```

This tells the **LENGTH** of a string.

```
LOWER(string)
```

LOWER converts every letter in a string to lowercase.

```
LPAD(string,length [,'set'])
```

LPAD stands for **L**eft **PAD**. It makes a string a specific length by adding a specified set of characters to the left.

```
LTRIM(string [,'set'])
```

LTRIM stands for **L**eft **TRIM**. It trims all the occurrences of any one of a set of characters off of the left side of a string.

```
NLS_INITCAP(string[,'NLS_SORT=sort'])
```

NLS_INITCAP stands for **N**ational **L**anguage **S**upport **INIT**ial **CAP**ital. This version of **INITCAP** uses the collating sequence *sort* to do the case conversion.

```
NLS_LOWER(string[,'NLS_SORT=sort'])
```

NLS_LOWER stands for **N**ational **L**anguage **S**upport **LOWER**case. This version of **LOWER** uses the collating sequence *sort* to do the case conversion.

```
NLS_UPPER(string[,'NLS_SORT=sort'])
```

NLS_UPPER stands for **N**ational **L**anguage **S**upport **UPPER**case. This version of **UPPER** uses the collating sequence *sort* to do the case conversion.

```
NLSSORT(string[,'NLS_SORT=sort'])
```

Oracle uses **N**ational **L**anguage **S**upport **SORT**. This gives the collating sequence value of the given string based on the collating sequence *sort* or, if omitted, the National Language Support option chosen for the site.

```
REGEXP_COUNT(source_string, pattern,
  [,position, match_parameter])
```

REGEXP_COUNT returns the number of occurrences of a specified regular expression pattern in a source string.

```
REGEXP_INSTR(source_string, pattern
  [,position,occurrence,return_option,match_parameter])
```

REGEXP_INSTR returns an integer indicating the start of the search pattern. **REGEXP_INSTR** extends the capabilities of **INSTR** by permitting searches of regular expression patterns.

```
REGEXP_REPLACE(source_string, pattern
  [,replace_string,position,occurrence,match_parameter])
```

REGEXP_REPLACE returns *source_string* with every occurrence of *pattern* replaced with *replace_string* (zero or more characters). **REGEXP_REPLACE** extends the capabilities of **REPLACE** by permitting searches of regular expression patterns.

```
REGEXP_SUBSTR(source_string, pattern
  [,position,occurrence,match_parameter])
```

REGEXP_SUBSTR returns a subset of *source_string* based on the results of a regular expression search. **REGEXP_SUBSTR** extends the capabilities of **SUBSTR** by permitting searches of regular expression patterns.

```
REPLACE(string, if [,then])
```

REPLACE returns *string* with every occurrence of *if* replaced with *then* (zero or more characters). If no *then* string is specified, then all occurrences of *if* are removed. *See* **TRANSLATE**.

```
RPAD(string,length [ ,'set'])
```

RPAD stands for **R**ight **PAD**. It makes a string a specific length by adding a specified set of characters to the right.

```
RTRIM(string [,'set'])
```

RTRIM stands for **R**ight **TRIM**. It trims all the occurrences of any one of a set of characters off the right side of a string.

```
SOUNDEX(string)
```

SOUNDEX converts a string to a code value. Names with similar sounds tend to have the same code value. You can use **SOUNDEX** to compare names that might have small spelling differences but are still the same.

```
SUBSTR(string, start [,count])
```

SUBSTRing clips out a piece of a string beginning at *start* position and counting for *count* characters from *start*.

```
TRANSLATE(string,if,then)
```

This **TRANSLATE**s a string, character by character, based on a positional matching of characters in the *if* string with characters in the *then* string. *See* **REPLACE**.

```
TREAT(expr AS [REF][user.]type)
```

TREAT changes the declared type of an expression.

```
TRIM
( [{ { LEADING | TRAILING | BOTH } [trim_character])
  | trim_character
  } from   ]   trim_source )
```

TRIM removes all the occurrences of any one of a set of characters off of the right side, left side, or both sides of a string.

```
UPPER(string)
```

UPPER converts every letter in a string into uppercase.

```
USERENV(option)
```

USERENV returns information about the **USER ENV**ironment, usually for an audit trail. Options include 'ENTRYID', 'SESSIONID', and 'TERMINAL'. **USERENV** is still supported but has been replaced by SYS_CONTEXT's UserEnv namespace.

```
VSIZE(string)
```

VSIZE gives the storage size of *string* in Oracle.

CHARTOROWID

SEE ALSO CONVERSION FUNCTIONS, **ROWIDTOCHAR**
FORMAT

```
CHARTOROWID(string)
```

DESCRIPTION This stands for **CHAR**acter **TO ROW ID**entifier. It changes a character string to act like an internal Oracle row identifier, or **ROWID**.

CHR

SEE ALSO **ASCII**, CHARACTER FUNCTIONS
FORMAT

```
CHR(integer)
```

DESCRIPTION **CHR** returns the character with the ASCII value of *integer*. (*integer* means an integer between 0 and 255 because the ASCII value of a character is an integer between 0 and 255.) Those between 0 and 127 are well defined. Those above 127 (called the extended ASCII set) tend to differ by country, application, and computer manufacturer. The letter *A*, for instance, is equal to the ASCII number 65, *B* is 66, *C* is 67, and so on. The decimal point is 46. A minus sign is 45. The number 0 is 48, 1 is 49, 2 is 50, and so on.

EXAMPLE

```
select chr(77), chr(46), chr(56) from dual;


C C C
- - -
M . 8
```

CLEAR (SQL*Plus)

SEE ALSO BREAK, COLUMN, COMPUTE
FORMAT

```
CL[EAR] option
```

DESCRIPTION
   CLEAR clears the option.
   BRE[AKS] clears breaks set by the **BREAK** command.
   BUFF[ER] clears the current buffer.
   COL[UMNS] clears options set by the **COLUMN** command.
   COMP[UTES] clears options set by the **COMPUTE** command.
   SCR[EEN] clears the screen.
   SQL clears the SQL buffer.
   TIMI[NG] deletes all timing areas created by the **TIMING** command.
EXAMPLES To clear computes, use this:

```
clear computes
```

To clear column definitions, use this:

```
clear columns
```

CLOB

CLOB is a datatype that supports character large objects. *See* Chapter 40.

CLOSE

SEE ALSO **DECLARE CURSOR, FETCH, FOR, OPEN**, Chapter 32
FORMAT

```
CLOSE cursor;
```

DESCRIPTION **CLOSE** closes the named cursor and releases its resources to Oracle for use elsewhere. *cursor* must be the name of a currently open cursor.

Even though a cursor has been closed, its definition has not been lost. You can issue **OPEN** *cursor* again, so long as the cursor was explicitly declared. A **FOR** loop will also implicitly **OPEN** a declared cursor. *See* **CURSOR FOR LOOP**.

CLUSTER_ID

FORMAT
cluster_id::=

cluster_id_analytic::=

mining_attribute_clause::=

mining_analytic_clause::=

DESCRIPTION This function is for use with clustering models that have been created using the DBMS_DATA_MINING package or with the Oracle Data Mining Java API. It returns the cluster identifier of the predicted cluster with the highest probability for the set of predictors specified in the *mining_attribute_clause*. The value returned is an Oracle NUMBER.

CLUSTER_PROBABILITY

FORMAT
cluster_probability::=

cluster_prob_analytic::=

mining_attribute_clause::=

mining_analytic_clause::=

DESCRIPTION   This function is for use with clustering models that have been created with the DBMS_ DATA_MINING package or with the Oracle Data Mining Java API. It returns a measure of the degree of confidence of membership of an input row in a cluster associated with the specified model.

CLUSTER_SET
FORMAT
cluster_set::=

cluster_set_analytic::=

mining_attribute_clause::=

mining_analytic_clause::=

DESCRIPTION   This function is for use with clustering models that have been created with the DBMS_DATA_MINING package or with the Oracle Data Mining Java API. It returns a varray of objects containing all possible clusters that a given row belongs to. Each object in the varray is a pair of scalar values containing the cluster ID and the cluster probability. The object fields are named CLUSTER_ID and PROBABILITY, and both are an Oracle NUMBER.

COALESCE
SEE ALSO   **DECODE**, Chapter 16
FORMAT

```
COALESCE(value1, value2, ...)
```

DESCRIPTION   **COALESCE** returns the first non-**NULL** value encountered in the list of values provided.

COLLECT
SEE ALSO   COLLECTION FUNCTIONS, **CAST**
FORMAT

```
COLLECT(column)
```

DESCRIPTION   **COLLECT** takes the input *column* value and creates a nested table of the input type out of the rows selected. To get the results of this function, you must use it within a **CAST** function.

COLLECTION FUNCTIONS
Collection functions operate on nested tables and varying arrays; *see* Chapter 39 for details. Collection functions available include **CARDINALITY**, **COLLECT**, **POWERMULTISET**, **POWERMULTISET_BY_CARDINALITY**, and **SET**.

COLUMN
SEE ALSO   **ALIAS**, Chapter 6
FORMAT

```
COL[UMN]    {column | expression}
   [ ALI[AS] alias ]
   [ CLE[AR] | DEF[AULT] ]
```

```
[ ENTMAP {ON|OFF}
[ FOLD_A[FTER]
[ FOLD_B[EFORE]
[ FOR[MAT] format ]
[ HEA[DING] text
    [ JUS[TIFY] {L[EFT]|C[ENTER]| R[IGHT]} ] ]
[ LIKE {expression | alias} ]
[ NEWL[INE] ]
[ NEW_V[ALUE] variable ]
[ NOPRI[NT]|PRI[NT] ]
[ NUL[L] text ]
[ OLD_V[ALUE] variable ]
[ ON | OFF ]
[ WRA[PPED]|WOR[D_WRAPPED]|TRU[NCATED] ]...
```

DESCRIPTION **COLUMN** controls column and column heading formatting. The options are all cumulative, and may be entered either simultaneously on a single line or on separate lines at any time; the only requirement is that the word **COLUMN** and the column or expression must appear on each separate line. If one of the options is repeated, the most recent specified will be in effect. **COLUMN** by itself displays all the current definitions for all columns. **COLUMN** with only a column or expression will show that column's current definition.

column or *expression* refers to a column or expression used in **SELECT**. If an expression is used, the expression must be entered exactly the same way that it is in the **SELECT** statement. If the expression in the **SELECT** statement is **AMOUNT * RATE**, then entering **RATE * AMOUNT** in a **COLUMN** command will not work. If a column or expression is given an alias in the **SELECT** statement, that alias must be used here.

If you **SELECT** columns with the same name from different tables (in sequential selects), a **COLUMN** command for that column name will apply to both. Avoid this by assigning the columns different aliases in the **SELECT** statement (not with the **COLUMN** command's **ALIAS** clause) and entering a **COLUMN** command for each column's alias.

ALIAS gives this column a new name, which then may be used to reference the column in **BREAK** and **COLUMN** commands.

CLEAR drops the column definition.

DEFAULT leaves the column defined and **ON**, but drops any other options.

ENTMAP allows entity mapping to be turned on or off for selected columns in HTML output.

FOLD_A[FTER] and **FOLD_B[EFORE]** instruct Oracle to fold a single row of output across multiple rows when printed. You can choose to fold the row either before or after the column.

FORMAT specifies the display format of the column. The format must be a literal like A25 or 990.99. Without **FORMAT** specified, the column width is the length as defined in the table.

A LONG column's width defaults to the value of the **SET LONG**. Both regular CHAR and LONG fields can have their width set by a format like **FORMAT A***n*, where *n* is an integer that is the column's new width.

A NUMBER column's width defaults to the value of **SET NUMWIDTH**, but is changed by the width in a **FORMAT** clause such as **FORMAT 999,999.99**. These options work with both **SET NUMFORMAT** and the **COLUMN FORMAT** commands:

Format	Result
,	Displays a comma.
.	Displays a period.

Format	Result
$99999	A dollar sign is placed in front of every number.
999990	Displays trailing zeroes, and a zero if the value is zero.
099999	Displays leading zeroes.
9999990	The count of nines and zeros determines the maximum digits that can be displayed.
999,999,999.99	Commas and decimals are placed in the pattern shown.
B99999	The display is blank if the value is zero.
C999	Displays the ISO currency symbol in this position.
99D99	Displays the decimal in the position indicated.
9.999EEEE	The display is in scientific notation (4 *E*s are required).
9G999	Displays the group separator in the position shown.
L999	Displays the local currency symbol.
99999MI	If the number is negative, a minus sign follows the number. The default is for the negative sign to be on the left.
99999PR	Negative numbers are displayed within **<** and **>**.
RN or rn	Displays uppercase or lowercase Roman numerals. Values are 1 to 3999.
S9999 or 9999S	Returns leading or trailing **+** for positive values, **–** for negative values.
TM	Displays the data in the smallest number of decimal characters possible.
U999	Displays the Euro or other dual currency symbol in the specified position.
999V99	Multiplies number by $10n$, where *n* is the number of digits to the right of V.
X	Displays the hexadecimal value for the rounded value of the specified number of digits.

HEADING relabels a column heading. The default is the column name or the expression. If text has blanks or punctuation characters, it must be in single quotes. The **HEADSEP** character (usually **|**) in text makes SQL*Plus begin a new line. The **COLUMN** command will remember the current **HEADSEP** character when the column is defined and continue to use it for this column unless the **column** is redefined, even if the **HEADSEP** character is changed.

JUSTIFY aligns the heading over the column. By default, this is **RIGHT** for number columns and **LEFT** for anything else.

LIKE replicates the column definitions of a previously defined column for the current one, where either the expression or label was used in the other column definition. Only those features of the other column that have not been explicitly defined in the current column command are copied.

NEWLINE starts a new line before printing the column value.

NEW_VALUE names a variable to hold the column's value for use in the **TTITLE** command. *See* Chapter 6 for usage information.

NOPRINT and **PRINT** turn the column's display off or on.

NULL sets text to be displayed if the column has a **NULL** value. The default for this is a string of blanks as wide as the column is defined.

OFF or **ON** turns all these options for a column off or on without affecting its contents.

OLD_VALUE names a variable to hold the column's value for use in the **BTITLE** command.

WRAPPED, **WORD_WRAPPED**, and **TRUNCATED** control how SQL*Plus displays a heading or string value too wide to fit the column. **WRAP** folds the value to the next line. **WORD_WRAP** folds similarly but breaks on words. **TRUNCATED** truncates the value to the width of the column definition.

COMMENT

SEE ALSO   Chapter 45
FORMAT

```
COMMENT ON
  { TABLE [schema.] { table | view | materialized view }
  | COLUMN [schema.] { table. | view. | materialized view. } column
  | OPERATOR [schema.] operator
  | INDEXTYPE [schema.] indextype
  }
  IS 'text';
```

DESCRIPTION   **COMMENT** inserts the comment text about an object or column into the data dictionary.

You drop a comment from the database by setting it to an empty string (set *text* to ' ').

As of Oracle Database 11*g,* **COMMENT** has a new MINING MODEL clause that lets you provide descriptive comments for a data mining model.

COMMIT

To commit means to make changes to data (INSERTs, UPDATEs, and DELETEs) permanent. Before changes are stored, both the old and new data exist so that changes can be made, or so that the data can be restored to its prior state ("rolled back"). When a user enters the Oracle SQL command **COMMIT**, all changes from that transaction are made permanent.

COMMIT

SEE ALSO   **ROLLBACK, SAVEPOINT**
FORMAT

```
COMMIT [WORK] [ COMMENT 'text' | FORCE 'text' [, integer] ];
```

DESCRIPTION   **COMMIT** commits any changes made to the database since the last **COMMIT** was executed implicitly or explicitly. **WORK** is optional and has no effect on usage.

COMMENT associates a text comment with the transaction. The comment can be viewed via the data dictionary view DBA_2PC_PENDING in the event a distributed transaction fails to complete. **FORCE** manually commits an in-doubt distributed transaction.

COMPOSE

SEE ALSO   CONVERSION FUNCTIONS, Chapter 11
FORMAT

```
COMPOSE(string)
```

DESCRIPTION   **COMPOSE** takes as its argument a string in any datatype and returns a Unicode string in its fully normalized form in the same character set as the input.

EXAMPLE   To display an *o* with an umlaut:

```
select compose ( 'o' || unistr('\0308') ) from dual;
```

```
C
-
ö
```

COMPUTE (SQL*Plus)

SEE ALSO **BREAK**, AGGREGATE FUNCTIONS
FORMAT

```
COMP[UTE] [AVG|COU[NT]|MAX[IMUM]|MIN[IMUM]|NUM[BER]|STD|SUM|VAR[IANCE]]...
    [function LABEL label_name
    OF {expression | column | alias} ...
    ON {expression | column | alias | REPORT | ROW}...]
```

DESCRIPTION *expression* is a column or expression. **COMPUTE** performs computations on columns or expressions selected from a table. It works only with the **BREAK** command.

By default, Oracle uses the function name (**SUM**, **AVG**, etc.) as the label for the result in the query output. **LABEL** allows you to specify a *label_name* that overrides the default value.

OF names the column or expression whose value is to be computed. These columns also must be in the **SELECT** clause or the **COMPUTE** will be ignored.

ON coordinates the **COMPUTE** with the **BREAK** command. **COMPUTE** prints the computed value and restarts the computation when the **ON** *expression*'s value changes, or when a specified ROW or REPORT break occurs. *See* **BREAK** for coordination details.

COMPUTE by itself displays the computes in effect.

AVG, **MAXIMUM**, **MINIMUM**, **STD**, **SUM**, and **VARIANCE** all work on expressions that are numbers. **MAXIMUM** and **MINIMUM** also work on character expressions, but not DATEs. **COUNT** and **NUMBER** work on any expression type.

All of these computes, except **NUMBER**, ignore rows with **NULL** values:

AVG	Gives average value
COUNT	Gives count of non-**NULL** values
MAXIMUM	Gives maximum value
MINIMUM	Gives minimum value
NUMBER	Gives count of all rows returned
STD	Gives standard deviation
SUM	Gives sum of non-**NULL** values
VARIANCE	Gives variance

Successive computes are simply put in order without commas, as in this case:

```
compute sum avg max of amount rate on report
```

This computes the sum, average, and maximum of both AMOUNT and RATE for the entire report.
EXAMPLE To calculate for each item classification and for the entire report, enter this:

```
break on report on industry skip 1
compute sum of volume on industry report
```

CONNECT

SEE ALSO **COMMIT**, **DISCONNECT**, Chapter 25
FORMAT

```
CON[NECT] [{user[/password] [@connect_identifier] |/} [AS SYSOPER|SYSDBA}]];
```

DESCRIPTION   You must be in SQL*Plus to use this command, although you don't need to be logged onto Oracle (*see* **DISCONNECT**). **CONNECT** commits any pending changes, logs you off of Oracle, and logs you on as the specified *user*. If the *password* is absent, you are prompted for it. It is not displayed when you type it in response to a prompt.

@connect_identifier connects to the named database. It may be on your host or on another computer connected via Oracle Net.

CONNECT BY

SEE ALSO   **SELECT**, Chapter 14
FORMAT
   hierarchical_query_clause::=

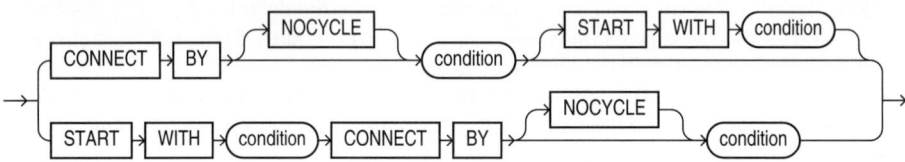

DESCRIPTION   **CONNECT BY** is an operator used in a **SELECT** statement to create reports on inheritance in tree-structured data, such as company organization, family trees, and so on. **START WITH** tells where in the tree to begin. These are the rules:

- The position of **PRIOR** with respect to the **CONNECT BY** expressions determines which expression identifies the root and which identifies the branches of the tree.

- A **WHERE** clause eliminates individuals from the tree, but not their descendants (or ancestors, depending on the location of **PRIOR**).

- A qualification in the **CONNECT BY** (particularly a not equal sign instead of the equal sign) eliminates both an individual and all of its descendants.

- **CONNECT BY** cannot be used with a table join in the **WHERE** clause.

EXAMPLE

```
select cow, bull, lpad(' ',6*(level-1))||offspring as offspring,
       sex, birth_date
from breeding
connect by offspring = prior cow
start with offspring = 'Della'
order by birth_date;
```

In this example, the clause

```
connect by offspring = prior cow
```

means the offspring is the cow **PRIOR** to this one.

CONSTRAINTS

SEE ALSO   CREATE TABLE, INTEGRITY CONSTRAINT, Chapter 17
FORMAT

constraint::=

inline_constraint::=

out_of_line_constraint::=

inline_ref_constraint::=

out_of_line_ref_constraint::=

references_clause::=

constraint_state::=

using_index_clause::=

index_properties::=

index_attributes::=

exceptions_clause::=

DESCRIPTION Constraints are defined with the **RELATIONAL_PROPERTIES** clause of the **CREATE TABLE** and **ALTER TABLE** commands. You use the constraints clauses to create a constraint or to alter an existing constraint. You can enable and disable constraints. If you disable a constraint and then try to re-enable it, Oracle will check the data. If the constraint cannot be re-enabled, Oracle can write the exceptions out to a separate table for review.

For PRIMARY KEY and UNIQUE constraints, Oracle creates indexes. As part of the constraint clause for those constraints, you can use the **USING INDEX** clause to specify the tablespace and storage for the index.

CONTAINS

CONTAINS is used to evaluate text searches that use CONTEXT indexes within Oracle Text. Supported text search operators for **CONTAINS** are shown in the following table:

Operator	Description
OR	Returns a record if either search term has a score that exceeds the threshold.
|	Same as **OR**.
AND	Returns a record if both search terms have a score that exceeds the threshold.
&	Same as **AND**.
ACCUM	Returns a record if the sum of the search terms' scores exceeds the threshold.
,	Same as **ACCUM**.
MINUS	Returns a record if the score of the first search minus the score of the second search exceeds the threshold.
-	Same as **MINUS**.
*	Assigns different weights to the score of the searches.
NEAR	Bases score on how near the search terms are to each other in the searched text.
;	Same as **NEAR**.
{}	Encloses reserved words such as **AND** if they are part of the search term.
%	Multiple-character wildcard.
_	Single-character wildcard.
$	Performs stem expansion of the search term prior to performing the search.
?	Performs a fuzzy match (allowing for misspellings) of the search term prior to performing the search.
!	Performs a **SOUNDEX** (phonetic) search.
()	Specifies the order in which search criteria are evaluated.

CONVERSION FUNCTIONS

SEE ALSO AGGREGATE FUNCTIONS, CHARACTER FUNCTIONS, NUMBER FUNCTIONS, Chapter 11
DESCRIPTION The following is an alphabetical list of all current conversion and transformation functions in Oracle version of SQL.

Function Name	Definition
ASCIISTR	Translates a string in any character set and returns an ASCII string in the database character set
BIN_TO_NUM	Converts a binary value to its numerical equivalent

Function Name	Definition
CAST	**CAST**s one built-in or collection type to another; commonly used with nested tables and varying arrays
CHARTOROWID	Changes a character string to act like an internal Oracle row identifier, or ROWID
COMPOSE	Translates a string in any datatype to a Unicode string in its fully normalized form in the same character set as the input
CONVERT	**CONVERT**s a character string from one national language character set to another
DECOMPOSE	Translates a string in any datatype to a Unicode string after canonical decomposition in the same character set as the input
HEXTORAW	Changes a character string of hex numbers into binary
NUMTODSINTERVAL	Converts a NUMBER to an INTERVAL DAY TO SECOND literal
NUMTOYMINTERVAL	Converts a NUMBER to an INTERVAL YEAR TO MONTH literal
RAWTOHEX	Changes a string of binary numbers to a character string of hex numbers
RAWTONHEX	Converts RAW to an NVARCHAR2 character value containing its hexadecimal equivalent
ROWIDTOCHAR	Changes an internal Oracle row identifier, or ROWID, to a character string
ROWIDTONCHAR	Converts a ROWID value to an NVARCHAR2 datatype
SCN_TO_TIMESTAMP	Converts a system change number to an approximate timestamp
TIMESTAMP_TO_SCN	Converts a timestamp to an approximate system change number
TO_BINARY_DOUBLE	Returns a double-precision floating-point number
TO_BINARY_FLOAT	Returns a single-precision floating-point number
TO_CHAR	Converts a NUMBER or DATE to a character string
TO_CLOB	Converts NCLOB values in a LOB column or other character strings to CLOB values
TO_DATE	Converts a NUMBER, CHAR, or VARCHAR2 to a DATE (an Oracle datatype)
TO_DSINTERVAL	Converts a character string of CHAR, VARCHAR2, NCHAR, or NVARCHAR2 datatype to an INTERVAL DAY TO SECOND type
TO_LOB	Converts a LONG to a LOB as part of an **INSERT AS SELECT**
TO_MULTI_BYTE	Converts the single-byte characters in a character string to multibyte characters
TO_NCHAR	Converts a character string, NUMBER, or DATE from the database character set to the national character set
TO_NCLOB	Converts CLOB values in a LOB column or other character strings to NCLOB values
TO_NUMBER	Converts a CHAR or VARCHAR2 to a number
TO_SINGLE_BYTE	Converts the multibyte characters in a CHAR or VARCHAR2 to single bytes
TO_TIMESTAMP	Converts a character string to a value of TIMESTAMP datatype
TO_TIMESTAMP_TZ	Converts a character string to a value of TIMESTAMP WITH TIME ZONE datatype
TO_YMINTERVAL	Converts a character string of CHAR, VARCHAR2, NCHAR, or NVARCHAR2 datatype to an INTERVAL YEAR TO MONTH type
TRANSLATE...USING	TRANSLATEs characters in a string into different characters
UNISTR	Converts a string into Unicode in the database Unicode character set

CONVERT
SEE ALSO   CONVERSION FUNCTIONS
FORMAT

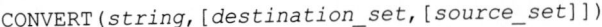

```
CONVERT(string,[destination_set,[source_set]])
```

DESCRIPTION   **CONVERT** is used to convert the characters in *string* from one standard bit representation to another, such as from US7ASCII (the default if either set isn't entered) to WE8DEC. This is typically done when data entered into a column on one computer contains characters that can't be properly displayed or printed on another computer. **CONVERT** allows a reasonable translation of one standard to the other in most cases. The most common sets include the following:

- **US7ASCII**   U.S. 7-bit ASCII character set
- **WE8ISO8859P1**   ISO 8859-1 West European 8-bit character set
- **EE8MSWIN1250**   Microsoft Windows East European Code Page 1250
- **WE8MSWIN1252**   Microsoft Windows West European Code Page 1252
- **WE8EBCDIC1047**   IBM West European EBCDIC Code Page 1047
- **JA16SJISTILDE**   Japanese Shift-JIS character set, compatible with MS Code Page 932
- **ZHT16MSWIN950**   Microsoft Windows Traditional Chinese Code Page 950
- **UTF8**   Unicode 3.0 Universal character set CESU-8 encoding form
- **AL32UTF8**   Unicode 5.0 Universal character set UTF-8 encoding form

COPY (SQL*Plus)

NOTE
*The SQL*Plus **COPY** command is not being enhanced to handle datatypes or features introduced with, or after, Oracle8i. The **COPY** command is likely to be made obsolete in a future release. Use Data Pump Export/ Import instead.*

SEE ALSO   **CREATE DATABASE LINK**, Chapter 25
FORMAT

```
COPY [FROM user/password@database]
     [TO user/password@database]
     {APPEND | CREATE | INSERT | REPLACE}
     table [ (column [,column]...) ]
     USING query
```

DESCRIPTION   **COPY** copies **FROM** a table **TO** a table in another computer using Oracle Net. **FROM** is the username, password, and database of the source table, and **TO** is the destination table. Either **FROM** or **TO** may be omitted, in which case the user's default database will be used for the missing clause. The source and destination databases must not be the same, so only one of the **FROM** and **TO** clauses may be absent.

    APPEND adds to the destination table; if the table does not exist, it is created. **CREATE** requires that the destination table be created; if it already exists, a "table already exists" error occurs. **INSERT** adds to the destination table; if the table does not exist, a "table does not exist" error occurs. **REPLACE** drops the data in the destination table and replaces it with the data from the source table; if the table does not exist, it is created.

table is the name of the destination table. *column* is the name(s) of the column(s) in the destination table. If named, the number of columns must be the same as in the query. If no columns are named, the copied columns will have the same names in the destination table as they had in the source table. *query* identifies the source table and determines which rows and columns will be copied from it.

SET LONG (*see* SET) determines the length of a long field that can be copied. LONG columns with data longer than the value of LONG are truncated. **SET COPYCOMMIT** determines how many sets of rows get copied before a commit. **SET ARRAYSIZE** determines how many rows are in a set.

EXAMPLE   This example copies BOOKSHELF_CHECKOUT from the EDMESTON database to the database that the local SQL*Plus user is connected to. The table LOCAL_CHECKOUT is created by the copy. The columns may be renamed at the destination. Note the use of the dash (-) at the end of each line. This is required. The command does not end with a semicolon (since it is a SQL*Plus command, not a SQL command). *See* the **SET** command for options related to the **COPY** command.

```
copy from practice/practice@LotsOfPractice79 -
create local_checkout (borrower, title) -
  using select name, title -
        from bookshelf_checkout
```

CORR

SEE ALSO   AGGREGATE FUNCTIONS
FORMAT

```
CORR ( expr1 , expr2 ) [OVER ( analytic_clause )]
```

DESCRIPTION   CORR returns the coefficient of correlation of a set of number pairs. Both *expr1* and *expr2* are number expressions. Oracle applies the function to the set of (*expr1*, *expr2*) after eliminating the pairs for which either *expr1* or *expr2* is **NULL**. Then Oracle makes the following computation:

```
COVAR_POP(expr1, expr2) / (STDDEV_POP(expr1) * STDDEV_POP(expr2))
```

The function returns a value of type NUMBER. If the function is applied to an empty set, it returns **NULL**.

CORR_K and CORR_S

SEE ALSO   CORR
FORMAT

```
{CORR_K | CORR_S }
  (expr1, expr2 [, { COEFFICIENT |ONE_SIDED_SIG|TWO_SIDED_SIG}])
```

DESCRIPTION   The **CORR_K** and **CORR_S** functions support nonparametric or rank correlations. Correlation coefficients take a value ranging from 1 to –1, where 1 indicates a perfect relationship and –1 a perfect inverse relationship. The arguments must be either numeric or implicitly converted to a numeric datatype. **ONE_SIDED_SIG** is for one-tailed significance of the correlation; **TWO_SIDED_SIG** is for two-tailed significance.

COS

SEE ALSO   ACOS, ASIN, ATAN, ATAN2, COSH, EXP, LN, LOG, SIN, SINH, TAN, TANH
FORMAT

```
COS(value)
```

DESCRIPTION   **COS** returns the cosine of a value, an angle expressed in radians. You can convert a degree angle into radians by multiplying it by pi/180.

COSH

SEE ALSO ACOS, ASIN, ATAN, ATAN2, COS, EXP, LN, LOG, SIN, SINH, TAN, TANH
FORMAT

```
COSH(value)
```

DESCRIPTION **COSH** returns the hyperbolic cosine of a *value*.

COUNT

SEE ALSO AGGREGATE FUNCTIONS, Chapters 9 and 12
FORMAT

```
COUNT ( { * | [ DISTINCT | ALL ] expr } ) [OVER ( analytic_clause )]
```

DESCRIPTION **COUNT** counts the number of rows in which *expression* is non-**NULL**, which is then returned by the query. With **DISTINCT**, **COUNT** counts only the distinct non-**NULL** rows. With *, **COUNT** counts all rows, whether **NULL** or not.

COVAR_POP

SEE ALSO AGGREGATE FUNCTIONS
FORMAT

```
COVAR_POP ( expr1 , expr2 ) [OVER ( analytic_clause )]
```

DESCRIPTION **COVAR_POP** returns the population covariance of a set of number pairs. You can use it as an aggregate or analytic function.

Both *expr1* and *expr2* are number expressions. Oracle applies the function to the set of (*expr1*, *expr2*) pairs after eliminating all pairs for which either *expr1* or *expr2* is **NULL**. Then Oracle makes the following computation:

```
(SUM(expr1 * expr2) - SUM(expr2) * SUM(expr1) / n) / n
```

where *n* is the number of (*expr1*, *expr2*) pairs where neither *expr1* nor *expr2* is **NULL**.

COVAR_SAMP

SEE ALSO AGGREGATE FUNCTIONS
FORMAT

```
COVAR_POP ( expr1 , expr2 ) [OVER ( analytic_clause )]
```

DESCRIPTION **COVAR_SAMP** returns the sample covariance of a set of number pairs. You can use it as an aggregate or analytic function.

Both *expr1* and *expr2* are number expressions. Oracle applies the function to the set of (*expr1*, *expr2*) pairs after eliminating all pairs for which either *expr1* or *expr2* is **NULL**. Then Oracle makes the following computation:

```
(SUM(expr1 * expr2) - SUM(expr1) * SUM(expr2) / n) / (n-1)
```

where *n* is the number of (*expr1*, *expr2*) pairs where neither *expr1* nor *expr2* is **NULL**.

CREATE CLUSTER

SEE ALSO **CREATE INDEX**, **CREATE TABLE**, Chapter 17

FORMAT
    create_cluster::=

physical_attributes_clause::=

parallel_clause::=

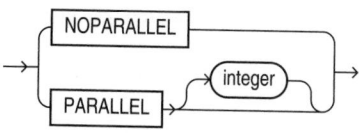

DESCRIPTION   CREATE CLUSTER creates a cluster for one or more tables. Tables are added to the cluster using **CREATE TABLE** with the **CLUSTER** clause. **CREATE CLUSTER** requires at least one cluster column from each of the tables. These columns must have the same datatype and size, but are not required to have the same name. For the tables in a cluster, rows with the same cluster column values are kept together on disk in the same area, in the same logical block(s). This can improve performance when the cluster columns are the columns by which the tables are usually joined.

Each distinct value in each cluster column is stored only once, regardless of whether it occurs once or many times in the tables and rows. This typically can reduce the amount of disk space needed to store the tables, but each table continues to appear as if it contains all of its own data. Tables with LONG columns cannot be clustered.

cluster is the name created for the cluster. *column* and *datatype* follow the method of **CREATE TABLE**, except that **NULL** and **NOT NULL** cannot be specified. However, in the actual **CREATE TABLE** statement, at least one cluster column in a cluster must be **NOT NULL**. **SIZE** sets the size in bytes for a logical block (not a physical block). **SPACE** is the cluster's initial disk allocation, as used in **CREATE TABLE**.

SIZE should be the average amount of space needed to store all the rows from all the clustered tables that are associated with a single cluster key. A small **SIZE** value may increase the time needed to access tables in the cluster, but can reduce disk space usage. **SIZE** should be a proper divisor of the physical block size. If not, Oracle will use the next larger divisor. If **SIZE** exceeds the physical block size, Oracle will use the physical block size instead.

By default, the cluster is indexed, and you must create an index on the cluster key before putting any data in the cluster. If you specify the hash cluster form, however, you don't need to (and can't) create an index on the cluster key. Instead, Oracle uses a hash function to store the rows of the table.

You can create your own hash value as a column of the table and use that for hashing with the **HASH IS** clause to tell Oracle to use that column as the hash value. Otherwise, Oracle uses an internal hash function based on the columns of the cluster key. The **HASHKEYS** clause actually creates the hash cluster and specifies the number of hash values, rounded to the nearest prime number. The minimum value is 2.

See **STORAGE** for details on the common storage clause parameters.

CREATE CONTEXT
FORMAT
    create_context::=

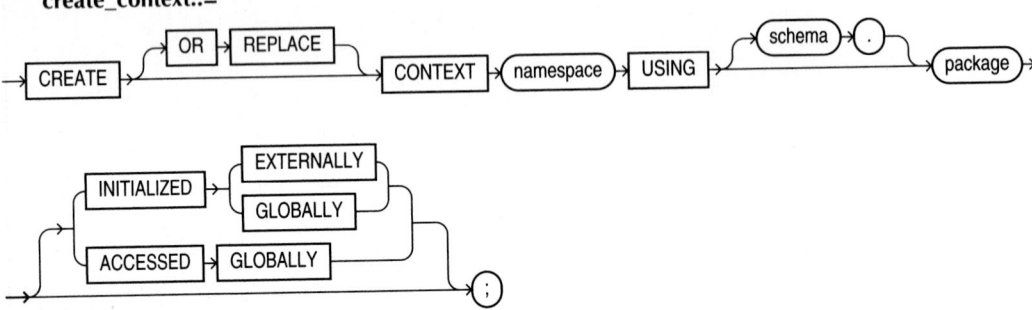

DESCRIPTION   A context is a set of attributes used to secure an application. **CREATE CONTEXT** creates a namespace for a context and associates the namespace with the externally created package that sets the context. To create a context namespace, you must have the CREATE ANY CONTEXT system privilege.

CREATE CONTROLFILE
SEE ALSO   **ALTER DATABASE, CREATE DATABASE**

FORMAT
   create_controlfile::=

   logfile_clause::=

   character_set_clause::=

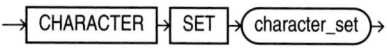

DESCRIPTION   You can use the **CREATE CONTROLFILE** command to re-create a control file if you have lost your current control file to media failure, if you want to change the name of your database, or if you want to change one of the options for the redo log file or a datafile. In general, this command should be used only by experienced database administrators.

NOTE
Perform a full offline backup of all of your database files before using this command.

   The **REUSE** option lets existing control files be reused. If you specify the name of an existing control file but do not use the **REUSE** option, the command will return an error. The **SET** option changes the name of the database, specified by the **DATABASE** clause. The **LOGFILE** clause specifies the redo log file groups, all of which must exist. The **RESETLOGS** versus **NORESETLOGS** clause tells Oracle to reset the current logs or not. The **DATAFILE** line specifies the datafiles for the database, all of which must exist.

The **MAXLOGFILES** option specifies the maximum number of redo log file groups that can be created. The **MAXLOGMEMBERS** option specifies the number of copies for a redo log group. The **MAXLOGHISTORY** option specifies the number of archived redo log file groups for Real Application Clusters. The **MAXDATAFILES** option specifies the maximum number of datafiles that can ever be created for the database. The **MAXINSTANCES** option gives the maximum number of Oracle instances that can mount and open the database. The **ARCHIVELOG** and **NOARCHIVELOG** options turn archiving of the redo log files on and off, respectively.

The **CREATE CONTROLFILE** command needed for an existing database can be generated via the **ALTER DATABASE BACKUP CONTROLFILE TO TRACE** command.

CREATE DATABASE
SEE ALSO   **ALTER DATABASE, CREATE CONTROLFILE, CREATE PLUGGABLE DATABASE, CREATE ROLLBACK SEGMENT, CREATE TABLESPACE, SHUTDOWN, STARTUP**, Chapters 2 and 51
FORMAT
create_database::=

database_logging_clauses::=

tablespace_clauses::=

default_tablespace::=

default_temp_tablespace::=

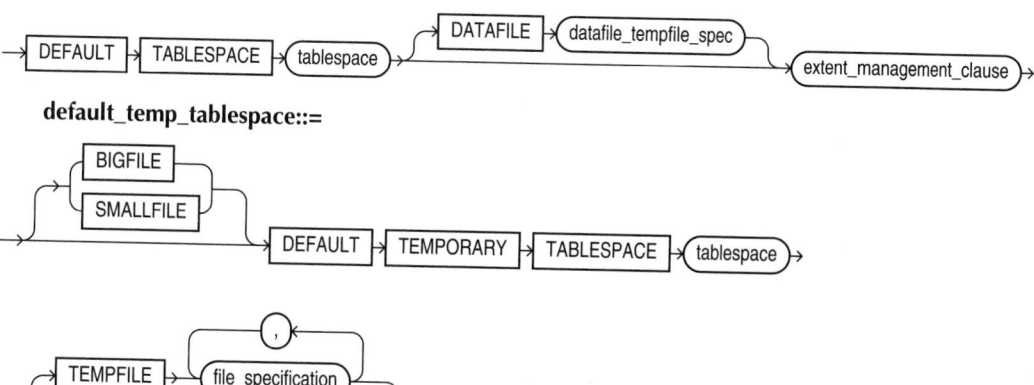

extent_management_clause::=

EXTENT → MANAGEMENT → LOCAL → AUTOALLOCATE / UNIFORM → SIZE → size_clause

undo_tablespace::=

BIGFILE / SMALLFILE → UNDO → TABLESPACE → tablespace → DATAFILE → file_specification

set_time_zone_clause::=

SET → TIME_ZONE → = → ' → (+ / −) → hh → : → mi / time_zone_region → '

enable_pluggable_database::=

ENABLE → PLUGGABLE → DATABASE →

SEED → file_name_convert → SYSTEM → tablespace_datafile_clauses → SYSAUX → tablespace_datafile_clauses

file_name_convert::=

FILE_NAME_CONVERT → = → (→ ' → filename_pattern → ' → , → ' → replacement_filename_pattern → ' →) / NONE

tablespace_datafile_clauses::=

DATAFILES → SIZE → size_clause / autoextend_clause

DESCRIPTION   *database* is the database name, which must have eight characters or fewer. DB_NAME in **init.ora** contains the default database name. In general, this command should be used only by experienced database administrators.

NOTE
Using this command in an existing database erases the specified datafiles.

file_definition defines the redo log file and datafile names and sizes.

```
'file' [SIZE integer [K | M] [REUSE]
```

SIZE is the number of bytes set aside for this file. Suffixing this with **K** multiplies the value by 1024; **M** multiplies it by 1048576 (G and T are also supported). **REUSE** (without **SIZE**) means destroy the contents of any file by this name and associate the name with this database. **REUSE** with **SIZE** creates the file if it doesn't exist, and checks its size if it does exist. **CONTROLFILE REUSE** overwrites the existing control files defined by the CONTROL_FILES parameter in the initialization parameter file.

LOGFILE names the files to be used as redo log files. If this parameter is not used, Oracle creates two by default. **MAXLOGFILES** overrides the LOG_FILES initialization parameter and defines the maximum number of redo log files that can ever be created for this database. This number cannot be increased later except by re-creating the control file. The minimum number for files is two. A high number only makes a somewhat larger control file.

DATAFILE names the files to be used for the database itself. **MAXDATAFILES** sets the absolute upper limit for files that can be created for this database and overrides the DB_FILES initialization parameter. A high number only makes a somewhat larger control file.

You can specify Automatic Storage Management files as well as file system files. When the **AUTOEXTEND** option is turned ON for a datafile, the datafile dynamically extends as needed in increments of **NEXT** size, to a maximum of **MAXSIZE** (or **UNLIMITED**).

MAXINSTANCES overrides the INSTANCES parameter in **init.ora** and sets the maximum number of simultaneous instances that can mount and open this database.

ARCHIVELOG and **NOARCHIVELOG** define the way redo log files are used when the database is first created. **NOARCHIVELOG** is the default and means that redo log files will get reused without saving their contents elsewhere. This provides instance recovery but not recovery from a media failure, such as a disk crash. **ARCHIVELOG** forces redo log files to be archived (usually to another disk or a tape), so you can recover from a media failure. This mode also supports instance recovery. This parameter can be reset by **ALTER DATABASE**.

The **MAXLOGMEMBERS** option specifies the maximum number of copies of a redo log file group. The **MAXLOGHISTORY** option specifies the maximum number of archived redo log files, useful only for the Real Application Clusters when you are archiving redo log files. The **CHARACTER SET** option specifies the character set used to store data, which depends on the operating system.

For more automated handling of undo (rollback) segments, you can specify the **UNDO TABLESPACE** clause to allocate a tablespace specifically to hold undo data. The database must be started in Automatic Undo Management (AUM) mode.

You can use the **DEFAULT TEMPORARY TABLESPACE** clause to designate a non-SYSTEM tablespace as the default temporary tablespace for all new users created in the database.

To create a container database (CDB), you specify the *enable_pluggable_database* clause. This clause initializes the seed and root container for hosting pluggable databases (PDBs).

CREATE DATABASE LINK
SEE ALSO   CREATE SYNONYM, SELECT, Chapter 25

FORMAT
create_database_link::=

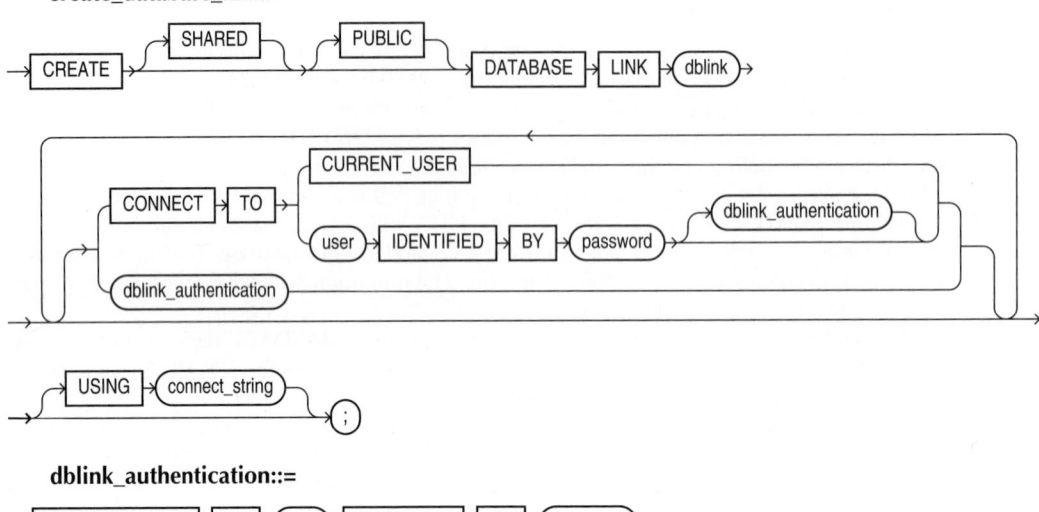

dblink_authentication::=

DESCRIPTION *dblink* is the name given to the link. *connect_string* is the definition of the remote database that can be accessed through Oracle Net and defines the link between a local database and a username on a remote database. **PUBLIC** links can be created only by a user with the CREATE PUBLIC DATABASE LINK system privilege, but are then available to all users except those who have created a private link with the same name. If **PUBLIC** isn't specified, the link is only available to the user who executed the **CREATE DATABASE LINK** statement. *connect_string* is the Oracle Net service name for the remote database.

Remote tables can be accessed just like local tables, except that the table name must be suffixed by *@link* in the **FROM** clause of the **SELECT** statement. Most systems set the maximum number of simultaneous links to four. The DBA can increase this number with the OPEN_LINKS parameter in **init.ora**.

Tree-structured queries are limited. They may not use the **PRIOR** operator except in the **CONNECT BY** clause. **START WITH** cannot contain a subquery. **CONNECT BY** and **START WITH** cannot use the function **USERENV**('ENTRYID'), or the pseudo-column ROWNUM.

To create a database link, you must have the CREATE DATABASE LINK privilege in the local database and the CREATE SESSION privilege in a remote database. To create a public database link, you must have the CREATE PUBLIC DATABASE LINK system privilege.

If you use the **CONNECT TO CURRENT_USER** clause, the link will attempt to open a connection in the remote database by using your current username and password. You therefore need to coordinate any password changes you make between the local database and the remote database, or else database links may stop working.

If you use the shared server architecture, you can create **SHARED** database links that eliminate the need for many separate dedicated connections via links. When you create a **SHARED** link, you must supply a valid username and password in the remote database to use as an authentication for the connection.

EXAMPLES The following defines a link named EDMESTON_BOOKS that connects to the PRACTICE username in the EDMESTON database:

```
create database link edmeston_books
connect to practice identified by practice
  using 'EDMESTON';
```

You now can query PRACTICE's tables like this:

```
select title, publisher
from bookshelf@edmeston_books;
```

A synonym could also be created to hide the remoteness of the tables:

```
create synonym bookshelf for bookshelf@edmeston_books;
```

CREATE DIMENSION

SEE ALSO **ALTER DIMENSION**, **DROP DIMENSION**, Chapter 26
FORMAT

create_dimension::=

level_clause::=

hierarchy_clause::=

dimension_join_clause::=

attribute_clause::=

extended_attribute_clause::=

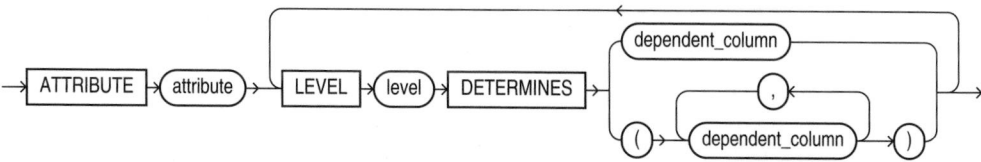

DESCRIPTION   **CREATE DIMENSION** creates hierarchies among related columns in tables for use by the optimizer. The optimizer uses dimension values when determining whether a materialized view will return the same data as its base table. To create a dimension, you must have the CREATE DIMENSION privilege; to create a dimension in another user's schema, you must have the CREATE ANY DIMENSION privilege.

LEVEL defines the level within the dimension. **HIERARCHY** defines the relationships among the levels. **ATTRIBUTE** assigns specific attributes to levels within the dimension. **JOIN_KEY** defines the join clauses between the levels.

EXAMPLES   Consider a geography dimension. Continents are divided into countries, so there is a hierarchy between country data and continent data. For a table named COUNTRY, with columns COUNTRY and CONTINENT, and a second table named CONTINENT, with a column named CONTINENT:

```
create table continent (
continent     varchar2(30));

create table country (
country       varchar2(30) not null,
continent     varchar2(30));

create dimension geography
   level country_id      is country.country
   level continent_id    is continent.continent
   hierarchy country_rollup (
      country_id            child of
      continent_id
   join key country.continent references continent_id);
```

CREATE DIRECTORY
SEE ALSO   BFILE, Chapters 28 and 40
FORMAT
   create_directory::=

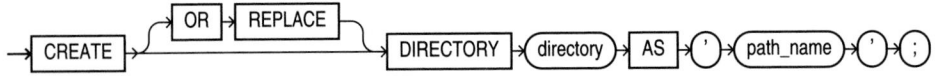

DESCRIPTION   Within Oracle, a "directory" is an alias for an operating system directory. You must create a directory prior to accessing BFILE datatype values or external tables.

CREATE DISKGROUP
SEE ALSO   **ALTER DISKGROUP**, **DROP DISKGROUP**, Chapter 51

FORMAT
    create_diskgroup::=

    qualified_disk_clause::=

NOTE
CREATE DISKGROUP *is valid only if you are using Automatic Storage
Management (ASM) and you have installed and started an ASM instance.*

DESCRIPTION   CREATE DISKGROUP creates a collection of disks. Oracle manages a diskgroup as a
logical unit and evenly spreads each file across the disks to balance I/O. Oracle automatically
distributes database files across the available disks in diskgroups and rebalances the storage when the
storage configuration changes. **CREATE DISKGROUP** creates a diskgroup, assigns disks to the
diskgroup, and mounts the diskgroup for the first time.

CREATE FLASHBACK ARCHIVE
SEE ALSO   ALTER FLASHBACK ARCHIVE, DROP FLASHBACK ARCHIVE
FORMAT
    create_flashback_archive::=

flashback_archive_quota::=

flashback_archive_retention::=

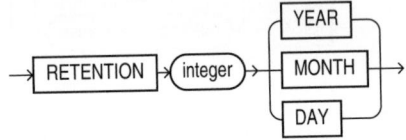

DESCRIPTION Use **CREATE FLASHBACK ARCHIVE** to create a flashback data archive, which provides the ability to automatically track and archive transactional data changes to specified database objects. A flashback data archive consists of multiple tablespaces and stores historic data from all transactions against tracked tables.

Flashback data archives retain historical data for the time duration specified using the RETENTION parameter. Historical data can be queried using the flashback query AS OF clause. Archived historic data that has aged beyond the specified retention period is automatically purged.

As of Oracle Database 12c, the **[NO] OPTIMIZE DATA** clause controls how the rows in an FDA are compressed. Oracle automatically chooses one of the following: Advanced Row Compression, Advanced LOB Compression, Advanced LOB Deduplication, segment-level compression tiering, or row-level compression tiering.

You must have the FLASHBACK ARCHIVE ADMINISTER system privilege to create a flashback data archive. In addition, you must have the CREATE TABLESPACE system privilege to create a flashback data archive, as well as a sufficient quota on the tablespace in which the historical information will reside. To designate a flashback data archive as the system default flashback data archive, you must be logged in as SYSDBA.

CREATE FUNCTION
SEE ALSO **ALTER FUNCTION**, BLOCK STRUCTURE, **CREATE LIBRARY**, **CREATE PACKAGE**, **CREATE PROCEDURE**, DATATYPES, **DROP FUNCTION**, Chapter 35
FORMAT
    create_function::=

plsql_function_source::=

invoker_rights_clause::=

accessible_by_clause::=

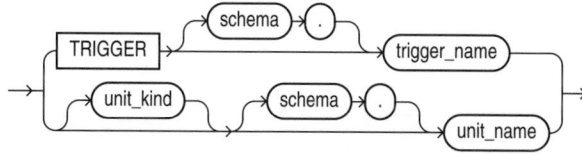

accessor_clause::=

parallel_enable_clause::=

streaming_clause::=

call_spec::=

java_declaration::=

c_declaration::=

external_parameter::=

property::=

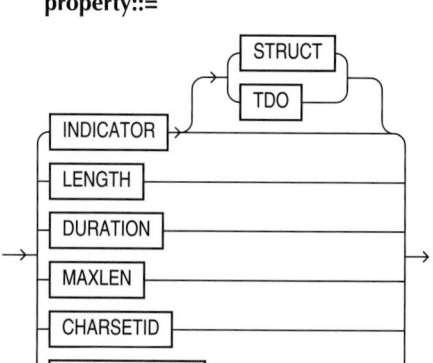

DESCRIPTION *function* is the name of the function being defined. A function may have parameters and named arguments of a certain datatype, and every function returns a value of a certain datatype as specified by the **RETURN** clause. The PL/SQL block defines the behavior of the function as a series of declarations, PL/SQL program statements, and exceptions.

The **IN** qualifier means that you have to specify a value for the parameter when you call the function, but since you always have to do this for a function, the syntax is optional. In a procedure, you can have other kinds of parameters. The difference between a function and a procedure is that a function returns a value to the calling environment.

To create a function, you must have the CREATE PROCEDURE system privilege. To create a function in another user's account, you must have the CREATE ANY PROCEDURE system privilege.

Your function can use C libraries that are stored outside of the database (see **CREATE LIBRARY**). If you use Java within your function, you can provide a Java declaration within the **LANGUAGE** clause. The **INVOKER_RIGHTS** clause lets you specify whether the function executes with the privileges of the function owner (the definer) or the current user (the invoker).

CREATE INDEX
SEE ALSO **ANALYZE**, **ALTER INDEX**, **DROP INDEX**, INTEGRITY CONSTRAINT, **STORAGE**, Chapters 17 and 46
FORMAT
  create_index::=

cluster_index_clause::=

table_index_clause::=

bitmap_join_index_clause::=

index_expr::=

index_properties::=

index_attributes::=

physical_attributes_clause::=

logging_clause::=

key_compression::=

domain_index_clause::=

local_domain_index_clause::=

XMLIndex_clause::=

local_XMLIndex_clause::=

global_partitioned_index::=

individual_hash_partitions::=

partitioning_storage_clause::=

LOB_partitioning_storage::=

hash_partitions_by_quantity::=

index_partitioning_clause::=

local_partitioned_index::=

on_range_partitioned_table::=

on_list_partitioned_table::=

segment_attributes_clause::=

on_hash_partitioned_table::=

on_comp_partitioned_table::=

index_subpartition_clause::=

parallel_clause::=

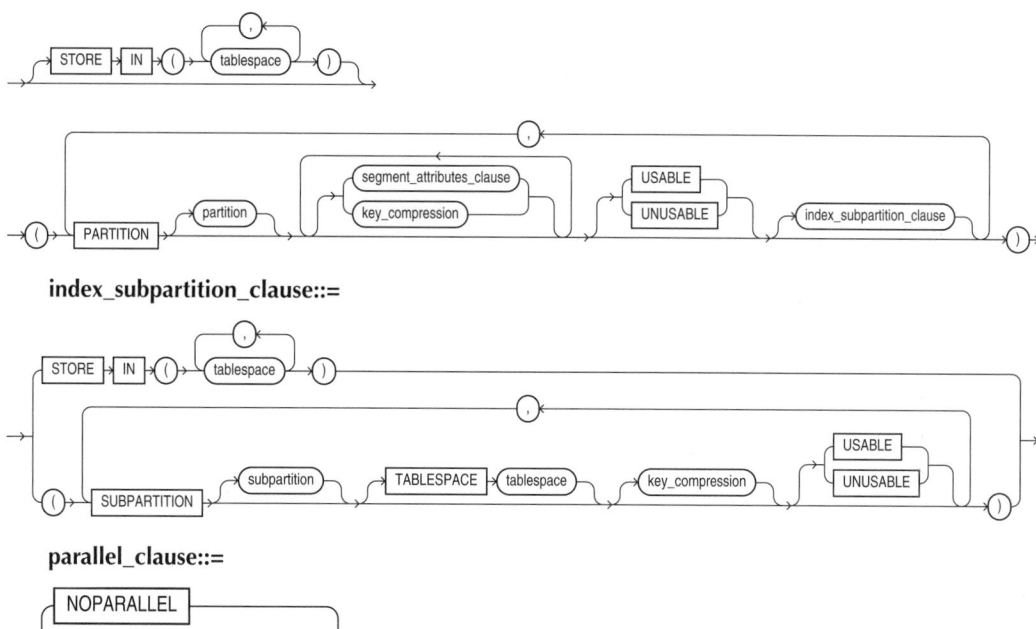

DESCRIPTION *index* is a name you assign to this index. It's usually a good idea to make it reflect the table and columns being indexed. *table* and *column(s)* are the table and column(s) for which the index is to be created. A unique index guarantees that each indexed row is unique on the values of the index columns. You can use the UNIQUE constraint on the columns to automatically create unique indexes. Specifying multiple columns creates a composite index. **ASC** and **DESC** mean ascending and descending. **CLUSTER** is the name of the cluster key that is indexed for a cluster. Clusters must have their keys indexed for their associated tables to be accessed. **PCTFREE** is the percentage of space to leave free in the index for new entries and updates. The minimum is zero.

TABLESPACE is the name of the tablespace to which this index is assigned. The physical attributes section contains subclauses that are described under **STORAGE**. **NOSORT** is an option whose primary value is in reducing the time to create an index if, and only if, the values in the column being indexed are already in ascending order. It doesn't harm anything if they later fall out of ascending order, but **NOSORT** works only if they are in order when the index is created. If the rows are not in order, **CREATE INDEX** returns an error message, does not damage anything, and allows you to rerun it without the **NOSORT** option.

PARALLEL, along with **DEGREE** and **INSTANCES**, specifies the parallel characteristics of the index. **DEGREE** specifies the number of query servers to use to create the index; **INSTANCES** specifies how the index is to be split among instances of Real Application Clusters for parallel query processing. An integer *n* specifies that the index is to be split among the specified number of available instances.

To create an index, you must own the indexed table, have INDEX privilege on the table, or have the CREATE ANY INDEX system privilege. To create a function-based index, you must have the QUERY REWRITE privilege.

BITMAP creates a bitmap index, which can be useful for columns with few distinct values. The **PARTITION** clauses create indexes on partitioned tables. Bitmap join indexes store index key values for multiple tables in a single index (usually for data warehouse applications). Bitmap join indexes use the **FROM** and **WHERE** clauses to specify the tables involved and the join conditions.

REVERSE stores the bytes of the indexed value in reverse order. You cannot reverse a bitmap index.

COMPRESS saves storage space by compressing non-unique, non-partitioned indexes. During data retrieval, the data is displayed as if it were uncompressed. You can turn off index compression; re-create the index using the **NOCOMPRESS** clause.

COMPUTE STATISTICS analyzes the index data as the index is created.

As of Oracle Database 11g, you can create a locally partitioned domain index, and you can create an XMLIndex index for XML data. You can use the *index_attributes* clause to create an index that is invisible to the optimizer.

CREATE INDEXTYPE
FORMAT
create_indextype::=

using_type_clause::=

array_DML_clause::=

storage_table_clause::=

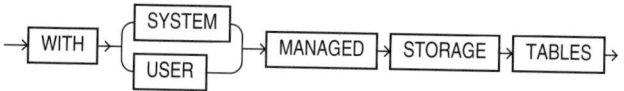

DESCRIPTION **CREATE INDEXTYPE** specifies the routines used by a domain index. To create an indextype, you must have the CREATE INDEXTYPE system privilege. To create an indextype in another user's schema, you must have the CREATE ANY INDEXTYPE system privilege.

As of Oracle Database 11g, you can specify that domain indexes be range-partitioned and that they have their storage tables and partition maintenance operations managed by the database.

CREATE JAVA

SEE ALSO   **ALTER JAVA, DROP JAVA,** Chapters 43 and 44
FORMAT
   create_java::=

invoker_rights_clause::=

DESCRIPTION **CREATE JAVA** creates a Java source, class, or resource. You must have the CREATE PROCEDURE system privilege or (to create the object in another user's schema) the CREATE ANY PROCEDURE system privilege. To replace such a schema object in another user's schema, you must have the ALTER ANY PROCEDURE system privilege.

The **JAVA SOURCE**, **JAVA CLASS**, and **JAVA RESOURCE** clauses load sources, classes, and resources, respectively.

The **AUTHID** lets you specify whether the function executes with the privileges of the function owner or the current user.

EXAMPLE The following command creates a Java source:

```
create java source named "Hello" as
   public class Hello (
     public static String hello() (
       return "Hello World";   ) );
```

CREATE LIBRARY

SEE ALSO **CREATE FUNCTION, CREATE PACKAGE BODY, CREATE PROCEDURE**, Chapter 35
FORMAT
   create_library::=

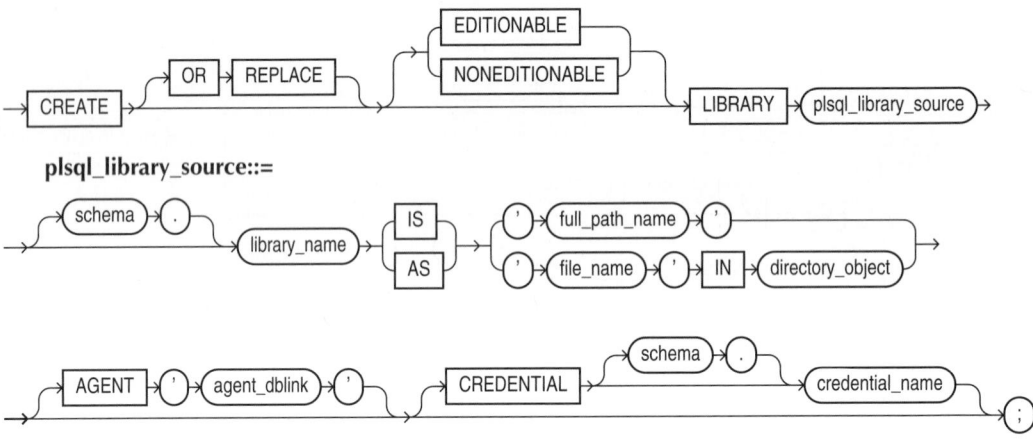

DESCRIPTION **CREATE LIBRARY** creates a library object, allowing you to reference an operating-system shared library, from which SQL and PL/SQL can call external 3GL functions and procedures. To use the procedures and functions stored in the library, you must have been granted EXECUTE privilege on the library. Specify the **AGENT** clause if you want external procedures to be run from a database link other than the server. Oracle uses the database link specified by *agent_dblink* to run external procedures. If you omit this clause, the default agent on the server (extproc) will run external procedures.

CREATE MATERIALIZED VIEW

SEE ALSO **ALTER MATERIALIZED VIEW, CREATE MATERIALIZED VIEW LOG, DROP MATERIALIZED VIEW, STORAGE**, Chapter 26

FORMAT
 create_materialized_view::=

physical_properties::=

materialized_view_props::=

scoped_table_ref_constraint::=

index_org_table_clause::=

key_compression::=

index_org_overflow_clause::=

create_mv_refresh:=

Deferred_segment_creation::=

segment_attributes_clause::=

physical_attributes_clause::=

logging_clause::=

table_compression::=

column_properties::=

object_type_col_properties::=

substitutable_column_clause::=

nested_table_col_properties::=

varray_col_properties::=

varray_storage_clause::=

LOB_storage_clause::=

LOB_storage_parameters::=

LOB_parameters::=

LOB_partition_storage::=

parallel_clause::=

build_clause::=

evaluation_edition_clause::=

query_rewrite_clause::=

unusable_editions_clause::=

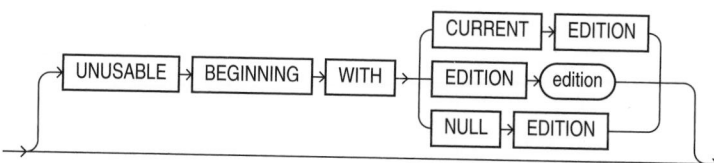

DESCRIPTION The keyword **SNAPSHOT** is supported in place of **MATERIALIZED VIEW** for backward compatibility.

CREATE MATERIALIZED VIEW creates a materialized view, a table that holds the results of a query, usually on one or more tables, called master tables. The master tables may be in a local database or in a remote database. You can have the data refreshed at intervals by using the **REFRESH** clause.

To enable a materialized view for query rewrite, you must have the QUERY REWRITE system privilege. If the materialized view is based on objects in other schemas, you must have the GLOBAL QUERY REWRITE privilege.

Materialized views cannot contain LONG columns or reference any objects owned by SYS.

A **FAST** refresh uses the materialized view log associated with the master table(s) to refresh the materialized view. A **COMPLETE** refresh re-executes the query. A **FORCE** refresh lets Oracle make the choice between a **FAST** and a **COMPLETE** refresh. Oracle first refreshes the materialized view on the **START WITH** *date*. If you give a **NEXT** *date*, Oracle refreshes the materialized view at intervals specified by the difference between the **START WITH** and **NEXT** dates.

A simple materialized view selects data from a single master table using a simple query. A complex materialized view selects data using a **GROUP BY**, **CONNECT BY**, subquery, join, or set operation in the query. Oracle can do a **FAST** refresh only on simple materialized views that have materialized view logs.

To create a materialized view in your schema, you must have the CREATE MATERIALIZED VIEW system privilege. To create a materialized view in another user's schema, you must have the CREATE ANY MATERIALIZED VIEW system privilege.

EXAMPLE

```
create materialized view local_bookshelf
storage (initial 100K next 100K pctincrease 0)
tablespace users
refresh force
start with sysdate next sysdate+7
with primary key
as
select * from bookshelf@remote_connect;
```

CREATE MATERIALIZED VIEW LOG

SEE ALSO **ALTER MATERIALIZED VIEW LOG**, **CREATE MATERIALIZED VIEW**, **DROP MATERIALIZED VIEW LOG**, **STORAGE**, Chapter 26

FORMAT

create_materialized_vw_log::=

physical_attributes_clause::=

logging_clause::=

parallel_clause::=

new_values_clause::=

mv_log_purge_clause::=

for_refresh_clause::=

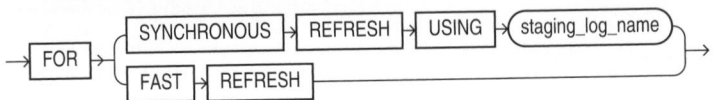

DESCRIPTION   The keyword **SNAPSHOT** is supported in place of **MATERIALIZED VIEW** for backward compatibility.

CREATE MATERIALIZED VIEW LOG creates a table associated with the master table of a materialized view that tracks changes to the master table's data. Oracle uses the materialized view log to **FAST** refresh the materialized views of a master table. The storage options specify the storage of the table. Oracle logs database changes only if there is a simple materialized view based on the master table.

You can have only one log for a given master table, and the log is stored in the same schema as the master table. To create a materialized view log on your own master table, you must have the CREATE TABLE system privilege. If the master table is in another user's schema, you must have the CREATE ANY TABLE and COMMENT ANY TABLE system privileges as well as the SELECT privilege on the master table.

CREATE OPERATOR

FORMAT

create_operator::=

binding_clause::=

implementation_clause::=

context_clause::=

using_function_clause::=

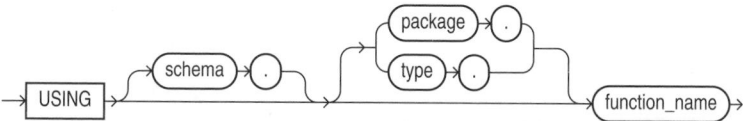

DESCRIPTION   CREATE OPERATOR creates a new operator and defines its bindings. You can reference operators in indextypes and in SQL statements. The operators, in turn, reference functions, packages, types, and other user-defined objects.

To create an operator, you must have EXECUTE privilege on the functions and operators referenced by the operator, and the CREATE OPERATOR system privilege. If the operator is created in another user's schema, you must have the CREATE ANY OPERATOR system privilege.

CREATE OUTLINE
SEE ALSO   Chapter 46

FORMAT
create_outline::=

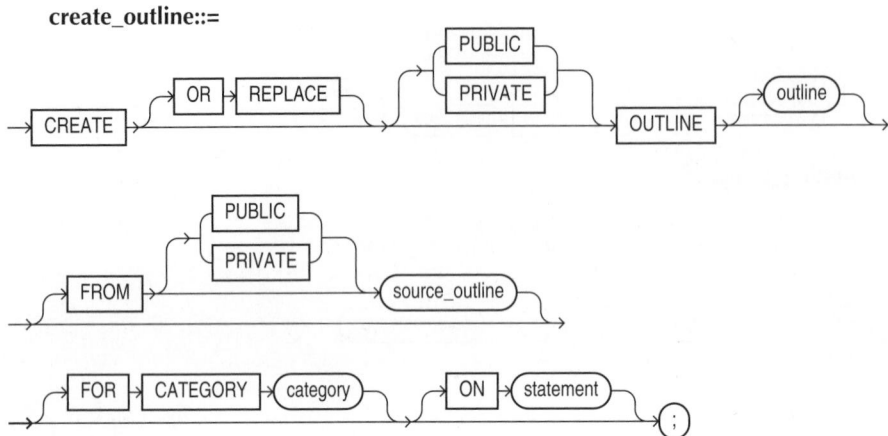

DESCRIPTION   **CREATE OUTLINE** creates a stored outline, which is a set of hints used to create the execution plan of the associated query. Later executions of the query will use the same set of hints. You can group stored outlines into categories.

To create an operator, you must have the CREATE ANY OUTLINE system privilege.

EXAMPLE

```
create outline test
   for category development
    on select author_name, count(author_name)
from bookshelf_author
group by author_name;
```

CREATE PACKAGE

SEE ALSO   **ALTER PACKAGE, CREATE FUNCTION, CREATE PACKAGE BODY, CREATE PROCEDURE,** CURSOR, **DROP PACKAGE,** EXCEPTION, RECORD, TABLE, VARIABLE DECLARATION, Chapter 35
FORMAT
create_package::=

plsql_package_source::=

invoker_rights_clause::=

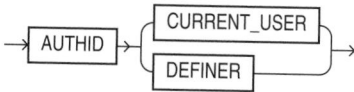

DESCRIPTION **CREATE PACKAGE** sets up the specification for a PL/SQL package, a group of public procedures, functions, exceptions, variables, constants, and cursors. Adding **OR REPLACE** replaces the package specification if it already exists, which invalidates the package and initiates a recompilation of the package body and any objects that depend on the package specification.

Packaging your procedures and functions lets them share data through variables, constants, and cursors. It enables you to grant the whole collection at once as part of a role. Oracle accesses all the elements of a package more efficiently than it would if they were separate. If you change the package body, which Oracle stores separately from the package specification, you do not have to recompile anything that uses the package.

To create a package, you must have the CREATE PROCEDURE system privilege; to create a package in another user's account, you must have the CREATE ANY PROCEDURE system privilege.

The **AUTHID** clause lets you specify whether the package code executes with the privileges of the package owner or the user who runs the package's code.

CREATE PACKAGE BODY

SEE ALSO **ALTER PACKAGE**, **CREATE FUNCTION**, **CREATE LIBRARY**, **CREATE PACKAGE**, **CREATE PROCEDURE**, CURSOR, **DROP PACKAGE**, EXCEPTION, RECORD, TABLE, VARIABLE DECLARATION, Chapter 35
FORMAT

create_package_body::=

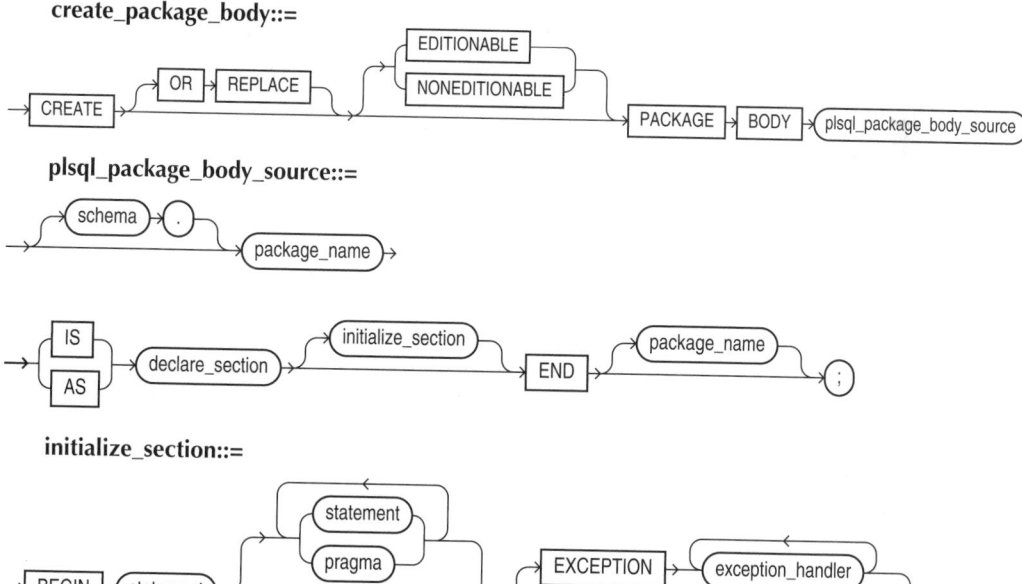

plsql_package_body_source::=

initialize_section::=

DESCRIPTION **CREATE PACKAGE BODY** builds the body of a previously specified package created with **CREATE PACKAGE**. Adding **OR REPLACE** replaces the package body if it already exists. You must have the CREATE PROCEDURE system privilege to create a package body; to create a package body in another user's account, you must have the CREATE ANY PROCEDURE system privilege.

CREATE PFILE

SEE ALSO **CREATE SPFILE**
FORMAT
    create_pfile::=

DESCRIPTION **CREATE PFILE** exports a binary server parameter file into a text-initialization parameter file (**init.ora**). Creating a text parameter file is a convenient way to get a listing of the current parameter settings being used by the database, and it lets you edit the file easily in a text editor and then convert it back into a server parameter file using the **CREATE SPFILE** statement. You can specify the name of both the source binary server parameter file and the target text parameter file.

As of Oracle Database 11g, you can create a parameter file from current system-wide parameter settings.

EXAMPLE

```
create pfile from spfile;
```

CREATE PLUGGABLE DATABASE

SEE ALSO **ALTER PLUGGABLE DATABASE**, **DROP PLUGGABLE DATABASE**, Chapter 49
FORMAT
    create_pluggable_database::=

file_name_convert::=

pdb_storage_clause::=

path_prefix_clause::=

tempfile_reuse_clause::=

create_pdb_clone::=

create_pdb_from_xml::=

source_file_name_convert::=

DESCRIPTION CREATE PLUGGABLE DATABASE creates a pluggable database (PDB) within a container database. You can create a PDB using a seed (default) database within the container database (CDB), copy an existing PDB within the CDB and plug it in, or plug in a PDB unplugged previously from this or another CDB.

CREATE PROCEDURE

SEE ALSO   ALTER PROCEDURE, BLOCK STRUCTURE, **CREATE LIBRARY**, **CREATE FUNCTION**, **CREATE PACKAGE**, DATATYPES, **DROP PROCEDURE**, Chapters 35 and 44

FORMAT

create_procedure::=

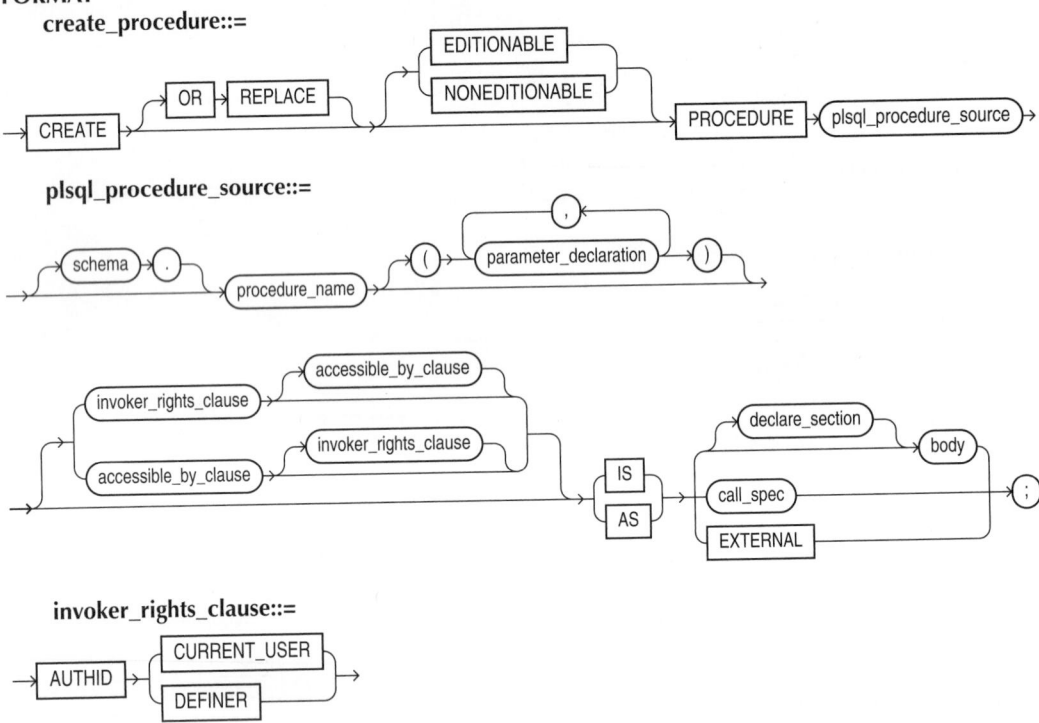

DESCRIPTION   CREATE PROCEDURE creates the specification and body of a procedure. A procedure may have parameters, which are named arguments of a certain datatype. The PL/SQL block defines the behavior of the procedure as a series of declarations, PL/SQL program statements, and exceptions.

The **IN** qualifier means that you have to specify a value for the argument when you call the procedure. The **OUT** qualifier means that the procedure passes a value back to the caller through this argument. The **IN OUT** qualifier combines the meaning of both **IN** and **OUT**—you specify a value, and the procedure replaces it with a value. If you don't have any qualifier, the argument defaults to **IN**. The difference between a function and a procedure is that a function returns a value to the calling environment in addition to any arguments that are **OUT** arguments.

The PL/SQL block can refer to programs in an external C library or to a Java call specification. The *invoker_rights* (**AUTHID**) clause lets you specify whether the procedure executes with the privileges of the function owner or the privileges of the user who is calling the function.

CREATE PROFILE

SEE ALSO **ALTER PROFILE, ALTER RESOURCE COST, ALTER SYSTEM, ALTER USER, CREATE USER, DROP PROFILE**, Chapter 19

FORMAT

create_profile::=

resource_parameters::=

password_parameters::=

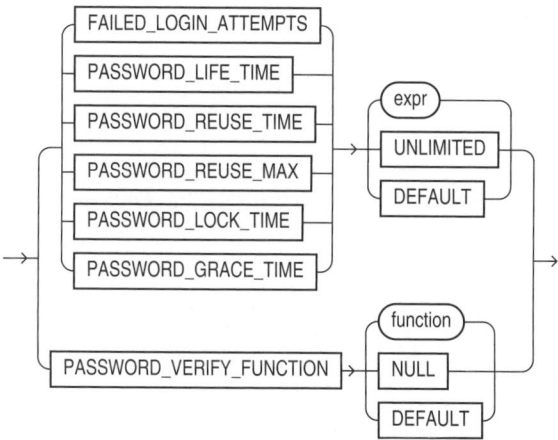

DESCRIPTION **CREATE PROFILE** creates a set of limits on the use of database resources. When you associate the profile with a user with **CREATE USER** or **ALTER USER**, you can control what the user does via those limits. To use **CREATE PROFILE**, you must enable resource limits through the initialization parameter *resource_limit* or through the **ALTER SYSTEM** command.

SESSIONS_PER_USER limits the user to *integer* concurrent SQL sessions. **CPU_PER_SESSION** limits the CPU time in hundredths of seconds. **CPU_PER_CALL** limits the CPU time for a parse, execute, or fetch call in hundredths of seconds. **CONNECT_TIME** limits elapsed time of a session in minutes. **IDLE_TIME** disconnects a user after this number of minutes; this does not apply while a query is running. **LOGICAL_READS_PER_SESSION** limits the number of blocks read per session; **LOGICAL_READS_PER_CALL** does the same thing for parse, execute, or fetch calls. **PRIVATE_SGA** limits the amount of space you can allocate in the SGA as private; the **K** and **M** options apply only to this limit. **COMPOSITE_LIMIT** limits the total resource cost for a session in service units based on a weighted sum of CPU, connect time, logical reads, and private SGA resources.

UNLIMITED means there is no limit on a particular resource. **DEFAULT** picks up the limit from the DEFAULT profile, which you can change through the **ALTER PROFILE** command.

If a user exceeds a limit, Oracle aborts and rolls back the transaction and then ends the session. You must have the CREATE PROFILE system privilege to create a profile. You associate a profile to a user with the **ALTER USER** command.

CREATE RESTORE POINT
SEE ALSO **FLASHBACK DATABASE, FLASHBACK TABLE, DROP RESTORE POINT**
FORMAT
    create_restore_point::=

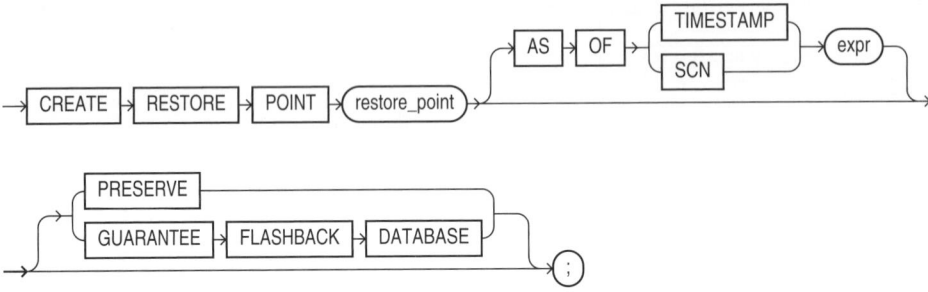

DESCRIPTION Use **CREATE RESTORE POINT** to create a restore point, which is a name associated with a timestamp or an SCN of the database. A restore point can be used to flash back a table or the database to the time specified by the restore point without needing to determine the SCN or timestamp. Restore points are also useful in various RMAN operations, including backups and database duplications. You can use RMAN to create restore points in the process of implementing an archival backup.

CREATE ROLE
SEE ALSO **ALTER ROLE, ALTER USER, CREATE USER, DROP ROLE, GRANT, REVOKE, SET ROLE,** Chapter 19

FORMAT
  create_role::=

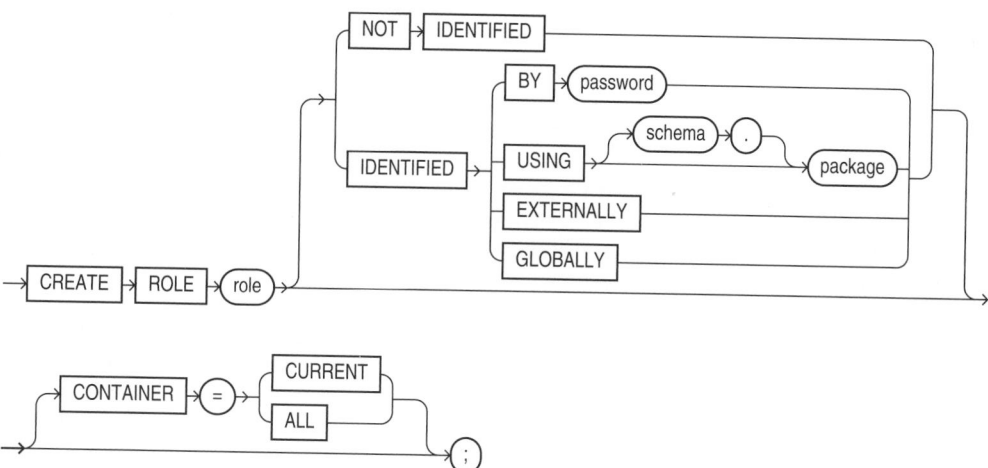

DESCRIPTION With **CREATE ROLE**, you can create a named role or set of privileges. When you grant the role to a user, you grant him or her all the privileges of that role. You first create the role with **CREATE ROLE**, and then you grant privileges to the role using the **GRANT** command. When a user wants to access something that the role allows, he or she enables the role with **SET ROLE**. Alternatively, the role can be set as the user's DEFAULT role via the **ALTER USER** or **CREATE USER** command.

If you put password protection on the role, the user who wants to use the privileges must supply the password in the **SET ROLE** command to enable the role. The **USING** *package* clause lets you create an application role, which is a role that can be enabled only by applications using an authorized package. If you do not specify *schema,* Oracle assumes the package is in your own schema.

CREATE ROLLBACK SEGMENT
SEE ALSO **ALTER ROLLBACK SEGMENT, CREATE DATABASE, CREATE TABLESPACE, DROP ROLLBACK SEGMENT, STORAGE,** Chapter 51
FORMAT
  create_rollback_segment::=

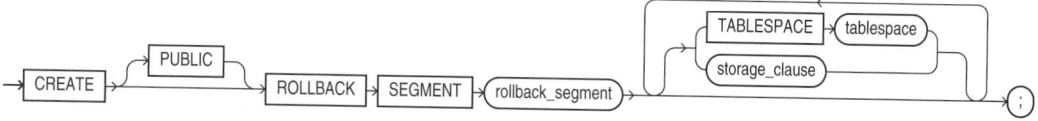

DESCRIPTION *rollback_segment* is a name assigned to this rollback segment. *tablespace* is the name of the tablespace to which this rollback segment is assigned. One tablespace may have multiple rollback segments.

storage_clause contains subclauses that are described under **STORAGE**. If **PUBLIC** is used, this rollback segment can be used by any instance that requests it; otherwise, it is available only to instances that named it in their initialization parameter files.

CREATE SCHEMA
SEE ALSO **CREATE TABLE, CREATE VIEW, GRANT**

FORMAT
    create_schema::=

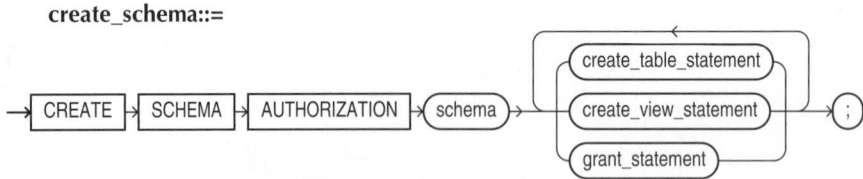

DESCRIPTION   The **CREATE SCHEMA** command creates a collection of tables, views, and privilege grants as a single transaction. The schema name is the same as your Oracle username. The **CREATE TABLE**, **CREATE VIEW**, and **GRANT** commands are the standard commands, and the order in which the commands appear is not important, even if there are internal dependencies.

CREATE SEQUENCE
SEE ALSO   ALTER SEQUENCE, AUDIT, DROP SEQUENCE, GRANT, REVOKE, NEXTVAL and **CURRVAL** under PSEUDO-COLUMNS, Chapter 17
FORMAT
    create_sequence::=

DESCRIPTION   *sequence* is the name given to the sequence. The default **INCREMENT BY** is 1. A positive number increments the sequence number in an interval equal to the integer. A negative number decrements (decrease the value of) the sequence in the same way. **START WITH** is the number with which the sequence begins. The default **START WITH** is **MAXVALUE** for descending sequences and **MINVALUE** for ascending; use **START WITH** to override this default.

MINVALUE is the lowest number the sequence will generate. The default is 1 for ascending sequences. **MAXVALUE** is the highest number the sequence will generate. For descending sequences, the default is –1. To allow sequences to progress without limitation, specify only **MINVALUE** for ascending sequences and **MAXVALUE** for descending sequences. To stop creating sequence numbers and force an error when an attempt is made to get a new one, specify a **MAXVALUE** on an ascending sequence, or a **MINVALUE** on a descending sequence, plus **NOCYCLE**. To restart either type of sequence where its **MAXVALUE** or **MINVALUE** made it begin, specify **CYCLE**.

CACHE allows a preallocated set of sequence numbers to be kept in memory. The default is 20. The value set must be less than **MAXVALUE** minus **MINVALUE**.

ORDER guarantees that sequence numbers are assigned to instances requesting them in the order the requests are received. This is required only in applications using Real Application Clusters.

To create a sequence in your own schema, you must have the CREATE SEQUENCE system privilege; to create a sequence in another user's schema, you must have the CREATE ANY SEQUENCE system privilege.

CREATE SPFILE

SEE ALSO   **CREATE PFILE**, **init.ora**
FORMAT
create_spfile::=

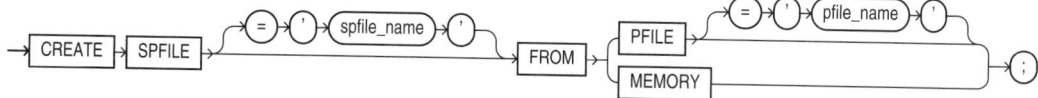

DESCRIPTION   **CREATE SPFILE** creates a server parameter file from a client-side text-based initialization parameter file. Server parameter files are binary files that exist only on the server and are called from client locations to start up the database. Server parameter files let you make persistent changes to individual parameters; parameter changes made via **ALTER SYSTEM** commands are retained across database shutdowns and startups even if no external parameter file is manually updated.

As of Oracle Database 11*g*, you can create a system parameter file from current systemwide parameter settings.

CREATE SYNONYM

SEE ALSO   **CREATE DATABASE LINK**, **CREATE TABLE**, **CREATE VIEW**, Chapters 17 and 25
FORMAT
create_synonym::=

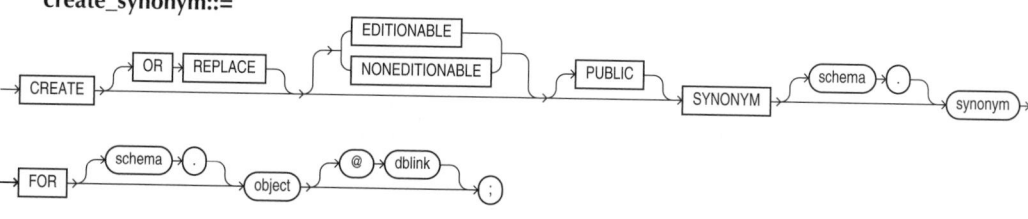

DESCRIPTION   **CREATE SYNONYM** creates a synonym for a table, view, sequence, stored procedure, function, package, materialized view, Java class object, or synonym, including those on a remote database. **PUBLIC** makes the synonym available to all users, but the synonym can be created only by a DBA or a user with the CREATE PUBLIC DATABASE LINK system privilege. Without **PUBLIC**, users must prefix the synonym with their username. *synonym* is the synonym name. *schema.object* is the name of the table, view, or synonym to which the synonym refers. You can have a synonym of synonym. @*database_link* is a database link to a remote database. The synonym refers to a table in the remote database as specified by the database link.

EXAMPLE

```
create synonym local_bookshelf for bookshelf@remote_connect;
```

CREATE TABLE

SEE ALSO   **ALTER TABLE**, **CREATE CLUSTER**, **CREATE INDEX**, **CREATE TABLESPACE**, **CREATE TYPE**, DATATYPES, **DROP TABLE**, INTEGRITY CONSTRAINT, OBJECT NAMES, **STORAGE**, Chapters 4, 17, 28, 38, 39, and 41

FORMAT

create_table::=

relational_table::=

object_table::=

XMLType_table::=

relational_properties::=

column_definition::=

identity_options::=

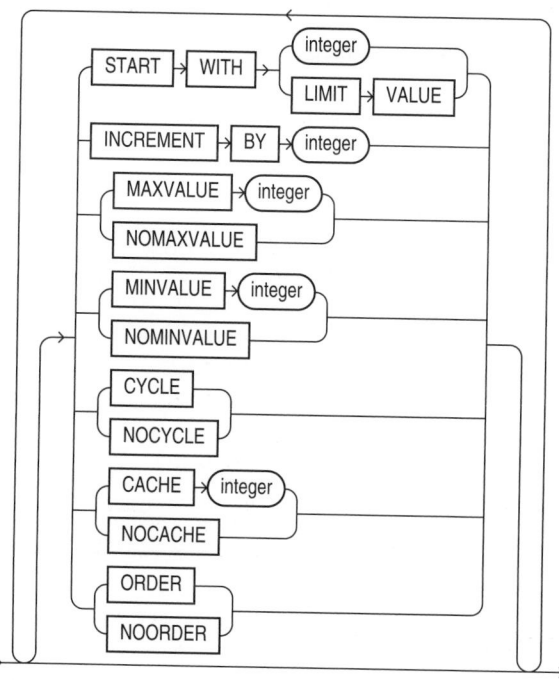

identity_clause::=

GENERATED → [ALWAYS | BY → DEFAULT → [ON → NULL]] → AS → IDENTITY → (→ identity_options →)

virtual_column_definition::=

column → datatype → [VISIBLE | INVISIBLE] → [GENERATED → ALWAYS] → AS → (→ column_expression →)

VIRTUAL → evaluation_edition_clause → unusable_editions_clause → inline_constraint

evaluation_edition _clause::=

EVALUATE → USING → [CURRENT → EDITION | EDITION → edition | NULL → EDITION]

unusable_editions_clause::=

UNUSABLE → BEFORE → [CURRENT → EDITION | EDITION → edition]

UNUSABLE → BEGINNING → WITH → [CURRENT → EDITION | EDITION → edition | NULL → EDITION]

period_definition::=

PERIOD → FOR → valid_time_column → (→ start_time_column → , → end_time_column →)

encryption_spec::=

USING → ' → encrypt_algorithm → ' → IDENTIFIED → BY → password

' → integrity_algorithm → ' → [NO] → SALT

object_table_substitution::=

object_properties::=

oid_clause::=

oid_index_clause::=

physical_properties::=

deferred_segment_creation::=

segment_attributes_clause::=

physical_attributes_clause::=

table_compression::=

ilm_clause::=

ilm_policy_clause::=

tiering_clause::=

table_properties::=

column_properties::=

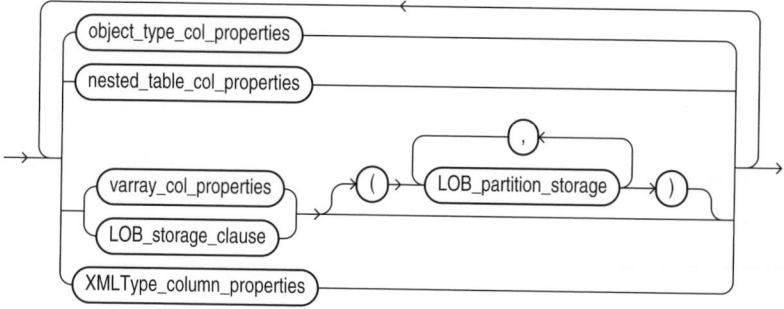

object_type_col_properties::=

substitutable_column_clause::=

nested_table_col_properties::=

varray_col_properties::=

varray_storage_clause::=

LOB_storage_clause::=

LOB_storage_parameters::=

LOB_parameters::=

LOB_retention_clause::=

LOB_deduplicate_clause::=

LOB_compression_clause::=

logging_clause::=

LOB_partition_storage::=

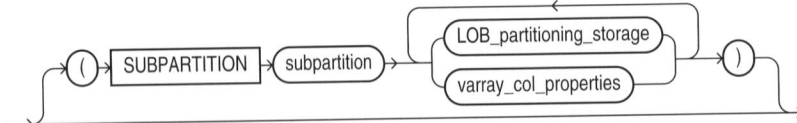

LOB_partitioning_storage::=

XMLType_column_properties::=

XMLType_storage::=

XMLType_virtual_columns::=

XMLSchema_spec::=

row_movement_clause::=

flashback_archive_clause::=

index_org_table_clause::=

mapping_table_clauses::=

key_compression::=

index_org_overflow_clause::=

supplemental_logging_props::=

supplemental_log_grp_clause::=

supplemental_id_key_clause::=

external_table_clause::=

external_data_properties::=

table_partitioning_clauses::=

range_partitions::=

hash_partitions::=

individual_hash_partitions::=

hash_partitions_by_quantity::=

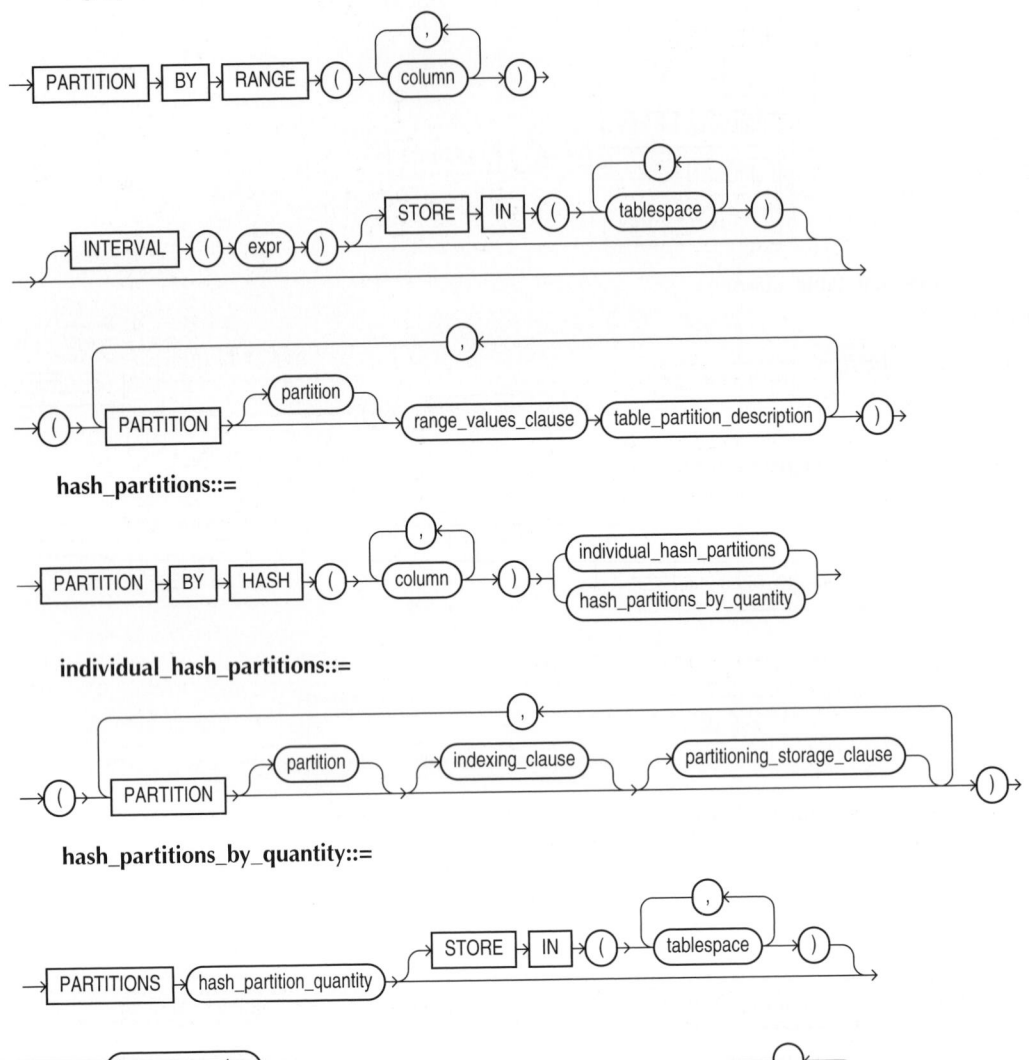

list_partitions::=

reference_partitioning::=

reference_partition_desc::=

composite_range_partitions::=

composite_hash_partitions::=

composite_list_partitions::=

system_partitioning::=

range_partition_desc::=

list_partition_desc::=

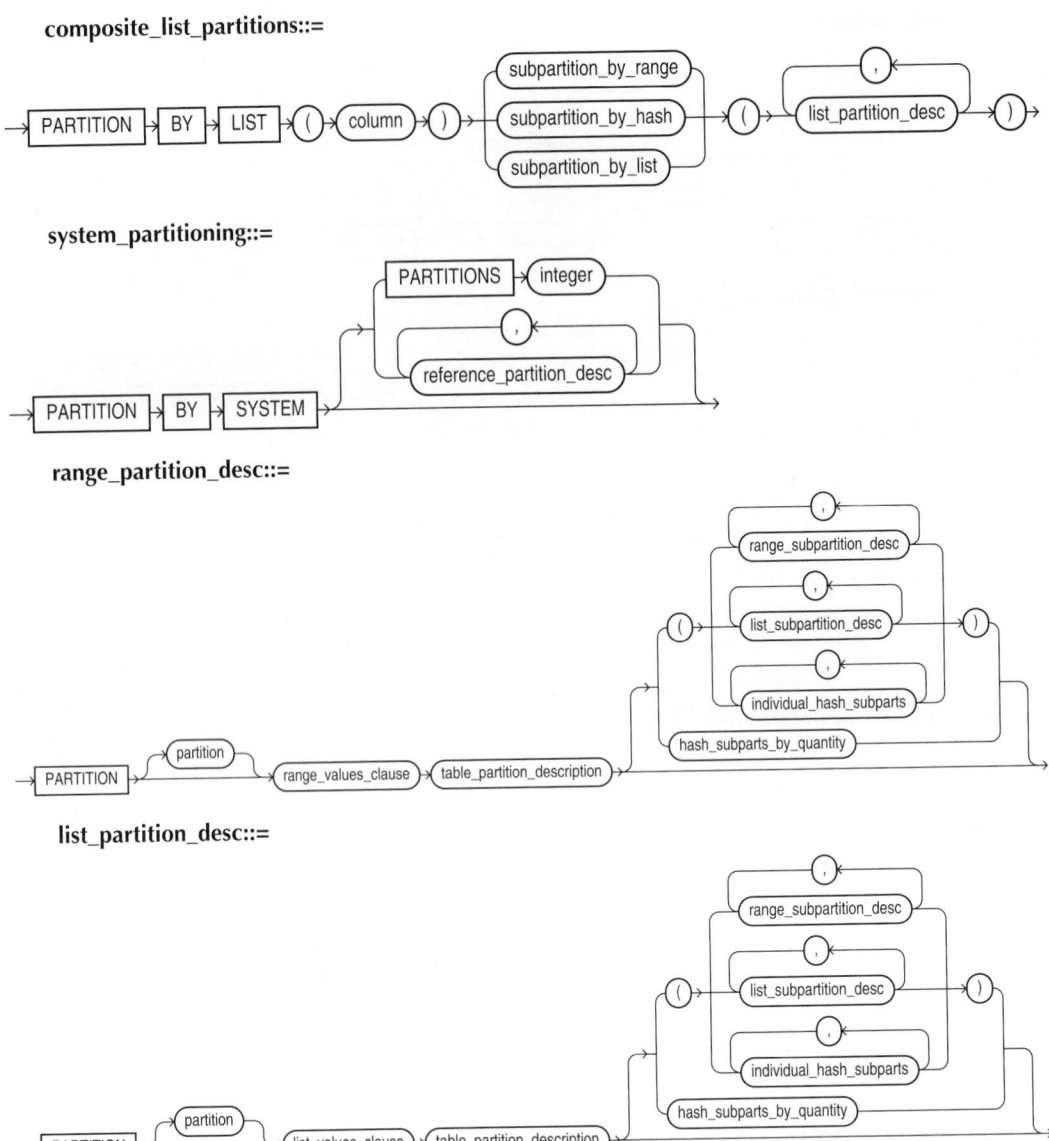

subpartition_template::=

subpartition_by_range::=

subpartition_by_list::=

subpartition_by_hash::=

range_subpartition_desc::=

list_subpartition_desc::=

individual_hash_subparts::=

hash_subparts_by_quantity::=

range_values_clause::=

list_values_clause::=

table_partition_description::=

partitioning_storage_clause::=

LOB_partitioning_storage::=

parallel_clause::=

enable_disable_clause::=

using_index_clause::=

index_properties::=

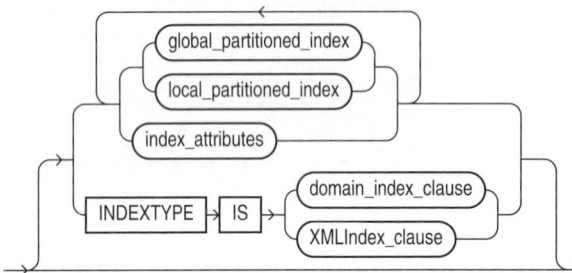

DESCRIPTION *user* is the table owner. If the table owner is absent, *user* defaults to the user issuing this command. *table* is the table name and follows Oracle naming conventions.

column is the name of a column, and *datatype* is one of the Oracle-supplied datatypes (*see* DATATYPES) or a user-defined type (*see* **CREATE TYPE**). **DEFAULT** specifies a value to be assigned to the column if a row is inserted without a value for this column. The value can be a simple literal or the result of an expression. The expression, however, cannot include a reference to a column, level, or ROWNUM.

For an existing abstract datatype, you can create an object table. The following example creates an object table called ANIMAL, based on the ANIMAL_TY datatype:

```
create table animal of animal_ty;
```

CLUSTER includes this table in the named cluster. The table columns listed must correspond in order and datatype to the cluster's cluster columns. The names need not be the same as the corresponding cluster's columns, although matching names can help the user to understand what is being done.

INITRANS specifies the initial number of transactions that can update a data block concurrently (**SELECT**s are not counted). **INITRANS** ranges from 1 to 255. 1 is the default. Every transaction takes space in the data block itself until the transaction is completed. When more than the **INITRANS** number of transactions are created for the block, space is automatically allocated for them. Transactions queuing up for execution occupy more and more free space in the block, although usually there is more free space than is needed for all concurrent transactions.

Whenever Oracle inserts a row into a table, it first looks to see how much space is available in the current block (the size of a block is operating-system dependent—see the *Oracle Installation and User's Guide* for your system). If the size of the row will leave less than **PCTFREE** percent in the block, Oracle puts the row in a newly allocated block instead. The default is 10; 0 is the minimum.

PCTUSED defaults to 40. This is the minimum percentage of available space in a block that will make it a candidate for insertion of new rows. Oracle tracks how much space in a block has been made available by deletions. If it falls below **PCTUSED**, Oracle makes the block available for insertions.

STORAGE contains subclauses that are described under **STORAGE**. **TABLESPACE** is the name of the tablespace to which this table is assigned.

The **ENABLE** and **DISABLE** clauses enable and disable constraints, respectively.

PARALLEL, along with **DEGREE** and **INSTANCES**, specifies the parallel characteristics of the table. **DEGREE** specifies the number of query servers to use; **INSTANCES** specifies how the table is to be split among instances of Real Application Clusters (RAC) for parallel query processing. An integer *n* specifies that the table is to be split among the specified number of available instances.

The **PARTITION** clauses control how the table's data is partitioned—by range, by hash, or by a composite of multiple partition methods. *See* Chapter 18 for details on partitioning. In Oracle Database 12*c*, a reference partitioned table can use an interval partitioned table as the parent (foreign key) partitioning strategy.

A temporary table contains data that is visible only to the session that creates it. If a temporary table is defined as **GLOBAL**, its definition may be seen by all users. Temporary tables may not be partitioned and cannot support many standard table features (such as varying array datatypes, LOB datatypes, and index organization). For example, the following command creates a table whose rows will be deleted at the end of the current session:

```
create global temporary table work_schedule (
   startdate date,
   enddate   date,
   payrate   number)
   on commit preserve rows;
```

The **AS** clause creates the rows of the new table through the returned query rows. The columns and types of the query must match those defined in the **CREATE TABLE** statement. The query used in the **AS** clause may not contain any LONG datatype columns. You can turn off logging during the **CREATE TABLE...AS SELECT** operation via the **NOLOGGING** keyword. This option disables the redo log entries that would normally be written during the population of the new table, thus improving performance while impacting your ability to recover that data if an instance failure occurs prior to the next backup.

The **LOB** clause specifies the out-of-line data storage used for internally stored LOB (BLOB, CLOB, and NCLOB) data. The object table definition section applies to object tables, in which each row has an object ID (OID).

As of Oracle Database 11*g*, **CREATE TABLE** has been enhanced as follows:

- The *flashback_archive_clause* lets you create the table with tracking of historical changes enabled.
- The *system_partitioning* clause lets you partition the table **BY SYSTEM**.
- You can create virtual columns.
- You can store XML data in binary XML format.
- You can partition a table by reference to another partitioned table.
- LOB storage now includes the SECUREFILE parameter, compression options, deduplication options, and encryption options.

CREATE TABLESPACE

SEE ALSO **ALTER TABLESPACE, DROP TABLESPACE**, Chapters 22 and 51
FORMAT

create_tablespace::=

permanent_tablespace_clause::=

logging_clause::=

tablespace_encryption_spec::=

extent_management_clause::=

segment_management_clause::=

flashback_mode_clause::=

temporary_tablespace_clause::=

tablespace_group_clause::=

undo_tablespace_clause::=

tablespace_retention_clause::=

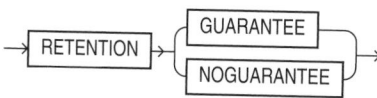

DESCRIPTION *tablespace* is the name of the tablespace and follows Oracle naming conventions. The DATAFILE is a file or series of files described according to a *file_specification*, which defines the file names and sizes:

```
'file' [SIZE integer [K | M | G | T] [REUSE]
```

The file format is operating system specific. **SIZE** is the number of bytes set aside for this file, in kilobytes (**K**), megabytes (**M**), gigabytes (**G**), or terabytes (**T**). **DEFAULT STORAGE** defines the default storage for all objects created in this tablespace, unless those defaults are overridden in the **CREATE TABLE** command itself. **ONLINE**, the default, indicates that this tablespace will become available to users as soon as it is created. **OFFLINE** prevents access to the tablespace until **ALTER TABLESPACE** changes it to **ONLINE**. DBA_TABLESPACES gives the status of all the tablespaces.

SIZE and **REUSE** together tell Oracle to reuse the file if it already exists (anything it contains will be wiped out) or create it if it doesn't already exist. **SIZE** without **REUSE** creates a file that does not exist but returns an error if it does. Without **SIZE**, the file must already exist.

The **MINIMUM EXTENT** size parameter specifies the minimum size for extents within the tablespace. The default is operating-system specific and database block–size specific.

When turned ON, the **AUTOEXTEND** option dynamically extends a datafile as needed in increments of **NEXT** size, to a maximum of **MAXSIZE** (or **UNLIMITED**). If a tablespace will be used only for temporary segments created during query processing, you can create it as a **TEMPORARY** tablespace. If the tablespace will contain permanent objects (such as tables), then you should use the default setting of **PERMANENT**.

EXTENT MANAGEMENT controls the manner in which the extent management data for a tablespace is recorded. By default, extent usage is **LOCAL**—the extent location information is stored in a bitmap within the tablespace's datafiles.

You can use the **BIGFILE** clause to create a bigfile tablespace. Also, you can assign a temporary tablespace to a temporary tablespace group (via the **TABLESPACE GROUP** clause). For undo tablespaces, you can guarantee that unexpired data will be preserved even at the expense of ongoing transactions requiring undo segment space (via **RETENTION GUARANTEE**).

As of Oracle Database 11g, you can use the **ENCRYPT** keyword to encrypt an entire tablespace. In Oracle Database 12c, entire tablespaces can be backed up from or recovered to specific PDBs.

CREATE TRIGGER

SEE ALSO **ALTER TABLE**, **ALTER TRIGGER**, BLOCK STRUCTURE, **DROP TRIGGER**, Chapters 34 and 38
FORMAT

create_trigger::=

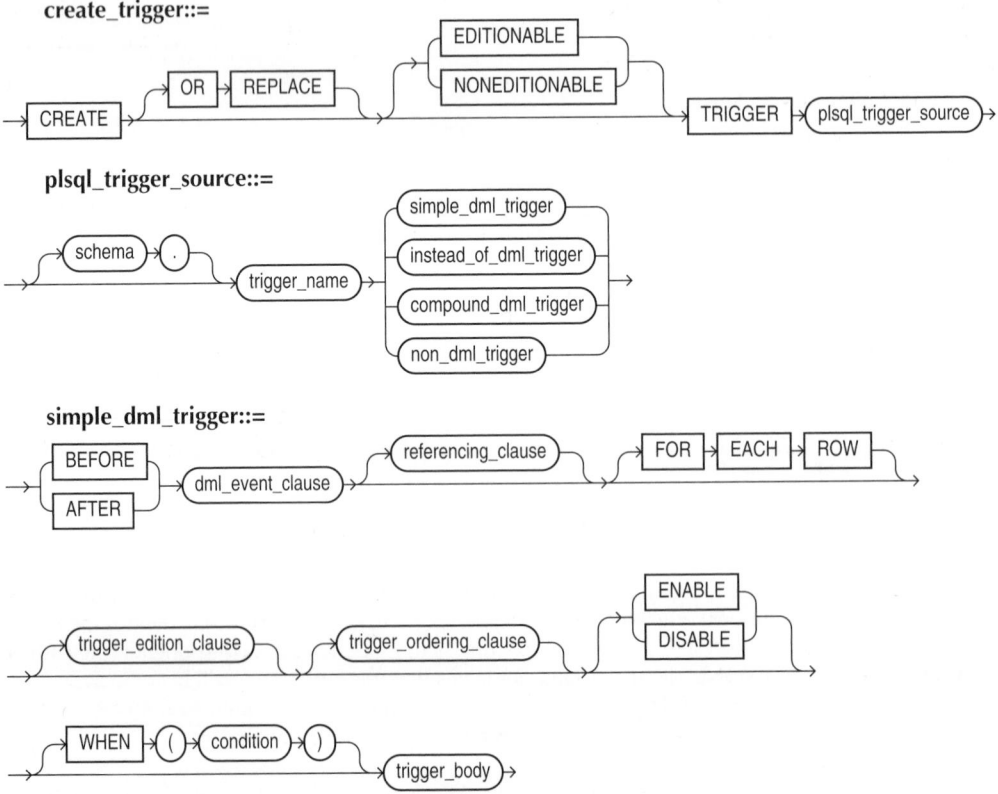

plsql_trigger_source::=

simple_dml_trigger::=

instead_of_dml_trigger::=

compound_dml_trigger::=

non_dml_trigger::=

dml_event_clause::=

referencing_clause::=

trigger_ordering_clause::=

trigger_body::=

compound_trigger_block::=

timing_point_section::=

timing_point::=

tps_body::=

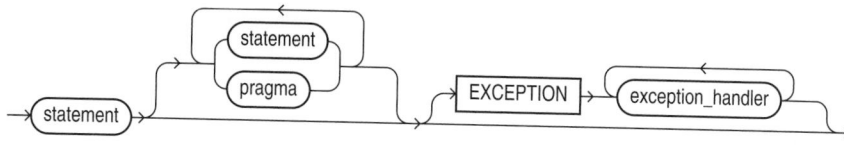

DESCRIPTION   CREATE TRIGGER creates and enables a database trigger, a stored procedure block associated with a table, specified in the **ON** clause, that Oracle automatically executes when the specified SQL statement executes against the table. You can use triggers to enforce complex constraints and to propagate changes throughout the database instead of in your applications. That way, you implement the triggered code just once, instead of having to implement it in every application.

The main clause of the **CREATE TRIGGER** command specifies the SQL operation that triggers the block (such as **DELETE**, **INSERT**, or **UPDATE**) and when the trigger fires (**BEFORE**, **AFTER**, or **INSTEAD OF** executing the triggering operation). If you specify an **OF** clause on an **UPDATE** trigger, the trigger fires only when you update one or more of the specified columns. Note that you can also create triggers that fire when DDL events occur (including **CREATE**, **ALTER**, and **DROP**) and when specific database events occur (logons, logoffs, database startups, shutdowns, and server errors).

The **REFERENCING** clause specifies a correlation name for the table for the OLD and NEW versions of the table. This lets you use the name when referring to columns, to avoid confusion, particularly when the table name is OLD or NEW. The default names are OLD and NEW.

The **FOR EACH ROW** clause specifies the trigger to be a row trigger, a trigger fired once for each row affected by the triggering operation. The **WHEN** clause restricts the execution of the trigger to happen only when the *condition* is met. This condition is a SQL condition, not a PL/SQL condition.

You can disable and enable triggers through the **ALTER TRIGGER** and **ALTER TABLE** commands. If a trigger is disabled, Oracle does not fire the trigger when a potential triggering operation occurs. The **CREATE TRIGGER** command automatically enables the trigger.

To create a trigger on a table you own, you must have the CREATE TRIGGER system privilege. To create a trigger on another user's table, you must have the CREATE ANY TRIGGER system privilege. The user must have been directly granted all privileges necessary to execute the stored procedure.

As of Oracle Database 11*g*, **CREATE TRIGGER** lets you create a compound trigger by specifying a multipart PL/SQL block. A new **FOLLOWS** clause lets you order multiple triggers. You can use the **ENABLE** and **DISABLE** clauses to create a trigger in enabled or disabled form.

CREATE TYPE

SEE ALSO **CREATE TABLE**, **CREATE TYPE BODY**, Chapters 38 and 39
FORMAT
create_type::=

plsql_type_source::=

object_type_def::=

invoker_rights_clause::=

sqlj_object_type::=

sqlj_object_type_attr::=

element_spec::=

inheritance_clauses::=

subprogram_spec::=

procedure_spec::=

function_spec::=

return_clause::=

constructor_spec::=

map_order_function_spec::=

sqlj_object_type_sig::=

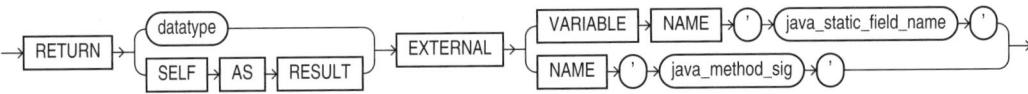

DESCRIPTION   CREATE TYPE creates an abstract datatype, named varying array (**VARRAY**), nested table type, or an incomplete object type. To create or replace a type, you must have the CREATE TYPE privilege. To create a type in another user's schema, you must have the CREATE ANY TYPE system privilege.

When creating an abstract datatype, you can base it on Oracle's provided datatypes (such as DATE and NUMBER) and on previously defined abstract datatypes.

An "incomplete" type has a name but no attributes or methods. However, it can be referenced by other object types, and so can be used to define object types that refer to each other. If you have two types that refer to each other, you must create one as an incomplete type, then create the second, and then re-create the first with its proper definition.

If you plan to create methods for the type, you need to declare the method names in the type specification.

EXAMPLES   This example creates a type that will have associated methods:

```
create or replace type animal_ty as object
(breed      varchar2(25),
```

```
name       varchar2(25),
birth_date  date,
member function age (birth_date in date) return number,
pragma restrict_references(age, wnds));
```

This example creates a varying array:

```
create or replace type tools_va as varray(5) of varchar2(25);
```

This example creates a type with no methods:

```
create type address_ty as object
(street  varchar2(50),
 city    varchar2(25),
 state   char(2),
 zip     number);
```

This example creates a type that uses another type:

```
create type person_ty as object
(name     varchar2(25),
 address  address_ty);
```

CREATE TYPE BODY

SEE ALSO **CREATE FUNCTION**, **CREATE PROCEDURE**, **CREATE TYPE**, Chapters 38, 39, and 41
FORMAT

create_type_body::=

plsql_type_body_source::=

subprog_decl_in_type::=

proc_decl_in_type::=

func_decl_in_type::=

parallel_enable_cl_In_type::=

streaming_cl_In_type::=

constructor_declaration::=

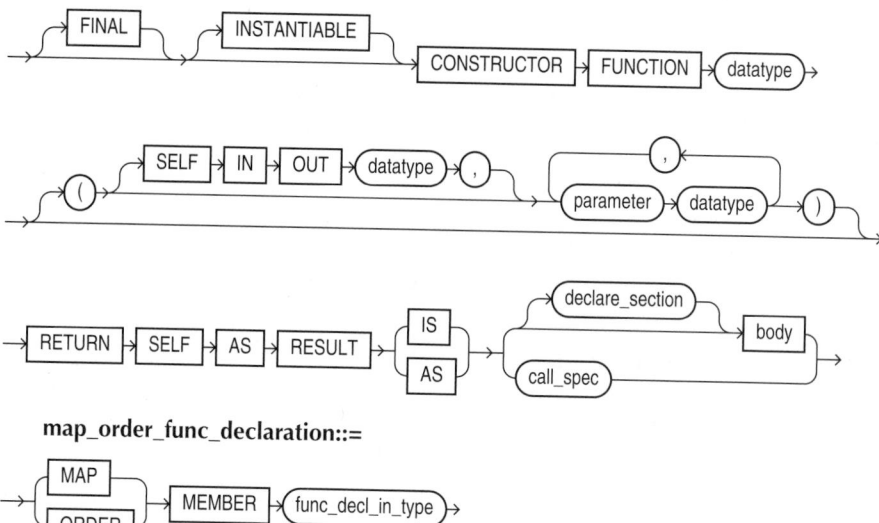

map_order_func_declaration::=

DESCRIPTION CREATE TYPE BODY specifies the methods to be applied to types created via **CREATE TYPE**. You must have the CREATE TYPE privilege to create type bodies. To create a type body in another user's schema, you must have the CREATE ANY TYPE privilege.

EXAMPLE

```
create or replace type body animal_ty as
member function age (birth_date date) return number is
  begin
     return round(sysdate - birth_date);
  end;
end;
```

CREATE USER

SEE ALSO   ALTER USER, CREATE PROFILE, CREATE ROLE, CREATE TABLESPACE, GRANT, Chapter 19

FORMAT
create_user::=

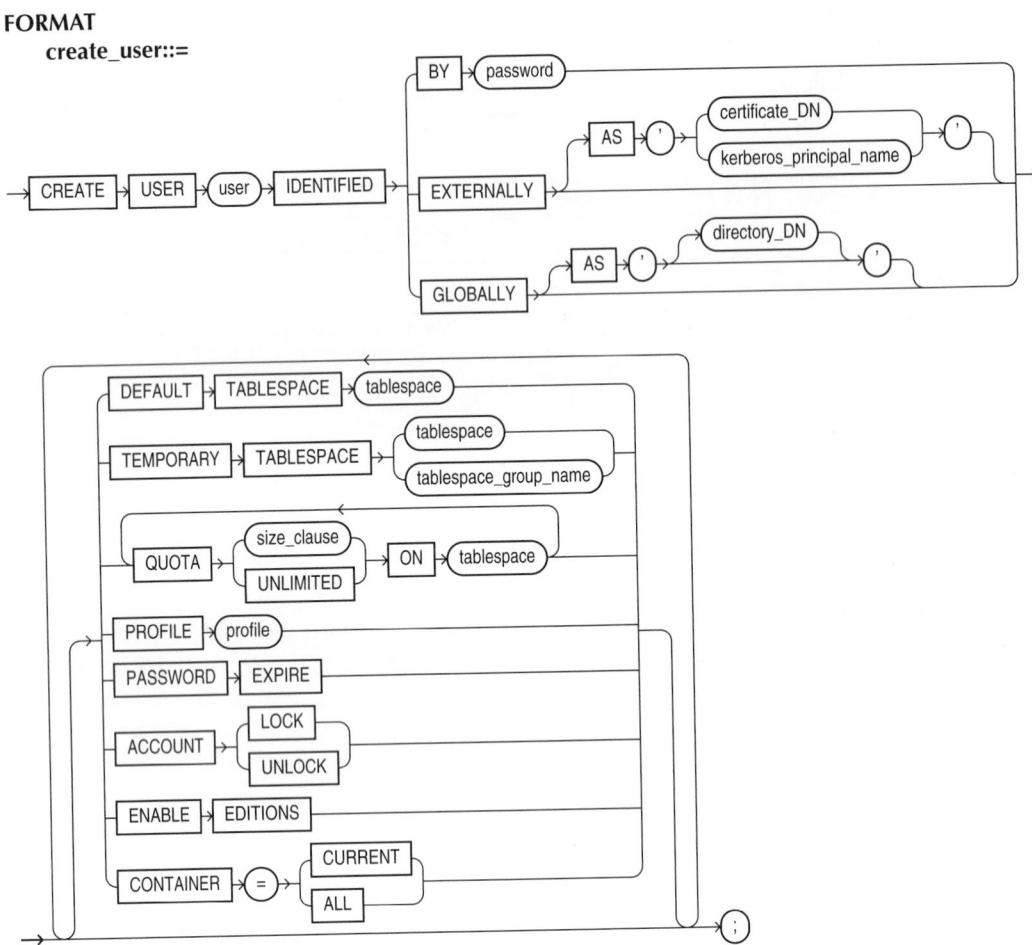

DESCRIPTION   **CREATE USER** creates a user account that lets you log into the database with a certain set of privileges and storage settings. If you specify a password, you must supply that password to log on; if you specify the **EXTERNALLY** option, access is verified through operating system security. External verification uses the OS_AUTHENT_PREFIX initialization parameter to prefix the operating system user ID, so the username you specify in **CREATE USER** should contain that prefix (usually OPS$).

The **DEFAULT TABLESPACE** is the tablespace in which the user creates objects. The **TEMPORARY TABLESPACE** is the tablespace in which temporary objects are created for the user's operations.

You can put a **QUOTA** on either of these tablespaces that limits the amount of space, in bytes (kilobytes or megabytes for **K** or **M** options, respectively), that a user can allocate. The **PROFILE** clause assigns a named profile to the user to limit usage of database resources. Oracle assigns the DEFAULT profile to the user if you don't specify a profile.

When you first create a user, the user has no privileges. You must use the **GRANT** command to grant roles and privileges to the user. You should usually grant CREATE SESSION as a minimal privilege.

For information on password expirations and account locking, see **CREATE PROFILE** and Chapter 19.

You can assign a user a temporary tablespace group as the designated temporary tablespace, thereby effectively assigning multiple temporary tablespaces to the user.

CREATE VIEW

SEE ALSO   **CREATE SYNONYM**, **CREATE TABLE**, **DROP VIEW**, **RENAME**, INTEGRITY CONSTRAINT,
Chapters 17 and 38
FORMAT

create_view::=

object_view_clause::=

XMLType_view_clause::=

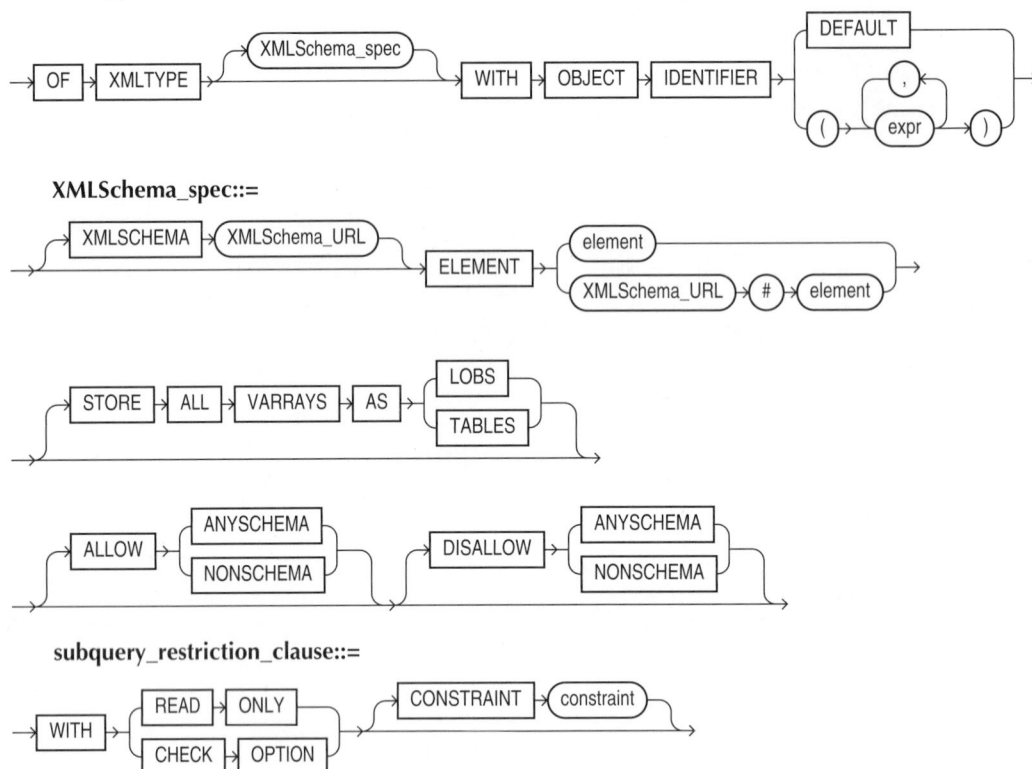

XMLSchema_spec::=

subquery_restriction_clause::=

DESCRIPTION CREATE VIEW defines a view named *view*. *user* is the name of the user for whom the view is created. The **OR REPLACE** option re-creates the view if it already exists. The **FORCE** option creates the view regardless of whether the tables to which the view refers exist or whether the user has privileges on them. The user still can't execute the view, but he or she can create it. The **NO FORCE** option creates the view only if the base tables exist and the user has privileges on them.

If an alias is specified, the view uses the alias as the name of the corresponding column in the query. If an alias is not specified, the view inherits the column name from the query; in this case each column in a query must have a unique name, one that follows normal Oracle naming conventions. It cannot be an expression. An alias in the query itself also can serve to rename the column.

AS *query* identifies the columns of tables and other views that are to appear in this view. Its **WHERE** clause determines which rows are to be retrieved.

WITH CHECK OPTION restricts **INSERT**s and **UPDATE**s performed through the view to prevent them from creating rows that the view cannot itself select, based on the **WHERE** clause of the **CREATE VIEW** statement. **WITH CHECK OPTION** may be used in a view that is based on another view; however, if the underlying view also has a **WITH CHECK OPTION**, it is ignored.

constraint is an optional name given to the **CHECK OPTION**. Without it, Oracle will assign a name in the form **SYS_C*n***, where *n* is an integer. An Oracle-assigned name will usually change during an import, whereas a user-assigned name will not change.

UPDATE and **DELETE** work on rows in a view if the view is based on a single table and its query does not contain the **GROUP BY** clause, the **DISTINCT** clause, group functions, or references to the pseudo-column ROWNUM. You may **UPDATE** views containing other pseudo-columns or expressions, as long as they are not referenced in the **UPDATE**.

You may **INSERT** rows through a view if the view is based on a single table and if its query does not contain the **GROUP BY** clause, the **DISTINCT** clause, group functions, references to any pseudo-columns, or any expressions; rows may also be inserted through a view with more than one table by using **INSTEAD OF** triggers. If the view is created **WITH READ ONLY**, then only **SELECT**s are allowed against the view; no data manipulation is allowed.

You can create object views to superimpose abstract datatypes on existing relational tables. To create a view, you must have the CREATE VIEW system privilege. To create a view in another user's schema, you must have the CREATE ANY VIEW system privilege.

CUBE

SEE ALSO **GROUPING, ROLLUP**, Chapter 12
FORMAT

```
GROUP BY CUBE (column1, column2)
```

DESCRIPTION **CUBE** groups rows based on the values of all possible combinations of expressions for each row, and returns a single row of summary information for each group. You can use the **CUBE** operation to produce crosstab reports. *See* Chapter 12.

CUBE_TABLE

SEE ALSO AGGREGATE FUNCTIONS
FORMAT

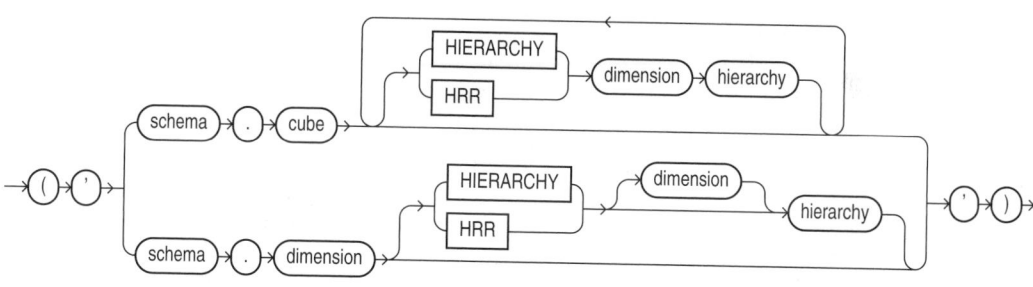

DESCRIPTION **CUBE_TABLE** extracts data from a cube or dimension and returns it in the two-dimensional format of a relational table, which can be used by SQL-based applications.

The function takes a single VARCHAR2 argument. The optional hierarchy clause enables you to specify a dimension hierarchy. A cube can have multiple hierarchy clauses, one for each dimension.

You can generate these different types of tables:

- **Cube table** Contains a key column for each dimension and a column for each measure and calculated measure in the cube. To create a cube table, you can specify the cube with or without a cube hierarchy clause. For a dimension with multiple hierarchies, this clause limits the return values to the dimension members and levels in the specified hierarchy. Without a hierarchy clause, all dimension members and all levels are included.

- **Dimension table** Contains a key column as well as a column for each level and each attribute. All dimension members and all levels are included in the table. To create a dimension table, specify the dimension *without* a dimension hierarchy clause.
- **Hierarchy table** Contains all the columns of a dimension table plus a column for the parent member and a column for each source level. Any dimension members and levels that are not part of the named hierarchy are excluded from the table. To create a hierarchy table, specify the dimension *with* a dimension hierarchy clause.

CUBE_TABLE is a table function and is always used in the context of a **SELECT** statement with this syntax:

```
select ... from table(cube_table('arg'));
```

CUME_DIST

SEE ALSO AGGREGATE FUNCTIONS
FORMAT For aggregates:
   cume_dist_aggregate::=

   cume_dist_analytic::=

DESCRIPTION **CUME_DIST** calculates the cumulative distribution of a value in a group of values. The range of values returned by **CUME_DIST** is >0 to <=1. Tie values always evaluate to the same cumulative distribution value.

CURRENT_DATE

SEE ALSO DATE FUNCTIONS
FORMAT

   → CURRENT_DATE →

DESCRIPTION **CURRENT_DATE** returns the current date in the session time zone, in a value in the Gregorian calendar of datatype DATE.
EXAMPLE

```
select current_date from dual;
```

CURRENT_TIMESTAMP

SEE ALSO DATE FUNCTIONS
FORMAT

DESCRIPTION CURRENT_TIMESTAMP returns the current date and time in the session time zone, in a value of datatype TIMESTAMP WITH TIME ZONE. The time zone displacement reflects the current local time of the SQL session. If you omit precision, the default is 6. The difference between this function and **LOCALTIMESTAMP** is that **CURRENT_TIMESTAMP** returns a TIMESTAMP WITH TIME ZONE value whereas **LOCALTIMESTAMP** returns a TIMESTAMP value. *precision* specifies the fractional second precision of the time value returned.

EXAMPLE

```
select CURRENT_TIMESTAMP from DUAL;
```

CURSOR (PL/SQL)

SEE ALSO **CREATE PACKAGE, CREATE PACKAGE BODY**, Chapter 32
FORMAT

```
CURSOR cursor [(parameter datatype[,parameter datatype]...]
   [IS query]
```

DESCRIPTION You can specify a cursor in a PL/SQL package and declare its body. The specification contains only the list of parameters with their corresponding datatypes, not the **IS** clause, while the body contains both. The parameters may appear anywhere in the query that a constant could appear. You can specify the cursor as part of the public declarations of the package specification and then the cursor body as part of the hidden package body.

CURSOR FOR LOOP

In FOR loops, the loop executes a specified number of times. In a Cursor FOR loop, the results of a query are used to determine dynamically the number of times the loop is executed. In a Cursor FOR loop, the opening, fetching, and closing of cursors is performed implicitly; you do not need to explicitly code these actions.

The following listing shows a Cursor FOR loop that queries the RADIUS_VALS table and inserts records into the AREAS table:

```
declare
   pi      constant NUMBER(9,7) := 3.1415927;
   area    NUMBER(14,2);
   cursor rad_cursor is
      select * from radius_vals;
begin
   for rad_val in rad_cursor
     loop
       area := pi*power(rad_val.radius,2);
       insert into areas values (rad_val.radius, area);
     end loop;
end;
```

In a Cursor FOR loop, there is no **OPEN** or **FETCH** command. The

```
for rad_val in rad_cursor
```

command implicitly opens the *rad_cursor* cursor and fetches a value into the *rad_val* variable. Note that the *rad_val* variable is not explicitly declared when you use a Cursor FOR loop. When there are no more records in the cursor, the loop is exited and the cursor is closed. In a Cursor FOR loop, you do not need a **CLOSE** command. *See* Chapter 32 for further information on cursor management within PL/SQL.

CV
FORMAT

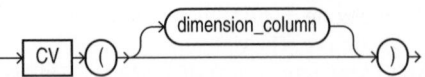

DESCRIPTION   **CV** can be used only in the **MODEL** clause of a **SELECT** statement. It returns the current value of a dimension column carried from the left side to the right side of a rule to provide relative indexing with respect to the dimension column.

DATA MINING FUNCTIONS
The data mining functions operate on models that have been built using the DBMS_DATA_MINING package or the Oracle Data Mining Java API. The SQL data mining functions are **CLUSTER_ID**, **CLUSTER_PROBABILITY**, **CLUSTER_SET**, **FEATURE_ID**, **FEATURE_SET**, **FEATURE_VALUE**, **PREDICTION**, **PREDICTION_BOUNDS**, **PREDICTION_COST**, **PREDICTION_DETAILS**, **PREDICTION_PROBABILITY**, and **PREDICTION_SET**.

DATATYPES
SEE ALSO   CHARACTER FUNCTIONS, CONVERSION FUNCTIONS, DATE FUNCTIONS, LIST FUNCTIONS, NUMBER FUNCTIONS, OTHER FUNCTIONS

DESCRIPTION   When a table is created and the columns in it are defined, they must each have a datatype specified. Oracle's primary datatypes are VARCHAR2, CHAR, DATE, LONG, LONG RAW, NUMBER, RAW, and ROWID, but for compatibility with other SQL databases, its **CREATE TABLE** statements will accept several versions of these. The following table summarizes the built-in Oracle datatypes:

Datatype	Definition
VARCHAR2(*size*)	Variable-length character string having a maximum of *size* bytes (up to 4000).
NVARCHAR2(*size*)	Variable-length character string having a maximum of *size* bytes (up to 4000) or characters, depending on the choice of national character set.
NUMBER(*precision, scale*)	For NUMBER column of specified *precision* with *scale* digits after the decimal point. *precision* can range from 1 to 38; *scale* can range from –84 to 127.
LONG	Character data of variable size up to 2GB in length.
DATE	Valid dates range from January 1, 4712 B.C., to December 31, 9999 A.D.
BINARY_FLOAT	32-bit floating-point number.
BINARY_DOUBLE	64-bit floating-point number.
TIMESTAMP (*precision*)	Date plus time, where *precision* is the number of digits in the fractional part of the SECONDS field (values range from 0 to 9, default is 6).
TIMESTAMP (*precision*) WITH TIME ZONE	TIMESTAMP plus time zone displacement value. *precision* is the number of digits in the fractional part of the SECONDS field (values range from 0 to 9, default is 6).
TIMESTAMP (*precision*) WITH LOCAL TIME ZONE	TIMESTAMP, normalized to local time zone.

Datatype	Definition
INTERVAL YEAR (*precision*) TO MONTH	Period of time in years and months, where *precision* is the number of digits in the YEAR datetime field (values range from 0 to 9, default is 2).
INTERVAL DAY (*day_ precision*) TO SECOND (*second_precision*)	Period of time in days, hours, minutes, and seconds, where *day_precision* is the number of digits in the DAY datetime field (values range from 0 to 9, default is 2) and *second_precision* is the number of digits in the fractional part of the SECONDS field (values range from 0 to 9, default is 6).
RAW(*size*)	Raw binary data, *size* bytes long. Maximum size is 2000 bytes.
LONG RAW	Raw binary data; otherwise, the same as LONG.
ROWID	Base 64 string representing the unique address of a row in its table.
UROWID (*size*)	Base 64 string for the logical address of a row in an index-organized table; maximum *size* is 4000 bytes.
CHAR(*size*)	Fixed-length character data, *size* characters long. Maximum size is 2000. Default is 1 byte. Padded on the right with blanks to full length of size.
NCHAR(*size*)	Multibyte character set version of CHAR.
CLOB	Character large object, up to 4GB in length.
NCLOB	Same as CLOB, but containing Unicode characters.
BLOB	Binary large object, up to 4GB in length.
BFILE	Pointer to a binary operating system file.

DATE

DATE is a standard Oracle datatype to store date and time data. Standard date format is 22-APR-04. A DATE column may contain a date and time between January 1, 4712 B.C., and December 31, 9999 A.D.

DATE FORMATS

SEE ALSO   DATE FUNCTIONS, Chapter 10

DESCRIPTION   Date format models are used in conversion functions. Date model components are listed here:

/,-:.;	Punctuation to be incorporated in display for **TO_CHAR** or ignored in format for **TO_DATE**.
A.D. or **AD**	AD indicator, with or without periods.
A.M. or **AM**	Displays A.M. or P.M., depending on time of day, with or without periods.
B.C. or **BC**	Same as **A.D.** or AD.
CC	Century (e.g., 21 for 2004).
SCC	Century, with BC dates prefixed with **-**.
D	Number of days in week, 1 to 7.
DAY	Day fully spelled out, padded to 9 characters.
DD	Number of days in month, 1 to 31.
DDD	Number of days in year (since January 1), 1 to 366.
DL	Date in local long format; in U.S. format, this is equivalent to fmDay, Month dd, yyyy.
DS	Date in local short format; in U.S. format, this is equivalent to MM/DD/RRRR.
DY	Three-letter abbreviation of day (FRI).

E	Abbreviated era name (Japanese Imperial, ROC Official, and Thai Buddha calendars).
EE	Full era name version of **E** format.
FF [1..9]	Fractional seconds; the number following **FF** specifies the number of digits in the fractional seconds portion displayed.
FM	Suppresses leading and trailing blanks; without **FM**, all months and days are displayed at same width.
FX	Format Exact, specifies exact format matching for the character argument and the date format model.
HH	Hour of day, always 1 to 12.
HH12	Same as **HH**.
HH24	Hour of day, 24-hour clock, 0 to 23.
I	One-digit year from ISO standard.
IW	Weeks in year from ISO standard, 1 to 53.
IY	Two-digit year from ISO standard.
IYY	Three-digit year from ISO standard.
IYYY	Four-digit year from ISO standard.
J	Julian; days since December 31, 4712 B.C.
MI	Minutes of hour, 0 to 59.
MM	Month of year, 01 to 12.
MON	Three-letter abbreviation of month (AUG).
MONTH	Month fully spelled out (AUGUST).
P.M.	Same effect as **A.M.**
Q	Quarter of year, 1 to 4.
RM	Roman numeral month.
RR	Last two digits of year relative to current date.
RRRR	Rounded year, accepting either two- or four-digit input.
SS	Seconds of minute, 1 to 60.
SSSSS	Seconds since midnight, always 0 to 86399.
TS	Short time format, for use with **DL** or **DS**.
TZD	Daylight savings time information.
TZH	Time zone hour.
TZM	Time zone minute.
TZR	Time zone region.
W	Number of weeks in month, where week 1 starts on the first day of the month.
WW	Number of weeks in year, where week 1 starts on the first day of the year.
X	Local radix character.
YEAR or SYEAR	Year spelled out; **S** marks BC dates with a leading minus sign.
YYYY or SYYYY	Full four-digit year; **S** marks BC dates with a leading minus sign.

Y,YYY	Year, with comma.
Y	Last one digit of year.
YY	Last two digits of year.
YYY	Last three digits of year.

Date formats that work only with **TO_CHAR** but not **TO_DATE** include:

"string"	*string* is incorporated in display for **TO_CHAR**.
TH	Suffix to a number: **ddTH** or **DDTH** produces 24th or 24TH. Capitalization comes from the case of the number—**dd** or **DD**—not from the case of the **TH**. Works with any number in a date: **YYYY, DD, MM, HH, MI, SS**, and so on.
SP	Suffix to a number that forces number to be spelled out: **DDSP, DdSP**, or **ddSP** produces THREE, Three, or three. Capitalization comes from case of number—**dd** or **DD**—not from the case of **SP**. Works with any number in a date: **YYYY, DD, MM, HH, MI**, SS, and so on.
SPTH	Suffix combination of **TH** and **SP** that forces number to be both spelled out and given an ordinal suffix: **Ddspth** produces Third. Capitalization comes from case of number—**dd** or **DD**—not from the case of **SP**. Works with any number in a date: **YYYY, DD, MM, HH, MI, SS**, and so on.
THSP	Same as **SPTH**.

DATE FUNCTIONS

SEE ALSO DATE FORMATS, Chapter 10

DESCRIPTION This is an alphabetical list of all current date functions in the Oracle version of SQL. Each of these is listed elsewhere in this reference under its own name, with its proper format and use.

- **ADD_MONTHS(date,***count***)** Adds *count* months to *date*.
- **CURRENT_DATE** Returns the current date in the session's time zone.
- **CURRENT_TIMESTAMP** Returns the current timestamp with the active time zone information.
- **DBTIMEZONE** Returns the current database time zone, in UTC format.
- **EXTRACT**(*datetime*) Extracts a portion of a date from a date value, such as extracting the month value from a date column's values.
- **FROM_TZ** Converts a timestamp value to a timestamp with timezone value.
- **LAST_DAY**(*date*) Gives date of last day of month that *date* is in.
- **LOCALTIMESTAMP** Returns the local timestamp in the active time zone, with no time zone information shown.
- **MONTHS_BETWEEN**(*date2,date1*) Gives *date2–date1* in months (can be fractional months).
- **NEW_TIME**(*date*, '*this*', '*other*') Gives the *date* (and time) in *this* time zone. *this* will be replaced by a three-letter abbreviation for the current time zone. *other* will be replaced by a three-letter abbreviation for the other time zone for which you'd like to know the time and date.

Time zones are as follows:

AST/ADT	Atlantic standard/daylight time
BST/BDT	Bering standard/daylight time
CST/CDT	Central standard/daylight time
EST/EDT	Eastern standard/daylight time

GMT	Greenwich mean time
HST/HDT	Alaska-Hawaii standard/daylight time
MST/MDT	Mountain standard/daylight time
NST	Newfoundland standard time
PST/PDT	Pacific standard/daylight time
YST/YDT	Yukon standard/daylight time

- **NEXT_DAY**(*date*,'*day*') Gives date of next day after *date*, where '*day*' is 'Monday', 'Tuesday', and so on.
- **NUMTODSINTERVAL**(*n*,'*value*') Converts a number or expression *n* to an INTERVAL DAY TO SECOND literal where *value* is the unit of *n*: 'DAY', 'HOUR', 'MINUTE', 'SECOND'.
- **NUMTOYMINTERVAL**(*n*,'*value*') Converts a number or expression *n* to an INTERVAL YEAR TO MONTH literal where *value* is the unit of *n*: 'YEAR', 'MONTH'.
- **ROUND**(*date*,'*format*') Without *format* specified, rounds a *date* to 12 A.M. (midnight, the beginning of that day) if time of *date* is before noon; otherwise, rounds up to next day. For use of *format* for rounding, *see* **ROUND**.
- **SESSIONTIMEZONE** Returns the value of the current session's timezone.
- **SYS_EXTRACT_UTC**(*datetime_with_timezone*) Extracts the Coordinated Universal Time (UTC) from a datetime field with time zone displacement.
- **SYSDATE** Returns the current date and time.
- **SYSTIMESTAMP** Returns the system date, including fractional seconds and time zone of the database.
- **TO_CHAR**(*date*,'*format*') Reformats *date* according to *format*.
- **TO_DATE**(*string*,'*format*') Converts a *string* in a given '*format*' into an Oracle date. Will also accept a *number* instead of a *string*, with certain limits. '*format*' is restricted.
- **TO_DSINTERVAL**('*value*') Converts *value* of CHAR, VARCHAR2, NCHAR, or NVARCHAR2 datatype to an INTERVAL DAY TO SECOND type.
- **TO_TIMESTAMP**('*value*') Converts *value* of CHAR, VARCHAR2, NCHAR, or NVARCHAR2 datatype to a value of TIMESTAMP datatype.
- **TO_TIMESTAMP_TZ**('*value*') Converts *value* of CHAR, VARCHAR2, NCHAR, or NVARCHAR2 datatype to a value of TIMESTAMP WITH TIMEZONE datatype.
- **TO_YMINTERVAL**('*value*') Converts *value* of CHAR, VARCHAR2, NCHAR, or NVARCHAR2 datatype to a value of INTERVAL YEAR TO MONTH datatype.
- **TRUNC**(*date*,'*format*') Without *format* specified, sets a *date* to 12 A.M. (midnight, the beginning of that day). For use of *format* for truncating, *see* **TRUNC**.
- **TZ_OFFSET**('*value*') Returns the time zone offset corresponding to the value entered based on the date the statement is executed.

DBTIMEZONE

SEE ALSO DATE FUNCTIONS
FORMAT

→| DBTIMEZONE |→

DESCRIPTION **DBTIMEZONE** returns the value of the database time zone.
EXAMPLE

```
select dbtimezone from dual;
```

DECLARE CURSOR (Form 1—Embedded SQL)
SEE ALSO **CLOSE, DECLARE DATABASE, DECLARE STATEMENT, FETCH, OPEN, PREPARE, SELECT, SELECT** (Embedded SQL), *Programmer's Guide to the Oracle Precompilers*
FORMAT

```
EXEC SQL [AT {database | :host_variable}]
   DECLARE cursor CURSOR
      FOR {SELECT command | statement}
```

DESCRIPTION The **DECLARE CURSOR** statement must appear before any SQL that references this cursor, and must be compiled in the same source as procedures that reference it. Its name must be unique to the source.

database is the name of a database already declared in a **DECLARE DATABASE** statement and used in a **CONNECT**; *host_variable* is a variable with such a name as its value. *cursor* is the name you assign to this cursor. The **SELECT** *command* is a query with no **INTO** clause. Alternatively, a SQL statement or a PL/SQL block already declared in a SQL **DECLARE STATEMENT** *statement* can be used.

When the **FOR UPDATE OF** clause is included in the **SELECT** statement, an **UPDATE** can reference the cursor with **WHERE CURRENT OF** *cursor*, although the cursor must still be open, and a row must be present from a **FETCH**.

DECLARE CURSOR (Form 2—PL/SQL)
SEE ALSO **CLOSE, FETCH, OPEN, SELECT...INTO**, Chapter 32
FORMAT

```
DECLARE
CURSOR cursor (parameter datatype [,parameter datatype]...)
   IS select_statement
   [FOR UPDATE OF column [,column]...];
```

DESCRIPTION A *cursor* is a work area that Oracle uses to control the row currently being processed. **DECLARE CURSOR** names a cursor and declares that it **IS** (the result of) a certain *select_statement*. The *select_statement* is required and may not contain an **INTO** clause. The cursor must be declared. It can then be **OPEN**ed and rows can then be **FETCH**ed into it. Finally, it can be **CLOSE**d.

Variables cannot be used directly in the **WHERE** clause of the *select_statement* unless they've first been identified as parameters in a list that precedes the select. Note that **DECLARE CURSOR** does not execute the **SELECT** statement, and the parameters have no values until they are assigned in an **OPEN** statement. Parameters have standard object names and datatypes, including VARCHAR2, CHAR, NUMBER, DATE, and BOOLEAN, all without size or scale, however.

FOR UPDATE OF is required if you wish to affect the current row in the cursor using either **UPDATE** or **DELETE** commands with the **CURRENT OF** clause.

DECLARE DATABASE (Embedded SQL)
SEE ALSO **CONNECT** (Embedded SQL), *Programmer's Guide to the Oracle Precompilers*
FORMAT

```
EXEC SQL DECLARE database DATABASE
```

DESCRIPTION   **DECLARE DATABASE** declares the name of a remote database for use in later **AT** clauses of SQL statements, including **COMMIT**, **DECLARE CURSOR**, **DELETE**, **INSERT**, **ROLLBACK**, **SELECT**, and **UPDATE**.

DECLARE STATEMENT (Embedded SQL)

SEE ALSO   **CLOSE, FETCH, OPEN, PREPARE,** *Programmer's Guide to the Oracle Precompilers*
FORMAT

```
EXEC SQL [AT {database | :host_variable}]
DECLARE STATEMENT {statement | block_name} STATEMENT
```

DESCRIPTION   *statement* is the name of the statement in a **DECLARE CURSOR** statement and must be identical to the statement name here. *database* is the name of a database previously declared with **DECLARE DATABASE**; *host_variable* may contain such a name as its value. This command is only needed if **DECLARE CURSOR** will come before a **PREPARE** command. When it is used, it should come prior to **DECLARE, DESCRIBE, OPEN,** or **PREPARE** and must be compiled in the same source as procedures that reference it.

DECLARE TABLE

SEE ALSO   **CREATE TABLE,** *Programmer's Guide to the Oracle Precompilers*
FORMAT

```
EXEC SQL DECLARE table TABLE
(column datatype [NULL|NOT NULL],
     ...);
```

DESCRIPTION   *table* is the name of the table being declared. *column* is a column name, and *datatype* is its datatype. This structure is nearly identical to that of **CREATE TABLE**, including the use of **NULL** and **NOT NULL**.

   You use **DECLARE TABLE** to tell precompilers to ignore actual Oracle database table definitions when running with SQLCHECK=FULL. The precompilers will regard the table description here as relevant to the program and ignore the table definitions in the database. Use this when table definitions will change or when a table has not yet been created. If SQLCHECK is not equal to FULL (which means tables and columns will not be checked against the database anyway), this command is ignored by the precompiler and becomes simply documentation.

EXAMPLE

```
EXEC SQL DECLARE COMFORT_TABLE (
            City          VARCHAR2(13) NOT NULL,
            SampleDate    DATE NOT NULL,
            Noon          NUMBER(3,1),
            Midnight      NUMBER(3,1),
            Precipitation NUMBER
            );
```

DECODE

SEE ALSO   **CASE,** OTHER FUNCTIONS, **TRANSLATE,** Chapter 16
FORMAT

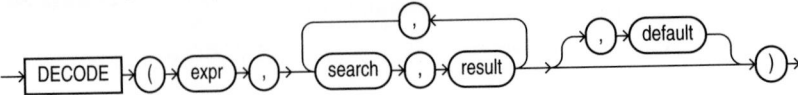

DESCRIPTION *value* represents any column in a table, regardless of datatype, or any result of a computation, such as one date minus another, a **SUBSTR** of a character column, one number times another, and so on. For each row, *value* is tested. If it equals *if1*, then the result of the **DECODE** is *then1*; if *value* equals *if2*, then the result of the **DECODE** is *then2*, and so on, for virtually as many if/then pairs as you can construct. If *value* equals none of the *if*s, then the result of the **DECODE** is *else*. Each of the *if*s, *then*s, and the *else* also can be a column or the result of a function or computation.

EXAMPLE

```
select distinct city,
    decode(city, 'San Francisco', 'City by the bay', city)
from comfort;

CITY            DECODE(CITY,'SA
-------------   ---------------
Keene           Keene
San Francisco   City by the bay
```

DECOMPOSE
SEE ALSO CONVERSION FUNCTIONS
FORMAT

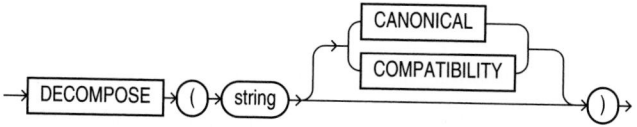

DESCRIPTION **DECOMPOSE** translates a string in any datatype to a Unicode string after canonical decomposition in the same character set as the input.

DEFINE (SQL*Plus)
SEE ALSO EDIT, SET
FORMAT

```
DEF[INE] [variable] | [variable = text]
```

DESCRIPTION *variable* is a user or predefined variable whose value you wish to assign or list. *text* is the new value for the variable; it must be a CHAR value and should be enclosed within single quotes if it contains punctuation or blanks. **DEFINE** without a variable will list all variables.

The following variables are predefined by Oracle for each session:

Variable	Description
_CONNECT_IDENTIFIER	Connection identifier used to make current connection
_DATE	Current date or a user-defined fixed string
_EDITOR	Specifies the editor to be used via the **EDIT** command
_O_RELEASE	Full release number of the database
_O_VERSION	Current version of the database
_PRIVILEGE	Privilege level of the current connection (for example, AS SYSDBA)
_SQLPLUS_RELEASE	Full release number of the SQL*Plus version in use
_USER	Username for current connection

DEL (SQL*Plus)

SEE ALSO APPEND, CHANGE, EDIT, INPUT, LIST, Chapter 6
FORMAT

```
DEL [n | n m | n* | n LAST | * | *n | * LAST | LAST]
```

DESCRIPTION **DEL** deletes the current line of the current buffer. You can delete multiple lines with a single **DEL** command. **DEL** is not available in iSQL*Plus.
EXAMPLE

```
del
```

deletes the current line in the SQL*Plus buffer.

To delete a range of lines with one command, specify the line numbers of the beginning and ending of the range in the **DEL** command. The following command would delete lines 2 through 8 in the current buffer:

```
del 2 8
```

To delete from line 4 to the end, use the * character:

```
del 4*
```

DELETE (Form 1—PL/SQL)

SEE ALSO DECLARE CURSOR, UPDATE, Chapter 32
DESCRIPTION In *PL/SQL*, **DELETE** follows the normal SQL command rules, with these added features:

- A PL/SQL function and/or variable can be used in the **WHERE** clause just as a literal could be.

- **DELETE...WHERE CURRENT OF** *cursor* can be used in conjunction with a **SELECT FOR UPDATE** to delete the last row **FETCH**ed. The **FETCH** can be either explicit or implicit from a FOR loop.

- Like **UPDATE** and **INSERT**, the **DELETE** command executes only within the SQL cursor. The SQL cursor's attributes can be checked for the success of the **DELETE**. SQL%ROWCOUNT contains the number of rows deleted. If this is 0, none were **DELETE**d. (Also, SQL%FOUND is FALSE if none were **DELETE**d.)

DELETE (Form 2—SQL Command)

SEE ALSO DROP TABLE, FROM, INSERT, SELECT, UPDATE, WHERE, Chapter 15
FORMAT
    delete::=

DML_table_expression_clause::=

partition_extension_clause::=

subquery_restriction_clause::=

table_collection_expression::=

where_clause::=

returning_clause::=

error_logging_clause::=

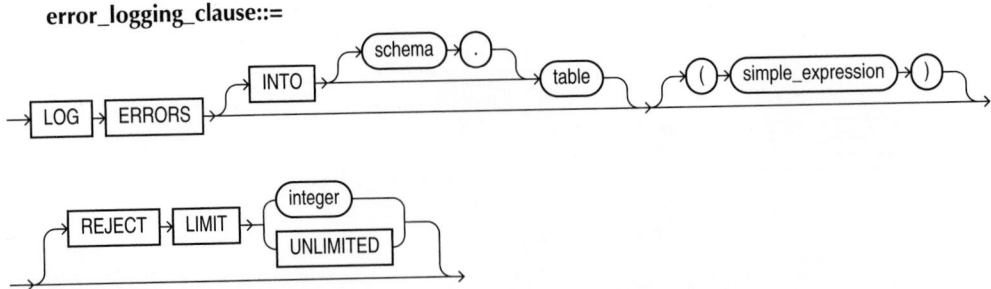

DESCRIPTION   **DELETE** deletes from *table* all rows that satisfy *condition*. The *condition* may include a correlated query and use the alias for correlation. If the table is remote, a database link has to be defined. *@link* specifies the link. If *link* is entered, but *user* is not, the query seeks a table owned by the same user on the remote database.

When using the **DELETE** command, you may specify a partition or subpartition. To delete rows from a table, you must have DELETE privileges on the table. If the SQL92_SECURITY initialization parameter is set to **TRUE**, then you must also have SELECT privileges if the **DELETE** refers to columns in the table itself.

EXAMPLE   This example deletes all rows for the city of Keene from the COMFORT table:

```
delete from comfort
where city = 'Keene';
```

DELETE (Form 3—Embedded SQL)
FORMAT

```
EXEC SQL [AT {db_name | :host_variable} ] [FOR :host_integer | integer]
  DELETE [FROM]
  [ (subquery)
  | [user.] {table | view } [@dblink |PARTITION (partition_name)] ]
[alias] [WHERE {condition | CURRENT OF cursor} ]
[{ RETURN | RETURNING } expr [, expr]... INTO
  :host_variable [[INDICATOR] :ind_variable]
  [, :host_variable [[INDICATOR] :ind_variable]]...]
```

DESCRIPTION   This form of the **DELETE** command allows you to delete rows (from a table, view, or index-only table) from within a precompiler program.

DELETEXML
FORMAT

→ DELETEXML → (→ XMLType_instance → , → XPath_string → , → namespace_string →) →

DESCRIPTION   **DELETEXML** deletes the node or nodes matched by the XPath expression in the target XML. The input variables are

- *XMLType_instance,* which is an instance of XMLType.
- The *XPath_string,* which is an XPath expression indicating one or more nodes that are to be deleted. You can specify an absolute *XPath_string* with an initial slash or a relative

XPath_string by omitting the initial slash. If you omit the initial slash, the context of the relative path defaults to the root node. Any child nodes of the nodes specified by *XPath_string* are also deleted.

■ The optional *namespace_string,* which provides namespace information for the *XPath_string*. This parameter must be of type VARCHAR2.

DENSE_RANK

SEE ALSO AGGREGATE FUNCTIONS, Chapter 12
FORMAT

dense_rank_aggregate::=

dense_rank_analytic::=

DESCRIPTION **DENSE_RANK** computes the rank of a row in an ordered group of rows. *See* Chapter 12 for related examples.

DEPTH

FORMAT

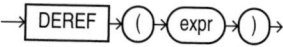

DESCRIPTION **DEPTH** is an ancillary function used only with the **UNDER_PATH** and **EQUALS_PATH** conditions. It returns the number of levels in the path specified by the **UNDER_PATH** condition with the same correlation variable. The *integer* value can be any NUMBER integer.

DEREF

FORMAT

→| DEREF |→(→(expr)→)→

DESCRIPTION The **DEREF** operator returns the value of a referenced object. *See* Chapter 41.

DESCRIBE (Form 1—SQL*Plus)

SEE ALSO CREATE TABLE

FORMAT

```
DESC[RIBE] {[user.]object[@connect_identifier]}
```

DESCRIPTION **DESCRIBE** displays a specified object's definition. If *user* is omitted, SQL*Plus displays the table owned by you. The definition includes the table and its columns, with each column's name, **NULL** or **NOT NULL** status, datatype, and width or precision. **DESCRIBE** can also be used on views, synonyms, and function and procedure specifications.

EXAMPLE

```
describe comfort
```

Name	Null?	Type
CITY	NOT NULL	VARCHAR2(13)
SAMPLEDATE	NOT NULL	DATE
NOON		NUMBER(3,1)
MIDNIGHT		NUMBER(3,1)
PRECIPITATION		NUMBER

DESCRIBE (Form 2—Embedded SQL)

SEE ALSO **PREPARE**

FORMAT

```
EXEC SQL DESCRIBE [ BIND VARIABLES FOR
                  | SELECT LIST FOR]
        statement_name INTO descriptor
```

DESCRIPTION The **DESCRIBE** command initializes a descriptor to hold descriptions of host variables for a dynamic SQL statement or PL/SQL block. The **DESCRIBE** command follows the **PREPARE** command.

DISASSOCIATE STATISTICS

SEE ALSO **ASSOCIATE STATISTICS**

FORMAT
  disassociate_statistics::=

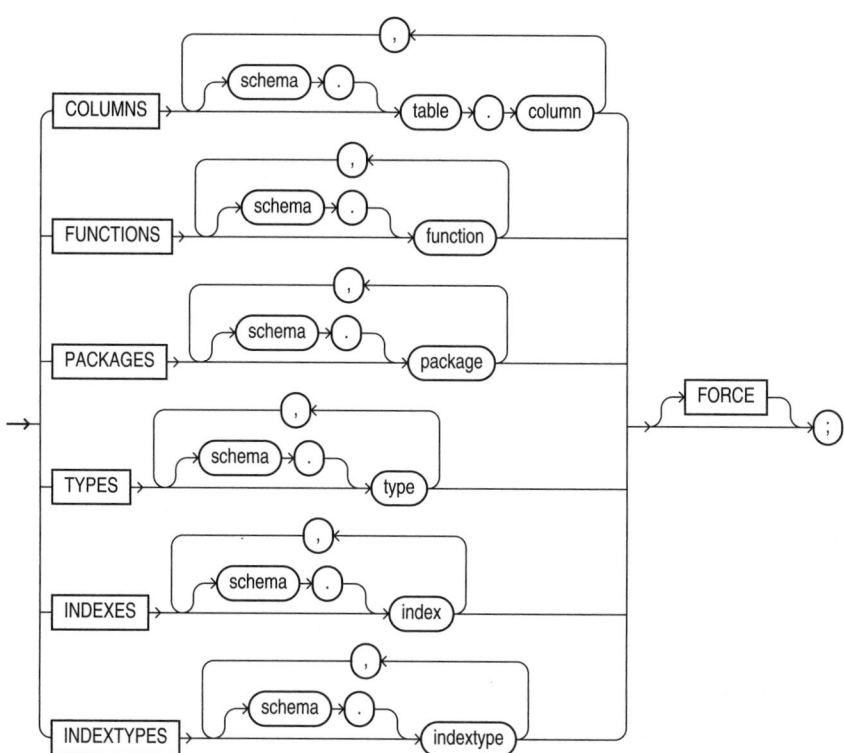

DESCRIPTION   ASSOCIATE STATISTICS associates a set of statistics functions with one or more columns, stand-alone functions, packages, types, or indexes. **DISASSOCIATE STATISTICS** revokes the associations. You must have the ALTER privilege on the base object.

DISCONNECT (SQL*Plus)
SEE ALSO   CONNECT, EXIT, QUIT
FORMAT

```
DISC[ONNECT]
```

DESCRIPTION   DISCONNECT commits pending changes to the database and logs you off of Oracle. Your SQL*Plus session remains active and the features of SQL*Plus continue to function, but without any connection to the database. You can edit buffers, use your own editor, spool and stop spooling, or connect to Oracle again, but until a connection is established, no SQL can be executed.

  EXIT or **QUIT** returns you to your host's operating system. If you are still connected when you **EXIT** or **QUIT**, you will be automatically disconnected and logged off of Oracle.

DISTINCT
Distinct means unique. It is used as a part of **SELECT** statements and group functions. *See* AGGREGATE FUNCTIONS, **SELECT**.

DROP CLUSTER

SEE ALSO   **CREATE CLUSTER**, **DROP TABLE**, Chapter 17
FORMAT
   drop_cluster::=

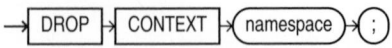

DESCRIPTION   **DROP CLUSTER** deletes a cluster from the database. You must have DROP ANY CLUSTER privilege if the cluster is not in your own schema. You cannot drop a cluster that contains tables. The tables must be dropped first. The **INCLUDING TABLES** clause drops all the clustered tables automatically. The **CASCADE CONSTRAINTS** option drops all referential integrity constraints from tables outside the cluster that refer to keys in the clustered tables.

   Individual tables cannot be removed from a cluster. To accomplish the same effect, copy the table under a new name (use **CREATE TABLE** with **AS SELECT**), drop the old one (this will remove it from the cluster), **RENAME** the copy to the name of the table you dropped, and then issue the appropriate **GRANT**s and create the needed indexes.

DROP CONTEXT

SEE ALSO   **CREATE CONTEXT**
FORMAT
   drop_context::=

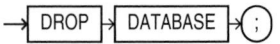

DESCRIPTION   **DROP CONTEXT** deletes a context namespace from the database. You must have the DROP ANY CONTEXT system privilege.

DROP DATABASE

SEE ALSO   **CREATE DATABASE**, Chapter 51
FORMAT
   drop_database::=

→ DROP → DATABASE → ;

DESCRIPTION   **DROP DATABASE** drops the current database (which must be mounted and closed) and deletes all control files and datafiles listed in the control file. Any related spfile is also deleted. Archived logs and backups are not removed. If the database is on raw disks, **DROP DATABASE** does not delete the actual raw disk special files.

DROP DATABASE LINK

SEE ALSO   **CREATE DATABASE LINK**, Chapter 25
FORMAT
   drop_database_link::=

DESCRIPTION **DROP DATABASE LINK** drops a database link you own. For a public link, the optional **PUBLIC** keyword must be used, and you must be a DBA to use it. **PUBLIC** cannot be used when dropping a private link. *link* is the name of the link being dropped. You must have the DROP PUBLIC DATABASE LINK system privilege to drop a public database link. You may drop private database links in your account.

EXAMPLE The following drops a database link named ADAH_AT_HOME:

```
drop database link ADAH_AT_HOME;
```

DROP DIMENSION

SEE ALSO CREATE DIMENSION, Chapter 26
FORMAT
    drop_dimension::=

DESCRIPTION **DROP DIMENSION** drops a dimension that you own. You must have the DROP ANY DIMENSION system privilege.

EXAMPLE The following drops the GEOGRAPHY dimension:

```
drop dimension geography;
```

DROP DIRECTORY

SEE ALSO **CREATE DIRECTORY**, Chapters 24, 28, and 40
FORMAT
    drop_directory::=

DESCRIPTION **DROP DIRECTORY** drops an existing directory. You must have the DROP ANY DIRECTORY privilege to drop a directory.

NOTE
Do not drop a directory while its files are in use.

EXAMPLE The following drops a directory called REVIEWS:

```
drop directory reviews;
```

DROP DISKGROUP

SEE ALSO **ALTER DISKGROUP, CREATE DISKGROUP**, Chapter 51
FORMAT
    drop_diskgroup::=

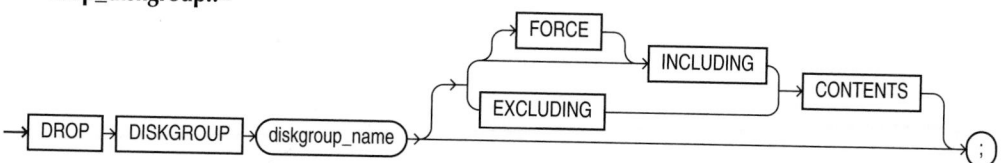

DESCRIPTION For databases using Automated Storage Management (ASM), **DROP DISKGROUP** drops an ASM diskgroup along with all the files in the diskgroup. ASM first ensures that no files in the diskgroup are open; if a file is open, the diskgroup is not dropped.

As of Oracle Database 11*g*, you can use the **FORCE** clause to drop a diskgroup that can no longer be mounted by an ASM instance. For Oracle Database 12*c*, the **DROP DISKGROUP** command works the same whether the ASM instance is local or is part of an Oracle Flex ASM server.

DROP FLASHBACK ARCHIVE
SEE ALSO   **ALTER FLASHBACK ARCHIVE, CREATE FLASHBACK ARCHIVE**
FORMAT
> **drop_flashback_archive::=**

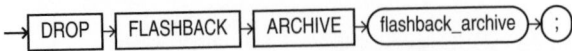

DESCRIPTION   Use **DROP FLASHBACK ARCHIVE** to remove a flashback data archive from the system. This statement removes the flashback data archive and all the historical data in it, but does not drop the tablespaces that were used by the flashback data archive. You must have the FLASHBACK ARCHIVE ADMINISTER system privilege to drop a flashback data archive.

DROP FUNCTION
SEE ALSO   **ALTER FUNCTION, CREATE FUNCTION**, Chapter 35
FORMAT
> **drop_function::=**

DESCRIPTION   **DROP FUNCTION** drops the specified function. Oracle invalidates any objects that depend on or call the function. You must have the DROP ANY PROCEDURE system privilege to drop a function that you do not own.

DROP INDEX
SEE ALSO   **ALTER INDEX, CREATE INDEX, CREATE TABLE**, Chapters 17 and 51
FORMAT
> **drop_index::=**

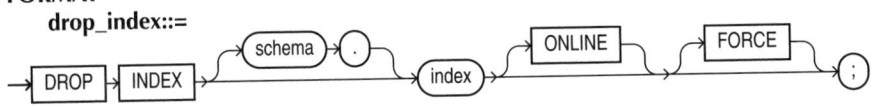

DESCRIPTION   **DROP INDEX** drops the specified index. You must either own the index or have the DROP ANY INDEX system privilege. **FORCE** applies only to domain indexes. This clause drops the domain index even if the indextype routine invocation returns an error or the index is marked **IN PROGRESS**.

DROP INDEXTYPE
SEE ALSO   **CREATE INDEXTYPE**
FORMAT
> **drop_indextype::=**

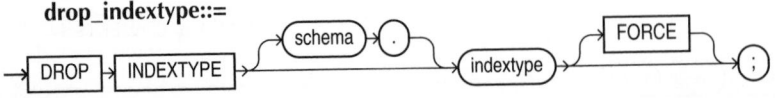

DESCRIPTION   **DROP INDEXTYPE** drops the specified indextype and any association with statistics types. You must have the DROP ANY INDEXTYPE system privilege.

DROP JAVA

SEE ALSO   **CREATE JAVA**, Chapter 42
FORMAT
    drop_java::=

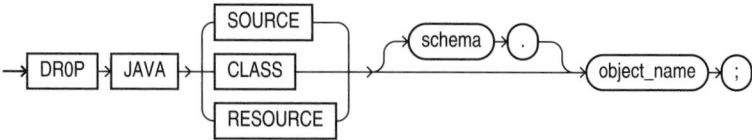

DESCRIPTION   **DROP JAVA** drops the specified Java class, source, or resource. You must have the DROP PROCEDURE system privilege. If the object is in another user's schema, you must have the DROP ANY PROCEDURE system privilege.

DROP LIBRARY

SEE ALSO   **CREATE LIBRARY**
FORMAT
    drop_library::=

DESCRIPTION   **DROP LIBRARY** drops the specified library. You must have the DROP ANY LIBRARY system privilege.

DROP MATERIALIZED VIEW

SEE ALSO   **ALTER MATERIALIZED VIEW, CREATE MATERIALIZED VIEW**, Chapter 26
FORMAT
    drop_materialized_view::=

DESCRIPTION   **DROP MATERIALIZED VIEW** drops the indicated materialized view. You must either own the materialized view or have the DROP ANY SNAPSHOT or DROP ANY MATERIALIZED VIEW system privilege. The keyword **SNAPSHOT** is supported in place of **MATERIALIZED VIEW** for backward compatibility. **PRESERVE TABLE** lets you retain the materialized view container table and its contents after the materialized view object is dropped. The resulting table has the same name as the dropped materialized view. The metadata associated with the materialized view is dropped but the indexes, nested table columns, and storage tables for those columns are preserved along with their metadata. If you drop a materialized view that was created on a prebuilt table, the database drops the materialized view and the prebuilt table reverts to its identity as a table.

DROP MATERIALIZED VIEW LOG

SEE ALSO   **ALTER MATERIALIZED VIEW LOG, CREATE MATERIALIZED VIEW LOG**, Chapter 26
FORMAT
    drop_materialized_view_log::=

DESCRIPTION   DROP MATERIALIZED VIEW LOG drops the indicated log table. To drop a materialized view log, you must have the privileges to drop a table. After dropping the log, any materialized views on the master table will get **COMPLETE** refreshes, not **FAST** refreshes.

The keyword **SNAPSHOT** is supported in place of **MATERIALIZED VIEW** for backward compatibility.

DROP OPERATOR
SEE ALSO   ALTER OPERATOR
FORMAT
  drop_operator::=

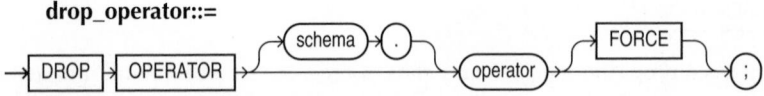

DESCRIPTION   DROP OPERATOR drops a user-defined operator. You must either own the operator or have the DROP ANY OPERATOR system privilege. Specify **FORCE** to drop the operator even if it is currently being referenced by one or more schema objects (indextypes, packages, functions, procedures, and so on), and mark those dependent objects **INVALID**.

DROP OUTLINE
SEE ALSO   CREATE OUTLINE
FORMAT
  drop_outline::=

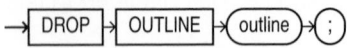

DESCRIPTION   DROP OUTLINE drops a stored outline from the database. You must have the DROP ANY OUTLINE system privilege. Subsequent executions of SQL statements that used the outline will have their execution paths evaluated at run time.

DROP PACKAGE
SEE ALSO   ALTER PACKAGE, CREATE PACKAGE, Chapter 35
FORMAT
  drop_package::=

DESCRIPTION   DROP PACKAGE drops the specified package. Using the optional **BODY** clause drops only the body without dropping the package specification. Oracle invalidates any objects that depend on the package if you drop the package specification, but not if you just drop the body. You must either own the package or have the DROP ANY PROCEDURE system privilege.

DROP PLUGGABLE DATABASE
SEE ALSO   ALTER PLUGGABLE DATABASE, CREATE PLUGGABLE DATABASE, Chapter 49
FORMAT
  drop_pluggable_database::=

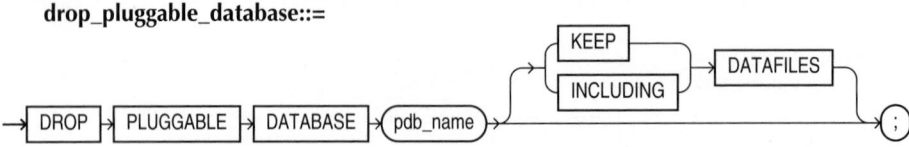

DESCRIPTION **DROP PLUGGABLE DATABASE** drops a pluggable database (PDB) and removes all references to the dropped PDB in the container database (CDB) controlfile. Archived redo logs and backups associated with the PDB are not automatically deleted but can be deleted using Recovery Manager (RMAN). You must have the SYSDBA or SYSOPER privilege on the PDB you want to drop and be connected to the root.

EXAMPLE The following command drops the pluggable database DATAPLUG from the container along with the PDB's associated datafiles:

```
drop pluggable database dataplug including datafiles;
```

DROP PROCEDURE
SEE ALSO **ALTER PROCEDURE, CREATE PROCEDURE**, Chapter 35
FORMAT
    drop_procedure::=

DESCRIPTION **DROP PROCEDURE** drops the specified procedure. Oracle invalidates any objects that depend on or call the procedure. You must either own the procedure or have the DROP ANY PROCEDURE system privilege.

DROP PROFILE
SEE ALSO **ALTER PROFILE, CREATE PROFILE**, Chapter 19
FORMAT
    drop_profile::=

DESCRIPTION **DROP PROFILE** drops the specified profile. You must have the DROP PROFILE system privilege. **CASCADE** unassigns the profile from any users to whom it has been assigned; they are automatically assigned the DEFAULT profile in its place. You must use **CASCADE** if the profile being dropped is currently assigned to users.

DROP RESTORE POINT
SEE ALSO **CREATE RESTORE POINT, FLASHBACK DATABASE, FLASHBACK TABLE**
FORMAT

DESCRIPTION Use the **DROP RESTORE POINT** statement to remove a normal restore point or a guaranteed restore point from the database.

You need not drop normal restore points. The database automatically drops the oldest restore points when necessary, as described in the semantics for *restore_point*. However, you can drop a normal restore point if you want to reuse the name.

Guaranteed restore points are not dropped automatically. Therefore, if you want to remove a guaranteed restore point from the database, you must do so explicitly using this statement.

To drop a normal restore point, you must have either the SELECT ANY DICTIONARY or the FLASHBACK ANY TABLE system privilege. To drop a guaranteed restore point, you must have the SYSDBA system privilege.

DROP ROLE

SEE ALSO   ALTER ROLE, CREATE ROLE, Chapter 19
FORMAT
    drop_role::=

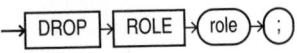

DESCRIPTION   DROP ROLE drops the specified role. You must either have been granted the role
WITH ADMIN OPTION or have the DROP ANY ROLE system privilege.

DROP ROLLBACK SEGMENT

**SEE ALSO   ALTER ROLLBACK SEGMENT, CREATE ROLLBACK SEGMENT, CREATE TABLESPACE,
SHUTDOWN, STARTUP, Chapter 51
FORMAT**
    drop_rollback_segment::=

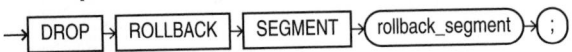

DESCRIPTION   *rollback_segment* is the name of an existing rollback segment to be dropped. The
segment must not be in use when this statement is executed. **PUBLIC** is required for dropping public
rollback segments.
    The STATUS column of the data dictionary view DBA_ROLLBACK_SEGS can reveal which rollback
segments are in use. If the segment is in use, you can either wait until it no longer is in use or
SHUTDOWN the database using **IMMEDIATE**, and then bring it up in EXCLUSIVE mode using
STARTUP. You must have the DROP ROLLBACK SEGMENT system privilege to drop a rollback
segment.

DROP SEQUENCE

SEE ALSO   ALTER SEQUENCE, CREATE SEQUENCE, Chapter 17
FORMAT
    drop_sequence::=

DESCRIPTION   *sequence_name* is the name of the sequence being dropped. To drop a sequence, you
must either own the sequence or have the DROP ANY SEQUENCE system privilege.

DROP SYNONYM

SEE ALSO   CREATE SYNONYM, Chapter 25
FORMAT
    drop_synonym::=

DESCRIPTION   DROP SYNONYM drops the specified synonym. To drop a public synonym, you must
have the DROP ANY PUBLIC SYNONYM system privilege. To drop a private synonym, you must own
the synonym or have the DROP ANY SYNONYM system privilege. You must specify **FORCE** if the
synonym has dependent tables or user-defined types.

DROP TABLE

SEE ALSO **ALTER TABLE, CREATE INDEX, CREATE TABLE, DROP CLUSTER**, Chapter 17
FORMAT
   drop_table::=

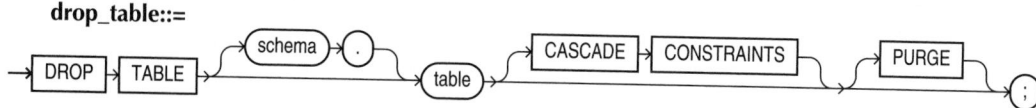

DESCRIPTION **DROP TABLE** drops the specified table. To drop a table, you must either own the table or have the DROP ANY TABLE system privilege. Dropping a table also drops indexes and grants associated with it. Objects built on dropped tables are marked invalid and cease to work.

   The **CASCADE CONSTRAINTS** option drops all referential integrity constraints referring to keys in the dropped table.

   You can drop a cluster and all of its tables by using the **INCLUDING TABLES** clause on **DROP CLUSTER**.

   Using the **DROP TABLE** statement moves a table or object table to the recycle bin or removes the table and all its data from the database entirely. Unless you specify the **PURGE** clause, the **DROP TABLE** statement does not result in space being released back to the tablespace for use by other objects and the space continues to count toward the user's space quota. Objects may be automatically purged from the recycle bin if the tablespace runs out of space for new objects.

DROP TABLESPACE

SEE ALSO **ALTER TABLESPACE, CREATE DATABASE, CREATE TABLESPACE**, Chapter 51
FORMAT
   drop_tablespace::=

DESCRIPTION *tablespace* is the name of the tablespace being dropped. The **INCLUDING CONTENTS** option allows you to drop a tablespace that contains data. Without **INCLUDING CONTENTS**, only an empty tablespace can be dropped. Tablespaces should be offline (*see* **ALTER TABLESPACE**) before dropping, or the drop operation will be prevented if any users are accessing data, index, rollback, or temporary segments in the tablespace. You must have the DROP TABLESPACE system privilege to use this command.

DROP TRIGGER

SEE ALSO **ALTER TRIGGER, CREATE TRIGGER**, Chapters 34 and 38
FORMAT
   drop_trigger::=

DESCRIPTION **DROP TRIGGER** drops the specified trigger. You must either own the trigger or have the DROP ANY TRIGGER system privilege.

DROP TYPE

SEE ALSO   **CREATE TYPE**, Chapter 38
FORMAT
    drop_type::=

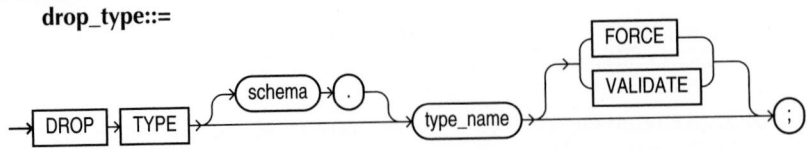

DESCRIPTION   **DROP TYPE** drops the specification and body of an abstract datatype. You must either own the type or have the DROP ANY TYPE system privilege. Unless you use **FORCE**, you cannot drop a type if a table or other object references it.

DROP TYPE BODY

SEE ALSO   **CREATE TYPE**, **CREATE TYPE BODY**, **DROP TYPE**, Chapter 38
FORMAT
    drop_type_body::=

DESCRIPTION   **DROP TYPE BODY** drops the body of the specified type. You must either own the type or have the DROP ANY TYPE system privilege.

DROP USER

SEE ALSO   **ALTER USER, CREATE USER**, Chapter 19
FORMAT
    drop_user::=

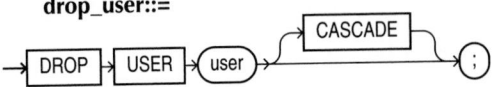

DESCRIPTION   **DROP USER** drops the specified user. You must have the DROP USER system privilege. The **CASCADE** option drops all the objects in the user's schema before dropping the user, and you *must* specify **CASCADE** if the user has any objects in the schema.

DROP VIEW

SEE ALSO   **CREATE SYNONYM, CREATE TABLE, CREATE VIEW**, Chapter 17
FORMAT
    drop_view::=

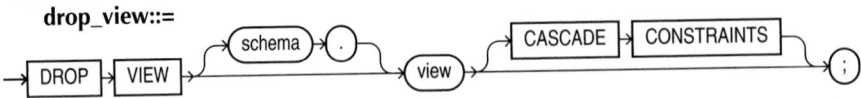

DESCRIPTION   **DROP VIEW** drops the specified view. To drop a view, either the view must be in your schema or you must have the DROP ANY VIEW system privilege.

DROPJAVA

DROPJAVA is a utility for removing Java classes from the database. *See* LOADJAVA.

DUAL

SEE ALSO   FROM, SELECT, Chapter 10

DESCRIPTION   DUAL is a table with only one row and one column in it. Because Oracle's many functions work on both columns and literals, it is possible to demonstrate some of its functionality by using just literals or pseudo-columns. When doing this, the **SELECT** statement doesn't care which columns are in the table, and a single row is more than sufficient to demonstrate a point.

EXAMPLE   The following shows the current USER and SYSDATE:

```
select user, sysdate from dual;
```

DUMP

SEE ALSO   RAWTOHEX

FORMAT

```
DUMP( string [,format [,start [,length] ] ] )
```

DESCRIPTION   DUMP displays the value of *string* in internal data format, in ASCII, octal, decimal, hex, or character format. *format* defaults to ASCII or EBCDIC, depending on your machine; 8 produces octal, 10 decimal, 16 hex, and 17 character (the same as ASCII or EBCDIC). *start* is the beginning position in the string, and *length* is the number of characters to display. *string* can be a literal or an expression.

EXAMPLE   The following shows how characters 1 through 8 are represented in hex for just the CITY in the first row of the COMFORT table:

```
select city, dump(city,16,1,8) from comfort where rownum < 2;

CITY            DUMP(CITY,16,1,8)
------------    ------------------------------------
San Francisco Typ=1 Len=13: 53,61,6e,20,46,72,61,6e
```

EDIT (SQL*Plus)

SEE ALSO   DEFINE, SET, Chapter 6

FORMAT

```
ED[IT] [file[.ext]]
```

DESCRIPTION   EDIT calls an external standard text editor and passes to it the name of the file. If *.ext* is omitted, the extension .sql is appended. If *file* and *.ext* are both omitted, the editor is called and passed the name of a file (constructed by SQL*Plus) that contains the contents of the current buffer. The local user variable *_editor* determines which text editor is used by **EDIT**. *_editor* can be changed with **DEFINE**, and this is usually best done in the **login.sql** file, which is read whenever SQL*Plus is invoked.

EDIT will fail if the current buffer is empty and **EDIT** is called without a filename. You can use the **SET EDITFILE** command to set the default name of the file created by the **EDIT** command.

EMPTY_BLOB

SEE ALSO   Chapter 40

FORMAT

```
EMPTY_BLOB()
```

DESCRIPTION   EMPTY_BLOB returns an empty LOB locator that can be used to initialize a LOB variable or, in an **INSERT** or **UPDATE** statement, to initialize a LOB column or attribute to EMPTY. EMPTY means the LOB is initialized, but not populated with data.

EXAMPLE

```
update book_text set blobcol = empty_blob();
```

EMPTY_CLOB

SEE ALSO   Chapter 40
FORMAT

```
EMPTY_CLOB()
```

DESCRIPTION   **EMPTY_CLOB** returns an empty LOB locator that can be used to initialize a LOB variable or, in an **INSERT** or **UPDATE** statement, to initialize a LOB column or attribute to EMPTY. EMPTY means the LOB is initialized, but not populated with data.

EXAMPLE

```
update book_text set clobcol = empty_clob();
```

END

SEE ALSO   **BEGIN**, BLOCK STRUCTURE, Chapter 32
FORMAT

```
END [block label] ;
```

DESCRIPTION   **END** is unrelated to the **END IF** and **END LOOP** statements. *See* **IF** and **LOOP** for details on either of them.

END is the closing statement of a PL/SQL block's executable section (and the entire block). If the block is named at the **BEGIN** statement, the name must also follow the word **END**. At least one executable statement is required between **BEGIN** and **END**.

EXCEPTION

SEE ALSO   BLOCK STRUCTURE, **RAISE**, Chapter 32
FORMAT

```
EXCEPTION
  {WHEN {OTHERS | exception [OR exception]...}
       THEN statement; [statement;]...}
 [ WHEN {OTHER | exception [OR exception]...}
       THEN statement; [statement;]...]...
```

DESCRIPTION   The EXCEPTION section of a PL/SQL block is where program control is transferred whenever an exception flag is raised. Exception flags are either user-defined or system exceptions raised automatically by PL/SQL. *See* **RAISE** for details on user-defined exception flags. The system exception flags are all, in effect, BOOLEAN variables that are either TRUE or FALSE. The **WHEN** clause is used to test these. For example, the NOT_LOGGED_ON flag is raised if you attempt to issue a command to Oracle without being logged on. You do not need to have **DECLARE**d an exception, or **RAISE**d this flag yourself. PL/SQL will do it for you.

When any exception flag is raised, the program immediately halts whatever it was doing and jumps to the EXCEPTION section of the current block. This section, however, doesn't know automatically which exception flag was raised, nor what to do. Therefore, you must code the EXCEPTION section first to check all of the exception flags that are likely to have occurred and then give action instructions for each. This is what the **WHEN...THEN** logic does. You can use **WHEN OTHERS** as a catch-all to handle unanticipated errors for which you have not declared exceptions.

EXAMPLE   Here, one exception flag is tested in the EXCEPTION section. The ZERO_DIVIDE flag is raised when any calculation attempts to divide by zero.

```
declare
   pi     constant NUMBER(9,7) := 3.1415927;
   radius INTEGER(5);
```

```
  area    NUMBER(14,2);
  some_variable   NUMBER(14,2);
begin
  radius := 3;
  loop
    some_variable := 1/(radius-4);
    area := pi*power(radius,2);
      insert into AREAS values (radius, area);
    radius := radius+1;
    exit when area > 100;
  end loop;
exception
  when ZERO_DIVIDE
    then insert into AREAS values (0,0);
end;
```

The system-raised exception flags are as follows:

Exception Flag	Description
ACCESS_INTO_NULL	Your program attempts to assign values to the attributes of an uninitialized (atomically null) object.
CASE_NOT_FOUND	None of the choices in the **WHEN** clauses of a **CASE** statement is selected, and there is no **ELSE** clause.
COLLECTION_IS_NULL	Your program attempts to apply collection methods other than **EXISTS** to an uninitialized (atomically null) nested table or varying array, or the program attempts to assign values to the elements of an uninitialized nested table or varying array.
CURSOR_ALREADY_OPEN	Your program attempts to open an already open cursor. A cursor must be closed before it can be reopened. A Cursor FOR Loop automatically opens the cursor to which it refers. So, your program cannot open that cursor inside the loop.
DUP_VAL_ON_INDEX	Your program attempts to store duplicate values in a database column that is constrained by a unique index.
INVALID_CURSOR	Your program attempts an illegal cursor operation such as closing an unopened cursor.
INVALID_NUMBER	In a SQL statement, the conversion of a character string into a number fails because the string does not represent a valid number. (In procedural statements, VALUE_ERROR is raised.) This exception is also raised when the **LIMIT**-clause expression in a bulk **FETCH** statement does not evaluate to a positive number.
LOGIN_DENIED	Your program attempts to log on to Oracle with an invalid username and/or password.
NO_DATA_FOUND	A **SELECT INTO** statement returns no rows, or your program references a deleted element in a nested table or an uninitialized element in an index-by table. SQL aggregate functions such as **AVG** and **SUM** always return a value or a **NULL**. So, a **SELECT INTO** statement that calls an aggregate function never raises NO_DATA_FOUND. The **FETCH** statement is expected to return no rows eventually, so when that happens, no exception is raised.
NOT_LOGGED_ON	Your program issues a database call without being connected to Oracle.
PROGRAM_ERROR	PL/SQL has an internal problem.

Exception Flag	Description
ROWTYPE_MISMATCH	The host cursor variable and PL/SQL cursor variable involved in an assignment have incompatible return types. For example, when an open host cursor variable is passed to a stored subprogram, the return types of the actual and formal parameters must be compatible.
SELF_IS_NULL	Your program attempts to call a MEMBER method on a NULL instance. That is, the built-in parameter SELF (which is always the first parameter passed to a MEMBER method) is NULL.
STORAGE_ERROR	PL/SQL runs out of memory or memory has been corrupted.
SUBSCRIPT_BEYOND_COUNT	Your program references a nested table or varying array element using an index number larger than the number of elements in the collection.
SUBSCRIPT_OUTSIDE_LIMIT	Your program references a nested table or varying array element using an index number (–1 for example) that is outside the legal range.
SYS_INVALID_ROWID	The conversion of a character string into a universal ROWID fails because the character string does not represent a valid ROWID.
TIMEOUT_ON_RESOURCE	A time-out occurs while Oracle is waiting for a resource.
TOO_MANY_ROWS	A **SELECT INTO** statement returns more than one row.
VALUE_ERROR	An arithmetic, conversion, truncation, or size-constraint error occurs. For example, when your program selects a column value into a character variable, if the value is longer than the declared length of the variable, PL/SQL aborts the assignment and raises VALUE_ERROR. In procedural statements, VALUE_ERROR is raised if the conversion of a character string into a number fails. (In SQL statements, INVALID_NUMBER is raised.)
ZERO_DIVIDE	Your program attempts to divide a number by zero.

The associated Oracle error numbers and SQLCODE values are as follows:

Exception	Oracle Error #	SQLCODE
ACCESS_INTO_NULL	ORA-06530	–6530
CASE_NOT_FOUND	ORA-06592	–6592
COLLECTION_IS_NULL	ORA-06531	–6531
CURSOR_ALREADY_OPEN	ORA-06511	–6511
DUP_VAL_ON_INDEX	ORA-00001	–1
INVALID_CURSOR	ORA-01001	–1001
INVALID_NUMBER	ORA-01722	–1722
LOGIN_DENIED	ORA-01017	–1017
NO_DATA_FOUND	ORA-01403	+100
NOT_LOGGED_ON	ORA-01012	–1012
PROGRAM_ERROR	ORA-06501	–6501
ROWTYPE_MISMATCH	ORA-06504	–6504
SELF_IS_NULL	ORA-30625	–30625
STORAGE_ERROR	ORA-06500	–6500
SUBSCRIPT_BEYOND_COUNT	ORA-06533	–6533
SUBSCRIPT_OUTSIDE_LIMIT	ORA-06532	–6532

Exception	Oracle Error #	SQLCODE
SYS_INVALID_ROWID	ORA-01410	−1410
TIMEOUT_ON_RESOURCE	ORA-00051	−51
TOO_MANY_ROWS	ORA-01422	−1422
VALUE_ERROR	ORA-06502	−6502
ZERO_DIVIDE	ORA-01476	−1476

OTHERS is the catch-all for any exception flags you did not check for in your EXCEPTION section. It must always be the last **WHEN** statement and must stand alone. It cannot be included with any other exceptions.

Exception Handling, particularly as it relates to exceptions you declare, should really be reserved for errors that are fatal—that means normal processing should stop.

If an exception flag is raised that is not tested for in the current block, the program will branch to the EXCEPTION block in the enclosing block, and so on, until either the exception raised is found or control falls through to the host program.

EXCEPTION sections can reference variables in the same manner that the execution block can. That is, they can reference local variables directly or variables from other blocks by prefixing them with the other block's name.

Use caution in testing for certain kinds of exceptions. For instance, if the EXCEPTION section takes the error message and inserts it into a database table, a NOT_LOGGED_ON exception would put the EXCEPTION section into an infinite loop. Design the statements that follow **THEN** not to duplicate the error that got the program there in the first place. You also may use **RAISE** without an exception name to will automatically pass control to the next outer EXCEPTION block or the main program. *See* **RAISE** for further details.

EXCEPTION_INIT

SEE ALSO **DECLARE CURSOR**, EXCEPTION, **SQLCODE**, *Programmer's Guide to the Oracle Precompilers*
FORMAT

```
PRAGMA EXCEPTION_INIT(exception,integer);
```

DESCRIPTION   The standard system exceptions, such as ZERO_DIVIDE, which are referenced by name, are actually no more than the association of a name with the internal Oracle error number. There are hundreds of these error numbers, and only the most common have been given names. Any that are not named will still raise an exception flag and transfer control to the EXCEPTION block, but they will all be caught by OTHERS, rather than by name.

You can change this by assigning your own names to other Oracle error numbers. **EXCEPTION_ INIT** allows you to do this. *exception* is the one-word name you assign to the integer error number (*see* Oracle's *Error Messages and Codes Manual* for a complete list). *integer* should be negative if the error code is negative (true for fatal errors), and *exception* must follow normal object naming rules.

Note that the format of this command requires the word **PRAGMA** before **EXCEPTION_INIT**. A pragma is an instruction to the PL/SQL compiler, rather than executable code. The pragma must be in the DECLARE section of a PL/SQL block, and must be preceded by an exception declaration.

EXAMPLE

```
DECLARE
    some_bad_error      exception;
    pragma              exception_init(some_bad_error, -660);
BEGIN
    . . .
```

```
EXCEPTION
    when some_bad_error
            then ...
END;
```

EXECUTE

SEE ALSO   **CALL, CREATE FUNCTION, CREATE PACKAGE, CREATE PACKAGE BODY, CREATE PROCEDURE, GRANT,** Chapter 35
FORMAT

```
EXECUTE procedural_object_name [arguments];
```

DESCRIPTION   **EXECUTE** executes a procedure, package, or function in SQL*Plus. To execute a procedure within a package, specify both the package name and the procedure name in the **EXECUTE** command, as shown in the following example. This example executes a procedure named NEW_BOOK, in a package named BOOKSHELF_PACKAGE; the value 'Tale Of Two Cities' is passed as input to the procedure.

```
execute bookshelf_package.new_book('Tale Of Two Cities');
```

To execute a procedural object, you must have been granted the EXECUTE privilege on that object. *See* **GRANT.**

EXECUTE (Dynamic Embedded SQL)

SEE ALSO   **EXECUTE IMMEDIATE, PREPARE,** *Programmer's Guide to the Oracle Precompilers*
FORMAT

```
EXEC SQL [FOR { integer | :array_size }]
  EXECUTE statement_id
  [USING
   { DESCRIPTOR SQLDA_descriptor
   | :host_variable [[INDICATOR] :indicator_variable]
     [, :host_variable [[INDICATOR] :indicator_variable]]... } ]
```

DESCRIPTION   *integer* is a host variable used to limit the number of iterations when the **WHERE** clause uses arrays. *statement_id* is the identifier for a prepared **INSERT, DELETE,** or **UPDATE** statement to be executed (**SELECT** is not allowed). **USING** introduces a list of substitutions into the host variables of the previously prepared statement.

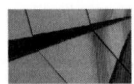

NOTE
See the Programmer's Guide to the Oracle Precompilers *for a full list of all commands. This reference does not contain all of the possible precompiler commands.*

EXECUTE IMMEDIATE (Dynamic Embedded SQL)

SEE ALSO   **EXECUTE, PREPARE,** *Programmer's Guide to the Oracle Precompilers*
FORMAT

```
EXEC SQL [AT {database | :host_variable}]
  EXECUTE IMMEDIATE {:string | literal}
```

DESCRIPTION   *database* is the name of a database connection other than the default; *host_variable* may contain such a name as its value. *string* is a host variable string containing a SQL statement. *literal* is a character string containing a SQL statement. The **EXECUTE IMMEDIATE** statement cannot contain host variable references other than an executable SQL statement in *string*. The SQL statement is parsed, put into executable form, and executed, and the executable form is destroyed. It is intended only for statements to be executed just once. Statements that require multiple executions should use **PREPARE** and **EXECUTE**, as this eliminates the overhead of parsing for each execution.

NOTE
See the Programmer's Guide to the Oracle Precompilers *for a full list of all commands. This reference does not contain all of the possible precompiler commands.*

EXISTS
SEE ALSO **ALL, ANY, IN, NOT EXISTS**, Chapter 13
FORMAT

```
SELECT ...
WHERE EXISTS (SELECT...)
```

DESCRIPTION **EXISTS** returns TRUE in a **WHERE** clause if the subquery that follows it returns at least one row. The **SELECT** clause in the subquery can be a column, a literal, or an asterisk—it doesn't matter. (Convention suggests an asterisk or an 'x'.)

Many people prefer **EXISTS** over **ANY** and **ALL** because it is easier to remember and understand, and most formulations of **ANY** and **ALL** can be reconstructed using **EXISTS**.
EXAMPLE
The query shown in the following example uses **EXISTS** to list from the BOOKSHELF table all PUBLISHERS that have had books checked out:

```
select publisher
from bookshelf b
where exists
        (select 'x' from bookshelf_checkout
          where bookshelf_checkout.title = b.title);
```

EXISTSNODE
SEE ALSO Chapter 47
FORMAT

```
EXISTSNODE ( XMLType_instance , Xpath_string )
```

DESCRIPTION **EXISTSNODE** determines whether traversal of the document using the path results in any nodes. It takes as arguments the XMLType instance containing an XML document and a VARCHAR2 string designating a path.

The return value is NUMBER: 0 if no nodes remain after applying the XPath traversal on the document and >0 if any nodes remain.

EXIT (Form 1—PL/SQL)
SEE ALSO **END**, LOOP, Chapter 32
FORMAT

```
EXIT [loop] [WHEN condition];
```

DESCRIPTION Without any of its options, **EXIT** simply takes you out of the current loop and branches control to the next statement following the loop. If you are in a nested loop, you can exit from any enclosing loop simply by specifying the loop name. If you specify a condition, you exit when the condition evaluates to TRUE. Any cursor within a loop is automatically closed when you **EXIT**.

EXIT (Form 2—SQL*Plus)
SEE ALSO   COMMIT, DISCONNECT, QUIT, START
FORMAT

```
{EXIT | QUIT} [SUCCESS|FAILURE|WARNING|integer|variable|:BindVariable]
[COMMIT|ROLLBACK]
```

DESCRIPTION   **EXIT** ends a SQL*Plus session and returns the user to the operating system, calling program or menu. Unless ROLLBACK is specified, **EXIT** commits pending changes to the database. A return code is also returned. SUCCESS, FAILURE, and WARNING have values that are operating-system specific; FAILURE and WARNING may be the same on some operating systems.

integer is a value that you can pass back explicitly as the return code; *variable* allows you to set this value dynamically. This can be a user-defined variable or a system variable, such as SQL.SQLCODE, which always contains the SQLCODE of the last SQL statement executed, either in SQL*Plus or an embedded PL/SQL block.

EXP
SEE ALSO   LN, NUMBER FUNCTIONS, Chapter 9
FORMAT

```
EXP(n)
```

DESCRIPTION   **EXP** returns *e* raised to the *n*th power; e = 2.718281828….

EXPLAIN PLAN
SEE ALSO   Chapter 46
FORMAT

```
EXPLAIN PLAN [SET STATEMENT_ID = 'name']
[INTO [schema.] table [@ dblink]]
FOR statement;
```

DESCRIPTION   *name* identifies this plan explanation for this *statement* when it appears in the output table and follows normal object-naming conventions. If *name* is not specified, the STATEMENT_ID column in the table will be **NULL**. *table* is the name of the output table into which the plan explanation will go. It must be previously created before this procedure can be executed. The start file **utlxplan.sql** contains the format and can be used to create the default table, named PLAN_TABLE. If *table* is not specified, **EXPLAIN PLAN** uses PLAN_TABLE. *statement* is the simple text of any **SELECT**, **INSERT**, **UPDATE**, or **DELETE** statement you wish to have analyzed for Oracle's execution plan for it.

EXTRACT (datetime)
SEE ALSO   DATE FUNCTIONS, Chapter 10
FORMAT

```
EXTRACT
( { { YEAR
    | MONTH
    | DAY
    | HOUR
    | MINUTE
    | SECOND    }
  | { TIMEZONE_HOUR
```

```
      | TIMEZONE_MINUTE      }
  | { TIMEZONE_REGION
      | TIMEZONE_ABBR
      }  }
  FROM { datetime_value_expression | interval_value_expression } )
```

DESCRIPTION   **EXTRACT** extracts and returns the value of a specified datetime field from a datetime or interval value expression.

EXAMPLE

```
select birthdate,
       extract(month from birthdate) as month
from birthday
where first_name = 'Victoria';

BIRTHDATE    MONTH
---------  ----------
20-MAY-79          5
```

EXTRACT (XML)

SEE ALSO   Chapter 52
FORMAT

```
EXTRACT ( XMLType_instance , Xpath_string )
```

DESCRIPTION   **EXTRACT** is similar to the **EXISTSNODE** function. It applies a VARCHAR2 XPath string and returns an XMLType instance containing an XML fragment.

EXTRACTVALUE

SEE ALSO   XMLType
FORMAT

```
EXTRACTVALUE(XMLType_instance, Xpath_string [,namespace_string])
```

DESCRIPTION   **EXTRACTVALUE** takes as arguments an XMLType instance and an XPath expression and returns a scalar value of the resultant node. The result must be a single node and must be a text node, an attribute, or an element. By comparison, the **EXTRACT** function returns an XML fragment; **EXTRACTVALUE** returns the scalar value of the XML fragment.

FEATURE_DETAILS

FORMAT
   feature_details::=

feature_details_analytic::=

mining_attribute_clause:=

mining_analytic_clause::=

DESCRIPTION Use this function with feature extraction models that have been created using the DBMS_DATA_MINING package or with the Oracle Data Mining Java API. It returns feature details for each row in the selection.

FEATURE_ID

FORMAT
   feature_id::=

   feature_id_analytic::=

mining_attribute_clause:=

mining_analytic_clause::=

DESCRIPTION Use this function with feature extraction models that have been created using the DBMS_DATA_MINING package or with the Oracle Data Mining Java API. It returns an Oracle NUMBER that is the identifier of the feature with the highest value in the row.

FEATURE_SET
FORMAT

feature_set::=

feature_set_analytic::=

mining_attribute_clause:=

mining_analytic_clause::=

DESCRIPTION Use this function with feature extraction models that have been created using the DBMS_DATA_MINING package or with the Oracle Data Mining Java API. It returns a varray of objects containing all possible features. Each object in the varray is a pair of scalar values containing the feature ID and the feature value. The object fields are named FEATURE_ID and VALUE and both are Oracle NUMBER.

The optional *topN* argument is a positive integer that restricts the set of features to those that have one of the top *N* values. If there is a tie at the *N*th value, the database still returns only *N* values. If you omit this argument, the function returns all features.

FEATURE_VALUE
FORMAT
feature_value::=

feature_value_analytic::=

mining_attribute_clause:=

mining_analytic_clause::=

DESCRIPTION Use this function with feature extraction models that have been created using the DBMS_DATA_MINING package or with the Oracle Data Mining Java API. It returns the value of a given feature. If you omit the *feature_id* argument, the function returns the highest feature value. You can use this form in conjunction with the **FEATURE_ID** function to obtain the largest feature/value combination.

FETCH (Form 1—Embedded SQL)
SEE ALSO **CLOSE, DECLARE CURSOR, DESCRIBE,** INDICATOR VARIABLE, **OPEN, PREPARE,**
Programmer's Guide to the Oracle Precompilers
FORMAT

```
EXEC SQL [FOR { integer | :array_size }]
  FETCH { cursor | :cursor_variable }
```

```
{ USING DESCRIPTOR SQLDA_descriptor
| INTO :host_variable [[INDICATOR] :indicator_variable]
  [, :host_variable [[INDICATOR] :indicator_variable]]... }
```

DESCRIPTION   *integer* is a host variable that sets the maximum number of rows to fetch into the output variables. *cursor* is the name of a cursor previously set up by **DECLARE CURSOR**. *:host_variable* is one or more host variables into which fetched data will be placed. If any of the host variables is an array, then all of them (in the **INTO** list) must be arrays. The **INDICATOR** keyword is optional.

NOTE
See the Programmer's Guide to the Oracle Precompilers *for a full list of all commands. This reference does not contain all of the possible precompiler commands.*

FETCH (Form 2—PL/SQL)
SEE ALSO   **%FOUND, %ROWTYPE, CLOSE, DECLARE CURSOR, LOOP, OPEN, SELECT ... INTO,** Chapter 32
FORMAT

```
FETCH cursor INTO {record | variable [,variable]...};
```

DESCRIPTION   **FETCH** gets a row of data. The named cursor's **SELECT** statement determines which columns are retrieved, and its **WHERE** statement determines which (and how many) rows can be retrieved. This is called the "active set," but it is not available to you for processing until you fetch it, row by row, using the **FETCH** statement. The **FETCH** gets a row from the active set and drops the row's values into the record (or string of variables), which has been defined in the **DECLARE**.

If you use the variable-list method, each column in the select list of the cursor must have a corresponding variable, and each of them must have been declared in the **DECLARE** section. The datatypes must be the same or compatible.

If you use the record method, the record is **DECLARE**d using the **%ROWTYPE** attribute, which declares the structure of the record to be the same (with the same datatypes) as the column list in the **SELECT** statement. Each variable within this record can then be accessed individually using the record name as a prefix and a variable name that is the same as the column name.
EXAMPLE

```
declare
    pi      constant NUMBER(9,7) := 3.1415927;
    area    NUMBER(14,2);
    cursor rad_cursor is
            select * from radius_vals;
    rad_val rad_cursor%ROWTYPE;
begin
  open rad_cursor;
    loop
      fetch rad_cursor into rad_val;
      exit when rad_cursor%NOTFOUND;
        area := pi*power(rad_val.radius,2);
        insert into areas values (rad_val.radius, area);
    end loop;
  close rad_cursor;
end;
```

FILE_SPECIFICATION

SEE ALSO ALTER TABLESPACE, CREATE CONTROLFILE, CREATE DATABASE, CREATE LIBRARY, CREATE TABLESPACE

FORMAT

file_specification::=

datafile_tempfile_spec::=

redo_log_file_spec::=

ASM_filename::=

fully_qualified_file_name::=

numeric_file_name::=

incomplete_file_name::=

alias_file_name::=

autoextend_clause::=

maxsize_clause::=

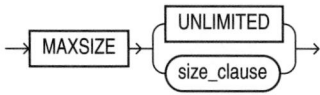

DESCRIPTION   *file_specification* defines the name, location, and size of a file used by the database. For example, when you create a tablespace, you must specify at least one datafile for the tablespace to use. *file_specification* provides the format for the datafile portion of the **CREATE TABLESPACE** command.

The file specification subclauses *datafile_tempfile_spec* and *redo_log_file_spec* let you specify Automatic Storage Management (ASM) files in addition to file system files.

FIRST
SEE ALSO   DENSE_RANK, LAST
FORMAT
> **first::=**

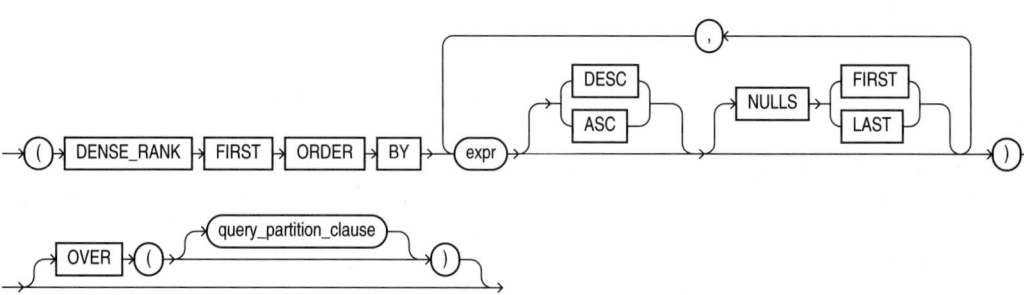

DESCRIPTION   **FIRST** is both an aggregate and analytic function that operates on a set of values from a set of rows that rank as the first with respect to a given sorting specification. *aggregate_function* is one of the standard numeric grouping functions (such as **MIN**, **MAX**, **AVG**, and **STDDEV**).

FIRST_VALUE

SEE ALSO **LAST_VALUE**
FORMAT

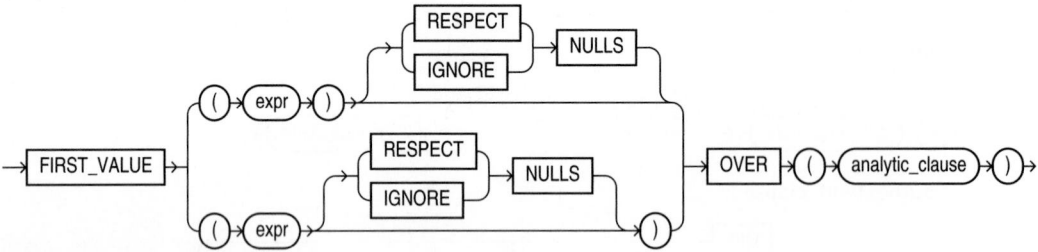

DESCRIPTION **FIRST_VALUE** is an analytic function. It returns the first value in an ordered set of values. If the first value in the set is **NULL**, then **FIRST_VALUE** returns **NULL** unless you specify **IGNORE NULLS**.

FLASHBACK DATABASE

SEE ALSO **FLASHBACK TABLE**, Chapter 30
FORMAT
  flashback_database::=

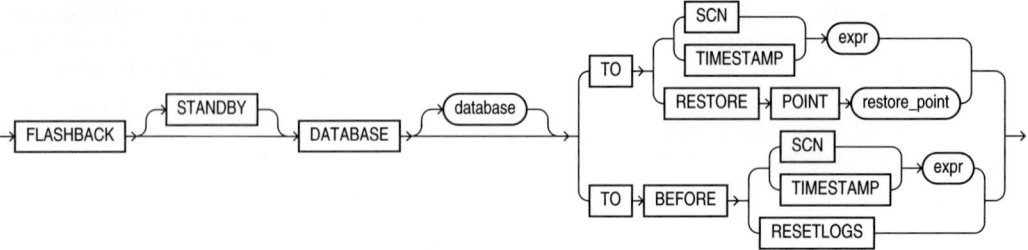

DESCRIPTION **FLASHBACK DATABASE** returns the database to a past time or system change number (SCN). This command provides a fast alternative to performing incomplete database recovery. Following a **FLASHBACK DATABASE** operation, in order to have write access to the flashed-back database, you must reopen it with an **ALTER DATABASE OPEN RESETLOGS** command.

NOTE
*The database must have been put in FLASHBACK mode with an **ALTER DATABASE FLASHBACK ON** command. The database must be mounted in EXCLUSIVE mode but not open.*

You can determine how far back you can flash back the database by querying the V$FLASHBACK_DATABASE_LOG view. The amount of flashback data retained in the database is controlled by the DB_FLASHBACK_RETENTION_TARGET initialization parameter and the size of the flash recovery area.
EXAMPLE

```
startup mount exclusive;
alter database flashback on;
alter database open;
```

With the database open for over an hour, flash it back:

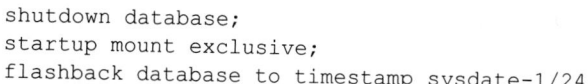

```
shutdown database;
startup mount exclusive;
flashback database to timestamp sysdate-1/24;
```

FLASHBACK TABLE

SEE ALSO   FLASHBACK DATABASE, Chapter 30
FORMAT
    flashback_table::=

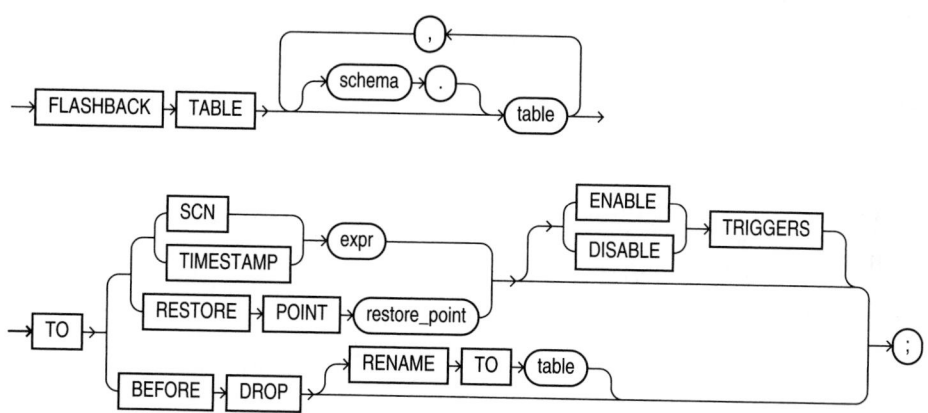

DESCRIPTION   FLASHBACK TABLE restores an earlier state of a table in the event of human or application error. Oracle cannot restore a table to an earlier state across any DDL operations that change the structure of the table.

NOTE
The database must be using Automatic Undo Management for
FLASHBACK TABLE *to work. The ability to flash back to old data is limited by the amount of undo retained in the undo tablespace and the UNDO_ RETENTION initialization parameter setting.*

You cannot roll back a **FLASHBACK TABLE** statement. However, you can issue another **FLASHBACK TABLE** statement and specify a time just prior to the current time.

NOTE
Record the current SCN before you issue a **FLASHBACK TABLE** *command.*

You must have either the FLASHBACK object privilege on the table or the FLASHBACK ANY TABLE system privilege. You must also have SELECT, INSERT, DELETE, and ALTER object privileges on the table. Row movement must be enabled for all tables in the flashback list. To flash back a table to before a **DROP TABLE** operation, you only need the privileges necessary to drop the table.

During a **FLASHBACK TABLE** operation, Oracle acquires exclusive DML locks on all tables specified. The command is executed in a single transaction across all tables; if any of them fails, then the entire statement fails.

NOTE
*FLASHBACK TABLE TO SCN or **TO TIMESTAMP** does not preserve ROWIDs. **FLASHBACK TABLE TO BEFORE DROP** does not recover referential constraints.*

When a table is flashed back, its statistics are not flashed back. Indexes that exist on the table are reverted and reflect the state of the table at the flashback point. Indexes dropped since the flashback point are not restored. Indexes created since the flashback point continue to exist and will be updated to reflect the older data.

To see the contents of your recycle bin, query USER_RECYCLEBIN.

EXAMPLE

```
flashback table emp to before drop;
```

FLOOR

SEE ALSO   **CEIL**, NUMBER FUNCTIONS, Chapter 9
FORMAT

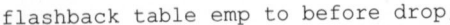

DESCRIPTION   **FLOOR** is the largest integer smaller than or equal to *value*.
EXAMPLE

```
FLOOR(2)    =   2
FLOOR(-2.3) = -3
```

FOR

See LOOP and CURSOR FOR LOOP.

FORMAT

See **BTITLE**, **COLUMN**, DATE FORMATS, **TO_CHAR**, **TO_DATE**, **TTITLE**.

FROM

SEE ALSO   **DELETE**, **SELECT**, Chapter 5
FORMAT

```
DELETE FROM [user.]table[@link] [alias]
WHERE condition

SELECT... FROM [user.]table[@link] [, [user.]table[@link] ]...
```

DESCRIPTION   *table* is the name of the table used by **DELETE** or **SELECT**. *link* is the link to a remote database. Both **DELETE** and **SELECT** commands require a **FROM** clause to define the tables from which rows will be deleted or selected. If the table is owned by another user, its name must be prefixed by the owner's username.

If the table is remote, a database link has to be defined. *@link* specifies the link. If *link* is entered but *user* is not, the query seeks a table owned by the user on the remote database. The *condition* may include a correlated query and use the *alias* for correlation.

FROM_TZ
SEE ALSO TIMESTAMP WITH TIME ZONE
FORMAT

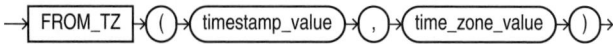

DESCRIPTION **FROM_TZ** converts a timestamp value at a time zone to a TIMESTAMP WITH TIME ZONE value. *time_zone_value* is a character string in the format 'TZH:TZM' or a character expression that returns a string in TZR with optional TZD format.

GET (SQL*Plus)
SEE ALSO **EDIT**, **SAVE**
FORMAT

```
GET file[.ext] [LIS[T] | NOL[IST]]
```

DESCRIPTION **GET** loads a host system file named *file* into the current buffer (whether the SQL buffer or a named buffer). If the file type is not included, **GET** assumes a file type of SQL. **LIST** makes SQL*Plus list the lines being loaded into the buffer. This is the default. **NOLIST** gets the file without listing its contents. If you do not specify a filename extension, .sql is the default value. To change the default filename extension, use the **SET SUFFIX** command; *see* **SET**.
EXAMPLE This **EXAMPLE** gets a file called work.sql:

```
get work
```

GOTO
SEE ALSO BLOCK STRUCTURE, Chapter 34
FORMAT

```
GOTO label;
```

DESCRIPTION **GOTO** transfers control to a section of code preceded by the named *label*. Such a label can be used to precede any legitimate statement within an execution block or within an EXCEPTION section. There are certain restrictions:

- A **GOTO** cannot transfer control to a block enclosed in the current block, or inside of a **FOR** loop or an **IF** statement.

- A **GOTO** cannot transfer to a label outside of its own block unless it is to a block that encloses its block.

EXAMPLE Here's an informal loop built from a GOTO that, without actually knowing ahead of time what the top number will be, INSERTs a geometric progression from 1 to about 10,000 into a table:

```
DECLARE
  ...
BEGIN
   x := 0;
   y := 1;
<<alpha>\>
   x := x + 1;
   y := x*y;
   insert ...
```

```
if y > 10000
    then goto beta;
goto alpha;
<<beta>\>
    exit;
```

GRANT

SEE ALSO   ALTER USER, **CREATE USER**, PRIVILEGE, **REVOKE**, ROLE, Chapter 19
FORMAT
grant::=

grant_system_privileges::=

grant_object_privileges::=

on_object_clause::=

grantee_clause::=

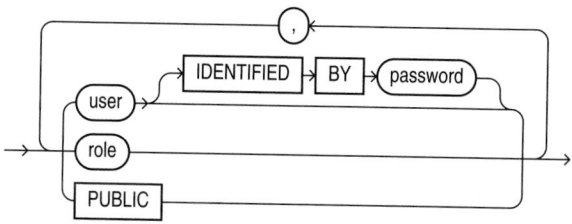

DESCRIPTION   The first form of **GRANT** extends one or more system privileges to users and roles. A system privilege is an authorization to perform one of the various data definition or control commands, such as **ALTER SYSTEM**, **CREATE ROLE**, or **GRANT** itself. *See* PRIVILEGE for details of these privileges. A user is created by **CREATE USER** and is then granted system privileges to enable logging into the database and other operations. A user without grants is unable to do anything at all in Oracle. A *role* is a collection of privileges created by **CREATE ROLE**. As with a user, a role has no privileges when created, but gets them through one or more **GRANT**s. One can grant one role to another role to create a nested network of roles, which gives the database administrator a great deal of flexibility in managing system security.

The **WITH ADMIN OPTION** lets the granted user or role (the grantee) grant the system privilege or role to other grantees. The grantee can also alter or drop a role granted **WITH ADMIN OPTION**.

The second form of the **GRANT** command grants *object privileges*, privileges that affect specific kinds of objects in Oracle databases, to any user or role. *object* can be a table, view, sequence, procedure, function, package, materialized view, or a synonym for one of these objects. **GRANT**s on a synonym actually become grants on the underlying object that the synonym references. *See* PRIVILEGE for a complete list of object privileges and a discussion of which can be granted for the various objects.

If you are granting INSERT, REFERENCES, or UPDATE privileges on a table or view, **GRANT** can also specify a list of columns of the table or view to which the **GRANT** applies. The **GRANT** applies only to those columns. If **GRANT** has no list of columns, the **GRANT** applies to all columns in the table or view.

PUBLIC grants the privileges to all users present and future.

The **WITH GRANT OPTION** passes along the right to grant the granted privileges to another user or role.

GREATEST

SEE ALSO   **LEAST**, LIST FUNCTIONS, **MAX**, Chapters 9 and 10
FORMAT

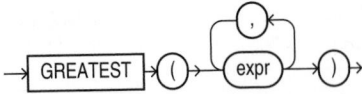

DESCRIPTION   **GREATEST** chooses the greatest of a list of values. These can be columns, literals, or expressions, and CHAR, VARCHAR2, NUMBER, or DATE datatypes. A number with a larger value is considered greater than a number with a smaller value. All negative numbers are less than all positive numbers. Thus, –10 is less than 10; –100 is less than –10. A later date is considered greater than an earlier date.

Character strings are compared position by position, starting at the leftmost end of the string, up to the first character that is different. Whichever string has the greater character in that position is considered the greater string. One character is considered greater than another if it appears after the other in the computer's collation sequence. Usually this means that a *B* is greater than an *A*, but the value of *A* compared to *a*, or compared to the number 1, will differ by computer.

If two strings are identical through to the end of the shorter one, the longer string is considered greater. If two strings are identical and the same length, they are considered equal. In SQL, it is important that literal numbers be typed without enclosing single quotes, as '10' is considered less than '6' because the quotes cause these to be regarded as character strings rather than numbers, and the '6' is seen as greater than the 1 in the first position of '10'.

Unlike many other Oracle functions and logical operators, the **GREATEST** and **LEAST** functions do not evaluate literal strings that are in date format as dates. For **LEAST** and **GREATEST** to work properly, the **TO_DATE** function must be applied to the literal strings.

GROUP BY

SEE ALSO   **CUBE**, **HAVING**, **ORDER BY**, **ROLLUP**, **WHERE**, Chapter 12
FORMAT

```
SELECT expression [,expression]...
GROUP BY expression [,expression]...
HAVING condition
    ...
```

DESCRIPTION   **GROUP BY** causes a **SELECT** to produce one summary row for all selected rows that have identical values in one or more specified columns or expressions. Each expression in the **SELECT** clause must be one of these things:

- A constant
- A function without parameters (SysDate, User)
- A group function such as **SUM**, **AVG**, **MIN**, **MAX**, or **COUNT**
- Matched identically to an expression in the **GROUP BY** clause

Columns referenced in the **GROUP BY** clause need not be in the **SELECT** clause, though they must be in the table.

You use **HAVING** to determine which groups the **GROUP BY** is to include. A **WHERE** clause, on the other hand, determines which rows are to be included in groups.

GROUP BY and **HAVING** follow **WHERE**, **CONNECT BY**, and **START WITH**. The **ORDER BY** clause is executed after the **WHERE**, **GROUP BY**, and **HAVING** clauses (which execute in that order). It can employ group functions or columns from the **GROUP BY** clause, or a combination. If it uses a group function, that function operates on the groups, and then the **ORDER BY** sorts the *results* of the function in order. If the **ORDER BY** clause uses a column from the **GROUP BY** clause, it sorts the rows that are returned based on that column. Group functions and single columns can be combined in the **ORDER BY** clause (so long as the column is in the **GROUP BY** clause).

In the **ORDER BY** clause, you can specify a group function and the column it affects even though they have nothing at all to do with the group functions or columns in the **SELECT**, **GROUP BY**, or **HAVING** clause. On the other hand, if you specify a column in the **ORDER BY** clause that is not part of a group function, it must be in the **GROUP BY** clause.

EXAMPLE

```
select title, count(*)
from bookshelf_author
group by title
having count(*) > 1;
```

GROUP_ID

SEE ALSO   AGGREGATE FUNCTIONS, **GROUP BY**, **GROUPING_ID**, Chapter 12
FORMAT

DESCRIPTION   **GROUP_ID** distinguishes duplicate groups resulting from a **GROUP BY** specification.

GROUPING

SEE ALSO   **CUBE**, **ROLLUP**
FORMAT

DESCRIPTION   **GROUPING** is a function used in conjunction with the **ROLLUP** and **CUBE** functions to detect **NULL**s.

GROUPING_ID

SEE ALSO   **ROLLUP**, **CUBE**, and Chapter 12
FORMAT

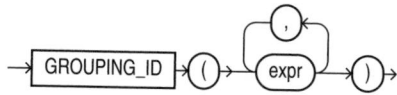

DESCRIPTION   **GROUPING_ID** returns a number corresponding to the **GROUPING** bit vector associated with a row.

HAVING

See **GROUP BY**.

HELP (SQL*Plus)

FORMAT

```
HELP | ? [topic]
```

DESCRIPTION   The **HELP** command accesses the SQL*Plus help system. **HELP INDEX** displays a list
of topics.

HEXTORAW

SEE ALSO   **RAWTOHEX**
FORMAT

DESCRIPTION   **HEXTORAW** (**HEX**adecimal **TO RAW**) changes a character string of hex numbers into
binary.

HINT

Within a query, you can specify hints that direct the cost-based optimizer in its processing of the query.
To specify a hint, use the following syntax. Immediately after the **SELECT** keyword, enter the following
string:

```
/*+
```

Next, add the hint, such as this:

```
full(bookshelf)
```

Close the hint with the following string:

```
*/
```

> *See* Chapter 46 for a description of the available hints and their impact on query processing.

HOST (SQL*Plus)

SEE ALSO $, !, @, @@, START
FORMAT

```
HO[ST] command
```

DESCRIPTION   A host is a computer on which the Oracle RDBMS is running. The **HOST** command in
SQL*Plus passes any **HOST** command back to the operating system for execution without exiting
SQL*Plus. SQL*Plus permits embedding local or PL/SQL variables in the **HOST** command string. This
doesn't work on all hardware or operating systems. **HOST** is not available within iSQL*Plus.

IF

SEE ALSO   LOOP, Chapter 32
FORMAT

```
IF condition
    THEN statement; [statement;]...
```

```
      [ELSIF condition THEN statement; [statement;]...
      [ELSIF condition THEN statement; [statement;]...]... ]
      [ELSE statement; [statement;]...]
      END IF;
```

DESCRIPTION The **IF** statement will execute one or more *statements* if *condition* evaluates to TRUE, after which the program branches to **END IF**. If the *condition* is FALSE, then any number of a series of optional **ELSIF** conditions are tested. If any statement is TRUE, the associated *statements* (following **THEN**) are executed, and then the program branches to **END IF**. If none of the **ELSIF** conditions is TRUE (and the original **IF** condition was not TRUE), then the statements following the optional **ELSE** are executed. Note that the final **ELSE** does not have a condition.

EXAMPLE

```
declare
    pi      constant NUMBER(9,7) := 3.1415927;
    area    NUMBER(14,2);
    cursor rad_cursor is
    select * from radius_vals;
    rad_val rad_cursor%ROWTYPE;
begin
    open rad_cursor;
    fetch rad_cursor into rad_val;
    area := pi*power(rad_val.radius,2);
      if  area > 30
        then
          insert into areas values (rad_val.radius, area);
      end if;
    close rad_cursor;
end;
```

IN

SEE ALSO ALL, ANY, LOGICAL OPERATORS, **WHERE**, Chapter 5

FORMAT

```
WHERE expression IN ({expression1[,expression2]... | select...})
```

DESCRIPTION **IN** is equivalent to **=ANY**. In the first option, **IN** means the expression is equal to any member of the following list of literals or expressions. In the second option, it means the expression is equal to any value in any row selected from the subquery. The two are logically equivalent, with the first giving a list made of expressions and the second building a list from a query.

INDEX

Index is a general term for an Oracle/SQL feature used primarily to speed execution and impose uniqueness on certain data. In general, indexes provide a faster access method to table data than doing a full table scan. An index has an entry for each value found in the table's indexed field(s) (except those with a **NULL** value) and pointer(s) to the row(s) having that value.

INDEX-ORGANIZED TABLE

An index-organized table keeps its data sorted according to the primary key column values for the table. An index-organized table allows you to store the entire table's data in an index. A normal index stores only the indexed columns in the index; an index-organized table stores all of the table's columns in the index.

To create an index-organized table, use the **ORGANIZATION INDEX** clause of the **CREATE TABLE** command, as shown in the following example:

```
create table trouble (
city           varchar2(13),
sample_date    date,
noon           number(4,1),
midnight       number(4,1),
precipitation number,
constraint trouble_pk primary key (city, sample_date))
organization index;
```

To create TROUBLE as an index-organized table, you must create a PRIMARY KEY constraint on it.

In general, index-organized tables are appropriate for associative tables in many-to-many relationships. Ideally, an index-organized table has few (or no) columns that are not part of its primary key.

See Chapter 17 and **CREATE TABLE**.

INDICATOR VARIABLE

SEE ALSO **:** (colon, the host variable prefix), *Programmer's Guide to the Oracle Precompilers*
FORMAT

```
:name [INDICATOR] :indicator
```

DESCRIPTION An indicator variable—used when both name and indicator are host language variable names—is a data field whose value indicates whether a host variable should be regarded as **NULL**. (The **INDICATOR** keyword is for readability and has no effect.)

name may be any legitimate host variable data name used in the host program and included in the precompiler's DECLARE section. *indicator* is defined in the precompiler's DECLARE section as a two-byte integer.

Few procedural languages directly support the idea of a variable with a **NULL** or unknown value, although Oracle and SQL do so easily. To extend languages for which Oracle has developed precompilers to support the **NULL** concept, an indicator variable is associated with the host variable, almost like a flag, to indicate whether it is **NULL**. The host variable and its indicator variable may be referenced and set separately in the host language code, but are always concatenated in SQL or PL/SQL.

EXAMPLE

```
BEGIN
    select Title, Author_Name into :Title, :Author_Name:Author_Name_Ind
    from BOOKSHELF_AUTHOR;

    IF :Author_Name:Author_Name_Ind IS NULL
        THEN :Author_Name:Author_Name_Ind := 'No Auth'
    END IF;
END;
```

Note that both the test to see whether the variable is **NULL** and, if it is, the assignment of 'No Auth' to it are done with the concatenated variable name. PL/SQL knows enough to check the indicator in the first case and set the variable value in the second case. The two variables together are treated just like a single Oracle column. These important points must be noted:

■ Within any single PL/SQL block, a host variable must either always stand alone or always be concatenated with its indicator variable.

■ An indicator variable cannot be referenced alone within PL/SQL, although it can be in the host program.

When setting host variables within the host program, but outside of PL/SQL, note these points:

■ Setting the indicator variable equal to –1 forces the concatenated variable to be regarded within PL/SQL as **NULL**, both in logic tests and for **INSERT**s or **UPDATE**s.

■ Setting the indicator variable greater than or equal to 0 forces the concatenated variable to be regarded as equal to the value in the host variable and **NOT NULL**.

■ PL/SQL tests the value of all indicator variables on entering a block and sets them on exiting the block.

When loading concatenated host variables within PL/SQL, via a SQL statement with an **INTO** clause, the following rules apply when checking the indicator variable within the host program, but outside of PL/SQL:

■ The indicator variable is equal to –1 if the value loaded from the database is **NULL**. The value of the host variable is uncertain and should be treated as such.

■ The indicator variable is equal to 0 if the value from the database is loaded completely and correctly into the host variable.

■ The indicator variable is greater than 0 and equal to the actual length of the data in the database column if only a portion of it could fit in the host variable. The host variable will contain a truncated version of what was in the database column.

init.ora

The **init.ora** file is a database system parameter file (in plaintext format) that contains settings and filenames used when a system is started using the **CREATE DATABASE**, **STARTUP**, or **SHUTDOWN** command. You can either use an **init.ora** file or create a system parameter file via the **CREATE SPFILE** command. *See* **CREATE PFILE** and **CREATE SPFILE**.

INITCAP

SEE ALSO CHARACTER FUNCTIONS, **LOWER**, **UPPER**, Chapter 7
FORMAT

→ INITCAP → (→ char →) →

DESCRIPTION **INITCAP** (**INIT**ial **CAP**ital) changes the first letter of a word or series of words into uppercase. It also notes the presence of symbols and will **INITCAP** any letter that follows a space or a symbol, such as a comma, period, colon, semicolon, !, @, #, $, and so on.
EXAMPLE

```
initcap('this.is,an-example of!how@initcap#works')
```

produces this:

```
This.Is,An-Example Of!How@Initcap#Works
```

INPUT (SQL*Plus)

SEE ALSO   APPEND, CHANGE, DEL, EDIT, Chapter 6
FORMAT

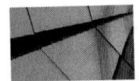

```
I[NPUT] [text]
```

DESCRIPTION   **INPUT** adds a new line of text after the current line in the current buffer. Using **INPUT** by itself allows multiple lines to be keyed in after the current line, which stops when the system encounters ENTER with nothing else on the line. The space between **INPUT** and *text* will not be added to the line but any additional spaces will be. *See* **DEL** for a discussion of the current line. **INPUT** is not available in iSQL*Plus.

INSERT (Form 1—Embedded SQL)

SEE ALSO   **EXECUTE**, CURSOR FOR LOOP, *Programmer's Guide to the Oracle Precompilers*
FORMAT

```
EXEC SQL [AT { db_name | :host_variable }]
  [FOR { :host_integer | integer }]
  INSERT INTO
  [ [schema.] { table | view }
    [ @db_link | PARTITION (part_name) ] ]
  [(column) [, (column)]...]
  { VALUES (expr [, expr]...) | subquery }
  [{ RETURN | RETURNING } expr [, expr]... INTO
  :host_variable [[INDICATOR] :ind_variable]
  [, :host_variable [[INDICATOR] :ind_variable]]...]
```

DESCRIPTION   *db_name* is a database other than the user's default, and *host_variable* contains the name of the database. *:host_integer* is a host value that limits the number of times the **INSERT** will be processed (*see* CURSOR FOR LOOP). *table* is any existing table, view, or synonym, and *db_link* is the name of a remote database where the table is stored. (*See* the **INSERT** Form 3 definition for a discussion of the **VALUES** clause, columns, and query.) *expression* here can be an expression or a host variable in the form *:variable[:indicator]*.

> **NOTE**
> *See* the Programmer's Guide to the Oracle Precompilers *for a full list of all commands. This reference does not contain all of the possible precompiler commands.*

INSERT (Form 2—PL/SQL)

SEE ALSO   SQL CURSOR, Chapter 32
FORMAT

```
INSERT INTO [user.]table[@db_link] [(column [,column]...)]
    VALUES (expression [,expression]...) | query...);
```

DESCRIPTION   PL/SQL's use of **INSERT** is identical to its general form (Form 3 in the following section), with these exceptions:

- You may use a PL/SQL variable in an expression for the value in the VALUES list.
- Each variable is treated in the same way that a constant, with the value of the variable, would be treated.
- If you use the *query...* version of the **INSERT**, you cannot use the **INTO** clause of the **SELECT**.

INSERT (Form 3—SQL Command)

SEE ALSO   **CREATE TABLE**, Chapters 5, 15, 38, and 39

FORMAT

insert::=

single_table_insert::=

insert_into_clause::=

values_clause::=

returning_clause::=

multi_table_insert::=

conditional_insert_clause::=

DML_table_expression_clause::=

partition_extension_clause::=

subquery_restriction_clause::=

table_collection_expression::=

error_logging_clause::=

DESCRIPTION INSERT adds one or more new rows to the table or view. The optional *schema* must be a user whose table you have been granted insert authority to. *table* is the table into which rows are to be inserted. If a list of columns is given, an expression (SQL expression) must be matched for each of those columns. Any columns not in the list receive the value **NULL**, and none of them can be defined **NOT NULL** or the **INSERT** will fail. If a list of columns is not given, values must be given for all columns in the table.

  INSERT with a subquery adds as many rows as the query returns, with each query column being matched, position for position, with columns in the column list. If no column list is given, the tables must have the same number and type of columns. The USER_TAB_COLUMNS data dictionary view shows these, as does **DESCRIBE** in SQL*Plus.

EXAMPLE The following inserts a row into the COMFORT table:

```
insert into comfort values ('Keene','23-SEP-13',99.8,82.6,NULL);
```

  The following inserts CITY, SAMPLE_DATE (both **NOT NULL** columns), and PRECIPITATION columns into COMFORT:

```
insert into comfort (city, sample_date, precipitation) values
                    ('Keene','22-DEC-13',3.9);
```

  To copy only the data for the city of Keene into a new table named NEW_HAMPSHIRE, use this:

```
insert into new_hampshire
select * from comfort
where city = 'Keene';
```

INSERTCHILDXML
FORMAT

→ INSERTCHILDXML →

DESCRIPTION INSERTCHILDXML inserts a user-supplied value into the target XML at the node indicated by the XPath expression.

INSERTCHILDXMLAFTER
FORMAT

→ INSERTCHILDXMLAFTER →

DESCRIPTION INSERTCHILDXMLAFTER inserts a user-supplied value into the target XML *after* the node indicated by the XPath expression.

INSERTCHILDXMLBEFORE
FORMAT

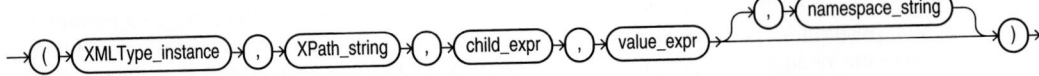

DESCRIPTION   INSERTCHILDXMLBEFORE inserts a user-supplied value into the target XML *before* the node indicated by the XPath expression.

INSERTXMLAFTER
FORMAT

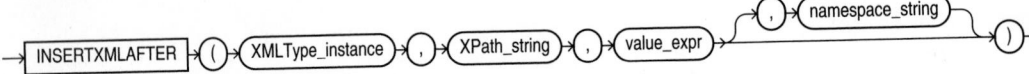

DESCRIPTION   INSERTXMLAFTER inserts a user-supplied value into the target XML *after* the node indicated by the XPath expression.

INSERTXMLBEFORE
FORMAT

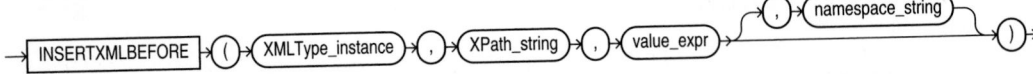

DESCRIPTION   INSERTXMLBEFORE inserts a user-supplied value into the target XML *before* the node indicated by the XPath expression.

INSTR
SEE ALSO   CHARACTER FUNCTIONS, **SUBSTR**, Chapter 7
FORMAT

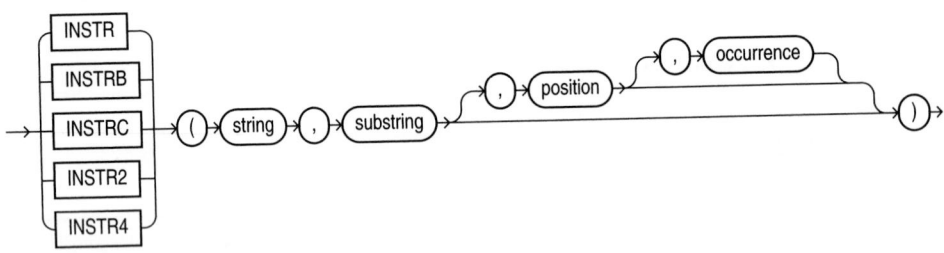

DESCRIPTION   INSTR finds the location of a *set* of characters in a *string*, starting at position *start* in the string, and looking for the first, second, third, and so on, *occurrence* of the *set*. This function also works with NUMBER and DATE datatypes. *start* also can be negative, meaning the search begins with the characters at the end of the string and searches backward.

EXAMPLE
To find the third occurrence of "Pi" in this string, use this:

```
instr('Peter Piper Picked a Peck of Pickled Peppers','Pi',1,3)
```

The result of this function is 30, the location of the third occurrence of "Pi."

INTEGRITY CONSTRAINT

An integrity constraint is a rule that restricts the range of valid values for a column. It is placed on a column when the table is created. For the syntax, see CONSTRAINTS.

If you do not name a constraint, Oracle assigns a name in the form SYS_C*n*, where *n* is an integer. An Oracle-assigned name will usually change during an import, whereas a user-assigned name will not change.

NULL permits **NULL** values. **NOT NULL** specifies that every row must have a non-**NULL** value for this column.

UNIQUE forces column values to be unique. There can be only one PRIMARY KEY constraint on a table. If a column is UNIQUE, it cannot also be declared the PRIMARY KEY (PRIMARY KEY also enforces uniqueness). An index enforces the UNIQUE or PRIMARY KEY, and the **USING INDEX** clause and its options specify the storage characteristics of that index. *See* **CREATE INDEX** for more information on the options.

REFERENCES identifies this column as a foreign key from [*user.*]*table* [*(column)*]. Omitting *column* implies that the name in the *user.table* is the same as the name in this table. Note that when REFERENCES is used in a *table_constraint* (described shortly), it must be preceded by FOREIGN KEY. This is not used here, as only this column is referenced; *table_constraint* can reference several columns for FOREIGN KEY. **ON DELETE CASCADE** instructs Oracle to maintain referential integrity automatically by removing foreign key rows in the dependent tables if you remove the primary key row in this table.

CHECK assures that the value for this column passes a condition such as this:

```
amount number(12,2) check (amount >= 0)
```

condition may be any valid expression that tests TRUE or FALSE. It can contain functions, any columns from this table, and literals.

The **EXCEPTIONS INTO** clause specifies a table into which Oracle puts information about rows that violate an enabled integrity constraint. This table must be local.

The **DISABLE** option lets you disable the integrity constraint when you create it. When the constraint is disabled, Oracle does not automatically enforce it. You can later enable the constraint with the **ENABLE** clause in **ALTER TABLE**.

You can also create constraints at the table level. Table constraints are identical to column constraints except that a single constraint can reference multiple columns—for example, in declaring a set of three columns as a primary or foreign key.

INTERSECT

SEE ALSO **MINUS**, QUERY OPERATORS, **UNION**, Chapter 13
FORMAT

```
select...
INTERSECT
select...
```

DESCRIPTION **INTERSECT** combines two queries and returns only those rows from the first **SELECT** statement that are identical to at least one row from the second **SELECT** statement. The number of columns and datatypes must be identical between **SELECT** statements, although the names of the columns do not need to be. The data, however, must be identical in the rows produced for the **INTERSECT**ion to pass them.

INTERVAL DAY TO SECOND

FORMAT

```
INTERVAL DAY [(day_precision)] TO SECOND [(second_precision)]
```

DESCRIPTION The INTERVAL DAY TO SECOND datatype stores the period of time in days, hours, minutes, and seconds. You can specify a *day_precision* as the number of digits in the DAY datetime field (default is 2) and a *second_precision* as the number of digits in the fractional part of the Seconds field (default is 6).

INTERVAL YEAR TO MONTH

FORMAT

```
INTERVAL YEAR [(year_precision)] TO MONTH
```

DESCRIPTION The INTERVAL YEAR TO MONTH datatype stores the period of time in years and months, where *precision* is the number of digits in the YEAR datetime field (default is 2).

IS A SET

SEE ALSO **IS EMPTY**, Chapter 39
FORMAT

DESCRIPTION Use an **IS A SET** condition to test whether a specified nested table is composed of unique elements. The condition returns TRUE if the nested table is a set, even if it is a nested table of length zero, and returns FALSE otherwise. It returns **NULL** if the nested table is empty.

IS ANY

SEE ALSO **SELECT**
FORMAT

```
dimension_column IS ANY
```

DESCRIPTION The **IS ANY** clause is relevant only for inter-row calculations and can be used only in the **MODEL** clause of a **SELECT** statement. Use this condition to qualify all values of a dimension column, including **NULL**. The condition always returns a Boolean value of TRUE to qualify all values of the column.

IS EMPTY

SEE ALSO **IS A SET**, Chapter 39
FORMAT

DESCRIPTION Use the **IS [NOT] EMPTY** conditions to test whether a specified nested table is empty, regardless of whether any elements of the collection are **NULL**. The condition returns a Boolean value: TRUE for an **IS EMPTY** condition if the condition is empty, TRUE for an **IS NOT EMPTY** condition if the condition is not empty. If you specify **NULL** for the nested table or array, the result is **NULL**.

IS NULL

SEE ALSO   LOGICAL OPERATORS, Chapters 5 and 9
FORMAT

```
WHERE column IS [NOT] NULL
```

DESCRIPTION   **IS NULL** tests a column (or an expression) for the absence of any data. A **NULL** test is distinctly different from a test for equality because **NULL** means that the value is unknown or irrelevant, and it, therefore, cannot be said to be equal to anything, including another **NULL**.

IS OF TYPE

SEE ALSO   **VALUE**, Chapter 38
FORMAT
   is_of_type_condition::=

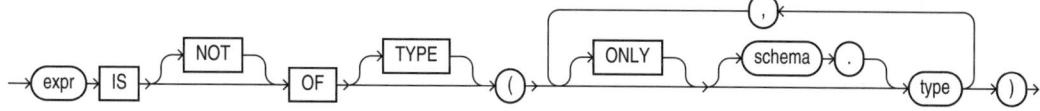

DESCRIPTION   Use the **IS OF** *type* condition to test object instances based on their specific type information. The condition evaluates to **NULL** if *expr* is **NULL**. If *expr* is not **NULL**, then the condition evaluates to TRUE (or FALSE if you specify the **NOT** keyword) under either of these circumstances:

- The most specific type of *expr* is the subtype of one of the types specified in the *type* list and you have not specified **ONLY** for the type.

- The most specific type of *expr* is explicitly specified in the *type* list.

- The *expr* frequently takes the form of the **VALUE** function with a correlation variable.

IS PRESENT

SEE ALSO   **SELECT**
FORMAT

DESCRIPTION   The **IS PRESENT** condition is relevant only for inter-row calculations and can be used only in the **MODEL** clause of a **SELECT** statement. Use this condition to test whether the cell referenced is present prior to the execution of the **MODEL** clause. The condition returns TRUE if the cell exists prior to the execution of the **MODEL** clause and returns FALSE if it does not.

ITERATION_NUMBER

SEE ALSO   **SELECT**
FORMAT

→| ITERATION_NUMBER |→

DESCRIPTION   The **ITERATION_NUMBER** function is relevant only for inter-row calculations. It can be used only in the **MODEL** clause of the **SELECT** statement and then only when ITERATE(*number*) is specified in the **MODEL RULES** clause. It returns an integer representing the completed iteration through the model rules. The **ITERATION_NUMBER** function returns 0 during the first iteration. For each subsequent iteration, the **ITERATION_NUMBER** function returns the equivalent of *iteration_number* plus one.

JOIN
SEE ALSO **SELECT**, Chapter 5
FORMAT

```
WHERE TableA.column = TableB.column
```

or

```
FROM TableA INNER JOIN TableB
    on TableA.Column = TableB.Column
```

or

```
FROM TableA INNER JOIN TableB
  using(Column)
```

or

```
FROM TableA NATURAL JOIN TableB
```

DESCRIPTION   A join combines columns and data from two or more tables (and, in rare cases, of one table with itself). The tables are all listed in the **FROM** clause of the **SELECT** statement, and the relationship between the two tables may be specified in the **WHERE** clause, usually by a simple equality, such as this:

```
where book_order.title = bookshelf.title
```

This relationship is often called an *equi-join* because it uses the equal sign in the **WHERE** clause. You could join tables using other forms of equality, such as \>=, \<, and so on, but the results are seldom meaningful. There also are cases in which one or both sides of the equal sign contain an expression, perhaps a **SUBSTR** or a combination of columns, which is used for equality with the other side. This usage is fairly common.

Joining two tables together without a join clause—either in the **FROM** clause or in the **WHERE** clause—produces a Cartesian product, which combines every row in one table with every row in the other table. An 80-row table combined with a 100-row table would produce an 8000-row result (which is usually quite meaningless).

An *outer join* is a method for intentionally retrieving selected rows from one table that don't match rows in the other table. You can use the ANSI standard outer join syntax options (CROSS JOIN, NATURAL JOIN, LEFT OUTER JOIN, RIGHT OUTER JOIN, and FULL OUTER JOIN).

LABEL (PL/SQL)
A label is a word associated with an executable statement, usually for the purpose of being the target of a **GOTO** statement.

LAG

SEE ALSO   LEAD
FORMAT

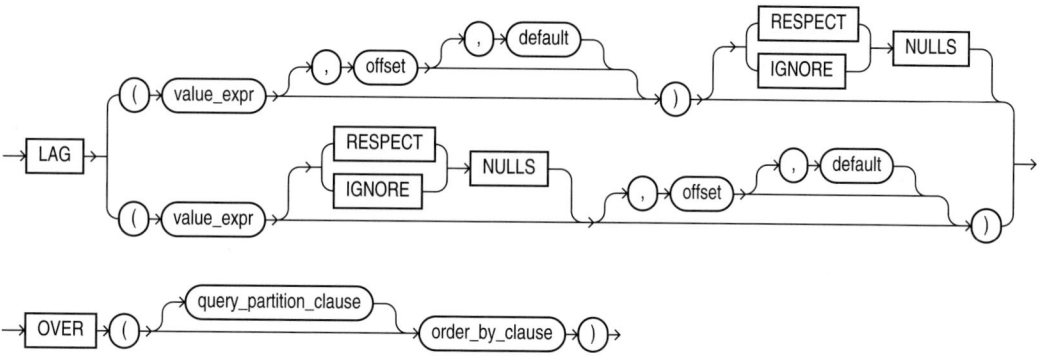

DESCRIPTION   LAG provides access to more than one row of a table at the same time without a self-join. Given a series of rows returned from a query and a position of the cursor, **LAG** provides access to a row at a given physical offset prior to that position.

LAST

SEE ALSO   DENSE_RANK, FIRST
FORMAT
  last::=

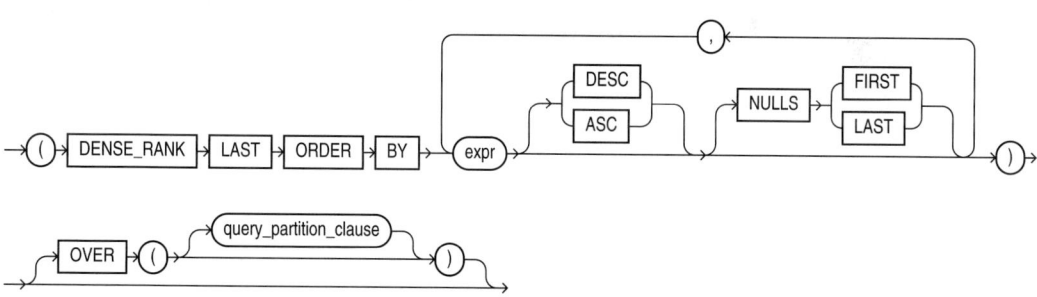

DESCRIPTION   LAST is both an aggregate and analytic function that operates on a set of values from a set of rows that rank as the last with respect to a given sorting specification. *aggregate_function* is one of the standard numeric grouping functions (such as **MIN, MAX, AVG**, and **STDDEV**).

LAST_DAY

SEE ALSO   ADD_MONTHS, DATE FUNCTIONS, **NEXT_DAY**, Chapter 10
FORMAT

DESCRIPTION   LAST_DAY gives the date of the last day of the month that *date* is in.

EXAMPLE

```
LAST_DAY ('05-NOV-08')
```

produces a result of 30-NOV-08.

LAST_VALUE
SEE ALSO   FIRST_VALUE
FORMAT

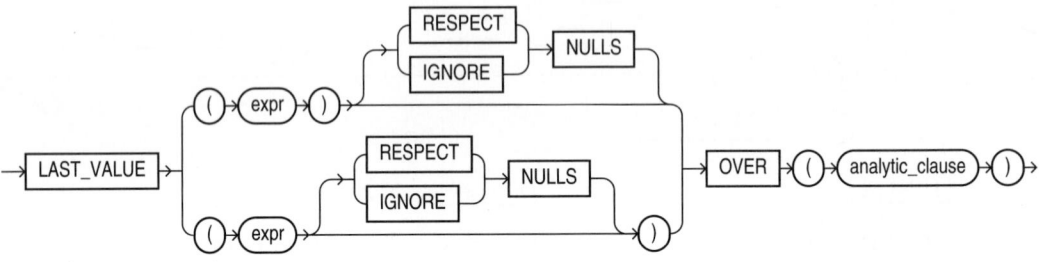

DESCRIPTION   LAST_VALUE is an analytic function. It returns the last value in an ordered set of values. If the last value in the set is **NULL**, then the function returns **NULL** unless you specify **IGNORE NULLS**.

LEAD
SEE ALSO   LAG
FORMAT

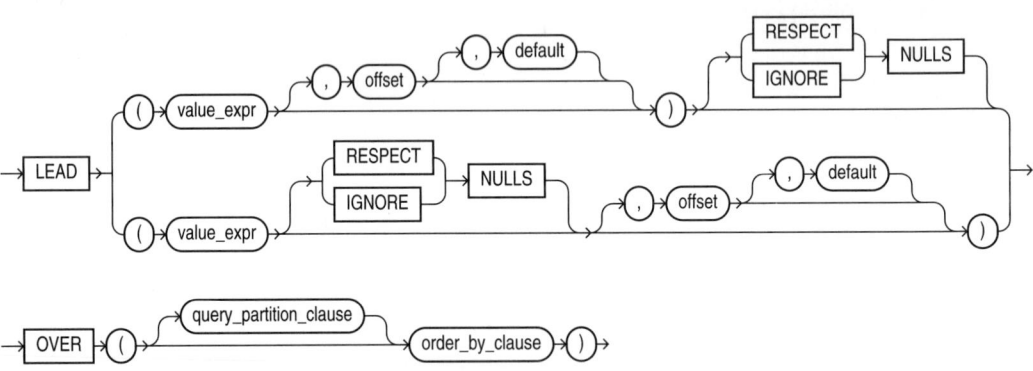

DESCRIPTION   LEAD provides access to more than one row of a table at the same time without a self-join. Given a series of rows returned from a query and the position of the cursor, **LEAD** provides access to a row at a given physical offset beyond that position.

LEAST
SEE ALSO   GREATEST, LIST FUNCTIONS, Chapter 10
FORMAT

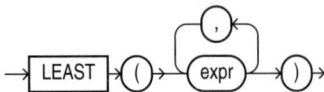

DESCRIPTION **LEAST** is the value of a list of columns, expressions, or values. Values may be VARCHAR2, CHAR, DATE, or NUMBER datatypes, although **LEAST** will not properly evaluate literal dates (such as '20-MAY-12') without the **TO_DATE** function. *See* **GREATEST** for a discussion of evaluating relative values.

LENGTH

SEE ALSO CHARACTER FUNCTIONS, **VSIZE**, Chapter 7
FORMAT

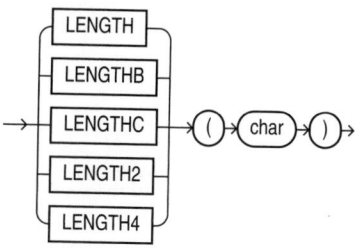

DESCRIPTION **LENGTH** tells the length of a string, number, date, or expression. The *string* can be CHAR (the returned length will include all trailing blanks), VARCHAR2, NCHAR, NVARCHAR2, CLOB, or NCLOB. There are several **LENGTH** functions, all following the same format:

- **LENGTH** calculates the length using characters as defined by the input character set.

- **LENGTHB** uses bytes instead of characters.

- **LENGTHC** uses Unicode complete characters.

- **LENGTH2** uses UCS2 code points.

- **LENGTH4** uses UCS4 code points.

LEVEL

SEE ALSO CONNECT BY, PSEUDO-COLUMNS, Chapter 14
FORMAT

```
LEVEL
```

DESCRIPTION
Level is a pseudo-column, used with **CONNECT BY**, that is equal to 1 for a root node, 2 for a child of a root, 3 for a child of a child of a root, and so on. Level tells how far down a tree you've traveled.

LIKE

SEE ALSO LOGICAL OPERATORS, Chapter 5
FORMAT
like_condition::=

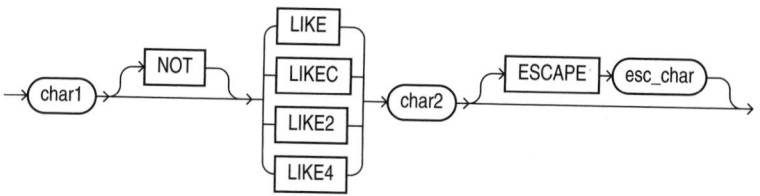

DESCRIPTION   **LIKE** performs pattern matching. An underline represents exactly one space. A percent sign represents any number of spaces or characters, including zero. If **LIKE** uses either the _ or % in the first position of a comparison (as in the following second and third examples), any index on the column is ignored.

EXAMPLES

```
feature like 'MO%'    "FEATURE begins with the letters MO."
feature like '__I%'   "FEATURE has an I in the third position."
feature like '%0%0%'  "FEATURE has at least two O's in it."
```

LIST (SQL*Plus)

SEE ALSO   **APPEND, CHANGE, EDIT, INPUT, RUN**, Chapter 6

FORMAT

```
L[IST] [n |n m|n*|n LAST|*|*n|*LAST|LAST]
```

DESCRIPTION   **LIST** lists lines of the current buffer starting at *n* and ending at *m*, both of which are integers. The end line becomes the current line of the buffer, and is flagged with an asterisk. **LIST** without *n* or *m* lists all lines. **LIST** with a single number displays just that line. The space between **LIST** and *n* is not necessary but it does help readability. **LIST n*** lists all lines from *n* to the end of the buffer. **LIST *n** lists all lines from the beginning to the specified line.

EXAMPLE   Use this to list the current SQL buffer:

```
list
```

An asterisk designates the current line. To list just the second line, use this:

```
list 2
```

This also makes 2 the current line in the current buffer.

LIST FUNCTIONS

SEE ALSO   All other functions, Chapter 10

DESCRIPTION   The following is an alphabetical list of all current list functions in the Oracle version of SQL. Each of these is listed elsewhere in this reference under its own name, with its proper **FORMAT** and use.

This gives the first non-**NULL** value in the set:

```
COALESCE(value1, value2, ...)
```

This gives the greatest value of a list:

```
GREATEST(value1, value2, ...)
```

This gives the least value of a list:

```
LEAST(value1, value2, ...)
```

LN

SEE ALSO   NUMBER FUNCTIONS, Chapter 9

FORMAT

DESCRIPTION   **LN** is the "natural," or base *e*, logarithm of a *number*. If *number* is BINARY_FLOAT, then the function returns BINARY_DOUBLE.

LNNVL

SEE ALSO   **SELECT**

FORMAT

DESCRIPTION   **LNNVL** provides a way to evaluate a condition when one or both operands of the condition may be **NULL**. The function can be used only in the **WHERE** clause of a query. It takes as an argument a condition and returns TRUE if the condition is FALSE or UNKNOWN and returns FALSE if the condition is TRUE. **LNNVL** can be used anywhere a scalar expression can appear, even in contexts where the **IS [NOT] NULL**, **AND**, or **OR** conditions are not valid but would otherwise be required to account for potential NULLs. **LNNVL** may show up in explain plans when Oracle internally requires **NOT IN** conditions as **NOT EXISTS** conditions.

EXAMPLES   If you want to retrieve all rows for which a column is greater than a given value, the standard **FORMAT** is

```
where column > value
```

To also return the rows for which *column* is **NULL**, use **LNNVL**:

```
where LNNVL(column > value)
```

LOB

A LOB is a large object. Oracle supports several large object datatypes, including BLOBs (binary large objects), CLOBs (character large objects), and BFILEs (binary files, stored outside the database). *See* Chapter 40 and the **LOB** clause of **CREATE TABLE**.

LOCALTIMESTAMP

SEE ALSO   DATE FUNCTIONS, Chapter 10

FORMAT

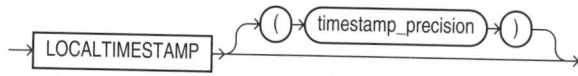

DESCRIPTION   **LOCALTIMESTAMP** returns the current date and time in the session time zone as a value of the TIMESTAMP datatype.

EXAMPLE

```
select localtimestamp from dual;
```

LOCK TABLE

SEE ALSO   COMMIT, DELETE, INSERT, ROLLBACK, SAVEPOINT, UPDATE

FORMAT
lock_table::=

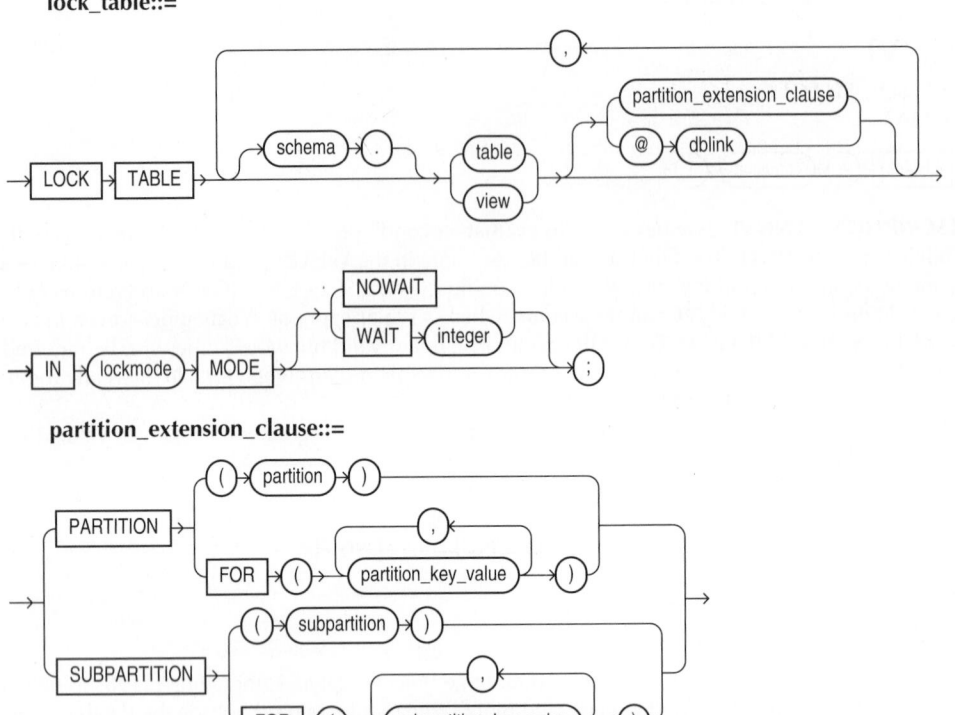

partition_extension_clause::=

DESCRIPTION   **LOCK TABLE** locks a table in one of several specified modes, allowing it to be shared, but without loss of data integrity. Using **LOCK TABLE** allows you to give other users continued but restricted access to the table. Regardless of which option you choose, the table will remain in that lock mode until you **COMMIT** or **ROLLBACK** your transactions.

Lock modes include ROW SHARE, ROW EXCLUSIVE, SHARE UPDATE, SHARE, SHARE ROW EXCLUSIVE, and EXCLUSIVE.

EXCLUSIVE locks permit users to query the locked table but not to do anything else. No other user may lock the table. SHARE locks permit concurrent queries but no updates to the locked table.

With a ROW SHARE or SHARE UPDATE lock, no user can lock the whole table for exclusive access, allowing concurrent access for all users to the table. The two types of lock are synonymous, and SHARE UPDATE exists for compatibility with previous versions of Oracle.

ROW EXCLUSIVE locks are similar to ROW SHARE but they prohibit shared locking, so only one user may access the table at a time.

If a **LOCK TABLE** command cannot be completed (usually because someone else has executed a prior and competing **LOCK TABLE** of some sort), then your **LOCK TABLE** will wait until it can complete. If you wish to avoid this, and simply have control returned to you, use the **NOWAIT** option. Note that you can lock specific partitions and subpartitions.

As of Oracle Database 11g, you can specify the maximum number of seconds the statement should wait to obtain a DML lock on the table.

LOG

SEE ALSO   NUMBER FUNCTIONS, Chapter 9
FORMAT

DESCRIPTION   **LOG** gives the logarithm of a *number* for a specified *base*.
EXAMPLE

```
LOG(EXP(1),3) = 1.098612   -- log(e) of 3
LOG(10,100)   = 2          -- log(10) of 100
```

LOGICAL OPERATORS

SEE ALSO   PRECEDENCE
FORMAT   The following lists all current logical operators in the Oracle version of SQL. Most of these are listed elsewhere in this reference under their own names with their proper **FORMAT** and use. All of these operators work with columns or literals.

Logical Operators That Test a Single Value

```
=    expression    is equal to expression
>    expression    is greater than expression
>=   expression    is greater than or equal to expression
<    expression    is less than expression
<=   expression    is less than or equal to expression
!=   expression    is not equal to expression
^=   expression    is not equal to expression
<>   expression    is not equal to expression

EXISTS (query)
NOT EXISTS (query)

LIKE expression
NOT LIKE expression

expression IS NULL
expression IS NOT NULL
```

Logical Operators That Test More Than a Single Value

```
ANY (expression [,expression]... | query)
ALL (expression [,expression]... | query)
```

ANY and **ALL** require an equality operator as a prefix, such as >**ANY**, =**ALL**, and so on.

```
IN (expression [,expression]... | query)
NOT IN (expression [,expression]... | query)

BETWEEN expression AND expression
NOT BETWEEN expression AND expression
```

Other Logical Operators

```
+           Addition
-           Subtraction
*           Multiplication
/           Division
**          Exponentiation
||          Concatenation
()          Overrides normal precedence rules, or encloses a
            subquery
NOT         Reverses logical expression
AND         Combines logical expressions
OR          Combines logical expressions
UNION       Combines results of queries
UNION ALL   Combines results of queries without eliminating duplicates
INTERSECT   Combines results of queries
MINUS       Combines results of queries
```

LONG DATATYPE

See DATATYPES.

LONG RAW DATATYPE

A LONG RAW column contains raw binary data, but is otherwise the same as a LONG column. Values entered into LONG RAW columns must be in hex notation.

LOOP

You can use loops to process multiple records within a single PL/SQL block. PL/SQL supports three types of loops:

Loop Type	Description
Simple loops	A loop that keeps repeating until an **EXIT** or **EXIT WHEN** statement is reached within the loop
FOR loops	A loop that repeats a specified number of times
WHILE loops	A loop that repeats until a condition is met

You can use loops to process multiple records from a cursor. The most common cursor loop is a Cursor FOR Loop. *See* CURSOR FOR LOOP and Chapter 32 for details on using loops for both simple and cursor-based processing logic.

LOWER

SEE ALSO   CHARACTER FUNCTIONS, **INITCAP, UPPER**, Chapter 7
FORMAT

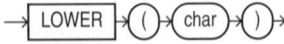

DESCRIPTION   **LOWER** converts every letter in a string to lowercase.
EXAMPLE

```
lower('PenINsulA') returns 'peninsula'
```

LPAD

SEE ALSO   CHARACTER FUNCTIONS, **LTRIM, RPAD, RTRIM**, Chapter 7
FORMAT

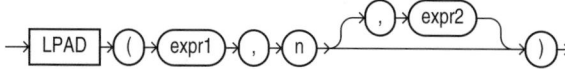

DESCRIPTION   Left **PAD** makes a *string* a certain *length* by adding a certain *set* of characters to the left of the string. If *set* is not specified, the default pad character is a space.
EXAMPLE

```
lpad('>',11,'- ')
```

produces

```
- - - - - >
```

LTRIM

SEE ALSO   CHARACTER FUNCTIONS, **LPAD, RPAD, RTRIM**, Chapter 7
FORMAT

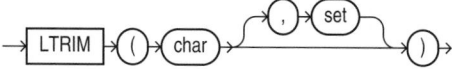

DESCRIPTION   Left **TRIM** trims all the occurrences of any one of a *set* of characters off of the left side of a *string*.
EXAMPLE

```
ltrim('NANCY','AN')
```

produces this:

```
CY
```

MAKE_REF

SEE ALSO   Chapter 41
FORMAT

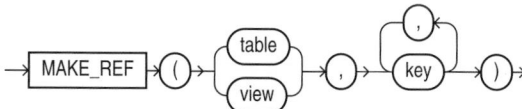

DESCRIPTION   **MAKE_REF** constructs a **REF** (reference) from the foreign key of a table that references the base table of an object view. **MAKE_REF** allows you to construct references superimposed on existing foreign key relationships. *See* Chapter 41 for examples.

MAX

SEE ALSO   AGGREGATE FUNCTIONS, **COMPUTE, MIN**, Chapter 9
FORMAT

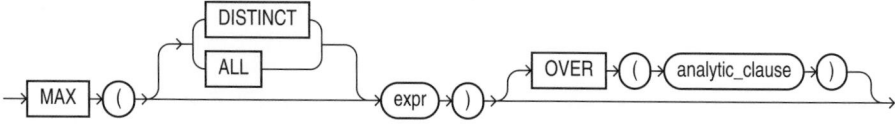

DESCRIPTION **MAX** is the maximum of all *values* for a group of rows. **MAX** ignores **NULL** values. The **DISTINCT** option is not meaningful because the maximum of all values is identical to the maximum of the distinct values.

MEDIAN
SEE ALSO **AVG, COUNT**
FORMAT

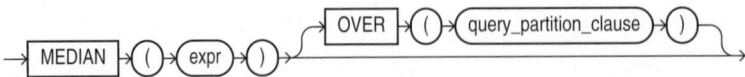

DESCRIPTION **MEDIAN** takes a numeric or datetime value and returns the middle value or an interpolated value that would be the middle value once the values are sorted. **NULL**s are ignored.

MERGE
SEE ALSO **INSERT, UPDATE,** Chapter 15
FORMAT
   merge::=

   merge_update_clause::=

merge_insert_clause::=

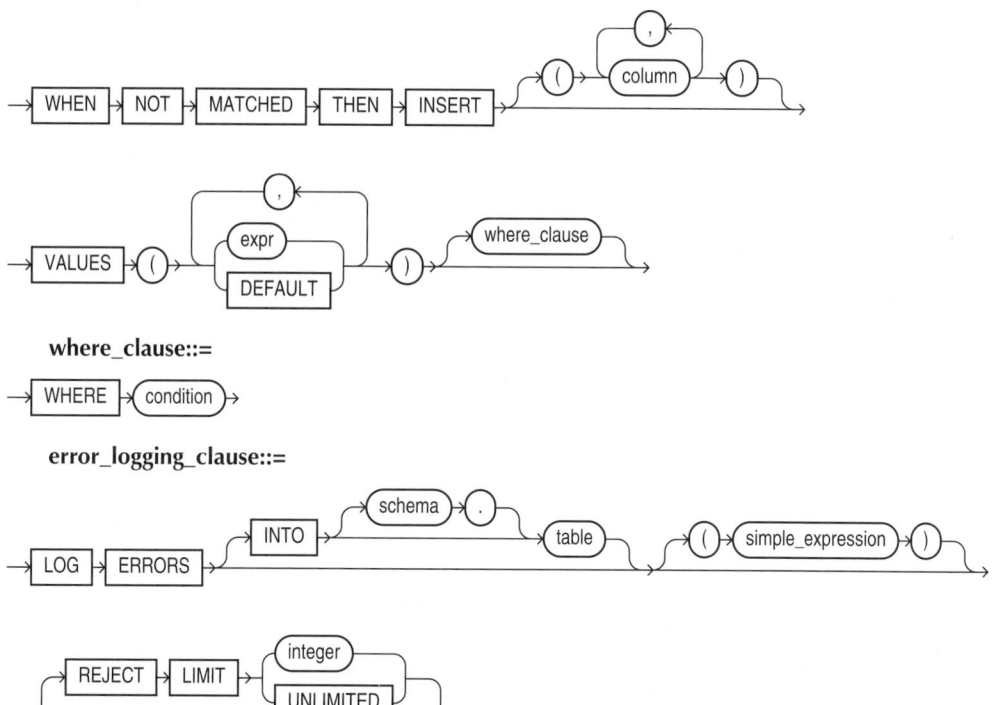

where_clause::=

error_logging_clause::=

DESCRIPTION **MERGE** performs updates and inserts of a target table in a single command, based on a selected set of rows. You specify the conditions to determine whether an **INSERT** or **UPDATE** is performed on a row-by-row basis.

NOTE
Since **MERGE** *performs queries, you can use hints.*

You can specify either the **UPDATE** or the **INSERT** operation, or both. Also, you can delete rows from the target table during the **UPDATE** operation.

As of Oracle Database 11g, you can use the **MERGE** command on tables with domain indexes.

MIN
SEE ALSO AGGREGATE FUNCTIONS, **COMPUTE, MAX**, Chapter 9
FORMAT

DESCRIPTION **MIN** is the minimum of all *values* for a group of rows. **MIN** ignores **NULL** values. The **DISTINCT** option is not meaningful because the minimum of all values is identical to the minimum of the distinct values.

MINUS

SEE ALSO **INTERSECT**, QUERY OPERATORS, **UNION**, Chapters 13 and 27
FORMAT

```
SELECT
MINUS
SELECT . . .
```

within Oracle Text queries against CONTEXT indexes:

```
SELECT column
FROM table
WHERE CONTAINS(text_column,'text MINUS text') > 0;
```

DESCRIPTION **MINUS** combines two queries. It returns only those rows from the first **SELECT** statement that are not produced by the second **SELECT** statement (the first **SELECT** MINUS the second **SELECT**). The number of columns and datatypes must be identical between **SELECT** statements, although the names of the columns do not need to be. The data, however, must be identical in the rows produced for the **MINUS** to reject them. *See* Chapter 13 for a discussion of the important differences and effects of **INTERSECT**, **MINUS**, and **UNION**.

Within text searches against CONTEXT indexes, **MINUS** tells the text search of two terms to subtract the score of the second term's search from the score of the first term's search before comparing the result to the threshold score.

MOD

SEE ALSO NUMBER FUNCTIONS, Chapter 9
FORMAT

DESCRIPTION **MOD** divides a *value* by a *divisor* and gives the remainder. **MOD(23,6) = 5** means divide 23 by 6. The answer is 3 with 5 left over, so 5 is the result of the modulus. *value* and *divisor* can both be any real number, except that *divisor* cannot be 0.
EXAMPLES

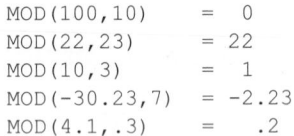

```
MOD(100,10)   =   0
MOD(22,23)    = 22
MOD(10,3)     =   1
MOD(-30.23,7) = -2.23
MOD(4.1,.3)   =   .2
```

The second example shows what **MOD** does whenever the divisor is greater than the dividend (the number being divided). It produces the dividend as a result. Also note this important case:

```
MOD(value,1)   = 0
```

if *value* is an integer. This is a good test to see if a number is an integer.

MODEL FUNCTIONS

Model functions are relevant only for inter-row calculations and can be used only in the **MODEL** clause of the **SELECT** statement. They are non-recursive. The model functions are **CV**, **ITERATION_NUMBER**, **PRESENTNNV**, **PRESENTV**, and **PREVIOUS**.

MONTHS_BETWEEN

SEE ALSO **ADD_MONTHS**, DATE FUNCTIONS, Chapter 10
FORMAT

DESCRIPTION **MONTHS_BETWEEN** gives *date2* minus *date1* in months. The result is usually not an integer.

NANVL

SEE ALSO **LNNVL**
FORMAT

DESCRIPTION **NANVL** is useful only for floating-point numbers of type BINARY_FLOAT or BINARY_DOUBLE. Oracle will return an alternative value *n* if the input value *m* is not a number; otherwise it returns *m*.

NCHAR

NCHAR is a multibyte version of the CHAR datatype. It stores fixed-length character data up to 2000 bytes in length. *See* DATATYPES.

NCHR

SEE ALSO **CHR**
FORMAT

DESCRIPTION **NCHR** returns the character having the binary equivalent to *number* in the national character set.

NCLOB

The NCLOB datatype is the multibyte version of the CLOB datatype. NCLOB stores character large objects containing Unicode characters, up to a maximum length of 4GB. *See* DATATYPES.

NEAR

SEE ALSO **CONTAINS**, Chapter 27
DESCRIPTION Within CONTEXT indexes, **NEAR** indicates that a proximity search should be executed for the specified text strings. If the search terms are "summer" and "lease," then a proximity search for the two terms could be

```
select sonnet_text
from sonnet
where contains(sonnet_text,'summer NEAR lease') >0;
```

When evaluating the text search results, text with the words "summer" and "lease" near each other will have higher scores than text with the words "summer" and "lease" farther apart.

NEW_TIME

See DATE FUNCTIONS.

NEXT_DAY

See DATE FUNCTIONS.

NEXTVAL

See PSEUDO-COLUMNS.

NLS_CHARSET_DECL_LEN

SEE ALSO   NCHAR
FORMAT

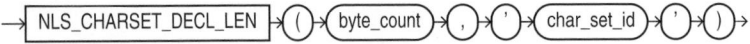

DESCRIPTION   **NLS_CHARSET_DECL_LEN** returns the declaration width (in number of characters) of an NCHAR column.

NLS_CHARSET_ID

SEE ALSO   NLS_CHARSET_NAME
FORMAT

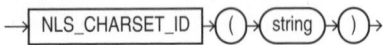

DESCRIPTION   **NLS_CHARSET_ID** returns the character set ID number corresponding to the character set name *text*.

NLS_CHARSET_NAME

SEE ALSO   NLS_CHARSET_ID
FORMAT

DESCRIPTION   **NLS_CHARSET_NAME** returns the name of the character set corresponding to ID number *number*.

NLS_INITCAP

SEE ALSO   CHARACTER FUNCTIONS, **INITCAP**, Chapter 7
FORMAT

DESCRIPTION   **NLS_INITCAP** is like the **INITCAP** function except with the addition of a parameter string. The *nls_parameters* string, enclosed in single quotation marks, gives a sort sequence for capitalizing special linguistic sequences. You would generally use **INITCAP** with the default sort sequence for the session, but this function lets you specify the exact sort sequence to use.

NLS_LOWER
SEE ALSO CHARACTER FUNCTIONS, **LOWER**, Chapter 7
FORMAT

DESCRIPTION **NLS_LOWER** is like the **LOWER** function except with the addition of a parameter string. The *nls_parameters* string, enclosed in single quotation marks, gives a sort sequence for lowercasing special linguistic sequences. You would generally use **LOWER** with the default sort sequence for the session, but this function lets you specify the exact sort sequence to use.

NLS_UPPER
SEE ALSO CHARACTER FUNCTIONS, **UPPER**, Chapter 7
FORMAT

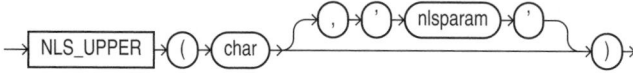

DESCRIPTION **NLS_UPPER** is like the **UPPER** function except with the addition of a parameter string. The *nls_parameters* string, enclosed in single quotation marks, gives a sort sequence for capitalizing special linguistic sequences. You would generally use **UPPER** with the default sort sequence for the session, but this function lets you specify the exact sort sequence to use.

NLSSORT
SEE ALSO **CREATE DATABASE**
FORMAT

DESCRIPTION **NLSSORT** (National Language Support **SORT**) gives the collating sequence value (an integer) of the given *character* based on the National Language Support option chosen for the site. The *nls_parameters* string, enclosed in single quotation marks, gives a sort sequence for special linguistic sequences if you do not want to use the session or database default.

NOAUDIT

SEE ALSO   AUDIT, PRIVILEGE
FORMAT
   noaudit::=

   audit_operation_clause::=

   auditing_by_clause::=

   audit_schema_object_clause::=

auditing_on_clause::=

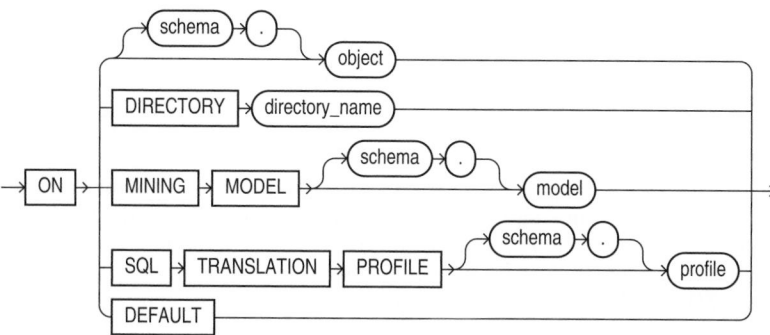

DESCRIPTION **NOAUDIT** stops auditing of SQL statements being audited as a result of the **AUDIT** command. It stops auditing either a statement (*see* **AUDIT**) or a statement authorized by a system privilege (*see* PRIVILEGE). If there is a **BY** clause with a list of users, the command stops the auditing of statements issued by these users. If there is no **BY** clause, Oracle stops auditing the statements for all users. The **WHENEVER SUCCESSFUL** option stops auditing only for those statements that successfully complete; **WHENEVER NOT SUCCESSFUL** stops auditing only for those statements that result in an error.

   NOAUDIT also stops the audit for an option of the use of a table, view, or synonym. To stop the audit of any table, view, or synonym, you must either own them or have DBA authority. *option* refers to the options described shortly. *user* is the username of the object owner. *object* is a table, view, or synonym. *option* specifies what commands the audit should be stopped for. **ON** *object* names the object being audited, and includes a table, view, or synonym of a table, view, or sequence. **ALL** stops the audits of all commands on the object.

EXAMPLES The following stops auditing of all attempts at UPDATE or DELETE on the BOOKSHELF table:

```
noaudit update, delete on bookshelf;
```

   This stops auditing of all unsuccessful access to BOOKSHELF:

```
noaudit all on bookshelf whenever not successful;
```

NOT
SEE ALSO LOGICAL OPERATORS, Chapter 5
DESCRIPTION **NOT** comes before and reverses the effect of any of these logical operators: **BETWEEN**, **IN**, **LIKE**, and **EXISTS**. **NOT** can also come before **NULL**, as in **IS NOT NULL**.

NOT EXISTS
SEE ALSO **ALL, ANY, EXISTS, IN**, Chapter 13
FORMAT

```
SELECT ...
WHERE NOT EXISTS (SELECT...);
```

DESCRIPTION **NOT EXISTS** returns false in a **WHERE** clause if the subquery that follows it returns one or more rows. The **SELECT** clause in the subquery can be a column, a literal, or an asterisk—it doesn't matter. The only part that matters is whether the **WHERE** clause in the subquery will return a row.
EXAMPLE NOT EXISTS is frequently used to determine which records in one table do not have matching records in another table. *See* Chapter 13 for examples using NOT EXISTS.

NTILE
SEE ALSO   WIDTH_BUCKET
FORMAT

DESCRIPTION   **NTILE** is an analytic function. It divides an ordered dataset into a number of buckets indicated by an expression and assigns the appropriate bucket number to each row. The buckets are numbered and the expression must resolve to a positive constant for each partition.

NULL (Form 1—PL/SQL)
SEE ALSO   BLOCK STRUCTURE
FORMAT

```
NULL;
```

DESCRIPTION   The **NULL** statement has nothing to do with **NULL** values. Its main purpose is to make a section of code more readable by saying, in effect, "do nothing." It also provides a means of having a NULL block (since PL/SQL requires at least one executable statement between **BEGIN** and **END**). It is generally used as the statement following one (usually the last) of a series of condition tests.
EXAMPLE

```
IF Age > 65 THEN
   ...
ELSEIF AGE BETWEEN 21 and 65 THEN
   ...
ELSE
  NULL;
ENDIF;
```

NULL (Form 2—SQL Column Value)
SEE ALSO   AGGREGATE FUNCTIONS, **CREATE TABLE**, INDICATOR VARIABLE, **NVL**, Chapter 5
DESCRIPTION   A **NULL** value is one that is unknown, irrelevant, or not meaningful. Any Oracle datatype can be **NULL**. That is, any Oracle column in a given row can be without a value (unless the table was created with **NOT NULL** for that column). **NULL** in a NUMBER datatype is not the same as zero.

Few procedural languages directly support the idea of a variable with a **NULL** or unknown value, although Oracle and SQL do so easily. In order to extend languages for which Oracle has developed precompilers to support the **NULL** concept, an indicator variable is associated with the host variable, almost like a flag, to indicate whether it is **NULL**. The host variable and its indicator variable may be referenced and set separately in the host language code, but are always concatenated in SQL or PL/SQL.

You use the **NVL** function to detect the absence of a value for a column and convert the **NULL** value into a real value using the datatype of the column. For instance, **NVL(Name,'NOT KNOWN')** converts a **NULL** value in the column NAME into the words NOT KNOWN. For a non-**NULL** value (that is, where a name is present), the **NVL** function simply returns the name. **NVL** works similarly with NUMBERs and DATEs.

Except for **COUNT(*)** and **COMPUTE NUMBER**, aggregate functions ignore **NULL** values. Other functions return a **NULL** value when a **NULL** is present in the value or values they are evaluating:

```
NULL + 1066 is NULL.
LEAST(NULL,'A','Z') is NULL.
```

Because **NULL** represents an unknown value, two columns that are each **NULL** are not equal to each other. Therefore, the equal sign and other logical operators (except for **IS NULL** and **IS NOT NULL**) do not work with **NULL**. For example,

```
where name = null
```

is not a valid **WHERE** clause. **NULL** requires the word **IS**:

```
where name is null
```

During **ORDER BY** sorts, **NULL** values always come first when the order is ascending and last when it is descending.

When **NULL** values are stored in the database, they are represented with a single byte if they fall between two columns that have real values, and no bytes if they fall at the end of the row (last in the column definition in the **CREATE TABLE**). If some of the columns in a table are likely to often contain **NULL** values, those columns can be usefully grouped near the end of the **CREATE TABLE** column list, saving a minor amount of disk space.

NULL values do not appear in indexes, except in the single case where all the values in a cluster key are **NULL**.

NULLIF

SEE ALSO   **COALESCE, DECODE, NULL**, Chapter 16
FORMAT

DESCRIPTION   **NULLIF** compares *expr1* and *expr2*. If they are equal, the function returns **NULL**. If they are not equal, the function returns *expr1*. You cannot specify the literal **NULL** for *expr1*.

The **NULLIF** function is logically equivalent to the following **CASE** expression:

```
CASE WHEN expr1 = expr2 THEN NULL
ELSE expr1 END
```

NUMBER DATATYPE

A NUMBER datatype is a standard Oracle datatype that may contain a number, with or without a decimal point and a sign. Valid values are 0 and positive and negative numbers. NUMBER datatypes are defined as having precision and scale. Precision can range from 1 to 38; scale can range from –84 to 127.

NUMBER FORMATS

SEE ALSO   **COLUMN**, Chapter 9
DESCRIPTION   The following options work with both the **SET NUMFORMAT** and **COLUMN FORMAT** commands:

Option	Description
9999990	The count of nines and zeros determines the maximum digits that can be displayed.
999,999,999.99	Places commas and decimals in the pattern shown.
999990	Displays trailing zeroes.
099999	Displays leading zeroes.
$99999	Places a dollar sign in front of every number.

Option	Description
B99999	Displays a blank for the integer portion of a fixed-point number when the integer is zero.
99999MI	If the number is negative, a minus sign follows the number. The default is for the negative sign to be on left.
S9999	Returns leading + for positive values, – for negative values.
9999S	Returns trailing + for positive values, – for negative values.
99999PR	Negative numbers are displayed within < and >.
99D99	Displays the decimal in the position indicated.
9G999	Displays the group separator in the position shown.
C9999	Displays the ISO currency symbol in this position.
9G999	Returns the group separator (the current value of the NLS_NUMERIC_CHARACTER parameter) in the specified position. You can specify multiple group separators in a number format model.
L999	Displays the local currency symbol in the position specified.
,	Displays a comma.
.	Displays a period.
9.999EEEE	The display will be in scientific notation (4 Es are required).
999V99	Multiplies number by 10n, where n is the number of digits to the right of V, so 999V99 turns 1234 into 123400.
9999RN	Displays Roman numeral values, for integer values between 1 and 3999. When lowercase "rn" is used, the Roman numerals are displayed in lowercase.
TM	Returns the smallest number of characters possible (text minimum).
U999	Returns the Euro or other dual currency symbol in the specified position.
X	Returns the hexadecimal value of the specified number of digits.

NUMBER FUNCTIONS

The following is an ordered list of all current single-value number (numeric) functions in the Oracle version of SQL. Each of these is listed elsewhere in this reference under its own name, with its proper format and usage. Each can be used as a regular SQL function as well as a PL/SQL function. *See* AGGREGATE FUNCTIONS and LIST FUNCTIONS.

Function	Definition
value1 + *value2*	Addition
value1 – *value2*	Subtraction
value1 * *value2*	Multiplication
value1 / *value2*	Division
ABS(*value*)	ABSolute *value*
ACOS(*value*)	Arc COSine of *value*, in radians
ASIN(*value*)	Arc SINe of *value*, in radians
ATAN(*value*)	Arc TANgent of *value*, in radians
ATAN2(*value1, value2*)	Arc TANgent of *value1* and *value2*, in radians

Function	Definition
BITAND (*value1, value2*)	BITwise AND of *value1* and *value2*, both of which must resolve to nonnegative integers; returns an integer
CEIL(*value*)	Numeric CEILing: the smallest integer greater than or equal to *value*
COS(*value*)	COSine of *value*
COSH(*value*)	Hyperbolic COSine of *value*
EXP(*value*)	e raised to *value* EXPonent
FLOOR(*value*)	Largest integer less than or equal to *value*
LN(*value*)	Natural Logarithm of value
LOG(*value*)	Base 10 LOGarithm of *value*
MOD(*value, divisor*)	MODulus
NANVL(*value1,value2*)	For BINARY_FLOAT and BINARY_DOUBLE numbers, returns *value2* if *value1* is not a number
POWER(*value, exponent*)	*value* raised to an *exponent* POWER
REMAINDER(*value1,value2*)	Remainder of *value1* divided by *value2*
ROUND(*value, precision*)	ROUNDing of *value* to *precision*
SIGN(*value*)	1 if *value* is positive, −1 if negative, 0 if zero
SIN(*value*)	SINe of *value*
SINH(*value*)	Hyperbolic SINe of *value*
SQRT(*value*)	SQuare RooT of *value*
TAN(*value*)	TANgent of *value*
TANH(*value*)	Hyperbolic TANgent of *value*
TRUNC(*value, precision*)	*value* TRUNCated to *precision*
WIDTH_BUCKET(*expr,min,max,num*)	Constructs equal-width histograms

NUMTODSINTERVAL

SEE ALSO DATATYPES, Chapter 11
FORMAT

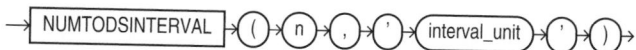

DESCRIPTION NUMTODSINTERVAL converts *n* to an INTERVAL DAY TO SECOND literal. *n* can be a number or an expression resolving to a number. *char_expr* can be a CHAR, VARCHAR2, NCHAR, or NVARCHAR2 datatype. The value for *char_expr* specifies the unit of *n* and must resolve to one of the following string values: 'DAY', 'HOUR', 'MINUTE', or 'SECOND'.

NUMTOYMINTERVAL

SEE ALSO DATATYPES, Chapter 11
FORMAT

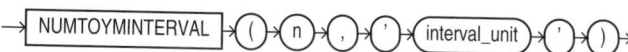

DESCRIPTION **NUMTOYMINTERVAL** converts number *n* to an INTERVAL YEAR TO MONTH literal. *n* can be a number or an expression resolving to a number. *char_expr* can be a CHAR, VARCHAR2, NCHAR, or NVARCHAR2 datatype. The value for *char_expr* specifies the unit of *n* and must resolve to either 'YEAR' or 'MONTH'.

NVARCHAR2

NVARCHAR2 is the multibyte equivalent of the VARCHAR2 datatype. Its maximum length is 32,767 bytes. *See* DATATYPES.

NVL

SEE ALSO AGGREGATE FUNCTIONS, **NULL**, OTHER FUNCTIONS, Chapter 9
FORMAT

DESCRIPTION If *value* is **NULL**, this function returns *substitute*. If *value* is not **NULL**, this function returns *value*. *value* can be any Oracle datatype. *substitute* can be a literal, another column, or an expression, but must be the same datatype as *value*.

NVL2

SEE ALSO AGGREGATE FUNCTIONS, **NULL**, OTHER FUNCTIONS, Chapter 9
FORMAT

DESCRIPTION **NVL2** is an extended form of **NVL**. In **NVL2**, *expr1* can never be returned; either *expr2* or *expr3* will be returned. If *expr1* is not **NULL**, **NVL2** returns *expr2*. If *expr1* is **NULL**, **NVL2** returns *expr3*. The argument *expr1* can have any datatype. The arguments *expr2* and *expr3* can have any datatypes except LONG.

OBJECT NAMES

These database objects may be given names: tables, views, synonyms, aliases, columns, indexes, users, sequences, tablespaces, and so on. The following rules govern naming objects:

- The name of an object can be from 1 to 30 characters long, except for database names, which are up to 8 characters, and host filenames, whose length is operating-system dependent.
- A name may not contain a quotation mark.
- A name must:
  Begin with a letter
  Contain only the characters A–Z, 0–9, $, #, and _
  Not be an Oracle reserved word (*see* RESERVED WORDS)
  Not duplicate the name of another database object owned by the same user

Object names are not case sensitive. Object names should follow a sensible naming convention.

OBJECT REFERENCE FUNCTIONS

Object reference functions manipulate REFs, which are references to objects of specified object types. The object reference functions are described under their individual entries in this reference. The functions are **DEREF**, **MAKE_REF**, **REF**, **REFTOHEX**, and **VALUE**.

OID

An OID is an object identifier, assigned by Oracle to each object in a database. For example, each row object within an object table has an OID value assigned to it; the OID is used to resolve references to the row objects. Oracle does not reuse OID values after an object is dropped. *See* Chapter 41.

OPEN

SEE ALSO   CLOSE, DECLARE CURSOR, FETCH, LOOP, Chapter 32
FORMAT

```
OPEN cursor [(parameter[,parameter]...]
```

DESCRIPTION   OPEN works in conjunction with **DECLARE CURSOR** and **FETCH. DECLARE CURSOR** sets up a **SELECT** statement to be executed and establishes a list of parameters (PL/SQL variables) that are to be used in its **WHERE** clause, but it does not execute the query.

OPEN cursor, in effect, executes the query in the named cursor and keeps its results in a staging area, where they can be called in, a row at a time, with **FETCH**, and their column values put into local variables with the **INTO** clause of the **FETCH**. If the cursor **SELECT** statement uses parameters, then their actual values are passed to the **SELECT** statement in the parameter list of the **OPEN** statement. They must match in number and position and have compatible datatypes.

There is also an alternative method of associating the values in the **OPEN** statement with those in the **SELECT** list:

```
DECLARE
    cursor mycur(title, publisher) is select ...
BEGIN
    open my_cur(new_book => title, 'Pandoras' => publisher);
```

Here, *new_book*, a PL/SQL variable, loaded perhaps from a data entry screen, is pointed to TITLE, and therefore loads it with whatever is currently in the variable *new_book*. PUBLISHER is loaded with the value 'PANDORAS', and these then become the parameters of the cursor *my_cur*. (*See* **DECLARE CURSOR** for more details on parameters in cursors.)

You also may combine pointed associations with positional ones, but the positional ones must appear first in the **OPEN** statement's list.

You cannot reopen an open cursor, though you can **CLOSE** it and re**OPEN** it, and you cannot use a cursor for which you have a current **OPEN** statement in a Cursor FOR Loop.

OPEN CURSOR (Embedded SQL)

SEE ALSO   CLOSE, DECLARE CURSOR, FETCH, PREPARE, *Programmer's Guide to the Oracle Precompilers*
FORMAT

```
EXEC SQL  [FOR { integer | :array_size }]
OPEN cursor
  [USING
  {DESCRIPTOR SQLDBA_descriptor
  | :variable[[ INDICATOR ]:indicator_variable
  [,:variable[ INDICATOR ]:indicator_variable]]... }]
```

DESCRIPTION   *cursor* is the name of a cursor previously named in a **DECLARE CURSOR** statement. The optional **USING** references either the host variable list of variables that are to be substituted in the statement in the **DECLARE CURSOR**, based on position (the number and type of variables must be the same), or a descriptor name that references the result of a previous **DESCRIBE**.

OPEN cursor allocates a cursor, defines the active set of rows (the host variables are substituted when the cursor is opened), and positions the cursor just before the first row of the set. No rows are retrieved until a **FETCH** is executed. Host variables do not change once they've been substituted. To change them, you must reopen the cursor (you don't have to **CLOSE** it first).

NOTE
See the Programmer's Guide to the Oracle Precompilers *for a full list of all commands. This reference does not contain all of the possible precompiler commands.*

OR
SEE ALSO   AND, CONTAINS, Chapters 5 and 27
DESCRIPTION   OR combines logical expressions so the result is TRUE if either logical expression is true.
EXAMPLE   The following produces data for both KEENE and SAN FRANCISCO:

```
select * from comfort
where city = 'Keene' OR city = 'San Francisco'
```

Within CONTEXT queries, an **OR** operator can be used for searches involving multiple search terms. If either of the search terms is found, and its search score exceeds the specified threshold value, the text will be returned by the search.

ORA_HASH
FORMAT

DESCRIPTION   ORA_HASH computes a hash value for a given expression. This function is useful for operations such as analyzing a subset of data and generating a random sample. *expr* is the data for which Oracle will compute a hash value (usually a column name). *max_bucket* determines the maximum bucket value (0 to 4294967295). The *seed_value* argument (0 to 4294967295) enables Oracle to produce different results with the same *expr*.

ORDER BY
SEE ALSO   FROM, GROUP BY, HAVING, SELECT, WHERE, Chapter 5
FORMAT

```
ORDER BY { expression [,expression]... |
          position [,position]... }
          alias [,alias]... }
[ ASC | DESC ]
```

DESCRIPTION   The **ORDER BY** clause causes Oracle to sort the results of a query before they are displayed. This can be done either by *expression*, which can be a simple column name or a complex set of functions, an *alias* (see the next Note), or a column *position* in the **SELECT** clause (see Note). Rows are ordered first by the first expression or position, then by the second, and so on, based on the collating sequence of the host. If **ORDER BY** is not specified, the order in which rows are selected from a table is indeterminate and may change from one query to the next.

NOTE
Oracle still supports the use of column positions in ORDER BY clauses, but this feature is no longer part of the SQL standard and is not guaranteed to be supported in future releases. Use column aliases instead.

ASC or **DESC** specifies ascending or descending order and may follow each expression, position, or alias in the **ORDER BY** clause. **NULL** values precede ascending and follow descending rows in Oracle.

ORDER BY follows any other clauses except **FOR UPDATE OF**.

If **ORDER BY** and **DISTINCT** are both specified, the **ORDER BY** clause may refer only to columns or expressions that are in the **SELECT** clause.

When the **UNION**, **INTERSECT**, or **MINUS** operator is used, the names of the columns in the first **SELECT** may differ from the names in subsequent **SELECT**s. **ORDER BY** must use the column name from the first **SELECT**.

Only CHAR, VARCHAR2, NUMBER, and DATE datatypes—and the special datatype ROWID—can appear in an **ORDER BY** clause.

EXAMPLE

```
select title, publisher
from bookshelf
order by title;
```

OTHER FUNCTIONS

This is an alphabetical list of all current functions in the Oracle version of SQL that do not readily fall into any other function category. Each of these is listed elsewhere in this reference under its own name, with its proper format and use.

BFILENAME, COALESCE, CV, DECODE, DEPTH, DUMP, EMPTY_BLOB, EMPTY_CLOB, EXISTSNODE, EXTRACT, EXTRACTVALUE, GREATEST, LEAST, LNNVL, NLS_CHARSET_DECL_LEN, NLS_CHARSET_ID, NLS_CHARSET_NAME, NULLIF, NVL, NVL2, ORA_HASH, PATH, PRESENTNNV, PRESENTV, PREVIOUS, SYS_CONNECT_BY_PATH, SYS_CONTEXT, SYS_DBURIGEN, SYS_EXTRACT_UTC, SYS_GUID, SYS_TYPEID, SYS_XMLAGG, SYS_XMLGEN, UID, UPDATEXML, USER, USERENV, VSIZE, XMLAGG, XMLCOLATTVAL, XMLCONCAT, XMLFOREST, XMLSEQUENCE, XMLTRANSFORM

PARAMETERS

SEE ALSO   **&, &&, ACCEPT, DEFINE**

DESCRIPTION   Parameters allow the execution of a start file with values passed on the SQL*Plus command line. These are simply spaced apart following the name of the start file. Within the file, parameters are referenced by the order in which they appeared on the command line. **&1** is the first, **&2** the second, and so on. Aside from this rule, the rules for use are the same as for variables loaded using **DEFINE** or **ACCEPT**, and they may be used in SQL statements in the same way.

There is one limitation, however. There is no way to pass a multiple-word argument to a single variable. Each variable can take only one word, date, or number. Attempting to solve this by putting the parameters in quotes on the command line results in the words being concatenated.

EXAMPLE   Suppose you have a start file named fred.sql that contains this SQL:

```
select title, publisher
from bookshelf
where title > &1;
```

Starting it with this command line:

```
start fred.sql M
```

produces a report of all titles that start with a character **> "M"**.

PASSWORD (SQL*Plus)

SEE ALSO ALTER USER, Chapter 19
FORMAT

```
PASSW[ORD] [username]
```

DESCRIPTION You can use the **PASSWORD** command in SQL*Plus to change the password on your account or another account (if you have the ALTER ANY USER privilege). If you use the **PASSWORD** command, your new password will not be displayed on the screen as you type. Users with DBA authority can change any user's password via the **PASSWORD** command; other users can change only their own password.

When you enter the **PASSWORD** command, you will be prompted for the old and new passwords.
EXAMPLE

```
connect angie/apple2000lb
password
Changing password for angie
Old password:
New password:
Retype new password:
```

When the password has been successfully changed, you receive the feedback:

```
Password changed
```

PATH

SEE ALSO DEPTH
FORMAT

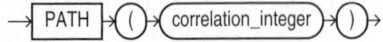

DESCRIPTION **PATH** is an ancillary function used only with the **UNDER_PATH** and **EQUALS_PATH** conditions. It returns the relative path that leads to the resource specified in the parent condition. The *correlation_integer* value can be any NUMBER integer. Values less than 1 are treated as 1.

PAUSE (SQL*Plus)

SEE ALSO ACCEPT, PROMPT
FORMAT

```
PAU[SE] [text];
```

DESCRIPTION **PAUSE** is similar to **PROMPT**, except **PAUSE** first displays an empty line, then a line containing *text*, and then waits for the user to press RETURN. If *text* is not entered, **PAUSE** displays two empty lines, then waits for user to press RETURN.

NOTE
*PAUSE waits for a RETURN from the terminal even if the source of command input has been redirected to be from a file, which means a start file with **SET TERMOUT OFF** could hang, waiting for a RETURN, with no message as to why it was waiting (or that it was waiting). Use **PAUSE** with caution.*

EXAMPLE

```
prompt Report Complete.
pause Press RETURN to continue.
```

PERCENT_RANK

SEE ALSO   AGGREGATE FUNCTIONS

FORMAT

For aggregates:

percent_rank_aggregate::=

For analytics:

percent_rank_analytic::=

DESCRIPTION   As an aggregate function, **PERCENT_RANK** calculates, for a hypothetical row R identified by the arguments of the function and a corresponding sort specification, the rank of row R minus 1 divided by the number of rows in the aggregate group. This calculation is made as if the hypothetical row R were inserted into the group of rows over which Oracle is to aggregate. The arguments of the function identify a single hypothetical row within each aggregate group. Therefore, they must all evaluate to constant expressions within each aggregate group. The constant argument expressions and the expressions in the **ORDER BY** clause of the aggregate match by position. Therefore, the number of arguments must be the same and their types must be compatible.

The range of values returned by **PERCENT_RANK** is 0 to 1, inclusive. The first row in any set has a **PERCENT_RANK** of 0.

As an analytic function, for a row R, **PERCENT_RANK** calculates the rank of R minus 1, divided by 1 less than the number of rows being evaluated (the entire query result set or a partition).

PERCENTILE_CONT
SEE ALSO   AGGREGATE FUNCTIONS, **PERCENTILE_DISC**
FORMAT

DESCRIPTION   **PERCENTILE_CONT** is an inverse distribution function that assumes a continuous distribution model. It takes a percentile value and a sort specification and returns an interpolated value that would fall into that percentile value with respect to the sort specification. Nulls are ignored in the calculation.

The first *expr* must evaluate to a numeric value between 0 and 1 because it is a percentile value. This *expr* must be constant within each aggregation group. The **ORDER BY** clause takes a single expression that must be a numeric or datetime value, as these are the types over which Oracle can perform interpolation.

PERCENTILE_DISC
SEE ALSO   AGGREGATE FUNCTIONS, **PERCENTILE_CONT**
FORMAT

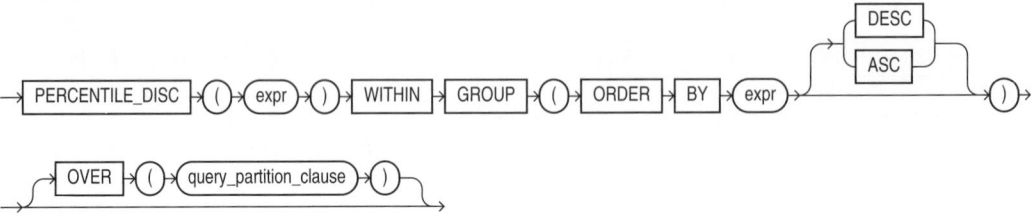

DESCRIPTION   **PERCENTILE_DISC** is an inverse distribution function that assumes a discrete distribution model. It takes a percentile value and a sort specification and returns an element from the set. Nulls are ignored in the calculation.

The first *expr* must evaluate to a numeric value between 0 and 1 because it is a percentile value. This expression must be constant within each aggregate group. The **ORDER BY** clause takes a single expression that can be of any type that can be sorted.

For a given percentile value P, **PERCENTILE_DISC** function sorts the values of the expression in the **ORDER BY** clause and returns the one with the smallest **CUME_DIST** value (with respect to the same sort specification) that is greater than or equal to P.

POWER
SEE ALSO   **SQRT**, Chapter 9
FORMAT

DESCRIPTION   **POWER** is *value* raised to an *exponent*.

POWERMULTISET

SEE ALSO   Chapter 39
FORMAT

DESCRIPTION   **POWERMULTISET** takes as input a nested table and returns a nested table of nested tables containing all nonempty subsets (called submultisets) of the input nested table. *expr* can be any expression that evaluates to a nested table; if that nested table is empty, an error is returned.

POWERMULTISET_BY_CARDINALITY

SEE ALSO   **POWERMULTISET**
FORMAT

DESCRIPTION   **POWERMULTISET_BY_CARDINALITY** takes as input a nested table and returns a nested table of nested tables containing all nonempty subsets (called submultisets) of the input nested table of the specified cardinality. *expr* can be any expression that evaluates to a nested table, and *cardinality* can be any positive integer; if that nested table is empty, an error is returned.

PRECEDENCE

SEE ALSO   LOGICAL OPERATORS, QUERY OPERATORS, Chapter 13
DESCRIPTION   The following operators are listed in descending order of precedence. Operators with equal precedence are on the same line. Operators of equal precedence are evaluated in succession from left to right. All **AND**s are evaluated before any **OR**. Each of these is listed and described separately under its own symbol or name in this Alphabetical Reference.

Operator	Function
-	SQL*Plus command continuation. Continues a command on the following line.
&	Prefix for parameters in a SQL*Plus start file. Words are substituted for **&1**, **&2**, and so on. *See* **START**.
& &&	Prefix for a substitution in a SQL command in SQL*Plus. SQL*Plus prompts for a value if an undefined **&** or **&&** variable is found. **&&** also defines the variable and saves the value; **&** does not. *See* **&** and **&&**, **DEFINE**, and **ACCEPT**.
:	Prefix for a host variable in PL/SQL.
.	Variable separator, used in SQL*Plus to separate the variable name from a suffix, so that the suffix is not considered a part of the variable name.
()	Surrounds subqueries or lists of columns.
'	Surrounds a literal, such as a character string or date constant. To use a **'** in a string constant, use two **'** marks (not a double quotation mark).
"	Surrounds a table or column alias that contains special characters or a space.
"	Surrounds literal text in a date format clause of **TO_CHAR**.
@	Precedes a database name in a **COPY** or a link name in a **FROM** clause.
()	Overrides normal operator precedence.
+ -	Prefix sign (positive or negative) for a number or number expression.

Operator	Function
* /	Multiplication and division.
+ -	Addition and subtraction.
| |	Char value concatenation.
NOT	Reverses result of an expression.
AND	Returns TRUE if both conditions are true.
OR	Returns TRUE if either condition is true.
UNION	Returns all distinct rows from both of two queries.
INTERSECT	Returns all matching distinct rows from two queries.
MINUS	Returns all distinct rows in the first query that are not in the second.

PREDICTION

SEE ALSO   PREDICTION_BOUNDS, PREDICTION_COST, PREDICTION_SET
FORMAT
   prediction::=

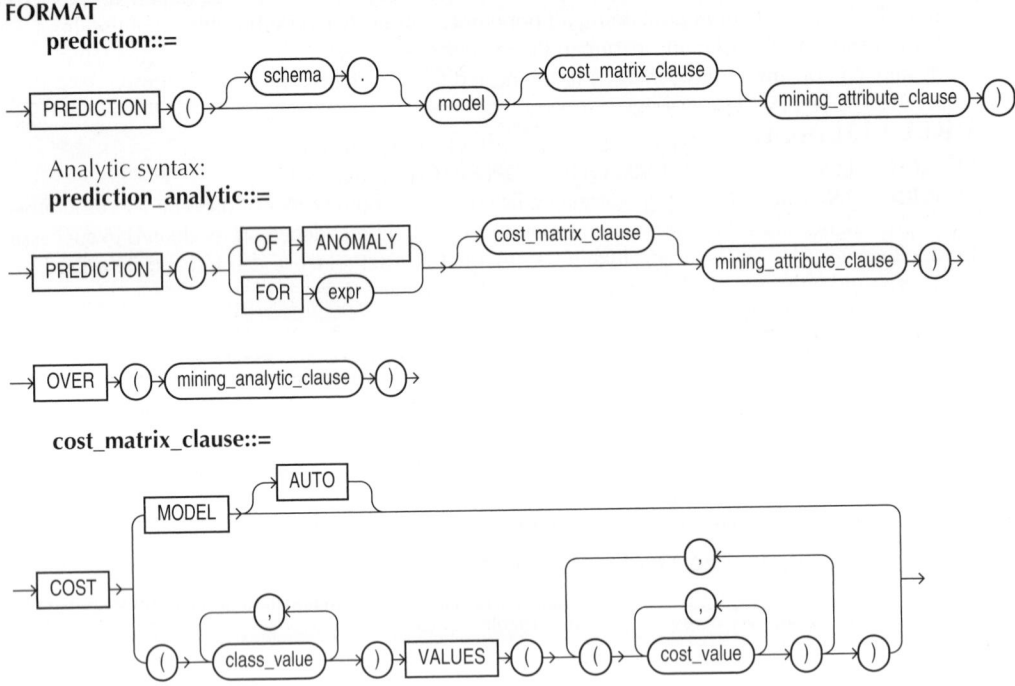

   Analytic syntax:
   prediction_analytic::=

   cost_matrix_clause::=

mining_attribute_clause::=

mining_analytic_clause::=

DESCRIPTION   The **PREDICTION** function is for use with models created by the DBMS_DATA_MINING package or with the Oracle Data Mining Java API. It returns the best prediction for the model. The datatype returned depends on the target value type used during the build of the model. For regression models, this function returns the expected value.

PREDICTION_BOUNDS

SEE ALSO   **PREDICTION, PREDICTION_COST, PREDICTION_SET**
FORMAT

mining_attribute_clause::=

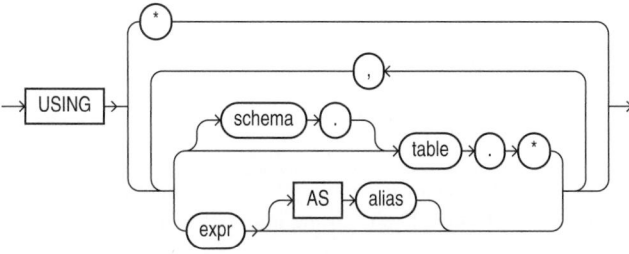

DESCRIPTION   The **PREDICTION_BOUNDS** function is for use only with generalized linear models. It returns an object with two NUMBER fields, LOWER and UPPER. For a regression mining function, the bounds apply to the value of the prediction. For a classification mining function, the bounds apply to the probability value. If the GLM was built using ridge regression, or if the covariance matrix is found to be singular during the build, then this function returns NULL for both fields.

PREDICTION_COST

SEE ALSO   PREDICTION
FORMAT
   prediction_cost::=

Analytic syntax:
prediction_cost_analytic::=

cost_matrix_clause::=

mining_attribute_clause::=

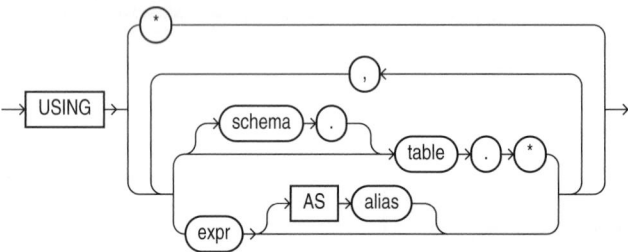

DESCRIPTION   The **PREDICTION_COST** function is for use with any classification model created by the DBMS_DATA_MINING package or with the Oracle Data Mining Java API. It returns a measure of cost for a given prediction as an Oracle NUMBER.

PREDICTION_DETAILS

SEE ALSO PREDICTION, PREDICTION_BOUNDS, PREDICTION_COST
FORMAT
    prediction_details::=

Analytic syntax:
prediction_details_analytic::=

    mining_attribute_clause::=

    mining_analytic_clause::=

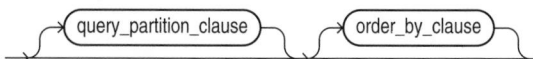

DESCRIPTION The **PREDICTION_DETAILS** function is for use with decision tree models and single-feature Adaptive Bayes Network (ABN) models created by the DBMS_DATA_MINING package or with the Oracle Data Mining Java API. It returns an XML string containing model-specific information related to the scoring of the input row.

PREDICTION_PROBABILITY
SEE ALSO PREDICTION, PREDICTION_BOUNDS, PREDICTION_COST
FORMAT

Analytic syntax:
prediction_prob_analytic::=

mining_attribute_clause::=

mining_analytic_clause::=

DESCRIPTION The **PREDICTION_PROBABILITY** function is for use with classification models created by the DBMS_DATA_MINING package or with the Oracle Data Mining Java API. It is not valid with other types of models. It returns the probability for a given prediction as an Oracle NUMBER.

PREDICTION_SET
SEE ALSO PREDICTION, PREDICTION_BOUNDS, PREDICTION_COST
FORMAT

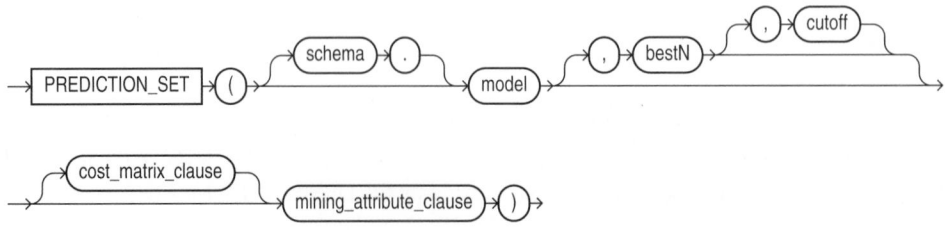

Analytic syntax:
prediction_set_analytic::=

PREDICTION_SET — (— OF → ANOMALY / FOR → expr — , → bestN — , → cutoff

cost_matrix_clause — mining_attribute_clause —) → OVER → (→ mining_analytic_clause →)

cost_matrix_clause::=

COST — MODEL → AUTO / (→ class_value →) → VALUES → (→ (→ cost_value →) →)

mining_attribute_clause::=

USING — * / schema . table . * / expr — AS → alias

mining_analytic_clause::=

query_partition_clause — order_by_clause

DESCRIPTION   The **PREDICTION_SET** function is for use with classification models created using the DBMS_DATA_MINING package or with the Oracle Data Mining Java API. It is not valid with other types of models. It returns a varray of objects containing all classes in a multiclass classification scenario. The object fields are named PREDICTION, PROBABILITY, and COST. The datatype of the PREDICTION field depends on the target value type used during the build of the model. The other two fields are both Oracle NUMBER. The elements are returned in the order of best prediction to worst prediction.

PREPARE (Embedded SQL)
SEE ALSO   CLOSE, CURSOR, DECLARE CURSOR, FETCH, OPEN, *Programmer's Guide to the Oracle Precompilers*
FORMAT

```
EXEC SQL [AT { db_name | :host_variable }] PREPARE statement_id
  FROM { :host_string | 'text' | select_command }
```

DESCRIPTION PREPARE parses SQL in the host variable *:host_string* or the literal *text*. It assigns a *statement_id* as a reference to the SQL. If the *statement_id* has been used previously, this reference replaces it. The SQL is a **SELECT** statement and may include a **FOR UPDATE OF** clause. *:host_string* is not the actual name of the host variable used, but a placeholder. **OPEN CURSOR** assigns input host variables in its **USING** clause, and **FETCH** assigns output host variables in its **INTO** clause, based on position. A statement needs to be **PREPARE**d only once. It can then be executed multiple times.

NOTE
See the Programmer's Guide to the Oracle Precompilers *for a full list of all commands. This reference does not contain all of the possible precompiler commands.*

EXAMPLE

```
query_string : string(1..100)
get(query_string);
EXEC SQL prepare FRED from :query_string;
EXEC SQL execute FRED;
```

PRESENTNNV
SEE ALSO PRESENTV
FORMAT

DESCRIPTION PRESENTNNV is relevant only for inter-row calculations. It can be used only in the **MODEL** clause of the **SELECT** statement and then only on the right side of a model rule. It returns *expr1* when, prior to the execution of the **MODEL** clause, *cell_reference* exists and is not Null. Otherwise it returns *expr2*.

PRESENTV
SEE ALSO PRESENTNNV
FORMAT

DESCRIPTION PRESENTV is relevant only for inter-row calculations. It can be used only in the **MODEL** clause of the **SELECT** statement and then only on the right side of a model rule. It returns *expr1* when, prior to the execution of the **MODEL** clause, *cell_reference* exists (but may be NULL). Otherwise it returns *expr2*.

PREVIOUS
SEE ALSO ITERATION_NUMBER
FORMAT

DESCRIPTION PREVIOUS is relevant only for inter-row calculations. It can be used only in the **MODEL** clause of the **SELECT** statement and then only in the **ITERATE ... [UNTIL]** clause of the **MODEL RULES** clause. It returns the value of *cell_reference* at the beginning of each iteration.

PRINT

SEE ALSO   **VARIABLE**, Chapter 32
FORMAT

```
PRI[NT] [variable...]
```

DESCRIPTION   **PRINT** displays the current value of the specified variable (which is created via the **VARIABLE** command). You can print the current values of multiple variables in a single command.

PRIOR

See CONNECT BY.

PRIVILEGE

A privilege is a permission granted to an Oracle user to execute some action. In Oracle, no user can execute any action without having the privilege to do so.

There are two kinds of privileges: *system privileges* and *object privileges*. System privileges extend permission to execute various data definition and data control commands, such as **CREATE TABLE** and **ALTER USER**, or even to log onto the database. Object privileges extend permission to operate on a particular named database object.

System privileges in Oracle include CREATE, ALTER, and DROP privileges for the various **CREATE**, **ALTER**, and **DROP** commands. Privileges with the keyword **ANY** in them mean that the user can exercise the privilege on any schema for which the privilege has been granted, not just his or her own schema. The standard privileges in the list following just give permission to execute the indicated command and don't require further explanation. Some of the privileges aren't intuitively clear; these are explained here.

System privileges include the following:

Privilege	Permission to...
ADVISOR FRAMEWORK	
ADVISOR	Access the advisor framework through PL/SQL packages including DBMS_ADVISOR and DBMS_SQLTUNE.
ADMINISTER SQL TUNING SET	Create, drop, select, load, and delete a SQL tuning set owned by the grantee through the DBMS_SQLTUNE package.
ADMINISTER ANY SQL TUNING SET	Create, drop, select, load, and delete a SQL tuning set owned by any user through the DBMS_SQLTUNE package.
CREATE ANY SQL PROFILE	Accept a SQL profile recommended by the tuning advisor.
DROP ANY SQL PROFILE	Drop an existing SQL profile.
ALTER ANY SQL PROFILE	Alter the attributes of an existing SQL profile.
CLUSTERS	
CREATE CLUSTER	Create clusters in grantee's schema.
CREATE ANY CLUSTER	Create a cluster in any schema. Behaves similarly to CREATE ANY TABLE.
ALTER ANY CLUSTER	Alter clusters in any schema.
DROP ANY CLUSTER	Drop clusters in any schema.

Privilege	Permission to...
CONTEXTS	
CREATE ANY CONTEXT	Create any context namespace.
DROP ANY CONTEXT	Drop any context namespace.
DATABASE	
ALTER DATABASE	Alter the database.
ALTER SYSTEM	Issue **ALTER SYSTEM** statements.
AUDIT SYSTEM	Issue **AUDIT** statements.
DATABASE LINKS	
CREATE DATABASE LINK	Create private database links in grantee's schema.
CREATE PUBLIC DATABASE LINK	Create public database links.
DROP PUBLIC DATABASE LINK	Drop public database links.
DEBUGGING	
DEBUG CONNECT SESSION	Connect the current session to a debugger.
DEBUG ANY PROCEDURE	Debug all PL/SQL and Java code in any database object. Display information on all SQL statements executed by the application.
DICTIONARIES	
ANALYZE ANY DICTIONARY	Analyze any data dictionary object.
DIMENSIONS	
CREATE DIMENSION	Create dimensions in the grantee's schema.
CREATE ANY DIMENSION	Create dimensions in any schema.
ALTER ANY DIMENSION	Alter dimensions in any schema.
DROP ANY DIMENSION	Drop dimensions in any schema.
DIRECTORIES	
CREATE ANY DIRECTORY	Create directory database objects.
FLASHBACK DATA ARCHIVES	
FLASHBACK ARCHIVE ADMINISTER	Create, alter, or drop any flashback data archive.
INDEXTYPES	
CREATE INDEXTYPE	Create an indextype in the grantee's schema.
CREATE ANY INDEXTYPE	Create an indextype in any schema.
ALTER ANY INDEXTYPE	Modify indextypes in any schema.
DROP ANY INDEXTYPE	Drop an indextype in any schema.
EXECUTE ANY INDEXTYPE	Reference an indextype in any schema.
INDEXES	
CREATE ANY INDEX	Create in any schema a domain index or an index on any table in any schema.
ALTER ANY INDEX	Alter indexes in any schema.
DROP ANY INDEX	Drop indexes in any schema.

Privilege	Permission to...
JOB SCHEDULER OBJECTS	
CREATE JOB	Create jobs, schedulers, or programs in the grantee's schema (using DBMS_SCHEDULER).
CREATE ANY JOB	Create, alter, or drop jobs, schedules, or programs in any schema.
EXECUTE ANY PROGRAM	Use any program in a job in the grantee's schema.
EXECUTE ANY CLASS	Specify any job class in a job in the grantee's schema.
MANAGE SCHEDULER	Create, alter, or drop any job class, window, or window group.
LIBRARIES	
CREATE LIBRARY	Create external procedure/function libraries in grantee's schema.
CREATE ANY LIBRARY	Create external procedure/function libraries in any schema.
DROP ANY LIBRARY	Drop external procedure/function libraries in any schema.
MATERIALIZED VIEWS	
CREATE MATERIALIZED VIEW	Create a materialized view in the grantee's schema.
CREATE ANY MATERIALIZED VIEW	Create materialized views in any schema.
ALTER ANY MATERIALIZED VIEW	Alter materialized views in any schema.
DROP ANY MATERIALIZED VIEW	Drop materialized views in any schema.
QUERY REWRITE	This privilege has been deprecated.
GLOBAL QUERY REWRITE	Enable rewrite using a materialized view when that materialized view references tables or views in any schema.
ON COMMIT REFRESH	Create a refresh-on-commit materialized view on any table in the database. Alter a refresh-on-demand materialized view on any table in the database to refresh-on-commit.
FLASHBACK ANY TABLE	Issue a FLASHBACK QUERY on any table, view, or materialized view in any schema.
MINING MODELS	
CREATE MINING MODEL	Create mining models.
CREATE ANY MINING MODEL	Create mining models in any schema.
ALTER ANY MINING MODEL	Alter any mining model.
DROP ANY MINING MODEL	Drop any mining model in any schema.
SELECT ANY MINING MODEL	Score or view any model in any schema.
COMMENT ANY MINING MODEL	Create a comment on any model in any schema.
OLAP CUBES	
CREATE CUBE	Create an OLAP cube.
CREATE ANY CUBE	Create an OLAP cube in any schema.
ALTER ANY CUBE	Alter an OLAP cube in any schema.
DROP ANY CUBE	Drop any OLAP cube.
SELECT ANY CUBE	Query or view any OLAP cube in any schema.
UPDATE ANY CUBE	Update any cube in any schema.

Privilege	Permission to...
OLAP CUBE MEASURE FOLDERS	
CREATE MEASURE FOLDER	Create an OLAP measure folder.
CREATE ANY MEASURE FOLDER	Create an OLAP measure folder in any schema.
DELETE ANY MEASURE FOLDER	Delete from an OLAP measure folder in any schema.
DROP ANY MEASURE FOLDER	Drop any measure folder in any schema.
INSERT ANY MEASURE FOLDER	Insert a measure into any measure folder in any schema.
OLAP CUBE DIMENSIONS	
CREATE CUBE DIMENSION	Create an OLAP cube dimension.
CREATE ANY CUBE DIMENSION	Create an OLAP cube dimension in any schema.
ALTER ANY CUBE DIMENSION	Alter an OLAP cube dimension in any schema.
DELETE ANY CUBE DIMENSION	Delete from an OLAP cube dimension in any schema.
DROP ANY CUBE DIMENSION	Drop an OLAP cube dimension in any schema.
INSERT ANY CUBE DIMENSION	Insert into an OLAP cube dimension in any schema.
SELECT ANY CUBE DIMENSION	View or query an OLAP cube dimension.
UPDATE ANY CUBE DIMENSION	Update an OLAP cube dimension in any schema.
OLAP CUBE BUILD PROCESSES	
CREATE CUBE BUILD PROCESS	Create an OLAP cube build process.
CREATE ANY CUBE BUILD PROCESS	Create an OLAP cube build process in any schema.
DROP ANY CUBE BUILD PROCESS	Drop an OLAP cube build process in any schema.
UPDATE ANY CUBE BUILD PROCESS	Update an OLAP cube build process in any schema.
OPERATORS	
CREATE OPERATOR	Create an operator and its bindings in the grantee's schema.
CREATE ANY OPERATOR	Create an operator and its bindings in any schema.
ALTER ANY OPERATOR	Modify an operator in any schema.
DROP ANY OPERATOR	Drop an operator in any schema.
OUTLINES	
CREATE ANY OUTLINE	Create public outlines that can be used in any schema that uses outlines.
ALTER ANY OUTLINE	Modify outlines.
DROP ANY OUTLINE	Drop outlines.
PROCEDURES	
CREATE PROCEDURE	Create stored procedures, functions, and packages in grantee's schema.
CREATE ANY PROCEDURE	Create stored procedures, functions, and packages in any schema.
ALTER ANY PROCEDURE	Alter stored procedures, functions, or packages in any schema.
DROP ANY PROCEDURE	Drop stored procedures, functions, or packages in any schema.
EXECUTE ANY PROCEDURE	Execute procedures or functions (stand-alone or packaged). Reference public package variables in any schema.

Privilege	Permission to...
PROFILES	
CREATE PROFILE	Create profiles.
ALTER PROFILE	Alter profiles.
DROP PROFILE	Drop profiles.
ROLES	
CREATE ROLE	Create roles.
ALTER ANY ROLE	Alter any role in the database.
DROP ANY ROLE	Drop roles.
GRANT ANY ROLE	Grant any role in the database.
ROLLBACK SEGMENTS	
CREATE ROLLBACK SEGMENT	Create rollback segments.
ALTER ROLLBACK SEGMENT	Alter rollback segments.
DROP ROLLBACK SEGMENT	Drop rollback segments.
SEQUENCES	
CREATE SEQUENCE	Create sequences in grantee's schema.
CREATE ANY SEQUENCE	Create sequences in any schema.
ALTER ANY SEQUENCE	Alter any sequence in the database.
DROP ANY SEQUENCE	Drop sequences in any schema.
SELECT ANY SEQUENCE	Reference sequences in any schema.
SESSIONS	
CREATE SESSION	Connect to the database.
ALTER RESOURCE COST	Set costs for session resources.
ALTER SESSION	Issue **ALTER SESSION** statements.
RESTRICTED SESSION	Log on after the instance is started using the SQL*Plus **STARTUP RESTRICT** statement.
SYNONYMS	
CREATE SYNONYM	Create synonyms in grantee's schema.
CREATE ANY SYNONYM	Create private synonyms in any schema.
CREATE PUBLIC SYNONYM	Create public synonyms.
DROP ANY SYNONYM	Drop private synonyms in any schema.
DROP PUBLIC SYNONYM	Drop public synonyms.
TABLES	
CREATE TABLE	Create tables in grantee's schema.
CREATE ANY TABLE	Create tables in any schema. The owner of the schema containing the table must have space quota on the tablespace to contain the table.
ALTER ANY TABLE	Alter any table or view in any schema.
BACKUP ANY TABLE	Use the Export utility to incrementally export objects from the schema of other users.

Privilege	**Permission to...**
DELETE ANY TABLE	Delete rows from tables, table partitions, or views in any schema.
DROP ANY TABLE	Drop or truncate tables or table partitions in any schema.
INSERT ANY TABLE	Insert rows into tables and views in any schema.
LOCK ANY TABLE	Lock tables and views in any schema.
SELECT ANY TABLE	Query tables, views, or materialized views in any schema.
FLASHBACK ANY TABLE	Issue a flashback query on any table, view, or materialized view in any schema.
UPDATE ANY TABLE	Update rows in tables and views in any schema.
TABLESPACES	
CREATE TABLESPACE	Create tablespaces.
ALTER TABLESPACE	Alter tablespaces.
DROP TABLESPACE	Drop tablespaces.
MANAGE TABLESPACE	Take tablespaces offline and online and begin and end tablespace backups.
UNLIMITED TABLESPACE	Use an unlimited amount of any tablespace. This privilege overrides any specific quotas assigned. If you revoke this privilege from a user, the user's schema objects remain but further tablespace allocation is denied unless authorized by specific tablespace quotas. You cannot grant this system privilege to roles.
TRIGGERS	
CREATE TRIGGER	Create a database trigger in grantee's schema.
CREATE ANY TRIGGER	Create database triggers in any schema.
ALTER ANY TRIGGER	Enable, disable, or compile database triggers in any schema.
DROP ANY TRIGGER	Drop database triggers in any schema.
ADMINISTER DATABASE TRIGGER	Create a trigger on DATABASE. (You must also have the CREATE TRIGGER or CREATE ANY TRIGGER privilege.)
TYPES	
CREATE TYPE	Create object types and object type bodies in grantee's schema.
CREATE ANY TYPE	Create object types and object type bodies in any schema.
ALTER ANY TYPE	Alter object types in any schema.
DROP ANY TYPE	Drop object types and object type bodies in any schema.
EXECUTE ANY TYPE	Use and reference object types and collection types in any schema, and invoke methods of an object type in any schema if you make the grant to a specific user. If you grant EXECUTE ANY TYPE to a role, users holding the enabled role will not be able to invoke methods of an object type in any schema.
UNDER ANY TYPE	Create subtypes under any nonfinal object types.

Privilege	Permission to...
USERS	
CREATE USER	Create users. This privilege also allows the creator to: Assign quotas on any tablespace. Set default and temporary tablespaces. Assign a profile as part of a **CREATE USER** statement.
ALTER USER	Alter any user. This privilege authorizes the grantee to: Change another user's password or authentication method. Assign quotas on any tablespace. Set default and temporary tablespaces. Assign a profile and default roles.
DROP USER	Drop users.
VIEWS	
CREATE VIEW	Create views in grantee's schema.
CREATE ANY VIEW	Create views in any schema.
DROP ANY VIEW	Drop views in any schema.
UNDER ANY VIEW	Create subviews under any object views.
FLASHBACK ANY TABLE	Issue a SQL flashback query on any table, view, or materialized view in any schema. The privilege is not needed to execute the DBMS_ FLASHBACK procedures.
MERGE ANY VIEW	If a user has been granted the MERGE ANY VIEW privilege, then for any query issued by that user the optimizer can use view merging to improve query performance without performing the checks that would otherwise be performed to ensure that view merging does not violate any of the view creator's security intentions.
MISCELLANEOUS	
ANALYZE ANY	Analyze any table, cluster, or index in any schema.
AUDIT ANY	Audit any object in any schema using **AUDIT** *schema_objects* statements.
BECOME USER	Allow users of the Data Pump Import utility and the original Import utility to assume the identity of another user in order to perform operations that cannot be directly performed by a third party. This system privilege allows Streams administrators to create or alter users in the Streams environment. By default, this privilege is part of the DBA role. Data Vault removes this privilege from the DBA role. Therefore, this privilege is needed by Streams only in an environment where Data Vault is installed.
COMMENT ANY TABLE	Comment on any table, view, or column in any schema.
EXEMPT ACCESS POLICY	Bypass fine-grained access control. This is a very powerful system privilege, as it lets the grantee bypass application-driven security policies. Database administrators should use caution when granting this privilege.
FORCE ANY TRANSACTION	Force the commit or rollback of any in-doubt distributed transaction in the local database. Induce the failure of a distributed transaction.
FORCE TRANSACTION	Force the commit or rollback of grantee's in-doubt distributed transactions in the local database.

Privilege	Permission to...
GRANT ANY OBJECT PRIVILEGE	Grant any object privilege.
GRANT ANY PRIVILEGE	Grant any system privilege.
RESUMABLE	Enable resumable space allocation.
SELECT ANY DICTIONARY	Query any data dictionary object in the SYS schema. This privilege lets you selectively override the default FALSE setting of the O7_DICTIONARY_ACCESSIBILITY initialization parameter.
SYSDBA	Perform STARTUP and SHUTDOWN operations. ALTER DATABASE: open, mount, back up, or change character set. CREATE DATABASE. ARCHIVELOG and RECOVER. CREATE SPFILE. Includes the RESTRICTED SESSION privilege.
SYSOPER	Perform STARTUP and SHUTDOWN operations. ALTER DATABASE OPEN | MOUNT | BACKUP. ARCHIVELOG and RECOVER. CREATE SPFILE. Includes the RESTRICTED SESSION privilege.

System Roles	Use
CONNECT, RESOURCE, and DBA	Provided for compatibility with previous versions of Oracle Database software.
DELETE_CATALOG_ROLE, EXECUTE_CATALOG_ROLE, SELECT_CATALOG_ROLE	These roles are provided for accessing data dictionary views and packages.
EXP_FULL_DATABASE, IMP_FULL_DATABASE	These roles are provided for convenience in using the Import and Export utilities.
AQ_USER_ROLE, AQ_ADMINISTRATOR_ROLE	These roles are needed for Oracle Advanced Queuing.
SNMPAGENT	This role is used by the Enterprise Manager Intelligent Agent.
RECOVERY_CATALOG_OWNER	This role is required for the creation of a recovery catalog schema owner.
HS_ADMIN_ROLE	Needed for support of Heterogeneous Services.
SCHEDULER_ADMIN	This role allows the grantee to execute the DBMS_SCHEDULER package's procedures.

NOTE
For external tables, the only valid privileges are CREATE ANY TABLE, ALTER ANY TABLE, DROP ANY TABLE, and SELECT ANY TABLE.

Object privileges apply only to certain kinds of objects. The following table shows the relationships and the grantable object privileges.

Object Privilege

	Table	View	Sequence	Procedures, Functions, Packages	Materialized View	Directory	Library	User-defined Type	Operator	Indextype
ALTER	X		X							
DELETE	X	X			X[b]					
EXECUTE				X[c]			X[c]	X[c]	X[c]	X[c]
DEBUG	X	X		X				X		
FLASHBACK	X	X			X					
INDEX	X									
INSERT	X	X			X[b]					
ON COMMIT REFRESH					X					
QUERY REWRITE	X									
READ						X				
REFERENCES	X	X								
SELECT	X	X	X		X					
UNDER		X						X		
UPDATE	X	X			X[b]					
WRITE						X				

[a] Oracle treats a Java class, source, or resource as if it were a procedure for purposes of granting object privileges.
[b] The DELETE, INSERT, and UPDATE privileges can be granted only to updatable materialized views.
[c] Job Scheduler objects are created using the DBMS_SCHEDULER package. Once these objects are created, you can grant the EXECUTE object privilege on Job Scheduler classes and programs. You can grant the ALTER privilege on Job Scheduler jobs, programs, and schedules.

For FLASHBACK ARCHIVE, MINING MODEL, and OLAP options, the available privileges are as follows:

FLASHBACK DATA ARCHIVE PRIVILEGE	The following flashback data archive privilege authorizes operations on flashback data archives.
FLASHBACK ARCHIVE	Used to enable or disable historical tracking for a table.
MINING MODEL PRIVILEGES	The following mining model privileges authorize operations on a mining model. These privileges are not required for models within the user's own schema.
ALTER	Used to change the mining model name or the associated cost matrix using the applicable DBMS_DATA_MINING procedures.

SELECT	Used to score or view the mining model. Scoring is done with the PREDICTION family of SQL functions or with the DBMS_DATA_MINING.APPLY procedure. Viewing the model is done with the DBMS_DATA_MINING.GET_MODEL_DETAILS_* procedures.
OLAP PRIVILEGES	The following object privileges are valid if you are using Oracle Database with the OLAP option.
INSERT	Used to insert members into the OLAP cube dimension or measures into the measures folder.
ALTER	Used to change the definition of the OLAP cube dimension or cube.
DELETE	Used to delete members from the OLAP cube dimension or measures from the measures folder.
SELECT	Used to view or query the OLAP cube or cube dimension.
UPDATE	Used to update measure values of the OLAP cube or attribute values of the cube dimension.

PROMPT (SQL*Plus)

SEE ALSO ACCEPT
FORMAT

```
PRO[MPT] [text]
```

DESCRIPTION **PROMPT** displays the *text* to the user's screen. If no *text* is specified, then a blank line is displayed. To display a variable, *see* **PRINT**.

PSEUDO-COLUMNS

DESCRIPTION A pseudo-column is a "column" that yields a value when selected but is not an actual column of the table. Here are the current Oracle pseudo-columns:

Pseudo-Column	Value Returned
COLUMN_VALUE	When you refer to an XMLTable construct without the **COLUMNS** clause, or when you use the **TABLE** function to refer to a scalar nested table type, the database returns a virtual table with a single column. The name of this pseudo-column is **COLUMN_VALUE**.
CONNECT_BY_ISCYCLE	Equal to 1 if the current row has a child that is also its ancestor, otherwise 0.
CONNECT_BY_ISLEAF	Equal to 1 if the current row is a leaf of the tree defined by the **CONNECT BY** condition, otherwise 0.
Level	Equal to 1 for a root node, 2 for a child of a root, and so on. Tells basically how far down a tree you've traveled.
sequence.CURRVAL	Current value for this sequence name.
sequence.NEXTVAL	Next value for this sequence name. Also increments the sequence.
VERSIONS_STARTTIME	For flashback version queries, returns the timestamp of the first version of the rows returned by the query.
VERSIONS_STARTSCN	For flashback version queries, returns the SCN of the first version of the rows returned by the query.

Pseudo-Column	Value Returned
VERSIONS_ ENDTIME	For flashback version queries, returns the timestamp of the last version of the rows returned by the query.
VERSIONS_ ENDSCN	For flashback version queries, returns the SCN of the last version of the rows returned by the query.
VERSIONS_XID	For flashback version queries, for each version of each row, returns the transaction ID of the transaction that created that row version.
VERSIONS_ OPERATION	For flashback version queries, for each version of each row, returns a single character for the operation that caused the row version: I (insert), U (update), or D (delete).
OBJECT_ID	Returns the object identifier of a column of an object table or view.
OBJECT_VALUE	Returns system-generated names for the columns of an object table, XMLType table, object view, or XMLType view.
ORA_ROWSCN	Returns the conservative upper-bound SCN of the most recent change to the row, showing approximately when the row was last updated (row-level dependencies should be created for more fine-grained auditing).
ROWID	Returns the row identifier for a row. Use the ROWID in the **UPDATE...WHERE** and **SELECT...FOR UPDATE**. This guarantees that only a certain row is updated, and no others.
ROWNUM	Returns the sequence number in which a row was returned when selected from a table. The first row ROWNUM is 1, the second is 2, and so on.
XMLDATA	Lets you access the underlying XMLType LOB data or object relational column.

PURGE

SEE ALSO Chapter 51
FORMAT
purge::=

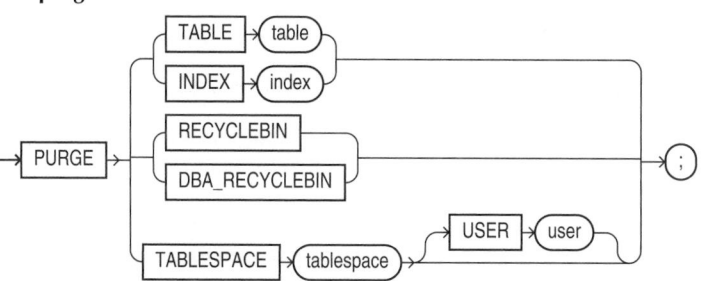

DESCRIPTION PURGE removes a table or index from your recycle bin and releases all of the space associated with the object, or removes the entire recycle bin, or removes part or all of a dropped tablespace from the recycle bin.

NOTE
*You cannot roll back a **PURGE** command. You cannot recover an object after it is purged.*

To see the contents of your recycle bin, query the RECYCLEBIN data dictionary view.
You can use the **TABLE** or **INDEX** keywords to specify the name of the object you wish to purge. Specifying **RECYCLEBIN** purges all objects in the user's recycle bin. **DBA_RECYCLEBIN** purges all users' recycle bins. **TABLESPACE** purges all objects residing in the specified tablespace from the recycle bin. **USER** *user* purges space within a tablespace for a particular user.

EXAMPLE   To purge an individual table:

```
purge table bookshelf;
```

To purge the current user's recycle bin:

```
purge recyclebin;
```

QUERY OPERATORS

The following is an alphabetical list of all current query operators in the Oracle version of SQL. Each of these is listed elsewhere in this reference under its own name, with its proper format and use. *See also* Chapter 13.

Operator	Purpose
INTERSECT	Returns all matching distinct rows from two queries
MINUS	Returns all distinct rows in first query that are not in the second
UNION	Returns all distinct rows from both of two queries
UNION ALL	Returns all rows from both of two queries

QUIT

SEE ALSO   COMMIT, DISCONNECT, EXIT, SET AUTOCOMMIT, START
FORMAT

```
QUIT
```

DESCRIPTION   QUIT ends a SQL*Plus session and returns the user to an operating system, calling program, or menu.

RAISE

SEE ALSO   EXCEPTION, EXCEPTION_INIT
FORMAT

```
RAISE [exception]
```

DESCRIPTION   **RAISE** names the exception flag you want to raise, based on a condition that is being tested. The exception must be either one you've explicitly **DECLARE**d, or an internal system exception such as DIVIDE_BY_ZERO (*see* EXCEPTION for a complete list). A **RAISE** statement causes control to be transferred to the EXCEPTION section of the current block, where you must test to see which exception was raised. If no EXCEPTION section is present, control is passed to the nearest EXCEPTION section of an enclosing block (basically backward through the nesting of the blocks). If no logic is found to handle the exception, control is passed from the PL/SQL to the calling program or environment with an unhandled exception error. (The use of OTHERS can avoid this. *See* EXCEPTION.) **RAISE** without an explicitly named exception can be used only in one circumstance: within an EXCEPTION section, to force the current exception to be handled by an enclosing block's EXCEPTION section, rather than the current one. If, for instance, a NOT_LOGGED_ON error had occurred and your local EXCEPTION section says this:

```
when not_logged_on
    then raise;
```

it would pass control back to the EXCEPTION section of the next enclosing block that had one or to the program if none was found. That EXCEPTION block could also test for NOT_LOGGED_ON. The benefit here is that for a certain class of errors, particularly where the recovery, tracing, or error-logging steps you want to take may be extensive, you can set every nested block's EXCEPTION section to simply hand the EXCEPTION backward to a single spot for disposition.

RANK

SEE ALSO ANALYTIC FUNCTIONS
FORMAT

Aggregate syntax:
rank_aggregate::=

Analytic syntax:
rank_analytic::=

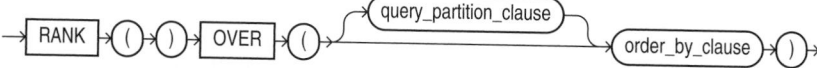

DESCRIPTION **RANK** calculates the rank of a value in a group of values. The return type is NUMBER. Rows with equal values for the ranking criteria receive the same rank.

RATIO_TO_REPORT

SEE ALSO AGGREGATE FUNCTIONS
FORMAT

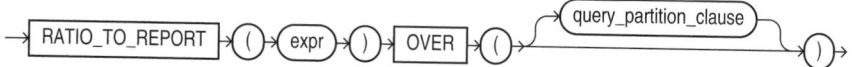

DESCRIPTION **RATIO_TO_REPORT** is an analytic function. It computes the ratio of a value to the sum of a set of values. If *expr* evaluates to **NULL**, the ratio-to-report value also evaluates to **NULL**.

RAW DATATYPE

A RAW column contains binary data in whatever form the host computer stores it. RAW columns are useful for storing binary (noncharacter) data.

RAWTOHEX

SEE ALSO HEXTORAW
FORMAT

DESCRIPTION **RAWTOHEX** changes a string of binary numbers to a character string of hexadecimal numbers.

RAWTONHEX

SEE ALSO   RAWTOHEX
FORMAT

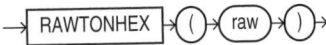

DESCRIPTION   **RAWTONHEX** converts *raw* to an NVARCHAR2 character value containing its hexadecimal equivalent.

RECORD (PL/SQL)

SEE ALSO   TABLE (PL/SQL), DATATYPES
FORMAT

```
TYPE new_type IS RECORD
  (field {type | table.column%TYPE}[NOT NULL]
  [,field {type | table.column%TYPE}[NOT NULL]...]);
```

DESCRIPTION   A **RECORD** declaration declares a new type that can then be used to declare variables of that type. The individual components of the record are fields, and each has its own datatype. That datatype can be either one of the standard PL/SQL datatypes (including another RECORD but not a TABLE), or a reference to the type of a particular column in a specific table. Each field also may have a **NOT NULL** qualifier that specifies that the field must always have a non-**NULL** value.

You can refer to the individual fields in a record by using dot notation.

RECOVER

RECOVER is a clause within the **ALTER DATABASE** command. It is also a command in Oracle Recovery Manager (RMAN). *See* the *Oracle Database 12c DBA Handbook* for details on RMAN.
SEE ALSO   **ALTER DATABASE**, Chapter 51
FORMAT

```
RECOVER {general | managed | BEGIN BACKUP | END BACKUP}
```

where the **GENERAL** clause has the following syntax:

```
[AUTOMATIC] [FROM location]
{ {full_database_recovery | partial_database_recovery |LOGFILE filename}
[ {TEST | ALLOW integer CORRUPTION | parallel_clause }
[TEST | ALLOW integer CORRUPTION | parallel_clause]...]
|CONTINUE [DEFAULT]|CANCEL}
```

where the **FULL DATABASE RECOVERY** clause has the following syntax:

```
[STANDBY] DATABASE
[ {UNTIL {CANCEL | TIME date | CHANGE integer} | USING BACKUP CONTROLFILE}
[UNTIL {CANCEL | TIME date | CHANGE integer} | USING BACKUP CONTROLFILE]...]
```

where the **PARTIAL DATABASE RECOVERY** clause has the following syntax:

```
{TABLESPACE tablespace [, tablespace]... | DATAFILE datafilename [, data-
filenumber]...
| STANDBY
{TABLESPACE tablespace [, tablespace]... | DATAFILE datafilename [, data-
filenumber]...}
UNTIL [CONSISTENT WITH] CONTROLFILE }
```

and the **PARALLEL** clause has the following syntax:

```
{NOPARALLEL | PARALLEL [integer]}
```

and the **MANAGED** clause has the following syntax:

```
MANAGED STANDBY DATABASE recover_clause | cancel_clause | finish_clause
```

and the **RECOVER** clause has the following syntax:

```
{{DISCONNECT [FROM SESSION]|{TIMEOUT integer | NOTIMEOUT}}
 |{NODELAY | DEFAULT DELAY | DELAY integer} | NEXT integer
 |{EXPIRE integer | NO EXPIRE} | parallel_clause
 | USING CURRENT LOGFILE | UNTIL CHANGE integer
 | THROUGH {[THREAD integer] SEQUENCE integer
    | ALL ARCHIVELOG | {ALL|LAST|NEXT} SWITCHOVER}}
[DISCONNECT [FROM SESSION] | {TIMEOUT integer | NOTIMEOUT}
 | {NODELAY|DEFAULT DELAY|DELAY integer}| NEXT integer
 | {EXPIRE integer | NO EXPIRE}| parallel_clause
 | USING CURRENT LOGFILE | UNTIL CHANGE integer
 | THROUGH {[THREAD integer]SEQUENCE integer
    | ALL ARCHIVELOG | {ALL|LAST|NEXT} SWITCHOVER}}
```

and the **CANCEL** clause has the following syntax:

```
CANCEL [IMMEDIATE] [WAIT | NOWAIT]
```

and the **FINISH** clause has the following syntax:

```
[DISCONNECT [FROM SESSION]] [parallel_clause]
FINISH [SKIP [STANDBY LOGFILE]][WAIT|NOWAIT]
```

DESCRIPTION

The **RECOVER** command, like the **RECOVER** clause of the **ALTER DATABASE** command, recovers a database using various options. **AUTOMATIC** recovery generates the redo log filenames automatically during recovery. The **FROM** clause specifies the location of the archived redo log file group and must be a fully qualified filename. The default is set by the initialization parameter LOG_ARCHIVE_DEST (or LOG_ARCHIVE_DEST_1).

The **DATABASE** option recovers the entire database and is the default. The **UNTIL CANCEL** alternative recovers the database until you cancel the recovery with the **CANCEL** option. The **UNTIL TIME** alternative recovers up to a specified date and time (in the format YYYY-MM-DD:HH24:MI:SS). The **UNTIL CHANGE** alternative recovers up to a *system change number* (SCN), which is a unique number assigned to each transaction) specified by an integer. The **USING BACKUP CONTROLFILE** alternative recovers by applying the redo log in a backup control file.

You can perform trial recoveries via the **TEST** option and **CONTINUE** a multi-instance recovery even after it has been interrupted. The **DELAY** parameters relate to the application of logs to standby databases during recovery; by default, they are delayed as defined via the LOG_ARCHIVE_DEST_*n* parameter values.

RECYCLE BIN

Dropped objects go into a recycle bin by default rather than being immediately dropped. The recycle bin allows for dropped objects to be restored without the need for a full database recovery. You can purge specific objects from the recycle bin via the **PURGE** command. *See* **PURGE**.

To see the objects presently in your recycle bin, query the RECYCLEBIN data dictionary view or use the **SHOW RECYCLEBIN** command.

REF

SEE ALSO   Chapter 41
FORMAT

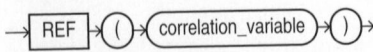

DESCRIPTION   **REF** is a reference function used with object tables; the input correlation variable is a table alias. **REF** returns the object instance for that variable. *See* Chapter 41 for detailed examples.

REFTOHEX

SEE ALSO   Chapter 41
FORMAT

DESCRIPTION   **REFTOHEX** converts argument *expr* to a character value containing its hexadecimal equivalent. *expr* must return a **REF**.

REGEXP_COUNT

SEE ALSO   **REGEXP_INSTR**, Chapter 8
FORMAT

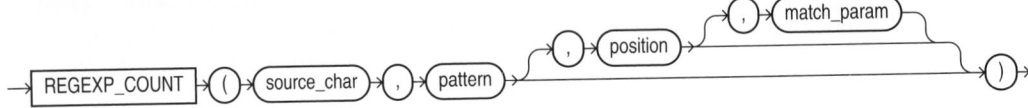

DESCRIPTION   **REGEXP_COUNT** complements the functionality of the **REGEXP_INSTR** function by returning the number of times a pattern occurs in a source string. The function evaluates strings using characters as defined by the input character set. It returns an integer indicating the number of occurrences of *pattern*. If no match is found, the function returns 0.

- *source_char* is a character expression that serves as the search value. It is commonly a character column and can be any of the datatypes: CHAR, VARCHAR2, NCHAR, NVARCHAR2, CLOB, and NCLOB.

- *pattern* is the regular expression. It is usually a text literal and can be any of the datatypes: CHAR, VARCHAR2, NCHAR, and NVARCHAR2. It can contain up to 512 bytes. If the datatype of *pattern* is different from the datatype of *source_char*, Oracle Database converts *pattern* to the datatype of *source_char*.

- **REGEXP_COUNT** ignores subexpression parentheses in *pattern*. For example, the pattern "(123(45))" is equivalent to "12345".

- *position* is a positive integer indicating the character of *source_char* where Oracle should begin the search. The default is 1, meaning that Oracle begins the search at the first character of *source_char*. After finding the first occurrence of *pattern,* the database searches for a second occurrence beginning with the first character following the first occurrence.

■   *match_param* is a text literal that lets you change the default matching behavior of the function. You can specify one or more of the following values for *match_param*:

　■   'i' specifies case-insensitive matching.

　■   'c' specifies case-sensitive matching.

　■   'n' allows the period (.), which is the match-any-character character, to match the newline character. If you omit this parameter, the period does not match the newline character.

　■   'm' treats the source string as multiple lines. Oracle interprets the caret (^) and dollar sign ($) as the start and end, respectively, of any line anywhere in the source string, rather than only at the start or end of the entire source string. If you omit this parameter, Oracle treats the source string as a single line.

　■   'x' ignores whitespace characters. By default, whitespace characters match themselves.

If you specify multiple contradictory values, Oracle uses the last value. For example, if you specify 'ic', Oracle uses case-sensitive matching. If you specify a character other than those just shown, Oracle returns an error.

If you omit *match_param*, then

■   The default case sensitivity is determined by the value of the NLS_SORT parameter.

■   A period (.) does not match the newline character.

■   The source string is treated as a single line.

REGEXP_INSTR

SEE ALSO   **INSTR**, Chapter 8
FORMAT

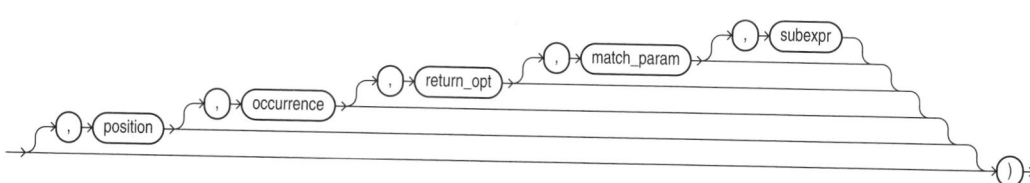

DESCRIPTION   **REGEXP_INSTR** extends the functionality of the **INSTR** function by letting you search a string for a regular expression pattern. The function evaluates strings using characters as defined by the input character set. It returns an integer indicating the beginning or ending position of the matched substring, depending on the value of the *return_option* argument. If no match is found, the function returns 0.

See Chapter 8 for examples of the **REGEXP** functions.

As of Oracle Database 11*g,* you can target a particular substring of the regular expression being evaluated.

REGEXP_LIKE

SEE ALSO   **LIKE**, Chapter 8

FORMAT
regexp_like_condition::=

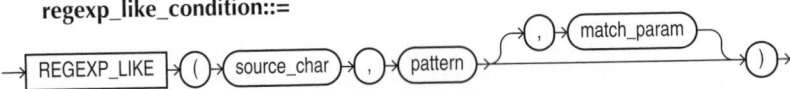

DESCRIPTION   **REGEXP_LIKE** extends the functionality of the **LIKE** operator by letting you search a string for a regular expression pattern. The function evaluates strings using characters as defined by the input character set. *See* Chapter 8 for examples of the **REGEXP** functions.

REGEXP_REPLACE
SEE ALSO   **REPLACE**, Chapter 8
FORMAT

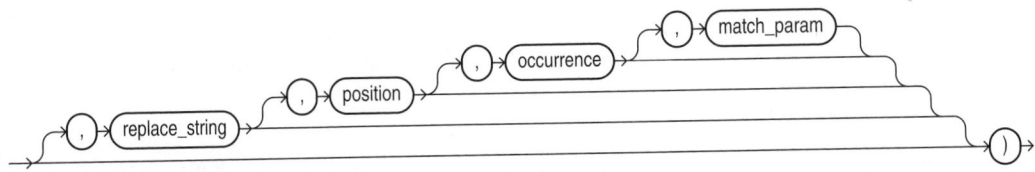

DESCRIPTION   **REGEXP_REPLACE** extends the functionality of the **REPLACE** function by letting you search a string for a regular expression pattern. By default, the function returns the *source_string* with every occurrence of the regular expression pattern replaced with *replace_string*. The string returned is in the same character set as *source_string*. The function returns VARCHAR2 if the first argument is not a LOB and returns CLOB if the first argument is a LOB. *See* Chapter 8 for examples of the **REGEXP** functions.

REGEXP_SUBSTR
SEE ALSO   **SUBSTR**, Chapter 8
FORMAT

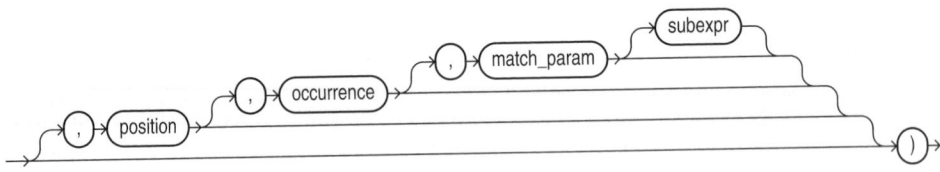

DESCRIPTION   **REGEXP_SUBSTR** extends the functionality of the **SUBSTR** function by letting you search a string for a regular expression pattern. It is similar to **REGEXP_INSTR**, but instead of returning the position of the substring, it returns the substring itself. The function returns the string as VARCHAR2 or CLOB data in the same character set as *source_string*.

See Chapter 8 for examples of the **REGEXP** functions.

As of Oracle Database 11*g*, you can target a particular substring of the regular expression being evaluated.

REGR_ (LINEAR REGRESSION) FUNCTIONS

SEE ALSO AGGREGATE FUNCTIONS
FORMAT

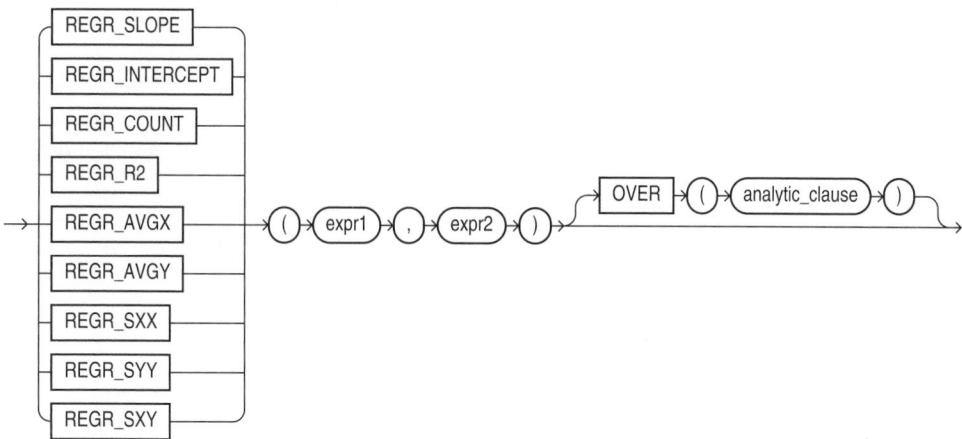

DESCRIPTION The linear regression functions fit an ordinary-least-squares regression line to a set of number pairs. You can use them as both aggregate and analytic functions. **REGR_SLOPE** returns the slope of the line. **REGR_INTERCEPT** returns the y-intercept of the regression line. **REGR_COUNT** returns an integer that is the number of non-**NULL** number pairs used to fit the regression line. **REGR_R2** returns the coefficient of determination for the regression. **REGR_AVGX** evaluates the average of the independent variable (*expr2*) of the regression line. **REGR_AVGY** evaluates the average of the dependent variable (*expr1*) of the regression line. **REGR_SXY**, **REGR_SXX**, and **REGR_SYY** are auxiliary functions used to compute various diagnostic statistics.

REMAINDER

SEE ALSO NUMBER FUNCTIONS
FORMAT

DESCRIPTION **REMAINDER** returns the remainder of *m* divided by *n*.

REMARK (SQL*Plus)

SEE ALSO /* */, --, Chapter 6
FORMAT

```
REM[ARK] text
```

DESCRIPTION **REMARK** begins a single line of remarks, usually documentation, in a start file. It is not interpreted as a command. **REMARK** cannot appear within a SQL statement.
EXAMPLE

```
REM Reduce the default column width for this data field:
column ActionDate format a6 trunc
```

RENAME

SEE ALSO COPY, **CREATE SEQUENCE, CREATE SYNONYM, CREATE TABLE, CREATE VIEW**
FORMAT
 rename::=

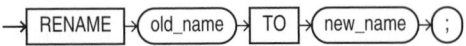

DESCRIPTION **RENAME** changes the name of a table, view, sequence, or synonym from its old name
to a new one. No quotes are used around the names, and the new name must be neither a reserved
word nor the name of an existing object for the user.
EXAMPLE The following changes the BOOKSHELF table to the BOOK table:

```
rename bookshelf to book;
```

REPFOOTER (SQL*Plus)

SEE ALSO **ACCEPT, BTITLE, DEFINE,** PARAMETERS, **REPHEADER**
FORMAT

```
REPF[OOTER] [PAGE][option [text|variable]... | OFF|ON]
```

DESCRIPTION **REPFOOTER** (**REP**ort **FOOTER**) puts a footer (may be multiline) on the last page of a
report. OFF and ON suppress and restore, respectively, the display of the text without changing its
contents. **REPFOOTER** by itself displays the current **REPFOOTER** options and *text* or *variable*. **PAGE**
begins a new page before printing the specified report footer. *text* is a footer you wish to give this
report, and *variable* is a user-defined variable or a system-maintained variable, including SQL.LNO, the
current line number; SQL.PNO, the current page number; SQL.RELEASE, the current Oracle release
number; SQL.SQLCODE, the current error code; and SQL.USER, the username.
 Valid values for *option* are

- **COL** *n* skips directly to position *n* from the left margin of the current line.

- **S[KIP]** *n* prints *n* blank lines. If no *n* is specified, one blank line is printed. If *n* is 0, no blank
  lines are printed and the current position for printing becomes position 1 of the current line
  (leftmost on the page).

- **TAB** *n* skips forward *n* positions (backward if *n* is negative).

- **LE[FT]**, **CE[NTER]**, and **R[IGHT]** left-justify, center, and right-justify data on the current line.
  Any text or variables following these commands are justified as a group, up to the end of the
  command, or a LEFT, CENTER, RIGHT, or COL. CENTER and RIGHT use the value set by the
  SET LINESIZE command to determine where to place the text or variable.

- **BOLD** prints data in bold print. SQL*Plus represents bold print on your terminal by repeating
  the data on three consecutive lines.

- **FORMAT** *string* specifies the FORMAT MODEL that will control the format of subsequent
  text or variables and follows the same syntax as FORMAT in a **COLUMN** command, such
  as FORMAT A12 or FORMAT $999,990.99. Each time a FORMAT appears, it supersedes the
  previous one that was in effect. If no FORMAT MODEL has been specified, the one set by **SET
  NUMFORMAT** is used. If NUMFORMAT has not been set, the default for SQL*Plus is used.

 Date values are printed according to the default format unless a variable has been loaded with a
date reformatted by **TO_CHAR**.

REPHEADER (SQL*Plus)

SEE ALSO **ACCEPT**, **BTITLE**, **DEFINE**, PARAMETERS, **REPFOOTER**
FORMAT

```
REPH[EADER] [PAGE] [option [text|variable]... | OFF|ON]
```

DESCRIPTION **REPHEADER** (**REP**ort **HEADER**) puts a header (may be multiline) on the first page of a report. OFF and ON suppress and restore, respectively, the display of the text without changing its contents. **REPHEADER** by itself displays the current **REPHEADER** options and *text* or *variable*. **PAGE** begins a new page after printing the report header.

text is a header you wish to give this report, and *variable* is a user-defined variable or a system-maintained variable, including SQL.LNO, the current line number; SQL.PNO, the current page number; SQL.RELEASE, the current Oracle release number; SQL.SQLCODE, the current error code; and SQL.USER, the username.

Valid values for option are

- **COL** *n* skips directly to position *n* from the left margin of the current line.

- **S[KIP]** *n* prints *n* blank lines. If no *n* is specified, one blank line is printed. If *n* is 0, no blank lines are printed and the current position for printing becomes position 1 of the current line (leftmost on the page).

- **TAB** *n* skips forward *n* positions (backward if *n* is negative).

- **LE[FT]**, **CE[NTER]**, and **R[IGHT]** left-justify, center, and right-justify data on the current line. Any text or variables following these commands are justified as a group, up to the end of the command, or a LEFT, CENTER, RIGHT, or COL. CENTER and RIGHT use the value set by the **SET LINESIZE** command to determine where to place the text or variable.

- **BOLD** prints data in bold print. SQL*Plus represents bold print on your terminal by repeating the data on three consecutive lines.

- **FORMAT** *string* specifies the FORMAT MODEL that will control the format of subsequent text or variables, and follows the same syntax as FORMAT in a **COLUMN** command, such as FORMAT A12 or FORMAT $999,990.99. Each time a FORMAT appears, it supersedes the previous one that was in effect. If no FORMAT MODEL has been specified, the one set by **SET NUMFORMAT** is used. If NUMFORMAT has not been set, the default for SQL*Plus is used.

Date values are printed according to the default format unless a variable has been loaded with a date reformatted by **TO_CHAR**.

REPLACE

SEE ALSO CHARACTER FUNCTIONS, **TRANSLATE**, Chapter 7
FORMAT

DESCRIPTION **REPLACE** replaces a character or characters in a string with zero or more characters. *char* is a character or characters. Every time *char* appears in *search_string*, it is replaced by the contents of *replacement_string*.
EXAMPLE

```
replace('BOB','BO','TA') = TAB
```

RESERVED WORDS

SEE ALSO OBJECT NAMES

DESCRIPTION A reserved word is one that has a special meaning to SQL and, therefore, may not be used as the name of an object. Contrast this to a keyword, which may be used as an object name, but may become a reserved word in the future. Not every word is reserved in all products, so this list is structured to show which products reserve which words. In the following table, the entries with an * are reserved in SQL and ANSI:

ACCESS	ADD *	ALL *	ALTER *	AND *
ANY *	AS *	ASC *	AUDIT	BETWEEN *
BY *	CHAR *	CHECK *	CLUSTER	COLUMN
COMMENT	COMPRESS	CONNECT *	CREATE *	CURRENT *
DATE *	DECIMAL *	DEFAULT *	DELETE *	DESC *
DISTINCT *	DROP *	ELSE *	EXCLUSIVE	EXISTS
FILE	FLOAT *	FOR *	FROM *	GRANT *
GROUP *	HAVING *	IDENTIFIED	IMMEDIATE *	IN *
INCREMENT	INDEX	INITIAL	INSERT *	INTEGER *
INTERSECT *	INTO *	IS *	LEVEL *	LIKE *
LOCK	LONG	MAXEXTENTS	MINUS	MLSLABEL
MODE	MODIFY	NOAUDIT	NOCOMPRESS	NOT *
NOWAIT	NULL *	NUMBER	OF *	OFFLINE
ON *	ONLINE	OPTION *	OR *	ORDER *
PCTFREE	PRIOR *	PRIVILEGES *	PUBLIC *	RAW
RENAME	RESOURCE	REVOKE *	ROW	ROWID
ROWNUM	ROWS *	SELECT *	SESSION *	SET *
SHARE	SIZE *	SMALLINT *	START	SUCCESSFUL
SYNONYM	SYSDATE	TABLE *	THEN *	TO *
TRIGGER	UID	UNION *	UNIQUE *	UPDATE *
USER *	VALIDATE	VALUES *	VARCHAR *	VARCHAR2
VIEW *	WHENEVER *	WHERE	WITH *	

The following table lists the reserved words in PL/SQL:

Begins With	Reserved Words
A	ALL, ALTER, AND, ANY, ARRAY, ARROW, AS, ASC, AT
B	BEGIN, BETWEEN, BY
C	CASE, CHECK, CLUSTERS, CLUSTER, COLAUTH, COLUMNS, COMPRESS, CONNECT, CRASH, CREATE, CURRENT
D	DECIMAL, DECLARE, DEFAULT, DELETE, DESC, DISTINCT, DROP
E	ELSE, END, EXCEPTION, EXCLUSIVE, EXISTS
F	FETCH, FOR, FORM, FROM
G	GOTO, GRANT, GROUP

Begins With	Reserved Words
H	HAVING
I	IDENTIFIED, IF, IN, INDEX, INDEXES, INSERT, INTERSECT, INTO, IS
L	LIKE, LOCK
M	MINUS, MODE
N	NOCOMPRESS, NOT, NOWAIT, NULL
O	OF, ON, OPTION, OR, ORDER, OVERLAPS
P	PRIOR, PROCEDURE, PUBLIC
R	RANGE, RECORD, RESOURCE, REVOKE
S	SELECT, SHARE, SIZE, SQL, START, SUBTYPE
T	TABAUTH, TABLE, THEN, TO, TYPE
U	UNION, UNIQUE, UPDATE, USE
V	VALUES, VIEW, VIEWS
W	WHEN, WHERE, WITH

The following table lists the keywords within PL/SQL:

Begins With	Keywords
A	A, ADD, AGENT, AGGREGATE, ARRAY, ATTRIBUTE, AUTHID, AVG
B	BFILE_BASE, BINARY, BLOB_BASE, BLOCK, BODY, BOTH, BOUND, BULK, BYTE
C	C, CALL, CALLING, CASCADE, CHAR, CHAR_BASE, CHARACTER, CHARSET, CHARSETFORM, CHARSETID, CLOB_BASE, CLOSE, COLLECT, COMMENT, COMMIT, COMMITTED, COMPILED, CONSTANT, CONSTRUCTOR, CONTEXT, CONTINUE, CONVERT, COUNT, CURSOR, CUSTOMDATUM
D	DANGLING, DATA, DATE, DATE_BASE, DAY, DEFINE, DETERMINISTIC, DOUBLE, DURATION
E	ELEMENT, ELSIF, EMPTY, ESCAPE, EXCEPT, EXCEPTIONS, EXECUTE, EXIT, EXTERNAL
F	FINAL, FIXED, FLOAT, FORALL, FORCE, FUNCTION
G	GENERAL
H	HASH, HEAP, HIDDEN, HOUR
I	IMMEDIATE, INCLUDING, INDICATOR, INDICES, INFINITE, INSTANTIABLE, INT, INTERFACE, INTERVAL, INVALIDATE, ISOLATION
J	JAVA
L	LANGUAGE, LARGE, LEADING, LENGTH, LEVEL, LIBRARY, LIKE2, LIKE4, LIKEC, LIMIT, LIMITED, LOCAL, LONG, LOOP
M	MAP, MAX, MAXLEN, MEMBER, MERGE, MIN, MINUTE, MOD, MODIFY, MONTH, MULTISET
N	NAME, NAN, NATIONAL, NATIVE, NCHAR, NEW, NOCOPY, NUMBER_BASE
O	OBJECT, OCICOLL, OCIDATE, OCIDATETIME, OCIDURATION, OCIINTERVAL, OCILOBLOCATOR, OCINUMBER, OCIRAW, OCIREF, OCIREFCURSOR, OCIROWID, OCISTRING, OCITYPE, ONLY, OPAQUE, OPEN, OPERATOR, ORACLE, ORADATA, ORGANIZATION, ORLANY, ORLVARY, OTHERS, OUT, OVERRIDING
P	PACKAGE, PARALLEL_ENABLE, PARAMETER, PARAMETERS, PARTITION, PASCAL, PIPE, PIPELINED, PRAGMA, PRECISION, PRIVATE

Begins With	Keywords
R	RAISE, RANGE, RAW, READ, RECORD, REF, REFERENCE, RELIES_ON, REM, REMAINDER, RENAME, RESULT, RESULT_CACHE, RETURN, RETURNING, REVERSE, ROLLBACK, ROW
S	SAMPLE, SAVE, SAVEPOINT, SB1, SB2, SB4, SECOND, SEGMENT, SELF, SEPARATE, SEQUENCE, SERIALIZABLE, SET, SHORT, SIZE_T, SOME, SPARSE, SQLCODE, SQLDATA, SQLNAME, SQLSTATE, STANDARD, STATIC, STDDEV, STORED, STRING, STRUCT, STYLE, SUBMULTISET, SUBPARTITION, SUBSTITUTABLE, SUBTYPE, SUM, SYNONYM
T	TDO, THE, TIME, TIMESTAMP, TIMEZONE_ABBR, TIMEZONE_HOUR, TIMEZONE_MINUTE, TIMEZONE_REGION, TRAILING, TRANSACTION, TRANSACTIONAL, TRUSTED, TYPE
U	UB1, UB2, UB4, UNDER, UNSIGNED, UNTRUSTED, USE, USING
V	VALIST, VALUE, VARIABLE, VARIANCE, VARRAY, VARYING, VOID
W	WHILE, WORK, WRAPPED, WRITE
Y	YEAR
Z	ZONE

REVOKE

SEE ALSO **GRANT**, PRIVILEGE, Chapter 19
FORMAT
   revoke::=

   revoke_system_privileges::=

   revoke_object_privileges::=

grantee_clause::=

on_object_clause::=

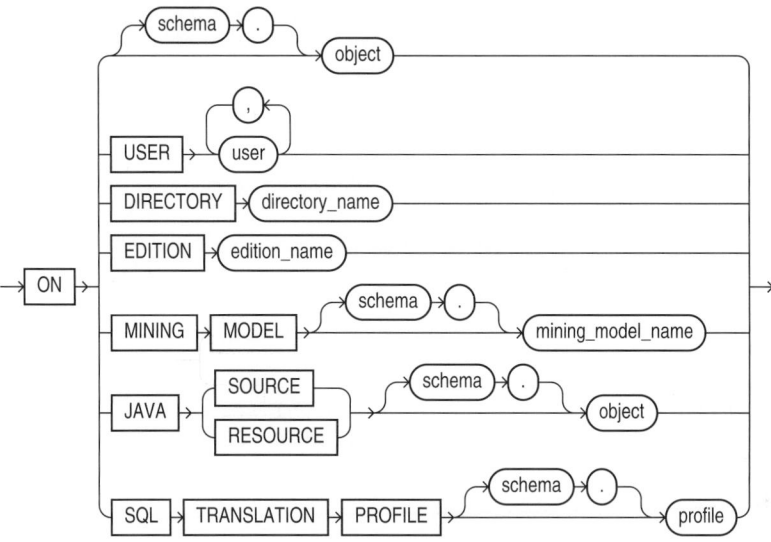

DESCRIPTION   The **REVOKE** command takes privileges and roles away from users, or privileges away from roles. Any system privilege may be revoked; *see* PRIVILEGE.

If you revoke a privilege from a user, the user can no longer execute the operations allowed by the privilege. If you revoke a privilege from a role, no user granted the role can execute the allowed operations, unless they are permitted by another role or directly as a user. If you revoke a privilege from PUBLIC, no user granted the privilege through PUBLIC can execute the operations allowed by the privilege.

If you revoke a role from a user, the user can no longer enable the role (*see* **ENABLE**) but may continue exercising the privilege in a current session. If you revoke a role from a role, users granted the role can no longer enable the role but may continue using the privilege during the current session. If you revoke a role from PUBLIC, users granted the role through PUBLIC can no longer enable the role.

For object access, the **REVOKE** command takes away object privileges on a specific object from a user or role. If a user's privileges are revoked, the user may not execute the operations allowed by the privilege on the object. If a role's privileges are revoked, no user granted the role may execute those operations unless they are granted through another role or directly to the user. If the PUBLIC's privileges are revoked, no user granted the privilege through PUBLIC may execute those operations.

The **CASCADE CONSTRAINTS** clause drops any referential integrity constraints defined by the user or by users granted the role. This applies to a REFERENCES privilege.

ROLLBACK (Form 1—SQL)

SEE ALSO   **COMMIT**, **SET AUTOCOMMIT**, Chapter 15
FORMAT

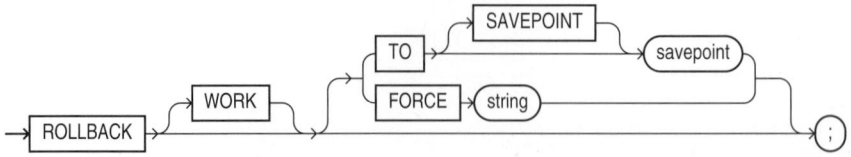

DESCRIPTION   **ROLLBACK** reverses all changes made to tables in the database since changes were last committed or rolled back and it releases any locks on the tables. An automatic rollback occurs whenever a transaction is interrupted, such as by an execution error, a power failure, and so on. **ROLLBACK** affects not just the last **INSERT**, **UPDATE**, or **DELETE** statement but any that have occurred since the last **COMMIT**. This allows you to treat blocks of work as a whole and only **COMMIT** when all of the changes you want are completed.

With **SAVEPOINT**, **ROLLBACK** goes to a specific, named place in the sequence of transactions being processed, the **SAVEPOINT**. It erases any interim **SAVEPOINT**s and releases any table or row locks that occurred after the **SAVEPOINT** was made.

With **FORCE**, **ROLLBACK** manually rolls back an in-doubt transaction identified by the literal text, which is a local or global transaction ID from the data dictionary view DBA_2PC_PENDING.

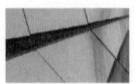

NOTE
*If **SET AUTOCOMMIT** is ON, every **INSERT**, **UPDATE**, or **DELETE**
immediately and automatically commits the changes to the database.
Typing the word **ROLLBACK** will produce a "ROLLBACK COMPLETE"
message, but this message won't mean anything since **ROLLBACK** only
rolls back to the last **COMMIT**.*

NOTE
*All DDL commands cause a **COMMIT**.*

ROLLBACK (Form 2—Embedded SQL)

SEE ALSO   **COMMIT**, **SAVEPOINT**, **SET TRANSACTION**, *Programmer's Guide to the Oracle Precompilers*
FORMAT

```
EXEC SQL [AT {database | :variable }]
ROLLBACK [WORK]
[TO [SAVEPOINT] savepoint] | [FORCE text] | [RELEASE] ]
```

DESCRIPTION   **ROLLBACK** ends the current transaction, reverses any changes resulting from the current transaction, and releases any locks being held, but does not affect host variables or program flow. *database* indicates the name of the database where the **ROLLBACK** should take effect. Its absence indicates the default database for the user. **SAVEPOINT** allows a rollback to a named *savepoint* that has been previously declared.

FORCE manually rolls back an in-doubt transaction specified by a literal text containing the transaction ID from the DBA_2PC_PENDING data dictionary view. **WORK** is entirely optional and is for readability only.

Both **ROLLBACK** and **COMMIT** have **RELEASE** options. **RELEASE** should be specified by one of them after the last transaction; otherwise, locks put on during the program will block other users. **ROLLBACK** occurs automatically (with a **RELEASE**) if the program abnormally terminates.

NOTE
See the Programmer's Guide to the Oracle Precompilers *for a full list of all commands. This reference does not contain all of the possible precompiler commands.*

ROLLUP

SEE ALSO   CUBE, **GROUPING**, Chapter 12
FORMAT

```
GROUP BY ROLLUP(column1, column2)
```

DESCRIPTION   **ROLLUP** generates subtotals for groups of rows within a query.

ROUND (Form 1—for Dates)

SEE ALSO   DATE FUNCTIONS, **ROUND** (NUMBER), **TRUNC**, Chapter 10
FORMAT
   round_date::=

DESCRIPTION   **ROUND** rounds *date* according to *format*. Without *format*, *date* is rounded to the next day if the time is 12:00:00 P.M. (exactly noon) or later, or to today's date if before noon; in other words, it is rounded to the nearest day. The resulting date has its time set to 12 A.M., the very first instant of the day.

The table lists the formats available for rounding:

Format	Meaning
CC, SCC	Century (rounds up to January 1 of next century, as of midnight exactly on the morning of January 1 of 1950, 2050, and so on)
SYEAR, SYYY, Y, YY, YYY, YYYY, and YEAR	Year (rounds up to January 1 of the next year as of midnight exactly on the morning of July 1)
IYYY, IYY, IY, I	ISO year
Q	Quarter (rounds up in the second month of the quarter as of midnight exactly on the morning of the 16th, regardless of the number of days in the month)
MONTH, MON, MM, RM	Month (rounds up as of midnight exactly on the morning of the 16th regardless of the number of days in the month)
WW	Same day of the week as the first day of the year
IW	Same day of the week as the first day of the ISO year
W	Same day of the week as the first day of the month
DDD, DD, J	Rounds up to the next day as of noon exactly; the same as **ROUND** with no format
DAY, DY, D	Starting day of week
HH, HH12, HH24	Hour
MI	Minute

When **WW** and **W** round, the time of the date being rounded is compared to a date that is set to 12 A.M., the very beginning of the day. The result of **ROUND** is a new date, which is also set to 12 A.M.

ROUND (Form 2—for Numbers)

SEE ALSO   **CEIL**, **FLOOR**, NUMBER FUNCTIONS, **ROUND** (DATE), **TRUNC**, Chapter 9
FORMAT
   round_number::=

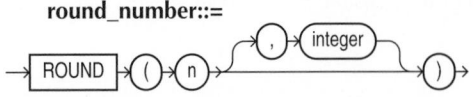

DESCRIPTION   **ROUND** rounds *value* to *precision*, which is an integer and may be positive, negative, or zero. A negative integer rounds to the given number of places to the left of the decimal point; a positive integer rounds to the given number of places to the right of the decimal point.
EXAMPLES

```
ROUND(123.456,0)   = 123
ROUND(123.456,-2)  = 100
ROUND(-123.456,2)  = -123.46
```

ROW_NUMBER

SEE ALSO   ROWNUM
FORMAT

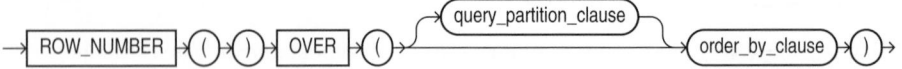

DESCRIPTION   **ROW_NUMBER** is an analytic function. It assigns a unique number to each row to which it is applied (either each row in the partition or each row returned by the query), in the ordered sequence of rows specified in the **ORDER BY** clause, beginning with 1.

ROWID

ROWID is the logical address of a row, and it is unique within the database.
   ROWID can be **SELECT**ed or used in a **WHERE** clause, but it cannot be changed by an **INSERT**, **UPDATE**, or **DELETE**. It is not actually a data column; it is the physical address of the table row on disk. ROWID is useful when used in a **WHERE** clause for rapid **UPDATE**s or **DELETE**s of rows. However, it can change if the table it is in is exported and imported.
   The ROWID datatype is a hexadecimal string representing the unique address of a row in a table. This datatype is primarily used for values returned by the ROWID pseudo-column.

ROWIDTOCHAR

SEE ALSO   **CHARTOROWID**, CONVERSION FUNCTIONS
FORMAT

DESCRIPTION   **ROWIDTOCHAR** (**ROW ID**entifier **TO CHAR**acter) changes an internal Oracle row identifier, or ROWID, to act like a character string. However, Oracle does this kind of conversion automatically, so this function isn't really needed. It seems to be a debugging tool that has made its way into general availability.

ROWIDTONCHAR

SEE ALSO   **CHARTOROWID**, CONVERSION FUNCTIONS, **ROWIDTOCHAR**
FORMAT

DESCRIPTION   **ROWIDTONCHAR** (**ROW ID**entifier **TO NCHAR**acter) changes an internal Oracle row identifier, or ROWID, to an NVARCHAR2 datatype.

ROWNUM

SEE ALSO   PSEUDO-COLUMNS
FORMAT

ROWNUM

DESCRIPTION   ROWNUM returns the sequence number in which a row was returned when first selected from a table. The first row has a ROWNUM of 1, the second has a ROWNUM of 2, and so on. Note, however, that even a simple **ORDER BY** in the **SELECT** statement may *disorder* the ROWNUMs, which are assigned to the rows before any ordering takes place.

RPAD

SEE ALSO   CHARACTER FUNCTIONS, **LPAD**, **LTRIM**, **RTRIM**, **TRIM**, Chapter 7
FORMAT

DESCRIPTION   **RPAD** (**R**ight **PAD**) makes a string a certain length by adding a certain *set* of characters to the right. If *set* is not specified, the default pad character is a space.
EXAMPLE

```
select rpad('HELLO ',24,'WORLD') from dual;
```

produces this:

```
HELLO WORLDWORLDWORLDWOR
```

RTRIM

SEE ALSO   CHARACTER FUNCTIONS, **LPAD**, **LTRIM**, **RPAD**, **TRIM**, Chapter 7
FORMAT

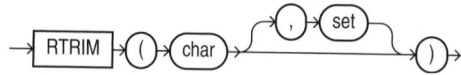

DESCRIPTION   **RTRIM** (**R**ight **TRIM**) trims all the occurrences of any one of a *set* of characters off of the right side of a string.
EXAMPLE

```
rtrim('GEORGE','OGRE')
```

produces *nothing*, an empty string with zero length! On the other hand,

```
rtrim('EDYTHE','HET')
```

produces this:

```
EDY
```

RUN
SEE ALSO   /, @, @@, **EDIT**, **START**
FORMAT

```
R[UN]
```

DESCRIPTION   **RUN** displays the SQL command in the SQL buffer and then executes it. **RUN** is similar to the / command, except that / doesn't display the SQL first.

SAVE (SQL*Plus)
SEE ALSO   EDIT, GET, Chapter 6
FORMAT

```
SAV[E] file[.ext] [ CRE[ATE] | REP[LACE] | APP[END] ]
```

DESCRIPTION   **SAVE** saves the contents of the current buffer into a host file with the name *file*. If no file type (extension) is specified, the file type .sql is added to the filename. This default extension can be changed with **SET SUFFIX**. **SAVE** commits pending work to the database.

If the file already exists, the **CREATE** option forces **SAVE** to abort and produces an error message. The **REPLACE** option replaces any existing file or creates a new one if none exists.

The **APPEND** option adds this file to the end of any existing file or creates a new one if none exists.
EXAMPLE   The following saves the contents of the current buffer into a file named **lowcost.sql**:

```
save lowcost
```

SAVEPOINT
SEE ALSO   **COMMIT**, **ROLLBACK**, **SET TRANSACTION**
FORMAT
     savepoint::=

DESCRIPTION   A savepoint is a point within a transaction to which you may roll back. Savepoints allow you to **ROLLBACK** portions of your current transaction.

The first version shown here is typical of SQL*Plus. The purpose of **SAVEPOINT** is to be able to assign a name to the beginning of a group of SQL statements and later, if necessary, roll back to that name, thus undoing the results of *just that group*. Savepoints can be nested or sequenced, allowing great control over recovery from errors. The idea here is to collect together a series of SQL statements that make up one logical transaction and hold the **COMMIT** until all the steps within it have been completed successfully. An attempted step may fail, but you'll want to be able to try it again without having to undo everything else prior to it. Here is an example:

```
insert into comfort
values ('Walpole', '22-APR-13',50.1, 24.8, 0);

savepoint a;

insert into comfort
values ('Walpole', '27-MAY-13',63.7, 33.8, 0);
```

```
savepoint b;

insert into comfort
values ('Walpole', '07-AUG-13',83.0, 43.8, 0);
```

You can roll back just the last **INSERT** by returning to savepoint B:

```
rollback to savepoint b;
```

This shows that SQL statements, or groups of them, can be collected together and undone in sets or singly. In a host program, or using PL/SQL or SQL*Plus, you may want to set up savepoints that you can roll back to, based on the results of your most recent SQL statement or condition test. **ROLLBACK** allows you to return to a specific step where you named a savepoint.

If a function, a section of logic, or an attempted SQL statement fails, you can return the data in the database back to the state it was in before the local step began. You can then try it again.

SAVEPOINT names must be unique to a transaction (defined by where it ends, with either a **COMMIT** or an unconditional **ROLLBACK**) but do not have to be unique to all of your database objects. You can give a **SAVEPOINT** the same name as a table, for instance (this might even result in more understandable code if the **SAVEPOINT** had the name of the table being updated). Names for **SAVEPOINT**s follow object naming conventions.

If you give a new **SAVEPOINT** with the same name as a previous one, the new one replaces the earlier one. The earlier one is lost, and you can no longer roll back to it.

Once a **COMMIT** or an unconditional **ROLLBACK** (not to a savepoint) is issued, all previous **SAVEPOINT**s are erased. Recall that all DDL statements (such as **DISCONNECT**, **CREATE TABLE**, **CREATE INDEX**, and so on) automatically issue an implicit **COMMIT**, and any severe failure (if the program terminates abnormally or the computer goes down) will result in an automatic **ROLLBACK**.

SCN_TO_TIMESTAMP
SEE ALSO   **ORA_ROWSCN** under PSEUDO_COLUMNS
FORMAT

$\rightarrow$ SCN_TO_TIMESTAMP $\rightarrow$ ($\rightarrow$ number $\rightarrow$) $\rightarrow$

DESCRIPTION   **SCN_TO_TIMESTAMP** takes as an argument a number that evaluates to a system change number (SCN) and returns the approximate timestamp associated with that SCN. The returned value is a TIMESTAMP datatype. This function is useful anytime you want to know the timestamp associated with an SCN. For example, it can be used in conjunction with the ORA_ROWSCN pseudo-column to associate a timestamp with the most recent change to a row.

SCORE
The **SCORE** function is used by CONTEXT indexes in Oracle Text to evaluate how well a text string meets the specified search criteria. You can display the score of an individual search; more often, the score is compared to a threshold value.

SELECT (Form 1—SQL)
SEE ALSO   **CONNECT BY**, **DELETE**, **DUAL**, **FROM**, **GROUP BY**, **HAVING**, **INSERT**, **JOIN**, LOGICAL OPERATORS, **ORDER BY**, QUERY OPERATORS, SUBQUERY, SYNTAX OPERATORS, **UPDATE**, **WHERE**
FORMAT
select::=

subquery::=

query_block::=

with_clause::=

plsql_declarations::=

subquery_factoring_clause::=

search_clause::=

cycle_clause::=

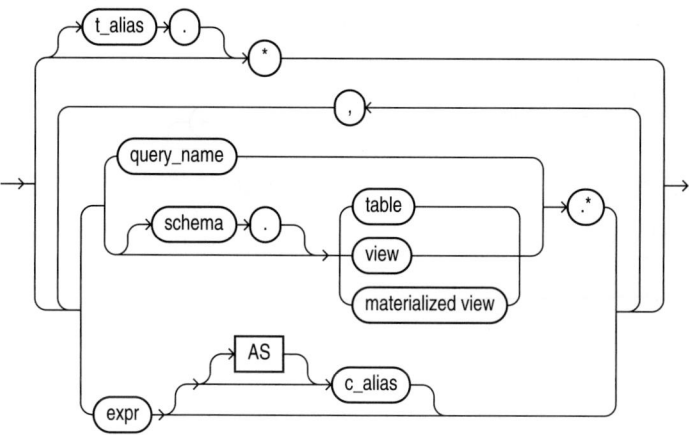

select_list::=

table_reference::=

flashback_query_clause::=

query_table_expression::=

pivot_clause::=

pivot_for_clause::=

pivot_in_clause::=

unpivot_clause::=

unpivot_in_clause::=

sample_clause::=

partition_extension_clause::=

subquery_restriction_clause::=

table_collection_expression::=

join_clause::=

inner_cross_join_clause::=

outer_join_clause::=

query_partition_clause::=

outer_join_type::=

cross_outer_apply_clause::=

where_clause::=

hierarchical_query_clause::=

group_by_clause::=

rollup_cube_clause::=

grouping_sets_clause::=

grouping_expression_list::=

expression_list::=

model_clause::=

cell_reference_options::=

return_rows_clause::=

reference_model::=

main_model::=

model_column_clauses::=

model_column::=

model_rules_clause::=

model_iterate_clause::=

cell_assignment::=

single_column_for_loop::=

multi_column_for_loop::=

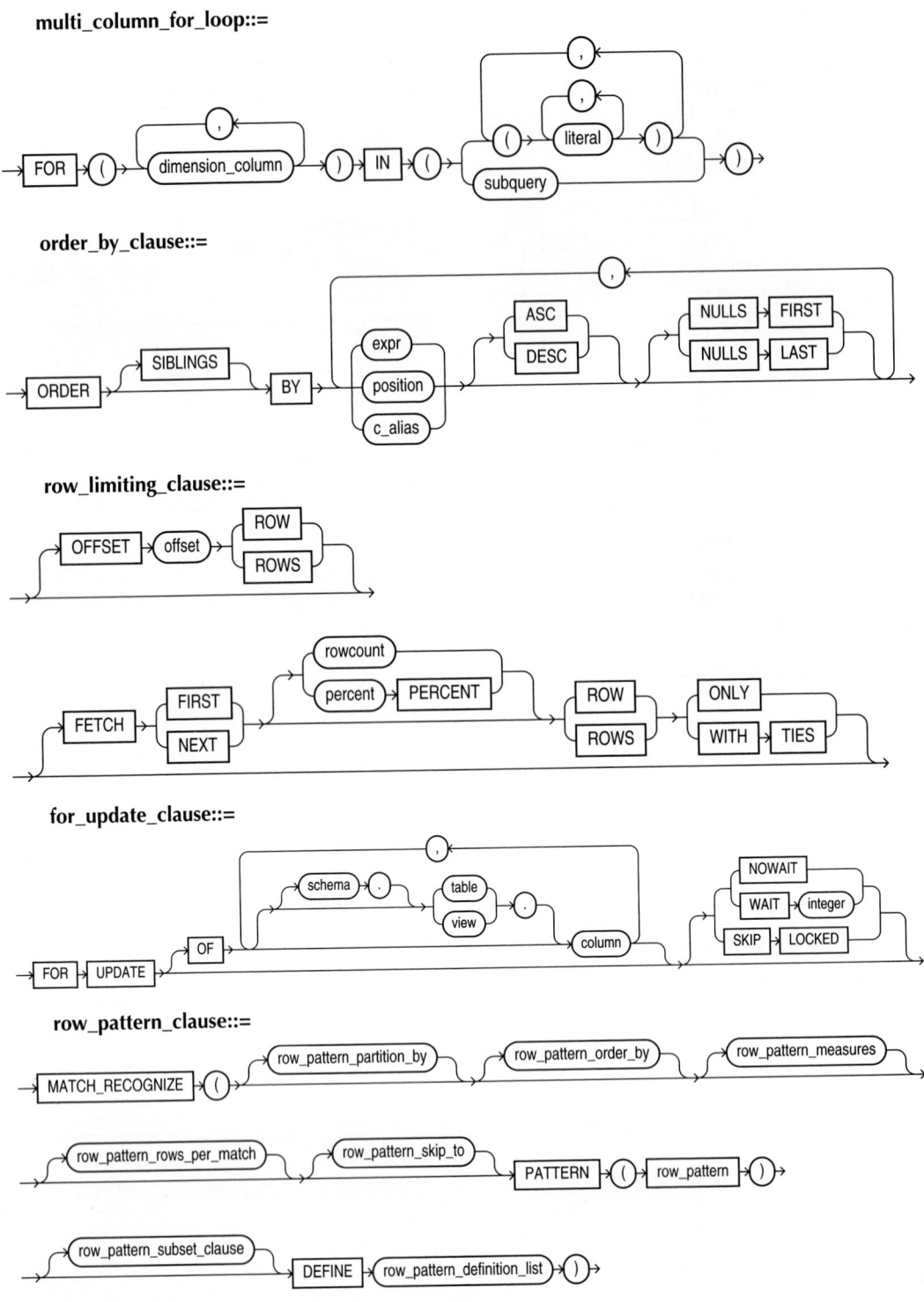

order_by_clause::=

row_limiting_clause::=

for_update_clause::=

row_pattern_clause::=

DESCRIPTION   **SELECT** retrieves rows from one or more tables or views, either as a command or as a subquery in another SQL command (within limitations), including **SELECT**, **INSERT**, **UPDATE**, and **DELETE**. **ALL** means that all rows that satisfy the conditions will be returned (this is the default). **DISTINCT** means that only rows that are unique will be returned; any duplicates will be weeded out first.

An * (asterisk) by itself results in all columns from all tables in the **FROM** clause being displayed. *table*.* means that all columns from this table will be displayed. An asterisk by itself cannot be combined with any other columns, but a *table*.* can be followed by column names and expressions, including ROWID.

select_list can include any form of a column. This could be a column name, a literal, a mathematical computation, a function, or several functions combined. The most common version is a simple column name or a column name prefixed by a table name or table alias. *c_alias* is a renaming of the column or expression. The column alias can be preceded by the word AS. The column alias will become the column heading in the display, and may be referenced by the **COLUMN**, **TTITLE**, and **BTITLE** commands in SQL*Plus. The column alias may be used in the **ORDER BY** clause. If it is more than one word, or will contain characters that are neither numbers nor letters, it must be enclosed in double quotation marks.

schema, *table*, and *dblink* denote the table or view from which the rows will be drawn. *schema* and *dblink* are optional, and their absence makes Oracle default to the current user. However, specifying the user in a query may reduce Oracle's overhead and make the query run more quickly. A subquery can be specified in the **FROM** clause. Oracle will execute the subquery and the resulting rows will be treated as if they came from a view.

A table *t_alias* here will rename the table for this query. This alias, unlike the expression alias, can be referenced elsewhere within the **SELECT** statement itself, for instance as a prefix to any column name coming from that table. In fact, if a table has an alias, the alias *must* be used whenever a column from that table has a table name prefix. Tables are typically aliased when two tables with long names are joined in a query, and many of their columns have the same name, requiring them to be unambiguously named in the **SELECT** clause. Aliases are also commonly used in correlated subqueries and when a table is being joined to itself.

condition may be any valid expression that tests true or false. It can contain functions, columns (from these tables), and literals. *position* allows the **ORDER BY** clause to identify the expressions based on their relative position in the **SELECT** clause, rather than on their names. This is valuable for complicated expressions. You should discontinue the use of ordinal positions in **ORDER BY** clauses; column aliases may be used in their place. The current SQL standard does not include support for ordinal positions in **ORDER BY** clauses, and Oracle may not support them in the future. **ASC** and **DESC** specify whether it is an ascending or descending sequence for each expression in the **ORDER BY** clause.

column is a column in a table listed in the **FROM** clause. This cannot be an expression but must be a real column name. **NOWAIT** means that a **SELECT ... FOR UPDATE** attempt that encounters a locked row will terminate and return immediately to the user, rather than wait and attempt to update the row again in a few moments.

The **FOR UPDATE OF** clause puts locks on the rows that have been selected. **SELECT ... FOR UPDATE OF** should be followed immediately by an **UPDATE ... WHERE** command, or, if you decide not to update anything, by a **COMMIT** or **ROLLBACK**. The **FOR UPDATE OF** clause also includes the actions of **INSERT** and **DELETE**. Once you have locked a row, other users cannot update it until you free it with a **COMMIT** command (or **AUTOCOMMIT**) or **ROLLBACK**. **SELECT ... FOR UPDATE OF** cannot include **DISTINCT**, **GROUP BY**, **UNION**, **INTERSECT**, **MINUS**, or any group function such as **MIN**, **MAX**, **AVG**, or **COUNT**. The columns named have no effect and are present for compatibility with other dialects of SQL. Oracle will lock only the tables that appear in the **FOR UPDATE** clause. If you don't have an **OF** clause listing any tables, Oracle will lock all the tables in the **FROM** clause for update. All the tables must be on the same database, and if there are references to a LONG column or a sequence in the **SELECT**, the tables must be on the same database as the LONG or the sequence.

If you are querying from a partitioned table, you can list the name of the partition you are querying as part of the **FROM** clause of the query. *See* Chapter 18.

The other individual clauses in the **SELECT** statement are all described under their own names elsewhere in this reference. The **AS OF {TIMESTAMP|SCN}** clause for flashback queries was introduced in Oracle9*i* Release 2. The **VERSIONS BETWEEN** clause for flashback version queries was introduced in Oracle Database 10*g*.

As of Oracle Database 11*g*, you can use the new **PIVOT** and **UNPIVOT** operations to rotate rows into columns. In Oracle Database 12*c*, you can include inline procedure and function definitions in the **WITH** clause. Also new in Oracle Database 12*c* is the *row_pattern_clause*, which makes it easy to use regular expression pattern matching across a sequence of rows in a table to partition a table logically based on something other than discrete values in the table.

OTHER NOTES   Clauses must be placed in the order shown, except for these:

- **CONNECT BY**, **START WITH**, **GROUP BY**, and **HAVING**, which may be in any order in relation to each other.

- **ORDER BY** and **FOR UPDATE OF**, which may be in any order in relation to each other.

SELECT (Form 2—Embedded SQL)

SEE ALSO   **CONNECT, DECLARE CURSOR, DECLARE DATABASE, EXECUTE, FETCH, FOR, PREPARE, UPDATE** (Form 1), **WHENEVER SQLERROR**, *Programmer's Guide to the Oracle Precompilers*

FORMAT

```
EXEC SQL [AT { db_name | :host_variable }]
 SELECT select_list INTO
 :host_variable [[INDICATOR] :indicator_variable]
 [, :host_variable [[INDICATOR] :indicator_variable]]...
 FROM table_list [WHERE condition]
 { [START WITH condition] CONNECT BY condition
 | CONNECT BY condition [START WITH condition]
 | GROUP BY expr [, expr]... [HAVING condition] }
 [ [START WITH condition] CONNECT BY condition
 | CONNECT BY condition [START WITH condition]
 | GROUP BY expr [, expr]... [HAVING condition] ]...
 [ WITH READ ONLY | WITH CHECK OPTION ]
 [{ UNION | UNION ALL | INTERSECT | MINUS } SELECT command]
[ ORDER BY
    { expr | position } [ ASC | DESC ]
    [, { expr | position } [ ASC | DESC ]]...
 | FOR UPDATE
    [OF [[schema.] { table. | view. | materialized view. }] column
    [, OF [[schema.] { table. | view. | materialized view. }] column]...  ]
      [NOWAIT] ]
 [ ORDER BY
    { expr | position } [ ASC | DESC ]
    [, { expr | position } [ ASC | DESC ]]...
 | FOR UPDATE
    [OF [[schema.] { table. | view. | materialized view. }] column
    [, OF [[schema.] { table. | view. | materialized view. }] column]...  ]
    [NOWAIT] ]...
```

DESCRIPTION *See* the description of the various clauses in **SELECT** (Form 1). The following are the elements unique to embedded SQL:

- **AT** *db_name* optionally names a database from a previous **CONNECT** statement, for a database name from a previous **DECLARE DATABASE** statement.

- **INTO** :*host_variable* [,:*host_variable*] is the list of host variables into which the results of the **SELECT** statement will be loaded. If any variable in this list is an array, all of the variables in the list must be arrays, though they need not all be the same size arrays.

- The **WHERE** clause may reference nonarray host variables.

- The **SELECT** clause may reference host variables anywhere a constant would have been used.

You can use the embedded **SQL SELECT** with variable arrays to return multiple rows with a single **FETCH**. You also can use it to either **DECLARE CURSOR** or **PREPARE** statements for use with a later **FETCH**, and it may include the **FOR UPDATE OF** clause. The later **UPDATE** statement can then reference the columns named in the **FOR UPDATE OF** clause using its own **CURRENT OF** clause. *See* **DECLARE CURSOR** and **UPDATE** (Form 2).

If the embedded **SELECT** returns no rows, SQLCODE is set to +100, and the host variables are left unchanged. In that case, **WHENEVER** lets you change the program flow.

All rows that meet the **SELECT** criteria are locked at the **OPEN**. **COMMIT** releases the locks, and no further **FETCH**ing is permitted. This means you must **FETCH** and process all of the rows you wish to update before you issue a **COMMIT**.

NOTE
See the Programmer's Guide to the Oracle Precompilers *for a full list of all commands. This reference does not contain all of the possible precompiler commands.*

SELECT ... INTO
SEE ALSO %ROWTYPE, %TYPE, DECLARE CURSOR, FETCH
FORMAT

```
SELECT expression [,expression]...
  INTO {variable [,variable]... | record}
  FROM [user.]table [,[user.]table]...
  [where...][group by... [having...]] [order by...];
```

DESCRIPTION This is not the form of the **SELECT** statement used in **DECLARE CURSOR**. This form utilizes the implicit cursor named SQL, executes within an execution section of a block (between **BEGIN** and **END**), and copies the values from a single row being returned into either a string of named variables or a record whose structure is declared by **%ROWTYPE** to be just like the columns being selected. If the form that uses variables is used, they must each be **DECLARE**d and have compatible datatypes with those being retrieved. The order in which they appear in the **INTO** clause must correspond to the order of the associated columns in the **SELECT** clause.

This **SELECT** may be used in a loop with PL/SQL variables appearing in the **WHERE** clause (or even acting like constants in the **SELECT** clause), but each time the **SELECT** executes, it must return only one row. If it produces more than one row, the TOO_MANY_ROWS exception is **RAISE**d, and SQL%ROWCOUNT is set to 2 (*see* EXCEPTION for details). SQL%FOUND will be TRUE.

If it produces no rows, the NO_DATA_FOUND exception is **RAISE**d, and SQL%ROWCOUNT is set to 0. SQL%FOUND will be FALSE.

SESSIONTIMEZONE
SEE ALSO   Chapter 10
FORMAT

DESCRIPTION   **SESSIONTIMEZONE** returns the value of the current session's time zone.
EXAMPLE

```
select sessiontimezone from dual;
```

SET (SQL*Plus)
SEE ALSO   **SET TRANSACTION**, **SHOW**, Chapter 6
FORMAT

```
SET feature value
```

where *feature* and *value* are from the following list. The default values are underlined.

- **APPI[NFO]{ON | OFF | text}** enables the registering of command files via the DBMS_
  APPLICATION_INFO package. The registered name appears in the MODULE column of the
  V$SESSION dynamic performance table.

- **ARRAY[SIZE] {15 | n}** sets the size of the batch of rows that SQL*Plus will fetch at one time.
  The range is 1 to 5000. Larger values improve the efficiency of queries and subqueries where
  many rows will be fetched but use more memory. Values greater than 100 generally do not
  produce much improvement. **ARRAYSIZE** has no other effect on the workings of SQL*Plus.

- **AUTO[COMMIT]{ON | OFF | IMM[EDIATE] | n}** makes SQL immediately commit any pending
  changes to the database on the completion of every SQL command. *n* allows you to specify
  the number of commands after which a commit occurs. **OFF** stops automatic committing,
  and you must instead commit changes intentionally with the **COMMIT** command. Many
  commands, such as **QUIT**, **EXIT**, and **CONNECT**, and all DDL commands will cause a
  COMMIT of any pending changes.

- **AUTOP[RINT] {ON | OFF}** sets whether SQL*Plus automatically displays bind variables used
  in a PL/SQL block or **EXECUTE**d procedure.

- **AUTORECOVERY [ON | OFF]** tells the **RECOVER** command to automatically apply the default
  filenames of archived redo log files needed during recovery.

- **AUTOT[RACE] {ON | OFF | TRACE[ONLY]} [EXP[LAIN]] [STAT[ISTICS]]** allows you to see the
  execution path for a query after the query has completed. To see the execution path, you first
  must have the PLAN_TABLE table created in your schema (it can be created by running the
  utlxplan.sql file in the **/rdbms/admin** directory under your Oracle software directory).

- **BLO[CKTERMINATOR] {. | c | ON | OFF}** sets the symbol used to denote the end of a PL/SQL
  block. This cannot be a letter or a number. To execute the block, use **RUN** or / (slash).

- **CMDS[EP] {; | c | ON | OFF}** sets the character used to separate multiple SQL*Plus commands
  entered on a line. **ON** and **OFF** control whether or not multiple commands may be entered on
  a line.

- **COLSEP {_ | text}** sets a value to be printed between columns.

- **COM[PATIBILITY]{V7 | V8 | NATIVE}** specifies the version of Oracle to which you are
  currently connected.

- **CON[CAT] {. | c | ON | OFF}** sets a symbol that may be used to terminate or delimit a user variable that is followed by a symbol, character, or word that would otherwise be interpreted as a part of the user variable name. Setting **CONCAT ON** resets its value to a period (.).

- **COPYC[OMMIT] {0 | n}** commits rows to the destination database on a cycle of *n* batches of rows (the number of rows in a batch is **SET** by **ARRAYSIZE**). Valid values are 0 to 5000. If the value is 0, a commit will occur only at the end of a **COPY** operation.

- **COPYTYPECHECK {ON | OFF}** enables the suppression of datatype checks when using the **COPY** command.

- **DEF[INE] {& | c | ON | OFF}** determines whether SQL*Plus will look for and substitute commands for substitution variables and load them with their **DEFINE**d values.

- **DESCRIBE [DEPTH {1 | n | ALL}][LINENUM {ON | OFF}][INDENT {ON | OFF}]** sets the depth of the level to which you can recursively describe an object. The valid range of the **DEPTH** clause is from 1 to 50.

- **ECHO {ON | OFF}** in SQL*Plus echoes (displays) commands to the screen as they execute from a start file. **OFF** makes SQL*Plus execute them without displaying them. The results of the commands, on the other hand, are controlled by **TERMOUT**.

- **EDITF[ILE]** *file_name*[.ext] sets the default filename created by the **EDIT** command.

- **EMB[EDDED] {ON | OFF}** allows a new report in a series of reports to begin anywhere on a page, just after the previous one ended. **OFF** forces the new report to start at the top of a new page.

- **ERRORL[OGGING] {ON | OFF} [TABLE [schema.]*tablename*] [TRUNCATE] [IDENTIFIER identifier]** enables error logging of SQL, PL/SQL, and SQL*Plus errors. Errors from queries are written to a default table, SPERRORLOG, in the current schema by default.

- **ESC[APE] {\ | c | ON | OFF}** defines the character you enter as the escape character. **OFF** undefines the escape character. **ON** enables the escape character. **ON** changes the value of *c* back to the default, \. You can use the escape character before the substitution character (set through **SET DEFINE**) to indicate that SQL*Plus should treat the substitution character as an ordinary character rather than as a request for variable substitution.

- **ESCCHAR [@ | ? | % | $ | OFF]** enables specific characters in filenames to be escaped.

- **FEED[BACK] {6 | n | ON | OFF}** makes SQL*Plus show "records selected" after a query if at least *n* records are selected. **ON** and **OFF** turn this display on and off, respectively. **SET FEEDBACK** to 0 is the same as **OFF**.

- **FLAGGER {OFF | ENTRY | INTERMED[IATE] | FULL}** sets the FIPS level for SQL92 compliance.

- **FLU[SH] {ON | OFF}** is used when a start file can be run without needing any display or interaction until it has completed. **OFF** lets the operating system avoid sending output to the display. **ON** restores output to the user's display. **OFF** may improve performance.

- **HEA[DING] {ON | OFF}** suppresses the headings, both text and underlines, that normally appear above columns. **ON** allows them to be displayed.

- **HEADS[EP] { | | c | ON | OFF}** defines the character you enter as the heading separator character. **ON** and **OFF** turn heading separation on and off, respectively.

- **INSTANCE [instance_path | LOCAL]** changes the default instance for your session to the specified instance path. Using the **SET INSTANCE** command does not connect to a database. The default instance is used for commands when no instance is specified.

- **LIN[ESIZE] {80 | n}** sets the line width, the total number of characters on a line that can be displayed before wrapping down to the next line. This number is also used when SQL*Plus calculates the proper position for centered or right-aligned titles. The maximum value of *n* is 999. In iSQL*Plus, the default is 150.

■ **LOBOF[FSET]** {**n** | **1**} sets the starting position from which CLOB and NCLOB data is retrieved and displayed.

■ **LOGSOURCE [pathname]** specifies the location from which archive logs are retrieved during recovery. The default value is set by the LOG_ARCHIVE_DEST initialization parameter in the Oracle initialization file. Using the **SET LOGSOURCE** command without a pathname restores the default location.

■ **LONG** {**80** | **n**} is the maximum width for displaying or copying (spooling) LONG, CLOB, and NCLOB values. *n* may range from 1 to 2GB.

■ **LONGC[HUNKSIZE]** {**80** | **n**} sets the size, in characters, of the increments in which SQL*Plus retrieves a LONG, CLOB, or NCLOB value.

■ **MARK[UP]** HTML [ON | **OFF**] [HEAD *text*] [*text*] [TABLE *text*] [ENTMAP {**ON** | OFF}] [SPOOL {ON | **OFF**}] [PRE[FORMAT] {ON | **OFF**}] outputs HTML marked-up text. **SET MARKUP** only specifies that SQL*Plus output will be HTML encoded. You must use **SET MARKUP HTML ON SPOOL ON** and the SQL*Plus **SPOOL** commands to create and name a spool file and to begin writing HTML output to it. **SET MARKUP** has the same options and behavior as **SQLPLUS -MARKUP**.

■ **NEWP[AGE]** {**1** | *n* | NONE} sets the number of blank lines to be printed between the bottom of one page and the top title of the next. A 0 (zero) sends a form feed at the top of each page. If the output is being displayed, this usually clears the screen.

■ **NULL** *text* sets the text that will be substituted when SQL*Plus discovers a **NULL** value. **NULL** without text displays blanks.

■ **NUMF[ORMAT]** *format* sets the default number format for displaying number data items. *See* NUMBER FORMATS for details.

■ **NUM[WIDTH]** {**10** | *n*} sets the default width for number displays.

■ **PAGES[IZE]** {**14** | *n*} sets the number of lines per page.

■ **PAU[SE]** {ON | **OFF** | *text*} makes SQL*Plus wait for you to press RETURN after it displays each page of output. **OFF** means no pause occurs between pages of display. *text* is the message SQL*Plus displays at the bottom of the screen as it waits for you to press the RETURN key. **PAUSE** waits before the very first page is displayed; you'll have to press RETURN to see it.

■ **RECSEP** {**WR[APPED?]** | EA[CH] | OFF} specifies the row wrapping rules for query results. Each row SQL*Plus brings back can be separated from other rows by a character, defined by **RECSEPCHAR**. By default, the character is a space, and this only happens for records (and therefore columns) that wrap.

■ **RECSEPCHAR** works with **RECSEP**. The default is a space, but you can set it to another symbol if you wish.

■ **SERVEROUT[PUT]** {ON | **OFF**} [SIZE *n*] [FOR[MAT] {WRA[PPED] | **WOR[D_WRAPPED]** | TRU[NCATED]}] allows you to display the output of PL/SQL procedures (from the DBMS_OUTPUT package—*see* the *Application Developer's Guide*). **WRAPPED**, **WORD_WRAPPED**, **TRUNCATED**, and **FORMAT** determine the formatting of the output text.

■ **SHIFT[INOUT]** {VIS[IBLE] | **INV[ISIBLE]**} allows correct alignment for terminals that display shift characters. Use **VISIBLE** for terminals that display shift characters as a visible character (for example, a space or a colon). **INVISIBLE** is the opposite and does not display any shift characters.

- **SHOW[MODE] {ON | OFF}** makes SQL*Plus display the old and new settings of a **SET** feature and its value when it is changed. **OFF** stops the display of both of these.

- **SQLBL[ANKLINES] {ON | OFF}** controls whether SQL*Plus allows blank lines within a SQL command or script. **ON** interprets blank lines and new lines as part of a SQL command or script. **OFF**, the default value, does not allow blank lines or new lines in a SQL command or script.

- **SQLC[ASE] {MIX[ED] | LO[WER] | UP[PER]}** converts all the text, including literals and identifiers, in either SQL or PL/SQL blocks, before it is executed by Oracle. **MIXED** leaves case just as it is typed. **LOWER** converts everything to lowercase; **UPPER** converts it all to uppercase.

- **SQLCO[NTINUE] {> | *text*}** sets the character sequence to be displayed as a prompt for a long line that must continue on the next line. When you enter a **-** (hyphen) at the end of a SQL*Plus command line, the **SQLCONTINUE** symbols or text will prompt you from the left of the next screen line.

- **SQLN[UMBER] {ON | OFF}** tells SQL*Plus that lines of SQL beyond the first one you enter will have line numbers as prompts. If this is **OFF**, the SQLPROMPT will appear only on additional lines.

- **SQLPLUSCOMPAT[IBILITY] {*x.y*[.*z*]}** sets the behavior or output format of VARIABLE to that of the release or version specified by *x.y*[.*z*], where *x* is the *version* number, *y* is the *release* number, and *z* is the *update* number. In later releases, **SQLPLUSCOMPATIBILITY** may affect features other than VARIABLE. Setting the value of **SQLPLUSCOMPATIBILITY** to a version less than 9.0.0 will result in the VARIABLE definition of NCHAR or NVARCHAR2 datatypes reverting to Oracle8*i* behavior, whereby the size of the variable is in bytes or characters depending on the chosen national character set.

- **SQLPRE[FIX] {# | *c*}** sets the SQL*Plus prefix character. When you are entering a SQL command or PL/SQL block, you can enter a SQL*Plus command on a separate line, prefixed by the SQL*Plus prefix character. SQL*Plus will execute the command immediately without affecting the SQL command or PL/SQL block that you are entering. The prefix character must be a nonalphanumeric character.

- **SQLP[ROMPT] {SQL> | *text*}** sets the SQL*Plus command prompt.

- **SQLT[ERMINATOR] {; | *c* | ON | OFF}** sets the character used to end and execute SQL commands to *c*.

- **SUF[FIX] {SQL | *text*}** sets the default file extension that SQL*Plus uses in commands that refer to command files. **SUFFIX** does not control extensions for spool files.

- **TAB {ON | OFF}** determines how SQL*Plus formats white space in terminal output. **OFF** uses spaces to format white space in the output. **ON** uses the tab character. Tab settings are every eight characters.

- **TERM[OUT] {ON | OFF}** enables or suppresses the display so you can spool output from a command file without seeing the output on the screen. **ON** displays the output.

- **TI[ME] {ON | OFF}** displays the current time before each command prompt. **OFF** suppresses the time display.

- **TIMI[NG] {ON | OFF}** displays timing statistics on each SQL command or PL/SQL block run. **OFF** suppresses timing of each command.

- **TRIM[OUT] {<u>ON</u> | OFF}** removes blanks at the end of each line, improving performance especially when you access SQL*Plus from a slow communications device. **OFF** allows SQL*Plus to display trailing blanks.

- **TRIMS[POOL] {ON | <u>OFF</u>}** removes blanks at the end of each line. **OFF** allows SQL*Plus to include trailing blanks.

- **UND[ERLINE] {<u>-</u> | c | <u>ON</u> | OFF}** sets the character used to underline column headings in SQL*Plus reports.

- **VER[IFY] {<u>ON</u> | OFF}** controls whether SQL*Plus lists the text of a SQL statement or PL/SQL command before and after SQL*Plus replaces substitution variables with values. **ON** lists the text; **OFF** suppresses the listing.

- **WRA[P] {<u>ON</u> | OFF}** controls whether SQL*Plus truncates the display of a **SELECT**ed row if it is too long for the current line width. **OFF** truncates the **SELECT**ed row; **ON** allows the **SELECT**ed row to wrap to the next line.

DESCRIPTION **SET** turns a SQL*Plus feature ON or OFF or to a certain value. All of these features are changed with the **SET** command and displayed with the **SHOW** command. **SHOW** will display a particular command if its name follows the word **SHOW**, or all commands if **SHOW** is entered by itself.

SET (function)
SEE ALSO **IS A SET**, Chapter 39
FORMAT

```
SET (nested_table)
```

DESCRIPTION **SET** converts a nested table into a set by eliminating duplicates. The function returns a nested table whose elements are distinct from one another. The returned nested table is the same type as the input nested table.

SET CONSTRAINTS
SEE ALSO INTEGRITY CONSTRAINT
FORMAT
  set_constraints::=

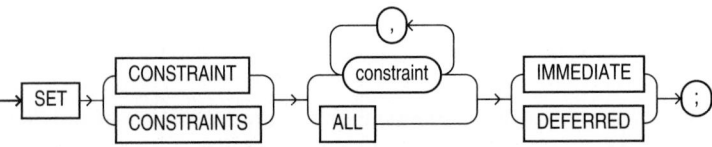

DESCRIPTION **SET CONSTRAINTS DEFERRED** tells Oracle not to check the validity of a constraint until the transaction is committed. This allows you to temporarily defer integrity checking of data. Deferred constraints are generally used when performing DML against multiple related tables when you cannot guarantee the order of the transactions. You must either own the table modified by the constraint or have the SELECT privilege on the table. The default setting is **SET CONSTRAINTS IMMEDIATE**, in which case the constraints are checked as soon as a record is inserted into the table.

SET ROLE
SEE ALSO **ALTER USER**, **CREATE ROLE**, Chapter 20

FORMAT
   set_role::=

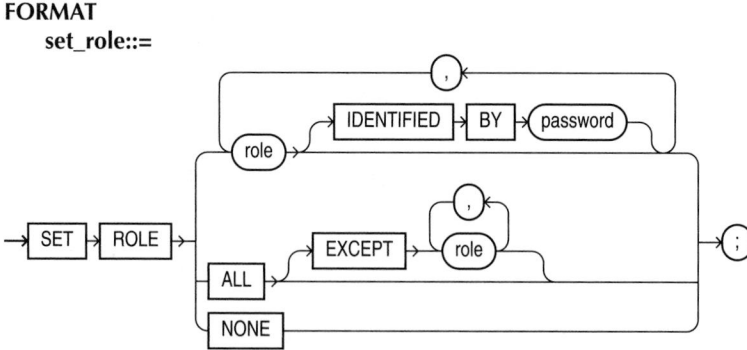

DESCRIPTION **SET ROLE** enables or disables roles granted to a user for the current SQL session. The first option lets the user enable specific roles, optionally giving a password if the role has one (*see* **CREATE ROLE**). The second option lets the user enable **ALL** roles **EXCEPT** for specific ones; these roles must be directly granted to the user, not roles granted through other roles. The **ALL** option does not enable roles with passwords. The third option, **NONE**, disables all roles for the current session.

SET TRANSACTION
SEE ALSO **COMMIT**, **ROLLBACK**, **SAVEPOINT**, TRANSACTION, Chapter 51
FORMAT
   set_transaction::=

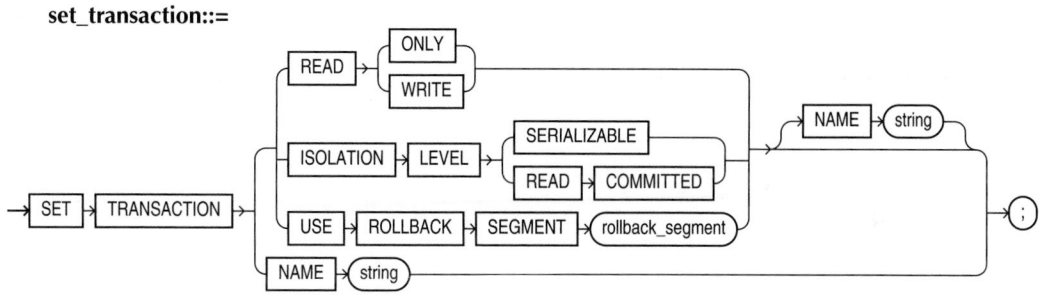

DESCRIPTION **SET TRANSACTION** starts a transaction. The standard SQL transaction guarantees statement-level read consistency, making sure the data from a query is consistent while the statement is executing. But some transactions need a stronger guarantee that a series of **SELECT** statements, accessing one or more tables, will see a consistent snapshot of all the data in one instant in time. **SET TRANSACTION READ ONLY** specifies this stronger read consistency. No changes to the queried data by other users will affect the transaction's view of the data. In a read-only transaction, you can use only the **SELECT**, **LOCK TABLE**, **SET ROLE**, **ALTER SESSION**, and **ALTER SYSTEM** commands.

    For transactions that include **INSERT**, **UPDATE**, or **DELETE** commands, Oracle assigns a rollback segment to the transaction. **SET TRANSACTION USE ROLLBACK SEGMENT** specifies that the current transaction will use a specific rollback segment.

    SET TRANSACTION must be the first SQL statement in a transaction. Placing a **COMMIT** just before **SET TRANSACTION** assures that this is true. The **COMMIT** at the end releases the snapshot of the data. This is important because the database needs to release the resources it has set aside to maintain consistency.

SHOW (SQL*Plus)
SEE ALSO **SET**

FORMAT

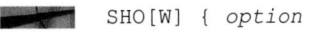

```
SHO[W] { option }
```

option may be any parameter set via the **SET** command or the following:

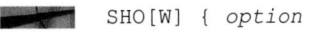

```
system_variable
ALL
BTI[TLE]
ERR[ORS] [ { FUNCTION | PROCEDURE | PACKAGE | PACKAGE BODY |
 TRIGGER| VIEW | TYPE | TYPE BODY | DIMENSION | JAVA CLASS } [schema.]name]
LNO
PARAMETERS [parameter_name]
PNO
RECYC[LEBIN] [original_name]
REL[EASE]
REPF[OOTER]
REPH[EADER]
SGA
SPOO[L]
SQLCODE
TTI[TLE]
USER
```

DESCRIPTION   SHOW displays the value of a feature of **SET**, or **ALL** features of **SET**, or of the other SQL*Plus items. More than one of these (including more than one **SET** feature) can follow the word **SHOW**, and each will be displayed on a separate line. The rows returned will be ordered alphabetically. The features that can be shown include the following:

- *system_variable* is any variable set with the **SET** command.
- **BTI[TLE]** displays the current **BTITLE** definition.
- **ERR[ORS]** shows the latest errors encountered with the compilation of a stored object.
- **LNO** shows the current line number (the line in the current page being displayed).
- **PARAMETERS** shows the setting of a specific parameter or all if none is specified.
- **PNO** displays the page number.
- **RECYC[LEBIN]** shows the names of objects in the recycle bin that can be reverted with the **FLASHBACK TABLE BEFORE DROP** command.
- **REL[EASE]** gives the release number of this version of Oracle.
- **REPF[OOTER]** shows the report footer.
- **REPH[EADER]** shows the report header.
- **SGA** shows the current memory allocations for the SGA.
- **SPOO[L]** tells whether output is being spooled (ON or OFF). *See* **SPOOL**.
- **SQLCODE** shows the error message number of the most recent Oracle error.
- **TTI[TLE]** displays the current **TTITLE** definition.
- **USER** shows the user's ID.

SHUTDOWN
SEE ALSO   **STARTUP**, **RECOVER**, Chapter 51
FORMAT

```
SHUTDOWN [ABORT|IMMEDIATE|NORMAL|TRANSACTIONAL [LOCAL]]
```

DESCRIPTION   **SHUTDOWN** shuts down an instance, optionally closing and dismounting it. If **ABORT** is used, uncommitted transactions are not rolled back. **NORMAL** (the default) prohibits further connections but waits for all current users to disconnect from the database. **IMMEDIATE** does not wait for current calls to complete or users to disconnect. **TRANSACTIONAL** performs a shutdown while allowing active transactions to complete. **TRANSACTIONAL LOCAL** specifies a transactional shutdown in the local instance only.
You must be connected AS SYSDBA or AS SYSOPER to use **SHUTDOWN**.

SIGN
SEE ALSO   +, PRECEDENCE, Chapter 9
FORMAT

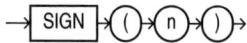

DESCRIPTION   **SIGN** equals 1 if *value* is positive, −1 if negative, 0 if zero.
EXAMPLE

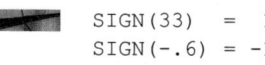
```
SIGN(33)   =   1
SIGN(-.6) = -1
SIGN(0)    =   0
```

SIN
SEE ALSO   **ACOS, ASIN, ATAN, ATAN2, COS, COSH**, NUMBER FUNCTIONS, **SINH, TAN**, Chapter 9
FORMAT

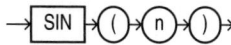

DESCRIPTION   **SIN** returns the sine of an angle *value* expressed in radians.
EXAMPLE

```
select sin(30*3.141593/180) Sine -- sine of 30 degrees in radians
from dual;
```

SINH
SEE ALSO   **ACOS, ASIN, ATAN, ATAN2, COS**, NUMBER FUNCTIONS, **SIN, TAN**, Chapter 9
FORMAT

DESCRIPTION   **SINH** returns the hyperbolic sine of an angle *value*.

SOUNDEX
SEE ALSO   **LIKE**, Chapters 7 and 27

FORMAT

DESCRIPTION **SOUNDEX** finds words that **SOUND** like an **EX**ample *string*. **SOUNDEX** makes certain assumptions about how letters and combinations of letters are usually pronounced. The two words being compared must begin with the same letter. You can perform **SOUNDEX** searches of individual words within text strings in CONTEXT indexes.

EXAMPLE

```
select lastname, firstname, phone
from address
where soundex(lastname)=soundex('SEPP');
```

```
LASTNAME                   FIRSTNAME                  PHONE
-------------------------  -------------------------  ------------
Szep                       Felicia                    214-555-8383
Sep                        Felicia                    214-555-8383
```

SPOOL (SQL*Plus)

SEE ALSO **SET**, Chapter 6
FORMAT

```
SPO[OL] [file[.ext][CRE[ATE]|REP[LACE]|APP[END]]|OFF|OUT]
```

DESCRIPTION **SPOOL** starts or stops spooling (copying) of SQL*Plus output to a host system file or the system printer. **SPOOL** *file* makes SQL*Plus spool all output to the named file. If the file type is not specified, **SPOOL** adds a default, similar to what **SAVE** does, usually .lst, but with some variation by host. OFF stops spooling. OUT stops spooling and sends the file to the printer. **REPLACE** replaces the contents of an existing file with the same name. To spool output to a file without displaying it, **SET TERMOUT OFF** in the start file prior to the SQL statement, but before the **SPOOL** command. **SPOOL** by itself shows the name of the current (or most recent) spool file.

SQL CURSOR

SEE ALSO **%FOUND**, **%ISOPEN**, **%NOTFOUND**, **%ROWCOUNT**, Chapter 32
DESCRIPTION *SQL* is the name of the cursor opened implicitly anytime the SQL statement being processed is not part of an explicitly named and opened cursor (*see* **DECLARE**). There is only one of these cursors at any time. The cursor attributes **%FOUND** and **%NOTFOUND** can be tested by checking **SQL%FOUND** and **SQL%NOTFOUND** before or after an **INSERT**, **UPDATE**, or **DELETE** (which are never associated with an explicit cursor) or a single-row **SELECT** that happened to be executed without an explicit cursor.

See **%FOUND** for details on these tests. *See* **%ROWCOUNT** for details on the values this attribute has under different conditions. **SQL%ISOPEN** always evaluates to FALSE because Oracle closes the SQL cursor automatically after executing the SQL statement.

SQLCODE

SEE ALSO EXCEPTION, SQLERRM
FORMAT

```
variable := SQLCODE
```

DESCRIPTION SQLCODE is an error function that returns the latest error number; however, outside of an exception handler (*see* EXCEPTION), it always returns 0. This is because the occurrence of an exception (that is, when SQLCODE would be nonzero) is expected to immediately transfer control to the EXCEPTION part of the PL/SQL block. Once there, SQLCODE can be tested for its value or used to assign a value to a variable.

SQLCODE cannot be used as part of a SQL statement (such as to insert the value of the error code into an error table). However, you can set a variable equal to SQLCODE and then use the variable in a SQL statement:

```
sql_error := sqlcode;
insert into PROBLEMLOG values (sql_error);
```

SQLERRM
SEE ALSO EXCEPTION, **EXCEPTION_INIT**, SQLCODE
FORMAT

```
SQLERRM[(integer)]
```

DESCRIPTION Without *integer* supplied, SQLERRM returns the error message related to the current SQLCODE. With an integer supplied, it returns the error message related to that integer value. Like SQLCODE, this function cannot be used directly in a SQL statement, but can be used in an assignment:

```
error_message := sqlerrm;
```

or to retrieve the error message associated with the error code 1403:

```
error_message := sqlerrm(1403);
```

Outside of an exception handler (*see* SQLCODE), this function without an integer argument always returns "normal, successful completion." In an exception handler, you get one of these messages:

- The message associated with an Oracle error
- The words "User-defined exception" for an explicitly raised user exception where you did not assign a message text
- A user-defined message text, loaded using the PRAGMA **EXCEPTION_INIT**

SQLLDR
SEE ALSO Chapter 24
FORMAT The following are the command-line parameters for the **SQLLDR** command:

USERID	Username and password for the load, separated by a slash.
CONTROL	Name of the control file.
LOG	Name of the redo log file.
BAD	Name of the bad file.
DATA	Name of the datafile.
DISCARD	Name of the discard file.
DISCARDMAX	Maximum number of rows to discard prior to stopping the load. Default is to allow all discards.

SKIP	Number of logical rows in the input file to skip prior to starting to load data. Usually used during reloads from the same input file following a partial load. Default is 0.
LOAD	Number of logical rows to load. Default is all rows.
ERRORS	Number of errors to allow. Default is 50.
ROWS	Number of rows to commit at a time. Use this parameter to break up the transaction size during the load. Default for conventional path loads is 64 and for Direct Path loads is all rows.
BINDSIZE	Size of conventional path bind array, in bytes. Default is operating-system dependent.
SILENT	Y/N flag to suppress messages during the load.
DIRECT	Uses Direct Path loading. Default is FALSE.
PARFILE	Name of the parameter file that contains additional load parameter specifications.
PARALLEL	Performs parallel loading. Default is FALSE.
FILE	File to allocate extents from (for parallel loading).
SKIP_UNUSABLE_INDEXES	Allows loads into tables that have indexes in unusable states. Default is FALSE.
SKIP_INDEX_MAINTENANCE	Stops index maintenance for Direct Path loads, leaving them in unusable states. Default is FALSE.
COMMIT_DISCONTINUED	Commits loaded rows when load is discontinued. Default is FALSE.
READSIZE	Size of the read buffer, in bytes; default is 1048576.
EXTERNAL_TABLE	Uses external table for load. Default is NOT_USED; other values are GENERATE_ONLY and EXECUTE.
COLUMNARRAYROWS	Number of rows for Direct Path column array. Default is 5000.
STREAMSIZE	Size of Direct Path stream buffer, in bytes. Default is 256000.
MULTITHREADING	Uses multithreading in Direct Path.
RESUMABLE	Enables or disables Resumable for current session; default is FALSE.
RESUMABLE_NAME	Text string used to identify resumable statements.
RESUMABLE_TIMEOUT	Wait time, in seconds, for Resumable. Default is 7200.
DATE_CACHE	Size (in entries) of data conversion cache. Default is 1000.

DESCRIPTION **SQLLDR** loads data from external files into tables in the Oracle database. *See* Chapter 23 for examples. The syntax for the control file is as follows:

options_clause::=

load_statement::=

infile_clause::=

concatenate_clause::=

into_table_clause::=

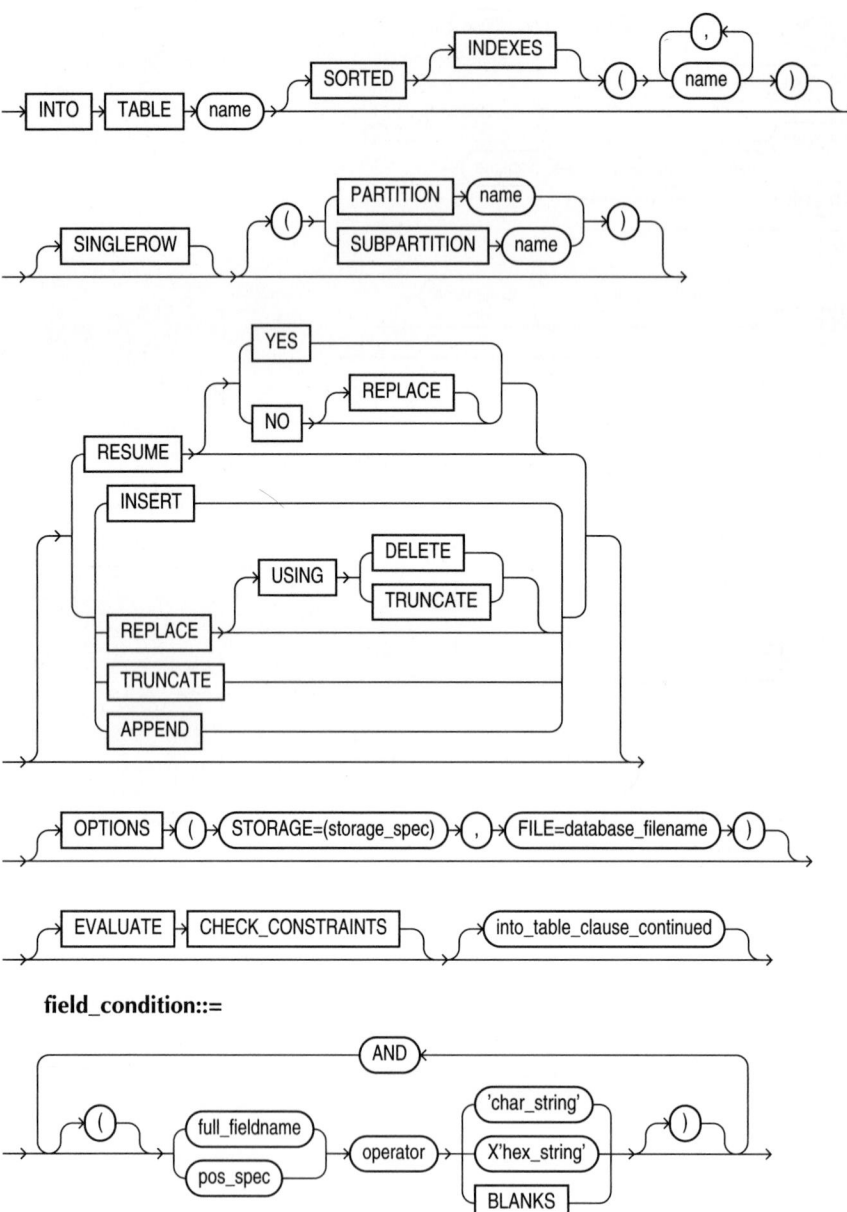

field_condition::=

delim_spec::=

full_fieldname::=

termination_spec::=

enclosure_spec::=

oid_spec::=

sid_spec::=

xmltype_spec::=

field_list::=

dgen_fld_spec::=

ref_spec::=

init_spec::=

bfile_spec::=

filler_fld_spec::=

scalar_fld_spec::=

lobfile_spec::=

pos_spec::=

datatype_spec::=

datatype_spec_cont::=

col_obj_fld_spec::=

collection_fld_spec::=

nested_table_spec::=

varray_spec::=

sdf_spec::=

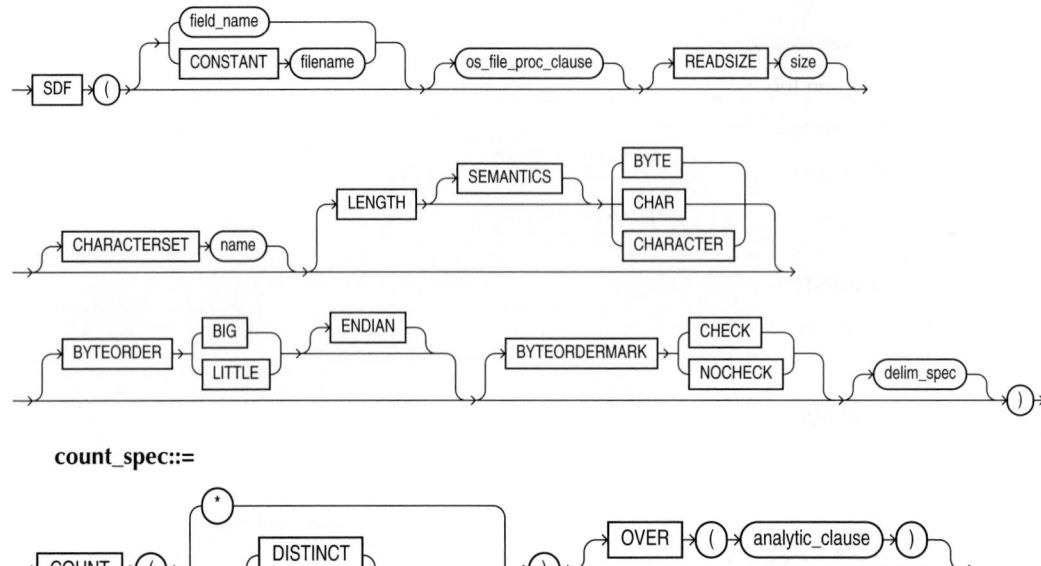

count_spec::=

SQLPLUS
SEE ALSO   Chapter 6
FORMAT

```
SQLPLUS [user[/password][@database] [@file] ] [-SILENT] |
  [/NOLOG] [-SILENT] | [-?]
```

DESCRIPTION   SQLPLUS starts up SQL*Plus. Entering both your username and password logs you onto your default database. Entering just your username causes SQL*Plus to prompt you for your password, which is not be displayed as you enter it. Entering @*database* connects you to the named database instead of your default. The @*database* can be anywhere, so long as the computer you are logging onto is connected to it through Oracle Net. There must be no space between *password* and @ *database*. For more information about Oracle Net, *see* Chapter 23. @*file* runs the start file immediately after SQL*Plus is loaded. There must be a space before @*file*. If the username and password are not entered on the command line with **SQLPLUS**, they must be the first line in the file. If they are in the file, and you enter them on the command line, you'll get an error message but the start file will run correctly anyway. To put *user* and *password* at the top of the file, separate them with a slash (/):

```
george/curious404
```

/NOLOG makes SQL*Plus start, but does not log you onto the Oracle database. You must then use **CONNECT** to attach to Oracle. (*See* **CONNECT**.)

-SILENT suppresses all of SQL*Plus's screen displays, including the command prompts and even the SQL*Plus logon and copyright information. It makes the use of SQL*Plus by another program invisible to the program's user.

-? displays the current version and level number for SQL*Plus without actually starting it.
EXAMPLE   Normal startup of SQL*Plus follows:

```
sqlplus george/curious404
```

To start up on the database EDMESTON, use this:

```
sqlplus george/curious404@EDMESTON
```

To start the report file REPORT6, which includes the name and password as its first line, use this:

```
sqlplus @report6
```

To start the report file REPORT6, which includes the name and password as its first line, on the database EDMESTON, use this:

```
sqlplus george/curious404@EDMESTON @report6
```

SQRT
SEE ALSO   **POWER**
FORMAT

DESCRIPTION   **SQRT** finds the square root of *value*.
EXAMPLE

```
SQRT(64)=8
```

The square root of negative numbers is not available in Oracle.

START (SQL*Plus)
SEE ALSO   **@, @@, ACCEPT, DEFINE, SPOOL**, Chapter 6
FORMAT

```
STA[RT] {url|file[.ext]} [parameter] [parameter]...
```

DESCRIPTION   **START** executes the contents of the specified start file (so called because it is started by this command). The file may contain any SQL*Plus commands. If no file type is specified, **START** assumes it is .sql. Any parameters following the filename are substituted into variables in the start file; the variables must be named *&1, &2, &3*, and so on, and will receive the parameters in order, from left to right. Every occurrence in the start file of &1 will get the first parameter. Parameters consisting of more than one word may be enclosed in single quotes (' '); otherwise, parameters are limited to a single word or number each.
EXAMPLE

```
start checkout INNUMERACY
```

where the file **checkout.sql** contains a variable named *&1*, into which the string 'INNUMERACY' will be substituted.

STARTUP
SEE ALSO   **SHUTDOWN**, **RECOVER**, Chapter 50
FORMAT

```
STARTUP options | upgrade_options
```

where *options* has the following syntax:

```
[FORCE][RESTRICT][PFILE=filename][QUIET][MOUNT[dbname]|
[OPEN [open_options][dbname]]|NOMOUNT]
```

where *open_options* has the following syntax:

```
READ {ONLY | WRITE [RECOVER]} | RECOVER
```

and *upgrade_options* has the following syntax:

```
[PFILE=filename]{UPGRADE|DOWNGRADE} [QUIET]
```

DESCRIPTION   **STARTUP** starts an instance. **FORCE** shuts down a running instance with
SHUTDOWN ABORT prior to starting it. **RESTRICT** allows only privileged users to log in. The **PFILE**
option allows you to specify an **init.ora** file to use during startup (in place of the standard spfile).
STARTUP RECOVER has the same effect as executing **RECOVER DATABASE** and starting an instance.
UPGRADE starts the database in **OPEN UPGRADE** mode and should be used only when a database is
first started with a new version of the Oracle software.

STANDARD_HASH
FORMAT

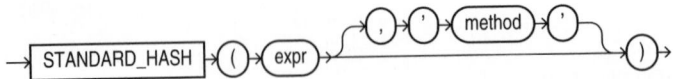

DESCRIPTION   **STANDARD_HASH** is a function that computes a hash value for any expression using
one of several algorithms. This function is useful for digital signatures, checksums, and other security
applications. Valid values for *method* are SHA1, SHA256, SHA384, and MD5. The default is SHA1.

STATS_BINOMIAL_TEST
FORMAT

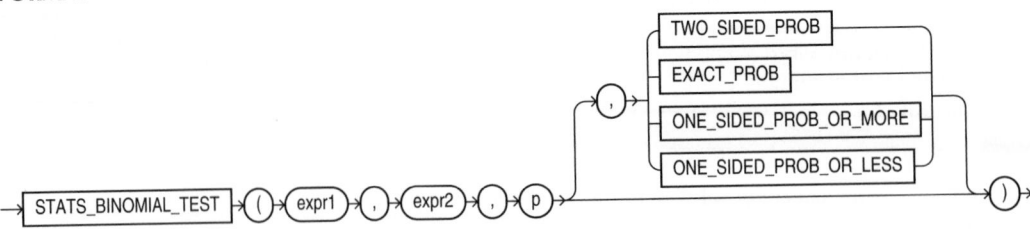

DESCRIPTION   **STATS_BINOMIAL_TEST** is an exact probability test used for dichotomous variables,
where only two possible values exist. It tests the difference between a sample proportion and a given
proportion.

STATS_CROSSTAB
FORMAT

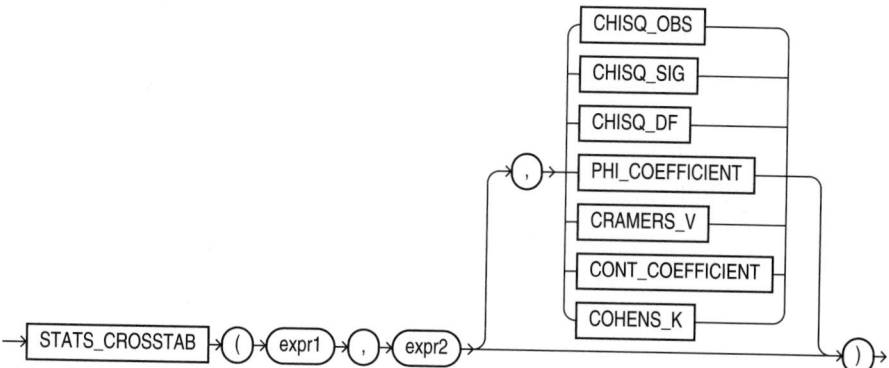

DESCRIPTION   **STATS_CROSSTAB** takes three arguments: two expressions and a return value of type VARCHAR2. *expr1* and *expr2* are the two nominal variables being analyzed. The function returns one number, determined by the value of the third argument. Values for the third argument are CHISQ_OBS, CHISQ_SIG, CHISQ_DF, PHI_COEFFICIENT, CRAMERS_V, CONT_COEFFICIENT, and COHENS_K.

STATS_F_TEST
FORMAT

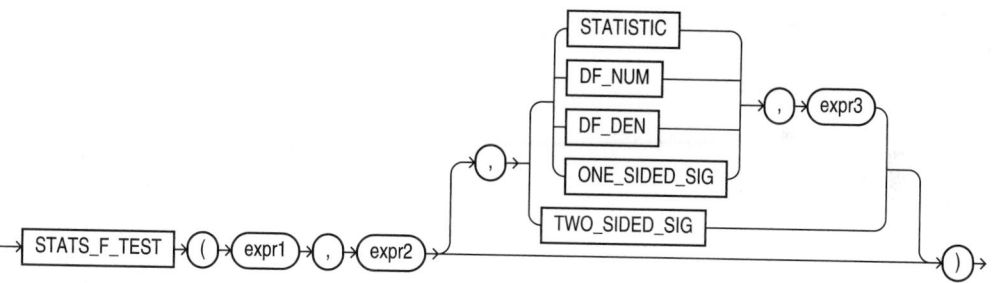

DESCRIPTION   **STATS_F_TEST** tests whether two variances are significantly different. The observed value of *f* is the ratio of one variance to the other, so values very different from 1 usually indicate significant differences.

STATS_KS_TEST
FORMAT

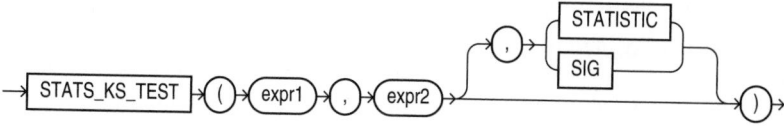

DESCRIPTION   **STATS_KS_TEST** is a Kolmogorov-Smirnov function that compares two samples to test whether they are from the same population or from populations that have the same distribution. It does not assume that the population from which the samples were taken is normally distributed.

STATS_MODE
FORMAT

DESCRIPTION   **STATS_MODE** takes as its argument a set of values and returns the value that occurs with the greatest frequency. If more than one mode exists, Oracle chooses one and returns only that one value.

STATS_MW_TEST
FORMAT

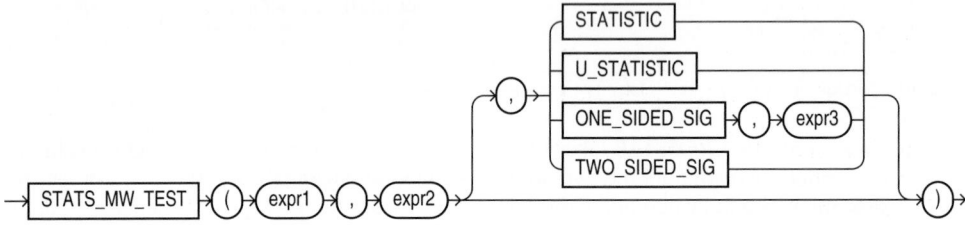

DESCRIPTION   A Mann-Whitney test compares two independent samples to test the null hypothesis that two populations have the same distribution function against the alternative hypothesis that the two distribution functions are different.

STATS_ONE_WAY_ANOVA
FORMAT

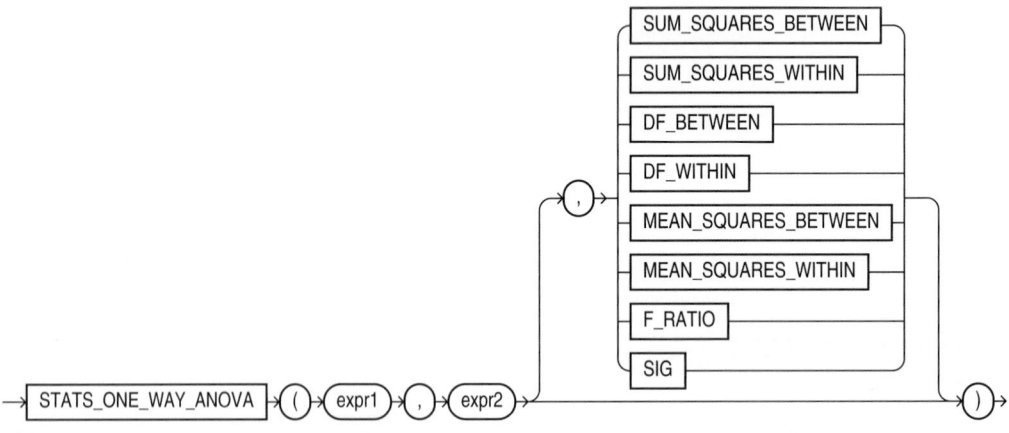

DESCRIPTION   **STATS_ONE_WAY_ANOVA** is a one-way analysis of variance function. It tests differences in means for statistical significance by comparing two different estimates of variance (mean square error and mean squares between). The function returns one number, determined by the value of the third argument (default is SIG, for significance).

STATS_T_TEST_* FUNCTIONS

FORMAT

    stats_t_test::=

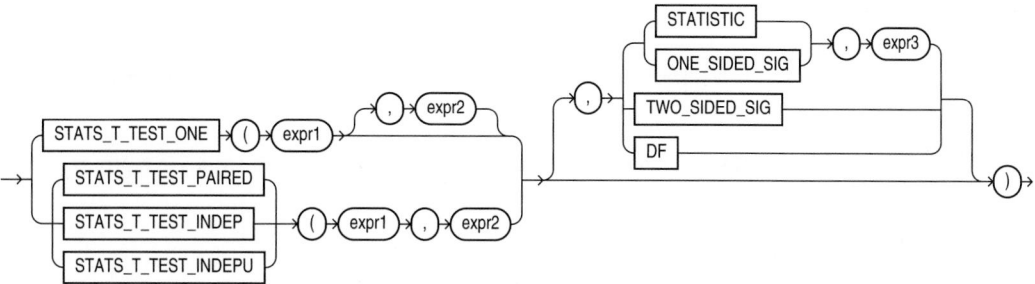

DESCRIPTION   The *t*-test measures the significance of a difference of means. You can use it to compare the means of two groups or the means of one group with a constant. The **STATS_T_TEST_*** functions take three arguments: two expressions and a return value of type VARCHAR2. The functions return one number, determined by the value of the third argument (default is TWO_SIDED_SIG).

    The tests are as follows:

- **STATS_T_TEST_ONE**   A one-sample *t*-test
- **STATS_T_TEST_PAIRED**   A two-sample, paired *t*-test
- **STATS_T_TEST_INDEP**   A *t*-test of two independent groups with the same variance
- **STATS_T_TEST_INDEPU**   A *t*-test of two independent groups with unequal variance

The values for the third argument are as follows:

- **STATISTIC**   The observed value of *t*
- **DF**   Degree of freedom
- **ONE_SIDED_SIG**   One-tailed significance of *t*
- **TWO_SIDED_SIG**   Two-tailed significance of *t*

STATS_WSR_TEST

FORMAT

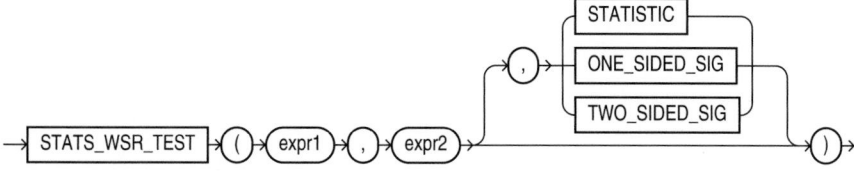

DESCRIPTION   **STATS_WSR_TEST** is a Wilcoxon Signed-Rank test of paired samples to determine whether the median of the differences between the samples is significantly different from zero. If you do not specify the third argument, it defaults to TWO_SIDED_SIG.

STDDEV
SEE ALSO   AGGREGATE FUNCTIONS, **VARIANCE**, Chapter 9
FORMAT

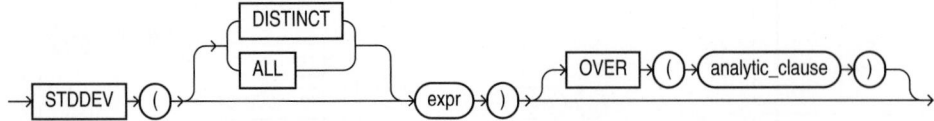

DESCRIPTION   **STDDEV** gives the standard deviation from the norm of values in a group of rows. It ignores **NULL** values in its calculation.

STDDEV_POP
SEE ALSO   AGGREGATE FUNCTIONS, **STTDEV, STDDEV_SAMP**
FORMAT

DESCRIPTION   **STDDEV_POP** computes the population standard deviation and returns the square root of the population variance.

STDDEV_SAMP
SEE ALSO   AGGREGATE FUNCTIONS, **STDDEV_POP, STTDEV,**
FORMAT

DESCRIPTION   **STDDEV_SAMP** computes the cumulative sample standard deviation and returns the square root of the sample variance.

STORAGE
SEE ALSO   **CREATE CLUSTER, CREATE INDEX, CREATE MATERIALIZED VIEW, CREATE MATERIALIZED VIEW LOG, CREATE ROLLBACK SEGMENT, CREATE TABLE, CREATE TABLESPACE**, as well as the **ALTER** statement for each of these

FORMAT
   storage_clause::=

   maxsize_clause::=

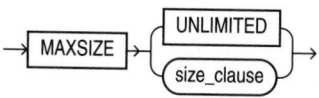

DESCRIPTION   The **STORAGE** clause is optional in any of the **CREATE** and **ALTER** statements listed under the preceding SEE ALSO section. **STORAGE** is not a SQL statement and cannot stand alone. In the following paragraphs, a *block* is a database block (*see* **BLOCK**) with a size depending on the operating system and the database initialization parameters.

   INITIAL allocates the first extent of space to the object. If **INITIAL** is not specified, it defaults to five data blocks. The smallest initial extent you can allocate is two data blocks and the largest depends on your operating system. You can express these numbers either as a simple integer or as an integer followed by **K** or **M** to indicate kilobytes or megabytes, respectively.

NEXT is the size of the extent allocated after the initial extent has been filled. If not specified, it defaults to five data blocks. The smallest next extent you can allocate is one data block and the largest depends on the operating system. You can use **K** and **M** for kilobytes and megabytes.

PCTINCREASE controls the rate of growth of extents beyond the second. If set to 0, every additional extent will be the same size as the second extent, specified by **NEXT**. If **PCTINCREASE** is a positive integer, each succeeding extent will be that percentage larger than the preceding one. For example, if **PCTINCREASE** is 50 (the default, if it is not specified), each additional extent will be 50 percent larger than the previous one. **PCTINCREASE** cannot be negative. The minimum **PCTINCREASE** is 0, and the maximum depends on the operating system. Oracle rounds the extent size up to the next multiple of the operating system block size.

MINEXTENTS defaults to 1 (or 2 for a rollback segment) if it is not specified, meaning that when the object is created, only the initial extent is allocated. A number greater than 1 will create that many total extents (which don't need to be contiguous on disk, as each extent itself does), and the size of each of them will be determined by the values set with **INITIAL**, **NEXT**, and **PCTINCREASE**. All of these will be allocated when the object is created.

MAXEXTENTS sets the limit on the total number of extents that can be allocated. The minimum limit is 1, with the default and maximum depending on the operating system. You can specify a **MAXEXTENTS** value of **UNLIMITED**.

OPTIMAL sets an optimal size in bytes for a rollback segment. Oracle dynamically deallocates extents in the rollback segment to maintain the optimal size. **NULL** means that Oracle never deallocates the rollback segment extents, and this is the default behavior. You must supply a size greater than or equal to the initial space allocated for the rollback segment by the **MINEXTENTS**, **INITIAL**, **NEXT**, and **PCTINCREASE** parameters.

FREELIST GROUPS gives the number of groups of free lists, with a default value of 1. This setting applies to the Real Application Clusters option of Oracle for tables, clusters, or indexes.

FREELISTS sets the number of free lists for each free list group.

BUFFER_POOL sets the buffer pool into which the table's blocks will be read. By default, all blocks are read into the **DEFAULT** pool. You can create separate pools for blocks you want to keep in memory longer (the **KEEP** pool) or for those you wish to age out of memory quickly (the **RECYCLE** pool).

For most applications, you should use Oracle's space management automation features, including locally managed tablespaces. In a locally managed tablespace, you define the storage parameters once and Oracle manages the space for the objects created within the tablespace.

STORE (SQL*Plus)
SEE ALSO   SAVE, START, Chapter 6
FORMAT

```
STORE SET file[.ext] [ CRE[ATE] | REP[LACE] | APP[END] ]
```

DESCRIPTION   **STORE** saves all of your SQL*Plus environment settings to a file.
EXAMPLE   The following command saves the current SQL*Plus environment settings to a file named settings.sql:

```
store settings.sql
```

SUBQUERY
A query (that is, a **SELECT** statement) may be used as a part of another SQL statement (called the parent, or outer statement), including **CREATE TABLE**, **DELETE**, **INSERT**, **SELECT**, and **UPDATE**, or in the SQL*Plus **COPY** command, in order to define the rows or columns that the parent will use in its execution. The results of the child query (also called a subquery) are not themselves displayed, but are passed to the parent SQL statement for its use. The following rules apply:

- In an **UPDATE** or **CREATE TABLE** command, the subquery must return one value for each column to be inserted or updated. The value or values are then used by the parent SQL statement to **INSERT** or **UPDATE** the rows.

- A subquery cannot contain **ORDER BY** and **FOR UPDATE OF** clauses.

- A "correlated" subquery is used in the **WHERE** clause of a **SELECT** statement and references an alias for the table used by the parent **SELECT** command. It is tested once for each row evaluated for selection by the parent **SELECT** statement (a standard subquery evaluated just once for the parent query). *See* Chapter 13 for further details.

Other than these restrictions, normal rules for a **SELECT** statement apply.

SUBSTITUTION
See **&**, **&&**, **ACCEPT**, and **DEFINE**.

SUBSTR
SEE ALSO   **||**, CHARACTER FUNCTIONS, **INSTR**, Chapter 7
FORMAT
　　substr::=

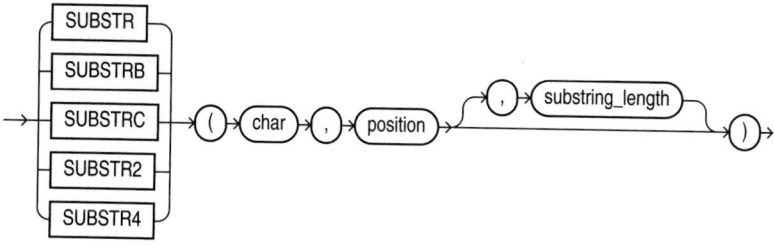

DESCRIPTION   **SUBSTR** clips out a piece of a string beginning at *start* and going for *count* characters. If *count* is not specified, the string is clipped from *start* and goes to the end of the string. There are multiple **SUBSTR** functions: **SUBSTR** calculates length using characters as defined by the input character set. **SUBSTRB** uses bytes instead of characters. **SUBSTRC** uses Unicode complete sets. **SUBSTR2** uses UCS2 code points. **SUBSTR4** uses UCS4 code points.
EXAMPLE

```
substr('Newspaper',5)
```

produces this:

```
paper
```

SUM
SEE ALSO   COMPUTE, AGGREGATE FUNCTIONS, Chapter 9
FORMAT

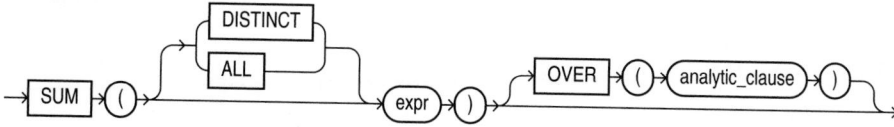

DESCRIPTION   **SUM** is the sum of all *values* for a group of rows. **DISTINCT** makes **SUM** add each unique value to the total only once; this is usually not very meaningful.

SYNTAX OPERATORS

SEE ALSO LOGICAL OPERATORS, PRECEDENCE

DESCRIPTION Syntax operators have the highest precedence of all operators and may appear anywhere in a SQL statement. Here, they are listed in descending order of precedence. Operators of equal precedence are evaluated from left to right. Most of these are listed and described separately under their own symbols.

Operator	Function
-	SQL*Plus command continuation. Continues a command on the following line.
&	Prefix for parameters in a SQL*Plus start file. Words are substituted for *&1*, *&2*, and so on. *See* **START.**
& &&	Prefix for a substitution variable in a SQL command in SQL*Plus. SQL*Plus prompts for a value if an undefined **&** or **&&** variable is found. **&&** also defines the variable and saves the value; **&** does not. *See* **&** and **&&**, **ACCEPT**, and **DEFINE**.
:	Prefix for a variable in SQL*FORMS and for a host variable in PL/SQL.
.	Variable separator, used in SQL*Plus to separate the variable name from a suffix so the suffix is not considered a part of the variable name, and used in SQL between user, table, and column names.
()	Surrounds subqueries and lists of columns, or controls precedence.
'	Surrounds a literal, such as a character string or date constant. To use a **'** in a string constant, use two **'** marks (not a double quotation mark).
"	Surrounds a table or column alias that contains special characters or a space.
"	Surrounds literal text in a date format clause of **TO_CHAR**.
@	Precedes a database name in a **COPY** or a link name in a **FROM** clause.

SYS_CONNECT_BY_PATH

SEE ALSO **CONNECT BY**, Chapter 14

FORMAT

DESCRIPTION **SYS_CONNECT_BY_PATH** is valid only in hierarchical queries. It returns the path of a column value from root to node, with column values separated by *char* for each row returned by the **CONNECT BY** condition.

SYS_CONTEXT

SEE ALSO **CREATE CONTEXT**

FORMAT

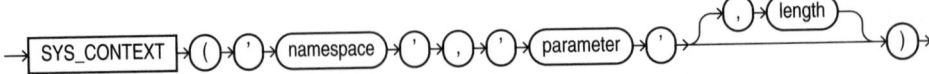

DESCRIPTION **SYS_CONTEXT** returns the value of *parameter* associated with the context *namespace*.

SYS_DBURIGEN

SEE ALSO   Chapter 52
FORMAT

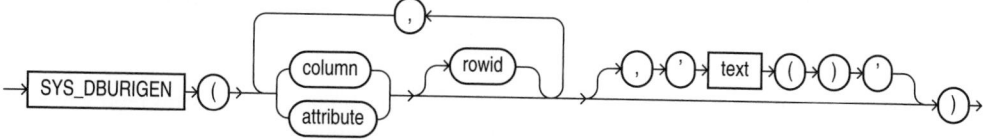

DESCRIPTION   SYS_DBURIGEN takes as its argument one or more columns or attributes, and optionally a ROWID, and generates a URL of datatype DBUriType to a particular column or row object. You can then use the URL to retrieve an XML document from the database.

All columns or attributes referenced must reside in the same table. They must perform the function of a primary key. That is, they need not actually match the primary keys of the table, but they must reference a unique value. If you specify multiple columns, all but the final column identify the row in the database, and the last column specified identifies the column within the row.

By default, the URL points to a formatted XML document. If you want the URL to point only to the text of the document, specify the optional **'text()'**. (In this XML context, the lowercase **'text'** is a keyword, not a syntactic placeholder.)

SYS_EXTRACT_UTC

SEE ALSO   Chapter 10
FORMAT

DESCRIPTION   SYS_EXTRACT_UTC extracts the UTC (Coordinated Universal Time) from a datetime with time zone displacement.

SYS_GUID

FORMAT

DESCRIPTION

SYS_GUID generates and returns a globally unique identifier (RAW value) made up of 16 bytes. On most platforms, the generated identifier consists of a host identifier and a process or thread identifier of the process or thread invoking the function and a nonrepeating value (sequence of bytes) for that process or thread.

SYS_TYPEID

SEE ALSO   Chapter 38
FORMAT

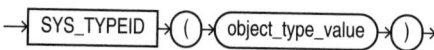

DESCRIPTION   SYS_TYPEID returns the type ID of the most specific type of the operand. This value is used primarily to identify the type-discriminant column underlying a substitutable column. For example, you can use the value returned by **SYS_TYPEID** to build an index on the type-discriminant column.

SYS_XMLAGG
SEE ALSO   SYS_XMLGEN, Chapter 45
FORMAT

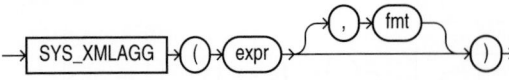

DESCRIPTION   **SYS_XMLAGG** aggregates all of the XML documents or fragments represented by *expr* and produces a single XML document. It adds a new enclosing element with a default name ROWSET. If you want to format the XML document differently, specify *fmt*, which is an instance of the SYS. XMLGenFormatType object.

SYS_XMLGEN
SEE ALSO   **SYS_XMLAGG**, Chapter 52
FORMAT

DESCRIPTION   **SYS_XMLGEN** takes an expression that evaluates to a particular row and column of the database and returns an instance of type SYS.XMLType containing an XML document. The *expr* can be a scalar value, a user-defined type, or an XMLType instance.

If *expr* is a scalar value, the function returns an XML element containing the scalar value. If *expr* is a type, the function maps the user-defined type attributes to XML elements. If *expr* is an XMLType instance, then the function encloses the document in an XML element whose default tag name is ROW.

By default, the elements of the XML document match the elements of *expr*. For example, if *expr* resolves to a column name, the enclosing XML element will be the same column name. If you want to format the XML document differently, specify *fmt*, which is an instance of the SYS.XMLGenFormatType object.

SYSDATE
SEE ALSO   Chapter 10
FORMAT

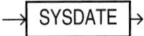

DESCRIPTION   **SYSDATE** returns the current date and time.
EXAMPLE

```
select sysdate from dual;
```

SYSTIMESTAMP
SEE ALSO   Chapter 10
FORMAT

DESCRIPTION   **SYSTIMESTAMP** returns the current date and time.
EXAMPLE

```
select systimestamp from dual;
```

TABLE (PL/SQL)

SEE ALSO DATATYPES, RECORD (PL/SQL)
FORMAT

collection_type_definition::=

assoc_array_type_def::=

varray_type_def::=

nested_table_type_def::=

datatype::=

collection_variable_dec::=

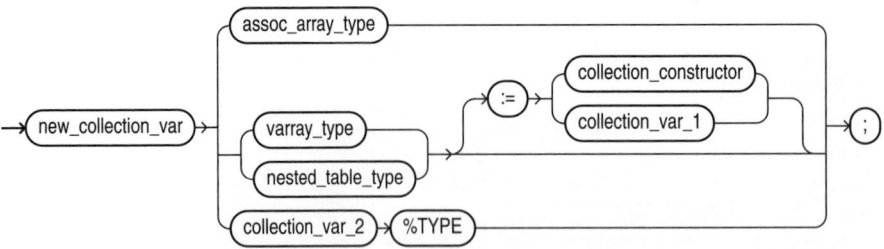

DESCRIPTION A TABLE declaration declares a new type that can then be used to declare variables of that type. A PL/SQL table has one column and an integer key and can have any number of rows. The datatype of the column can be either one of the standard PL/SQL datatypes (including another RECORD but not a TABLE) or a reference to the type of a particular column in a specific database table. Each field may also have a **NOT NULL** qualifier that specifies the field must always have a non-**NULL** value.

The **INDEX BY BINARY_INTEGER** clause is required and reminds you that the index is an integer. You can refer to any row of the table with the index in parentheses.

If you refer to an index to which you have not assigned any data, PL/SQL raises the NO_DATA_FOUND exception.

TAN

SEE ALSO ACOS, ASIN, ATAN, ATAN2, COS, COSH, NUMBER FUNCTIONS, SIN, TANH, Chapter 9
FORMAT

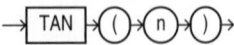

DESCRIPTION TAN returns the tangent of an angle *value* expressed in radians.
EXAMPLE

```
select tan(135*3.141593/180) tan -- tangent of 135 degrees in radians
from dual;
```

TANH

SEE ALSO ACOS, ASIN, ATAN, ATAN2, COS, COSH, NUMBER FUNCTIONS, SIN, TAN, Chapter 9
FORMAT

DESCRIPTION TANH returns the hyperbolic tangent of an angle *value*.

TIMESTAMP

The TIMESTAMP (*fractional_seconds_precision*) datatype records year, month, and day values of date, as well as hour, minute, and second values of time, where *fractional_seconds_precision* is the number of digits in the fractional part of the SECOND datetime field. Accepted values of *fractional_seconds_precision* are 0 to 9. The default is 6. *See* DATATYPES and Chapter 10.

TIMESTAMP WITH TIME ZONE

The TIMESTAMP (*fractional_seconds_precision*) WITH TIME ZONE datatype records year, month, and day values of date, as well as hour, minute, and second values of time, where *fractional_seconds_* *precision* is the number of digits in the fractional part of the SECOND datetime field. Accepted values of *fractional_seconds_precision* are 0 to 9. The default is 6.

TIMESTAMP WITH LOCAL TIME ZONE

The TIMESTAMP (*fractional_seconds_precision*) WITH LOCAL TIME ZONE datatype records the TIMESTAMP WITH TIME ZONE values, normalized to the database time zone when the data is stored. When the data is retrieved, users see the data in the session time zone.

TIMING (SQL*Plus)

SEE ALSO   CLEAR, SET
FORMAT

```
TIMI[NG] [ START area | STOP | SHOW ];
```

DESCRIPTION   **TIMING** keeps track of elapsed time from **START** to **STOP** by area name. **START** opens a timing area and makes *area* its title. *area* must be a single word. Several areas may exist at once. The most recently created one is the current timing area until it is deleted, when the previously created one becomes current. Timing areas are, in effect, nested. The most recently created will always show the least amount of time because the elapsed time of those before it will be, by definition, longer. Total time for any timing area is its own net time plus those of all the timing areas that followed it.

SHOW gives the current timing area's name and elapsed time.

STOP gives the current timing area's name and elapsed time, deletes the area, and makes the one previous to it (if there is one) the current timing area. *See the SQL*Plus User's Guide and Reference* for your host operating system for details on the precise meaning of time on your machine.

EXAMPLE   To create a timing area named 1, you enter this:

```
timing start 1
```

To see the current timing area's name and time, but to allow it to continue running, enter the following:

```
timing show
```

To see the current timing area's name and accumulated time, to stop it, and to make the previous one current, use this:

```
timing stop
```

TIMESTAMP_TO_SCN

SEE ALSO   SCN_TO_TIMESTAMP
FORMAT

DESCRIPTION   **TIMESTAMP_TO_SCN** takes a timestamp value as an argument and returns the system change number (SCN) closest to that timestamp.

TO_BINARY_DOUBLE

SEE ALSO   TO_BINARY_FLOAT
FORMAT

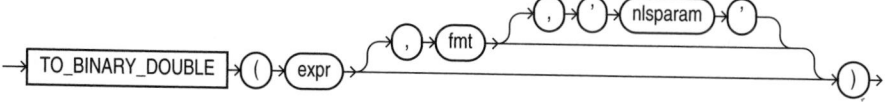

DESCRIPTION **TO_BINARY_DOUBLE** returns a double-precision floating-point number. *expr* can be a character string or a numeric value of type NUMBER.

TO_BINARY_FLOAT
SEE ALSO TO_BINARY_DOUBLE
FORMAT

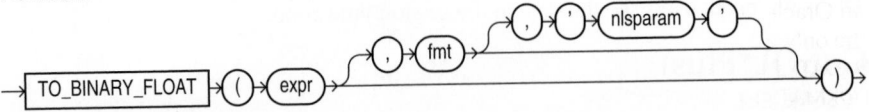

DESCRIPTION **TO_BINARY_FLOAT** returns a single-precision floating-point number. *expr* can be a character string or a numeric value of type NUMBER.

TO_BLOB
SEE ALSO Chapter 40
FORMAT
    to_blob::=

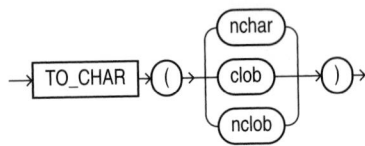

DESCRIPTION **TO_BLOB** converts LONG RAW and RAW values to BLOB values. All RAW datatypes are deprecated and either CLOBs or BLOBs should be used instead.

TO_CHAR (character formats)
SEE ALSO **TO_CHAR** (date and number formats)
FORMAT
    to_char_char::=

DESCRIPTION The **TO_CHAR** (*character*) function converts NCHAR, NVARCHAR2, CLOB, or NCLOB data to the database character set.
EXAMPLE

```
select to_char(title) from bookshelf;
```

TO_CHAR (date and number formats)
SEE ALSO DATE FORMATS, DATE FUNCTIONS, NUMBER FORMATS, **TO_DATE**, Chapter 10
FORMAT
    to_char_date::=

to_char_number::=

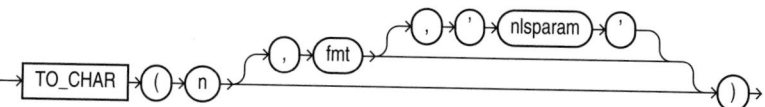

DESCRIPTION **TO_CHAR** reformats *number* or *date* according to *format*. *date* must be a column defined as an Oracle DATE datatype. It cannot be a string even if it is in the default date format of DD-MON-YY. The only way to use a string in which *date* appears in the **TO_CHAR** function is to enclose it within a **TO_DATE** function. The formats possible for this function are numerous. They are listed under NUMBER FORMATS and DATE FORMATS.

EXAMPLE Note the **FORMAT** in the following example. This is necessary in SQL*Plus to avoid the current default date width produced by TO_CHAR, which is about 100 characters wide:

```
column Formatted format a30 word_wrapped heading 'Formatted'

select birthdate, to_char(birthdate,'mm/dd/yy') Formatted
from birthday
where firstname = 'Victoria';

BIRTHDATE Formatted
--------- ------------------------------
20-MAY-79 05/20/79
```

TO_CLOB
SEE ALSO Chapter 40
FORMAT
  to_clob::=

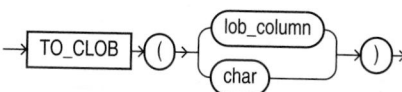

DESCRIPTION **TO_CLOB** converts NCLOB values in a LOB column or other character strings to CLOB values. *char* can be any of the datatypes CHAR, VARCHAR2, NCHAR, NVARCHAR2, CLOB, or NCLOB. Oracle executes this function by converting the underlying LOB data from the national character set to the database character set. Note that LONG values can be converted directly to CLOB columns via **ALTER TABLE**.

TO_DATE
SEE ALSO DATE FORMATS, DATE FUNCTIONS, **TO_CHAR**, Chapter 10
FORMAT

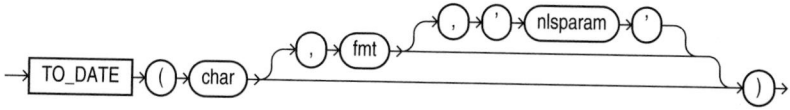

DESCRIPTION **TO_DATE** converts a *string* in a given format into an Oracle date. It also will accept a number instead of a string, with certain limits. *string* is a literal string, a literal number, or a database column containing a string or a number. In every case but one, the format must correspond to that which is described by *format*. Only if a string is in the format 'DD-MON-YY' can the format be omitted. Note that *format* is restricted. *See* DATE FORMATS for a list of acceptable formats for **TO_DATE**.

EXAMPLE

```
select to_date('02/22/13','mm/dd/yy') from dual;

TO_DATE('
---------
22-FEB-13
```

TO_DSINTERVAL

SEE ALSO DATATYPES
FORMAT

sql_format::=

ds_iso_format::=

DESCRIPTION **TO_DSINTERVAL** converts a character string of CHAR, VARCHAR2, NCHAR, or NVARCHAR2 datatype to an INTERVAL DAY TO SECOND type. *char* is the character string to be converted. The only valid NLS parameter you can specify in this function is NLS_NUMERIC_CHARACTERS. This argument can have the form NLS_NUMERIC_CHARACTERS = "*dg*" where *d* and *g* represent the decimal character and group separator, respectively. ISO duration format is compatible with the ISO 8601:2004 standard.

TO_LOB

SEE ALSO **INSERT**, Chapter 40
FORMAT

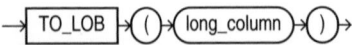

DESCRIPTION **TO_LOB** converts LONG values in *long_column* to LOB values. You can apply this function only to a LONG column and only in the **SELECT** list of a subquery in an **INSERT** command.

TO_MULTI_BYTE

SEE ALSO   CONVERSION FUNCTIONS, Chapter 11
FORMAT

DESCRIPTION   TO_MULTI_BYTE converts the single-byte characters in a character *string* to their multibyte equivalents. If a character has no multibyte equivalent, the function returns the character unconverted.

TO_NCHAR (character)

SEE ALSO   CONVERSION FUNCTIONS, **TRANSLATE ... USING**
FORMAT
   to_nchar_char::=

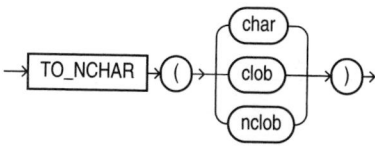

DESCRIPTION   TO_NCHAR (*character*) converts a character string, CLOB, or NCLOB from the database character set to the national character set. This function is equivalent to the **TRANSLATE ... USING** function with a **USING** clause in the national character set.

TO_NCHAR (datetime)

SEE ALSO   CONVERSION FUNCTIONS
FORMAT
   to_nchar_date::=

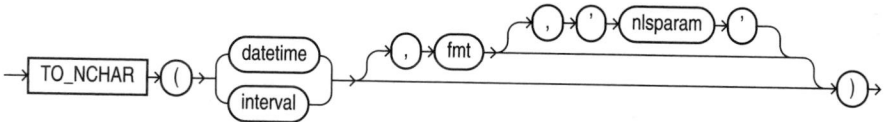

DESCRIPTION   TO_NCHAR (*datetime*) converts a character string of DATE, TIMESTAMP, TIMESTAMP WITH TIME ZONE, TIMESTAMP WITH LOCAL TIME ZONE, INTERVAL MONTH TO YEAR, or INTERVAL DAY TO SECOND datatype from the database character set to the national character set.

TO_NCHAR (number)

SEE ALSO   CONVERSION FUNCTIONS
FORMAT
   to_nchar_number::=

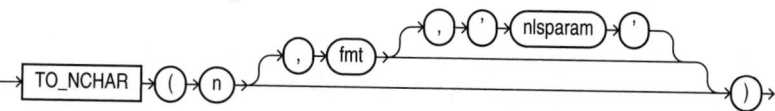

DESCRIPTION   TO_NCHAR (*number*) converts a number to a string in the NVARCHAR2 character set. The optional *fmt* and *nlsparam* corresponding to *n* can be one of these datatypes: DATE,

TIMESTAMP, TIMESTAMP WITH TIME ZONE, TIMESTAMP WITH LOCAL TIME ZONE, INTERVAL MONTH TO YEAR, or INTERVAL DAY TO SECOND datatype.

TO_NCLOB
SEE ALSO CONVERSION FUNCTIONS, Chapter 40
FORMAT

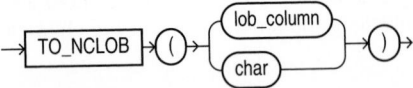

DESCRIPTION **TO_NCLOB** converts CLOB values in a LOB column or other character strings to NCLOB values. *char* can be any of these datatypes: CHAR, VARCHAR2, NCHAR, NVARCHAR2, CLOB, or NCLOB. Oracle implements this function by converting the character set of the LOB column from the database character set to the national character set.

TO_NUMBER
SEE ALSO CONVERSION FUNCTIONS, Chapter 11
FORMAT

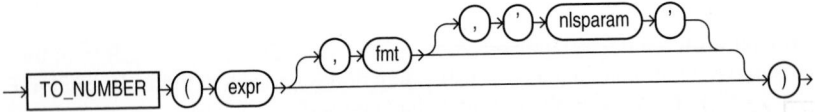

DESCRIPTION **TO_NUMBER** converts a character *string* to a NUMBER datatype. It requires that the characters in the string be a properly formatted number with only the characters **0–9**, **–**, **+**, and **.** included. This function is largely unnecessary due to the automatic data conversion done by Oracle, except when used for a character column containing numbers in an **ORDER BY** or a comparison.
EXAMPLE

```
to_number('333.46')
```

TO_SINGLE_BYTE
SEE ALSO CONVERSION FUNCTIONS, Chapter 11
FORMAT

DESCRIPTION **TO_SINGLE_BYTE** converts the multibyte characters in a character *string* to their single-byte equivalents. If a multibyte character has no single-byte equivalent, the function returns the character unconverted.

TO_TIMESTAMP
SEE ALSO CONVERSION FUNCTIONS, TIMESTAMP, **TO_CHAR**, **TO_TIMESTAMP_TZ**
FORMAT

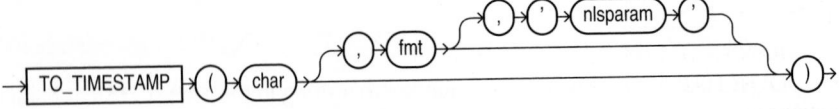

DESCRIPTION **TO_TIMESTAMP** converts the *char* of CHAR, VARCHAR2, NCHAR, or NVARCHAR2 datatype to a value of the TIMESTAMP datatype, using a *fmt* format if *char* is not in the default format of the TIMESTAMP datatype. The optional *nlsparam* has the same purpose in this function as in the **TO_CHAR** function for date conversion.

TO_TIMESTAMP_TZ

SEE ALSO CONVERSION FUNCTIONS, TIMESTAMP WITH TIME ZONE, **TO_TIMESTAMP**
FORMAT

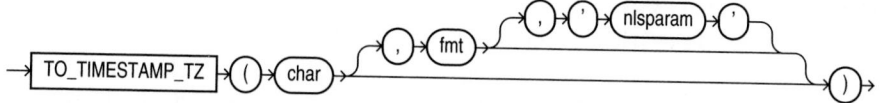

DESCRIPTION **TO_TIMESTAMP_TZ** converts *char* of the CHAR, VARCHAR2, NCHAR, or NVARCHAR2 datatype to a value of TIMESTAMP WITH TIME ZONE datatype.

TO_YMINTERVAL

SEE ALSO CONVERSION FUNCTIONS, INTERVAL YEAR TO MONTH
FORMAT

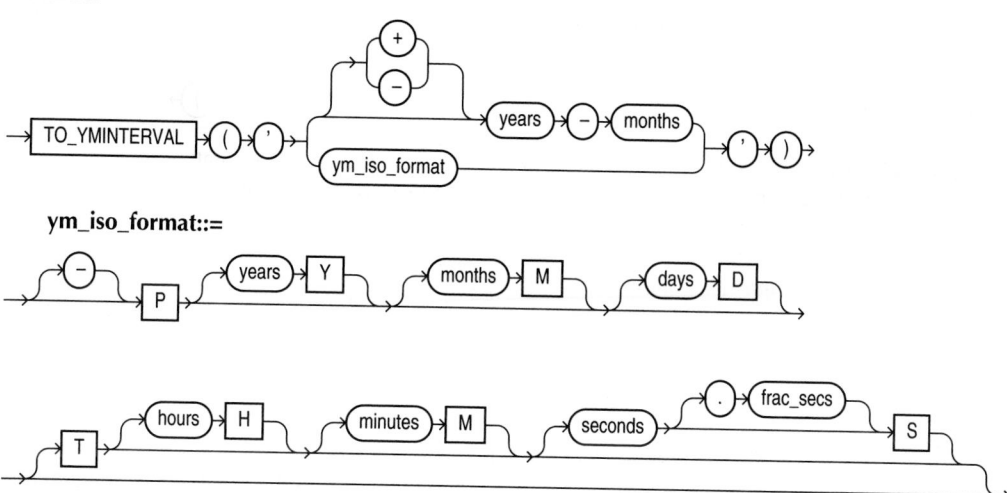

ym_iso_format::=

DESCRIPTION **TO_YMINTERVAL** converts a character string of the CHAR, VARCHAR2, NCHAR, or NVARCHAR2 datatype to an INTERVAL YEAR TO MONTH type, where *char* is the character string to be converted.

TRANSLATE

SEE ALSO REPLACE, Chapter 11
FORMAT

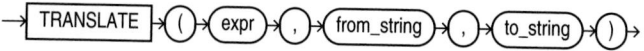

DESCRIPTION **TRANSLATE** looks at each character in *string* and then checks *from* to see if that character is there. If it is, **TRANSLATE** notes the position in *from* where it found the character and then looks at the same position in *to*. Whatever character it finds there, it substitutes for the character in *string*.

EXAMPLE

```
select translate('I Love My Old Thesaurus','AEIOUY','123456')
from dual;

TRANSLATE('ILOVEMYOLDTH
----------------------
3 Love My 41d Thesaurus
```

TRANSLATE ... USING

SEE ALSO CONVERSION FUNCTIONS, **CONVERT, TO_NCHAR, UNISTR**
FORMAT

DESCRIPTION **TRANSLATE ... USING** converts *text* into the character set specified for conversions between the database character set and the national character set. The *text* argument is the expression to be converted.

Specifying the **USING CHAR_CS** argument converts *text* into the database character set. The output datatype is VARCHAR2.

Specifying the **USING NCHAR_CS** argument converts *text* into the national character set. The output datatype is NVARCHAR2.

This function is similar to the Oracle **CONVERT** function, but must be used instead of **CONVERT** if either the input or the output datatype is being used as NCHAR or NVARCHAR2. If the input contains UCS2 code points or backslash characters (\), use the **UNISTR** function.

TREAT

SEE ALSO **DEREF, REF**, Chapter 41
FORMAT

DESCRIPTION **TREAT** changes the declared type of an expression.

If the declared type of *expr* is *source_type*, then *type* must be some supertype or subtype of *source_type*. If the most specific type of *expr* is *type* (or some subtype of *type*), then **TREAT** returns *expr*. If the most specific type of *expr* is not *type* (or some subtype of *type*), then **TREAT** returns **NULL**.

If the declared type of *expr* is **REF** *source_type*, then *type* must be some subtype or supertype of *source_type*. If the most specific type of **DEREF**(*expr*) is *type* (or a subtype of *type*), **TREAT** returns *expr*. If the most specific type of **DEREF**(*expr*) is not *type* (or a subtype of *type*), then **TREAT** returns **NULL**.

TRIM

SEE ALSO **LTRIM, RTRIM**, Chapter 7

FORMAT

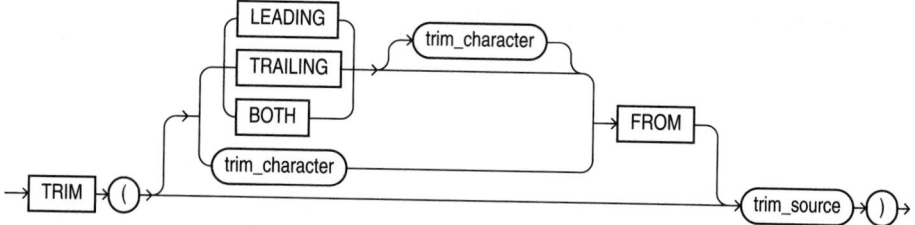

DESCRIPTION   **TRIM** enables you to trim leading or trailing characters (or both) from a character string. If *trim_character* or *trim_source* is a character literal, you must enclose it in single quotes.

If you specify **LEADING**, Oracle removes any leading characters equal to *trim_character*. If you specify **TRAILING**, Oracle removes any trailing characters equal to *trim_character*. If you specify **BOTH** or none of the three, Oracle removes leading and trailing characters equal to *trim_character*.

If you specify only *trim_source,* Oracle removes leading and trailing blank spaces. If either *trim_source* or *trim_character* is a **NULL** value, then the **TRIM** function returns a **NULL**.

EXAMPLE

```
select TRIM('"' from Title) from magazine;
select TRIM(leading '"' from Title) from magazine;
select TRIM(trailing '"' from Title) from magazine;
```

TRUNC (Form 1—for Dates)

SEE ALSO   **COLUMN**, DATE FUNCTIONS, **TRUNC** (Form 2), Chapter 10

FORMAT

   trunc_date::=

DESCRIPTION   **TRUNC** truncates *date* according to *format*. Without a *format, date* is truncated to 12 A.M. (midnight), with the first moment of the new day, today's date, for any time up to and including 11:59:59 P.M. (just before midnight). *See* **ROUND** (Form 1) for valid date *format* values.

The result of **TRUNC** is always a date with its time set to 12 A.M., the first moment of the day.

TRUNC (Form 2—for Numbers)

SEE ALSO   **COLUMN**, NUMBER FUNCTIONS, **TRUNC** (Form 1), Chapter 9

FORMAT

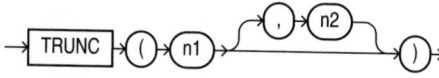

DESCRIPTION   **TRUNC** is *value* truncated to *precision*.

EXAMPLES

```
TRUNC(123.45,0)  = 123
TRUNC(123.45,-1) = 120
TRUNC(123.45,-2) = 100
```

TRUNCATE CLUSTER

SEE ALSO **CREATE CLUSTER, DELETE, DROP TABLE,** Chapter 17
FORMAT
  truncate_cluster::=

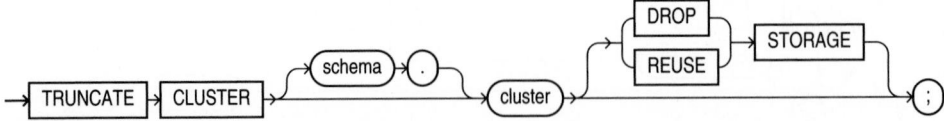

DESCRIPTION Use the **TRUNCATE CLUSTER** statement to remove all rows from a cluster. By default, Oracle Database also performs the following tasks:

- Deallocates all space used by the removed rows except that specified by the **MINEXTENTS** storage parameter
- Sets the **NEXT** storage parameter to the size of the last extent removed from the segment by the truncation process

Removing rows with the **TRUNCATE** statement can be more efficient than dropping and re-creating a cluster. Dropping and re-creating a cluster invalidates dependent objects of the cluster, requires you to re-grant object privileges on the cluster, and requires you to re-create the indexes and cluster on the table and re-specify its storage parameters. Truncating has none of these effects. Removing rows with the **TRUNCATE CLUSTER** statement can be faster than removing all rows with the **DELETE** statement, especially if the cluster has numerous indexes and other dependencies. To truncate a cluster, the cluster must be in your schema or you must have the DROP ANY TABLE system privilege.

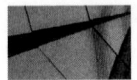

NOTE
You cannot roll back a TRUNCATE statement.

TRUNCATE TABLE

SEE ALSO **CREATE TABLE, DELETE, DROP TABLE,** Chapter 17
FORMAT
  truncate_table::=

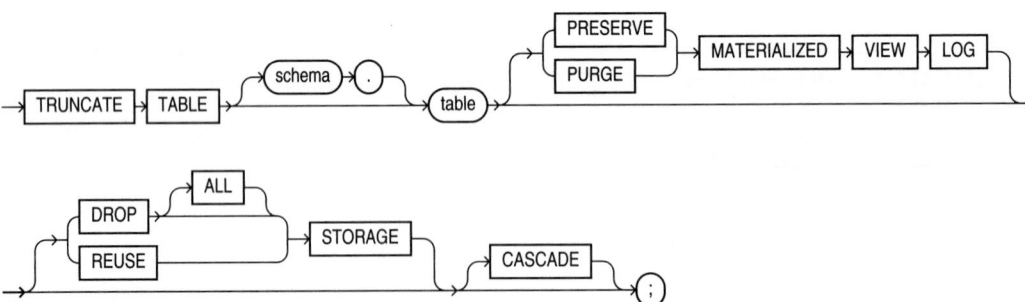

DESCRIPTION **TRUNCATE** removes all the rows from a table. If you add the **DROP STORAGE** option, **TRUNCATE** deallocates the space from the deleted rows; if you add the **REUSE STORAGE** option, **TRUNCATE** leaves the space allocated for new rows in the table. **DROP STORAGE** is the default.

The **TRUNCATE** command is faster than a **DELETE** command because it generates no rollback information, does not fire any **DELETE** triggers (and, therefore, must be used with caution), and does not record any information in a materialized view log. In addition, using **TRUNCATE** does not invalidate the objects depending on the deleted rows or the privileges on the table.

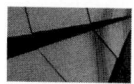

NOTE
You cannot roll back a TRUNCATE statement.

TTITLE (SQL*Plus)

SEE ALSO   ACCEPT, **BTITLE**, **DEFINE**, PARAMETERS, **REPFOOTER**, **REPHEADER**
FORMAT

```
TTI[TLE] [option [text|variable]... | OFF | ON]
```

DESCRIPTION   **TTITLE** (Top **TITLE**) puts a title (may be multiline) at the top of each page of a report. OFF and ON suppress and restore the display of the text without changing its contents. **TTITLE** by itself displays the current TTITLE options and *text* or *variable*.

text is the title you wish to give this report, and *variable* is a user-defined variable or a system-maintained variable, including SQL.LNO, the current line number; SQL.PNO, the current page number; SQL.RELEASE, the current Oracle release number; SQL.SQLCODE, the current error code; and SQL.USER, the username.

SQL*Plus uses **TTITLE** in the new form if the first word after **TTITLE** is a valid option. The valid options are

- **COL *n*** skips directly to position *n* from the left margin of the current line.

- **S[KIP] *n*** prints *n* blank lines. If no *n* is specified, one blank line is printed. If *n* is 0, no blank lines are printed and the current position for printing becomes position 1 of the current line (leftmost on the page).

- **TAB n** skips forward *n* positions (backward if *n* is negative).

- **BOLD** prints the output data in bold print.

- **LE[FT]**, **CE[NTER]**, and **R[IGHT]** left-justify, center, and right-justify data on the current line. Any text or variables following these commands are justified as a group, up to the end of the command, or a LEFT, CENTER, RIGHT, or COL. CENTER and RIGHT use the value set by the **SET LINESIZE** command to determine where to place the text or variable.

- **FORMAT *string*** specifies the FORMAT MODEL that will control the format of subsequent text or variables and follows the same syntax as FORMAT in a **COLUMN** command, such as FORMAT A12 or FORMAT $999,990.99. Each time a FORMAT appears, it supersedes the previous one that was in effect. If no FORMAT MODEL has been specified, the one set by **SET NUMFORMAT** is used. If NUMFORMAT has not been set, the default for SQL*Plus is used.

Date values are printed according to the default format unless a variable has been loaded with a date reformatted by **TO_CHAR**.

Any number of options, pieces of text, and variables may be used in a single **TTITLE**. Each is printed in the order specified, and each is positioned and formatted as specified by the clauses that precede it.

TYPE (Embedded SQL)

SEE ALSO   *Programmer's Guide to the Oracle Precompilers*

FORMAT

```
EXEC SQL TYPE type IS datatype
```

DESCRIPTION   PL/SQL lets you assign an Oracle external datatype to a user-defined datatype. The datatype may include a length, precision, or scale. This external datatype is mapped to the user-defined type and assigned to all host variables assigned to the type. For a list of external datatypes, see the *Programmer's Guide to the Oracle Precompilers.*

NOTE
See the Programmer's Guide to the Oracle Precompilers *for a full list of all commands. This reference does not contain all of the possible precompiler commands.*

TZ_OFFSET
SEE ALSO   DBTIMEZONE, SESSIONTIMEZONE
FORMAT

DESCRIPTION   TZ_OFFSET returns the time zone offset corresponding to the value entered based on the date the statement is executed. You can enter a valid time zone name, a time zone offset from UTC (which simply returns itself), or the keyword **SESSIONTIMEZONE** or **DBTIMEZONE**. For a listing of valid values, query the TZNAME column of the V$TIMEZONE_NAMES dynamic performance view.

UID
FORMAT

DESCRIPTION   **UID** returns an integer that uniquely identifies the session user (the user who logged on).

UNDEFINE (SQL*Plus)
SEE ALSO   ACCEPT, DEFINE, PARAMETERS
FORMAT

```
UNDEF[INE] variable
```

DESCRIPTION   UNDEFINE deletes the definition of a user variable that has been defined by **ACCEPT, DEFINE,** or as a parameter to the **START** command. You can **UNDEFINE** the current values of multiple variables in a single command. The format is shown in the following listing:

```
undefine variable1 variable2 ...
```

EXAMPLE
To UNDEFINE a variable named TOTAL, use this:

```
undefine total
```

UNION
SEE ALSO **INTERSECT**, **MINUS**, QUERY OPERATORS, Chapter 13
FORMAT

```
SELECT...
  UNION [ALL]
SELECT...
```

DESCRIPTION **UNION** combines two queries. It returns all distinct rows for both **SELECT** statements or, when ALL is specified, all rows regardless of duplication. The number of columns and datatypes must be identical between **SELECT** statements, although the names of the columns do not need to be. *See* Chapter 13 for a discussion of the important differences and effects of **INTERSECT**, **UNION**, and **MINUS**, and the role that precedence plays in the results.

UNISTR
SEE ALSO CONVERSION FUNCTIONS, **CONVERT, TRANSLATE ... USING**
FORMAT

DESCRIPTION **UNISTR** takes as its argument a string in any character set and returns it in Unicode in the database Unicode character set. To include UCS2 codepoint characters in the string, use the escape backslash (\\) followed by the next number. To include the backslash itself, precede it with another backslash (\\\\).

This function is similar to the **TRANSLATE ... USING** function, except that **UNISTR** offers the escape character for UCS2 codepoints and backslash characters.

UPDATE (Form 1—Embedded SQL)
SEE ALSO **EXECUTE IMMEDIATE, FOR, PREPARE, SELECT** (Form 2), *Programmer's Guide to the Oracle Precompilers*
FORMAT

```
EXEC SQL [AT { dbname | :host_variable }]
  [FOR { :host_integer | integer }]
  UPDATE
  [ (subquery)
  | [schema.] { table | view } [ @db_link | PARTITION (part_name) ] ]
  SET
  { column = { expr | (subquery_2) }
  | (column [, column]...) = (subquery_1) }
  [, { column = { expr | (subquery_2) }
     | (column [, column]...) = (subquery_1)     } ]...
  [WHERE { condition | CURRENT OF cursor }]
  [{ RETURN | RETURNING } expr [, expr]... INTO
  :host_variable [[INDICATOR] :ind_variable]
  [, :host_variable [[INDICATOR] :ind_variable]]...]
```

DESCRIPTION   *See* **UPDATE** (Form 3) for a description of the various clauses. The elements unique to Embedded SQL follow:

- **AT *dbname*** optionally names a database from a previous **CONNECT** statement for a database name from a previous **DECLARE DATABASE** statement.

- **FOR :*host_integer*** sets the maximum number of rows that can be fetched. *integer* is a named host variable.

- *expr* may include a host :*variable*[:*indicator*].

- The **WHERE** clause may include host variables or arrays.

- **CURRENT OF** updates the last row fetched for the named *cursor*. However, the cursor must be open and positioned on the row. If it isn't, the **CURRENT OF** clause, which is a part of the **WHERE** clause, causes the **WHERE** to find no rows, and none will be updated. The cursor must have previously been named in a **DECLARE CURSOR** statement with a **SELECT ... FOR UPDATE OF**.

If any host variable in either the **SET** or **WHERE** is an array, then all host variables in both must be arrays, though they do not all need to be the same size arrays. If they are arrays, **UPDATE** is executed once for each set of components in the array, and may update zero or more rows. The maximum number depends on either the size of the smallest array or the integer value in the **FOR** clause, if one is specified. *See* CURSOR FOR LOOP for additional details.

NOTE
See the Programmer's Guide to the Oracle Precompilers *for a full list of all commands. This reference does not contain all of the possible precompiler commands.*

UPDATE (Form 2—PL/SQL Extensions)
SEE ALSO   **DECLARE CURSOR**, SUBQUERY
FORMAT
    update_set_clause::=

    where_clause::=

DESCRIPTION   **UPDATE** in PL/SQL works identically to the normal SQL **UPDATE** statement, with the exception of the alternative **WHERE** clause—**WHERE CURRENT OF** cursor. In this instance, the

UPDATE statement affects just the single row currently in the cursor as a result of the last **FETCH**. The cursor **SELECT** statement must have included the words **FOR UPDATE**.

Like **INSERT**, **DELETE**, and **SELECT ... INTO**, the **UPDATE** statement always uses the implicit cursor named SQL. This is never declared (although the **SELECT ... FOR UPDATE** statement must be **DECLARE**d in a cursor for the **WHERE CURRENT OF** cursor to be used). Its attributes are set as follows:

- **SQL%ISOPEN** is irrelevant.
- **SQL%FOUND** is TRUE if one or more rows are updated and FALSE if no rows are updated. **SQL%NOTFOUND** is the opposite of SQL%FOUND.
- **SQL%ROWCOUNT** is the number of rows updated.

UPDATE (Form 3—SQL Command)

SEE ALSO **DELETE**, **INSERT**, **SELECT**, SUBQUERY, **WHERE**, Chapter 15
FORMAT
   update::=

   DML_table_expression_clause::=

   partition_extension_clause::=

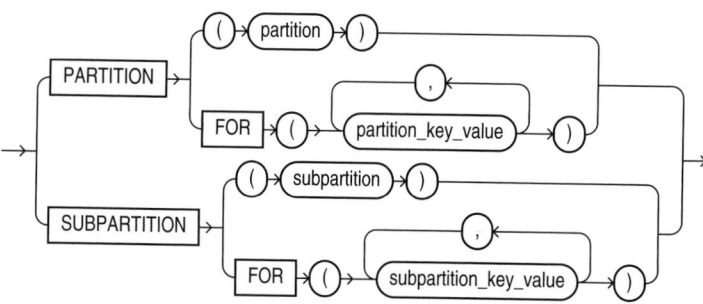

subquery_restriction_clause::=

table_collection_expression::=

update_set_clause::=

where_clause::=

returning_clause::=

error_logging_clause::=

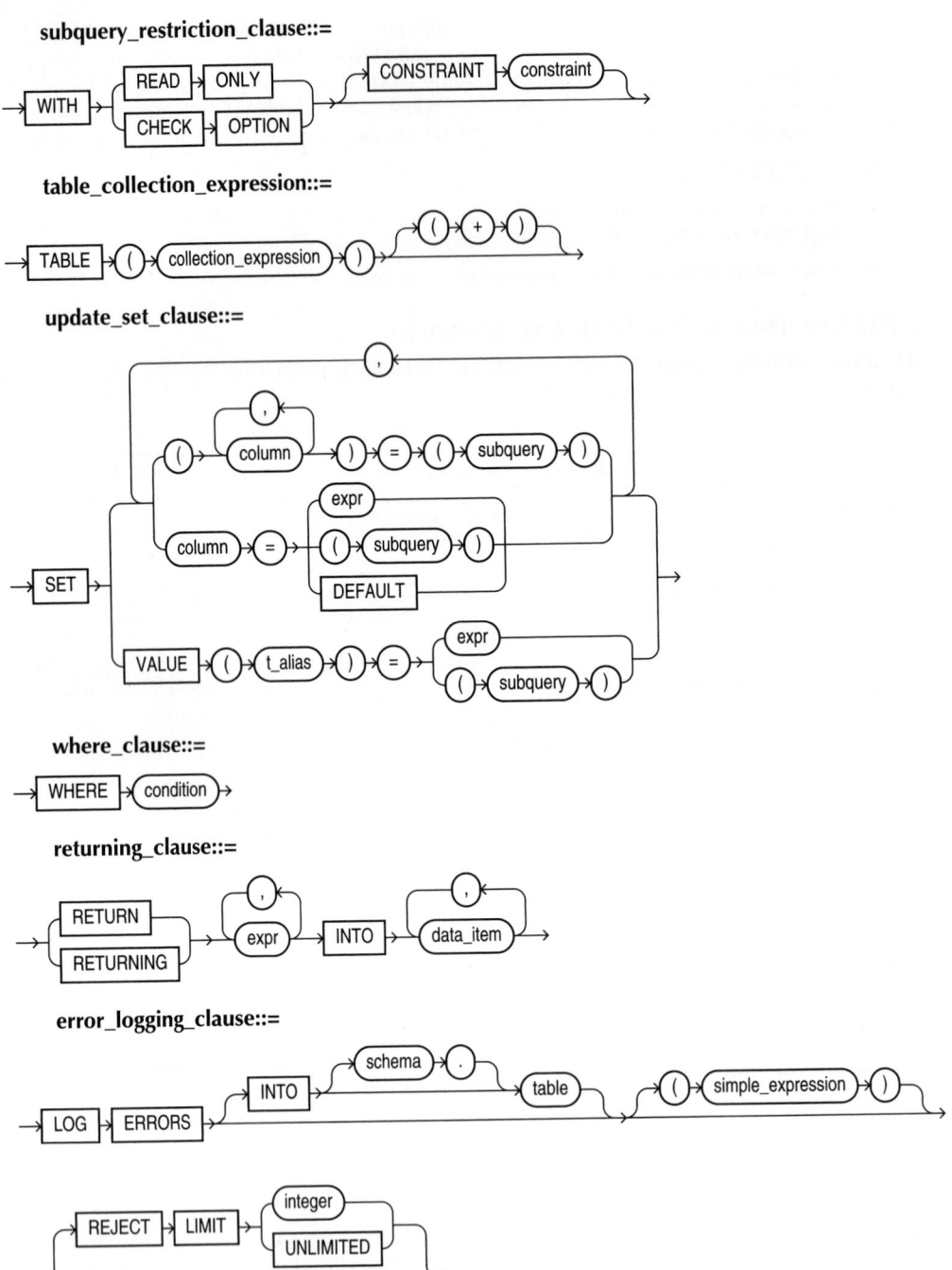

DESCRIPTION **UPDATE** changes the values in the listed columns in the specified table. The **WHERE** clause may contain a correlated subquery. A subquery may select from the table that is being updated, although it must return just one row. Without a **WHERE** clause, all rows will be updated. With a **WHERE** clause, only those rows it selects will be updated. The expressions are evaluated as the command is executed, and their results replace the current values for the columns in the row(s).

A subquery must select the same number of columns (with compatible datatypes) as are in parentheses on the left side of the **SET** clause. Columns that are set to equal an expression may precede columns in parentheses set equal to a subquery, all within a single **UPDATE** statement.

EXAMPLE   To set all PUBLISHER values to NULL:

```
update bookshelf set publisher = null ;
```

The following updates the city of Walpole in the COMFORT table, setting the precipitation for all Walpole rows to **NULL**, the noon temperature equal to that in Manchester, and the midnight temperature equal to the noon temperature minus 10 degrees:

```
update comfort set precipitation = null,
            (noon, midnight) =
        (select temperature, temperature - 10
         from weather
         where city = 'Manchester')
    where city = 'Walpole';
```

UPDATEXML
SEE ALSO   Chapter 52
FORMAT

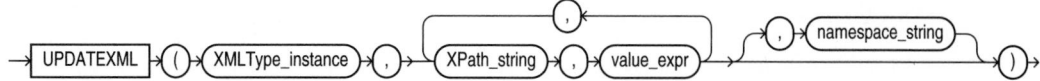

DESCRIPTION   **UPDATEXML** takes as arguments an XMLType instance and an XPath value pair and returns an XMLType instance with the updated value. If *Xpath_string* is an XML element, then the corresponding *value_expr* must be an XMLType instance. If *Xpath_string* is an attribute or text node, then the *value_expr* can be any scalar datatype. The datatypes of the target of each *Xpath_string* and its corresponding *value_expr* must match. The optional *namespace_string* must resolve to a VARCHAR2 value that specifies a default mapping or namespace mapping for prefixes, which Oracle uses when evaluating the XPath expressions.

UPPER
SEE ALSO   **LOWER**, Chapter 7
FORMAT

DESCRIPTION   **UPPER** converts every letter in *string* into uppercase.
EXAMPLE

```
select upper('Look what you''ve done!') from dual;
```

produces this:

```
LOOK WHAT YOU'VE DONE!
```

UROWID

UROWID (Universal **ROWID**) is the datatype for index-organized tables' primary keys. The maximum and default size is 4000 bytes. *See* DATATYPES and **CREATE TABLE**.

USER

SEE ALSO UID
FORMAT

→| USER |→

DESCRIPTION **USER** is the name by which the current user is known to Oracle. **USER** is a function and, as such, can be queried in any **SELECT** statement.
EXAMPLE

```
select user from dual;
```

USERENV

SEE ALSO CHARACTER FUNCTIONS
FORMAT

DESCRIPTION **USERENV** is a legacy function, replaced by SYS_CONTEXT's UserEnv namespace. Use SYS_CONTEXT for all new development. The options and their return values are as follows:

'CLIENT_INFO'	Returns up to 64 bytes of user session information that can be stored by an application using the DBMS_APPLICATION_INFO package.
'ENTRYID'	Returns available auditing entry identifier. You cannot use this attribute in distributed SQL statements. To use this keyword in USERENV, the initialization parameter AUDIT_TRAIL must be set to TRUE.
'ISDBA'	Returns 'TRUE' if the user has been authenticated as having DBA privileges through either the operating system or a password file.
'LANG'	Returns the ISO abbreviation for the language name, a shorter form than the existing 'LANGUAGE' parameter.
'LANGUAGE'	Returns the language and territory currently used by your session along with the database character set in this form: *language_territory.characterset*.
'SESSIONID'	Returns your auditing session identifier. You cannot use this attribute in distributed SQL statements.
'TERMINAL'	Returns the operating system identifier for your current session's terminal. In distributed SQL statements, this attribute returns the identifier for your local session. In a distributed environment, this is supported only for remote **SELECT** statements, not for remote **INSERT**, **UPDATE**, or **DELETE** operations.

VALUE

SEE ALSO **DEREF**, **REF**, Chapter 41
FORMAT

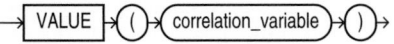

DESCRIPTION   In a SQL statement, **VALUE** takes as its argument a correlation variable (table alias) associated with a row of an object table and returns object instances stored in the object table. The type of the object instances is the same type as the object table. *See* Chapter 41.

VAR (Embedded SQL)

SEE ALSO   **SELECT** (Form 2), VARIABLE DECLARATION, *Programmer's Guide to the Oracle Precompilers*
FORMAT

```
EXEC SQL VAR host_variable
 { IS dtyp [({ length | precision, scale })]
   [CONVBUFSZ [IS] (size)]
 | CONVBUFSZ [IS] (size) }
```

DESCRIPTION   PL/SQL lets you override the default datatype assignment of a variable via the **VAR** command. Once a variable has been declared, it uses the datatype assigned to it in the **DECLARE** command. **VAR** allows you to change the datatype of a declared variable within a PL/SQL block.

NOTE
See the Programmer's Guide to the Oracle Precompilers *for a full list of all commands. This reference does not contain all of the possible precompiler commands.*

VAR_POP

SEE ALSO   AGGREGATE FUNCTIONS, **VAR_SAMP**, **VARIANCE**
FORMAT

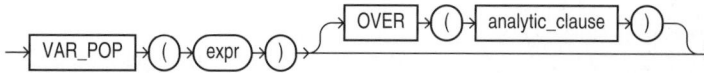

DESCRIPTION   **VAR_POP** returns the population variance of a set of numbers after discarding the **NULL**s in this set.

VAR_SAMP

SEE ALSO   AGGREGATE FUNCTIONS, **VAR_POP**, **VARIANCE**
FORMAT

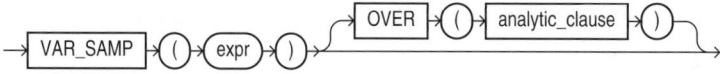

DESCRIPTION   **VAR_SAMP** returns the sample variance of a set of numbers after discarding the **NULL**s in this set.

VARCHAR2

See DATATYPES.

VARIABLE
SEE ALSO   PRINT
FORMAT

```
VAR[IABLE] [variable_name [NUMBER|CHAR|CHAR (n{CHAR|BYTE})|NCHAR|NCHAR(n)
|VARCHAR2 (n[CHAR|BYTE]) | NVARCHAR2(n) | CLOB | NCLOB | REFCURSOR
|BINARY_FLOAT | BINARY_DOUBLE
```

DESCRIPTION   **VARIABLE** declares a bind variable that can be referenced in PL/SQL. Each variable is assigned a *variable_name* and a type (NUMBER or CHAR). For CHAR variables, a maximum length (*n*) can be specified. **VARIABLE** followed by a variable name lists that variable.

EXAMPLE   In the following **EXAMPLE**, a variable named bal is created and is set equal to the result of a function:

```
variable bal NUMBER
begin
  :bal := LATE_FEE('DORAH TALBOT');
end;
```

VARIABLE DECLARATION (PL/SQL)
FORMAT

```
variable [CONSTANT]
{type | identifier%TYPE | [user.]table%ROWTYPE}
 [NOT NULL]
 [{DEFAULT | :=} expression];
```

DESCRIPTION   PL/SQL lets you declare variables in a PL/SQL block. If you declare the variable to be CONSTANT, you must initialize the variable with a value in the declaration and you cannot assign a new value to the variable.

   The type of the variable can be a PL/SQL type (*see* DATATYPES), the type of another PL/SQL variable or database column given by an identifier, or a ROWTYPE (*see* %ROWTYPE) that lets you refer to a record corresponding to a database table.

   If you add **NOT NULL** to the declaration, you cannot assign a **NULL** to the variable and you must initialize the variable. The initialization (following a DEFAULT or assignment **:=**) expression is any valid PL/SQL expression that results in a value of the type declared.

VARIANCE
SEE ALSO   ACCEPT, AGGREGATE FUNCTIONS, **COMPUTE**, **DEFINE**, PARAMETERS, **STDDEV**, **VAR_POP**, **VAR_SAMP**, Chapter 9
FORMAT

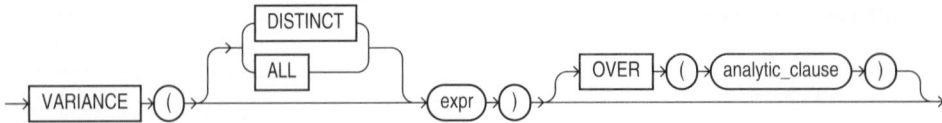

DESCRIPTION   **VARIANCE** gives the variance of all *values* for a group of rows. Like other group functions, **VARIANCE** ignores **NULL** values.

VARRAY

VARRAY is a clause within the **CREATE TYPE** command that tells the database the limit to the number of entries within the varying array. *See* **CREATE TYPE** for syntax information.

VSIZE

SEE ALSO CHARACTER FUNCTIONS, **LENGTH**, NUMBER FUNCTIONS, Chapter 9
FORMAT

DESCRIPTION **VSIZE** is the storage size of *value* in Oracle. For numbers it is usually smaller than the apparent length because less space is required to store numbers in the database.

WHENEVER

SEE ALSO EXECUTE, FETCH
FORMAT

```
EXEC SQL WHENEVER {NOT FOUND | SQLERROR | SQL WARNING}
    {CONTINUE |
     GOTO label |
     STOP |
     DO routine |
     DO BREAK |
     DO CONTINUE}
```

DESCRIPTION **WHENEVER** is not an executable SQL statement, but rather an instruction to the Oracle language processor to embed an **IF** *condition* **THEN GOTO** *label* statement after every SQL statement to follow. As each SQL statement executes, its results are tested to see if they meet the *condition*. If they do, the program branches to the *label*.

WHENEVER may be used with **CONTINUE** or a different label for each of the three possible conditions. Each of these will be in effect for all subsequent SQL statements. A new **WHENEVER** with one of these conditions will completely replace its predecessor for all subsequent SQL statements.

The **NOT FOUND** condition is raised any time the SQLCODE is 100, meaning, for instance, that a **FETCH** failed to return any rows (this includes subqueries in **INSERT** statements).

SQLERROR occurs whenever SQLCODE is less than 0. These are typically fatal errors and require serious error handling.

SQLWARNING occurs when a nonfatal "error" occurs. These include truncation of character strings being loaded into host variables, a select list of columns that doesn't match the INTO list of host variables, and **DELETE** or **UPDATE** statements without **WHERE** clauses.

Usually, initial branching, continuation, stopping, or routine execution is set up at the very beginning of a program before any executable SQL statements. However, within particular blocks of logic in the body of the program, any or all of these could be replaced depending on local needs. Note that **WHENEVER** knows nothing about the host language's scoping rules, calls, or branching. From the moment a **WHENEVER** is asserted, its rules remain in effect until another **WHENEVER** (with the same condition) replaces it. On the other hand, your program must obey language scoping rules with regard to the **GOTO** and label.

The **STOP** option stops program execution; the **DO** option calls a host language routine of some kind, the syntax of which depends on your host language. **DO BREAK** performs a break from a loop; **DO CONTINUE** performs a continue statement from a loop when the condition is met.

Lastly, in an error-handling routine, particularly one that may contain SQL statements, **WHENEVER SQLERROR** should probably contain **CONTINUE** or **STOP** or should call an exit routine in order to avoid an infinite loop back into the same error-handling routine.

WHENEVER OSERROR (SQL*Plus)

SEE ALSO   WHENEVER SQLERROR
FORMAT

```
WHENEVER OSERROR
{EXIT [SUCCESS|FAILURE|n|variable|:BindVariable] [COMMIT|ROLLBACK]
|CONTINUE [COMMIT|ROLLBACK|NONE]}
```

DESCRIPTION   **WHENEVER OSERROR** handles processing logic within SQL*Plus if an operating system error occurs. **EXIT** directs SQL*Plus to exit, and **CONTINUE** turns off **EXIT**. **COMMIT** tells SQL*Plus to issue a **COMMIT** prior to exiting, and **ROLLBACK** tells it to issue a **ROLLBACK** before exiting. The default behavior is **NONE**.

WHENEVER SQLERROR (SQL*Plus)

SEE ALSO   WHENEVER OSERROR
FORMAT

```
WHENEVER SQLERROR
{EXIT [SUCCESS|FAILURE|WARNING|n|variable|:BindVariable]
[COMMIT|ROLLBACK]|CONTINUE [COMMIT|ROLLBACK|NONE]}
```

DESCRIPTION   **WHENEVER SQLERROR** handles processing logic within SQL*Plus if a SQL command or a PL/SQL block encounters an error. **EXIT** directs SQL*Plus to exit, and **CONTINUE** turns off **EXIT**. **COMMIT** tells SQL*Plus to issue a **COMMIT** prior to exiting, and **ROLLBACK** tells it to issue a **ROLLBACK** before exiting. The default behavior is **NONE**.

NOTE
*SQL and PL/SQL errors initiate **WHENEVER SQLERROR** processing. SQL*Plus errors do not.*

You may place **WHENEVER SQLERROR** in a start file in front of as many SQL statements as you wish. Each **WHENEVER SQLERROR** will supersede the one before and will remain in effect until it is itself superseded.

EXAMPLE   When the CREATE TABLE command in the following example fails because the literal 'Keene' is not enclosed in single quotation marks, the subsequent UPDATE and SELECT will never even execute. The WHENEVER SQLERROR will exit SQL*Plus immediately and pass the SQL.SQLCODE back to the host:

```
WHENEVER SQLERROR EXIT SQL.SQLCODE;

create table keene as
select * from comfort
where city = Keene; -- will cause an error

update keene set noon = 75;

select * from keene;
```

WHERE

SEE ALSO **DELETE**, LOGICAL OPERATORS, PRECEDENCE, **SELECT**, SYNTAX OPERATORS, **UPDATE**
FORMAT

```
DELETE FROM [user.]table ...
   [ WHERE condition ]
SELECT ...
   [ WHERE condition ]
UPDATE [user.]table [alias] ...
   [WHERE condition ]
```

DESCRIPTION **WHERE** defines those logical conditions that control which rows a **SELECT** statement
will return, a **DELETE** statement will delete, or an **UPDATE** statement will update.
   A condition may be defined in one of several ways:

- ◼ A comparison between expressions (=, \>, !=, and so on)

- ◼ A comparison between an expression and a query

- ◼ A comparison between a list of expressions and a list of expressions from a query

- ◼ A comparison between an expression and **ANY** or **ALL** members of a list or between an
  expression and the values brought back from a query

- ◼ A test to see if an expression is **IN** or **NOT IN** a list or the results of a query

- ◼ A test for being **BETWEEN** or **NOT BETWEEN** one value and another

- ◼ A test to see if an expression **IS NULL** or **IS NOT NULL**

- ◼ A test to see if there **EXISTS** (or **NOT EXISTS**) any results for a query

- ◼ A combination of any of the above, using the conjunctions **AND** and **OR**

EXAMPLE

```
where section = any ('A','C','D');
where city != all (select city from location);
where section in ('A','C','D');
where city not in (select city from location);
where page between 4 and 7;
where skill is null;
where exists (select * from worker where age < 90);
where section = 'A' or section = 'B' and page = 1;
```

WHILE (PL/SQL)
See **LOOP**, Chapter 34

WIDTH_BUCKET
SEE ALSO NTILE
FORMAT

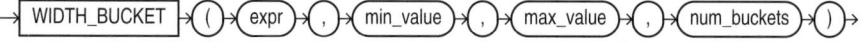

DESCRIPTION **WIDTH_BUCKET** constructs equiwidth histograms, in which the histogram range is
divided into intervals that have identical size. (Compare this function with **NTILE**, which creates

equiheight histograms.) Ideally, each bucket is a "closed-open" interval of the real number line. For a given expression, **WIDTH_BUCKET** returns the bucket number into which the value of this expression would fall after being evaluated. *expr* is the expression (a number or datetime value) for which the histogram is being created. If *expr* evaluates to **NULL**, the expression returns **NULL**. *min_value* and *max_value* are expressions that resolve to the end points of the acceptable range for *expr*. Both of these expressions must also evaluate to number or datetime values and neither can evaluate to **NULL**. *num_buckets* is an expression that resolves to a constant that indicates the number of buckets. This expression must evaluate to a positive integer.

XMLAGG
SEE ALSO   SYS_XMLAGG
FORMAT

DESCRIPTION   **XMLAGG** is an aggregate function. It takes a collection of XML fragments and returns an aggregated XML document. Any arguments that return **NULL** are dropped from the result.

   XMLAGG is similar to **SYS_XMLAGG** except that **XMLAGG** returns a collection of nodes. **XMLAGG** does not accept formatting using the XMLFORMAT object. Also, **XMLAGG** does not enclose the output in an element tag as **SYS_XMLAGG** does.

XMLCAST
SEE ALSO   Chapter 52
FORMAT

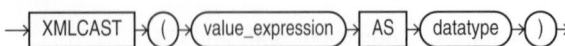

DESCRIPTION   **XMLCAST** casts *value_expression* to the scalar SQL datatype specified by *datatype*. The *value_expression* argument is a SQL expression that is evaluated. The *datatype* argument can be of datatype NUMBER, VARCHAR2, or any of the datetime datatypes.

XMLCDATA
SEE ALSO   Chapter 52
FORMAT

DESCRIPTION   XMLCData generates a CDATA section by evaluating *value_expr*. The *value_expr* must resolve to a string.

XMLCOLATTVAL
SEE ALSO   Chapter 52

FORMAT

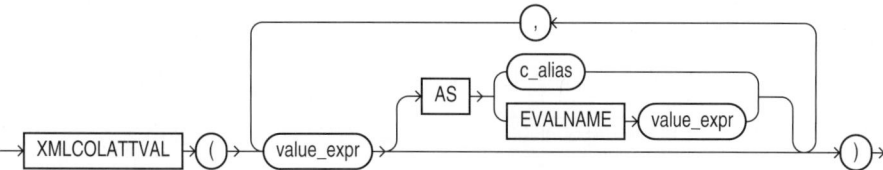

DESCRIPTION **XMLCOLATTVAL** creates an XML fragment and then expands the resulting XML so that each XML fragment has the name *column* with the attribute *name*. You can use the **AS** *c_alias* clause to change the value of the *name* attribute to something other than the column name.

You must specify a value for *value_expr*. If *value_expr* is **NULL**, no element is returned.

XMLCOMMENT

SEE ALSO   *Oracle XML DB Developer's Guide*
FORMAT

DESCRIPTION **XMLCOMMENT** generates an XML comment using the evaluated result of *value_expr*.

XMLCONCAT

SEE ALSO   XMLSEQUENCE
FORMAT

DESCRIPTION **XMLCONCAT** takes as input a series of XMLType instances, concatenates the series of elements for each row, and returns the concatenated series. **XMLCONCAT** is the inverse of **XMLSEQUENCE**.

XMLDIFF

SEE ALSO   Chapter 52
FORMAT

→ XMLDiff →

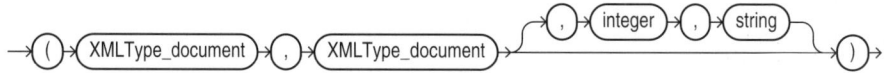

DESCRIPTION   The **XMLDiff** function is the SQL interface for the XmlDiff C API. This function compares two XML documents and captures the differences in XML conforming to an Xdiff schema. The diff document is returned as an XMLType document.

XMLELEMENT

SEE ALSO   SYS_XMLGEN
FORMAT

XML_attributes_clause::=

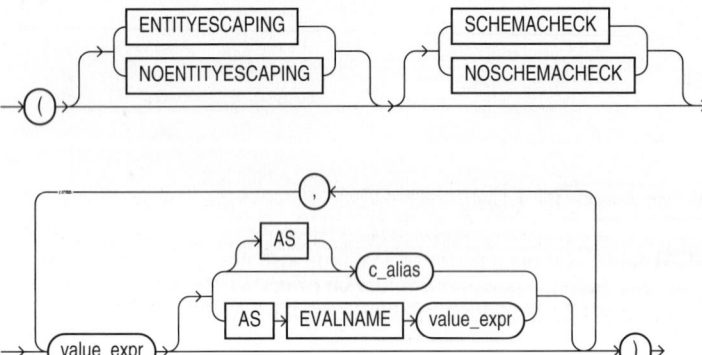

DESCRIPTION   XMLELEMENT takes an element name for *identifier*, an optional collection of attributes for the element, and arguments that make up the content of the element. It returns an instance of XMLType. **XMLELEMENT** is similar to **SYS_XMLGEN** except that **XMLELEMENT** can include attributes in the XML returned. **XMLELEMENT** does not accept formatting using the XMLFORMAT object.

XMLEXISTS

SEE ALSO   Chapter 52
FORMAT

XML_passing_clause::=

DESCRIPTION   XMLEXISTS checks whether a given XQuery expression returns a nonempty XQuery sequence. If so, the function returns TRUE; otherwise, it returns FALSE. The argument *XQuery_string* is a literal string, but it can contain XQuery variables that you bind using the *XML_passing_clause*.

The *expr* in the *XML_passing_clause* is an expression returning an XMLType or an instance of a SQL scalar datatype that is used as the context for evaluating the XQuery expression. You can specify only one *expr* in the PASSING clause without an identifier. The result of evaluating each *expr* is bound to the corresponding identifier in the *XQuery_string*. If any *expr* is not followed by an AS clause, the result of evaluating that expression is used as the context item for evaluating the *XQuery_string*.

XMLFOREST
SEE ALSO   XMLCONCAT
FORMAT

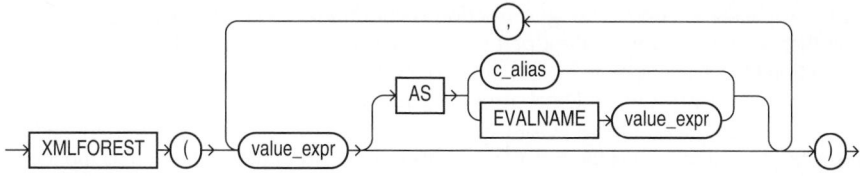

DESCRIPTION   XMLFOREST converts each of its argument parameters to XML, and then returns an XML fragment that is the concatenation of these converted arguments.

XMLISVALID
SEE ALSO   Chapter 52
FORMAT

DESCRIPTION   XMLISVALID parses the *XMLType_instance* and checks conformity with the relevant XML schema. If it's valid, it returns 1, otherwise 0.

XMLPARSE
SEE ALSO   Chapter 52
FORMAT

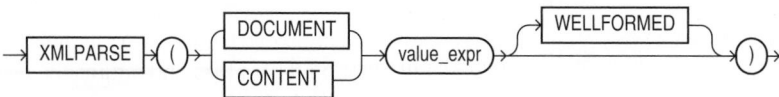

DESCRIPTION   XMLPARSE parses and generates an XML instance from the evaluated result of *value_expr*. The *value_expr* must resolve to a string. If *value_expr* resolves to NULL, the function returns **NULL**.

XMLPATCH
SEE ALSO   Chapter 52
FORMAT

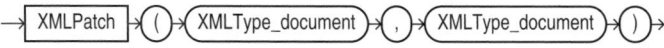

DESCRIPTION The **XMLPATCH** function is the SQL interface for the XmlPatch C API. This function patches an XML document with the changes specified. A patched XMLType document is returned.

XMLPI

SEE ALSO Chapter 52
FORMAT

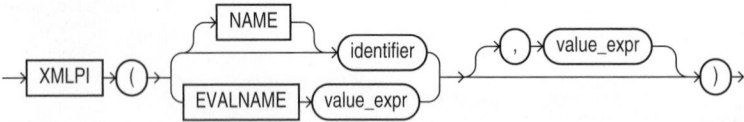

DESCRIPTION **XMLPI** generates an XML processing instruction using *identifier* and optionally the evaluated result of *value_expr*. A processing instruction is commonly used to provide to an application any information that is associated with all or part of an XML document. The application uses the processing instruction to determine how best to process the XML document.

You must specify a value for Oracle Database to use the enclosing tag. You can do this by specifying *identifier*, which is a string literal, or by specifying EVALNAME *value_expr*. In the latter case, the value expression is evaluated and the result, which must be a string literal, is used as the identifier. The identifier can be up to 4000 characters and does not have to be a column name or column reference. It cannot be an expression or NULL.

XMLQUERY

SEE ALSO Chapter 52
FORMAT

XML_passing_clause::=

DESCRIPTION **XMLQUERY** lets you query XML data in SQL statements. It takes an XQuery expression as a string literal, an optional context item, and other bind variables and returns the result of evaluating the XQuery expression using these input values.

XMLROOT

SEE ALSO   Chapter 52
FORMAT

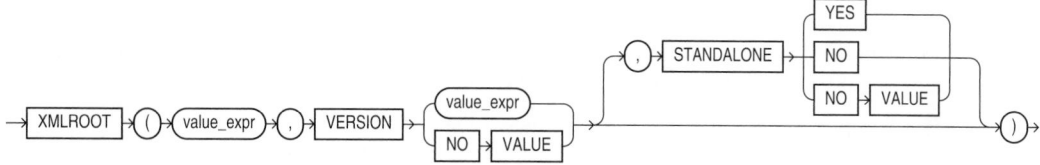

DESCRIPTION   **XMLROOT** lets you create a new XML value by providing version and stand-alone properties in the XML root information (prolog) of an existing XML value. If the *value_expr* already has a prolog, the database returns an error. If the input is NULL, the function returns NULL.

XMLSEQUENCE

SEE ALSO   **XMLCONCAT**
FORMAT

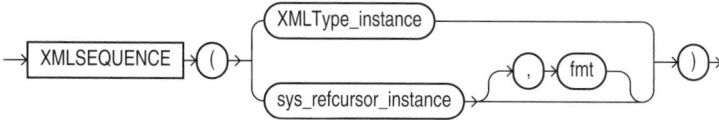

DESCRIPTION   **XMLSEQUENCE** has two forms:

- The first form takes as input an XMLType instance and returns a varying array of the top-level nodes in the XMLType.

- The second form takes as input a REFCURSOR instance, with an optional instance of the XMLFORMAT object, and returns as an **XMLSEQUENCE** type an XML document for each row of the cursor.

XMLSERIALIZE

SEE ALSO   Chapter 52
FORMAT

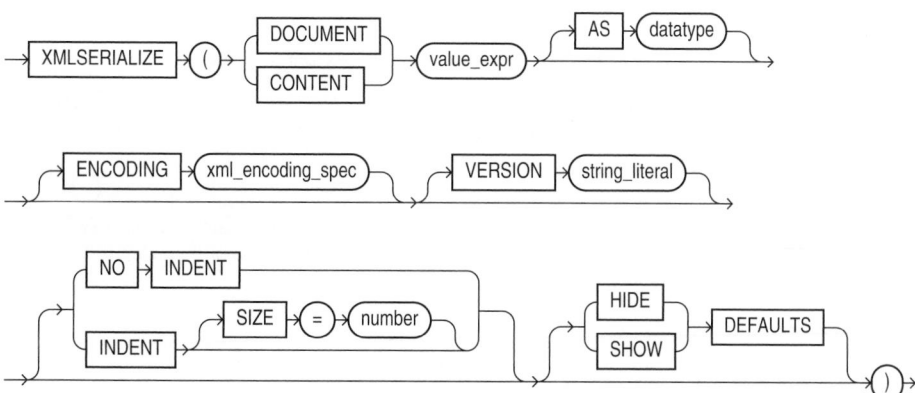

DESCRIPTION **XMLSERIALIZE** creates a string or LOB containing the contents of *value_expr*.

- If you specify **DOCUMENT**, then the *value_expr* must be a valid XML document.

- If you specify **CONTENT**, then the *value_expr* need not be a singly rooted XML document. However it must be valid XML content.

- The *datatype* specified can be a string type (VARCHAR2 or VARCHAR, but not NVARCHAR or NVARCHAR2), BLOB, or CLOB. The default is CLOB.

- If *datatype* is BLOB, then you can specify the **ENCODING** clause to use the specified encoding in the prolog.

- Specify the **VERSION** clause to use the version you provide as *string_literal* in the XML declaration (\<?xml version="..." ...?\>).

- Specify **NO INDENT** to strip all insignificant whitespace from the output. Specify **INDENT SIZE** = *N*, where *N* is a whole number, for output that is pretty-printed using a relative indentation of *N* spaces. If *N* is 0, then pretty-printing inserts a newline character after each element, placing each element on a line by itself, but omitting all other insignificant whitespace in the output. If **INDENT** is present without a **SIZE** specification, then two-space indenting is used. If you omit this clause, then the behavior (pretty-printing or not) is indeterminate.

- **HIDE DEFAULTS** and **SHOW DEFAULTS** apply only to XML schema–based data. If you specify **SHOW DEFAULTS** and the input data is missing any optional elements or attributes for which the XML schema defines default values, then those elements or attributes are included in the output with their default values. If you SPECIFY **HIDE DEFAULTS**, then no such elements or attributes are included in the output. **HIDE DEFAULTS** is the default behavior.

XMLTABLE

SEE ALSO   Chapter 52
FORMAT

XMLnamespaces_clause::=

XMLTABLE_options::=

XML_passing_clause::=

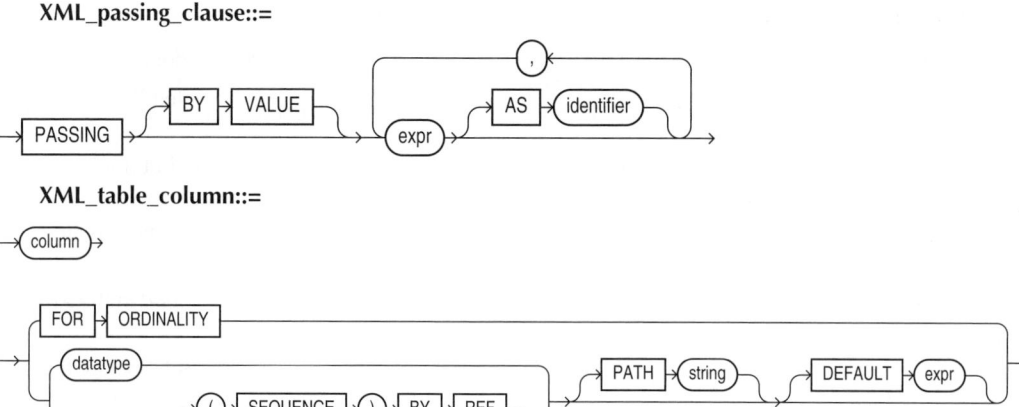

XML_table_column::=

DESCRIPTION **XMLTABLE** maps the result of an XQuery evaluation into relational rows and columns. You can query the result returned by the function as a virtual relational table using SQL.

The **XMLNAMESPACES** clause contains a set of XML namespace declarations. These declarations are referenced by the XQuery expression (the evaluated *XQuery_string*), which computes the row, and by the XPath expression in the **PATH** clause of *XML_table_column*, which computes the columns for the entire **XMLTABLE** function. If you want to use qualified names in the **PATH** expressions of the **COLUMNS** clause, then you need to specify the **XMLNAMESPACES** clause.

XQuery_string is a complete XQuery expression and can include prolog declarations.

The *expr* in the *XML_passing_clause* is an expression returning an XMLType or an instance of a SQL scalar datatype that is used as the context for evaluating the XQuery expression. You can specify only one *expr* in the **PASSING** clause without an identifier. The result of evaluating each *expr* is bound to the corresponding identifier in the *XQuery_string*. If any *expr* is not followed by an **AS** clause, then the result of evaluating that expression is used as the context item for evaluating the *XQuery_string*.

The optional **COLUMNS** clause defines the columns of the virtual table to be created by **XMLTABLE**.

XMLTRANSFORM
SEE ALSO Chapter 52
FORMAT

DESCRIPTION **XMLTRANSFORM** takes as arguments an XMLType instance and an XSL style sheet, which itself is a form of XMLType instance. It applies the style sheet to the instance and returns an XMLType.

XMLTYPE

XMLType is a datatype available to store and query XML data in the database. As a type, XMLType has member functions to access, extract, and query XML data using a class of operations known as XPath expressions. The SYS_XMLGEN, SYS_XMLAGG, and DBMS_XMLGEN packages create XMLType values from existing object-relational data. When you designate a column as using the XMLType datatype, Oracle internally stores the data in a CLOB datatype.

The following listing shows the creation of a table using the XMLType datatype:

```
create table MY_XML_TABLE
(Key1       NUMBER,
Xml_Column  SYS.XMLTYPE);

insert into MY_XML_TABLE (Key1, Xml_Column)
values (1, SYS.XMLTYPE.CREATEXML
 ('<book>
  <title>Complete Reference</title>
  <chapter num= "48">
     <title>Ending</title>
     <text>This is the end of the book.</text>
  </chapter>
</book>'));

select M.Xml_Column.GETCLOBVAL() as XML_Data
from MY_XML_TABLE M
where Key1 = 1;
```

See Chapter 52 for additional details on XMLType and its related methods.

About the CD-ROM

How to Use the *Oracle Database 12c: The Complete Reference* CD-ROM

The CD-ROM that accompanies this book contains an Adobe Acrobat PDF edition of *Oracle Database 12c: The Complete Reference*. With this electronic version, you can easily transport all of the valuable information contained in the book to your computer while the printed version of the book remains in your office or home.

NOTE
To view the electronic edition of the book, you will need the Adobe Acrobat Reader program. If you do not already have it pre-installed on your computer, go towww.adobe.com or http://get.adobe.com/reader/to download it for free.

Using the Code

The tables used in this book are available for you to access and use without retyping! You can use these to easily work your way through the examples and experiment with the many techniques illustrated in this book. Simply open the files **Tables.sql** and **Examples.sql** included on this CD. You can freely select, copy, and paste the desired text from these files.

NOTE
No technical support is provided with this CD-ROM.

Index

Hardware and Software
Engineered to Work Together

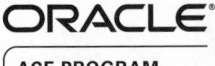

ORACLE®

⌐ ACE PROGRAM

Need help? Need consultation?
Need an informed opinion?

Stay Connected

oracle.com/technetwork/oracleace

 oracleaces

 @oracleace

B blogs.oracle.com/oracleace

You Need an Oracle ACE

Oracle partners, developers, and customers look to
Oracle ACEs and Oracle ACE Directors for focused
product expertise, systems and solutions discussion,
and informed opinions on a wide range of data center
implementations.

Their credentials are strong as Oracle product and
technology experts, community enthusiasts, and
solutions advocates.

And now is a great time to learn more about this
elite group—or nominate a worthy colleague.

For more information about the
Oracle ACE program, go to:
oracle.com/technetwork/oracleace

ORACLE®

Can I copy Java
code to an HTML
extension?

I want to improve
the performance of
my application...

Here's where you
can find the
latest release.

I coded it
this way...

Is the app
customizable?

How does
restricted task
reassignment
work?

Just watch the
live webcast on
virtualization.

The best way to migrate
Oracle E-Business
Application Suite Tier
servers to Linux is...

Where can I find
technical articles on
logging in Java ME?

Oracle Technology Network. It's code for sharing expertise.

Come to the best place to collaborate with other IT professionals.

Oracle Technology Network is the world's largest community of developers, administrators, and architects using industry-standard technologies with Oracle products.

Sign up for a free membership and you'll have access to:

- Discussion forums and hands-on labs
- Free downloadable software and sample code
- Product documentation
- Member-contributed content

Take advantage of our global network of knowledge.

JOIN TODAY ▷ Go to: oracle.com/technetwork

ORACLE®
TECHNOLOGY NETWORK

ORACLE®